Foreword

I've had a long love affair with strategy guides and hintbooks for games. I love flipping through them, seeing all the maps and hidden stuff I never knew about. It's like peering into the soul of a game. A look at what's really in it. And I think there are two great ways to experience *Fallout 3*; one, obviously, is to play the game. The next way is to read this book. Pick a chapter or page at random and start reading. I guarantee you'll see something you didn't know about it. It could be something big, like a reward you missed out on due to your choices, or a hidden weapon.

Over the last four years, the *Fallout 3* team put everything they had into this game. I think it's hard for someone playing the game for the first time to really appreciate how much has gone into it; how many big things there are and just how many small things. In some respects, this book represents the totality of the game—better than the actual game. I love seeing the work of so many passionate and creative people packed into a large tome. It becomes something tangible, a record of all that has been made.

The world of *Fallout* allows so many great ideas, whether they be dramatic, action packed, or darkly humorous, to come together in a new way. The journey in creating all of this has been a shared experience, and one that has proven to be the most fun I've ever had making a game. I hope reading about it is as much.

Todd Howard
Game Director: *Fallout 3*

Chapter 1 TRAINING

Welcome to the Capital Wasteland

You've escaped Vault 101, and you're frightened, alone, there's desolation in every direction, and a large, hairless rat creature is nipping at your heels. Welcome to the Capital Wasteland, survivor! You've chanced upon this strategy guide, and it should provide you with everything you require to thrive in this most inhospitable of environments. The current section you're reading offers a variety of tried and tested plans for spending your Statistic, Skill, and Perk points proficiently, offers some example characters to galvanize your imagination, details some general and advanced training, and showcases all of the important weapons, armor, and aid you should look for during this gigantic excursion.

Tip

Please read through the Instruction Manual that came with the copy of your game, so you're somewhat familiar with the tenets of this adventure. Now continue....

YOU'RE EXTRA S.P.E.C.I.A.L.!

S.P.E.C.I.A.L. is an acronymn that stands for your seven Primary Statistics: Strength, Perception, Endurance, Charisma, Intelligence, Agility, and Luck. These Primary Statistics (also known as "Attributes") serve as the foundation of all characters, from your own adventurer to people inhabiting the Wasteland and even creatures. They are measured from 1 (pitiful) to 10 (incredible).

What do the Primary Statistics Do?

Generally speaking, the higher your Primary Statistic, the higher your associated ability and skill bonuses are, as this table shows:

S.P.E.C.I.A.L. Effects Table I

S.P.E.C.I.A.L.	ASSOCIATED ATTRIBUTE	SKILLS MODIFIED
Strength	Carry Weight	Melee Weapons
Perception	Compass Markers	Energy Weapons, Explosives, Lockpick
Endurance	Health, Resistances	Big Guns, Unarmed
Charisma	Disposition	Barter, Speech
Intelligence	Skill Points per Level	Medicine, Repair, Science
Agility	Action Points	Small Guns, Sneak
Luck	Critical Chance	All Skills

Furthermore, when a S.P.E.C.I.A.L. statistic affects a skill, it does so by the amount shown in the following table. Luck is the exception, because it affects all skills, but at a much lower rate.

S.P.E.C.I.A.L. Effects Table II

S.P.E.C.I.A.L.	SKILL MODIFIER (%)	LUCK MODIFIER (%)
1	Skill +2	Skill +1
2	Skill +4	Skill +1
3	Skill +6	Skill +2
4	Skill +8	Skill +2
5	Skill +10	Skill +3
6	Skill +12	Skill +3
7	Skill +14	Skill +4
8	Skill +16	Skill +4
9	Skill +18	Skill +5
10	Skill +20	Skill +5

PRIMA GAMES

AN IMPRINT OF RANDOM HOUSE, INC.

3000 Lava Ridge Court, St. 100

Roseville, CA 95661

www.primagames.com

Senior Product Manager: Mario De Govia
Associate Product Manager: Shaida Boroumand
Design & Layout: Jamie A. Knight, James Knight (no relation)
Maps: 99 Lives Design
Manufacturing: Stephanie Sanchez

Originally hailing from Manchester in the United Kingdom, David left his role as a writer of numerous British video game magazines (including *Mean Machines*, *Computer & Video Games*, and the *Official Nintendo* and *Sega Saturn* magazines) and a bohemian lifestyle on a rusting, condemned dry-docked German fishing trawler to work on the part-fraternity, part-sanitarium known as *GameFan* magazine in 1996.

David helped to launch the fledgling GameFan Books and form Gamers' Republic in 1998, authoring many strategy guides for Millennium Publications, including *The Official Metal Gear Solid Mission Handbook*. After launching the wildly unsuccessful *incite* Video Gaming and Gamers.com, David began authoring guides for Prima Games in 2000. He has written over 60 strategy guides, including: *The Legend of Zelda: Twilight Princess*, *Assassin's Creed*, *Crysis*, *Spore*, *Half-Life: Orange Box*, and *Mario Kart Wii*. He lives in the Pacific Northwest with his wife, Melanie, and an eight-foot statue of Great Cthulhu.

We want to hear from you! E-mail comments and feedback to dhodgson@primagames.com.

Author thanks and Acknowledgements:
To my wonderful and loving wife Melanie; Miguel Lopez; Bryn, Rachel, and young Samuel; Mum, Dad, Ian and Rowena; The Moon Wiring Club, Laibach, Ladytron, Kraftwerk, The Knife, and Ron & Fez (noon to three). And C for Cthulhu, who lies in Ryleth a'dreaming; One sight of whom leaves most; Gibbering, drooling or screaming.

Thanks to all at Prima, especially Julie Asbury and Andy Rolleri for allowing me to tackle this project, and their patience during the process. Cheers too, to Mario DeGovia for steering the ship through choppy waters; monumental thanks to Shaida Boroumand for her incredible organization and level-headedness; to ace-designers Jamie Knight and Jim Knight; and Oliver and Sonja at 99 Lives for their spectacular cartography.

ISBN: 978-07615-5996-2
Library of Congress Control Number: 2008927755
Printed in the United States of America

08 09 10 11 LL 10 9 8 7 6 5 4 3 2 1

Bethesda Softworks Credits

Written By:
David S.J. Hodgson

Additional Writing:

Joel Burgess	Alan Nanes
Erik Caponi	Bruce Nesmith
Brian Chapin	Emil Pagliarulo
Jon Paul Duvall	Fred Zeleny
Kurt Kuhlmann	Nathan Purkeypile

Concept Artist:
Adam Adamowicz

Editors-in-Chief:

Jeff Gardiner	Pete Hines

Fallout 3 created by:
Bethesda Game Studios

Fallout 3 Executive Producer:
Todd Howard

Special Thanks to:
Istvan Pely, Noah Barry, Kevin Kaufmann, Chris Krietz, Natalia Smirnova, Jeff Browne, Daryl Brigner, Phil Nelson, Ryan Redetzky, Jesse Tucker, Craig Lafferty, Gavin Carter, Tim Lamb, Ashley Cheng, Nathan McDyer, and, of course, everyone at Bethesda Softworks, Bethesda Game Studio and ZeniMax Media, Inc.

TABLE OF CONTENTS

During your character's creation, your S.P.E.C.I.A.L. points are allotted automatically based on the decisions you make during the first three Main Quests: Baby Steps, Future Imperfect, and just before you leave Vault 101 for the first time in Escape! During the latter two quests, you can redistribute points manually to lay the foundation for exactly the type of adventurer you want to be.

You have 40 points to spend across the seven Primary Statistics. Seven of these points are automatically allocated (you must have a minimum of 1 point in every statistic), but the rest are freely distributed as you like. The following information reveals what associated skills and perks are affected by each statistic.

 Tip

Go and read up on some skills and perks that particularly interest you, then check what statistic affects them and bump up the points in that statistic accordingly.

Note

Each of the statistics has a collectible Bobblehead associated with it. Find the Bobblehead, and you automatically (and permanently) receive +1 to that statistic.

Primary Statistics

 ## STRENGTH

Strength is a measure of your raw physical strength. It determines how much you can carry, and the extra damage done with in unarmed combat.

STRENGTH	CARRY WEIGHT (LBS) †	MELEE DAMAGE (HP) ‡	SKILL MODIFIERS ††
1	160	0.5	Melee Weapons +2
2	170	1	Melee Weapons +4
3	180	1.5	Melee Weapons +6
4	190	2	Melee Weapons +8
5	200	2.5	Melee Weapons +10
6	210	3	Melee Weapons +12
7	220	3.5	Melee Weapons +14
8	230	4	Melee Weapons +16
9	240	4.5	Melee Weapons +18
10	250	5	Melee Weapons +20

† Carry Weight: Every item you scavenge in the Wasteland has a weight associated with it. The stronger you are, the more you can carry without becoming over-encumbered (which means you cannot run).

‡ Unarmed Damage: If you're going to primarily use your fists or a hand weapon such as a Power Fist, expect to add this amount of damage to every strike.

†† Skill Modifiers: You instantly (and permanently) add this percentage to your Melee Weapons skill.

ASSOCIATED SKILL (AND DERIVED STATISTIC)

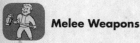 **Melee Weapons**   **Carry Weight**

ASSOCIATED PERKS

PERK	MIN. STRENGTH NEEDED	LEVEL AVAILABLE
Little Leaguer	4	2
Iron Fist	4	4
Strong Back	5	8

PERCEPTION

Perception determines how well you use your five senses, and also pertains to an almost superhuman "sixth sense." The higher your Perception, the sooner the compass markings appear on your compass to indicate a threat.

PERCEPTION	SKILL MODIFIERS (%) †
1	Energy Weapons +2, Explosives +2, Lockpick +2
2	Energy Weapons +4, Explosives +4, Lockpick +4
3	Energy Weapons +6, Explosives +6, Lockpick +6
4	Energy Weapons +8, Explosives +8, Lockpick +8
5	Energy Weapons +10, Explosives +10, Lockpick +10
6	Energy Weapons +12, Explosives +12, Lockpick +12
7	Energy Weapons +14, Explosives +14, Lockpick +14
8	Energy Weapons +16, Explosives +16, Lockpick +16
9	Energy Weapons +18, Explosives +18, Lockpick +18
10	Energy Weapons +20, Explosives +20, Lockpick +20

† Skill Modifiers: You instantly (and permanently) add this percentage to these skills.

ASSOCIATED DERIVED STATISTIC

• **Easier to detect enemies on compass**

ASSOCIATED SKILLS

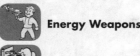 **Energy Weapons**   **Explosives**

 **Lockpick**

ASSOCIATED PERKS

PERK	MIN. PERCEPTION NEEDED	LEVEL AVAILABLE
Thief	4	2
Sniper	6	12
Light Step	6	14
Contract Killer	6	14
Lawbringer	6	14
Better Criticals	6	16
Infiltrator	7	18

 # ENDURANCE

Endurance is your Health and overall physical fitness. The higher your Endurance, the better your Health and Poison and Radiation Resistance are.

ENDURANCE	INITIAL HEALTH †	SKILL MODIFIERS (%)
1	120	Big Guns +2, Unarmed +2
2	140	Big Guns +4, Unarmed +4
3	160	Big Guns +6, Unarmed +6
4	180	Big Guns +8, Unarmed +8
5	200	Big Guns +10, Unarmed +10
6	220	Big Guns +12, Unarmed +12
7	240	Big Guns +14, Unarmed +14
8	260	Big Guns +16, Unarmed +16
9	280	Big Guns +18, Unarmed +18
10	300	Big Guns +20, Unarmed +20

† Initial Health: Because this is the amount of damage you can take before dying, it is worth figuring out what type of combat you're planning. For example, you need more Health if you're planning to fight hand-to-hand instead of long-range sniping.

ASSOCIATED DERIVED STATISTICS

 Poison resistance   **Radiation resistance**

ASSOCIATED SKILLS

 Big Guns   **Unarmed**

ASSOCIATED PERKS

PERK	MIN. ENDURANCE NEEDED	LEVEL AVAILABLE
Toughness	5	6
Lead Belly	5	6
Strong Back	5	8
Rad Resistance	5	8
Size Matters	5	8
Life Giver	6	12
Solar Powered	7	20

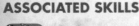 # CHARISMA

Charisma defines your overall attractiveness and likeability. Having a high Charisma will improve people's disposition toward you, although it can't overcome a particular high or low Karma. Prefer talking and shooting to just shooting? Read on....

CHARISMA	SKILL MODIFIERS (%)
1	Barter +2, Speech +2
2	Barter +4, Speech +4
3	Barter +6, Speech +6
4	Barter +8, Speech +8
5	Barter +10, Speech +10
6	Barter +12, Speech +12
7	Barter +14, Speech +14
8	Barter +16, Speech +16
9	Barter +18, Speech +18
10	Barter +20, Speech +20

ASSOCIATED SKILLS (AND OTHER INFORMATION)

 Barter   **Speech**

- **Disposition of others toward you**

ASSOCIATED PERKS

PERK	MIN. CHARISMA NEEDED	LEVEL AVAILABLE
Scoundrel	4	4
Child at Heart	4	4
Impartial Mediation	5	8
Animal Friend	6	10
Master Trader	6	14

INTELLIGENCE

This measures your basic intellect, curiosity in the world, and adeptness at critical thinking. The higher your Intelligence, the more skill points you can distribute when you level up.

INTELLIGENCE	SKILL POINTS	SKILL MODIFIERS (%)
1	11	Medicine +2, Repair +2, Science +2
2	12	Medicine +4, Repair +4, Science +4
3	13	Medicine +6, Repair +6, Science +6
4	14	Medicine +8, Repair +8, Science +8
5	15	Medicine +10, Repair +10, Science +10
6	16	Medicine +12, Repair +12, Science +12
7	17	Medicine +14, Repair +14, Science +14
8	18	Medicine +16, Repair +16, Science +16
9	19	Medicine +18, Repair +18, Science +18
10	20	Medicine +20, Repair +20, Science +20

ASSOCIATED SKILLS (AND OTHER INFORMATION)

 Medicine

Repair

Science

• Skill points per level up

ASSOCIATED PERKS

PERK	MIN. INTELLIGENCE NEEDED	LEVEL AVAILABLE
Swift Learner	4	2
Gun Nut	4	2
Daddy's Boy	4	2
Educated	4	4
Entomologist	4	4
Comprehension	4	6
Nerd Rage!	5	10
Computer Whiz	7	18

AGILITY

Agility is a measure of your quickness and dexterity. Agility affects your total number of Action Points, which are used to perform specialized combat actions in V.A.T.S. mode.

AGILITY	ACTION POINTS (APS)	SKILL MODIFIERS (%)
1	67	Small Guns +2, Sneak +2
2	69	Small Guns +4, Sneak +4
3	71	Small Guns +6, Sneak +6
4	73	Small Guns +8, Sneak +8
5	75	Small Guns +10, Sneak +10
6	77	Small Guns +12, Sneak +12
7	79	Small Guns +14, Sneak +14
8	81	Small Guns +16, Sneak +16
9	83	Small Guns +18, Sneak +18
10	85	Small Guns +20, Sneak +20

ASSOCIATED SKILL (AND DERIVED STATISTIC)

 Small Guns

Sneak

• Action Points

ASSOCIATED PERKS

PERK	MINIMUM AGILITY NEEDED	LEVEL AVAILABLE
Gun Nut	4	2
Thief	4	2
Silent Running	6	12
Sniper	6	12
Light Step	6	14
Action Boy	7	16

LUCK

Luck is a slightly different statistic, because it affects every other skill. Raising your Luck raises all of your skill values by a small amount. Having a high Luck will also improve your chance of a critical hit.

LUCK	SKILL MODIFIERS (%)
1	Critical 1%, All Skills +1
2	Critical 2%, All Skills +1
3	Critical 3%, All Skills +2
4	Critical 4%, All Skills +2
5	Critical 5%, All Skills +3
6	Critical 6%, All Skills +3
7	Critical 7%, All Skills +4
8	Critical 8%, All Skills +4
9	Critical 9%, All Skills +5
10	Critical 10%, All Skills +5

ASSOCIATED DERIVED STATISTIC

 Critical Chance

ASSOCIATED PERKS

PERK	MINIMUM LUCK NEEDED	LEVEL AVAILABLE
Fortune Finder	5	6
Scrounger	5	8
Finesse	6	10
Mysterious Stranger	6	10
Better Criticals	6	16

APPENDICES — COMPLETION — TOUR — MISC. QUESTS — MAIN QUEST — BESTIARY — TRAINING

Derived Statistics

Derived Statistics are a second, related set of values determined automatically, based on the Primary Statistics (S.P.E.C.I.A.L.) and skills that you can allocate points to, or certain perks. There are different ways to increase (and decrease) these Derived Statistics; they aren't just affected by your Primary Statistics.

For example, imagine you want to modify your Carry Weight. This is affected by the following:
- You could increase or decrease your Strength,
- Or, you could take the Strong Back perk.

Here are all the Derived Statistics and what they do:

ACTION POINTS

As the name might suggest, the higher the number, the more actions you can accomplish before another entity (whether friend or foe) reacts back. Your total number of Action Points (APs) is visible only on your Pip-Boy's Stats screen. Otherwise, APs are represented by a bar on your H.U.D. Your AP bar is constantly in motion, retracting as you shoot weapons or access your inventory, and filling back up when not engaged in these types of moves. Don't worry about running out of APs unless you are engaged in combat, and specifically, in V.A.T.S. mode.

So, why not act in "real time" and ignore V.A.T.S. mode? Because V.A.T.S. allows easier takedowns, advantageous combat, and more pronounced effects. That Raider in the distance may be difficult to manually decapitate, but enter V.A.T.S., and expend some Action Points, and you're playing at your full potential; you're as proficient as your points allocations allow. Most of all, V.A.T.S. gives you an additional +15% chance of a critical hit. That's a four times improvement for a character with a Luck of 5.

AGILITY	ACTION POINTS
1	67
2	69
3	71
4	73
5	75
6	77
7	79
8	81
9	83
10	85

PERKS THAT MODIFY ACTION POINTS (PERMANENTLY)

 Action Boy/Girl, +25 Action Points

TEMPORARY MODIFIERS TO ACTION POINTS: CHEMS

 Jet Action Points +30

UltraJet Action Points +40

Fire Ant Nectar Agility +4 (AP +8)

Nuka-Cola Quantum Action Points +20

 NukaLurk Meat Action Points +20

TEMPORARY MODIFIERS TO ACTION POINTS: ADDICTIONS

Alcohol Addiction: Agility -1 (AP -2)

Jet Addiction: Agility -1 (AP -2)

Med-X Addiction: Agility -1 (AP -2)

TEMPORARY MODIFIERS TO ACTION POINTS: RADIATION POISONING

400 Rads: Agility -1 (AP -2)

600 Rads: Agility -2 (AP -4)

800 Rads: Agility -2 (AP -4)

ACTION POINT COSTS

You can perform a number of actions in both regular "run and gun" and V.A.T.S. modes. These actions consume Action Points. Attack with any kind of weapon except a Rifle or Big Gun and it takes 10 APs. Crouching or standing takes 10 APs. Firing a Rifle takes 25 APs. Firing a Big Gun with a projectile takes 75 APs.

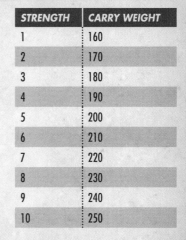 CARRY WEIGHT

Your Carry Weight, shown on your Pip-Boy's Inventory menu, determines how much you can carry before you become over-encumbered, slow down, and eventually stop. It is determined by your Strength:

STRENGTH	CARRY WEIGHT
1	160
2	170
3	180
4	190
5	200
6	210
7	220
8	230
9	240
10	250

PERKS THAT MODIFY CARRY WEIGHT (PERMANENTLY)

 Strong Back, +50 Carry Weight

Solar Powered, ST +2 in sunlight (+40 Carry Weight)

TEMPORARY MODIFIERS TO CARRY WEIGHT: CHEMS

 Any alcoholic beverage, ST +1 (Carry Weight +20)

Buffout, ST +1 (Carry Weight +20)

 Mississippi Quantum Pie, ST +1 (Carry Weight +20)

TEMPORARY MODIFIERS TO CARRY WEIGHT: ADDICTIONS

Nectar Withdrawal: ST -2 (Carry Weight -40)

Buffout Withdrawal: ST -1 (Carry Weight -20)

TEMPORARY MODIFIERS TO CARRY WEIGHT: RADIATION POISONING

600 Rads: ST -1 (Carry Weight -20)

800 Rads: ST -2 (Carry Weight -40)

CRITICAL CHANCE

Every time you strike an opponent (or receive a hit yourself) there's a chance that hit will inflict Critical Damage. The exact amount of Critical Damage varies depending on the weapon, whether or not it's a sneak attack, and whether or not you are in V.A.T.S. In most cases Critical Damage is double normal damage and the chance of a critical hit is simply your Luck as a percentage.

LUCK	BASE CHANCE OF CRITICAL DAMAGE
1	1%
2	2%
3	3%
4	4%
5	5%
6	6%
7	7%
8	8%
9	9%
10	10%

 Note

With certain weapons, such as the Laser Rifle, additional effects occur when a critical is successful, such as the enemy being immolated into a pile of dust!

PERKS THAT MODIFY CRITICAL CHANCE (PERMANENTLY)

 Finesse, +5% Critical Chance

Ninja, +15% Critical Chance (only with Unarmed and Melee Weapons)

DAMAGE RESISTANCE

If you are struck while in combat, you receive damage. The amount of damage you are spared, with bonuses from employing armor or perks, is your Damage Resistance. This can be between 0 and 85%. You might see a number greater than 100 in the HUD, but a max of 85 is actually used. If you have a Damage Resistance of 30, you take 30% less damage when you're struck. The most common way to increase your DR is to wear armor. Helmets also add to your overall DR. Wear both for maximum protection.

PERKS THAT MODIFY DAMAGE RESISTANCE (PERMANENTLY)

 Toughness, +10 Damage Resistance

Cyborg, +10 Damage Resistance

Nerd Rage, +50 Damage Resistance, but only with low health

TEMPORARY MODIFIERS TO DAMAGE RESISTANCE: CHEMS

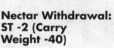 **Med-X, +25 Damage Resistance**

HEALTH

Your general well-being is governed by your Health, as indicated both in your Pip-Boy, and on-screen. When you reach 0 Health, you are dead. Your Endurance statistic determines your starting Health and you gain 10 more each time you level up. Naturally, the more Health you have, the better your chances at survival (at least initially) are.

In addition, you and your enemies' Health represent the total health of your entire body. You can refer to the Factions and Bestiary chapter (page 46) to discover the Health of every foe. However, each body part of an enemy (and yourself) has an approximate percentage of the total Health. This means (for example), that shooting a 100 Health Raider in the torso requires you to damage him for 46 points before the body part is crippled. Remember that the Raider's armor also stops some of the incoming damage. The following table shows the player's and an NPC's body part Health as a percentage of the NPC's total Health. Creatures all have unique body part Health distributions. Notice that the player has very high body part Health. You are the hero. You're a pretty tough guy.

ENDURANCE	STARTING HEALTH
1	120
2	140
3	160
4	180
5	200
6	220
7	240
8	260
9	280
10	300

BODY PART	NPC HEALTH	PLAYER HEALTH
Head	20%	75%
Torso	60%	255%
Left Arm	25%	100%
Right Arm	25%	100%
Left Leg	25%	150%
Right Leg	25%	150%

This is one reason why limb shots are favored by professional Wasteland killers. As long as your aim is good, you only need inflict a percentage of a foe's total Health to cripple that limb.

Tip

In most cases you inflict double damage if you aim at the head too; make cranial destruction an essential part of your combat repertoire!

Also note that if you fall a great distance, or you're shot or wounded in a specific area, you may lose the use of that body part. For example, a fall from the balcony over the Atom Bomb in Megaton cripples a leg. Seek a doctor, or inject yourself with a Stimpak to heal yourself.

PERKS THAT MODIFY HEALTH (PERMANENTLY)

 Life Giver, +30 Health

TEMPORARY MODIFIERS TO HEALTH: CHEMS

 Buffout, EN +3 (Health +60)

 ## MELEE AND UNARMED DAMAGE

These two types of "close quarter" damage are sometimes difficult to distinguish, so follow this rule: If you're inflicting Melee Damage, you are using a weapon in one or both hands that is designed to strike directly into a foe, such as a Lead Pipe. Unarmed Damage is punishment inflicted by just your fists, and by specialized Unarmed weapons such as Brass Knuckles. Unarmed Damage is determined strictly by your Unarmed skill. Your Unarmed Damage is 25% of your Unarmed skill. So if you have a skill of 60, you do 15 points of damage. Any Unarmed Weapon Damage is added to this.

STRENGTH	MELEE DAMAGE
1	+0.5
2	+1.0
3	+1.5
4	+2.0
5	+2.5
6	+3.0
7	+3.5
8	+4.0
9	+4.5
10	+5.0

PERKS THAT MODIFY MELEE OR UNARMED DAMAGE (PERMANENTLY)

 Iron Fist, +5 Unarmed Damage

 Nerd Rage!, ST set to 10 (Melee Damage 5.0), but only with low Health

TEMPORARY MODIFIERS TO MELEE DAMAGE: CHEMS

 Any alcoholic beverage, ST +1 (Melee Damage +0.5)

 Buffout, ST +1 (Melee Damage +0.5)

 Mississippi Quantum Pie, ST +1 (Melee Damage +0.5)

TEMPORARY MODIFIERS TO MELEE DAMAGE: ADDICTIONS

 Nectar Withdrawal: ST -2 (Melee Damage -1)

Buffout Withdrawal: ST -1 (Melee Damage -0.5)

TEMPORARY MODIFIERS TO MELEE DAMAGE: RADIATION POISONING

 600 Rads: ST -1 (Melee Damage -0.5)

 800 Rads: ST -2 (Melee Damage -0.5)

 ## POISON AND RADIATION RESISTANCE

Certain foes and weapons inflict a poisonous attack on you, and Poison Resistance reduces how much the poison hurts you. So, if you have a Poison Resistance of 20%, you take that much less damage. Because poison ignores your armor and Damage Resistance, this is the only defense you have against poison.

Certain areas of the Wasteland are irradiated; this includes all water sources, muddy pools, and areas where bombs were dropped long ago. Your Radiation Resistance indicates how adept your body is at ignoring exposure. You cannot become completely immune to radiation; there are highly irradiated areas in the Wasteland that kill you in seconds, even if you take every precaution.

Such precautions include wearing specialized armor, a Radiation Suit, consuming Rad-X, or choosing the Rad Resistance perk.

Your Endurance helps you tough out poison or radiation. Although you can't see it in your Pip-Boy, you can calculate it.

ENDURANCE	POISON RESISTANCE	RADIATION RESISTANCE
1	0	0
2	5%	2%
3	10%	4%
4	15%	6%
5	20%	8%
6	25%	10%
7	30%	12%
8	35%	14%
9	40%	16%
10	45%	18%

Exposure to radiation is calculated in "Rads" on your Pip-Boy, and the exposure you receive (without visiting a doctor or taking the Chem RadAway) results in appalling poisoning that is detrimental to your well being. Specifically, the following effects occur:

APPROX. RADS EXPOSURE	EFFECTS
0	No effect
200	-1 Endurance
400	-2 Endurance, -1 Agility
600	-3 Endurance, -2 Agility, -1 Strength
800	-3 Endurance, -2 Agility, -2 Strength
1,000	Instant death

PERKS THAT MODIFY POISON OR RADIATION RESISTANCE (PERMANENTLY)

Rad Resistance, +25% Radiation Resistance

Cyborg, +10% to both Poison and Radiation Resistance

MOVEMENT SPEED

How quickly you move around the Wasteland is governed by a three factors:

1. How much you are carrying: If your inventory weighs more than your Carry Weight, you become over-encumbered, essentially slowing yourself down to a crawl. Discard items so you can move more quickly, or live with it.

2. The armor you are wearing: Heavy Power Armor slows you down, but provides excellent protection. Dirty Pre-War Business Suits provide quick mobility, and no protection whatsoever. Switch your outfits accordingly, as the situation arises. There's no penalty for carrying both types of outfits (or more) as long as your Carry Weight allows it.

3. Remain unarmed. Flick between carrying a Combat Shotgun, and stowing it, and you'll see a difference in your speed.

Skills Overview

Skills are the backbone of any character. They determine whether you're a dumb-as-nails brute or a well-educated computer genius, an accomplished sharpshooter or a martial arts master. Many skills also serve as prerequisites for certain perks. They are rated between 0 and 100.

TAG SKILLS

When you complete your G.O.A.T. for the first time, you get to choose three Tag skills. These start with a +15 higher score than other skills.

SKILLS: LEARNING THE BASICS

Each Skill is affected by only one S.P.E.C.I.A.L. statistic (as previously listed, and shown below). The higher the statistic, the higher your starting bonus in the related skill. Each point in the statistic gives you two points in the skill. The following chart shows the starting values of all the different skills, based on a minimum statistic rank of 1, and an average of 5.

SKILL	LOWEST STARTING VALUE	STARTING VALUE W/ ATTR. OF 5	RELATED S.P.E.C.I.A.L.
Barter	7	15	Charisma
Big Guns	7	15	Endurance
Energy Weapons	7	15	Perception
Explosives	7	15	Perception
Lockpick	7	15	Perception
Medicine	7	15	Intelligence
Melee Weapons	7	15	Strength
Repair	7	15	Intelligence
Science	7	15	Intelligence
Small Guns	7	15	Agility
Sneak	7	15	Agility
Speech	7	15	Charisma
Unarmed	7	15	Endurance

Tip

Here's the plan: Check the skills you're most interested in, bump up the associated statistic, and for skills you really want to specialize in, select them as one of your three Tag skills.

Note

Each of the skills has a collectible Bobblehead associated with it. Find the Bobblehead, and you automatically (and permanently) receive +10 to that skill.

SKILL POINTS AWARDED

When you receive enough Experience Points (XP) to level up, you earn Skill points that can be "spent" to increase the exact skills you wish to advance, one point at a time. The number of Skill points the player gets each level is governed by Intelligence as depicted in the following table:

INTELLIGENCE	SKILL POINTS PER LEVEL
1	11
2	12
3	13
4	14
5	15
6	16
7	17
8	18
9	19
10	20

AVAILABLE SKILLS

BARTER

S.P.E.C.I.A.L. Statistic: Charisma

The Barter skill affects the prices you get for buying and selling items. In general, the higher your Barter skill, the lower your prices on purchased items. Use this whenever you trade with a scavenger or merchant.

REQUIRED SKILL LEVEL	AVAILABLE PERK	REQUIRED CHARACTER LEVEL
60	Master Trader	14

BIG GUNS

S.P.E.C.I.A.L. Statistic: Endurance

The Big Guns skill determines your combat effectiveness with all oversized weapons, specifically the Flamer, Gatling Laser, Minigun, Fat Man, Missile Launcher, Rock-it Launcher, and any unique variants of these weapons. As this skill increases, so does your accuracy and damage with all of these weapons, both in and out of V.A.T.S. mode.

REQUIRED SKILL LEVEL	AVAILABLE PERK	REQUIRED CHARACTER LEVEL
60	Concentrated Fire	18

ENERGY WEAPONS

S.P.E.C.I.A.L. Statistic: Perception

The Energy Weapons skill determines your combat effectiveness with all energy-based weapons, specifically the Alien Blaster, Laser Pistol, Mesmetron, Plasma Pistol, Laser Rifle, Plasma Rifle, and any unique variants of these weapons. As this skill increases, so does your accuracy and damage with all of these weapons, both in and out of V.A.T.S. mode.

REQUIRED SKILL LEVEL	AVAILABLE PERK	REQUIRED CHARACTER LEVEL
60	Concentrated Fire	18

EXPLOSIVES

S.P.E.C.I.A.L. Statistic: Perception

The Explosives skill is used to successfully set or disarm Mines. When setting a Mine (Frag, Pulse, Plasma, or Bottlecap varieties), the higher your skill, the more you automatically "overload" the explosive and increase its damage output. For disarming purposes, whenever you approach an armed Mine, a "countdown beep" increases in speed until the Mine explodes. The higher your Explosives skill, the more time you have to disarm it before detonation.

In addition, Explosives governs the care and accuracy you take when throwing a weapon such as a Frag Grenade, Plasma Grenade, Pulse Grenade, or Nuka-Grenade, as well as the damage they do. With a high Explosives skill, a well-aimed Grenade will land right at an opponent's feet, won't roll away, and will explode immediately.

REQUIRED SKILL LEVEL	AVAILABLE PERK	REQUIRED CHARACTER LEVEL
60	Demolition Expert	6
60	Pyromaniac	12

LOCKPICK

S.P.E.C.I.A.L. Statistic: Perception

The Lockpick skill is used to open locked doors and containers. If you don't have a high enough skill, you won't even be allowed to try. The higher your Lockpick skill, the easier it will be to pick the lock, because the "sweet spot" where the tumblers fall into place is larger. Or, if you choose the lockpicking minigame's "auto attempt" function, your Lockpick skill largely determines your automatic chance of success.

LOCK DIFFICULTY	REQUIRED LOCKPICK SKILL
Very Easy	0
Easy	25
Average	50
Hard	75
Very Hard	100

REQUIRED SKILL LEVEL	AVAILABLE PERK	REQUIRED CHARACTER LEVEL
80	Infiltrator	18

Tip

Attempt a Lockpick carefully, and with gentle touches. Line your Bobby Pin up anywhere in the 180 degree arc. Try the lock. If there's give, move it slightly in one direction. If there's more give, you're moving the Bobby Pin the correct way. If there's less give, move it in the opposite direction. Let the lock reset after each try. On the third turn, the lock should open. If it doesn't, the Bobby Pin snaps. Try again, remembering where there was most give, and place the Bobby Pin there to start with. Continue with this until the lock opens. Patience is a virtue!

MEDICINE

S.P.E.C.I.A.L. Statistic: Intelligence

The higher your Medicine skill, the more Health you replenish when using a Stimpak or any other medicinal item such as Rad-X, RadAway, etc. If you maximize your Medicine skill at 100, your Stimpak effectiveness is doubled.

REQUIRED SKILL LEVEL	AVAILABLE PERK	REQUIRED CHARACTER LEVEL
60	Cyborg	14
60	Chem Resistant	16

MELEE WEAPONS

S.P.E.C.I.A.L. Statistic: Strength

The Melee Weapons skill determines your combat effectiveness with all melee weapons, specifically the Police Baton, Chinese Officer's Sword, Combat Knife, Lead Pipe, Ripper, Rolling Pin, Knife, Switchblade, Tire Iron, Repellent Stick, Baseball Bat, Nail Board, Pool Cue, Sledgehammer, Super Sledge, Shishkebab, and any unique variants of these weapons. As this skill increases, so does your damage inflicted with all of these weapons, both in and out of V.A.T.S. mode. The Melee Weapons skill also allows you to use a melee weapon to block an attack; the higher the skill, the more damage is absorbed.

REQUIRED SKILL LEVEL	AVAILABLE PERK	REQUIRED CHARACTER LEVEL
80	Ninja	20

REPAIR

S.P.E.C.I.A.L. Statistic: Intelligence

The Repair skill allows you to maintain any weapons and apparel, which degrade during combat. This makes it one of the most useful skills in the game. Anyone can repair a weapon to about 50% condition. The higher your Repair skill, the higher condition you can get it to. With a Repair of 100, you can fully repair any item. Before attempting a repair, look at how much you will get from it. If the percentage is low, don't bother. You are probably wasting the repair because you are already close to the max you can fix it up. Wait for the item to wear out a little more and then repair it.

When you repair an item, you essentially destroy one just like it. As a rule, always repair your highest condition item using the lowest condition one in your inventory. Those really low condition items aren't much use to you, and can't be sold for very many Caps, so they are most useful as spare parts. That said, scavenging a higher condition item will effect a larger repair.

SCIENCE

S.P.E.C.I.A.L. Statistic: Intelligence

The Science skill represents your combined scientific knowledge. Science is primarily used during the hacking minigame, to determine your chance of accessing restricted computers, also known as terminals. The Science skill is a requirement for more perks than any other skill.

REQUIRED SKILL LEVEL	AVAILABLE PERK	REQUIRED CHARACTER LEVEL
40	Entomologist	4
50	Nerd Rage!	10
50	Robotics Expert	12
60	Cyborg	14
80	Computer Whiz	20

Tip

Hacking is delightfully simple, as long as you perform this neat trick: Assuming your Science allows you to hack, bring up the garbled code, locate the "real words," select a word with your cursor, and try it. Continue this until you have one try left. Then back out of the terminal without finishing the hack, and start again. This way you can "infinitely" hack the terminal until you choose the correct word. Each hacking attempt will reset the password and all the words you can guess. Use this technique, and you'll never lock a terminal again!

SMALL GUNS

S.P.E.C.I.A.L. Statistic: Agility

The Small Guns skill determines your combat effectiveness with all conventional projectile weapons, specifically the 10mm Pistol, Silenced 10mm Pistol, 1mm Submachine Gun, .32 Pistol, Scoped .44 Magnum, Chinese Pistol, Sawed-Off Shotgun, Chinese Assault Rifle, Assault Rifle, BB Gun, Combat Shotgun, Hunting Rifle, Lincoln's Repeater, Sniper Rifle, Dart Gun, Railway Rifle, and any unique variants of these weapons. As this skill increases, so does your accuracy and damage with all of these weapons, both in and out of V.A.T.S. mode.

REQUIRED SKILL LEVEL	AVAILABLE PERK	REQUIRED CHARACTER LEVEL
60	Concentrated Fire	18

SNEAK

S.P.E.C.I.A.L. Statistic: Agility

The higher your Sneak skill, the more likely you are to remain undetected while crouched. When you're crouched, and stationary or moving slowly, you're even harder to spot. Sneak is also used to successfully steal an item or pick someone's pocket, and the skill is incredibly useful in a combat situation. Any attack made while you are hidden is a Sneak attack critical, which can do more than twice as much damage as a regular critical.

REQUIRED SKILL LEVEL	AVAILABLE PERK	REQUIRED CHARACTER LEVEL
60	Mister Sandman	10
50	Silent Running	12
80	Ninja	20

SPEECH

S.P.E.C.I.A.L. Statistic: Charisma

The Speech skill governs how much you can influence someone through dialog, and gain access to information they might otherwise not want to share. Generally, the higher your Speech, the more likely you are to succeed at Speech challenges, or extract information from someone who has a low disposition toward you.

UNARMED

S.P.E.C.I.A.L. Statistic: Endurance

The Unarmed skill is used for fighting without a weapon, or with the few weapons specifically designed for hand-to-hand combat, such as the Brass Knuckles, Power Fist, Spiked Knuckles, Deathclaw Gauntlet, and any unique variants of these weapons. As a general rule, if you're close enough to an opponent, you'll always hit them; your Unarmed skill and unarmed weapon combined determines how much Unarmed Damage you inflict. Unarmed also allows you to use your bare hands to block an attack. The higher the skill, the more damage is absorbed.

REQUIRED SKILL LEVEL	AVAILABLE PERK	REQUIRED CHARACTER LEVEL
70	Paralyzing Palm	18
80	Ninja	20

Perks Overview

Perks are benefits that are more specific to your character development, and allow much more focused specialization in a chosen field. Perks vary greatly in their benefit, and between four and seven perks are added to the available list every two levels, as well as a "substitute" perk called Intense Training (see below). In many cases, you also have to have certain minimum attributes or skills to be able to pick a perk. Remember that when you level up, you can always choose a perk you could have picked at an earlier time. You can also choose to enhance some perks an additional "rank" instead of picking a new one. The following chart shows what perks are awarded, and when:

LEVEL	AVAILABLE PERK #1 (RANKS)	AVAILABLE PERK #2 (RANKS)	AVAILABLE PERK #3 (RANKS)	AVAILABLE PERK #4 (RANKS)	AVAILABLE PERK #5 (RANKS)	AVAILABLE PERK #6 (RANKS)	AVAILABLE PERK #7 (RANKS)
2	Black Widow (1) / Lady Killer (1)	Daddy's Boy / Daddy's Girl (3)	Gun Nut (3)	Intense Training (10)	Little Leaguer (3)	Swift Learner (3)	Thief (3)
4	Child at Heart (1)	Comprehension (1)	Educated (1)	Entomologist (1)	Iron Fist (3)	Scoundrel (3)	—
6	Bloody Mess (1)	Demolition Expert (3)	Fortune Finder (1)	Gunslinger (1)	Lead Belly (1)	Toughness (1)	—
8	Commando (1)	Impartial Mediation (1)	Rad Resistance (1)	Scrounger (1)	Size Matters (3)	Strong Back (1)	—
10	Animal Friend (2)	Finesse (1)	Here and Now (1)	Mister Sandman (1)	Mysterious Stranger (1)	Nerd Rage! (1)	Night Person (1)
12	Cannibal (1)	Fast Metabolism (1)	Life Giver (1)	Pyromaniac (1)	Robotics Expert (1)	Silent Running (1)	Sniper (1)
14	Adamantium Skeleton (1)	Chemist (1)	Contract Killer (1)	Cyborg (1)	Lawbringer (1)	Light Step (1)	Master Trader (1)
16	Action Boy (1)	Better Criticals (1)	Chem Resistant (1)	Tag! (1)	—	—	—
18	Computer Whiz (1)	Concentrated Fire (1)	Infiltrator (1)	Paralyzing Palm (1)	—	—	—
20	Explorer (1)	Grim Reaper's Sprint (1)	Ninja (1)	Solar Powered (1)	—	—	—

Tip

Look down the following list of perks before you begin adventuring, and look at the perks that require the same prerequisites. For example, Child at Heart and Scoundrel both require Charisma of 4+, so you should seriously look at both of them. To know the requirements for a higher-level perk is to be forward-thinking, allowing you to obtain associated perks at the earliest possible time.

INTENSE TRAINING

Level Available: 2
Ranks Available: 10
Requirements: None (Always available)

With the Intense Training perk, the player can sacrifice a standard, ability-enhancing perk and instead choose to put a single point into any of his/her S.P.E.C.I.A.L. statistics. This is usually done to qualify for a perk, although it can be done for any reason.

Tip

A possible plan is to figure out the two or three Primary Statistics you want to focus on, keep them at around 7 so you can balance out the rest of your stats, and then locate the Bobblehead for your preferred stats, as well as employing this Intense Training perk. A few levels in, you could have bumped your stats up to 9+, and be seeing the benefits. Naturally, these are at the cost of taking the available perks.

Raising a S.P.E.C.I.A.L. point can sometimes be very useful, and sometimes not. You must figure out what the "knock-on" effects are. Remember that raising a S.P.E.C.I.A.L. point also increases corresponding Skill points, so consider that an bonus.

Recommended examples of using Intense Training is to raise Luck (increased criticals and sometimes increased Skill points), Intelligence (extra Skill point every time you level up) and Strength (additional Carry Weight).

Some experts believe that Intense Training isn't worth bothering about because the benefits of raising a statistic aren't as profound as other perks. The notable exception is raising a statistic to make a particular perk available to you. Some of the perks have requirements. For example, if you really want Mysterious Stranger, that requires a Luck of six or higher. If you have a Luck of five, use Intense Training to raise that Luck score so that next time, Mysterious Stranger is an option.

BLACK WIDOW/ LADY KILLER

Ranks Available: 1
Requirements: None

With the Black Widow perk, a female player inflicts an extra 10% damage to all male NPCs encountered and gains access to special dialog options with them.

With the Lady Killer perk, a male player inflicts an extra 10% damage to all female entities encountered and gains access to special dialog options with them.

There are more male NPC enemies than female ones, so Black Widow is generally more useful than Lady Killer.

DADDY'S BOY/ DADDY'S GIRL

Ranks Available: 3
Requirements: Intelligence 4+

Just like dear old dad, you've devoted your time to intellectual pursuits. You gain an additional 5% to both the Science and Medicine skills.

- Rank 1: +5 Science skill increase, +5 Medicine skill increase
- Rank 2: +10 Science skill increase, +10 Medicine skill increase
- Rank 3: +15 Science skill increase, +15 Medicine skill increase

GUN NUT

Ranks Available: 3
Requirements: Agility 4+

You're obsessed with using and maintaining a wide variety of conventional firearms. With each rank of the Gun Nut perk, you gain an additional 5% to the Small Guns skill and Repair skill.

- Rank 1: +5 Small Guns increase, +5 Repair increase
- Rank 2: +10 Small Guns increase, +10 Repair increase
- Rank 3: +15 Small Guns increase, +15 Repair increase

Because Small Guns and Repair are two of the most popular skills, this perk is a favorite of most new players.

LITTLE LEAGUER

Ranks Available: 3
Requirements: Strength 4+

Years of playing little league baseball in the Vault have honed a couple of related abilities. You gain an additional 5% to both the Melee and Explosives skills.

- Rank 1: +5 Melee skill increase, +5 Explosives skill increase
- Rank 2: +10 Melee skill increase, +10 Explosives skill increase
- Rank 3: +15 Melee skill increase, +15 Explosives skill increase

SWIFT LEARNER

Ranks Available: 3
Requirements: Intelligence 4+

With the Swift Learner perk, you gain an additional 10% to Experience Points (XP) whenever they are earned. Obviously, this perk is best taken at an early level. Although this seems like a great idea, there are downsides. You need to employ this early, to become a little more powerful a little quicker. The other issue is that you have a variety of more exciting perks to choose from, with a variety of superb abilities.

- Rank 1: Modify experience +10%
- Rank 2: Modify experience +20%
- Rank 3: Modify experience +30%

THIEF

Ranks Available: 3
Requirements: Agility 4+, Perception 4+

With each rank of the Thief perk, you gain a one-time bonus of 5% to the Sneak and Lockpick skills.

- Rank 1: Modify Sneak skill +5, Modify Lockpick skill +5
- Rank 2: Modify Sneak skill +10, Modify Lockpick skill +10
- Rank 3: Modify Sneak skill +15, Modify Lockpick skill +15

Level 4 Perks

CHILD AT HEART

Ranks Available: 1
Requirements: Charisma 4+

With this perk, you are much more likely to receive a friendly greeting when dealing with children. This opens special dialogue options when dealing with them. "Children" are characters under the age of 16, and are found in Little Lamplight, Grayditch, Tranquility Lane, Rivet City, Canterbury Commons, the Republic of Dave, and other scattered locales.

Are you planning on using your Speech challenges a lot, and doing as little fighting as possible? Then take this perk. It's only useful in a few places, such as Little Lamplight.

COMPREHENSION

Ranks Available: 1
Requirements: Intelligence 4+

With this perk, you gain one additional Skill point bonus when reading Skill Books. This is thoroughly recommended if you plan on searching every nook and cranny for Skill Books. Because there are 13 different types of Skill Books, you could theoretically raise your skills by +50 points instead of +25 if you find all 324; an incredible amount!

Take this as early as you can. Because you receive +2 when you read each Skill Book instead of +1, save your Skills Books until after you learn this perk.

Are you finding Skill Books, but haven't chosen Comprehension yet? Stop! Wait until you level up and choose more perks, and pick it!

EDUCATED

Ranks Available: 1
Requirements: Intelligence 4+

With the Educated perk, you gain +3 more Skill points every time you advance in level. You can spend these points on anything; perhaps placing them in skills you normally wouldn't choose. Choose this only at Level 4, because there are diminishing returns the longer you leave it. Seriously consider taking this now.

Although +3 Skill points may not seem like a lot at first, these add up quickly. By Level 20, you'd have 48 additional points.

ENTOMOLOGIST

Ranks Available: 1
Requirements: Intelligence 4+, Science 40+

With the Entomologist perk, you inflict an additional 50% damage every time you attack an insect: normal, giant, mutated, or otherwise. Affected creatures are Giant Ant, Giant Ant Queen, Radroach, Radscorpion (all genuses).

When you first encounter Giant Radscorpions, you'll soon learn to fear them. If you plan on wandering the Capital Wasteland and finding everything out this, these perk can come as a major relief.

IRON FIST

Ranks Available: 3
Requirements: Strength 4+

With this perk, you inflict an additional 5 points of Unarmed damage per rank.

- Rank 1: Modify Unarmed damage +5
- Rank 2: Modify Unarmed damage +10
- Rank 3: Modify Unarmed damage +15

The damage you inflict makes this a must-have for Unarmed specialists only.

SCOUNDREL

Ranks Available: 3
Requirements: Charisma 4+

You use your wily charms to influence people. Each rank in Scoundrel perk raises your Speech and Barter skills by 5%.

- Rank 1: Speech skill +5, Barter skill +5
- Rank 2: Speech skill +10, Barter skill +10
- Rank 3: Speech skill +15, Barter skill +15

Level 6 Perks

BLOODY MESS

Ranks Available: 1
Requirements: None

With the Bloody Mess perk, you inflict an extra 5% damage with any weapon to any opponent, and explode them spectacularly upon death.

The benefits of this perk are more visually appealing (or unappealing) than useful, but the spectacular gore-ballets are a sight to see!

DEMOLITION EXPERT

Ranks Available: 3
Requirements: Explosives 50+

With each rank of this perk, your Mines, Grenades, and Missile Launcher inflicts +20% damage.

As expected, if you're concentrating on Explosives as a Secondary skill, or you use the Big Gun Missile Launcher, take this perk. A true expert can place a series of Bottlecap Mines in the path of a Behemoth and bring it down single-handedly, without resorting to a Fat Man!

FORTUNE FINDER

Ranks Available: 1
Requirements: Luck 5+

With the Fortune Finder perk, you gain a keen sense of locating Nuka-Cola Caps. These are located in safes, desks, cabinets, and the usual places to look.

Although this is tempting (as it's great to find approximately twice the normal number of Caps in containers), it might be worth waiting a couple of levels until you can take Scrounger, and begin to collect a large amount of ammo. Ammo nets you a lot more Caps when you sell it, and you can also use it in combat.

GUNSLINGER

Ranks Available: 1
Requirements: None

With the Gunslinger perk, you gain a 25% better chance to hit in V.A.T.S. with any one-handed ranged weapon. These include the Alien Blaster, Laser Pistol, Mesmetron, Plasma Pistol, 10mm Pistol, Silenced 10mm Pistol, 10mm Submachine Gun, .32 Pistol, Scoped .44 Magnum, Chinese Pistol, Sawed-Off Shotgun, Dart Gun, and any unique variants of these weapons.

Consult the Weapons chart (page 41), and view the stats for some of the more powerful one-handed weapons, like Sydney's 10mm Submachine Gun or the .44 Scoped Magnum.

Your V.A.T.S. hit percentage rises considerably (for example, a 40% chance becomes a 50% chance), and you can drop foes at a distance with easily, reliably, and without wasting ammunition.

LEAD BELLY

Ranks Available: 1
Requirements: Endurance 5+

With the Lead Belly perk, you take 50% less radiation poisoning when drinking from an irradiated water source. These include sinks, toilets, faucets under water towers, and any lakes and rivers such as the Potomac.

If you're ignoring the Medicine skill in favor of others, you'll end up drinking a lot of irradiated water to survive (using sinks to drink from, for example). Take this perk to lessen the rad poisoning you receive as a result. This is also good if you don't stock up on Stimpaks, and you're wandering the Wasteland. There's always a nearby faucet, toilet, or pool to sip from.

TOUGHNESS

Ranks Available: 1
Requirements: Endurance 5+

With the Toughness perk, you gain +10 to overall Damage Resistance. However, this cannot exceed the normal maximum of 85.

+10 to Damage Resistance of any kind? This is like having free armor! Is there any reason not to immediately take this perk? No!

Level 8 Perks

COMMANDO

Ranks Available: 1
Requirements: None

With the Commando perk, you gain a 25% better chance to hit in V.A.T.S. with any rifle. For example, a 40% chance becomes a 50% chance. These include the Plasma Rifle, Laser Rifle, Chinese Assault Rifle, Assault Rifle, Hunting Rifle, Sniper Rifle, Railway Rifle, and any unique variants of these weapons.

This is arguably advantageous over Gunslinger (so you may wish to wait and choose this) if you're using rifles and other two-handed weaponry. Later in the adventure, two-handed weapons tend to be much more powerful, and this perk becomes even more advantageous. For now, are you using V.A.T.S. and guns? Then take this perk!

IMPARTIAL MEDIATION

Ranks Available: 1
Requirements: Charisma 5+

If you have the Impartial Mediation perk, you gain an extra 30% to Speech, so long as you can maintain a neutral Karma.

The bonus to your Speech is massive, but maintaining neutral Karma is more difficult than you might think. You must be careful to weigh up your actions, and check the guide for advice during a quest.

Certain clothing items also increase proficiency in Speech challenges (such as Button's Wig and Grimy Pre-War Business-wear), so by changing your clothes, combined with this perk, you could boost your Speech when you need to.

RAD RESISTANCE

Ranks Available: 1
Requirements: Endurance 5+

The Rad Resistance perk allows you to—what else?—resist radiation. You receive 25% to Radiation Resistance.

If you're ignoring Rad-X before you go wading into water, simply take this perk once instead, and sell the Rad-X you find.

SCROUNGER

Ranks Available: 1
Requirements: Luck 5+

Just as the Fortune Finder perk increased the Caps you find, the Scrounger perk grants access to more ammunition from safes, desks, cabinets, etc.

This is generally thought to be a better option than Fotune Finder, because you have the flexibility of finding more ammunition, which can be sold or expended in battle, instead of simply finding Caps. You will find much more ammunition though, and the exact number varies depending on the type.

SIZE MATTERS

Ranks Available: 3
Requirements: Endurance 5+

With the Size Matters perk, you gain +15 to Big Guns skill for every rank.

- Rank 1: Big Guns +15
- Rank 2: Big Guns +30
- Rank 3: Big Guns +45

This is the biggest permanent Skill point bonus of any perk, and you can take it three times! Employ it if you're focusing on Big Guns, or if you want to use them later in your adventure, and want to quickly add up to +45 points.

Remember! You can add fewer points to Big Guns with the knowledge that when this perk becomes available, you can quickly increase it. Use this perk to raise your Big Guns skill, and assign Skill points to other abilities.

STRONG BACK

Ranks Available: 1
Requirements: Strength 5+, Endurance 5+

With the Strong Back perk, you can carry 50 more pounds of equipment.

Do you enjoy Big Guns, Bartering, or stealing everything you come across? Or perhaps you like wearing heavy armor? Then employ this so you can hold more, fire more, and make more Caps, and can take the punishment while you're at it!

Level 10 Perks

ANIMAL FRIEND

Ranks Available: 2
Requirements: Charisma 6+

With the Animal Friend perk, you never have to worry about being attacked by an animal (normal, mutated, or otherwise) again; unless of course, you attack first! The animals in question are Brahmin, Dogs, Mole Rats, and Yao Guai. If you're adventuring in the Wasteland, don't want the problem of being overrun by animals, and are willing to forfeit the XP for killing animals, then take this. The second rank is worth taking just to coax a band of Raiders into following you to a Yao Guai den!

This is very useful when you're playing the game on Very Hard, and need all the help you can get; especially in areas with Deathclaws and Yao Guai. Great for mid-level and higher characters. It's like having your own pet Yao Guai in the wasteland to help fight the Enclave!

- Rank 1: Animals won't attack unless provoked.
- Rank 2: Animals attack your adversary with you (but not against another animal).

FINESSE

Ranks Available: 1
Requirements: None

With the Finesse perk, you have a higher chance to score a critical hit on an opponent in combat; by 5% (or five Luck points). Or, to put it another way, this increases your critical hit chance as if your Luck were five points higher. Usually this doubles the base chance of a critical.

Do you enjoy inflicting critical hits during combat? Then always take this, and combine it with Better Criticals and a high Luck statistic.

HERE AND NOW

Ranks Available: 1
Requirements: None

The Here and Now perk immediately grants you an additional experience level, complete with all the advantages that brings.

This is useful if you're only two levels away from a perk you really must have, or you're simply impatient. The downside is that by the time this is available, there are many incredible perks to choose from instead. Note you have to be lower than Level 20 to take this perk.

MISTER SANDMAN

Ranks Available: 1
Requirements: Sneak 60+

With the Mister Sandman perk, you can instantly kill any adult human you encounter while they're sleeping. This includes Ghouls, and it is advantageous to be Sneaking. You receive the associated XP for each throat-slit.

Can't seem to fathom why anyone would take this perk? Then you haven't heard the legends of a stealthy man who killed an entire city of sleeping inhabitants in a single night. That man had a Mister Sandman perk. Unfortunately, there are only a limited number of places where you might find this useful.

MYSTERIOUS STRANGER

Ranks Available: 1
Requirements: Luck 6+

When you possess this perk, a Mysterious Stranger occasionally appears during V.A.T.S. combat. The Mysterious Stranger remains long enough kill that opponent, and then departs as mysteriously as he arrived. You only see the Mysterious Stranger in V.A.T.S. mode.

If at the end of a V.A.T.S. attack, your opponent has less than 150 points of health, there is a 10% chance the Mysterious Stranger will show up and finish him off. This perk is most useful if your game is set to a higher difficulty.

This is also a perk to take for sheer entertainment value, but it's useful in battle nevertheless; you save on ammo and APs, and he takes the head-shot for you.

NERD RAGE!

Ranks Available: 1
Requirements: Intelligence 5+, Science 50+

You've been pushed around for long enough! When your Health drops to 20% or less overall, your Strength is raised to 10, and you gain +50 to Damage Resistance. This is an impressive amount, so don't just think of this perk being for those skilled in non-combative abilities. It can get you out of an otherwise tight jam.

If you have a high Endurance, you naturally have a fair amount of Health, so this perk lasts a lot longer. This is good if you're playing this adventure on a higher difficulty.

Life Giver is another perk that works well with this, giving you more Health and thus making the effects of Nerd Rage! last longer.

NIGHT PERSON

Ranks Available: 1
Requirements: None

With the Night Person perk, you gain +2 to Intelligence and +2 to Perception (up to a maximum of 10) when the sun is down, technically between 6 PM and 6 AM. This benefit continues into areas that aren't outside. Check your Pip-Boy's Clock for the correct time.

This perk does not affect Skill points earned when you level up.

Level 12 Perks

CANNIBAL

Ranks Available: 1
Attribute Requirements: None

With the Cannibal perk, you can feed on corpses to regain health. You must be Sneaking to attempt this, and every time you feed, you lose Karma. If this disgusting act is witnessed, expect to be attacked.

For each Corpse Eaten: Health [+25], Karma [-1]

The delicious flavor of human flesh is perfect if you're planning on creating a character with a large negative Karma. This is a great way to gain Health without having to increase your radiation poisoning. Make sure you're not being watched, as you might be attacked for being...well, a disgusting freak.

FAST METABOLISM

Ranks Available: 1
Requirements: None

With the Fast Metabolism perk, you receive 20% more healing when using a Stimpak.

When used with the Medicine skill, you can increase your Health by a spectacular amount. If you're focusing on Unarmed or Melee skills, this perk is especially useful.

LIFE GIVER

Ranks Available: 1
Requirements: Endurance 6+

With the Life Giver perk, you gain an additional 30 Health immediately.

PYROMANIAC

Ranks Available: 1
Requirements: Explosives 60+

With the Pyromaniac perk, you inflict 50% more damage with fire-based weapons. These weapons are the Flamer (and unique variant), "Firelance" Alien Blaster, Zhu-Rong v418 Chinese Pistol, Nuka-Grenade, and Shishkebab.

You must take this perk if you have a character focused on any of these weapons.

This basically turns the Flamer into an even-more-deadly weapon, Nuka-Grenades into one-hit-kill projectiles, and makes the Shiskebab the finest Melee weapon in the Wasteland.

ROBOTICS EXPERT

Ranks Available: 1
Requirements: Science 50+

With the Robotics perk, you gain 25% damage against any robot. But, even better, if you can manage to Sneak up on a hostile robot undetected, activating that robot will permanently shut it down.

Employ this if you have a very high Sneak skill, so you can easily disrupt any mechanoids. Remember to destroy it afterward for the XP and loot! You gain a few conversation options when speaking with more friendly robots, too.

SILENT RUNNING

Ranks Available: 1
Requirements: Agility 6+, Sneak 50+

With the Silent Running perk, speed no longer factors into a successful Sneak attempt, and you gain an additional +10 percent to Sneak. Before this perk, moving quickly while crouching made more noise than moving slowly while crouching. After this perk, you can crouch and move in for the kill without any noise problems whatsoever. Remember you still have to Sneak for this to be effective.

If you're focused on Unarmed, Sneak, or Melee, this is a must-have choice.

SNIPER

Ranks Available: 1
Requirements: Perception 6+, Agility 6+

With the Sniper perk, your chance to hit the opponent's head is 25% higher in V.A.T.S.

If you're always attempting headshots, make sure to combine this with Commando or Gunslinger to create a lethal long-range killing machine.

ADAMANTIUM SKELETON

Ranks Available: 1
Requirements: None

With the Adamantium Skeleton perk, your limbs receive only 50% of the damage they normally would. Your overall Health isn't affected. It allows you to heal with Stimpaks longer before you have to find a bed.

This isn't as useful as it first appears, because most adventurers aren't constantly crippling themselves. However, if you're falling from rocks and hurting your limbs, take this perk.

CHEMIST

Ranks Available: 1
Requirements: Medicine 60%+

With the Chemist perk, any Chems you take last twice as long. The Chems in question are: Ant Queen Pheromones, Buffout, Jet, Mentats (all flavors), Med-X, Psycho, RadAway, Rad-X, Stealth Boy, and Ultrajet.

If you're focusing on the use and abuse of Chems, you must take this perk.

Try combining Jet, Psycho, and Med-X with this perk and you can take on the toughest of foes, until the Chems wear off.

CONTRACT KILLER

Ranks Available: 1
Requirements: None

Once you have the Contract Killer perk, you can loot an ear from the corpse of any good character (human or Ghoul). You can then sell this ear to an "evil" vendor for Caps.

The vendor in question is Littlehorn and Associates. They have a field office—actually, more of a shack—in the Scrapyard [Location 6.03]. A very low proportion of the following enemies are classified as "good": Wastelander, Brotherhood of Steel member, inhabitant of a settlement, slave or abolitionist, scavenger, trader, doctor, repairer, non-feral Ghoul.

There aren't that many good characters around here, unfortunately.

Ear   5 Caps (per ear)

CYBORG

Ranks Available: 1
Requirements: Science 60%+, Medicine 60%+

You have used your amazing scientific and medical knowledge to make permanent enhancements to your body. The Cyborg perk instantly adds +10% to Damage Resistance, Poison Resistance, and Radiation Resistance, plus Energy Weapons skill. This is arguably one of the most generally useful perks around; it's like having free armor, too!

Even if you're concentrating on a violent fighter, it is almost worth raising your Medicine and Science skills enough to obtain this perk. Definitely take this if you're using Energy Weapons.

LAWBRINGER

Ranks Available: 1
Requirements: None

Once you have the Lawbringer perk, you can loot a finger from the corpse of any defeated evil human or Ghoul character. You can then sell this finger to a "good" vendor for Caps. Speak to Sheriff Lucas Simms in Megaton [Location 8.03] about this.

The vendor in question resides in the Regulator Headquarters [Location 6.A]. The following enemies are classified as "evil": Enclave Officer, Enclave Scientist, Enclave Soldier, Raider, Slaver, and Talon Company Mercenary. There are lots of evil sorts.

 Finger   5 Caps (per Finger)

LIGHT STEP

Ranks Available: 1
Requirements: Agility 6+, Perception 6+

When you have the Light Step perk, you never set off enemy Mines or Traps.

If the prospect of treading into one more Mine, Bear Trap, or Trip Wire infuriates you, take this perk. It is useful if you're Sneaking about, too.

Of course, you can simply take extra care, and read this guide to find out where the majority of Traps are. Forewarned is forearmed!

MASTER TRADER

Ranks Available: 1
Requirements: Charisma 6+, Barter 60+

With the Master Trader perk, prices of all bought items from vendors (including Scavengers, traveling Merchants, and Traders in settlements) are reduced by 25%.

If you are still having Caps problems by Level 14, take this perk. Otherwise make another choice.

Level 16 Perks

ACTION BOY/GIRL

Ranks Available: 1
Requirements: Agility 6+

With the Action Boy perk, you gain an additional 25 Action Points that can be used in V.A.T.S.

An extra 25 APs is a huge increase, and can often mean an extra attack in V.A.T.S. with your favorite weapon. Everyone that uses V.A.T.S. should consider taking this perk.

BETTER CRITICALS

Ranks Available: 1
Requirements: Perception 6+, Luck 6+

With the Better Criticals perk, critical hits do 50% more damage. Note that this does not mean you score critical hits more frequently.

If you're concentrating on delivering particularly adept killing blows, of if your character has a high Luck or has taken the Finesse perk, this is an essential addition.

CHEM RESISTANT

Ranks Available: 1
Requirements: Medicine 60+

With the Chem Resistant perk, you are 50% less likely to get addicted to Chems. The Chems in question are: Buffout, Jet, Mentats (all flavors), Med-X, Psycho, and Ultrajet.

This perk is an obvious choice for the Chem user and abuser. Pair this with Chemist and you can really enhance your attacks!

TAG!

Ranks Available: 1
Requirements: None

The Tag! perk allows you to select a fourth skill to be a Tag skill, which instantly raises it by 15 points.

If you've ignored a skill for too long that you really want to try, or want to raise a skill to a higher level (such as Lockpicking, so you can go from unlocking Average to Hard locks), take this.

Level 18 Perks

COMPUTER WHIZ

Ranks Available: 1
Requirements: Intelligence 7+, Science 70%+

With the Computer Whiz perk, you receive a special bonus whenever hacking a computer. If you are locked out of a computer, you can attempt to hack it one more time. This includes terminals you've locked yourself out of.

Because you can quit out of any terminal before you run out of chances and start again, this is of limited value.

CONCENTRATED FIRE

Ranks Available: 1
Requirements: Small Guns 60+, Energy Weapons 60+

With the Concentrated Fire perk, you gain an automatic +5% to hit a body part, when that body part is targeted again, your hit chances are further increased, until you run out of Action Points or stop aiming at that limb.

Take this if your character has a large number of Action Points, and the weapon you're using has a low AP rating.

If you've already taken Commando, Gunslinger, and/or the Sniper perks (which shorten your foes' life expectancy severely), the usefulness of this perk comes into question.

- Targeting 1st Time: normal %
- Targeting 2nd Time: +5%
- Targeting 3rd Time: +10%, et cetera.

INFILTRATOR

Ranks Available: 1
Requirements: Perception 7+, Lockpick 70+

With the Infiltrator perk, you gain a special bonus whenever you pick a lock. If a lock is broken, and can't normally be picked again, you can attempt to pick it one more time. This includes locks you've broken with a "Force Lock" attempt. You can't do this a third time, though!

You might simply wish to perfect the Lockpicking minigame instead of taking this perk. This is of limited value.

It also saves you precious Bobby Pins. Force the lock once, and if that doesn't work, try to pick it, rather than the other way round.

PARALYZING PALM

Ranks Available: 1
Requirements: Unarmed 70+

With the Paralyzing Palm perk, you can access a special unarmed V.A.T.S. palm strike. A hit with the palm strike paralyzes the opponent for 30 seconds. You must be completely unarmed to perform this strike, although you can have Brass Knuckles or even the Deathclaw equipped.

Essentially a death sentence for the enemy, freezing them for 30 seconds allows you to re-equip, and bring down a foe at your leisure. Excellent! This is a must-have perk for Unarmed-based characters.

Level 20 Perks

EXPLORER

Ranks Available: 1
Requirements: None

With the Explorer perk, every Primary Location on your World Map is revealed, and you can Fast Travel to it.

Although slightly less necessary because you have complete maps of the Wasteland in this guide, this perk allows you to quickly find every major location. It also makes a great reference if you plan on playing through again with a new character.

NINJA

Ranks Available: 1
Requirements: Sneak 80+, Melee Weapons 80+

The Ninja perk grants you the power of the fabled shadow warriors. When attacking with either Melee or Unarmed, you gain a +15% critical chance on every strike. Sneak attack criticals do 25% more damage than normal.

If you're planning a Melee / Unarmed and Sneak character, this is the zenith of your capabilities.

GRIM REAPER'S SPRINT

Ranks Available: 1
Attribute Requirements: None

Slay a target in V.A.T.S. and all your Action Points are restored when you exit.

If your character already has a high number of Action Points, you could easily clear a room of foes with this perk. Superb!

SOLAR POWERED

Ranks Available: 1
Requirements: Endurance 7+

With the Solar Powered perk, you gain an additional 2 points of Strength when in direct sunlight, and the ability to slowly regain Health.

Don't underestimate the sheer impressiveness of Health regeneration! If you're exploring the Wasteland at length, and can find a mattress to sleep on each night, this is a fine perk to take.

You regenerate 1 point every 10 seconds in sunlight. This does not heal limb damage. It is excellent in combination with Adamantium Skeleton.

Quest-Related Perks

The following perks are available only once you've succeeded impressively—or failed spectacularly—in a specific quest.

POWER ARMOR TRAINING

MAIN QUEST: Picking up the Trail

Ranks Available: 1
Requirements: Learn the subtleties of Power Armor maneuvering from Paladin Gunny at the Citadel.

You are now skilled in Power Armor, and can wear the following Armor types: Outcast Power Armor, Brotherhood Recon Armor, Brotherhood Power Armor, Enclave Power Armor, Tesla Armor, and any unique variants of these items.

DREAM CRUSHER

MISC QUEST: The *Wasteland Survival Guide*

Ranks Available: 1
Requirements: Convince Moira Brown to stop writing her survival guide

No high-minded ideal or frivolous dream can stand before your cold, unfeeling logic. The road to Hell may be paved with good intentions, but the express lane is paved with ruthless efficiency.

- Enemy attackers' critical hit chances are reduced by 50%.
- You get a 30% discount on Moira's trade items.

RAD LIMB HEALING

MISC QUEST: The *Wasteland Survival Guide*

Ranks Available: 1
Requirements: Achieve critical rad poisoning during one of your research chapter field studies.

Something Moira did during the operation changed you. When suffering from advanced radiation poisoning (400+), crippled limbs automatically regenerate.

JUNIOR SURVIVOR

MISC QUEST: The *Wasteland Survival Guide*

Ranks Available: 1
Requirements: Complete fewer than 5 bonus objectives in this quest. Answer Moira's questions in one of five different ways to obtain one of the five different variants to this perk.

- Standard: +2% Poison Resistance, +2% Radiation Resistance, +5 Health
- Smart: +2% Poison Resistance, +2% Radiation Resistance, +2 Medicine, +2 Science
- Tough: +2% Poison Resistance, +2% Radiation Resistance, +2 Damage Resistance
- Sly: +2% Poison Resistance, +2% Radiation Resistance, +2 Sneak, +2 Speech
- Snide: +2% Poison Resistance, +2% Radiation Resistance, +1% Critical Chance

SURVIVOR EXPERT

MISC QUEST: The *Wasteland Survival Guide*

Ranks Available: 1
Requirements: Complete between 5 and 8 bonus objectives in this quest. Answer Moira's questions in one of five different ways to obtain one of the five different variants to this perk.

- Standard: +4% Poison Resistance, +4% Radiation Resistance, +10 Health
- Smart: +4% Poison Resistance, +4% Radiation Resistance, +4 Medicine, +4 Science
- Tough: +4% Poison Resistance, +4% Radiation Resistance, +4 Damage Resistance
- Sly: +4% Poison Resistance, +4% Radiation Resistance, +4 Sneak, +4 Speech
- Snide: +4% Poison Resistance, +4% Radiation Resistance, +2% Critical Chance

SURVIVOR GURU

MISC QUEST: The *Wasteland Survival Guide*

Ranks Available: 1
Requirements: Complete 9 or more bonus objectives in this quest. Answer Moira's questions in one of five different ways to obtain one of the five different variants to this perk.

- Standard: +6% Poison Resistance, +6% Radiation Resistance, +15 Health
- Smart: +6% Poison Resistance, +6% Radiation Resistance, +6 Medicine, +6 Science
- Tough: +6% Poison Resistance, +6% Radiation Resistance, +6 Damage Resistance
- Sly: +6% Poison Resistance, +6% Radiation Resistance, +6 Sneak, +6 Speech
- Snide: +6% Poison Resistance, +6% Radiation Resistance, +3% Critical Chance

TRAINING — BESTIARY — MAIN QUEST — MISC. QUESTS — TOUR — COMPLETION — APPENDICES

ANT MIGHT

 MISC QUEST: Those!

Ranks Available: 1
Requirements: Choose this from Doctor Lesko upon successful completion of this quest.

Your body has been genetically enhanced with the strength and flame resistance of the Grayditch Fire Ants! Your Strength has increased by 1 and you are now 25% resistant to fire.

ANT SIGHT

 MISC QUEST: Those!

Ranks Available: 1
Requirements: Choose this from Doctor Lesko upon successful completion of this quest.

Your body has been genetically enhanced with the perception and flame resistance of the Grayditch Fire Ants! Your Perception has increased by 1 and you are now 25% resistant to fire.

WIRED REFLEXES

 MISC QUEST: The Replicated Man

Ranks Available: 1
Requirements: Rewarded by Doctor Zimmer for siding with him during this quest.

Advanced technology from the Commonwealth has increased your reaction speed, giving you a higher chance to hit in a V.A.T.S. Your chance to hit is now 10% higher.

HEMATOPHAGY

 MISC QUEST: Blood Ties

Ranks Available: 1
Requirements: Learn the ways of the Family under the tutelage of Vance.

This perk allows you to regain 20 Health (instead of 1) by consuming Blood Packs.

BARKSKIN

 MISC QUEST: Oasis

Ranks Available: 1
Requirements: Shoot an exposed heart in an underground cavern so it sprays on you.

You've been infected by Harold's strain of F.E.V. and your skin is now as hard as tree bark. Your Damage Resistance is now +10, and Endurance is +1.

Plans for Successful Character Development

 Tip

First, make the most important Game Save of all; complete the Main Quest: Escape! up to the point where you're just about to leave the Vault, but haven't exited the door at the end of the natural tunnel. Save your game now! Then, when you're ready to try a second character, simply begin at this point, without replaying your childhood. You can change all your stats and skills, and even your face, hair, and gender, before you leave.

In order to create the most proficient and well-rounded character you can, follow this in-depth tactical advice:

1. CROSS-REFERENCE YOUR STATISTICS WITH YOUR SKILLS

Your seven S.P.E.C.I.A.L. attributes obviously affect your Skill points and allocations, so make sure you're placing points in the correct Primary Statistic. Are you planning on using Small Guns? Then bump up your Agility to 7 or higher. Thinking about using Repair, Medicine, or Science? Increase your Intelligence to the same level.

Tip

Every point added to a S.P.E.C.I.A.L. attribute raises its associated skills by two points. However, the Luck attribute is different. It affects all skills, but only at half its value. Try to keep your Luck at an odd number to take advantage of this.

LOWERING STATISTICS

One way to get extra points for your statistics is to lower them. Confused? Don't be: By lowering statistics you don't care about, you gain extra points to add to the ones you do. However, make sure you are willing to live with the consequences!

For each statistic, look at the associated skills and the derived characteristics. If you don't care about them, consider lowering that statistic to a three or even a one.

The one statistic you should never lower is Strength. How much you can carry is critical to all types of characters. Even if you aren't planning on fighting much (good luck with that!), you'll need Strength to carry your ill-gotten gains back from the various lairs and hidey-holes.

Similarly, think twice before lowering Endurance or Intelligence. The first controls your Health, which means you die more easily with a lower Endurance. The second controls how many Skill points you get to distribute when you go up in level. Your character will advance slower with a low Intelligence.

RAISING STATISTICS

You'll get five extra points to add to statistics. While it may sound great to add all five to a single statistic such as Strength or Endurance, it's rarely a good idea. There are just too many benefits to the other statistics to ignore them.

Don't pick the statistics to raise based on their associated skills; pick them based on the Derived Characteristics or perks you may want. These are much more important. The fact that your Big Guns skill goes up by a few points when you raise Endurance pales in

comparison to your Health going up by 20 points for each point of Endurance.

The "big three" Statistics for most character types are Strength, Endurance, and Intelligence. Not that the others aren't good too, but these are important for all characters. Consider raising each of them to at least a seven. If you have points left over, Agility or Luck are the next best choices for combat-oriented characters.

2. CHOOSE A PRIMARY COMBAT SKILL

"You must be proficient at something. That something should be Small Guns, if you're a newcomer to the Capital Wasteland."

- Choose one skill and make it your primary means of defeating foes.
- Make sure it is one of your three Tag skills.
- Raise it very quickly at early levels.
- Later in your adventure, this skill may not be your main combat choice, so always have a Secondary Combat skill you're adding to as well.
- If you are playing your first few characters, Small Guns is an excellent (and recommended) choice.
- With Small Guns, there are plentiful weapons you can use throughout your adventure.
- Unarmed or Melee Weapons skills are also viable. However, there are very few truly effective melee weapons at higher levels; so be prepared to bolster a Secondary Combat skill in the future.
- Unarmed and Melee Weapons are excellent skills because you can sell the ammo you pick up, but don't use, for a large number of Caps.

The following chart should help you decide a good Primary Combat skill to take:

COMBAT SKILL	PRACTICALITY	ADVANTAGES	DISADVANTAGES
Small Guns	Extremely	Guns and ammo are plentiful.	None, really.
Melee Weapons	Very	Weapons are plentiful, no ammo required.	You have to get close to use them.
Unarmed	Moderate	No weapon needed.	Until you get Brass Knuckles, you don't do a lot of damage.
Energy Weapons	Moderate	Highly accurate.	Guns and ammo are hard to find early in the game.
Big Guns	Poor	Weapons do lots of damage.	These suckers are heavy! Ammo can be hard to find.
Explosives	Poor	Lots of damage to multiple opponents.	Can't use them up close.

Tip

If you want to use Unarmed, Energy Weapons, Big Guns, or Explosives as a Tag skill, choose a Secondary Combat skill as well to support it.

APPENDICES — COMPLETION — TOUR — MISC. QUESTS — MAIN QUEST — BESTIARY — TRAINING

3. PRIMARY AND SECONDARY COMBAT SKILL COMBINATIONS

"Focus and figure out your key statistics, and three Tag skills before you begin, or you face the prospect of wasted Skill points."

You should be adding points to a Secondary Combat skill as a back-up, in case you (for example) run out of ammunition, or you're facing a very tough opponent.

This should complement your Primary Combat skill, with the potential to "overtake" it (in terms of points allocated) later in your adventure. Most characters who specialize in Small Guns end up pouring points into Energy Weapons at higher levels. Laser Rifles and Plasma Rifles are wickedly powerful, but not readily available at low levels.

Some recommended Primary and Secondary Combat skill combinations are:

Small Guns and Explosives:

- If your Assault Rifle just isn't cutting it against those tougher Mutants, throw in a few Grenades.

Sneak / Melee / Unarmed and Explosives:

- A much more tactical battle plan involves Sneaking around (optionally utilizing a Stealth Boy), and attempting to land a devastating Melee, Unarmed, or Sneak attack.
- Laying plenty of Mines along your escape route allows you to flee if you're overwhelmed or outclassed.
- Remember to disarm and pick up unused Mines afterward.
- The Custom Weapon: Dart Gun is an extremely useful weapon for this combination.

Unarmed and Energy Weapons:

- Energy Weapons are expensive, but often have a faster rate of fire and lower Action Point cost than Small Guns.
- Punch weaker enemies and collect all the bullets so you can afford the Energy Weapon Ammo and quality armor for your unarmed skirmishes.
- High Agility with this combination is helpful, as you can land four punches and laser shots in while in V.A.T.S.

"Anything" and Big Guns:

- "Anything" includes any of the previously listed skills used in combinations.
- Be sure to pick the Strong Back perk for this build, because Big Guns are heavy.
- Big Guns tend to eat up ammo quickly, but inflict a lot of damage.
- Big guns are extremely satisfying to shoot, and the Flamer is excellent against armored enemies.
- Unless you start making the Custom Weapon: Rock-it Launchers very early, you won't find much use for this skill for a while, however.

4. THE THIRD TAG SKILL: REPAIR YOUR OWN ORDNANCE

Repair is the best skill available to you. You can construct better quality weapons and armor. This in turn, allows you to withstand and inflict more damage, thus spending fewer Caps on costly Stimpaks. You also tend to run into groups of enemies that carry the same gun; so managing your loot becomes much easier. Are you seeing scattered Assault Rifles everywhere, and don't know what to do with them? Then use them to Repair your own Assault Rifle, so you have at least two of your favorite weapons in great condition.

Now you've figured out a Primary Combat, Secondary Combat, and Repair as the recommended skills to add points to, make these your three Tag skills.

To sum up:

COMBAT SUPPORT SKILL	MOST USEFUL WITH	NOTES
Repair	Small Guns, Melee Weapons, Energy Weapons, Big Guns	Weapons in good repair do more damage. They also sell for more caps.
Sneak	All skills	Getting close to (or getting past) an opponent without begin detected is always an advantage.
Medicine	Melee Weapons, Unarmed	If you have to take a few hits to make the kill, being able to heal yourself better becomes very important.
Explosives	Melee Weapons, Unarmed	It's handy for all combat skills, but particularly for these. Gives you some ability to attack at a distance, or to plant devastating Mines.

5. ADVICE ON OTHER SKILLS

The flexibility and wide variety of skills means there are no "correct" skills to choose. Every skill has its own set of benefits. Below are skills that aren't so obvious, but are worth taking a serious look at.

MEDICINE

This increases the effectiveness of Stimpaks, Rad-X, and RadAway. When you only have to use half the Stimpaks it would normally take to heal yourself, you have more Caps to purchase cooler items. You also get to employ that Medical knowledge during quests, and unlock some excellent perks.

SNEAK

Sneak is another highly useful combat support skill. Attacks on unsuspecting targets do extra damage, not to mention the advantage of not being shot at yourself. Unless you like playing the guns-a-blazing kind of character, you should give serious consideration to Sneak as a Tag skill.

Unarmed or Melee attacks while using Sneak are difficult to complete successfully, but the Sneak critical hit bonus is massive.

It is easiest to Sneak up on an opponent that's unaware (rather than alert), then enter V.A.T.S. and "line up" Sneak attacks on multiple enemies.

Think Sneak isn't devastating enough? A headshot from a Combat Shotgun is likely to drop a Deathclaw if your skill is high enough, and you're close enough.

SPEECH

Are you adventuring with a more cerebral plan in mind? Then succeeding in Speech challenges when interacting with others can be very useful. It can also halt hostile posturing in those you're speaking with (and occasionally create them!).

A high Speech skill opens interesting doors (both verbal and literal) that allow you to complete quests in ways that would otherwise by difficult or impossible to accomplish.

Check the Main and Miscellaneous Quests in this guide for all the examples of Speech challenges. And if you want to witness the results, load up points on this skill. It is used often.

SCIENCE

You can occasionally find interesting outcomes to your problems by using Science to hack terminals or pass skill checks.

Want to witness a turret malfunction where it sprays the enemies it was designed to protect with gunfire? Need to unlock certain doors or safes with a connected terminal? This is your skill, and you'll use it often. It also unlocks some useful perks.

The difference between this and Lockpick is that there are fewer terminals to hack than there are locks to pick. Also the rewards for hacking a terminal tend to be less immediate or tangible.

LOCKPICK

Lockpick is clearly the most advantageous non-combat skill.

Do you hate being locked out of an area you're exploring? Want to know what every storage room or secret area contains? Then thoroughly read through this guide, or place some points into Lockpick.

This guide also flags the difficulty level of every major lock on safes, doors, footlockers and Ammo Boxes.

You can open the majority of these if your Lockpick skill is 50. Relatively few locks require 100 Lockpick skill.

This chart summarizes some key points:

NON-COMBAT SKILL	USEFULNESS	ADVANTAGES
Lockpick	Extremely	Loot is frequently locked away.
Science	Moderate	Terminals control turrets, which can then fight for you. They may also reveal important information.
Speech	Moderate	You can sometimes persuade people to do your bidding, thereby avoiding more difficult choices, or getting better rewards for you actions.
Barter	Fair	Caps are always useful. You can buy better guns and more ammo. However, if Caps are what you want, it's always possible to clean out everything in a lair and sell it, or to steal the items you need.

6. ALLOCATING SKILL POINTS

A recommended plan for newcomers to the Wasteland is to increase your Primary Combat, and Repair skills up to around 75 points as soon as possible. Then add to your Secondary Combat skill and all other preferred skills as needed.

Although specific situations vary, a good rule to follow is to spend around 60–75% of your Skill Point allowance on your Primary Combat and Repair skills until they reach around 75.

A common mistake is to raise your skills all the way to 100 as soon as possible. Certain collectible items (Bobbleheads and Skill Books) and perks permanently raise your skills, and these become useless if your skills are already at the maximum.

Consult this guide; learn where a nearby Bobblehead and a few Skill Books related to your preferred skills are, so you can obtain them as early as possible to further increase your Skill points.

7. DRESS FOR SUCCESS

"When attempting to Repair a weapon, massacure a Mutie camp, or Barter with a merchant, you must dress appropriately."

Another excellent point to remember is that some outfits increase skills (including Repair, Lockpick, and Science). Change into these outfits before attempting adventuring that requires these specific skills.

A good example: Raise your Lockpick skill to 45. Then wear apparel that gives you +5 to Lockpick (such as the Vault 101 Utility Jumpsuit). You can now pick Average locks.

Also remember that every point of Perception adds +2 to Lockpick. Remember to check your statistics to ensure you've placed enough points to help enhance your associated skills.

The Vault 101 Utility Jumpsuit adds +5 to Repair as well, and you find it during **Main Quest: Escape!**, so don't forget to pick it up!

8. GROWING YOUR CHARACTER

As your character gains levels, you get a chance to add more Skill points. The best part about this is that if you made a mistake when creating your character, you can correct it very quickly. If you put points into Melee Weapons because you wanted to beat your opponents to a pulp, but then discovered that you had more fun shooting them, within a level or two you can switch over to being skilled with Small Guns instead.

ADDING SKILL POINTS

Most characters will have at least 15 points to spread around. Think about what kinds of actions you attempted since the last time you leveled up. Think about the actions you want to do. Place your points into those skills.

For the most part, split your points relatively evenly between your three Tag skills until Level 5 or 6. You chose these Tag skills because you wanted to use them, so make sure they're at least above 50.

Two important skills to raise are Lockpick and Science. These skills have threshold values that are important. Every 25 points opens up a new class of locks or terminals. So you want Lockpick to be 25 early in the game to access those locks. Science isn't quite as important, but you should get it to 25 early on as well.

Between Levels 5 and 10, keep focusing on your Tag skills, getting them into the 70s. Good secondary skills to put some points into are Lockpick and Medicine. Getting Lockpick up to 50 will

make the majority of the locks available to you. Medicine gives you more benefit from Stimpaks, which is important for combat.

Above level 10, stop raising your skills when they get into the 80s. You will find clothing or armor that will give you bonus points. You may find Bobbleheads or Skill Books that can raise your skills. Most skills can be raised with perks more efficiently than with Skill points. It can be frustrating to raise a skill to 100, and then find something that gives a bonus you can't use. The difference between a 90 and a 100 in a skill isn't enough to be worth wasting the points.

Character Examples

Here are some examples of character archetypes, where a series of complementary statistics, skills, and perks help create a well-rounded and extremely adept character.

PART 1: CHARACTER ARCHETYPES

ARCHETYPE #1: THE QUICK-HANDED ASSASSIN
Statistics Focus: Agility, Luck
Skills Focus: Unarmed
Perks Focus: Iron Fist (Rank 3), Action
Boy, Ninja, Finesse, Better Criticals, Paralyzing Palm.

Slot a Power Fist on this berserker, and watch him inflict massive amounts of crushing damage! The Paralyzing Palm is useful here too, if you want to simply use your fists. V.A.T.S. is extremely effective using this archetype, and if you paralyze a foe, there's a chance you'll kick him while he's crumpled on the floor.

ARCHETYPE #2: TWISTED FIRESTARTER
Statistics Focus: Endurance
Skills Focus: Big Guns
Perks Focus: Pyromaniac

A simple combination to achieve, as long as you're carrying a Flamer. Burn hordes of Ghouls in seconds, or keep your fire concentrated and topple a larger, more vicious foe in moments. Locate the Unique Weapon: Burnmaster Flamer in the Franklin Metro for even more power!

ARCHETYPE #3: HOTTER POTATO
Statistics Focus: Perception
Skills Focus: Explosives
Perks Focus: Demo Expert, Pyromaniac

Once you learn how to build Custom Weapon: Nuka-Grenades, use them to take down just about any foe with a single toss. Clustered foes are great to flambé, as the splash damage sets them on fire, too. Don't get over-eager; you'll feel a world of pain if you're caught in your own explosion!

ARCHETYPE #4: THE PHANTOM DARTER
Statistics Focus: Agility
Skills Focus: Sneak, Small Guns
Perks Focus: Gunslinger, Silent Running

This often-overlooked combination requires you to build a Custom Weapon: Dart Gun. This weapon cripples the legs on any foe that isn't a robot. Better yet, it fires silently, which is perfect for keeping foes away from you. However, the dart impact alerts

enemies. This means you can shoot a dart at a wall, cause a guard to leave his post to investigate, and Sneak on by.

ARCHETYPE #5: CONDITION CRITICAL
Statistics Focus: Luck
Skills Focus: Small Guns, or Energy Weapons
Perks Focus: Finesse, Better Criticals

Many of the Energy Weapons have a higher critical hit percentage than Small Guns, although the Sniper Rifle and Custom Weapon: Railway Rifle are excellent choices too. Become an adept shot at inflicting critical hits with this archetype. Complete **Miscellaneous Quest: The Wasteland Survival Guide** with Snide responses to obtain the Survival Guru with a critical hit bonus as well.

PART 2: CHARACTER UBER-ARCHETYPES

Below are three example characters that are completely tweaked for easy Wasteland survival:

"SNIPER"
Theme: Sneaks around and shoots guys from a distance.
Tag Skills: Repair, Small Guns, Sneak
S.P.E.C.I.A.L.: ST 6, PE 7, EN 5, CH 1, IN 7, AG 7, LK 7
Notable Perks: Gun Nut, Bloody Mess, Commando, Finesse

"THUG"
Theme: Runs up and smacks foes around the head.
Tag Skills: Explosives, Melee Weapons, Repair
S.P.E.C.I.A.L.: ST 7, PE 7, EN 7, CH 3, IN 6, AG 5, LK 5
Notable Perks: Little Leaguer, Toughness, Strong Back

"BOXER"
Theme: Runs up and smacks foes around the head...with his fist.
Tag Skills: Big Guns, Unarmed, Sneak
S.P.E.C.I.A.L.: ST 7, PE 4, EN 7, CH 3, IN 7, AG 5, LK 7
Notable Perks: Iron Fist, Toughness, Size Matters

General Training and Advice

Now that you've built the ultimate Wasteland survivor, it's time to detail some information on other facets to your adventure, primarily related to your Pip-Boy, and the challenges you face during your expedition.

INITIAL MENU INFORMATION

Assuming you've read the Instruction Manual, you should have a basic grasp of how your Pip-Boy, game menus, and basic maneuvering all works. However, there are a couple of additional pieces of information you may find useful:

GAME DIFFICULTY

You can choose to increase or decrease the game difficulty. Higher difficulty means opponents do more damage and you do less damage in combat. You also get more Experience Points for kills at higher difficulty levels. Lower difficulty means opponents do less damage and you do more. However, lowering the difficulty does not change your Experience Point awards for kills.

DIFFICULTY	OPPONENT'S DAMAGE	PLAYER'S DAMAGE
Very Easy	50%	200%
Easy	75%	150%
Normal	100%	100%
Hard	150%	75%
Very Hard	200%	50%

SETTINGS TWEAKS

If you're seeing blue, you might pick out foes a little more easily, depending on your eyes.

Saving: It is usually better to Save your game often and constantly. But it also benefits you greatly if you save just before you attempt an epoch-making change to your fate. If you read one of the quests, and learn there's an upcoming Speech challenge, you should Save just before the challenge, so you can try again if you fail. This is also advisable before any large-scale confrontations or explorations take place. Aim to have dozens of Saved Game slots used up. Well over 400 were used in the creation of this guide alone!

Display Tweaks: Although most of this is to your preference, there's a lot to be said for fiddling with your brightness (although technically, this could be seen as cheating). If you're in a darkened tunnel filled with Ghouls, you may wish an ultra-bright image so you can pick out every movement. For the best gameplay, set it as dark as you can while still seeing a difference between the two darkest blocks. Your H.U.D. opacity and color are also strictly related to preference, but some find the blue H.U.D. color to be superior, as the target crosshairs are easier to see during bright light situations. Increase the opacity if you're relying on the crosshairs, too.

KARMA: TWO SIDES OF THE SAME SCALE

OVERVIEW

The General Stats part of your Pip-Boy displays what you have accomplished, along with your Karma. Your Karma is another vital part of your adventuring, as it measures how pleasant or unpleasant you're being, based on previous actions. In short, it's how "good" or "evil" you're being. Karma affects a variety of elements, from how you're treated by others, to the Followers who agree to join you, to areas of the Wasteland you can visit.

Although you can't see it, you begin your adventure with a "value" of zero. This value increases with positive actions, and decreases with negative ones, on a sliding scale. Karma can range from -1,000 (true evil) to +1,000 (an absolute saint). Here's how you're judged, based on your Karma value:

KARMA VALUE	TYPE	
-1,000 to -750		Very Evil
-749 to -250		Evil
-249 to +249		Neutral
+250 to +749		Good
+750 to +1,000		Very Good

> **Caution**
>
> You can't check specifically on your Karma "value"; your character title is the only clue you have (outside of reactions by others).

HOW TO RAISE AND LOWER YOUR KARMA

Numerous actions affect your Karma:

ACTION	KARMA EFFECT
Killing an Evil character or creature	None
Killing a Very Evil character or creature	+100 Karma
Murdering† a Neutral or Good creature	-25
Murdering† a Neutral or Good character	-100 Karma
Stealing from a Neutral or Good character, or from a non-evil faction	-5 Karma per item
Donating Caps to any church	Dependent on Caps donated
Performing a "good" action in a Freeform Quest	At least +50 Karma
Performing an "evil" action in a Freeform Quest	At least -50 Karma

† "Murder" is defined as an unprovoked attack.

HOW TO RAISE AND LOWER YOUR KARMA (QUESTS)

Your actions throughout the course of your adventuring allow you an infinite number of choices, and many have a Karmic element to them. Consult the Main and Miscellaneous Quest chapters to see the most important actions you can take.

TRAINING — BESTIARY — MAIN QUEST — MISC. QUESTS — TOUR — COMPLETION — APPENDICES

DAY-TO-DAY CHANGES IN PERCEPTION

Karma affects you in four general ways:

- It modifies the reactions and dialogue options of certain individuals you meet.
- It determines the accessibility to certain locations within the Wasteland. For example, you can enter the Slaver stronghold of Paradise Falls without problems with a low enough Karma.
- If you are Very Evil or Good, you may be attacked by enemies of the opposing Karmic range. For example, if you're Very Good, expect to be stalked by Talon Company Mercs.
- Be warned: Your Karma also influences the type of ending you receive when your expedition is over!

RAMIFICATIONS OF HAVING EVIL KARMA

The Slavers of Paradise Falls welcome you and your unpleasant ways into their fold.

Any player who reaches a Karma of -250 or below—and is thereby considered "evil"—should expect some unique occurrences. These are:

- Access to Paradise Falls, including all services offered there.
- Ability to purchase the schematics for the Dart Gun, from Pronto in Paradise Falls.
- Ability to hire two "evil" Followers: Jericho (Megaton), and Clover (from Paradise Falls).
- Easier Speech challenges with "evil" characters you speak with.
- Access to "evil" Karma titles and corresponding achievements.
- Three Dog the D.J. has some specific words for you.
- General characters you meet may react to your Karma during conversations.

RAMIFICATIONS OF HAVING NEUTRAL KARMA

Although it is sometimes difficult to stay on this path, if you maintain a neutral Karma of between -249 and +249, you should expect some different unique occurrences:

- Raiders will always attack you.
- Ability to hire two "neutral" Followers: Butch (from Vault 101, but met in Rivet City), and Sergeant RL-3 (bought from Tinker Joe in the Wasteland near Tenpenny Tower).
- No chance of getting attacked by either a "good" or "evil" hit squads.
- Access to "neutral" Karma titles and corresponding achievements.

RAMIFICATIONS OF HAVING GOOD KARMA

A faultless and Vaultless existence still involves the taking of life, specifically scummy Raider life.

Any player who reaches a Karma of 250 or more is considered "good" and can benefit from the following:

- Ability to hire two "good" Followers: Fawkes (Vault 87) and Star Paladin Cross (the Citadel).
- Raiders will always attack you.
- More difficult Speech challenges with "evil" characters you speak with.
- Access to "good" Karma titles and corresponding achievements.
- Three Dog the D.J. has some specific words for you.
- General characters you meet may react to your Karma during conversations.
- Very Good: Access to small gifts given out by "good" characters (such as Caps, Ammo, Food, and other common items).

EXPERIENCE POINTS AND KARMA

Finally, here are all the titles based on your character's level and Karma.

LEVEL	XP REQUIRED	EVIL KARMA TITLE (-250 OR LESS)	NEUTRAL KARMA TITLE (-250 TO +250)	GOOD KARMA TITLE (+250 OR MORE)
1	0	Vault Delinquent	Vault Dweller	Vault Guardian
2	200	Vault Outlaw	Vault Renegade	Vault Martyr
3	550	Opportunist	Seeker	Sentinel
4	1,050	Plunderer	Wanderer	Defender
5	1,700	Fat Cat	Citizen	Dignitary
6	2,500	Marauder	Adventurer	Peacekeeper
7	3,450	Pirate of the Wastes	Vagabond of the Wastes	Ranger of the Wastes
8	4,550	Reaver	Mercenary	Protector
9	5,800	Urban Invader	Urban Ranger	Urban Avenger
10	7,200	Ne'er-do-well	Observer	Exemplar
11	8,750	Capital Crimelord	Capital Councilor	Capital Crusader
12	10,450	Defiler	Keeper	Paladin
13	12,300	Vault Boogeyman	Vault Descendant	Vault Legend
14	14,300	Harbinger of War	Pinnacle of Survival	Ambassador of Peace
15	16,450	Urban Superstition	Urban Myth	Urban Legend
16	18,750	Villain of the Wastes	Strider of the Wastes	Hero of the Wastes
17	21,200	Fiend	Beholder	Paragon
18	23,800	Wasteland Destroyer	Wasteland Watcher	Wasteland Savior
19	26,550	Evil Incarnate	Super-Human	Saint
20	29,450	Scourge of Humanity	Paradigm of Humanity	Last, Best Hope of Humanity

EXPERIENCE POINTS

GAINING XP

From the smallest victory to the most terrifying feat, your experience is the key to a happy future.

You gain Experience Points (XP) by defeating opponents, completing quests, and performing a few other types of action, such as unlocking doors and safes, hacking terminals, completing a difficult or impressive conversation, and the like. You'll know when you've received XP because it appears on your H.U.D., and you can view your current XP total in your Pip-Boy screen. The previous chart revealed the number of XP it takes to level up from 1 to 20. Once you reach Level 20, your XP reads as "Maxed."

Should you complete the entire series of Main Quests in the advantageous manner described in this book, you're likely to reach Level 13–14 by the end of it.

QUEST	EXPERIENCE POINTS AWARDED
Baby Steps	0
Growing Up Fast	0
Future Imperfect	0
Escape!	300
Following in His Footsteps	200
Galaxy News Radio	400
Scientific Pursuits	500
Tranquility Lane	600
The Waters of Life	700
Picking up the Trail	800
Rescue from Paradise	900
Finding the Garden of Eden	1,000
The American Dream	1,100
Take It Back!	1,200 ‡

‡ Because your expedition ends once this quest is over, this value is irrelevant.

This means you should be thinking about augmenting your XP by attempting the 16 different Miscellaneous Quests. These usually award you 300 XP for each one you complete.

Furthermore, you occasionally gain a small amount of XP from Freeform Quests.

Locate each of the World Map markers (each showing a Primary Location) for another 10 XP per location.

THOSE OTHER WAYS TO EARN XP

The most common method of earning XP, aside from quests, is by killing something before it kills you. How much XP you earn varies with the difficulty of your opponent. Values range from 1 point for a Radroach to 50 points for a Deathclaw. Killing NPCs can also get you up to 50 XP each.

You also receive experience points for performing other actions. The following chart details the XP you are likely to gain from completing other actions, and the difficulty of those actions:

ACTION #1	ACTION #2	ACTION #3	ACTION #4	DIFFICULTY	XP AWARDED
Kill an Opponent	Pick a Lock	Hack a Computer	Speech Challenge	Very Easy	0
Kill an Opponent	Pick a Lock	Hack a Computer	Speech Challenge	Easy	10
Kill an Opponent	Pick a Lock	Hack a Computer	Speech Challenge	Average	20
Kill an Opponent	Pick a Lock	Hack a Computer	Speech Challenge	Hard	30
Kill an Opponent	Pick a Lock	Hack a Computer	Speech Challenge	Very Hard	50

GETTING THE MOST OUT OF YOUR XP

There are a few ways to increase how many experience points you get. Playing the game at a higher difficulty level gives you bonus XP. Although it's a low-down, dirty-rotten trick, raising the difficulty level before fighting an easy-to-kill creature or NPC will give you extra XP from it. Just don't forget to set it back, or the next Yao Guai may take you out!

Getting the well-rested bonus earns +10% XP. You can only get this bonus by sleeping in a rented bed or a bed in a place you own, such as your house in Megaton or your room in Tenpenny Tower. The bonus lasts for 12 hours of game time.

The Swift Learner perk can get you 10% extra XP for every rank of it you take. This bonus applies to all XP rewards, not just killing things.

Note

Experience Points do not "scale" with your level, as all of the entities and challenges you encounter offer roughly the same degree of challenge no matter when you attempt them.

Tip

Double-shot XP: Many doors and safes can be unlocked by Lockpicking or using Science to hack a nearby terminal. Obtain extra XP by hacking the terminal, but do not disengage the lock. Then pick the lock on the door to get a "double shot" XP from it.

Mapping the Capital Wasteland

This section deals with how to maneuver around this vast and frightening landscape without turning up dead in a drainage ditch 20 feet from Springvale. Use the following plans, and make sure you're already familiar with Fast Travel and plotting your own route markers.

The World Map: every single Primary Location is revealed once you discover it, or obtain a specific perk.

The Local Map provides more detail and some entrances you don't see on the World Map.

Because you have a large Guide Poster, and a Tour chapter dedicated to revealing every single location in the Wasteland, you have a distinct advantage when you decide to explore. However, the benefits of Fast Travel and locating new areas are dependent on employing some specific cunning tactics:

1. Always use Vault 101 or the nearby settlement of Megaton as your "base" until you familiarize yourself with your surroundings. Figure

TRAINING — BESTIARY — MAIN QUEST — MISC. QUESTS — TOUR — COMPLETION — APPENDICES

out how far a location is from Megaton, as this is the safest place you can return to.

2. Start to use visual cues to instantly figure out where you are. That large skyscraper to the south? That's Tenpenny Tower [Location 7.14]. Now that you know this, you can learn what adjacent locations there are, and if any of them interest you.

3. Begin to use smaller visual cues to figure out specifically where you are. That crashed monorail with small Raider Camp and the bathtub [Location 2.N]? That's just north of Germantown Police Headquarters [Location 5.01]. Begin to "fill in" the topography of the area to prevent you from getting lost.

4. Use the compass. It's there for a reason, and that reason is to show you where you're generally headed. Make sure you use your Pip-Boy's Route Marker, too.

5. It's a sound plan to race to discover a single location, explore it before backtracking to a safer environment, and when you wish to return, Fast Travel back to that location and explore in a concentric circle out from this "secondary base camp."

6. The guide refers to Primary and Secondary Locations with a latitude and longitude position, and a number. These don't appear

in the game; they are simply there so you can keep track of the hundreds of locations in the Wasteland.

INSIDE THE D.C. RUINS

Matters take a turn for the complicated when you enter the massive derelict ruins of D.C. itself. Here, the only way to reach the more significant internal locations, such as the Mall and Arlington Cemetery, is to head underground through a series of linked underground tunnels that were part of the old Metro and sewage systems. The Tour chapter separates these so you know which areas are accessible from the "outside" Wasteland, and which aren't.

Tip

You might wish to visit Reilly and complete her quest because she awards you a GeoMapper that rewards you with 20 Caps for each location you uncover. It's a great way to add Caps for doing something you're already attempting!

Other Pip-Boy Functionality

A QUICK NOTE ON NOTES

You should know by now that your Pip-Boy's Note section is more than just a collection of texts; there are Holotapes to listen to, and some quests don't update until you read or listen to a Note you've picked up.

RADIO WAVES

Tuning in to hear the latest in Enclave Propaganda or the howls of mad Three Dog can provide comfort during those long treks across a darkened Wasteland (and can also attract attention; switch off your Radio when Sneaking). But are you aware of the other Radio Stations you can pick up on your Pip-Boy?

Recon Craft Theta Beacon
5,000m radius. Garbled static and odd chatter serve only to bewilder and enthrall.

Chinese Radio Beacon
3,000m radius. A random mini-encounter.

People's Republic of America Radio
16,000m radius. The voice of Red China, operating out of Mama Dolce's.

Vault 101 Emergency Frequency
25,000m radius. Assuming a catastrophic issue with Vault 101, this crackles into life.

Agatha's Station
Entire Wasteland. Complete the Agatha's Song quest, and listen to sweet, lilting violin music.

Ranger Emergency Frequency
7,000m radius. A mayday for Reilly's remaining Rangers, stuck on top of the Statesman Hotel.

Radio Tower Signal (9)
Dotted across the landscape are shut-down radio masts. Activate them, and some may have a signal (usually Morse code stating the name of the mast and an S.O.S.) you can triangulate to locate a hidden area.

THE FLASHLIGHT

The benefits of a Flashlight far outweigh the negatives, unless you like stumbling around Ghoul-infested tunnels in the dark.

If you're having difficulty seeing where you're going, ensure your safety by switching on your Pip-Boy's Flashlight. It allows you to see your surrounding area much more clearly, but at the expense of stealth. Keep this off if you're Sneaking.

The Battle for Wasteland Supremacy

V.A.T.S. AND RUNNING AND GUNNING

V.A.T.S. or run-and-gun? There are benefits using either method, but the real winners employ both to great complementary effect.

Your Vault-Tec Assisted Targeting System is a work of genius. It allows you to pause the action, take in your surroundings without penalty, locate most of your threats—and then kill them. Before you try large-scale battles, perfect the art of flicking between enemies, and enemy parts, learn when to enter V.A.T.S. (as soon as you see an opening, and usually when a head is available to target), and what benefits there are for tagging the various appendages. Best of all, there is a +15% chance of a critical hit with V.A.T.S.

Head: Damage is usually doubled. If the chance to hit the head is more than half that of other limbs, aim there, unless the foe is extra-tough. Otherwise, you are better off aiming for the arms or legs.

Weapon: If your foe is damaging you with a nasty weapon, remove it from play. With an Unarmed Attack in return, you can shrug this off as you rain in the free hits.

Arms: If an opponent needs two hands to hold a dangerous weapon, such as a Minigun, cripple one of them. He will drop the weapon. Even if he picks it up again, his aim will be horrible.

Legs: If you want a more leisurely takedown, strike the legs of foes that are apt to flee, and remain quicker than they are. Dispose of them as you wish. This is a great tactic for Mirelurks, Yao Guai, and Deathclaws.

Control Boxes and Antennae: Robots, turrets, and some insects have these. Once it is destroyed, they will frenzy and attack anything nearby, even their friends. Don't bother with this if you are fighting the creature one on one, because it will just come after you anyway. It's a great tactic for turrets though.

Running-and-gunning also has its benefits. Some weapons are easier to employ in real-time, such as the Flamer. You can also circle-strafe around an enemy, make quick evasive maneuvers in and out of cover, and use your dexterity more easily. However, it is sometimes more difficult to precisely aim, especially at range.

 Tip

• If you're out of Action Points, you can still use V.A.T.S. to excellent effect. Use it to center your aim on a target, even if you have no APs left. Then, without firing, exit V.A.T.S. Your run-and-gun manual aim is now dead-center on your foe. Fire away!

• If you're quick entering V.A.T.S., you can often target an adversary before they throw a Grenade. Shoot the Grenade, either when it's in the air or in the enemy's hand. Detonation in the air causes no harm to you. Detonating in the enemy's hand causes it to explode, resulting in an instant kill if you're battling a Raider.

• Are you trying to avoid confrontation with a foe, and don't want to kill it? Target the legs in V.A.T.S., cripple them both, then out-run the foe. The Custom Weapon: Dart Gun does this to all non-robotic foes and is useful against Yao Guai and Deathclaws. If you are running away, try closing any doors between you and your foes; this slows them down, and prevents them from shooting you.

 Tip

• Hot Key: Your Pip-Boy's Hot Key function, allowing you to place one of eight objects for quick access, is an incredible benefit. Stick your three or four favorite weapons, a variety of Chems, Stimpaks, and Rad-X, and you'll cut down on the time spend raising and lowering your left arm.

WEAPON TYPES

BIG GUNS

Just relying on Big Guns may be stretching your scavenging and combat skills to the limit, but the amusement and devastation these weapons bring makes up for any shortcomings. However, it's always best to leave your Fat Man at home when trudging through narrow interiors; Miniguns and Flamers are a much better bet. Also remember that Missiles take time to strike their target. Judge where your foe will be when your Missile arrives, not where he is at the moment.

ENERGY WEAPONS

The technology of tomorrow, here today! Energy Weapons allow you to dispatch your foes into a pile of dust (which fortunately still yields the same loot). These are very expensive to keep in ammunition. Aside from the Unique variants, the Plasma Rifle is a highly impressive and damaging weapon; when you've upgraded from the Laser Rifle and Pistol you'll see a marked difference in the time it takes to topple a target. Most Energy Weapons are more accurate than old-fashioned guns.

GRENADES OR MINES

Lobbing Grenades as a back-up for your Small Gun fire is an effective combat strategy, and judging distance by checking the hit chances in V.A.T.S. first is always a good plan. Don't forget to pack Pulse varieties, because they dispatch robot adversaries in seconds. Setting up ambushes using mines (of any kind) is always entertaining.

In interior locations, look for a doorway and set a couple there, then provoke an enemy (usually with a 10mm Pistol) and run back past the doorway. You don't set off your own Mines, but your enemy does! A similar trick is available in the city by setting Mines around corners. Finally, for the ultimate kill, place a Mine with Grenades around it; when the Mine detonates the Grenades also explode.

Tip

It is also incredibly satisfying to use Grenades that are attached to enemies (or being held in their hands) against them: Take careful aim, and use V.A.T.S. to check if your target has Grenades hanging from a weapon belt. Then manually hit these for an amusingly violent explosion. Is a Super Mutant or Raider holding a Grenade just prior to lobbing it? Not for long; blast it from their hands, and watch the gore fly!

MELEE WEAPONS

Guns for show; knives for a pro. Take your pick, and test them out on Mole Rats as some of these hand-carried weapons and blades have a slower swing than others. Your first weapon, the Baseball Bat, is reasonably effective. Try it out until you can churn body parts with the Ripper, or graduate to something heavy like the Super Sledge. Don't bother with pool cues, rolling pins, police batons, or nailboards. They just aren't tough enough. As stated previously, you should be attempting the element of surprise using these weapons, not wading in from a distance into a barrage of fire.

SMALL GUNS

A wide variety of Small Guns present copious takedown opportunities for every occasion. Begin with Pistols, before graduating to the 10mm Submachine Gun, a stalwart piece only superseded by the two Assault Rifle types. Ignore the .32 Caliber Pistol and the Chinese Pistol. You are better off selling them than using them. If you're on the Wasteland plains, bring your Hunting Rifle; it's a great long-distance shot. When you find your first Combat Shotgun, treasure it; this is a mid- to close-range monster of a weapon, and fantastic at headshots, as is the .44 Magnum.

If you are using long distance weapons like the Sniper Rifle, it's sometimes better to aim manually rather than using V.A.T.S. The V.A.T.S. chance to hit will be lower than what you can probably do manually. However, you will be giving up the +15% bonus chance for a critical that V.A.T.S. provides. Also, for all long-range attacks, you should be stealthed to get the stealth attack critical bonus.

UNARMED WEAPONS

Due to the small variety of Unarmed Weapons, using Unarmed combat can be challenging. You'll get Spiked Knuckles pretty easily. If you find a Power Fist, you're set for a while. Do what you must to keep it repaired. At higher levels, attempt to construct the Deathclaw Gauntlet as soon as you can. V.A.T.S. is entertaining when you use these weapons, because it is easier to hit, providing you can wade through enemy gunfire. Employ Sneaking to ensure that your attacks land with additional (and critical) force.

Tip

Attack from higher ground; it's always easier to slink back behind ground cover than flee with foes descending after you.

VEHICULAR MANSLAUGHTER

Blowing up vehicles (specifically cars with engines, truck engines, and city coach liners) creates a large and satisfying explosion, and possible chain-reaction if a second vehicle catches fire. This is both useful and problematic—you can catch enemies in the splash damage the explosion generates, but you may accidentally destroy (or move) an item placed nearby. Generally though, attract enemy attention with this technique, or create a cluster of burning metal parts to show you've been here before.

TRAPS

You haven't lived until you've almost died being bombarded by baseballs, or receiving a Brahmin-skull-on-a-chain to the happy sack. Throughout the Wasteland, the more enterprising (and psychotic) of enemies have left a variety of Traps waiting for you. Most can be disarmed if you have a decent Repair skill—yet another reason why Repair is your go-to skill when you're not shooting stuff.

RADIATION

Take a Rad-X before you go wading into any water, or investigating any craters, and you'll shrug off the light radiation. Visiting a wider radiation zone? Then pack a Radiation Suit. Heading over to Vault 87? Then carve your tombstone now; you'll never reach the surface entrance. Let Fawkes do the work and then backtrack.

MINES

Tread slowly and lightly, looking down and rotating until you find your Mine, then disarm it. The Mine is added to your inventory. If you are crouched in the Sneak mode, you can grab them from slightly farther away. If you're happy Sneaking, place Mines in a foe's path, then hide and fire at them to attract their attention. The results are messily effective.

CHAIN TRAPS

Mostly activated by a trip wire, these Traps are mostly set by Super Mutants and Raiders so you know where to look for them. Simply find the trip wire (sometimes difficult if you're being manhandled by these brutes) to deactivate them.

RIGGED SHOTGUNS

These activate two ways: pressure plate or trip wire. Avoid either, or duck in locations you suspect of having these Traps. Or, move around the plate or trip wire, and disarm from the side. You receive a Combat Shotgun and ammo for your troubles.

GRENADE BOUQUETS

Although vicious, the Grenades take a few seconds to detonate, giving you time to flee (usually into a second Trap!). Either disarm the trip wire, or look up and reach the Grenade cluster to bag three Frag Grenades. Or, shoot them from a safe distance.

RIGGED TERMINALS

Always take extra time to inspect terminals, especially ones with a small antenna on the back, used to detonate a Frag Grenade hidden

on the unit itself. This only happens when you try to use the terminal, so approach from the side or rear to disarm it and pocket a Frag Grenade.

BEAR TRAPS

An ancient form of crippling, Bear Traps are nasty and quick to snap, although you can disarm them relatively easily too. There's little point in rearming them; either avoid them completely or risk the injury.

GAS LEAKS

Prevalent in underground tunnels, these are extremely problematic if you employ Energy Weapons. The Shiskebab will also trigger them. Either step around the corner and lob in a Grenade to clear the path, or get up close and personal.

BABY CARRIAGES

Baby carriages are perhaps the scariest Trap of all. A frightening robot head is encased inside, rigged to explode. Disarm it quickly, as soon as you hear the baby cry. There's nothing to take afterward. Another tactic is to retreat—quickly!

BASEBALL PITCHERS

Step up to the plate (in this case, a pressure plate, although trip wires are also common), and expect a dozen baseballs in the guts. These are more of a nuisance than a threat; sidestep to avoid them. Or swing back with a Baseball Bat!

Going on Maneuvers

One of the most important aspects of staying alive in this desolate jungle is to employ a wide variety of tactics: many offensive, some defensive, and all cunning. This section details how to go from subsistence living to thriving.

SNEAKING AND THE STEALTH BOY

Stay hidden, and you can investigate the most dangerous of locations without becoming cannon fodder.

One of the key skills to use when you don't want to attack enemies, or can't (due to a lack of ammunition, low Health, or as part of a quest fulfillment), Sneaking requires you to duck then shuffle around silently, the slower the better. Practice doing this around folks who won't bludgeon you to death with a Sledgehammer, such as the fine people of Megaton. Perfect the technique before creeping around Ghouls, Mirelurks, or other, more hideous abominations. The key is to notice where your foes are facing, and maneuver around so they don't see you, by staying 180 degrees to their rear or behind cover.

If you see the Caution warning on your H.U.D., don't panic. If the target is close by, combat is probably imminent, and you should just shoot him first. If the target is farther away or may have difficulty getting to your position, just sit tight. If you don't move for a while, eventually the warning will return to Hidden and you can resume moving.

Tip

• While Sneaking, if you need to encourage an enemy to move or turn around so you can Sneak past an enemy or light source, try tossing a Grenade or shooting your gun at a distant wall. This causes the enemies to investigate that area. The Silenced 10mm works perfectly for this, because it doesn't give your position away. Remember, you're shooting at the wall, not the foe!

• The Stealth Boy, a device you pick up then activate via your Pip-Boy, turns you almost invisible for a limited amount of time. It's the perfect companion to Sneaking, as it allows temporary invisibility. However, you're still audible!

STEALING

Try stealing a bottle of whiskey at Moriarty's Saloon during the evening drinking session, and see how one light-fingered prank can turn into outright mayhem!

This may lower your Karma slightly, but Stealing items is a great way to add to your inventory. However, it's also a great way to get kicked out of town! With this in mind, you might wish to combine Stealing with Sneaking or a Stealth Boy for really important items. It's only considered Stealing in places where a person or group "owns" the property you have your eye on. Usually you can get away with opening a cabinet and closing it again while being watched, as long as you don't take anything. Otherwise, Steal only if no one is looking. So long as the H.U.D. reads Hidden, you are safe to Steal stuff.

HOSTILE SETTLEMENTS

Outstayed your welcome? You can stand and fight, or fall back, wait three days, and return to the site of the carnage.

If matters start to get out of hand while you're Stealing, or you bring weapons out and begin to take out residents in a settlement, expect a full-on battle, and a massive loss in Karma. If you manage to survive, and flee the area, wait three days.

This is how long it takes for the residents to forget your description and allow you back into town. The only difference is the Slaver township of Paradise Falls. If you start problems there, you'll never end up on friendly terms with the scum that inhabit this place. They will constantly attack you until every last one is wiped from the Wasteland.

APPENDICES — COMPLETION — TOUR — MISC. QUESTS — MAIN QUEST — BESTIARY — TRAINING

PICKPOCKETING

Whether you're planning to become a Psychotic Prankster, or you just want to take a valuable item (usually a key) without killing the individual, Pickpocketing (which is part of your Sneak skill) is the way to go. Start hidden, so you aren't making a fool of yourself, and approach from behind for best results. The value of the item affects the chances of discovery. Don't try to Pickpocket expensive stuff unless you are highly skilled. If you really need to pick a pocket or two, and your Sneak skill isn't so great, use a Stealth Boy. Note that some enemies have to "give" you their preferred items; they aren't available through Pickpocketing. Also, you can't Pickpocket anything the guy has equipped, like his gun or his clothes.

You must try placing a Grenade into the pocket of an unassuming victim. There's a guaranteed (and very messy) death soon after!

SCAVENGING

Objects are hidden is some rather odd, out-of-the-way places. Look everywhere, be vigilant, and master the art of refuse-sifting!

The Wasteland is full of detritus, objects rusting in the irradiated winds, and odd little trinkets. The valuable ones are known as collectibles (and are listed later in this chapter). The rest of them vary in their usefulness. As there are hundreds of items to find, only the most impressive are listed at the end of this chapter. However, you'll need to figure out where to look, and know which more common items are just as essential to your needs.

Any item that appears visibly in the world stays there until you pick it up. Any Ammunition, Health, Chems, and rare items are flagged for collecting during the Tour of the Wasteland chapter.

Any items that appears inside another storage device are almost always randomly generated. This means that if you open the same desk during two different scavenger hunts, you won't find the same items. However, the items you do find are likely to be what you need, such as Ammo, Health, or Custom Weapon parts.

Always check the VAL (Value) of the item you're grabbing, as well as its weight. A Carton of Cigarettes, for example, is worth 50 Caps, and well worth stuffing into your pockets.

Check every desk, filing cabinet, footlocker, shelf, bookcase, safe (on desks, floors, in walls, or floors), dead body or corpse; peer into bathtubs and behind cabinets; and conduct a thorough sweep of your location.

If you're having a hard time finding Ammunition, take the Scrounger perk at Level 8, or Fortune Finder at Level 6.

The main objects to locate are Ammo Boxes and First Aid Boxes. They always contain what they say on the tin! In fact, First Aid Boxes are likely to contain Chems and Bobby Pins too. Remember that some of these boxes are locked.

Aiding and Abetting the Vault Dweller

Now that you've learned some offensive techniques, the final part of this training showcases the benefits you can receive for your hard-earned running, gunning, scavenging, and fast-talking.

TRADING, HEALING, AND REPAIRING

Wandering merchant caravans plod through the massive Wasteland, stopping some impressive settlements along the way. And Arefu.

Now you've collected a pocket-full of Cherry Bombs, and don't want the tart after-taste and radiation poisoning, what are you going to do with them? Well, certain objects are used to create Custom Weapons. Others net you more Caps if sold to a specific Wasteland resident. But most of the time, you'll be trading items with merchants in settlements, dotted around the landscape as scavengers, or wandering in caravans. Certain traders also have rare or unique items to purchase. Or steal!

Your Barter skill reduces the number of Caps an item costs, and increases the Caps an item sells for. If trading is a major part of your plan, you know what to specialize in! Because prices change depending on your skill and the condition of the item, they aren't referenced in this guide.

Almost every trader can also Repair your items up to about 50%. This may sound like a great plan, but this is something you should (and can) do for yourself. It is much more cost-effective if you're

Repairing your own equipment; especially if the nearest trader is miles away from the Deathclaw Sanctuary you've stumbled into! Some Wastelanders can Repair items but aren't interested in trading.

If you're crippled, unhealthy, suffering from radiation poisoning, or addicted to Chems, it's time to seek a doctor. Almost every large settlement has one, and they'll help you out, for the correct (Bartered) price. Or you can do it yourself: any bed heals your crippled limbs and missing Health, and RadAway fixes radiation poison. Unfortunately, only a doctor can cure your addiction to Chems.

> **Tip**
>
> If you can, dispatch the wandering vendors (and their guards) who have Custom Weapon Schematics in their "for sale" inventory. You'll take a Karma hit, but the amount of supplies you get from the vendor, his Brahmin, and his guard will make it worthwhile. Also, you'll get a Roving Trader Outfit [+5 Barter] and sometimes a Roving Trader Cap [also +5 Barter], which you can then wear when you're dealing with other vendors you don't plan on killing...just yet.

TINKERING AT WORK BENCHES

There are 46 Work Benches throughout the landscape. Use these to build a Custom Weapon, providing you have the necessary Schematic and Repair skill. Consult the section on Custom Weapons (page 39) for more information.

SLEEPING (AND WAITING)

There's nothing as refreshing as a few hours' kip on the blood-stained, gore-splattered mattress of a man you just killed; you can't sleep or rest with foes present.

Why sleep? Because you gain Health and heal limb damage, and you can quickly add hours to your day. This is important if you want to travel across the Wasteland during daylight hours, or you're waiting 12 hours for a small child to return with some stolen ammunition. Note that if you pay for a night's rest (at Moriarty's in Megaton or the Weatherly Hotel in Rivet City), or you're using a bed in a residence you own, you receive a "well-rested" bonus, which gives you an additional +10% XP for 12 hours. Finally, remember there are numerous types of beds: from a blood-soaked mattress to a naval cot.

> **Tip**
>
> The best place to quickly heal up is Big Town. There is a bed about two steps from where you land when you Fast Travel there. You can Fast Travel in, rest for a hour, and Fast Travel back.

Why wait? Well, if there are no enemies nearby, and you're not being damaged by radiation (which is the same when sleeping), you can wait around in a location and choose how long (in hours). While you don't gain the Health you would for a sleep, you can "skip time," which is useful if you want to travel during daylight (or night) hours, or you want to enter a store or meet someone who keeps specific hours. Check your Instruction Manual for the key or button to press.

ARMOR AND CLOTHING

Create an outfit for any occasion. This occasion? Hunting down and caving in the skulls of Super Mutants.

In the same way that you created one or two "sets" of weapons for different combat occasions, make sets of armor. The chart at the end of this chapter lists all armor variants and their effects, so you can see whether what you're wearing is the most helpful to your cause. Further augment your armor by Repairing it, adding a helmet, and placing any additional clothing to complete the look.

Once you have your "combat" outfit complete, move on to a secondary one that helps you when speaking to individuals, Bartering, or some other social activity you often attempt. As you can tell, it is important to view the items you pick up on your Pip-Boy to work out their abilities.

> **Tip**
>
> If you're heading into combat, and you're sure you won't get shot, replace heavy armor with something lightweight that gives you bonuses to skills such as Small Guns.

Carrying around some extra outfits can be an immense help, especially as many items weigh next to nothing but have excellent extra effects, such as the Vault 101 Utility Jumpsuit. It only weighs 1, but gives you Lockpick +5 and Repair +5. Many adventurers carry this around the entire time. Whenever combat is over, try switching outfits and Repairing all your items while wearing the jumpsuit at a decent bonus. Try to locate the fabled Button's Wig, too.

HEALTH AND CHEMS

Broaden your palate spectrum with this brave new choice, a particularly gamey taste known as Strange Meat....

By now, you've probably used a Stimpak once or twice, and are wondering what kind of other ingestible items can benefit you. The table out at the end of this chapter shows the statistics for all food, liquor and Chems available in the Wasteland. From here, you can see which of them are best-suited to your style of play, and which cause addiction.

ADDICTION

You ingest a Chem by clicking on it in the inventory, and the effects are immediate. As soon as you become addicted, you must seek a doctor to cure you of your dependency. If you don't, you'll suffer Attribute penalties from withdrawal unless you take more of that Chem. Each time you ingest a Chem, it builds up in your system, increasing the chance of addiction. You can get away with taking it twice before there is a chance for addiction. After that, you need to wait 30 hours for the Chem to be flushed from your system. Then you can take it again safely. This only becomes a problem if you don't have a large supply of that particular Chem, so you might wish to figure out your closest doctor, and have enough Chems, using them only when the situation arises.

Alcohol works differently. Each time you swig beer or wine, there is a 5% chance of addiction, regardless of how many times you drank or how long you waited between drinks. Scotch, whiskey and vodka have a 10% chance of addiction.

STACKING

Although addiction may put you off employing Chems, the "stacking" nature of Chems should let you see the benefits. If you take two Buffouts, for example, the effects last twice as long. Chems don't "stack" with each other, but they do stack with other items. Here's a particularly awesome example:

Swallow a Psycho and some Yao Guai Meat. It increases your damage by +25 and +10 equaling a total of +35 damage. Because same-drug effects don't stack (such as taking 2 doses of Psycho at once), the Psycho+Yao Guai Meat combination is as powerful as you can get for increasing overall damage percentage. If using Unarmed or Melee Weapons, add Buffout to the mix, and your Strength will temporarily increase, resulting in devastating attacks from the combination of drugs.

With this in mind, cross-reference the chart, and you should begin to experiment with different concoctions of Chems, alcohol, and food.

AN ACQUIRED TASTE

Ready for some more exotic food than the Fancy Lads Snack Cakes? Well, aside from stealing fresh fruit in Rivet City's Science Lab, you may wish to head out with a Hunting Rifle and bring down a Mirelurk or two. Four different types of Mirelurk food replenish Health: Hatchling Mirelurk Meat and Mirelurk Cakes add +6 to Health. Mirelurk Meat adds +24, and Softshell Mirelurk Meat add 36. Softshell Mirelurk Meat is the best Health restoring food in the Wasteland. The second best? Human flesh....

A PLACE TO CALL "HOVEL"

Some of the more unhinged Wasteland survivors decorate their rooms entirely in refuse, scavened parts, and even gore and body parts. These people aren't well.

There are two places in the Wasteland where you can become a permanent resident: Megaton and Tenpenny Tower. Unfortunately, to get the Tenpenny Tower suite, you have to blow up Megaton, so you can only own one of them at a time.

However, once you acquire the deeds to your shack (or penthouse suite), you can purchase items and themes for your digs. Consult the Tour chapter for more information.

 Tip

• Top of the list of essential house items is a Nuka-Cola machine. This allows you to insert Nuka-Colas into it, and it then cools them to Ice Cold Nuka-Cola, which give you twice the Health restoration of regular Nuka-Colas.

• Also remember to sleep in your own bed; you receive a "well-rested" bonus to your XP every time!

 Tip

• Travel back to your house routinely to drop off loot and items you may wish to use or sell later. Use different containers in your house for weapons, apparel, and components (for Custom Weapons); this makes it easier to find what you need. If you purchase a Work Bench, having a cache of components readily available means you can make (and profit from) Custom Weapons quickly and easily.

FOLLOWERS

There's no point in becoming a Wasteland hero if no one is there to listen to your excitable ramblings. This is where Followers come in. There are eight individuals, located across the land, that you can hire as a bodyguard, mercenary, supporting fire expert, or scavenger (if they're able to search for you). Remember you have to have a particular Karma level for certain Followers to join you.

The mighty Ghoul Charon (left) and a Wasteland hero (middle) play dress-up together, while Roy Phillips (right) looks on in bemused silence.

As soon as you have a Follower, you can tell them to stay where they are (if you need to explore by yourself), come with you, move closer or farther away during fights, scavenge for different items (if applicable), or leave your service. During their time with you, Followers can (and should) use your weapons, armor, Stimpaks, and anything else you would normally need. Treat them as a trusted companion. Or, try out one of these more esoteric uses for a Follower....

 Tip

• Use a Follower as a "pack-mule." They can carry a large quantity of supplies, so gather as much as you can loot or kill, and load them up. For example, massacre a camp of Raiders, scavenge all their armor and weapons, Repair it all, then hand it over to your Follower. As Assault Rifles and Hunting Rifles are fairly common, have your Follower carry around four of each, before you sell them at a settlement or wandering vendor.

• You can't wear Power Armor yet, can you? But your Follower can, so equip it on them as soon as possible. Then, as soon as you acquire another piece, "trade" and take back the Power Armor, Repairing it with the newly acquired piece. Then "trade" it back in this new condition. Followers take amazing care of this armor. It always remains in the condition it was in when first given and never deteriorates, so it becomes more protective each time you Repair it using a newly looted piece.

FOLLOWER #1: BUTCH

The Serpent King of the Tunnel Snakes

Complete **Miscellaneous Quest: Trouble** on the Homefront and be sure Butch is alive, and the Overseer has stepped down or died, or you've sabotaged the Vault. Journey to the Muddy Rudder bar in Rivet City, and easily convince your old "friend" to join your cause.

FOLLOWER #2: SERGEANT RL-3

Purchase Sergeant RL-3 from a traveling robot salesman called Mister Tinker who randomly roams the Wasteland near the RobCo factory. But the robot follows you only if you're neutral: a soldier can't afford to be too clean or too dirty.

Mechanoid Gutsy reporting for duty

FOLLOWER #3: FAWKES

Although not able to join you immediately, once you're back in the Wasteland after visiting Vault 87, Fawkes is waiting for you, assists in battling adversaries keen on your destruction, and then offers to swing his giant hammer as often as you'll let him.

A hulking great guy to be around

FOLLOWER #4: STAR PALADIN CROSS

Head into the Citadel for the first time and speak with her. If you're suitably Karmic, she agrees to accompany you on a special detachment mission. If you become a little less honorable, and drop to neutral Karma or lower, she returns to base.

An old family friend and combat queen

FOLLOWER #5: JERICHO

Jericho is moping around Megaton, whining about the good old days of killing, and only lightly threatening the patrons of Moriarty's Saloon. If you're evil, you can talk him into resuming his previous career as a "terror of the wastes." He needs "supplies" though.

Old man Raider, and combat veteran

FOLLOWER #6: CLOVER

Gain entrance to Paradise Falls by nonviolent means, speak to Eulogy Jones, and he offers to sell his companion to you. Her near-brainwashed condition enables her to believe you're Eulogy's replacement, and her love is transferred to you.

Lady of the night, putting up a fight

FOLLOWER #7: CHARON

This large Ghoul has nothing to say, until his contract with Ahzrukhal in Underworld is either sold or bought. This either costs you in Caps or Karma. Once the contract is in your possession, you might want to stand well back, because the two Ghouls don't get along.

Indentured killing machine

FOLLOWER #8: DOGMEAT

Barking is heard in the Scrapyard. Raiders are savaged by this hound, who mourns the passing of his previous master. Approach the canine, and Dogmeat follows. Who's a good boy? You are! Who's going to find me some Stimpaks? You are! Woof!

The irradiated man's best friend

> *Note*
>
> You can have Dogmeat plus one other Follower. Hiring a second Follower forces the first one to leave.

SCHEMATICS: CREATING A CUSTOM WEAPON

Your tinkering in the Wasteland shouldn't be limited to fixing your weapon. There are seven truly spectacular (not to mention crazy) weapons available if you have the Repair skill necessary to create them. To do this, you require the Schematic, a Work Bench (46 are dotted across the Wasteland, and all are listed in the Tour chapter), and the proper components for that weapon. The components are listed below, allowing you to collect the part prior to finding the schematic if you wish.

Anyone can create a Custom Weapon. However, you want one that doesn't fall apart after an embarrassingly short amount of time. The weapon's condition is based on your Repair skill, and how many copies of that weapon's schematic you have acquired:

- 1 Schematic: Condition is half your Repair skill
- 2 Schematics: Condition is equal to your Repair skill
- 3 Schematics: Condition is 125% of your Repair skill (up to 100%)

Custom Weapon Schematics are very rare. Only three of each schematic exist for most Custom Weapons (Bottlecap Mine and Rock-It Launcher have four). Generally, one can be bought from a merchant, one can be found in a Wasteland location, and one is given as a reward at the end of a quest. The exact locations are revealed in the Tour chapter.

> *Tip*
>
> Remember to make additional weapons when your original begins to wear out.

BOTTLECAP MINE

A mixture of Cap shrapnel and explosive power makes this deadly. Lay it in the path of an advancing foe for excellent results.

- **Lunch Box**
- **Sensor Module**
- **Cherry Bomb**
- **10 Bottle Caps**

DART GUN

Incredibly powerful and great when facing Deathclaws: As it cripples the legs, you can move faster, and attack without being mauled.

- **Paint Gun**
- **Toy Car**
- **Radscorpion Poison Gland**
- **Surgical Tubing**

APPENDICES — COMPLETION — TOUR — MISC. QUESTS — MAIN QUEST — BESTIARY — TRAINING

DEATHCLAW GAUNTLET

Punching straight through armor and inflicting nasty damage, this is a must for the Unarmed aficionado.

- **Wonderglue**
- **Medical Brace**
- **Leather Belt**
- **Deathclaw Hand**

NUKA-GRENADE

Quantums aren't just for sipping; fashion them into a Grenade with tremendous damage and area of effect.

- **Nuka-Cola Quantum (1)**
- **Turpentine**
- **Tin Can**
- **Abraxo Cleaner**

RAILWAY RIFLE

Aside from impressive damage, this can pin a hapless foe (or a body part) to a nearby surface. Amusement is guaranteed!

- **Crutch**
- **Fission Battery**
- **Steam Gauge Assembly**
- **Pressure Cooker**

ROCK-IT LAUNCHER

When you've run out of ammunition, use whatever is lying around as projectiles. Remember to pick them up and reuse them!

- **Vacuum Cleaner**
- **Firehose Nozzle**
- **Leaf Blower**
- **Conductor**

Tip

If you're using the Rock-it Launcher, look in certain containers to find useful items. There's nothing like firing an Office Fan (somewhat rarely found in Metal Crates) or some Mutilated Skulls and Organs (found only in Gore Bags) into your enemy's face in V.A.T.S. mode! And with the Bloody Mess perk, the entertainment value only increases.... Other entertaining Ammo includes Nuka-Cola Trucks, Garden Gnomes, Toilet Plungers, and of course, the Teddy Bear (especially the extra rare Giant kind).

SHISHKEBAB

If slicing body parts off your foe isn't enough, how about setting them on fire as you do it? The Shiskebab is another vicious close-range beast of a blade!

- **Motorcycle Gas Tank**
- **Lawnmower Blade**
- **Pilot Light**
- **Motorcycle Handbrake**

Tip

Have you thought about selling your creations for a large number of Caps?

COLLECTIBLES

There are many "collectible" items scattered about. These give you an instant bonus to a statistic or skill, can be returned to a specific character in return for Caps, or provide an impressive combat potential. Other items (such as Cartons of Cigarettes or Cave Fungus) simply provide Caps, but these are more general, and aren't related to a specific character. The Tour chapter has the location of each of these collectibles (providing they don't randomly appear).

Note

You can also collect Chinese Assault Rifles to please Pronto, a Slaver merchant.

BLOOD PACKS

Number Available: N/A
Character: Vance, leader of The Family [Location 5.05]

Not particularly useful unless you've taken the Hematophagy perk after completing **Miscellaneous Quest: Blood Ties** (which allows you to receive +20 HP for each Blood Pack consumed instead of +1 HP), or you're bringing them back for Vance, who pays you 15 Caps per Blood Pack. These are scattered about, and randomly placed.

BOBBLEHEADS

Number Available: 20
Character: None

Limited Edition Vault-Tec Bobbleheads have been secreted away in some interesting and out-of-the-way locations, and it's up to you to find them. Seven of them add a point to each of your Primary Statistics. The other 13 add 10% to each of the Skills you can choose. If you own a dwelling, you can even display those you've collected in a rather impressive cabinet!

FAT MEN

Number Available: 9
Character: None

Aside from the Unique "Experimental MIRV" Fat Man, there are 9 of these astonishingly devastating weapons to locate across the blasted countryside. You can occasionally buy one from Flak and Shrapnel's in Rivet City. Naturally, you don't need to find them all, but it helps to use the parts to Repair your main weapon, or you can sell these for around 1,000 Caps per weapon.

FAT MAN MINI-NUKES

Number Available: 71
Character: None

As with the Fat Man itself, the Mini-Nukes that slot into the chute and are fired from the weapon are also in short supply. Fortunately, we've pinpointed where all 71 of them are, so you can locate them and keep your Fat Man handy for the more devastating combat situations, usually involving Behemoths.

FIRE ANT NECTAR

Number Available: N/A
Character: Doctor Lesko, Grayditch / Marigold Station [Location 9.10]

The nectar from a particular strain of Giant Ant has some interesting properties, and the doctor who discovered and genetically engineered the species is hoping to further his research with it. The more he has, the larger the batches of tests he can attempt. He'll pay you Caps for each nectar you bring him, once **Miscellaneous Quest: Those!** is complete.

HOLOTAGS: THE BROTHERHOOD OF STEEL

Number Available: N/A
Character: Scribe Jameson, the Citadel [Location 9.11]

Each of the Brotherhood of Steel Paladins, Initiates, Knights, Captains, and Scribes has their own set of holotags, and Scribe Jameson is keeping track of those unfortunate enough to have died fighting for the cause. As the Wasteland (specifically the D.C. Metro Area) is expansive, you're tasked with finding these holotags, and returning them for a Caps reward.

HOLOTAPES: THE REPLICATED MAN

Number Available: 19
Character: Doctors, the technologically minded, sympathizers, and Slavers

During your adventuring, you may run into a secret underground Holotape that's been copied and is making the rounds, being passed around different notable inhabitants. It concerns a strange android and an operation to wipe his memory. A certain Doctor Zimmer in Rivet City needs this Replicated Man back for some reason.

NUKA-COLA QUANTUMS
Number Available: 94
Character: Sierra Petrovita, Girdershade nutcase [Location 7.05]

Not content with wowing (and irradiating) the populace with Nuka-Cola, the Nuka-Cola Company had just finished shipping its brand new, highly addictive beverage: Nuka-Cola Quantum! Only 94 of these bottles are known to exist. They are vital to the manufacture of Nuka-Grenades, and a madwoman in Girdershade goes giddy every time you bring one back to her.

SCHEMATICS: CUSTOM WEAPONS
Number Available: 23
Character: None

As previously detailed, there are seven different Custom Weapons you can construct on a Work Bench, and they provide countless hours of extreme delight and satisfaction when employed in the combat zone. More importantly, the quality of your Custom Weapon depends on whether you're building it with all three of its Schematics, and your Repair skill.

SCRIBE PRE-WAR BOOKS
Number Available: 98
Character: Scribe Yearling, Arlington Public Library [Location 9.18]

Down at the Arlington Public Library, Brotherhood Scribe Yearling is desperately trying to save as much information as possible, and is seeking out any pre-war (undamaged) books you can find. Nothing scorched, burned, or otherwise tampered with will do. Skill Books are out of the question; just the clean, green pre-war tomes. There's Caps in it for every one you return to her.

SKILL BOOKS
Number Available: 324
Character: None

Skill Books are by far the most plentiful of all the collectibles in the Wasteland. Scattered from one corner of this tundra-scape to the other are a total of 324 Skill Books, each granting you a +1 (or +2 with the Comprehension perk) to a chosen skill. As Skill Books provide essentially free augmentations to your character, you owe it to yourself to track down every last one.

SUGAR BOMBS
Number Available: N/A
Character: Murphy, Ghoul Scientist [Location 5.02]

A lumpy-skin scientist holed up in the Northwest Seneca Station thinks he's found a way to tweak Jet into an even more violently addictive concoction. The result is Ultrajet, and it's as potent as the name suggests. Unfortunately, he needs Sugar Bombs to complete the experiment. If you find any, be sure to drop in on him. You can even use the proceeds to buy his Chem!

SHEET MUSIC BOOKS
Number Available: 5
Character: Agatha, sweet old-lady violinist [Location 5.06]

An old widow wistfully remembers a time when she and her husband used to listen to the calming music wafting through the air from her violin. Now that she's old and gray, she wants to write down the tunes she remembers playing on Sheet Music. That's where you come in. There's an impressively violent and Unique .44 Magnum if you're keen enough.

UNIQUE WEAPONS AND ITEMS
Number Available: 89
Character: None

Perhaps the most important (and certainly the most impressive) collection to find, there are 89 Unique Weapons and Items to discover on your travels. These are enhanced versions of the "regular" item they are based on, and should be employed as the Primary version when found. Cannibalize all parts from the "common" version of this item to keep it functional.

The Wasteland Weapons, Armor, & Items Table

WEAPONS

BIG GUN NAME	VALUE	WEIGHT	CLIP	AMMO	AP	DMG	AUTO	ROF	SPREAD	CRIT % MULT	CRIT. DMG	NOTES	RARITY
Flamer	500	15	60	Flamer Fuel	50	16	Yes	8	0.5	4	1	Sets enemies on fire	
"Burnmaster" Flamer	500	15	60	Flamer Fuel	50	24	Yes	8	0.5	4	1	Sets enemies on fire	Unique
Gatling Laser	2000	18	240	Electron Charge Pack	30	8	Yes	20	0.5	1	6		
"Vengeance" Gatling Laser	2400	18	240	Electron Charge Pack	30	11	Yes	20	0.5	1	12		Unique
Minigun	1000	18	240	5mm Round	30	5	Yes	20	2	1	5		
"Eugene" Minigun	1500	18	240	5mm Round	30	7	Yes	20	2	1	7		Unique
Fat Man	1000	30	1	Mini Nuke	65	10	No	4.5	2	0			Collectible
"Experimental MIRV" Fatman	2500	30	8	Mini Nuke	65	10	No	4.5	13	0		Launches multiple nukes simultaneously	Unique
Missile Launcher	500	20	1	Missile	55	20	No	5.5	0.5	0			
"Miss Launcher" Missile Launcher	400	15	1	Missile	55	20	No	5.5	0.5	0		Missiles arcs like a grenade, explodes after three seconds.	Unique

ENERGY WEAPON NAME	VALUE	WEIGHT	CLIP	AMMO	AP	DMG	AUTO	ROF	SPREAD	CRIT % MULT	CRIT. DMG	NOTES	RARITY
Alien Blaster	500	2	10	Alien Power Cell	20	100	No	3	0	1	40	Chance to Disintegrate on death	
"Firelance" Alien Blaster	750	2	10	Alien Power Cell	20	80	No	3	0	3	40	Sets enemies on fire	Unique
Laser Pistol	320	3	30	Energy Cell	17	12	No	6	0	1.5	12		
Col. Autumn's Laser Pistol	420	2	20	Energy Cell	0	15	No	6	0	1	22		Unique
"Protectron's Gaze" Laser Pistol	320	3	20	Energy Cell	17	24	No	3	2.5	1	24	Fires two shots at once	Unique
"Smuggler's End" Laser Pistol	450	2	30	Energy Cell	17	18	No	6	0	1.5	18		Unique
Mesmetron	500	2	5	Mesmetron Power Cell	65	1	No	1	0	1	0	Weapon and ammo from Grouse at Paradise Falls	Unique
Plasma Pistol	360	3	16	Energy Cell	21	25	No	3	0.5	2	25		
Laser Rifle	1000	8	24	Micro Fusion Cell	17	23	No	2	0	1.5	22		
"Wazer Wifle" Laser Rifle	900	8	30	Micro Fusion Cell	17	28	No	2	0	1.5	28		Unique
Plasma Rifle	1800	8	12	Micro Fusion Cell	25	45	No	4	0.2	2	44		
A3-21's Plasma Rifle	2200	8	12	Micro Fusion Cell	25	50	No	4	0.2	2.5	50		Unique

GRENADE OR MINE NAME	VALUE	WEIGHT	CLIP	AMMO	AP	DMG	AUTO	ROF	SPREAD	CRIT % MULT	CRIT. DMG	NOTES	RARITY
Frag Grenade	25	0.5			24	100				0		20 ft. radius	
Plasma Grenade	50	0.5			24	150				0		20 ft. radius	
Pulse Grenade	40	0.5			24	10				0		20 ft. radius, 200 dmg to robots, 8 second disable	
Frag Mine	25	0.5			35	100				0		20 ft. radius	
Plasma Mine	50	0.5			35	150				0		20 ft. radius	
Pulse Mine	40	0.5			35	10				0		20 ft. radius, 200 dmg to robots, 8 second disable	

MELEE WEAPON NAME	VALUE	WEIGHT	CLIP	AMMO	AP	DMG	AUTO	ROF	SPREAD	CRIT % MULT	CRIT. DMG	NOTES	RARITY
Police Baton	70	2			25	4				1	4		
Chinese Officer's Sword	75	3			28	10				2	15		
"Vampire's Edge" Chinese Officer's Sword	400	1			28	15				3	20		Unique
Combat Knife	50	1			17	7				3	13		
"Occam's Razor" Combat Knife	65	1			17	10				3	13		Unique
"Stabhappy" Combat Knife	65	1			17	10				4	15	slightly more damage to limbs	Unique
Lead Pipe	75	3			24	9				1	18		
Ripper	100	6			65	30				0			
"Jack" Ripper	200	6			65	30				1	15	50% exta limb damage	Unique
Rolling Pin	10	1			24	3				0			
Knife	20	1			20	4				1	4		
"Ant's Sting" Knife	30	1			20	4				1	4	poisons enemies, 40 dmg/10 sec.	Unique
Switchblade	35	1			18	5				2	9		
"Butch's Toothpick" Switchblade	50	1			18	10				2.5	13		Unique
Tire Iron	40	3			27	6				1	6		

MELEE WEAPON NAME	VALUE	WEIGHT	CLIP	AMMO	AP	DMG	AUTO	ROF	SPREAD	CRIT % MULT	CRIT. DMG	NOTES	RARITY
"Highwayman's Friend" Tire Iron	75	5			27	10				1	10		Unique
Repellent Stick	120	3			40	1				0		Explodes Mole Rats after 5 seconds	
Baseball Bat	55	3			25	9				1	9		
Nail Board	30	4			27	8				0			
"Board of Education" Nail Board	60	4			27	12				1	12		Unique
Pool Cue	15	1			27	3				0			
"The Break" Pool Cue	50	1			27	6				1	6		Unique
Sledgehammer	130	12			38	20				1	10		
"The Tenderizer" Sledgehammer	230	12			38	30				1	15		Unique
Super Sledge	180	20			38	25				1	25		
Fawkes' Super Sledge	300	18			38	32				1	32	Attacks faster than regular Sledgehammer	Unique

SMALL GUN NAME	VALUE	WEIGHT	CLIP	AMMO	AP	DMG	AUTO	ROF	SPREAD	CRIT % MULT	CRIT. DMG	NOTES	RARITY
10mm Pistol	225	3	12	10mm Round	17	9	No	6	0.5	1	9		
Col. Autumn's 10mm Pistol	325	3	12	10mm Round	17	13	No	6	0.5	1	13		Unique
Silenced 10mm Pistol	250	3	12	10mm Round	21	8	No	6	0.5	2	5		
10mm Submachine Gun	330	5	30	10mm Round	20	7	Yes	10	1.5	1	7		
Sydney's 10mm "Ultra" SMG	430	5	50	10mm Round	20	9	Yes	10	1.5	1	9		Unique

SMALL GUN NAME	VALUE	WEIGHT	CLIP	AMMO	AP	DMG	AUTO	ROF	SPREAD	CRIT % MULT	CRIT. DMG	NOTES	RARITY
.32 Pistol	110	2	5	.32 Caliber Round	20	6	No	6	0.5	1	6		
Scoped .44 Magnum	300	4	6	.44 Round, Magnum	32	35	No	2.25	0.3	2	35	Scoped	
"Blackhawk" Scoped .44 Magnum	500	4	6	.44 Round, Magnum	32	55	No	2.25	0.3	2	45	Scoped	Unique
Chinese Pistol	190	2	10	10mm Round	17	4	No	6	1	1	4		
"Zhu-Rong v418" Chinese Pistol	290	2	10	10mm Round	17	4	No	4.5	1	2	4	Chance of setting enemies on fire.	Unique
Sawed-Off Shotgun	150	4	2	Shotgun Cell	37	50	No	2.25	7	0			
"The Kneecapper" Sawed-Off Shotgun	350	5	2	Shotgun Cell	37	75	No	1.9	4	0			Unique
Chinese Assault Rifle	500	7	24	5.56mm Round	23	11	Yes	8	1.5	1	10		
"Xuanlong" Assault Rifle	400	7	36	5.56mm Round	23	12	Yes	8	1.5	1	12		Unique
Assault Rifle	300	7	24	5.56mm Round	23	8	Yes	8	1.5	1	8		
BB Gun	36	2	100	BB	28	4	No	0.75	0.5	1	4		
Combat Shotgun	200	7	12	Shotgun Cell	27	55	No	1.5	3	1	27		
The Terrible Shotgun	250	10	12	Shotgun Cell	27	80	No	1.5	6	1	40		Unique
Hunting Rifle	150	6	5	.32 Caliber Round	25	25	No	0.75	0.3	1	25		
"Ol' Painless" Hunting Rifle	250	6	5	.32 Caliber Round	23	30	No	1.1	0	1	30		Unique
Lincoln's Repeater	500	5	15	.44 Round, Magnum	25	50	No	0.75	0	2	50		
Sniper Rifle	300	10	5	.308 Caliber Round	38	40	No	1	0	5	40	Scoped	
"Reservist's Rifle" Sniper Rifle	500	10	3	.308 Caliber Round	32	40	No	1.6	0	5	40	Scoped	Unique
"Victory Rifle" Sniper Rifle	450	10	5	.308 Caliber Round	38	40	No	1	0	3	40	Scoped, knocks enemy down on critical hit	Unique

UNARMED WEAPON NAME	VALUE	WEIGHT	CLIP	AMMO	AP	DMG	AUTO	ROF	SPREAD	CRIT % MULT	CRIT. DMG	NOTES	RARITY
Brass Knuckles	20	1			18	6				1	6		
Power Fist	100	6			28	20				1	20		
"Fisto!" Power Fist	100	6			25	25				1.5	25		Unique
"The Shocker" Power Fist	150	6			25	20				1	20	additional 25 damage to robots	Unique
Spiked Knuckles	25	1			19	9				1	9		
"Plunkett's Valid Points" Spiked Knuckles	30	1			15	12				2	12		Unique

CUSTOM WEAPON NAME	VALUE	WEIGHT	CLIP	AMMO	AP	DMG	AUTO	ROF	SPREAD	CRIT % MULT	CRIT. DMG	NOTES	RARITY
Rock-It Launcher	200	8	12	Misc. objects	32	50	No	3.3333	1	1	25	Big Guns	
Nuka-Grenade	50	0.5			24	500		0	0	0		20 ft. radius, Radiation and Fire	
Bottlecap Mine	75	0.5			35	500		1	0	0			
Shishkebab	200	3			28	35		0	0		24	Melee Weapon, Ignites target	
Dart Gun	500	3	1	Dart	25	6	No	8.3333	0	2.5	12	Small Guns, Poison: 64 dmg/8 sec & cripples legs	
Railway Rifle	200	9	8	Railway Spikes	24	30	No	2	0.75	3	30	Small Guns	
Deathclaw Gauntlet	150	10			26	20		0		5	30	Unarmed weapon, Ignores DR from armor	

ARMOR AND APPAREL

ARMOR NAME	VALUE	POWERED	WEIGHT	HEALTH	DR	EFFECT LIST
Advanced Radiation Suit	100	N	7	25	8	Rad Resist +40%
Armored Vault 101 Jumpsuit †	180	N	15	100	12	Energy Weapons +5, Small Guns +5
Combat Armor	390	N	25	400	32	
Combat Armor, Talon	275	N	25	300	28	
Enclave Power Armor	780	Y	45	1200	40	Rad Resist +15%, AG -1, ST +1
Leather Armor	160	N	15	150	24	
Linden's Outcast Power Armor †	740	Y	45	1000	40	Rad Resist +10%, AG -1, ST +1, Big Guns +5
Merc Adventurer Outfit	50	N	8	100	12	Small Guns +2, Melee Weapons +2
Merc Charmer Outfit	50	N	8	100	12	Small Guns +2, Melee Weapons +2
Merc Cruiser Outfit	50	N	8	100	12	Small Guns +2, Melee Weapons +2
Merc Grunt Outfit	50	N	8	100	12	Small Guns +2, Melee Weapons +2
Merc Troublemaker Outfit	50	N	8	100	12	Small Guns +2, Melee Weapons +2
Merc Veteran Outfit	50	N	8	100	12	Small Guns +2, Melee Weapons +2

ARMOR NAME	VALUE	POWERED	WEIGHT	HEALTH	DR	EFFECT LIST
Metal Armor	460	N	30	500	36	AG -1
Outcast Recon Armor	180	N	20	400	28	Sneak +5
Power Armor	740	Y	45	1000	40	Rad Resist +10%, AG -2, ST +2
Prototype Medic Power Armor †	1000	Y	45	1000	40	Rad Resist +25%, AG -1, auto dispense Med-X
Radiation Suit	60	N	5	15	6	Rad Resist +30%
Raider Armor, Badlands	180	N	15	100	16	
Raider Armor, Blastmaster	180	N	15	100	16	
Raider Armor, Painspike	180	N	15	100	16	
Raider Armor, Sadist	180	N	15	100	16	
Ranger Battle Armor	430	N	27	1100	39	Small Guns +10, AP +5, LK +1
Recon Armor	180	N	20	400	28	Sneak +5
Rivet City Security Uniform	330	N	20	400	24	Small Guns +5
T-51b Power Armor †	1000	Y	40	2000	50	Rad Resist +25
Tenpenny Security Uniform	180	N	20	100	24	Small Guns +5
Tesla Armor	820	Y	45	1500	43	Rad Resist +20%, Energy Weapons +10
The AntAgonizer's Costume †	120	N	15	100	20	AG +1, CH -1

† Unique

APPENDICES — COMPLETION — TOUR — MISC. QUESTS — MAIN QUEST — BESTIARY — TRAINING

ARMOR NAME	VALUE	POWERED	WEIGHT	HEALTH	DR	EFFECT LIST
The Mechanist's Costume †	30	N	15	100	20	EN +1, CH -1
Vault 101 Security Armor	70	N	15	100	12	
Wanderer's Leather Armor †	160	N	15	150	24	Small Guns +10

HELMET NAME	VALUE	POWERED	WEIGHT	HEALTH	DR	EFFECT LIST
Boogeyman's Hood †	110	N	3	100	8	
Combat Helmet	50	N	3	50	5	
Combat Helmet, Talon	60	N	3	40	4	
Crow's Eyebot Helmet †	20	N	10	25	5	PE +1
Enclave Power Helmet	110	Y	5	75	9	Rad Resist +5%, CH -1
Eyebot Helmet	20	N	3	25	5	
Hockey Mask	10	N	1	15	3	Unarmed +5
Ledoux's Hockey Mask	100	N	1	25	4	AP +25
Metal Helmet	70	N	3	50	5	
Motorcycle Helmet	6	N	1	10	5	
Outcast Recon Helmet	40	N	3	40	4	PE +1
Power Helmet	110	Y	5	75	8	Rad Resist +3
Raider Helmet, Archlight	20	N	3	15	2	
Raider Helmet, Blastmaster	20	N	3	15	2	Explosives +5, Big Guns +5
Raider Helmet, Psycho-Tic	20	N	3	15	2	
Raider Helmet, Wastehound	20	N	3	15	2	
Ranger Battle Helmet	60	N	5	50	6	
Recon Armor Helmet	40	N	3	40	4	
Rivet City Security Helmet	50	N	3	25	4	
T-51b Power Helmet †	120	Y	4	100	10	Rad Resist +8%, CH +1
Tenpenny Security Helmet	50	N	1	25	4	
Tesla Helmet	120	Y	5	100	9	Rad Resist +5%, CH -1
The AntAgonizer's Helmet †	60	N	5	50	6	
The Mechanist's Helmet †	60	N	5	50	6	
Torcher's Mask	20	N	3	15	2	Explosives +5, Big Guns +5
Vault 101 Security Helmet	30	N	3	25	3	

CLOTHING NAME	VALUE	POWERED	WEIGHT	HEALTH	DR	EFFECT LIST
Brahmin-Skin Outfit	6	N	2	100	2	EN +1, AG +1
Brotherhood Scribe Robe	6	N	2	100	2	
Chinese Jumpsuit	10	N	2	100	6	Small Guns +5
Colonel Autumn's Uniform †	12	N	3	100	10	Energy Weapons +5, Small Guns +5
Dirty Chinese Jumpsuit	6	N	2	50	6	Small Guns +5
Dirty Pre-War Businesswear	8	N	2	100	3	Speech +5
Dirty Pre-War Casualwear	6	N	2	100	3	AG +1
Dirty Pre-War Parkstroller Outfit	5	N	10	100	3	AG +1
Dirty Pre-War Relaxedwear	6	N	5	100	3	AG +1
Dirty Pre-War Spring Outfit	5	N	2	100	3	AG +1
Elder Lyons' Robe †	8	N	2	100	3	
Enclave Officer Uniform	8	N	3	100	5	Energy Weapons +5, Small Guns +5
Enclave Scientist Outfit	8	N	2	100	3	Science +5

CLOTHING NAME	VALUE	POWERED	WEIGHT	HEALTH	DR	EFFECT LIST
Environment Suit	100	N	5	25	6	Rad Resist +30%, Medicine +5
Eulogy Jones' Suit †	6	N	3	100	2	CH +1
Grimy Pre-War Businesswear	6	N	2	100	3	Speech +5
Handyman Jumpsuit	6	N	1	100	2	Repair +5
Lab Technician Outfit	8	N	2	100	3	Science +5
Lesko's Lab Coat †	10	N	1	100	5	Science +10, Rad Resist +20%
Maple's Garb †	6	N	2	100	4	PE +1, AG +1
Modified Utility Jumpsuit	30	N	2	100	1	Repair +5, Rad Resist +10, LK +1
Naughty Nightwear	30	N	1	100	1	CH +1, LK +1, Speech +10
Negligee	6	N	1	100	1	CH +1
Negligee	10	N	1	100	1	CH +1
Oasis Robe	30	N	3	100	4	
Oasis Villager Robe	6	N	2	100	4	
Pre-War Casualwear	8	N	2	100	3	AG +1
Pre-War Parkstroller Outfit	6	N	2	100	3	AG +1
Pre-War Relaxedwear	8	N	2	100	3	AG +1
Pre-War Spring Outfit	8	N	2	100	3	AG +1
Red Racer Jumpsuit	6	N	1	100	2	Repair +5
Red's Jumpsuit	40	N	1	100	3	Small Guns +5
Regulator Duster	70	N	3	150	10	Small Guns +5, CH +1
RobCo Jumpsuit	6	N	1	100	2	Repair +5
Roving Trader Outfit	6	N	2	100	2	Barter +5
Scientist Outfit	8	N	2	100	3	Science +5
Sheriff's Duster †	35	N	3	150	5	Small Guns +5, CH +1
Tenpenny's Suit	8	N	2	100	3	
The Surgeon's Lab Coat †	30	N	1	100	2	Science +5, Medicine +10
Tunnel Snake Outfit	8	N	2	100	4	Melee Weapons +5
Vance's Longcoat Outfit †	100	N	4	100	10	Small Guns +10, CH +1, PE +1
Vault Jumpsuit	8	N	1	100	1	Small Guns +2, Melee Weapons +2
Vault Lab Uniform	6	N	1	100	2	Science +5
Vault Utility Jumpsuit	10	N	1	100	1	Repair +5, Lockpick +5
Wasteland Doctor Fatigues	6	N	2	100	2	Medicine +5
Wasteland Settler Outfit	6	N	2	100	2	EN +1, AG +1
Wasteland Surgeon Outfit	6	N	2	100	2	Medicine +5
Wasteland Wanderer Outfit	6	N	2	100	2	EN +1, AG +1

HAT NAME	VALUE	POWERED	WEIGHT	HEALTH	DR	EFFECT LIST
Ballcap with Glasses	6	N	1	10	1	PE +1
Bandana	6	N	1	10	2	PE +1
Biker Goggles	6	N	1	10	1	
Button's Wig †	20	N	1	100	1	Speech +10, Barter +5, IN +1, PE -1
Chinese Commando Hat	6	N	1	15	1	PE +1
Enclave Officer Hat	6	N	1	15	1	Energy Weapons +5
Eulogy Jones' Hat †	6	N	1	15	1	CH +1
Ghoul Mask †	50	N	1	100	3	Causes Feral Ghouls to ignore you
Lincoln's Hat †	40	N	1	50	1	Speech +5, IN +1
Lucky Shades †	40	N	1	150	1	LK +1
Makeshift Gas Mask †	40	N	2	25	3	
Oasis Druid Hood	6	N	1	10	2	

† Unique

HAT NAME	VALUE	POWERED	WEIGHT	HEALTH	DR	EFFECT LIST
Poplar's Hood	6	N	1	25	2	AG +1, Sneak +10
Pre-War Baseball Cap	8	N	1	15	1	PE +1
Pre-War Bonnet	8	N	1	15	1	PE +1
Pre-War Hat	8	N	1	15	1	PE +1
Red's Bandana †	30	N	1	10	2	PE +1
Roving Trader Hat	6	N	1	10	1	Barter +5
Shady Hat †	40	N	1	50	1	Sneak +5, PE +1
Sheriff's Hat †	35	N	1	40	1	PE +1
Stormchaser Hat	6	N	1	10	1	PE +1
Surgical Mask	6	N	1	10	1	Medicine +5, Poison Resist +5%, Rad Resist +5%
Takoma Park Little Leaguer Cap †	60	N	1	15	1	Melee Weapons +5, Explosives +5, Melee Damage +5
Three Dog's Head Wrap †	200	N	0	15	2	CH +1, LK +1

† Unique

COMESTIBLES AND CHEMS

FOOD NAME	WEIGHT	COST	QUEST	ADDICTION	EFFECT LIST
Ant Meat	1	4			Health +5, Rads +3
Ant Nectar	0.25	20		Yes	IN +2, CH +2, ST +4, 4 min.
Blamco Mac and Cheese	1	5			Health +5, Rads +3
Bloatfly Meat	1	4			Health +5, Rads +3
Blood Pack	1	5	Yes		Health +1
Brahmin Steak	1	5			Health +5, Rads +3
Bubblegum	1	1			Health +1, Rads +1
Cave Fungus	1	50			Health +5, Rads +10
Cram	1	5			Health +5, Rads +3
Crispy Squirrel Bits	1	5			Health +5, Rads +3
Crunchy Mutfruit	1	5			Health +5, Rads +3
Dandy Boy Apples	1	5			Health +5, Rads +3
Dirty Water	1	10			Health +10, Rads +6
Dog Meat	1	4			Health +5, Rads +3
Fancy Lads Snack Cakes	1	5			Health +5, Rads +3
Fire Ant Nectar	1	20	Yes		AG +4, IN -3, Fire Resist +25%, 2 min.
Fresh Apple	1	5			Health +10
Fresh Carrot	1	5			Health +10
Fresh Pear	1	5			Health +10
Fresh Potato	1	5			Health +10
Gum Drops	1	2			Health +1, Rads +1
Hatchling Mirelurk Meat	1	4			Health +5, Rads +3
Human Flesh	1	0	Yes		Health +25, Rads +10
Ice Cold Nuka-Cola	1	20	Yes		Health +20, Rads +3
Iguana Bits	1	5			Health +5, Rads +3
Iguana on a Stick	1	5			Health +5, Rads +3
InstaMash	1	5			Health +5, Rads +3
Junk Food	1	5			Health +5, Rads +3
Mirelurk Cakes	1	5			Health +5, Rads +3
Mirelurk Meat	1	20			Health +20, Rads +3
Miss. Quantum Pie	1	20	Yes		ST +1, IN -1, AP +20, Rads +5, 4 min.
Mole Rat Meat	1	4			Health +5, Rads +3
Mole Rat Wonder Meat	1	20	Yes		Health +20, Rads +3
Mutfruit	1	5			Health +5, Rads +3
Noodles	1	5			Health +5, Rads +3
Nuka-Cola	1	20			Health +10, Rads +3
Nuka-Cola Quantum	1	30	Yes	Yes	AP +20, Rads +10, 4 min.
NukaLurk Meat	1	7	Yes		Health +20, Rads +5, AP +10, 4 min.

FOOD NAME	WEIGHT	COST	QUEST	ADDICTION	EFFECT LIST
Pork N' Beans	1	5			Health +5, Rads +3
Potato Crisps	1	5			Health +5, Rads +3
Purified Water	1	20			Health +20
Radroach Meat	1	4			Health +5, Rads +3
Salisbury Steak	1	5			Health +5, Rads +3
Softshell Mirelurk Meat	1	30			Health +3, Rads +3
Squirrel on a Stick	1	5			Health +5, Rads +3
Squirrel Stew	1	5			Health +5, Rads +3
Strange Meat	1	2	Yes		Health +5, Rads +3
Strange Meat Pie	1	2	Yes		Health +5, Rads +3
Sugar Bombs	1	5			Health +5, Rads +3
Yao Guai Meat	1	30			Health +10, Rads +10, Damage +10%, 2 min.
YumYum Deviled Eggs	1	5			Health +5, Rads +3

ALCOHOL NAME	WEIGHT	COST	QUEST	ADDICTION	EFFECT LIST
Beer	1	2		Yes	IN -1, ST +1, CH +1, 4 min.
Scotch	1	10		Yes	IN -1, ST +1, CH +1, 4 min.
Vodka	1	20		Yes	IN -1, ST +1, CH +1, 4 min.
Whiskey	1	10		Yes	IN -1, ST +1, CH +1, 4 min.
Wine	1	10		Yes	IN -1, ST +1, CH +1, 4 min.

CHEM NAME	WEIGHT	COST	QUEST	ADDICTION	EFFECT LIST
Ant Queen Pheromones	1	75	Yes		CH +3, IN -3, PE -3, 4 min.
Buffout	0	20		Yes	ST +2, EN +3, Health +60, 4 min.
Jet	0	20		Yes	AP +30, 4 min.
Mentats	0	20		Yes	IN +5, PE +5, 4 min.
Mentats, Berry	0	20	Yes	Yes	IN +5, 4 min.
Mentats, Grape	0	20	Yes	Yes	CH +5, 4 min.
Mentats, Orange	0	20	Yes	Yes	PE +5, 4 min.
Med-X	0	20		Yes	DR +25, 4 minutes
Psycho	0	20		Yes	Damage +25%, 4 min.
RadAway	0	20			Restore Rads +50
Rad-X	0	20			Rad Resist +25%
Stealth Boy	1	100			Stealth Field, Sneak +100, 2 min.
Stimpak	0	25			Health or Limb Condition +30
Ultrajet	0	50	Yes	Yes	AP +40, 4 min.

Chapter 2 FACTIONS AND BESTIARY

This chapter reveals the major factions across the violent and warring Wasteland, and then reveals all of the adversaries lurking behind well-defended encampments, charging out of caves, or swooping down from the skies.

> ## Note
> **Genus Note:** Throughout this guide, whenever a type of entity is encountered, the suffix "Genus" may be employed. This means you should expect enemies from that entire species to be at a location, and the exact type changes depending on your character's level. For example, early on in your adventure, you might stumble into a Super Mutant camp with two Super Mutant Brutes. Later on, stumble into that same camp, and they might now be Super Mutant Masters.

Part 1: Wasteland Factions

THE ENCLAVE

In the recent past, the Enclave—the remains of the United States government—were evacuated to an oil rig off the coast of California. Little is known about what happened to these forces, although the country has new commander-in-chief: President John Henry Eden. However, recent reports and chatter have pinpointed the resurgence of the Enclave, with their base centered on a secure underground facility known as Raven Rock. Initial contact was made there 35 years ago.

During this time, the new President Eden has been slowly rebuilding his resources, thanks in part to the technology already available at the Raven Rock military base. Vertibirds, weapons, and robots were easy to construct, but human followers were more difficult to find. The answer was to rely on Colonel Autumn, who controls the Enclave soldier forces, as well as creating a propaganda-spewing series of Eyebots to roam the Wasteland, spreading hope. Eden could spout his pro-government rhetoric, and promise a return of the pre-war America of legend: a land of white picket fences, baseball, apple pie, and good, old-fashioned American global supremacy.

President Eden's secretive plan all along has been to rule over an America of the "pure," free from any mutation. He has learned of a ridiculously ambitious experiment known as Project Purity, and knew the time to strike had come: His Enclave forces would "reclaim" the Jefferson Memorial. By controlling the purified water, Eden would control the Capital Wasteland, and the rest of the country eventually. What better way to administer modified F.E.V.— which kills anyone infected with any form of mutation—than through the water supply?

THE BROTHERHOOD OF STEEL

The Brotherhood of Steel is a neo-knightly order that rose from the ashes of the American military of the West Coast in the years following the devastation of 2077. The organization's tenets include the eradication of mutants and worship of technology, and the Brotherhood has never been very keen on sharing their resources with their fellow Wastelanders (who they generally consider too ignorant and irresponsible to deserve such advanced technology).

The Brotherhood is generally beneficial to humanity, but they have their faults: They don't care for mutants; they worship technology

(and in many cases put it above human life); and they don't like to share their choicest technological discoveries, despite the obvious benefits their technology could bring to the Wasteland. It's commonly accepted within the Brotherhood that the people of the Wasteland are not responsible enough to use (and maintain) all of the technology the B.O.S. has at their disposal. They are known for trading some of their technologies with frontier communities and N.C.R. states, but they keep the more sensitive technologies to themselves.

Unlike the chivalrous knights of old, members of the Brotherhood are not interested in justice for the obviously weaker and less fortunate around them, but instead in keeping their secrecy and preserving and developing technology. Their motives are often unclear, and Brotherhood members are not people to be trifled with. The east coast contingent of the Brotherhood has "gone native" under the leadership of Elder Owyn Lyons. Lyons believes he has a responsibility to protect the people of the Capital Wasteland from the Super Mutant threat. His knights have forgone the mission to recover new technology, and instead acts as a kind of security force. Lyons runs operations from a stronghold christened the Citadel, a heavily defended structure built from the ruins of an ancient building known as "the Pentagon."

TALON COMPANY MERCENARIES

The Talon Company is the largest of the mercenary groups in the Wasteland. They can be found almost anywhere. They put cash and loot ahead of almost anything, and will attack most groups on sight in the hopes of taking their stuff. Currently an unknown benefactor has hired the Talon Company to hunt down do-gooders. The reasons for this are unknown, but the effect is to keep the Wasteland a lawless place where the guys with the biggest guns make the rules. The Talon Company frequently has the biggest guns.

BROTHERHOOD OUTCASTS

The Brotherhood Outcasts are a contingent of Brotherhood of Steel soldiers who split from Elder Lyons' group at the Citadel (stealing technology and weapons in the process). The reason for the split? They felt like Elder Lyons had "gone native," and concerned himself too much with the needs of the locals. Yes, he was supposed to discover the breeding ground of the Super Mutants, but not to the exclusion of the original, "greater" mission—the acquisition of technology. In their eyes, Lyons is a joke, possibly even a traitor. He hasn't even bothered to get his giant robot working, let alone continue the search for technology.

In their eyes, they are the true Brotherhood of Steel, carrying on the mission of the main West Coast contingent. They proudly wear the name "Outcast"; anything to further disassociate them from Lyons. It's also important to note that the Brotherhood's concentration on acquiring advanced technology means they have their obsessions—including the procurement of alien weapons from anywhere in the Capital Wasteland, including possible crashed U.F.O. and pre-war government installations.

VAULT DWELLERS

Vault 101 was actually part of an unscrupulous social experiment. All of the other Vaults were intended to be opened at one point or another when the "all clear" signal was sent from Vault-Tec or the appropriate regulatory agency, and this indeed, did transpire, with almost universally horrific results. But Vault 101's secret plans were different: The doors were never scheduled to open. Ever. In fact, the Vault was supplied with just the type of equipment it would need to keep functioning indefinitely—like spare parts for the water processor. But this was just the beginning:

The true experiment was even more devious and cunning. Although Vault 101 was about testing the human condition when a Vault never opened, this was only the first part of the plan. The "actual" experiment went far beyond that, and a select few knew the true nature; that this was to test the role of the Overseer. While the Overseer was able to interact (and even visit) the outside world via radio transmissions, and a secret tunnel from his sealed office, the rest of the inhabitants faced a much more dismal future: As far as they knew, Vault 101 was never sent an "all clear" signal, and faked radio transmissions described a nuclear-ravaged world gone mad, with absolutely no hope of existence outside of a Vault. The radio transmissions were actually recorded before the bombs even fell, and in many cases described a world even more horrible than the reality of the nuclear wasteland. The Vault 101 Overseer, like his counterparts in the other Vaults, was actually a planted Vault-Tec operative whose job it was to control the experiment from the inside.

Aside from keeping up this ruse, the Overseer's other important role was to reinforce to the dwellers of Vault 101 that the outside world would never be habitable again, and that their only salvation was in the Vault. The Overseer prevented anyone from leaving the Vault, and made sure the Vault dwellers received their regular "transmission" from the outside world. People entered Vault 101 in 2077, just before the bombs fell.

The Overseer died of natural causes 50 years later (in 2127), at the age of 84, after grooming a subordinate to continue the clandestine plan. The new Overseer led his people according to the same isolationist doctrine preached by his predecessor, but also attempted to garner as many senior Vault Dwellers to become complicit in this plan as possible. By 2277, the descendants of the Overseer had an entire generation of Vault Dwellers who were playing along with this plan, keeping the secrets from their children.

The Overseer and his cronies continued to receive periodic information from the outside world, while those not in the know were told that things had gotten so bad that whoever was sending transmissions was no longer able to do so; reinforcing the thought that leaving the Vault was sheer suicide. The final piece of this grand experiment only truly began when the Vault Dwellers living in blissful ignorance finally realized the world outside could be accessed, and there was a possibility of life above ground. The experiment only really commenced when the Vault 101 door first opened, and a young dweller fled into the light.

RAIDERS

Chaos and anarchy. Or if you prefer, anarchy and chaos. Raiders revel in both. Numerous Raider groups dot the wasteland. Most are no more than a handful of people scraping out a living by preying on anything weaker than them. They have no driving purpose or goal, other than to live to see tomorrow and raise as much hell as possible today.

The largest known band of Raiders has set up a crude city in Evergreen Mills. This well-defended canyon gives them a base of operations. Rumor has it that they trade with Slavers, selling their captives for cash.

SUPER MUTANTS

The Super Mutants that infest the urban ruin of Washington D.C. originated in Vault 87. Those unlucky enough to have reserved space in Vault 87 soon found themselves forcefully taken to a secure part of the vault, where they were locked in airtight chambers and exposed to a concentrated form of the F.E.V. The Overseer and his security force had no real idea what to expect; they were simply following the "plan." When the exposed vault dwellers started transforming into Super Mutants, nearly the entire vault population had been exposed. Those who hadn't yet metamorphosed knew what was coming, and, well…it didn't end well for humanity.

The dwellers of Vault 87 were turned into Super Mutants in 2078, and have been a presence in the Capital Wasteland ever since. Most of those original Super Mutants have long since been killed. But whether it's because of the nature of the F.E.V. they were exposed to, or a simple underlying human instinct, the Super Mutants of the Capital Wasteland are obsessed with the preservation of their own species. Super Mutants are asexual and incapable of procreation, so their only way of reproducing is to kidnap other humans, drag them back to the Vault 87 chambers, and infect them with F.E.V. And so they have done, for nearly 200 years.

Super Mutant society is loosely hierarchical, with the weaker (most recently transformed) Super Mutants generally giving way to the stronger. The Super Mutant hierarchy, as defined by the Capital Wasteland contingent of the Brotherhood of Steel, is as follows: Grunt, Brute, Master, and Behemoth. Generally speaking, the Super Mutants of the Capital Wasteland get bigger, stronger, and dumber as they age. The Behemoths are so strong and savage that they're the only thing feared by the other Super Mutants.

REILLY'S RANGERS

Reilly grew up in the ruins of Washington D.C. not even knowing what happened to her parents. When she was only 10, she encountered a man who had formal military training and took her in. Throughout the years, as she grew from a girl to a woman, this man taught her everything there was to know about combat, tactics, and survival. Finally, when she was 22, he died of natural causes. To honor him, Reilly bravely carried his body all the way to Arlington Cemetery, where she interred his body and gave him the best military burial she could provide.

After that, she wandered the Wasteland, doing odd mercenary-related jobs, and building up a reputation as a tried and true soldier who gets the job done. When she was 26, she founded Reilly's Rangers and undertook the biggest mission of her career: mapping all of the ruins of Washington D.C. It's unknown if Reilly undertook this mission of her own accord or was hired to do so, but she attacked this task with everything in her arsenal. Taking several other mercenaries with her, she formed "Reilly's Rangers" and set out to accomplish this dangerous feat.

WASTELANDERS

Wastelander is a catch-all term for anyone living in the Wasteland who is not affiliated with some other group. Most are not aggressive but will defend themselves if attacked. When that happens, they usually die. Quickly.

SLAVERS

The Slavers of the Capital Wasteland are headquartered at the compound of Paradise Falls and led by the charismatic and ruthless Eulogy Jones. Slavery has nothing to do with race, and everything to do with the subjugation of the weak for profit. The Slavers have a pretty limited clientele, and sell mostly to their return customers, the Raiders. Other customers are residents of the Wasteland, including Allistair Tenpenny, creator of Tenpenny Tower.

SLAVES (ABOLITIONISTS)

Slaves are not so much a faction as a collection of victims. No one is safe from slavery in the Wasteland. If you are weak or vulnerable, you may be taken as a slave.

There is a band of abolitionist slaves deep in the Wasteland. They are all escaped slaves, seeking to end slavery for all time. You can learn more about them in **Miscellaneous Quest: Head of State**.

UNDERWORLD GHOULS (NON FERAL)

The Underworld Ghouls are a group of refugees who have taken up residence in the remains of the Museum of American History. They mostly keep to themselves, doing their best not to draw attention from the outside world and its prejudices. They are known to welcome visitors, so long as those visitors behave themselves. But even as they welcome newcomers, the Ghouls of Underworld are cautious and wary of strangers. Each was subject to abuses by humans in the past, and as a result, their trust is easily revoked.

CHINESE REMNANT ARMY

The Chinese Remnant faction is just that: the last, scattered remnants of Chinese military operations in the United States. These spies, intelligence agents, and special-ops soldiers were abandoned on foreign soil and have been kept alive these long years as irradiated Ghouls. There numbers are extremely few, and you are unlikely to encounter them in any numbers unless you should stumble across their cover operation from years ago, somewhere in the bowels of DC...

THE FAMILY

The Family is a group of cannibals who have banded together thanks to the efforts of Vance, their leader. Living under the ruins of Meresti Trainyard, the group keeps out of public view, staying away from larger towns and settlements and only surfacing to feed. Realizing that the cannibal is both feared and hated even in the lawless Wasteland, Vance has decided to teach his people the way of the vampire as he interprets it from classic literature. He's convinced most of the Family that they are indeed true vampires, teaching them to drink the blood of their prey and not to feed upon their flesh. Vance believes this gives them a sense of belonging and purpose in a world that doesn't understand their unusual trait. Although the Family may truly believe they are like the vampires in traditional works of fiction, they retain no abilities or "powers" that distinguish them from any other cannibal in the Capital Wasteland.

THE REGULATORS

The Regulators are a relatively new group in the Capitol Wasteland, having appeared only in the last 10 years or so. They take it upon themselves to punish troublemakers and do their best to keep a semblance of peace wherever they are.

LITTLEHORN AND ASSOCIATES

Almost nothing is known about the mysterious Littlehorn and Associates. They occasionally employ individuals who they feel suit their ends, although neither Daniel Littlehorn nor his glass-eyed associates will divulge anything about what those ends actually are.

Part 2: The Bestiary— Human Foes with Higher Functions

This Bestiary is segmented into two separate sections; adversaries that are human in form, and enemies that are more creature-like.

Humans have a different set of statistics than creatures, and it is important to note what each entails.

HUMAN STATISTICS

NAME: The name your Pip-Boy gives to the humanoid in question.

LEVEL: Although they can appear at any time, this foe is commonly encountered when you reach this level.

PERCEPTION: What Perception statistic rating the human has (1–10), measured the same way as your Perception. The higher the Perception, the quicker you're spotted.

HEALTH: The full Health of the human, prior to combat.

BIG GUNS: The enemy's Big Guns Skill (0–100), measured in the same way as yours.

ENERGY WEAPONS: The enemy's Energy Weapons Skill (0–100), measured in the same way as yours.

MELEE WEAPONS: The enemy's Melee Weapons Skill (0–100), measured in the same way as yours.

SMALL GUNS: The enemy's Small Guns Skill (0–100), measured in the same way as yours.

ARMOR: The type of armor the foe wears, and what to expect to find when looting the corpse. There may be other (random) items, but the noted item is always present.

PRIMARY WEAPON(S): The preferred weapon the adversary first attacks with. There may be back-up weapons to worry about, too.

XP: XP gained from defeating the human.

TYPE 1: BROTHERHOOD OF STEEL †

NAME	LEVEL	PERCEPTION	HEALTH	BIG GUNS	ENERGY WEAPONS	MELEE WEAPONS	SMALL GUNS	ARMOR	PRIMARY WEAPON(S)	XP
Brotherhood of Steel Initiate	1	7	70	44	46	14	44	Brotherhood Power Armor	Flamer	10
Brotherhood of Steel Initiate	1	5	70	44	14	44	44	Brotherhood Power Armor	Laser Pistol / Laser Rifle	10
Brotherhood of Steel Initiate	1	6	65	14	16	43	47	Brotherhood Power Armor	Power Fist, Frag Grenades	10
Brotherhood of Steel Knight	7	7	95	57	59	14	57	Brotherhood Power Armor	Laser Pistol / Laser Rifle	20
Brotherhood of Steel Knight	7	6	90	14	16	57	61	Brotherhood Power Armor	Ripper, Frag Grenades	20
Brotherhood of Steel Paladin	11	7	125	74	76	14	74	Brotherhood Power Armor	Minigun / Gatling Laser	30
Brotherhood of Steel Paladin	11	7	125	74	76	14	74	Brotherhood Power Armor	Laser Pistol / Laser Rifle	30
Brotherhood of Steel Paladin	11	6	120	14	16	75	79	Brotherhood Power Armor	Super Sledge, Frag Grenades	30
Brotherhood of Steel Paladin	11	7	125	74	76	14	74	Brotherhood Power Armor	Missile Launcher	30
Brotherhood of Steel Scribe	n/a	5	55	13	15	11	13	Brotherhood Scribe Robe	10mm Submachine Gun	varies

† Brotherhood members are usually neutral or friendly toward you, unless you provoke them.

Brotherhood forces are tough to take down (especially because your father has sided with them!), and you might wish to wait to battle them until they train you to wear Power Armor. Each fallen soldier (whether killed by you or not) holds a holotag, which can be traded for Caps if you find Scribe Jameson in the Citadel. If you're interested in Energy Weapons, fire away!

TYPE 2: CHINESE REMNANT SOLDIER

NAME	LEVEL	PERCEPTION	HEALTH	BIG GUNS	ENERGY WEAPONS	MELEE WEAPONS	SMALL GUNS	ARMOR	PRIMARY WEAPON(S)	XP
Chinese Remnant Soldier †	1	5	25	28	15	28	30	Dirty Chinese Jumpsuit	Chinese Pistol	10
Chinese Remnant Sergeant †	6	5	40	41	15	41	43	Dirty Chinese Jumpsuit	Chinese Assault Rifle	10
Chinese Remnant Officer †	10	5	55	54	15	54	56	Dirty Chinese Jumpsuit	Chinese Assault Rifle	20

† may flee

Very few Chinese Remnant Soldiers are left 200 years after being stranded here. All are Ghouls, and although they fire an excellent Small Gun, they are prone to fleeing. The Sergeant and Officer class are better at combatting your attacks.

APPENDICES — COMPLETION — TOUR — MISC. QUESTS — MAIN QUEST — **BESTIARY** — TRAINING

TYPE 3: ENCLAVE

NAME	LEVEL	PERCEPTION	HEALTH	BIG GUNS	ENERGY WEAPONS	MELEE WEAPONS	SMALL GUNS	ARMOR	PRIMARY WEAPON(S)	XP
Enclave Soldier	1	6	45	16	45	14	47	Enclave Power Armor	Laser Pistol	10
Enclave Soldier	1	6	45	16	45	47	12	Enclave Power Armor	Ripper, Frag Grenades	10
Enclave Soldier	7	6	80	16	68	14	70	Enclave Power Armor	Laser Rifle	20
Enclave Soldier	7	6	80	16	68	70	12	Enclave Power Armor	Ripper, Plasma Grenades	20
Enclave Soldier	11	6	125	87	87	16	12	Enclave Power Armor	Flamer, Plasma Grenades	30
Enclave Soldier	11	6	125	16	83	16	16	Enclave Power Armor	Laser Rifle	30
Enclave Soldier	18	6	170	100	100	16	12	Enclave Power Armor	Minigun / Gatling Laser	50
Enclave Soldier	18	6	170	16	100	16	16	Enclave Power Armor	Plasma Rifle	50
Enclave Soldier	18	6	170	100	100	16	12	Enclave Power Armor	Missile Launcher	50
Enclave Officer	n/a	6	125	16	100	16	16	Enclave Officer Uniform	Plasma Pistol, Plasma Grenades	50
Enclave Scientist †	n/a	6	20	11	17	11	17	Enclave Scientist Outfit	Laser Pistol	10

† Will flee

The other way to claim a lot of Energy Weapons is to take on these well-armored and powerful foes. They are one of the few sources of Plasma Weapons. Unlike the Brotherhood, these well-trained foes attack you on sight, and they are highly accurate and skilled. They also have robots and Modified Deathclaws on occasion.

TYPE 4: BROTHERHOOD OUTCAST †

NAME	LEVEL	PERCEPTION	HEALTH	BIG GUNS	ENERGY WEAPONS	MELEE WEAPONS	SMALL GUNS	ARMOR	PRIMARY WEAPON(S)	XP
Brotherhood Outcast	1	5	70	44	14	44	44	Outcast Power Armor	Assault Rifle / 10mm Submachine Gun / Chinese Assault Rifle	10
Brotherhood Outcast	1	6	70	14	16	47	51	Outcast Power Armor	Power Fist, Frag Grenades	10
Brotherhood Outcast	1	7	70	44	46	14	44	Outcast Power Armor	Flamer	10
Brotherhood Outcast	7	7	95	57	59	14	57	Outcast Power Armor	Laser Pistol / Laser Rifle	20
Brotherhood Outcast	7	6	90	14	16	57	61	Outcast Power Armor	Ripper, Frag Grenades	20
Brotherhood Outcast	11	7	125	74	76	14	74	Outcast Power Armor	Minigun / Gatling Laser	30
Brotherhood Outcast	11	7	125	74	76	14	74	Outcast Power Armor	Laser Pistol / Laser Rifle	30
Brotherhood Outcast	11	6	120	14	16	75	79	Outcast Power Armor	Super Sledge, Frag Grenades	30
Brotherhood Outcast	11	7	125	74	76	14	74	Outcast Power Armor	Missile Launcher	30

† Outcast members are usually haughty and unpleasant, but not violent toward you, unless provoked.

Should you engage Outcast Soldiers in combat, they are just as tough as the Brotherhood and Enclave forces, although their weapons are more antiquated. They sometimes trundle into a fight with a rusting robot to help them.

TYPE 5: RAIDER †

NAME	LEVEL	PERCEPTION	HEALTH	BIG GUNS	ENERGY WEAPONS	MELEE WEAPONS	SMALL GUNS	ARMOR	PRIMARY WEAPON(S)	XP
Raider	1	5	25	13	15	32	34	Raider Armor	.32 Pistol / Chinese Pistol / 10mm Pistol	10
Raider	1	5	30	15	15	34	32	Raider Armor	Pool Cue / Knife / Baton / Tire Iron, Frag Grenades	10
Raider	1	5	25	13	15	32	34	Raider Armor	Hunting Rifle	10
Raider	4	5	55	13	15	45	47	Raider Armor	Hunting Rifle / Sawed Off Shotgun / Assault Rifle	10
Raider	4	5	60	15	15	47	45	Raider Armor	Lead Pipe / Baseball Bat / Combat Knife, Frag Grenades	10
Raider	4	5	55	13	15	45	47	Raider Armor	Hunting Rifle	10
Raider	4	5	55	41	15	45	45	Raider Armor	Flamer	10
Raider	7	5	85	13	15	66	68	Raider Armor	Assault Rifle / Combat Shotgun / 10mm Submachine Gun	20

† Raiders may flee

NAME	LEVEL	PERCEPTION	HEALTH	BIG GUNS	ENERGY WEAPONS	MELEE WEAPONS	SMALL GUNS	ARMOR	PRIMARY WEAPON(S)	XP
Raider	7	5	90	15	15	68	66	Raider Armor	Lead Pipe / Knife / Sledgehammer/ Chinese Sword, Frag Grenades	20
Raider	7	5	85	13	15	66	68	Raider Armor	Hunting Rifle	20
Raider	7	5	85	62	15	66	66	Raider Armor	Missile Launcher	20

For the accomplished combat specialist, Raiders are the least-troubling enemies, as long they are encountered in small groups of four or less. They shout, aren't particularly Perceptive, and carry low-to-mid quality loot. Build up your XP hunting these freaks.

TYPE 6: SLAVER †

NAME	LEVEL	PERCEPTION	HEALTH	BIG GUNS	ENERGY WEAPONS	MELEE WEAPONS	SMALL GUNS	ARMOR	PRIMARY WEAPON(S)	XP
Slaver	n/a	4	75–110	13	13	41–74	41–74	Merc Outfit	Various Pistols / Rifles / 10mm Submachine Gun / Combat Shotgun	varies

† Slaver may flee

Slavers are slightly more battle-tested than Raiders, but just as merciless. As with Raiders, they are prone to fleeing, so aim for their legs to ensure a slow getaway.

TYPE 7: TALON COMPANY MERCENARY

NAME	LEVEL	PERCEPTION	HEALTH	BIG GUNS	ENERGY WEAPONS	MELEE WEAPONS	SMALL GUNS	ARMOR	PRIMARY WEAPON(S)	XP
Talon Company Merc ‡	1	7	75	15	64	17	62	Talon Combat Armor	Laser Pistol / Hunting Rifle / Assault Rifle	10
Talon Company Merc ‡	1	7	80	17	19	62	62	Talon Combat Armor	Police Baton / Combat Knife / Frag Grenades	10
Talon Company Merc ‡	1	7	75	15	64	17	62	Talon Combat Armor	Sniper Rifle	10
Talon Company Merc ‡	8	7	105	15	77	17	75	Talon Combat Armor	Laser Pistol / 10mm Submachine Gun / Assault Rifle / Combat Shotgun	20
Talon Company Merc ‡	8	7	110	17	19	75	75	Talon Combat Armor	Police Baton / Combat Knife, Frag Grenades	20
Talon Company Merc ‡	8	7	105	15	77	17	75	Talon Combat Armor	Sniper Rifle	20
Talon Company Merc ‡	8	7	105	73	19	17	75	Talon Combat Armor	Flamer / Missile Launcher	20
Talon Company Merc	12	7	135	15	90	17	68	Talon Combat Armor	Laser Rifle / Combat Shotgun / Chinese Assault Rifle	30
Talon Company Merc	12	7	140	17	19	88	88	Talon Combat Armor	Police Baton / Combat Knife, Frag Grenades	30
Talon Company Merc	12	7	135	86	19	17	88	Talon Combat Armor	Missile Launcher	30
Talon Company Merc	12	7	135	15	90	17	88	Talon Combat Armor	Sniper Rifle	30

‡ May flee

Tougher than Raiders, but not on par with those enemies clad in Power Armor, these thugs are more "professional" and don't flee the combat arena, but they aren't wearing enough protection to cause consternation.

TYPE 8: WASTELANDER AND GHOUL (NON-FERAL) †

NAME	LEVEL	PERCEPTION	HEALTH	BIG GUNS	ENERGY WEAPONS	MELEE WEAPONS	SMALL GUNS	ARMOR	PRIMARY WEAPON(S)	XP
Caravan Guard	n/a	6	290	14	17	91	93	Leather Armor	Assault Rifle, Frag Grenades	50
Megaton Settler ‡	n/a	5	35	12	14	16	45	Various Clothing	.32 Pistol / Chinese Pistol / 10mm Pistol / Knife / Combat Knife / Lead Pipe	10
Rivet City Security ‡	n/a	6	55–85	14	16	52–76	54–78	Rivet City Security Uniform	Submachine Gun	varies
Scavenger ‡	n/a	5	140–170	13	15	15	55	Roving Trader Outfit	Various Pistols / Rifles / 10mm Submachine Gun / Sawed-off Shotgun	10
Tenpenny Resident ††	n/a	5	40	12	14	16	45	Various Clothing	None	10
Tenpenny Security Guard	n/a	6	65	14	16	61	63	Tenpenny Security Uniform	Assault Rifle	20

† These are Ghouls that are either neutral toward you, or hostile but still attack with weapons, not their bare claws.

†† Will flee

‡ May flee

TRAINING — BESTIARY — MAIN QUEST — MISC. QUESTS — TOUR — COMPLETION — APPENDICES

NAME	LEVEL	PERCEPTION	HEALTH	BIG GUNS	ENERGY WEAPONS	MELEE WEAPONS	SMALL GUNS	ARMOR	PRIMARY WEAPON(S)	XP
Underworld Resident ‡	n/a	5	45	12	14	16	49	Various Clothing	.32 Pistol / Chinese Pistol / 10mm Pistol / Knife / Combat Knife / Lead Pipe	10
Wastelander ‡	n/a	5	25	12	14	31	31	Wasteland Apparel	Various Pistols / Melee Weapons / Hunting Rifle, Frag Grenades	varies
Wastelander (Ghoul) ‡	n/a	5	25	12	14	31	31	Wasteland Apparel	Various Pistols / Melee Weapons / Hunting Rifle, Frag Grenades	varies

‡ May flee

Wastelanders come in a wide variety, ranging from the Tenpenny Tower civilian to the well-trained Rivet City guard. A good rule to follow is to check whether your Wastelander is apt to flee; they're more of a push-over. Ghouls wear shabby but recognizable clothes, speak rather than snarl, immediately charge you, and have deep suspicions about "smoothskin" humans. They similar to Raiders as a threat.

Part 3: The Bestiary—
Creatures and Wild Abominations

Creatures have a different set of statistics than human enemies, and it is important to learn what each means.

CREATURE STATISTICS

NAME: The name your Pip-Boy gives to the entity in question.

LEVEL: Although they can appear at any time, a creature is commonly encountered when you reach this level.

INVENTORY: What the creature has when you inspect the corpse. There may be other (random) items, but the noted item is always present.

PERCEPTION: What Perception statistic rating the creature has (1–10), measured the same way as your Perception. The bigger the Perception number, the quicker you're spotted.

HEALTH: The full health of the creature, prior to combat.

DAMAGE: What damage it inflicts with its usual, regular weapon.

SPECIAL WEAPON: Whether the creature has a special or unique attack.

DAMAGE: What damage the special or unique attack inflicts.

WEAPON NOTES: Any pertinent data regarding damage, or special damage caused.

XP: XP gained from defeating the creature.

NOTES: Specific notes particular to the creature; useful tactical information.

TYPE 1: MUTATED INSECTS

NAME	LEVEL	INVENTORY	PERCEPTION	HEALTH	DAMAGE	SPECIAL WEAPON	DAMAGE	WEAPON NOTES	XP	NOTES
Giant Worker Ant	1	Ant Meat	3	30	7	Fire Spit	16/sec.	—	5	Frenzies if antennae are destroyed. Legs take 50% damage.
Giant Soldier Ant	8	Ant Meat	4	150	24	Fire Spit	32/sec.	—	10	Frenzies if antennae destroyed. Legs take 50% damage.
Giant Ant Queen	n/a	Ant Meat	4	1,000	—	Acid Spit	40	—	10	Legs take 50% damage.

There are a few sub-genres of Ants, including ones that breathe fire, and "Invader" Ants that are extremely aggressive. However, the trick with all of the Workers and Soldiers is to shoot off the antennae if you're facing more than one; the antenna-less Ant attacks its friend while you sit back. Otherwise, target the head or torso because the legs take half damage

| Bloatfly | 1 | Bloatfly Meat | 5 | 15 | — | Larva Spit | 5 | — | 1 | Flying enemy. |

This disgusting, bloated fly has a ranged attack that is difficult to sidestep. Pop these easily. If ammo is tight, run up and whack them with a Melee Weapon.

| Radroach | 1 | Radroach Meat | 3 | 5 | 3 | — | — | — | 1 | Flees easily. |

Offering disgusting meat, these are simple to kill, but keep coming back. They are good enemies to practice attacking , particularly with Melee Weapons. Don't waste ammo on them unless you have to.

| Radscorpion | 1 | Radscorpion Poison Gland | 4 | 150 | 22 | Stinger | 22 | 15 dmg/5 sec. Poison | 10 | Legs take 50% damage. |
| Giant Radscorpion | 13 | Radscorpion Poison Gland (4) | 6 | 350 | 60 | Stinger | 60 | 40 dmg/5 sec. Poison | 25 | Legs take 50% damage. |

Radscorpions are a problem, especially because their attacks are poisonous. Attacking and crippling the legs may let you finish them off out of stinger range. However, their legs only take half damage. If they are already in close, aim for the stinger, head, or torso.

TYPE 2: MUTATED ANIMALS

NAME	LEVEL	INVENTORY	PERCEPTION	HEALTH	DAMAGE	SPECIAL WEAPON	DAMAGE	WEAPON NOTES	XP	NOTES
Brahmin	n/a	Brahmin Steak	3	40	8	—	—	—	1	Heads take 50% damage.

Offering nothing more than some steak, you can easily drop these grazing animals if you're hungry. Aim for the heads for a quick takedown.

NAME	LEVEL	INVENTORY	PERCEPTION	HEALTH	DAMAGE	SPECIAL WEAPON	DAMAGE	WEAPON NOTES	XP	NOTES
Mirelurk	1	Mirelurk Meat	4	120	28	—	—	—	10	Torso takes half damage
Mirelurk Hunter	9	Mirelurk Meat	6	250	50	—	—	—	25	Torso takes half damage
Mirelurk King	13	Mirelurk Meat, Softshell Mirelurk Meat	7	375	35	Shriek	10	50 dmg ignores armor, PE -10/10 sec.	50	—

The trick to tackling a Mirelurk is not to aim at the well-protected torso, but hit the small face, or failing that, the pincer arms or legs. Mines are a great way to slow them down. Beware the King as his shriek attack ignores all armor; sidestep the shriek shockwave if you can. Also note that Mirelurk Meat is the tastiest treat around!

NAME	LEVEL	INVENTORY	PERCEPTION	HEALTH	DAMAGE	SPECIAL WEAPON	DAMAGE	WEAPON NOTES	XP	NOTES
Mole Rat	1	Mole Rat Meat	3	40	15	—	—	—	5	Will explode if hit with Repellent Stick

Annoying, ankle-biting mutant rodents are easy to dispatch, and entertainingly defeated if you have Moira Brown's Repellent Stick, given during **Miscellaneous Quest: The Wasteland Survival Guide**.

NAME	LEVEL	INVENTORY	PERCEPTION	HEALTH	DAMAGE	SPECIAL WEAPON	DAMAGE	WEAPON NOTES	XP	NOTES
Yao Guai	12	Yao Guai Meat	7	220	75	—	—	—	10	Very fast!

These furry mutations are fast, meaning it's almost impossible to out-run one; stand your ground and fight to the bitter end! If you encounter them at a distance, aim for their legs.

TYPE 3: ABOMINATIONS

NAME	LEVEL	INVENTORY	PERCEPTION	HEALTH	DAMAGE	SPECIAL WEAPON	DAMAGE	WEAPON NOTES	XP	NOTES
Centaur	7	—	9	100	27	Radioactive Spit	30	50 rads/10 sec.	5	Legs take 75% damage, tongues take 25% damage

Slow-moving, but spitting a highly dangerous radioactive poison, this is an abomination in the true sense of the word. This crime against nature is usually the sign of nearby Super Mutants. Aim at the head or torso to quickly stop it.

NAME	LEVEL	INVENTORY	PERCEPTION	HEALTH	DAMAGE	SPECIAL WEAPON	DAMAGE	WEAPON NOTES	XP	NOTES
Deathclaw	13	Deathclaw Hand	8	500	100	—	—	—	50	Very fast!

Deathclaws are arguably the fiercest creatures in the game aside from a Behemoth, with a tough hide, a quickness that overwhelms, and massive damage from their swiping claws. Attack from range, preferably with Sniper Rifles or Plasma Weapons, and switch to powerful closer combat weapons as they close. If you get a chance, drop some Mines before the combat begins. There are also Modified Deathclaws, controlled by the Enclave, that are identical aside from metal headgear.

NAME	LEVEL	INVENTORY	PERCEPTION	HEALTH	DAMAGE	SPECIAL WEAPON	DAMAGE	WEAPON NOTES	XP	NOTES
Super Mutant	1	Hunting Rifle, .32 Caliber Ammo	3	100	4	Hunting Rifle	See weapon	—	10	—
Super Mutant	1	Nail Board	3	100	4	Nail Board	See weapon	—	10	May carry grenades
Super Mutant Brute	10	Assault Rifle, 5.56mm Ammo	5	250	5	Assault Rifle	See weapon	—	25	—
Super Mutant Brute	10	Sledgehammer	5	250	5	Sledgehammer	See weapon	—	25	May carry Grenades
Super Mutant Brute	10	Minigun, 5mm Ammo	5	250	5	Minigun	See weapon	—	25	—
Super Mutant Brute	10	Missile Launcher, Missiles	5	250	5	Missile Launcher	See weapon	—	25	—

NAME	LEVEL	INVENTORY	PERCEPTION	HEALTH	DAMAGE	SPECIAL WEAPON	DAMAGE	WEAPON NOTES	XP	NOTES
Super Mutant Master	13	Chinese Assault Rifle, 5.56mm Ammo	6	360	6	Chinese Assault Rifle	See weapon	—	50	—
Super Mutant Master	13	Super Sledge	6	360	6	Super Sledge	See weapon	—	50	May carry Grenades
Super Mutant Master	13	Minigun, 5mm Ammo	6	360	6	Minigun	See weapon	—	50	—
Super Mutant Master	13	Missile Launcher, Missiles	6	360	6	Missile Launcher	See weapon	—	50	—
Super Mutant Behemoth	n/a		5	2,000		Fire Hydrant	100	Loaded with loot	50	Very fast!

Super Mutants are perhaps the biggest threat to your existence, as they are scattered in numerous areas, are as violent as they are ugly, and have a large amount of Health. They sometimes employ Grenades, never flee, and are always aggressive, meaning you need to finish them off with everything you've got. Use arm shots to force them to drop their weapons. Once their arms are crippled, their aim is horrible. Occasionally, large groups of Super Mutants (also known as "Muties") bring a stupid but stupendously powerful Behemoth; it inflicts colossal damage from its fire hydrant pole, and is best tackled using a Fat Man and Mini-Nuke.

TYPE 4: ANIMALS

NAME	LEVEL	INVENTORY	PERCEPTION	HEALTH	DAMAGE	SPECIAL WEAPON	DAMAGE	WEAPON NOTES	XP	NOTES
Dog	1	Dog Meat	8	20	5	—	—	—	1	—
Vicious Dog	1	Dog Meat	8	60	12	—	—	—	5	Fast
Raider Guard Dog	1	Dog Meat	8	60	12	—	—	—	5	Fast

Minimally affected by radiation, Dogs, whether the property of a Scavenger or more feral varieties, are quick, but no match for your latest hardware. You might want to aim at their legs to slow them down.

TYPE 5: FERAL GHOULS

NAME	LEVEL	INVENTORY	PERCEPTION	HEALTH	DAMAGE	SPECIAL WEAPON	DAMAGE	WEAPON NOTES	XP	NOTES
Feral Ghoul	1	—	3	25	5	—	—	—	5	—
Feral Ghoul Roamer	6	—	4	80	16	—	—	—	10	—
Glowing One	13	—	5	240	32	Radiation Burst	5	50 Rads	25	Healed by radiation

Feral Ghouls are humans that have slowly turned into Ghouls, and then lost all sanity and become completely mad. They exist to shriek, tear flesh from humans, and consume it afterward. They are easy to sneak up on and susceptible to headshots. As long as you're not overwhelmed, you can tackle them methodically without issues. That is, until you come across a Glowing One! This fearsome beast is a radioactive mutation that gives off pulses of Radiation that actually heals itself and any nearby Feral Ghouls; tackle this first, and be swift about it! Mines laid in a path are a great way to wound a Glowing One, before finishing it at close quarters. Finally, if you're given a Ghoul Mask by Roy Phillips at the conclusion of **Miscellaneous Quest: Tenpenny Tower**, you can maneuver around Ghouls with impunity, as long as you don't attack them.

TYPE 6: ROBOTS †

NAME	LEVEL	INVENTORY	PERCEPTION	HEALTH	DAMAGE	SPECIAL WEAPON	DAMAGE	WEAPON NOTES	XP	NOTES
Enclave Eyebot	1	ó	5	30		Electrical Zap	5	ó	0	Flies, explodes on death
Protectron	1	ó	4	75	ó	Laser gun (head or hand)	23	May incinerate on death	5	Frenzies if control unit is destroyed
Robobrain	6	Energy cells	5	200	5	Laser gun	30	ó	10	Head takes 50% extra damage
Robobrain	6	Energy cells	5	200	5	Mesmetron	1	100 dmg to head	ó	—
Mister Handy	ó	Flamer Fuel	5	100		Buzzsaw	12	ó	5	Frenzies if control unit is destroyed
Mister Handy	ó	Flamer Fuel	5	100	5	Flamer	28	Burn 10 dmg/ 5 sec.	ó	—

† Most opponents take double damage if hit in the head. There is no bonus damage to targeting a robot's cranial area. All robots are immune to poison and radiation.

NAME	LEVEL	INVENTORY	PERCEPTION	HEALTH	DAMAGE	SPECIAL WEAPON	DAMAGE	WEAPON NOTES	XP	NOTES
Mister Gutsy	9	Flamer Fuel	6	350	ó	Flamer	41/sec.	Burn 10 dmg/ 5 sec.	25	Frenzies if control unit destroyed
Mister Gutsy	9	Energy cells	6	350	ó	Plasma gun	51	May gooify on death	ó	—
Sentry Bot	13	Electron Charge Pack	7	500	22	Gatling laser	108/sec.	May incinerate on death	50	Frenzies if control unit is destroyed
Sentry Bot	13	5mm bullets	7	500	22	Minigun	108/sec.	—	ó	Armored head takes 50% damage, armored legs take 75% damage
Sentry Bot	13	Missiles	7	500	22	Missile Launcher	18	135 dmg explosion	ó	—

Robots have a variety of imposing and dangerous weaponry, and since they generally don't take bonus damage for headshots it might be a good plan to target the weapons specifically. Also check the weapon types before engaging; for example; if a Mister Handy has a Buzzsaw and Flamer, back out of range to conduct combat. With the Sentry Bot, target the Missile Launcher first.

If you encounter them with other opponents, try to destroy its control unit first. Then it will turn on any nearby target, friend or foe. Employ Pulse Grenades or Mines exclusively when dealing with robots; they are highly susceptible to the pulse that occurs when these weapons explode.

Mark I Turret (ceiling) ‡	1	—	10	40	1	5.56mm gun	23/sec.	—	1	Frenzies if control unit destroyed, explodes on death
Mark II Turret (floor) ‡	1	—	10	50	1	Laser gun	18/sec.	May incinerate on death	1	Frenzies if control unit destroyed, explodes on death
Mark III Turret (ceiling) ‡	7	—	10	60	1	5.56mm gun	36/sec.	—	5	Frenzies if control unit destroyed, explodes on death
Mark IV Turret (floor) ‡	7	—	10	75	1	Laser gun	31/sec.	May incinerate on death	5	Frenzies if control unit destroyed, explodes on death
Mark V Turret (ceiling) ‡	11	—	10	75	1	5.56mm gun	57/sec.	—	10	Frenzies if control unit destroyed, explodes on death
Mark VI Turret (floor) ‡	11	—	10	100	1	Laser gun	48/sec.	May incinerate on death	10	Frenzies if control unit destroyed, explodes on death

Turrets are stationary, aside from their pivoting, and can be avoided most of the time. Or, you can hack into a nearby terminal (usually Average in difficulty for your Science skill), and cause the terminal to attack anything that moves. Pulse weapons are highly advantageous to use against turrets, too.

‡ Most turrets have a nearby terminal. Hack this, and switch off the turret instead of attacking it.

Chapter 3 · MAIN QUEST

QUEST FLOWCHART

	MAIN PATH	MAIN PATH 2	MAIN PATH 3	MAIN PATH 4	MAIN PATH 5
Main Characters	Your father, James; Your mother, Catherine; Nurse Madison Li	Your father, James	Your father, James; Amata Almodovar; Paul Hannon; Officer Gomez; The Overseer; Lucy "Old Lady" Palmer; Butch DeLoria; Wally Mack; Stanley Armstrong; Mister Handy "Andy"; Beatrice; Officer Kendall; Jonas Palmer	Your father, James; Jonas Palmer; Stanley Armstrong; Mister Handy "Andy"; Butch Deloria; Paul Hannon; Wally Mack; Amata Almodovar; Edwin Brotch; Freddie Gomez; Susie Mack; Christine Kendall	Amata Almodovar, Butch DeLoria, Ellen DeLoria, Grandma Taylor, Officer Gomez, Mister Handy "Andy", Stanley Armstrong, Tom Holden, Mary Holden, Allen Mack, Floyd Lewis (Deceased), Jonas Palmer (Deceased)
Locations	Jefferson Memorial, Gift Shop area		Vault 101		
Adv. Items/Abilities	—	—	Small Guns, BB Gun	Speech	Science, Sneak, Speech
Possible enemies	—	—	Radroach	—	Radroach, Officer Kendall, Officer O'Brian, Officer Richards, Officer Wolfe, Officer Park, Security Chief Paul Hannon, Officer Steve Mack, The Overseer
Karma Influence	—	—	—	Neutral	Neutral

• Main Quest: Birth

Cry, and manipulate features

• Main Quest: Baby Steps

Walk to Dad.

Learn to Turn and Move

Open the playpen's gate.

Exit the playpen.

Learn to Open

Look at the "You're SPECIAL" book.

Choose your Statistics

Learn to Pick up and Throw objects. Listen to Dad. Memorize the Biblical Passage number

Follow Dad.

• Main Quest: Growing Up Fast

Enjoy the party and speak with the guests.

Receive presents; Learn to use your Inventory

Fight with Butch

Speak to other partygoers

• Pip-Boy 3000, Vault 101 PA System Signal, Grognak the Barbarian, Sweet Roll, Kid's Baseball Cap

Enter the Overseer's office.

Speak with Amata. Take or refuse her father's 10mm Pistol

• Bobby Pins (10), 10mm Pistol, Your room items

Navigate your way to Butch and Ellen DeLoria

Rescue Ellen, or [Speech] Convince Butch to rescue Ellen

Gun everyone down

• Tunnel Snake Outfit

Fight your way to the Security Room

Help Amata

Interrogate The Overseer

Leave Amata

Enter Overseer's Bedroom

Overseer's Office Key

Use the Overseer's computer to access the secret tunnel.

Access Overseer's Terminal in his Office

Continued on next page

From next page

Color code: | Objective | Action | Rewards |

From previous page

Meet Jonas on the Reactor Level.

Listen to Beatrice

• A Birthday Poem

Locate Jonas, wait for Dad

• BB Gun and Ammo

Shoot all three targets with the BB Gun.

Use manual aiming or V.A.T.S.. Stand for photo with Dad

Main Quest: Future Imperfect

Get to class and talk to Mr. Brotch about the G.O.A.T.

Speak to Dad about the G.O.A.T.

Locate your Dad's Bobblehead

• Bobblehead: Medicine

No need for Speech Challenge

Locate Amata and the Tunnel Snakes

[Speech] Convince Butch to back off

Convince Wally Mack to depart or tease Amata about her weight

Punch Butch down to half health

Let Butch Punch you down to half health

Sit down and take the G.O.A.T.

Speak to Mr. Brotch, get him to fill in the answers or take the G.O.A.T.

Turn in the G.O.A.T. to Mr. Brotch.

Choose Tag Skill and Skills, or talk to Brotch and change them

Exit the Classroom.

Main Quest: Escape!

Escape the Vault.

Flee using the secret tunnel, exit into the Capital Wasteland

• Last Chance to change Character stats

• Main Quest: Following in His Footsteps

Birth

Your birth is a moment of great joy and sadness for your father. A name is chosen, your sex is checked, and a **Project Purity [9.14]** Gene Projection unit reveals what you'll eventually look like as an adult. This happy time is but a fleeting moment. Something terrible is happening to your mother....

WHAAAA! AH-WAAAA!

Welcome to the world, little mite. That's your daddy, little guy (or sweetheart).

There's a blinding white light. Your vision is blurred. A woman lies to your left, panting. "Well?" asks a man's voice. "Is it a boy or a girl?" Choose your sex, and your father peers down and exclaims his joy at your birth. Your father and mother have been thinking of a name for you. Type it in when prompted.

Your father brings forward the Gene Projection, allowing you to see what you'll look like in 20 years or so. You can now change your Race, Face, and Hair. Whatever the outcome, you're very much like your father in appearance. The nurse wheels you out of the operating room while your father can be heard shouting "she's in cardiac arrest!" Everything fades to white....

One Year Later...

Baby Steps

You're alone in your room, playing with your teddy, truck, rattle, and big red ball. Open the playpen gate and make a break for it, inspect your toys, and read your extra-S.P.E.C.I.A.L. book. Then listen to Daddy. Follow Daddy outside; he knows where to go. You should always follow Daddy.

DADA? DAAH-DA? DADDA!

Your father is proud of your first faltering steps, you little tear-away!

NEW OBJECTIVE
"Walk to Dad" begins.

Everything fades from white. You're looking around a rather cold chamber with metal walls and a mesh gate in front of you. Your father is standing on the other side of a playpen gate. You're taking your first steps, so stagger east through the open gate and into your father's arms.

NEW OBJECTIVE
"Open the playpen's gate" begins.

NEW OBJECTIVE
"Exit the playpen" begins.

Your father closes the playpen gate, trapping you with only a big red ball for company. You can run into the ball to push it, but the real trick is planning an escape from the pen. Move to the Gate Door, and open it when the prompt appears on-screen. Toddle back to the rug or check the hatch door. Your Lockpick skill isn't quite that developed yet....

NEW OBJECTIVE
"Look at the 'You're S.P.E.C.I.A.L.' book" begins.

Make a quick reconnoiter of the room. Your crib with the missile mobile is to the north, the Vault-Tec code of ethics is framed on the wall above the bed. But the big news is the toy box; scamper over, following the on-screen instructions for grabbing a toy from the box, and letting go. Sit on the chair if you wish. When you're bored of the toy-throwing, crawl to the "You're S.P.E.C.I.A.L." book, and open it.

Spend the next few minutes assigning points to your seven S.P.E.C.I.A.L. abilities. Remember that you can reduce an ability as well as increase it. Every ability, how points affect them, and recommended "types" of character based on point allocation, are shown in the Character Development section of this guide (starting on page 24). When you've finished assigning points, close the book. You have another option to change your scores after you take your G.O.A.T. exam.

Catherine's favorite biblical verse comforts your father. That Nuka-Cola truck comforts you.

Once the book has been closed, your father returns, and sits down on the rug to explain Catherine's favorite biblical verse to you. After the comforting talk, your father gets up and leaves. Follow him through the open hatch door, through a living room, and into a metallic passageway. Continue to follow. Everything fades to white....

Nine Years Later...

Growing Up Fast

You are 10 years old. Surprise! Welcome to your birthday party. Your father has a nice surprise for you down in the Reactor Level if you're good. Wait, Andy appears to have obliterated the cake. No matter, there are still some presents to receive, and people to chat with. You also receive your most important present of all: your very own Pip-Boy 3000!

PARTY, STREAMERS, AND A PIP-BOY

Everything fades from white. Your father is congratulating you on your 10th birthday, while your best friend Amata, Officer Gomez, and Paul Hannon applaud. They've thrown a surprise party and everyone's here! One of the invited guests is Amata's father, the Overseer. He greets you with his usual stern expression and gives you an extra-special gift: your very own Pip-Boy 3000! It isn't the

latest model, but Stanley reckons it's more reliable than the newfangled unit.

 **Pip-Boy 3000**

 Vault 101 PA System Signal found

NEW OBJECTIVE
"Enjoy the party and speak with the guests" begins.

Amata knew you'd be surprised by this party, but it was your dad who organized most of it. Chat with Amata, and you're presented with a number of dialog choices, depending on how friendly or unpleasant you want to be to her. Amata's gift is a real doozy: a *Grognak the Barbarian*, issue 14, with no missing pages! Take the present, then optionally speak with Paul Hannon before he returns to sit with Butch and his gang.

Amata's a real sweetheart and you may be developing a crush on her. You know, if girls weren't so weird and gross.

 Grognak the Barbarian
Skill Book: +1 Melee Weapons (when read)

 Tip

Immediately bring up your Pip-Boy and run through its basic functionality, as detailed in the section of this guide called General Training (page 29). Read the Grognak the Barbarian comic and your Melee Weapons skill is immediately increased by 1! You can also check out the Vault 101 PA transmissions by selecting the Radio option on your Pip-Boy.

Buttersaw! Andy the robot may have the depth perception of a Radroach, but he means well. Just as long as doesn't go into field surgery....

Officer Gomez offers some nice platitudes, there's no response from the intercom, and the notice board offers some light reading. You can talk to anybody you like, in any order. The following people are closest to you. Begin with the Overseer, who's a real stickler for the rules. Old Lady Palmer seems much nicer, and no matter how rude you are to her, she still offers you one of her delicious Sweetrolls. It appears in your Pip-Boy's Item > Aid screen. This might be the only food you're eating; Andy's cutting arm appears to have malfunctioned, and your cake looks like it's been attacked! Take a Party Hat from the counter to cheer yourself up.

 Party Hat   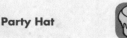 **Sweetroll**
+5 HP (when eaten)

Next stop is Butch and his table of miscreants. Butch demands that you give him the Sweetroll now that the cake is ruined. You have many responses, and the farther down the dialog list you go, the more angry Butch's response is likely to be. Butch actually gets off his seat to punch you if you mention his mother and her alcohol

problems, and the fight is broken up by Officer Gomez. You can then blame Butch, but any choice is fine, although you might want to stand up for yourself. Butch's boys are Wally Mack and Paul Hannon.

Wally asks whether you enjoyed his last party, but then remembers you didn't, because you weren't invited. Paul offers some half-hearted jibes, then Amata runs over to ask what happened with Butch. After that, make sure you speak with Stanley at the bar; he's the one that fixed up your A-Series Pip-Boy, and he also has a birthday gift for you. Take the Kid's Baseball Cap, then speak with your dad. He wants you to follow him out of the diner because someone has another present for you. Your dad speaks to his friend Jonas on the intercom; they've been cooking up something special for you!

 Kid's Baseball Cap

NEW OBJECTIVE
"Meet Jonas on the Reactor Level" begins.

SUFFOCATION! LITTLE HANDS, GROPING IN SUBTERRANEAN UNCERTAINTY.

Your dad opens the diner door to the west (be sure you use the Pip-Boy's compass, shown all the time at the screen's bottom left). Before you can depart, Beatrice beckons you over. She gives you A Birthday Poem; read it in your Pip-Boy's Data > Note screen. When you're ready, head north out of the diner, along the corridor, and make the first left (west) turn. Walk west, looking for the sign pointing right (north) down to the reactor. You can speak to Officer Kendall coming down from the upper level, but he isn't very pleasant.

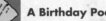 **A Birthday Poem**

Instead, descend to the connecting room near the reactor, where Jonas is waiting for you. He's a bit of a joker, so answer his questions with a bit of wit. When your father arrives, he gives you his birthday gift: an old BB Gun he and Jonas spent the last three months scavenging pieces for. Take it graciously (or ungraciously), then follow your father into the side corridor. Your dad tells you to come down here any time you want to practice. In fact, he's set up a few targets right now!

 BB Gun    **50 BBs**

NEW OBJECTIVE
"Shoot all three targets with the BB Gun" begins.

Test your aiming abilities on some metal, and greasy, irradiated insect targets.

Move to the southern end of this side corridor, between the crates, and peer ahead; there are three targets. Bring out your BB Gun and fire, optionally using the Aim functionality to get a better view.

Remember to shoot the center target, not the outer metal area, or the target won't swing back. If you have any problems, read the on-screen instructions. When all targets are struck, a Radroach scuttles out from the right.

It is time for your first live kill! Bring your BB Gun to bear on the Radroach, or enter the Vault-Assisted Targeting System (V.A.T.S.), which allows you to pinpoint the Radroach's different appendages for a slower, but cleaner kill. When the Radroach has been peppered with ball-bearings, head back to your father, who beckons Jonas over to take a picture. Whoa, that flash is white...very white....

Six Years Later...

Future Imperfect

You're not a kid any more. You're 16 years old, and ready (but somewhat unwilling) to take the first transitional step into adulthood. The step in question is the Generalized Occupational Aptitude Test, or G.O.A.T. The way you respond to this official Vault-Tec aptitude test determines your future career inside the Vault. This becomes important as your three Tag skills are also determined, but don't worry; you can adjust and choose the skills you want after the test is over. Before then, though, there's the mildly threatening presence of the bully Butch and his thug friends.

GREASER TEASERS

Everything fades from white. Your father is examining you, and the prognosis is good. You can take your G.O.A.T. today. The Generalized Occupational Aptitude Test is completed by every 16-year-old in the Vault, and it determines what jobs they're most suited for. Stalling doesn't help, so speak to your father about other matters if you wish before you leave. You can even read the confidential profiles on your father's Vault 101 Medical Data System. His patients make interesting reading:

It seems Freddie Gomez is suffering from VDS (Vault Depressive Syndrome).

Stanley has chronic head-pain, probably due to the schedule the Overseer has given him.

Amata is the picture of health, but her father insists on being with her for her medical examination.

His "other work" makes extremely interesting reading:

There's an entry about somebody's cells replicating normally. Has someone your dad knows been outside the Vault? Impossible!

There's a cryptic entry about your dad and Jonas working with "water chips" on some weird experiment.

Leave your dad's surgery, but not before a quick check of the area. There's a Bobblehead: Medicine on the table. Pick it up, and then inspect the wall plaque with your mother's favorite biblical passage. It is locked. Perhaps you should head back here later? Say hello to Jonas on the way out. Stanley is waiting to see the doctor (those headaches again?), and Andy is performing maintenance in the corridor outside. Head west and take your test!

Bobblehead: Medicine: "The smart man knows a bandage only hides his wounds."

Bobblehead: Medicine
Your Medicine skill is permanently increased by 10 points.

Note
There are 19 more of these Vault-Tec Limited Edition Bobbleheads scattered throughout this world, each giving you a substantial (and permanent) bonus to a particular ability. Each location is shown in the Inventory section of this guide, on page 455.

Your decisions have wide-reaching implications, so keep your (good or bad) Karma in check!

Head down the corridor where the Tunnel Snakes—a gang of greasers led by Butch—are harassing Amata. You can ignore this petty squabble, step in to help Amata, or join in the bullying. Your choices are as follows:

 Sidle in, speak with Butch, and convince him the Overseer is going to come down hard on the Tunnel Snakes. If successful, he agrees to "deal with her later". Note this option doesn't require a **Speech** challenge if you already fought Butch during "Growing Up Fast."

 Or, you can ignore Butch and convince Wally Mack that the Vault's opinion of Butch is far less flattering than his own. Wally and Paul bail, you cut down the Tunnel Snakes leader without direct conflict, and class can begin.

You can give Butch some verbal ammunition—and the taunting gets worse. Amata runs off crying, and the Tunnel Snakes saunter off into class.

> You can let your **fists** do the talking for you ("raise" your fists before starting the dialog), and punch Butch down to half his health (concentrate on him, not the other Tunnel Snakes). He stops the fight, and the Tunnel Snakes shuffle off into class.

You can let your less capable fists do the pleading for you and begin to fight but let the gang batter you down to half health. You're no challenge, so the gang swaggers into class.

Or simply ignore the teasing altogether. Amata will get over it. Whatever your choice, head north and then turn left, into the classroom.

GETTING YOUR G.O.A.T.

Step into the classroom, and speak with Mr. Brotch, your teacher. You can try to wheedle out of sitting this test, but Brotch assures you there are no wrong answers! However, if you ask him whether you have to take "this stupid test," you can ignore the G.O.A.T. entirely, Brotch fills out the answers for you, and you can pick the conclusion to your test yourself! Otherwise, spend some moments locating your desk, and

The Overseer wants to see your skills, so answer the G.O.A.T. as accurately as possible. Or cheat, afterward!

chatting with the assembled classmates, including Freddie (who's looking rather pale), and the girls over by the chalkboard. Then take your seat as Brotch moves to the front of the class.

> **NEW OBJECTIVE**
> **"Sit down and take the G.O.A.T." begins.**

The G.O.A.T. consists of 10 multiple-choice questions, based mainly on moral or skill-based situations. You can answer the questions carefully or quickly, but whatever your decisions, question 10 is by far the easiest! Once the G.O.A.T. is over, approach Mr. Brotch at his desk, and he tells you the job you've been chosen to undertake. You can agree with the choice or not, it doesn't matter; Brotch says you can tweak your test results to your choosing, anyway!

> **NEW OBJECTIVE**
> **"Turn in the G.O.A.T. to Mr. Brotch" begins.**

The Skills menu now appears from your Pip-Boy. Thirteen skills are listed here, with three skills chosen to allocate G.O.A.T. points to. If the chosen skills are to your liking, click "Done." If they are not, you can change them. When you've finished allocating Skill points, you can leave the classroom or stay and listen to how everyone else did. Once you leave the room, everything fades to white.

> **NEW OBJECTIVE**
> **"Exit the Classroom" begins.**

>
> *Tip*
> Are you having problems deciding what skills to give points to? Then read the descriptions on-screen, or access the Skills and Perks section of the Training chapter of this guide (page 11), for more advice.

Three Years Later...

Escape!

You are now 19 years old. The passage to adulthood has been anything but smooth. However your world is completely turned upside down after you're awakened by Amata. Your father has left the Vault! It gets worse: the Overseer's overzealous security team has killed Jonas for helping in the escape, and the Vault has been put on lockdown to prevent any other inhabitants from trying the same plan. This has also cut some of the power to the Vault, causing Radroaches to scuttle into the building, attacking anything they encounter. You're tasked with finding some way out of this chaos, as the Overseer will soon turn to you for answers. Fortunately, your oldest and dearest friend—Amata Almodovar, the Overseer's own daughter—is here to help.

WHAT'S THE MATTER, AMATA?

Amata shakes you from your slumber and informs you that all hell has broken loose. Jonas is dead, your dad has escaped, and you've slept through the turmoil. Amata's father's men are likely to be heading your way in seconds, and you need an escape plan. The following options are available:

You can agree to let Amata help you escape. A secret tunnel leads directly from the Overseer's office to the Vault exit, although you'll need to hack into a computer to open it. You're given 10 Bobby Pins to help you access this room. Amata also pushes her father's 10mm Pistol into your hands (which you can refuse, which helps her out during a subsequent interrogation). She then leaves, recommending that you gather belongings and start to flee.

Or you can dismiss her help completely. You aren't given any items and may need to return to her later to apologize and request her help. This, as you might have gathered, isn't the recommended option! Instead, you can proceed directly to the Overseer's Office, and escape using Bobby Pins (in Amata's room) or the key from the Overseer himself.

Now ransack your desk. Take the Baseball Bat, Baseball, Glove, BB Gun, and BBs (50), then raid the First Aid Box for a Med-X and Stimpaks (10).

Bobby Pins (10)

10mm Pistol

Baseball Bat

Baseball and Glove

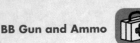 **BB Gun and Ammo** **First Aid Box Health and Chems**

NEW OBJECTIVE
"Enter the Overseer's office" begins.

 Tip

Take the BB Gun and Baseball Bat, then set your Pip-Boy's Hot Key functionality so you can quickly switch to the 10mm Pistol, Baseball Bat, or BB Gun, depending on the situation.

Head north, into the corridor from your apartment, and try to Sneak briefly; you can circumvent some guards and Radroaches if you employ this skill. However, it is beneficial to move to the junction and watch a Radroach attack Officer Kendall.

The most cunning plan? Keep the Radroaches alive until they savage Officer Kendall, then snag his armor!

The following options are available:

 Watch combat begin, then open the door to the left, behind Kendall, that leads into the gentlemen's restroom. **Sneak** into here, and completely avoid being spotted.

Let the Radroaches win, then pepper them with BB Gun fire until they splatter. Don't use the 10mm Pistol; save the ammo.

If you help Kendall, he turns and attacks you anyway, because he's been sent to tackle you as a traitor.

Or, you can flee, heading west and leaving Kendall to his fate, but without watching it unfold.

If you let the Radroaches kill Kendall, you can raid his corpse, taking a Police Baton (useful only after your Baseball Bat breaks) and his armor. Quickly place the weapon into the fourth Hot Key location, then wear the armor; it provides protection for the fighting to come, and helps conserve Stimpaks.

 Police Baton **Vault 101 Security Armor**

Vault 101 Security Helmet

Ellen DeLoria has a few unwanted drinking partners. Help her or leave her or massacre the bums.

Turn the corner, or if you're continuing to Sneak, break into the ladies restroom, and you're soon spotted by Butch. He's conveniently forgotten the last 10 years of teasing, and he pleads for you to help his mother, who's trapped in her apartment under Radroach attack. There are a few available options, here:

You can agree (either immediately, or after letting Butch stew with your dialog choices, although action needs to be immediate once the conversation ends). Follow Butch to the south end of the corridor, then turn right, armed with your preferred gun. Ellen DeLoria is surrounded by three Radroaches and is in danger of dying; quickly enter V.A.T.S., aim at a single enemy, and destroy it. Then manually blast the remaining foes. This is the most adept way of dealing with the infestation. Don't hit Ellen, or the DeLorias turn hostile!

You can tell Butch exactly what you think of him and his alcoholic mother, and he calls for guards to come. Run to the next section of the Vault and leave Butch and Ellen to their fates.

 Or, you can use **Speech** to convince Butch to get in there and stamp the menace out himself, gaining respect from his mother.

Or, you can get Butch to save his mom himself; give him your BB Gun or Baseball Bat.

Or, you can gun Butch and his mother down; this gives you a few minor additional items, and a sting of regret.

If you helped Butch (and all three Radroaches were killed by someone), and his mother survived, you receive Karma, and Butch displays actual gratitude and offers you his jacket. Whatever the outcome, head north, then west from Butch's apartment, toward the diner.

 Tunnel Snake Outfit

Follow the only open corridor in the Vault, moving north past the diner (you can enter it and uncover the body of Grandma Taylor), and follow the signs to the atrium. At the top of the stairs, you bump into Officer Gomez. He's just as confused as you are but doesn't want to fight because he was a good friend of your father's.

You can leave him alone, continuing to a fire up ahead.

Or, you can shoot him (and any other innocents you meet from this point on).

Continue east toward the atrium, but stop at the laboratory area to watch Andy do something right; cooking Radroaches with his flamer! Step into the lab area, briefly chat with Stanley, who goes out to mend Andy, and rummage around in your father's ransacked office. His terminal turns out to be locked, but your real reason for being here is to grab an extra-special Vault-Tec Limited Edition Bobblehead; take this if you didn't during "Future Imperfect." Now head out to the corridor, and east to the Door to Vault 101 Atrium.

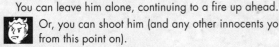 **Bobblehead: Medicine**
Your Medicine Skill is permanently increased by 10 points.

 Note

There is something behind the wall plaque in here, but you'll need Lockpick 50 to open it. Return during **Miscellaneous Quest: Trouble on the Homefront** to claim it.

"I DON'T WANT YOU TO FOLLOW ME."

Tom and Mary flee in a state of confusion. Tom heads into a dead-end, literally.

Enter the lower level of the atrium, and you bump into Tom and Mary Holden, Tom sprints off toward the door to the Vault exit in fear and confusion. The lights are on emergency back-up, so try switching your Pip-Boy's Flashlight on. A computer room to the northeast holds some minor items, but the real shock comes from heading to the locked Vault exit corridor. Tom Holden is viciously shot down by power-mad Officers O'Brian and Richards (they both have 10mm Pistols; a great reward if you can defeat them)! Seek vengeance by battering the two guards yourself. The Door to Vault 101 Entrance is locked, so move to the door with the locker preventing it from closing, and head to the upper level.

Security Chief Hannon is no pushover...unless you slam him over the gantry!

Move to the corridor at the top of the stairs where Security Chief Hannon (and Paul Jr.'s dad) spots you. Bring the fight to him, retreating onto the gantry above the atrium's lower level, and knocking him unconscious or worse. Continue west, past the circular window (which is where the Overseer's office is), and pass Alan Mack (Wally's dad) knocking on the window. You can't reach him, so run into the admin area and the server room. The remains of Floyd Lewis, the technician, lie in a heap. You can optionally grab his Tinted Reading Glasses and Vault 101 Utility Jumpsuit, but only if you're collecting outfits!

Continue into the atrium corridor, then look left (west) through the security room window. Amata is being tortured by her own father and his lackey, Officer Mack (Wally's brother)! You have a variety of choices here:

You can leave them to interrogate Amata and continue to escape.

You can open the door and storm inside. Amata immediately flees, while the Overseer backs up and lets Officer Mack attack. Beat or shoot him down, and then approach the Overseer.

If you let Amata keep the 10mm Pistol earlier, she uses it on Officer Mack.

 Or, you can **Sneak** in and pickpocket the Overseer's key and password from him. Run for the Overseer's office if they catch you in the act!

Once you're alone with the Overseer, you can talk or attack him.

If you talk, he reveals nothing. Threaten to harm Amata though, and the Overseer's Office Key and Overseer's Terminal Password are yours!

You can (foolishly) surrender to him, and he takes your weapons, using them on you!

A better plan is to leave him be. Search the lockers to find Batons and security uniforms, if you haven't lifted them from guards you've dispatched. There's some 10mm Ammo inside one of the lockers, too.

Or, you can kill the Overseer and take the key and password from the body. This won't make Amata happy, though!

10mm Rounds **Overseer's Office Key**

Overseer's Terminal Password

Run north from the Overseer, and turn right (east), into the Overseer's office. Amata was right; your dad's friend Jonas has been killed! Search his body to uncover Eyeglasses, a Stimpak, and a Vault Lab Uniform, as well as a Note from Dad. Play this on your Pip-Boy in the Data > Note area. It is a farewell message, telling you that it was best for you not to know, it was something your father needed to do, and that he doesn't want you to follow him. Turn north, and enter the Overseer's living quarters.

Note from Dad

If you freed Amata, she's crying on a chair to your right. She tells you to get going, and she'll meet you at the Vault Door. If she has the 10mm Pistol, she gives it to you now. Now investigate the chamber to the north: the Overseer's bedroom. Open the dresser in the corner, and grab 10mm Rounds and the Overseer's Office Key, but leave the three Jumpsuits, which simply weigh you down. Then enter Amata's bedroom, locate her dresser (with a picture on top), and grab the Bobby Pins inside. Now you can finally enter the Overseer's office.

10mm Rounds (and Pistol) **Overseer's Office Key**

Bobby Pins (5)

NEW OBJECTIVE
"Use the Overseer's computer to access the secret tunnel" begins.

Enter the Overseer's office, and move quickly over to the lockers in the far right corner. One of them contains the Overseer's Terminal Password. Now move over to the terminal behind the Overseer's curved desk. The following options are available:

 Use your **Science** skill to hack into the terminal, if you don't have the Overseer's Terminal Password. Follow the on-screen instructions. If you're successful, you can access the computer records. If you fail, move to the locker and take the password.

APPENDICES — COMPLETION — TOUR — MISC. QUESTS — MAIN QUEST — BESTIARY — TRAINING

Or, access the terminal using the password.

You have four attempts to hack into the terminal. However, if you quit out of the terminal when you have one attempt left, then access the Terminal again, the number of attempts resets. Use this trick across the Wasteland, when hacking into every terminal you find!

The Overseer's terminal makes fascinating reading. There are four sets of entries to pour through:

Security Dossiers

The Tunnel Snakes: They have been providing a "service" for the Overseer but are getting unruly.

Beatrice: Her mind is getting feeble, and the Overseer is seeking a long-term pharmaceutical "solution" for her.

Jonas: He's a fine medic, but he's being filled with "idealistic non-sense" by your father.

Amata: She's becoming increasingly distant, despite the Overseer raising her on his own since she was an infant.

Scouting Reports

You thought there was no contact with the outside world! However, Anne Palmer (Jonas's mother) presented a scouting report that it's safe to head outside without radiation suits. Springfield township is in ruins and the team was attacked by Giant Ants, but civilization seems to have survived! A settlement called "Megaton" is mentioned, and pictured, as is a Giant Ant.

Vault-Tec Instructions

Letter from Doctor Stanislaus Braun: This tells the Overseer his Vault has been selected for "experimental protocols." Something about G.E.C.K. is mentioned. Vault 101 doesn't have one.

The G.E.C.K.: This appears to be a wondrous terraforming module that can create life from lifelessness.

Open Overseer's Tunnel: Do this immediately!

Take a look out at that Wasteland, adjust your glasses and Tunnel Snake jacket (optional), and start to explore!

Watch the Overseer's desk rise up and a hidden staircase appear! Descend into the secret passage, using the electrical switch to open the hatch door, then run down the passageway, turning left (east) and ending up at another hatch door. This leads to a small room with a hidden door in front of you. Press the switch and the wall panel slides up, allowing you to clamber to the entrance chamber. Use the Vault Door Control Pod to activate the giant piston that plugs into the massive "cog" door, spinning it out and allowing your first glimpse into the outside world!

NEW OBJECTIVE

"Escape the Vault" begins.

As the door grinds open, Amata appears and wishes you the best of luck. She refuses your offer to come along. As the guards charge in, run east, toward the gate with the light streaming in. Before you leave Vault 101 for good, you have a final opportunity to edit your Name, Race, Sex, S.P.E.C.I.A.L. Abilities, and Skills before you open the gate and step out into the dangerous wilds of a radioactive waste-land. What remains of civilization? You'll find out soon enough!

Following in His Footsteps

You've escaped from **Vault 101 [8.01]**, and must track down your fugitive father across a massive and terrifying Wasteland! You need to plan ahead. Surviving out in the Wasteland, especially with darkness falling, isn't easy. The Overseer's Terminal notes mentioned the nearby town of **Megaton [8.03]**. Head into town, and speak to the inhabitants: they point you to a speakeasy called Moriarty's. Inside the saloon, seek out the proprietor himself; Moriarty tells you your father was headed into the ruins of Washington D.C., seeking out a DJ named Three Dog who is sympathetic to his cause. Travel there yourself, either via Ghoul-filled underground tunnels that were once the city subway, or over ground, avoiding pockets of vicious entities, mercenaries, and mutations. Once you near the **Galaxy News Radio [10.03]** station where Three Dog broadcasts from, you meet a haughty band of well-equipped humans clad in impressive Power Armor. These are the Brotherhood of Steel, and you embark on a hard-fought street-by-street cleansing, all the way to the G.N.R. Plaza, ridding the area of Super Mutants! Only then will the Wasteland's last DJ beckon you in to fight the Good Fight for the pockets of human resistance, trying to survive against these overwhelming odds....

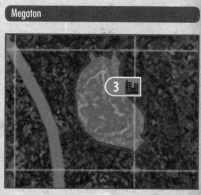

Megaton

3

QUEST FLOWCHART

	MAIN PATH	OPTIONAL PATH 1
Main Characters	President John Henry Eden, Three Dog, Sheriff Lucas Simms, Nova, "Gob" Gobtholemew, Moriarty, Silver, Sentinel Sarah Lyons	Moriarty, Silver
Locations	Silverlake, Megaton, Farragut West Metro Station, Friendship Health Metro Station, Chevy Chase North Metro Station, Galaxy News Radio	Megaton, Silverlake
Adv. Items/Abilities	Lockpick, Repair, Science, Speech, Sneak	Speech
Possible enemies	Enclave Eyebot, Protectron, Mole Rat, Ghoul Genus, Super Mutant Genus, Radroach, Raider, Deathclaw, Robot Genus, Talon Company Mercenary, Brotherhood of Steel, Centaur, Super Mutant Behemoth	
Karma Influence	Neutral	Neutral

Visit Springvale, checking Mailboxes

• Ammo and Chems, Your first Skill Book: Pugilism Illustrated

Exit Vault 101

• Enclave Radio Signal, Galaxy News Radio Signal

Investigate the nearby town of Megaton for information about Dad.

Locate and enter Megaton

[Optional] Begin any Freeform Quest or Miscellaneous Quest you wish

Speak to Sheriff Lucas Simms or any Megaton Settler about Dad

Speak to Colin Moriarty about Dad.

Plan A: The Fast-Talk Challenge: [Speech] Lie to his face

Plan B: The Fast-Hack Attack: [Science] Hack into Moriarty's Terminal

Plan C: 300 Pieces of Silver

Pay Moriarty 100 Caps

Agree to shake down Silver

[Optional] Deal with Silver in Springvale.

Locate Silver's Ranch House in Springvale

Continued on next page

Color code: | Objective | Action | Rewards |

APPENDICES — COMPLETION — TOUR — MISC. QUESTS — MAIN QUEST — BESTIARY — TRAINING

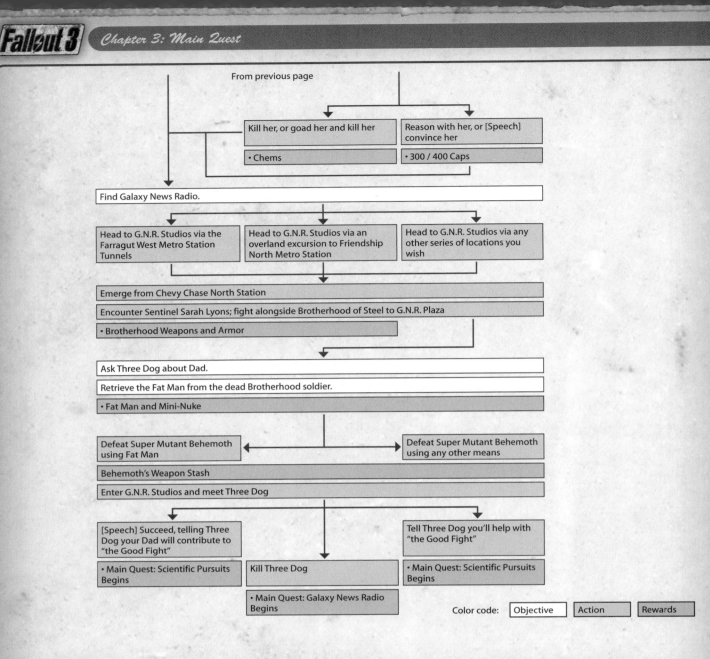

From previous page

Kill her, or goad her and kill her	Reason with her, or [Speech] convince her
• Chems	• 300 / 400 Caps

Find Galaxy News Radio.

Head to G.N.R. Studios via the Farragut West Metro Station Tunnels	Head to G.N.R. Studios via an overland excursion to Friendship North Metro Station	Head to G.N.R. Studios via any other series of locations you wish

Emerge from Chevy Chase North Station

Encounter Sentinel Sarah Lyons; fight alongside Brotherhood of Steel to G.N.R. Plaza

• Brotherhood Weapons and Armor

Ask Three Dog about Dad.

Retrieve the Fat Man from the dead Brotherhood soldier.

• Fat Man and Mini-Nuke

Defeat Super Mutant Behemoth using Fat Man	Defeat Super Mutant Behemoth using any other means

Behemoth's Weapon Stash

Enter G.N.R. Studios and meet Three Dog

[Speech] Succeed, telling Three Dog your Dad will contribute to "the Good Fight"		Tell Three Dog you'll help with "the Good Fight"
• Main Quest: Scientific Pursuits Begins	Kill Three Dog	• Main Quest: Scientific Pursuits Begins
	• Main Quest: Galaxy News Radio Begins	

Color code: | Objective | Action | Rewards |

WELCOME TO THE WASTELAND

As soon as you step from Vault 101 into the late afternoon sun, you're likely to reach Level 2. Consult the Character Development chapter (page 27) for examples of how and why to allocate points to your skills. Immediately, a new quest begins; you're tasked

In the distance are skeletons of the Capitol Building and Washington Monument. Southeast lies a corrugated junk-town named Megaton.

with reaching the nearby town of Megaton to investigate where your father might have gone. Step to the scenic overlook, and you can actually see Megaton; it's the large mound of tin and rusting metal glinting to the southeast.

NEW OBJECTIVE
"Investigate the nearby town of Megaton for information about Dad" begins.

 Tip

Bring up your Pip-Boy, and enter the Data > World Map screen. Megaton is already located on your map as an arrow point. This arrow point also appears under your on-screen compass, giving you an instant idea where to travel.

 Note

At this point, you can literally go anywhere and do anything you want! As there are infinite numbers of routes to and from the various locations across the Wasteland, the following routes are simply the optimal paths to take.

The rocket's red glare: Begin to remember certain landmarks, such as the Red Rocket Gas Stations.

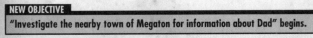

The easiest way to Megaton is to travel east along the remains of the tarmac road. As you head out into the open, two new radio signals are picked up through your Pip-Boy. The first is the Enclave Radio Signal, which is an official transmission from President Eden. A mixture of patriotic tunes of the ancients and information on creating a brave new world. The second is a broadcast from Galaxy News Radio in the D.C. Ruins; tunes are spun and rants are recorded by your DJ Three Dog. Both give clues to your adventure ahead. Switch one of them on by accessing the Data > Radio menu.

 Enclave Radio Signal   **Galaxy News Radio Signal**

Head down into the ruins of a small development called Springvale. Check the mailbox for some hidden items. This should clue you in that everywhere in town might contain useful items and objects. Some are junk, some can be sold, some can be combined to make customized weapons, and some augment your abilities, health, or skills. For now, make a quick sweep of the area. Also floating around here is an Enclave Eyebot, a recon droid that relays the Enclave Radio Signal and isn't harmful unless you fire at it. Move to the Red Rocket Gas Station where a corrugated sign points toward Megaton.

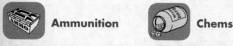 **Ammunition**   **Chems**

Tip

There's a junkie named Silver who fled from her "care-giver" in Megaton, and she lives just north of here in a small ranch house. You can't know this information yet, but you might wish to investigate her abode to save a back-and-forth visit later. Skip to "Conversing with Moriarty: Plan C" if you want to know more.

When you've finished rummaging around, follow the road south out of town and up a rocky path. To the south is an airplane tail rudder and other metal sections pointing skyward. This is Megaton, and you should head to the

Howdy partner, and welcome to Megaton. Don't shoot the Protectron Deputy!

front gate immediately. Lower your weapon, or simply don't fire it. The Protectron guarding the gate—Deputy Weld—is a friendly sort. Solomon the sniper sits in a nest above the gate too. As the diagonal metal slats grind upward, head inside this hold-out town of Wastelanders, weirdos, and human flotsam and jetsam.

Note

You may pass or interact with a thirsty man named Mickey, or one of a few Traders that traverse the Wasteland with a bodyguard and Brahmin in tow. For information on how to interact with these people, part of a series of tasks known as Freeform Quests, turn to the Tour of the Wasteland chapter, beginning on page 253.

MEGATON AND MORIARTY'S: THE RECONNOITER

Enter the ramshackle outpost called Megaton, and head south down the main pathway. Speak with, and remain civil to, the man with the cowboy hat; that's Sheriff Lucas Simms, and he's the law in these parts. At this point, you can begin **Miscellaneous Quest: The Power of the Atom** if you wish. However, you should definitely ask him if he has any information about the whereabouts of your father. If you agree to disarm the bomb, he directs you to a saloon on the southern "balcony" overlooking the town, a place called Moriarty's.

NEW OBJECTIVE
"Speak to Colin Moriarty about Dad" begins.

Now make a thorough exploration of the town, gaining backstory on the settlement about the different inhabitants. When you're done, head toward Moriarty's Saloon, ideally via the rusting ramp and over the roof of the clinic, past the Craterside Supplies store (where you can begin **Miscellaneous Quest: The Wasteland Survival Guide,** and around to the "top of the town." You can't miss Moriarty's Saloon! Enter via the front door; it's a lot more practical and safer than trying to Lockpick the back door.

Caution

Just for fun, try grabbing a bottle of whiskey that doesn't belong to you (the information appears in red) from the bar. The inhabitants turn on you, and the situation quickly gets out of control, violent, and actually rather entertaining! However, in this case, you'll get no clues about where to look for your father and you must simply stumble across the information on your own. This happens if you accidentally shoot anyone or threaten them.

Step into the gloomy interior of Moriarty's, and you have a host of inhabitants to quiz. The two most relevant to your quest are just to your right (southwest). A redhead named Nova doesn't take kindly to unpleasant dialog, but if you're civil, she can point you to the barkeep, Gob, who might know more about your dad. It looks like Gob's seen better days, but his amazing skin conditions are the results of the background radiation; he's a Ghoul, and they're usually treated like second-class citizens.

Also seated to your right is Lucy West. She has a sealed envelope she'd like you to deliver to a town called Arefu. Accept, and you begin **Miscellaneous Quest: Blood Tie**s.

 Buck this trend, and speak to him with politeness. He offers you cut-price drinks as a result!

 Continue to be polite, and ask about your father. If you succeed with your **Speech** challenge, Gob reveals that Moriarty has a computer terminal in the back of his office, which has all the goings-on in town.

If you fail the Speech challenge, you're simply pointed in the direction of Colin Moriarty.

TRAINING — BESTIARY — MAIN QUEST — MISC. QUESTS — TOUR — COMPLETION — APPENDICES

Tip

This is possibly the first time outside of Vault 101 that you've had chance to perform a Speech challenge. If you want to succeed every time (and the same rule applies to Lockpicking), simply save your game before you begin the conversation. If the Speech challenge fails, reload the game and try again. Or, simply face the consequences instead.

CONVERSING WITH COLIN MORIARTY

There are three separate ways you can glean information about your father's whereabouts from Moriarty.

PLAN A: THE FAST-TALK CHALLENGE

He's a brutal bar-owner with a no-nonsense attitude. Fight Moriarty's falsehoods with your own lies!

This plan quickly and succinctly resolves the problem of learning what Moriarty knows. Step up to the salt-and-pepper haired man with the swarthy complexion, and ask him about your father. Moriarty blusters on about you staying with him here, as a baby, and your dad's Brother-hood of Steel friend. Could this be true? You can't remember.

 However, when you get the chance, lie to his face, and say that Dad talked about him all the time. Succeed with your **Speech**, and Moriarty is slightly taken aback, and explains your dad headed southeast, into the city. He said he needed information from "the loonies" at Galaxy News Radio. A Pip-Boy Map Marker is placed, and you can leave Megaton and begin "Coming in from the Countryside" right away.

NEW OBJECTIVE
"Find Galaxy News Radio" begins.

PLAN B: THE FAST-HACK ATTACK

You can try his plan if you fail the Speech challenge, or don't want to complete Plan C, although it is more dangerous. Step into Moriarty's back room, just behind Gob, and make sure no one is in the room with you.

Sidle up to Moriarty's Terminal, and use **Science** to hack into it. Once at the Server Menu, there are three sub-menus to read through; Residents, Visitors, and Tabs. The first two are of most interest to you:

Residents:

Jericho: He has some dirt on the "Jenny incident." Perhaps you can use this on Jericho, too!

Leo Stahl: He's a junkie, and part of the Stahl clan with Andy and Jenny.

Andy Stahl: Hated for opening up a rival bar in town. Fortunately, Moriarty still has the best draw around for customers looking for a good time, and it isn't Gob.

Billy Creel: He swigs Nuka-Cola and looks after little orphan Maggie. Moriarty is suspicious of his motives.

Doc Church: The town quack has a secret: he used to tend the wounds of the hated Slavers at Paradise Falls.

Visitors:

Mr. Burke: Some weirdo in a sharp suit staying at the saloon, waiting for an "opportunist."

James (Vault 101): He made contact! He's heading to Galaxy News Radio. Shockingly, he met Moriarty 20 years ago, then sought out and entered Vault 101. You thought he'd been here all his life!

Exit the terminal, and leave town. You can follow the Pip-Boy's Map Marker directions, and begin "Coming in from the Countryside."

NEW OBJECTIVE
"Find Galaxy News Radio" begins.

Tip

When you're hacking, time stands still, so you can take as long as you like to read the information on a terminal. When you're choosing phrases as a password, and you're down to your last attempt, quit out and start again.

PLAN C: FREEFORM QUEST: 300 PIECES OF SILVER

A ramshackle ranch house on the northwest side of town is where Silver the junkie shoots up.

Try this plan if you fail your Speech challenge. It takes a while and involves a short search of Springvale, but nets a few Caps. Speak with Moriarty, and keep asking for information on your father. Finally, Moriarty agrees to let you know where he went...for 100 Caps! You have three options:

You can find your own way to your father, and locate Galaxy News Radio without it being pinpointed on your World Map. Simply locate Galaxy News Radio from the guide map, manually pinpoint it, and leave town without paying this snake!

You can pay him 100 Caps, and he pinpoints Galaxy News Radio on your map. Begin "Coming in from the Countryside."

If you have less than 100 Caps, Moriarty has a proposition for you. A "junkie bitch" named Silver borrowed some Caps from Mori-arty, promising to funnel Jet and Psycho for a good price. Agree, and Moriarty instantly raises the price to 300 Caps! With little to bargain with, grudgingly accept the proposal, and head out of town.

NEW OBJECTIVE [OPTIONAL]
"Deal with Silver in Springvale" begins.

Silver is an ex-prostitute, current junkie, and thief. She's the most pitiful (and only) resident of Springvale.

Head north out of Megaton, passing the Red Rocket Gas Station as you reach Springvale, and continue northward up the road, until you spot the small ranch house on your left (northwest). Either entrance allows access to the residence. Silver wants to know what you're doing in her home.

 You can simply kill her, ransack her home, and return to Moriarty.

 You can goad her into attacking you, and then kill her, then return to Moriarty. With either of the first two choices, you can grab Jet and Psycho, plus Health and Chems from a First Aid Box.

You can reason with her, and ask her to give you enough Caps to pay off Moriarty (300), so she can live in peace. Well, until her next hit, anyway.

 Or, you can use **Speech** to convince her to hand over what she owes, and you'll convince Moriarty she left town. She agrees, and hands over 400 Caps. Things are looking up! Return to Moriarty, and speak with him again. You only need give him 100 Caps and tell him Silver has left town. In return, he tells you where your father went: to the Galaxy News Radio offices in the city.

Caps (300)
If you reasoned with Silver.

Caps (400)
If you Speech challenged Silver.

 Tip
Plan C is actually the best of the bunch, as you can net 300 Caps in a few minutes!

NEW OBJECTIVE
"Find Galaxy News Radio" begins.

COMING IN FROM THE COUNTRYSIDE

With concrete evidence of your father's trail, you can now leave Megaton. However, before you go, you should visit Craterside Supplies, and speak with Moira Brown. You can optionally begin **Miscellaneous Quest: The Wasteland Survival Guide** during your conversation, but the main reason you're here is to sell and buy items, and use her Work Bench if you want to begin to customize your weaponry. Depending on how much other exploring you've done, you may have enough versions of the same weapon to Repair it. Refer to the Weapons Training section (page 33) for a complete understanding. When you've tooled up with a good-size arsenal of two or three good quality weapons, some ammunition, and a set of sturdy armor, head out of town.

Leave the relative safety of Megaton, and travel roughly east-northeast over the rocky outcrops, until the land becomes a more gentle slope of dead grass and rusting outbuildings. Pass the low fence, keep left of the water tower, and move to the left (north) side

of the Super-Duper Mart. Head to a small bridge to the northeast. However, instead of running along the top of the bridge, drop under it. It's safer, and on the far side is a booby-trapped Ammo Box, usually filled with Grenades.

 To reach it, move toward the prepped Frag Mine, and quickly disarm it. The larger your **Repair** skill is, the more time you have to react. Claim the loot, then continue northeast.

Ammunition

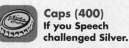 **Tip**
You now have two main options:

Going Underground: Locate the Galaxy News Radio offices via the fastest route through the linked Underground Metro Tunnels (recommended).

Finding Friendship: Continue overland, looking for the Friendship North Metro Station.

There's a third option of course: trek on one of an infinite number of routes, exploring the city. This is recommended only if you aren't worried about completing this quest.

The former plan is slightly shorter and safer, and it begins to unlock the labyrinth of sewers, passages, and train tracks that still exist under the D.C. Ruins, allowing you to Fast Travel to these destinations in the future.

GOING UNDERGROUND

PART A: DIRECT PATH TO CHEVY CHASE

Head down here if you're more agoraphobic than claustrophobic!

From the bridge, turn slightly more southeast, prep your weapon for possible combat, and move under the remains of the freeway overpass. Unless you're Sneaking, you may encounter a few Raiders in this area; especially if you continue past the Metro Station entrance into the flat, riverside courtyard just beyond. Attack them if you wish, but your best bet is to locate Farragut West Metro Station quickly and nonviolently. Enter the chain gate, and head into the underground. Immediately enter the metal door marked "Authorized Personnel Only" if you want to thoroughly search the station.

Enter the small office area, and begin a quick search for items inside the lockers, filing cabinets, and desks. You should find some Caps and Ammo in small quantities. Of more interest is a Metro Security Terminal, mounted to one of the walls.

 Use your **Science** skill to hack into the terminal. Here, you can Activate Metro Protectron (the other choices are offline). This boots up the Protectron standing in the nearby pod. It starts off neutral but becomes hostile if you fire your weapon. There's no other reason to activate this, other than to destroy it for XP and Energy Cell ammunition.

When you're done here, move down the entrance concourse to the turnstiles, and begin dropping Mole Rats exiting from a doorway to your right (northwest). Ransack this office, then locate the maintenance tunnel entrance on the northwest wall.

Head northeast down the tunnel steps, blasting Mole Rats as you go. Pass the flaming barrel, enter the generator pit area, and climb the metal stairs to the top. To the northwest is a mesh gate with some disgusting-looking humanoids roaming around. Ignore them for the moment, and open the metal door to the southeast. Inside this office there's a First Aid Box on the desk, next to a terminal, and a safe on the floor. Ransack the First Aid Box for a Metro Utility Gate Key.

Enjoy melee combat? Then open the gates, and begin the Ghoul bludgeoning! Otherwise, try a more cunning plan....

Activate the MDCTA Service Access Terminal (no hacking or Science skill is needed), and stop the gas flow test. This shuts off escaping gas farther into this tunnel structure, which means you can fire weapons without the surrounding area exploding! You can unlock the floor safe from this terminal, too.

 Or if you have enough Bobby Pins, you can use **Lockpick** on the safe for a small XP boost.

The safe contains various items (such as Caps and weaponry), plus a few interesting objects:

 First Aid Box Health and Chems

 Utility Gate Key

 Holotape: DCTA Laser Firearms Protocol
Notes about firing Laser Weapons near flammable pipes.

Nikola Tesla and You
+1 Energy Weapons (when read)

Head northwest, toward the utility gate, and unlock it using the key you just found. If you didn't find the key, try your Lockpick skill. The moment the gates swing open, four unsavory characters race in to maul you. These are "Feral" Ghouls, once-humans driven mad by radiation. Naturally, you can wade in, get mauled, and hopefully survive. Or, you can shut the gate, and pop their skulls from safety (just make sure you're on the right side of the gate!). Or, you can shoot out the generators to your right, catching the Ghouls in the explosion, and severely weakening them.

> ## Note
> "Flaming barrels" usually direct you to the correct route, so look out for them!
>
> Also note, Ghouls vary in strength and type depending on your Player Level. Hostile entities with different "versions" display this, and are referenced as "Genus" in the Hostiles Overview at the beginning of this quest.

Not only can you continue your Coffee Mug collection, but there's a host of valuable ordnance in here, too!

With the threat of drooling lumpyskins abated, stop and check out this chamber. Stairs heading down from the gantry end at a door in the southwest wall, under your feet. Descend there.

 If you can, jimmy open the hatch door using your **Lockpick** skill. Inside is a treasure trove of armaments. Ignore the Coffee Mugs (they simply add to your encumbrance unless you have room to spare and can sell them quickly), and instead open up the four Ammo Boxes, grab Missiles, take the U.S. Army: *30 Handy Flamethrower Recipes*, Assault Rifle, 10mm Pistol, Baseball Bat, and Frag Grenades.

Then head up the stairs to the metal door in the northwest wall, use Lockpicking or the Utility Gate Key to open it, and ascend the stairs. At the top, open the Door to Tenleytown/Friendship Station.

Ammo Box Ammunition (4)

Missiles

U.S. Army: 30 Handy Flamethrower Recipes
+1 Big Guns (when read)

Assault Rifle

10mm Pistol

Baseball Bat

Frag Grenades

Step onto the train tracks, and look east. There's a carriage in the distant gloom, and the tunnel curves around and continues (for information on this route, check out Part B: Indirect Path to Chevy Chase, below), but your preferred direction is to head south into the connecting tunnel. Note the daubed graffiti on the left corner of the wall, near the Nuka-Cola machine; this points the way to the G.N.R. Building. Head past the machine, and make a right, moving west. You're on the Red Line, heading toward the Tenleytown Station.

Continue along the tunnel as it bends around to the south, into a station mezzanine. Expect both Ghouls and a huge, eight-foot-tall hulking Super Mutant to be waiting for you here. If possible, stay away so the Ghouls and Super Mutant attack each other, and mop up survivors. The other tunnels here are blocked, so ascend one of the broken escalators, pass the ticket booth, and head east, then blast (or ignore) the Radroach problem. Follow the exit tunnel left (north), all the way to the metal gates; note the next "G.N.R. graffiti" daubed on the floor.

PART B: INDIRECT PATH TO CHEVY CHASE (VIA FRIENDSHIP STATION)

Ghouls have gruesome, elongated fingernails and a persistent attack. Try Hunting Rifle headshots at range to avoid close-up blasting.

Return to the spot where you spotted the first G.N.R. graffiti, and check out the tunnel to the east that you haven't visited before. This allows you to pinpoint another station on your map, so you can Fast Travel to it later. Pass the train carriage, then look right (east), and look out! There's a Ghoul problem in this connecting tunnel. Once you've eradicated the Ghouls, inspect the generator in the alcove. The shelves to the left of it hold a First Aid Box and other items.

 First Aid Health and Chems

Then step into the other tunnel, or continue along the one you were in; both emerge into another mezzanine, complete with waiting Ghoul fiends. Then climb up the escalator, pass the Wastelander's burning shack, and head east, then north, out of the underground station. On the way, prepare for at least four more Ghouls and a couple of Radroaches. Grab a few items from a small office to your left (west). Hack into the terminal or use Lockpick skill to open the wall safe for more ammo and some Caps. Now emerge into Friendship Heights station. A small Raider party is camped out behind you; if you want to learn how to deal with them, and what items they're guarding, check out the end of "Finding Friendship." Now return to finish Part A and exit Tenleytown Station, emerging at Chevy Chase North.

Note

Friendship Heights Station allows you access into the Wasteland, and the outskirts of the D.C. Ruins. It's useful for escaping, but is the wrong way to go if you're heading to Galaxy News Radio.

FINDING FRIENDSHIP

Tip

The following route shows the quickest route to take, heading along the northern outskirts of the D.C. Ruins. Alternately, you can make a very long, looping clockwise semicircle north from the Super-Duper Mart, into the Wasteland wilderness, and then head south directly into Friendship Station, to avoid a high concentration of Super Mutants. Of course, the Wasteland has its own share of beasts to fear!

If you decided to explore the more dangerous "over-ground" around the D.C. Ruins, head up the tarmac road from the bridge near the Super-Duper Mart, and ready yourself for Raider combat as you reach the ruined freeway overpass. Be very careful around here. Sometimes a Deathclaw heads down from the northern wilds of the Wasteland to attack, and if one does, prepare to launch everything you have at it. These are deadly predators! Once immediate

threats have been nullified, continue vaguely eastward, following the tarmac sections of road that remain.

A swipe from one of these monstrosities can cause a real Stimpak shortage; you've been warned!

Up ahead is a parked big-rig truck, and guarding it is a small band of Talon Company Mercenaries, along with a single robot protector. You can head north, skirting this dangerous area, or (if you want to test out your Hunting Rifle), bring down the Talon Merc with your favored gun. A good place to hide is inside the back of the container the truck was attached to. Sidestep out, blast, and then head back to cover. Rummage through the three Ammo Boxes inside the container before you continue.

 Ammo Box Ammunition (3)

Tip

You may wish to save your game before tackling the eight-foot-tall cannibal Super Mutants roaming this next city block.

Charging a Minigun-wielding Super Mutant, and you're carrying a plank of wood? Not your finest hour....

Ready yourself for some brutal combat (or Sneak north and around to miss this mayhem) by continuing east, toward and under a bridge, and locate two Super Mutants, and their "pet," a disgusting mishmash of skin and bone known as a Centaur. This may be the moment to use the Grenades you found under the bridge earlier. Finish off your trio of mutations with a Hunting Rifle, and finally an Assault Rifle as you reach closer combat.

Complete your Super Mutant execution by continuing east, around the horribly sharp spikes, and enter a Super Mutant "bonfire." A couple of these are scattered around the city, and on a central platform near a fire, a strong Super Mutant lies in wait. Introduce him to a Grenade or two, tearing him apart, and then pick through the corpses of the Super Mutants, and the items stacked by the wall, once you've finishing healing yourself. The following is available, and well worth picking up:

TRAINING — BESTIARY — MAIN QUEST — MISC. QUESTS — TOUR — COMPLETION — APPENDICES

First Aid Box Health and Chems (2)

 Ammo Box Ammunition (3)

 Mini-Nuke

The way east is blocked, so head north, between the bridge and rubble pile, then turn right (east), and skirt the ruined buildings until you reach a patch of open ground with a Red Rocket Gas Station ahead of you. Pass to the right of the gas station, and continue east-southeast until you spot the signs for the Friendship Heights Station! Unfortunately, you're not welcomed particularly enthusiastically by the small band of Raiders here.

There are around four Raiders here, including one armed with a Flamer: another exciting weapon to add to your collection! First though, you need to get it off the Raider's hands. Try a long-range Hunting Rifle or lob Grenades. Crouch and use the low wall and metal barricades as cover. A great plan is to aim for the motorbike propped up behind the Raiders engaging you. When the motorbike explodes, the splash damage wounds multiple foes at once! When everyone with bondage gear has gasped their last, inspect this Raider camp. They've been busy little collectors—grab any from the following list. You can sleep on a bed inside their tent for a great way to replenish your health without Stimpaks.

 Ammo Box Ammunition (2)

 10mm Pistols and Submachine Guns

 First Aid Box Health and Chems

 Chems

It's official. Flamer fuel works wonders on those fast-moving fiends!

You can now open the metal gate to Tenleytown/Friendship Station. You've arrived at a location linked to during "Going Underground"; for a more thorough exploration, read that section of this quest. For a quick route to Chevy Chase North, head south and then west, into the station mezzanine, burning Ghouls that race to meet and eat you. Head down the escalator by the burning Wastelander shack, and face south. Run down the train tunnel, following it west as it curves around. Once you reach the connecting tunnel with the graffiti and arrows pointing to the G.N.R. Building, follow them all the way to Chevy Chase North.

 Tip

At around this point, you should be able to Fast Travel. Consult the Mapping the Capital Wasteland section (page 31) to read up on the benefits of this, and use it when you can!

ON THE PROWL WITH LYON'S PRIDE

Super Mutants are active near the radio station (note the G.N.R. radio mast). Fortunately, so are the Brotherhood of Steel.

Head up the steps, and turn left (south), walking out into the open and crossing the debris-strewn crossroads, toward a large indentation in the ground. You're close to the G.N.R. Building, but first deal with two lunging Super Mutants attempting to pepper you with Hunting Rifle fire! Return the favor. As you strike, you should be aware of a group of armored humans aiding you in this battle.

Hold your fire, and move to the flaxen-haired woman and engage her in conversation. This is Sentinel Sarah Lyons, and she isn't taking any crap, especially from the likes of you. You can tag along as she provides back-up to her brethren

The first member of the Brotherhood of Steel is actually a sister: a combat veteran named Sentinel Lyons.

guarding the G.N.R. Building. She can provide more information on the building, but she soon cuts off the conversation. Follow her and Initiate Reddin into a covered passage and around a corner. On a bloody mattress lies Initiate Jennings, the latest casualty of the Brotherhood's battle against the Super Mutants. You can scavenge Energy Cells and Power Armor from her corpse without incurring the Brotherhood's wrath. Unfortunately, you aren't trained in the use of Power Armor yet, so you might wish to discard or sell it until you've visited the Citadel.

 Energy Cells

 Laser Pistol

 Power Armor

 Power Helmet

There's little time to pause, because gunfire erupts from the ruins of a school to the west of you, and Lyons orders her pride forward to take over the building. Head west, staying to the left and the cover it affords you, and bring your ordnance to bear on a trio of Super Mutants at the entrance. If you're trying to conserve ammunition, let the Brotherhood do the firing. Then enter the doorway to the remains of the Early Dawn Elementary School, and follow the Brotherhood as they weave through the building.

Stay on the ground floor as you systematically check every room for Super Mutants, and then Ammo Boxes and stashes of items on shelving. Spend some time checking each area, or wait until after the subsequent battle and return here to completely pick the area clean. Or, you can run up the stairs, and use the connecting planks to head south across to the other side of the school, raining hot lead on the Super Mutant scum below.

BRINGING DOWN A BEHEMOTH

Push out into the G.N.R. Building Plaza, where a Super Mutant attack squad is firing on some Brotherhood Knights dug in behind sandbags, guarding the building entrance. Here are a few of many possible tactics:

Wade in and circle-strafe around the biggest "Brute" threat, then move to a subsequent target, and so on. Expect to soak up damage but end the combat quickly.

Stay behind the relative safety of the school wall, either on the ground or upper floor, and snipe at foes using a weapon such as the Hunting Rifle. Mix this up with Grenades lobbed at the feet of the biggest Brutes.

Or, you can simply let the Brotherhood secure the area. This results in more casualties, but you expend less ordnance. Whatever the plan, make sure you search the corpses after this battle is over.

Behold the behemoth! Attacking this monstrosity with small arms fire usually gets you killed.

You have little time to regroup after the last of the Super Mutants falls to your teamwork, when the biggest Super Mutant you've ever seen lumbers into the plaza! This is the fearsome Super Mutant Behemoth, and he's a grave threat to the surviving members of the Brotherhood. Just before the Behemoth arrives, move to the remains of the fountain at the center of the plaza, and locate the dead Brotherhood soldier. Loot the corpse, and obtain the greatest invention in the history of ordnance: the Fat Man!

NEW OBJECTIVE
"Retrieve the Fat Man from the dead Brotherhood soldier" begins.

NEW OBJECTIVE
"Help defeat the Super Mutant Behemoth" begins.

The Fat Man is a just-portable nuclear bomb launcher that fires Mini-Nukes at its target. Although you can defeat the Behemoth with other weaponry (providing you hide in the school, keep moving, and don't care about Brotherhood casualties), a far more entertaining plan is to retreat at least 20 feet from the Behemoth, and then launch a Mini-Nuke into its leathery, 20-foot-tall hide! Then hit it again to ensure that it goes down. Once the dust has cleared, and you've searched the Behemoth corpse for a huge stash of items, you can speak with Lyons again. She thanks you for your help, and you commiserate about Initiate Reddin's demise, if you weren't fast enough to help out.

 Behemoth's Weapon Stash

 Note

This Fat Man is one of 9 located in the Capital Wasteland. The Mini-Nuke is one of 71. Consult the Tour of the Wasteland chapter for the locations of these collectible items.

As soon as the Behemoth has been destroyed, you can leave the pride, and move southeast to the main doors at the foot of the G.N.R. Building. Use the intercom to get the Brotherhood Knights to unlock the door for you. Enter the building, and optionally speak with Knight Dillon (he's the one brandishing the Minigun). He tells you that Three Dog is expecting you.

NEW OBJECTIVE
"Ask Three Dog about Dad" begins.

Heya, buddy! It's your friend in the wilderness, now in the flesh! Is he the best in the business? Agatha's fans might disagree....

Climb either set of stairs to the balcony, and optionally loot the empty rooms for the odd Bottle Cap, before moving to the middle corridor. Head east, opening the Door to G.N.R. Studios, and head up the stairs to your right (south). Anything you loot is now stealing, so keep your fingers out of any cabinets or desks, at least until Three Dog tells you what you want to hear. Head upstairs to meet the man himself!

Three Dog isn't what you'd call self-deprecating, and as long as you can listen through his grand entrance, he mentions that he's talked with your father. Then he impresses on you how vital his services are. After all, people out there are barely making it day-to-day, and a whole host of factions attempt to muscle in on different territories. It's a chaotic mess out there!

 At this point, you can mention that Three Dog fights the good fight with his voice and radio station. Your **Intelligence** impresses him more than standard answers.

Keep the conversation civil, and Three Dog tells you that to know more about your Dad's location, you'll have to contribute to the "Good Fight." You have two main choices at this point:

You can use **Speech** to reason with him that once you find your Dad, he can help with the good fight. If successful, Three Dog asks whether he would really help the cause. Answer "I know he will. He's always talked about doing what's right." Three Dog immediately tells you where your father is! This allows you to completely skip the next **Main Quest: Galaxy News Radio**, and move to begin Scientific Pursuits.

If you choose any other conversation, or fail your Speech challenge, or pass the challenge, but choose the other answer, Three Dog begins to tell you exactly how you can help him with the good fight. A signal needs boosting, and you've just volunteered to drag a dish to the top of the biggest structure in the region. **Main Quest: Galaxy News Radio** begins now!

TRAINING — BESTIARY — MAIN QUEST — MISC. QUESTS — TOUR — COMPLETION — APPENDICES

Galaxy News Radio

You're currently trying to relax inside the compound of the **Galaxy News Radio [10.03]** station as a guest of Three Dog. He reveals that your father did indeed pass through, and in fact, he'll even reveal where your father went (mentioning a contact called Doctor Li and "Project Purity"). But first you must help Three Dog: a battle for the hearts and minds of the remaining humans fighting to survive in this nightmare. Three Dog's most pressing concern is the satellite booster dish that was attached to the **Washington Monument [17.05]** until it fell off under heavy Super Mutant fire. The dish needs to be replaced so Three Dog can yell at the entire Wasteland. You'll need to embark through the D.C. Ruins interior, remaining calm as you search for a ruined **Metro station [11.05]** that allows you access to **the National Mall [Zone 17]**. Only then can you reach the **Museum of Technology [17.10]**, secure it from Super Mutants, and retrieve a small communications dish. From there, the battle continues across the Mall, to the Washington Monument itself; currently under Brotherhood of Steel protection. Ascend to the top of the monument, and get that radio station up and running!

Galaxy News Radio

QUEST FLOWCHART

	MAIN PATH	OPTIONAL PATH
Main Characters	Three Dog, Brotherhood of Steel	Three Dog, Brotherhood of Steel
Locations	Galaxy News Radio, Collapsed Car Tunnel, Dupont Circle Station, Museum Station, Museum of Technology, The Washington Monument	Galaxy News Radio, Collapsed Car Tunnel, Dupont Circle Station, Museum Station, Museum of Technology, The Washington Monument, Hamilton's Hideaway
Adv. Items/Abilities	Lockpick, Science, Small Guns	Lockpick, Science, Small Guns
Possible enemies	Ghoul Genus, Raider, Vicious Dog, Super Mutant Genus	Ghoul Genus, Raider, Vicious Dog, Super Mutant Genus
Karma Influence	Positive	Neutral

MAIN PATH:

G.N.R. Building; Three Dog's Room

Kill Three Dog (–Karma)

Find the Museum of Technology.

Speak to Three Dog

• Note: Virgo II Lunar Lander
• Washington Monument Access

• Main Quest: The Search Continues

Head out of the rear entrance. Move to Metro Central, then to the Mall

Locate The Mall by any other route

Enter Museum of Technology

Discover Rivet City

Retrieve the Communications Relay Dish.

Secure the Atrium, work your way to the Virgo II exhibit

• Virgo II Dish

Find the Washington Monument.

OPTIONAL PATH:

Complete Main Quest: Scientific Pursuits first

You are offered an alternate reward

Museum Information Terminal

• Tech Museum Note

Freeform Quest: Jiggs' Loot

• Jiggs' Loot Passcode
• Gun Locker Key
• 200 Caps
• Note to find Prime in Jury St. Metro

Continued on next page

Continued on next page

Color code: | Objective | Action | Rewards |

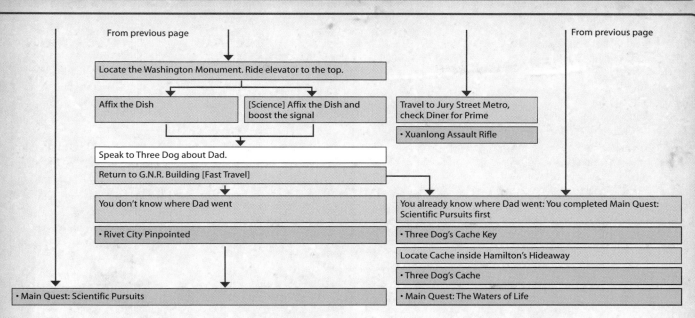

From previous page

From previous page

Locate the Washington Monument. Ride elevator to the top.

Affix the Dish

[Science] Affix the Dish and boost the signal

Travel to Jury Street Metro, check Diner for Prime

• Xuanlong Assault Rifle

Speak to Three Dog about Dad.

Return to G.N.R. Building [Fast Travel]

You don't know where Dad went

You already know where Dad went: You completed Main Quest: Scientific Pursuits first

• Rivet City Pinpointed

• Three Dog's Cache Key

Locate Cache inside Hamilton's Hideaway

• Three Dog's Cache

• Main Quest: Scientific Pursuits

• Main Quest: The Waters of Life

DODGING GHOULS NEAR DUPONT CIRCLE

If this isn't your view as you leave Galaxy News Radio, you're going the wrong way!

Conclude your conversation with Three Dog. If you failed your previous Speech challenge, or decided to stay and fight the "Good Fight," Three Dog has a mission for you. Some Super Mutant scum recently took a potshot at Three Dog's broadcast relay, mounted high atop the Washington Monument. Without this relay, Three Dog can be heard only in the D.C. Ruins area. A Brotherhood soldier mentioned that he saw a dish in one of D.C.'s old museums. Three Dog wants you to find this dish, bring it to the top of the Washington Monument, and jerry-rig it so Three Dog's banter can be heard across the entire Wasteland!

NEW OBJECTIVE
"Find the Museum of Technology" begins.

You're now given two notes. One is a password ("Renfield") allowing you into the Washington Monument, while the other gives you photograph of the dish you're stealing; it's from the Virgo II Lunar Lander. You also receive a Map Marker showing the route to take to reach the museum. Head out of the rear entrance, go north down the stairs to the wooden door, then down the stairs to the Door to Dupont Circle.

 Caution

Three Dog is your friend, and it's not advisable to piss him off, especially because he's friendly with the three Brotherhood of Steel Paladins who rush in to his aid; good luck with your impending slaughter! If you do kill Three Dog, even though he doesn't have much to steal, you begin a quest called The Search Continues. This ends once you discover Rivet City.

Note: Virgo II Lunar Lander

Washington Monument Access

Aside from Fast Travel to a nearby Mall building or station you may have previously visited, there are dozens of different routes from here to the Mall, where the Museum of Technology is located. However, the following route is optimal. Follow the route closely, because it's very easy to get lost in the rabbit warren of underground tunnels!

If you kill Three Dog, you won't be given any clues and must chance upon your dad's location, or follow the directions in this guide!

Carefully drop from the ledge, onto the rubble, and peer down to the lower ground area below. There's no way back to the G.N.R. Building door, so the only way is onward. Head down to the sloping dirt near a walkway overpass. To the east is a station entrance down to Metro Junction. Do not take this route! Instead, ignore the overpass, and prepare for combat with around three Ghouls prowling the remains of a sunken roadway.

You can try to Sneak, shoot each Ghoul with a favored weapon, or aim for the rusting coach liner, causing it to explode and hit all three Ghouls with a shockwave of splash damage! This causes nearby vehicles to catch fire and explode in a chain reaction; make sure you're away from the explosions! Pick through the rubble-strewn sunken roadway until you reach the metal door with a "Mall Outpost" graffiti sign daubed next to it. Dupont Circle is just ahead (south) of you, but you can't climb up the rubble to reach it (although the circle itself isn't necessary to investigate). A detour is called for: open the Door to Collapsed Car Tunnel.

TRAINING — BESTIARY — MAIN QUEST — MISC. QUESTS — TOUR — COMPLETION — APPENDICES

After a short connecting tunnel, the chamber opens up into a large tunnel with concrete debris and mangled beams jutting everywhere. Of the two exit doors here, the optimal one to run to is southwest, behind sandbags. Or, you can turn south, and venture farther into the Collapsed Car Tunnel.

 Try **Sneaking** along the western edge of the tunnel, without attracting the attention of any nearby Ghouls. There's a First Aid Box on the wall to open, too. Continue until you reach the door on the western wall, at the tunnel's far end.

Or, you can begin to slaughter the quartet of Ghouls roaming this tunnel. However, you must be extremely careful with your gunfire. One stray bullet can hit any of the rusting vehicles, causing them to burn and explode, usually killing you if you're not out of the blast radius. Try using V.A.T.S. to pinpoint your foes.

Or, you can remain at the tunnel entrance, blast the nearest car, stand well back, and let the entire tunnel explode before you pick through the debris and mop up any surviving Ghouls.

 First Aid Box Health and Chems

Two doors lead out. The southern one leads to a set of steps (watch for a waiting Ghoul!), and a Door to Dupont Circle. Exit this, and you're out in the open again, at the base of the escalators leading up to Dupont Circle itself. Although

A pair of fearsome mutations await you in Dupont Circle Station. Use the nearby office filing cabinets as cover.

you can head across here—investigating a Raider encampment in the circle's center and nearby ruined homes, and then locating Foggy Bottom Station entrance to the west—this is a much longer and more dangerous route. Instead, immediately turn right, and enter Dupont Circle Station.

Assuming you took the northern of the two doors, head down a short passage to a metal door that opens to Dupont Circle Station. A graffiti daub signifies that you're on the right track. Stride through the connecting office, pausing only to rifle through some filing cabinets for the odd Cap or two, and optionally release a Protectron using the security terminal. It may distract the two Super Mutants in the station concourse; shoot them down or flee in fear. Locate the alcove in the southwest wall, and open the metal door to flee to the maintenance tunnel and beyond. Onward and downward!

UTILITY CAVERN TO METRO CENTRAL

Descend the maintenance tunnel steps to the hatch door, and step into a train tunnel. Head left (south), but immediately turn right and cross onto the other tracks, turning north to investigate a small alcove with metal barricades propped up. If you're quick, you can

startle a Raider awake, and kill the fool while he or she sleeps. Loot the corpse and the shelves near the bed for some Ammo and other items. Then continue south to the door with the red light near it. Step into a connecting chamber, heading down the steps to slay another Raider, then look right (north) and grab more items (including Blood Pack and Chems) from a small alcove stash.

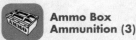

Ammo Box Ammunition (3)   **First Aid Box Health and Chems**

Your move, punk! Expect crossfire, angry Raiders, and little room to maneuver.

Follow the corridor south and down to a small office that opens up into an underground cavern.

 Before you dash into combat, you may wish to employ your **Science** skill to hack into the wall terminal and disarm the turrets.

Now head onto a gantry that winds downward, and stay back while you tag two ceiling turrets and a number of Raiders running about this area. Toss Grenades at the mohawked band of psychopaths ahead or below you. When the coast is clear, continue heading downward, through a low zigzag gantry, to a utility gate at ground level. This leads to a small connecting sewer tunnel, where the remains of Ghoul bodies lie decomposing. Head south to the Door to Metro Central.

METRO CENTRAL TO THE MALL

After a small connecting corridor, step into a subterranean chamber and watch a pitched battle between two Raiders and Ghouls that just keep on coming! Fortunately, you can wait until the Ghouls overpower the Raiders, and then slay the bony fiends yourself, or just mow everything down if time and XP are factors. When the room is cleared (watch for more Ghouls heading your way), inspect the weapon caches here. Then head east, out to a rubble-filled metro tunnel, where radiation levels are higher than normal. Another graffiti daub points out that the Mall is to your right. Continue along either of the parallel tunnels toward the mezzanine section, dropping some isolated Ghouls on the way.

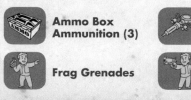

Ammo Box Ammunition (3)   **Chems**

Frag Grenades   **10mm Pistol**

Chinese Assault Rifle

Continue pressing southward, ignoring the escalators, and looking for the tunnels marked "Museum Station." Head down the rubble-filled tunnel, to the right of the half-buried carriages, and bring out your canine-killing weaponry as a pack of Vicious Dogs dashes out to bite you. Leave them to fight with a Ghoul, or slay them all. Check the nearby tripod light for some Ammo Boxes, then press on to the tunnel's southern end and the graffiti pointing to a short passageway. This leads to the Door to Museum Station.

Ammo Box Ammunition (3)

A rooftop Raider takedown is easier than looking up, feeling exposed, and getting shot at from foes you can't pinpoint.

Exit the small storage room, and head for the illuminated stairs, attacking a Ghoul in the process. The graffiti on the wall verifies your direction. The top of the stairs are blocked by a trap door that opens upward; activate the electrical switch on the right wall to open the door. This leads to a fancy pool table room, with a Raider keen to keep this area "members only." Slay him, and scrabble about looking for items; among the Cherry Bombs and Chems is a comic you might wish to read.

Grognak the Barbarian
+1 Melee Weapons (when read)

Head east, onto more metro tunnel tracks and the Red Line, and ignore the area to the left (north) of you. Cross between the metal columns, continuing up toward the Museum Station mezzanine, killing Raiders as you go. When you reach the escalator area, prepare for a small band of Raiders, including one standing on top of the rusting carriages. Drop down from the mezzanine balcony and slaughter him (as pictured), then take out any remaining Raiders on the escalators. Head east and out the metal gate to the Mall.

Tip

Make a mental note that the Museum Station is the one with wooden planks connecting the rusting carriage roofs. The more spatially aware you are, the less confusing your exploration will be.

Head up and out into the Mall. Ahead and in the distance is the Capitol Building, a haven for Super Mutants. To the left are the Mall's grounds, a warren of open trenches with Super Mutant horrors at every corner. You can remain outside, under Super Mutant gunfire, or turn right (southeast) and immediately run to the wooden double doors of the Museum of Technology. Your quest for the Virgo II dish now begins in earnest. Head inside to the main foyer.

The true extent of the damage to the D.C. Ruins is now apparent. Super Mutants rule, and the Capitol is in shambles.

MAYHEM IN THE MUSEUM: SECURING THE ATRIUM

Dive to the left or right as you enter the atrium, and use any of the crumbling columns as cover. There's Super Mutant activity in this zone. Drop the lumbering beast ahead of you, and the one heading down the balcony stairs to your left (east). Once the place is silent, investigate the area, passing the destroyed biplane and the stairs to all the exhibits (where you'll head shortly). In the western corner, read the Research Lead's Terminal for some messages he left to other staff members hundreds of years ago. Then move to the ground floor entrance desk. There's a small amount of food, but all the computers are destroyed. Of more interest is the Museum Information Terminal kiosk, with the curved plastic dome surrounding the terminal. Access this now.

NEW OBJECTIVE
"Retrieve the Communications Relay Dish" begins.

FREEFORM QUEST
Jiggs' Loot (Part 1 of 4)

The Museum Information Terminal has background data on all the exhibits, a list of forthcoming lectures (now cancelled indefinitely), and an odd little menu item marked "#000." There's a strange message from a person named Prime to a compadre called Jigg. Apparently, Prime left a series of clues to unlock a weapons cache somewhere in this building! Return to the main menu, and item has now changed to "#001." Select this, and you're presented with a little brain-teaser. There are four additional numbers to choose from. Pick the one you think is correct.

Tech Museum Note

Tip

If you're having trouble figuring out the puzzle, check the answer in the spoiler alert later in the quest walkthrough.

Continue your sweep for goods by entering the doorway in the northwest corner. Spin around and open the First Aid Box on the wall, then ignore the two bathrooms, unless you're determined to collect every plunger in the Wasteland! You can now head up the stairs to a small security room, where two terminals can be accessed (the wall terminal requires hacking). You can activate or deactivate the museum's turrets (the latter being the best option), and read more on the workings of the museum back in 2077. With the atrium ground floor fully explored, head up the stairs to the exhibits. The double doors on the eastern wall lead to two Halls of Today. These are blocked by rubble. Pass the two terminal kiosks (there are no odd numbers to access in these), and head into the corridor to the Vault tour. The remainder of the balcony is impassible.

 First Aid Box Health and Chems

Head south, and begin your Vault-Tec–approved official tour! Much of the exhibit is still functioning, so take the tour, stepping through the Vault door, listening to the narrator extol the virtues of this fantastic survival bunker! Continue south, down the stairs, and press the interactive buttons on the walls Exit the exhibit and you're now back on the atrium balcony, across from the rubble you couldn't navigate past. Open the Door to Museum of Technology West Wing.

MAYHEM IN THE MUSEUM: THE WEST WING

View your compass and investigate everywhere thoroughly. There's usually a Super Mutant to tag, too.

Step into a large balcony area. Ahead (to the west), through the collapsed ceiling and rubble pile, you can make out the Virgo II Lunar Lander, but the debris prevents you from reaching it. The model of the Enclave VTOL vehicle to your left is adjacent to a short hallway leading to the Delta IX exhibit. If you don't have competent Lockpick or Science skills, this is the place to head to, once you sweep the area for items and information. Expect to cut down another couple of Super Mutants in this area.

FREEFORM QUEST
Jiggs' Loot (Part 2 of 4)

Before you continue, access the Museum Information Terminal kiosk on this balcony. The relevant terminal is on the right. The menus are familiar to you, but there's an "#002" to

access. You're presented with four numbers. Choose the correct one, and continue. If you choose incorrectly, the puzzle resets and you have to return to the first kiosk and begin again.

Now begin a thorough search of the area. Below you is a desk with four terminals, and the functioning ones give you the same series of Far Out Space Facts! Check the doorway in the northwest corner. This leads to the planetarium. This automatically whirs into action, displaying a spectacular view of the night sky. Two Suuper Mutants will try to ambush you, relying on the darkness and the noise of the looped narration to confuse you. Take them out, and continue exploring.

To the east is a planetarium office area, complete with two terminals and a locked gun cabinet. "Mayhem in the Museum: Dish of the Day" reveals what's contained in the cabinet (although you can unlock it now if you've poured most of your points into Lockpick, or if you've already solved Prime's puzzle and collected the key). There is a Nuka-Cola Quantum, a delicious (but irradiated and collectible) drink on a high shelf in this chamber, as well. Save this if you're going to attempt **Miscellaneous Quest: The Nuka-Cola Challenge**.

 With a modicum of hacking (**Science**), you can access the wall terminal, and unlock the planetarium exit on the opposite (western) side of the chamber. This allows you to quickly reach the Virgo II Lunar Lander exhibit after a quick run down a narrow passageway, passing a metal door on your right (west). "Dish of the Day" also reveals what's through this metal door

 Or, you can try picking the planetarium exit door; the effect is the same.

 Tip

To complete Freeform Quest: Jiggs' Loot, don't take this shortcut; move to the Delta IX exhibit instead.

 Nuka-Cola Quantum †

† Collectible: Consult Appendix 6 (page 458) for all locations.

Head through into the Delta IX exhibit, a massive relic from the 21st century, and begin a vicious firefight with the Super Mutants on the multi-floor balcony here. Expect attacks from above and below; hug the wall to avoid most of the gunfire. You can access any of the balcony terminals, which give you a brief history of the exhibit and allow you to fiddle with the lights and other exhibit elements. After you've nullified the Super Mutant threat, thoroughly explore this exhibit room.

You can head down the balcony steps to the base of the rocket. There's scattered food on the balcony. If you're feeling adventurous, you can jump to the chassis of the rocket, and drop down. You might cripple yourself in the process, though! Then move through the double doors, readying your weapon for a firefight up the slight incline corridor, and up into the Virgo II exhibit.

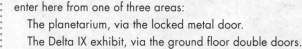

Or, you can head all the way to the top of the Delta IX exhibit chamber, and use **Lockpick** to open the metal door. This leads to small storage alcove and stairs down. Enter the small maintenance office, where you can access previously read notes on a terminal. More importantly, you can open the desk and grab the Custodian Key for Tech Museum from here! Open the nearby door, and head out onto a balcony overlooking the Virgo II exhibit.

Custodian Key for Tech Museum

Note

The key unlocks the metal door at the top of the Delta IX gallery, which provides an optional (but quicker) route back to the gallery when you are returning from the Virgo display.

FREEFORM QUEST
Jiggs' Loot (Part 3 of 4)

Prior to leaving the Delta IX exhibit room, make sure you access the kiosk on the ground floor, near the double doors, for the next part of Prime's puzzle. Choose "#003" and input the correct number. If you're successful, you receive a new menu option: "#Get Passcode." Choose this, and you're given a congratulatory message from Prime. The loot is stored in the security office, and you'll head there in a moment. Prime mentions that Jiggs should meet him at the Jury Street Metro Station.

Jiggs' Loot Passcode Confirmed

Tip

If you travel to the Jury Street Metro Station (map 8.A, page 372; due west of Vault 101), you may find Prime's remains, along with some interesting items. Check **Freeform Quest: The Jiggs' Up** for details.

MAYHEM IN THE MUSEUM: DISH OF THE DAY

Slay the Super Mutant, grab the dish, and you're almost done.

You should now be in the Virgo II Lunar Lander chamber. You can enter here from one of three areas:

The planetarium, via the locked metal door.

The Delta IX exhibit, via the ground floor double doors.

The Delta IX exhibit, via the upper balcony and maintenance room.

Commence firing on any Super Mutants in the vicinity, and once they're downed, move over to the Virgo II Lunar Lander itself. Take the communications dish from the exhibit at once! You can now exit this building, or stay and secure the loot that Prime left behind.

  Virgo II Dish

NEW OBJECTIVE
"Find the Washington Monument" begins.

FREEFORM QUEST
Jiggs' Loot (Part 4 of 4)

The Jiggs is up! Locate the door in the north wall of the Virgo II exhibit that leads to the planetarium. Step into the narrow corridor and enter the metal door to the west. Climb the stairs and enter the security office. Ignore the wall terminal, grab the 10mm Pistol on the counter, then move to the far end, and access the Museum of Tech Security Terminal. If you've completed Prime's puzzle, you can unlock the adjacent wall safe. Grab the items listed below. The Gun Locker Key unlocks the gun cabinet back in the planetarium office, so head there immediately. Use the key, and grab the large selection of Ammo, Assault Rifles, and other ordnance, including a Missile Launcher!

Gun Locker Key

Bottle Caps (200)

Chems

Gun Locker Ammo and Weapons

Spoiler Alert

Numbers Game: Solving Prime's Puzzle

The solution is to choose the prime number each time. The clue is in the puzzle-creator's name! Here's what to input, and where:

TERMINAL NUMBER	NUMBER TO INPUT
#000	Read Menu option
#001	#019
#002	#053
#003	#113
#003	#Get Passcode

Exiting the building is quick and easy if you plan your route. From the planetarium, head south, into the room with the large balcony, and move up the stairs (east) to the Door to Museum of Technology Atrium. Once on the balcony, simply drop down and head north, out to the Mall.

TRAINING — BESTIARY — MAIN QUEST — MISC. QUESTS — COMPLETION — TOUR — APPENDICES

AN EXPRESS ELEVATOR FROM HELL: GOING UP

Expect some gunfire from the Super Mutant warrens in the middle of the Mall grounds as you exit. Turn and head west, passing (but not entering) the Metro Station you used earlier. Try Sneaking if you want to avoid combat.

Unless you're geared up for a supreme struggle in the trenches, ignore the Super Mutants, and head here.

You're heading for the most prominent landmark of all: the giant obelisk known as the Washington Monument. Continue to skirt the trenches, either running from, or engaging and retreating from the Super Mutants. There are numerous enemies here, so you might wish to attempt a tactical withdrawal!

Continue west, and move to the Washington Monument gates, which are guarded by two Brotherhood of Steel soldiers. They help you if Super Mutants are attacking, so head there at once, and access the wall terminal by the gate. You automatically use the passcode that Three Dog gave you earlier (otherwise, this monument is impenetrable), and open the outer security gate. Head west to the Door to the Washington Monument.

Tip

For an extra stash of items, check out "Freeform Quest: Caching In with Three Dog" at the end of this section before repairing the radio dish.

Activate the elevator control once you're inside the monument, and step into the elevator. Hit the control again, and look up as you're buffeted slightly and the elevator ascends to the very top! You're actually quite safe up here, so inspect the area around the central elevator. There's Ammo and a bed to sleep on. Once you awake refreshed, move to the Galaxy News Radio Relay. Choose to install the Virgo Dish and activate the relay.

With an impressive **Science** skill, you can boost the signal past the default setting, allowing you to listen to Three Dog from anywhere in the Wasteland. Nice work!

NEW OBJECTIVE
"Speak to Three Dog about Dad" begins.

Tip

Stop! Before you go, you can optionally begin either of the Miscellaneous Quests that start in this area, such as Head of State or You Gotta Shoot 'Em in the Head. You can also investigate the Museum of History to locate quest-critical items for Stealing Independence.

Before you descend the elevator again, you can elect to Fast Travel back to the Galaxy News Radio Plaza. This is thoroughly recommended, because you can almost instantly complete this quest. If you don't, you must travel all the way back to Friendship Station or Chevy Chase North. You can't retrace the route you took for this quest, because the rear entrance to G.N.R. you used is inaccessible from the sunken roadway near the Collapsed Car Tunnel.

Back at Three Dog's room, the man is truly impressed at your determination and skill. He reveals that your father was heading to a place called Rivet City, south of here. He pinpoints this on your map. That floating rustbucket moored near the Jefferson Memorial is your next port of call.

Note

Additional: You're Out of Order!

You can grab the dish in the museum without ever having to speak to Three Dog, and you can find out about Dad by "other means" (see below), but you can't get into the Washington Monument without Three Dog's authorization.

FREEFORM QUEST: CACHING IN WITH THREE DOG

If you plan your routes a little differently, you can attempt an exceptionally recommended Freeform Quest. Here's how:

Find out about your dad's progress by visiting a place other than Galaxy News Radio. You have several options:

1. Head to Rivet City and speak with Doctor Li.
2. Head to Vault 112 and enter Tranquility Lane.

Or, agree to complete this quest and obtain the Virgo Lander Dish, but before you repair the dish at the top of the Washington Monument, execute plans 1 and 2 (above). Because Three Dog's "reward" (where your Dad is) is now unimportant, he sweetens the deal. He doesn't want you to leave empty handed, so he offers you the cache as compensation. Head to Hamilton's Hideaway [5.03]. Follow the map and instructions in the Tour chapter, and locate the barred gate. Open it using Three Dog's Cache Key, and stagger out with any or all of the following:

Three Dog's Cache Key	**Ammo Box Ammunition (7)**
First Aid Box Health and Chems (3)	**Frag Grenades (4)**
Stealth Boy	**Guns and Bullets**
Assault Rifle	**Mini-Nuke**

Note

This is the only way you can retrieve this loot, so plan ahead!

Scientific Pursuits

While there is a chance you may have discovered **Rivet City [9.15]** independently, it is now imperative that you leave **Galaxy News Radio [10.03]** and Fast Travel southward to a gigantic aircraft carrier slowly rusting away in the Potomac River, near the **Jefferson Memorial [9.14]**. You're here to see Doctor Madison Li, proves less than hospitable. She says your dad did indeed come to convince her to rejoin Project Purity, but she thought his idea was madness. Doctor Li gives you the details on Project Purity and says your father claimed he was close to gaining the information he needed to get it running. Right before your dad disappeared with his newborn baby (you), he talked about the "missing puzzle piece," that he was sure he could find in the scientific journals of one of pre-war America's most eminent scientists, Doctor Stanislaus Braun. But when you were born, your dad left Project Purity stranded. Now he wants to set things right and has set off to find Doctor Braun's journals. But Doctor Li has no idea just where he was going. Perhaps he left Holotapes with clues to his whereabouts? Indeed he did, but they are scattered about the interior of the Jefferson Memorial, where Project Purity resides. Find the Holotapes, and you'll have the location to **Vault 112 [7.03]**, the last known whereabouts of Doctor Braun.

Rivet City

QUEST FLOWCHART

	MAIN PATH	OPTIONAL PATH
Main Characters	Three Dog, Harkness, Garza, Doctor Janice Kaplinski, Doctor Anna Holt, Doctor Madison Li	Doctor Madison Li
Locations	Galaxy News Radio, Anacostia Crossing Station, Rivet City, Jefferson Memorial, Smith Casey's Garage, Vault 112	Rivet City, Jefferson Memorial
Adv. Items/Abilities	Science, Sneak, Stealth Boy	
Possible enemies	Raider, Centaur, Super Mutant Genus, Mole Rat, Radroach	Super Mutant Genus, Centaur, Radroach
Karma Influence	Neutral	

Talk to Doctor Li about Dad and Project Purity.

Head to Rivet City via Anacostia Crossing or by following the Potomac River

Move to the Rivet City Science Lab, and speak with Doctor Li

Engage in any Miscellaneous Quest or Freeform Quest related to Rivet City

[Optional] Uncover Doctor Li's Holotapes in her quarters

• Three Holotapes: Project Purity Journal: Entry 1, Entry 3, Entry 5

Look for Dad in Project Purity's Control Room.

Locate the Gift Shop Entrance at the Jefferson Memorial

Search Dad's Holotapes for clues to his location.

Locate your first three Holotapes in the Rotunda at Project Purity

• Three Holotapes: Project Purity Personal Journal: Entry 5, Entry 8, Entry 10

[Optional] Collect all available Holotapes

Enter the Sub-Basement Medical Room

• Two Holotapes: Project Purity Journal: Entry 7, Entry 8

Color code: | Objective | Action | Rewards

Continued on next page

TRAINING — BESTIARY — MAIN QUEST — MISC. QUESTS — TOUR — COMPLETION — APPENDICES

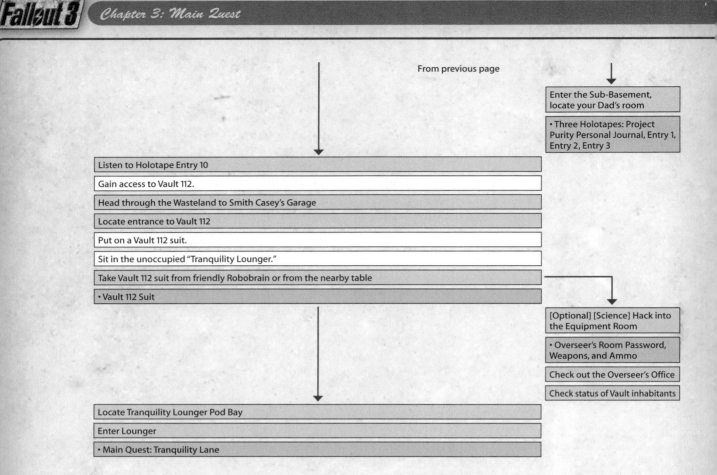

From previous page

Enter the Sub-Basement, locate your Dad's room

• Three Holotapes: Project Purity Personal Journal, Entry 1, Entry 2, Entry 3

Listen to Holotape Entry 10

Gain access to Vault 112.

Head through the Wasteland to Smith Casey's Garage

Locate entrance to Vault 112

Put on a Vault 112 suit.

Sit in the unoccupied "Tranquility Lounger."

Take Vault 112 suit from friendly Robobrain or from the nearby table

• Vault 112 Suit

[Optional] [Science] Hack into the Equipment Room

• Overseer's Room Password, Weapons, and Ammo

Check out the Overseer's Office

Check status of Vault inhabitants

Locate Tranquility Lounger Pod Bay

Enter Lounger

• Main Quest: Tranquility Lane

A RIVETING EXPLORATION

Note

After receiving the information from Three Dog, you have a number of routes you can take to reach Rivet City:

NEW OBJECTIVE
"Talk to Doctor Li about Dad and Project Purity" begins.

PATH A: ADVANCING TO ANACOSTIA CROSSING

Unless you've spent the last few hours (and few dozen Stimpaks) eradicating Super Mutants, dive into cover here!

Tip

This is the preferred route, because it unlocks another station for you to Fast Travel to at your leisure, and is shorter than the other route.

Leave the Galaxy News Radio Building via any exit. Instead of traipsing around the Metro Tunnels and getting lost, immediately Fast Travel to the Museum of Technology, where you just came from (and where you located the Virgo II dish). You land outside, near the Super Mutant trenches in the Mall. Immediately run west and enter the Museum Metro Station. If you've been following the optimal route, you explored this location during **Main Quest: Galaxy News Radio**.

Follow the winding concourse west to the mezzanine area, and peer left, looking south down an escalator with the sign reading "Southbound to Anacostia Crossing this Platform." Head down the escalator, or jump to the carriage roofs then down by the flaming barrel, and enter the left tunnel, heading south. The train tunnel curves east, leading to a small Raider confrontation, then continues south to an opening on your left. The door is busted open, allowing you to head around the corner, and open the Door to Anacostia Crossing Station.

Head out onto the Red Line, and turn right (west). Run forward, brandishing your weapon, and turn to use it as you reach an opening on the right wall. A couple of Raiders provide a distraction; gun them down and steal the small amount of Health and Chems on the table. Sleep here if you wish, then continue west. The tunnel bends around to the south and opens to a large mezzanine. Move to the southwest, and climb the nearest escalator. At the top is a small Raider camp, complete with another 10mm Pistol and Ammo, and four Raiders to cull. Head west, up into the entrance tunnel, ignoring the empty restrooms, and exit to the Capital Wasteland via the metal gate.

PATH B: GUN AND RUN DOWN THE POTOMAC

Farragut Station. Head south, following the river from here, and ready yourself for numerous firefights.

Caution

This route is optional but not recommended. It takes longer but allows more exploring.

Head out of any of the Galaxy News Radio Building exits, and immediately Fast Travel to Farragut West Station, Friendship Station up at the north area, or any station or location where you have access back to the Wasteland. From Farragut, follow the Potomac River south, staying on the eastern side, moving through the Anchorage Memorial, around Dukov's Place, and finally around to view Rivet City in all its dilapidated glory.

A LIAISON WITH DOCTOR MADISON LI

This is a stop-off point for Traders, thirsty travelers, and those seeking the best in scientific knowledge.

No matter which direction you came from, you're headed to the gigantic aircraft carrier, slowly rusting into the Potomac River in the very southwestern part of the Wasteland. Access to the ship is via a long gantry plank, which is accessed via the entrance ramp. Carlos, a thirsty traveler, waits near to a security intercom switch. Click the switch, and you're told to wait while the bridge extends. Once it has clicked into place (you can chance a jump if you're feeling reckless), head across.

You're stopped by Harkness, the head of security. He wants to know what your business is. Simply tell him you're here to see either your father or Doctor Li, and he finally lets you past. You can also pester him for information on this ship, including the location of a large Marketplace. You are encouraged to go here and sell what you've scavenged and meet some of the vessel's interesting inhabitants. If this quest is of paramount importance though, turn left (northeast) at the two hatch doors, and enter the Door to Stairwell.

Once inside the stairwell, stay on this level, and open the hatch Door to Midship Deck, to the northwest. You appear inside the belly of the boat, which is initially confusing. However, follow the signs to "Science Lab," and there shouldn't be any problems. Head forward (northwest), all the way to the T-junction where the motorbike is parked. Turn right (northeast), walk forward a few steps, then turn left (north) at either of the next two junctions. There are two entrances to the Science Lab (located in the Aft Hangar); pick either and head inside.

The Science Lab is a large chamber, with a variety of scientific equipment to refrain from touching. Here, you can speak with Christie Young (who's here to clean the place) and Garza, a mysterious man with strong arms. Over to the southwest is a cluster of scientists. Among them is Janice Kaplinski, the chief botanist. She's seen your dad, but doesn't feel like imparting any more information. Doctor Li herself is watching an argument between her fellow scientist Doctor Anna Holt and an old, suited man named Doctor Zimmer, here with a tough-looking bodyguard known only as Armitage. If you're staying on this quest, it's best not to get involved....

You do remember Doctor Li, don't you? This isn't the first time she's assisted you. She cut your cord!

Tip

But if you're not worried, take a detour and speak to Doctor Zimmer. He's one of many Miscellaneous Quests you can begin or continue while on this vessel.

Talk with Doctor Li, and her initial annoyance melts away as she recognizes you as your father's offspring. Your father isn't here now; he insisted that the old team (Li included) restart Project Purity in the old laboratory, inside the Jefferson Memorial building, northwest of here. You can ask Li about your mother, and what your father was like in his youth.

NEW OBJECTIVE
"Look for Dad in Project Purity's Control Room" begins.

The nearby Jefferson Memorial is your father's last known location. Ready for another Mutie hunt?

Doctor Li tells you that your father journeyed to the old laboratory, sometimes known as Project Purity, after their last conversation. This is where you should head next. Retrace your steps to the the Rivet City entrance.

If you're low on Ammo and Health, drop to the lower deck and grab items from a First Aid Box and two Ammo Boxes hidden below, near where Harkness is standing. Exit Rivet City and head west toward the dome of the Jefferson building.

TRAINING — BESTIARY — MAIN QUEST — MISC. QUESTS — TOUR — COMPLETION — APPENDICES

First Aid Box
Health and Chems

 **Ammo Box**
Ammunition (2)

Move to the metal ramp surrounding the Memorial steps (which cannot be accessed), and kill your first Super Mutant of the quest. Then head up the ramp, as this higher ground allows you to spot a few more Super Mutants guarding the perimeter raised gantry. Move southwest, wiping each of them out, and descend the ramp on the other side. Just to the left of this ramp, near a tripod worker lamp and red cone, is the Door to Jefferson Museum and Gift Shop. Head inside.

PROJECT PURITY— HOLOTAPE RECONNOITER

Expect a mixture of Super Mutants and their "pet" Centaurs as you proceed through this gift shop. Begin by cutting down a frothing foe as you head east to the first junction (Jefferson Memorial). You need not continue to the end of this corridor, because it leads to a sift pump that cannot be activated yet. Instead, turn right (south) at the junction, and watch as the automated turret attacks a couple of enemies in the main foyer. Hacking a wall terminal just before you enter doesn't yield much in the way of advantages; it just turns the turrets on and off.

Coax a trio of thick, sinewy mutated cannibals into your firing line, and drop them. Mines work well here.

With the immediate threats in the foyer abated, turn east and enter the gift shop. There's a First Aid Box on the outer wall, and two Ammo Boxes on the shelves inside. Take what you need, then head south to an area of scattered lab equipment, and exits to your left and right. Head left (east) to a door in the corner. It's one of two that allows access to the rotunda.

 First Aid Box
Health and Chems

 **Ammo Box**
Ammunition (2)

Head here next, but only after you've coaxed three Super Mutants out to battle you, securing the area. Before you head into the rotunda, carefully explore the remaining parts of the gift shop. There's a door to the sub-basement and a manhole to Taft Tunnels. The manhole cannot be entered but is vital for a subsequent quest. Head into the rotunda via either door.

Holotapes vital to your progress are on the Auxiliary Filtration Input, just behind this bloodthirsty brute.

Head west, then up the stairs to the right, as you enter the rotunda (the door opposite leads back to the gift shop). Your father was a busy man; his team built this gigantic tank and surrounding structures inside the rotunda, and called it Project Purity. Ironically, the water

inside the transparent tank is extremely radioactive. You've reached the control room, but your father is nowhere to be seen. There's equipment you can press, but none of it works.

NEW OBJECTIVE
"Search Dad's holotapes for clues to his location" begins.

There's also the small matter of two hulking Super Mutants. Make sure they don't ambush you. You may have to back down to the gift shop doors and use the columns as cover. Don't get caught in a dead-end! When the control room is a Mutie-free zone, step back up to the entrance, and look west at the Auxiliary Filtration Input. There are three Holotapes on it. Grab them all. The only vital Holotape to listen to is Journal Entry 10. Your father mentions another Vault, 112, which is hidden under some kind of garage deep in the Wasteland. That's your next destination! Exit this building the same way you entered.

 Project Purity Personal Journal: Entry 5

 Project Purity Personal Journal: Entry 8

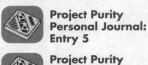 **Project Purity Personal Journal: Entry 10**

NEW OBJECTIVE
"Gain access to Vault 112" begins.

> **Note**
> You can begin the search for Vault 112 immediately ("Dealing with Pests out West"), or you can stay and search for more Holotapes. The end of the next section also lists what each Holotape contains.

[OPTIONAL] PROJECT PURITY HOLOTAPES—THE COMPLETE COLLECTION

> **Tip**
> It isn't necessary to complete this, but it does clear out more Super Mutants, facilitating a return trip.

Head back into the gift shop, and move to the south wall, looking for the door with the three signs to the left of it: the Door to Memorial Sub-Basement. Bring out your favored Super Mutant hunting weapon. Head down the stairs, into the initial chamber, with a mesh fence in front of you. A sewer pipe, which can't be accessed from this point, is ahead (north) of you, and a utility door to your left is currently sealed. The only way onward is to head right, past the Gore Bag, to the doorway just before the stairs.

 Project Purity Journal: Entry 7

 **Project Purity Journal: Entry 8**

Enter this small room with medical equipment and other electronics, and prepare to battle a Super Mutant or three. When you've defeated the ambushers, look for the small table in the northeast corner. Grab the two Holotapes, then head out and down the stairs to a dormitory. Kill any foes, then push forward (west).

Head down the corridor, and make your first turn left (south), at a crossroads. There's likely to be another Super Mutant to deal with here, too.

Ignore the generator room the Super Mutant was in, and make your first turn right (west), to a hatch door that opens up into an office with a bed and a burnt-out terminal. Swing around and deal with a Super Mutant intrusion, and then inspect the chamber. On the table with the terminal are four Holotapes. On the side table near the entrance is a single Holotape, with different markings: "Better Days." Now that all relevant Holotapes have been collected, you can exit the sub-basement, despite not having

visited every room. A complete search is only necessary during **Main Quest: The Waters of Life**. Now return to the outside Wasteland, backtracking through the gift shop.

 Project Purity Personal Journal: Entry 1

 **Project Purity Personal Journal: Entry 2**

 Project Purity Personal Journal: Entry 3

Project Purity Personal Journal

Better Days

HOLOTAPE SCRUTINY

The following information is imparted on each of the Holotapes you collect. You must listen to Holotape 10 to know where your father went. All others are optional. Note that this is a complete list, including Holotapes found in Doctor Li's Science Lab aboard Rivet City. There are two types: those recorded 20 years ago, and those just recorded:

The 20-year-old Holotapes are collectively known as "Project Purity Journal: Entry [x]"

HOLOTAPE	LOCATION	DESCRIPTION
Project Purity Journal: Entry 1	Located in Doctor Li's quarters in Rivet City	Work has resumed after a week of delays. Brotherhood soldiers are defending the lab, but not everyone is comfortable having them around. Full analysis of the last three small-scale purification tests are due, and Catherine hasn't been feeling well.
Project Purity Journal: Entry 3	Located in Li's quarters	Catherine's not ill, she's pregnant! Everyone has taken a renewed interest in making the purifier work, and they might finally be on the right track. Catherine refuses to rest; she's determined to resolve the power problems before the baby is born.
Project Purity Journal: Entry 5	Located in Li's quarters	The Mutant attacks are increasing, and the project is not progressing as it should. The Brotherhood soldiers are starting to question the value in defending the project at the cost of their men.
Project Purity Journal: Entry 7	Located in Project Purity, memorial sub-basement, on table in the medical room where, incidentally, you were born	Catherine has died during childbirth. In her place is you. Vault 101 is no place for an infant.
Project Purity Journal: Entry 8	Located with Entry 7	Progress has come to a halt. Mutant attacks occur several times a day. Madison Li is not happy with the Brotherhood's involvement. Your father must leave. He must put your needs before his own.

The following Holotapes were recorded by your dad in the recent past, both before and after visiting Rivet City and attempting to convince Li to return to the project. They are labeled "Project Purity Personal Journal: Entry [x]":

HOLOTAPE	LOCATION	DESCRIPTION
Project Purity Personal Journal	Located on Dad's desk in Project Purity, memorial sub-basement	It has been close to 20 years since his last entry, and since he left this all behind. Vault 101 wasn't perfect, but it was safe. You don't need your daddy any more, so he fled to begin the experiment again.
Project Purity Personal Journal: Entry 1	Located on Dad's desk	Your father is back where it all began, 19 years after stopping his work. He still believes Project Purity can and will be operational!
Project Purity Personal Journal: Entry 2	Located on Dad's desk	He needs help powering up the mainframe; Madison in Rivet City should provide support.
Project Purity Personal Journal: Entry 3	Located on Dad's desk	Li thinks he's mad. She's got her own life and team, while he is a paragon of failure and false promises. He needs her.
Project Purity Personal Journal: Entry 5	Located in Project Purity Rotunda	After hacking the Overseer's computer, your father comes across a name: Doctor Stanislaus Braun, Vault-Tec's sorcerer scientist. He was involved in the G.E.C.K., or Garden of Eden Creation Kit.
Project Purity Personal Journal: Entry 8	Located in Project Purity Rotunda	G.E.C.K. is nothing short of a miracle: a terraforming module that works! They were distributed to Vaults to be used after the atomic bomb. Braun was on the reservation list for Vault 112.
Project Purity Personal Journal: Entry 10	Located in Project Purity Rotunda	Your father requires equipment to get the purifier up and running. Project Purity is an eternity of "almost theres." He hopes Braun may have the missing puzzle piece.
Additional: Better Days	Located on Dad's side table in Project Purity, memorial sub-basement	A woman's voice; you're sure it is your mother. She's hoping to "recalibrate the equipment." James (your father) interrupts her. She giggles and stops the recording. Did you just hear your mother's voice? More importantly, was it just before the moment of your conception?!

TRAINING — BESTIARY — MAIN QUEST — MISC. QUESTS — TOUR — COMPLETION — APPENDICES

DEALING WITH PESTS OUT WEST

As soon as you head outside to the Jefferson Memorial exterior, deal with any nearby enemies and then Fast Travel, because Vault 112 has appeared on your World Map. It's underneath Smith Casey's Garage, so don't be confused that the Vault itself doesn't appear. Depending on how many areas you've uncovered, you may be able to Fast Travel to Evergreen Hills or another nearby location. However, it's more likely that your nearest explored area is Megaton, which is also a great place to trade, stock up on provisions, and repair your equipment. When you're tooled up and ready to go, head west.

Cross the rocky terrain, under the freeway skeleton, and follow the remains of the road before straightening out and continuing due west. Pass the radio antenna on the outskirts of the Jury Street Metro Station area, and plow on ahead, using the distant chapel spire to guide you. Cross a small ravine, dealing with a vicious band of Raiders as you see fit. As you reach the chapel, be sure you're ready for the Rigged Shotgun and quintet of Raiders that ambush you once you step inside. Switch from a Hunting Rifle to something useful in close combat, like a Shotgun or Minigun, and waste them all! Continue your trek west, until you locate the sprawling Evergreen Hills area. Stay on the upper ground, and skirt around it.

A long-abandoned garage and gas station is the unassuming entrance to the infamous Vault 112.

Once you're around and on top of Evergreen Hills, continue west, as Smith Casey's Garage appears through the rocks and dusty trail. Step onto the tarmac road remains, and continue to the garage, where piles of rusting cars and a truck lie exposed to the harsh elements. The metal door on the western (left) side of the building is the only entrance. Head inside. In one corner of the first chamber is a small container with a Nuka-Cola Quantum to be grabbed and kept. You can sleep here if you wish, but only after you deal with the Mole Rats and a Radroach.

Step into the garage area and check the Gun Cabinet on the western wall; you may find a new weapon in there. Also grab items from the First Aid Box on the eastern wall. Finally, move to the northwest corner, activate the electrical switch, and wait for the horizontal trap flaps to open. Stairs lead down to a small generator room, and a couple more Mole Rats. Dispatch them, and head down the stairs to the Door to Vault 112.

 First Aid Box Health and Chems

LOUNGING AROUND AT TRANQUILITY BASE

The familiar cog door of a Vault-Tec tomb rumbles. What fresh hell lies beyond? Oh, it's quite nice down here....

Head down the short set of underground steps to a doorway, and head on through to the massive, sealed cog door of Vault 112. Locate the Vault Door Control Pod, and activate it. Klaxons blare as the door depressurizes and slowly grinds open. Step inside the Vault, which appears to be in perfect condition, although it seems a lot less expansive than Vault 101. Head east through the hatch door, and through another at the corridor's far end. Put your weapons away.

Stop yourself from shooting as a Robobrain addresses you, stating that you're just a tad late for a "Tranquility Lounger." You're given a Vault 112 Jumpsuit and asked to wear it. Do so, and then head through the door behind the Robobrain. There are no more threats in this Vault...at least, none in the actual world! Now descend the stairs, and reach the T-junction. Explore the entirety of Vault 112; it doesn't take long.

 Vault 112 Jumpsuit

NEW OBJECTIVE
"Put on a Vault 112 suit" begins.

NEW OBJECTIVE
"Sit in the unoccupied 'Tranquility Lounger'" begins.

 Caution

Yes, you can shoot the Robobrains. No, they don't fire back. Yes, this is a pointless exercise.

Turn right (west) at the bottom of the entrance stairs, and locate the "Clinic" sign. This leads to a balcony overlooking a strange sight: a cluster of large pods, all linked to a central processing column, administered by two Robobrains. Head down there in a moment. For now, check both rooms for goods. The far room (south) has a First Aid Box, and both have items in the lockers. Now head down the stairs, or leap off the balcony, and land on the Tranquility Lounger chamber.

 First Aid Box Health and Chems

Move to the eastern side of the chamber, to the locked equipment room door. There are some very exciting items to uncover in here!

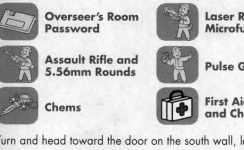

To enter this room, you need to use **Science** to hack the wall terminal. If you're proficient enough, you can step into the room and gather a load of armaments, plus other items in the lockers. Among the goodies is a Holotape with the Overseer's Room Password. Be sure you grab this!

Overseer's Room Password

Laser Rifle and Microfusion Cells

Assault Rifle and 5.56mm Rounds

Pulse Grenades

Chems

First Aid Box Health and Chems

SUBJECT	STRESS LEVEL
Unknown (your father)	Elevated
M. Henderson	Nominal
M. Simpson	Elevated
W. Foster	Nominal
G. Neusbaum	Nominal
P. Neusbaum	Nominal
J. Rockwell	Elevated
R. Rockwell	Elevated
T. Dithers	Extreme

Turn and head toward the door on the south wall, leading to stairs heading up to a junction. Head left (west), following the sign to the Overseer's office. At the wall terminal (which is normally inaccessible), you automatically use the Overseer's Room Password to open the door. The terminal thinks you're a Doctor Braun. Could this be Doctor Stanislaus Braun who your father was searching for, and who the Vault 101 Overseer was communicating with? Inside the room is a single Tranquility Lounger, with a man inside, seemingly mesmerized by a series of flickering images. He can't be awakened, but his room can be ransacked; check the locker, desk, and a wall safe before you leave.

The good news: You've found your dad. The bad news: He's sealed inside one of these evil-looking pods....

Inspect the Tranquility Lounger chamber a little more closely. All but two of them have a Vault resident inside. Inspect the terminals at the center of the chamber, and you can read the vital signs for each of the residents, including the "anomalous" one. Check that pod a little more closely; it's your father in there! No amount of banging can wake him, so there's only one plan to try. You need to access whatever program he's trapped in, and try to free him! Before this occurs, note the stress levels of each inhabitant:

This gives you a clue to the emotional state of the inhabitants of whatever strange program you're about to launch yourself into. Find the only working (and empty) Tranquility Lounger, then activate and sit in it. The hatch slowly closes, and a monitor surrounds your vision. You begin to see a sepia-toned leafy lane. What the hell is going on?! And who was that frightening little girl's face you glimpsed? Welcome to Tranquility Lane. You'll Never Leave!

This seems to be a rather pleasant simulation of pre-apocalyptic suburbia...oh my god, who was that?!

Tranquility Lane

Your father came to **Vault 112 [7.03]** in search of pre-war scientific records from Doctor Stanislaus Braun. As your father is trapped inside a Tranquility Lounger, you must enter the virtual reality world. You appear in Tranquility Lane, a perfect little cul-de-sac, where a slice of American life (before the bombs dropped) is ready to explore. But something isn't right here. A sinister little girl named Betty seems to know more than she's letting on. It only takes a few torturous minutes to realize the truth. Doctor Braun, in his Betty guise, is quite simply evil, or deranged, or both. To make matters worse, he's bored. Having spent his previous years dismantling the perfect existence of the residents of Tranquility Lane, he wants you to help with the tasks. In return, you're promised an exit from this place. You have the moral choice to follow Betty's pranks, which soon turn to fully realized mass murder, or to find another way out of this deranged simulation: a Failsafe hidden from all but the most logical and cunning inhabitants. Can you crack the code and crack open your Tranquility Lounger, before it becomes your tomb?

Vault 112

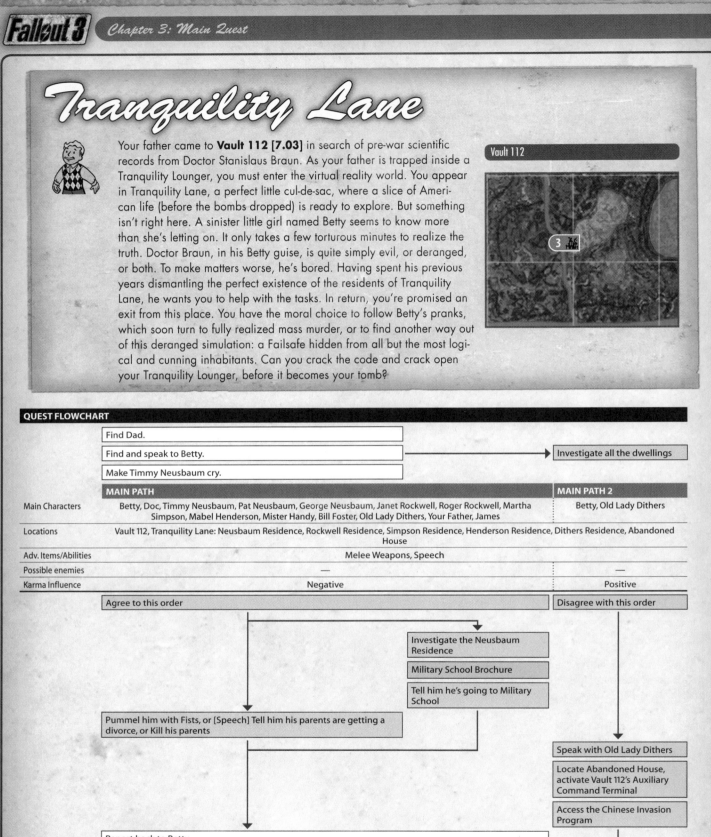

QUEST FLOWCHART

Find Dad.
Find and speak to Betty.	→ Investigate all the dwellings
Make Timmy Neusbaum cry.

	MAIN PATH	MAIN PATH 2
Main Characters	Betty, Doc, Timmy Neusbaum, Pat Neusbaum, George Neusbaum, Janet Rockwell, Roger Rockwell, Martha Simpson, Mabel Henderson, Mister Handy, Bill Foster, Old Lady Dithers, Your Father, James	Betty, Old Lady Dithers
Locations	Vault 112, Tranquility Lane: Neusbaum Residence, Rockwell Residence, Simpson Residence, Henderson Residence, Dithers Residence, Abandoned House	
Adv. Items/Abilities	Melee Weapons, Speech	
Possible enemies	—	—
Karma Influence	Negative	Positive

Agree to this order	Disagree with this order

Investigate the Neusbaum Residence

Military School Brochure

Tell him he's going to Military School

Pummel him with Fists, or [Speech] Tell him his parents are getting a divorce, or Kill his parents

Speak with Old Lady Dithers

Locate Abandoned House, activate Vault 112's Auxiliary Command Terminal

Access the Chinese Invasion Program

Report back to Betty.

Break up the Rockwell's marriage without killing either of them.

Color code: Objective   Action   Rewards

Continued on next page

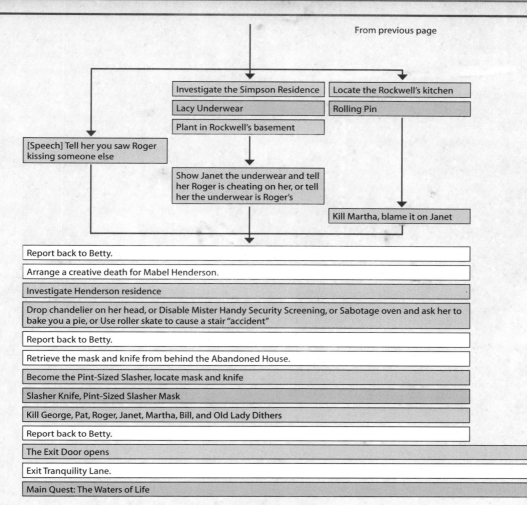

From previous page

Investigate the Simpson Residence	Locate the Rockwell's kitchen
Lacy Underwear	Rolling Pin
Plant in Rockwell's basement	

[Speech] Tell her you saw Roger kissing someone else

Show Janet the underwear and tell her Roger is cheating on her, or tell her the underwear is Roger's

Kill Martha, blame it on Janet

Report back to Betty.

Arrange a creative death for Mabel Henderson.

Investigate Henderson residence

Drop chandelier on her head, or Disable Mister Handy Security Screening, or Sabotage oven and ask her to bake you a pie, or Use roller skate to cause a stair "accident"

Report back to Betty.

Retrieve the mask and knife from behind the Abandoned House.

Become the Pint-Sized Slasher, locate mask and knife

Slasher Knife, Pint-Sized Slasher Mask

Kill George, Pat, Roger, Janet, Martha, Bill, and Old Lady Dithers

Report back to Betty.

The Exit Door opens

Exit Tranquility Lane.

Main Quest: The Waters of Life

IT'S A BEAUTIFUL DAY IN THIS NEIGHBORHOOD

A leafy lane, little Timmy selling lemonade, and the friendliest of neighbors: this must be paradise.

Welcome to Tranquility Lane. There's no exit off this street, and everything's tinged in sepia. You quickly figure that you're in an alternate virtual reality simulation of some kind, and for some reason, you've taken the form of a small child. You're the same gender and about age 10. Get up off the bench. It isn't long before you're greeted by George Neusbaum. He tells you to run and say hello to Betty, over on the playground. She'll love to meet you!

NEW OBJECTIVE
"Find Dad" begins.

NEW OBJECTIVE
"Find and speak to Betty" begins.

Before you head over to see what this "Betty" wants, you should check your Pip-Boy to see...ah. It's now a Vault-Tec approved watch! Without mapping, rely solely on your compass and make a quick circuit of the "lane." At any point you can speak with any resident, and enter any house. Every single person loves it here, and laughs off your crazy talk about this being some sort of virtual reality simulation. Well, almost everyone.... For now though, memorize the road crossing marking to your right (south), and start a counterclockwise tour.

The first house (all on your right) is the Neusbaum Residence (where George, Pat, and Timmy live): It has the bench, lamppost, and the lemonade stand.

Pass the tricycle, and look at your next house; the Rockwell Residence (where Roger and Janet live). There's no fence, but there is a gnome on the front step, and a speed limit sign and lamppost on the sidewalk out front.

The next house is the Simpson Residence (where Martha lives). This house has a fence.

Then comes the Henderson Residence (where Mabel and her Mister Handy robot live). There's a lamppost, no fence, and a single car.

TRAINING — BESTIARY — MAIN QUEST — MISC. QUESTS — TOUR — COMPLETION — APPENDICES

Over on the shady side of the street is where Old Lady Dithers lives. The house has a picket fence, two cars, and a fire hydrant out in front.

The final house is the Abandoned House. It's on the shady side of the street too, with a lamppost and speed limit sign in front, and no name on the mailbox.

Bill Foster, Betty, and Doc the dog don't have a fixed address. Everyone wanders around the neighborhood, moving from house to house. Except that shut-in, Old Lady Dithers.

Tip

You can tell which residence is which by looking at the names on the mailboxes; there's no need to move to the front door.

You can optionally peer around the rear of each house (two of them have kennels), and enter each place if you want. When you're confident you know your way around Tranquility Lane, head to the central playground.

Betty's hobbies include watering her daffodils, making boys cry, insanity, and proving complex mathematical theorems.

Speak with Doc the dog if you want. He makes a familiar "woof." Play on the slide, then locate Betty, the odd-looking little girl who is watering her daffodils by the climbing frame. She asks if you want to play a game. Answer in the affirmative, and she tells you all you have to do is make little Timmy Neusbaum cry. Accept, or refuse, without penalty.

Note

Stop! At this point (actually, from the moment you appeared here), you have two possible scenarios you can play out:

The first is to agree to Betty's games. There are four, each taxing your cunning and morals more than the last. Begin "It's a Terrible Time for Timmy in This Neighborhood."

The second is to disagree with Betty's cruel fun, and find help (and your dad) by other means. Start "It's a Communist Invasion in This Neighborhood."

IT'S A TERRIBLE TIME FOR TIMMY IN THIS NEIGHBORHOOD

NEW OBJECTIVE

"Make Timmy Neusbaum cry" begins.

Timmy is usually at his lemonade stand, although he sometimes wanders or heads into the Neusbaum Residence. He's easy to spot because he's the only child on the lane, aside from yourself and Betty. You can make Timmy cry using any of the following methods:

A Bunch of Fives: Step up to Timmy with your fists raised, and begin to pummel him. He yells, and runs off weeping!

A Broken Home: Speak to Timmy, and win a **Speech** challenge, convincing him that his parents are getting a divorce, and it's all his fault. He blubbers, and sprints off.

Short Sharp Shock: Investigate the Neusbaum Residence, and enter the kitchen. On the table is a Military School Brochure from the Hoffman Training Academy. Return to Timmy, and lie to him, telling him he's being sent there. Produce the brochure when Timmy tells you he doesn't believe you, and start the waterworks!

Military School Brochure

Mommy Dearest: Locate either of Timmy's parents, ideally on their own and inside the Neusbaum Residence. Instead of giving pleasantries, swing your fists, and pummel the parent to death. Keep the chase going until the parent keels over, covered in blood. Exit the residence. Timmy runs in, so follow him, and watch with glee as the crybaby finds his parent collapsed in a pool of blood.

NEW OBJECTIVE

"Report back to Betty" begins.

Return to the demon child. Your prize is a single question; choose any of the ones she lists, but perhaps the most useful is "Just who are you?" Betty's voice suddenly changes to an older European man's tone. It appears you're talking to Doctor Stanislaus Braun's avatar! He/she has a second task that she wants you to complete: breaking up the Rockwell's marriage, without punching either of them to death!

Caution

Don't taunt Betty more than once with your answers, or you'll find she wields more than just a watering can. You'll be zapped and stand in agony if you attempt to hurt or backchat her. If you aren't enjoying being her helper, start "It's a Communist Invasion in This Neighborhood" instead.

THERE'S A ROCKY MARRIAGE TO BREAK APART IN THIS NEIGHBORHOOD

NEW OBJECTIVE

"Break up the Rockwell's marriage without killing either of them" begins.

As you might imagine, Roger and Janet Rockwell are usually in their residence. Head there after pondering which of the devious schemes you'd like to try, and before you act, you might wish to snoop around upstairs, in the Rockwell's bedroom. They sleep in separate beds, and Janet Rockwell's diary makes interesting reading. Here are some highlights:

Roger is always in his "stupid basement."

Or, he's "sweet-talking" Martha Simpson, but claims there's nothing between them.

She found a pendant on Roger's basement workbench once.

Some days, she wishes she beat Martha to death instead of just "scaring" her.

Oh, she feels such a fool!

You can receive hints that back up this information from general talk among the lane's inhabitants. Now plot a marriage break-up:

 Martha the Trollop: Locate Janet Rockwell, and begin to speak with her. Complete a **Speech** challenge, telling her that you saw Roger kissing another woman. Janet is furious and immediately thinks it's Martha Simpson. She screams at Roger and leaves the house. Roger appears a little dazed.

Martha the Hussy: Head over to the Simpson Residence. Martha is insulted if you try to pry the truth from her, but don't worry; you can plan a little surprise for Janet. Head to Martha's upstairs bedroom, and locate the Lacy Underwear on her bed. Head to the Rockwell's Residence, and enter the basement (it's the metal door between the front room and kitchen). Place the Lacy Underwear on Roger's desk, and return upstairs to Janet. Tell her there's something she needs to see in the basement. When she inquires what is it, tell her to trust you. Feign shock that the underwear isn't Janet's, and exclaim that he's cheating on her. She storms off upstairs, and the argument begins!

Lacy Underwear

Roger the Transvestite: For this variation on "Martha the Hussy," locate and place the Lacy Underwear on Roger's desk, but instead of convincing Janet that her husband is cheating on her, tell her the outfit is probably Roger's. For those times when no one is looking…. Janet races upstairs, and the argument rages! As always, Roger is bewildered by this planted evidence and shocking insinuations!

Martha the Mangled: Head inside the Rockwells' abode, and head into the kitchen. Take the Rolling Pin from the kitchen table, and depart the house, heading for the Simpson Residence. Enter, and then bludgeon Martha to death with the Rolling Pin. Exit and locate Roger Rockwell, and tell him he's married to a psychopath. After he nervously laughs off your remarks, tell him again, and he heads over to Martha's house. It doesn't end well….

Rolling Pin

NEW OBJECTIVE
"Report back to Betty" begins.

When you've chosen your favored method of wrenching apart Janet and Roger, return to that pug-nosed scamp, and speak to her again. As you're heading down a dark path, it's best to be sycophantic with your dialog choices. For your next task, Betty wants to raise the stakes a little, and have you kill Mabel Henderson. The death can't simply be by your fists though; you need to be creative!

IT'S TIME TO MURDER MABEL IN THIS NEIGHBORHOOD

NEW OBJECTIVE
"Arrange a creative death for Mabel Henderson" begins.

Your murderous impulses to deal with Mabel occur inside her house, but you can ask the locals if they have any information on her before you arrive. For example, Bill Foster mentions Mabel has a real fondness for gadgets. Bill can't count the number of times he's had to fix "that newfangled robot" of hers. Most interesting…. Now head inside the Henderson Residence.

Chain Reaction: After being greeted by the slightly creepy Mister Handy, look for objects you can use to snuff the life from Mabel. The chandelier in the front room is a good example. Look up at it, and you notice that it's supported by an old metal chain. Execute a quick fiddle, so the chandelier becomes unstable. Don't wait under it; instead, head to the corner of the room. Patiently wait for Mabel to walk under the chandelier, which promptly comes crashing down on her head!

Twisted Mister: That Mister Handy looks docile enough, but you're sure it has a screw loose somewhere. Head into the kitchen and access the wall terminal. Two menu options look promising: "Initialize Security Program," and "Disable Security Screening." This essentially turns Mister Handy into a robotic killing machine, with no failsafe mechanism. Keep out of its sight until you hear Mabel's screams. Then watch as she's killed with a mixture of flame-thrower and circular saw attacks: Messy, but creative!

Burn, Baby, Burn: That Mabel bakes some delicious pies, and if you ask nicely, she'll make one especially for you. Of course, before you ask her, head into her kitchen, and inspect the oven. You can fiddle with the pilot light, filling the room with gas. Now locate Mabel, and ask her for a pie. She walks over to light the oven and is consumed by a massive gas explosion!

Stepping Out: There's a roller skate at the top of Mabel's staircase. Give the skate a hearty push, so it trundles to the top of the first step, and leave it alone. Then patiently wait for Mabel to head down from upstairs (which is the best time to attempt this, or you'll have to wait for her to ascend the stairs, then come back down). She treads on the roller skate, and breaks her neck in the proceeding tumble.

NEW OBJECTIVE

"Report back to Betty" begins.

Once Mabel has met her maker, return to Betty the bully once more. She tells you that after this next task, you'll receive a wish for whatever you want. Hopefully you'll be able to finally rendezvous with your dad, especially as you haven't seen him around here. Well, not in human form, at any rate. Your final mission is to head to the dog kennel at the side of the Abandoned House, and search it for a (previously unobtainable) mask and knife. You are to become the Pint-Sized Slasher!

THERE GOES THE NEIGHBORHOOD

NEW OBJECTIVE

"Retrieve the mask and knife from behind the Abandoned House" begins.

The stuff of your neighbors' nightmares is both real, and frightening! Here comes the Pint-Sized Slasher!

Everyone must die! Everyone! Well, not everyone; Timmy has disappeared, Mister Handy doesn't count, the dog can live, and you can't kill Betty. But everyone else is fair game! The residents will run in fear. Go forth, and make Betty proud.

 **Slasher Knife**   **Pint-Sized Slasher Mask**

 With Mabel (and possibly Martha) already dead, there's only seven (or possibly six) inhabitants that need to taste your cold steel. They are: George and Pat Neusbaum, Roger and Janet Rockwell, (Martha Simpson), Bill Foster, and strange Old Lady Dithers. Your plan is straightforward: run up and slice them once! The trick is to keep your killing indoors wherever possible, because your residents have less room to flee. Chasing down George Neusbaum in his backyard is hard work; that guy can move! You'll know when you've finished your bloodletting, because your quest updates.

NEW OBJECTIVE

"Report back to Betty" begins.

Betty—or should that be Doctor Stanislaus Braun—has found your bloodshed thoroughly enjoyable. In return for your murderous run, she grants you your wish of leaving Tranquility Lane, and she actually obliges you: a door appears behind her! You can spend extra time here, attempting to justify your actions, but in the end, you should exit via the door. Activate EXIT now!

IT'S A COMMUNIST INVASION IN THIS NEIGHBORHOOD

Note

Attempt this if you want to save all the inhabitants of Vault 112. You can attempt it any time after you begin this quest, but it's most advantageous to start it immediately.

The only resident with a modicum of sanity is the ironically named Old Lady Dithers.

To help the Vault 112 inhabitants trapped in this infinite reality program, and go against Doctor Stanislaus Braun, you must find the only individual who knows the truth. That's Old Lady Dithers, who never leaves her house. Head there immediately and find her inside. She immediately starts babbling about none of this being real, and that "the suffering must end!" Immediately respond that you want to get out of here, and Dithers starts (what else?) dithering about a Failsafe device she knows Braun is accessing. She hints that you'll find more at the Abandoned House.

Dithers was correct! After tinkering with some objects, a portal appears.

Head through the front door of the Abandoned House, and step into the gloom. This place is different from the others. It's almost pitch black, and has a variety of common objects scattered about the front room. If you activate a certain number of them, you hear a strange chime. Upon further deducing, you come to realize that these objects must be activated in a specific sequence. Through trial and error, or simply reading the following sentence, you can create a portal to Vault 112's Auxiliary Command Terminal!

The sequence is as follows; radio, pitcher, gnome, pitcher, cinder block, gnome, and bottle.

The Red Chinese spill crimson across Tranquility Lane, although you're seeing it as more of a deep sepia.

Access the terminal, and bring up a series of five options:

Access "Chinese Invasion" Program: Documents show that this routine was never activated, because it would kill everyone but keep Braun in this simulation for eternity. For the actual program activation, see below.

Access Version Control. This shows a series of overrides programmed in by Braun, effectively giving him a god-like status.

Entry: Toucan Lagoon. The endless beating sun and lagoon waves no longer entrance Braun. Only watching Simpson wither away from scurvy or Neusbaum being eaten by a mako shark entertain him now. But it's not enough. He resets the simulation.

Entry: Slalom Chalet. Braun enthuses about Dithers impaling herself on a fence, and the contrast of the blood on the snow. After 23 years in the Swiss Alps, Braun fancies a change, something more domestic.

Entry: Tranquility Lane. Braun notes that this simulation reminds him of his childhood home town of Kronach. He is eager to twist this reality to his whim, as his subjects are "at home," making his illusions all the more callous.

Activate the Chinese Invasion Program, and quickly head outside to see a squad of Chinese commandos rampage through Tranquility Lane, slaying all the residents. Although harsh, this ending is much more humane than an eternity with Braun, who can remain here and suffer. Head to Betty, who you can tell is extremely annoyed about this outcome. You can press her/Braun for information on the G.E.C.K., and the location of your father. When you're ready, activate EXIT!

NEW OBJECTIVE

"Exit Tranquility Lane" begins.

You meet your father, finally, and he thanks you for saving him from that infernal machine. Speak to him, and he tells you Braun's technology is unstable and potentially dangerous, but it can be adapted for Project

Your father is back! You can finally team up, and save what remains of the world together!

Purity. He needs to return to Rivet City and speak with Doctor Li. If a G.E.C.K. can be found, Project Purity can become a reality. Agree to accompany your father on the trip back; you're edging closer to creating humanity's biggest advancement since the atomic bomb....

XP +600

The Waters of Life

Spoiler Alert

The information below contains some major developments in the lives of you and your friends. If you don't wish to know what the future holds, be careful where your eyes wander!

When your father escapes from **Vault 112 [7.03]** and returns to **Rivet City [9.15]**, he and Doctor Li agree that it is time to complete Project Purity. At the **Jefferson Memorial [9.14]**, your father finds the control room partially operational, but before you can test the machine, the complex is overrun with Enclave Soldiers. The facility is being claimed in the name of President Eden. Your father buys you time to escape, but he pays a very high price. Escort Doctor Li's team out of the complex via the underground tunnels; the goal is to reach the safety of the Brotherhood of Steel's main base: a five-sided fortification once called the Pentagon, and now known by friend and foe alike as the **Citadel [9.11]**.

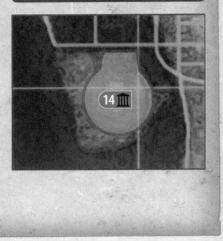

Jefferson Memorial

14 🏛

QUEST FLOWCHART

MAIN PATH		
Main Characters	Your father, James, Doctor Madison Li, Doctor Janice Kaplinski, Daniel Agincourt, Alex Dargon, Garza, Paladin Bael	
Locations	Smith Casey's Garage, Rivet City, Jefferson Memorial, Taft Tunnels, The Citadel	
Adv. Items/Abilities	Energy Weapons, Lockpick, Small Arms, Sneak, Speech, Stimpaks (5+), Buffout (5+)	
Possible enemies	Super Mutant Genus, Enclave Soldier, Colonel Autumn, Enclave Eyebot, Ghoul Genus	
Karma Influence	Negative	Positive

Exit Vault 112

Go to the Rivet City Science Lab.

[Optional] Speak with Doctor Zimmer, if you haven't already

• Miscellaneous Quest: The Replicated Man

Meet up with Doctor Li

Join the scientists at Project Purity.

Clear Project Purity of any remaining Mutant threat.

Clear the entire area of threats

Tell Dad it's safe to enter Project Purity.

Escort the scientists inside Project Purity.

Speak to your father about your past

• Note: Revelation 21.6

Turn on the Flood Control Pump Power.

Head into the Sub-Basement, locate the Flood Control

Get the fuses from Dad.

Return to your Dad

• Fuses (3)

Replace the damaged fuses.

Locate the Fuse Room, insert Fuses

Boot up the mainframe.

Color code: | Objective | Action | Rewards |

Continued on next page

From previous page

Locate Mainframe Room in Sub-Basement

Speak with Dad over the intercom.

Drain the intake pipes.

Enter Pump Control

Return to the control room.

Enter Sub-Basement, and battle to Rotunda. Watch altercation with Colonel Autumn and your father

Escort Doctor Li to the evacuation point.

Locate the Manhole to Taft Tunnels, inside the building

Escort Doctor Li through Taft Tunnels to the Citadel.

Battle through Taft Tunnels, keeping everyone alive or keeping only Doctor Li alive

Locate locked Utility Door

[Sneak] Sneak past the open doorway, or [Science] Hack the door Terminal

Engage the foes while Li hacks the door

• Chinese Army: Spec. Ops. Training Manual

Garza becomes ill

Deal with the Garza "situation".

Shoot him; or Ignore the problem, clear the way, then return; or [Speech] Convince Li or Garza he's a liability; or [Speech] Convince Li that Buffout is needed, give Li Buffout (3)

Give Li or Garza Stimpaks (5)

[Lockpick] Investigate side tunnel

• Safe Items

Clear the rest of the Tunnels

• Nuka-Cola Quantum

Enter Brotherhood-controlled Tunnels

Doctor Li orders advancement into The Citadel

• Main Quest: Picking Up The Trail

Color code: | Objective | Action | Rewards

MEETING OF THE MINDS

As soon as you finish speaking with your father in Vault 112 and agree to accompany him back to Rivet City, you can begin this quest and the return journey. Weave through the Vault's stairs and corridors, passing

Don't delay in your return to Rivet City; your father certainly isn't waiting around!

the Robobrains, and up through Smith Casey's Garage, into the Wasteland wilderness. Before you scramble out, following your

father who runs at an impressive pace, remove your Vault 112 Jumpsuit and replace it with your preferred armor, helmet, and weapon.

NEW OBJECTIVE

"Go to the Rivet City Science Lab" begins.

After you depart from the garage, it's almost certain that you'll run into a number of Wasteland pests, such as Raiders or a group of Radscorpions. Wait here and make sure you kill everything before it overwhelms your father's fighting skills. As soon as all nearby foes are nullified, bring up your Pip-Boy's World Map, and Fast Travel all the way back to Rivet City.

APPENDICES — COMPLETION — TOUR — MISC. QUESTS — MAIN QUEST — BESTIARY — TRAINING

Note

Although you can both traipse across the entire Wasteland, down the Potomac, and finally into Rivet City, this is only advisable if you save often, have enough Stimpaks, and want the additional hassle (and XP).

You arrive at the far end of the Rivet City drawbridge. Run across, past Harkness, and enter the Market-place if you wish to stock up on supplies, or simply head into the Midship Deck, fol-lowing the same route

Madison and James are back and bantering again, like an old married couple.

to the Science Lab as you did before. Depending on your point of entry, you may run into Doctor Zimmer and Armitage. Zimmer stops and asks if you'd be interested in a quick mission, if you haven't spoken to him already. If you want to begin **Miscellaneous Quest: The Replicated Man**, do so now. Otherwise, rendezvous back with Doctor Li, who is already having a heated discussion with your father.

Interrupt their talk by speaking with Doctor Li. You can ask her about Rivet City, your father, and even that odd Doctor Zimmer. When you're done, talk to Dad, who immediately wants to get back to Project Purity. The computer inside the Jefferson Memorial is the best chance to locate a G.E.C.K. You're asked to scout on ahead, so leave the Science Lab, head out of Rivet City, and proceed immediately to the Jefferson Memorial.

NEW OBJECTIVE
"Join the scientists at Project Purity" begins.

Tip

There's no need to Fast Travel to the Jefferson Memorial. It's close enough, and you want to clear the area of enemies first.

SAFE AND PURE

These blasted Mutants need expunging from the darkest recesses of the memorial sub-basement, too!

Drop down from the Rivet City entrance, or dive into the water, and move to the grounds of the Jefferson Memorial. The worst possible result would be the death of a member of Li's science team, or the unthinkable, the demise of your father, so scour the exterior of the building for any Super Mutants you may have missed during your earlier sortie. You're heading for the gift shop entrance, where you entered earlier.

NEW OBJECTIVE
"Clear Project Purity of any remaining Mutant threat" begins.

The doctor's team and your father now wait outside the gift shop entrance. Speak with your father, and he asks you to clear the interior of the memorial (that's the gift shop, rotunda, and sub-base-ment) of all possible threats. You may have completed this during the **Main Quest: Scientific Pursuits**, when you optionally searched for all your father's Holotapes. Explore every nook and cranny of the place, until there are no further enemies. You'll know the area is secured when the objective appears on your screen. Simply return to the surface, and speak with your dad. He thanks you, and you can now begin to escort the scientists inside the building.

NEW OBJECTIVE
"Tell Dad it's safe to enter Project Purity" begins.

NEW OBJECTIVE
"Escort the scientists inside Project Purity" begins.

Doctor Li has brought some of the most impressive (surviving) minds with her to help your father's cause, and it's important that they all reach their specific locations. Move south then east

The search for a G.E.C.K. won't begin until everyone is at the appropriate stations, so chaperone them there.

to the northern of the two rotunda entrances, and wait for Doctors Madison Li and Janice Kaplinski to reach you. Behind them strides your father. Make sure all three of them enter the rotunda door. Optionally, you can speak with two more of Li's team, waiting at specific scientific equipment in the gift shop.

The first is Daniel Agincourt, who's very annoyed at you and your father for not sticking with Li during the development of Project Purity. Don't worry; he'll get over it. You can also speak to the far less grumpy Alex Dargon, who's thrilled to be working with two of the most brilliant minds in the world. That's more like it! Now move to the rotunda, via either door.

THE ALPHA AND OMEGA

As soon as your father is in the rotunda, enter the area yourself, and head up the steps to the giant transparent vat. Your father is suitably excited, and asks you if you remember Catherine's favorite Biblical passage. This experiment is the water; the purifier. This is your mother's dream! Revelation 21:6 is added to your Pip-Boy. Now you can speak to your father about your past, your mother,

Project Purity, and anything else you feel like. Do this now, because you may not get the chance once this experiment starts. When you ask what needs to be done next, your father tells you that the project was abandoned shortly after your birth. Some floodwater needs pumping out. You're tasked with this job!

 Note: Revelation 21:6

NEW OBJECTIVE
"Turn on the Flood Control Pump Power" begins.

Head southeast down the stairs, and take the right side (south) exit back into the gift shop. This gives you a straight shot southwest, to the Door to the Sub-Basement (Jefferson Memorial) only a few steps away. There's an intercom in every room; use these to contact your father for directions if you get lost. Wind down the stairs, passing the sewer tunnel exit, and turn right (east), moving past the Gore Bag and following another tunnel staircase down. If you miss a turn, look for the signs pointing to the Flood Control. Head straight ahead (west), passing the bunk beds, and make your first turn left (south) at the very next junction. Follow the passage to the very end to a rusting, floor-level flood pump, and locate the two devices on the eastern wall, behind the floor pump. There's an intercom, and a Flood Control Power Switch. Activate the switch, and the pump begins to remove the floodwater. You need additional power now, because the fuse box is malfunctioning. Your father has the fuses.

NEW OBJECTIVE
"Get the fuses from Dad" begins.

Retrace your steps to the gift shop area, and enter the rotunda near where Alex Dargon is standing. Run up the steps and contact your father once again. You can get emotional with dear old dad, or you can ask him about the fuses. Apparently, the flooding shorted out the fuse boxes downstairs, including one that controls an automatic door (the one near the Gore Bag, in fact). When the fuses are replaced, you should be able to power up the mainframe computer. You're given the fuses.

 Fuses (3)

NEW OBJECTIVE
"Replace the damaged fuses" begins.

A tiny chamber with two entrances is the Fuse Access A1. Slot your fuses in here.

Return to the sub-basement, using exactly the same route as before, all the way down to the bunk bed area. Move forward (west), through the doorway, and at the first junction, turn right (north) this time. You enter a larger chamber with two small ponds. Ignore this, and head west to the doorway, just left of the white sofa, into a corridor marked "Fuse Access A1." Look for this sign if you get lost. This is the quicker of the two routes to the fuse room. The fuse box is on the north wall. Place the fuses in here, and listen for another intercom message.

NEW OBJECTIVE
"Boot up the mainframe" begins.

You must now access the mainframe computer and reboot it. Find the mainframe chamber on your map; it's almost exactly above the fuse room. Backtrack up the stairs to the initial room with the sewer pipe and the Gore Bag, and continue west to the large utility hatch door you couldn't access before. The "Mainframe" sign indicates the chamber behind this door. Step into the mainframe room through the door, which is now flashing green as it is powered up. Once inside the room, locate the Mainframe Power Switch on the mainframe itself, and activate it.

NEW OBJECTIVE
"Speak with Dad over the intercom" begins.

As soon as the mainframe has booted up, wait for your dad's response from the intercom, and wait again until the objective appears. Then locate a nearby intercom (there's one or more in every chamber), and see what errand he wants you to attempt next. On your way to an intercom, move up and out of the sub-basement, and exit into the gift shop. Optimally, use the intercom just to the right (east) of this exit. Janice has found a blockage in one of the intake pipes. You're tasked with draining it.

NEW OBJECTIVE
"Drain the intake pipes" begins.

Secure the Pipe Controls, and remove the build up of scum blocking your progress.

The pipe itself is located at the opposite end of the gift shop entrance chamber. To reach it, head north, around the debris and through the entrance doorway, passing the wall terminal, but make a right (east) turn, moving up the slowly rising corridor to a collapsed chamber with steam rising from an exposed grating in the ground. Open this grate, and enter a confined tunnel to the Pump Control. At the end of the first section of pipe, open the Grate to the Capital Wasteland.

Move to the section of pipe that rusted away, exposing a mesh fence and the Jefferson Memorial gantry. The Pipe Control is on the east side of the broken pipe. Spin the faucet valve to drain the intake pipe. Suddenly, you see an explosion in the distance! Radio chatter erupts as two Vertibirds drop on the gantry and Power Armored soldiers exit! It's pandemonium at the rotunda,

TRAINING — BESTIARY — MAIN QUEST — MISC. QUESTS — TOUR — COMPLETION — APPENDICES

with dad sealing the grate behind you and preparing for infiltration by unknown forces! You need to get back there and help defuse tensions!

NEW OBJECTIVE
"Return to the control room" begins.

THE BEGINNING AND THE END

Spoiler Alert

Do not read any further, because a major, life-changing moment is about to occur. You have been warned!

These troops are from the Enclave. What does President Eden's forces want with Project Purity?

The Grate to Sift Pump is now unlocked, so the only way is north, through the grate, and down the pipe, landing on each grate platform to break your fall. The sewer pipe winds down and around, and ends at another grate, this one leading to the sub-basement. You appear on the other side of the mesh wall, facing the Gore Bag and mainframe door. A figure clad in Power Armor is firing at you, so drop down immediately (as you're currently a sitting duck). You land in the large chamber with two pools and the white sofa.

Head forward (south), then make the first left (east) turn you can. You're back at the bunk bed room. Ready your favored weapon and attack the Enclave Soldier at the top of the steps, until he yields. Move back into the gift shop area, where you can defeat three or more additional Enclave Soldiers. As the door back outside to the Wasteland is firmly sealed from the other side, the only doors you can try lead into the rotunda. Head there at once.

Tip

You're close to the point of being able to use Power Armor, so you might want to pick up a suit and helmet from one of your downed foes. Take the least-damaged one you can find.

Senseless violence and the ultimate sacrifice; your father hides his pet project to the bitter end.

Muffled sounds of commotion are coming from the containment vat, and Doctor Li is locked outside, trying in vain to open the sealed emergency bulkhead. On the other side is a military man clad in a thick overcoat and flanked by two Enclave Soldiers. The man is Colonel Autumn, and he's demanding that your father hand over the secrets of Project Purity and bring the experiment online immediately.

Autumn shows he's not messing around by tagging Janice Kaplinski right in the heart! Try as you might, you can't open the emergency bulkhead! Autumn tells your father again to reveal his secrets, and he tries reasoning with the man, turning to his computer to type in some keystrokes. This actually releases a massive burst of radioactivity. Your father slumps to the bulkhead, mouthing for you to flee, before collapsing himself. Turn and speak to a shocked Doctor Li. She tells you the only way out is through an escape tunnel they've used before. Doctor Li and three survivors from her team have fled down a manhole. Head out of the rotunda via the door to the north, then turn south, and dash into the small alcove. Locate the Manhole to Taft Tunnels and descend.

NEW OBJECTIVE
"Escort Doctor Li to the evacuation point" begins.

TROUBLE IN THE TUNNELS

Doctor Li's life is of paramount importance. The other three guys? Not so much.

Speak with Doctor Li, who's certainly not about to trek through this highly dangerous area without you to guide her and her three colleagues: Alex Dargon, Daniel Agincourt, and Garza. Bring out your favorite tunnel-blasting weapon, and speak to Doctor Li again. Tell her to follow you, and head west, to the Taft Tunnels first junction. Ignore the tunnel to the southwest, which is filled with radioactive barrels, but take the Stimpaks and Chems from the nearby wall First Aid Kit, and the Buffout atop the barrel. Shoot the Enclave Eyebot as it whistles by you.

NEW OBJECTIVE
"Escort Doctor Li through Taft Tunnel to the Citadel" begins.

First Aid Box Health and Chems

Tip

You have two options: tell Doctor Li to follow you, or ask her to wait so you can scout ahead. The following route details the critical moments for the scientists to hold back. Otherwise, assume Doctor Li's group is following closely behind you.

Not everyone has to live. That Agincourt guy, he wasn't nice to your Dad, was he? Garza? He's always complaining about his "heart trouble." Alex Dargon? He's a sycophant of the worst kind. Pop a quick bullet in all three of their heads. Not the doctor though because she's important to your cause. Stifle your maniacal laughter as their brains go pop.

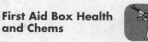 **Tip**

Save your progress often during this route so you can reload a particularly ham-fisted battle.

Head right, to the northwest, and then straight out (west) as the tunnel slopes down to a doorway. Step into a narrow passage that leads to a hatch door. Stop and optionally Sneak, then open the door. In the room beyond, a couple of Enclave Soldiers are running left to right, along an upper balcony. Stay until they leave via an upper exit and the coast is clear. Then stand up, and move into the chamber, avoid the dripping radioactive acid, and head through the doorway to the right (west). Stop at the next doorway, and blast a second Eyebot as it floats left to right.

This is a good opportunity to halt Doctor Li and tell her to wait. Head into the corridor, turning right (north). You could venture left (south), but the room and a small alcove up here are filled with radioactive barrels (and a Rad-X), meaning it can be ignored. Instead, head north around the corner and face west. Ahead is an open doorway to your left (south), a wall terminal, and a utility door ahead of you. To the right is a First Aid Box on the wall. Snag the items inside, once you've navigated the following area using a plan listed below:

 You can **Sneak** (optionally using a Stealth Boy) past the open doorway to the left (south).

Or, you can simply walk to the doorway. Peer inside, and you'll see a two-tier chamber with patrolling Enclave Soldiers. There's a chance you'll be spotted, so don't stay at the doorway for long (unless you want to engage them; see below).

 If you have an incredibly high **Science** skill, hack into the wall terminal. Once at the menu, you can open the utility door ahead. Sneak back to the doctor, tell her to follow you, and run through the doorway before you're spotted.

The other plan requires simple brute force. Either bring the doctor and her team with you, so she can hack the wall terminal (and her brethren face the odd laser fire), or just bring yourself. Either way, make sure you're the Enclave's main target. Storm into the room to the left (south), and use the cylinders and pipes to your left or the girders on your right as cover. Deal with a quartet of foes streaming out of the door at the opposite end of this room, and another two or three on the balcony above.

This battle requires good aiming, cunning tactics (such as lobbing a Frag Grenade through the doorway before all the enemies exit), and well-aimed balcony shots. Do not let the Enclave Soldiers into the tunnel to rake fire on your team! Once the Enclave Soldiers are defeated in this area, inspect the bodies for

ammunition and armor, then grab some junk from the small table, including a Chinese Assault Rifle, and the *Chinese Army: Spec. Ops. Training Manual*. Read it when you can! Now return to Doctor Li, who has opened the utility door if you had her follow you. If not, bring her to the wall terminal, and let her do the hacking.

First Aid Box Health and Chems	**First Chinese Assault Rifle**

Chinese Army: Spec. Ops. Training Manual

Head through the utility door, and then turn and tell Doctor Li to remain where she is. Then weave through the two junk piles to a sloping tunnel structure, where a Ghoul is ready to snap your neck and savage your throat! Gun it down, then head to the small barricade and barrels. Another feral, once-human fiend comes screaming out of the small chamber ahead of you; shoot it in the head. Then turn right (north), and make a circuit around the central column, blasting anything with an exposed rib-cage. When you're sure all the Ghouls are dead, return for Doctor Li, and bring the team around and past the bathtub, and through the hatch door near the baby carriage.

GAME OVER FOR GARZA?

 **Note**

This is only available if Garza is still alive, although he may not be for much longer....

One of the team is holding you up. Sacrifice is the key here: either his or yours!

Head through into a small connecting passage, and out into a tiny cross-shaped junction, with only skeletal remains and a hatch door to the north to investigate. You're interrupted by Doctor Li, who tells you the team can't continue any longer. It appears Garza is suffering from heart trouble, and he needs medicine. Li isn't moving until he gets the care and attention he deserves. Garza needs Stimpaks.

NEW OBJECTIVE

"Deal with the Garza 'situation'" begins.

Some solutions to this problem include:

 Step up to Garza, and shoot him until he falls over. Problem solved! Li isn't happy, but she's not the one with the Assault Rifle, is she?

 You can continue your search in the remainder of the tunnels without the team, although you need Doctor Li to leave. When you return, Garza has passed away. Oh, well.

 You can give either Doctor Li or Garza five of your hard-earned Stimpaks. This heals him right up, and he's ready to go.

TRAINING — BESTIARY — MAIN QUEST — MISC. QUESTS — TOUR — COMPLETION — APPENDICES

You can speak with Garza, and convince him that he's only going to slow everyone down, and it's better if he stays behind. Succeed in your **Speech** challenge, and he agrees.

 You can talk to Doctor Li, and convince her that Garza is a liability. Succeed in your **Speech** challenge, and she agrees, talks to him, and he agrees to stay behind.

Or, you can convince Doctor Li that Buffout is the best medicine for Garza. She takes three from you if you have them. Succeed in your **Speech** challenge, and have three Buffouts, and Garza is given this concoction.

INTO THE LYONS DEN

Enclave Soldiers aren't lobotomized like Ghouls. They try cunning tactics to thwart you.

Now that Garza is feeling better (or much worse), press onward, opening the hatch door to the north, and moving to another small passageway, with a door on your left (west). Tell Doctor Li to remain here while you investigate the room with the metal gantry steps. Step into the room, and once on the metal platform, swing around to face behind you (east); two Enclave Soldiers on a balcony you cannot reach are attempting an ambush. Dispatch them, then climb the stairs to the upper exit, and grab the rather natty-looking Eyebot Helmet on the desk.

 Eyebot Helmet

Head into another chamber with gantry steps, and brace yourself for a Ghoul attack at the top. Creep forward (west), as another Ghoul charges in, and step to a T-junction, looking right (north) and bracing for another Ghoul attack. Now that the coast is clear, investigate the small medical bay on the left, with a First Aid Box in one corner. Then return and speak with Doctor Li, bringing her up the stairs, then north and west to the exit passageway.

You might want to keep Doctor Li back in the medical bay for this next section. Open the hatch, and immediately rattle off some rounds into a couple of nearby Ghouls as you step into another large tunnel. Once the Ghouls are down, grab the delicious Nuka-Cola Quantum on the picnic table to the southwest, but don't drink

it. You need it for **Miscellaneous Quest: The Nuka-Cola Challenge**. Head north up the tunnel, pausing to cut down another Ghoul to your left (west), and another ahead of you. Now halt Doctor Li one final time.

 Nuka-Cola Quantum

 At the northern end of the tunnel is a locked hatch door. Once you jimmy it open, you can enter a smaller tunnel leading down and east. This, in turn leads to a Ghoul-filled staircase with another doorway at the bottom, and a tiny tunnel section to a half-buried safe. Blast any remaining Ghouls, and crack open the safe with **Lockpicking** skill, and take the items inside.

 Caution

Don't take your scientist friends into this area, as it's very easy for them to get mauled, which is particularly galling as you're almost out of this labyrinth!

 Items from the safe

Hold your fire, and use the switch to open the utility door by the skeletal corpses. You're entering an area controlled by the Brotherhood of Steel, and a Flamer Initiate is ready to beckon you in. Quickly run around the sandbags, as a group of Ghouls attempts to breach this security point. Join in and dispatch them, with the help of the Flamer Initiate and automatic turret system. To minimize casualties, head up the tunnel so the scientists don't mill about the entrance. When combat has ended, check the shelving behind you (west); grab the weapons and items from the shelves, the two Ammo Boxes, and the First Aid Box.

Ammo Box Ammunition (2) **First Aid Box Health and Chems**

You can make good your escape, heading up the final tunnel section, turning left (west) at the bathtub, inspecting the small table for some Med-X, and then accessing the Ladder to the Capital Wasteland. You scramble up onto a rocky outcrop, west of the Jefferson Memorial. The Brotherhood of Steel's main base on the East Coast, in a structure you think used to be called "the Pentagon," is just ahead. Listen to the Red Chinese's attempts to convert you before their signal is jammed, if you wish.

 People's Republic of America Radio Signal Found

You can reach the entrance to the Brotherhood's base first, and encounter a Sentry Bot, a soldier, and Paladin Bael. Although you can speak to him, he refuses you access into the building. That is, until Doctor Li strides over, punches the intercom, and shouts through to someone named Elder Lyons that she needs access into the building. The massive metal gate grinds upward, and your chaperoning adventure is over. Welcome to the Citadel.

Picking up the Trail

Although you succeeded in escorting Doctor Li to the **Citadel [9.11]**, all is not well. Your father never had the chance to track down the a G.E.C.K. Inquire among the Brotherhood Scribes to point you in the right direction. After you meet with Elder Lyons to discuss Power Armor training, ask Scribe Rothchild where to look, and dig around in some Vault-Tec records. You learn that G.E.C.K.s were issued to several Vaults, including one relatively close-by: Vault 87. Current Brotherhood maps suggest the area around the ground entrance is shrouded in deadly radiation, but the Lamplight Caverns may have another entrance. When you reach **Little Lamplight [4.08]**, you're confronted by a no-nonsense 10-year old named Mayor MacCready, who doesn't trust adults and won't let you pass. Convince him you're harmless, and you're let inside a strange underground settlement run by children. After some spelunking, you discover two possible entrances to the Vault.

Little Lamplight

QUEST FLOWCHART

	MAIN PATH 1	**OPTIONAL PATH 1**	**OPTIONAL PATH 2**
Main Characters	Elder Lyons, Sentinel Sarah Lyons, Paladin Gunny, Scribe Rothchild, Mayor MacCready, Princess, Joseph		
Locations	The Citadel, Little Lamplight		
Adv. Items/Abilities	Lockpick, Science, Sneak, Speech, Child at Heart		
Possible enemies	Super Mutant Genus		
Karma Influence	Neutral		

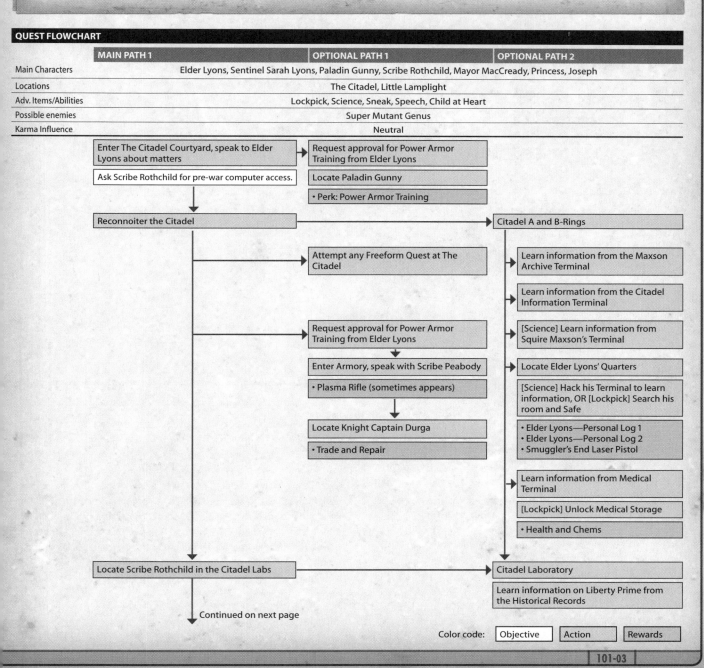

- Enter The Citadel Courtyard, speak to Elder Lyons about matters
- Ask Scribe Rothchild for pre-war computer access.

- Request approval for Power Armor Training from Elder Lyons
- Locate Paladin Gunny
- • Perk: Power Armor Training

- Reconnoiter the Citadel
- Citadel A and B-Rings

- Attempt any Freeform Quest at The Citadel

- Learn information from the Maxson Archive Terminal
- Learn information from the Citadel Information Terminal

- Request approval for Power Armor Training from Elder Lyons
- Enter Armory, speak with Scribe Peabody
- • Plasma Rifle (sometimes appears)
- Locate Knight Captain Durga
- • Trade and Repair

- [Science] Learn information from Squire Maxson's Terminal
- Locate Elder Lyons' Quarters
- [Science] Hack his Terminal to learn information, OR [Lockpick] Search his room and Safe
- • Elder Lyons—Personal Log 1
- • Elder Lyons—Personal Log 2
- • Smuggler's End Laser Pistol

- Learn information from Medical Terminal
- [Lockpick] Unlock Medical Storage
- • Health and Chems

- Locate Scribe Rothchild in the Citadel Labs
- Citadel Laboratory
- Learn information on Liberty Prime from the Historical Records

Continued on next page

Color code: | Objective | Action | Rewards |

Main Characters | Elder Lyons, Sentinel Sarah Lyons, Paladin Gunny, Scribe Rothchild, Mayor MacCready, Princess, Joseph

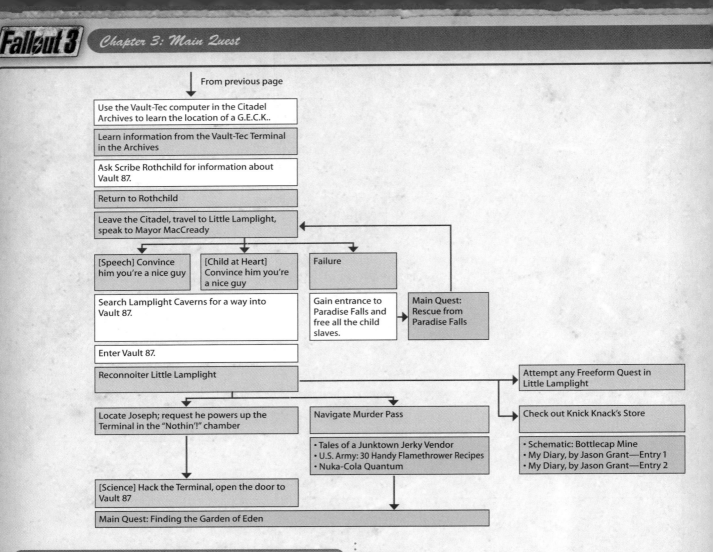

From previous page

```
Use the Vault-Tec computer in the Citadel
Archives to learn the location of a G.E.C.K..

Learn information from the Vault-Tec Terminal
in the Archives

Ask Scribe Rothchild for information about
Vault 87.

Return to Rothchild

Leave the Citadel, travel to Little Lamplight,
speak to Mayor MacCready
```

[Speech] Convince him you're a nice guy	[Child at Heart] Convince him you're a nice guy	Failure

```
Search Lamplight Caverns for a way into
Vault 87.
```

Gain entrance to Paradise Falls and free all the child slaves.	Main Quest: Rescue from Paradise Falls

```
Enter Vault 87.

Reconnoiter Little Lamplight                           →  Attempt any Freeform Quest in
                                                          Little Lamplight
```

Locate Joseph; request he powers up the Terminal in the "Nothin'!" chamber	Navigate Murder Pass	Check out Knick Knack's Store
	• Tales of a Junktown Jerky Vendor • U.S. Army: 30 Handy Flamethrower Recipes • Nuka-Cola Quantum	• Schematic: Bottlecap Mine • My Diary, by Jason Grant—Entry 1 • My Diary, by Jason Grant—Entry 2

```
[Science] Hack the Terminal, open the door to
Vault 87

Main Quest: Finding the Garden of Eden
```

THE PRIDE OF LYONS

This old veteran warrior is wise and commands respect. Yes, but what about my Power Armor training?

Once you and Doctor Li's team step into the main Citadel courtyard, you are hastily greeted by an old man, flanked by his young daughter Sarah, who you previously assisted during the Super Mutant hunt near Galaxy News Radio. Doctor Li (who impressively managed to survive a Ghoul- and Enclave-infested tunnel run wearing high heels) tells you not to trust these people. "They're the Brotherhood" she whispers. You can now converse with the Citadel's leader:

You can ask about the Enclave, an organization Lyons deems the most threatening to the Capital Wasteland of all. He fought them back in California, 30 years ago. He says they seek to control and destroy, and by recent evidence, Lyons may have a point.

You can inquire about the Brotherhood, and there's a wealth of knowledge here. Lyons lets you know about the Brotherhood's orders to acquire all advanced technology, and Lyons' supervisors and his Pride's split from the main Brotherhood.

You can seek Elder Lyons' advice on the Super Mutant threat.

You can also ask whether someone in the Citadel can train you to wear Power Armor. He recommends Paladin Gunny, who trains Initiates in the bailey.

Finally, you are instructed to meet with Scribe Rothchild, who may be able to help you locate information on a G.E.C.K., tucked away in pre-war archives.

NEW OBJECTIVE

"Ask Scribe Rothchild for pre-war computer access" begins.

You can optionally speak with Sarah Lyons, and she echoes her father's thoughts on the Enclave (the Brotherhood had no idea such well-equipped Enclave forces operated in this area), Super Mutants, Power Armor, and Lyons' Pride. Bid Sarah farewell, and head into the bailey, which is the central part of this courtyard. Here, you'll see Initiates blasting effigies of Super Mutants with a variety of weapons. Hand-to-hand combat and push-ups are all part of the training. Locate Paladin Gunny, and ask him to train your in Power Armor. He says he doesn't like it, but he has to go along with it. Moments later, you're trained!

Power Armor Training

Finally, you can don the most impressive, cool-looking, and downright useful armor available. Remember that you must follow this two-step plan to receive this perk:

1. Speak to Elder Lyons, requesting Power Armor Training.
2. Speak to Paladin Gunny, and request Power Armor Training.

Both Brotherhood members are in the courtyard, so this should take no time at all. Then, as the nearby slides show, you can wear any of the Power Armor outfits you've collected. You can mix and match, too, such as wearing a Brotherhood suit and Enclave Helmet (slide #1), or an Enclave suit and Brotherhood Helmet (slide #2), or even the fabled Tesla Armor (not pictured)....

Tip

Need a suit of Power Armor in a hurry, but forgot to pack one in your Pip-Boy's Inventory? Then Fast Travel to the Galaxy News Radio Plaza, and search through the ruined school and the surrounding area for a recently deceased soldier.

Note

Before you explore the area below the courtyard, you can try climbing the outside balcony, checking the Initiate's open-air sleeping quarters, and even attempt some target practice, shooting Nuka-Cola bottles off the trays of the stuffed Super Mutant mannequins.

Note

You can tour the Citadel at your leisure, picking up background info and meeting members of the Brotherhood. For more detail on the various chambers, the Freeform Quests, and the Brotherhood personnel that dwell within, consult the Tour of the Wasteland chapter (starting at page 380).

RENDEZVOUS WITH SCRIBE ROTHCHILD

With your tour of the Citadel complete, continue with your quest progress. You are to rendezvous with Scribe Rothchild, who is usually on the lower floor of the laboratory. Ask him if he has any information regarding the G.E.C.K. He doubts the kit even exists, but says Archive records may hold a clue; specifically the Vault-Tec terminal located in the A-Ring.

One of the senior members of the Order of the Scribes, Rothchild almost helps you locate Vault 87.

NEW OBJECTIVE

"Use the Vault-Tec computer in the Citadel Archives to learn the location of a G.E.C.K." begins.

The optimal route to the Citadel Archives is to head up any of the gantry stairs to the upper lab balcony, and run to the southeast corner, then enter the corridor leading to the Citadel—A Ring. At the top of the stairs, turn right (south), and run straight into the Archives, and locate the terminal straight in front of you, marked Vault-Tec Terminal. Quickly access DC Area Vault Listings > Vault 87 > Equipment Issuances. As soon as the information spools down, your quest is updated. You've found a G.E.C.K. location!

NEW OBJECTIVE

"Ask Scribe Rothchild for information about Vault 87" begins.

Sprint back to Rothchild by the same route, and tell him you've found information on a G.E.C.K. inside Vault 87, but aren't able to pinpoint it. Rothchild reveals the locations of five Vaults in the nearby vicinity (which now appear on your Pip-Boy). Unfortunately, no one has managed to enter Vault 87 due to an extremely high radiation content. The exterior is sealed, and Super Mutants prowl the area.

All is not lost though; Rothchild recommends you visit the Lamplight Caverns, which the Vault may be accessible from. Rothchild can't spare any men (although a woman named Star Paladin Cross can accompany you if you locate her and ask her to). Set off for Lamplight Caverns immediately.

NEW OBJECTIVE

"Search Lamplight Caverns for a way into Vault 87" begins.

LET THERE BE LAMPLIGHT

Ascend to the bailey (courtyard), and look for the double metal doors that lead out to the Wasteland. Exit via this location, and immediately Fast Travel before you leave the outer defenses of the Citadel. Although you can't directly travel to Little Lamplight (unless you've previously explored the Western Wasteland sector), you can Fast Travel closer than your current location. Two possible options that you may have uncovered en route to Vault 112 are the Jury Street Metro Station, or the Smith Casey Garage. Assuming you move to Smith Casey Garage, head north-northwest, avoid the Military Checkpoint, and run through Radio Antenna Papa November.

This is more than just a hole in the ground. It's a hole with fairy-lights strewn everywhere.

From there, it's a short jog across the blasted heath, and a possible confrontation with Raiders, Radscorpions, and Super Mutant hunting parties, until you spot Little Lamplight's large water tower in the distance. As you get close, pass the rusting coach liner and vehicles, and step into the entrance kiosk. Rummage around to uncover three Ammo Boxes on the back shelf, and some food. Then head west, down and into the cave, to the Door to Lamplight Caverns.

Ammo Box Ammunition (3)

Wind through the entrance tunnel until it widens out and leads to a sturdy but rusting gate constructed from cannibalized metal parts. Before you can step forward, you're ordered to halt in no uncertain terms by a kid wearing a combat helmet three sizes too big for him. This tyke is Mayor MacCready, and he doesn't take any guff, especially from Mungos like you! Little Lamplight, you see, is completely inhabited by children, and they don't trust grown-ups. You'll have to convince MacCready you can be trusted. First, ask about Vault 87, and if you can come in. "No, Mungos aren't allowed!" is the response. The following choices are now available:

> You can **Speech** challenge MacCready and convince him that you're a nice guy, really. If this fast-talking works, you're let into the place.
>
> If you have the **Child at Heart** perk, you can reason much more easily with MacCready, and he lets you in.

If your Speech fails, and you don't have Child at Heart, or you just want to ask MacCready how to enter Little Lamplight, he refuses.

No amount of reasoning, gunfire, or threats change his mind. After you speak to MacCready and ask how you can prove yourself, he tells you about three kidnapped kids—Penny, Sammy, and Squirrel—who've been held by Slavers in Paradise Falls. If you can find and bring them back alive, he'll know you're a trustworthy Mungo. You must now complete **Main Quest: Rescue from Paradise Falls** before returning here.

NEW OBJECTIVE
"Gain entrance to Paradise Falls and free all the child slaves" begins.

NEW OBJECTIVE
"Enter Vault 87" begins.

 Note
Remember! You don't need to begin Rescue from Paradise Falls, and you can attempt it even if you're allowed into Little Lamplight, but it is mandatory if you fail to sweet-talk Mayor MacCready.

A GLOOMY TOUR OF LITTLE LAMPLIGHT

 Note
This assumes you've entered the main gate at Little Lamplight, either through fast-talking or kid-rescuing. If you don't want to investigate Little Lamplight, talk to Mayor MacCready immediately, and skip to "Two Ways to Vault 87." It is also possible that you may have stumbled across Paradise Falls, and completed Rescue from Paradise, in which case you can tell MacCready you rescued the kids. Little Lamplight is a little easier to find too, because Sammy will have marked it on your World Map.

This is completely optional. For more detail on the various chambers, the Freeform Quests, and the Little Lamplighters that dwell within, consult the Tour of the Wasteland Chapter (page 298).

 **Note**
If you've already gained entry to Little Lamplight before visiting the Citadel and attempting this part of the Main Quest, you can't speak to MacCready about Vault 87, or have the way opened for you.

KID'S STUFF PART A: ENTRANCE AND ESSENTIALS

Would you trust your sutures to this pint-sized physician? You should; she's really good.

Now that you're inside the main gate, you can explore this settlement thoroughly. Head under the gate and speak to the assembled kids who seem to be holding a party for someone named Sticky; he's the teenager with the party hat. Speak to him if you wish to begin **Miscellaneous Quest: Big Trouble in Big Town**. Otherwise, the rest of the Lamplight's inhabitants roam the tunnels, moving to specific locations (listed below) from time to time.

Before you follow the two signs to Spelunker's and Great Chamber, move east to the front of a small wooden structure. Open the Door to Little Lamplight Office Building. Inside is a three-room area, and a small girl named Lucy. The first room is a disused school room; Joseph holds class here, and you can talk to him about the history of this odd little place. The second is Lucy's office, where "The Doctor Is In!", and also where you can steal Ammo Box Ammunition. The third room is where Lucy sleeps. Speak with Doctor Lucy, and she can heal, sell your medical supplies, talk about life here, give you directions, or talk about an android if you're investigating the whereabouts of a Replicated Man (a Miscellaneous Quest).

Lamplighters: Mayor MacCready, Lucy, Sticky Hands, and Joseph†.

KID'S STUFF PART B: SOUVENIR SHOP CAVERN

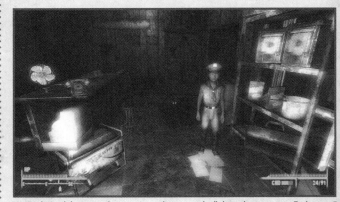

Knick Knack lives up to his name, providing you with all the junk you want to Trade.

Follow the tunnel to a junction, allowing you to continue west to Spelunker's Cafe and the Great Chamber, or north, following the signs to "Souvenirs." You may encounter a couple of Lamplight dogs on your travels. Exit to the Souvenir Chamber, and ignore the restrooms unless you need water, or want to look at the dead Mungo skeleton in there. The bigger attraction is the souvenir shop, although you need to pick the lock if it isn't open.

The proprietor of the shop is Knick Knack, who can Repair and Trade with you. One of his items is a sought-after Schematic for the Bottlecap Mine. The shop itself is stacked with some food and Ammo Box Ammunition you can grab. The cabinet requires a key, which you can take if you Pickpocket Knick Knack; it holds the entire inventory! Of more interest are three Holotapes. The one on the counter begins **Miscellaneous Quest: The Replicated Man**. The other two on the shelves are diary entries of a 10-year old boy named Jason Grant. Exit the shop, and you have two additional tunnels to explore; one to the west, linking up to the Great Chamber, and a tunnel to the north, to the rear entrance.

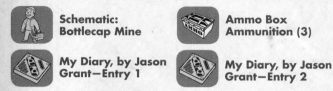

Schematic: Bottlecap Mine	**Ammo Box Ammunition (3)**
My Diary, by Jason Grant—Entry 1	**My Diary, by Jason Grant—Entry 2**

Lamplighters: Knick Knack, Squirrel, Bumble, Stan, Zip†.

KID'S STUFF PART C: REAR ENTRANCE GATE

Choose the northern tunnel, and you reach the back entrance. This is where Mayor MacCready moves to when you request access to Murder Pass, as this is the entrance to it. Here you'll find nothing except the prim and petulant Princess, who has an attitude to match her name. Move to this area when you wish to continue this quest and are ready to brave Murder Pass.

KID'S STUFF PART D: SPELUNKING AREA

Move back to the junction, and check out the tunnel to Spelunker's and the Great Chamber. Spelunker's is a small cafe on the calm cavern water, which you can dive into if you want to view some sunken picnic tables

Spelunker's Cafe is the main eatery around here. Ask Eclair how he got his nickname.

and your own radiation burns, but of greater interest is Eclair's counter, where the cafe proprietor offers food for sale. There are some nearby Ammo Boxes to raid, too. When you're ready, head north, into the Great Chamber.

 Ammo Box Ammunition (3)

Lamplighters: Eclair

KID'S STUFF PART E: THE GREAT CHAMBER

Welcome to the Great Chamber: a natural wonder, augmented by the hard work of small children.

The most impressive cave area by far in Little Lamplight is the Great Chamber. It is a massive cavern, with rope bridges connecting different platforms and sleeping areas. The following exploration

begins at the platform linking the southern and eastern entrances. First, you can head down a few different ramps to ground level. The floor of this chamber has a burning pile of refuse to the west, but little else of use (except, perhaps, a Lamplighter you're trying to find). Stay on the platforms for the rest of the exploration.

Head northwest to the first giant rock column, with a motorbike propped up against it. Move left (clockwise) around the column to uncover (all on your left) a shack with a bed, a ramp to the ground, two bridges leading north, and a small zigzag ramp to an upper shack room with a bed.

Choose the bridge that curves to the right (northeast). This leads to a floating junction. Turn left and head into the outhouse shack, with a privacy screen and a short "pondering plank" with a chair at the end. Continue east to a rocky alcove with a bed in it.

Select the other bridge that curves to the right (north), and move to the next rock column. Turn left (west), and follow another bridge section to a shack on your right (north) containing a pool table, an impressive Intact Garden Gnome, and a Holotape on the table's edge. Grab and listen to it. Then continue westward to a rocky alcove, with a Work Bench, and an impressive Bottlecap Mine to take. Now return to the stone column.

January 2077— Little Lamplight!	**Bottlecap Mine**
Holotape: The First Mayor of Lamplight	

Lamplighters: Pete, Bandit, Ginger (all dogs), Joseph, Penny, Biwwy, Knock Knock.

†The Lamplighters move around the different areas, so you may need to look thoroughly to find the child you wish to converse with.

KID'S STUFF PART F: NOTHIN'!

Traipse over the debris, and there's the back entrance to Vault 87. Find a tiny teacher to help you.

Move counterclockwise around the rock column, passing the blue outhouse roof on your right, and stopping at the exit junction. There's a ramp down to the ground to the west, but the most interesting area is the bridge to the north. This leads to a debris-filled cavern called "Nothin'!" However, this isn't quite the case; at the northwestern corner of this cavern is a small metal room with a reactor inside. This looks like an entrance to Vault 87! Unfortunately, the terminal isn't powered. This is the alternate way to enter the Vault, if you don't want to face Murder Pass.

TWO WAYS TO VAULT 87

PATH A: THE SAFE AND SHORT WAY

The first method of gaining entry into Vault 87 is to ignore Murder Pass completely, and use the rear entrance. For this, you need to find Joseph, the eldest of the kids. Find him, and begin a conversation. Request that he power up the terminal in the chamber called "Nothin'!", and he obliges. Follow him to this chamber, and move up to the terminal. He quickly powers it back on.

 Now use your **Science** skill to open the hatch door to the right of the terminal. If you're successful, you open the door, move into the Reactor Chamber of Vault 87, and immediately begin **Main Quest: Finding the Garden of Eden**, without a furious firefight through Murder Pass.

PATH B: THE LONG AND EXTREMELY DANGEROUS WAY

It's called Murder Pass for a reason! Prepare to repel a gang of Super Mutants out for blood.

The usual method of reaching Vault 87 is to navigate north through Little Lamplight to the rear entrance, where Princess is usually on guard. You must speak with Mayor MacCready (ideally straight after he lets you into Little Lamplight at the first entrance), and inform him you wish to enter Vault 87. He grudgingly agrees to open the northern gate and lowers the weights with Princess. Head on through and enter the Door to Murder Pass.

Walk forward (north) a few steps until you reach a junction with a tunnel to your left (west), or the continuation straight ahead. You face a lot fewer problems staying straight ahead, but you can pick up more items from corpses if you turn left. Continue straight on to a shack and a wider opening, with a couple of nearby Super Mutants to Sneak past or engage, and another farther up, around the corner to the north. When combat is over, be sure to check the shack for two Ammo Boxes on the bed frame, and another by a small outhouse. The toilet itself has some light reading, too. Now continue up the tunnel to the north as it winds around, and eventually meets at a small, circular junction where a large stack of sandbags have fallen.

 Ammo Box Ammunition (3)

 Tales of a Junktown Jerky Vendor +1 Barter (when read)

If you took the left path, expect a much heavier resistance. First, there's usually a foe on the bridge in front of you (west). A second Super Mutant on the opposite side carries a Missile Launcher, and he doesn't care who he hits, as long as some of the splash damage strikes you! Back up, dealing with the first foe, then edge forward and tag the heavy weapons Mutie with a sniper shot, a lobbed Grenade, or a Missile of your own. Then sprint across the bridge, so you aren't winged by the foes down below. Keep going west, down the dead-end tunnel toward the flaming barrel.

It illuminates a table where you can grab two First Aid Kits' worth of goods, Ammo from two Ammo Boxes, and a copy of U.S. Army: 30 Handy Flamethrower Recipes.

 Missile Launcher

 First Aid Box Health and Chems (2)

 Ammo Box Ammunition (2)

U.S. Army: 30 Handy Flamethrower Recipes +1 Big Guns (when read)

The main cavern chamber itself is a deadly place, where three Super Mutants ready their weaponry to fire, and one is armed with a Minigun. You can head down the planks to the ground below, moving to the campfire, and staying mobile with a Combat Shotgun, or you can backtrack to the circular junction, and access the stilt huts from the same height as the Super Mutants, using the rock walls as cover. Assuming the battle is successful, the spoils are reasonable. Two stilt shacks contain the following items:

Minigun

Ammo Box Ammunition (2)

First Aid Box Health and Chems (5)

The only remaining path heads north at the circular junction, so follow the tunnel as it winds around to a fork. On the left is a dead-end, and a Brahmin-head-on-a-chain Trap that can seriously wound you

The detour is finally over; you can at last enter Vault 87, and begin locating the G.E.C.K.

if you let it. Move to the side and shoot it loose, or ignore the left fork and continue north up the right side. Ready yourself for another trap as you reach a wider area. Run through the gap in the mesh fence, and don't dawdle because a Grenade Trap drops here.

Not only that, but a Super Mutant waits to crush you, popping out of an alcove to your right (east). When everything has quieted down, you can finally step to the hatch door, and enter a small outer monitoring chamber. To the right are two burned-out terminals and a desk with a Grenade Trap nearby. On the left is a shelf with Ammo Boxes, a First Aid Box, and a Nuka-Cola Quantum; collect it for the **Miscellaneous Quest: The Nuka-Cola Challenge**. Stagger out the other side of the room and weave to the Door to the Reactor Room, then congratulate yourself; Vault 87 awaits! Your G.E.C.K. search begins now.

 Nuka-Cola Quantum

 Ammo Box Ammunition (3)

 First Aid Box Health and Chems

Rescue from Paradise

Little Lamplight's Mayor MacCready is a foul-mouthed little tyke, but he knows how to access **Vault 87 [4.06]**, and he won't let you through. You can't resort to infanticide, but you can make the mayor trust you. You must help the village of **Little Lamplight [4.08]** by rescuing a trio of captured kids from the Slaver compound known ironically as **Paradise Falls [2.08]**. When you reach the compound, a Slaver named Grouse refuses you entry. He's open to bribery, a Miscellaneous Quest, or a bullet through his skull. Assuming you remain on neutral terms and are allowed safe passage, you're greeted by a fleeing slave. He doesn't get far; his head explodes. Slavers have found a novel and inhumane way to keep their commodities in line: Slave Collars.

Once inside this place of butchery, misery, and anarchy, you need to speak to a bright little cherub named Squirrel. He's got a plan, involving the deactivation of the Slave Collars, a quick guard distraction, and a quick dash to the toilets, where a kid-sized sewer tunnel allows them access to the Wasteland. Agree to help, then optionally save a third child named Penny with a crush on a Mungo, and report back to Little Lamplight for your reward: access into Vault 87. Finally!

Paradise Falls

QUEST FLOWCHART

Request for entering Little Lamplight is denied by Mayor MacCready, or Begin this quest of your own volition

Gain entrance to Paradise Falls.

Locate Grouse at the entrance to Paradise Falls

Complete Miscellaneous Quest: Strictly Business, rounding up Slaves for him; or Have an extremely low Karma, your reputation precedes you; or [Speech] Bribe Grouse to let you in, give him 500 Caps

Attack the Slavers

Watch the Slaver execution of Carter; speak to Sammy

Find and speak with the kidnapped Lamplighters.

Thoroughly investigate Paradise Falls

	MAIN PATH	MAIN PATH 2	MAIN PATH 3
Main Characters	Mayor MacCready, Grouse, Carter, Sammy, Squirrel, Penny, Forty, Clover, Crimson, Eulogy Jones, Rory Maclaren		
Locations	Little Lamplight, Paradise Falls		
Adv. Items/Abilities	Lockpick, Repair, Science, Sneak, Speech, 2,500+ Caps, Very Low Karma	Speech, 2,500+ Caps, Low Karma	Big Guns, Energy Weapons, Small Guns
Possible enemies	—		Slavers
Karma Influence	Neutral	Neutral	Positive

Begin to search for the Slaves, and commence Squirrel's Secret Plan

Speak to Eulogy Jones about purchasing the Slaves

Locate Quantum Stash and Bobblehead in Eulogy's Pad

• Bobblehead: Speech, Paradise Falls Box Key, Nuka-Cola Quantum (5), Eulogy's Hat

Speak to Squirrel

Slay the man

Eulogy Jones agrees to sell them for 2,000 Caps

Leave no Slaver alive

Color code: Objective   Action   Rewards

Continued on next page

TRAINING — BESTIARY — MAIN QUEST — MISC. QUESTS — TOUR — COMPLETION — APPENDICES

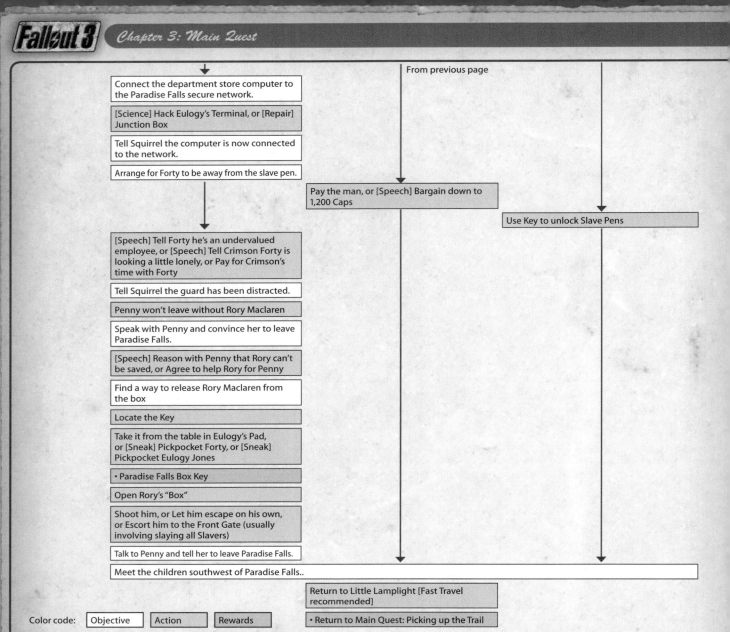

From previous page

Connect the department store computer to the Paradise Falls secure network.

[Science] Hack Eulogy's Terminal, or [Repair] Junction Box

Tell Squirrel the computer is now connected to the network.

Arrange for Forty to be away from the slave pen.

Pay the man, or [Speech] Bargain down to 1,200 Caps

Use Key to unlock Slave Pens

[Speech] Tell Forty he's an undervalued employee, or [Speech] Tell Crimson Forty is looking a little lonely, or Pay for Crimson's time with Forty

Tell Squirrel the guard has been distracted.

Penny won't leave without Rory Maclaren

Speak with Penny and convince her to leave Paradise Falls.

[Speech] Reason with Penny that Rory can't be saved, or Agree to help Rory for Penny

Find a way to release Rory Maclaren from the box

Locate the Key

Take it from the table in Eulogy's Pad, or [Sneak] Pickpocket Forty, or [Sneak] Pickpocket Eulogy Jones

• Paradise Falls Box Key

Open Rory's "Box"

Shoot him, or Let him escape on his own, or Escort him to the Front Gate (usually involving slaying all Slavers)

Talk to Penny and tell her to leave Paradise Falls.

Meet the children southwest of Paradise Falls..

Return to Little Lamplight [Fast Travel recommended]

• Return to Main Quest: Picking up the Trail

Color code: Objective   Action   Rewards

ON THE OUTSKIRTS OF PARADISE

Note

This entire quest is completely optional, unless you fail to enter Little Lamplight during **Main Quest: Picking up the Trail**.

This quest begins not in Paradise Falls, but during your conversation with Mayor MacCready as you attempt to gain entrance into Little Lamplight. If you fail a Speech challenge and don't have the Child at Heart perk for another fast-talking attempt, you aren't getting into this place unless you can prove to MacCready you're a trustworthy Mungo. For this, you need to ask what happened to Sammy, Squirrel, and Penny. It seems they were captured by Slavers. Offer to rescue them, and the quest begins. Your next stop is Paradise Falls. Fast Travel to the closest place you've previously explored.

NEW OBJECTIVE

"Gain entrance to Paradise Falls" begins.

If you've been strictly following the Main Quest, your best place to Fast Travel to is Vault 101. Head around the rocky outcrop, and trek north. The Wasteland now has Enclave Soldiers dotted about the landscape, so prepare to attack small groups of them, and optionally blow up any Vertibirds that have landed. Continue northward, and head up the main road through Big Town. Head across the bridge, and skirt the Hallowed Moors Cemetery, because the place is crawling with Super Mutants. Pass under the monorail, and you can see Paradise Falls over the next rise; there's a giant Big Burger Boy you can use as a landmark.

Welcome to the Slaver settlement of Paradise Falls. It's well-guarded by evil men.

Head north-northwest, keeping your eye on the Big Burger Boy which is within the Paradise Falls settlement, then skirt the perimeter, moving clockwise around until you're facing a sandbag and makeshift barricade entrance. This is the only entrance (except for a child-size drainage hole you can't fit into, which is inside the place). You're greeted by the gruff, no-nonsense, and thoroughly unpleasant Grouse.

The following options are available when speaking with Grouse at the entrance to Paradise Falls:

Bribery and Corruption

Request entry, and continue to ask until you can try a **Speech** challenge. Ask "everyone has a price; what's yours?" If you're unsuccessful, Grouse doesn't even entertain your question, and you must try another option. If you succeed, Grouse needs a bribe; 500 Caps should cover it. Pay the man, and you're allowed into the place.

Strictly Business

If your fast-talking fails, you can always fall back on a secondary plan. Grouse needs some Slaves rounded up and will split the profits with you. If you agree to this, you must begin (and complete) **Miscellaneous Quest: Strictly Business**. Once Grouse is satisfied with your captures, he lets you in.

Grouse Shooting

You can use threatening language, simply annoy Grouse to the point that he snaps, or begin by planting a bullet into Grouse's skull without giving him the satisfaction of speaking to you. Naturally, this launches you into a full battle with you and the dozen or two Slavers in town. Skip ahead to "Slaver Slaughter" for more information on taking Paradise Falls by force.

Or, with chillingly low Karma, you can simply walk into the place, spit verbally back at Grouse, and use your reputation as a disgusting human being to win over the Slavers instantly.

Note

Grouse has a Holotape by his feet: This is part of a **Miscellaneous Quest: The Replicated Man**, which activates if you take the Holotape and listen to it.

When you finally get past Grouse (assuming you aren't in combat), head southward along the pathway flanked with barricades on either side, and as you near the entrance, you see a slave running at you. This is Carter, and he's attempting to make a break for it. A second later Carter's head explodes! Quickly run forward (southeast) to the interior entrance.

Here, a small boy named Sammy was also trying to run; he just had the foresight to stop before he became a casualty. He tells you he needs to speak to you, then quickly backs away. Near him is a Slaver named Forty. Keep it civil, and he tells you Carter was wearing a special collar that caused the cranial implosion. This is why it's so difficult for slaves to escape. With this knowledge, enter through the shopping center doors.

NEW OBJECTIVE
"Find and speak with the kidnapped Lamplighters" begins.

Before investigating the entire settlement, check in with Sammy again, in the slave pens.

Inside, you can begin a thorough search of Paradise Falls, or you can move all the way to the far end (east) of the settlement, and speak with Sammy, who's behind the mesh fencing with the other slaves. From here, you can begin one of three different plans to free Sammy and his friends:

Jonesing for Some Slaves

This involves finding the settlement's leader and bartering for the children.

Squirrel's Secret Plan

Or, you can speak to Sammy's friend Squirrel, and follow his ideas for a break-out.

Slaver Slaughter

Or, you can engage all the Slavers in a mad and dangerous ballet of bullets.

Note

All other settlements in the Capital Wasteland tend to calm down, allowing you access back in after three days if you're violent to the inhabitants inside. The same isn't true of Paradise Falls; Slavers never forget, and will shoot you on sight indefinitely. You've been warned, cowboy!

PARADISE FALLS: THOROUGH INVESTIGATION

Note

This optional investigation gives you a good idea of what's inside this settlement. It is written assuming you are on friendly or neutral terms with the Slavers.

Pass the stand with a "Stow Your Piece" sign, which is only an optional idea, and then move around and head east to an abandoned mart, which now houses a place called "Lock and Load." Enter the double doors, and you reach a counter with a number of different weapons to steal, including Ammo from boxes, and melee weapons, rifles, and pistols on the counter. There's a Work Bench near the caged party skeleton, too. You can Trade and Repair items with the proprietor, Pronto. You could also explore a small (and empty) basement.

 Ammo Box Ammunition

 Small Guns (Various)

Melee Weapons (Various)

Move over to the western side of the initial courtyard, and enter the barracks. In the middle is a pool table, where the classic, antique game of beer pong has recently been played. Explore the kitchenette area for some minor items, or grab a drink from the vending machine. Then check upstairs, which has a ruined floor. There are some beds you can sleep in, and a bathtub that's tricky to reach (shimmy along the edge of the floor) for a whiskey bottle. Nothing else is available in this chamber.

Step out into the refuse-strewn courtyard, and move south to the adjacent building to the barracks. This was once Velma's emporium but is now Cutter's Clinic. The lady in question is either in her adjacent back bedroom, or in the clinic itself, and she offers to heal you, cure radiation, or sell you Stimpaks and Chems. She has keys to Chem and Health Supplies, which you can steal or kill her for. The Holotape atop the filing cabinet in the southwest corner is part of **Miscellaneous Quest: The Replicated Man**.

Pass the hanging cages, optionally head up the gantry steps to the east for a better view of Eulogy's Pad (an old cinema), then turn right at the fire hydrant and check out the open-air remains of an old RobCo Store. This is apparently where "food" is served, but the clientele is unpleasant. There's Carolina Red, a wretched young woman with daddy issues, and a pair of lunatics called Jotun and his father Ymir. They don't like their vodka watered down. When you tire of the insults, head southeast, and inspect the old cinema behind the roasting Brahmin.

Head inside Eulogy's Pad. There's an entrance area with a few items to steal, and an expansive projector room where Eulogy Jones has his heart-shaped bed. The man himself is usually on the roof balcony with his female slaves, walking in his home, or wandering around town. Speak to him about the kidnapped kids, or you can start a Freeform Quest (see page 278) and steal children from Little Lamplight. You can also purchase one of his ladies from him...eventually.

When the coast is clear, make sure you steal Eulogy's Hat and the key on the table, then check the southeast corner of the projector room for a Bobblehead and Paradise Falls Main Terminal. The stairs lead up to the balcony overlooking town. Behind the stairs is the largest stash of Nuka-Cola Quantums in the Wasteland! Grab them all, but don't drink them if completing **Miscellaneous Quest: The Nuka-Cola Challenge** is part of your plans.

Eulogy's Hat	**Paradise Falls Box Key**
Bobblehead: Speech†	**Nuka-Cola Quantum (5)**

† "Let your words be your weapon." +10 Speech (when picked up).

Tip

As always, only steal something if no one is watching you!

The final areas of Paradise Falls are the slave pens to the east. Head there, and you can see a Pulowski Preservation Shelter to the west, in which is a slave named Rory Maclaren. He doesn't escape, even if you unlock "The Box" (if you have the Paradise Falls Box Key); he's petrified of a head explosion. Nearby is the Paradise Falls Coffee Shop, now the toilets, with a grating that leads outside Paradise Falls. It's too small to squeeze into, but looks just the right size for a child.

Near the toilets are two slave pens and you can unlock either with the Paradise Falls Box Key, although the Slavers will turn hostile if they see you do this. On the left is the child slave pen and house, and on the right are the adults. The children are Sammy, Squirrel, and Penny. The adults are Miss Jeanette, Breadbox, Bleak, and Bronson. Check out the Freeform Quest (page 278) to save the adults.

JONESING FOR SOME SLAVES

Note

You can try this optional task if you have enough Bottle Caps.

A Big Burger Boy may tower over the settlement, but everyone knows who the big man in town is.

It doesn't matter whether you speak with Sammy and Squirrel or not; you can head directly for Eulogy's Pad, the cinema in the middle of the settlement, and locate the man with the long red coat. He introduces himself as Eulogy Jones, head of the Slavers. Mention that you want to buy some kids. Then talk about a price, because threatening Eulogy results in the Slavers becoming hostile. Eulogy offers to sell Sammy and Penny for 500 Caps each, but the price on Squirrel is 1,000 Caps because the kid's talented. That's 2,000 Caps total. At this point, you can:

Stop and ponder the decision, or (if you don't have the funds) leave Paradise Falls, secure the Caps, and return.

Or, you can pay Eulogy Jones 2,000 Caps.

Or, you can bargain Jones down to 1,200 Caps for all three. If you succeed in your **Speech** challenge, he agrees.

Tip

If you're after a bargain, make sure you grab the Bobblehead inside Eulogy's Pad before you speak with him!

When the purchase is complete, all three children are ushered to the Paradise Falls entrance, where you met Forty and watched Carter's head explode. You can walk with them to the outskirts of Paradise Falls, and then run with them all the way back to Little Lamplight, or Fast Travel there. Mayor MacCready now lets you through the entrance gate.

SQUIRREL'S SECRET PLAN

Note

This plan is optional but recommended if you don't feel equipped (or don't want) to defeat the Slavers in combat.

Squirrel's got a sound plan to turn off those Slave Collars; he doesn't want to get "chunkified"!

Move to the slave pens, open the only unlocked gate, and walk to the mesh fence to speak with Sammy. Ask him about a plan to free the children, and he reckons that his friend Squirrel might be able to use a computer in the settlement to turn off the collars. Squirrel is summoned, and he tells you there's a terminal inside Eulogy's Pad. If you don't think you can manage this, Squirrel recommends you find the junction box near the food area. Halt the conversation with Squirrel, and then nonchalantly walk into Eulogy's Pad.

NEW OBJECTIVE

"Connect the department store computer to the Paradise Falls secure network" begins.

Once inside the pad, you can Sneak or simply wander around, making sure you know where Eulogy and both his female slaves are at all times. When they are well away from the projector room, move to the southeast corner, and locate the table with the Bobble-head, Holotape, and whiskey on it. Next to that is the Paradise Falls Main Terminal—the only computer you can access in this settlement.

 Use **Science** to hack into this terminal. If you can't, you must try Squirrel's other plan. You have three menu options:

Update Network Connections

This option is available only after you speak with Squirrel. This connects the terminal to the network.

Unlock Safe

This allows you to pilfer the Bottle Caps and other items from Eulogy's floor safe, to the left of the terminal.

Personal Restraint Systems

Access is denied.

If you can't access the wall terminal, or you have a better Repair skill, move to the food area opposite Eulogy's Pad. Near where Ymir is sometimes sitting is a cable junction box on the northern wall. Once you Repair the junction box, you can return to Squirrel. If you can't access the terminal or the junction box, you have to either fight for the children or buy them. Once either plan has been successful, you can return to Squirrel.

NEW OBJECTIVE

"Tell Squirrel the computer is now connected to the network" begins.

When you're fast-talking Forty, appeal to his greedy, needy side. It isn't difficult.

When you return to Squirrel, he hasn't finished with his grand plan yet. He can access the terminal, turn off the collars, and open the gate, but the Slavers aren't just going to let everyone walk out of here. Squirrel suggests you wait until midnight, when there's only one guard, that guy named Forty. Optionally oblige the little tyke, and head to the barracks for a sleep, wake up at midnight, and return to the slave pen area, although you can simply find Forty on his patrol path through town, and holler at him, no matter what the time of day.

NEW OBJECTIVE

"Arrange for Forty to be away from the slave pen" begins.

The following conversation is available:

 Use **Speech** skill to prompt Forty into thinking he's an undervalued employee of Eulogy's. Keep up the pretense, and Forty walks away to see Eulogy about a raise.

If Forty is proving to be more of a hassle that you'd imagined, there's another, more creative method of getting him away from his post. Visit Crimson, one of Eulogy's two female slaves, making sure Jones isn't nearby when you speak with her. The following options are available:

 You can mention that Forty is looking a little lonely, and he'd benefit from some company. Crimson agrees if your **Speech** is successful, and slips away to find him.

Or, you can simply purchase Crimson's "services" for Forty in a cold, hard transaction; it'll cost you 100 Caps.

NEW OBJECTIVE

"Tell Squirrel the guard has been distracted" begins.

Two down, and one to go. Penny wants her Mungo friend out of here, too. This one's tricky!

Time to leave, kiddies! What? Penny won't go?! Yes, when you return to Squirrel, he's ready to head into the toilets and escape via the child-sized sewer pipe that leads to the southwest of the settlement. But Penny won't leave. She's befriended a Mungo named Rory Maclaren, and won't abandon him.

 Try reasoning with Squirrel that you can't save everyone, and leave her behind. If your **Speech** succeeds, Squirrel agrees, the two boys bolt for the coffee shop, and you leave Penny behind. They open the slave pen gates in the process.

Or, you can agree to help, and they head for freedom. It seems Penny is the one to ask, so enter the child slave pens, and run over to her.

NEW OBJECTIVE

"Speak with Penny and convince her to leave Paradise Falls" begins.

Penny is a sweet girl, but she's stubborn, and she won't leave until her friend Rory is out of his "box." The box in question is the Pulowski Shelter just outside the pens. Speak to Penny first, and she tells you Forty has a key for the box, and she thinks there's one in Eulogy's place, too. The following options are available:

 Use **Speech** to convince Penny that Rory can't be saved. Penny says Rory was going to be sold, and she'd never see him again. She's sad. Still, she'll get over it.

Or, you can detour your main mission still further, and agree to figure out a way to release that Rory character from his solitary confinement.

TRAINING — BESTIARY — MAIN QUEST — MISC. QUESTS — TOUR — COMPLETION — APPENDICES

"Find a way to release Rory Maclaren from the box" begins.

The only nonviolent way of grabbing the Box Key is from this table. Although you might want to pick a pocket or two.

Freeing Rory is a straightforward affair. For this to occur, you need to obtain one of three Paradise Falls Box Keys. They are in three locations around the settlement:

On a table inside Eulogy's Pad. Steal it when no one is looking.

 In the pocket of Forty the guard. Use **Sneak** to Pickpocket him, or loot it from his corpse after slaying the entire settlement.

 In the coat of Eulogy Jones. Use **Sneak** to Pickpocket him, or loot it from his corpse after slaying the entire settlement.

🔑 **Paradise Falls Box Key**

Head to the box, and activate it using the key. Speak with the rough-looking man in this sweltering cylindrical prison, and tell him he's got three options:

You can escort him to the front gate. Unless you Sneak, it's dark, and the Slavers are mainly in the barracks, this results in bloodshed—his, mainly. However, you aren't targeted unless you fire back, and there's no Karma penalty if you leave him to die.

 If you must keep him alive, massacre all the Slavers first, and then open the box. That way, he can escape with ease, while you hobble to the nearest First Aid Box.

You can tell him he's on his own. He tries to escape, and is gunned down in seconds.

You can shoot him. Although this is a little harsh, it's no less horrific than what's in store for him if you leave him on his own.

"Talk to Penny and tell her to leave Paradise Falls" begins.

Back at Rory's best buddy, you can tell her either that Rory has been freed (whether it's true or not is a different story), or that he died. She thanks you whatever the outcome, and moves to the grate inside the toilets and escapes using Sammy and Squirrel's route.

"Meet the children southwest of Paradise Falls" begins.

SLAVER SLAUGHTER

 Note

This is optional, but adds valuable Karma for each Slaver you defeat, and is a more direct approach.

As you might imagine, the violent option involves you being ready for an all-out war with more than a dozen highly armed Slavers, complete with a heavy-weapons guy on the gantry near Eulogy's Pad, and a couple of melee weapon–wielding lunatics stationed at the food area. The action begins easily enough. Kill Grouse and his friend, then strafe Forty if he hasn't retreated into the settlement, and take up refuge in the Lock and Load store. Naturally, this is a great place to re-arm, exit, blast a couple of foes, then return when you need to re-arm.

Eulogy's eulogy: He was a sharp dresser, but not quite enough of a sharpshooter. He won't be missed.

Continue the fracas, and once you've tooled up with weapons, sprint for the clinic. Gun down Cutter, then rifle through her Health and Chems for some narcotics to soothe your wounds, and shake off combat strikes from the Slavers. Then press onward, mopping up the remaining foes, but don't wade into the open fire pit and food area. Instead stay back and use the "Crap" as cover and retreat to any store.

Finally, step in and blast Eulogy, using the walls as cover, because he's carrying a nasty Scoped Magnum that really dishes damage. You rid the Wasteland of this blight in minutes! Don't forget the corpse-looting. Then simply take the Paradise Falls Box Key from the body of Jones or Forty, or pick it up from Jones' bedside table, and unlock the slave pens. Sammy and Squirrel both escape. Unlock Rory from the box, then speak to Penny, and she escapes too.

Don't lose sleep worrying over Rory; he's not essential to this quest. In fact, he's likely to be dead in the box. Also note that if you start combat with the Slavers before you enter Paradise Falls, Sammy remains at the entrance to the interior part of the settlement; look for him there, not the slave pen.

"Meet the children southwest of Paradise Falls" begins.

 Caution

Watch out! Eulogy's slave girls fight for their master, so you'll have to slaughter them too. However, don't gun down the slaves in the pens!

RETURN FROM PARADISE

Head out of Paradise Falls the same way you came in, and meet up with Sammy, Squirrel, and perhaps Penny, and they thank you for all your help before racing off to Little Lamplight. Although you can follow and chaperone them, it is far easier to Fast Travel directly back to Little Lamplight, where Mayor Mac-Cready is amazed at your helpfulness. He opens the gate and allows you into his settlement, but just this once! You can now rejoin **Main Quest: Picking up the Trail** already in progress.

Finding the Garden of Eden

FINDING THE GARDEN OF EDEN

Spoiler Alert

The information below contains some major developments in your adventure. If you don't wish to know what the future holds, be careful where your eyes wander!

Vault 87 [4.06] was a breeding ground for the first generation of Super Mutants. You're searching for the Garden of Eden Creation Kit: a device that's needed to kick-start Project Purity. Strains of mutation were once cultivated in Vault 87's Test Labs using F.E.V. All test subjects died horrific deaths, except a single survivor named Fawkes, who deviates from the norm by being civil, loyal, and intelligent. Fortunately, he's still got the strength of his brethren, and you can use this in your push to the chamber where the G.E.C.K. resides. Alas, when you find the G.E.C.K., Colonel Autumn is claiming the device as United States property. You end your search as a prisoner of the Enclave....

Vault 87

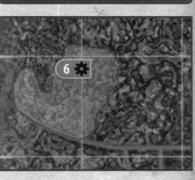

QUEST FLOWCHART

	MAIN PATH	OPTIONAL PATH
Main Characters	—	Fawkes
Locations	Little Lamplight, Vault 87	
Adv. Items/Abilities	Energy Weapons, Lockpick, Science, Small Guns, Sneak Rad-X, RadAway, Radiation Suit	Energy Weapons, Lockpick, Science, Small Guns, Sneak
Possible enemies	Radroach, Centaur, Super Mutant Genus, Enclave Soldier, Colonel Autumn	Centaur, Super Mutant Genus, Sid
Karma Influence	Negative	Neutral

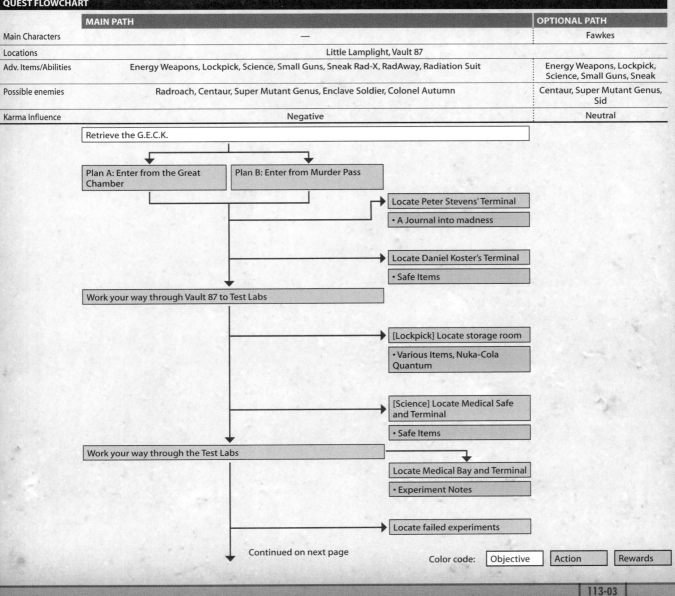

Retrieve the G.E.C.K.

Plan A: Enter from the Great Chamber

Plan B: Enter from Murder Pass

Locate Peter Stevens' Terminal
• A Journal into madness

Locate Daniel Koster's Terminal
• Safe Items

Work your way through Vault 87 to Test Labs

[Lockpick] Locate storage room
• Various Items, Nuka-Cola Quantum

[Science] Locate Medical Safe and Terminal
• Safe Items

Work your way through the Test Labs

Locate Medical Bay and Terminal
• Experiment Notes

Locate failed experiments

Continued on next page

Color code: Objective | Action | Rewards

TRAINING — BESTIARY — MAIN QUEST — MISC. QUESTS — TOUR — COMPLETION — APPENDICES

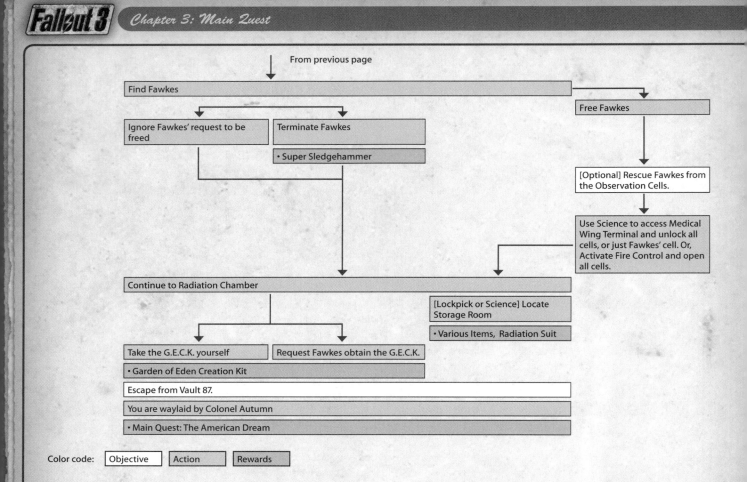

From previous page

Find Fawkes

Free Fawkes

Ignore Fawkes' request to be freed

Terminate Fawkes
- Super Sledgehammer

[Optional] Rescue Fawkes from the Observation Cells.

Use Science to access Medical Wing Terminal and unlock all cells, or just Fawkes' cell. Or, Activate Fire Control and open all cells.

Continue to Radiation Chamber

[Lockpick or Science] Locate Storage Room
- Various Items, Radiation Suit

Take the G.E.C.K. yourself

Request Fawkes obtain the G.E.C.K.
- Garden of Eden Creation Kit

Escape from Vault 87.

You are waylaid by Colonel Autumn
- Main Quest: The American Dream

Color code: | Objective | Action | Rewards |

PETER STEVENS'S VOICES

NEW OBJECTIVE
"Retrieve the G.E.C.K." begins.

PATH A: ENTERING FROM THE GREAT CHAMBER

Note

This assumes that you gained entry to the reactor room via the Little Lamplight chamber called "Nothin'!" using Joseph's technical know-how to open the door.

A refuse-strewn reactor room basement with the typing of a rapidly degenerating mental case

You enter facing west, looking at a small reactor. Turn left (south), and exit into a secondary chamber, where you'll find a small, half-hearted attempt to barricade the southern doorway, some minor Chems on the table, and Peter Stevens's Personal Journals Terminal next to his safe. Access this computer to see seven entries:

Journal Entry 06A01
Data Corrupted.

Journal Entry 06A02
This entry of Peter Stevens, Technician Class 3, details the loss of his boy, Jason, and his wife's mental breakdown. He believes he's sealed inside this "permanent tomb."

Journal Entry 06A03
Data Corrupted.

Journal Entry 06A04
Data Corrupted.

Journal Entry 06A05
Peter thinks he hears children laughing when he's in the outer tunnels. The doctors recommended pills. Everything is so pointless.

Journal Entry 06A06
Data Corrupted.

Journal Entry 06A07
A snapped mind in text form: "Iamsanelammelamforever!"

Before you leave this chamber, use **Lockpick** to open the floor safe, and grab the Caps and other optional items contained within.

Safe Items

Exit through the southern doorway, ignore the left corridor for a second, and open the hatch door ahead of you (south). This leads to a rock wall and dead end. At the foot of the mannequin is a small crate of whiskey. Better yet, there's a copy of *Nikola Tesla and You*. Read it, then step back to the corridor to the east, and run along and up the stairs. You reach the other rear entrance to Vault 87. From here, the paths merge, although you can head south, out of the Vault, and take down Super Mutants in Murder Pass (if you're after the experience and items).

 **Whiskey**

Nikola Tesla and You
+1 Energy Weapons (when read)

PATH B: VENTURING IN FROM MURDER PASS

Note

This assumes that you headed up Murder Pass, collecting the numerous items and health, found many Super Mutants, and accessed the other rear entrance to this Vault.

Step around the "Not Part of Tour" sign, open the hatch door, and step into a rusting corridor with another passage heading west and some skeletons at your feet. You've spotted the corridor down to the reactor room, and Peter Stevens's Terminal; the location of the other rear entrance. Head down Path A in reverse to obtain any items you deem necessary. You can't exit into the Great Chamber unless you hacked the terminal after Joseph powered it up. Backtrack to the initial junction, and the paths merge.

KNEE-DEEP IN THE DEAD

Scoped *Magnum* shots to the face cripple even hulking eight-foot green Muties!

Head north, into a connecting chamber, with windows on either side showing a rocky wall. Head to the door on the opposite wall, but make sure you clear the western area of Radroaches, feast-

ing on the long-dead corpses of Vault workers. Don't let your Radroach exterminations get too loud, or you attract the attention of three Super Mutants waiting at the top of the next set of stairs. Sneak or use a Stealth boy to approach the bottom of the steps and eavesdrop on two of them. They plan to search for more of the "green stuff" and use it to make more Super Mutants. Apparently, there is F.E.V. in this facility, and the Super Mutants are using it to reproduce. Head up the stairs, and into a small reactor chamber. Unless you're collecting whiskey, quickly exit the reactor chamber and head up the stairs to the south, and open the Door to Living Quarters.

Tip

Preferred corridor takedown methods include the following:

Sneak forward, plant mines, then make noise, and watch Super Mutant legs fly off before mopping up the survivors.

Blast, back up behind cover, and blast again.

Learn the layout of the Vault so you can backpedal and run at the same time as shooting Super Mutants.

Grenades work well in enclosed spaces, as long as you're outside the blast radius.

Step around more corpses as you pass another small reactor, and head toward the hatch door to the east. Back up when you see a staircase directly ahead; there's a toughened Super Mutant ready to bludgeon you! Back up and blast, then climb the stairs, passing the corpses as the corridor bends around and up. Head west to the door, and step into the lower level of a rusting Atrium area. The exit to this room is on the same wall, to the north of you. Go there, or spend some time investigating the Atrium.

Make a quick, clockwise sweep of the Atrium. Along the left (south) wall, there's a small storage room and a projector room. Both contain some minor food and other items, but the projector room also houses a vicious Super Mutant. Deal with him as soon as you can. On the west wall is a hatch door, which opens up into a blocked-off storage area with a flaming barrel in the middle of it. Scour the shelves for First Aid Boxes, Ammo, and other essentials. There are two delicious Gore Bags to sift through, too! Return to the Atrium. Now check the north wall for two final chambers: a storage room with some minor items, and a medical room with an operating stretcher holding disgusting body parts. Find some Med-X and a Stimpak in here.

 **Ammo Box Ammunition (2)**

Frag Grenades

First Aid Box Health and Chems

Head east, along a corridor with a room to your right (south) that you can't enter. Instead, head around the corner and up the stairs to a corridor parallel to the upper Atrium. At the top of the stairs, prepare for a series of Super Mutant attacks. In fact, you're wise to move very slowly through this section, dealing with them one or two at a time. Assuming you do, here's what a quick search of the area uncovers:

At the top of the stairs are two doors. The one on the left is locked, so check the door to the right (north) which leads to a small restroom. Continue west along the corridor, blasting a Mutie or two, to the next set of doors left and right. The left door leads to the gantry above the lower Atrium, where the majority of the Super Mutants appear from. Keep this closed to avoid getting swamped. On the right is another small restroom. Sip toilet water if you dare, then continue to the end of this corridor, which has a door to the left (also leading to the upper Atrium gantry area), and a blockade you can't maneuver through, You can see stairs beyond, though. Step into the Atrium gantry, and the two doors on the opposite side open to reveal around four Super Mutants. Back up, and start strafing!

 If you're relying on **Sneaking** rather than combat prowess, use **Lockpick** to open the initial left-side door. This allows you to Sneak to the door opposite and out to a parallel corridor, where you can turn west, catch Super Mutants unaware, and have fewer to deal with.

The engineering room is filled with foes, but there's evidence on what went so wrong in this Vault, too.

Once the general Atrium area is secure, you can inspect the parallel corridor running along the outside of the gantry area. Head east to the end of the corridor, where a door leads to the connecting room with the locked door. Of more interest are the stairs heading down and around to another small engineering room. If they haven't stormed the Atrium, expect another three Super Mutants in here! Aside from the lumps of flesh on a mattress, and items on the shelves, there's Engineer Daniel Koster's Terminal. This has six entries:

Service Issue Entry V87-002

Dormitory water dispensers have a foul aftertaste. This should clear up in a few days.

Service Issue Entry V87-003

Power spikes had darkened areas of the Vault; the reactor was malfunctioning. Whatever is powering the reactor is way over the acceptable power consumption limits.

Service Issue Entry V87-004

Vault-Tec's substandard build quality has resulted Koster having to patch and re-patch the radiation purge system.

Service Issue Entry V87-005

There's a major problem with the tapioca pudding color matrix!

Service Issue Entry V87-006

The EEP Chamber has failed. Koster mentions a "strange device," but the entry has been heavily edited.

Service Issue Entry V87-007

Something is terribly wrong in the experimental section of the Vault. Koster's wife quickly died from an unknown disease. Medical records are missing. Many are dead. Accessing this message opens the nearby wall safe.

 You can read Entry 007 on the terminal, or use **Lockpick** on the wall safe, which contains Koster's weapon and other items. Grab what you need, and return to the upper Atrium area.

 Koster's Safe Items

 Move to the locked door on the left (south) side of the corridor, and **Lockpick** it open. Search the storage room for various items. Jimmy open a wall safe inside here, too.

 First Aid Box Health and Chems

 Laser Rifle and Cells

Nuka-Cola Quantum

Pugilism Illustrated +1 Unarmed (when read)

 Wall Safe Items

The upper Atrium is explored, so continue up the corridor (west), to the top of the next set of stairs. On your right (north) is a barricade, with Super Mutants behind it. Lob a couple of Grenades in there, then continue forward, ignoring the blocked passageway on your left (south). Turn the corner, walk past a window on your right, and turn again, dealing with the Super Mutants you softened up with Grenades. Then turn right (south) and inspect the room you saw through the window. This small laboratory has a few items to take, a medical wall safe, and a Medical Records Terminal.

 Use **Science** to access this terminal. Inside are four menu options, the first of which is to unlock the Medical Safe.

All Employees Must Read!

Vault members deceased from contact in the EEP section are designated an unexplained or undefined death.

Deceased Listing

Everybody is dead. Of the 93 Vault inhabitants, 87 (coincidentally) have "unexplained" deaths.

Death Code Definitions

Some revised "death code" definitions. Criminal deaths and suicides are never listed.

 The medical wall safe can also be opened with **Lockpick** skill, but this is much more difficult. Inside, expect a number of items such as Purified Water and Stimpaks.

 Wall Safe Items

With the medical room ransacked, exit, and ignore the stairs down to the barricade you couldn't get through earlier. Instead, turn south and locate the door in the left (east). This leads to a corridor that bends around to more stairs heading upward. Pass up around two landings, one with another collection of corpses, and reach the Door to Test Labs.

THE TEST LABS: MUTILATED MUTATIONS

This stomach-churning mutation has a body wracked with elongated twists and snapped, sinewy growths.

Bring a strong stomach, and tougher weaponry up to the test labs, where the realization of exactly what went on in this Vault begins to dawn on you. Look into the room on your right (west), where a Super Mutant is standing. Once he's lying down, inspect the room, and grab Ammo from two boxes (one requires Lockpicking to uncover the Missiles within), and then wrench open (with Lockpicking) more items from the floor safe. Grab any additional items you want, then blast a waddling Centaur back in the main corridor.

 Ammo Box Ammunition (2)   **Floor Safe Items**

The next door is on your left, labeled Test Chamber 01. There's a wall terminal, but the functionality is broken, so either peer through the window or open the door and brave some light radiation as you inspect the dingy insides. There's nothing too horrible until you reach the medical lounger in the middle of the room, upon which lies a truly horrific sight: a mangled mutation with growths and sickeningly elongated arms. This is a test subject who's been doused with F.E.V. (Forced Evolutionary Virus). This is the real reason no detailed deaths were given on the medical records you inspected earlier.

Turn the corner so you're facing west, and inspect Test Chamber 02, which is where the Centaur waddled in from. Was this the location where the first Centaur was spawned? Continue past Test Chamber 03, which is empty, and turn the corner of the main corridor again, to face north. Another F.E.V. test subject lies rotting on the floor, but this one is being watched by a Super Mutant, which turns its attention on you. Blast it to smithereens, then continue to the pair of doors left (west) and right (east) of you. The left door is barricaded from the inside and cannot be entered. The right door leads to a small experimental medical bay with a First Aid Box on a stretcher, and the Chief Physician's Terminal on a desk. There are five entries:

Entry V87-34190

There are five test subjects exposed to the modified F.E.V., and all are showing progress after a single exposure. They hope to have an answer as Vault-Tec and the military at Mariposa are becoming bothersome.

Entry V87-34224

The male and female specimens are becoming almost asexual in appearance and transformation in upper body strength.

Entry V87-34233

Mary Kilpatrick (one of the female specimens) died of a massive loss of brain function, a usual test pattern and an expected result.

Entry V87-24265

All remaining test subjects' skin is becoming thick and resilient. Doctor Filo's skin engineering was a success!

Entry V87-34335

After two weeks, all test subjects began exhibiting severe rage and anxiety, and were put to death. This happens every time....

 First Aid Kit Health and Chems

THE TEST LABS: FIREWORKS WITH FAWKES

As you reach a junction where the corridor splits at a corner, you hear a guttural, growling voice asking for help. Stop immediately, and study Isolation Room 05, in front of you. A large Super Mutant wearing blue overalls

What a guy! Fawkes is a true anomaly: a friendly Super Mutant, loyal to anyone who rescues him. Yes, that's a hint.

is attempting to make contact with you! He identifies himself as Fawkes, and asks you to help him free himself. The following possibilities become available:

You can ignore him and continue toward the G.E.C.K. Head west, ignoring the northern corridor.

You can speak with Fawkes, another "failed experiment" in the medical wing of this Vault. He pleads for you to release him, and in return, he'll help you secure the G.E.C.K.; he can endure the radiation of the chamber it's in. To free him, you need to trip the Fire Console Control at the end of the northern corridor. This releases him, and all the experiments located in this medical wing!

You can speak with Fawkes and refuse to aid him in any way whatsoever. He pleads and then gets angry. You'll be back!

> You can use **Science** to access Isolation Room 05's wall terminal. The three menu options are to check Fawkes' subject identification (Subject D624), to unlock the door (which is jammed, and unable to budge), or to terminate specimen.

Terminate Fawkes, and (in the same way his namesake was commemorated in ancient times, over in England) a blast of fire burns him up, and he collapses. Congratulations; you've murdered one of only two friendly Super Mutants in the Wasteland! Make sure you take his Super Sledgehammer, though!

 Super Sledgehammer

NEW OBJECTIVE [OPTIONAL]
"Rescue Fawkes from the Observation Cells" begins.

If you detour your mission for a moment to help free Fawkes, move north past Isolation Rooms 01, 04, 02, and 03. Each of them has a locked hatch door and wall terminal, which you can optionally use, although this isn't necessary, as you'll see in a moment. After passing Sid in Isolation Room 03, turn the corner (east), and face a Super Mutant or two in the medical wing's reactor room. Drop these foes, then inspect the Fire Console Control in the middle of the east wall. There's a wall terminal too. The following options are available:

Option 1: Freeing everything

Simply activate the Fire Console Control, and choose to Activate Fire Alarm. Klaxons blare, and all five isolation room doors open.

Alternately, use **Science** to access the Medical Wing Terminal adjacent to the control, and unlock all five isolation rooms.

Option 2: Freeing Only Fawkes

 Ignore the Fire Console Control, and use **Science** to hack the Medical Wing Maintenance Terminal. When the five menu options appear, unlock only Isolation Room 05.

 Return to Fawkes's cell, and dispatch any enemies you may have released. There are Sid and two Centaurs to contend with, while Isolation Room 01 simply contains the bodies of a Wastelander and a Raider, pitted against each other. During the battle, Fawkes comes stomping down the corridor, brandishing his Super Sledgehammer, and wallops anything attacking you. He thanks you, and tells you to follow him; he's now going to keep his end of the bargain!

THE TEST LABS: GETTING TO THE G.E.C.K.

Note
This can be attempted on your own, or with Fawkes helping you battle the remaining Super Mutants. The latter option is recommended.

Caution
Watch your fire! Ensure you're mainly using V.A.T.S., and don't spray Fawkes with your gunfire, or he turns on you. He's much better as an ally.

Tip
Have you teamed up with Fawkes? There are two ways to secure the remaining rooms:
Let Fawkes go in front of you, soaking up the damage and blasting foes.Or, run ahead (optionally telling Fawkes to wait), engage the enemy, back up, and let Fawkes deal with them as they advance.

The tag-team of yourself and Fawkes is a winning combination.

Head west from Fawkes's cell and climb up some steps to a hatch door. This leads to a connecting chamber with a sunken middle, and a couple of foes for Fawkes to bludgeon. Continue west, passing another Gore Bag, and locate the junction chamber. The door ahead (west) of you is sealed and requires a key (which isn't currently available). The only way onward is through the door to the north, and up another set of steps to the final upper floor. Turn the corner, and open the door on the north wall. Execute the Super Mutant near this green-hued laboratory, then halt your progress for a moment. Head back to the corridor, and continue around the corner to a locked door to the south. This leads to a storage room, and there are two ways in:

 You can, of course, use **Lockpick**, and enter. Or, you can enter the laboratory, and use **Science** to hack the Lab Technician's Terminal. Inside, are four options, the first of which is to unlock the storage room door. The remaining entries are as follows:

Notice #009
    The storage room has been stocked with Rad Suits.
Notice #012
    Radiation expulsion ducts from the G.E.C.K. are venting radiation directly into this area.
Notice #018
    Doctor Merrick has ordered the F.E.V. subjects terminated. The area must be scrubbed to avoid cross-contamination when new subjects begin testing.

Move to the storage room at the end of the corridor, and rummage around inside. Be sure you grab the items you need, as well as the Advanced Radiation Suit because this area is highly contaminated.

 Use **Lockpick** to open a wall safe and take a few additional items.

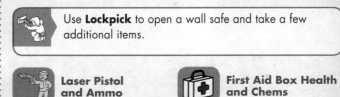

Laser Pistol and Ammo   **First Aid Box Health and Chems**

Advanced Radiation Suit and Chems   **Wall Safe Items**

Push forward, into the lab room with the window on the right, through which you can see an inner corridor that's glowing with massive radiation seepage. Concentrate on the two doors ahead of you; choose the right one, which leads to a small server room and a Super Mutant. Drop that so it doesn't ambush you from behind, then open the connecting doors to a new corridor. Move north, and follow the corridor right (east), through another hatch door, into a maintenance room with a sunken area, and more Muties to kill! Take the junk parts from the shelves if you need to, and open the door opposite.

Check your Local Map. You're making a clockwise circle around the middle chamber of this level. Follow the corridor around to the south, through a door, and into a second laboratory. Scour the locker for goods, then press on, through the south door to a storage room empty except for a Super Mutant. Finally push through to the radiation chamber entrance, where you can grab Health and Chems from a First Aid Box on the table, then curse the malfunctioning wall terminal that doesn't allow you to purge the radiation. If you head through the door in the northwest, you'll face radiation damage of well over +100 RAD/SEC. How will you access the G.E.C.K. inside this chamber? There are three options:

 ### First Aid Box Health and Chems

Option 1: Head inside, unprotected, after gobbling down some Rad-X. Head northeast, north, and immediately turn left (west) at the door and open it, then dart in, open the G.E.C.K. container. Sprint back

If you want something done properly, do it yourself. Or have Fawkes do it for you.

to the radiation chamber entrance, and gobble down RadAway to return your radiation poisoning to an acceptable level. Then sprint back in, and take the G.E.C.K. You absorb less radiation backing up and waiting for the container to open in safety.

Option 2: You can struggle into the Advanced Radiation Suit that you stole from the previous storage room, swallow a Rad-X, and then trudge into the container room and take the G.E.C.K. that way.

Option 3: Or, you can speak to Fawkes, who offers to shrug off the radiation and stomp his way to the container. You can watch from a nearby window if you wish. He soon returns, gives you the G.E.C.K., and you part ways because Fawkes wants to find his own way out. Perhaps you'll meet again?

Caution

When you reach the G.E.C.K. yourself, you're asked if you want to Pick Up, or Activate the G.E.C.K. Always choose the former, as the latter begins terraforming right there in Vault 87, killing you instantly in the process!

Garden of Eden Creation Kit

NEW OBJECTIVE

"Escape from Vault 87" begins.

It seems you may have underestimated the guile (and radiation proof overcoat) of Colonel Autumn.

Aside from the door you couldn't open, you've thoroughly explored Vault 87. The only way back to the Citadel is the way you came, so backtrack through the laboratory, down the stairs, and into the junction chamber...wait, what's that blipping noise? You're engulfed in static electricity and white light! You slowly collapse to the ground in paralytic shock as two Enclave Soldiers carrying Miniguns and wearing fabled Tesla Power Armor stride in. They are followed by Colonel Autumn. He commends the soldiers on your capture, and orders the G.E.C.K. to be secured on his Vertibird. You're to be prepared for transportation immediately! But where...?

TRAINING — BESTIARY — MAIN QUEST — MISC. QUESTS — TOUR — COMPLETION — APPENDICES

The American Dream

Spoiler Alert

Your forthcoming adventure knowledge becomes shockingly clear if you read any further through this section. Do not proceed unless you've come to accept this fact!

You wake up in Cell 4, deep inside **Raven Rock [1.01]**. Colonel Autumn and President Eden both want you to serve their own ends. Either give Autumn the Project Purity activation code, or make your way to meet President Eden. Eden gives you a vial of Modified F.E.V.; he wants you to place it in the Project Purity apparatus to solve the "mutation problem." After that, you need to escape the base, and find the Brotherhood at the **Citadel [9.11]** before they're completely over-whelmed by Autumn's Enclave forces.

Raven Rock

QUEST FLOWCHART

	MAIN PATH	OPTIONAL PATH
Main Characters	Colonel Autumn, President John Henry Eden, Lieutenant Williams, Fawkes, Sentinel Sarah Lyons, Elder Owyn Lyons, Scribe Reginald Rothchild, Liberty Prime	Nathaniel Vargas, Fawkes
Locations	Raven Rock, The Citadel	Raven Rock
Adv. Items/Abilities	Big Guns, Energy Weapons, Small Guns, Speech	—
Possible enemies	Enclave Soldier, Enclave Officer, Enclave Vertibird, Colonel Autumn	
Karma Influence	Neutral	Positive

Colonel Autumn Interrogation

Ignore his threats → President Eden intervenes: Raven Rock is friendly

Reveal the correct code → You are shot to death

Retrieve equipment from the locker.

• Your entire Inventory

Meet President Eden in his office.

You are stopped by Lieutenant Williams: Stop him with words or actions

Colonel Autumn disobeys Eden's orders: Raven Rock is hostile (Robot forces excluded)

Fight your way to the President's Office

Take the vial of modified F.E.V..

Locate Cell 3: Nathaniel Vargas
• Housekey — Nathan and Manya

Locate Colonel Autumn's Quarters
• Bobblehead: Energy Weapons
• Colonel Autumn's 10mm Pistol
• Holotape: Self-Destruct Code

Discuss matters with the President
• Modified F.E.V. Vial

Escape the Enclave base.

Fight your way to the Capital Wasteland

Report to Elder Lyons at the Citadel.

Meet Fawkes
• Follower: Fawkes

Report back to Elder Lyons. Rothchild powers up Liberty Prime. You receive an honorary membership of Lyons' Pride

Accept
• Power Armor Or Recon Armor
• Main Quest: Take it Back!

Refuse

Color code: | Objective | Action | Rewards |

RAVEN ROCK LEVEL 3—A PRESIDENTIAL PARDON

EXPLORATION: FLOOR 3A CELLS

Colonel Autumn has you right where he wants you. But the commander-in-chief wants you somewhere else.

You wake with a start. You're in some kind of cell (Cell 4, in fact), you've been stripped of all your weapons, armor, and other supplies, and you're staring at Colonel Autumn, who immediately gets to the point: You're going to tell him the code to activate the Purifier, and you're going to tell him now! The following options are therefore possible:

You can tell him, using all manner of expletives, where he can stick that information. Keep it going, and rile him up!

You can simply play dumb, which also infuriates the Colonel.

You can play along with his questions, and give him the code 7-0-4. This is the incorrect code, but Autumn contacts his men at the Jefferson Memorial Project Purity chamber, and they input it. This is perhaps, the most furious you've seen the Colonel....

You can surrender and give him the code 2-1-6. This is the correct code, and Autumn contacts his men at the Project Purity chamber, and they input it. They report the success, and the colonel is pleased. You're no longer useful, so he draws his pistol and guns you down. You don't stand a chance; perhaps not the wisest move!

 **Note**

How do you know that 2-1-6 is the correct code? Do you remember the number of the Biblical verse that your father has framed in his Vault 101 clinic?

Choose any of the previous options except the last one, and before Colonel Autumn can start a more forceful interrogation, a voice booms out around the room: "Colonel, I have need of you!" The voice sounds familiar. It is President Eden's, and he removes Autumn from the chamber. He apologizes for the colonel's attitude and wants to meet you face-to-face. He'll be waiting in his office; you can retrieve your possessions from the nearby locker. Notice that the president's blue eyeball camera pivots to watch your every move, and he has numerous eyes all over the facility you're trapped in. It is wise to see what the president has to say. Leave Cell 4, entering a connecting corridor.

NEW OBJECTIVE
"Retrieve equipment from the locker" begins.

NEW OBJECTIVE
"Meet President Eden in his office" begins.

 Caution

You can begin a crazed firefight as soon as you grab your stuff, but it's more cunning to reason with the slightly confused Enclave personnel. The following tactics have you hold off on gunfire until the very last possible moment.

 **Tip**

Grab your equipment from the locker, but don't forget to wear your armor and reassign your Hot Keys. Wandering around in just your Vault 101 undergarments is not recommended!

Open the cell door, and step into the corridor. You're automatically stopped by an Enclave Officer, who says you aren't going anywhere, and he's got a full complement of guards to back up his threat. The following options are available:

 You can use **Speech** to tell him to calm down, as you're supposed to be here. Fail, and he gets violent. Succeed, and you tell him you're meeting with the president. The lieutenant strides over to the eye opposite your cell door, and checks directly with President Eden, who requests "no questions, and no interference." The officer is to report to his superior for "reassignment." How the tables have turned!

If you have a high **Charisma**, you can tell the guard you're off to the president, and you'll put in a good word for him. He's suitably excited and leaves you alone.

With high enough **Strength**, you can intimidate him with your bulging muscles, and he sheepishly backs away, remembering that he needs to be elsewhere.

Or, you can simply start a fight.

Assuming you used an ability, you're free to explore Level 3 of Raven Rock.

You are now free to move to Level 2 of Raven Rock's interior. However, it is interesting, if not essential, to quickly check out the entirety of Level 3 right now, because the president comes on the intercom to tell his subjects and troops not to impede your progress. Although you can go anywhere, begin with a quick march south to a second cell on your left (east). Imprisoned inside Cell 3 is Nathan. Wasn't he the guy in town who was convinced the Enclave would save everyone? He's changed his tune now; frantically telling you they "aren't what they seem." Leave him, or Pickpocket him to take the Housekey—Nathan and Manya.

 Housekey—Nathan and Manya

EXPLORATION: 3A CELLS AND CONCOURSE

Continue to wander around the cells, weaving around to face west, and check Cell 2, which is under a sign pointing to Sector 3B. Inside is an Enclave Guard, who tells you to get over to see President Eden immediately; he's still suspicious. The same goes for an Enclave Soldier you pass if you continue west along this corridor. Head out of the corridor, into a larger concourse, with a sign reading Sector 3A. This is the Bio Lab and cells and you're in the cells part. There's a map in front of you, too. If you want, you can turn and make a long counterclockwise run around the cell corridor where you came from, and explore Cells 5 and 6 to the north. This is the correct route, as President Eden tells you. You appear at the northern end of the concourse.

Although you're never far from a fracas, you look completely intimidating wearing Tesla Armor!

Impressively armored Enclave Soldiers patrol this area, and if you want a suit of Tesla Armor and a helmet, this is one time to attack (but not the best time). Remember that the Tesla Armor is bulky and thick, with electrical discharge coming off it; it's not the regular Enclave Armor. You have two other doors to investigate. But first, you can head down into the lower area under the concourse via steps at either end of the corridor. These lead to a set of three blue lasers. Run through them, and a flame shoots out (so keep moving!). This is the Enclave's attempt at dealing with a Radroach infestation, although a couple of the critters still scuttle about down here.

EXPLORATION: 3B MESS HALL

The optimal route to Level 2 is via the Bio Lab, but you can optionally explore the Mess Hall instead, which is opposite the southern exit from the cells. Open the door, climb the stairs, and inspect the Mess Hall. Amid the precisely placed cutlery are two Enclave Soldiers, and a back larder/kitchen with some meticulously arranged food to take. There are two First Aid Boxes attached to a locker, too. For fun, head down the steps here to the area under the grating. There are no Radroaches, but the floor's design flaws are showcased, as you discover numerous dropped knives and forks down here! You can backtrack to the cells, then head north to the lab, or head east, up the stairs to the Door to Raven Rock Level 2. This brings you out farther into the Tech and Cryo Labs, at the south area of Level 2.

 Food

First Aid Box Health and Chems (2)

> **Note**
> By about this time, Colonel Autumn has disobeyed the president's orders, and told his Soldiers to shoot you on sight; you must now begin to battle the Enclave!

EXPLORATION: 3A BIO LAB

Head to the middle point of the north-south corridor, and locate the door on the eastern wall marked "Bio Lab." Enter this place, where Enclave Scientists (who run for cover if Colonel

Among mutations encased in vats, and scattering Enclave Scientists, combat in this maze begins now!

Autumn has his troops fire on you) are inspecting various captured mutations. Expect around three Enclave Soldiers to attack when prompted by Autumn's intercom speech. When you've purged the area, you can check out the four specimen rooms on the lower level; each contains a vat with a Ghoul or Brahmin double-head in it. The middle vat holds a Super Mutant. Turn north and head up the stairs to the upper four rooms. The southwest one has a First Aid

Box and an Enclave Crate to ransack. The southwest medical bay has another First Aid Box, and the northwest experiment room has two Enclave Crates and a First Aid Box. Grab what you need, then exit through the door in the northwest room to Sector 2A: Tech Lab.

Enclave Crate Ammunition (3)

First Aid Box Health and Chems (4)

RAVEN ROCK LEVEL 2—BATTLE TO THE WAR ROOM

EXPLORATION: FLOOR 2A TECH LAB

Enter the Tech Lab at the exit of the Bio Lab on Level 3. Spend a moment or two defeating the Enclave Soldiers in these eight small chambers (four up, four down), and then inspect them. Encased in vats are

Grafting large brain matter into mechanical parts is only part of the experimentation going on in the Tech Lab.

Enclave Eyebots, a fused brain inside a metal surround, and a large rocket device in the middle of the lab. Proceed around the upper rooms and you'll find more Ammo inside two Enclave Crates in the northwest storage room. There are two exits. The one is in the upper southwest room leads to the Cryo Lab or back to the Mess Hall. The other, in the northern part of the lower area, also leads to the Cryo Lab, or (if you continue north) to the main L-shaped concourse for this level. Both lead to a pillared atrium area. It's slightly confusing, so check your Local Map.

Enclave Crate Ammunition (2)

EXPLORATION: FLOOR 2A CRYO LAB

The Cryo Lab's upper quartet of rooms are of similar size to the previous lab chambers, and frozen Ghouls are dotted around the place. The northwest room hosts one of these experiments, along with two Enclave Crates and a First Aid Box. Move to the downstairs area, scaring a couple of Enclave Scientists, and you can inspect the four identically sized chambers underneath, where Ghouls, Deathclaws, and a Yao Guai are preserved. There are three exits to the Cryo Lab. One is on the upper floor (northeast room) leading back to the atrium. The one on the southern wall of the lower level leads back to the Mess Hall and Tech Lab. The one to the west leads to storage and living quarters areas. Head there, stepping out into the concourse.

Enclave Crate Ammunition (2)

First Aid Box Health and Chems

EXPLORATION: FLOOR 2B STORAGE AND QUARTERS

Move to the south end of the L-shaped concourse, and inspect the storage area, which is open to the concourse itself. Here are the remains of a few Deathclaw cages, used to transport these ferocious beasts from their capture in the Wasteland. Fortunately, none are occupied, and the entire area is deserted. Grab what you need from a bank of lockers, grab Energy Cells from either

Enclave Crate, and optionally head down the steps to the area under the floor grating if you want to set off the Radroach fire system, or Sneak around along here.

Ideally though, head north to the doors on either side of you. Check the left (west) living quarters out first; there's little else but a First Aid Box to snag here. Over on the right (east) side, look for another First Aid Box on top of a locker, then inspect a nearby Security Barrier Terminal.

 Use **Science** to access this terminal, and you can disarm the security barrier at the north end of this room. Behind the barrier are three Enclave Crates; each holding a variety of armor and weaponry. Grab what you need, then continue north along the concourse.

 First Aid Box Health and Chems (2)

 Enclave Grenade Crate Items

Enclave Armor Crate Items

Enclave Gun Crate Items

 Note

The east-west concourse houses a Soldier or two, and a larger door to access as you head west. A small alcove to the north leads to stairs down to the area under the floor grating. This allows you to Sneak all the way to the storage area, which is purely optional. Continue on your route to President Eden by heading toward Sector 2C.

EXPLORATION: FLOOR 2C WAR ROOM

Continue northward up the western concourse, opening the door, stepping through to a concourse section with two doors at the end. Swing right (east) and lob a Grenade at the opening door that leads to 2C; you'll catch three Enclave Soldiers on their way out to ambush you. Then aim for their heads and dispatch them. With combat over, make sure to inspect the room opposite, to the west. This is Colonel Autumn's personal chamber and there's a Bobblehead: Energy Weapons on the table! Then open the gun cabinet for a unique 10mm Pistol, a Holotape (which has President Eden's self-destruct code, which could come in handy later!). Grab the First Aid Kit atop one locker, then inspect the wall terminal.

 Use **Science** to access this terminal, and you can disarm the security barrier near the entrance to this room. Behind the barrier are three Enclave Crates; each holding a variety of Ammo and Health.

 Bobblehead: Energy Weapons
"Arrive at peaceful resolutions by using superior firepower." +10 Energy Weapons (when picked up)

 Colonel Autumn's 10mm Pistol

 **Holotape: Self-Destruct Code**

 First Aid Box Health and Chems

 Enclave First Aid Box Health and Chems

 Enclave Ammo Crate Ammunition (2)

EXPLORATION: FLOOR 2C WAR ROOM

Head through the door where the three Enclave Soldiers who forgot their helmets stormed in from, and climb the metal stairs to the War Room. It is empty, save for a large holomap in the middle of the chamber. Study it if you wish, then access the door in the west wall, leading to 1A Access. This leads to the Raven Rock Control Room.

RAVEN ROCK LEVEL 1— AN AUDIENCE WITH EDEN

EXPLORATION: FLOOR 1A CONTROL ROOM ENTRANCE

Enter the Control Room, and you're immediately blasted by two Enclave Soldiers. However, nanoseconds later, President Eden's two Enclave Sentry Bot guards receive orders from the president to nullify

Sentry Bot slaughter: It's Autumn versus Eden in the Control Room and those hulking great Sentry Bots are on your side!

all threats to your personage, and rip apart the Enclave Soldiers. After that, they request that you "have a nice day," and unlock the door to the Control Room. It is sealed prior to combat ending. Don't shoot the Sentry Bots, because they're helping you! Grab what you need from the corpses, and head into the Control Room.

EXPLORATION: FLOOR 1A CONTROL ROOM

Move to the northwest corner of the Control Room, gazing at a long central pillar of computer servers, girders, and other technology, and find the metal steps leading up and southward. Follow the steps and gantries onward and upward as they weave through the structure, until you reach a small platform with a door to the east. President Eden doesn't seem to be about...but there's a large console screen near a vase of daffodils to inspect. As you close, the deep booming voice of Eden resonates across the chamber. He welcomes you to his office. The trip here was not quite what he intended, but it was an adequate test of your abilities.

President Eden is behind this console, and he has plans to purge the Wasteland of abominations.

Begin to speak with President Eden. You soon realize his true nature, and you have numerous dialog choices where you can use your Science and Intelligence to add thoughtful responses to Eden's answers. Continue the conversation until Eden requests that you help him. No matter what your intent is, allow him to explain. While mutation runs rampant, Eden's Soldiers cannot stem this tide, especially when they are tied up fighting the Brotherhood of Steel. Super Mutants and Ghouls—all abominations—must be purged from this land. For this, your father's experiments can help.

TRAINING — BESTIARY — MAIN QUEST — MISC. QUESTS — TOUR — COMPLETION — APPENDICES

"Take the vial of modified F.E.V." begins.

It seems the president has made a few modifications to the F.E.V., which could be inserted into the water supply when Project Purity is turned on. In the future, whenever mutations would drink, they would be eradicated—and humans will no longer share the world with monsters! The F.E.V. can be inserted directly into part of Project Purity just before it is activated. A vial of it is released from the president's console. Whether you agree or not, continue the conversation until you can access the following dialog options:

 With enough **Speech** skill, tell Eden his work must stop, and the base must be destroyed.

 If you have a high enough **Science** skill, you can tell Eden he is an abortion of science, and needs to die.

You can ask Eden more about the plan for the Purifier, and the president itself.

If you found the self-destruct code Holotape in Colonel Autumn's quarters, you can open a new line of dialog placing you in a more advantageous position.

You can ask what the problem is with Colonel Autumn.

Or, you can leave without any more conversation.

The important choices are the Speech challenge, Science challenge, or the simple agreement and leaving. The first two options, when spoken to completion, give President Eden more information than he can take, and he agrees to power down and destroy Raven Rock. The last option simply reinforces his stature, as despite the rift between Eden and Autumn, the Enclave will prevail! Snatch the Modified F.E.V. from the Zax Panel, and make your exit before Autumn's men get a lock on you. Turn, and open the Door to Raven Rock—Level 1 behind President Eden. You can't leave until you take the F.E.V.

 Modified F.E.V.

"Escape the Enclave base" begins.

RAVEN ROCK LEVEL 1—EXIT CONCOURSE

Head out onto the exit concourse, and turn south. Run to the concourse door, and when it opens, stay between or behind two Mark VI Turrets as they rake fire over two Enclave Soldiers. Back up the turrets if you wish, and watch as Eden's robotic help allows you progress and supports your battle against the Enclave. Ahead (south) another concourse door slams and shorts out. You can't enter the area beyond it, leaving the only exit path to your right (west). Run down this corridor, and just before the left corner, peer out of the window to your right. There's a hangar lift and a Vertibird departing. Autumn is sending everything he's got to shore up the Jefferson Memorial!

Turn the left corner (to face south), and venture forward. Up ahead are more Enclave Soldiers, but two Sentry Bots roll out from a left alcove and demolish them while you can take a leisurely look at another ascending Vertibird on

Add to the mayhem by releasing a captured Deathclaw, and watch the Sentry Bots do their job.

your right. A better use of your time is to look left (east). Move to the desk and Delivery Terminal. Grab the First Aid Box items from the desk.

 Use **Science** to hack into the terminal, and you can unlock the Delivery Crate.

There is a note to read, which mentions that the creature inside needs transportation to the Bio Lab, and that "domestication units" must be brought in, and quickly.

 First Aid Box Health and Chems

Unlock the crate, and a Deathclaw emerges, picks at its teeth, and then attacks anything human; you or the Enclave Soldiers! Quickly back up, and let the Enclave Sentry Bots cut the beast down, then continue down the main concourse.

Continue along the main concourse to another door that slides open, revealing more Enclave Soldiers under turret (and side panel flame-thrower) fire. These Soldiers are armed with Plasma Rifles, and they make short work of the turrets, so fire back at a distance. Now inspect the stairs to the area under the floor grating by the electrified door to your right (north). There's an Enclave stash down here; grab the items from the boxes. The two doors to the north can't be breached, so stay on the main concourse, pushing forward as two more Enclave Sentry Bots strafe the remaining Soldiers at the far end. Meanwhile, locate the Security Barrier Terminal, switch off the barrier, and claim more weaponry.

 First Aid Box Health and Chems (2)

 Enclave Mine Box Ammunition (2)

 **Enclave Ammo Crate Ammunition**

 Enclave Gun Box Weaponry (2)

 Enclave Grenade Box Ammunition (3)

You're making out like a bandit! Continue west down the concourse, pausing only to grab the Minigun and Tesla Armor from the last fallen Soldier, and exit via the Door to the Capital Wasteland.

"Report to Elder Lyons at the Citadel" begins.

PRELUDE TO THE FINAL ASSAULT

Colonel Autumn's forces fly southward en masse to deliver a critical killing blow to the Brotherhood...

Down in the lab, there's a heated exchange between the Brotherhood's leaders.

Once outside, prepare for chaos, the type of which depends on how the conversation with President Eden went. If you took the F.E.V. without questioning the president's plan, Vertibirds are already taking off,

Or, they scatter into the air, some Vertibirds burning, if President Eden ordered Raven Rock's destruction!

flying to support the troops currently holed up in and around Project Purity. If you're extremely quick, you can blast the Vertibird that's about to take off with Plasma fire (or a Missile), and it flies off burning, or blows up on the ground.

However, if you used the president's own logic against him, and Eden agreed to end it all, as you exit Raven Rock, the entire facility begins to rock as massive plumes of fire begin to escape from the rocky outcrops, and Vertibirds tumble out of the sky, crashing into the rock face as the entire base collapses in on itself!

If you freed Fawkes from his confinement in Vault 87, you'll find him out at the entrance, happily mowing down Enclave troops with a procured Gatling Laser. He waves hello, and you can briefly chat again before he goes on his merry way.

A Super Mutant in a tattered Vault 87 jumpsuit is sometimes spotted, putting his bloodlust to good use...

 If you have Good Karma, and aren't using a Follower already, he can join you as a valued team member!

No matter what the final fate of Raven Rock is, you need to reach the Citadel immediately! Clear any remaining Enclave troops from the vicinity, and Fast Travel back to the Citadel at once; the final Brotherhood battle against the Enclave begins now!

 Fawkes

Return to the Citadel, and head southwest into the middle of the courtyard, then head right slightly (west-southwest) to the door leading into the Laboratory. Descend the steps, then leap down to the gantry stairs, and descend to the floor, where Sarah Lyons, Rothchild, and Elder Lyons are engaged in a rather heated discussion. Sarah wants to hit now rather than later, but her father states that the risk isn't worth the reward. Sarah isn't happy and doesn't like this edict. Elder Lyons replies that she doesn't have to like it, but she does have to follow orders!

Elder Lyons turns to you, and asks if you've been successful. You can speak to Elder Lyons using any dialog choice, as you reveal that the Enclave now has the G.E.C.K., and they wish to use it for their own ends. Elder Lyons is troubled and wants more information from you. You can tell him:

That Eden wanted you to sabotage the project.

That the Enclave is fractured.

That the Enclave lacks the activation code, and can't start the Purifier.

That you have the F.E.V., and decide whether to turn it in or not. You can keep it, and make the decision later without any Karma penalties.

Rothchild powers up Liberty Prime. The robot thinks it's attacking Alaska in an effort to save Anchorage!

Elder Lyons's tactics now change. He agrees to send the Pride in, but only with some extra firepower. "Is it ready?" Lyons asks a startled Rothchild. Rothchild goes to power up the robot, while Sentinel Lyons heads toward you. She has her father's blessing to make you an honorary member of Lyons' Pride! Which Power Armor will you choose?

The full suit of Power Armor has more damage absorption, but less mobility.

The Recon Power Armor is light armor, with extra speed and agility.

Or, you can tell Sarah to keep her Power Armor.

Or, you can tell Sarah that you don't want to be part of her little club.

Although some responses are more offensive than others, Sarah asks you whether you're ready for this attack. You can elect to wait a minute, or tell her you can accompany her for the final push. The attack to save Project Purity begins now!

TRAINING — BESTIARY — MAIN QUEST — MISC. QUESTS — TOUR — COMPLETION — APPENDICES

Take It Back!

Spoiler Alert

The ultimate end to your adventure becomes far less cloudy if you rest your eyes a while on the following pages. Do not continue unless this presents little or no problem to you!

This is it! Liberty Prime is up and running. The Brotherhood of Steel is prepped for battle, and only a battalion of Enclave troops stand between you and your goal. Battle to the **Jefferson Memorial [9.14]**, fight to the rotunda, and enter the **Project Purity Control Room [9.14]**. After the area is finally secured, Sarah Lyons gives you grave news about the experiment. The Enclave sabotaged the main water flow control system. The Purifier must be activated manually (and fatally). Whether you choose to sacrifice yourself, or that fate falls on Sentinel Lyons, the people of the Wasteland have just been saved…or will soon fall victim to the deadly effects of the modified F.E.V., if you poisoned the water supply….

Project Purity

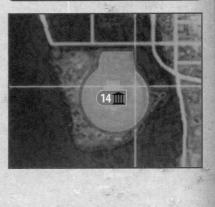

QUEST FLOWCHART

MAIN PATH	
Main Characters	Sentinel Sarah Lyons, Knight Captain Gallows, Knight Captain Dusk, Paladin Vargas, Paladin Glade, Paladin Kodiak, Liberty Prime
Locations	The Citadel, Jefferson Memorial (Project Purity)
Adv. Items/Abilities	Big Guns, Energy Weapons, Small Guns, Speech
Possible enemies	Enclave Soldier, Enclave Vertibird, Colonel Autumn
Karma Influence	Neutral

Prepare for battle, and then report to Sarah Lyons.

Prepare for the final battle; stock up on Ammunition and Weaponry, Stimpaks and Chems, Armor and Helmet, Items are in a good state of Repair

Follow Liberty Prime as he makes his way to the Purifier.

Locate Jefferson Memorial Gift Shop Entrance [Once entered, you cannot exit]

Reach the Project Purity Control Room.

Secure the Project Purity Control Room.

Engage in combat with Colonel Autumn and his bodyguards	[Speech] Mediate a truce with Colonel Autumn and his bodyguards
• Colonel Autumn's Uniform, Colonel Autumn's 10mm Pistol	

Activate Project Purity.

Project Impurity: Infect the Project Purity water supply…or not.

Ignore the Auxiliary Filtration Input	Activate the Auxiliary Filtration Input, place the Modified F.E.V. Vial inside

Agree to start the Purifier	Order Sarah Lyons into the Purifier	Refuse to start the Purifier	Agree to start the Purifier, then wait

Up to 3 minutes pass

Project Purity Activates	Project Purity Explodes

Color code: Objective   Action   Rewards

ROTHCHILD, FIRE IT UP!

NEW OBJECTIVE
"Prepare for battle, and then report to Sarah Lyons" begins.

Lyons' Pride is ready for action: Gallows, Dusk, Vargas, Glade, and Kodiak are standing by!

Before agreeing to begin the final push on the Enclave, make sure you have the following:

• A large supply of ammunition and weaponry for urban take-downs and close-quarters fighting.
• All the Stimpaks and Chems you depend upon.
• A good set of armor and a helmet.
• Everything repaired to a good or exceptional degree.

Return to Sentinel Lyons when you are fully equipped, healthy, and ready to end this power struggle once and for all. Agree to her readiness question, and she turns to her troops. The Pride is on

Liberty Prime is online! Weapons are hot! Mission: The destruction of all Chinese communists!

her, and the goal is to enter Project Purity. The robot is responsible for destroying the Enclaves' energy fields, while the Pride provides fire-support. The robot will keep the Enclave scum busy, while Lyons relies on the element of surprise to turn the battle in their favor. Move quickly, and meet up in the bailey. Rothchild activates the central lift, and Liberty Prime crackles into life. Its vocal programming is still tuned to American propaganda during a proposed assault in Anchorage Alaska, 200 years ago, but the sentiments are still relevant!

NEW OBJECTIVE
"Follow Liberty Prime as he makes his way to the Purifier" begins.

Even Enclave Vertibirds are no match for the latest in 2077 technology.

Head back up to the courtyard outside, passing Paladin Gunny as he fist-pumps the air in excitement! A large crane is lifting Liberty Prime out of the bailey, narrowly missing an exterior wall, and positioning it for the attack! Head past the initiates, and locate the Door to the Capital Wasteland. Follow Lyons' Pride out of the Citadel, and turn northeast, as Liberty Prime activates, and immediately begins blasting Vertibirds out of the sky with its head laser! Score one for democracy!

> ### Note
> You can ignore Lyons' orders, break away from Liberty Prime and the Pride, and head southwest, swimming over to the road leading to the Jefferson Memorial, where you're likely to be overwhelmed by well-armed Enclave shock troops.

Standing next to an exploding car is never a good idea, as this Brotherhood Initiate found, to his cost.

Follow Liberty Prime at a distance so you aren't stomped on or hit by the missiles lobbed from the Jefferson Memorial. The route Liberty Prime is taking isn't direct, but it is drawing most of the Enclave's firepower. Fortunately, the robot looks like it can stand it. Follow it cautiously up the bridge ramp, staying away from any exploding vehicles (or shooting them yourself from range, so you know you're safe.) Prime reaches the first magnetic resonance field, and draws the energy: Probability of mission interference: Zero Percent!

GIVE ME LIBERTY, DON'T GIVE ME DEATH!

Liberty's prime directive: Kill anything that looks even vaguely hostile!

The first barricade is through! Head up onto the bridge and provide support fire for Liberty Prime, such as launching attacks on Vertibirds that swoop overhead or any enemies you can see in the distance. Liberty Prime has his own ordnance however, and he lobs a gigantic Mini-Nuke that clears a parked Vertibird. Prime finishes the bridge stomp by clearing and exploding more Vertibirds, before turning, growling more democratic cheer on the hapless Enclave forces, and stomping down the main street.

The robot has functioned far more brilliantly than Rothchild had thought possible. Excellent work, Prime!

Stay a little farther back from Liberty Prime as he continues to demolish a squad of Enclave Soldiers on the overpass walkway, then stomps under it, past the irradiated metro, and up the other side, moving relatively quickly around to the road to the Jefferson Memorial. Keep your eyes peeled for Enclave forces that have slipped by Prime's lasers, and stay bunched with Lyons' Pride and you'll have no problems tearing through the stragglers. Once on the final stretch of road, Liberty Prime lobs another massive grenade at a parked Vertibird near the gift shop entrance, then absorbs the final resonance field.

NEW OBJECTIVE

"Reach the Project Purity Control Room" begins.

ULTIMATE CONTROL

The Enclave Soldiers put up a valiant attempt, but you should and must prevail. Cut them down!

Tip

You can remain outside, blasting Vertibirds landing nearby or keeping Liberty Prime company, but you've got a job to do. Head straight for the Jefferson Memorial Gift Shop entrance, and begin to retrace your steps back to the Project Purity Control Room. Turn right (south) at the junction, optionally lobbing in a Grenade to soften up the couple of Soldiers behind the sandbags, and then push forward into the pillared room, cutting down two more foes before heading to either of the rotunda doors. Enter the Project Purity Control Room.

Caution

Once you enter here, you cannot leave: If you wish to explore any more of the Capital Wasteland, do so before you head inside!

NEW OBJECTIVE

"Secure the Project Purity Control Room" begins.

You again! Colonel Autumn is waiting for you in the Control Room. Unfortunately, he's brought friends...

Step into the Control Room, and you're greeted by Colonel Autumn once more. He isn't surprised to see you; after all, you seem hell-bent on destroying everything the government has worked to achieve. Once you've uttered the final words he'll ever hear, engage Autumn and his two Tesla Armored bodyguards.

 Or, you can use **Speech** to convince Autumn to halt his violence against you. If you succeed, his forces depart the facility.

The trick here is to stay behind the pillars, backing out of the room if you're becoming too close to death. Start with a Grenade lob as soon as the conversation with Autumn is over, then concentrate

Mow the bodyguards down immediately, followed by the colonel himself.

on blasting one bodyguard at a time. Autumn usually picks up a dropped Minigun that either bodyguard carried; take it from the corpse during battle to prevent this. Once Autumn and his overcoat are a pile of ash or a crumpled corpse (for an extra optional fun task, try to cut him down so he falls backward, and into the irradiated water vat!), Sentinel Lyons joins you. Your father's project can finally begin!

Note

You can take a unique Uniform from Colonel Autumn. Of course, you don't have much time to enjoy its Energy Weapons and Small Guns bonuses!

Colonel Autumn's Uniform

NEW OBJECTIVE

"Activate Project Purity" begins.

NEW OBJECTIVE

Project Impurity "Infect the Project Purity water supply...or not" begins.

The jubilation is short-lived. One of you must make a supreme sacrifice.

Once Colonel Autumn is dead, move up to the intercom near the airlock control, and listen as Doctor Li gives detailed instructions on how this is going to power up. Sarah speaks to Li directly. Li says that because of the damage, the entire complex will overload shortly, unless the water is rerouted through the purification tanks. This can only be done by turning the Purifier on...now. If the Purifier isn't activated within three minutes, the pipes will burst and the Purifier will essentially implode. It should be clear by now what must be done: someone has to go into the irradiated control core and sacrifice their own life to save the Purifier.

The following options are available:

You can agree to start the Purifier.

You can order Sarah Lyons into the Purifier.

You can refuse to start the Purifier altogether.

You can agree to start the Purifier, then stand where you are or not enter the airlock. The countdown continues until you make a decision, damnit!

Note

You can change your mind about who's going in, but only once.

Before you enter the Purifier itself, you have the option of activating the Auxiliary Filtration Input. Slide in the Modified F.E.V. Vial if you want the G.E.C.K. to lace the water with special bacterial agents that destroy mutations.

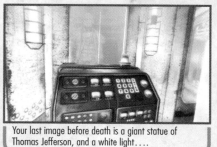

Have you allied with the clockwork president? Then execute his bidding, and place the F.E.V. in his contraption first.

Whether or not you activated the Auxiliary Filtration Input, you have three possible conclusions to this quest:

PROJECT PURITY COMMENCEMENT: PLAN A

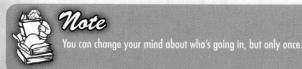

Your last image before death is a giant statue of Thomas Jefferson, and a white light....

You decide to enter the airlock. Sarah waits until you're inside, then leaves you to your fate. Move to the Purity Machine and hit the three digits of your mother's favorite Bible verse (2-1-6) and then Enter. The Purifier, linked to G.E.C.K., activates, filling the room with a brilliant white light. You are lost in the expansion of creation. Everything fades to white....

PROJECT PURITY COMMENCEMENT: PLAN B

You convince Sarah Lyons to enter the airlock. Sarah agrees, and waits in the airlock until you seal it off. She moves to the Purity Machine, and inputs the code you just told her. She types it in, and collapses as the room fills with a brilliant light. Everything fades to white....

PROJECT PURITY COMMENCEMENT: PLAN C

You convince Sarah Lyons to enter the airlock. Sarah agrees, and waits in the airlock until you seal it off. She moves to the Purity Machine, and waits for you to tell her the input code. You refuse, and after three minutes of waiting, the Project Purity machine expands in a sea of brilliant light. Everything fades to white....

There are several ways to cause Plan C to begin:

1. Refuse to give Sarah the code when you speak with her.

2. Give her the code, but then don't cycle the airlock.

3. Tell her you'll go, but then don't ever enter the airlock.

4. Tell her you'll go, let her cycle the airlock, but don't approach the console.

Basically, the more inactive you are, the better your chances for this embarrassment of an ending.

NEW OBJECTIVE

The Main Quest has concluded. You now watch the ending. If you require further information on the various endings, turn to the Completion section on page 453.

Chapter 4 MISCELLANEOUS QUESTS

Big Trouble in Big Town

On a visit to the settlement of children known as **Little Lamplight [4.08]**, you meet a boy named Sticky, who has just come of age. Sticky needs a chaperone to **Big Town [5.10]**, and assuming one or both of you survive, you soon realize Big Town is a poorly guarded settlement that's constantly being overrun by Super Mutants. The Super Mutants are staging raids from the abandoned **Germantown Police Headquarters [5.01]**, where they are currently holding a group of Big Town residents. Your role is to rescue as many survivors as you can, and teach the rest how to defend themselves from the next Super Mutant raid.

Big Town

10 🏠

QUEST FLOWCHART

	MAIN PATH 1	MAIN PATH 2	MAIN PATH 3	OPTIONAL PATH
Main Characters	Sticky, Pappy, Red	Pappy, Red	Red	Sticky, Pappy, Red, Shorty
Locations	Little Lamplight, Big Town, Germantown Police Headquarters	Big Town, Germantown Police Headquarters	Big Town, Germantown Police Headquarters	Little Lamplight, Big Town, Germantown Police Headquarters
Adv. Items/Abilities	Explosives, Lockpick, Melee Weapons, Science, Small Guns, Sneak, Speech			
Possible Enemies	Radroach, Super Mutant Genus			
Karma Influence	Negative	Positive	Positive	Positive

Locate and speak with Sticky at Little Lamplight
- Party Hat

Locate Big Town

Locate Red

Escort Sticky OR leave Sticky and head to Big Town

Ask the people of Big Town about their captured friends.

Rescue the Big Town captives from the Super Mutants.

Clear path OR sneak between Big Town and Germantown Police HQ

Germantown Police HQ: Unlock side entrance OR enter rear entrance

Locate ground floor cells

Rescue the Big Town captives from the Super Mutants.

Locate the Basement Kitchen

[Optional] Rescue Shorty.

Escort Shorty safely back to Big Town.

Red survives

Red and Shorty survive

Neither Red nor Shorty survive

Speak to Red for your reward
- 300 or 500 Caps

Speak to Pappy for your reward
- 200 Caps

Repel Super Mutant attack
- Radiation Healing (Red)
- Medical Supplies (Red)
- Items Repaired (Pappy)

Ignore attack and leave

Color code: Objective   Action   Rewards

Try starting this quest either after exploring and locating Big Town (if Sticky is unimportant), or during **Main Quest: Picking Up the Trail**, which places you in Little Lamplight on other matters.

YOU'VE GOT TO BE KIDDING

Sticky's grown up to become a real petulant liability.

Once you've negotiated an entrance into Little Lamplight with Mayor MacCready (which you should read about first during **Main Quest: Picking Up the Trail**), locate Sticky. He's easy to spot, because he's easily the tallest human in town besides you, and he has his party hat on. He's standing to the left of the entrance gate. When you're ready, choose "I'll escort you to Big Town, but it'll cost you." He's fine with this, as his girlfriend—Red—has the Caps. You can get him to remove that ridiculous headgear (or not, as it makes him easy to spot in the Wasteland). Meet him outside when you're ready to leave.

Party Hat

Optionally give Sticky a weapon to help fend off the monsters that lurk in the Wasteland, and begin the trek. If you're finding this hard going, you can simply ignore Sticky, and visit Big Town on your own. Here's fun: Speak to Sticky in Little Lamplight, then forget about him. He waits a week, then heads to Big Town on his own. He doesn't quite make it, and you can find his corpse in the vicinity if you want; he's more *Stinky* than *Sticky*.

 Or he can be silenced with a **Speech** persuasion to keep quiet.

 A bullet to the back of the skull also works well.

Follow your map target, and keep going until you reach Big Town. It takes a real saint to keep from throttling Sticky, so pat yourself on the back if you both make it. Try the trek during daylight hours.

When you manage to stagger into Big Town, it isn't quite as expansive as its name might suggest. There's only one, badly defended entrance, which is where Dusty the town guard is sitting. All it takes is vague politeness to be allowed to wander unchecked around town. Your quest formally begins now. You're encouraged to ask people in town about the friends of theirs that Dusty said had been carried off by roving Super Mutants. You're about to discover the true extent of this town's troubles....

NEW OBJECTIVE
"Ask the people of Big Town about their captured friends" begins.

Pappy's the old timer around here, but he's still in his awkward phase.

One of the best choices to speak with is Pappy, a morose young man who's resigned himself to death by Super Mutant chopping implement. Keep your offensive comments to a minimum, and you'll instill a slight glimmer of hope, and Pappy offers to help Repair some of your equipment. He also mentions where the Super Mutants took their human food during the last raid; they're holed up in the Germantown Police Headquarters to the north. Your Pip-Boy and quest now update. Talk to others if you wish.

NEW OBJECTIVE
"Rescue the Big Town captives from the Super Mutants" begins.

HORROR AT HALLOWED MOORS CEMETERY

 You can maneuver through these areas using your **Sneak** ability, your weapons fire, or a combination of both.

When you've satisfied your curiosity with the townsfolk, leave Big Town via the rope bridge, and head north, ideally following the remains of the road to the bridge, and across to the moors on the other side. The ominous Hallowed Moors Cemetery church's tumble-down steeple provides a landmark. Head here, or around to the east, if you want to avoid the Super Mutants and a Centaur prowling the vicinity. If you do engage the enemies outside the church, remain at a distance, and use the rocky outcrops as cover.

Enter the remains of the chapel when you've dealt with the Super Mutant menace by the front entrance, and expect at least two hardened Super Mutants (one usually carrying a Minigun) to ambush you in this area. Use the walls for cover. When you've demolished this advance party, check the building for Ammunition and First Aid Boxes. There's also a Wasteland Captive tied up at the rear (northeast) end of the chapel interior. Untie or leave her; numerous other Captives (all are unrelated to this quest) all over the Wasteland are being held by these abominations.

 Gain Karma by letting your untied Wastelander leave with her supplies. You gain less Karma by taking the supplies the Wastelander offers as thanks for rescuing her.

Ammo Box Ammunition

First Aid Health and Chems

EXTERIOR POLICE HQ PROTOCOL: SNEAK OR STRIKE

Once the church is secure (which helps you on your way back with Red, as you don't need to worry about the Super Mutants killing her), make a vaguely north-northeast trek across the rocky terrain, heading for the ruined building on the higher ground; this is the remains of Germantown. The Super Mutants patrol this area, and the only entrance into the Police Headquarters is around the back. You can

TRAINING — BESTIARY — MAIN QUEST — MISC. QUESTS — TOUR — COMPLETION — APPENDICES

skirt the perimeter using Sneak, or attack via the front gate (as shown), and drop the Super Mutant with a Combat Shotgun, or other excellent close-assault weapon.

To clear the building's exterior, head into the mesh-fenced pen area, winding around the narrow entrance, and enter the area with the tents, dropping another Super Mutant en route to inspecting the tents themselves. The tent to the north houses a First Aid Box, while the rest simply house scattered dirty mattresses. You can also check the terminal on the table next to the delightful empty Gore Bag, and read some rather disturbing log entries by a long-dead member of the N.C.R.A.R.U. (National Catastrophe Relief Auxiliary Response Unit), Nancy Kroydon. She charts her experience as the bombs dropped, the response, the desertion of her team (who fled to the nearby Vault 87), her care for those with radiation poisoning, and her final, hopeless end.

 First Aid Health

Whether or not you choose to investigate the tents, you can head to the rear (north) of the building exterior, either inside or outside the mesh fence, and head through the gap to the half-demolished back of the building. Find the exterior steps leading to the edge of a broken floor, and move to the Door to Police HQ Top Floor. This is the only way into the premises. Before you enter, it's a good idea (but not mandatory) to wait until sunrise so you can time your leaving (with Red) to coincide with daylight, if you haven't learned the terrain.

 Another door, on the ground floor just after the mesh gate, leads directly to Red's cell. However, it requires a very high **Lockpick** skill to open. If you happen to have mastered this skill, unlock this door, turn left and unlock Red's cell, ignore Shorty, and leave (skipping to "Better Red than Dead") in about 10 seconds!

LOOKING FOR THE LOCKDOWN HOLOTAPE

PATH A: ROOMS TO THE SOUTH

Doorways are excellent places for side-stepping out to gun down grunting Muties.

 Caution

Watch out! This place is crawling with Super Mutants, and Frag Mines are placed for maximum damage. Save your game often, and keep your eyes open for these types of trap! Remember you can employ Sneak throughout this building!

 You can follow the main "spine" corridor to the door leading to the stairs heading down (see the map on page 307 for the layout), or you can search the top floor of this place. Remember that a good **Sneak** skill allows you to navigate around enemies instead of attacking them.

 The room directly to your right (south) has a terminal you can hack into using your **Science** skill. There are two violations listed to a Danielle Faye and a Jennifer Wilkins.

They're long-dead, so move to the middle of the floor, and check the door to your right; it leads to a room with chemical beakers and burned-out terminals. There's nothing of real value here, so use this room if you're employing Sneak, and exit out to a side corridor. Immediately, there's a door in the eastern wall. Enter this wrecked office, turn south, and deactivate the Frag Mine on the ground by the terminal and safe. If the Frag Mine explodes, Super Mutants are attracted to your location. Expect an attack from the open doorway to the north.

 Inspect this room closely. On the desk with the terminal is a handy item: a Holotape with the Password for Lockdown Computer on it. If you want to open the safe, use either **Science** to hack into the terminal, or **Lockpicking** to open the safe directly.

Grab everything. Now move to the exit doorway, or optionally inspect the rooms to the north side of this building.

 Safe Items   **Password for Lockdown Computer**

PATH B: ROOMS TO THE NORTH

If you're not using V.A.T.S., attack when they reload, or run around and strike from behind.

If you're prowling the north rooms on this floor, expect at least one Super Mutant confrontation. Step through the doorway into this open-plan office and rummage around. Watch out for a Frag Mine at the eastern desk cubicle, along with some minor Ammo, and a First Aid Box on the northern wall. Grab anything you wish (including that Frag Mine once you deactivate it), and return to the main west-to-east corridor.

Continue down it to a room with some green leather chairs, and a Frag Mine trap just inside the doorway. Deactivate it, and grab the First Aid Box from the table. Now return to the corridor, head east, and make a left (north) turn. This last chamber has an Ammo Box, a First Aid Box, an Assault Rifle, a Sledgehammer, and a full Gore Bag. If you're intending on losing Karma and acquiring the taste for human flesh, this is a great place to start! Collect what you need, then head for the door to the ground floor.

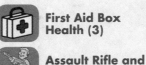 **First Aid Box Health (3)**   **Sledgehammer**

Assault Rifle and Ammo Box

GROUND FLOOR: SUPER MUTANT SLAUGHTERHOUSE

Open the door, and be very careful descending the steps; if you let off the Frag Mine on the landing, two toughened Super Mutants come gunning for you. A third patrols this area, too. You can Sneak past here if combat is problematic! When you're done, move from the stairwell into the first corridor, turn east, and locate the doorway leading into the dispatch room.

 You can hack into three working terminals here with **Science** skill. Read notes on past 911 calls. Remember: "That's how you get to llama school!"

Caution

Beware! There's a Frag Mine in the middle of this room, and each terminal has the option to activate the station alarm. Either alerts all the Super Mutants, so employ these "mistakes" only if you want a vicious shoot-out instead of a sneaky exploration.

When you're done in the dispatch room, head out of the other doorway (which you haven't been through yet) into the debriefing room. This contains a number of tables, a lot of rubble, and not much else, except for a copy of *Lying: Congressional Style* on the remains of the front podium. Grab and read it for a boost to your stats. Exit to the main corridor. If you turn north, you can reach another staircase leading to the basement. Hold on for the moment; you should scour the remaining rooms on this floor first.

 Lying: Congressional Style
+1 Speech Skill (when read).

Move to the south end of this floor, and inspect a couple of bathrooms, a larger foyer with a single table, and four crumbling columns. Deal with the Radroach infestation (don't worry, those readings aren't all Super Mutants!),

I got signals! I got readings, in front and behind! Fortunately, these may be Radroaches; squish them hard.

and head west, crossing the main corridor and into the armory.

 This room has one working terminal, and a locked door behind the desk. First, deactivate the Frag Mine on the floor, and choose either of your skills (**Lockpicking** the door is less difficult, but both that and **Science** require high skill points) to unlock the door to the weapons closet. The closet is well worth ransacking. Inside you'll find the following:

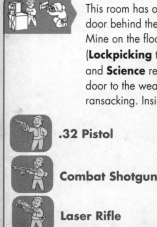

.32 Pistol	**Silenced 10mm Pistol**
Combat Shotgun	**Frag Grenades**
Laser Rifle	**Ammo Box Ammunition**

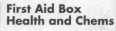 **First Aid Health**

NO ONE COMES BACK FROM THE KITCHEN

Red has been living in the worst sanitary conditions ever seen...until you meet Shorty.

The only other rooms you haven't visited on the ground floor are the holding cells. Here you find a solitary figure clad in a red jacket and bandana. Your powers of deduction tell you this must be Red. The cell door is locked. You can try an extremely difficult Lockpick, but it is better to move to the adjacent terminal, and release all the cell doors using the Password for Lockdown Computer that you found on the desk back on the top floor. Before you do this, kill all the Radroaches in the cell room; you need Red as healthy as possible!

 Once the cell door swings open, speak with Red. Keep the chat civil, and she tells you a second human might still be alive: Shorty, who was recently dragged down to the kitchen. Offer to find him if you want (or, if Shorty doesn't concern you, skip to "Better Red Than Dead"). Although Red can accompany you, it is safer for her to remain in the cell. Tell her to wait, then enter the main corridor. Travel east, then north to the stairs, and descend to the Door to Police HQ–Basement. Open it!

NEW OBJECTIVE
"Escort Red safely back to Big Town" begins.

NEW OBJECTIVE [OPTIONAL]
"Rescue Shorty" begins.

Once you're in the basement, you can add to your inventory by stepping eastward through the first doorway, into a horrific gun range, filled with hanging Gore Bags and strung-up human targets. They're all dead, so concentrate on the First Aid Box, Ammo Box, and Gun Cabinets.

 **Chinese Pistol and Ammo**	**First Aid Box Health and Chems**
Ammo Box Ammunition	

 Before you go, check the gun range doorway to the north. The area of interest is a locked door. Use an accomplished **Lockpick** skill to open this door and ransack a weapons storage area, where you'll find the following:

 **Ammo Box Ammunition (3)**	**Fat Man**
Assault Rifle and Ammo	

APPENDICES — COMPLETION — TOUR — MISC. QUESTS — MAIN QUEST — BESTIARY — TRAINING

Head back to the main corridor, and move into the large empty room, cutting down a few Radroaches. Step through the doorway to the south, and head west into the kitchen (there's another exit in this room, but it leads to the locker rooms that have little in the way of items, and a Radroach or two to defeat). The kitchen is a scene of horror, with gore across almost every surface, and an enraged Super Mutant ready for battle. Stay at the entrance doorway and don't throw in grenades; there's a small lad tied up in here!

 Untie Shorty, and he expresses his extreme thanks, and extreme need to get the hell out of here! Grab any Abraxo Cleaner you need from the galley behind the kitchen, and retrace your steps to Red's cell. After the reunion, optionally give each of them a weapon, and exit via the door to the west, just outside Red's cell.

NEW OBJECTIVE
"Escort Shorty safely back to Big Town" begins.

If you're determined to keep Red and Shorty alive, save your progress now, because this could take a couple of tries! However, all is not lost if either Shorty or Red die; they aren't critical to your quest completion.

BETTER RED THAN DEAD

With both Big Town residents armed and ready to flee, begin the chaperoning process by retracing your steps out of the Police Head-quarters, down the rocky hill, across the moors away from the cha-pel, toward the bridge, and south into Big Town. Along the way, you're advised to leave Shorty and Red and scout ahead, then return and move southward in 300-400 foot dashes. Destroy any-thing vaguely mutated, then return quickly, when the coast is clear, and continue. Save constantly to avoid disappointment. Take care when you reach the bridge; Raiders to the east may spot you and open fire with long-range weapons.

 Tip
A much more cunning plan at this point is to Fast Travel back to Big Town as soon as you leave the Police Headquarters. Both Red and Shorty make the trip with you, and their safety is assured.

Pat yourself on the back if both Red and Shorty survive: Then fleece Red for up to 500 Caps if the mood takes you!

When you return to Big Town, speak with Red (or if she's dead, try Dusty or Pappy). You can attempt the following conversations:

 Refuse any Caps reward, and end the quest.

- Take 300 Caps from Red for rescuing her.
- Take 200 Caps from another Big Town inhabitant if Red died (regardless if Shorty is alive or not).
- Sticky is a liability; there's no additional reward for bringing him to Big Town.

  Use **Speech** to take 200 additional Caps that Red was saving to buy medicine for the town's people; you make out like a bandit, because essen-tially, that's what you are!

The quest is now complete, but you can attend to a couple of post quest antics.

QUEST REWARDS

You receive the following rewards for finishing **Big Trouble in Big Town**:

 300 Bottle Caps
for returning to Big Town†.

 200 Bottle Caps
for returning to Big Town if Red died.

 200 Bottle Caps
from Red for using Speech and demanding more Caps.

 + KARMA
when Red and/or Shorty return to Big Town.

XP **300 XP**

† Sticky and Shorty do not need to survive for this reward, but Red does.

Tip
It's optimal to keep as many Big Town residents alive as you can. After the quest, you can return here whenever you need the following:
- Radiation healing (from Red).
- Medical supplies (from Red).
- Items Repaired (from Pappy).

POST-QUEST ANTICS

BIG TOWN STRIKES BACK

Tip
Whatever skill you teach the Big Town folk, an excellent plan is to place a number of Frag Mines around and on the bridge where the Super Mutants storm in; if they are far enough apart to explode one at a time, you can really curtail the Mutie threat. Also make sure you have a variety of weapons at the ready using your Pip-Boy's Hot Key function.

As soon as the quest is over, Red (or any surviving Big Town inhabitant) tells you that the Super Mutants are planning an attack right now, and they need your help to survive the massacre. Depending on your skillset, you have the following options:

In this option, a quick training session at the shooting range helps in the forthcoming fracas.

You can ignore the townsfolk, end the conversation, and leave before trouble arrives. When you next visit Big Town, everyone is dead.

 With a good **Science** skill, you can program the town's robot defenders to help defeat the attack.

 With a proficient **Explosives** skill, you show them how to plant mines.

 If you can **Sneak**, you can turn this into a ghost town, fooling the Super Mutants into leaving.

 With **Small Guns** skills, you can give basic weapons training so the townsfolk hold the Super Mutants off at the bridge.

 Use **Melee Weapons**, and the townsfolk swarm the attackers to batter them.

Or, if you're unable to use any of these abilities, you can choose to simply deal with the attack by yourself.

Victory! Hey, wait a minute...is that Bittercup's crumpled body behind Red? Noooo...!

The moment you can leave the townspeople to their training, move and prep the bridge area (the only place where the four incoming Super Mutants are attacking from), and wait for them to arrive. As mentioned previously, lay mines to slow down the initial charge, lob Frag Grenades to wound them before they reach the end of the bridge, and quickly flip (using your Hot Key function). Or, you could simply fire a Mini-Nuke from your Fat Man before the Super Mutants get to close! Whatever you decide, any surviving townspeople thank you for your help once the threat is over.

 Note

Freeform Quest: Bittercup Runneth Over and Freeform Quest: Ticking Timebomb can also be completed in this area. Consult the "Tour of the Wasteland" chapter for details.

The Superhuman Gambit

The trading town of **Canterbury Commons [6.02]** was once a bustling little community. That changed one day, when the AntAgonizer emerged from her **Lair [6.01]**, leading an army of Giant Ants. After the first attack, the town's mechanic snapped. After losing his favorite robot to this so-called super-villain, he became the self-dubbed "Mechanist," fortified himself in the nearby **Robot Repair Center and Forge [6.H]**, and began creating an army to fight the AntAgonizer. Sadly, when they eventually fought in the town, they were more dangerous than the Ants alone had ever been. Now, the head of the town now just wants rid of them. Can a new kind of hero–preferably one with a sane and functioning mind–come to the rescue? Read up on the AntAgonizer at **Hubris Comics Publishing [20.01]** and enter the fray.

Canterbury Commons

QUEST FLOWCHART

	MAIN PATH 1	MAIN PATH 2	OPTIONAL PATH 1	OPTIONAL PATH 2
Main Characters	Ernest "Uncle" Roe, AntAgonizer, The Mechanist	Ernest "Uncle" Roe, AntAgonizer, The Mechanist	None	Derek Pacion, Joe Porter
Locations	Canterbury Commons, Canterbury Tunnels, AntAgonizer's Lair, The Forge	Canterbury Commons, The Forge, Canterbury Tunnels, AntAgonizer's Lair	Hubris Comics Publishing	Canterbury Commons
Adv. Items/Abilities	Lockpick, Science, Speech, Child at Heart	Lockpick, Science, Speech, Child at Heart	Science	Child at Heart
Possible enemies	Giant Ant Genus, Robot Genus	Giant Ant Genus, Robot Genus	D.C. Area Entities	None
Karma Influence	Positive and/or Negative	Positive and/or Negative	None	None

Find the Mechanist or AntAgonizer and stop their rivalry.

Read up on the AntAgonizer at Hubris Comics Publishing

[Optional] Ask Derek for information about the Mechanist and AntAgonizer.

Locate the Basement Kitchen

Find the AntAgonizer and stop her.

Investigate the Canterbury Tunnels

Find the Mechanist and stop him.

Investigate the Forge (Barry's Electronics Store)

Access the Desk Terminal

• Pulse Grenade (6)

Access the Mechanist's Lair

Reveal her "Secret Identity" (-Karma)

"Unmask his Alter Ego" (+Karma)

Team up as a "Dynamic Duo" (-Karma)

Team up as "Mechano-Lad" (-Karma)

"Costume Change"; deliver Mechanist outfit (-Karma)

"Outfit Outreach"; deliver AntAgonizer outfit (-Karma)

Antagonize the AntAgonizer (neutral Karma)

"Manhandle the Mechanist" (neutral Karma)

• AntAgonizer's Costume
• AntAgonizer's Helmet
• Ant Sting

• Mechanist's Costume
• Mechanist's Helmet
• Protectron's Gaze

Report back to town for your reward.

• 200 or 400 caps

Color code: | Objective | Action | Rewards

COMMOTION IN THE COMMONS

When exploring the eastern Wastelands (north of the Convega Factory, and east of Wheaton Armory, enter what's left of the road to Canterbury Commons, a once-thriving market town that's currently in more disarray than most. If you spot Crow, or one of the other traveling merchants, they complain about the two costumed superheroes disrupting business. Sure enough, they're fighting in the main street. One of them has a Protectron robot, while the other has Giant Ants scurrying about her. Let them fight it out until they flee, and deal with any Ants that remain.

Tip

Call yourself a comic book fan? Then head on over to Hubris Comics Store and read up on your female adversary in a Letter to the Editor at the terminal there. It could come in handy later into this quest...

When all threats are gone, the few remaining townsfolk emerge from their hiding places. One in particular is eager to meet you. He introduces himself as Ernest "Uncle" Roe, and explains the town's two problem citizens—now known as the Mechanist and the AntAgonizer—and

Despite the superhero insanity, you're greeted warmly by the town mayor, Ernest "Uncle" Roe.

their antics are playing havoc with the traders that the town relies on to survive. Your help is requested, and there's 200 Caps in it for you. Try this option, too:

If you have a high **Speech** skill, offer to help, then ask for double the pay. If you succeed, expect a return of 400 Caps.

Now follow Uncle Roe's advice, and locate his nephew Derek, who's the biggest (and only) fan of the superheroes.

> **NEW OBJECTIVE**
> "Find the Mechanist or AntAgonizer, and stop their rivalry" begins.

> **NEW OBJECTIVE [OPTIONAL]**
> "Ask Derek for information about the Mechanist and AntAgonizer" begins.

> **NEW OBJECTIVE [OPTIONAL]**
> "Find the AntAgonizer and stop her" begins.

> **NEW OBJECTIVE [OPTIONAL]**
> "Find the Mechanist and stop him" begins.

THE WORD ON THE STREET

When you've agreed to the quest, (assuming you haven't accidentally gunned down all the town's inhabitants, searched their corpses, ransacked the two open buildings and the diner, and then fled, which is a possible plan if you're uninterested in the quest, don't care about Karma, and can carry a huge amount of junk and items that aren't yours), speak to the other townsfolk. These two bruisers, Machete and Dominic "Dom" D'Ellsadro, are in charge of roughing up thieves, so try not to threaten them and you'll accrue

a little more information on the Mechanist; apparently he and Dom were buddies.

Move toward the diner, across from the town hall (which you can explore, but there's nothing there of value unless you're stealing), and talk to the two townsfolk here: the barkeep Joe Porter, and Ernest's nephew, Derek. When you speak with both of them, the following useful options are available (as well as a lot of backstory on the rivalries between the heroes):

Joe: Ask him specifically about the superheroes, and he tells you he might know who the AntAgonizer is: a girl named Tanya Christoff, whose family was wiped out by Ants shortly before the AntAgonizer turned up in town.

Derek: Inquire about the AntAgonizer, and he tells you she's got a lair to the north of the town. It now appears on your map.

Derek: Inquire about the Mechanist, and he tells you he's got a Forge in the robot shop on the hill to the south of the town. It now appears on your map. Derek is also a fan of comic books, which you'll discover if you pick his pocket.

If you have the **Child at Heart** perk, you can acquire an additional bit of information: that "Scott" the Mechanist used to look out for Derek. This may come in handy later.

Note

Your next steps are to challenge either the AntAgonizer, or the Mechanist, after finding them in their lairs. You can approach the remainder of this quest in any order you like, although some minor outcomes are affected.

ANTAGONIZER: ENGAGE! (SLOWER THAN A SPEEDING BULLET)

Not exactly the hollowed-out shell of a dormant volcano, but this super-villain's underground lair is still fraught with danger....

Head west to the end of the main street, turn north, and locate the large rocky outcrop that matches your Pip-Boy's entrance locator. Is your Lockpick skill not up to par? Then ignore the Sewer Grate at the top of the outcrop, head to the foot of the outcrop, and locate the metal door. This leads to a man-made sewer system. Head down the stairs, and stop at the first junction. Turn right, head east, and rummage around the small storeroom at the end of the corridor. Find two First Aid Boxes, and avoid tripping a Rigged Shotgun.

Tip

If the darkness scares you, remember your Pip-Boy has a built-in Flashlight; activate it if you need to (although it attracts Ants!).

 First Aid Box Health and Chems

APPENDICES — COMPLETION — TOUR — MISC. QUESTS — MAIN QUEST — BESTIARY — TRAINING

Back up to the main corridor, head to the filtering chamber, and descend the stairs. Locate the doorway in the northwest corner. Follow the corridor down steps, turn a corner, and when facing south, look for another junction. The narrow storage corridor to your right usually contains some Frag Mines. Move quickly and pick them up to disarm them; you can optionally use them to blow Ants up if you wish.

 Tip

Remember you'll inflict 50 percent more damage on any Ant if you have the Entomologist perk!

 Frag Mines

Collect any items you want from here (there's nothing special), and move to the Generator Room. Activate the Electrical Switch (face west), and a metal trapdoor opens. Descend the steps. Open the door, brandish your favored Ant-killing weapon, and tackle two Giant Worker Ants at the threshold of the sewer tunnel. Move out into the sewer, and immediately enter the hole in the southern wall; you're now in the AntAgonizer's Lair!

Wind along the tunnel until you reach the U-shaped junction. Both passages reconnect after you pass the lanterns, and the trail continues to a door. Enter it, appearing near the inner lair where the AntAgonizer herself resides. There's a small wooden platform with shelves and chairs, but the AntAgonizer herself is flanked by two white sewer basins in an adjacent area. You can now choose an option during "An Audience with the AntAgonizer.".

Tip

If you want an Ant adversary to go crazy and attack others, shoot it in the antenna (ideally in V.A.T.S.). Do this only if other enemies are present; otherwise it still attacks you!

ANTAGONIZER: ENGAGE! (FASTER THAN A SPEEDING BULLET)

Climb to this Sewer Grate to survey the scenery, and for a quicker route into the AntAgonizer's Lair.

The entire hillside has been washed away, leaving only this rocky outcrop. Clamber up the trail of jutting rocks to the top, and spy the rusting Sewer Grate. It is locked, preventing you from accessing the lair beneath. The following options are available:

If you have a reasonable **Lockpick** skill, attempt to pick the lock.

If you fail to pick the lock, or don't have a high enough skill, employ the tactics from "Slower than a Speeding Bullet" and head down to enter the metal door.

Once down the ladder from the Sewer Grate, pass the AntAgonizer's bed, and head roughly south, and pivot around the basin to your left to reach her throne.

AN AUDIENCE WITH THE ANTAGONIZER

 **Note**

When facing the AntAgonizer, the tactics are slightly different depending on whether you've already dealt with the Mechanist or not. These specific tactics are noted.

Taming Tanya: Either play along with her antics, or give her a stern talking to if you know her secret identity.

Approach the rickety throne, where the AntAgonizer is sitting. "Why shouldn't I have my pretties kill you where you stand?" she inquires. Respond with one of the following:

 The "Secret Identity" Response: Tell her that her days of terrorizing the town are over, and she mocks you. You have three possible plans from this point:

Try to argue her point without the benefit of knowledge, which only leads to the Antagonizing the AntAgonizer response.

If you have enough **Speech** skill, and you've talked with Joe Porter, you use her real name in a response. If you're successful, she realizes what suffering she's caused, and agrees to leave, reveals her human form, and gives you her suit and helmet.

If you've visited the Hubris Comics Store and read the Letter to the Editor at one of the terminals (see page 437 for exact details), you also know the AntAgonizer's true identity. Use this knowledge now, and her responses are the same; she takes off her costume, and stops her super-villain antics.

As long as you don't then kill her, she leaves her lair, and wanders the Wastes. You may even see her much later into your wanderings, by chance. If you do decide to kill her now, no Ants join the fight, but you lose Karma.

 The AntAgonizer's Costume   The AntAgonizer's Helmet

 **Note**

This is only available if you haven't already conversed with the Mechanist.

The "Dynamic Duo" Response: Tell her you're here to help her rid the world of the Mechanist, and she stops her threatening talk. You have one more chance to stop the conversation (if you want to side with the Mechanist, or visit him, or stall this quest). Or, agree again: You are fortunate that the Mechanist chooses this moment to raid the lair! Follow and watch the Giant Soldier and Worker Ants swarm the Mechanist's Protectrons, and (if you aren't doing any shooting) see the AntAgonizer finish off the Mechanist with her incredible laser power! You find the following on the corpse:

 Laser Pistol

 The Mechanist's Helmet

 The Mechanist's Costume

After the combat, talk to the AntAgonizer again, and she requests the Mechanist's suit for a memento. Pry it off the corpse and hand it to her; if you're simpering rather than threatening, she gives you a special melee weapon: the Ant's Sting! Then, she leaves. If you're more forceful, she agrees to leave anyway, but without giving you her prize. Of course, you can murder her in cold blood afterward, but you won't get that blade!

 Ant's Sting

The "Antagonizing the AntAgonizer" Response: If you've had enough of this weirdo, simply keep threatening her, ignoring her dire warnings, and then start a fight, fending off her close-range attacks by backing off. Optionally shoot the antennae of the Giant Soldier Ants attacking you, and they turn on each other. The AntAgonizer's metal costume doesn't offer her much protection. After she drops, you can loot the corpse, and return to Canterbury Commons.

 AntAgonizer Lair Key

 Ripper

 The AntAgonizer's Costume

The AntAgonizer's Helmet

> ### Note
> This is available only if you have already conversed with the Mechanist, ideally looting his corpse and keeping his outfit.

The "Costume Change" Response: If you have the Mechanist's suit, the AntAgonizer demands you hand over his costume as proof that her opponent is dead. The following options now become available:

You can agree, receive the Ant's Sting, and let her be on her way.

You can refuse, and she angrily summons her Ants to begin combat.

> You can succeed in a **Speech**, and negotiate her leaving while keeping the suit.

NEW OBJECTIVE
"Report back to town for your reward" begins.

Now return to Canterbury Commons. If you looted or Pickpocketed the AntAgonizer, you can use her Key to unlock the Sewer Grate at the top of her ladder, or try Lockpicking. Otherwise, you need to head through the tunnels to the sewer; check the guide map for the route in reverse (in case you want to search for items).

FINGER ON THE PULSE GRENADES

If you're heading for the Mechanist's hideout (either before or after searching for the AntAgonizer) you may find the parking lot near the Robot Repair Center to be filled with foes. Detonate a car or two to help in the fight, but watch for the Radiation. The building itself is on a rocky ridge above Canterbury Commons, and features only one entrance; face south to spot it. All other entrances are boarded shut and firmly sealed.

Spin and face west when you enter the Robot Repair Center, as there's a malfunctioning Protectron in the offices to your left. Use the wall as cover, and bring it down (remember to search it; there may be Energy Cells you can use). Now that the coast is clear, check every desk and office cabinet in this room; but pay special attention to the two desks in the southwest corner:

One has an active RobCo Industries Desk Terminal. Read the Note from Frank: It's a letter to Bob, telling him how Frank and Snake smuggled in some Pulse Grenades to help with some wayward turrets. The Key is stuck to the back of this terminal. Grab it!

 **Frank's Key**

> An Ammo Box under the corner desk contains six Pulse Grenades, perfect for instantly defeating any robots you'll meet! Either use the Key, or try **Lockpicking**. Take all six Grenades; they don't weigh you down that much. Optionally now check the two doors north of here; one leads to a bathroom, while the other is locked. If your **Lockpick** skill is high enough, try jimmying it open, and step into the Pulse Chamber (AKA Sector A); watch for turrets as you enter!

 Pulse Grenades (6)

RAMPAGE THROUGH THE ROBOT REPAIR CENTER

You now have two ways to enter the Pod Bay (AKA Sector B) and Pulse Chamber (AKA Sector A) of the Robot Repair Facility, and a third elevator door that's locked. This accesses the Forge directly. The unlocked method is detailed now; the locked door to the Pulse Chamber was mentioned previously. Move to the cargo door and step through it when it opens. You enter a dark Pod Bay; quickly climb the stairs, and lob a Pulse Grenade at the robots clanking about up here. You can use the same type of Grenade to silence the two Mk II Turrets here as well. Or, you can run west, up to the control room door for a more Science-based turret takedown.

When the coast is clear, stay on the upper gantry, and locate the Repair Sector Terminal. There's a message there about a malfunctioning main platform. If you peer into the middle of the chamber, you see that the platform is indeed broken. Now inspect the two rows of pods, one on each side of the chamber. Activate an open pod, and you simply get a small electrical crackle. Activate the switch to the left of the pod, and it opens up. Most of the pods have broken or missing Protectrons, but a couple have fully functional models.

TRAINING — BESTIARY — MAIN QUEST — MISC. QUESTS — TOUR — COMPLETION — APPENDICES

You can throw a Pulse Grenade at them (as shown), but a more amusing plan is to leave them to activate their program; they walk toward where the main platform is supposed to be, and fall off! Then they pick themselves up, climb the stairs, and repeat! They pose no threat, but it's best to destroy them so you can collect any items they may be carrying. Now move to the Control Room. Move to the wall terminal, and try the following:

 With a reasonable **Science** skill, you can enter a password-protected menu, where you can read the same management message about the malfunctioning platform. In addition, you can shut down the Security in Sector B (the turrets in the Pod Bay). This is good if you entered the Pulse Chamber first, or fled to the Control Room without defeating the turrets.

> **Tip**
> Are you trying to hack into a password-protected terminal? Then save your game first, so that you can reload if you didn't choose the correct password. You can also back out of a terminal before using your last hack attempt and click it again to retry the hack from scratch.

Look west and locate the two doors, both leading to different metal gantries overlooking the Pulse Chamber. If you took the right door, leading to the stairs, run down to the ground level, and lob in a Pulse Grenade to deal with the Robobrain. As for the two

Deal with a Robobrain by shorting its circuits. Or, find a way to defeat every robot in the building with a single pulse charge!

Mk II Turrets, they're difficult to catch in a Pulse Grenade explosion, so either shoot them, backtrack and take the other door back in the Control Room, or run through the door directly below the two turrets, into a small Workshop.

 With a reasonable **Science** skill, you can enter a password-protected menu, read the management message, and shut down the turrets in Section A (above you).

While you're in this room, open the First Aid Box on the wall, and grab the health supplies inside. Then (or when the coast is clear), check this entire chamber for supplies. There's junk you can use to build weaponry, and Energy Weapon Ammunition scattered about in Metal Boxes, Protectrons, a Skill Book, and three Ammunition Boxes (the locked one has a large amount of Charge Packs and Cells). A final sortie around the ground floor reveals a shallow loading ramp and a locked door; this is the one you could have accessed from the front office where you found the Pulse Grenades (detailed previously). Now head back up to the middle Control Room, take the other exit door, and wander to the door on the south wall leading to the Forge.

 Valuable Junk

 Stimpaks and Narcotics

 Ammo Box Ammunition

 Nikola Tesla and You +1 Energy Weapons (when read).

A FINGER FIRMLY ON THE PULSE

Use scientific know-how at this terminal to cripple the out-of-control robots in this chamber.

A more stealthy way to deliver a crippling blow to the Mechanist's metal friends is to quietly unlock the door in the front office, and (optionally) use Sneak to creep up the stairs to the middle Control Room. Then move along the upper gantry (you may have been tagged by the turrets by this time), and enter the small manager's office, near the Forge door. There's ammo in the filing cabinets and desk, but the real prize is in the small safe.

 With a reasonable **Lockpick** skill, fiddle with the mechanism, and take some Caps, other items, and (importantly), the Sector A Encryption Key.

With a reasonable **Science** skill, you can access the password protected wall terminal to the right of it, shutting down the turrets, reading the management note, but also charging a massive pulse storm! You automatically use the Encryption Key to enter the code; the one already in the terminal's system is incorrect. After a few moments, a massive burst of electrical energy surges through the building! All robots in the Pulse Chamber are toasted (but not the ones in the Pod Bay)! Now you can visit the Forge.

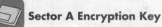 **Sector A Encryption Key**

FORCING FORWARD TO THE FORGE

PLAN A: PICKING LOCKS AT THE ELEVATOR

Pick the lock, move through the enclosed corridor, and this is the view of the Mechanist's Lair; he's on your right.

This plan is viable only if you have a good **Lockpick** skill. Move to the elevator doors, and begin fiddling with the lock. You can do this without investigating either Sector A or B at all. Succeed, and you step through into a rusting entrance chamber; rummage in the Metal Boxes and Filing Cabinets for some minor ammo additions. Then head down the L-shaped corridor, and into the Mechanist's hiding spot.

PLAN B: BREWING COFFEE IN THE BACK OFFICE

This assumes you maneuvered through most, if not all, of the Robot Repair Center. Without Lockpick skills, or if you fail Plan A, move to the Forge Door, and open it. This leads to the back office.

The Mechanist has lived up to his name; he's created a cunningly convoluted way to reach him. He's on your left.

There's a fallen Protectron, which you can raid for Energy Cells, but all other objects in this chamber are broken or empty, except for that Coffee Brewer. Activate it, and the red corrugated wall slides back, revealing a set of cogs and gears. Activate the Door Gear, and the cogs spin back, revealing an additional four security measures that all rotate open. This small secret corridor leads right to the Mechanist's hiding spot!

A MEETING WITH THE MECHANIST

> **Note**
>
> When viewing the Mechanist, the following plans differ depending on whether you've checked out or fought with the AntAgonizer. These specific tactics are noted.

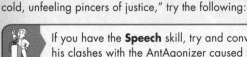

Settling down Scott: He's much harder to convince than his nemesis, but it's still possible for him to reveal all.

Approach the Mechanist, who's at his work bench. "Speak now citizen, or I'll be forced to detain you until I can ascertain your true motives!" he cries. Respond with any of the following:

The "Unmasked Alter Ego" Response: Tell him that you're here to talk and find a peaceful outcome. After he spouts on about "the scaly claw of tyranny being destroyed by the cold, unfeeling pincers of justice," try the following:

> If you have the **Speech** skill, try and convince him that his clashes with the AntAgonizer caused more trouble for Canterbury Commons than when it was just one nutcase terrorizing the area.

> If you have the **Child at Heart** perk, you can play on his idealism, and he agrees to give up his harmful ways.

Use this knowledge now, and he takes off his costume, leaves his base, and wanders the Wastes. You may even see him later in your wanderings. You can murder Scott "Bean" Woliniski (the alter ego) now, but you lose Karma.

 The Mechanist's Costume

 The Mechanist's Helmet

> **Note**
>
> This is available only if you haven't already conversed with the AntAgonizer.

 **The "Mechano-Lad Is Born" Response**: Tell him you're here to rid the world of the AntAgonizer. You have one additional chance to stop the conversation (if you want to side with the AntAgonizer, visit her, or stall this quest). Or, agree again, and you're christened "Mechano-Lad"! Just then, the AntAgonizer raids the base; follow the Mechanist, and make sure you bear the brunt of a Giant Worker Ant's attacks. Open the elevator doors, and defend the Mechanist from a quartet of Worker and Soldier Ants, plus the AntAgonizer's nasty Ripper attacks.

 **AntAgonizer Lair Key**

The AntAgonizer's Costume

Ripper

The AntAgonizer's Helmet

> **Note**
>
> The AntAgonizer's Lair Key allows you to unlock the Sewer Grate; the quick and top entrance to her lair.

After the combat, speak with the Mechanist again, and he orders you to give him the AntAgonizer's outfit. Remove it from the corpse and give it to him. By staying on friendly terms, you're then rewarded with a special laser weapon: the Protectron's Gaze! He then departs. If you're more threatening, he agrees to leave regardless, but without giving you the gun. If you try cold-blooded murder now, you're left with two superhero outfits, but no gun!

 Protectron's Gaze

The "Man-handing the Mechanist" Response: If this bucketheaded psychotic has driven you into a rage, simply keep threatening him, and begin to battle, backing away from his Laser Pistol fire. The Protectron in the corner of the room activates for this battle, too; so deal with it (you can try shooting its Combat Inhibitor so it goes haywire). The Mechanist's outfit isn't the strongest armor around, so you should defeat him easily. Loot the corpse, then return to Canterbury Commons.

 **Laser Pistol**

The Mechanist's Helmet

The Mechanist's Costume

> **Note**
>
> This is available only if you have already conversed with the AntAgonizer, ideally looting her corpse and keeping her costume.

APPENDICES — COMPLETION — TOUR — MISC. QUESTS — MAIN QUEST — BESTIARY — TRAINING

The "Outfit Outreach" Response: If you have the AntAgonizer's suit, the Mechanist demands you hand over her costume as proof that his adversary is dead. The following options now become available:

You can agree, receive the Protectron's Gaze, and let him be on his way.

You can refuse, and he activates his Protectron minder, and combat begins.

 You can succeed in a **Speech**, and negotiate for him to leave while keeping the suit.

NEW OBJECTIVE
"Report back to town for your reward" begins.

Now return to Canterbury Commons. If you didn't use the elevator, you can access the doors from the Mechanist's side, so escaping the Robot Repair Center is straightforward.

FANFARE FOR THE CANTERBURY COMMONS MAN

Find Uncle Roe wandering the main street or in the City Hall, and inform him of your superhuman heroics.

Return to Canterbury Commons, and explain what you've done to Ernest "Uncle" Roe (he rewards you when one or both superheroes are dead or dismissed). If by some chance Roe is dead, locate Derek to claim your prize. Your quest is now complete, and the traders return; this is a good spot to return to if you're in need of supplies. If you have a high Repair skill, the Forge's Work Bench is an exceptional place to fix or build weapons and armor.

QUEST REWARDS

You receive the following rewards from Ernest "Uncle" Roe:

 Bottle Cap (400 total)
if Speech was successful at start of quest and both superheroes were stopped.

 Bottle Cap (200 total)
if Speech wasn't employed at start of quest and both superheroes were stopped.

 Ant's Sting
if you fought the Mechanist and brought his outfit to the AntAgonizer.

 Protectron's Gaze
if you fought the AntAgonizer and brought her costume to the Mechanist.

 AntAgonizer's Costume
if you fought her and kept the outfit. +1 AGL and -1 CHA plus Armor benefits when wearing the costume. The helmet simply has Armor benefits.

 The Mechanist's Costume
if you fought him and kept the outfit. +1 END and -1 CHA plus Armor benefits when wearing the costume. The helmet simply has Armor benefits.

 300 XP

Optionally fight crime as the Bizarro-world hero "The AntMechanist." Your special powers? The ability to instantly look foolish.

 Tip

Do you favor Melee combat, or Energy weapons? If it's the former, side with the AntAgonizer (and end up with the Ant's Sting). If it's the latter, side with the Mechanist (and end up with the Protectron's Gaze). You can collect one, but not both.

Also try wandering the Wasteland in either superhero costume. You may be accosted...by a small child (see Mini-Encounter 4 on page 254)!

The Wasteland Survival Guide

Inside Craterside Supply in **Megaton [8.03]**, meet Moira Brown. She speaks very rapidly and excitedly about her pet project: the Wasteland Survival Guide. Like many guide authors, she's a little eccentric. After asking you to provide a foreword about your life in Vault 101, she asks whether you'll help test the other theories and ideas behind this book. She presents her hypotheses one at a time, allowing you to choose which task to pursue. Travel the Wastelend (to the **Super-Duper Mart [9.01]**, **Minefield [3.09]**, **Tepid Sewer [9.07]**, the **Anchorage War Memorial [9.06]**, **Rivet City [9.15]**, the **RobCo Production Facility [7.10]**, and the **Arlington Public Library [9.18]**) to complete the tasks and help Moira finish her guide. Once you've finished a task, your services are rewarded with a prize, plus a bonus offering if her instructions are carried out to the letter. You can also provide responses dependent on your favored S.P.E.C.I.A.L. Abilities. Unless you convince Moira otherwise, after nine separate tasks, the guide is complete, and handed out to survivors across the Wasteland.

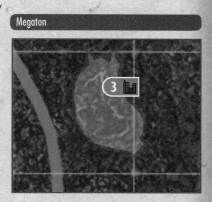

Megaton

QUEST FLOWCHART

	MAIN PATH 1	MAIN PATH 2	OPTIONAL PATH 1
Main Characters	Moira Brown, Bannon, Vera Weatherly	Moira Brown, Arkansas, Bannon, Vera Weatherly, Belle Bonny, Seagrave Holmes, Mr. Pinkerton, Scribe Yearling	Moira Brown
Locations	Megaton, Super-Duper Mart, Minefield, Tepid Sewer, Anchorage War Memorial, Rivet City, RobCo Production Facility, Arlington Public Library		Megaton
Adv. Items/Abilities	Strength, Perception, Endurance, Charisma, Intelligence, Agility, Explosives, Lockpick, Medicine, Science, Sneak, Speech, Robotics Expert		Speech
Possible enemies	Raider, Protectron, Radroach, Mole Rat, Mirelurk Genus		None
Karma Influence	Negative	Negative	Negative

CHAPTER 1.1

Locate Moira Brown's Craterside Supply Store, and speak to her. Begin work on the Wasteland Survival Guide.

• Armored Vault 101 Jumpsuit

Find Food in the Super-Duper Mart.

Locate Food in either refrigerator

• Food

[Optional] Find medicine in the Super-Duper Mart.

Open Pharmacy Door by hacking or lockpicking	Open Pharmacy Door by using the Key
	• Super-Duper Pharmacy Key

• Pharmacy Supplies, Health and Chems

Return to Moira.

Convince Moira to give up on the book and become a trader

Give Moira an Answer (Lie, Standard, Snide, Smart, Tough, or Sly)

• Iguana Bits

Give Moira an Answer (Standard, Snide, Smart, Tough, or Sly)

• Bonus Awarded: Food Sanitizer

CHAPTER 1.2

Contract radiation sickness (200 rads).

Science: Explain radiation to Moira

Locate a radiation source

[Optional] Contract more severe radiation sickness (600 rads).

Locate a radiation source

• Advanced Rad Poisoning (200 rads)

• Critical Rad Poisoning (600 Rads).

Color code: Objective | Action | Rewards

Continued on next page

Continued on next page

TRAINING — BESTIARY — MAIN QUEST — MISC. QUESTS — TOUR — COMPLETION — APPENDICES

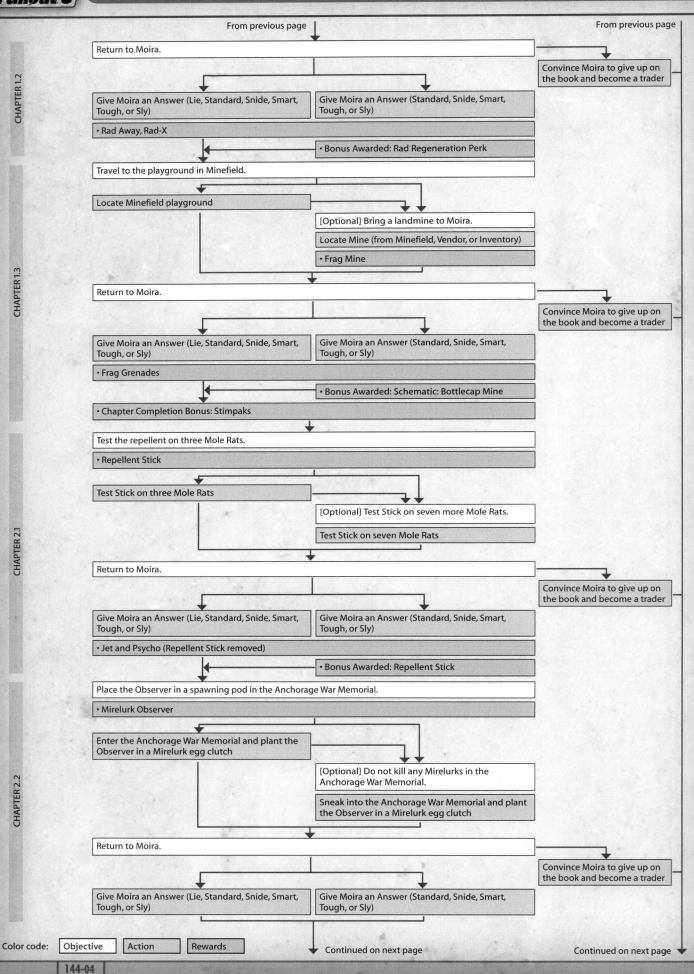

From previous page ↓   From previous page ↓

CHAPTER 1.2

Return to Moira.

Convince Moira to give up on the book and become a trader

Give Moira an Answer (Lie, Standard, Snide, Smart, Tough, or Sly)

Give Moira an Answer (Standard, Snide, Smart, Tough, or Sly)

• Rad Away, Rad-X

• Bonus Awarded: Rad Regeneration Perk

CHAPTER 1.3

Travel to the playground in Minefield.

Locate Minefield playground

[Optional] Bring a landmine to Moira.

Locate Mine (from Minefield, Vendor, or Inventory)

• Frag Mine

Return to Moira.

Convince Moira to give up on the book and become a trader

Give Moira an Answer (Lie, Standard, Snide, Smart, Tough, or Sly)

Give Moira an Answer (Standard, Snide, Smart, Tough, or Sly)

• Frag Grenades

• Bonus Awarded: Schematic: Bottlecap Mine

• Chapter Completion Bonus: Stimpaks

CHAPTER 2.1

Test the repellent on three Mole Rats.

• Repellent Stick

Test Stick on three Mole Rats

[Optional] Test Stick on seven more Mole Rats.

Test Stick on seven Mole Rats

Return to Moira.

Convince Moira to give up on the book and become a trader

Give Moira an Answer (Lie, Standard, Snide, Smart, Tough, or Sly)

Give Moira an Answer (Standard, Snide, Smart, Tough, or Sly)

• Jet and Psycho (Repellent Stick removed)

• Bonus Awarded: Repellent Stick

Place the Observer in a spawning pod in the Anchorage War Memorial.

• Mirelurk Observer

CHAPTER 2.2

Enter the Anchorage War Memorial and plant the Observer in a Mirelurk egg clutch

[Optional] Do not kill any Mirelurks in the Anchorage War Memorial.

Sneak into the Anchorage War Memorial and plant the Observer in a Mirelurk egg clutch

Return to Moira.

Convince Moira to give up on the book and become a trader

Give Moira an Answer (Lie, Standard, Snide, Smart, Tough, or Sly)

Give Moira an Answer (Standard, Snide, Smart, Tough, or Sly)

Color code: Objective   Action   Rewards

Continued on next page ↓   Continued on next page ↓

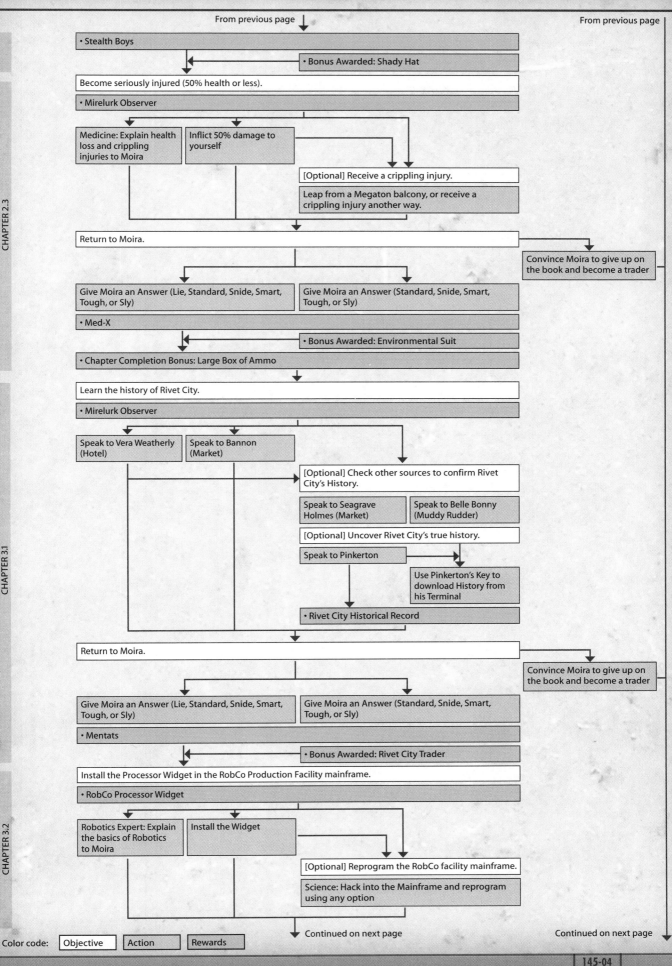

CHAPTER 2.3

- Stealth Boys

- Bonus Awarded: Shady Hat

Become seriously injured (50% health or less).

- Mirelurk Observer

Medicine: Explain health loss and crippling injuries to Moira

Inflict 50% damage to yourself

[Optional] Receive a crippling injury.

Leap from a Megaton balcony, or receive a crippling injury another way.

Return to Moira.

Convince Moira to give up on the book and become a trader

Give Moira an Answer (Lie, Standard, Snide, Smart, Tough, or Sly)

Give Moira an Answer (Standard, Snide, Smart, Tough, or Sly)

- Med-X

- Bonus Awarded: Environmental Suit

- Chapter Completion Bonus: Large Box of Ammo

CHAPTER 3.1

Learn the history of Rivet City.

- Mirelurk Observer

Speak to Vera Weatherly (Hotel)

Speak to Bannon (Market)

[Optional] Check other sources to confirm Rivet City's History.

Speak to Seagrave Holmes (Market)

Speak to Belle Bonny (Muddy Rudder)

[Optional] Uncover Rivet City's true history.

Speak to Pinkerton

Use Pinkerton's Key to download History from his Terminal

- Rivet City Historical Record

Return to Moira.

Convince Moira to give up on the book and become a trader

Give Moira an Answer (Lie, Standard, Snide, Smart, Tough, or Sly)

Give Moira an Answer (Standard, Snide, Smart, Tough, or Sly)

- Mentats

- Bonus Awarded: Rivet City Trader

Install the Processor Widget in the RobCo Production Facility mainframe.

- RobCo Processor Widget

CHAPTER 3.2

Robotics Expert: Explain the basics of Robotics to Moira

Install the Widget

[Optional] Reprogram the RobCo facility mainframe.

Science: Hack into the Mainframe and reprogram using any option

Continued on next page

Continued on next page

Color code: Objective | Action | Rewards

TRAINING — BESTIARY — MAIN QUEST — MISC. QUESTS — TOUR — COMPLETION — APPENDICES

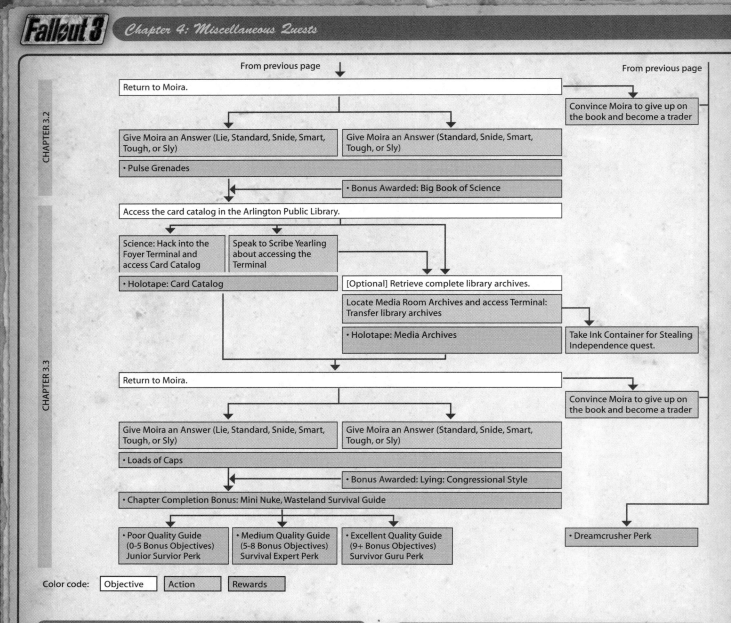

CHAPTER 3.2

Return to Moira.

Convince Moira to give up on the book and become a trader

Give Moira an Answer (Lie, Standard, Snide, Smart, Tough, or Sly)

Give Moira an Answer (Standard, Snide, Smart, Tough, or Sly)

• Pulse Grenades

• Bonus Awarded: Big Book of Science

Access the card catalog in the Arlington Public Library.

Science: Hack into the Foyer Terminal and access Card Catalog

Speak to Scribe Yearling about accessing the Terminal

• Holotape: Card Catalog

[Optional] Retrieve complete library archives.

Locate Media Room Archives and access Terminal: Transfer library archives

• Holotape: Media Archives

Take Ink Container for Stealing Independence quest.

CHAPTER 3.3

Return to Moira.

Convince Moira to give up on the book and become a trader

Give Moira an Answer (Lie, Standard, Snide, Smart, Tough, or Sly)

Give Moira an Answer (Standard, Snide, Smart, Tough, or Sly)

• Loads of Caps

• Bonus Awarded: Lying: Congressional Style

• Chapter Completion Bonus: Mini Nuke, Wasteland Survival Guide

• Poor Quality Guide (0-5 Bonus Objectives) Junior Survior Perk

• Medium Quality Guide (5-8 Bonus Objectives) Survival Expert Perk

• Excellent Quality Guide (9+ Bonus Objectives) Survivor Guru Perk

• Dreamcrusher Perk

Color code: | Objective | Action | Rewards |

VISITING MISS BROWN, IN TOWN

Your quest starts in the sunken hole of an unexploded atom bomb: Megaton. There are numerous corrugated sheets of metal with the town's name daubed on it for you to follow en route to the entrance, with its sliding defense panels, and Protectron guard: Deputy Weld.

Initially bewildering, the route to Craterside Supply is right at the grazing Brahmin, and up, over the Clinic.

You can talk with Sheriff Lucas Simms, begin **Miscellaneous Quest: The Power of the Atom**, or wander around Megaton engaging in conversations, but when you're ready, follow the signposts. You can see the letters "SUPPLY" protruding from a rusting airplane cockpit; follow this to the shack underneath with the words "The Craterside Supply" scratched above the door. Make sure you visit between 8 a.m. and 8 p.m., or the place will be closed.

 Tip

Before you meet Moira, don your Vault 101 Jumpsuit (the Laser Pistol is purely optional); these help you strike up an initial conversation, and grab an initial prize.

Locate the red-haired woman with the RobCo Jumpsuit inside Craterside Supply, who introduces herself as Moira Brown. She runs the place, but what she really does is some tinkering and research (a Work Bench across from her proves this point). She's heard you're from the Vault, and she's very interested in using your story as a foreword for her book all about the Wasteland. Do you have a comment? Answer in the affirmative (or don't, and stop the quest), then choose your favored response about your time in Vault 101, and let Moira know. The truth is optional. Whatever your response, you're

Moira is a strategy guide author: diligent, hardworking, and providing a valuable service... a truly spectacular human being.

awarded an Armored Vault 101 Jumpsuit from Moira, for your troubles.

Armored Vault 101 Jumpsuit

Moira notes down your foreword, and asks if you'd be interested in helping her write a *Wasteland Survival Guide*. Answer in the affirmative, and the quest begins. You're her assistant, here to test her theories. She's beginning with the first chapter, and wants to write about where it's safe and unsafe to find food, the dangers of radiation, and using landmines for fun and profit. Refuse, and the quest remains in stasis until you choose an area you want to help her with.

You now have a series of objectives to undertake. Each has an optional bonus objective to complete, too. You are able to give Moira Standard (straightforward and to the point), Snide (humorous and nasty), or Attribute-based responses to each of her tasks. The responses available depend on whether you complete just the basic objective, or the basic and the bonus objectives. There are three types of Attribute-based responses:

[7+] A "smart" response: Highbrow and detailed.

[7+] A "tough" response: Physical and blunt.

[7+] A "sly" response: Charming and manipulative.

The types of answers you choose influence the specific bonuses of your final reward (the Survival perk). Check page 158 for all the information.

Tip

Moira Brown is writing nine entries, covering three chapters, in her *Wasteland Survival Guide*. You can complete the Chapter 1 entries in any order. However, all three entries (1.1, 1.2, and 1.3) must be finished before you can begin the next chapter, and so on. Each "entry" has a regular and optional aspect to it. The "optional" aspect is harder to achieve and isn't necessary, but it adds to the quality of the final guide.

CHAPTER 1.1: SUPER-DUPER FOOD FORAGING

MEETING THE BASIC REQUIREMENTS

Choose Moira's first option (the location of safe and unsafe food-stuffs), and you're given a Pip-Boy map location to travel to: the Super-Duper Mart. Tool up with some armor and your preferred Raider-killing weaponry, and

There's Super-Duper devastation, roving Raiders, and a severe food shortage to contend with here.

leave Megaton, traveling roughly east. The remains of the Washington Monument make a good landmark to follow. After you pass the water tower, the Super-Duper Mart is just ahead and below you.

NEW OBJECTIVE
"Find food in the Super-Duper Mart" begins.

NEW OBJECTIVE [OPTIONAL]
"Find medicine in the Super-Duper Mart" begins.

Train your weapon on a few Raiders who are roaming the forecourt and parking lot in front of the entrance; they've jazzed up the Mart's awnings with strung-up bodies to announce that this is a Raider stronghold. Set upon the enemies. Remember that you can fire on the vehicles so they catch fire and blow up, ideally hitting a Raider with splash damage. When the outside enemies are taken care of, check the Nuka-Cola machine, and enter the northern doors, which are closer to your food.

Amid the gloom and violent Raider scum is a small fridge bearing delicious comestibles. Bring these back!

Tip
If you're low on ammo, or want to employ stealth, use Sneak (and optionally, a Stealth Boy or two) to enter and exit this place without being spotted.

Enter the Super-Duper Mart, moving from the entrance area into the huge Mart floor itself. Make a swift right turn (this can be done without attracting the attention of the Raiders patrolling the ground and on top of the shelves). Leap over the desk near the intercom, and quickly rummage through a bunch of Energy Cell ammo, a Bottlecap Mine, and some Laser Pistols. Your real prize however, is the contents of the Food Storage refrigerator. There's a second fridge sitting in one of the waist-high freezers in the wide aisle at the back of the Mart. Open it up, and grab the Blamo Mac and Cheese, Noodles, and Salisbury Steaks. You can now return to Moira with it.

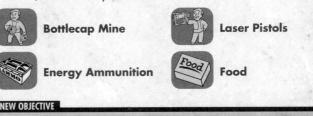

Bottlecap Mine **Laser Pistols**

Energy Ammunition **Food**

NEW OBJECTIVE
"Return to Moira" begins.

MEETING THE OPTIONAL REQUIREMENTS

The Pharmacy isn't open to the general public, unless you're sporting the "post-apocalyptic punk" look.

Don't leave yet. there's still the optional part: obtain medicine from the Mart. The area to investigate is across the Mart's rows of scattered shelving, slaying Raiders as you go. You can tread on top of the shelves, but you're a bigger target. Instead, use the shelving as cover, and continue to the opposite corner of the Mart, where a high concentration of Raiders are holed up. Ideally,

TRAINING — BESTIARY — MAIN QUEST — MISC. QUESTS — TOUR — COMPLETION — APPENDICES

head west, jump the counter, and battle your way south, through a small rear corridor to the pharmacy entrance.

There are a lot of Ammo Boxes to raid and dropped weapons to snag, but no medicine on the store floor. Instead, you need to break into the Pharmacy storeroom, which is sealed from this side. Three possible options are available:

 Use your **Science** skill to hack into the terminal next to the door and unlock the door from the list of menu commands.

Or, if you have a slightly higher **Lockpick** skill, you can break a few Bobby Pins and open up the door via the lock itself.

Or, locate the Super-Duper Pharmacy Key hidden in one of the three metal boxes in the center western alcove, north of the Pharmacy door. The box is on the counter next to the table with the Bottlecap Mine, and unlocks the door without a skill check.

 Super-Duper Pharmacy Key

Once inside the Pharmacy storeroom, begin a slow, methodical ransack of the masses of Metal Boxes, Ammo Boxes, and other crates. Among the debris are some extremely useful and important items; on the back desk is a Mini-Nuke, Frag Grenades, and a load of Ammo Boxes. On the wall is what you came for: Pharmacy Supplies inside the First Aid Box. Empty this, which completes the objective. Then check the northern wall; amid the Chems and Blood Packs are crates of Nuka-Cola Bottles, and (much more importantly) three bottles of Nuka-Cola Quantum! These are invaluable! Grab (but don't drink) them; there are only 90 in the entire Wasteland.

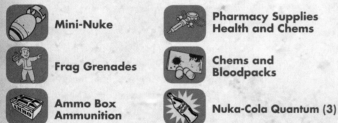

Mini-Nuke

Pharmacy Supplies Health and Chems

Frag Grenades

Chems and Bloodpacks

Ammo Box Ammunition

Nuka-Cola Quantum (3)

Nuka-Cola Quantum bottles are vital to **Miscellaneous Quest: The Nuka-Cola Challenge**. Do not consume them!

Before you go, hack into the terminal by the locked RobCo Pod. You can choose to start a Maintenance Program. Moments later, the pod opens, and a Protectron trudges out. It slowly wanders out onto the storeroom floor, where it gets easily overwhelmed and destroyed by any remaining Raiders! You can fight with the Protectron, shoot it, or flee while the Raiders are preoccupied. Once outside, you can instantly Fast Travel back to Megaton, and meet back with Moira.

MEETING WITH MOIRA

Return to Moira, and speak to her specifically about your recently completed task. The following dialog options are open to you:

 You can wait 24 game hours from the moment you received the objective, return to Moira, and lie to her about what you found.

Or, you can choose to answer in the following manner:

Standard: Tell her you found the Raiders and robot, and the Mart is no place to scavenge.

Snide: Or, you can give her a rather sarcastic remark about the party atmosphere down at the Mart.

Or, you can give an Attribute-based reponse. Three are available if you completed just the basic objective, and three if you completed the bonus objective.

 [7+] Smart (Basic Objective)
[7+] Smart (Bonus Objective)

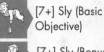 [7+] Sly (Basic Objective)

 [7+] Tough (Basic Objective)

[7+] Sly (Bonus Objective)

[7+] Tough (Bonus Objective)

Whatever your answer, Moira is most thankful for your help, and gives you some Iguana Bits from a shipment she just received. If you completed the optional objective, you receive a Food Sanitizer, which automatically activates. When you're ready to complete the next part of Chapter 1, agree to it with Moira.

 At this point, you can also (via **Speech** persuasion) convince Moira that she's wasting her time writing this book, and she should simply become a trader instead. The quest ends if you're successful.

Iguana Bits
(amount depends on your level at the time of completion)

Food Sanitizer
+20% HP regained for eating any food.

Note: Sanitizer Instructions

CHAPTER 1.2: CONTEMPLATING CONTAMINATION

MEETING BOTH REQUIREMENTS

Come on in, the water's…slowly dissolving your mutated innards.

When you want to help Moira figure out just how long a human can survive exposure to the radiation that plagues the Wasteland's landscape, agree to this objective. You have the following options:

 If you have a high **Science** skill, you can explain to Moira exactly how the human body reacts to this type of radiation. The short answer: not well. Attempt this if you're not interested in the optional reward.

Or, you can agree to test Moira's theories out in the field. She only needs you to irradiate yourself with a radiation rating of 200 rads. However, if you're willing to really get sick, she'd love a specimen to observe with 600 rads of poisoning, or more!

NEW OBJECTIVE
"Contract radiation sickness (200 rads)" begins.

"Contract more severe radiation sickness (600 rads)" begins.

Although you're putting yourself at extreme risk, this part of Chapter 1 is actually rather easy to accomplish. Just outside of Craterside Supply, in the middle of town, is a half-submerged A-bomb lodged into the crater it made years ago. The town's sewage also deposits into this pool, and the resulting mass gives you a light bathing of radiation when you step into it. Stand here, and expect a +2 Rad/Sec affliction. This means that to claim the basic rewards, just stand in the water for 200 or 600 seconds. That's 3:34, or 10:00 minutes of real time waiting. Or, you can simply drink the bomb water and speed up this process.

NEW OBJECTIVE
"Return to Moira" begins.

Caution

Naturally, you can also traverse the landscape and gradually increase your radiation level, but you may be far from Moira when you receive Critical Rad Poisoning. It also takes longer than 10 real-time minutes to reach another radiation hot-spot, wade around, and return. Make sure you still have radiation poisoning when you return to Moira.

MEETING BACK WITH MOIRA

When you've reached "Advanced Rad Poisoning" (one segment beyond the second stage in your rad poisoning meter), you've completed the basic objective.

When you've reached "Critical Rad Poisoning" (at three stages in your rad poisoning meter), you've completed the optional objective.

Return to Moira. Moira is giddy with the results you're giving her. Give a Standard, Snide, or Attribute-based response:

	[7+] Smart (Basic Objective) [7+] Smart (Bonus Objective)
	[7+] Tough (Basic Objective) [7+] Tough (Bonus Objective)
	[7+] Sly (Basic Objective) [7+] Sly (Bonus Objective)

No matter what the response, she begins her "experimental tricks." After you wake up, Moira removes your rad poisoning and awards you with some radiation Chems as a way of saying thanks. If you completed the optional objective, she pulled out all the experimental stops, and accidentally left you with the Rad Regeneration Perk. When you're ready to complete the last part of Chapter 1, let Moira know.

 RadAway
(amount depends on your level at the time of completion)

 Rad-X
(amount depends on your level at the time of completion)

 Rad Regeneration Perk
When suffering from Advanced Radiation Poisoning, crippled limbs automatically regenerate.

CHAPTER 1.3: MINE, ALL MINE

MEETING BOTH REQUIREMENTS

Moira needs to make a little money, and she knows that landmines are a danger she can benefit from researching, and you know you can profit from. Disarming mines before they explode, then selling them, is an excellent way to bring in the Caps. Moira's heard about a ghost town that the traders call Minefield because of the large number of unexploded mines lying around. You're tasked with investigating the area, locating the playground in the middle of the booby-trapped place, and coming home with a mine memento, if you can deactivate one without crippling yourself, or worse.

NEW OBJECTIVE
"Travel to the playground in Minefield" begins.

NEW OBJECTIVE [OPTIONAL]
"Bring a landmine to Moira" begins.

Use a mixture of darting from cover to cover, a Stealth Boy, or simple running and retreating to avoid the sniper fire.

Minefield is a long trek across the Wasteland traveling in a roughly northerly direction. Detour northeast if you hit a dangerous area or impassible rocks. Keep on trekking until you spot the cluster of ruined buildings in the distance. Although it is tempting to head straight up the main road of Minefield, try sidestepping left (west), to a road on slightly higher ground that runs parallel, and finally bends around to meet the lower street. There are fewer hazards up here.

 Look on the road for a circular Frag Mine, and quickly stoop and deactivate it when you hear it ticking. The greater your **Explosives** skill, the longer you have to deactivate each mine before it explodes. Only one mine needs to be deactivated and picked up.

Or, if Minefield is just too far away, simply return to Moira with a mine; you could have picked it up anywhere, or even bought it from a store; she won't know the difference!

Continue along the upper road, moving quickly down and onto the playground, until your objective updates as you near the swings. Shrug off any sniper fire from the lone gunman atop the ruined concrete structure to the northeast. Then go back the way you came, and Fast Travel back to Moira, once you've reached a safe spot, away from Arkansas's sniper fire.

 Frag Mine

NEW OBJECTIVE
"Return to Moira" begins.

Tip

Arkansas is the lone gunman in this area. He's set up in a great vantage point and plugs away at trespassers. Resist the temptation to shoot back or hunt him down and kill him. There's a Slaver bounty on his head, and if you can mesmerize him, affix a Slaver Collar around his neck, and instruct him to run to Paradise Falls, you stand to make some real Caps. Check **Miscellaneous Quest: Strictly Business** for all the information.

MEETING BACK WITH MOIRA

Return to Moira, and talk to her about your light-footed Minefield experience. The following dialog options are open to you:

You can wait 24 game hours from the moment you received the objective, return to Moira, and lie to her about what you found.
Standard: Tell her the truth, there's a crazy sniper at this death trap.
Snide: A smart mouth may be hilarious to you.
Or, you can give an Attribute-based response:

[7+] Smart (Basic Objective)

[7+] Smart (Bonus Objective)

[7+] Tough: (Basic Objective)
[7+] Tough: (Bonus Objective)

[7+] Sly: (Basic Objective)
[7+] Sly: (Bonus Objective)

No matter what the answer is, Moira is excited about how her book is progressing; she might even give you a co-author credit! You're given some Frag Grenades, and if you finished the optional objective, Moira reveals Schematics for creating the ultra-powerful Bottlecap Mine. After telling you the chapter's almost written (there's just the section on how to cook rat properly), she hands you some Stimpaks to patch yourself up with, and you can start Chapter 2.

Frag Grenades
(amount depends on your level at the time of completion)

Schematic: Bottlecap Mine
At a Work Bench, combine Lunch Box, Cherry Bomb, Sensor Module, and 10 Bottle Caps.

 Stimpaks
(amount depends on your level at the time of completion)

CHAPTER 2.1: WHACK-A-MOLE RAT

MEETING THE BASIC REQUIREMENT

Take one branch with green goo at one end, and connect it with Mole Rat heads. The results are...unexpected.

The second chapter of Moira's guide is mostly about the mutated creatures that roam the Wasteland, and how they live. The first involves the Mole Rat. Due to a Mole Rat's burrowing tendencies, which can be annoying

or cause the ground to become unstable, Moira has crafted a chemical Repellent Stick. Before she writes the recipe in her guide, she needs to field test it on three Mole Rats. For the optional objective, Moira suggests you travel downtown, to the Tepid Sewers, where there's a high concentration of Mole Rats.

 Repellent Stick

NEW OBJECTIVE
"Test the repellent on three Mole Rats" begins.

NEW OBJECTIVE [OPTIONAL]
"Test the repellent on seven more Mole Rats" begins.

The initial part of the task is straightforward. Head out of Megaton brandishing the Repellent Stick, turn left (southwest), and search the rocky, debris-filled area west of Megaton, below the freeway overpass remains, for your initial pack of Mole Rats. Swing your stick at each one. It strikes, and a few seconds later, the Mole Rat's head explodes in a shower of greasy chunks. Moira won't be happy with those field results! When you've tested this out on three Mole Rats, you can return to Moira.

NEW OBJECTIVE
"Return to Moira" begins.

MEETING THE OPTIONAL REQUIREMENT

To complete the optional task, you need to test the Repellent Stick on seven additional Mole Rats. The way Moira recommends is to locate the Tepid Sewer in the D.C. Wasteland, which is near one of the Georgetown Metro Stations. Travel east from Megaton, and enter the Tepid Sewers from the metal door near the water.

 Tip

Employ your Pip-Boy's Hot Key function, so that you can quickly switch between the Repellent Stick (for Mole Rat combat) and your preferred weapon (for attacking anything else).

Once inside the Tepid Sewers, engage any Mole Rats you can. The problem here is that Raiders are also exploring this area, and they've massacred most of your test subjects. Carefully edge along the labyrinth of corridors and Metro tunnels, taking each opportunity to strike a Mole Rat, while using other means to tackle the Raiders. When 10 Mole Rats have exploded, you can return to Moira.

Dog-sized, hairless vermin are a dime a dozen down at the RobCo Production Facility.

Although you can continue with other quests, remembering to bring out your Repellent Stick whenever you encounter a Mole Rat, another, better plan is to leave Megaton, and journey southwest across the Wastes, using the Tenpenny Tower skyscraper as a landmark. You're heading to the factory adjacent to the tower, which has a large RobCo sign on it. Enter this place, and begin systematically clearing the interior, which is filled with Radroaches and Mole Rats. Naturally, switch to another weapon when you're killing Radroaches. Why is this a preferred plan? Because you need to return to this facility later in the quest (chapter 3.2), and prior knowledge of the layout (and dealing with threats before you return) is a better use of your time and resources.

MEETING BACK WITH MOIRA

Head back to Craterside Supply, and speak to Moira about her decapitation stick. The following dialog options can be chosen:

 You can wait 24 game hours from the moment you received the objective, return to Moira, and lie to her about what you found.

Standard: Tell Moira the truth, that her weapon is less of a repellent, and more of a "Massacre Stick."

Snide: Or, you be slightly less understanding about her aversion to harming the creatures, which she doesn't take kindly to.

 [7+] Smart (Basic Objective)
[7+] Smart (Bonus Objective)

 [7+] Tough (Basic Objective)
[7+] Tough (Bonus Objective)

 [7+] Sly (Basic Objective)
[7+] Sly (Bonus Objective)

When you've answered the questions, Moira tells you to hold onto the Repellent Stick (only if you complete the optional objective here), and (if you tested the stick on 10 Mole Rats) she also gives you the leftover Chems used to make the repellent. You can progress to either of the next two parts of the chapter.

Repellent Stick
One hit, instant kill to Mole Rats.

Jet
(amount depends on your level at the time of completion)

Psycho
(amount depends on your level at the time of completion)

CHAPTER 2.2: THE MIRELURKING HORROR

 Tip

It might be wise to explore the Anchorage War Memorial first, to get the lay of the land. You can whittle down the Mirelurks without killing all of them, and chart a path to the spawning pods. Also make sure you have at least three Stealth Boys before you agree to this objective.

MEETING BOTH REQUIREMENTS

When you're ready to spend time crouched in a damp tunnel, inches away from gigantic Mirelurk pincers, all in the name of scientific discovery, talk to Moira about her next harebrained scheme. She needs you to Sneak into the Mirelurk lair at the Anchorage War Memorial and plant an Observer in one of their spawning pods. She also hopes you can contain your bloodlust, leaving all

Mirelurks alone. Attacking them could ruin the validity of the study! Take the Observer and leave town. The Anchorage War Memorial is near the Potomac River. Trudge there, or Fast Travel to an adjacent area, such as Dukov's Place or one of the Georgetown Stations.

Finding a Mirelurk spawning ground is relatively easy; head to the Anchorage War Memorial.

 Observer

NEW OBJECTIVE
"Place the observer in a spawning pod in the Anchorage War Memorial" begins.

NEW OBJECTIVE [OPTIONAL]
"Do not kill any Mirelurks in the Anchorage War Memorial" begins.

Use **Sneak** throughout this objective, if you want to remain in one piece, with the Mirelurks none the wiser.

Be very, very quiet. You're trying not to get your arm mangled by these mutated crustaceans!

Use the entrance pictured previously, rather than the tunnel entrance, because it is easier to complete the objectives from this direction. Enter the tunnel stairs. Stay straight, ignoring the corridor to your left (west). Continue down and left to the door with the red lights at the base. Before you open this door, Sneak, use a Stealth Boy, and keep your Pip-Boy's Flashlight off and your gun out (so you can see whether you're still cloaked or not). Enter a hub room, with doors and stairs, and a prowling Mirelurk (or Hunter if you're at a higher level). Sneak around the Mirelurk without alerting it, heading east to the Door to Anchorage Memorial Facility Bay.

Once you're through to the Facility Bay, make a clockwise circle around the outside of the chamber, which is open to the spawning pools below. Continue around the perimeter until you're heading south, and creep down the stairs in the floor. Turn right immediately, as you're at the flooded area. To the north stands a Mirelurk (or Hunter), although he may be waddling around. Ensure that your Stealth Boy is on, then move toward the gantry bridge, turn and head west, and look for an opening in the railings to your right.

You're looking for a Mirelurk Egg Clutch like this one to stick your Observer into.

Land in the water, and wade a couple of feet to a Mirelurk Egg Clutch. You're prompted to hide the observation device inside the spawning ball. Do so, and then retreat out of this place. Use the metal steps in front of you, then turn and head east, while still Sneaking or using the Stealth Boy, and head north, up the stairs, across to the hub room, and back out to the memorial. If you're caught by Mirelurks on the way out, you can (and should) outrun them and still claim both objectives.

Tip

Did it all go horribly wrong, and you were spotted? Then flee this area, back out to the D.C. Wasteland, and re-enter it. Both objectives can be retried.

NEW OBJECTIVE

"Return to Moira" begins.

MEETING BACK WITH MOIRA

Trek back to Craterside Supply, and converse with Moira about your frightening outing under the War Memorial. The following options are available:

Standard: Tell Moira about your experiences and give out correct information; that the Mirelurks are definitely vicious and highly territorial. This doesn't give you a bonus.

Snide: Or, you can fib and explain that they've got a little bubbling castle that they spend all day circling. It doesn't grant a bonus.

 [7+] Smart (Basic Objective)

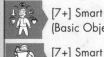 [7+] Smart (Bonus Objective)

 [7+] Tough (Basic Objective)
[7+] Tough (Bonus Objective)

[7+] Sly (Basic Objective)
[7+] Sly (Bonus Objective)

Once you've responded, and assuming you didn't fire a shot at any Mirelurk (it doesn't matter if you're spotted; only that you didn't fight them), Moira suggests they should be avoided, and awards you with Stealth Boys to ensure that you can in the future. If only she'd given them to you earlier! Complete the optional objective, and a rather natty Shady Hat is all yours.

At this point and from now on, you can also (via a **Speech** persuasion) convince Moira again that she's not cut out to be an author, and should concentrate on trading instead. The quest ends if you're successful.

 Stealth Boy
(amount depends on your level at the time of completion)

 Shady Hat
+1 Perception, +5 Sneak.

CHAPTER 2.3: A PAINFUL LESSON

MEETING BOTH REQUIREMENTS

Next up in your co-authoring capacity are some bench tests Moira wants to run on you when you've been injured: badly injured. The next time you're hobbling around, close to death, think of Moira, and return to her shack so she can stitch you up and observe your girlish screams. Naturally, there are easy ways and hard ways of completing both objectives:

NEW OBJECTIVE

"Become seriously injured (50% health or less)" begins.

NEW OBJECTIVE [OPTIONAL]

"Receive a crippling injury" begins.

If you have a high **Medicine** skill, you can explain how health loss and crippling injuries work to Moira, and complete both the regular and optional objectives without self-harm.

Otherwise, you can crawl around the Wasteland looking for something to injure you, which is highly unwise. Instead, try heading outside, moving up to Moriarty's Saloon, then leaping over the flimsy iron railing, and landing on the shack roof of the Children of the Atom's church. This isn't the painful part; that comes after you peer over the edge and look at the A-bomb in the radioactive pool below. Now jump off, and land by the bomb, aiming for the water, which is ankle deep. This almost always cripples a leg, and solves both objectives! Now drag yourself back to Moira before you pass out.

NEW OBJECTIVE

"Return to Moira" begins.

MEETING BACK WITH MOIRA

Meanwhile, back at Craterside Supply, the increasingly zany Moira studies your injuries, and asks how you feel:

Standard: Tell the truth. Your fear of death is counterbalanced by the adrenaline rush you're experiencing. Or it could be terror.

Snide: Or you can murmur under your breath about a vicious payback on your co-author.

 [7+] Smart (Basic Objective)
[7+] Smart (Bonus Objective)

 [7+] Tough (Basic Objective)
[7+] Tough (Bonus Objective)

 [7+] Sly (Basic Objective)
[7+] Sly (Bonus Objective)

Once Moira has scarred you for life with her inventive stitching, she hands over two rewards: Med-X if you simply returned with half-health or less, and an Environment Suit if you crippled yourself as well. Chapter 2 has come to a close. Are you ready to research Chapter 3? If so, you're awarded a giant box of ammunition, just in case your research takes a turn for the horrific.

Med-X
(amount depends on your level at the time of completion)

 Environment Suit
AR 6, Rad Resistance +30%, +5 Medicine Skill.

Ammo (amount and type depends on your level at the time of completion)

CHAPTER 3.1: A RIVETING HISTORY

MEETING THE BASIC REQUIREMENT

Moira's last chapter has taken a turn for the more esoteric, and the research she needs is mainly about the back-ground and forma-tion of Rivet City, the gathering of lost archival materials, and even tinkering

Your history lesson begins by boarding this gigantic rust-bucket. Mind your manners here!

with elderly robot technologies. Any can be chosen. This section involves finding out the origins of Rivet City. It's the most successful survivor settlement of all, but nobody knows how it started. When you're ready, head out into the D.C. Wasteland, and move to the southeast corner. You can't miss Rivet City; it's the gigantic iron air-craft carrier rusting in the harbor east of the Jefferson Monument.

NEW OBJECTIVE
"Learn the history of Rivet City" begins.

Note

You may have visited Rivet City a number of times during the Main Quest or a Miscellaneous Quest. Be mindful of your previous activities. If you gunned down everyone, you may not think you'd be able to finish this quest; however, you can if you find the City Founders Log in Pinkerton's Private Computer, in his hideaway in the Broken Bow. Or, you can just lie! You may wish to complete this portion of the quest during **Main Quest: Scientific Pursuits.**

Once you're aboard, you can begin conversations with any of the inhabitants. Most clue you in on four members of Rivet City who have a better knowledge of the boat than them. They are Vera Weatherly (owner of the hotel bearing her name), Bannon (a provider of fine clothing in the Marketplace), Seagrave Holmes (another Marketplace vendor), and Belle Bonny (manager of the basement bar, the Muddy Rudder). Run into any of them at their workplace, usually during daylight hours.

Speak with Bannon, (usually at Potomac Attire in the Marketplace) and ask about Rivet City's history. Bannon tells you he was personally responsible for setting up the settlement 12 years ago.

With a quick **Speech** challenge, Bannon admits the boat has been moored here far longer than 12 years, but that there wasn't much to the place before he boarded.

You can also continue without a Speech challenge. If you're after ancient history, he suggests you visit "that old crone" Belle Bonny.

Or, speak with Vera Weatherly, (usually at the hotel bearing her name) and ask about Rivet City's history. Vera tells you she doesn't know that type of information. She suggests you speak with Seagrave Holmes, who's been living on the boat since he was a boy.

When you finish speaking with either of these Rivet City patrons, you complete the basic requirements for this quest. You can return to Moira, or complete a new (and optional) objective:

NEW OBJECTIVE [OPTIONAL]
"Check other sources to confirm Rivet City's history" begins.

Track down Seagrave Holmes (either at Rivet City Supply in the Marketplace, or his bunk), and ask him about the history of the place. He's been constantly keeping the boat from collaps-ing since he could walk, and the only other feller he can remember from all those years ago was Mr. Pinkerton. He left Rivet City a decade ago, though, after a spat with the science team. He directs you to the Broken Bow of the vessel, where Pinkerton kept a storage chamber. This might have some evidence on the origins of the vessel.

Head down to the basement, and follow the signs for the Muddy Rudder pub. Running the place is Belle Bonny, who can impart some information:

In this **Speech** challenge, you can request that Bonnie regale you with a story.

You can also keep going with information about Bannon, who told you he organized the entire place himself.

Bonnie scoffs at Bannon's tall stories, and tells you to speak with Mr. Pinkerton, who's holed up in the Broken Bow of the vessel.

When you complete your chat with either Seagrave or Bonnie, a new (and optional) objective starts:

NEW OBJECTIVE [OPTIONAL]
"Uncover Rivet City's true history" begins.

Tip

It might be wise to combine your next move with the conclusion of *Miscellaneous Quest: The Replicated Man.*

Exit to the Flight Deck, or the entrance, and jump into the water, swimming roughly southwest. Switch on your Pip-Boy's Flashlight, then swim down to the entrance between the two parts of the boat. Open the door, swim forward to the room half-filled with debris. Continue in a south-southwest direction through the open door. Ignore the open hatchway to the left (unless you're desperate for air), and continue to open the bulkhead door ahead. This leads to some underwater gantry steps and a sliver of air you can inhale to avoid drowning. Turn southeast, unlock the underwater bulkhead door, then surface in the same spot again.

With a lungful of air, swim southeast, and surface in a water-logged chamber. Move to the next chamber through a half-sub-merged doorway, and clamber onto the dry corner near an open doorway that leads to a debris-filled blockage, and a possible Mirelurk assailant. Spin around and look northwest; you should spot gantry stairs (on the far left of the previous picture) that lead up to the dry deck of this vessel. Climb to the top, and peer around; there should be a vent with the number "7" etched onto it.

You can investigate the adjacent chamber of the boat, or continue to Pinkerton.

TRAINING — BESTIARY — MAIN QUEST — MISC. QUESTS — TOUR — COMPLETION — APPENDICES

Quickly open the hatch door, and check out the adjacent room. Search this chamber; there's a First Aid Kit, two Ammo Boxes full of .44 Magnum rounds along with the gun itself, and an exit bulkhead door. Deactivate a Frag Mine and collect the Magnum and Ammo on the table to the right of the door, then flick the lever so you can come and go into the Broken Bow from the rusting gangplank near the Jefferson Memorial.

 .44 Magnum and rounds   **First Aid Kit items**

The exit chamber, in the opposite direction from Pinkerton's hidey-hole, is still worth trekking to.

Head roughly southeast down the corridor, then duck down, and open the bulkhead door on your right. This allows you to enter an item-filled room without being shot in the chest by two Rigged Shotguns. Deactivate the Frag Mine, grab the Purified Water, and open the Ammo Box with more Frag Mines inside.

Purified Water   **Frag Mines**

Deactivate the Shotguns or duck and exit, turn southeast, heading to a blocked gantry staircase, and a wandering Mirelurk. Back completely out of this room to start combat, as seeping gas causes the chamber to be engulfed in flame and burn you. When the Mirelurk meets its match, continue to the door and open it; there's little here to grab, so move southwest into a refuse-strewn room. The door ahead is sealed; don't make the mistake of accessing the booby-trapped terminal to the right of the door. Instead deactivate the trap on the rear panel, or ignore it. Open the door by activating the switch on the northeast wall behind you.

The reclusive Pinkerton is ready to reveal the real history of Rivet City. Or, his version, at least.

Enter Pinkerton's chamber, and locate the man himself. He's initially reluctant to talk to a "topsider" like yourself. Lightly pressure him to spill the beans and he helps you, if only to set the record straight. It began 40 years ago, when the remnants of the Naval Research Institute cleared Mirelurks off the shipwreck, looking for lab space. The Science Lab was the result, and the team was led by H. Pinkerton, the man you're speaking with. That was, until 18 years ago when Doctor Li began her work on Project Purity, and the staff sided with her. He hands you the Rivet City Historical Record and Rivet City Council Minutes as proof. If Pinkerton is dead for some reason, check his corpse; it holds a key to unlock his private computer, where you can obtain the same information.

 Rivet City Historical Record   **Rivet City Council Minutes**

NEW OBJECTIVE
"Return to Moira" begins.

MEETING BACK WITH MOIRA

Your sleuthing work is over for the moment. Back at Craterside Supply, wow Moira with your Rivet City knowledge:

 You can wait 24 game hours from the moment you received the objective, return to Moira, and lie (using **Speech**) that Rivet City is the remains of an ancient underwater civilization.

You can tell Moira the truth, depending on whether you obtained the initial information from Bannon, or all the information from Pinkerton:

Standard.
Snide: Sarcasm has its place.

 [7+] Smart (Basic Objective)   [7+] Tough (Basic Objective)

[7+] Smart (Bonus Objective)   [7+] Tough (Bonus Objective)

[7+] Sly (Basic Objective)

[7+] Sly (Bonus Objective)

When you've replied to Moira's questioning, she gives you some Mentats for future actions involving your wits. If you uncovered the entire history from Pinkerton, you receive a bonus discount every time you buy and sell in Rivet City, thanks to Moira's favorable review of their stores in her tome. Your penultimate chapter challenge awaits; what shall it be?

 Mentats
(amount depends on your level at the time of completion)

 Rivet City Trader Bonus
Anyone in Rivet City grants you a 10% discount for buying, and 10% improvement in selling. This doesn't apply to medical services, renting a room, or other types of trade.

CHAPTER 3.2: TOYING WITH ANTIQUATED TECHNOLOGY

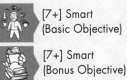 *Note*
You may have already visited and cleared the enemies from the RobCo Facility during Chapter 2.1.

MEETING THE BASIC REQUIREMENT

Moira explains she's recently been traded a RobCo Processor Widget, and according to the seller, if it's attached to the mainframe at the RobCo Facility, all the robots inside could be reprogrammed to obey your command! Take the RobCo Processor Widget, agreeing to the following objective, and set off for the facility. Exit Megaton, and head southwest across the Wasteland, tackling the odd pack of Raiders, and (at higher levels) a wandering Sentry Bot or Robobrain or two. Continue, using Tenpenny Tower as a landmark, and the facility is nearby. It has massive "ROBCO" lettering on it that you can't miss.

 If you have the **Robotics Expert** perk, you can forgo your outing to the RobCo Facility, and instead use your knowledge by explaining the basics to Moira. You are awarded the basic and optional rewards for imparting such wisdom.

RobCo Processor Widget

NEW OBJECTIVE

"Install the Processor Widget in the RobCo production facility mainframe" begins.

Head around to the remains of the parking lot, and face north; the only door into this facility is here. Enter it, and begin to traverse the maze of chambers, bays, and offices making up this factory. The entrance foyer has some display model Protectrons. They aren't functional, so ignore them. You can enter the small storage room and office to the northwest, and rummage around for some Ammo Boxes, and check behind the front desk, while fending off Radroaches and Mole Rats. However, you must progress by heading east, onto the factory floor.

If you stay at ground level, you can head east, into an adjacent chamber where there's a collection of broken terminals and factory computers. This isn't the mainframe, but there's some First Aid on the interconnecting wall, and Ammo Boxes in the connecting chamber. Your way forward is up the gantry steps, then east, through an L-shaped connecting passage, before turning right. You're above the ground floor computer terminals. Continue east, and you can see a door ahead of you. This is where you must go. However, you can head south into another L-shaped passage that connects you to a third factory floor. This leads down to a Work Bench area, and a ground-level connecting passage. Ignore this unless you're exploring; you want that Door to Offices and Cafeteria.

Ammo Box Ammunition

First Aid Box Health and Chems

This is the all-powerful computer mainframe you're readying your Widget for.

The offices and cafeteria level can be a flummoxing maze, but not if you follow these directions (and if you're not interested in the Ammo, Health, and other items scattered about in the ancillary parts of this building).

Step into the recreation room, and open the door on the left (east), next to the Protectron pod. This leads to a short, winding tunnel, infested with Radroaches. Open the door at the opposite end, step through and turn left (south) if you want to slay more Mole Rats and Radroaches in the dead-end office.

A better plan, if you're not systematically destroying the vermin inside this structure, is to turn right (north), and run around the left corner to the stairs. Climb them, expecting more Mole Rats to waylay you. The mainframe chamber is directly ahead (north), through the door. Pick the First Aid Box lock, and grab the Stealth Boy from the table. Although the computer terminal inside the mainframe is locked, the Widget fits in without any Science skill being needed. Moira's trader was wrong, as you might have expected; the Widget turns all of the Protectrons in the building hostile!

Stealth Boy

First Aid Box Health and Chems

NEW OBJECTIVE [OPTIONAL]

"Reprogram the RobCo facility mainframe" begins.

MEETING THE OPTIONAL REQUIREMENT

Alert! All Protectrons are now hostile! Before you have time to think, destroy the Protectron that's clanking its way out from the pod in the mainframe chamber. Once it has been destroyed, you can complete the optional part of this outing:

> This terminal has a Hard lock on it, so use your **Science** skill to hack into the mainframe computer you just inserted the Widget into, and you're greeted with these relevant options:
>
> • Orientation Guide: This tells you about the two relevant programming routines you can load into the facility's Protectrons.
> • Basic Operation: This cannot be activated because the power supply to the facility isn't large enough.
> • Initiate/Cease Pest Extermination: This causes all Protectrons to activate and begin to attack the Mole Rat and Radroach infestation. This is an excellent plan, and one that rewards you with the optional objective.
> • Initiate/Cease Total Liquidation: This causes all Protectrons to attack anything on sight; you, other Protectrons, and the infestation!
> • Initiate/Cease Stress Testing: This causes all Protectrons to attack each other.

NEW OBJECTIVE

"Return to Moira" begins.

The best plan is to Initiate Pest Extermination and Cease Total Liquidation. (Although any option you choose will satisfy your objective, these two options will make things easiest on you.) This enables you to head back the way you came without fighting the Protectrons, and you can watch them zap the Mole Rat and Radroach menace. Retrace your steps back to the Wasteland, and then trek all the way to Moira at Megaton.

MEETING BACK WITH MOIRA

After attaching the Widget and reprogramming the Protectrons, tell Moira all about your adventure:

> Standard: Tell Moira the truth, that the robots became docile once you reprogrammed them.
> Snide: Or, tell Moira you caused massive robotic carnage.
>
>
> [7+] Smart (Basic Objective)
> [7+] Smart (Bonus Objective)
>
> [7+] Tough (Basic Objective)
> [7+] Tough (Bonus Objective)
>
> [7+] Sly (Basic Objective)
> [7+] Sly (Bonus Objective)

Any answer is fine, so long as you completed both objectives. She recommends that you carry some Pulse Grenades in the future; these deactivate anything robotic with a single explosion. She gives you some, and (if you completed the optional objective) hands over the *Big Book of Science*, a helpful tome that you should instantly locate in your Pip-Boy's inventory and read. Your final task now awaits you.

TRAINING — BESTIARY — MAIN QUEST — MISC. QUESTS — TOUR — COMPLETION — APPENDICES

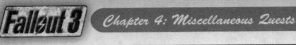
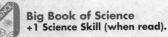

Pulse Grenades
(amount depends on your level at the time of completion)

Big Book of Science
+1 Science Skill (when read).

CHAPTER 3.3: DANGER AND THE DUODECIMAL SYSTEM

Tip

You may wish to read one of the optional objectives in *Miscellaneous Quests: Stealing Independence* and *The Nuka-Cola Challenge* before you embark on the assault inside the Arlington Public Library. You can search for the critical items in both quests during this one outing. The optional objectives for these two other quests are noted here, too.

MEETING THE BASIC REQUIREMENT

Your final field investigation takes place here, at the dilapidated Arlington Public Library.

For your final task, Moira tells you a little bit about "books." Apparently, these receptacles are where the old world kept knowledge, and there's a library stacked full of them in Arlington. The computer records found inside would be invaluable, and you're to download them to your Pip-Boy. Moira prefers that you find the archives, but even the card catalog would be useful; perhaps the information contained within could help rebuild humanity. When you are ready for this task, agree to it, and leave town.

NEW OBJECTIVE
"Access the card catalog in Arlington Public Library" begins.

NEW OBJECTIVE [OPTIONAL]
"Retrieve complete library archives" begins.

An excellent idea is to Fast Travel to Mason District South Station, or Rivet City. Both locations are relatively close to the Arlington Public Library. You're looking for the tall, imposing Georgian structure with the decaying columns.

All hail the Brotherhood of Steel! They provide valuable help as "bullet sponges" in the assault to come!

There is only one entrance, but watch the streets to the south of the building. There's a well-armed and dug-in squad of Talon Company Mercs, and they're as mean as they are tough. Circumvent them, and enter the entrance foyer. Hold your fire! This area is under the protection of the Brotherhood of Steel!

The Paladins on patrol don't say much, but Scribe Yearling, dressed in her red robe, is more talkative, providing you with information, and even asking you to help her locate books for her own records (a Freeform Quest detailed on page 393 of this book). She can also pinpoint the library archives on your Pip-Boy, which is

handy. Move toward the curved main desk, and move to the check-in station terminal.

It is a simple matter to hack into this terminal using **Science** (remember to quit out before your third attempt, so you can hack again without penalty), and bring up the main menu. Two options are worth noting: Access Card Catalog and Access Library Archives. The first option should be highlighted and completed. Due to signal disruption, the second option is unavailable.

 Card Catalog Holotape

Tip

If you speak with Scribe Yearling, she grants you the password for the front terminal. If she's dead, you could always lie about completing this to Moira.

MEETING THE OPTIONAL REQUIREMENT

Tip

To reach a computer that can access library archives, you need to head up and into this building, which is overrun by Raiders. Brotherhood Paladins are clearing this zone; join them in eliminating the Raider threat! The following route is preferred, but is only one way to travel and doesn't show any side chambers, which can also be investigated.

Follow the radio chatter and bravado of the Brotherhood Paladins, if you haven't explored this building already, and stay on the ground floor, moving west through the doorway between the two staircases. Turn south, ignoring the restrooms, and follow around, and into another large foyer, where a fierce firefight flares up. Don't just stand there—offer fire support to the Paladins. The longer they last, the safer you are!

When the fracas is over, check the Raiders and upstairs for items, but to progress, stay on the ground floor, move to the northwest corner of the second foyer, through the doorway, and open the Door to Arlington Library Media Archive.

Climb the stairs, and venture south down a corridor, avoiding the annoying baseball-pitching machine, which announces your arrival to a trio of hilariously coiffed Raider scum that need to die screaming. When the threat has subsided, check the side chambers for items, move past the pitching machine, and up the stairs to the next floor. At the top of these stairs, turn southwest, and open the door opposite, just right of the headless corpse on the mattress. This leads to more stairs heading up. You can head back here in a moment.

First though, head east down the corridor, backing up or deactivating the Frag Mines laid as a trap at your feet, and turning left at the corner. You have just enough time to dive into a storage room with a Turret Control Terminal.

Take down gimp-boy, then all his friends, and locate an antique Ink Container; a future quest may depend on it!

Use your **Science** skill to hack into the terminal, turning off the turrets in the media room to the north.

Or, you can grin and burst through the double doors, into the media room, blasting the Raiders inside, and shooting out both turrets, or ignoring them if you deactivated them. Once the Raider threat is temporarily nullified, head into the room, moving counterclockwise around the perimeter. On the north wall near two Ammo Boxes is a Metal Box labeled "Restoration Supplies" on your Pip-Boy when you move close to it. Open this up, and take the following:

Ink Container

 Note

This Ink Container is vital for completing an optional objective in **Miscellaneous Quest: Stealing Independence**. Don't sell it or throw it away; keep it safe!

Now let's concentrate on the current quest: Leave the media room and head through the door, southward down a rubble-strewn corridor. Turn right, moving into a collapsed room. You can use the ceiling of this room as a ramp to run up to the upper floor. Beware of Raiders in the connecting chambers, here. Open the door to the west.

If you head south, into the Children's Archive, you can collect books for the Squire, battle Raiders, and collect items. However, for this quest, move through the door to the west, into a wrecked chamber. Grab health from a First Aid Box, then head south toward a barrel and blocked-off corridor. An opening on your right leads to a second Media Room. Brandish your weapon, and slaughter the remaining Raider force in here. Once you're done, there are two areas of interest in this chamber.

First Aid Box Health and Chems

The first is the terminal in the middle of the room. Don't confuse this with the terminal in the corner that opens the safe, giving you some Caps and other items. This one is called the Arlington Public Library Terminal. When you hack in, choose the "Transfer Library Archives" option, and all the records are downloaded onto your Pip-Boy in seconds. Your optional (and final) objective is over!

Media Archives Holotape

NEW OBJECTIVE
"Return to Moira" begins.

The second is on the small circular table in the southwest corner of the room. Hidden behind two artfully placed skulls is a Nuka-Cola Quantum, a must-have item if

you're undertaking the Nuka-Cola Challenge quest! Grab this, but don't sell, drink, or otherwise dispose of this bottle because a lunatic woman living under a freeway craves this concoction!

MEETING WITH MOIRA ONE LAST TIME

Retrace your steps, all the way to the D.C. Wasteland outside the library, and Fast Travel to Moira, revealing that the final chapter of her guide can be completed. Try one of the following:

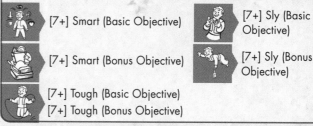 You can wait 24 game hours from the moment you received the objective, return to Moira, and lie to her that the library is a hole in the ground.

Standard: You can actually complete the task, and tell her you found both the library, and (if you did both tasks) the archives.

Snide: Or, you can completely fabricate a story about librarians, and bringing her a present, but say you forgot your library card.

[7+] Smart (Basic Objective)

[7+] Smart (Bonus Objective)

[7+] Tough (Basic Objective)
[7+] Tough (Bonus Objective)

[7+] Sly (Basic Objective)

[7+] Sly (Bonus Objective)

Your answers may matter to the overall quality of the book, but whatever response you give, Moira is very excited at your help, and rewards you with a load of Caps, as well as a book.

At this point, you can once again convince Moira that she's wasting her time writing this book, and she should simply become a trader instead. The quest ends if you're successful.

 Caps
(amount depends on your level at the time of completion)

Lying: Congressional Style
+1 Speech (when read).

THE *WASTELAND SURVIVAL GUIDE*

Here's the finished guide. What will those who wander the Wastes think of your hard work? You find out soon enough!

Your deadline has been met, and Moira only needs to add the final touches before she's ready to print and distribute! You're given a Mini-Nuke that's been giving her the creeps, and fortunately, she's got traders she can rely on to help distribute the guide to survivors everywhere! Moira's excitement is almost infectious no matter how badly or well you performed the 18 different objectives she requested, but—as is always the way with strategy guides—the readers soon give their own responses on the usefulness of your tome! The quest is complete, and you can return to Moira if you need to buy items, make items, or purchase her Rock-it Launcher Schematic.

Mini-Nuke

Wasteland Survival Guide

TRAINING — BESTIARY — MAIN QUEST — MISC. QUESTS — TOUR — COMPLETION — APPENDICES

A QUALITY READ, OR HORRENDOUS RUSH-JOB?

As you may have realized, the care and attention you take in creating this guide affects the final product.

DETERMINING FACTOR	POINTS
Each Basic Requirement met	+0
Each Optional Requirement met	+1
Each time you lie about information	-1
Each time a skill or perk is used to explain a theory, without needing to complete a Requirement	+1
Poor Quality *Wasteland Survival Guide* Produced	5 or less
[+ KARMA] Good Quality *Wasteland Survival Guide* Produced	6–8
[+ KARMA] Excellent Quality *Wasteland Survival Guide* Produced	9+

Note

Random Mini-Encounters depend on the quality of work that was published. Expect a Survival Failure, Survivalist, or Survival Expert sometime in your future.

SURVIVAL PERK

There are 15 variations of this perk, depending on the quality of the finished tome, and the most common style you used to answer the questions.

Junior Survivor

- Fewer than 5 Bonus Objectives completed.
- Standard: +2% Poison Resistance, +2% Radiation Resistance, +5 Health
- Snide: +2% Poison Resistance, +2% Radiation Resistance, +1% Critical Chance
- Smart: +2% Poison Resistance, +2% Radiation Resistance, +2 Medicine, +2 Science
- Tough: +2% Poison Resistance, +2% Radiation Resistance, +2 Damage Resistance
- Sly: +2% Poison Resistance, +2% Radiation Resistance, +2 Sneak, +2 Speech

Survival Expert

- 5–8 Bonus Objectives completed.
- Standard: +4% Poison Resistance, +4% Radiation Resistance, +10 Health
- Snide: +4% Poison Resistance, +4% Radiation Resistance, +2% Critical Chance
- Smart: +4% Poison Resistance, +4% Radiation Resistance, +4 Medicine, +4 Science
- Tough: +4% Poison Resistance, +4% Radiation Resistance, +4 Damage Resistance
- Sly: +4% Poison Resistance, +4% Radiation Resistance, +4 Sneak, +4 Speech

Survival Guru

- 9+ Bonus Objectives completed.
- Standard: +6% Poison Resistance, +6% Radiation Resistance, +15 Health
- Snide: +6% Poison Resistance, +6% Radiation Resistance, +3% Critical Chance
- Smart: +6% Poison Resistance, +6% Radiation Resistance, +6 Medicine, +6 Science
- Tough: +6% Poison Resistance, +6% Radiation Resistance, +6 Damage Resistance
- Sly: +6% Poison Resistance, +6% Radiation Resistance, +6 Sneak, +6 Speech

THE DREAM CRUSHER

At three times during this quest, you can perform a difficult Speech conversation with Moira, and convince her that writing this guide is useless, a waste of time, or that her idealistic goal of "helping humanity" is better spent fixing caravan carts, cleaning up Brahmin droppings, and offering a better service to the Megaton locals. If successful, Moira is heartbroken, but resolved to her new, more mundane life. You receive the Dream Crusher Perk, lose Karma, but can visit Moira for a 30% discount on trading. Her Repair skill also increases significantly, so take items to her if they need fixing.

Dream Crusher Perk

Something about your presence dampens others' desires to excel. While it can be a drag at parties, it has the happy coincidence of lowering an enemy's chance of a Critical Hit on you by 50%. A dull bore is a safe bore.

QUEST REWARDS

This extensive collection of interesting and useful goods is awarded depending on your performance in this quest:

Causing Moira to Quit the Guide
- Dream Crusher Perk

Chapter 1.1
- Basic: Iguana Bits (3–15 depending on your level)
- Optional: Food Sanitizer
- Chapter 1.2
- Basic: RadAway (5)
- Basic: Rad-X (7)
- Optional: Rad Regeneration Perk

Chapter 1.3
- Basic: Frag Grenades (9)
- Optional: Schematic: Bottlecap Mine
- Basic: Stimpaks (7)

Chapter 2.1
- Basic: Repellent Stick
- Optional: Jet (5)
- Optional: Psycho (5)

Chapter 2.2
- Basic: Stealth Boy (6)
- Optional: Shady Hat

Chapter 2.3
- Basic: Med-X (5)
- Optional: Environment Suit
- Basic: Ammo (varies depending on level)

Chapter 3.1
- Basic: Mentats (6)
- Optional: Rivet City Trader Bonus

Chapter 3.2
- Basic: Pulse Grenades (6)
- Optional: Big Book of Science

Chapter 3.3
- Basic: Caps (400)
- Optional: Lying: Congressional Style

Completion
- Basic: Mini-Nuke
- Basic: *Wasteland Survival Guide*
- Basic: Survival Perk (Perk's effect depends on guide's quality and style.)

Those!

A shell-shocked, disheveled boy emerges from the Wasteland and stumbles into your path. He looks at you and manages to blurt out a single word: "Those!" The boy's township—a medium-sized settlement called **Grayditch [9.09]**—was recently attacked by Giant "Fire Ants," and his entire family was killed (along with pretty much all the other inhabitants). You can help revenge the child (named Bryan Wilks) and his loss by locating the Ants' nest and obliterating the menace. After some sleuthing, you learn of a Doctor Lesko, and some breeding experiments he is performing inside the **Marigold Metro Station [9.10]**. After exploring, you run across Lesko, whose befuddlement doesn't allow him to realize the havoc his creations have caused. The doctor then enlists you to halt an out-of-control experiment, and your path leads to a confrontation with the gigantic Queen of the colony. Once the threat has subsided, you can find a good (or horrific) home for Bryan, the young orphan.

Grayditch

QUEST FLOWCHART

	MAIN PATH 1	OPTIONAL PATH 1	OPTIONAL PATH 2	OPTIONAL PATH 3
Main Characters	Bryan Wilks, Fred Wilks, William Brandice, Lug-Nut, Doctor Lesko	Doctor Lesko, Bryan Wilks, Fred Wilks, William Brandice, Lug-Nut	Doctor Lesko, Bryan Wilks	Doctor Lesko, Bryan Wilks
Locations	Grayditch, Marigold Station Tunnels			
Adv. Items/Abilities	Lockpick, Science, Speech, Child at Heart, Entomologist	Lockpick, Science, Speech, Child at Heart, Entomologist	Science	Science
Possible enemies	Fire Ant Genus, Fire Ant Queen			
Karma Influence	Positive and/or Negative			

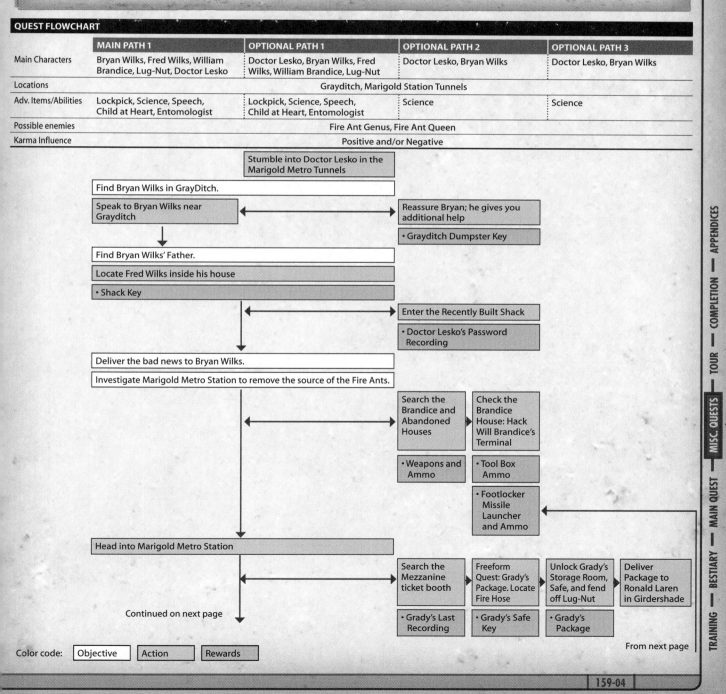

Stumble into Doctor Lesko in the Marigold Metro Tunnels

Find Bryan Wilks in GrayDitch.

Speak to Bryan Wilks near Grayditch → Reassure Bryan; he gives you additional help

• Grayditch Dumpster Key

Find Bryan Wilks' Father.

Locate Fred Wilks inside his house

• Shack Key

→ Enter the Recently Built Shack

• Doctor Lesko's Password Recording

Deliver the bad news to Bryan Wilks.

Investigate Marigold Metro Station to remove the source of the Fire Ants.

Search the Brandice and Abandoned Houses → Check the Brandice House: Hack Will Brandice's Terminal

• Weapons and Ammo → • Tool Box Ammo

• Footlocker Missile Launcher and Ammo

Head into Marigold Metro Station

Search the Mezzanine ticket booth → Freeform Quest: Grady's Package. Locate Fire Hose → Unlock Grady's Storage Room, Safe, and fend off Lug-Nut → Deliver Package to Ronald Laren in Girdershade

• Grady's Last Recording → • Grady's Safe Key → • Grady's Package

Continued on next page

From next page

Color code: Objective | Action | Rewards

TRAINING — BESTIARY — MAIN QUEST — MISC. QUESTS — TOUR — COMPLETION — APPENDICES

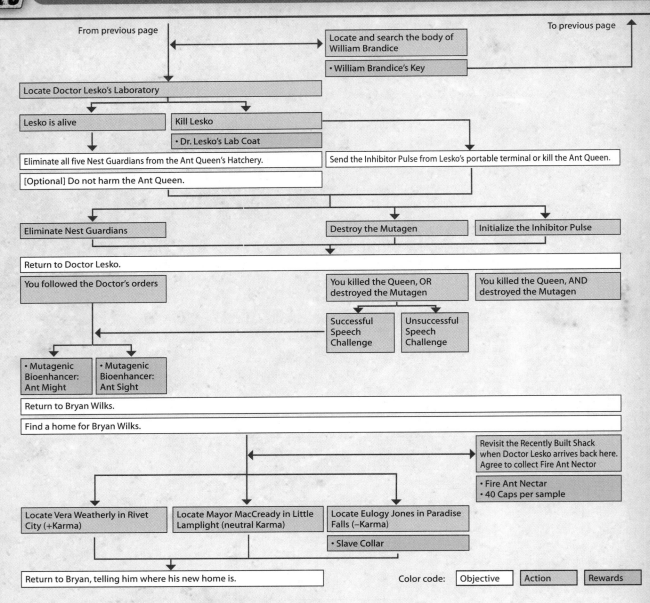

From previous page

To previous page

Locate and search the body of William Brandice
- William Brandice's Key

Locate Doctor Lesko's Laboratory

Lesko is alive

Kill Lesko
- Dr. Lesko's Lab Coat

Eliminate all five Nest Guardians from the Ant Queen's Hatchery.

[Optional] Do not harm the Ant Queen.

Send the Inhibitor Pulse from Lesko's portable terminal or kill the Ant Queen.

Eliminate Nest Guardians

Destroy the Mutagen

Initialize the Inhibitor Pulse

Return to Doctor Lesko.

You followed the Doctor's orders

You killed the Queen, OR destroyed the Mutagen

You killed the Queen, AND destroyed the Mutagen

Successful Speech Challenge

Unsuccessful Speech Challenge

- Mutagenic Bioenhancer: Ant Might

- Mutagenic Bioenhancer: Ant Sight

Return to Bryan Wilks.

Find a home for Bryan Wilks.

Revisit the Recently Built Shack when Doctor Lesko arrives back here. Agree to collect Fire Ant Nectar

- Fire Ant Nectar
- 40 Caps per sample

Locate Vera Weatherly in Rivet City (+Karma)

Locate Mayor MacCready in Little Lamplight (neutral Karma)

Locate Eulogy Jones in Paradise Falls (–Karma)
- Slave Collar

Return to Bryan, telling him where his new home is.

Color code: | Objective | Action | Rewards

AN INSECT INFESTATION: ANT ATTACK!

PATH A: MEETING BRYAN WILKS FIRST

Locate Grayditch on the guide map, and head there. Around a mile away from the outskirts of town (it could be when you near an adjacent locale, such as the Super-Duper Mart to the north or the Scavenger on the bridge to the south, or as you approach Grayditch along one of the thoroughfares), a small child appears and chases you down. His name is Bryan Wilks, and he's scared witless. Here are some beneficial conversation options:

 If you have high enough **Strength**, you can tell Bryan you'll protect him.

If you have a **Speech** skill, you can try to tell Bryan he'll be okay.

This allows you to gain more information about the threat. In this case, the threat is from giant Fire Ants, or as Bryan's father explained

to him: "F–kin' Ants." Bryan's father also knew how to confuse them, by "shooting for their antenner [*sic*]". Keep questioning him, and he reveals he's the last of seven inhabitants, which include a Doctor Lesko, Will Brandice, and his mother and father. More questions yield specific information about each of these individuals.

Bryan finishes by describing his house, which he's too afraid to enter; it's the one closest to the old diner.

 If you succeed in your **Speech** skill, Bryan gives you additional help.

 If you have **Child at Heart**, you can comfort Bryan, and he automatically gives you additional help.

This "help" takes the form of a Grayditch Dumpster Key. With that, Bryan rushes off to hide in the Pulowski Preservation Shelter located next to the diner, and you're free to explore Grayditch. Draw your favored insect-culling weapon, and head into town.

 Grayditch Dumpster Key

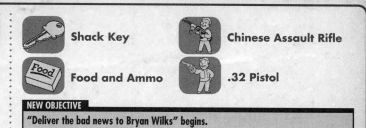
NEW OBJECTIVE
"Find Bryan Wilks's Father" begins.

PATH B: MEETING DOCTOR LESKO FIRST

There is a chance that you may run across Doctor Lesko, a scientist carrying out slightly deranged experiments in the Marigold Metro Tunnels, prior to being waved down by Bryan. This occurs if you're exploring the tunnels (from Falls Church Metro Station, for example) and if you run into the doctor. In fact, you can completely rid the subterranean areas of Fire Ants and resolve the insect infestation before surfacing to find Bryan Wilks. The doctor considers him a nuisance; find the kid in the Pulowski Preservation Shelter and get his side of the story.

NEW OBJECTIVE
"Find Bryan Wilks in Grayditch" begins.

GONE, DADDY, GONE

Have your finest Ant-killing implement handy as you maneuver through the ruined streets. Ideally locate these Fire Ants at range, and blast them to their close attack—a devastating cone of fiery breath—never comes close

Search the rear of this fine dining establishment for an ammo stash. Bryan stays hidden in the adjacent Personal Shelter.

to hitting you; the Hunting Rifle is a good option here. Work your way over to the diner, and the Pulowski Preservation Shelter, which is where Bryan is hiding from this point on. If you met Doctor Lesko before Bryan, speak to the youngster using the dialog choices listed previously. Now head around the back of the diner to a dumpster that requires the key Bryan gave you. Grab the contents if you need them. The type and amount of guns, ammo, grenades, and chems inside depends on your XP level.

Note

Depending on your level of experience, the type of Fire Ants you encounter varies. Three main types roam Grayditch and the tunnels: Workers, Soldiers, and Warriors. Each is tougher than the next. If you want the least trouble tackling these insects, head over here early in your adventure.

Fred's dead: It looks like the "F–king Ants" got to him before help could arrive. Don't forget to search him.

Head east down the main street from the diner. Ignore the shack to your left, and instead look for the door to the end row-house with the large Nuka-Cola advertisement on the outside wall. The door is unlocked. Step inside, and you're greeted by a smattering of dead Ants, some small fires, and the body of Fred Wilks. Take the Shack Key from his corpse, then rummage around the house; there's ammo, two guns, food in the refrigerator, and a queen-sized bed to sleep on if you need it.

 Shack Key   Chinese Assault Rifle

Food and Ammo   .32 Pistol

NEW OBJECTIVE
"Deliver the bad news to Bryan Wilks" begins.

GRAYDITCH RECONNOITER: A GRAY DAY

Step back into the town's street and take care of any additional Fire Ants that you can hear or see; it's worth exterminating them now to clear a safer path for yourself later, and you can collect Fire Ant Nectar in the process. If you wish, search the entire town now for Fire Ants to hunt down, and other evidence and items to help you. First, locate the shack adjacent to the Wilks's residence, and use the Shack Key to get inside. Inside this tiny building is some Abraxo Cleaner, two cans of Turpentine, and Doctor Lesko's Password Recording. Take this, bring up your Pip-Boy, and listen to the message.

Doctor Lesko's Password Recording

This allows you to activate Doctor Lesko's terminal without any issues. Ignore the Robot Pod because no mechanoids are nearby. Highlight the Doctor's Personal Notes (because activating the Science Robot is fruitless). These notes make interesting reading. You'll find out about Batch A27 (a formula that failed to shrink Giants Ants back to regular size), and a good experiment location: the Marigold Metro Station. Your quest log is updated. It looks like this is where the source of the Ants is coming from.

NEW OBJECTIVE
"Investigate Marigold Metro Station to remove the source of the Fire Ants" begins.

> Both the dumpster and the shack door can also be rattled open with a high **Lockpick** skill.

Return to speak with Bryan at any time; he's saddened by the loss of his father, and he demands your promise to stop whatever was responsible. Agree, then continue to search the town. Opposite the Wilks residence is the entrance to the Brandice residence. Search the place for some useful items, including a Frag Grenade between one desk and a wall, a Baseball Bat on the living room shelf, and a liquor cabinet to ransack. Check the bathroom wall for a First Aid Box. There's also a footlocker that needs a special key to open (which you can locate in the Metro Station). The more interesting information is upstairs. If the darkness is scaring you, turn on your Pip-Boy's Flashlight.

> With a good **Science** skill, you can hack into this terminal, and read Will Brandice Senior's entries. There are six to scan through. It charts the general hopelessness he and his wife Sheila felt as the Ants closed in. One entry makes reference to Will leaving a place called Navarro. With some historic knowledge, you may be able to deduce that Will could be an Enclave soldier.

TRAINING — BESTIARY — MAIN QUEST — MISC. QUESTS — TOUR — COMPLETION — APPENDICES

In his third entry, he details a gun he bought at Megaton; it's behind the fridge in a tool box, so be sure to search for it! Entry #5 gives clues that Will Brandice was a wanted fugitive, because he freaks out when listening to Enclave Radio, and President Eden's dulcet tones; he thought President Richardson was still in charge. Once done, collect the weapon, and leave.

.32 Pistol and Ammo	**First Aid Box**
Frag Grenade	**Baseball Bat**

With a favored weapon in hand, begin a thorough inspection of the entire town of Grayditch. There are two main types of building. The first is burnt-out or half-demolished shells that you can move through or up to a second floor (which is great for long-range sniping of Fire Ants). The other consists of two abandoned buildings. Search both thoroughly for Ammo Boxes and First Aid Boxes. The second building also has a Hunting Rifle propped up by the low bookcase on the ground floor. Then navigate the various streets to the collapsed overpass, tear Fire Ants apart at the playground, and continue your eradication.

Ammunition Box	**Hunting Rifle**
First Aid Box	

When you think you've defeated all the surface Fire Ants, it's time to locate Doctor Lesko's laboratory in the Metro Tunnels. Look for the stone city hall building (which you can't enter), and walk to the Marigold Station entrance. Rattle the chain gate open, and head into the turnstile area. There's an Ant to nullify here, and another just after you hop over the turnstiles, before the path splits into two choices as you head on down.

> **💡 Tip**
>
> Are you searching every dead Ant you kill? You should because there's the possibility of collecting Ant Meat and Fire Ant Nectar. The first is a reasonably edible foodstuff, while the second can rake in the Caps in the days after this quest is completed.

NAVIGATING TO THE BLUE LINE

> **💡 Tip**
>
> If you haven't tried this before, now is an exceptional time to make use of your Pip-Boy's Hot Key functionality: Select a great rapid-fire Assault Rifle—style armament, a complement of Frag Grenades, a close-assault Shotgun, a Melee Weapon, and a number of Frag Mines you can lay as you retreat. This way, you can instantly switch weapons without navigating your Pip-Boy's Items Menu.

PATH A: THROUGH THE MAINTENANCE ROOMS

Just after you've hopped over the turnstiles and you're looking south, there are two possible routes to take. The first is the door to the east. This is a more dangerous path, so be sure you have enough ammunition for a fight. Head through the door into a small generator chamber, and pump bullets into a waiting Fire Ant. Head

down the passage, turning south, and stop at the door to a second, longer room. Defeat the Ant, then aim at another; this one is extra-tough, and you might want to back up and lay a Mine. Now search the room; there's the usual detritus, but also some health from a First Aid Box. When you're done, exit via the southwest doorway, onto the Blue Line tracks.

 First Aid Box

PATH B: THROUGH THE MEZZANINE AND DOWN THE ESCALATOR

The alternate route offers an interesting item, and more room to maneuver. Move onto the mezzanine level, and cut down the two roaming Ants. Watch out because one is tougher than the other. After combat is over, search the stall and look on the bench. There's a Holotape to pick up, some ammo, a .32 Pistol and a skeleton (who you deduce is the long-dead Grady) near a Lunch Box. Bring up your Pip-Boy, and in the Notes, highlight Grady's Last Recording. It seems there's a locked chamber with a package inside, hidden somewhere down here. First you need to find Grady's Key. Your Map Marker is updated. Now descend the escalator, head east, and choose the left tunnel if you want to reach the Blue Line track sign and Path A's exit.

 Grady's Last Recording

> **NEW OBJECTIVE [OPTIONAL]**
> **Freeform Quest: "Grady's Package" begins.**

While you're scouting around Marigold Metro Station, make sure you move to the last fenced-off linking corridor between the subway tunnels, just before you encounter Doctor Lesko. A body is propped up against an old generator and the wall here.

These are the desiccated remains of William Brandice, a military man whose terminal diary you may have read. You can tell this corpse is Will's because there's a Laser Pistol, ammunition, and some Ant Meat and Ant Nectar. But the real giveaway is William Brandice's Key; this unlocks a special footlocker back at his house.

Laser Pistol and Ammunition	**William Brandice's Key**

LOCATING DOCTOR LESKO

PART A: THE CONNECTING TUNNELS

Continue east along the Blue Line, or navigate around to the parallel tunnel to the south. For a speedy wander, continue east until you reach the gap in the right side of the tunnel, and prepare for a Fire Ant fight. After the insects are destroyed, check this alcove area between the two tunnels. The corpse has ammo and a scoped .44 Magnum near it, and there's a Nuka-Cola machine to raid as well as a First Aid Box. There's also a Sledgehammer and a Silenced 10mm Pistol to grab. You can head south to check out the maintenance corridor door, or continue east. The tunnel branches to the right. If you continue east, you end up in Falls Church Metro Station, and away from this quest. If you take the branching path to the right, you can locate Grady's Chamber, but you need another key first; ignore this area for the moment.

Weapons and Ammo

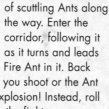
First Aid Box

PART B: INTO THE MAINTENANCE CORRIDORS

Danger! This room has a gas leak! As long as nothing gives off a spark or breathes fire, you're quite safe....

The preferred path (if you're after every valuable item) is to join the parallel tunnel, and move to the maintenance corridor door. Battle a couple of scuttling Ants along the way. Enter the corridor, following it as it turns and leads you to a long maintenance room with a tough Fire Ant in it. Back away at once! There's a gas leak here, and if you shoot or the Ant breathes fire, there'll be a highly damaging explosion! Instead, roll in a Grenade to clear the gas, and then begin the fight.

Grady mentioned hiding a key behind a fire hose before he committed suicide. Look what we found here....

After the Ant is tackled, check for two Frag Grenades in an open locker; don't overlook the door in the eastern wall. It leads to a storage closet and Grady's Fire Hose Box. If you're concerned about this quest, rummage around in the box and uncover Grady's Safe Key, as well as Stimpaks and Ammunition. Grab all you need, then head out of the maintenance room's only unexplored exit.

After descending and turning a couple of times, you reach the lower maintenance room; there are two Fire Ant Soldiers to deal with here, and a load of scattered junk in Metal Boxes. When you've searched enough, continue roughly east to the maintenance corridor exit. From here, you can step across to the opposite doorway leading to the Doctor's Chamber, or move north and across to Grady's Chamber, hidden behind a train carriage.

Note
Check the guide map to find a second connecting area between the two north-south subway tunnels, and some Frag Mines in an Ammo Box: perfect for the combat to come!

Tip
Unlocking the "package" inside Grady's Chamber can be attempted at any time.

Grady's Safe Key

LET'S GO TO LESKO: MEETING THE DOCTOR

Just east and slightly north from the maintenance corridor exit is another closed door. Head there, and you startle a gray-haired man wearing a lab coat. This is Doctor Lesko; if you want the quest to continue, talk to him about his experiments, and try any of the following plans:

"The mutagen caused a bio-defensive reaction metamorphosing the ant's venom glands." In short, the doc's the fire-starter.

Simply remain civil to him, and use your **Intelligence** to realize that the doctor is trying to shrink the Fire Ants back to normal size by lacing their eggs with a mutagen. Do this a second time to admonish the doctor for not using a controlled environment.

Or, you can simply follow along as best you can. The doctor informs you that his experiment caused the Ants to display an unforeseen reaction: the ability to breathe fire. His laboratory is now overrun with a quintet of Nest Guardians and a Queen; if he can reach the Hatchery Chamber he can launch an Inhibitor Pulse, causing the removal of Grayditch's insect problem.

When prompted, respond with "This is a hefty task, Doc. I'm going to need serious incentive" to sway the doctor into giving you his old lab coat, and a Mutagenic Bioenhancer.

If you have a good **Science** skill, you can ask how Lesko got his results so quickly, and he admits he used the F.E.V. in his work. No wonder the Ants have mutated!

When the conversation ends, you should have agreed to dispatch the five Nest Guardians, spare the Queen (although you can always go back on your word), and started to rummage around the lab room for three Ammo Boxes (one is easily unlocked with Lockpick skill), two 10mm Pistols on shelves, a First Aid Box, and some Ant Meat. There's Doctor Lesko's Terminal too, but don't access it unless you're being violent toward the doctor, which isn't advisable yet. Instead, head east out of the Doctor's Chamber, turn south, and move down the subway tracks until the ground falls away and you descend to the Hatchery Door.

Weapons and Ammo

First Aid Box

Has Doctor Lesko been killed, either accidentally or otherwise? If this occurs prior to you resolving the Guardian problem in the Hatchery, you no longer receive the two quest updates below. Instead, a new option appears: Send the Inhibitor Pulse from Lesko's portable terminal or Kill the Ant Queen. Pick one or the other, and don't expect a Mutagenic Bioenhancer!

NEW OBJECTIVE
"Eliminate all five Nest Guardians form the Ant Queen's Hatchery" begins.

NEW OBJECTIVE
OR "Send the Inhibitor Pulse from Lesko's portable terminal or Kill the Ant Queen" begins (if Doctor Lesko is dead).

APPENDICES — COMPLETION — TOUR — MISC. QUESTS — MAIN QUEST — BESTIARY — TRAINING

BUTCHERY IN THE HATCHERY

Step through the Hatchery Door, and into an almost black and extremely winding rock cavern. Switch on your Pip-Boy's Flashlight, and venture slowly forward, learning the layout of the only pathway. You need to be able to quickly back up, because there comes a point where you attract a few of the Fire Ant Nest Guardians. They are even more deadly than the Warrior type. Try dropping a Frag Mine, and slowly back up, lobbing Frag Grenades so each Guardian is peppered with explosives. Then finish with a Hunting or Assault Rifle. Keep this up!

Behold the Marigold Ant Queen: 12 feet of horrific mutation. Either save or savage this behemoth!

Continue edging down the cavern tunnel until you reach a gap to your right. The final Guardians are here, along with a massive Ant Queen! You can keep your word to Doctor Lesko and resist the temptation to strike her; if you do, attract the remaining Guardians, back up the cavern tunnel away from the Queen, and take them down. Make sure all five Guardians are dealt with. As soon as the last one drops, try one of the following options:

Do exactly what the doctor ordered; ignore the main cavern chamber, and return to the doctor, leaving the Ant Queen alone.

Or, kill the Queen as well as the Guardian Ants, then return to the doctor.

 Or, if you have a good **Science** skill, you can hack into Doctor Lesko's Portacomp in the cavern after activating the mutagen tank, and destroy the mutagen.

Or, you can hack into Doctor Lesko's Portacomp and initialize the Inhibitor Pulse without the doctor's help.

No matter what you choose to do, return to the doctor to tell him. Before you leave, grab the *Big Book of Science*, select it in your Pip-Boy, and read it.

 ## Caution

The doctor's Science Protectron is idling around this cavern, waiting for its master. It's is quite harmless unless you shoot it. So don't!

Big Book of Science
+1 Science (when read).

NEW OBJECTIVE
"Return to Doctor Lesko" begins.

LET'S GO TO LESKO

Backtrack to Doctor Lesko's laboratory room in the subway tunnels, tell him you're done, and reveal how well you did, or how badly you screwed up. Navigate the following options:

1. If you did exactly what the doctor ordered:

You receive the Mutagenic Bioenhancer of your choice, and Lesko's Lab Coat (if this second item was agreed upon).

2. If you killed the Queen Ant or you destroyed the mutagen:

 Lesko is furious, and you must reason with him using either your **Science** or **Speech** abilities. If you're successful, the previous rewards are given. If not, you receive nothing.

3. If you killed the Queen Ant and you destroyed the mutagen:

Lesko is hopping mad, and you are denied any sort of prize.

In the case of option 1, the doctor walks down to the Hatchery to begin the pulse initialization; you can follow and watch if you wish.

 Mutagenic Bioenhancer (1 of 2)   **Lesko's Lab Coat**

If you decide to kill the doctor (either before or after completing your Ant antics), you can search his twitching corpse, grab his 10mm Pistol, Ammo, Lab Technician Outfit, a Holotape of Lesko's Portable Terminal Access (which you should listen to), and his Reading Glasses. You can then easily access the terminal in his lab, and read his notes, where his worries are saved in digital format. Once this stage of your quest is over, all the remaining surface Ants in Grayditch go into a frenzy and destroy themselves, thanks to the Inhibitor Pulse.

Caution

Keep that trigger finger off your weapon. Lesko is worth more to you alive than dead. Check the end of this quest for more information.

Note

As soon as the Inhibitor Pulse is executed (by you or Lesko), the Ants in Grayditch are no longer a threat. Don't expect any more on the surface, although they still occupy the Marigold vicinity of the Metro Tunnels.

NEW OBJECTIVE
"Return to Bryan Wilks" begins.

WE INTERRUPT YOUR REGULARLY SCHEDULED QUEST TO BRING YOU...

Meet Lug-Nut, the numb-nut with a fetish for naughty night-attire. He's less enthusiastic about a bullet in the head.

 If you've discovered Grady's Holotape and Safe Key, now's the time to find out what incredible prize he's squirreled away for safe-keeping. Move to the entrance to Grady's Chamber, half-hidden by the subway carriage (but easy to spot because there's a rotating beacon flashing by the entrance).

(continued)

Use either **Lockpicking** or Security (**Science**) to disengage the door, and enter. Aside from some junk, there's a Ripper to grab, as well as a First Aid Box. The real prize though, is locked in Grady's Safe. Use the Key you found in the Metro Station (or Lockpick skill) and claim the Naughty Nightwear!

Ripper

First Aid Box

 Naughty Nightwear

As you're leaving, you're accosted by a Raider called Lug-Nut, who tries to force you to hand the Nightwear over. If you have a high Speech skill, you can tell him to back off in a low growling tone, and he stammers an apology and leaves. Any other outcome results in a fight. Claim any items you want from his corpse. Now take a moment to check your map. Grady's Holotape note should have flagged the hamlet of Girdershade as the location where the "package" needs to be delivered. The Freeform Quest is detailed in the "Tour of the Wasteland" chapter.

THE LIFE OF BRYAN

Backtrack out of the Metro Tunnels, across Grayditch, and north to the diner where Bryan is still hiding in his Pulowski Preservation Shelter. He thanks you with glee at your heroics, and begins to wander the streets if you don't talk to him about finding him a permanent home. He excitedly remarks that he has a cousin Vera who lives on a giant rusting ship called Rivet City.

While you're away looking for his accommodation, he buries his father and cleans up the mess in his house. You now have a choice of endings to this quest:

NEW OBJECTIVE
"Find a home for Bryan Wilks" begins.

1. You can stay in Grayditch, telling Bryan you don't want to look for a home he can move to, and end the quest now (without the Karma bonus or penalty of options 2 and 4).

 2. You can travel to Rivet City, as Bryan suggests, and seek out Vera Weatherly at the Weatherly Hotel. She's more than happy to take Bryan in. Return to Grayditch and tell him; he moves there soon after you depart (you don't need to accompany him). The quest ends.

3. You can journey to Little Lamplight, and meet with Mayor MacCready. Use Speech or Child at Heart to convince him to let Bryan stay with him. Head back to Grayditch, and speak with Bryan; he's moderately happy, and moves to Lamplight. The quest ends.

4. Or, you can befriend the Slavers in Paradise Falls by successfully completing **Miscellaneous Quest: Strictly Business**, gain an audience with Eulogy Jones, and sell Bryan to him! Jones offers 100 Caps, but you can use Speech and raise the price to 300 Caps. Take the Collar from Jones, return to Grayditch, and convince Bryan to wear it. The quest ends, and a little piece of your soul dies.

5. Finally, once you find a home for Bryan, you can visit him and ask how he likes his new life. Depending on where you placed him, is responses range from joyful to heart-wrenchingly less than joyful. If you sent him to Paradise Falls, you won't find him if you try to visit. Perhaps Eulogy sold him?

POST-QUEST ANTICS

BRANDISHING BRANDICE'S BIG GUN

There's a major weapon to grab from the home of the long-dead Will Brandice.

Remember the rotting corpse in the Marigold Metro Station? Be sure you searched the body and uncovered William Brandice's Key. Before you leave Grayditch, return to the Brandice residence, and unlock the footlocker in here.

Inside is a Missile Launcher and Ammunition. Thanks, Will!

Will Brandice's Missile Launcher (and Ammunition)

> **Note**
> There are two Freeform Quests you can complete during this quest: **Nectar Collecting for Fun and Profit** and **Grady's Package**. Details are given at Location [7.05] and [9.09] in the "Tour of the Wasteland" chapter.

QUEST REWARDS

You receive the following rewards for finishing Those! (assuming you followed Lesko's instructions):

Ant Might Perk
+1 Strength, +25% Resistance to Fire.

OR

Ant Sight Perk
+1 Perception, +25% Resistance to Fire.

 Lesko's Lab Coat
+%20 Resistance to Radiation, +%10 Science when worn.

XP 300 XP

The Nuka-Cola Challenge

In the isolated two-hut settlement of **Girdershade [7.06]** resides Sierra Petrovita; Sierra is addicted to good old Nuka-Cola, the odd soft drink that once dominated the beverage market. She's acquired a map showing the location of Washington D.C.'s **Nuka-Cola Bottling Facility [8.10]**; a place she's certain contains the holy grail for Nuka-Cola drinkers everywhere: Nuka-Cola Quantum. This is where you come in: Sierra promises a reward for every intact bottle of Nuka-Cola Quantum you can find. She needs 30 to fill her pristine Nuka-Cola vending machine. After agreeing to become a bottle collector, you run into Ronald Laren, who tries to convince you to sell Quantum to him instead. Scour the landscape, finding Nuka-Cola Quantums wherever you can, and selling them to either of these two nut-balls: Sierra or Ronald. You can even try a swig of the stuff yourself, although it's altogether more profitable to collect than quaff.

Nuka-Cola Bottling Facility

10

QUEST FLOWCHART

	MAIN PATH 1	MAIN PATH 2	OPTIONAL PATH 1	OPTIONAL PATH 2
Main Characters	Sierra Petrovita, Ronald Laren, Milo	Sierra Petrovita, Ronald Laren, Milo	Grady, Sierra Petrovita, Ronald Laren, Milo	Sierra Petrovita, Ronald Laren, Milo, Winger Mercier, Goalie Ledoux, Winger Gervais, Centre Dubois
Locations	Girdershade, Nuka-Cola Bottling Facility, Wasteland		Marigold Metro Tunnels, Grayditch, Girdershade	Girdershade, Nuka-Cola Facility, Red Racer Tricycle Factory, Wasteland
Adv. Items/Abilities	Lockpick, Science, Speech, Black Widow			
Possible enemies	Radroach, Nuka-Cola Security Protectron, Nukalurk			
Karma Influence	Positive	Negative	Neutral	

Locate Grady's Package in Marigold Train Tunnels
- Grady' Package

Find Sierra's Shack in Girdershade ⬅

Take Sierra's Nuka-Cola Tour.

Ice Cold Nuke Cola

Speak to Sierra Petrovita.

Speak with Ronald Laren

Deliver Grady's Package
- 300 Caps

Recover 30 bottles of Nuka-Cola Quantum and bring them to Sierra Petrovita.

[Optional] Recover 30 bottles of Nuka-Cola Quantum and bring them to Ronald Laren..

[Optional] Find the ruins of the Nuka Cola Bottling Facility.

Enter the Bottling Facility

[Optional] Recover the Nuka-Cola Quantum shipping manifests.

Investigate the Mechanic's area
- Employee ID

Begin Freeform Quest: Sudden Death Overtime. Search the facility
- Note: Finding the Formula

Locate Milo, the shipping foreman; either fool him or kill him
- Terminal Data Module

- Research Dept. Safe Key (Kill)

Open Research Dept. Safe
- Nuka-Cola Clear Formula

Continued on next page

Color code: Objective   Action   Rewards   Continued on next page

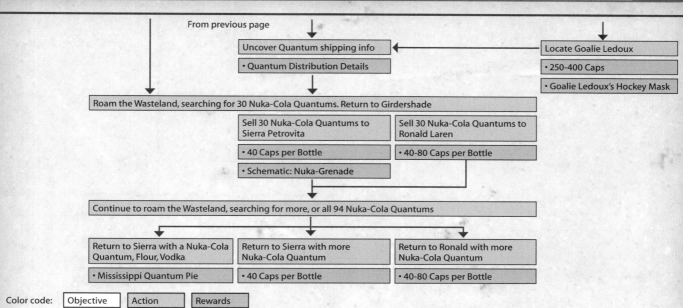

From previous page

Uncover Quantum shipping info
• Quantum Distribution Details

Locate Goalie Ledoux
• 250-400 Caps
• Goalie Ledoux's Hockey Mask

Roam the Wasteland, searching for 30 Nuka-Cola Quantums. Return to Girdershade

Sell 30 Nuka-Cola Quantums to Sierra Petrovita
• 40 Caps per Bottle
• Schematic: Nuka-Grenade

Sell 30 Nuka-Cola Quantums to Ronald Laren
• 40-80 Caps per Bottle

Continue to roam the Wasteland, searching for more, or all 94 Nuka-Cola Quantums

Return to Sierra with a Nuka-Cola Quantum, Flour, Vodka
• Mississippi Quantum Pie

Return to Sierra with more Nuka-Cola Quantum
• 40 Caps per Bottle

Return to Ronald with more Nuka-Cola Quantum
• 40-80 Caps per Bottle

Color code: Objective | Action | Rewards

COME FOR THE NUKA-COLA, STAY FOR THE INSANITY

 Tip

You can begin this quest at any time, but it helps to pack enough health and ammo to make the trek to this desolate part of The Wasteland. Try completing **Freeform Quest: Grady's Package** during **Miscellaneous Quest: Those!** first.

The quaint hamlet of Girdershade consists of two shacks sitting under an increasingly unstable freeway skeleton.

When you're ready, make a lengthy trek across the Wasteland to Girdershade; a half-hidden pair of shacks under the remains of the freeway overpass. The western shack is empty (for the moment), so head down the slight slope, and open the door to Sierra Petrovita's house. You can tell which is her abode due to the scattered Nuka-Cola bottles, and the buzzing neon sign affixed to the right of her door. Holster your weapon, unless you want to forego this quest in favor of shooting innocents, accidentally or otherwise.

Enter this ramshackle hut, and prepare to be amazed! That is, if you're a fan of everyone's favorite slightly irradiated soft-drink, Nuka-Cola! You may be a fan, but you're not Nuka-Cola's biggest fan. That dubious award goes to the blonde-haired woman sitting on her Nuka-Cola stool. She introduces herself as Sierra Petrovita, and providing you're not too rude, she goes on about winning the Nuka-Cola Fan Club Collection Award for the last 10 years! You're too polite to point out that she's probably the only entrant, and the competition is probably only in her head.

Continue the conversation, and you find out the fan club actually consists of two members: young Sierra here, and Ronald, her "neighbor and protector." He's protected her from fights (particularly when a Raider called Lug-Nut threatened him), and is, apparently, a cross

between a guardian angel and a super-hero. He sounds great. When she asks whether you want a guided tour of her collection, answer in the affirmative, even if this sounds like a terrible idea; it's the only way to begin this quest!

NEW OBJECTIVE
"Take Sierra's Nuka-Cola Tour" begins.

NEW OBJECTIVE
"Speak to Sierra Petrovita" begins.

After her tour, you must immediately (and perhaps, unfortunately) speak to her again. It's thirsty work, listening to this headcase; fortunately, you're given an Ice Cold Nuka-Cola for listening to this drivel, before Sierra begins to speak to you about Nuka-Cola Quantum, an all-new drink with extra kick, thanks to the inclusion of a mildly radioactive isotope. "No ill effects were ever recorded," Sierra informs you. Anyway, she needs Nuka-Cola Quantums delivered to her so she can fill that pristine dispensing machine.

 However, if you challenge her with **Speech**, she admits she has a Schematic for the Nuka Grenade, and if you bring her 30 bottles, the Schematic is all yours.

You're instructed to visit the Nuka-Cola Bottling Facility on the outskirts of the D.C. Ruins; shipping manifests inside can tell you where to search. Your Pip-Boy is updated, so agree to this quest. You can also speak to her about the Grenade (if you succeeded in your Speech), Grady (if you found his note during Those!), and other general matters.

 Ice Cold Nuka-Cola

NEW OBJECTIVE
"Recover 30 bottles of Nuka-Cola Quantum and bring them to Sierra Petrovita" begins.

NEW OBJECTIVE [OPTIONAL]
"Find the ruins of the Nuka-Cola Bottling Facility" begins.

Exit Sierra's shack, and you immediately run into Ronald Laren, who asks what the hell you're doing speaking with his woman. He backs off a bit if you're polite, telling you he's infatuated with her (at least if "plowing her bean field" means what you think it means). He's also got a proposition for you, but fortunately, it isn't the horizontal kind; he wants you to give him the Quantums, so he can present them to Sierra, and "seal the deal." He'll pay you 40 Caps per bottle (the same as Sierra).

 He also carries a Unique Sawed-off Shotgun you can pry from his corpse. If you have the Black Widow perk, you can obtain it without Karma loss.

 Kneecapper Sawed-Off Shotgun

Or, if you succeed in using **Speech** to verbally barter with him, he raises the price to 80 Caps.

Agree to this for the moment, as it doesn't affect your Karma, and you don't have to make the choice yet (if you're rude, he won't be so pleasant next time you speak to him). Your next stop is the Nuka-Cola Bottling Facility; you're looking for shipping manifests. You can also deliver Grady's Package (a Freeform Quest) to Ronald at this point, too.

If you're female, and have the **Black Widow** perk, when Ronald asks you whether you'd help secure Quantums, you can offer your own horizontal proposition: a "plow in both bean fields" if you like. The look on Ronald's face is priceless, and he sprints off out of town immediately. It looks like he's doing Quantum searching too, for the "extra incentive"!

NEW OBJECTIVE [OPTIONAL]
"Recover 30 bottles of Nuka-Cola Quantum and bring them to Ronald Laren" begins.

 Tip

Because you possess all the information contained in the shipping manifests in this guide, you don't actually need to visit the Nuka-Cola Bottling Facility at all. In fact, if you turn up at Girdershade for the first time, and already have 30 Nuka-Cola Quantums, you can sell them to either Sierra or Ronald immediately, once you've met them. Simply refer to the Tour of the Wasteland chapter of this guide for all the Quantum locations.

DON'T LOSE YOUR BOTTLE

The place where a taste sensation rocked a nation. Before that nation burned in radioactive fires.

Tip

Before (or after) you enter the facility, you can grab a Quantum from a container truck, parked at the rear. This is #86 of the 94 available Quantum bottles.

Journey to the Nuka-Cola Bottling Facility, on the southwestern outskirts of the D.C. Ruins. There's only one entrance; move and open the double metal doors, and head straight into the foyer. Check the

First Aid Box on the west wall behind the large desk. If you previously used your feminine charms on Ronald Laren (the Black Widow perk), you'll find his body in this general area; he should have packed more than his libido for this mission! Liberate the Unique "Kneecapper" Shotgun, Leather Armor, and Shotgun Shells from his corpse. You now have two routes to take through this building—one involves a massive amount of exploration, while the other requires opening a door....

 First Aid Box Health and Chems

NEW OBJECTIVE [OPTIONAL]
"Recover the Nuka-Cola Quantum shipping manifests" begins.

The quick route is to simply head forward (north) to the pair of metal doors with the red light above them and use your **Lockpick** skill. If you can catch this very difficult lock, you can head straight into the shipping bay on the other side, and skip all exploration to the end of "Take the Leap...Enjoy Quantum!" then work backward to Milo if you wish.

Otherwise, prepare for a thorough investigation of these premises! Begin by heading east through the doorway, down a short corridor, and turn left (north) into an executive office. Beware of the Nuka-Cola Security Protectron; blast it before you continue (a Shotgun or Pulse Grenades are a good plan), then search the room. There are two Nuka-Cola machines to empty (and a 10 percent chance you'll find a Quantum in each—these are your chances at every machine in the entire Wasteland). Step back into the foyer, then run west, following the two signs marked "Offices" and "Shipping."

Step into the research office, and blast the Protectron in this chamber. Then activate either of the working research terminals; you can read some rather sensitive information on Nuka-Cola Clear (a new flavor with minimal fatalities!), and on how the Nuka-Cola Quantum tests went. Hint: Nuka "Condolences" fruit and cheese packages were shipped on multiple occasions! There's no manifest yet, so head north, out into the loading bay. There's a safe on the west wall, but it only opens with a key. Enter the bay, bringing two Protectrons crashing down, and watching for escaping gas on the ramp area. Then run up the ramp and open the metal door on the west wall.

It has the same great mandible-ripping and soft-head cavity, but with an all-new luminosity! Fend off the NukaLurk now!

Head down the stairs, readying yourself for a close-quarters fight with an all-new mutation; the NukaLurk. Feeding off the soft drink chemicals still leaking throughout this facility, these Mirelurk hybrids have a luminous tone to them, but are otherwise just as vicious. Kill the first one, then move into a small mechanic's chamber and kill a second NukaLurk near some stairs. Then inspect the mechanic's area; there are some items and health to grab, including a Laser Pistol. Also on the table is a sheet of paper, the Employee ID. Pick it up!

 Optionally, you can use **Science** to hack into the terminal, and once successful, run the maintenance routine. This activates a Protectron that can fight alongside you, but it takes a while to reach the next section of the facility.

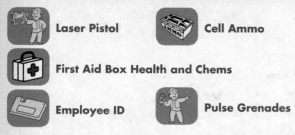

Laser Pistol

Cell Ammo

First Aid Box Health and Chems

Employee ID

Pulse Grenades

Descend the stairs, moving around the U-shaped tunnel, and exiting into a flooded vats chamber. Although the radiation hit you're taking is low, you might wish to head out of the water, but not at the expense of being struck by any of the four NukaLurks wading around this area. Deliver a killing blow to each of them, then move northwest, to the U-shaped metal stairs (the other one leads to a gap in the gantry). Follow the gantry eastward, then turn north (left), and drop down to another set of metal steps, resting on rubble underneath. Turn and look southeast; the exit doorway is just in front of you, at water level. Ascend the stairs to the door leading to the offices, then continue up the staircase, tackling Radroaches as you go.

TRY SOMETHING NEW...GO BLUE! OR CLEAR?

Climb to the floor of offices, and immediately swing right (south). Defeat two NukaLurks, and deal with a number of Radroaches. When immediate threats have been neutralized, concentrate on a sweep of this floor: Head south, and enter the group of offices with the missing interior walls. Two terminals in here are worth activating; they have the Nuka-Cola Company's marketing campaign for the introduction of Quantum, including some spectacular tag-lines! Check the nearby desk because there are usually Magnum rounds in here, and the Magnum is another great NukaLurk-dispatching weapon.

The rest of this floor is a maze of almost-empty offices, devoid of interest except for some irritating Radroaches. Locate the base of the stairwell with the "Shipping" sign near it, and check the office adjacent to it, toward the middle of the floor, and locate the locked door in this room.

 Assuming your **Lockpick** skills are good enough, break into a storage chamber with two First Aid Boxes in it.

Return to the main corridor, and follow the "Shipping" signs to the next set of stairs, and ascend them.

First Aid Box Health and Chems (2)

Thinking about corporate espionage? Then locate Winger Mercier's corpse in this office space.

Up on the next floor, you can continue up the stairs to "Shipping," or head around to the left (west), and investigate this floor. Bag a Radroach or two, then check the large middle chamber. Take care not to fall through the hole in the floor, or you'll end up back in the lower office area. Grab a few Caps and check another marketing terminal, but the real goodies are

to the east. Head into the adjacent office for more First Aid Box items, an easy-to-open safe with some Caps, and a copy of *Lying: Congressional Style*.

 First Aid Box Health and Chems

Bottle Caps

 Lying: Congressional Style
+1 Speech (+2 with Comprehension perk).

The rest of this floor is quiet, except for the odd Radroach, and the NukaLurk in the southwestern office area. Be sure to challenge the enemies here, as there's an interesting corpse to ransack lying in the corner. These are the partially digested remains of Winger Mercier, a Raider from the Sudden Death Overtime gang. He's got an odd collection of the usual items, and a rather intriguing note called Finding the Formula. Read this, then head northward, through the hole in the wall to a machine room, where you can find the *Big Book of Science* on the table. Read that, too! Now head back to your main plan; heading up the stairs following the "Shipping" signs to the door to the factory floor.

Note: Finding the Formula

Big Book of Science
+1 Science (+2 with Comprehension perk).

> *Note*
>
> The Finding the Formula note mentions the location of Nuka-Cola Clear (somewhere in the R&D floor), and a rendezvous point (the Red Racer Tricycle Factory not far from here). This is the beginning of **Freeform Quest: Just for the Taste of it.**

TAKE THE LEAP...ENJOY QUANTUM!

Meet Milo, the jolly Mister Handy foreman. He's less jovial if he has to award you three demerits.

Enter the factory floor, which is actually a series of three gantry-ways with lower chambers to investigate. Run eastward along the gantryway, but don't head into the connecting passage just yet. Instead, descend to the doorway at ground level (**Waypoint #8**), where you're stopped in your tracks by the robotic Shipping Foreman Milo. He immediately requests your identification. There are a number of actions to take:

 You can refer to yourself as John-Caleb Bradberton, owner of the place. If your **Speech** succeeds, Milo gives detailed instructions to the shipping manifests and more Quantum information. Ask for the key, too.

Or, you can present the Employee ID that you found earlier in your exploration of this place. This satisfies Milo, and you can ask for the Shipping Computer Login Code and Key.

Otherwise, you'll need to quickly retreat before you're toasted by Milo's flamer attack. Fight back, and claim the Login Code from Milo's remains. You can also claim the Research Dept. Safe Key.

 Shipping Computer Login Code

 Research Dept. Safe Key

APPENDICES — COMPLETION — TOUR — MISC. QUESTS — MAIN QUEST — BESTIARY — TRAINING

Move into Milo's quarters, and pick apart the furniture for some Caps, and a First Aid Box on one wall. The real find is the Nuka-Cola Shipping Terminal. Through hacking, or the Data Module, you can finally download the shipping manifests! There are three locations for the Quantum test market:

1. Paradise Falls Shopping Mart
2. Super-Duper Mart
3. Old Olney Grocery

When you're done at the terminal, unlock the safe high on a shelf behind a door on the south wall. Inside is a load of Caps, making this quite a fruitful five minutes!

 Caps

 **First Aid Box
Health and Chems**

Note: Quantum Distribution Details

Tip

The exact number of bottles and locations didn't quite go as the Nuka-Cola Company planned. Although these shipments left for the three test markets, only two trucks arrived. The Tour of the Wasteland chapter shows you exactly where to find these shipments, and many more Quantum bottles.

Don't leave without activating the packing line and grabbing three Quantums the rusting conveyor leaves behind.

Ascend to the gantry and head south, along a corridor with a Protectron at the far end. Demolish it, but look for the stairs down on your right (east), and descend to another Protectron; this one is guarding a packing terminal and large conveyor belt on the floor. Use Science to easily hack into the packing line terminal, and choose "Load Quantum into Sorting Unit" followed by "Activate Packing Line." The line grinds for a moment, then shorts out. Scour the office for a few Caps, then head onto the packing line itself. Three Quantums have dropped out of the pods. Grab these before ascending.

 Nuka-Cola Quantum (3)

Move back to the gantry, and continue into the last chamber, pausing by the gantry desk before you descend to rifle through a First Aid Box. Launch a salvo at a Protectron, as you move down to ground level, enter the only available exit doorway, and wind back to a chamber devoid of enemies, but cluttered with machinery. This leads to a pair of double doors—the same double doors you could have picked at the start of the facility exploration! Before you go, don't forget to return to the Research Dept. Safe, and use the key found with Milo. The safe contains items vital to your rendezvous with the Sudden Death Overtime Gang! When you've grabbed the Formula, leave, and start to locate Quantum Bottles until your total exceeds 30.

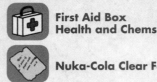 **First Aid Box
Health and Chems**

 **RadAway**

Nuka-Cola Clear Formula

[OPTIONAL] SUDDEN DEATH, OR SUDDEN CASH INFUSION?

If you want a quick way to add Caps to your collection, and you've found the Nuka-Cola Clear Formula inside the Research Dept. Safe, travel in a roughly northern path toward the Red Racer Tricycle Factory. Ignore the Raiders in the lower

Goalie Ledoux is a fan of "icegangs," where shaggy-haired men used to beat each other with sticks.

parking lot, and hold your fire as you reach the factory entrance. You're stopped by a mask-wearing Raider called Goalie Ledoux and his two guards, Winger Gervais and Centre Dubois. He's wistful for the days when men traded blows on the icy arena, but he's more interested in the Nuka-Cola Clear Formula. Agree to the sale, the following options are available:

You can use **Speech** to increase the price to 400 Caps, and Ledoux can grin through his gap teeth and bear it.

Or, you can settle on 250 Caps.

Or, you can shoot everybody on Ledoux's team, and grab the formula back. There's no Karma loss, but no one else wants to buy the formula. This has the added benefit of allowing you to ransack Goalie Ledoux's corpse. Pry his Hockey Mask off; it's well worth it!

When you're done collecting Caps, begin the Quantum hunt.

**Goalie Ledoux's Hockey Mask
+25 Action Points (when worn).**

QUANTUM DEPOSITS: SIERRA

When you've collected some Quantum bottles, return to Girdershade and speak with Sierra. She comments differently when you bring 1, 5, 10, 20, 25, or 30 Quantums. You only need return with 30 Quantums, however. Engage in conversation with her. Despite your best efforts, you can't convince her Ronald isn't thinking about a quantum leap into bed with Sierra, but no matter. When you hand over the 30th bottle, she excitedly remarks that her machine is full, and awards you the Schematic for the Nuka Grenade. She also buys Quantums from you at 40 Caps per bottle, making this an excellent (if long) quest to complete!

 **1,200 Caps
For 30 Quantum bottles.**

 Schematic: Nuka Grenade

Nuka Grenade

QUANTUM DEPOSITS: RONALD

 Alternately, you can head to Ronald's hut (assuming he's still alive), and sell the Quantums to him instead, at the price you bargained for at the beginning of this quest. Ronald takes everything you have, and then sets out to present them to Sierra, perhaps fooling the easily led girl into an evening of canoodling. Whatever the results, your Karma takes a hit for siding with this seedy predator. However, Ronald also warns you about the mysterious Dunwich Building; he reckons there's some weird stuff going on in there; unspeakable, even!

1,200 Caps
For 30 Quantum bottles.

2,400 Caps
For 30 Quantum bottles and Speech success.

POST QUEST ANTICS

THE GREAT NUKA-COLA QUANTUM HUNT

There are 94 Nuka-Cola Quantum bottles across the Wasteland. Of those, 93 are in crates, on tables and shelves, or hidden behind boxes; each location is detailed in the Tour of the Wasteland Chapter. Also, there is a single Quantum bottle you can purchase off a Wandering Merchant, one of the Random Mini-Encounters you can stumble across. It's extremely overpriced at 100 Caps, but worth it if you simply must collect every single bottle. Also, if you need directions to Girdershade, he provides them.

Additionally, you have a chance to find even more each time you search one of 178 Nuka-Cola vending machines. Single bottles of Quantum are found in machines only 10 percent of the time (the other 90 percent, they don't contain Quantum, but may contain regular Nuka-Cola). Once you search a machine, you can't search it again. The machines are not pinpointed on maps, because they're everywhere.

> **Tip**
>
> Save yourself yet another trip to Girdershade by locating flour and vodka before you finish this quest. Bring the ingredients to Sierra and you can complete **Freeform Quest: Mississippi Quantum Pie**, detailed in the Tour of the Walkthrough chapter (Zone 7).

QUITTING NUKA-COLA QUANTUM

There are only a finite number of Quantums in this world, so remember to expend them in the ways you think are best. Here's what you can do with them:

Drink them: Rads +10, AP +20

Sell them to Sierra: 40 Caps

Sell them to Ronald: 40 or 80 Caps

Customize them to Nuka Grenades

Have Sierra create a pie: Rads +5, AP +20, INT -1, STR +1

Head of State

Deep in the Wasteland is a small settlement known as the **Temple of the Union [3.10]**. This fortified village is centered around the severed stone head of Abraham Lincoln, and a chunk of stone long ago removed from the **Lincoln Memorial [17.01]**. The stone is part of the inscription that was once displayed over the statue of Lincoln in the memorial; the only remaining decipherable words are "Temple of the Union." For centuries, slaves have told the story of the Great Emancipator, Abraham Lincoln. When escaped slaves found the statue's head, they were inspired to begin an underground railroad to help others fleeing from the Slavers of Paradise Falls. Abraham Lincoln has become a symbol for these abolitionists. They want to restore the Lincoln Memorial as a beacon of hope and freedom, and they're searching for relevant artifacts in the **Museum of History [17.07]**. Meanwhile, the Slavers have heard of these plans, and seek to destroy both the temple and the head. They have fortified the Lincoln Memorial in readiness for a fight.

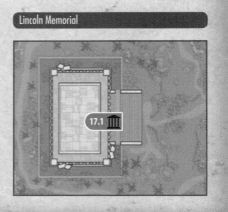

Lincoln Memorial

QUEST FLOWCHART

	MAIN PATH 1	MAIN PATH 2
Main Characters	Simone Cameron, Hannibal Hamlin, Caleb Smith	Silas, Leroy Walker
Locations	Temple of the Union, Lincoln Memorial, Museum of History	Lincoln Memorial, Museum of History, Temple of the Union
Adv. Items/Abilities	Lockpick, Speech, Small Arms, Big Guns, Energy Weapons	
Possible enemies	Super Mutant Genus, Feral Ghoul Genus, Silas, Leroy Walker, Slavers	Super Mutant Genus, Feral Ghoul Genus, Simone Cameron, Caleb Smith, Hannibal Hamlin, Bill Seward, Alejandra Torres
Karma Influence	Positive	Negative

Abolitionist Path A

Find Hannibal Hamlin and the Temple of the Union.

Gain entry into The Temple of the Union

→ By civil conversation
 • Temple of the Union Key

→ By Lockpick

Agree to become a Temple Member, assist Hannibal

Make sure the Lincoln Memorial is free of Super Mutants.

Talk to Caleb Smith.

Get a picture of the Lincoln Memorial.

→ Locate Lincoln Memorial; slay all Slavers
 • Nuka-Cola Quantum

→ Locate the Museum of History; secure artifacts
 • Nuka-Cola Quantum, Lincoln's Diary, Action Abe, Lincoln's Hat, John Wilkes Booth Wanted Poster, Civil War Draft Poster, Lincoln Memorial Poster, Lincoln's Voice, Lincoln's Repeater, Chinese Army: Spec. Ops. Training Manual, Antique Lincoln Coin Collection

Tell Hannibal the Memorial is free of Super Mutants.

Take the picture of the Lincoln Memorial to Caleb.

Return to The Temple of the Union

Accompany The Abolitionists on the journey to the Lincoln Memorial

Abolitionists successfully capture Lincoln Memorial
 • Schematic: Dart Gun

Slaver Path A

Speak to Silas, enter Lincoln Memorial. Hear what Leroy Walker has to say
 • Nuka-Cola Quantum

→ Lose, or ignore Challenge

→ [Speech] Win Challenge

Find at least one Lincoln artifact in Museum of History.

Locate the Museum of History; secure artifacts

Find Hannibal Hamlin and the Temple of the Union.

Locate The Temple of the Union. Report back to Leroy Walker
 • 100 Caps

Join Leroy Walker in attacking the Temple of the Union.

Slavers successfully capture The Temple of the Union

Hannibal is killed by you	Hannibal is killed by Leroy
• 50 Caps	• 100 Caps

Color code: Objective | Action | Rewards

RUMORS AND SCUTTLEBUTT

 Tip

You can begin this quest at any time, but a good time to begin the Slaver section is on your first trip to the Mall, during **Main Quest: Galaxy News Radio**. Or, a good time to begin the Abolitionist section is after finishing up **Miscellaneous Quest: The Superhuman Gambit**, then journeying north to find the Temple of the Union. The rest of the quest (reaching either conclusion) can then be completed at your leisure.

You begin this quest by stumbling upon one of two locations; the Lincoln Memorial (guarded by Slavers), or the Temple of the Union (home to the Abolitionists). They are sworn enemies of each other. However, before you find either of these locations, the following characters provide hints about this quest:

Three Dog speaks about the Temple of the Union, but doesn't know the location of the building.

Scattered randomly in The Wasteland (near Big Town, Canterbury, the RobCo Factory, Metro Center, and Paradise Falls) are the bodies of five dead slaves. Each carries a map, and on this map is marked the Temple of the Union.

If you speak to Mei Wong in Rivet City, and complete her Freeform Quest (page 391), she reveals the location of the Temple of the Union.

Three Freeform Quests in The Wasteland involve slaves, and dialog with them can reveal the location of the Temple of the Union. Bronson, a slave in Paradise Falls, also has a map.

KEEPING THIS QUEST IN ORDER

The majority of this quest is almost completely freeform, but there are two plans to choose from: the Abolitionist or the Slaver. Here are the following paths through the plans you can take. If you don't mind how you complete this quest, the easiest way is to choose a side and follow Path A.

Abolitionist (Path A):

Talk to Hannibal and Caleb, begin the quest.
Hear what Leroy Walker has to say.
Kill all the Slavers.
Acquire the Lincoln Memorial Poster.

 Finish the quest.

Abolitionist (Path B):

Kill all the Slavers.
Acquire the Lincoln Memorial Poster (or the other way around).
Talk to Hannibal and Caleb, begin the quest, then complete Objective 3 immediately.

 Finish the quest.

Abolitionist (Path C):

Talk to Hannibal and Caleb.
[Optional] Talk to the Slavers.
Acquire the Lincoln Memorial Poster.
Lead the Abolitionists to the memorial.
Kill all the Slavers (either alone or with the Abolitionists).

Slaver (Path A):

Hear what Leroy Walker has to say. Win Speech challenge. Begin quest.
Talk to Hannibal and Caleb.

 Inform Leroy Walker of Hannibal's location and finish the quest.

Slaver (Path B):

Hear what Leroy Walker has to say. Lose Speech challenge. Begin quest.
Acquire the Lincoln Memorial Poster.
Talk to Hannibal and Caleb.

 Inform Leroy Walker of Hannibal's location and finish the quest.

Slaver (Path C):

Acquire the Lincoln Memorial Poster.
Hear what Leroy Walker has to say. Begin quest.
Talk to Hannibal and Caleb.

 Inform Leroy Walker of Hannibal's location and finish the quest.

Slaver (Path D):

Talk to Hannibal and Caleb.
Hear what Leroy Walker has to say. Attempt Speech challenge and begin quest.
Acquire the Lincoln Memorial Poster (if required).

 Inform Leroy Walker of Hannibal's location and finish the quest.

ADVANCING THE ABOLITIONISTS' CAUSE

North of Canterbury Commons, along the remains of the road and amid the ruins of a settlement, is the Temple of the Union. Head toward the western side of the building, and you're greeted by a sniper named Simone Cameron. Make sure you approach during daylight hours, because the Abolitionists head into their concrete bunker rooms at night. If Simone isn't there, ring the bell. Respond by saying you're here to rest and perhaps to trade. Simone doesn't like it, but she's under orders from the group's leader, Hannibal Hamlin, to let people like you inside.

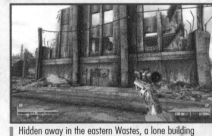
Hidden away in the eastern Wastes, a lone building protects the real home of the brave.

 Caution

You can inspect each of the rooms in this structure: Caleb's Room, which has Health to take from a First Aid Box; Simone's Room, which is filled with minor food and Chem items, and Hannibal's Home, which has similar foodstuffs and junk. However, if you attempt to unlock the storeroom, you're viciously attacked by the entire crew. Watch your thievery!

Meet Hannibal Hamlin and Abe Lincoln's head—the real and symbolic heads of the Abolitionists.

Head up to the next floor of the ruined building, and locate the guy clad in recon armor, patrolling the roof next to a large stone head. He introduces himself as Hannibal Hamlin. He immediately requests that you solemnly promise not to betray these people to Paradise Falls or the Slavers. Swear to protect the Temple of the Union, or face admonishment or combat. Once you agree, you're given the Temple of the Union Key; allowing you to pass in and out of the front gate unimpeded. Of course, you don't have to keep your word! If you don't want to keep this secret, you can also just jump out of the window and avoid the question—but you'll have to wait at least three days before trying to befriend these people again!

 Temple of the Union Key

Continue to speak with Hamlin, and he tells you he's set this motley crew up to help escaped slaves. He'd let them stay, but they are out of room and clean water. His real plan is to take over a place, a "shining beacon of hope." He wants to move his people to the Lincoln Memorial. The problem is that this monument is overrun by Super Mutants. You're tasked to clear the area, and then report back here to Hamlin. You must also speak to Caleb Smith. He's been ordered to restore the Lincoln Memorial—it needs its head back, for a start!

NEW OBJECTIVE
"Make sure the Lincoln Memorial is free of Super Mutants" begins.

NEW OBJECTIVE
"Talk to Caleb Smith" begins.

 Note
If you're interested in listening to a humorously distorted version of Lincoln's life, assemble by the head at noon and listen to Hamlin.

Don't fail to speak with Caleb Smith, or you'll have a lot of backtracking to do! Head down to the ground floor, and look for the man hammering stone near the Temple of the Union façade. Ask him what he needs, and Caleb tells you Hannibal wants to restore Lincoln's Memorial, and Caleb has the masonry skill to make this happen. Unfortunately, he doesn't have a reference picture to work with, but he knows where to find one: he believes one still survives in the Museum of History. Add that to your tasks, and leave the temple, using the key to unlock the front gate.

NEW OBJECTIVE
"Get a picture of the Lincoln Memorial" begins.

 Note
If you've already retrieved the Lincoln Memorial Poster, hand it over right now!

SIDING WITH THE SLAVERS

Under the Lincoln Memorial exists an ex-President's worst nightmare (aside from a nuclear conflagration, obviously).

To get the Slavers' requests as well as (or instead of) the Abolitionists', begin by exiting to the Mall, ideally from the Georgetown/ The Mall Metro Station, or Fast Travel to a nearby location. Walk in a vaguely westerly path toward the imposing and partially ruined Lincoln Memorial at the opposite end of the Mall from the Capitol Building. After you step over the partially exploded remains of some Super Mutants, Silas hollars at you. He wants to know what the hell you're doing here!

Whether you're here for the first time or you've been sent from Hannibal, tell Silas you're not looking for trouble, because this relaxes his guard. Move up toward the sandbags he's stationed behind, and either follow him around and into the Door to Memorial Maintenance Room, or begin to slay Slavers. Assuming you want to hear the Slavers' plans, head inside to meet Leroy Walker. Lower your weapon; there's no need to fire. Speak with Leroy and he tells you he's taken some Slavers from Paradise Falls to help him search for escaped slaves.

Succeed in a **Speech** challenge, and you can bargain with Leroy. He tells you he's only interested in securing the leader of the escaped slaves: Hannibal Hamlin. There's a 100 Cap bounty if you can find him (but leave the killing to Leroy). He warns you to stay off the Lincoln Memorial steps, as his men have orders to fire. You can now skip "Longing for Lincoln's Belongings" completely, and begin "A New Home for the Brave."

NEW OBJECTIVE
"Find Hannibal Hamlin and the Temple of the Union" begins.

If you fail the Speech challenge, you can either tell him you haven't seen any slaves recently, or that you wouldn't tell him anyway. Try the former dialog option, and Leroy takes a shine to you, and asks if you're for hire. He needs you to head into the museum and bring back an artifact; afterward, he'll allow you a closer look at the memorial. Head to the Museum of History at once.

NEW OBJECTIVE
"Find at least one Lincoln artifact in Museum of History" begins.

 Tip
There's a Nuka-Cola Quantum bottle resting on one of the shelves in this chamber. Don't forget to snag it if you're trying to complete **Miscellaneous Quest: The Nuka-Cola Challenge!**

Nuka-Cola Quantum

SLAUGHTERING THE SLAVERS

If you've been sent by Hannibal Hamlin to clear the Lincoln Memorial of Super Mutants, you'll find the Slavers have done this job for you. Of course, as the Slavers' *raison d'etre* is diametrically opposed to the Abolitionists', you'll need to clear the memorial of Slavers, too! This is best carried out with a modicum of cunning; when you're challenged by Silas at the front sandbag area, tell him you're not looking for trouble. Then move so you're directly behind him, and gun him down! This allows you to use the walls and sides as cover.

The next five minutes consist of fraught combat to remove the remaining Slavers from the memorial. Leroy is one of them, and he appears from the Maintenance Door under the memorial. Don't wait for him; use the walls as cover, then Sneak or run around the rear of the structure, gaining the higher ground, and use the walls as cover. Lob a Grenade or two, then employ your favorite weapon (a Hunting Rifle from range, a Combat Shotgun while charging, V.A.T.S., or any number of other possible takedown measures) until around eight Slavers lie dead and bleeding. Alternately, you can Sneak around the outside of the memorial and pick off Slaver patrols, but watch out for the large number of Frag Mines and Grenade Bouquets. Search the bodies, ransack the Maintenance Room for items, then return to Hannibal, making sure you've obtained the Lincoln Memorial Poster before you go.

NEW OBJECTIVE

"Tell Hannibal the memorial is free of Super Mutants" begins.

LONGING FOR LINCOLN'S BELONGINGS

Located on the north side of the Mall is this once-grand building, now home to dozens of lumpy-skinned Ghouls.

Travel into the D.C. Ruins, using the linking Metro and over-land areas to reach the Mall, or Fast Travel to the nearest location off the Mall's general area. Head to the ruins of a once-imposing structure just north of the Washington Monument, say hello to Willow the ghoulish guard, and enter the ground level (not the basement Metro) of the Museum of History. Make a left turn at the mammoth; you're looking for the Door to Museum of History Lower Levels.

Tip

Have you acquired the Ghoul Mask, given to you by Roy Phillips for your help during **Miscellaneous Quest: Tenpenny Tower**? Then you'll find the subsequent searching a lot less fraught!

Don't want to risk your life searching for Lincoln trinkets? Then choose the Slaver's way, and win a Speech conversation with Leroy Walker to skip this stage completely.

Begin a room-by-room search of these floors. Although most of the Lincoln artifacts are on the upper level, be sure to grab Lincoln's Diary from the display in the northwest corner of the big room at the top of the stairs. At the foyer, move southeast, around the left staircase, and into a small office. There are Caps in the filing cabinet, a First Aid Box on the wall, and items in the desk, but the real find is inside the wall safe.

Lincoln Artifact Acquired: Lincoln's Diary

Use your **Lockpick** skill to force the safe open, and grab the loot inside.

Begin a quick sweep of the ground floor, remembering to back up and employ your favored Ghoul-culling weapon when you see these gaunt creatures rushing you. Move southward, into the remains of a cafeteria, then turn right (north), and search the body of a dead Wastelander for any items you can collect. The long counters hold only junk, so move to the northeast doorway, and shoot down an advancing Ghoul.

Search the room behind the back of the counter area and secure some Health from a First Aid Box. Then move to the southeast corner of the floor, ransack the Nuka-Cola machines, and grab a Quantum from the small crate under the table, plus a Jet or two from the table above. The rest of this floor is filled with junk. Head back out to the foyer, and up the stairs.

First Aid Box Health and Chems

Lincoln's Diary

Nuka-Cola Quantum

Jet (2)

The second floor has a few unwashed sub-humans to gun down. Or draw them into the turret room and lock them inside by hacking into the wall terminal. A better plan is to move slowly forward, lay down some Mines between you and your bony foes, then attract them, backing up to the office where you found the wall safe. Or, you can run south, making a beeline for the Door to Museum of History Offices.

Head carefully up the stairs, and start a room-by-room search of this floor. Rushing in usually gets you killed by at least four Feral Ghouls, and there's at least one Glowing One too. Deal with it by Sneaking around, laying Mines, and letting it run over them en route to you. When all Ghoul threats in the vicinity are contained, make a sweep of the area. Just east of the exit doorway is a small alcove with a Nuka-Cola machine. Across from that is a locked door.

There's no need to use Lockpick to open the door, because you can access the room by heading south down the corridor, swinging left (east) into a room of bookcases, and heading through the hole in the wall. Ready your weapon for a couple more Ghouls, and then make a sweep of this office. There's an Assault Rifle and Ammo in the Gun Cabinet, more Ammo in the boxes on the wall shelves, Health and Chems in the First Aid Box, and a stash of Caps, Pre-War Money, and a Stealth Boy in the safe (use Lockpick). You can also deactivate the turrets in the Archives Room from here, too. But the real prize is the Action Abe Action Figure. Leroy or Hannibal might pay some Caps for that!

Lincoln Artifact Acquired: "Action Abe" Action Figure.

First Aid Box Health and Chems

TRAINING — BESTIARY — MAIN QUEST — MISC. QUESTS — TOUR — COMPLETION — APPENDICES

Assault Rifle and Ammo

Action Abe Action Figure

Note

You can now return to Leroy Walker without investigating the rest of this building, if you wish (and you're siding with the Slavers).

NEW OBJECTIVE

"Sell Lincoln artifacts to Leroy Walker" begins.

Roam the remainder of this floor. There are two desks, each in front of a barred gate. The southeast one has Ammo, while the southwest desk holds a Combat Knife. The rest of this floor has only minor items, but you can collect a stovepipe hat that belonged to the ex-President in a half-collapsed side room. Head back to either of the desks in the southeast or southwest corners of this floor.

Lincoln Artifact Acquired: Lincoln's Hat

Make sure you don't break both locks, or there's no other way to progress! **Lockpick** either of the Cell Doors, and enter the archive chamber.

If you collect ruined books, you've come to the right place! There is also some Ammo in the filing cabinets on the lower level,

Lincoln Artifact Acquired: Lincoln Memorial Poster.

Lincoln Artifact Acquired: Lincoln's Voice.

but your main concern is shooting out the turret before it detects you. Search the bookcases in the southern corners for two more artifacts. Now climb the stairs, and turn left (north). Behind the desk is the Lincoln Memorial Poster that Caleb Smith needs. Take this immediately, even if you've aligned with the Slavers; it'll fetch a price with Leroy, too. The other desk to the left has a phonograph of Lincoln's Voice, another excellent artifact!

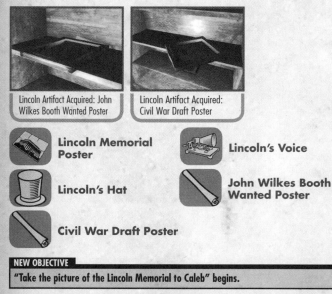
Lincoln Artifact Acquired: John Wilkes Booth Wanted Poster

Lincoln Artifact Acquired: Civil War Draft Poster

Lincoln Memorial Poster

Lincoln's Voice

Lincoln's Hat

John Wilkes Booth Wanted Poster

Civil War Draft Poster

NEW OBJECTIVE

"Take the picture of the Lincoln Memorial to Caleb" begins.

Enter the hole between the two desks, and search the large crumbling office, making sure you take Ghoul-preparedness measures. When the threat has subsided, move to the northwest corner of this middle chamber, and open the glass display case, taking Lincoln's Repeater from inside. Also look for a First Aid Box and a Skill Book at the back of this chamber. Then head to the east corridor, heading north or south, and enter the eastern doorway nearest the desk where you found the Lincoln Memorial Poster. Search the small library. On one of the shelves is yet another artifact: Antique Lincoln Coin Collection. Then prepare for a final sweep of the rooms up here. A room to the north has a hole in the floor; navigate the edges of it to reach an Ammo Box with .44 Magnum Rounds in it. Now that this building has given up all its treasures, head back to the faction of your choice: the Abolitionists or the Slavers.

Lincoln Artifact Acquired: Lincoln's Repeater.

Lincoln Artifact Acquired: Antique Lincoln Coin Collection.

First Aid Box Health and Chems

.44 Magnum Rounds

Lincoln's Repeater

Antique Lincoln Coin Collection

Chinese Army Spec. Ops Training Manual +1 Sneak (when read).

A NEW HOME FOR THE BRAVE

Tip

This ends the Abolitionist path of this quest. For this, you need to have secured the Lincoln Memorial Poster from the National Museum and killed all the Super Mutants and Slavers from the Lincoln Memorial.

Fast Travel back to the Temple of the Union. Use the key to open the gate, and once inside, meet Caleb again. He thanks you kindly for the Lincoln Memorial Poster, and directs you to Hannibal. Speak with Hannibal, telling him that the memorial is clear of both Super Mutants and Slavers. He is ecstatic, and tells you he'll start out on the trek to the memorial within the hour. You are told to meet Hannibal at the Lincoln Memorial. Fast Travel there at once.

Note

If you want a frantic and lengthy journey to the Lincoln Memorial with all the members of the Temple of the Union, wait for them to gather outside the building, and watch the procession leave. Now accompany them through the Wasteland, the numerous Metro and surface routes, fighting off Super Mutants and other threats as you go. You can tell Hannibal to wait while you scout ahead, or leave them to walk (slowly) toward their destination. This is purely optional, and not recommended, because if Hannibal dies, your quest fails.

A much better plan (and one ensuring quest completion) is to Fast Travel to the Lincoln Memorial and move inside the structure. This is also a good opportunity to rid the area of any outstanding foes. Then choose one of the mattresses inside the building, and sleep for six hours. Hannibal's train of slave survivors should arrive at the Mall Northwest Metro station entrance around this time (or you can keep sleeping until they show up). Escort them up and into the memorial. Now speak to Hannibal, who is ecstatic. He thanks you profusely and gives you a Dart Gun Schematic for your troubles. If you check back at the memorial from time to time, Lincoln's head is back on his body, a new plaque has been fitted, and the Abolitionists have set up tents in the forecourt. Caleb is busy fixing the walls. Alejandra Torres sweeps the floor. Every day at noon, Hannibal recites the Gettysburg Address.

 Schematic: Dart Gun   **XP** **300 XP**

AN OLD FATE FOR THE SLAVES

 Tip

This ends the Slaver path of this quest. For this, you need to have secured any artifact from the National Museum and sold it to Leroy Walker, found the Temple of the Union, and told Leroy where it is.

This first section assumes you failed your Speech challenge during "Siding with the Slavers." Once you've found any of the Lincoln Artifacts in the museum, return to Leroy Walker and sell him one or all of them. Remember he is only one of three inhabitants who will pay good Caps for these treasures!

 Try a **Speech** challenge to double your selling price.

Once you've sold an artifact, Leroy asks whether you'd be interested in information about an escaped band of slaves and their leader, Hannibal Hamlin. Answer that you're interested, then search for the Temple of the Union. Complete the "Advancing the Abolitionists' Cause" part of this quest, and remain on friendly terms with the Abolitionists. Return to Leroy Walker again (remember to Fast Travel!), and tell him you've made contact with Hannibal. Leroy claps politely, and rewards you justly.

 Caps (100)

NEW OBJECTIVE
"Join Leroy Walker in attacking the Temple of the Union" begins.

You can follow Leroy Walker and his merry band of Slavers throughout the D.C. Ruins, weaving underground and over rubble, and tackling multitudes of Muties along the way. Unfortunately, your quest fails if Leroy dies, so keep that in mind. A far shorter and less dangerous plan is to Fast Travel back to the Temple of the Union, and check your Pip-Boy's map for the location of the Slavers. Go and meet them on the outskirts of the derelict township, then follow them in as they charge the temple itself, slaying Abolitionists with ruthless aggression.

 Note

Before you fire on either side, you have a final opportunity to switch to the Abolitionists, help them slay the Slavers at the temple, and then help the remaining ex-slaves hobble to the Lincoln Memorial.

 A more likely solution is that you'll engage the Abolitionists in a fierce firefight, ripping innocents apart, or keeping back and saving your ammunition. Open the gate using the key Hannibal gave you to add insult to injury...and there's a whole lot of injury to inflict. Any of the ex-slaves are fair game, except for Hannibal Hamlin; leave him for Leroy to kill. Once the bloodshed has subsided, meet up with Leroy Walker again, and he gives you some final blood money. Satisfied, he heads back to Paradise Falls.

Caps (50)
If you killed
Hannibal Hamlin.

Caps (100)
If Leroy killed
Hannibal Hamlin.

XP **300 XP**

ALL THE FACTS ON THE ARTIFACTS

During this quest, you can sell any of the artifacts you find in the Museum of History to Leroy Walker or Hannibal Hamlin. Alternately, you can seek out the Capitol Preservation Society in Rivet City, where Abraham Washington is more than happy to take these priceless heirlooms of your hands. Consult **Miscellaneous Quest: Stealing Independence**.

Caution

Beware! Some items are critical to complete other Miscellaneous Quests!

ARTIFACT	PRICE (Hannibal Hamlin)	PRICE (Leroy Walker)	RELATED MISC. QUEST
Lincoln's Hat	25	25	Head of State
Action Abe	10	10	Head of State
John Wilkes Booth Wanted Poster	50	75	Head of State
Civil War Draft Poster	75	50	Head of State
Lincoln's Diary	100	75	Head of State
Antique Lincoln Coin Collection	15	15	Head of State
Gift Shop Poster of the Lincoln Memorial	—	100	Head of State
Lincoln's Voice (Phonograph)	50	50	Head of State
Lincoln's Repeater Rifle	150	100	Head of State
Emancipation Proclamation	150	150	Stealing Independence
Gettysburg Address	75	50	Stealing Independence

TRAINING — BESTIARY — MAIN QUEST — MISC. QUESTS — TOUR — COMPLETION — APPENDICES

The Replicated Man

When you first arrive in the rusting ship known as **Rivet City [9.15]**, you gradually realize that Doctor Li and her assistants are being harassed by another doctor known as Zimmer. He seems frustrated, and although discussions are hushed and never devolve to fisticuffs, the other scientists seem unwilling or unable to help him. Zimmer and his no-nonsense body-guard named Armitage have traveled to Rivet City from the Commonwealth (formerly known as Massachusetts). He professes to be a representative of "The Institute," a Commonwealth-based university that has made amazing scientific advances in recent decades. In fact, this is the reason Zimmer has come to the Capital Wasteland.He is discreetly searching for an escaped experiment—a lifelike android indistinguishable from a normal human—and he needs your help to find him. This begins an epic search for clues to the whereabouts and identity of the replicant, and finally a meeting with the android itself. Do you turn this monstrosity in to Zimmer, or do synthetic humans have feelings too?

Rivet City

15

QUEST FLOWCHART

	MAIN PATH 1	OPTIONAL PATH
Main Characters	Doctor Zimmer, Armitage, Harkness, various optional Capital Wasteland residents	
Locations	Rivet City, Capital Wasteland (various optional locations)	
Adv. Items/Abilities	Medicine, Science, Speech, Lockpick, Child at Heart, Radiation Suit, Rad-X, 100+ Caps	
Possible enemies	None	
Karma Influence	Positive and/or Negative	

Uncover strange Holotapes throughout the Wasteland

Learn more about the escaped android.

Visit Rivet City to learn more about the android from the Commonwealth.

Visit Rivet City's Science Lab, locate Doctor Zimmer

- Note: Missing Android
- Clue #1: Self-determination is not a malfunction

[Optional] Discover what Doctor Preston at Rivet City might know about the Android.

Search for clues about Zimmer's missing Android.

Locate any relevant Medical Professional:
- Doctor Preston (Rivet City)
- Doc Church (Megaton)
- Doctor Banfield (Tenpenny Tower)
- Doctor Barrows (Underworld Chop Shop)
- Lucy (Little Lamplight)
- Cutter (Paradise Falls)
- Red (Big Town)

Locate any relevant technologically-minded Wastelander:
- Seagrave Holmes (Rivet City)
- Moira Brown (Megaton)
- Winthrop (Underworld)
- Scribe Bowditch (Citadel)
- Knick Knack (Little Lamplight)

Locate any relevant sympathizer:
- Father Clifford (Rivet City)
- Manya (Megaton)
- Herbert Dashwood (Tenpenny Tower)
- Tulip (Underworld Outfitters)

Locate any relevant slaver:
- Grouse (Paradise Falls)
- Eulogy Jones (Paradise Falls)
- Sister (Rivet City or Paradise Falls)

- Holotape
- Holotape
- Holotape
- Holotape

- Clue #1: Self-determination is not a malfunction

- Clue #2: A request for help
- Clue #3: We got the tech, now we need the doc
- Clue #4: A free man, a new man

Chance of a visit by Victoria Watts (+Karma)

- Internal Component

Find out what Pinkerton at Rivet City knows about the Android.

Color code: Objective   Action   Rewards

Continued on next page

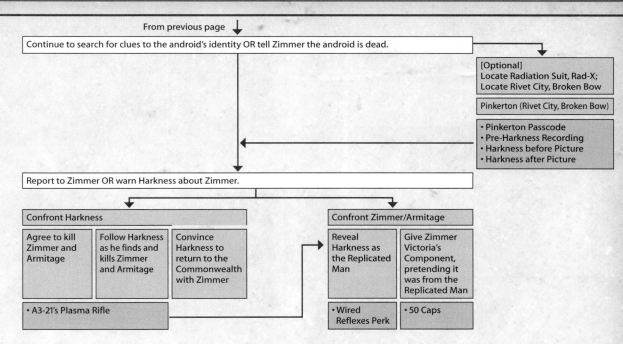

From previous page ↓

Continue to search for clues to the android's identity OR tell Zimmer the android is dead.

[Optional]
Locate Radiation Suit, Rad-X;
Locate Rivet City, Broken Bow

Pinkerton (Rivet City, Broken Bow)

• Pinkerton Passcode
• Pre-Harkness Recording
• Harkness before Picture
• Harkness after Picture

Report to Zimmer OR warn Harkness about Zimmer.

Confront Harkness

Agree to kill Zimmer and Armitage	Follow Harkness as he finds and kills Zimmer and Armitage	Convince Harkness to return to the Commonwealth with Zimmer

• A3-21's Plasma Rifle

Confront Zimmer/Armitage

Reveal Harkness as the Replicated Man	Give Zimmer Victoria's Component, pretending it was from the Replicated Man

• Wired Reflexes Perk
• 50 Caps

AN ESTEEMED COLLEAGUE FROM THE COMMONWEALTH

Rivet City Map: Page 386

During a visit to Rivet City, look over the schematic of the floating township in this book's Tour of the Wasteland Chapter, and locate Doctor Li's laboratory. A heated discussion occurs in the chamber (either before or after you speak with your father and Doctor Li), and listen in. Approach Dr. Zimmer, taking care not to make threatening moves that would cause problems with Armitage, Zimmer's bodyguard. Speak with Zimmer, and agree to find the wayward replicant his "Institute" has mislaid. Your incentive? "Advanced technology from the Commonwealth."

 Note: "Missing Android" **Note: "Self determination is not a malfunction"**

Continue to press the doctor for information. He tells you to search the offices of doctors or "techies" for android information because it may have contacted these people. Zimmer recommends you start with Rivet City's practicing physician, Doctor Preston. Keep pressing Zimmer, and he reveals the replicant was actually in charge of hunting other escaped androids, and believed he'd done something immoral. While you ponder just what the hell is going on inside the "Institute," set off to search for Doctor Preston, if you wish.

NEW OBJECTIVE
"Search for clues about Zimmer's missing android" begins.

NEW OBJECTIVE [OPTIONAL]
"Discover what Doctor Preston at Rivet City might know about the android" begins.

Your quest now becomes completely freeform; you must scour the Wasteland for additional clues to the location and name of this android. Depending on when you start collecting clues and when you first speak with Zimmer, you may need to collect three or four clues.

Clues may be uncovered in one of two ways: Find a Holotape in someone's room, or speak with them and convince them to give you more information. It doesn't matter who you speak with, or which

Holotape you find first; you always receive the clues in the correct order. Collect information from the four closest characters. You can question the android itself, but you won't be able to talk abou this specific quest until you've solved it.

Keep the following in mind as you search for clues:

 For many, you can use a **Speech** challenge to receive the information (instead of finding their Holotape).

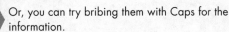 Or, you can try bribing them with Caps for the information.

 For doctors, you can rely on your **Medicine** to help you garner the information.

 For those characters deemed "technically minded," use your **Science**.

Before Doctors and techies give you clues through dialog, you must have first received a clue alluding to surgery or a mind wipe, or have spoken with Zimmer.

Some folks (sympathizers and Slavers) talk to you only after you've found their Holotape.

You get the same clue from finding the Holotape as you do by talking to its owner.

Except for Doctor Preston, everyone here has a Holotape stashed somewhere.

Note
Have you already found a Holotape on your travels? Now that you've met Doctor Zimmer, you can listen to it with a new understanding. Or, simply locate the characters most convenient to you.

Tip
Your replicant hunt begins now: The next four sections of this quest walkthrough showcase (in alphabetical order) the Wasteland characters with Holotapes, and information to impart.

DOCTORS' ORDERS: HOLOTAPES AND THE MEDICAL PROFESSION

The following medical professionals (and Cutter) have a Holotape to give, or one that you can find (your choice):

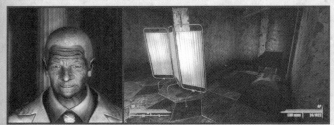

Cutter: Located in Paradise Falls [2.08]. The Holotape is on top of a corner file cabinet.

Doc Church: Located in Megaton [8.03]. Find the Holotape on the desk near his terminal in the clinic.

Doctor Banfield: Located in Tenpenny Tower [7.14]. The Holotape is on the floor, in the corner of the examination alcove.

Doctor Barrows: Located in Underworld [17.07]. The Holotape is near the terminal on the desk of Nurse Graves.

Doctor Preston: Located in Rivet City [9.15]. Speak with Doctor Preston (he has no Holotape lying around) in the clinic or the Weatherly Hotel.

Lucy: Located in Little Lamplight [4.08]. The Holotape is on her desk, below "The doctor is in!" sign, in her Essentials clinic.

Red: Located in Big Town [5.10] (assuming survival after Miscellaneous Quest: Home Sweet Home). The Holotape is on the desk inside her clinic.

FANS OF THE FUTURE: HOLOTAPES AND THE TECHNOLOGICALLY MINDED

These technically savvy inhabitants offer a copy of a Holotape after a chat, or you can rummage for it (your choice):

Knick Knack: Located in Little Lamplight [4.08]. The Holotape is on the desk near the phone, in his "Miner Mole" store.

Moira Brown: Located in Megaton [8.03]. Find the Holotape on the round table behind her counter.

Seagrave Holmes: Located in Rivet City [9.15]. The Holotape is on the floor, to the right of his desk, near his bunk.

Scribe Bowditch: Located in the Citadel [9.11]. The Holotape is by the Scribe's terminal. (Star Paladin Cross is nearby, but isn't knowledgeable about the replicant.)

Tulip: Located in Underworld [17.07]. The Holotape is on the Work Bench to the left (north) of her shop desk.

Wintrop: Located in Underworld [17.07]. Find the Holotape on his desk, in his room.

SECOND-CLASS SYNTHETICS: HOLOTAPES AND THE SLAVERS

A few of the thug-like Slavers have heard the android's tapes and are hoping to capture some replicants:

SYNTHETIC SYMPATHIZERS: HOLOTAPES AND THOSE FRIENDLY TO THE CAUSE

Whispers tell about an underground railroad helping to free androids from their programming:

Eulogy Jones: Located in Paradise Falls [2.08]. The Holotape is on the desk in Eulogy's main bedroom.

Manya: Located in Megaton [8.03]. The Holotape is on the table in her home, entered via the concertina door.

Grouse: Located in Paradise Falls [2.08]. Find the Holotape on the ground next to him, near the sandbags.

Father Clifford: Located in Rivet City [9.15]. The Holotape is at the base of his pulpit.

Sister: Located in Paradise Falls or Rivet City [9.15]. The Holotape is on the desk in his Rivet City room.

Once you've heard the fourth clue (whether through dialog or finding a Holotape), you learn the identity of the person who operated on the android: a crotchety rogue doctor named Pinkerton, who's holed up somewhere on the Broken Bow of the Rivet City ship. You must find him before you can continue.

NEW OBJECTIVE

"Find out what Pinkerton at Rivet City knows about the android" begins.

Herbert Dashwood: Located in Tenpenny Tower [7.14]. Find the Holotape in the corner of his central bookcase.

TRAINING — BESTIARY — MAIN QUEST — MISC. QUESTS — TOUR — COMPLETION — APPENDICES

THE ANDROID EVANGELIST

You can return to Zimmer at any time to update him, but he's only interested after you've found two or three clues, and it is only necessary to see him once all four clues are collected. However, before this happens (and usually while you're wandering Rivet City en route to Zimmer, or after you receive the third clue), you're flagged down by an imposing female wanderer with an impressive sword. She accuses you of meddling in matters that don't concern you. Her name is Victoria Watts.

Remain cordial, and she offers some advice. She's part of a group that helps androids escape along an underground railroad, and she says that the replicant you're chasing should be left in peace. She asks you to return to Zimmer, stop your searching, and present the doctor with a fake Internal Component (a Neuro Servo). Agree to her plan (unless you want less Karma, and want her dead); you don't have to carry it out, though! If you do as Victoria instructs you, skip to "Rendezvous with a Replicant," and return to Zimmer.

 Internal Component

NEW OBJECTIVE

"Continue to search for clues to the android's identity OR tell Zimmer the android is dead" begins.

BRAVING THE BROKEN BOW

Rivet City (Broken Bow) Map: Page 386

After your fourth clue, your sleuthing reveals that the doctor responsible for the android's new form is named Pinkerton. He's a hard guy to track down, because he's holed up in the dangerous and murky Broken Bow section of Rivet City, which has an underwater entrance. Various Rivet City residents might share rumors that will clue you in to his whereabouts. Grab some Mirelurk-killing weaponry and some Rad-X, and head to the underwater entrance.

Switch on your Pip-Boy's Flashlight, pop a Rad-X or wear a Radiation Suit, then swim down to the entrance. Open the door, swim forward to the room half-filled with debris. Continue in a south-southwest direction through the open door. Ignore the open hatchway to the left (unless you're desperate for air), and continue to open the bulkhead door ahead. This leads to some underwater gantry steps and a sliver of air you can inhale to avoid drowning. Turn southeast, unlock the underwater bulkhead door, then surface in the same spot again.

With a lungful of air, swim southeast and surface in a waterlogged chamber. Move to the next chamber through a half-submerged doorway, and clamber onto the dry corner near an open doorway that leads to a debris-filled blockage, and a possible Mirelurk assailant. Spin around and look northwest; you should spot gantry stairs (on the far left of the previous picture) that lead up to the dry deck of this vessel. Climb to the top, and peer around to see a vent with the number "7" etched onto it. Ahead is a hatch door room with a door leading outside to a rusting gangplank, which is only accessible from this side. Pull the switch to unlock the door so you can come and go as you please. Quickly look down and left, and deactivate the Frag Mine before it explodes! Now search this chamber; there's a First Aid Kit, two Ammo Boxes, and a Scoped .44 Magnum.

 **Scoped .44 Magnum**

 Ammo Box Ammunition (2)

 First Aid Box Health and Chems

TO PINKERTON'S HIDEY-HOLE

Continue roughly southeast, then duck down, and open the bulkhead door on your right. This allows you to enter an item-filled room without being shot in the chest by two Rigged Shotguns. Deactivate the Frag Mine, grab the Purified Water, and open the Ammo Box with more Mines inside.

 Purified Water   **Frag Mines**

Deactivate the Shotguns or duck and exit, turn southeast, and head to a blocked gantry staircase and a wandering Mirelurk. Back completely out of this room to start combat; otherwise seeping gas engulfs the chamber in flame and burns you. When the Mirelurk meets its match, continue to the door and open it. You're in the connecting chamber to Pinkerton's hidey-hole. There's little here to grab, so move southwest into a refuse-strewn room. The door ahead is sealed. Don't make the mistake of accessing the booby-trapped terminal to the right of the door. Instead, deactivate the trap on the rear panel, or ignore it. Open the door by activating the switch on the northeast wall behind you.

THE ANDROID ENABLER: MEETING PINKERTON

> **Caution**
>
> Remember, you need to have collected all the clues that point to Pinkerton before you have proof of his involvement!

Limp into this trap-master's inner sanctum, and begin interrogating Pinkerton. Without resorting to violence, go along with his explanations, and he reveals the android's true identity: it's Harkness the Security Chief! Because even Harkness doesn't know his true identity, you require yet more proof, and Pinkerton is happy to provide it. He gives you his terminal password, as well as pictures and a Holotape. Keep pestering him, and he reveals Harkness's recall code; "Activate A3-21 Recall Code Violent."

You can continue to ask about the Commonwealth, and Pinkerton even offers complete facial reconstruction, with a death-by-infection rate of only 35 percent. Fortunately, it's quite safe when you're under the plasma knife! Change your appearance, then check his hidey-hole. You can read Pinkerton's notes on his terminal, steal a *Big Book of Science*, *Dean's Electronics*, a Stimpak, a Stealth Boy, and other sundry goods, if you wish. There is also a Work Bench for repairing or building weapons.

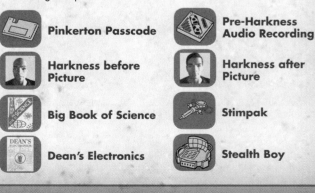

Pinkerton Passcode   **Pre-Harkness Audio Recording**

Harkness before Picture   **Harkness after Picture**

Big Book of Science   **Stimpak**

Dean's Electronics   **Stealth Boy**

NEW OBJECTIVE
"Report to Zimmer OR warn Harkness about Zimmer" begins.

RENDEZVOUS WITH A REPLICANT

PATH A: CONFRONTING HARKNESS

There's a choice of paths to end this quest, and the first involves meeting Harkness himself; he's usually guarding the exterior of Rivet City. If you don't have Pinkerton's proof, Harkness won't even acknowledge your

Straight from the synthman's lips: Harkness needs to hear what you (and he) have to say.

line of questioning. If you present all of Pinkerton's evidence in your dialog choices, Harkness's memory jolts back, and he realizes his true identity. You can now help Harkness decide what to do:

 He can authorize you to kill Zimmer. Search and destroy him and his bodyguard Armitage.

 Or you can leave Harkness to his own devices to deal with Zimmer. If you don't try to talk him out of violence, follow him as he finds Zimmer and has a showdown with him and Armitage.

 You can convince Harkness to return to the Commonwealth with Zimmer, and to grudgingly accept his fate. Security Guard Danvers takes charge.

With either positive outcome, Harkness (AKA A3-21) gives you his modified Plasma Rifle as a gift. Try it out on Zimmer, if you want!

 A3-21's Plasma Rifle

PATH B: CONFRONTING ZIMMER

Alternately, you can return to Zimmer, making sure to bring either Pinkerton's proof or Victoria's fake Internal Component. Figure out your plan, then talk to Zimmer:

 You can reveal everything. Zimmer thanks you, and gives you a special Combat Module perk. You can follow Zimmer to watch him "reclaim" his property.

 You lie and tell him Victoria's Neuro Servo is from an android you killed. He grudgingly accepts this, gives you 50 Caps, and leaves.

 Zimmer's Combat Module

PATH C: CLAIMING BOTH REWARDS

 Simply complete Path A, telling Harkness "your secret is safe with me," take the Plasma Rifle, and then head straight to Zimmer, rat out Harkness, and claim the Combat Module!

Tip
Do you want a V.A.T.S. boost, or a customized Energy Weapon? If it's the former, side with Zimmer (and receive the Combat Module). If it's the latter, side with Harkness (and end up with A3-21's Plasma Rifle). You can collect one, or both.

QUEST REWARDS

You receive the following rewards depending on how you react to Zimmer and Harkness:

 Bottle Cap (50 total)
If you gave Zimmer the fake Neuro Servo from Victoria Watts.

 Combat Enhancer: Wired Reflexes
(Hit Chance x1.1 in V.A.T.S.): If you reveal the truth to Zimmer.

 A3-21's Plasma Rifle
If you reveal the truth to Harkness.

XP **+300 XP**

Armitage is a wickedly accurate shot with that weapon. Those skills are almost inhuman....

Tip
Did you open fire on Zimmer, Armitage, Victoria Watts, or Pinkerton and kill them? Then search their bodies. You may find more than just flesh and bone on these corpses....

Blood Ties

Lucy West is a recent arrival to the bustling town of **Megaton** [8.03]. Although happy here, she's starting to worry. It's been over a month (she thinks) and she's lost all contact with her mother, father, and brother, and her last two letters have gone unanswered. Enlisting your help, she promises a reward from her father once the message is delivered. When you press her, she reveals that her shanty hamlet of **Arefu** [5.07] was having trouble with a marauding "gang." When you reach Arefu, the only resident not barricaded indoors is Evan King, who nervously explains that the place has been terrorized by "the Family," a group of crazies who've been spotted at the **Northwest Seneca Station** [5.02] and **Meresti Trainyard** [5.05], and sometimes hang out at **Hamilton's Hideaway** [5.03] and the **Moonbeam Outdoor Cinema** [5.09]. When you explore the shacks, Lucy's worst fears are confirmed. Her parents' hut reeks of putrid and decaying flesh. However, there appear to be only two victims from Lucy's family. Where is Ian, Lucy's younger brother? Perhaps Vance, the leader of the Family knows. And is Lucy telling you everything she knows about her brother? By all accounts, he was an odd little boy, said to love the taste of red meat. He couldn't stop gorging himself on the stuff, apparently....

Arefu

QUEST FLOWCHART

	MAIN PATH	OPTIONAL PATH 1	OPTIONAL PATH 2
Main Characters	Evan King, Ken Ewers, Brailee Ewers, Karen Schenzy, Davis West, Matilda West, Murphy, Robert, Brianna, Alan, Justin, Karl, Holly, Vance, Ian West		Lucy West, Ian West
Locations	Arefu, Hamilton's Hideaway, Moonbeam Cinema, North Seneca Station, Meresti Trainyard Tunnels		Megaton, Meresti Trainyard Tunnels
Adv. Items/Abilities	Strength, Intelligence, Charisma, Speech, Lockpick, Medicine, Black Widow, Cannibal, Impartial Mediation, Ladykiller, Scoundrel, 100+ Caps	Lockpick	—
Possible enemies	Radroach, Mole Rat, Mirelurk Genus	The Family	Radroach, Mole Rat, Mirelurk Genus
Karma Influence	Positive	Negative	Positive

Locate Evan King in Arefu ← Locate Lucy West in Megaton

• Lucy's Sealed Envelope

Discover what the Family did in Arefu. — Deliver Lucy's Message.

Check the Schenzy Residence.

Chech the Ewers Residence.

[Optional] Break into Evan King's Residence

• Bobblehead: Repair

Discover the bodies of David and Matilda West; use Medicine to determine extact cause of death

Report to Evan King.

King informs you of four possible locations for the Family

Locate the Family.

Hamilton's Hideaway | Moonbeam Cinema

The Family aren't here | The Family aren't here

Freeform Quest: Caching in with Three Dog: Open barred gate using key he gave you

• Three Dog's Weapon Cache

From previous page

Continued on next page   Color code: Objective | Action | Rewards

184-04

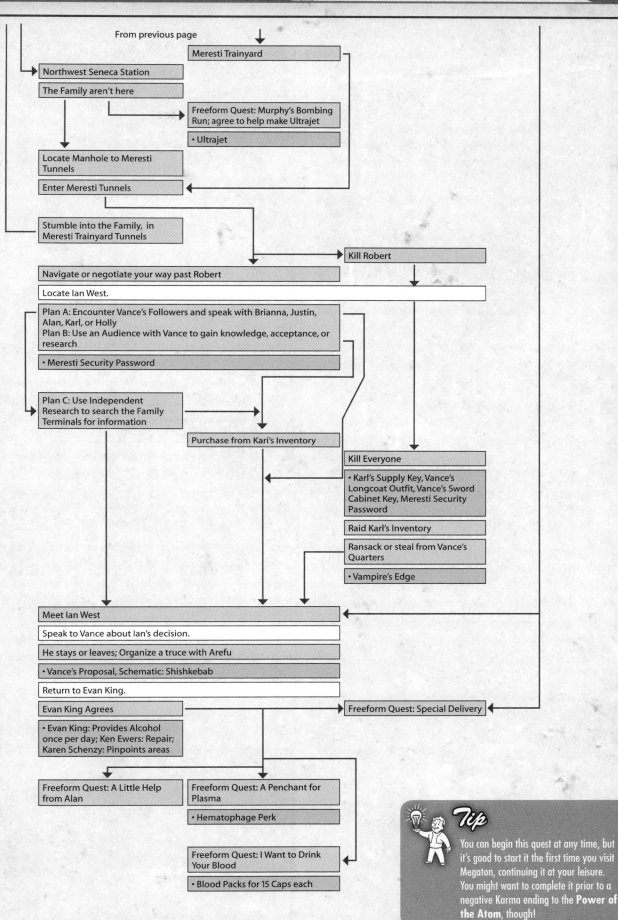

From previous page

Meresti Trainyard

Northwest Seneca Station

The Family aren't here

Freeform Quest: Murphy's Bombing Run; agree to help make Ultrajet

• Ultrajet

Locate Manhole to Meresti Tunnels

Enter Meresti Tunnels

Stumble into the Family, in Meresti Trainyard Tunnels

Kill Robert

Navigate or negotiate your way past Robert

Locate Ian West.

Plan A: Encounter Vance's Followers and speak with Brianna, Justin, Alan, Karl, or Holly
Plan B: Use an Audience with Vance to gain knowledge, acceptance, or research

• Meresti Security Password

Plan C: Use Independent Research to search the Family Terminals for information

Purchase from Kari's Inventory

Kill Everyone

• Karl's Supply Key, Vance's Longcoat Outfit, Vance's Sword Cabinet Key, Meresti Security Password

Raid Karl's Inventory

Ransack or steal from Vance's Quarters

• Vampire's Edge

Meet Ian West

Speak to Vance about Ian's decision.

He stays or leaves; Organize a truce with Arefu

• Vance's Proposal, Schematic: Shishkebab

Return to Evan King.

Evan King Agrees

Freeform Quest: Special Delivery

• Evan King: Provides Alcohol once per day; Ken Ewers: Repair; Karen Schenzy: Pinpoints areas

Freeform Quest: A Little Help from Alan

Freeform Quest: A Penchant for Plasma

• Hematophage Perk

Freeform Quest: I Want to Drink Your Blood

• Blood Packs for 15 Caps each

Tip
You can begin this quest at any time, but it's good to start it the first time you visit Megaton, continuing it at your leisure. You might want to complete it prior to a negative Karma ending to the **Power of the Atom**, though!

TRAINING — BESTIARY — MAIN QUEST — MISC. QUESTS — TOUR — COMPLETION — APPENDICES

GO TO WEST, YOUNG MAN

The town of Megaton, in the Southern Wastes, is perhaps the best (and safest) place to visit after you emerge from Vault 101. Use your Pip-Boy and trek southward from your hole in the ground. Once through the entrance defense panels and Deputy Weld, head into the settlement itself, and locate Moriarty's Saloon, spot-welded to the far end of town, commanding an impressive view of the settlement. This town is the setting for the **Miscellaneous Quest: The Power of the Atom**. You may wish to start that quest before entering the saloon.

When you've met Gob, and the other (slightly more attractive) members of Moriarty's staff, take the opportunity to look around and locate a young, blonde woman, who tells you she needs someone to make a delivery. If you're interested

Lucy is tough, attractive, and straight to the point, but her furrowed brow reveals her worry.

(which would be handy if you want to start this quest), she gives you Lucy's Sealed Envelope to give to her father Davis West, who has not responded to her missives for a month or more. He lives in Arefu, and he'll pay for your traveling expenses when you arrive.

 Lucy's Sealed Envelope

NEW OBJECTIVE
"Deliver Lucy's Message" begins.

Press her with additional questions about the town, and she mentions the sheriff, Evan King, and the safety aspects of the place. Apart from the Wasteland critters, Slaver trading parties, Raider hit squads, and an occasional landmine, the place is a real tourist hotspot. Take your leave (and her letter), and when you're ready, set off in a northwesterly direction, crossing the Wasteland to Arefu.

THE KING OF AREFU

 ## Note

You can begin this quest from this point, if you aren't near Megaton, or you've reached the more cataclysmic conclusion to **Miscellaneous Quest: The Power of the Atom**. However, not all dialog choices are available. Also, try not to even lightly wound any of Arefu's inhabitants: They're on edge as it is, and this will also fail your quest!

Expect this journey to feature occasional battles with a variety of enemies, including Mole Rats and Raiders. Continue past burnt-out shells of houses and crumbling freeway overpass columns as the rocks give way to a large open plain. Head past ruined farm settlements, along the southwest bank of what remains of the Potomac River. Look for the remains of the next freeway bridge, with the abandoned house at the foot of it. The remains of the freeway sign indicate you're nearing Arefu.

Evan King's duties are less regal, and more despondent. He spends his day guarding the ramp and waiting to die.

Head north, up the broken freeway sections, and stop as an explosion rocks the ground in front of you. An old man pokes his head above a section of sandbags. Evan King notices you aren't one of "them," and beckons you over. Tell him that you're delivering the letter to the West family. He isn't that interested; he's more concerned with raiding parties in the area; the most recent one slaughtered all their Brahmin. At this point you can ask:

 Use **Speech** to ask, "What's got you so spooked?"

King explains that there's something weird about the attackers; he doesn't know why they don't just attack, instead of picking off cattle from a distance. Offer to help (King has no Caps to reward you with, though), and King asks you to check on Arefu's residents while he guards the ramp.

NEW OBJECTIVE
"Check the West Residence" begins.

NEW OBJECTIVE
"Check the Schenzy Residence" begins.

NEW OBJECTIVE
"Check the Ewers Residence" begins.

Just behind Evan King on the left side of the road is the Ewers residence. Although it requires a key to open (which you don't have), simply knock on the door, and a woman answers, excited about her "catalog." Step in, and you receive an

The radiation in the Mirelurk Cakes may have gone to Brailee Ewer's brain. This also might explain Ken's curtness.

altogether colder reception from Ken Ewers. If you explain that his wife let you in, he berates her, then lets off steam about his predicament. Mention to him that Evan King asked you to check on them. Talk to Brailee, and she speaks as if the bombs haven't dropped; she's obviously in a state of psychosis. Without the necessary doctorate to treat her, mine both residents for information, then leave.

Karen Schenzy's cabin fever hasn't manifested itself as derangement, but she still isn't happy.

Continue north a few steps, then turn left, and swing to face south, and look for the shack adjacent to the Ewers's, and knock on the door to the Schenzy residence. Don't tell her you're with the Family, or she won't let you in. Once inside, you can extract additional information on Evan King ("that asshole"), and the Family ("no one wants to set foot outside"). Once again, make sure you let her know that Evan King asked you to look in on her. Karen

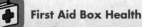

has resigned herself to an eventual death at the hands of marauders. When you've heard enough, leave.

The north end of Arefu is where Evan King's residence is, as well as the West's tiny shack and a couple of outhouses overlooking the end of the freeway span and a long drop into the river below.

You can break and enter Evan's house using **Lockpick** if you wish. Although it's trespassing, nobody is there to witness your behavior. Unless you're interested in increasing your spork collection, the ground floor doesn't feature items of value, except a Bobblehead: Repair. Climb the steps to the top floor though, and there are three Ammo Boxes on the shelf, and another four near Evan's bed. Grab this haul (if you want to take the small Karma hit) before departing.

Bobblehead: Repair

Ammo Box Ammunition (7)

You can't knock on the door of the West's residence. The reason for this becomes apparent when you step inside. There are no Wests, at least, none living. Although Lucy mentioned her parents and brother, only father Davis and mother Matilda are here, lying strewn across the shack. Figuring out their cause of death depends on your **Medicine** competency (which can affect future conversations, but is mainly to clue you in on where to search next):

[0–29] Your pathetic knowledge of this carnage extends only to confirming that, yes, these two aren't going to be dancing a jig anytime soon.

[30–49] You realize the bodies of the Wests have bite marks on the neck area that go to the bone.

[50–69] In addition, the lack of bloodstains on the sheets is strange, because any bite or wound of that depth should have caused massive bleeding.

[70–89] Furthermore, the bite marks on the necks appear to be from a human or humans with sharpened incisors or canines.

[90+] And finally, you smugly postulate that the blackish powdery residue on the bodies is not unlike that found in old trainyards.

Note

If you don't have the necessary Medicine skill, you can return with your rating boosted (with Mentats or other items) and see these clues. There's also a large and less-than-subtle clue on the wall: "The Family" scrawled in blood.

NEW OBJECTIVE
"Report to Evan King" begins.

Head back to the old coot, and explain the holes in his defenses. He's shocked at the Family's brazen attack, and worried for the safety of Ian West. King mentions he caught Ian and "that weirdo

leader" of the Family talking down by the river. Has Ian been carried off, or worse? King then tells you three possible locations where the Family has been spotted; he can't pinpoint where they are because they travel only at night. He tells you to search Hamilton's Hideaway, the old Moonbeam Cinema, or Northwest Seneca Metro Station. If you found the powdery residue on the Wests' bodies, you can ask if there's a nearby trainyard. King tells you of a fourth place to try: the Meresti Trainyard, almost due east of here.

NEW OBJECTIVE
"Locate the Family" begins.

CHASING PHANTOMS (WHERE THE FAMILY ISN'T)

All you have is a list of three (or four if your Medicine skill provided the trainyard clue) places to search, where Evan King believes the Family might reside. Fortunately, all are a few minutes' hike from Arefu. Hamilton's Hideaway and the Moonview Cinema are completely optional to explore, and do not result in any progression to your quest. Enemies, maps, and any associated Freeform Quests for these two areas are shown in the Tour of the Wasteland Chapter (page 309 for Hamilton's Hideaway, and page 314 for Moonbeam Cinema).

CHASING VAMPIRES (WHERE THE FAMILY IS): SENECA

You can now choose either of the following locations to gain entrance to the Family's sprawling underground lair. The first location is quicker, but the entrance is more difficult to find and it features more dangerous enemies.

Northwest Seneca Station is a ghost town, complete with its own ghoulish residents down in the darkness.

As soon as you're down the freeway ramp and by the abandoned house, turn and face north. Squint into the distance, and you'll spot a cluster of tenement blocks on the opposite side of the river. It's time to get wet (and a little radioactive)! Clamber over the rocks and dirt, and swim across to another area of rocky ground with the freeway sections to your left. Turn northeast, circling around the rocky outcrop, and then northwest, between the two clusters of buildings. Congratulations! You've discovered Northwest Seneca Station.

Before you investigate the station entrance, you can optionally enter the Cornucopia Fresh Groceries Store. Watch your footing, or the Stimpaks you'll find inside the First Aid Box on the wall will be immediately needed for Bear Trap injuries. There's a safe on the floor behind the counter, where you can grab a few Caps. Otherwise, expect the usual store items and junk to collect, if you wish. Exit the store, and head south, down the steps to the Chain Gate to Northwest Seneca Station.

Caps

First Aid Box Health

Flick on your Pip-Boy's Flashlight as you descend the ramp, but stifle your gunfire because the two disfigured forms in front of you are friendly, if not human. Unless you're itching for a fight, converse with Murphy. He's perfecting a new

Interested in Ultrajet? Meet Murphy and Barrett: one enterprising Ghoul and his tough-and-nails bodyguard.

Chem called Ultrajet, and he needs Sugar Bombs to complete the recipe. He's looking for a scavenger and will pay 15 Caps for each box of Sugar Bombs you bring him.

 Wait, did he say 15? He meant 30, if your fast-talking **Speech** is successful!

Murphy now waits for you to return to sell Sugar Bombs (these items are scattered randomly throughout the Wasteland); you've discovered **Freeform Quest: Murphy's Bombing Run**. For more information (including what benefits Ultrajet has), consult page 308. If you arrived here after completing your tour of Arefu, Murphy can also clue you in on the location of the Family.

Another damnable dead-end! Wait...where does that manhole lead?

Continue into Seneca Station, and you'll find the main path to the mezzanine completely blocked (this area can never be accessed). The only way onward is the door to your right, just past the turnstiles. Brandish your best Mole Rat–hunting weapon, and deliver a killing blow to this bloated beast and its companion. After a quick search of the office, where a few Caps, an Ammo Box with Frag Mines, and other refuse lie collecting dust, try the "authorized personnel" door to the south. In front of the badly deteriorating radioactive barrels is a manhole to Meresti Service Tunnel!

 Ammo Box with Frag Mines

This is an often-overlooked shortcut, so drop into an underground cave system with your preferred Mirelurk-killing weapon. Pass the Brahmin corpse and bones, and wind along the tunnel, continuing north and defeating two Mirelurks along the way. Watch for a Grenade Trap (back up until the explosion occurs) as you emerge from a hole linking the cavern corridor to the Meresti Tunnel system. You can continue heading north to exit out to the Meresti Trainyards, or follow the flaming barrels at the junction on your left, all the way to the Family's lair entrance.

CHASING VAMPIRES (WHERE THE FAMILY IS): MERESTI

If you choose to ignore the hidden entrance from Seneca to Meresti Station, you can try an overland route that takes a vaguely eastern path from Arefu. Pass the river, go up and over the Moonbeam Cinema area, and head toward the two bridges just north of Big

Town. Continue eastward, bringing out a scoped rifle to drop a group of Raiders that spot you from the river's edge, just below (and west of) the Meresti Trainyards.

Head up the hill continuing eastward, and look for the two tunnel entrances and the rusting carriages on the flat area of ground. These are the Meresti Trainyards, and you're likely to be attacked by Giant Ants, Radscorpions, or other multi-legged mutations. When the coast is clear, or if you wish to flee, run to either tunnel entrance; each has a service door that leads to a parallel Meresti Service Tunnel.

No matter which tunnel entrance you select, head through the connecting chamber and into the main tunnel, with the parallel one running next to it. Head south. If you chose the western Trainyard entrance, you need to head east through a connecting chamber. Watch out for the Baby Carriage Trap, which blows up a small generator. It seems the Family has set up a few dissuasions to prevent looters.

Locate the rusting carriage with the flaming barrels nearby, and head south, weaving between the carriages (watching out for a Rigged Shotgun Trap and a Brahmin-hide-on-a-Chain Trap), and staying slightly right of the baseball-thrower to avoid a fastball to the back of the head! Head south as the tunnel slopes downward, but ignore the red lights and stay to the right at the junction; straight ahead is a hole leading to a Mirelurk Tunnel and the secret entrance up to Seneca Station.

 Tip
Flaming barrels indicate a preferred route to take, usually ending in a place you want to travel to.

Robert is the Family's gate-keeper, but he isn't above bribery or persuasion. Or a hole in the head.

Farther around the tunnel, after you wind between two carriages, are a pair of flaming barrels and a gate guarded by a muscular man with a slightly glazed expression. Robert stops you in your tracks, and asks what you're up to in the Family's tunnels. It looks like you've found the gang responsible for the keeping Arefu's residents up at night! Here are some conversation tactics:

 You can vaguely impress him with a sense that it's important for him to let you by. If your **Speech** is successful, he does just that.

 If you've craved human flesh in the past, Robert recognizes the twinkle of the **Cannibal** perk in your eyes, and lets you through.

You can employ a spot of good old-fashioned bribery, offering 100 Caps in return for entrance into the settlement. This is agreeable, as long as you have the funds.

If these funds are not present, wave Lucy's Sealed Envelope for Ian West, and he figures out you should speak to the Family's leader, Vance.

Or, you can start a protracted and dangerous firefight, turn the entire Family hostile, and gun Robert down in cold blood. If you employ Sneak (Stealth Boy optional), you can maneuver around Robert and enter the Family's lair, but you face a fierce firefight; you must kill them if you use this tactic.

Or if you're being combative and inventive, you can coax Robert away without attacking him and let something else do the dirty work (for example, if a Mirelurk follows you in). You can then Lockpick the gate and hack the terminal, but the Family is likely to be hostile; if murder is on your mind, drop Robert and work through the rest of these death punks.

The following tactics assume you didn't employ this option, because it reduces all your future options considerably. If you do try gunplay, simply storm the station concourse, and keep firing until everyone without the first name "Ian" is dead.

The gate to Robert's living area is locked and will automatically unlock if you drop him or if he lets you in. He also has the key to the terminal that unlocks the door around the corner to the Family's living areas.

NEW OBJECTIVE

"Locate Ian West" begins.

If you choose to rampage through the Family, or attempt this once the quest is over, you can take the collection of items that Robert is storing in the connecting tunnel just behind his gate. Here, there's a computer terminal (one of three you can access later if you wish) Ammo Boxes, an Assault Rifle, Sledgehammer, Mentats, a couple of First Aid Boxes, a Pistol and Ammo, and a book called *Tumblers Today*. This last item is important, because it's the only one you can take without turning the Family hostile. Don't forget to pick it up, and read it from your Pip-Boy's Inventory immediately.

Tumblers Today
+1 Lockpick (+2 with Comprehension perk)

FIGURING OUT THE FAMILY: ADVANCING TO VANCE

PART A: ENCOUNTERING VANCE'S FOLLOWERS

Head west, then turn south and move through the connecting door to enter Meresti Metro Station itself. Step out into the tunnel and swing west. All other junctions or tunnel areas are dead-ends. The only way onward is west and into the Metro Station mezzanine itself. The place is in surprisingly good condition, and some pale, dark-clothed humans are walking the concourses. You can speak to any of them. Depending on your abilities, you can convince any of Vance's followers to impart the Meresti Security Password, which allows you to access the secured chamber where Ian is residing, without speaking to Vance. Here are your options:

Meet Brianna; she provides a vital "service" to the Family (well, the male members, anyway). She's tagged along with Vance. As well as taking care of the men, she can help you, too.

 If you have the **Lady Killer** perk, you can use your charms on her, and snag the password this way.

Or, try Justin, the new recruit who's been trying to talk to Ian and make him feel better about his "abilities." Try out one of the following:

 With the **Impartial Mediation** perk, you can convince Justin that an outside perspective is needed: yours.

Or, try a **Speech** about Ian, and then tell Justin that Ian needs some perspective from somebody on the outside.

Justin also tells you the origin of the name Meresti; apparently it's a town in a European country once known as Romania.

 Alan is Vance's longest serving member, and he's a little more wary of you. Your skills aren't helpful to wheedle out information, and Alan points to Justin as someone who might assist you.

 Over by the western edge of the concourse, below the mezzanine, is a workshop brimming with items and a Work Bench. Here you'll sometimes find Karl, if he's not sleeping upstairs. He's susceptible to one of the following:

 If you're female, and have the **Black Widow** perk, you can provocatively charm him into revealing the password.

Or, if you have a high **Strength**, Karl is impressed with your mettle, and agrees to give you the note.

 The final member of the Family who might help you is Holly, Vance's wife. It takes a like-minded or silver-tongued adventurer to get the better of her:

 If you've chosen the **Scoundrel** perk, your natural charm convinces her Ian needs to speak with you.

 The same effect is available if you're a naturally **Charismatic** person, and can influence Holly with your chutzpah.

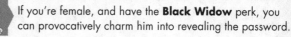 Meresti Security Password

PART B: AN AUDIENCE WITH VANCE

Tip

This initial (and more difficult) conversation with the leader of the Family is necessary only if you haven't already gleaned the Meresti Security Password from one of Vance's followers, or if you're intent on using one of the three terminals to find out more about this clan.

Vance is a charismatic leader, filled with slightly pretentious thoughts about his kind: Indulge him.

TRAINING — BESTIARY — MAIN QUEST — MISC. QUESTS — TOUR — COMPLETION — APPENDICES

Ignore the rest of Vance's followers, and speak to the man himself. He's up on the mezzanine level, in front of the sleeping quarters, and he's easy to spot: he's in the long coat, carrying what looks like a very impressive melee weapon. Let him speak, and keep your comments mostly courteous (unless you want to start combat). At the end of the conversation, you can try one of the following options:

 Although this is hard to pull off, you can use **Speech** to tell Vance him exactly what you think his kind are: a variation on the ancient myth of the vampire, except in this case, they're suffering from the Hematophage disorder.

 If you're afflicted with the **Cannibal** perk, and you've already feasted on the remains of your vanquished victims (along with the negative Karma associated with this), you know immediately what Vance is, and you're greeted warmly.

Or, you can find out more about the Family by understanding and researching their Laws.

Succeed in any of these three options to gain access to Ian West and receive the Meresti Security Password.

If Vance tells you to learn more about his kind, descend to the concourse area, and speak with his followers. For a faster option, access any of the computer terminals in this area, and read about The Five Laws of the Family:

1. "Feast not on the flesh, consume only the blood. This is our strength."

2. "Bear not the child; welcome only the exile. This is our fate."

3. "Feed not for pleasure; partake only to nourish. This is our dignity."

4. "Seek not the sun's light; embrace only the shadows. This is our refuge."

5. "Kill not our kindred; slay only the enemy. This is our justice."

You can also read Vance's proclamations about Feeding Grounds, and "the Arefu Incident," which he personally feels sorrow for. Return with this knowledge sloshing around in your brain, and Vance deems that you've learned enough to speak with Ian.

PART C: INDEPENDENT RESEARCH

Vance won't let you see Ian unless you satisfy the conditions listed below. Because it is very difficult to convince Vance to let you talk to Ian, make sure you know the following:

Vance's speeches about his clan's nature can be accessed at any time (whether you're here to see Ian or you stumbled in on the place). It allows you to read what a "vampire" is; basically that Vance has taken in a group of Cannibals and given them purpose and a place to belong. If you complete the vampire research elements, Vance respects you enough to let you see Ian, and you can negotiate a proposal from Vance to Evan King at the end of this quest (although skills and perks aren't available).

 Other possible plans to seeing Ian West include chatting with Vance after the research is over and completing a **Speech** challenge.

 Or, you can have the **Cannibal** perk already. You're spotted as "one of the brood," and can head up to meet Ian.

🗒️ **Meresti Security Password**

MAKING FRIENDS WITH THE FAMILY

Ian West is going through changes, although these involve a rare disorder, not puberty.

However you acquired the Meresti Security Password, once you have it, head south up the mezzanine exit tunnel, over the turnstiles and past Vance's personal quarters, and enter the alcove with the security door. Assuming you have the password, simply activate the terminal here, and step through into a makeshift "cell": the chamber where Ian West is sitting. You can be as rude or understanding as you like, until the matter of him staying or leaving is brought up. Now you have options:

You can simply end the conversation, and leave him to stay with the Family, which he does automatically.

 Or, you can attempt to persuade Ian (with **Speech**) to face his nightmares, and return home.

Or, if you have Lucy's Sealed Envelope, you can finally deliver it to Ian. He gets a little emotional and vows to return to be closer to his sister.

NEW OBJECTIVE
"Speak to Vance about Ian's decision" begins.

🏃 *Caution*

If you engage in combat with the Family after speaking with Ian (regardless of whether Ian has decided to leave or stay), he realizes what a maniac you are and the quest fails. If you are intent on massacring the Family, make sure everyone is dead before you open the door to Ian's cell. You have been warned!

Return to Vance, intending to speak to him about Ian's decision (no matter whether he decides to stay or not). Before you speak about Ian, there's the small matter of Arefu (and the terrified residents) to consider. You can implore Vance using one of your abilities:

At this point, you can earn big Karma, learn how to make a mighty melee weapon, or both.

 Use **Speech** to work on Vance's sense of morality (after all, he considered the raid on Arefu to be a mistake, if you believe the notes on the terminal).

 With a **Medicine** skill, you have two options. Both ideas involve the way Vance and his crew seek sustenance: Instead of Brahmin or humans, they can use Blood Packs with far less horrific consequences.

📖 Or, with enough **Intelligence**, you can suggest an alternative source of blood that Vance can survive on; again, this refers to the Blood Packs.

There's no need to utilize abilities if you've done your detective work and previously researched the Family's Laws.

Vance is amenable to this idea, but he hasn't found many Blood Packs, which drove him to his vampiric ways in the first place. You propose another fine plan, from the choices below:

Arefu donates Blood Packs, and the Family leaves the town alone.

Arefu donates Blood Packs, and the Family protects the town from Raiders and other marauders.

Arefu sells Blood Packs, and the Family leaves the town alone. Vance doesn't agree to this, and you're allowed to choose again.

Vance agrees, and gives you a proposal to give to Evan King, back at Arefu. You can now tell Vance of Ian's decision. It doesn't matter whether Ian stays or leaves; Vance still thanks you for taking the time to know him and his kin. You're awarded the schematics for the weapon Vance carries: the mighty Shishkebab!

Vance's Proposal   **Schematics: Shishkebab**

NEW OBJECTIVE
"Return to Evan King" begins.

You can leave the Family now (Ian will be in Arefu when you arrive there). Trek all the way back to Arefu (or Fast Travel once you reach the surface), and speak to Evan King (who also seems to have just arrived) about that proposal. He's happy to accept whatever you and Vance decided on, and he tells you to return to Vance to seal the deal. The quest is now complete. If you ask for reward, Evan King hands you ta few random items: a chem, a grenade, a mine, some ammo, or a bottle of vodka or scotch. Don't expect a Caps reward! If Ian decided to leave the Family, he has disposed of mom and pop, cleaned up the place, and taken up residence in the family home.

ADDITIONAL: OTHER WAYS TO PLAY THIS QUEST

PLAN A: BEGINNING AT AREFU

You can ignore Lucy West at Megaton altogether, and chance upon Arefu on your travels, speaking to Evan King instead. The quest is completed in exactly the same manner, although because you don't have Lucy's Sealed Envelope, you can't use it to dissuade Ian from remaining with the Family.

PLAN B: BEGINNING AT MERESTI

Did you stumble on Robert guarding the gate to the Family's station compound before hearing anything about Arefu or the Wests? Then you can head past Robert if he lets you. You don't know about Ian West, so either overhear a conversation between two Family members or read about "The Arefu Incident," and then receive a new objective:

NEW OBJECTIVE [ADDITIONAL]
"Discover what the Family did in Arefu" begins.

This of course, requires you to check out Arefu before finding out about Ian. Fortunately, you'll know where the Family is based!

PLAN C: BEGINNING WITH BLOODLUST

Whether you began at Lucy, Arefu, or Meresti, there's another way to finish this quest; and that's by slaughtering every last one of those bloodsucking parasites! Your massacre of the Family should begin with Robert. After gunning him down in cold blood, steal all his supplies, hotfoot it up to the station concourse, and set about demolishing the rest of these nightcrawlers! Use the vertical pillars as cover. You might want to begin with a thrown Grenade and close-up Combat Shotgun fire.

Hoping that Vance is noting the irony of his demise, continue the bloodletting by scampering upstairs and cleaving the Family's leader, wife, and anyone else who gets in your way. Once the red mist has ascended, you can search the bodies of the fallen. Karl has a Supply Key that unlocks an absolutely massive haul of Ammo and Weapons (and junk). You can find that in his workshop under the mezzanine. Vance has the password you need to free Ian, and that sword is a Shishkebab; so there's no need to build one! Finally, use Vance's Sword Cabinet Key to unlock the sword cabinet in Vance's quarters, and claim the powerful Vampire's Edge weapon. Then speak with Ian; if you're threatening, he fights to the death. If you're not, you can use Lucy's Sealed Envelope or the Speech persuasion to get him to return to Arefu.

Karl's Supply Key   **Massive Amounts of Ammo**

A Number of Weapons   **Multiple First Aid Box Health and Chems**

Meresti Security Password   **Schematic: Shishkebab**

Shishkebab   **Vance's Longcoat Outfit**

Vance's Sword Cabinet Key   **Vampire's Edge**

Caution

You fail this quest if you try any of the following:

Hurting or killing anyone in Arefu.

Hurting or killing Ian West.

Hurting or killing the Family after obtaining Ian's decision on what to do. Not nice!

QUEST REWARDS

You receive the following rewards for finishing Blood Ties:

Schematic: Shishkebab†   **Hematophage Perk‡**

XP **300 XP**

† For negotiating with the Family. You gain extra items if you slaughter the Family, at a cost to your Karma.

‡ For brokering a deal between Arefu and the Family: The perk allows you to gain 20 Health (instead of 1) by consuming Blood Packs.

Karma [+300]
For successfully dealing with Ian and remaining on good terms with Arefu and the Family.

KARMA [-100]
For killing each citizen of Arefu or Family member.

POST-QUEST ANTICS

Choose to broker a "Blood Pack for Protection" scheme, and you can finally enter that abandoned house...;

FREEFORM QUEST: A LITTLE HELP FROM ALAN

Meanwhile, back in the tunnels, Vance is waiting patiently for you to finish your yo-yo trekking between the two camps. He's happy to finally bring the Family's reign of terror to an end! Once the quest ends with a final chat with Evan King, return to Vance. He agrees to any of your three proposals. If you chose to have the Family guard Arefu in exchange for Blood Packs, Alan sets off immediately, and if you return to Arefu, he's set up in the abandoned house, which is now called Alan's residence. You can now enter this structure (it's the only way to do this), but there's little to claim inside.

FREEFORM QUEST: A PENCHANT FOR PLASMA

Return to Vance for the final conversation, and look for a new dialog option. He can teach you his vampiric ways, and you can learn the Hematophage perk!

FREEFORM QUEST: I WANT TO DRINK YOUR BLOOD

If you managed a proposal, you can return to Vance and sell him Blood Packs for 15 Caps each.

FREEFORM QUEST: SUGAR BOMBING RUN

Remember that you can continue this quest with Murphy at Seneca Station.

FREEFORM QUEST: SPECIAL DELIVERY

Finally, you can return to Megaton and speak with Lucy herself, telling her of her parents' fate, and Ian's situation (and condition).

OTHER ANTICS

Of more interest are some accoutrements for yourself, courtesy of those you helped:

Ken Ewers can Repair items for you at a cut-price rate.

Karen Schenzy has some interesting knowledge of the surrounding area, and she pinpoints some areas for you to explore.

If you didn't already give Ian West Lucy's Sealed Envelope, and want it out of your Inventory, you can visit his shack and hand it over.

Oasis

While wandering the northern Wastes, you stumble across a hidden settlement called **Oasis [2.01]**, an amazingly fertile, verdant dot hidden among the desolation. As you enter this secret vale, you're greeted by a strange tribal people calling themselves the Treeminders. Welcoming you with open arms, their leader, Tree Father Birch, invites you to meet their god. Should you oblige and indulge in the ceremony, you awake in front of a bizarre, yet oddly familiar monstrosity. He's the cause of this greening of the landscape, but he wants to die. Meanwhile, Tree Father Birch wants these effects to halt, while another of the tribe, Leaf Mother Laurel, sees larger parts of the Wasteland becoming green pastures for all to live on. Do you side with Birch, Laurel, or the rarest tree of all, the Herbert? Harold is counting on you….

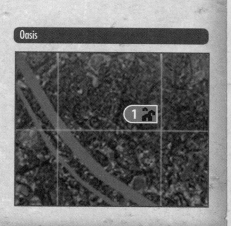

Oasis

QUEST FLOWCHART

	MAIN PATH 1	MAIN PATH 2	MAIN PATH 3	OPTIONAL PATH
Main Characters	Harold, Tree Father Birch	Tree Father Birch, Branchtender Cypress, Branchtender Maple, Sapling Yew	Leaf Mother Laurel, Branchtender Linden, Bloomseer Poplar, Sapling Yew	Harold
Locations	Oasis, The Grove, Sunken Cavern	Oasis, The Grove, Sunken Cavern	Oasis, The Grove, Sunken Cavern	Oasis, The Grove
Adv. Items/Abilities	Speech Skill, Child at Heart Perk	Speech Skill, Child at Heart Perk	Speech Skill, Child at Heart Perk	Flamer and Fuel
Possible enemies	Mirelurks	Mirelurks	Mirelurks	Treeminders
Karma Influence	None	Positive	Positive	Negative

Undertake the Treeminder's Ceremony.

Drink Sap from Basin of Purification and speak with Harold

Agree to Help Harold | Ignore Harold

↓

Obtain the key to the caves from Branchtender Cypress. | Kill Harold by burning him.

• Key to Oasis Caves

↓

Enter the caves below and destroy Harold's heart.

Listen to Tree Father Birch and Leaf Mother Laurel's discussion

• Birch's Sap Container
• Laurel's Liniment

↓

[Optional] Apply Birch's Sap to Harold's heart and stop his growth. | [Optional] Apply Laurel's Liniment to Harold's heart and accelerate his growth.

Shoot Harold in the heart | Apply Sap to heart | Apply Liniment to heart

• Barkskin Perk

Speak with Tree Father Birch. | Speak with Tree Father Birch. | Speak with Leaf Mother Laurel.

• Missile Launcher and Ammo	• Brotherhood Outcast Power Armor	• –Karma
• Druid's Outfit	• Villager's Hood	• Hostile Treeminders
• Bear Charm	• Bear Charm	

Color code: | Objective | Action | Rewards |

TRAINING — BESTIARY — MAIN QUEST — MISC. QUESTS — TOUR — COMPLETION — APPENDICES

AN OASIS IN THE DESERT

Note

The lush Oasis, its Treeminder denizens, and a tree named Harold have interesting back stories. These are located in the Tour of the Capital Wasteland Chapter (beginning on page 271).

When you're trekking through the very northern edge of the Wastelands, either following the monorail northwest, or navigating the rocky terrain across from the Power Station, look for the oddly shaped mountain shown in the nearby picture. If you're heading eastward, cross the rickety rope bridge on your way to the foot of the mountain. As you reach a narrow gorge, heading almost southeast, weave through the faint trails until you spot something odd; there are small clumps of green vegetation poking out of the soil. This is the first living plant life you've seen!

The mountainous terrain may be treacherous, but the secrets hidden in this oddly shaped outcrop are worth reaching.

Wander up through the winding path to discover more and more green vegetation. This strangeness continues as you reach a copse of live trees, flanking a wooden gate. An old man clad in a brown tunic and hood, with small branches protruding from his outfit, approaches you. He extends a friendly welcome, even though you're an Outsider. This is Tree Father Birch, and it's very difficult to get him to dislike you. He wants you to meet "Him," and (assuming you don't simply leave) tells you to hasten to the Pavilion, where all will be explained.

Meet Tree Father Birch and Branchtender Maple guarding the Oasis: Have you twigged what's going on?

NEW OBJECTIVE
"Undertake the Treeminder's Ceremony" begins.

THE PURIFICATION RITUAL

You're beckoned to a central Pavilion inside the Tree-minders' Oasis, and Tree Father Birch beckons you over to talk. You can wander this vibrant woodland, talking to each of the different Treeminders in turn; they all point you to their leader. Move to his throne when you're ready, and he begins to speak about Him: the "One Who Grows," the "One Who Gives," and the "One Who Guides."

If you have a high **Speech** skill, you can demand a straight answer.

If not, you still receive information about this group, who shun technology and embrace nature.

Caution

Watch your mouth in the presence of Tree Father Birch; if you are consistently rude to him, he gives you a warning. Should you continue, you are charged with Blasphemy, and Excommunicated. You are asked to leave within 10 minutes. Failure results in the Treeminders turning hostile. If the Treeminders turn hostile, you fail the quest.

Continue the conversation, and resist the temptation to insult the Father as he continues to speak about Him. Finally he wants you both to meet, but this can only happen if you perform the Purification Ritual. This involves drinking the Sap from the Basin of Purification, in the center of the Pavilion. You are assured that the Sap is quite safe. When you're ready, agree to the ritual, and all the Treeminders are summoned. This is the last chance to back out before a black out! After Tree Father Birch chants on about His Frondescence, you collapse at the end of the prayer, and are sent to meet Him.

PART MAN, PART TREE: SAY HELLO TO HAROLD

You come to in a beautiful forest glade, with a large central tree standing proud. The specimen is interesting for two reasons: you can't determine the species, and it has a humanoid figure fused into the side of it. This Talking Tree introduces itself, and one of the most bizarre conversations ever begins! The Talking Tree informs you that he's been hoping you'd stop by for weeks, and that Bob (AKA Herbert), the tree-like mutation that's been growing inside him for years, has completely taken over his once-human body. The tree thinks it all started when he was exploring a military base called Mariposa. He can't be sure. Anyway, he wants you to kill him.

Don't just bring out the Flamer, because it's slightly more complicated than that. He wants you to destroy his heart, which—thanks to Bob—hangs underneath him like a dangling hernia. Continue the conversation if you wish, but finally agree to his undertaking. When you're ready, exit via the Wooden Gate to Oasis.

Note

Harold seems to be suffering from a form of F.E.V., or Forced Evolutionary Virus.

NEW OBJECTIVE
"Obtain the key to the caves from Branchtender Cypress" begins.

NEW OBJECTIVE
"Enter the caves below and destroy Harold's Heart" begins.

THE ELDERS' ARGUMENT

Move back to the Pavilion hub of the Oasis, and walk down the southwest branch corridor. Just after the glade, Tree Father Birch and Leaf Mother Laurel are having a fierce discussion. Although they remain civil, their argument results in an impasse that they deem you important enough to solve. Tree Father Birch turns to you; converse until you hear his plan for keeping Oasis away from prying eyes. He wants you to rub Sap on his god's heart to slow the spread of greenery. Leaf Mother Laurel, meanwhile, sees the spreading as a great miracle, and she wants all of the Wasteland to benefit from it. She hands you a Liniment to increase Harold's mutation.

 **Note**

Although Treeminders would never resort to factions, Branchtender Cypress and Branchtender Maple take Tree Father Birch's view. Branchtender Linden and Bloomseer Poplar are pre-disposed to agreeing with Leaf Mother Laurel.

Birch's Sap Container   **Laurel's Liniment**

NEW OBJECTIVE [OPTIONAL]
"Apply Birch's Sap to Harold's Heart and stop his growth" begins.

NEW OBJECTIVE [OPTIONAL]
"Apply Laurel's Liniment to Harold's Heart and accelerate his growth" begins.

After hearing both sides to the argument, prepare to find Harold's Heart by heading to the entrance of the Oasis Caves, a decidedly less serene environment. Before you go, you may wish to speak to each of the Treeminders in turn about their personal feelings on who is right. Bloomseer Poplar, Branchtender Cypress, Branchtender Linden, Branchtender Maple, and even little Sapling Yew can provide information to help sway you to either side. Then simply ask Branchtender Cypress for the Key to Oasis Caves; he simply gives it to you (although Pickpocketing has the same result). Move to the mesh gate at the cave entrance.

Key to Oasis Caves

MURDERING MIRELURKS IN THE OASIS CAVES

 Caution

Beware! If you are at a higher Experience Level, you may encounter more Mirelurk Hunters instead of Mirelurks, and additional Mirelurk Kings, during your cavern expedition.

Arm yourself with your favored Mirelurk-hunting weapon, and step past the glowing fungi, moving to a shallow wading stream that would be picturesque except for the radiation and the giant crab-like beast charging you. Take the left tunnel, as the way ahead leads to a hole too high to reach. Stop at the higher ground and look over a large underground pond. You are wise to aim projectiles from this point; Mirelurks swim the pond, and one roams an alcove on the opposite side.

Deal with all enemies before diving into the pond and swimming through an opening under the alcove. Find a Mirelurk Egg Clutch and some hapless backpacker's last meal in a bag before you dive. Surface and scramble up the wet rocks, following the tunnel farther along to another Mirelurk. Squash a small infestation of Radroaches here also. Check the nearby Egg Clutch if Mirelurk meat is on your menu, then pass the dripping stalactites and find the door leading to the Sunken Chambers.

THE HEART OF THE MATTER

Don't get temporarily hypnotized by the streaming sunlight and junk collection; the dead-end passage can be a trap!

The Sunken Chambers are less soggy, and seem to have supported some Wasteland Settlers and Raiders until the Mirelurks moved in. At the first junction, edge forward, because there are two Mirelurks to defeat ahead of you. This is better than scurrying up the side tunnel to a sunlit-filled stash of junk, as you have nowhere to run from the Mirelurks who follow you. There's a small amount of Ammunition here. Now move onward to the crimson pool area. Tackle a nearby Mirelurk, then dive into the pool if your radiation level isn't too high; in this pool, search Raider bodies and grab a Mini-Nuke.

Climb out of the pool (which you can also visit on your way out of here, or after you cleanse the area of foes), and zigzag through the narrow gaps as the cave system once again becomes soggy. Beware the two Mirelurks ready to savage you in this area. After combat, carefully tread along the continuation of the tunnel system, pausing to check behind nearby rocks for a skeleton still clinging to a Missile and Blood Pack. Then continue all the way to the dead-end cave, which is directly under Harold's forest glade.

NEW OBJECTIVE [OPTIONAL]
"Apply Birch's Sap to Harold's Heart and stop his growth" begins.

NEW OBJECTIVE [OPTIONAL]
"Apply Laurel's Liniment to Harold's Heart and accelerate his growth" begins.

NEW OBJECTIVE [OPTIONAL]
"Kill Harold by burning him" begins.

You have three choices, and they involve massaging or mangling Harold's Heart.

You may wish to save your game before you begin your open-heart surgery; you're prompted to Destroy Harold's Heart, Apply Birch Sap to stop Harold's growth, or Apply Laurel's Liniment to accelerate Harold's growth. Or, you can do nothing. There are pros and cons of each plan, and the choice is entirely up to you. If you want the earliest possible prize, opt for Harold's plan, and shoot the heart after activating it. Unfortunately, some of Harold's blood spills onto you, and you become infected with F.E.V. (Harold's Strain). Your skin becomes hard as tree bark! Your rewards for rubbing either Birch Sap or Laurel Liniment become apparent when you return to Oasis.

NEW OBJECTIVE
"Speak with Tree Father Birch" begins (if you destroyed Harold's Heart, or applied the Sap).

NEW OBJECTIVE
"Speak with Leaf Mother Laurel" begins (if you applied the Liniment).

DOWN IN THE DAMP CAVE

You can now retrace your steps to Oasis. However, if you want some additional XP, and your Small Arms ordnance is a lot healthier than your Missiles, you can negotiate another subterranean system: the Damp Cave. It offers a slightly quicker exit, but untouched enemies. The route to the Damp Cave is an easy-to-miss path heading south-west from Harold's Heart. This passage ends at a door. Head through to a promontory overlooking a waterlogged cave. Up here is a small collection of junk, and a Missile.

Stay on this promontory so you can snipe the three Mirelurks that roam the watery area. Or, drop down and engage in a more danger-ous firefight (or use Melee attacks, or simply flee). When you wish to leave, head roughly northwest, diving underwater and swimming northward along a water-filled passage to a submerged door. This takes you back to Harold's Grove directly.

TREEMINDERS REJOICE!

Make your way to Harold's Grove. If you killed Harold, or applied the Sap, Tree Father Birch will be waiting nearby. If you applied the Liniment, Leaf Mother Laurel is here. Converse with either of them. If you killed Harold at his

Whether you destroyed or invigorated Harold's Heart, move to the Treeminder watching him, in the glade.

heart, Father Tree Birch feels no ill-will, as this is what Harold wished. If you applied the Sap or Liniment, Father Tree Birch or Leaf Mother Laurel are ecstatic, and inform you that gifts are available for your troubles. Wander around Oasis, looking for specific Treeminders to claim them (remember that one is likely to be guarding the entrance, in the Wasteland).

[OPTIONAL] TREE-HUGGERS? BURN!

 Despite Harold specifically telling you he wants to die from a heart attack, you can ignore this mutated crackpot and burn him with your Flamer! You could also use a Nuka Grenade, Missile Launcher, Shishkebab, Plasma Rifle, Plasma Pistol, or Fat Man to do the job. Of course, This doesn't sit well with the hippie folk, and they bring out their weapons to attack you. Forcing the Treeminders to attack means you're never welcomed here again, and your Karma plummets to devilish levels, especially if you turn your Flamer on them all! Remember, this can be done so you don't have to enter the caves (although you fail the quest); or you can complete the quest, claim the reward, and then torch the place!

QUEST REWARDS

COMPLETION PLAN 1: DESTROYING HAROLD'S HEART

 Barkskin Perk
Endurance +1, Damage Resistance +10.

COMPLETION PLAN 2: APPLYING FATHER TREE BIRCH'S SAP

Need a heavy weapon, but want to keep that back-to-nature look? Choose the Sap.

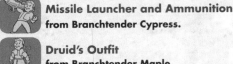 **Missile Launcher and Ammunition**
from Branchtender Cypress.

Druid's Outfit
from Branchtender Maple.

COMPLETION PLAN 3: APPLYING LEAF MOTHER LAUREL'S LINIMENT

Crave a special variant of Power Armor, but want to look mysterious, too? Choose the Liniment.

 Brotherhood Outcast Power Armor
from Branchtender Linden.
+10 Rad Resist, +5 Big Guns, +1 Strength, -1 Agility.

Villager's Hood
from Bloomseer Poplar.

FREEFORM QUEST: BLOOMSEER POPLAR'S VISIONS

Once you've completed the Oasis quest, you can speak to Bloom-seer Poplar. She will give you a clue to a Miscellaneous Quest that you haven't yet completed. You can receive a new clue once every 24 hours. Refer to the Zone 2 section of the Tour of the Wasteland chapter for details.

FREEFORM QUEST: YEW GOT A NEW FRIEND

Before you complete either Father or Mother's Quest, be sure to speak with Sapling Yew for her opinion on what should be rubbed into Har-old's Heart. She doesn't have a strong opinion either way, but as long as Harold doesn't die (by burning or a shot to the heart), the following options are available:

If you succeed in using this skill when speaking to her, she gives you her Bear Charm.

If you have this skill, she gives you this Bear Charm, if you want it.

 Bear Charm
from Sapling Yew
+10 Speech.

The Power of the Atom

When you first arrive at **Megaton [8.03]**, it becomes terrifyingly obvious that this ramshackle town was constructed around the crater left by a half-embedded, and currently unexploded Atom Bomb. Before inspecting the hazardous device, you meet Sheriff Lucas Simms, who has his own thoughts on these dangers. If you explore the town further, a visit to Moriarty's Saloon reveals an oddly out-of-place businessman named Mister Burke, who represents clandestine interests residing in the fortified **Tenpenny Tower [7.14]**, southwest of the town. These businessmen require a more...spectacular removal of the bomb (as well as the surrounding area). The choice is yours: turn Megaton into a safe refuge for its Wastelander inhabitants, or into a smoking hulk of scorched earth and radiation....

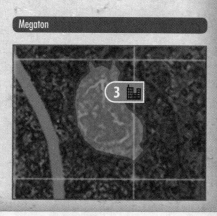

Megaton

QUEST FLOWCHART

	MAIN PATH 1	OPTIONAL PATH	MAIN PATH 2
Main Characters	Lucas Simms	Leo Stash	Lucas Simms, Mister Burke
Locations	Megaton	Megaton	Megaton, Tenpenny Tower
Adv. Items/Abilities	Speech Skill, Explosives Skill,	Speech Skill, 29 Bottle Caps	Speech Skill, Black Widow Perk, Explosives Skill
Karma influence	Positive	Positive and/or negative	Negative
Possible enemies	None	None	Mole Rats, Bloatflies, Raiders

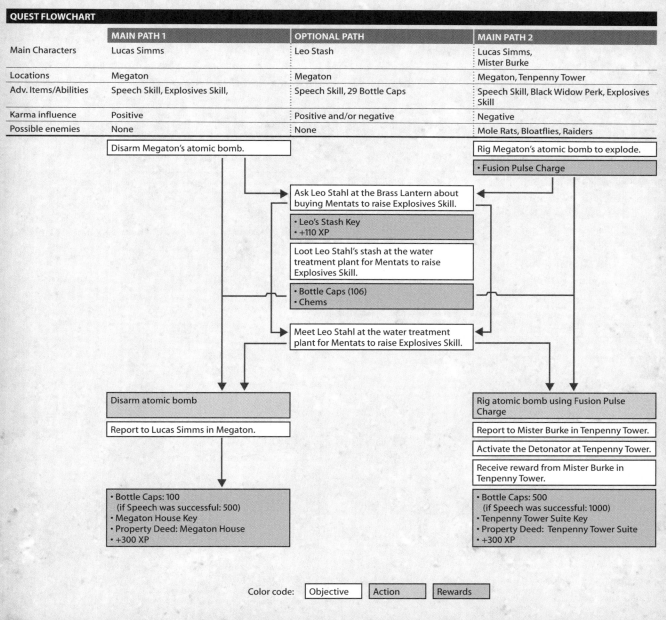

Disarm Megaton's atomic bomb.

Rig Megaton's atomic bomb to explode.

• Fusion Pulse Charge

Ask Leo Stahl at the Brass Lantern about buying Mentats to raise Explosives Skill.

• Leo's Stash Key
• +110 XP

Loot Leo Stahl's stash at the water treatment plant for Mentats to raise Explosives Skill.

• Bottle Caps (106)
• Chems

Meet Leo Stahl at the water treatment plant for Mentats to raise Explosives Skill.

Disarm atomic bomb

Report to Lucas Simms in Megaton.

• Bottle Caps: 100
  (if Speech was successful: 500)
• Megaton House Key
• Property Deed: Megaton House
• +300 XP

Rig atomic bomb using Fusion Pulse Charge

Report to Mister Burke in Tenpenny Tower.

Activate the Detonator at Tenpenny Tower.

Receive reward from Mister Burke in Tenpenny Tower.

• Bottle Caps: 500
  (if Speech was successful: 1000)
• Tenpenny Tower Suite Key
• Property Deed: Tenpenny Tower Suite
• +300 XP

Color code: | Objective | Action | Rewards |

APPENDICES — COMPLETION — TOUR — MISC. QUESTS — MAIN QUEST — BESTIARY — TRAINING

WELCOME FROM DEPUTY WELD: ENTERING MEGATON

Megaton is reasonably close to Vault 101, in the Southern Wastes, and is usually trekked to in a vaguely southerly route on your Pip-Boy's compass. The town's entrance is easy to spot, not least because of the large scrawled name on one of its sliding defense panels. After passing by Deputy Weld, a sentry robot, step under the turbine powering the opening gates, and into a small entrance chamber, then open the inner doors.

Sheriff Lucas Simms sizes you up.

Stockholm moves to a balcony above these doors to keep an eye on you. Ignore him, and greet that large, imposing cowboy, who introduces himself as Sheriff (and sometime Mayor) Lucas Simms. Strike up any type of conversation you like, but to begin this quest, say "Let's discuss this bomb." Try to stay on the civil side of Simms, and let him know that "I can see about disarming that bomb for you."

Simms agrees, telling you there's 100 Caps for you if you succeed in disarming the bomb. The following options are available:

> With a high **Speech** skill, you can persuade Lucas that the demolition won't be cheap, and demand 500 Caps. If your greed succeeds, Simms agrees to your fleecing.

You can agree to this quest without a financial benefit to you. Unless you're weighed down with Caps, this isn't a recommended option.

 You do get a Karma reward if you decline the Caps and disarm the bomb.

You can agree to Simms's financial incentive of 100 Caps, which is also the best option if you fail your Speech conversation.

Or, you can ignore this deadly problem and be on your way (come back to speak with Simms if you wish to start this quest later).

NEW OBJECTIVE

"Disarm Megaton's atomic bomb" begins.

MEGATON RECONNOITER: OTHER WAYS TO LEARN ABOUT THE BOMB

If you didn't bring up the subject of the bomb with Lucas Simms when you entered Megaton, you can also learn about it in a number of other ways:

Spotting a giant, unexploded bomb is easy. Disarming or detonating it is more difficult.

Locate a mysterious man called Mister Burke, who talks about the bomb.

Wander close to the bomb, which is sticking out of a waterlogged crater in the middle of town.

Strike up a conversation with a named Megaton inhabitant, who mentions the bomb.

After that, report back to Sheriff Lucas Simms to begin this quest.

I SHOT THE SHERIFF (AND I ALSO SHOT THE DEPUTY)

 Caution

If this quest is unimportant to you, simply open fire on Lucas Simms, and begin a highly dangerous gun battle that rages throughout the entire town. This is usually fatal if you aren't highly skilled in the arts of war. Bring all your ammunition, weapons, mood-altering narcotics, and Stimpaks; you're in for a long night of bloodshed. Everyone grabs a gun and hunts you down, from lowly Megaton Settlers to the sharpshooter Colin Moriarty.

If you're a maniac with a death wish, and you want to complete this quest, concentrate on agreeing to disarm the bomb with Lucas prior to strafing his corpse with bullets. Or better yet, finish the quest, obtain your reward, and then massacre the entire town. As you might expect, your Karma plummets after such behavior…if you're still alive!

THE SAFE OPTION: DISARM MEGATON'S BOMB

As soon as you're tasked with disarming the bomb, you can move down the earthen steps to the middle of the settlement, and inspect this deadly device yourself. Optionally, you can speak to Confessor Cromwell about the cult—sorry, bona fide religion—called the Children of the Atom. This isn't strictly necessary, but it gives you more background and helps with your main quest. When you're ready, and if a massive explosion doesn't interest you, approach the bomb itself, and begin Disarming the Bomb.

Moriarty's Saloon is not the classiest of establishments, and the clientele range from the slightly weird to massively irradiated.

If you require an alternative to saving Megaton, trudge southwest and up to the shacks perched on the south side of town. Locate the watering hole known as Moriarty's Saloon, and enter through the front door. Inside, mingle with the patrons, obtaining further information if you wish. Then turn westward, to a ramshackle sitting area just right of Gob, the ghoulish bartender banging on the radio. An oddly dressed gentleman beckons you over.

THE SLY OPTION: DISARM OR RIG MEGATON'S BOMB

Not the Mysterious Stranger, but this guy is certainly oddly out of place for this run-down shack. Say hello to Mister Burke.

Speak with Mister Burke, a well-mannered but slightly threatening man with an odd cadence. He makes his feelings on Megaton rather clear early on, comparing it unfavorably with a "putrescent cesspool." With this in mind, he requests that you rid the Wasteland of this eyesore, and he has just the Fusion Pulse Charge you need to get the job done. The following options are available:

 With a high **Speech** skill, you can request that Burke sweeten the deal with an additional 500 Caps. If he agrees, you receive a Fusion Pulse Charge, with the full amount to be paid later.

You can grudgingly or enthusiastically agree to an undisclosed "base fee" and receive a Fusion Pulse Charge.

You can consistently refuse his offer and tell him off, letting him know Megaton is under your protection. He brushes you aside and leaves.

NEW OBJECTIVE

"Disarm Megaton's atomic bomb...or rig it to explode" begins.

 Fusion Pulse Charge

> 📖 *Note*
> You can speak to Mister Burke and receive the Fusion Pulse Charge without any negative Karma consequences; you now have two choices instead of one.

LOVE LETTERS STRAIGHT FROM HIS HEART

 If you're female and possess the **Black Widow** perk, you and your succubus-like skills allow two additional options when speaking with Mister Burke. Choose to let him know you have a "proposition" of your own for him. The following options now become available:

You can explain that you live here, and he wouldn't want to hurt you. He stammers and blusters, and tells you he'll send for you soon, before he leaves Megaton for good.

You can laugh at his paltry "base fee" and demand he pay you a lot more Caps for your loyalty. He promptly offers you 500 additional Caps.

The first choice allows you to concentrate on disarming the bomb only.

The second choice enables you to choose whether to disarm or rig the bomb.

The first choice also results in Mister Burke pleading for you to retrieve a series of love letters that he sends to Colin Moriarty. Pick up all four if you're interested; a new one arrives at the saloon every seven days.

TATTLETALE TACTICS

Sheriff Lucas Simms has little time for bomb threats; if you inform on Mister Burke, a swift confrontation ensues.

At any time before the bomb is disarmed or rigged, you can tell either Sheriff Lucas Simms or Mister Burke of the other side's plans, and your subsequent thoughts on the next course of action. The following options are possible:

Agree or talk with Mister Burke. Then locate Lucas Simms, and inform him of the threat. The sheriff immediately brandishes his weapon, storms up to Moriarty's Saloon, and attempts to arrest Mister Burke. Burke responds with quick and deadly force, killing Simms! You can still disarm the bomb, but you must seek out Simms's son, Harden. Harden lives in Simms's house.

Agree or talk with Mister Burke. Then find Lucas Simms, and tell him you're siding with Burke's business associates. The Sheriff despises your underhanded plan and draws his weapon on you. The entire town engages in this firefight. If by some miracle you survive, you can only rig the bomb.

Agree or talk with Sheriff Simms. Then locate Mister Burke. If you tell him of the sheriff's request, and you're sticking by Simms, Mister Burke verbally threatens you, then leaves. You can now only disarm the bomb.

Finally, if for any reason you begin to distrust Burke (especially after the threat), you can draw your weapon and gun him down. He fights back, so use V.A.T.S. or shoot first to get the jump on him. The bar patrons are rather...philosophical about the murder. You can now only disarm the bomb, but wearing Dirty Pre-War business attire is now an attractive (if lightly armored) option.

Hitman about town: Slay Burke in Moriarty's if you find his plans particularly distasteful, but his outfit particularly stylish.

 Dirty Pre-War Businesswear

 Pre-War Hat

Tortoiseshell Glasses

10mm Pistol, Silenced

LEARNING ABOUT, AND LEANING ON, LEO STAHL

> 💡 *Tip*
> Do you already have Mentats in your inventory? Then you can skip this stage completely, and disarm or rig the bomb.

Whether you're siding with Sheriff Lucas Simms or Mister Burke, your next plan of action is to inspect the bomb itself.

 With **Explosives**, you can skip to the section marked "Finally Disarming or Rigging the Bomb."

If your Explosives skill is too low, you won't be able to touch the bomb. Return to Burke and explain that your bomb-defusing technique is a little lacking. Burke advises you attempt to locate a man named Leo Stahl, who may have some Chems to steady your hand, and increase your Explosives prowess. You need to complete the optional objectives related to Leo Stahl only if you require such drug-based help.

> 💡 *Tip*
> Make sure Simms references Chems, or Burke mentions Leo Stahl by name, and the Optional Quest Stage is activated before you find Leo Stahl, or you won't be able to interrogate him about his habits.

NEW OBJECTIVE [OPTIONAL]

"Ask Leo Stahl at the Brass Lantern about buying Mentats to raise Explosives skill" begins.

Immediately move to the Brass Lantern, an eatery adjacent and just north of the bomb itself. Enter the shack via the door under the neon sign, and locate Leo Stahl behind the bar. After a brief introduction, pick a new dialog choice: "I understand you have quite a Chem habit…." From this point on, you have the following options:

 Choose "It's okay, Leo. I want to help." Then attempt to play on his emotions by telling him he's hurting his family, Jenny and Andy. If your **Speech** is successful, and you don't choose "Never mind, Leo. It's not my business," either of the other options causes Leo to renounce his destructive lifestyle. He hands you a key to his private stash in the water treatment plant.

 Leo's Stash Key

NEW OBJECTIVE [OPTIONAL]

"Loot Leo Stahl's stash at the water treatment plant for Mentats to raise Explosives skill" begins.

If you failed in your Speech, you can still score a hook up, and the next option occurs:

Choose "What's it worth to you to keep it out of the public eye?" Leo quickly tells you he can hook you up, but only after his shift at the Lantern is over. He tells you to meet him at the water treatment plant. Further hassling yields nothing from Leo.

NEW OBJECTIVE [OPTIONAL]

"Meet Leo Stahl at the water treatment plant for Mentats to raise Explosives skill" begins.

Choose "Never mind, Leo. It's not my business anyway." Leo agrees with you, and refuses to talk any more about the habit. You need to procure Mentats elsewhere.

A TREAT AT THE TREATMENT PLANT

If you procured Leo's Stash Key after making the man feel bad about hurting his loved ones, head directly to the water treatment plant, on the upper rim of the crater, just up the ramp to the north of Craterside Supplies. Open the unlocked door, and saunter through to the back room. Old man Walter says hello, but it isn't necessary to chat; simply look for the locked desk and open it (use the key). There's a treasure trove inside, and a nice unhealthy drop in your Karma for your thievery:

 Bottle Caps (usually 100+ total)

 Chems and Stimpaks

You can now choose to either disarm or rig the bomb.

The delightful Nova does her level best to keep you comfortable.

If Leo Stahl has agreed to sell you some Mentats after his shift at the Brass Lantern, you must wait until eight o'clock in the evening (20:00) for him to arrive at his desk. Head there any

earlier, and you're greeted by an old worker called Walter, who's friendly enough but lacks the dangerous narcotics you crave. If you need to sleep to pass the time, an excellent plan is to head to Moriarty's Saloon, and locate one of his "special" staff members: Nova. This redhead sells a sleeping arrangement you might want to try. Her room is straight ahead at the top of the stairs. The cost is a little steep: 120 Caps.

Once you've passed the time, exit out onto the gloomy balcony overlooking Megaton, and head down to Craterside Supply. Then walk up the ramp heading north, and with the fuselage pile ahead of you, look right at the watering plant shack. Head inside. Don't mind Walter; he's a harmless old coot. Leo is sitting at his desk, at the back of the plant, and once you request a hook up, he offers Buffouts, Jets, Mentats, Med-X, and Stimpaks. Mentats are 29 Caps each, and (if you're here strictly to increase your Explosives skill) one bottle is all you need.

You can now choose to either disarm or rig the bomb.

FINALLY DISARMING OR RIGGING THE BOMB

You're hopped up on Mentats, and the safety of this ramshackle community is in your twitchy fingers.

Whether you procured the Mentats or not, you must now focus on the bomb. Move to it, and begin one of the following plans:

 Disarm (naturally or chemically): You automatically succeed in disarming it, if you choose this option and your **Explosives** skill is high enough. Once the bomb is disarmed, it cannot be rigged, and you cannot blow up Megaton.

Tip

Is your Explosives skill completely deficient? Then rise a level and place your points into this skill before returning with Mentats in hand.

NEW OBJECTIVE

"Report to Lucas Simms in Megaton" begins.

 Rig: You must have obtained the Fusion Pulse Charge from Mister Burke. If so, you can use your **Explosives** skill to access the bomb and connect the charge to it.

NEW OBJECTIVE

"Report to Mister Burke in Tenpenny Tower" begins.

LOCATING LUCAS SIMMS

When the bomb is safely defused, seek out the sheriff, who's ecstatic about the lack of gigantic live bombs in his town. In fact, his gratitude extends to rewarding you with the key and deed to your own piece of real estate, high in the northwestern corner of town. The digs aren't exactly palatial, but they're a place to rest your head and store your belongings. If Lucas Simms is dead, but the inhabitants of Megaton haven't turned hostile (usually because Burke shot the sheriff), look for Simms's son Harden to reward you.

SLINKING OFF TO TENPENNY TOWER

Tip

Remember: If you didn't make a deal with Burke, or you disarmed the bomb, there's no need (or point) to visit Tenpenny Tower!

If you rigged the bomb to explode, there's nothing you can do to change this (except leave this quest incomplete). You must leave Megaton, and rendezvous with Mister Burke in an impressively well-guarded tower southwest of Megaton. Head out, passing Deputy Weld for the last time, and head in a vaguely southwesterly direction, using the guide map or your Pip-Boy directional arrow to help you. Pass under the broken section of freeway. At the top of the next rise, you can spot Tenpenny Tower in the distance.

With more than 10 floors of brownstone and a well-defended concrete perimeter, this is luxury living, Wasteland style!

Continue in this vaguely southwestern path. Your likely adversaries are Mole Rats, Bloatflies, and the odd Raider. Continue through the valley and up to a second area of broken freeway flyover sections. Clamber across to flatter ground, and you'll get a better glimpse of the imposing Tenpenny Tower. Join the crumbling road heading west, and pass the RobCo Facility to your right. As the tower looms up before you, move left (or south) around its concrete slab perimeter; this is quicker than circling around to the right.

As you approach the rather elaborate gates, there's a man standing by the intercom, arguing that he's got some Caps to trade. On closer inspection, half his face seems to have melted away. This is Roy Phillips, a Ghoul who's having terrible trouble entering the facility. You can let him finish his argument, muttering under his breath as he steps away, or drop him where he stands if you like losing Karma and simply must kill anything with lumpy skin. Press the security intercom, and tell them you're here to see Mister Burke. The gate creaks open, and you receive a curt warning from Chief of Security Gustavo.

Tip

If you want to complete **Miscellaneous Quest: Tenpenny Tower**, you may want to hold off on Ghoul disposals for the moment.

You can wander the exterior, noting the numerous guards and chatting with them. When you're done, head north to the metal door leading to the Tenpenny Tower lobby. Inside is a lush, almost pre-apocalyptic building, with what look like real plants, and soft music emanating from the walls. You can investigate the Boutique Le Chic, Cafe Beau Monde, or other well-to-do areas, and generally hang around the toffs, trying not to stink up the joint. Your main plan though, is to locate the elevator between the staircases, behind the foyer desk. Ride it up to the penthouse suites.

Exit the elevator, and optionally roam the penthouse suites, chatting with any of the inhabitants you want. If you cause any problems (bullets to the head, for example), your destination becomes impenetrable, so hold your fire. Just to the east (left) of the elevator is a door with a security guard sitting by it. Approach the guard, and he tells you that Mister Burke is expecting you on the balcony. Wait for him to open the door, then enter, passing what could actually be some real plants. Step through the double doors, and onto a balcony featuring the most dynamic Wasteland vista you've ever witnessed....

MEGATON GOES BOOM

Moira Brown. Maggie and Billy. Lucy West. Even good old Gob. Vaporized by your hand. No more Megaton quests for you!

After gazing at the incredible panorama for a moment, you can optionally turn right and talk with the eccentric old Brit Allistair Tenpenny, who's able to waffle for England about his "jewel of the Wasteland." When he finally stops, talk with Mister Burke, who's happy you've rigged and arrived. He allows you the honor of pushing the detonator, located inside the suitcase on the table next to Burke. Open the case, and you can rid Tenpenny of the blot on the landscape that he and his investors had longed to remove. The resulting explosion is horrifyingly impressive. Try it during the day or night if you wish.

NEW OBJECTIVE
"Activate the Detonator at Tenpenny Tower" begins.

NEW OBJECTIVE
"Receive reward from Mister Burke in Tenpenny Tower" begins.

Tip

Did you make a mistake, and still have outstanding quests in Megaton that you need to complete? Then finish all of them before pushing that button!

TRAINING — BESTIARY — MAIN QUEST — MISC. QUESTS — TOUR — COMPLETION — APPENDICES

As the mushroom cloud (or as Burke calls it, "transcendent beauty") begins to dissipate, Mister Burke quickly moves on to the small matter of your payment. Based on your Speech skills, you're given a hefty number of Caps, and a more impressive prize still: a penthouse master suite. Lydia Montenegro in the Boutique Le Chic is the perfect interior decorator for your new pad. Rest your head in style, and keep your belongings as safe as they can possibly be.

QUEST REWARDS

Note

Information on themed housing and each abode you can access is located in the Tour of the Wasteland Chapter (Locations 7.14 and 8.03).

IF YOU DISARMED THE BOMB

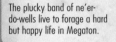

The plucky band of ne'er-do-wells live to forage a hard but happy life in Megaton.

You receive the following rewards for disarming the bomb:

 Bottle Cap (500 total):
If Speech was successful at start of quest.

 Bottle Cap (100 total):
If Speech wasn't employed at start of quest.

My Megaton House Key

Deed: Megaton House

 300 XP

 Karma [+200]
If you disarmed the bomb for free.

Receive Wadsworth the reprogrammed butler, a mildewed mattress to sleep on, a view of rusting tin from your shared balcony, and a second-hand Bobblehead Collector stand. Locate themes for your place by speaking with Moira Brown at Craterside Supplies.

IF YOU DESTROYED MEGATON

Twisted wreckage, heavy radiation, and a big hole in the ground. No more Megaton.

For destroying the town of Megaton, the following is awarded to you:

 Bottle Cap (1,000 total):
If Speech was successful at start of quest.

 Bottle Cap (500 total):
If Speech failed, or wasn't employed at start of quest.

 **My Tenpenny Tower Suite Key**

Property Deed: Tenpenny Tower Suite

 300 XP

Karma [-1,000]
If Megaton is destroyed.

Receive Godfrey the polished butler robot, a king-sized bed to sleep in, a magnificent view from your shared balcony, and the latest in Bobblehead Collector stands. Locate themes for your palace by speaking with Lydia Montenegro at Boutique Le Chic.

Tenpenny Tower

Rising from the dust in the middle of the southern Wastelands is **Tenpenny Tower [7.14]**, a towering skyscraper that stands as a beacon of humankind's ability to survive and thrive among chaos. At least, that's the gist of the marketing campaign. The tower is the brainchild of British entrepreneur Allistair Tenpenny,. While traversing the Wasteland, he discovered an abandoned but salvageable monolithic brownstone, and claimed it for King and Country. He made repairs, named it after himself, and hired a private mercenary security detail, renting out rooms to those who could afford it. All was well until the subway tunnels under the tower became populated with Ghouls that wandered in from the **Warrington Trainyard [7.12]**, and an arrogant Tenpenny refused them admittance. He wants to be rid of them all. The Ghouls want in. You're here to choose a solution that satisfies the humans, Ghouls, or both sides, depending on your moral compass.

Tenpenny Tower

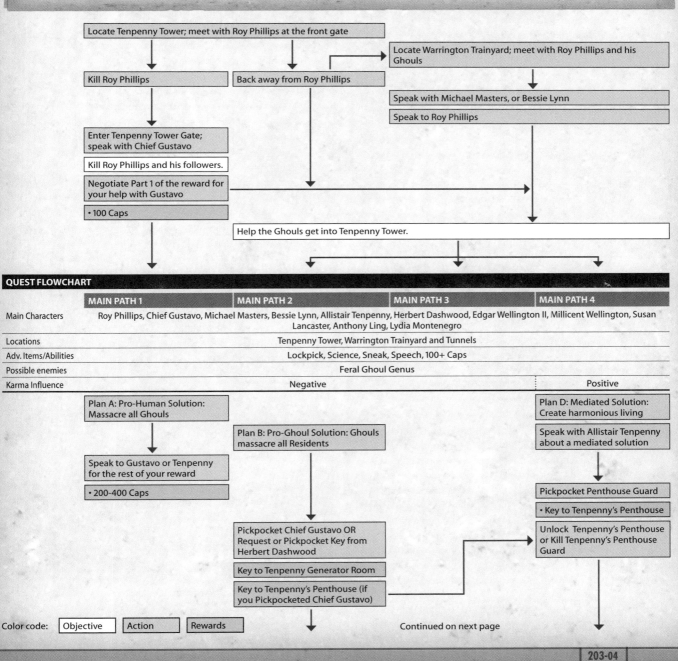

Locate Tenpenny Tower; meet with Roy Phillips at the front gate

↓

Kill Roy Phillips

Back away from Roy Phillips → Locate Warrington Trainyard; meet with Roy Phillips and his Ghouls

↓

Speak with Michael Masters, or Bessie Lynn

Speak to Roy Phillips

↓

Enter Tenpenny Tower Gate; speak with Chief Gustavo

Kill Roy Phillips and his followers.

Negotiate Part 1 of the reward for your help with Gustavo

• 100 Caps

Help the Ghouls get into Tenpenny Tower.

QUEST FLOWCHART

	MAIN PATH 1	MAIN PATH 2	MAIN PATH 3	MAIN PATH 4
Main Characters	Roy Phillips, Chief Gustavo, Michael Masters, Bessie Lynn, Allistair Tenpenny, Herbert Dashwood, Edgar Wellington II, Millicent Wellington, Susan Lancaster, Anthony Ling, Lydia Montenegro			
Locations	Tenpenny Tower, Warrington Trainyard and Tunnels			
Adv. Items/Abilities	Lockpick, Science, Sneak, Speech, 100+ Caps			
Possible enemies	Feral Ghoul Genus			
Karma Influence	Negative			Positive

Plan A: Pro-Human Solution: Massacre all Ghouls

↓

Plan B: Pro-Ghoul Solution: Ghouls massacre all Residents

Plan D: Mediated Solution: Create harmonious living

Speak with Allistair Tenpenny about a mediated solution

Speak to Gustavo or Tenpenny for the rest of your reward

• 200-400 Caps

Pickpocket Chief Gustavo OR Request or Pickpocket Key from Herbert Dashwood

Key to Tenpenny Generator Room

Key to Tenpenny's Penthouse (if you Pickpocketed Chief Gustavo)

Pickpocket Penthouse Guard

• Key to Tenpenny's Penthouse

Unlock Tenpenny's Penthouse or Kill Tenpenny's Penthouse Guard

Color code: Objective | Action | Rewards

Continued on next page

TRAINING — BESTIARY — MAIN QUEST — MISC. QUESTS — TOUR — COMPLETION — APPENDICES

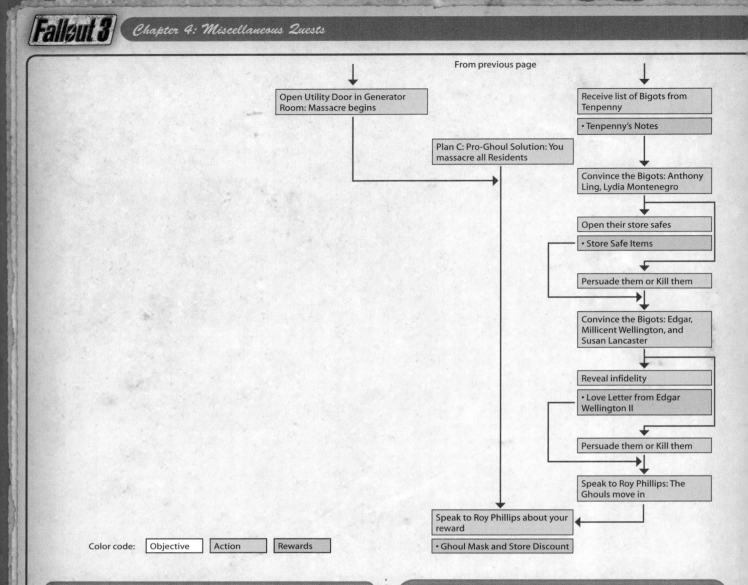

From previous page

Open Utility Door in Generator Room: Massacre begins

Plan C: Pro-Ghoul Solution: You massacre all Residents

Receive list of Bigots from Tenpenny
- Tenpenny's Notes

Convince the Bigots: Anthony Ling, Lydia Montenegro

Open their store safes
- Store Safe Items

Persuade them or Kill them

Convince the Bigots: Edgar, Millicent Wellington, and Susan Lancaster

Reveal infidelity
- Love Letter from Edgar Wellington II

Persuade them or Kill them

Speak to Roy Phillips: The Ghouls move in

Speak to Roy Phillips about your reward
- Ghoul Mask and Store Discount

Color code: Objective Action Rewards

ARRIVAL AT TENPENNY TOWER

Caution

If you are also engaged in **Miscellaneous Quest: The Power of the Atom**, and have chosen the bad Karmic path of meeting with Mister Burke, you can choose any option during the Tenpenny Tower quest; Mister Burke is still waiting for you on the balcony.

A monument to excess or the seeds of a brand new world? Tenpenny Tower looms over the southern Wastes.

To begin this quest, you must travel to Tenpenny Tower, the tallest structure in the southern Wasteland area. There are two possible ways you might stumble across this structure: The first is if you went out wandering due southwest of Megaton, passed the RobCo Facility, and spotted a 10-story brownstone skyscraper that's in remarkably good shape. Or, you could somehow have missed or ignored the tower on your overland travels, entered the Warrington Trainyard, and appeared out of the Warrington Station exit. Either way, head to the south side of the tower, to the pillared entrance. Here, you'll find an argument between a Ghoul and a wall.

LISTEN TO THE PRO-HUMAN AND PRO-GHOUL AGENDAS

On closer inspection, it appears that the Ghoul isn't Feral, and is therefore unlikely to savage you. The Ghoul's name is Roy Phillips, and he's being refused entry into Tenpenny Tower. After arguing with a guard on the intercom, Roy stands there, fuming. He isn't taking questions, especially from a smooth-skin like you. The following actions are now available:

You can talk to Roy, but he won't answer.

You can cut Roy down before he has chance to speak. This doesn't begin the quest either, but it deals with a Ghoul leader if you're a Ghoul hater.

If you've explored the Warrington Tunnels, accessed via the trainyard, and you've talked to either Michael Masters or Bessie Lynn near their makeshift hidey-hole, Roy's name came up in those previous conversations, and Roy actually speaks with you. Agree with his plan to storm the tower, choosing either to talk to Tenpenny, or kill the "elitists" (you can change hearts and minds later). You can skip to the "Metro Tunnel Massacre" section of this quest.

NEW OBJECTIVE

"Help the Ghouls get into Tenpenny Tower" begins. †

† (If you already visited Michael Masters and Bessie Lynn in the tunnels)

Ignore Roy, and instead activate the intercom. Chief Gustavo mistakes you for Roy initially, but after you put him straight, the following options become available:

If you're here to see Mister Burke as part of The Power of the Atom quest, Gustavo opens the security gate immediately.

 With a high **Speech** skill, you can fast-talk Gustavo into thinking you have a lucrative offer for Allistair Tenpenny. Gustavo hurriedly lets you in.

If you fail your Speech, or don't have this option, your pleading falls on deaf ears. Gustavo only wants cold, hard Caps. 100 of them to be exact. Agree to pay him, and he opens the door.

 **Note**
You must gain entry into Tenpenny Tower from this location, even if it means a 100 Cap payment to Gustavo.

On this side of the fence is Chief of Security Gustavo: His hatred of flappy-skinned folk is legendary.

Step into the exterior courtyard, and look left, at the stern Chief Gustavo. Start up a conversation, and you soon discover he's not a huge fan of Ghouls; in fact, he wants every one wiped from the face of the earth. To gain some useful information, you first need to speak with Roy Phillips, activate the objective "Help the Ghouls get into Tenpenny Tower," then return to Gustavo and ask him about the basement, which seems to link to a set of old subway tunnels running under the tower. Then bring the conversation around to the Ghoul problem. Ask where they are hiding out, and Gustavo tells you they have a base in the Warrington Station Metro Tunnels, living near packs of Feral Ghouls. Gustavo offers a 500 Cap incentive for slaying Roy and his followers (actually a 400 Cap incentive if it took 100 Caps to get in to see him). You now have the following options:

 With **Speech**, you can siphon an additional 200 Caps, plus a gun (usually a Submachine Gun or Hunting Rifle) and ammunition!

Otherwise, simply agree to a negotiation or slaughter on behalf of the Tenpenny Tower humans.

 10mm Submachine Gun or Hunting Rifle   **Rounds**

 Tip
You can tell both Roy and Gustavo anything you like, such as that you're working on a peaceful negotiated settlement, or you're going to murder the opposite faction. You can always change your mind later.

NEW OBJECTIVE
"Kill Roy Phillips and his followers" begins.

NEW OBJECTIVE
"Help the Ghouls get into Tenpenny Tower, OR Kill Roy Phillips and his followers" begins.†

† (If you spoke to both Roy Phillips and Chief Gustavo)

 Note
The following options are now available (beginning with the most likely):

If Roy wasn't in a chatty mood, Gustavo gave you a quest, and you want to slay Roy's ragtag team, head for the Metro Tunnels.

If Roy wasn't in a chatty mood, Gustavo gave you a quest, and you want to get Roy's side of the story, also head for the Metro Tunnels.

If you talked and sided with Roy, (and optionally Gustavo) and want to storm Tenpenny Tower, begin a massacre.

If you talked with Roy and Gustavo, and want to negotiate a coexistence, enter the tower.

INVESTIGATE WARRINGTON STATION

Derelict and eerie, Warrington Station (viewed looking northeast) has a gate even a Lockpick of 100 won't open; it must be locked from the inside. Try it from the Metro Tunnels side instead.

Travel due southwest from Tenpenny Tower, past a couple of ruined homesteads on your right, and continue toward the familiar wreckage of a train station entrance. This is the Warrington Station entrance, and it's completely blocked off; it can only be accessed from the other side. If you already explored the Warrington Metro Tunnels, this is the exit. If you explore the tunnels and unlock the gate from the other side, you can use this area (a couple of battered buildings) without any problems. For now, though, you should locate the Warrington Trainyard.

INVESTIGATE WARRINGTON TRAINYARD

When you wish to investigate the Metro Tunnels, begin to trek due west from the Tenpenny Tower entrance. Pass through a cluster of ruined homesteads, and the familiar tunnel entrance is just ahead. Encroach into the trainyard itself, and prepare to be set upon by Ghouls that lack their higher brain functions, and crave sweet, smooth meat—yours! Deal with a hardened Feral Ghoul by the tunnel entrance, and then dash inside the door, entering the Metro Tunnels immediately.

TRAINING — BESTIARY — MAIN QUEST — MISC. QUESTS — TOUR — COMPLETION — APPENDICES

Tip

Take all the panic out of your ranged combat by jumping on the roof of the tunnel entrance, stepping to the edge above the tunnel arch, and pop rotting heads from complete safety. Other safe areas include the tops of the carriages, accessed via the rusting walkway.

If you want to rummage around this area more, then take advantage of the metal bridges and rusting walkways to gain height on your enemy, in this case around six hostiles, usually a mixture of Feral Ghouls and Roamers. Bring their savagery to an (ideally messy) end from a favored vantage point. Once the area is devoid of Ghouls, take a quick look into the L-shaped rusting structure near the train carriages. Inside, expect to find a First Aid Box and an Ammunition Box, with some supplies to grab before your tunnel adventure begins.

 Ammo Box
Ammunition

First Aid Box
Health and Chems

WANDERING THE METRO TUNNELS

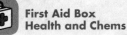

Note

The following strategies presuppose that you're exploring these tunnels for the first time, but after you've met Roy Phillips at the Tenpenny gates. If you explored the tunnels already, make sure you didn't actually kill Roy's friends!

Tip

Before you begin, think about how to approach your tunnel wander. You can go in with a gun at the ready, and tackle each hostile you find, or you can employ your Sneak skill and shuffle past them invisibly (as long as each Ghoul doesn't spot you). If you choose the first option, switch on your Pip-Boy's Flashlight function so you can see your initial footing.

Enter the tunnel via the side door under the trainyard arch, and once inside the tunnel, head down the sloping tunnel, following the bend around to the right to avoid a radioactive dead-end to your left. Bring out your favored Ghoul-hunting weapon, or Sneak around three enemies as soon as you spot them running over the track debris. Keep heading down the long, left bend until you reach a Metro Access door on your left. Open it and step back. There's a frenzied quartet of whipping-clawed abominations to cut down!

Once the Ghoul menace is temporarily halted, explore doorways to the north or northeast of the "Authorized Personnel Only" door. Both lead to two doors on either side of each other, and the start of the Blue Line subway track in this area. A second sign points to Eastbound Warrington Station. Drop the Ghoul lolloping toward you, then move past the derelict carriages. Stay right, as there's a side tunnel leading southward, through two more Ghouls, past a cluster of radioactive barrels, to a locked door. You now have the following options:

 With a **Lockpick** skill and a Bobby Pin or three, you can pick this storage room's door.

Otherwise, you cannot breach this cubbyhole. Inside, there's a load of Ammo and Health.

 Ammunition Boxes

First Aid Boxes

 Stimpaks

Assuming you snagged the storage room's goods, exit and head on a roughly northeastern path, passing the wrecked carriages, and continue to the rock fall blocking your tunnel progress. You may be accosted by another Feral Ghoul

Open wide and say "Arrgh!" Although the Shotgun is great in tight passages, try the Hunting Rifle for tunnel takedowns.

Roamer, so bring your close-assault weapon to bear, then tackle another nasty at the entrance to the pump chamber. Turn east. You have two routes to reach the next tunnel section (and around three Feral Ghouls to hunt):

Short and sweet: By far the better of the two routes is to pass the passage to your left, and head down the stairs to the east, clocking the Feral Ghoul on the way. Stop as you reach the small chamber with the pump. The doorway to the left leads you to the "Long and Sour" route. The door to your right takes you to Warrington Station, and should be accessed immediately.

Tip

The fire extinguishers lying on the floor in this small chamber make reasonable facsimiles of grenades if you shoot them. Pick them up if you have the room, then drop them on a Ghoul's attack path, retreat, and fire!

Long and sour: The other way is to take an immediate left, heading north, then east, down the stairs to a long corridor. See the shimmering vapor? That's methane gas escaping from the ground all around you, so you must cut down the couple of Ghouls you face with weapons that don't create heat. Try the Combat Knife or a Baseball Bat. Or, lob a Grenade in, then back up the steps. Fire while you're standing at the base of the steps or in the room, and you're consumed by a fireball of gas. This damages you, and slays the Ghoul. Your reward for getting toasty? A desk of junk and a longer route to the small chamber's exit door, and Warrington Station.

GHOUL ON GUARD: WARRINGTON STATION ENTRANCE (INTERIOR)

The only way onward is to the east, so head down the tracks to the mezzanine until you hear someone hollering at you. A Ghoul is shouting for you to put your weapons away. "No funny business unless you want to get shot!" he yells. The following options become available:

Michael Masters, PhD? The Ghoul guarding the station was a Tenpenny Tower vacationer, and also a scientist.

Familiar faces: If you've already been here, and met Michael Masters, the place is silent. You don't actually need to be here; return to Tenpenny Tower and talk to Roy Phillips at the gate.

No funny business: Holster your weapon and climb the escalator to meet Michael Masters. Choose dialogs to reveal Michael's past life as a scientist and frequenter of Tenpenny Tower, before his current "affliction." He tells you Roy is expecting you; that's all you need to hear.

Yes, funny business: Keep your weapon ready, and blow sinewy chunks out of Michael Masters if you're on a pro-human rampage through the tunnels. This is the first of your targets. Now for Bessie and Roy!

Michael's mezzanine guard post is filled with an impressive collection of nearly useful junk. Stay on the top floor, and there's an exit slope. Head roughly south through the turnstiles, and open the gates to the Capital Wasteland. This leads to Warrington Station (topside); you visited the locked gates on the other side of this exit while you were exploring the Metro Tunnels. This is a great place to maneuver on your way back from meeting Roy.

A GATHERING OF GHOULS: WARRINGTON STATION (TUNNELS)

Often easy to miss, the entrance to the Warrington Station Tunnels is directly under the mezzanine. Descend the escalator, and turn 180 degrees around, to face east. Open the mesh gate and head through the right-side, rubble-filled train tunnel (the left one is completely blocked with fallen concrete). If you've watched Michael Masters as he patrols the area, simply follow him. Pass to the right of the wrecked train, and follow him up to the doorway before the tunnel barricades. Check the desk inside for Caps.

As with many tunnel explorations, the flaming barrels are of significance; follow the trail of them to a desired location; in this case, an audience with grumpy Ghoul Roy Phillips. Head down the steps, turn right, and enter

Bless this mess: Don't judge Bessie by her interesting collection of skin conditions; she's got a heart of gold.

the Ghouls' hidey-hole. You're safe from the Ferals here, and you can meet and converse with Bessie Lynn. She's quite chipper, all things considered, and seems to have a soft spot for Roy (although it could be a case of the creeping buboes). Move farther into the hidey-hole, past the desk with the Steel Gauge Assembly on it, through the door, and down the stairs to the sleeping quarters. There are items here (and Bessie plus Roy, depending on the time of day), but it isn't wise to steal them if you're trying to keep the Ghouls on your side.

Your search for Roy should now come to an end: He may be sleeping in the Ghouls' hidey-hole area. If he isn't, exit through the door in the north wall, and follow the winding corridor, passing the flaming barrels, until you reach a small, relatively empty room. The door to the north leads to a small storage room, which you should ransack at once, for some Ammunition and a copy of *Dean's Electronics*, which makes very interesting reading (access it from the Aid section of your Pip-Boy's inventory).

Ammunition

Dean's Electronics
+1 Repair (when read).

Check the metal boxes in the two rooms you're in, and then move southward before winding along another snaking tunnel, all the way to the next door. Check the suitcase on the desk for some minor items, then eye the three doors. There's the one you came from, and a second one to the west leads to the area of Metro Tunnels beyond the barricades you didn't head through when you followed Masters. Expect around three Feral Ghouls to attack you if you explore here, which only brings you back to the hidey-hole.

The door that's most interesting is the one marked "to Metro Access and Generator"; the last place Roy Phillips may be waiting for you, and an important position if you try a pro-Ghoul solution to this quest. Open the door, and head up into the Generator Room. There are two areas of interest here: a massive Containment Door, and a narrow window showing a room on the other side (this is accessed from Tenpenny Tower, and can't be moved to). When you finally meet Roy, stay on his good side if you want to try helping the Ghouls. Agree to a mediation or to slaughtering the humans; any plan can be changed later (prior to any blood being spilled, naturally).

NEW OBJECTIVE
"Help the Ghouls get into Tenpenny Tower" begins.†

† (If Roy didn't speak to you at the Tenpenny Tower gate)

Note
Now that you've met both the warring sides, it's time to pick a plan from the following:

Plan A: Pro-Human: Gunning Down the Ghouls: Metro Tunnel Massacre.

Plan B: Pro-Ghoul: Unleashing the Feral Ghouls: The Tenpenny Tower of Terror!

Plan C: Pro-Ghoul: Pure, Anti-Human Hatred: The Tenpenny Tower Takedown.

Plan D: Mediated: Harmonious Living for the Lumpy and Smooth Skins.

PRO-HUMAN: GUNNING DOWN THE GHOULS: METRO TUNNEL MASSACRE

Now that you've found Roy, Bessie, and Michael, you can follow Chief Gustavo's thought process, and wipe them out... all of them! This is best achieved by gunning down Michael at his mezzanine outpost, and dealing with Roy next, as Bessie is the least adept at combat. Congratulations on becoming another Ghoul-hating bigot; now return to Gustavo and collect your blood money!

PRO-GHOUL: UNLEASHING THE FERAL GHOULS: THE TENPENNY TOWER OF TERROR!

This plan takes a little longer to gestate, but it's much more thrilling, and it turns Tenpenny Tower into a real house of horrors! When you talk to Roy, he mentions a door that leads from the tower's basement directly to Generator Room. His novel idea is to summon a horde of Feral Ghouls and Roamers, get the Containment Door open, and flood the tower with rampaging fiends! If this massacre of innocents is agreeable to your soul, head to the main gate, and follow Chief Gustavo into the Tower Lobby). Wait for a quiet moment, and then Pickpocket the Key to Tenpenny Generator Room from him. You receive the Key to Tenpenny's Penthouse, too!

Gustavo is almost as grumpy as Roy, and he really doesn't want you visiting the tower's basement. You know what that means....

 Key to Tenpenny Generator Room

 Key to Tenpenny's Penthouse

 Note

When you're in the lobby, turn west and look for the door marked "Metro Access and Generator." This leads to a storage room (rummage for minor items), and stairs down to the other side of the Containment Door. This is where your Ghoul horde enters the building.

Mr. Dashwood, I presume? He's a retired hunter, bon vivant, and a man with a twinkle still in his eye—the good one.

If you can't get to Gustavo's pockets, don't despair; instead, head up the stairs from the lobby, and up to the Tenpenny Suites. Move to the western corner and investigate the grand room of ancient explorer, Herbert "Darling" Dashwood. He's had a GNR radio play named after his exploits, don't you know. Butter him up, and when he mentions he has a copy of the basement key, suggest that he give it to you. Or, engage in his little game, and Pickpocket it from him (although this isn't necessary).

 Key to Tenpenny Generator Room

 Head out of the main lobby doors, and move around to the exterior of the tower, but inside the perimeter wall. Back here, some steps lead to a locked door, which can be opened only with the key you just snagged. Follow the basement corridor down to the Generator Room (tower side); Look through the narrow window and Roy waves back, with the promised tide of foaming fiends at the ready. Open the Containment Door using one of the following ideas:

With a reasonable **Science** skill, you can access the OCTA Emergency Access Terminal, and choose the "Open Containment Door" option. This immediately lets in the horde!

Or, you can simply brandish a favored weapon, and shoot either generator to your left, which also causes the door to open.

Head back up and outside, then around to the lobby doors, where Roy is waiting for you. His smile tells it all; either his lockjaw is back, or he's gibbering with excitement at this impending tower take-over! He gives you the fabled Ghoul Mask, which fools the Ferals into thinking you're one of them—essentially giving you immunity to Ghouls unless you're inches from them—and then beckons you to help bring down the hoity-toities. Put it on, now!

 Ghoul Mask

 Pandemonium has broken out! The lights are off, and a steady stream of unwashed flesh-rippers pours into the building! Watch the carnage unfold, and take part if you wish (remember; you're shooting innocent guards and residents, not Ghouls!), but don't forget to wear your Mask! Check that every single room on the ground floor is devoid of residents, and that optionally includes Shakes the robo-bartender!

The bloodshed gradually moves up to the suites above the lobby; follow the Ghouls up the stairs if you wish, and continue to help out, but watch for pockets of resistance. Dashwood—possibly discontent with his decision to give up his key—usually puts up a valiant, but ultimately doomed effort. Then move to the elevator and take it up to the penthouse suites, where the richest residents are regretting the lack of a fire escape. This includes Allistair Tenpenny, who's slaughtered with everyone else.

Note

You can meet up with Roy Phillips (who usually survives the encounter), and he gives you a final thanks, but no additional reward. Of course, you can now turn on all the Ghouls—if you have the firepower—to earn some extra XP!

PRO-GHOUL: PURE, ANTI-HUMAN HATRED: THE TENPENNY TOWER TAKEDOWN

Have you developed a fondness for homicidal massacres? Then gain entry to the tower, and begin to correct every single patron you see, from the guards to Chief Gustavo, to the snooty residents, and even dear old Dashwood; he's the only one who puts up a real fight, as he's carrying a Combat Shotgun. When everyone is corrected, including those outside, head up to Tenpenny's penthouse suite, where you have two choices:

Plan C, Option 1: Talk to Tenpenny, and he agrees to let the Ghouls live (and gives you Caps!); after all, he's got to receive rental payment from someone! Now return to Roy Phillips, tell him the good news, and he agrees to the plan. The next time you visit, the place is awash with the nouveau rotting. The time after that? Well, Tenpenny probably needed to hire a few more human bodyguards....

Plan C, Option 2: Simply gun Tenpenny down as well, and once all living things (and Shakes) are crumpled heaps, head back to Roy, who's happy to take over this tower. He moves in with his friends, and gives you the Ghoul Mask as a prize.

Your Karma takes a massive nosedive after this kind of madness!

Tip

Survive the slaughter by employing a number of cunning plans.
- Start on the penthouse level, where there are fewer residents, and gradually work your way down.
- Use the available cover, whether it's corners of doorways, sandbags outside, desks, or other places.
- Don't move into dead-ends, and keep pressing forward.
- Aim at one victim and ensure they are dead before moving to the next.
- Search every body for goodies, or keys to safes, andopen them, too.

MEDIATED: HARMONIOUS LIVING FOR THE LUMPY AND SMOOTH SKINS

If you're trying for a neutral Karma solution, this is your best bet. Head past Gustavo after being let into the tower, either before or after meeting Roy Phillips and getting his quest-related take on the situation. Gustavo is vehemently opposed to human/Ghoul cohabitation, so you need to speak to the organ grinder, not the monkey. In this case, it's an elderly British man named Allistair Tenpenny. He stays in his penthouse suite all day, and there are a variety of ways to meet him:

First, you can talk to all the bigoted residents, and then head to see Tenpenny, meaning you only need find him once.

Or, you can begin **Miscellaneous Quest: The Power of the Atom**, agree to place a Fusion Charge on Megaton's dormant Atom Bomb, and head to Tenpenny's tower balcony where he sits with Mister Burke, who represents Tenpenny's interests. Simply move to the guard sitting at Tenpenny's penthouse door, and tell him you're here to see Burke, and he lets you in. Then speak to Tenpenny.

 If you aren't interested in irradiating Megaton, challenge the guard at the penthouse door, and if your **Speech** is successful, he opens the door for you.

 If you're highly skilled in both **Sneak** and **Lockpick** (if you don't have the Penthouse Key), you can quickly navigate around the guard without being spotted, and then unlock the door.

The guard is carrying one of the same type of keys as Chief Gustavo, which opens the penthouse door. Pickpocket it, then **Sneak** past him to use it.

Or, wait until the guard gets up to stretch his legs, then steal the key from the pedestal near the door.

If you previously Pickpocketed Chief Gustavo, he has a key that unlocks the penthouse suite door. Deal with the guard at your discretion.

Or, you'll have to take down the guard with **Small Guns**, grab the key from his body, and use it to unlock the door.

Key to Tenpenny's Penthouse

Once the puzzle to enter Tenpenny's suite has been resolved, head in to find the man, and talk with him. Naturally, you can kill him if you quickly change your mind to a pro-Ghoul solution, but it's better to feign interest, and ask what it would take for him to agree to Ghoul/human habitation of the Tower. Tenpenny gives you a Note, listing the residents he needs to have convinced.

 ### Tenpenny's Note

Tenpenny will allow the Ghouls to move in, if the following tower residents are convinced:
- Mr. and Mrs. Wellington
- Ms. Montenegro
- Mr. Ling
- Ms. Lancaster

Anthony Ling needs you to "upgrade to fabulous." You need him to "downgrade to Ghoul."

Lydia Montenegro sells refined items in her shop, but her polite exterior changes when you mention your plans.

Either before or after you speak to Tenpenny, you can begin to convince the tower's residents that living with Ghouls won't be so bad. The plan here is simply to converse with the bigots outlined in Tenpenny's Note. Inhabitants not important enough to have their own names can be ignored. Inhabitants listed in this book at the beginning of this quest can easily be talked into agreeing to your solution, and put in a good word to Tenpenny. But you must concentrate on convincing the five bigots. They are randomly scattered about the Tower. All of them can be corrected in a few different ways:

 Succeed in your powers of persuasion, and each bigot whines and throws a variety of hissy fits but ultimately yields to this new plan. They pack their bags and skedaddle. This is the preferred, nonviolent solution; however, you must succeed with your **Speech** for each specific bigot.

Both Lydia Montenegro and Anthony Ling are shopkeepers. If you enter their stores (Boutique Le Chic and New Urban Apparel), and open their safes, they're taken aback by the tower's lax security, and leave the building.

Was your Speech not convincing enough? Then the bigot won't budge, and refuses to agree. Bring out a weapon, and end his life. Harsh, but unfair; that's the Wasteland way!

The remaining three bigots can be convinced using any of the previous plans, but there's another, secret layer to these snobs that you can uncover with a bit of detective work. First, enter the suites floor, and locate the entrance to Susan Lancaster's room. Turn right as you enter her room, and inspect her desk. Steal *Tales of a Junktown Jerky Vendor* and read it, then uncover a shocking Love Letter from Edgar Wellington II! The details are more than a little saucy; remember to read it on your Pip-Boy's Note section!

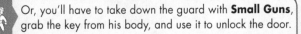

Tales of a Junktown Jerky Vendor
+1 Bargain (when read).

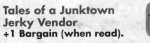

Love Letter from Edgar Wellington II

If you're after an easy way to deal with three bigots at once, locate Millicent and Edgar, and speak to Millicent. In your dialog, bring up the Love Letter, and watch the sparks fly! Step back as Millicent goes certifiably bonkers and kills her husband, then rampages through

TRAINING — BESTIARY — MAIN QUEST — MISC. QUESTS — TOUR — COMPLETION — APPENDICES

the tower and brings down Susan. She then flees the tower, never to be seen again! Or will she? There are a few more parts to complete before this quest is over:

Return to Allistair Tenpenny, and inform him that all five bigots have been "convinced." He agrees to your negotiated settlement.

Is Allistair Tenpenny dead? Then locate Chief Gustavo, and tell him the news. He states that Ghouls can move in "over his dead body." Oblige him.

Now go and find Roy Phillips (he's likely at the other side of the window in the basement, and tell him to pack his bags; the Ghouls are moving in!

Tip

Susan Lancaster isn't just "the other woman"; she has more issues than a Grognak the Barbarian compendium. Find out more about her (and perhaps keep her alive) if you plan to complete **Miscellaneous Quest: Strictly Business.**

If you forced Lydia Montenegro or Anthony Ling to leave via thievery, and caused Millicent to commit murder, there's a very small chance you'll run into them later in your Wasteland exploration, looking a shadow of their former selves....

Each resident has a large number of items, Caps, and other secrets hidden in different stashes and on their persons; be sure you snag and bag it all. The Tenpenny Tower section in the Tour of the Capital Wasteland chapter (page 349) reveals all!

AFTERMATH

Kill all the Ghouls, and life goes on as normal in the tower. However, if you opt for a mediated plan, when you return to the tower lobby, there's an uneasy truce between Roy Phillips and his Ghoul-friends and the previous human inhabitants. If you explore further, checking Tenpenny's bathtub, you may find that the tower could be looking for a new owner...ask Roy what happened. Head away from the Tenpenny Tower for 48 or more hours, and then return, checking the tower thoroughly for humans. It appears one party may have been unable to hold up their end of the bargain. A quick visit to the basement confirms your worst fears.... Still, you can buy the finest frocks and other supplies from Bessie, who's taken over Lydia's shop. Michael Masters has taken over in Anthony Ling's shop.

If you attacked with the Ghouls, try returning to the tower after 48 or more hours later, and the clean-up operation has occurred. Where have all the bodies been piled? Somewhere cool and secure....

Note

If you are trying to complete **Miscellaneous Quest: The Power of the Atom,** don't worry about the mysterious Mister Burke; even if you release the Feral Ghouls, you can still meet Burke on the balcony. In fact, Roy is there, becoming slightly intimidated by Burke's presence, and Roy lets Burke finish wiping Megaton off the map.

QUEST REWARDS

PLAN A COMPLETE: PRO-HUMAN GHOUL MASSACRE

Succeed in your tunnel massacre, and once the quest is over, speak to Gustavo or Tenpenny for the following:

 Bottle Cap (400 total)
If Speech was successful when quest was given.

 Bottle Cap (200 total)
If Speech wasn't employed when quest was given.

 XP 300 XP

PLAN B COMPLETE: PRO-GHOUL TERROR

Once the Ferals take control, savor the reward of finishing the quest, and the item Roy already gave you:

 Ghoul Mask†   **Store Discount‡**

 XP 300 XP

† (Ghouls won't attack unless provoked, if worn)

‡ (Bessie Lynn and Michael Masters only; when they "take over" Lydia Montenegro and Anthony Ling's stores)

PLAN C COMPLETE: PRO-GHOUL TAKEDOWN

If you mowed down all the humans in and around the tower, expect the same result as Plan B, whether Tenpenny survives or not. If you also kill all the Ghouls, you and your itchy trigger-finger receive only XP.

 **Ghoul Mask†**   **Store Discount‡**

XP 300 XP

† (Ghouls won't attack unless provoked, if worn)

‡ (Bessie Lynn and Michael Masters only; when they "take over" Lydia Montenegro and Anthony Ling's stores)

PLAN D COMPLETE: MEDIATED TRUCE

If you mediated between the two factions, all the service providers still alive (for all shops, repairs, and services) offer cut-price bargains, and the Ghoul Mask.

 **Ghoul Mask†**   **Store Discount‡**

XP 300 XP

† (Ghouls won't attack unless provoked, if worn)

‡ (Bessie Lynn and Michael Masters only; when they "take over" Lydia Montenegro and Anthony Ling's stores)

CUT-PRICE LIQUOR: THANKS, SHAKES!

 If Shakes the Protectron barkeep survives any of the plans, he refuses to give you a discount. That is, until you use your **Science** skill to hack into the terminal in his place of business! Then, it's drinks aplenty!

Strictly Business

The Slaver camp of **Paradise Falls [2.08]** is a location where the more uncaring and psychotic adventurer can win favors with a despicable band of lowlifes. If you're in the mood for human trafficking, head on over to the perimeter, where Grouse the sentry guard orders you to gather him up some specific inhabitants for his own personal (and undoubtedly sick) reasons. You're awarded Caps for every slave you deliver. Return one to gain access to the settlement itself. You can extend your deviant work to anyone you meet in the Wasteland, although the four high-value targets are the only ones critical to this quest. Leave your Hunting Rifle, and your moral scruples, at the door of Paradise Falls; it's human-hunting time!

Paradise Falls

QUEST FLOWCHART

	MAIN PATH
Main Characters	Roy Phillips, Chief Gustavo, Michael Masters, Bessie Lynn, Allistair Tenpenny, Herbert Dashwood, Edgar Wellington II, Millicent Wellington, Susan Lancaster, Anthony Ling, Lydia Montenegro
Locations	Paradise Falls, Minefield, Tenpenny Tower, Big Town, Germantown Police Headquarters, Rivet City
Adv. Items/Abilities	Sneak, Speech, Lockpick, 700+ Caps, -KARMA, Mesmetron, Slave Collar (4)
Possible enemies	—
Karma Influence	Negative

Locate Grouse in Paradise Falls

Agree to hunt VIPs for Grouse (and in order to access Paradise Falls)

• Note: List of "recruits" for Paradise Falls, Mesmetron (and Manual), Slave Collar (and instructions), Mesmetron Power Cells (50), Additional Mesmetron Power Cells (10 for 200 Caps)

Enslave the sniper Arkansas from Minefield.

Locate Arkansas in Minefield

Sneak close enough		Fight and dodge until close enough	
Rob him blind	Affix Slave Collar	Kill him	Leave him alone
• Ridgefield Gate Key, Sniper Rifle		• Ridgefield Gate Key, Sniper Rifle	

Head back to Grouse or continue

Slave captured	Slave not captured
• 250 Caps, Slave Collar	

Enslave Susan Lancaster from Tenpenny Tower.

Enter Tenpenny Tower, locate Susan Lancaster

Rob her blind	Affix Slave Collar	Kill her	Leave her alone
• Mirelurk Cakes		• Mirelurk Cakes	

Escape by battling the inhabitants	Escape undetected

Head back to Grouse or continue

Slave captured	Slave not captured
• 250 Caps, Slave Collar	

Continued on next page

Color code: Objective   Action   Rewards

APPENDICES — COMPLETION — TOUR — MISC. QUESTS — MAIN QUEST — BESTIARY — TRAINING

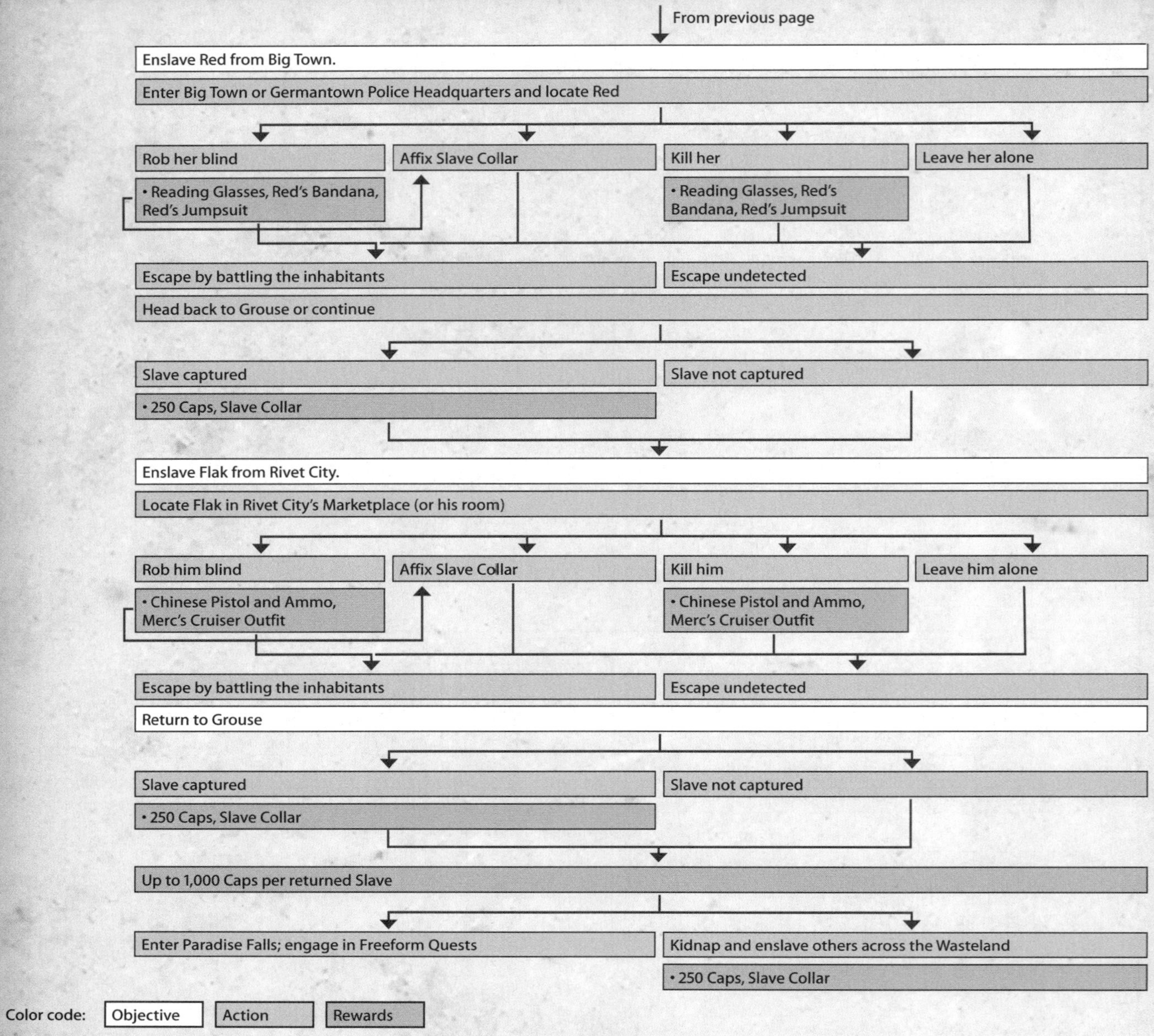

From previous page

Enslave Red from Big Town.

Enter Big Town or Germantown Police Headquarters and locate Red

Rob her blind	Affix Slave Collar	Kill her	Leave her alone
• Reading Glasses, Red's Bandana, Red's Jumpsuit		• Reading Glasses, Red's Bandana, Red's Jumpsuit	

Escape by battling the inhabitants | Escape undetected

Head back to Grouse or continue

Slave captured	Slave not captured
• 250 Caps, Slave Collar	

Enslave Flak from Rivet City.

Locate Flak in Rivet City's Marketplace (or his room)

Rob him blind	Affix Slave Collar	Kill him	Leave him alone
• Chinese Pistol and Ammo, Merc's Cruiser Outfit		• Chinese Pistol and Ammo, Merc's Cruiser Outfit	

Escape by battling the inhabitants | Escape undetected

Return to Grouse

Slave captured	Slave not captured
• 250 Caps, Slave Collar	

Up to 1,000 Caps per returned Slave

Enter Paradise Falls; engage in Freeform Quests	Kidnap and enslave others across the Wasteland
	• 250 Caps, Slave Collar

Color code: | Objective | Action | Rewards |

SPEAKING WITH THE SLAVER SENTRY

When you're ready to lose a few hundred Karma points, set off through the Wasteland, and locate the sprawling settlement of Paradise Falls. These stores have been turned into a well-guarded center of trade and operations for the Slavers—a thoroughly unscrupulous collection of thugs who deal in human suffering. You can approach from any direction, but the only entrance is on the west side of town, so enter heading east. Make a left turn at the giant "Paradise Falls" sign.

Move to the stop sign near the sandbags, and locate Grouse, the curt sentry who has no time for strangers. A little power-mad, he's certainly not falling for your silver tongue, and he refuses to let you into Paradise Falls under any circumstances, except over his dead body. That's a possibility, but not a wise one if you want to begin this quest. Instead, try one of the following plans:

Ask him what his price is. If you succeed in your **Speech** challenge, Grouse tells you 500 Caps should be a big enough bribe. Pay it immediately, or return with the funds, and you can roam Paradise Falls. This won't start the quest though; you have to return to Grouse and talk to him again.

If you sided with the Slavers and completed **Miscellaneous Quest: Head of State**, you can enter Paradise Falls without completing this quest; however, you can attempt it for fun and profit!

Or, you could have led a thoroughly despicable career thus far and have huge negative Karma (-250 or less). You're ushered right in!

Or, continue the conversation and steer it around to talking about slaves. Offer to get him some and be as rude as you want about it. Apparently, Eulogy Jones (the Slaver leader) has a few special contracts out on VIPs, and the money's good. If you find each of the targets and return them mostly unscathed to Grouse, he'll split the reward. If you herd one to Grouse, he'll let you into Paradise Falls without the Caps expenditure.

Grouse? Grouch, more like. Grin and bear his verbal barbs if you want to keep the Slavers sweet.

You won't just be relying on fast-talking or threats to bring the targets back. Grouse gives you a Mesmetron. This weapon (now available in your Inventory) stuns each "recruit," causing them to become dazed and docile. Then you can affix a Slave Collar around the target's neck, and instruct him or her to walk back to Paradise Falls. The Collar is set to explode if the wearer drifts too far from a direct route back. You only have one Collar at a time, though, so you need to return to Grouse each time you want to tag your next victim. Although you shouldn't need it, you can also purchase additional Mesmetron Power Cell ammo for the ludicrously high price of 10 for 200 Caps. Take it or leave it!

 Note: List of "recruits" for Paradise Falls

 Mesmetron (and Manual Summary)

 Slave Collar (1, and Instructions)

 Mesmetron Power Cells (50)

Tip

Remember to bring up your Pip-Boy and check out the four different targets, and read all the Notes you've received, including the information on the Mesmetron, Slave Collar, and targets. You can also ask Grouse to give you background on each target, which he does under verbal protest.

NEW OBJECTIVE
"Enslave the sniper Arkansas from Minefield" begins.

NEW OBJECTIVE
"Enslave Susan Lancaster from Tenpenny Tower" begins.

NEW OBJECTIVE
"Enslave Red from Big Town" begins.

NEW OBJECTIVE
"Enslave Flak from Rivet City" begins.

TARGET ACQUIRED: ARKANSAS

The nearest target to Paradise Falls is Arkansas, an old sniper whose sharpshooting skills are really starting to piss the Slavers off. The madman in Minefield is holed up in the high ruins to the left. You are wise to approach Minefield heading east, toward the rocky cliffs overlooking the booby-trapped settlement. This way, you're closer to Arkansas' location and you won't trip as many mines. If you wish, use a scoped weapon from the top of the cliffs to pan the ruins of the large concrete structure. You should see a series of planks and a couple of Ammo Boxes. Arkansas is hiding out here.

Naturally, you can storm the concrete ruins, shrugging off the Frag Mines underfoot, but a slightly safer option is to drop down to the dirt path, weave through the rocky outcrop, and tread into the concrete ruins, attracting minimal attention.

One option is to utilize your **Sneak** skill or a Stealth Boy to reach the location with minimal contact.

Arkansas still has exceptional hearing and reflexes though, so expect him to spot you. Use the ruined concrete pillars to hide from his shots, wait for him to step out, and then zap him with the Mesmetron.

Arkansas is a good initial candidate, because he's a crazy old hermit and your kidnap attempt won't be seen by others. Once he's dozy, you have 30 seconds to choose one of the following plans, accessed via a conversation with your bewildered victim:

Wobbling and burbling quietly, Arkansas is open to the power of your suggestions.

You can rob him blind, requesting that he give you all his stuff.

You can offer him the Slave Collar, which he takes without any problem, and places it on his neck. You inform Arkansas that he's now a slave and must move immediately to Paradise Falls, or risk his head separating from his body in a shower of chunky skull pieces. He's still groggy and duly obliges.

You can have a slight change of heart, and tell him to snap out of his malaise, then leave him be.

Seeing as you're going to hell anyway, you might as well enjoy the ride. The truly evil kidnap merchant should rob each subject, and then affix the Slave Collar. That way, you take all the victim's goods (the choicest couple of items are listed below) before sending them back to Grouse!

What's worse than forcing an elderly geezer into a life of enforced servitude? "Accidentally" firing the Mesmetron at him when he already has a Slave Collar on! The result is a horrific and spectacular explosion of bone and brain. The Slave Collar explodes, too. Grouse won't be happy....

If you decided to enslave Arkansas, take your Karma hit, then search his sniper spot, where there are three Ammo Boxes to rifle through. The Ridgefield Key opens all the intact homes in this deathtrap hamlet.

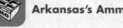 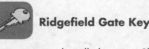 **Arkansas's Ammo Boxes**

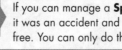 **Ridgefield Gate Key**

 Sniper Rifle

Have you accidentally lost your Slave Collar? Or lost your slave after a "mistaken" beheading? Then return to Grouse, and try a couple of purchasing options:

If you can manage a **Speech** conversation, you tell him it was an accident and take another Slave Collar for free. You can only do this once!

Or, you can purchase another from him for 100 Caps; he isn't happy about it, because these devices are difficult to obtain from unscrupulous dealers in the Commonwealth.

TRAINING — BESTIARY — MAIN QUEST — MISC. QUESTS — TOUR — COMPLETION — APPENDICES

Caution

Did you encounter Arkansas during part of **Miscellaneous Quest: The Wasteland Survival Guide**? Then make sure he was kept alive, or this kidnap attempt (and the 250 Caps) cannot be claimed.

NEW OBJECTIVE

"Return to Grouse" begins.

As soon as you order Arkansas to rush back to Paradise Falls, he duly obliges. The good news is that you don't need to accompany him back. In fact, even if you use Fast Travel (which is recommended after each enslavement), the victim beats you to Grouse. Speak to Grouse, and he's as enthusiastic as he can muster. He gives you the reward, and another Slave Collar, and your second kidnap attempt can now begin.

Note

When you've successfully enslaved one victim who returns to Paradise Falls, Grouse will let you explore the Slaver settlement if you wish. However, this quest ends only when all four victims are dead or steered back to Grouse.

 **250 Caps**   **Slave Collar**

TARGET ACQUIRED: SUSAN LANCASTER

Your next target (although you can choose them in any order) is Susan Lancaster, an ex-whore who cut the throat of her Slaver overlord and vanished a few months back. Reports have surfaced that she's ingratiated herself with the upper-class snobs who live in the Tenpenny Tower, in the southern Wasteland area. Trudge there when you want to tackle her, but be mindful of other intersecting quests that she is part of:

She has an active role in **Miscellaneous Quest: Tenpenny Tower**.

She has a passive role in **Miscellaneous Quest: The Power of the Atom**.

So, depending on your actions in those quests, Tenpenny Tower may be hostile or full of Ghouls, or Susan may be dead. If you enslave her, she can't play an active role in **Main Quest: Tenpenny Tower** (although that quest is still easily completed). Stay on good terms with the Tenpenny Tower security and patrons during this quest if you wish to complete the other quests more easily.

Enter Tenpenny Tower using one of these techniques:

 Simply use the intercom and succeed in a **Speech** challenge, telling Security Chief Gustavo you seek an audience with Allistair Tenpenny. You're let in.

Or, offer a 100 Cap bribe.

If you've already started the Power of the Atom Quest, say "I'm here to see Mr. Burke," and Gustavo will let you right in.

Enter the lobby, and spend some time going from room to room. Susan is likely to be in her chamber on the first-floor suites, accessed via the stairs, or wandering between the Cafe Beau Monde and the doctor's surgery. Don't talk to her or even come too close. Instead, stalk

her until she moves to a location where you can't be observed, such as a bedroom. Close the door behind you, then bring out the Mesmetron.

Susan carries no redeeming items. Simply tag her, and leave her to wander.

Once she's wobbling, you have 30 seconds to choose one of the following enslavement methods, accessed via a conversation:

You can rob her blind, requesting that she hand over her possessions. This isn't recommended, because her belongings are unimpressive. Remember to use the Slave Collar afterward.

 Offer her this fine fashion accessory: the Slave Collar.

You can locate your scruples, and leave her alone.

 **Mirelurk Cakes**   **Susan Lancaster's Outfit**

NEW OBJECTIVE

"Return to Grouse" begins.

Once Lancaster begins to run out of the building, holster your weapon and leave. Use Fast Travel to return to Grouse, claim your Caps, and begin the third enslavement outing.

 250 Caps   **Slave Collar**

TARGET ACQUIRED: RED

Find Red about to get a whole lot bloodier at the hands of the Super Mutants.

Your next target (if you're collecting them strictly in the order Grouse requested, which isn't necessary) is Red. She's an accomplished surgeon that the Slavers are in desperate need of. This quest to locate and enslave Red now intersects with **Miscellaneous Quest: Big Trouble in Big Town**. Trudge to Big Town in the central wastes when you wish to find her. Then, either begin the previously mentioned quest, complete it, or enslave her at her cell inside the Germantown Police Headquarters. All tactics related to locating Red are shown in the previous quest.

Or, you can complete **Miscellaneous Quest: Big Trouble in Big Town**, gain the benefits of Red's accomplishments as a doctor, and then locate her in this settlement. Unless you want a firefight and additional Karma losses, follow her into a building with no other people around, so you don't attract suspicion. Once Red is unsteady on her pins, choose an enslavement method within 30 seconds, accessed via a conversation:

Steal from her: This isn't recommended, as her belongings are sparse. Remember to use the Slave Collar afterward.

Offer her this brand new medical device: the Slave Collar.

You can think better of it, and tell her to snap out of the daze.

 Reading Glasses

 **Red's Bandana**

 Red's Jumpsuit

NEW OBJECTIVE
"Return to Grouse" begins.

When Red has turned and run away, you need not follow her; simply head back to Grouse, who offers you the same deal as before: 250 Caps, a new Slave Collar, and instructions on locating the last of the enslavement victims, Flak.

250 Caps

Slave Collar

TARGET ACQUIRED: FLAK

The final target is Flak, an ex-Slaver who double-crossed Grouse and his gang and must be brought back to face "consequences." He's easy to spot if you've visited Rivet City. Trudge to the southeastern corner of the D.C. Wasteland, near the Jefferson Monument, gain entry into the giant rusting ship, and locate the marketplace, where all the shanty-stores are positioned. Flak is the co-owner of his guns and ammo store. He's easy to spot; look for that intimidating handlebar moustache.

However, he's the most difficult to pin down, although it is still relatively easy. You need a modicum of patience and quick reactions. First, be sure no one else is nearby (especially security guards) when you quickly use the Mes-

Keep your Mesmetron holstered, and quickly tag and bag Flak when no one's looking.

metron. It's wise to save your game before trying anything, because you don't need Rivet City going hostile. Flak is occasionally found in the Muddy Rudder bar, and he also wanders the flight deck and takes a meal at Gary's Galley. Check these locations if he isn't at his shop. Remember that the map of Rivet City is on page 386. When you're zapping Flak, try one of the following:

Offer to carry his equipment because he looks tired. Then use the Collar afterward for more negative Karma.

 Tell him to hold still; you're affixing a Collar on him.

You can stop this human trafficking now, and stop this quest, telling Flak to be on his way.

 **Chinese Pistol and Ammo**

 Merc's Cruiser Outfit

NEW OBJECTIVE
"Return to Grouse" begins.

When Flak has vanished from the boat, make yourself scarce, and Fast Travel back to Paradise Falls. Grouse congratulates you on bagging this deserter, and offers up his usual reward. However, the quest now ends, providing all four targets have been enslaved (or have died).

Have circumstances led to all four of the Slaver targets being deceased before you get here? Then this quest isn't available, although you can claim the Mesmetron—from Grouse's corpse!

250 Caps (per slave)

Slave Collar (once slave is returned)

QUEST REWARDS

You receive the following rewards for finishing Strictly Business:

1,000 Bottle Caps for returning all four Slaves

-KARMA [400] for enslaving all four victims

XP 300 XP

POST-QUEST ANTICS: KEEPING UP WITH THE JONES

Although the Tour of the Wasteland chapter reveals some of the disturbing antics the Slavers get up to in Paradise Falls, when you've successfully herded one or more victims to Grouse, or paid that ludicrous toll, you can explore this large pile of garbage masquerading as a shopping center. Among the Freeform Quests you can try are kidnapping for Eulogy Jones, or the purchase of Clover, a bodyguard you can dress and have odd conversations with. For more information, check page 275. You can also try to redeem yourself, and rescue the children kept in this location, as a part of your **Main Quest: Rescue from Paradise**.

Remember that you can continue collecting Slaves (and adding Caps to your collection) with Grouse for as long as you like. There are a variety of options that occur when trying this; some targets react by being docile and "mezzed," others go into a frenzy and attack you, while the heads of others explode! For best results, try enslaving Wastelanders, Raiders, the Enclave, and Talon Company Mercs. You can't enslave Slavers!

You Gotta Shoot 'Em in the Head

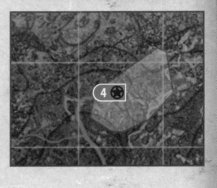

Fort Constantine

Twenty years ago, Allistair Tenpenny (**Tenpenny Tower [7.14]**) hired five people to raid **Fort Constantine [1.04]**, looking for experimental military gear. The team consisted of Tara Fields, Jeff Strayer, and three men paranoid enough to use only a single name, Dave, Dukov, and Crowley. Fields was savaged by Feral Ghouls. The rest left Crowley for dead in an irradiated Ghoul pen inside the facility. The surviving three found three security keys that bypassed the fort's security, and divided them up so none could return to risk death just to give Tenpenny his prototype armaments, then went their separate ways (**Dukov's [9.08]**, **Rivet City [9.15]**, **Republic of Dave [3.03]**). Jeff died a few years later, giving the key to his son. Unbeknownst to the survivors, their fourth team member made it out alive. And now he seeks revenge…or is it the latest experimental hardware? In a decaying, but once-opulent bar in the strange realm known as **Underworld [17.07]**, a cynical old Ghoul plots revenge on those he's been wronged by, and thinks they deserve a taste of their own medicine. Let's see whether they survive a headshot!

QUEST FLOWCHART

	MAIN PATH 1	MAIN PATH 2	OPTIONAL PATH 1	OPTIONAL PATH 2
Main Characters	Mister Crowley, Allistair Tenpenny, Dukov, Ted Strayer, Dave		Greta, Charon, Doctor Barrows, Quinn	Tara Fields (Deceased)
Locations	Underworld, Tenpenny Tower, Dukov's Place, Rivet City, The Republic of Dave		Underworld	Fort Constantine
Adv. Items/Abilities	Lockpick, Sneak, Science, Speech, Weapons, Black Widow, Lady Killer, Toughness, 500+ Caps		Speech	Lockpick, Science
Possible enemies	None			Robot Genus
Karma Influence	Positive	Negative	Neutral	

Locate and speak to Mister Crowley in Underworld (9th Circle Bar, or Carol's)

Kill Allistar Tenpenny.

Kill Dukov and get his key.

Kill Ted Strayer and get his key.

Kill Dave and get his key.

• Sniper Rifle and Ammo

Inquire about Mr. Crowley to: Greta Charon, Doctor Barrows, Quinn

Sweeten the deal with Mr. Crowley

• 100 Caps

Begin the hunt

Head to Tenpenny Tower

Excute with a Headshot

Double cross; agree to assassinate Crowley

• 100 Caps

Triple-cross!

Tell Mr. Crowley Allistair Tenpenny is dead.

Continued on next page

Continued on next page

Color code: Objective | Action | Rewards

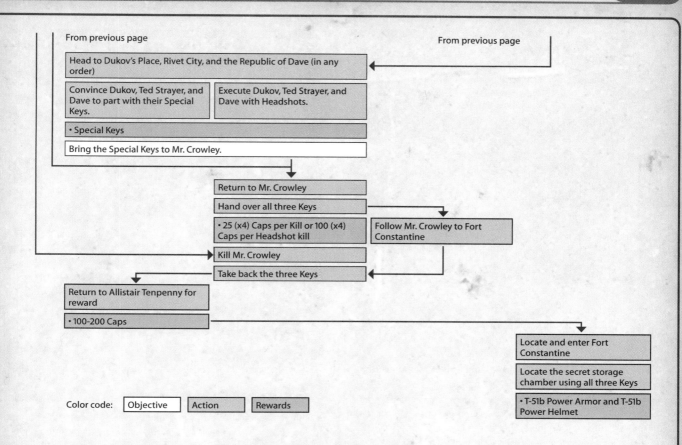

From previous page · From previous page

Head to Dukov's Place, Rivet City, and the Republic of Dave (in any order)

Convince Dukov, Ted Strayer, and Dave to part with their Special Keys.	Execute Dukov, Ted Strayer, and Dave with Headshots.

• Special Keys

Bring the Special Keys to Mr. Crowley.

Return to Mr. Crowley

Hand over all three Keys

• 25 (x4) Caps per Kill or 100 (x4) Caps per Headshot kill	Follow Mr. Crowley to Fort Constantine

Kill Mr. Crowley

Take back the three Keys

Return to Allistair Tenpenny for reward

• 100-200 Caps

Locate and enter Fort Constantine

Locate the secret storage chamber using all three Keys

• T-51b Power Armor and T-51b Power Helmet

Color code: Objective · Action · Rewards

MISTER CROWLEY, WHAT WENT ON IN YOUR HEAD?

Willow's the name: Information and friendly put-downs are her game.

When you've found the path through the Mall Tunnels, and you're trudging near the remains of the Washington Monument, look for Willow the sentry. She's the first person to direct you toward the Underworld, located behind her in the Museum of History. After a chat, head north into the museum and keep going; you can't miss the gigantic stone skull enveloping the entrance. Once inside the Underworld concourse, the Ninth Circle Bar is up the left stairs, at the far end of the upper walkway. You may need to explain your presence to Winthrop on the Underworld Concourse before you continue.

 Tip

Mister Crowley keeps somnambulist hours, so look for him in the Ninth Circle Bar no earlier than 10 PM (20:00 hours). At other times, he may be wandering elsewhere in Underworld, or be at Carol's place.

A Ghoul in here wants to speak with you. Engage Mister Crowley in conversation. If you're anything other than pleasant, he stops the chatter; he doesn't have time for bigots. When you get on his good side, he says he has some human targets—foes that wronged him in

the past or simply Ghoul haters—that need executing. The money is good: 100 Caps if executed with a headshot, and 25 if killed a little less "professionally." Crowley tells you to bring back a souvenir of each kill, a key for example. He's particularly insistent on an ironic headshot; this is, apparently, the only way most uninformed humans think Ghouls can be killed. Your targets are marked, and you receive a Sniper Rifle to aid you.

Mister alarming, in nocturnal rapport: Crowley's got a plan for you.

🔫 **Sniper Rifle and .308 Caliber Rounds**

NEW OBJECTIVE
"Kill Allistair Tenpenny" begins.

NEW OBJECTIVE
"Kill Dukov and get his key" begins.

NEW OBJECTIVE
"Kill Ted Strayer and get his key" begins.

NEW OBJECTIVE
"Kill Dave and get his key" begins.

Note

There is an inherent tension in this quest. On the one hand, you receive a good bounty (but lose Karma) for killing Crowley's targets. If you're worried about losing Karma, go for persuasion, trickery, purchasing, or stealing to obtain the keys; it isn't necessary to kill anyone.

MISTER CROWLEY, DID YOU TALK WITH THE DEAD?

Don't take Crowley's word for it. Do a bit of snooping yourself to understand just why the Ghoul wants these particular humans nullified. Although every Ghoul and their grandmother has an opinion, focus on four specific Ghouls who know Crowley better than most: Greta, Charon, Doctor Barrows, and Quinn. Greta is the only one who will give you the clue you need without a Speech challenge. The plans are identical for the other three:

Inquire about Mister Crowley, and when the Ghoul responds, fast-talk or bluster your way to a successful **Speech**, gain XP, and listen to some interesting extra details about Crowley.

Usually saying little except slightly menacing murmurs, Charon (who can also become your Follower, but doesn't need to be for the clue) can also give you information, as long you're successful in your Speech challenge. He answers that you're the third human Crowley has attempted to persuade to kill those guys. Charon is slightly put out that he wasn't asked, to be honest. He thinks that's strange.

Doctor Barrows tells you at first that he hasn't heard anything, but your Speech fools him into telling you Crowley's been spreading a pack of lies. He hopes whoever's agreed to being his hitman speaks to the victims first.

Quinn, who is a bit mercenary, asks for 50 Caps for his information. You can persuade him without expenditure using Speech. He doesn't believe Crowley's story and knows Dave personally. Dave's mighty strange, but he's no Ghoul hater.

Most other Ghouls, such as Patchwork the drunk, say Crowley doesn't buy any drinks. After you offer Patchwork 3 Caps, he tells you Crowley hires outsiders to do his killing.

Return to Ninth Circle and question Crowley. He's annoyed, but agrees that the keys on three of the four victims are what's important to him. Bring them back, and make up your own mind whether to assassinate the targets. Except Tenpenny, because that guy really is a bigot, apparently. You're given 100 Caps to sweeten the deal. Now head off to meet and greet or beat your first target.

 100 Caps

Note

You can approach the four targets in any order you like, including Tenpenny. They are presented in alphabetical order, beginning with Dave.

LAND OF THE FREE, HOME OF THE DAVE

A new utopia to some. A bunch of rusting shacks ruled over by a lunatic to others.

The Republic of Dave is a long trek to the northeastern corner of the Wastes, so pack provisions (Stimpaks and ammo) before you go, and perhaps conclude other quests en route. When you reach the gate, one of Dave's children is guarding it. Be sure you arrive no earlier than 10 AM, as Dave keeps business hours. Request an audience with President Daddy, and accompany the kid up to the largest shack at the far end the compound. Head inside, and locate Dave in his private chamber.

Note

There's a Freeform Quest in the Republic of Dave; don't forget to check it out on page 286.

When you've met Dave's wives, taken part in an election, or toured the compound to your satisfaction, figure out how you're going to tackle the small matter of Dave's key:

 Make three successful **Speech** conversations to find out that Crowley and Dave were part of an expedition to Fort Constantine, and Dave believes Crowley died locked in a room filled with Feral Ghouls. Convince Dave that parting with his key would be of strategic and diplomatic importance, and he agrees.

 If you have **Luck**, you can simply ask for the key, and Dave gives it to you; he has no use for it, except as a bargaining chip. Still, too late for that now....

 Or, you can threaten and attack him. This is messy, so it is better to wait until he's alone, and take careful aim at his head with your **Sniper Rifle**. Once his cranium has exploded, fight your way out of the compound, or massacre everyone.

 Pickpocket the key from Dave (using **Sneak**) and he'll be none the wiser.

Dave's Special Key

"Bring Dave's key to Mister Crowley" begins.

PUTTING DUKOV IN HIS PLACE

An imposing façade greets you when you find Dukov's building, and the man himself.

Dukov is a straightforward man to find; he's currently having his own private sex festival in the aptly titled Dukov's Place, which is adjacent to the Tepid Sewer. Your closest Metro is Georgetown; turn up any time. As you approach either side of the building (there are two entrances), read the signage and holster any weapons. Once inside, Dukov automatically hollers at you, wanting to know your business. He's got a loaded submachine gun, and two ladies in tow.

Dukov's harder to intimidate, perhaps because he insists on calling you "clown shoes."

When you've located Cherry and Fantasia (in case matters take a turn for the violent), make your move on Dukov. There are several methods to claim his key, his life, or both:

 Listen to Dukov's potty-mouth, and when he asks for Caps, lightly threaten him with a **Speech** intimidation. He laughs at the prospect, but he doesn't want to chance anything. He gives you the key.

You can convince Cherry to steal the key for you. Persuading her is an easier **Speech** challenge than persuading Dukov to surrender the key. However, she wants something in return: Escort her to Rivet City so she can leave life as Dukov's playmate behind. This takes some considerable time, so you might want to dump her body somewhere…if you're truly despicable!

 If you're female, and possess the **Black Widow** perk, Dukov won't be able to resist your advances, and perks up himself. Like putty in your hands, he readily hands over the key.

If you lack the social or sexual fortitude to play hardball (so to speak) with Dukov, you can agree to purchase the key for 200 Caps. Slap the money on the table, and leave.

 If you are male and possess the **Lady Killer** perk, Fantasia will steal the key for you. Unlike Cherry, she doesn't want anything in return.

 Dukov has a big mouth, and you may want to shut it up. Instead of starting a ruckus, politely end the conversation, retire to the upstairs balcony, and aim your **Sniper Rifle** at his head. Keep firing until his skull bursts, then search the corpse. For extra bad Karma, the truly psychotic would slay the hookers afterward. What are the voices in your head telling you?

You can just **Pickpocket** him for the key. He won't miss it until you're long gone.

🔑 **Dukov's Special Key**

NEW OBJECTIVE
"Bring Dukov's key to Mister Crowley" begins.

TED STRAYER'S RIVETING LIFE

Ted Strayer is the closest to Underworld, as he's recently arrived as a deckhand at Rivet City. Locate this floating township near the Jefferson Memorial, and move to the Common Room. Ted is likely to be asleep on one of the beds, or wandering around the vessel. Close the door behind you before you begin your interrogation:

 Ted tells you his father Jeff knew Crowley, and they investigated an old fort together. Ted has "needs," and refuses to hand over the key. Use **Speech** and insinuate that you'll cut him. Your thug-like behavior saves Ted's life, and he hands the key over.

If your threats are met with a much less intimidated response, you can always buy the key from Ted. Give him 25 Caps and be on your way.

 If you're more than merely intimidating, and have the **Toughness** perk, Ted becomes very fearful, and immediately hands over the key.

 As Ted wanders the boat, and doesn't already see you on his territory (unlike Dave and Dukov), try a swift **Pickpocket** to nab the necessary item.

 Crowley was right; humans are simply fleshbags and this one's the most tiresome of them all. He must be executed, but without alarming the entire population of the city. Exercise your **Small Guns** skill: Wait until he's in a room by himself, close the door, and decapitate him. Or follow him to a remote area of the ship, like the Flight Deck. Your mixture of patience and murderous rage yields the key.

🔑 **Ted Strayer's Special Key**

NEW OBJECTIVE
"Bring Ted Strayer's key to Mister Crowley" begins.

TRAINING — BESTIARY — MAIN QUEST — **MISC. QUESTS** — TOUR — COMPLETION — APPENDICES

TAKING DOWN TENPENNY

Caution

This stage is purely optional (assuming you've uncovered Crowley's real motives), and can affect two other Miscellaneous Quests (The Power of the Atom and Tenpenny Tower). Be mindful of this before you act!

Allistair Tenpenny really is a bigot, and Crowley's request to kill him isn't clouded by his key-collection expansion plans. To gain some extra Caps, travel to Tenpenny Tower, and use the tactics presented in **Miscellaneous Quest: Tenpenny Tower** (Listen to the Pro-Human and Pro-Ghoul Agendas) to get past the front gate, and Chief of Security Gustavo. Don't forget to bring 100 Caps, in case your fast-talking isn't up to par. Ascend to the penthouse level from the lobby and use one of the tactics from the "Mediated: Harmonious Living…" section of the Tenpenny Tower quest to navigate the guard, and enter Tenpenny's locked chamber.

Bring out your weapon as you move to the metal doors leading to Tenpenny's balcony (unless he's in his sleeping quarters), and corner the elderly Brit. Begin the conversation, but ignore the request for the key; Tenpenny doesn't know what the heck you're talking about. The following options are now available:

 Tenpenny is all business, and he tells you that double-crossing Crowley would be worth your while. Use **Speech** to increase your costs to 300 Caps, and you're awarded 100. You'll get the other 200 is when the deed is done.

If all you can muster is an agreement to this, you get 100, and another 100 when the Ghoul has been dispatched.

 Or, you can ignore this old man's proper mannerisms and accent, and pop him in the head with your **Sniper Rifle**. Try it twice, just to make sure. Make sure you're fine with other quests ending at this point, too.

Tip

Everyone likes free Caps, right? Then agree to assassinate Crowley, and then shoot Tenpenny; execute with a headshot, and you'll gain 100 Caps for the initial agreement with Tenpenny, and another when you return to Crowley!

NEW OBJECTIVE
"Kill Mister Crowley" begins (if you agreed to Tenpenny's plan).

NEW OBJECTIVE
"Tell Mister Crowley that Allistair Tenpenny is dead" begins (if you executed him).

CONCLUSIONS WITH CROWLEY

When your travels take you there, return to the Ninth Circle bar (remembering the 10 PM optimal time), and catch up with Crowley. He asks you how your search is going, and expects results. The following options are available, assuming you completed the previous stages:

Give each of the three Special Keys over to Crowley. He then pays you 100 Caps per kill with a headshot, or 25 if the victim

wasn't shot in the head, or you kept them alive. You can turn over individual keys one at time. You don't have to wait for all three (or four) to be completed before returning to Crowley, but it's more efficient that way.

 You may have heard of Fort Constantine on your travels. If you succeed in this difficult **Speech** persuasion, Crowley reveals that the complex is to the northwest. It should now appear on your map.

 Or, you can use your **Small Guns** and shoot Crowley (in the head, obviously, for the ultimately ironic kill). You are wise to give him the keys first, collect the Caps reward, then follow him out of Underworld to a location (such as the museum entrance hall) where no other Ghouls are present. Shoot him in Underworld, and you'll be savaged by flappy-skinned claws before you can retreat effectively.

 (up to) 300 Caps

Tip

If you dispatch Crowley, be sure to return to Allistair Tenpenny to collect your (up to) 200 Cap reward, if you agreed to kill Crowley for him.

Remember that you can turn over the individual keys one at a time, or all at once; the former is useful if you're near Underworld, want to pop round to see Crowley, and need the Caps. Otherwise, try the latter (and recommended) plan.

 (up to) 200 Caps

POST-QUEST PLAN: RAIDING FORT CONSTANTINE

Tip

Fort Constantine is a massive complex, filled with the latest military hardware. Although this is a search for Crowley's treasure, be sure to search adjacent corridors and locked chambers for massive weapon caches. Take all you can stagger out with!

When Crowley has the keys, your best bet is to follow him, and kill him in a quiet corner. You can trail him all the way to Fort Constantine, but this takes a long time, and it is much better to drop him before he disappears. Be sure you grab all three Special Keys from his corpse, and journey vaguely northwest, across the great Wasteland. Be sure you've stocked up on essentials, including a large amount of ammunition, well-repaired weapons, and Stimpaks. Clamber into your best armor, and hone your Security skill as proficiently as you can; you need to do all of this to survive the journey, and the roaming Brotherhood Outcast squads you may encounter at the fort's vicinity.

There are three large structures (two on the hill to the east), and a small cabin that once housed the commanding officer. Although you can (with an incredibly high Lockpick skill) enter any of the two higher buildings (leading to a munitions depot), or enter via the roof on the lower building (all of which is detailed in the Tour of the

Wasteland chapter), by far the easiest route is to open the cabin's door, and enter the CO quarters. Along the way, you encounter robots on the roof. Once inside, battle through a couple more robots, then turn west and head down to the basement. The bunker door is the area you need to get to, but remember to scour the house for goods beforehand. Take ammo and a special Bobblehead from the open safe.

Bobblehead: Big Guns

Sit down at the terminal, and use your Security skill to hack in; this is the only way to breach the bunker door. Remember to quit out on your last password attempt so you can retry until you get it right! Once through, there's a secondary door to the launch control bunker. Unlock this using Ted Strayer's Special Key (or a perfect 100 Lockpick skill and a number of bobby pins). Follow the corridor down the stairs, turning south to open a gate, and pillage the collection of ammunition in the desk area.

Open the nearby door, descend again to a locker room, and catch a robot near the restroom. Detonate him, then locate the stairs in the floor to the south. Descend again, following the corridor to a small junction with a locked door to your right. If you're successful, make a thorough search of the metal boxes and First Aid Box for a number of Stimpaks. Return to the corridor, and enter a gloomy office space. Deal with the robot threat here immediately.

Stimpaks

You can search the office space for a few clips of ammunition, but the key plan is to head to the staircase in the ground to the south. Descend to a rec room and swing left to drop another lolloping, rotting fiend. Make another quick search of the premises, but don't dawdle. Find more stairs to the south, leading down to the door to warhead storage. Unlock this with Dukov's Special Key, or some incredibly deft Lockpicking.

If you're ready to test your supreme Security or Lockpicking skills, you can investigate the two very well sealed doors to your right. If you can manage to get through, expect an incredibly large haul of armaments—more

The blue room: Home to the latest in health-assisted Medic Armor and Mini-Nukes.

than you can carry. But the real prize is through the sealed door to the south. Open it using Dave's Special Key and check the skeletal remains of Tara, one of the explorers originally tasked with rifling through this place with Crowley. She holds a Warhead Storage Key, which allows access into the large Warhead Storage Building via the inside or exterior doors.

For now, step over the corpse and enter a special experimental chamber. It is here you can grab a portable Mini-Nuke launcher: the Fat Man. Also up for grabs at the Armor R&D terminal (once you disable the stasis field at the terminal) is a suit of Experimental T-51b Power Armor! Don't forget the helmet!

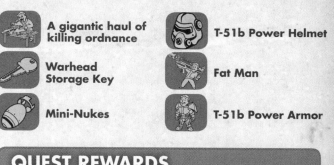

A gigantic haul of killing ordnance		T-51b Power Helmet	
Warhead Storage Key		Fat Man	
Mini-Nukes		T-51b Power Armor	

QUEST REWARDS

You receive the following rewards assuming you completed the optional Medic Armor hunt through Fort Constantine:

Bottle Cap (400 total):
If all four of Crowley's targets were assassinated with headshots. OR:

Bottle Cap (100 total):
If all four of Crowley's targets weren't assassinated with headshots.

Bottle Cap (300 total):
If Crowley was assassinated at the request of Tenpenny, and you succeeded in Speech. OR:

Bottle Cap (200 total):
If Crowley was assassinated at the request of Tenpenny.

 Fat Man, Mini-Nukes, T-51b Armor †
If you stole Crowley's three Special Keys, and explored Fort Constantine.

XP 300 XP

† Armor: DR 50, WG 40, VAL 869, Rad. Res. +25
† Helmet: DR 10, WG 4, VAL 120, CHR +1, Rad. Res. +8

The T-51b Tactical Armor grants you incredible damage resistance when worn, giving exceptional combat protection. Even better, it has no agility penalty, compared to other Power Armor types available, such as Brotherhood or Outcast Armor, Enclave Power Armor, and even the fabled Tesla Armor! This is the ultimate combat Power Armor suit. You need Power Armor Combat Training (achieved by visiting the Citadel during **Main Quest: Picking up the Trail**) to use it.

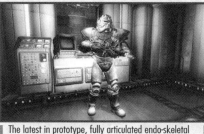

The latest in prototype, fully articulated endo-skeletal personal protection outfits? Yes please!

TRAINING — BESTIARY — MAIN QUEST — MISC. QUESTS — TOUR — COMPLETION — APPENDICES

Stealing Independence

Abraham Washington collects and catalogs District of Columbia antiquities for the Capitol Preservation Society, located deep in the bowels of **Rivet City [9.15]**. The collection is missing a crucial piece of DC history: the Declaration of Independence. You're tasked with entering the ruins of the **National Archives [17.11]** to attempt to retrieve this priceless original document; Washington will reward you with a fortune in Caps if you succeed. When you reach the Archive basement where the document is kept, you meet the eccentric Button Gwinnett, who is single-mindedly protective of the Declaration of Independence. After an optional side trip to the **Arlington Public Library [9.18]**, you must convince him of your loyalty: You're not a spy sent by King George, are you? You're not an agent of the abdicator, the plunderer of our seas, the ravager of our coasts, the burner of our towns, and the destroyer of the lives of our people, are you? Are you?!

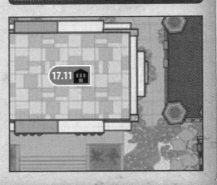

National Archives

17.11

QUEST FLOWCHART

	MAIN PATH 1	MAIN PATH 2	OPTIONAL PATH
Main Characters	Abraham Washington, Sydney, Button Gwinnett, Thomas Jefferson		Scribe Yearling
Locations	Rivet City, The National Archives		Arlington Library
Adv. Items/Abilities	Lockpick, Repair, Science, Speech		—
Possible enemies	Super Mutant Genus, Robot Genus, Turrets		Raiders
Karma Influence	Positive and/or Negative		Positive and/or Negative

Locate the Capitol Preservation Society in Rivet City → Consult the Society's Terminal
• America's History

Speak with Abraham Washington → Sell him any recovered Artifacts
• Caps

Retrieve the Declaration of Independence from the National Archives.

Locate and enter the National Archives → Play Guess and Win!
• Fruit Mentats

Enter the Archives Sub-Basement

Defend the Rotunda. | Ignore the Rotunda

Partner with Sydney | Ignore Sydney | Kill Sydney
• Sydney's 10mm Submachine gun

Use Rotunda Elevator to reach Sub-Basement | Take long route to Sub-Basement

Assault the Archives Passageways

[Science] The Quick Route | [Lockpick] The Slower Route | The Slowest Route

Locate Button Gwinnett's chamber → Raid side chambers
• Bill of Rights
• Magna Carta

→ [Repair] Inspect the Turret Generator
• Shut down Turrets

Continued on next page

Color code: Objective | Action | Rewards

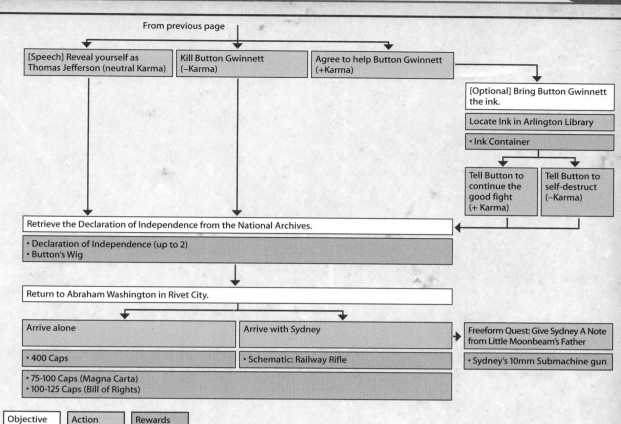

From previous page

[Speech] Reveal yourself as Thomas Jefferson (neutral Karma)

Kill Button Gwinnett (–Karma)

Agree to help Button Gwinnett (+Karma)

[Optional] Bring Button Gwinnett the ink.

Locate Ink in Arlington Library

• Ink Container

Tell Button to continue the good fight (+ Karma)

Tell Button to self-destruct (–Karma)

Retrieve the Declaration of Independence from the National Archives.

• Declaration of Independence (up to 2)
• Button's Wig

Return to Abraham Washington in Rivet City.

Arrive alone

Arrive with Sydney

Freeform Quest: Give Sydney A Note from Little Moonbeam's Father

• 400 Caps

• Schematic: Railway Rifle

• Sydney's 10mm Submachine gun

• 75-100 Caps (Magna Carta)
• 100-125 Caps (Bill of Rights)

Color code: | Objective | Action | Rewards |

WASHINGTON'S PROCLAMATION

Rivet City is home to the Capitol Preservation Society; look for the plane on the chain!

Begin this quest by trekking to Rivet City and following the signs throughout the interior midship deck that point to the Capitol Preservation Society. Look at the ceiling signs too, as the entrance is just in front of a door to the Science Lab. Walk into the society chamber, and you're greeted with a P-51 Mustang hanging from the ceiling. Turn southeast, and descend the metal steps to the Society's Terminal. Log on to find out a little more about America's history. You can read about:

• The Constitution of the U.S.A. (drafted, 1786).

• The Emancipation Proclamation (issued in 1862).

• The Gettysburg Address (speech by Lincoln, 1863).

• The Monroe Doctrine (presented in 1823).

• The U.S. Declaration of War on Germany (declared by Roosevelt, 1941).

• The U.S. Declaration of War on China (date unknown; either 2066 or 2067).

These documents are also framed on the wall to the left of the terminal, but some frames are empty, awaiting a missing document. Search this chamber for the curator and owner, Abraham Washington.

Investigate the room, but don't steal anything. You're here to meet Abraham Washington. When you find the old man, try to keep your offensive comments to a minimum, so you can easily ask about "the greatest prize" of all the documents, which is missing. He explains it is the Declaration of Independence, and Washington wants you to find it. He promises to reward you highly if you return with the document. He continues spouting knowledge, and you can further yours if you ask him more about it.

Washington hopes that you're up for this relic hunt. If you're not, he sits, wanders, and sips whiskey.

 In addition, you can use **Speech** to press Washington to reveal how he obtained all this information on the Declaration of Independence. He tells you he sent another relic hunter off to find the item. She reported back the information but lost contact a couple of months back.

Don't forget to have Washington pinpoint the National Archives (where Washington believes the Declaration is located) on your Pip-Boy.

NEW OBJECTIVE

"Retrieve the Declaration of Independence from the National Archives" begins.

If asked, Washington says he's also looking to branch out in his collecting, and if you find any other documents of historical significance, he'll pay you handsomely. When you're finished talking, tool up with your finest in Super Mutant–abatement weaponry, and exit to the D.C. Wasteland.

APPENDICES — COMPLETION — TOUR — MISC. QUESTS — MAIN QUEST — BESTIARY — TRAINING

The National Archives is near the Mall, and the Pennsylvania Ave./ The Mall Metro Station is the nearest link point. The building itself has two entrances. The rear entrance is quick to reach; head up the rusting escalator from the Pennsylvania Ave./The Mall Metro, turn right (southwest), and the entrance is just ahead, by the collapsed rubble. The front entrance is approached from the Mall itself, heading north. Either way, you need to cut down a group of Super Mutants. Once inside, your search begins.

TO THE ROTUNDA: SUPER MUTANT SEARCH AND DESTROY

 Note
There are two ways to reach a mysterious relic hunter, holed up in the central rotunda, who is helpful, but not mandatory to your quest. There's the short way, which involves ignoring most of the rooms, and heading in from the front entrance. There's also the long way, which involves heading in from either entrance, but clearing most of the building of Super Mutants.

PATH A: THE SHORT WAY (MAIN ENTRANCE)

Literally seconds away from the main entrance is your destination: the rotunda.

From the main entrance, step through into the once-opulent entrance foyer, and head around the central wall. On the other side is a Guess and Win! Terminal. Play the quiz if you wish, then inspect the three separate exits.

There are metal doors to the east and west, but head to the double wooden doors under the rotunda signage, next to the flaming barrel (a visual clue that this is the way to go). If you want to explore either metal door, you emerge on Path B.

Activate a National Archives Guess and Win! Terminal, and you get eight quiz questions about American history:

Question 1: The Declaration of Independence was an act of what body?
Answer: Second Continental Congress.

Question 2: How many North American Colonies rebelled against Great Britain in 1776?
Answer: Thirteen.

Question 3: Who was the first person to sign the Declaration of Independence?
Answer: John Hancock.

Question 4: How many delegates signed the Declaration of Independence?
Answer: 56.

Question 5: Which one of the following is NOT a written section of the Declaration of Independence?
Answer: Ratification.

Question 6: Who was the ruler of Great Britain when the Declaration was enacted in 1776?
Answer: King George III.

Question 7: Complete this famous phrase from the Declaration: "Life, Liberty, and the pursuit of..."
Answer: Happiness.

Question 8: Who was the principal author of the Declaration of Independence?
Answer: Thomas Jefferson.

Your rewards for correctly answering all eight questions in a row (start again if you get one answer wrong, the questions you previously got correct remain highlighted) is an Archives Prize Voucher, which can be cashed in for fabulous prizes. The prize terminal is immediately to the right of the Guess and Win! Terminal (and there's a safe in the nearby administration office with six more Prize Vouchers), and you can redeem vouchers for Fruit Mentats.

Archives Prize Voucher

Glamorously Grape Mentats (3)
+5 CHA for 240 minutes.

Brilliantly Berry Mentats (3)
+5 INT for 240 minutes.

Observantly Orange Mentats (3)
+5 PER for 240 minutes.

PATH B: THE LONG WAY (REAR ENTRANCE)

 **Note**
This is one way to explore the Archives, and you can head here from the front entrance too. Also shown is a highly dangerous and alternate way to the East Wing of the Archives, where the Declaration is said to reside.

Begin from the outside rear entrance, and enter the National Archives basement library, facing south. You can head left or right, but there are usually Super Mutant murmurings from the east; head left, around the bookcase, and slay anything yellowish-green and eight feet tall. After a brief fracas, head to the northeast corner of this chamber where a desk and safe reside.

Use **Lockpick** on the safe and the desk. There are some Caps, a First Aid Box to raid, and Ammo, plus a Scoped .44 Magnum inside the safe!

 Caps

Scoped .44 Magnum and Ammo

Pass through the wrecked wall into a connecting room, and east to a corridor. Swing south, readying yourself for Super Mutants. A classroom on your left can provide cover. Move to the pillar, where two more corridors stretch off. Head east, and you reach a locked door with a wall terminal. This leads to the sub-basement and is the alternate way to your goal, if you don't rendezvous with (or you accidentally kill) Sydney, the relic hunter in the rotunda. For the purposes of this particular route through the building, choose the corridor heading south, ignore the second classroom (although it contains a few items and Caps) and avoid the Brahmin Head-on-a-chain Trap at the base of the stairs to your left.

Climb the stairs, and when you reach the ground floor, look west at the metal door; this leads directly to the entrance foyer and the rotunda. Or, you can continue up the stairs to an office with a long hole in the western wall. This overlooks the rotunda interior, and you can actually make out a human female behind some defenses. Get down there and help her! Or, you could spend some time at the terminal, or unlocking the safe.

If you decide to use **Science** to hack the terminal, or **Lockpick** to open the wall safe, you receive these fine items:

.32 Pistol and Ammo

Pre-War Money (5)

Archive Prize Voucher (6)

These two giants are the reason Stimpaks were invented. Drop them before they get this close!

Descend to the corridor leading to the metal door, and step through into the entrance foyer. This is where you came in if you used Path A. Continue the quest by heading into the rotunda on your right (north). Or, continue on Path B by opening the other metal door opposite and going through a hole in the wall into a large chamber with a couple of brutish mutations to cut down. This area was once a library, but all the shelves are pushed away or gone, leaving a good-sized space and a couple of interesting places to investigate.

Begin by turning south and finding the metal door in the chamber's southeast corner. This leads to some stairs that lead to single chamber, a filing room with a portion of the floor collapsed. Two Super Mutants roam this area, so prepare for them, and once they're dispatched, spend some time collecting the items around the room's perimeter. There are two Ammo Boxes with Grenades, another two with Mines, a First Aid Box, and Caps plus Ammo in the desks. Grab what you can, then retrace your steps or fall through the floor.

Continue west, into the large chamber you came from, then turn south and head into a chamber the same size as the upstairs one. This chamber is a good source of items, but don't fall for the booby-trapped terminal:

 Use your **Repair** skill to disarm the bomb on the back of the terminal for XP. Or, leave it alone. Or shoot it!

Farther into the room are two Ammo Boxes, Mentats, and more Caps in the filing cabinets. At the west end of the chamber is an elevator to the archival strongroom, but it's locked and can't be accessed from this direction. Backtrack to the large room.

Frag Grenades

Frag Mines

Ammo Box Ammunition

Mentats

First Aid Box Health and Chems

The final part of this destructive clockwise rampage through this part of the Archives begins back in the big room. Ignore the restrooms, inspect the various pieces of scenery for the odd item, then look for the entrance to the stairs leading down. Before you head down, look

for the Combat Shotgun and Shells on the shelving. This is a great alternative to your current ordnance, unless you're already tearing through Super Mutant flesh with close-assault weaponry!

 Combat Shotgun and Ammo

Head downstairs, taking care not to get hit in the face by a falling engine-on-a-chain! Turn left (west) at the first doorway, checking out another classroom for items. There are a couple of Super Mutants down here, so prepare for them. Then check the desk and two Ammo Boxes for more esoteric bullets (Missiles and Cells), grab the Frag Grenades, then head down the corridor, turning left (west) and entering a second classroom. This one has a First Aid Box and other scattered items. Cross the corridor, and you end up in the basement library where you started! With this current area secure, either move to the rotunda (with Sydney) or head to the locked door to the sub-basement (without Sydney).

 Caution

Beware! There are two Frag Mines to deactivate, and a Brahmin-skull-on-a-railway-sleeper-on-a-chain Trap to dodge if you open the wooden door to the south, in this chamber.

Frag Grenades

 **Frag Mines**

Ammo Box Ammunition

First Aid Box Health and Chems

TO THE ARCHIVAL SECURE WING EAST: SLAUGHTERING WITH SYDNEY

When you've finished messing around, move into the rotunda, and try not to step on the half-dozen Mines scattered about the floor. You hear a female voice shouting to you. You haven't exactly been silent (unless you used Sneak and didn't kill anything), but there's no time for chit-chat; the Muties are coming! Proper introductions will have to wait. Spin around and train weapon at the door, and fire off your favorite ordnance into a trio of Super Mutants. Sydney must survive!

NEW OBJECTIVE
"Defend the Rotunda" begins.

You might want to lay a few Mines just as you open the double doors, before meeting Sydney, to waylay your adversaries. Fewer Super Mutants attack if you already wiped them from the Archives (if you took Path B). Lob in Grenades (away from Sydney!), rattle off Minigun shots or Missiles, and keep up the pressure until everything large and green is gurgling on the ground. Expect a second wave to arrive shortly after; don't let your guard up until your second objective displays as "completed."

Begin to speak with Sydney. She quickly realizes you're in the same line of work and have the same employer as her. She suggests you team up, find the Declaration, then bring it back to Washington and split the reward. Because you have this guide, her knowledge of the area isn't as critical, but you're still encouraged to agree to this;

especially because she has an interesting Post-Quest Antic to uncover. Isn't that right, Moonbeam? Assuming you agree, Sydney tells you the Declaration is secured in the archival strongroom underground. However, Sydney's found a concealed cargo lift in the center of the rotunda that takes you straight there.

Meet Sydney. She's been holding off Super Mutants since you left your daddy's vault.

Continue to get to know Sydney. Ask about how she got into this line of work, her impressive and customized submachine gun (which isn't available if you try Pickpocketing her), and her father, who she hopes to receive a message from. When you're ready, search the desk and filing cabinets for Ammo, then move to Sydney's Remote Terminal (near the flaming barrel), and "Unlock Rotunda Cargo Lift" using the password she supplies. The center of the rotunda raises slightly. Step on the lift, wait for Sydney, then look down and activate the lift. Your route continues in "Assault on the Archives Passageways."

 If Sydney was shot, or worse yet, was gunned down by your hand, expect a Karma loss. Without Sydney, you cannot use the rotunda cargo lift; you'll have to take the long way to the East Wing.

TO THE ARCHIVAL SECURE WING EAST: ALONE AGAINST THE MUTIES

 Caution

Ready for third-degree burns and a squad of Super Mutants that just don't know when to quit? Then take this highly dangerous route!

If Sydney is dead, or you don't want to share Washington's reward, or you just want a different method of reaching the archival strongroom, head to the locked door with the wall terminal.

Use **Science** to hack the terminal, or **Lockpick** to unlock the door, to access a set of crumbling stairs leading down into the sub-basement.

If you can't get through this door, and Sydney is dead, return here after placing more points into your Lockpick skill and locating more Bobby Pins. Once through, head down the stairs to a tiny book repository, and begin a battle through the shelving; use it to shield you from the Super Mutant attacks. Wait for another to open the door, then attack it, but stay back in this room.

There's a gas leak in the maintenance chamber beyond, and any sparks engulf you in fire. Stay in the book repository, and let the Super Mutants come to you. When immediate threats are cleared, roll in a Grenade and retreat. When the Grenade explodes, clearing the haze of gas, step into the maintenance chamber, and engage a Mutie who sometimes comes in with a Missile Launcher over on the south side of the chamber. Cross the small connecting bridge, but expect around six Super Mutants in this area from the

time you headed downstairs; they don't stop coming! When everything quiets down, inspect the southern room, where Ammo Boxes and a First Aid Box are available.

 Ammo Box Ammunition   **First Aid Box** Health and Chems

Once this cavalcade of carnage has temporarily halted, drop down from the small bridge, or turn and look for the tunnel to the east, which curves right and down to a pit room under the bridge and maintenance room. Exit via the doorway in the northwest corner, moving to a tunnel heading west, which ends in a T-junction. Hold your fire; there's another gas leak here! Turn south (north is a dead-end), and bound up the stairs. There's a locked gate to the east.

After a small struggle to jimmy open the lock using your **Lockpick** skill, you can enter this tiny storage area, complete with a collection of rarer items.

Bag these, then head west, to the Door to Archival Secure Wing East. Head through, and you're in the sub-basement directly under the rotunda. The paths for "Slaughtering with Sydney" and "Alone Against the Muties" now merge.

Metal Armor   **Metal Helmet**

Mini-Nuke   **Stealth Boy**

ASSAULT ON THE ARCHIVES PASSAGEWAYS

 **Tip**

It might be wise to bring out the Pulse Grenades at this point. If you want Sydney to survive, take a slow and steady approach to the exploration, or tell her to stay put in a safe place.

REACHING THE STAIRWELL WAYPOINT

If you must open the main hatch door, make sure the mechanized threat is contained!

Note

During the following search through the East Wing toward the archival strongroom, you hear the voice of Button Gwinnett "spurring the troops"; he sounds a little odd, as if commanding soldiers from an ancient Revolutionary War fortress.

Move northward, through the hatch door, and begin your descent into the passageways that lead to the archival strongroom. If you've spoken at length to Sydney, she has mentioned "short" and "long" routes throughout this particular area. For now, though, head into the initial chamber, turn left (west), and lob a Pulse Grenade at the waiting robot before he has chance to attack you. Back up out of range, and don't continue until oily's guts are clanking out over the concrete floor. Now pick one of three routes to reach the next chamber:

 The Quick Route: Move north to the utility gate. It is jammed, but if your **Science** skill is high enough, you can mend the door. It swings open, and you have a moment to react to the robot in the next chamber. Dispatch it!

The Slower Route: The second route involves moving west, toward the narrow corridor. Battle a second robot, then turn right (north) at the metal door. Use **Lockpick** to open the door, and step through into a very long, straight corridor. Run to the opposite end, open the other metal door, and step out into the original corridor as it reaches the next chamber, on your right (east).

The Slowest Route: If you're lacking Lockpick and Science skills, or if you want additional combat and pick-up opportunities, take the long way around to. Head west, poking your head through the first doorway on your left (south) to uncover some Pulse Mines, a Laser Rifle, and some Cell Ammo. Return to the corridor and continue to another doorway on your left, uncovering some more Cell Ammo and a skeleton. Follow the corridor around to a well-lit room, checking the shelves for another two Pulse Mines inside an Ammo Box, and optionally try your Laser Rifle or Pulse Mines out on a robot on the other side of the wall. Beware; there's a gas leak here! Then follow the corridor east as it connects to. All paths now merge at the rubble pile near a stairwell leading down.

 Pulse Mines   **Laser Rifle**

Energy Cell Ammo

 At the rubble pile, before you head down the steps, make sure you inspect the turret generator, between the two metal wall sections. **Repair** this and you can shut down all the turrets in the floor below, which guard some major archival materials!

 Tip

If you're partnered with Sydney, she's more than just a pretty face offering fire-support. She also shouts out some tactical advice, including shortcuts that can help in sections to come. Listen, then act on her advice.

RANSACKING TO THE BILL OF RIGHTS

Descend to the floor below, and locate the hatch door in the north wall. Step through, and you're greeted with a door in an alcove on your left, one on the right wall, and one at the end of a corridor with a wall terminal. Deal with the left door first:

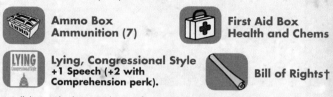 Bring out your Bobby Pins, and **Lockpick** open the hatch door that's locked. This leads to a secondary hatch door to **Lockpick** open if you want to ransack what's behind here.

Assuming you pick both locks, you can enter a narrow storeroom, filled with useful items. Grab the following (which includes the exceptionally valuable Bill of Rights inside the security safe), then head back to the corridor you just came from:

Ammo Box Ammunition (7)   **First Aid Box Health and Chems**

 Lying, Congressional Style +1 Speech (+2 with Comprehension perk).   **Bill of Rights†**

† Sell this to Abraham Washington for 100–125 Caps (depending on Barter skill level), or during Miscellaneous Quest: Head of State.

CARTING OFF THE MAGNA CARTA

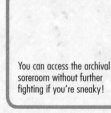 Either **Lockpick** the door in the initial corridor at the bottom of the stairs, or head forward, then double-back east and south into an archival room with an easily overlooked hatch door in the east wall. Open that, then **Lockpick** a second locked door.

Watch out for two turrets, and inspect another narrow storeroom that contains telephones, five Ammo Boxes, and another valuable object: the Magna Carta!

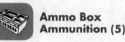 **Ammo Box Ammunition (5)**   **Magna Carta ‡**

‡ Sell this to Abraham Washington for 75–100 Caps (depending on Barter skill level), or during Miscellaneous Quest: Head of State.

TO THE ARCHIVES STRONGROOM: NO COMBAT

You can access the archival soreroom without further fighting if you're sneaky!

 Before you check the door on the east wall, move to the wall terminal, and use **Science** to hack into the computer. You can switch off the turret right beyond the door in the next chamber.

There are three robots in the area beyond the doors, but you don't have to avoid them; you can use your **Lockpick** skill on the door on the east wall.

 Once through, follow the small corridor into a room with large microfiche monitors, then continue north. The junction on the left leads to the robot threats, so **Sneak** (and optionally use a Stealth Boy) to continue on and around to the left, and quickly move to the north wall and the door to the archival strongroom. Open it before you're sensed by the robots.

TRAINING — BESTIARY — MAIN QUEST — **MISC. QUESTS** — TOUR — COMPLETION — APPENDICES

TO THE ARCHIVAL STRONGROOM: NO MERCY!

If turning mechanoids into rusting hulks of steaming metal appeals to you, open the unlocked hatch door. Enter the filing chamber, pausing to rifle through the filing cabinets for some minor Ammo and Caps. Then move to the T-junction ahead. You're spotted by two robots on either side of you, so back up from this ambush, and lay Pulse Mines or perform your preferred method of robot destruction. Once everything metal is crumpled, move around to the next chamber, which has the door to the archival strongroom on the north wall, and enter.

YIELDING TO THE DISTINGUISHED GOVERNOR OF GEORGIA

Holster your weapon (at least temporarily) as you emerge into the strongroom, and you're greeted by… why, I'd recognize that fellow anywhere. The powdered wig, the blue coat, the metal mandible appendages—this

The floor recognizes the second signer of the Declaration of Independence…isn't this loopy rustbucket!

must be Button Gwinnett, second governor of Georgia! Look closer, and you may spot some tiny discrepancies in this fellow: the pulsing brain module, the clanking sound Button makes, and the fact that this is actually a Protectron! It's been more than two hundred years, and Button's AI began to get a bit loopy a long time ago. He started to repair and reprogram the robots to accept new functionality, allowing them to believe he was their "leader" and they had to defend the ideals of freedom as laid out in the Declaration (a corrupted version of their original programing which was to defend the treasures of the archives and reenact the signing of the Declaration). Button now believes you to be a Redcoat spy. Set him straight on a few issues:

You can dismiss this foolishness, but Button doesn't fall for it. He keeps up the pretense until you either play along or seek violence. Your options are as follows:

Continue to play along, asserting that you're not a Redcoat spy but from the United States congress. At this point you have two options:

 Use **Speech** and declare yourself to be Thomas Jefferson (or his agent, if you're female), and that you've returned to liberate the Declaration. Button is overjoyed and eventually hands over the document.

You can seek to prove your honesty by tricking the Redcoats. The only option Button deems appropriate is to craft a "fake" Declaration of Independence, and for this, he needs ink from 500 years ago. There's only one place you can get this: Arlington Public Library!

NEW OBJECTIVE [OPTIONAL]
"Bring Button Gwinnett the ink" begins.

 Or, you can attempt your best Lachlan McIntosh impression, and gun down this maniac hunk of junk, powdered wig and all. You may be seen as a cad of the highest order, but you won't need to embark on a wild goose chase into a Raider stronghold to find some ink for a deranged droid! When Gwinnett is destroyed, he drops the password to the Strongroom Security Terminal. Collect it along with a few Cells.

Strongroom Security Terminal Password   **Energy Cell Ammo**

AN INK TO THE PAST

That nut-and-bolt case needs this Ink Container, does he? You'll find it here, under heavy Raider protection.

If you're the patient sort, set off for Arlington Public Library. The route through the library that you take is identical to the one presented during **Miscellaneous Quest: The Wasteland Survival Guide**. Check page 159 for the tactics to reach the Ink Container, then bring it all the way back to the strongroom!

GIVE IT UP, GWINNETT!

If you haven't destroyed Button Gwinnett, you can hand over the Ink Container when you return, or convince him you're Thomas Jefferson. Either way, you receive the Declaration of Independence from Button Gwinnett, and a passcode for the Archives Security Terminal. Copy or not, this is going straight back to Abraham Washington. Whether you're a "congress member" or "Thomas Jefferson," Button asks what his next orders should be:

 You can keep up the charade, telling him to continue to fight the good fight, or keep the Declaration.

You can tell him to do what he likes; you're leaving this deranged rustbucket immediately!

 Or you can tell Button to self-destruct. It's a cruel end to the co-signer of the Declaration of…oh wait. This is an insane droid that's taken up far too much of your time already!

NEW OBJECTIVE
"Return to Abraham Washington in Rivet City" begins.

Now that you have a Declaration, you can further explore this chamber. Use the Archives Secure Terminal Password, or the passcode that Button gave you, to access Button's Terminal. Here, you can unlock all the strongroom, East Wing, and mag-sealed doors (recommended). You can also steal (if Button is still alive) Cells and a Stealth Boy from his wooden desk and wardrobe. Behind Button's desk is a door to three safes; the middle one has the real Declaration of Independence. The others have Ammo and a few Caps. Don't forget Button's Wig also; it's one of the finest unique items in the Wasteland!

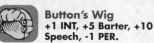 **Declaration of Independence**

 Button's Wig
+1 INT, +5 Barter, +10 Speech, -1 PER.

You can now open the door in the west wall, and head into a pod chamber, a maintenance bay where all the ancient Protectron tour guides resided for tune-ups and reprogramming. The only functional Protectron is in the northwest pod. Download the only available sub-routine (Thomas Jefferson), and another deranged reenactor stomps around the sub-basement, this one broadcasting the dulcet tones of Three Dog!

You can also access the Maintenance Terminal, where you can read about BGWIN009's system memory leak, an automated turret lock, a long-deactivated Nightingale, and other entries by the long-dead P. Brantseg of the Robotics Team. When you've finished larking about, locate Sydney and agree to return to Rivet City. Take the now-functional cargo elevator and leave the building. Fast Travel to Abraham Washington.

QUEST REWARD: HANDING OLD RELICS TO THE OLD RELIC

Washington is suitably excited to receive the document, and any others you may have stolen!

Return to the Capitol Preservation Society, where Old Man Washington is quite giddy about receiving the documents you've risked your life for. You're awarded a Railway Rifle Schematic for your troubles, and some Caps if you turn in any other documents or relics. The following table shows antiquities that Washington will readily purchase from you. He locates Sydney and awards her prize after you've left.

 Schematic: Railway Rifle
+400 Caps if you arrive alone.

 75–100 Caps
If Magna Carta delivered.

100–125 Caps
If Bill of Rights delivered.

POST-QUEST ANTICS

Assuming Sydney survived the quest, you can speak to her either in the National Archives, in Rivet City, or in the 9th Circle drinking establishment in Underworld (where she emigrates after this quest). Bring the following object:

 A Note from Little Moonbeam's Father

Find this Holotape in the Statesman Hotel; the exact location (a bed by a desiccated corpse) is shown during **Miscellaneous Quest: Reilly's Rangers** (page 251). Speak with Sydney about her father. You need to figure out that her father's "sappy" name for her ("Little Moonbeam") is the one used in the Holotape message, if you listened to it. Sydney is shocked and taken aback that her father didn't leave when she was 14, but rather tried to help her. She presents her customized one-of-a-kind SMG as a token of her appreciation.

Sydney's 10mm "Ultra" SMG
Holds 50 rounds, with higher crit and per shot damage.

Items that can be Sold to Abraham Washington

ARTIFACT	LOCATION	PRICE (Abraham Washington)	RELATED MISC. QUEST
Declaration of Independence	National Archives	Railway Rifle Schematics	Stealing Independence
(Faked) Declaration of Independence	National Archives	Railway Rifle Schematics	Stealing Independence
Bill of Rights	National Archives	100–125 Caps	Stealing Independence
Magna Carta	National Archives	75–100 Caps	Stealing Independence
Lincoln's Rifle	Museum of History	100–125 Caps	Head of State
Lincoln's Hat	Museum of History	70 Caps	Head of State
Action Abe	Museum of History	10 Caps	Head of State
John Wilkes Booth Wanted Poster	Museum of History	70–90 Caps	Head of State
Civil War Draft Poster	Museum of History	60 Caps	Head of State
Lincoln's Diary	Museum of History	100 Caps	Head of State
Lincoln's Head Penny Collection	Museum of History	15–30 Caps	Head of State
Lincoln's Voice (Phonograph)	Museum of History	60–80 Caps	Head of State
Agatha's Soil Stradivarius Violin*	Vault 92	200–300 Caps with Speech challenge	Agatha's Song

*This item is required to complete **Miscellaneous Quest: Agatha's Song**

Trouble on the Homefront

It has been roughly two weeks since you left the confines of **Vault 101 [8.01]**. Travelers across the Wastes have begun to speak of a faint radio signal looping over and over again. After listening to it on your Pip-Boy, you realize it is a message from Amata, telling you the situation inside your previous home has deteriorated. The Overseer has the entire fccility in lockdown, inhabitants are dead or missing, and there's trouble with the Vault's water-cooled reactor. When you return, the place is in a state of chaos. Your freedom had unforeseen consequences. Some wanted to leave with you, but the Overseer sealed the Vault, to ensure its "purity." The security staff terrorizes the residents who don't agree. There is talk of rebellion, but those who threaten to stand up to the Overseer disappear in the night. You have a mixture of emotions and are torn between making Amata the new Overseer; agreeing to keep the residents safe, but under the rule of a tyrant; or forcing the residents into this brave, new (and highly radioactive) world. Or, you could kill them all....

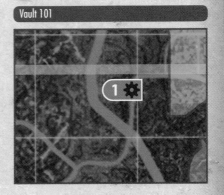

Vault 101

QUEST FLOWCHART

	MAIN PATH	OPTIONAL PATH 1	OPTIONAL PATH 2	OPTIONAL PATH 3
Main Characters	Amata, Jim Wilkins, Officer Gomez, Officer Armstrong, Overseer Almodovar (Overseer Mack), Butch, Officer Taylor, Freddy Gomez, Chip Taylor, Wally Mack, Ellen DeLoria, Pepper Gomez, Security Chief Hannon, Vikki Hannon, Mr. Brotch, Old Lady Palmer, Christine Kendall, Andy, Miss Beatrice, Stanley			
Locations	Vault 101			
Adv. Items/Abilities	Lockpick, Science, Sneak, Speech			
Possible enemies	Radroach			
Karma Influence	Neutral			

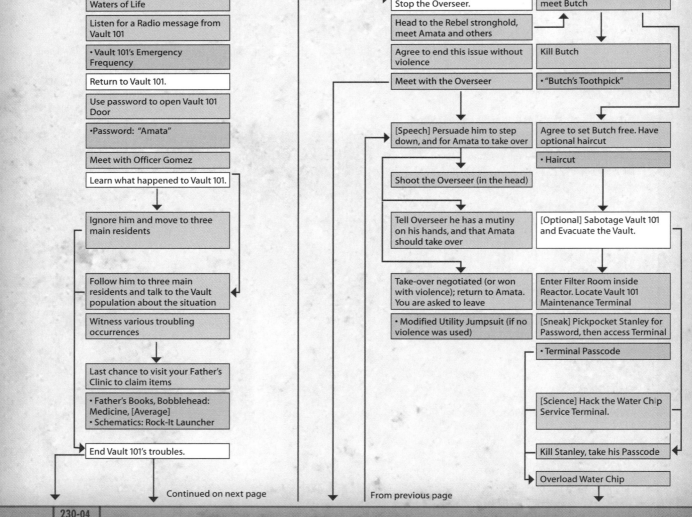

MAIN PATH

- Complete Main Quest: The Waters of Life
- Listen for a Radio message from Vault 101
  - • Vault 101's Emergency Frequency
- Return to Vault 101.
- Use password to open Vault 101 Door
  - •Password: "Amata"
- Meet with Officer Gomez
- Learn what happened to Vault 101.
- Ignore him and move to three main residents
- Follow him to three main residents and talk to the Vault population about the situation
- Witness various troubling occurrences
- Last chance to visit your Father's Clinic to claim items
  - • Father's Books, Bobblehead: Medicine, [Average]
  - • Schematics: Rock-It Launcher
- End Vault 101's troubles.

OPTIONAL PATH 1

- [Optional] Talk to the Rebels and Stop the Overseer.
- Head to the Rebel stronghold, meet Amata and others
- Agree to end this issue without violence
- Meet with the Overseer
- [Speech] Persuade him to step down, and for Amata to take over
- Shoot the Overseer (in the head)
- Tell Overseer he has a mutiny on his hands, and that Amata should take over
- Take-over negotiated (or won with violence); return to Amata. You are asked to leave
  - • Modified Utility Jumpsuit (if no violence was used)

OPTIONAL PATH 2

- Head to the Rebel stronghold, meet Butch
- Kill Butch
  - • "Butch's Toothpick"
- Agree to set Butch free. Have optional haircut
  - • Haircut

OPTIONAL PATH 3

- [Optional] Sabotage Vault 101 and Evacuate the Vault.
- Enter Filter Room inside Reactor. Locate Vault 101 Maintenance Terminal
- [Sneak] Pickpocket Stanley for Password, then access Terminal
  - • Terminal Passcode
- [Science] Hack the Water Chip Service Terminal.
- Kill Stanley, take his Passcode
- Overload Water Chip

Continued on next page

From previous page

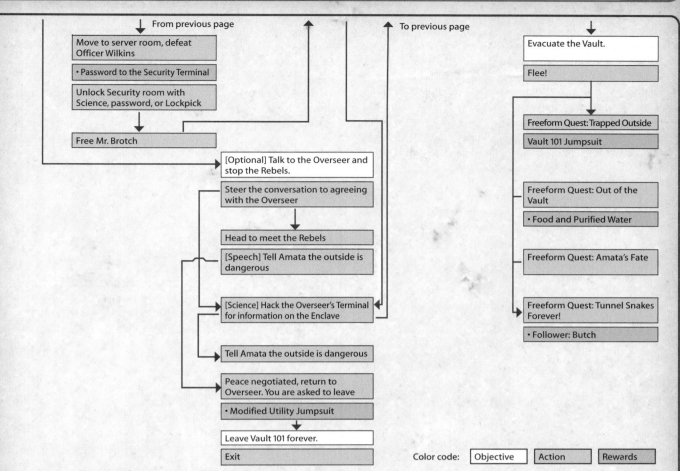

From previous page

- Move to server room, defeat Officer Wilkins
  - • Password to the Security Terminal
- Unlock Security room with Science, password, or Lockpick
- Free Mr. Brotch

[Optional] Talk to the Overseer and stop the Rebels.

Steer the conversation to agreeing with the Overseer

Head to meet the Rebels

[Speech] Tell Amata the outside is dangerous

[Science] Hack the Overseer's Terminal for information on the Enclave

Tell Amata the outside is dangerous

Peace negotiated, return to Overseer. You are asked to leave
- • Modified Utility Jumpsuit

Leave Vault 101 forever.

Exit

To previous page

Evacuate the Vault.

Flee!

Freeform Quest: Trapped Outside

Vault 101 Jumpsuit

Freeform Quest: Out of the Vault
- • Food and Purified Water

Freeform Quest: Amata's Fate

Freeform Quest: Tunnel Snakes Forever!
- • Follower: Butch

Color code: | Objective | Action | Rewards |

SOMETHING'S AMATA AT VAULT 101

Hidden deep beneath this rocky outcrop is Vault-Tec's latest failed experiment: Vault 101.

Continue your main journey without access to this quest, until you've completed **Main Quest: The Waters of Life**. Soon afterward, your Pip-Boy begins to pick up transmissions from Vault 101's Emergency Frequency.

Tune your radio to listen to a frantic message from Amata. She seems troubled, telling you that life in the Vault has taken a turn for the worse; the Overseer has gone insane! She's set the main door's password to "Amata" and hopes you can come and help as soon as possible.

 Vault 101's Emergency Frequency
Only audible from locations near Vault 101.

NEW OBJECTIVE
"Return to Vault 101" begins.

NEW OBJECTIVE
"Learn what happened to Vault 101" begins.

Enter the gate in the rock wall, and move to the Vault door. At the door controls, automatically use "Amata" as the password (you need to have listened to the radio message to know this), and the door rumbles open. Step through into the door security zone. Here, you can see the first shocking event. Jim Wilkins lies dead by the door controls! Optionally kill the Radroach scuttling about, then open the door to the west.

You step through into the generator room and are accosted by Officer Gomez (or Officer Armstrong if Gomez died in "Escape!"), who's really on edge. Converse with him (you might want to leave Amata's name out of your chat, because he doesn't know about the radio message). He then tells you that the night your father left, "everything went crazy." Radroaches scuttled in, inhabitants began to realize humans could survive outside, and the Overseer started to crack down on such talk. The Vault seems to be split; some favor the Overseer, while others side with Amata and the "Rebels."

The following options become available before the end of the conversation with Gomez:

If you don't want to explore or use the guide map, you can follow Gomez to either the Overseer or Amata (the choice is yours).

You can give up on solving the troubles, and leave Vault 101 forever. If you actually choose this, the quest ends, and you cannot return (the password changes, sealing you in the Wasteland).

If you want to explore and talk to other inhabitants, start investigating on your own.

NEW OBJECTIVE
"End Vault 101's troubles" begins.

THE 411 ON 101

Note

Speak to three main people at your earliest convenience:
- • The Overseer (located in his office).
- • Amata (found in the western wing of Vault 101).
- • Butch (found in the corridor near Amata).
- • Or, you can roam the Vault, speaking to the residents, and hearing their explanation of events.

Whatever your plan, move into the ground floor of the atrium, and watch Officer Taylor shoot at Freddie Gomez! Speak with him, and he tells you he's afraid of the Rebels and doesn't know what to do. Leave him to wander in a general state of senile paranoia, and face south. You can head anywhere you like, but to talk to a number of residents, open the door marked "storage." There's another dead resident in here! Officer Taylor's son, Chip, lies by the connecting door!

Continue your search through the inhabitants' quarters, and you'll find a number of survivors wandering the halls, including Wally Mack (who's left the Tunnel Snakes, and hates the Rebels), Ellen DeLoria (who can't quite remember what went on, but still blames your father), and young Pepper Gomez (who hates that her brother got involved with the Rebels, and can't stand you). Once you get a flavor of the problems plaguing this place, pay a visit to one of the three people listed previously, and plan one of four conclusions to this quest:

- Respecting Authority: Siding with the Overseer.
- The New Queen of Vault 101: Siding with Amata.
- Hair-brained Evacuation: Siding with Butch.
- Everybody's Gotta Die Sometime....

Note

You can also roam the basement reactor room area; the items you can grab are all listed in the "Siding With Butch" section of this quest.

Also remember you can choose to conclude this quest by speaking to people in any order; the following stages show the quickest way to resolve your plans.

You can also choose to leave Vault 101 and never return, when you speak to either the Overseer or Amata. Banishment isn't a recommended option until you finish the quest.

RESPECTING AUTHORITY: SIDING WITH THE OVERSEER

Travel to the Atrium/Upper Level of the Vault, head north along the main corridor to the door on your right, where you found the Overseer's office during **Main Quest: Escape!**, and enter. You may bump into Security Chief Hannon on your travels; his hatred of the Rebels and other trouble-making kids stems from the loss of his wife Vikki and their child. Don't antagonize him unless you plan to kill him later, and enter the Overseer's office to the south. Save your progress before you go in.

NEW OBJECTIVE [OPTIONAL]
"Talk to the Overseer and Stop the Rebels" begins.

Depending on your previous gunplay, the Overseer is either Amata's dad (left), or Wally's pop (right).

Enter the Overseer's office, and speak to him. If you killed the original Overseer (Amata's father) during **Main Quest: Escape!**, the new Overseer is Allen Mack (Wally's father). Whoever is running the show, you have the following options to try to get "on side" with the Overseer:

Ignore all other dialog choices, and steer the chat into agreeing to stop the Rebels. You need to read the dialog choices carefully, and choose answers that place this dictator in the shining light he thinks he's bathed in.

Travel to meet Amata, in the west wing of the Vault. Access the door to the lower levels just west of the Overseer's area. Head down the stairs, passing the turning for the Reactor, and make a left at the T-junction. Head up the steps following the signs to the atrium, navigate around Butch, and head northeast to Amata.

 Or, you can head to the Overseer's Office, and use **Science** access his terminal. Since your escape, the Overseer was contacted by the Enclave. They want access to Vault 101, claiming they're here to help. The Overseer seems to have denied them access, because he doesn't trust them; this could be the wisest move the man has made in a long time!

 Use your **Speech** skill to convince Amata to stop her rebellious plans by telling her the outside area is very dangerous. If you fail, you need to return to the Overseer, and speak with him. If you fail again, the only option is to leave.

Or, if you read the Overseer's information in his terminal, you can convince Amata to back down, as the Overseer is keeping the Vault safe from very real and deadly threats. You can attempt this without a Speech challenge.

Now return to the Overseer, who is surprised and pleased by your negotiating skills, especially because the Rebels were disbanded without bloodshed. Vault 101 continues to be ruled under the Overseer's iron fist. You are presented with a specially Modified Utility Jumpsuit for your troubles, and asked to leave; permanently. Your past escape has caused ill-will among the inhabitants.

 Modified Utility Jumpsuit

NEW OBJECTIVE
"Leave Vault 101 forever" begins.

THE NEW QUEEN OF VAULT 101: SIDING WITH AMATA

Before you chat with the Rebels, it helps your cause to investigate the admin area, accessed via the gantry area in the atrium. Step into the server room, and you may encounter Officer Wilkins, who's the most vehement of the Overseer's supporters. He opens fire after a brief threat, so be prepared to drop him. Search his corpse to obtain the Password to the Security Terminal. Then investigate the locked security room. Step inside, and head to the locked cell door with the terminal to the left.

Access the locked cell door with the password that you found on Wilkins' corpse.

 When successful, you can use **Science** to unlock the cell door, and read a memo marked CONFIDENTIAL. It details a midnight raid on the Rebels' stronghold by one of the more "enthusiastic" guards, and stresses the importance of not telling the Overseer.

If your **Lockpicking** is successful, the cell door opens, and you can release your old teacher, Mr. Brotch, from confinement. He moves to the Rebel area after telling you more about the raid, and the Rebels' plans.

NEW OBJECTIVE
"Talk to the Rebels and Stop the Overseer" begins.

Head to the Rebels' stronghold in the west wing of the Vault. Speak with Butch (optionally beginning "Siding with Butch"), then chat with Old Lady Palmer, Christine Kendall, and any other inhabitant you want to gain information from.

The plucky young Rebel leader, Amata, seeks to keep Vault 101 a democracy, not a dictatorship.

When you speak with Amata, agree to the following:

Choose the dialog option "I swear, I'll stop the Overseer and his guards. Just watch." Then agree not to use violence to solve this issue. You must now head to the Overseer, and bring this violent bickering to a (hopefully) peaceful conclusion.

Before you leave the Rebel stronghold, you can quickly check your father's old clinic, which has been taken over by Andy. He seems to have made rather a pig's ear of a sprained toe operation on Miss Beatrice, as the blood hasn't even been scraped off the walls yet. Leave this malfunctioning mechanoid, head out past Butch, down the stairs, and turn right (west), passing the stairs down to the reactor. You're headed up the atrium steps to speak with the Overseer. Before you speak with him, try this option:

Use **Science** to hack into the Overseer's terminal, and read the comments in there; there's evidence that the Overseer has been in contact with the outside world. Now speak with him.

The following plans can occur:

Steer the conversation toward this **Speech** challenge, telling the Overseer he doesn't have enough people to stay cooped up down here forever. This persuasion is easier if you've read his terminal log entries.

If this works, the Overseer agrees to step down and let Amata take over. If this fails, return to Amata and try again. Fail again, and there are two other ways to end this:

If you've read the cell terminal, or spoken to Mr. Brotch, you can tell the Overseer his security guards are planning a raid without his knowledge.

Or, you can shoot him in the head; that definitely stops him! Search him, grab the Pistol, and report back to Amata. Remember you can also activate the secret tunnel (that you used in **Main Quest: Escape!**) from the Overseer's office, too.

If you killed the original Overseer, Overseer Mack knows exactly what happens to those who try to reason with you, and begins combat as soon as you attempt to talk him out of his position. Your only option is to kill him too. Your past violent actions have come back to haunt you!

Return to Amata, who is suitably excited and astonished if your diplomacy succeeded, and tearfully regretful if you killed the Overseer. She thanks you profusely, but due to the delicate situation with the other inhabitants, you must still leave the Vault. To soften the blow, Amata gives you a special Modified Utility Jumpsuit, but only if you didn't use violence.

 Modified Utility Jumpsuit

NEW OBJECTIVE
"Leave Vault 101 forever" begins.

HAIR-BRAINED EVACUATION: SIDING WITH BUTCH

Butch is a little bitter at his lot in life, although he can sculpt a mean coif.

There's a third alternative to siding with the Overseer or the Rebels, and this is for those with a soft spot for Butch, or who have failed to convince either party and don't want to resort to violence. Seek out Butch, who's in the corridor close to the Rebel stronghold, and begin a conversation with him. You can keep chatting to him, exhausting all options, and he reveals he's desperate to escape his life as a hairdresser! You can request a change in your own hair at this point, if you wish. Then you're presented with a new option:

NEW OBJECTIVE [OPTIONAL]
"Sabotage Vault 101 and Evacuate the Vault" begins.

This terminal is the key to Butch's life on the outside; set the Tunnel Snake free!

It seems that the Water Chip Terminal downstairs is susceptible to a bit of espionage, so follow the signs down to the Reactor Room and sub-level, and enter the Filter Room. You can talk with Stanley, who's tinkering with the Water Chip, because it's in a pretty delicate state and shouldn't be used. This is a clue to your plan of sabotage; move past the First Aid Box, through the room with the Frag Grenades on the table, and locate the Vault 101 Maintenance Terminal.

 **Frag Grenades** **First Aid Box Health and Chems**

This is a hard terminal to hack into with **Science** skill. If you accomplish this, select "Begin Water Chip Service," then "Begin Manual Service," and finally (after the warning) "Run Systems Purge." This overloads the Water Chip and shuts down the reactor.

Stanley also has the password to the system on him, which you can Pickpocket from him using **Sneak**.

TRAINING — BESTIARY — MAIN QUEST — MISC. QUESTS — TOUR — COMPLETION — APPENDICES

Or, you can simply kill him and take the password.

For a gory bonus, overload the Water Chip while Stanley is working on the system. Messy as his demise is, it is probably faster than his doomed destiny should he flee into the Wasteland.

NEW OBJECTIVE

"Evacuate the Vault" begins.

 The klaxons wail as the Vault begins to power down and evacuation measures begin. This is your cue to leave, fast! However, you're accosted by the Overseer on your way out of the reactor (if you haven't killed him). You can tell him he no longer has the option to stay in the Vault, or:

> You can use **Speech** to try an exceedingly difficult lie, telling him Rebels were responsible.

If you encounter Overseer Mack, no matter which choice you make the Overseer attacks and must be neutralized.

> If Overseer Almodovar is still alive, you can attempt to challenge his reasoning. Succeed in your **Speech** and he blames himself for pushing his people too hard, and resigns himself to his fate, without fighting you.
>
> Now flee the scene. You bump into Amata at the exit, and her apprehension is palpable. You can tell her you caused the evacuation, and watch as she flees in disgust away from you. Or you can try a difficult lie, telling her the Overseer was responsible.

This still causes Amata to flee, but she doesn't blame you, and hopes you'll see her again: Having spent time in the Wastes, the chances of that occurring are slim to none, and slim's just run out of her protective fallout shelter.

If Amata flees, you cannot find her. However, you may later stumble across an Enclave checkpoint that Amata has reached; she approaches soldiers that she believes are helpful to her cause. After letting the Enclave know where Vault 101 is, they gun her down. Perhaps not the ending you were hoping for....

EVERYBODY'S GOTTA DIE SOMETIME...

 There's a final method to "help" out the inhabitants of Vault 101, to ensure they don't escape the Vault and die a slow, lingering death in the Wastes, or gradually turn deranged in this underground tomb. Draw your favorite weapon, and begin a systematic massacre, culling all your past acquaintances (you fail your quest, however). Old Man Taylor? A bullet between those twitchy eyes. Butch? Introduce this Tunnel Snake to your Combat Shotgun. The negative Karma you receive is so strong, it's a wonder you don't burst into flames....

QUEST REWARDS

You receive the following rewards:

 Modified Utility Jumpsuit:
If you sided with either the Overseer or Amata, only if you used no violence.

 300 XP

TRUTH AND CONSEQUENCES

Depending on your actions, the following consequences occur:

You killed the Overseer:

Amata becomes the new Overseer and bars you from returning to the Vault. She's shocked at the murdering monster you've become out in the Wastes.

You should ransack the entire Vault, finding a variety of supplies, and some unique items such as your Father's Books (check the laboratory for them), before you leave.

 Father's Books

You worked with the Overseer:

Vault 101 is sealed again, and permanently this time; you cannot return.

As a reward for your loyalty to the Overseer, you are awarded with the following:

 **Stealth Boy**    **Radiation Suit**

 Chems

You ended the lockdown:

Amata becomes the new Overseer but keeps the base closed and sealed, banishing you forever! This does allow Butch to flee from his life of hairdressing and shame.

 If you've led a neutral Karmic existence to this point, you can locate Butch at the Muddy Rudder in Rivet City and convince him to become your Follower (see location 9.15 in the Tour of the Wasteland chapter for details). The Tunnel Snakes are reborn! He acts as a Bodyguard from this point on, and you can dress him, order him around, or leave him near the Deathclaw Sanctuary in just his pants; it's your call.

You also receive low-radiation Food and Water whenever you return, thanks to the Water Chip functioning.

 Food and Water

You forced Vault 101's inhabitants to flee:

Some actually do flee, and you may encounter them again randomly, in other locales, such as Megaton. Those few remaining in Vault 101 hold a grudge against you and don't want to see your face around here again. You can ransack the place, grabbing your Father's Books and anything else you wish.

 Father's Books

Agatha's Song

Agatha's House [5.06] is a small single dwelling situated deep in the Wasteland. Her ancestors were all classically trained musicians, and although those days are long gone, she spent her entire life teaching herself how to play the violin until she matched their caliber. The problem is she's never actually held a true violin, only a makeshift replacement that has been kitbashed out of found goods. Agatha tells you a story (whether you like it or not): Her great-grandmother was "lucky" enough to be evacuated to a Vault in 2077 before the bombs fell. A violinist of some renown, she possessed the rare Soil Stradivarius violin (Soil is pronounced Swah). Agatha wants you to locate the Vault and recover the famous violin for her. Recover the records of the violin's location from the **Vault-Tec Corporation [12.02]** in downtown D.C., then slog to **Vault 92 [3.01]**. When you finally find this fabled violin, you can, at last, return a family heirloom to a frail but happy old woman. Or sell the artifact for some quick Caps....

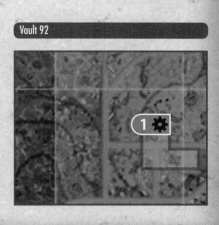

Vault 92

QUEST FLOWCHART

	MAIN PATH 1	OPTIONAL PATH 1	OPTIONAL PATH 2	OPTIONAL PATH 3
Main Characters	Agatha	Masterbrain	Abraham Washington, Ahzrukhal	Agatha
Locations	Agatha's House, Vault 92	Vault-Tec Corporation	Rivet City, Underworld	Vault 92, Arlington Library, Springvale School, Statesman Hotel, National Archives
Adv. Items/Abilities	Intelligence, Lockpick, Repair, Science, Sneak, Speech		Speech	—
Possible enemies	Mirelurk Genus	Science	—	—
Karma Influence	Positive	Neutral		Negative

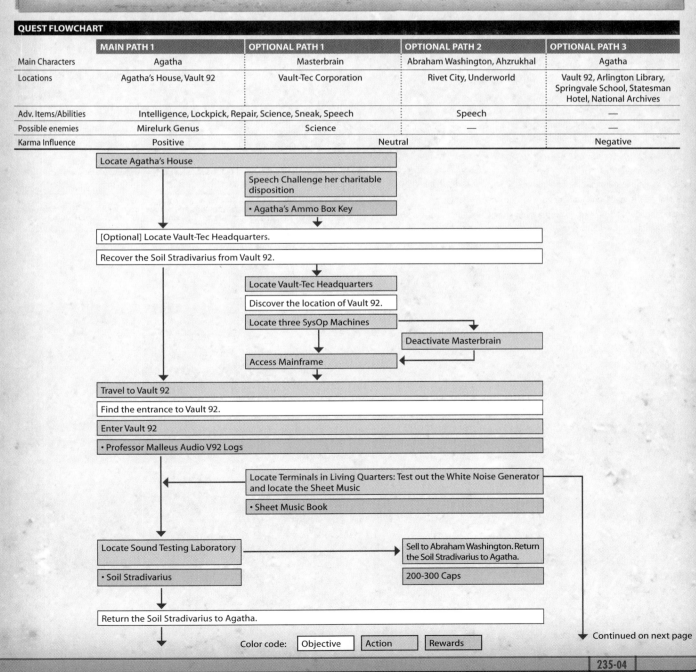

Locate Agatha's House

Speech Challenge her charitable disposition

• Agatha's Ammo Box Key

[Optional] Locate Vault-Tec Headquarters.

Recover the Soil Stradivarius from Vault 92.

Locate Vault-Tec Headquarters

Discover the location of Vault 92.

Locate three SysOp Machines

Deactivate Masterbrain

Access Mainframe

Travel to Vault 92

Find the entrance to Vault 92.

Enter Vault 92

• Professor Malleus Audio V92 Logs

Locate Terminals in Living Quarters: Test out the White Noise Generator and locate the Sheet Music

• Sheet Music Book

Locate Sound Testing Laboratory

Sell to Abraham Washington. Return the Soil Stradivarius to Agatha.

• Soil Stradivarius

200-300 Caps

Return the Soil Stradivarius to Agatha.

Color code: Objective | Action | Rewards

Continued on next page

TRAINING — BESTIARY — MAIN QUEST — MISC. QUESTS — TOUR — COMPLETION — APPENDICES

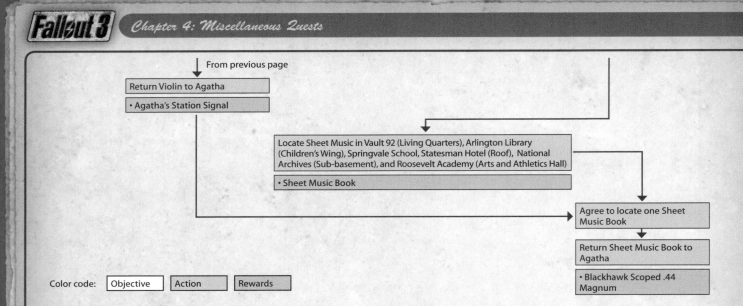

From previous page

Return Violin to Agatha

• Agatha's Station Signal

Locate Sheet Music in Vault 92 (Living Quarters), Arlington Library (Children's Wing), Springvale School, Statesman Hotel (Roof), National Archives (Sub-basement), and Roosevelt Academy (Arts and Athletics Hall)

• Sheet Music Book

Agree to locate one Sheet Music Book

Return Sheet Music Book to Agatha

• Blackhawk Scoped .44 Magnum

Color code: Objective | Action | Rewards

FINDING THE FIDDLER

Just northeast of the Meresti Trainyard, near the remnants of the monorail line, is a small rocky valley offering protection from the elements, as well as from roving bands of Raiders. Traders often stop here, and you may find one at the western end of a rope bridge. Cross this bridge, passing the remains of a white picket fence. You've found Agatha's House, a place where music and laughter once echoed around the corrugated shack and radio mast. That mast is massive. In fact, it looks like it could transmit across the entire Wasteland! Enter the shack.

The compact shack is the home of an old woman named Agatha. She greets you warmly. Continue the conversation, steering toward vaguely complimentary dialog choices at the very least, to begin this quest. Agatha tells you she's a widow, and her husband decided to cut off contact with the outside world, except for the Trader caravans. She entertains the caravans by playing her old and battered violin, usually through the radio mast her husband erected. It can broadcast across the entire Capital Wasteland.

 Your **Intelligence** tells you that an old, homemade violin is never quite in tune.

Ask how you can help, and she says that she knows of a location where a professionally made instrument could still reside.

At this point, you have two **Speech** options (one ruder than the other), a **Charisma** option, and a **Ladykiller** option stating that this search is going to take more than a charitable disposition. If you succeed in any challenge, she gives you the key to a small amount of ammunition that her husband left behind.

 Agatha's Ammo Box Key

She then recalls her great, great grandmother Hilda, who was alive back in 2077 before the bombs first fell. She was a classically trained violinist who was invited into Vault 92 during the war, because the Vault would be dedicated to preserving musical talent. She was never heard from again. You're not sure the violin is still intact 200 years later, never mind functional, but Agatha insists it was kept in a special pressurized case. The violin has a name, too:

The Soil Stradivarius. Made in 1714, it is priceless. Or it was when art and culture mattered. Agree to the quest, snag the items from the Ammo Box under the Ham Radio, speak to Agatha about the Vault-Tec Headquarters (which is then pinpointed on your map), and set out to find Vault 92.

Agatha is not only an accomplished violinist, but a huge fan of Captain Cosmos.

NEW OBJECTIVE [OPTIONAL]

"Locate Vault-Tec Headquarters" begins.

NEW OBJECTIVE

"Recover the Soil Stradivarius from Vault 92" begins.

 Agatha's Ammo
This contains ammunition for almost every type of weapon. Take what you need, and come back for more at your convenience.

ASSAULT ON VAULT-TEC HEADQUARTERS

Tip

This assault is purely optional. If you know the whereabouts of Vault 92 (which you will if you follow the tactics in this guide!), you can travel (or Fast Travel) there from Agatha's. The following is completely optional. You can also complete this before you meet Agatha.

GUEST RELATIONS ACTIVITIES

Too bad Vault-Tec didn't build their corporate headquarters underground....

Climb out of either of the Vernon Square Stations (Fast Travel here, or to the location nearest here). A Super Mutant prowls the area. Deal with him, move east toward the imposing Vault-Tec building, and enter

the double doors to the left of the Nuka-Cola machine. Enter the main foyer, and bring your favored Super Mutant and robot-hunting equipment with you. Ignore the northern side of the foyer. It contains the crumpled remains of a Super Mutant, and a Protectron (or Robobrain) roams the upper balcony, which you can't reach.

NEW OBJECTIVE [OPTIONAL]
"Discover the location of Vault 92" begins.

Instead, move to the southern part of the foyer, passing the front desk (which is good to use as cover). All the terminals are fried, so tackle a Super Mutant and climb up the stairs. At the top, lob a Pulse Grenade, or choose another favored attack method for neutralizing the Mister Gutsy (or other robotic menace) patrolling here. When you've searched this upper area, cross the balcony heading east, and open the Door to Vault-Tec Corporate Offices.

CORPORATE OFFICE ACTIVITIES

This level is a maze of wrecked office chambers, with a robot around almost every corner. You can execute an impressively thorough search for useful items, but except for the odd few Caps and Ammo rounds, this area has

At lower levels, your foes are mainly Robobrains. At higher levels, expect toughened Sentry Bots to waylay you.

a limited number of rewards. At the top of the stairs, look slightly left (northeast), and enter the ruined office. There's a hole on the left (north) wall. Head into the section of room with a completely collapsed ceiling. There's a First Aid Box on the floor to your right. On the left is a safe.

 First Aid Box Health and Chems

Leave this floor by the following route: From the top of the stairs, turn right (south), then immediately left (east), and pass the restrooms and small alcove on the right. Turn right (south), make another left (east), run to the end of the short corridor, turn left (north), and the stairs up to the next level are in the first opening on your right (east). Battle Robobrains or Sentry Bots and Mister Gutsys to reach this point.

The next level up has the familiar run-down walls (and Robobrains, Protectrons, and Sentry Bots at every turn), but the main chamber in front of you is lacking a floor completely, and the corridor to the left (south) is blocked. Instead, turn right (north), and run to the corner of the corridor, and turn left (west). Find some Shotgun Rounds in a filing cabinet half-buried in the rubble. Continue west until you reach a doorway on your left and right. Turn right, and enter a chamber with some shelves on the north wall. Grab the Nuka-Cola Quantum here; it's vital for **Miscellaneous Quest: The Nuka-Cola Challenge.**

 Nuka-Cola Quantum

Head back out to the main corridor, and move to the next rubble-filled corner, turning left (south). At the next doorway to your right (west), step in, and move to the area where the floor has given way. You're above the room where you found the safe earlier. Shimmy around the edge of the floor to the door, and enter a tiny storage room brimming with Cell ammunition, a Laser Pistol and a Stealth Boy on the metal shelves, and some First Aid Box Health. Continue southward along

the main corridor, popping into the women's restrooms to the west, near a Nuka-Cola Machine alcove, and check a toilet for a Magnum and Ammo. Return to the main corridor; the stairs up to the next level are just ahead of you. Climb them, then open the Door to Vault-Tec Administration.

Energy Cell Ammo

Stealth Boy

Laser Pistol

First Aid Box Health and Chems

Scoped .44 Magnum and Ammo

ADMINISTRATION ACTIVITIES

Find three SysOp machines, deactivate a Masterbrain, access the Mainframe, and don't get shot!

Step around the corner looking left (west), and immediately train your weapon on the ceiling, taking out a Mark V Turret before it strafes you. Then investigate the office to the north. Or, you can run past the turret, into this office. Immediately investigate two working terminals. Activate System Operation Station (SysOp) 3 first (you don't need to hack into this terminal). Three menus are available:

Important Bulletins:

These include a Security Notice, informing you that the VTMB01 Masterbrain requires authorization from three SysOp Terminals.

There's a message about the treatment of vending machines; apparently one Vault-Tec employee thought daubing a "messy protest" into the coin slot was a good idea....

There's a message about employee abuse of bathroom breaks, with a time limit reduced from 2.37 to 2.25 minutes.

There are messages about Vault 112 (it has been completed) and Vault 92 (it has been fitted with WNB Type Noise Generators).

Station 3 Mainframe Access: Approve this.

Station 3 Masterbrain Shutdown: Approve this.

 You can now hack the Turret Control Terminal if you wish, and deactivate all remaining turrets. This is advisable, if your **Science** skill is high enough.

Exit the office via the gate to the north, which leads into the mainframe chamber. You can wander around, but the Mainframe Terminal appears to be on the next floor above you. Retrace your steps, make a right, then journey south and turn left (east) to ascend another flight of stairs.

EXECUTIVE AND MAINFRAME ACTIVITIES

Ignore or blast the Mark V Turret at the top of the stairs. Face west, and open the metal door in front of you. This leads to an L-shaped balcony with System Operation Station 1. You can re-read the Important Bulletins, but make sure you:

Approve Station 1 Mainframe Access.

Approve Station 1 Masterbrain Shutdown.

Leave this room, and proceed down the corridor. At the wooden door to your right (east), optionally enter this office, and activate the Vault-Tec Employee Terminal. This doesn't shut down anything, but you can pretend to buy Vault-Tec merchandise from the online store!

TRAINING — BESTIARY — MAIN QUEST — MISC. QUESTS — TOUR — COMPLETION — APPENDICES

Move along the corridor to the corner and face northwest. Through the open doorway across from you is a turret. Blast it, and watch for the Masterbrain, an enhanced Robobrain that trundles along the corridor to the west of you. Explode the turret if you didn't deactivate it, then deliver a killing blow (with a Pulse Grenace or Mine) to the robot in here. Then turn and access the System Operation Station 2 in the chamber's southeast corner. Your final shutdown plan is now available:

Approve Station 2 Mainframe Access.

Approve Station 2 Masterbrain Shutdown.

 First Aid Box Health and Chems

The executive office is home to Vault-Tec propaganda, but this overpaid suit was a secret comic book fan at heart....

Step back into the corridor, move to this hunk of junk you just deactivated, and search it. Choose "Destroy Security Uplink," and the remaining robots and turrets in this building deactivate. Now that they're no longer a threat, search them for Energy Cells! Ignore or blast the turret on the ceiling ahead of you. Turn left (south), ignoring the stairs that descend (use them to escape this place after you visit the Mainframe). Open the next door on your right (west), and enter the executive office. Blast the Sentry Bot guarding the large curved desk, then ransack this room, and the two smaller offices behind it. One of them contains a *Grognak the Barbarian* Comic Book. What a result!

 **Grognak the Barbarian**
+1 Melee Weapons (when read).

Move back to the main corridor, ignoring the metal doors to the left (they lead to an L-shaped viewing chamber with no vital items). Blast the last of the turrets, open the barred gate, and move to the hatch door. It opens only once you have accessed all three SysOp Terminals. If you haven't operated all three, return and do so. Step across the balcony to the Mainframe itself, and "Download Vault Locations and Access Codes." Not only does this reveal the location of Vault 92 (and allows you to access the sealed door), but this also applies to all the other Vaults (87, 101, 108, and 112) operational in the Wasteland, too! Check the Tour of the Wasteland chapter for information on what horrors lurk inside these tombs....

Take the stairs down to the foyer of the Vault-Tec Guest Relations, then drop down, head outside, and Fast Travel to the location nearest to Vault 92, and trek the rest of the way there.

Tales of a Junktown Jerky Vendor
+1 Barter (when read).

MINES, MUSIC, AND MIRELURKS

 Note
You could explore Vault 92 before meeting Agatha, although without this guide, you wouldn't immediately know who would want the instrument (or that there was one inside the vault to begin with).

Trek up to the wilds of the northeast territories, lock and load, then let yourself in Vault 92.

Vault 92 is in the Northeast Wasteland territories, close to the Death-claw-infested town of Old Olney. It is imperative to bring a large selection of weaponry, as well as Stimpaks, Chems, and a good set of your preferred armor.

 Stealth Boys are also recommended if you attempt to **Sneak** through this entire base, which can get you far, but not all the way to your goal. Expect to face creatures at some point during this excursion.

 Tip
Follow the route detailed below, but employ Stealth Boys and Sneaking where necessary, to reach your goal with minimal combat, or to save ammunition.

Vault 92's entrance is in the gap between this clump of rocks, west of Old Olney. There are ruined buildings on the ground above and nearby. Open the gate and step inside. As you reach the main door, you see that it's already open—not a good sign. Step through into the door and maintenance room, and check the nearby table for some Fission Batteries, a Laser Pistol, Blood Pack, Energy Cell, and two lots of Health and Chems from First Aid Boxes. Grab these, and a mysterious Holotape on the upper gantry among the rusting terminals: Professor Malleus Audio Log V92-01. Now the exploration can take place.

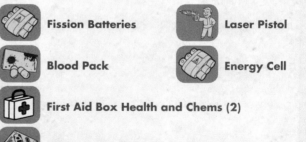

Fission Batteries **Laser Pistol**

Blood Pack **Energy Cell**

First Aid Box Health and Chems (2)

Professor Malleus Audio Log V92-01

Note
You now have two options: a complete exploration of Vault 92, or a direct route to the Soil Stradivarius. For the direct route, head to sound testing, following the signs to "Classroom."

UTILITY AREA WEST: COMPLETE EXPLORATION

Head southward, through the only available door, into a small utility generator room. Disarm the Frag Mine at your feet before it explodes. Begin to tag the Bloatflies that infest this dilapidated tomb, and then check the doors in this junction; the ones to the east and west are both locked. If you want to explore, or take a longer route to the violin, opt for the unlocked door to the atrium. The quickest route to the Soil Stradivarius is via the laboratory and classrooms, to the east.

To see how the reactor is doing, **Lockpick** the door on the right (west) wall.

Step through into a passageway (watch for another exploding Mine!), open the door at the opposite end of the connecting corridor, and enter two rusting chambers, devoid of items (unless you love collecting tin cans), but with a couple of Bloatflies to pop into disgusting showers of entrails. Continue west to a staircase leading down to the Vault's living quarters. For a look at the reactor room, head north.

UTILITY AREA EAST: COMPLETE EXPLORATION

Examine the eastern part of the utility area by unlocking the door with the "Classroom" and "Lab" signs above it. Disarm the Frag Mine thoughtfully placed on the threshold, then move through another narrow corridor to a second hatch door. Open that, and enter another generator room with two doors. The one straight ahead (east) leads directly down to the classroom and lab area, and is the quickest way to your target. The door to your left (north) leads down to the reactor.

REACTOR ROOM: COMPLETE EXPLORATION

 Tip
Investigate here only if you want to slay Mirelurks!

The downstairs reactor corridors are ankle deep in water, so expect a radioactive bath if you venture down here, which isn't necessary to the quest. Access the corridors from the west or the east; the exploration is similar. Wade through the water, then halt and kill each Mirelurk you encounter. Keep this up until you reach a working computer marked "Engineering Logs Terminal."

There follows a series of log entries from Carl Maynard, who's generally ranting about the incompetence of his co-workers, the slight issue with the air-conditioning and effluent tubes, a more severe issue with groundwater, and a real emergency involving the Overseer's chair needing an oiling.

Now struggle through the rest of the waterlogged tunnels and back up to the east or west utility area (depending on which entrance you used).

 Tip
Having problems slaying Mirelurks and Hunters? Try Sneaking, using a Stealth Boy, or striking them in the face with long-range weapons like the Sniper or Hunting Rifles. Keep your distance; only use guns with a narrow spread of fire.

ATRIUM: COMPLETE EXPLORATION

 Tip
Investigate here only if you want to collect items, or you can't pick the lock on the door with the "Classroom" and "Lab" signs.

The central atrium area is a maze. Leave an object here so you remember where you've been!

From the utility generator room, head south, through the only unlocked door (with the Atrium sign). Step into the connecting room.

 Use **Repair** skill to disarm a Rigged Shotgun, or duck under it so it fires over your head.

Head through the door diagonally opposite, pass the skeleton and metal box, and watch for the Frag Mine at the base of the stairs.

 Continue around to the south and **Lockpick** the next sliding door.

Once through, you appear on the ground floor of the Vault's atrium. There are many passageways off this area (and there's an upper gantry you can explore later; look up to study it). Let's take a clockwise tour of each passageway:

The "Lab" and "Classroom" passage: This has a skeleton at the threshold. Head north and enter the Door to Sound Testing. This is precisely where you need to go to complete this quest!

Southeast Corner Doorway: This simply leads to an empty room, picked clean by Raiders a long time ago.

Southern Passage: This curves around to stairs leading up to the atrium gantry. An exploration of this area, which leads to the Overseer's office, is detailed next.

Clinic: The western doorway leads to the Vault clinic, now devoid of anything except some Bloatflies and empty lockers.

Northwest Corner Passage: This leads to the living quarters, which are detailed after the atrium exploration.

UPPER ATRIUM: COMPLETE EXPLORATION

 Tip
Investigate here if you want to get items and listen to the Overseer's notes on this Vault's experimental procedures.

Head to the upper gantry, where there are only two places of interest. Head to the locked door in the northeast corner.

 Pry it open with your Bobby Pins and **Lockpick** skill. Inside are the remains of a weapons storage room. On the floor to the left, there are Energy Cells, Ammo Boxes with more Energy Cells and 10mm Ammo, a 10mm Submachine Gun, Darts, and a book called *Tales of a Junktown Jerky Vendor*. Open the unlocked safe for some Ammo, a (random) pistol, and some Healing items.

TRAINING — BESTIARY — MAIN QUEST — **MISC. QUESTS** — TOUR — COMPLETION — APPENDICES

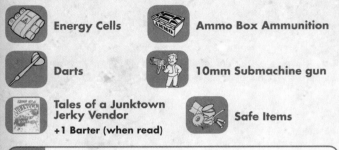

Use **Science** to access the terminal on the counter to read some Intra-Vault Mail. Topics include a curt request for headphones and the arrival of strawberry pudding at the shop. Gordie Sumner, the proprietor of the store, issued a final mail regarding "half the residents going crazy," and mentions leaving a gun in the safe. That must be the Laser Pistol you just took! Finally, you can open the safe, which was easy to do without accessing the terminal! Exit this room, and head to the southeast room with a door at the back marked "Overseer's Office."

Energy Cells

Ammo Box Ammunition

Darts

10mm Submachine gun

Tales of a Junktown Jerky Vendor
+1 Barter (when read)

Safe Items

 Open the door, then use **Lockpick** to easily disengage the lock on another door.

Step into the hub room where the Overseer appears to have made his final stand. Step over the upturned tables, and make an inspection of the various side doors and passages:

Southeast door: This leads to an empty bedroom. Take the whiskey from the footlocker if you wish.

Southwest door: Enter another bedroom. This one, however, holds some clues regarding the fate of the Vault dwellers in this place. Take the Holotape inscribed Professor Malleus Audio Log V92-02. Listen to it (although you might want to collect them all and listen in order).

Professor Malleus Audio Log V92-02

North door: This bedroom contains Metal Armor in a footlocker, and a few other items. As with any of these rooms, you can sleep on the beds to replenish your Health Points. Do this before or after you locate the Stradivarius, if you wish.

Now for the Overseer's office. Head west, following the short curved corridor into Overseer Rubin's office. Grab the Stealth Boy from the circular desk first, then take the Holotape from the side desk. Check the wooden shelves for a Skill Book, a Laser Rifle, and some Ammo Boxes on the floor against the wall. Finally inspect the terminal. There are four Personal Entries to read:

The first details how a "white noise generator" has been rerouted through to the Vault's loudspeaker system, and triggered via the security consoles. The password is mentioned, and noted in your Pip-Boy.

The second details "successes" in the field testing, although the Overseer's choice in test subjects is slightly worrying!

The third mentions deaths, and long-term "crazy" effects. The Overseer brushes this off, but employs a command word in their suggestion implants, just in case....

The fourth: The Overseer has lost control and is about to order the death of Professor Malleus, the head of the experiment.

When you've read all the information, return to the lower atrium, and locate the Door to the Living Quarters at the end of the northwest corner passage. Save your progress before you enter!

Professor Malleus Audio Log V92-03

Ammo Box Ammunition

Overseer Rubin Personal Entry 00897332

Laser Rifle

 Duck and Cover!
+1 Explosives (when read)

LIVING QUARTERS: COMPLETE EXPLORATION

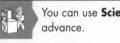 *Tip*

Investigate here if you wish to test out the white noise generator on the Mirelurks, and collect items in the process!

Head around the corner, and brace for a Mirelurk attack! If you've been following the "Complete Exploration" path, you should turn immediately right (west), and locate the Women's Dorm Security Terminal.

You can use **Science** to hack in as the Mirelurks advance.

A much better plan is to use the password you read from Overseer Rubin Personal Entry 00897332. This automatically logs you on without any hacking being necessary. All options are offline except one; execute the Noise Flush now!

Whoooph! The eight Mirelurks wandering this area are instantly charged with white noise, and their heads explode in unison! This is a far better way of defeating these clawed menaces, and it also allows you to explore this level unhindered. Begin with the female dorm:

 *Note*

This Mirelurk head explosion is not Vault-wide; it is only confined to this floor of the living quarters.

Female Dorm (north): There are four rooms, the first of which contains a First Aid Box. The closed door leads to a storage room with a safe that's already been ransacked. There are some Frag Mines, Bobby Pins, and Darts to grab though.

First Aid Box
Health and Chems

Frag Mines

Darts

Bobby Pins

Recreation room (opposite female and male dorms): There's little except a pack of Darts and other junk items here.

Male Dorm (west): A wall terminal is also available here, and can generate white noise just like the one by the female dorm. All the rooms are empty except the restroom (which contains a Sheet Music Book; grab it!) and a storage room to the south. Duck to avoid the Rigged Shotgun, then grab the Laser Pistol and unlock the Ammo Box for Energy Cells and a Stealth Boy.

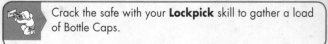 Crack the safe with your **Lockpick** skill to gather a load of Bottle Caps.

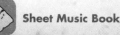 **Sheet Music Book**

 Laser Pistol

Energy Cell Ammo

 Stealth Boy

Bottle Caps

The lower living quarters are a little more serene once all Mirelurks are dribbling their brain matter out of their faces....

Head south to the stairs heading down to the lower living quarters area, shooting Mirelurks if you haven't popped their craniums. Pass a window on your right and peer in; you can see a Nuka-Cola Quantum on the other side. Head through two more doors, and begin a sweep of this area, once all threats have abated:

Terminal and Storage Room (west of entrance): Turn west, just as you enter this place, and head into the small storage room. The terminals may be broken, but there's a delicious and luminous Nuka-Cola Quantum to take! Don't chug this down; it's an important item to keep for **Miscellaneous Quest: The Nuka-Cola Challenge**. The real area of interest is the Security Terminal. If you've already accessed the upper terminals, you can quickly execute a Noise Flush, and defeat all Mirelurks in this area too! Unlock all the doors on this level via another option before you leave.

 Nuka-Cola Quantum

Terminal and Storage Room (east of entrance): Move back into the main corridor, and head east. Open the door and grab Pulse Grenades, Pulse Mines, and Combat Armor with a Helmet from this small chamber.

 Pulse Grenades

Pulse Mines

Combat Armor

Combat Helmet

Lower Hub Room: The chamber you first entered is L-shaped, and has some minor items hidden in an Ammo Box and Locker. But the real find is on the desk to the southwest; grab Professor Malleus Audio Log V92-04. You almost have a complete set!

 Professor Malleus Audio Log V92-04

Locked Weapons Storage: Over on the eastern wall is a terminal and a locked door.

 Use either **Lockpick** or **Science** to open this door; the time taken is worth it, because this chamber is a treasure trove of items. Grab what you need.

 Nikola Tesla and You
+1 Energy Weapons (when read).

Electron Charge Pack
(Locked Ammo Box)

 Energy Cells

 **Fission Batteries**

Stealth Boy

Microfusion Cells

Stimpak and Chems

Blood Pack

Darts

Power Armor and Helmet

Medical Bay: The final room is the medical bay, where you can snag items from the First Aid Box, and turn to the Laboratory Terminal to read four missives by Professor John Malleus to his lab assistants and Overseer Richard Rubin:

The first gives kudos to the team for the great successes.

The second regards a test subject that went insane. The scientists are puzzled as to why.

The third is a plea to the Overseer, telling him to call off his guards, and recognize the "problems."

The fourth is ominous; the Vault is under heavy guard, Rubin isn't responding to Malleus, and the Professor wants answers.

Now move to any of the three entrances that lead to the sound testing area of this Vault.

SOUND TESTING: COMPLETE EXPLORATION

The preferred route to enter this area is from the atrium, because it's close to the stairs down to the sound laboratory, your final destination. Thus, the exploration of this level begins here. Head right, around the corner. The stairs down to the lab are on your right (south). Continue around to the junction with the "Classroom" sign pointing east. Head down here, and enter the first door on your left (north).

Maintenance Storage: This two-room chamber contains a Mirelurk and has some minor items and tools to optionally rummage through. Head to the end of the corridor, and turn south. The door back to the utility area should be behind you. Move to the junction with doorways on either side. Check the left (east) area out first.

Office and Server Room: This two-room chamber features a Mirelurk and some minor junk with a server room behind it. The server area has an unlocked terminal, next to a Pre-War Book. It has Zoe Hammerstein's diary entries, which make interesting (if rather sombre) reading:

Zoe's Thoughts

Zoe is thrilled to be surrounded by all the musical talent; she's spending her life among the world's greatest musicians!

More of Zoe's Thoughts

She's recording Haydn's Symphony No. 3 in D Minor; and she got to play along with the orchestra! The best part was that you can hear yourself play on the studio's speakers. Perhaps Dvorak tomorrow?

More of Zoe's Thoughts

She's feeling sick; woozy because the studio is so stuffy. The other violinists are giving her pointers. Tonight is the Rec Hall dance; she's hoping that dreamy guy Parker asks her out.

morre of Zoes Thoughts

Mental confusion is beginning to take its toll: "I cant concentrate I wen t to Doctoor Bennisons offfice but he jusst said its stress and too take iit easy for a whil I think al the timee I am spendng inn the soundd sttudo is makd in g me tired I can barele type anymoor I am shaking so muc."

TRAINING — BESTIARY — MAIN QUEST — MISC. QUESTS — TOUR — COMPLETION — APPENDICES

klkhi plEAsse.HF puu HeLP meeLp

It doesn't end well.

Projector and Music Room: Opposite (west) is a projector room. There's Leather Armor in the closet, and the penultimate Holotape on the desk. The door leads to a music room devoid of useful items. Exit to the main corridor and follow it south, around the corner, to the west, passing a jammed door you can't enter. Follow the corridor all the way around, heading north past the windows of the music room. This floor has been explored; now head down to the laboratory.

 **Leather Armor**

 Professor Malleus Audio Log V92-05

SOUND LABORATORY: COMPLETE EXPLORATION

 Tip

Investigate here if you wish grab that violin and finish this quest!

This is it! Trek down and around to the crossroads, facing west. Start with an exploration to the right (north).

Kitchen and Recreation Room: This small chamber with a prowling Mirelurk offers some sustenance in the refrigerator, some Darts, a Nuka-Cola or two, and Three Dog's latest disc spinning if you activate the Jukebox (which also alarms Mirelurks, so make sure they're headless before you try this!).

 Locked Storage: Move west from the crossroads, and use **Lockpick** to jimmy open the door to this well-stocked storage room. Locate the following, grabbing anything you want. Then head out to the crossroads, go south, then turn left (east).

Darts   **Chems**

Stealth Boy   **Energy Cells**

Microfusion Cells   **Stimpaks**

Bottle Caps (Locked Safe)

Recording Studio: Enter the studio. There's the violin! Alas, it's behind glass in a chamber you can't access from here. Instead, search this room for your last Holotape. Then access the Security Terminal, and choose the option marked "Open Recording Studio." There are three other missives to read, too:

The first is regarding an odd sound bleeding issue.

The second is actually sent to Agatha's great, great grandmother Hilda! The studio engineer is enthralled by Hilda's music...and her other charms!

The third is...both saucy and shocking! Were people really that forward back in 2077?

 Professor Malleus Audio Log V92-06

Session Studio: Move west, then south to the final door in this Vault, unlocked only via the computer in the previous chamber. Grab the Laser Pistol from the floor, then open the wall safe for more items, including Bottle Caps, Energy Cells, and another Laser Pistol. The real prize is on the table behind the music stands: the Soil Stradivarius is intact! Take the violin, and retrace your steps, all the way back to the surface.

This astonishingly well-crafted instrument is over 600 years old. How much would Abraham Washington pay for it?

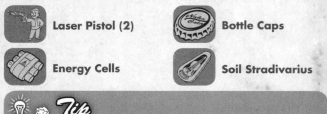

Laser Pistol (2)   **Bottle Caps**

Energy Cells   **Soil Stradivarius**

 *Tip*

Seal your triumph by listening to all six of the Holotapes marked "Professor Malleus Audio Log," detailing Vault 92's descent into aural madness!

THE SOUND OF MUSIC

Oh my goodness gracious! Seems like you've been gone forever. Please tell me you have good news.

The kindness of strangers knows no bounds. Unless you've sold the violin to a Ghoul named Ahzrukhal....

NEW OBJECTIVE

"Return to Agatha" begins.

NEW OBJECTIVE

"Find a buyer for the Soil Stradivarius" begins.

Your tumultuous trek for the Soil Stradivarius is over! Head back to Agatha's House with the violin in your Inventory, and speak with her again. She asks whether you've brought the instrument to her:

You can give her the Soil Stradivarius. She is suitably delighted and in your debt. She can't think of anything she could do to repay you, but she does have a small gift to impart. She gives you the Radio Frequency you can use to tune in and listen to Agatha play, no matter where in the Wasteland you are (simply access Data > Radio on your Pip-Boy, and choose it)! It's a truly beautiful gift, and far more classy than a shovelful of Caps!

You can lie, and tell her you haven't got it yet. The only reason to do this is to sell the violin to a couple of Traders you know...

Agatha's Station Signal   **XP** 300 XP

SELLING ON THE STRADIVARIUS

 Note

Sell the violin to either of these gentlemen, and the quest ends without the positive Karma or Agatha's Station accessible. You don't receive negative Karma, however.

Journey to Rivet City, perhaps beginning or continuing **Miscellaneous Quest: Stealing Independence**, and locate Abraham Washington, curator of the Capitol Preservation Society. Let him take a look at the violin. He offers you 200 Caps.

 Bargain with him using **Speech**, and he ups his offer to 300 Caps.

If you have a change of heart after the quest is over, you can return to Abraham Washington and attempt to buy back the violin. His offer is 300 Caps. Take it or leave it.

Head to the 9th Circle bar, perhaps beginning **Miscellaneous Quest: You Gotta Shoot 'Em in the Head**, and seek out the bar owner, a Ghoul named Ahzrukhal. Offer him the Stradivarius. He'll take it off your hands for 200 Caps.

 Bargain with him using **Speech**, and he ups his offer to 300 Caps.

If you're feeling pangs of guilt after the quest is over, you can return to Ahzrukhal, and attempt one of the following plans to take the violin back:

 Try to pickpocket (**Sneak**) the violin from him.

Or, you can kill him, and loot the violin from his corpse. This will, naturally, cause a riot in Underworld.

Or, you can hire Charon, send him to kill Ahzrukhal, and you can pick the violin off his corpse without dirtying your hands.

With either vendor, bring the violin back to Agatha to receive the Karma and Radio Station bonus. You cannot repeat the process after one selling and buying back has taken place.

POST QUEST ANTICS: GOING FOR A SONG

The kindness of strangers knows no bounds. Unless you're after a hand cannon; then let the bartering begin!

After the quest is over, speak to Agatha again. In your dialog choices you should tell her to write her music down, and keep it preserved for the future. Naturally, Agatha needs a Sheet Music Book in order to properly record the notes. Agree to this. If you found the one in Vault 92, you can give it to Agatha now, and ignore the other locations. Or you may have already found the Sheet Music Book. Otherwise, there are six places to try:

1. Vault 92 [3.01]
Living Quarters: In a stall in the men's restroom.

2. Arlington Library [9.18]
Children's Wing: In one of the office cubicles, below a sheet music stand.

3. Springvale School [5.14]
Inside a classroom in the southeast corner of the interior, inside the foot-well of an overturned desk.

4. Statesman Hotel [12.08]
Roof: The remains of a string-quartet's placing, on the ground next to a chair.

5. National Archives [17.11]
Sub-Basement: In the large storage area lined with shelves, north wall. It is standing on the end of the bottom-most shelf.

6. Roosevelt Academy [1.16]
Roosevelt Arts and Athletics Hall: On the far right of the stage, among the discarded music stands.

 Sheet Music Book

When you've found one of these Sheet Music Books, return to Agatha with it. The following options are now available:

 Simply give the Sheet Music Book without asking for a reward. You're awarded additional Karma.

Or, you can bargain with her for a reward. She remembers a special weapon she has, and gives you the Blackhawk .44 Scoped Magnum. No Karma is awarded.

 Blackhawk: Unique Scoped .44 Magnum
Higher damage, critical damage, and health.

APPENDICES — COMPLETION — TOUR — MISC. QUESTS — MAIN QUEST — BESTIARY — TRAINING

Reilly's Rangers

Reilly is an attractive patient lying in a coma in Doctor Barrow's clinic. She's the leader of a mercenary group called Reilly's Rangers. Her latest sortie from the **Ranger Compound [18.05]** ended badly after her team was jumped by Super Mutants. Retreating into **Our Lady of Hope Hospital [12.07]** to grab supplies, they were further compromised because the place was swarming with Muties. They backed into the nearby **Statesman Hotel [12.08]**, losing a team member in the firefight. Entrenched on the roof of the hotel, their ammo was all but depleted, and what was left sat in their weapons. Reilly hatched a plan, activated her Stealth Boy, and crept out of the hotel to find help. She was viciously attacked and left for dead, but she staggered onward and eventually lost consciousness and fell into an old culvert near **Underworld's [17.07]** entrance. Now it falls to you to help Reilly's Rangers in their hour of need.

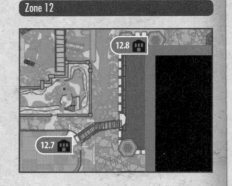

Zone 12

QUEST FLOWCHART

	MAIN PATH 1	MAIN PATH 2	OPTIONAL PATH 1	OPTIONAL PATH 1
Main Characters	Doctor Barrows, Reilly, Theo, Brick, Donovan, Butcher		—	Brick, Donovan, Butcher
Locations	Underworld, (Dry Sewer), Our Lady of Hope Hospital, Statesman Hotel, Ranger Compound	(Dry Sewer), Our Lady of Hope Hospital, Statesman Hotel, Ranger Compound	Ranger Compound	Statesman Hotel Roof
Adv. Items/Abilities	Explosives, Lockpick, Medicine, Science, Sneak, Speech, Gun Nut		—	Repair
Possible enemies	Talon Company Merc, Centaur, Super Mutant Genus			Super Mutant Genus
Karma Influence	Neutral			Negative

Receive Ranger Emergency Signal

Find Reilly in Underworld inside the Museum of History.

Wake up Reilly; Agree to assist her

• Ammo Box Code and Password to Ranger Compound

Find Our Lady of Hope Hospital.

[Optional] Locate the Ranger's ammo crate.

[Optional] Gear up at Ranger Compound.

Locate Reilly's Ranger Compound

• Guns and Ammunition

Enter Our Lady of Hope Hospital (via Vernon Square or Dry Sewer)

Locate Reilly's Rangers.

Enter Statesman Hotel via fallen radio antenna

Locate Theo's body

• Ranger's Ammo Crate

Battle to the Alfresco Lounge

• Ammo Cache

Find Little Moonbeam's Father (Quest: Stealing Independence)

• Note from Little Moonbeam's Father

Locate a Fission Battery.

Continued on next page

Color code: Objective | Action | Rewards

From previous page

Locate fallen Protectron in Alfresco Lounge
• Fission Battery

Head to the Roof

Search the roof balcony (Miscellaneous Quest: Agatha's Song)
• Sheet Music Book

Ignore or Kill Rangers
• Donovan's Wrench

Give out Ammunition to ensure Rangers survive
Give a Fission Battery to Donovan.
[Optional] Repair Elevator, or use Donovan's Wrench

Lead Reilly's Rangers to safety.
Provide covering fire for Rangers, and defeat threats in Lobby
Get to the Statesman Hotel exit.
Return to Reilly at the Ranger Compound.

Receive reward from Reilly
• Ranger Battle Armor, OR Eugene

Speak to Reilly again
• GeoMapper; Donovan can now Repair; Butcher can now Heal you

Color code: | Objective | Action | Rewards |

BEDSIDE WITH DOCTOR BARROWS

Begin this quest by visiting Underworld, negotiating with Willow the sentry, and opening the door to the Museum of History. You're looking for Doctor Barrows's Chop Shop, which is at the southern end of the ground concourse. Head inside, and inspect the woman lying on the bed in the southwest corner, behind the blinds. She can't be awakened, so speak with Doctor Barrows. He explains that her combat armor bears the insignia of a band of mercenaries based in the D.C. Ruins; she's their leader. You now have only two options:

If you have a suitably high **Speech** skill, you can firmly request that Barrows wake her up. If you succeed, he warns you how dangerous this is, but obliges. If you fail, he refuses completely.

With a competent **Medicine** skill, you can actually revive Reilly yourself. Wait until the conversation with Barrows ends, then do the deed. Reilly slows lifts herself to her feet.

Tip
These two methods are the only way to revive Reilly, so make sure you allocate points during previous level-ups to begin this quest. Or, you can go directly to the Statesman Hotel and find her at the Ranger Compound; she'll arrive before you do.

Induced waking from a coma can be deadly. But Reilly's made of tough stuff.

Begin to converse with Reilly. She quickly realizes she's left her men out in the field. Carry on the conversation with the following options:

Your **Medicine** skill tells you she's in no condition to be up and about, and you can say so. This doesn't affect the conversation compared to normal chatter.

If you have the **Gun Nut** perk, you've heard of Reilly's Rangers; they pack some serious firepower!

Continue to talk, and you'll hear that Reilly's unit was mapping Vernon Square when they were jumped by Super Mutants. They fought to Our Lady of Hope Hospital to seek cover. They moved to the Statesman Hotel, and ascended to the roof, losing a teammate—Theo—along the way, somewhere inside the hotel.

At this point, if your **Explosives** skill is proficient, you can ask if traps or mines were laid. She says yes, meaning you'll need to watch your step during the subsequent investigation.

The talk continues. Agree to rescue the Rangers (or refuse, incur Reilly's immediate wrath, and come back later when you're ready). She gives you the code to the Ammo Box Theo dropped, so you can snag the contents. She explains that the best way to reach the team is to head north to Metro Central, before looking for tunnels to Dupont Circle Station. From there, enter the Dry Sewers, and after another trek, you end up at Our Lady of Hope Hospital. Or, you weave through the tunnels and surface at Vernon Square. She notes that the hospital has storage rooms to raid for supplies, too.

Now ask: "Can you think of anything that will help me get there?" She responds, telling you they have a compound not far from here. You're given the access code to enter the gate—Reilly0247—and a marker on your Pip-Boy. Close the conversation by learning where Theo's body is (a second floor stairwell inside the Statesman Hotel). You can now head to the Ranger's Compound ("Stocking Up for the Slaughter"), or ignore the health and ammo in there and move straight to the hotel and hospital.

Note: Ammo Box Code

Note: Password to Ranger Compound

NEW OBJECTIVE
"Find Our Lady of Hope Hospital" begins.

NEW OBJECTIVE [OPTIONAL]
"Locate the Ranger's ammo crate" begins.

NEW OBJECTIVE [OPTIONAL]
"Gear up at Ranger Compound" begins.

STOCKING UP FOR THE SLAUGHTER

The direct, but deadly route is to head directly through the Capitol's Super Mutant stronghold.

Tip
Although this is optional, finding the Ranger Compound before the hotel assault allows you to stock up on ammunition and Fast Travel back once the quest is over.

Before slogging through the linked network of tunnels and streets to reach the Our Lady of Hope Hospital, stock up at the Ranger Compound. The quickest way to reach the compound from Underworld is to exit the Museum of History, pass Willow, and head Quest along the Mall toward the Capitol Building. Expect heavy resistance from bands of Super Mutants, Talon Company Mercenaries, and Raiders. Once

through the West Entrance, head to the Seward Square exit, engage more Super Mutants, and flee south and then east, passing Seward Square North Metro Station. You can also take the longer—but safer—underground route to this station, if you wish.

Reilly's Ranger Compound is tricky to locate; it's close to the Seward Square South Metro Station.

Continue heading southeast, until you reach the ruins of the Cornucopia Fresh Groceries store. The side street is the place to turn; continue northward until you spot some sandbags and a Reilly's Rangers insignia daubed on the wall, to your right. Turn and weave through the narrow concrete passage eastward. The Ranger Compound is just to the left (north) of the statue in the circle. Head up to the security door, input the code Reilly gave you, and you're automatically let in.

The place is empty (as all the Rangers are holed up in the Statesman Hotel under heavy Super Mutant fire), so check out the radio room if you want. You can use the Ranger's terminal and read the evaluations on Reilly, Brick, Butcher, Donovan, and Theo.

Inspect the storage room next; amid the copious amount of alcohol, there's an Ammo Box. Next, move to the sleeping and eating quarters, where the real ammunition is. There's food in the fridge, beer to swig, Stimpaks, a First Aid Box, two Ammo Boxes, a Frag Grenade, some Chems, Combat Knives, and a Scoped .44 Magnum and Ammo. After you leave, clamber up on the ruined concrete building above the compound for more five more Ammo Boxes and two First Aid Boxes. Now use the underground tunnels to reach either of the starting locations to reach the hospital.

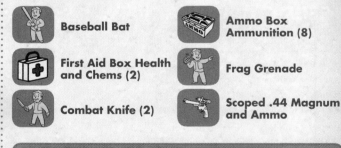
Baseball Bat

First Aid Box Health and Chems (2)

Combat Knife (2)

Ammo Box Ammunition (8)

Frag Grenade

Scoped .44 Magnum and Ammo

HEADING TO THE HOSPITAL

Choose one of the two paths to reach Our Lady of Hope Hospital.

PATH A: FROM VERNON SQUARE STATION

The first way to reach Our Lady of Hope Hospital is to use the Metro Tunnels throughout the city, and emerge at Vernon Square Station. If you fire off your weapon, expect a few Super Mutants to investigate. Otherwise, head past the wrecked vehicles, out of the gate, and turn south. With the Statesman Hotel on your left, head down the rubble-filled path. The double doors to Our Lady of Hope Hospital (complete with bloody handprint) are ahead, to your right. Before you enter, continue south, and inspect the truck and a table in the outside entrance; raid two First Aid Boxes from here.

There is a second way of entering the hospital from this area: the ruined building to the west. Beware Super Mutants and Frag Mines. Peel off from the main path and locate the single, ground floor door in the side of the hospital, leading to a small filing room, adjacent to the initial lobby.

First Aid Box Health (2)

The Statesman Hotel has an open door on the ground level, but entering the foyer now isn't advisable; there's no way to continue to the top of the building because the elevator isn't working.

> **Note**
> Switch your Pip-Boy's Radio to the Ranger Emergency Broadcast frequency, and listen to Reilly's remaining crew as they inform you where they are (on the roof). To get there, you need to cross from the hospital to the hotel, via the crumpled antenna girder that has fallen across the road above the hospital entrance.

Ranger Emergency Broadcast

PATH B: STUMBLING INTO THE RANGER'S EMERGENCY BROADCAST

If you're wandering in the Vernon Square area, or in the northeast part of the Pennsylvania Avenue Zone, you can flick on your Pip-Boy's Radio and listen to the Ranger Emergency Broadcast frequency without having to visit Reilly first. You can immediately enter the hospital, or leave the area, speak to Reilly, and return; your dialog choices are slightly different with Butcher if you haven't spoken to Reilly first.

PATH C: FROM THE DRY SEWER

This second route allows you to enter Our Lady of Hope Hospital from the interior basement.

This is a longer route, but it allows you to enter from the hospital itself. It's also a good way to reach the hospital in the future, if you need any health. Begin by using the linked Metro Tunnels, and surface at Dupont Station. Climb the rusting escalator, and head east across the concrete bridge. Step right, around the building, and head east down an alley. Turn north, tackling a few Raiders and watching for Frag Mines, and locate the small, half-demolished brick house. To the right of it, half-hidden behind a rough barricade, are steps heading down to a door marked "Hospital Maintenance." Enter here.

You're now in the Dry Sewer. Begin by following the tunnel to a pump chamber. Deploy lethal gunfire into two Talon Mercenaries on your way down, and open the door heading to the main tunnels. Head south to the junction (shown in the nearby slide), and watch the Talon Mercs fighting a losing battle against the Super Mutants. Back off and deliver killing blows to any remaining Super Mutants, then open the door in the south wall, by the junction. This leads to a dead-end generator room, but there's a First Aid Box to take on the wall.

 First Aid Box Health and Chems

Head east, past the cluster of irradiated barrels (don't fire here or you'll get caught in a massive fireball), and up the large tunnel where more Super Mutants and Talon Mercs are battling. Slay anyone who attacks you, including the Mister Gutsy (which can be dispatched with a well-aimed Pulse Grenade). Ignore the dead-end area, unless you want some specific pieces of junk to make a customized weapon, and instead head north into the side door. Follow the corridor up to the door, and open it.

Once through and into the generator room, you have a split-second choice to make: You can turn west, and sprint to the door that leads into the hospital basement, or you can stay and weave among the pipes, and tackle

Three's company, but four's a crowd; especially among these pipes. Stay and slay, or flee to the hospital door.

three Super Mutants in close proximity. If you try the latter, stay away from the generators you can detonate; but fire at them so the enemies are caught in the blast. Whether you fight or not, enter the Our Lady of Hope Hospital door, and emerge at the foot of the basement steps.

HOSPITAL GROUND FLOOR: MUTIE MASSACRE!

 **NEW OBJECTIVE**

"Locate Reilly's Rangers" begins.

HOSPITAL OVERVIEW

You begin in one of three locations, depending on the paths you took to get here. Heading in from the double doors and/or the single door to the filing room (Path A) is covered first. Entering from the basement (Path B) is covered second.

Only the mission-critical chambers are shown in the following route information. If you require medical attention, locations of the safes, or the Mister Handy, consult the Tour of the Wasteland Chapter map (page 406) for all item locations on this floor. There are Skill Books here, too.

First Aid Box Health (14)

D.C. Journal of Internal Medicine

There are usually around eight Super Mutants of varying toughness and two Centaurs; four Super Mutants and a Centaur in the waiting lobby, and another four and a Centaur scattered around the perimeter corridor with the patient rooms on either side.

There are also three Nurses' Terminals (shown on the map) throughout the hospital. If you use your Science skill to hack into them, you can unlock adjacent Chem supplies, read about numerous complaints, and learn about a patient named Harold Worthington III, and his bizarre predilection for pillows....

PLAN A: LEGGING IT THROUGH THE LOBBY

You may need a shot of your favorite Chems before bursting through into the waiting lobby.

With the double doors behind you, rummage through the entrance lobby; the filing cabinets hold a load of ammo. Head out the exit door in the western corner; the ones to the left lead to a long corridor that runs the perimeter of the floor. Deal

TRAINING — BESTIARY — MAIN QUEST — MISC. QUESTS — TOUR — COMPLETION — APPENDICES

with the Centaur, then weave around and into the massive waiting room). There are four Super Mutants to Sneak by or slay in a barrage of gunfire. The Combat Shotgun is thoroughly recommended for corridors, but try something a little more long-range, such as Grenades or a Missile when you're in the waiting room. When the dust clears, check the disgusting Gore Bags (including the hanging ones all around the room) for loot. There's a cache (three Ammo Boxes and two Frag Grenades) on the southeast corner desk, and a Scribe Pre-War book to find, too.

 Ammo Box Ammunition (3)　　 **Frag Grenade (2)**

 Scribe Pre-War Book

 Note

If you entered the hospital via the western door, step through the computer room and into the waiting room, and apply the same tactics.

PATH B: CORRIDOR DASH

If you entered from the Dry Sewer, prepare for Mutie combat as soon as you reach the top of the stairs. When all Super Mutants in your vicinity are dropped, you can investigate the various rooms for First Aid Boxes, watching for additional enemies. If you're after a quick escape, sprint northward into the waiting lobby where the paths merge. Turn west, and dash up the stairs, and open the Door to Our Lady of Hope Hospital 2nd Level.

HOSPITAL SECOND FLOOR: TAKE IT TO THE BRIDGE

Enter the second floor, and immediately turn left. Head east down the corridor, because the doorways on your right are blocked. Prepare to Sneak past or slaughter a Super Mutant or two as you reach a safe. Then enter the cafeteria to your left, where you have a couple of Super Mutants and a leaky gas line to worry about. Stay to the west, light the gas, and tackle the enemies from here. Then move forward, heading east toward the kitchen.

Enter the door at the east end of the cafeteria, moving into the kitchen and storage area. Use the central island as cover, and remember you always have the option to back out.

> Remember that you can employ **Sneak** to stealthily circumvent any combat, or to ambush Super Mutants from behind.

Head through the doorway opposite, into a small corridor where the last of the Super Mutants in the hospital await. When they've been slain, or coaxed out into the kitchen and blown apart with Mines or Grenades, move to the door with the "Exit" sign over it. This leads to a staircase. Open the door at the top and step out onto Vernon Square.

A precarious bridge is the only way to reach Reilly's Rangers. Try not to put a foot wrong!

You appear high above the ground, adjacent to the fallen radio antenna section that links the hospital to the Statesman Hotel. Beware of Super Mutants sniping at you from the north; raid the nearby wooden crate for a Psycho, Ammo Box, and First Aid Kit, and then drop down onto the metal bridge section. Rush across without falling, and drop down to the only unlockable entrance to the Hotel Mid Level on the other side.

 First Aid Box Health and Chems　　 **Ammo Box Ammunition**

 Caution

Once you cross the fallen antenna, enter the Statesman Hotel and drop down into the first room. Once you're inside, you are effectively trapped in this hotel. There is no way out until the roof elevator is repaired!

HOTEL MID LEVEL: ONWARD AND UPWARD

Tip

The Statesman Hotel is a labyrinthine series of confusing rooms, so keep an eye on your compass, and if you're getting lost, try the "Theseus" plan: Drop an expendable item from your inventory on a bed, or in an easy-to-spot location, so you know if you're accidentally backtracking.

Drop down through the ceiling into a wrecked hotel room. Try sleeping in the bed if you need to. Then exit, check a fire hose and First Aid Box next to it, then follow the corridor north, then east to the next hotel door. Back away from the Grenade Trap as you reach this door! Step into the interior bedroom closet area, and through to a rampaging Super Mutant and Centaur. Dispatch them both, step through the hole into a second bedroom, ignore the bathroom doors, and head into the main corridor.

 First Aid Box Health and Chems†

† Next to every fire hose in this hotel

Check the First Aid Box to the right of the fire hose. To the right is a small alcove with an Eat'o'tronic 3000 vending machine. The stairs to the west lead up and out. Head up the stairs, but pause when you reach the landing and inspect a couple of corpses. One of them is Theo, who's seen better days, but his Ammo Crate is intact. Open it automatically, using the code Reilly supplied you earlier, and claim the contents.

 **Ranger's Ammo Crate**　　 **Merc Charmer Outfit**

Stride up to the next floor, without continuing up the stairs to the dead-end and releasing the Grenade Trap. Instead, head through the door, and open the first door on your right; visit a couple of vending machines farther along the corridor if you're feeling peckish). Ready your Super Mutant takedown weapon, and head south toward the window, engaging a Super Mutant.

Turn left (east), and head through three separate hotel rooms, using the Super Mutant–sized holes until you find the hotel door in the north wall, and another Super Mutant to pepper with gunfire. All the other rooms off this route house items of limited use. Move across the main corridor into the hotel room opposite, and turn right at the gigantic hole in the wall. Face southeast and deal with another charging Super Mutant, then step forward and climb up the next set of stairs, all the way to the hotel's upper level.

MEETING LITTLE MOONBEAM'S DESICCATED DAD

You're still some way from the roof, so methodically pace yourself, and save your progress before venturing northward down the main corridor until you reach your first set of hotel doors to the left and right. Deliver a killing blow to the Centaur, then try the following:

 Use **Lockpick** to wrestle the storage door open to find some useful items: two Ammo Boxes, a First Aid Kit, and some Abraxo Cleaner.

Continue a few steps down the corridor and claim the items from the First Aid Kit box adjacent to the fire hose. Then backtrack to the door opposite the one you just unlocked.

Head west into the remains of a hotel bedroom, and move farther into the chamber. Begin a thorough search; in the midst of the junk is a small bed in the northwest corner with a skeletal corpse on it. Beside it is a Holotape with A Note from Little Moonbeam's Father. If you listen to it on your Pip-Boy, you can hear the final words of a man to his daughter as he lies dying from a bullet wound. Check under the bed for an Assault Rifle and nearby ammo, too. Dry your eyes, and proceed northeast, back into the corridor. Move to the pillar at the far end, grab more health from the First Aid Kit on the wall, and choose the left of the two doorways as you head west, to avoid a Grenade Trap.

Tip

A Note from Little Moonbeam's Father is meant for Sydney, a ruins delver you meet during **Miscellaneous Quest: Stealing Independence**. Return to Sydney with this Note for a prize, which is detailed in the other quest.

Continue west around the pillars, dealing with a Super Mutant by using the vertical columns to hide and outflank, and optionally check the elevator, which is currently broken.

 You can **Repair** the elevator and ascend to the Alfresco Lounge entrance. This is a good tactic for avoiding roving Super Mutants.

Head into the main corridor, pass another First Aid Kit on the wall, step over Super Mutant corpses, and deal with a live one at the far end, where the penultimate main staircase is.

Just to your left is a half-demolished bedroom; you can climb the debris to the stairs, or sleep in the bed (to heal any bones and gain

an XP bonus when the fighting continues) before you go. Check a nearby storage room to take a Skill Book. At the top of the stairs is another door. Prepare for Mutie massacring as you gun down another foe, then head east, all the way to the end of the main corridor. Don't head into the staircase yet.

 You can use **Lockpick** on the door on the western wall around the corner. Inside are two First Aid Kits and an Ammo Box.

Now leave the room, ready yourself for more Super Mutant combat, and climb the stairs all the way up to the Door to the Hotel Statesman Restaurant. On the way, listen for grenades detaching, and retreat immediately until they've exploded.

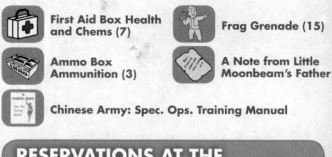

First Aid Box Health and Chems (7)	Frag Grenade (15)
Ammo Box Ammunition (3)	A Note from Little Moonbeam's Father
Chinese Army: Spec. Ops. Training Manual	

RESERVATIONS AT THE ALFRESCO LOUNGE

Two paths lead to the Alfresco Lounge: the long way or the short way (requiring a door unlock).

PATH A: THE LONG WAY

Investigate the alcove for a First Aid Kit and vending machines, then continue around the corner, and head south past two columns to a junction, fighting a foe as you go. At the corridor T-junction make a quick right, then left, and continue south along a very long corridor with a Centaur to cut down at the far end. This leads to the Alfresco Lounge entrance.

Now this is a real critical strike! Turning a Super Mutant into a small pile of ash means less corpse looting, though.

Move into the room with the collapsed floor, and strike a Super Mutant down before descending. Then head east and north to an adjacent chamber with a broken floor, and climb back up. Beware of the enemy patrolling up here. Check the lockers for a few Caps, then step into the kitchen. Don't fire your weapon, because there's a gas leak. Check the wall for the First Aid Kit, and finally enter the main bar area through either of the two wooden doors.

PATH B: THE SHORT WAY

Instead of turning right at the T-junction corridor, turn left where a corridor heads to a locked door. Choose one of the following methods of entry:

 Use **Science** to hack into the wall terminal and unlock the door.

TRAINING — BESTIARY — MAIN QUEST — MISC. QUESTS — COMPLETION — TOUR — APPENDICES

Or, use **Lockpick** to wrestle with the door itself.

Step through into the bar area. Be ready to retreat here when the Super Mutants spot you and charge your location.

INSIDE THE ALFRESCO LOUNGE

If you don't want to backtrack, make a thorough search of this restaurant, including this mechanoid.

The restaurant has at least four Super Mutants ready to man-handle you, including those prowling the upper balcony. Use pillars, doors, and corners as cover, and systematically drop them all. Once the place is quiet, begin a thorough search. There's a Nuka-Cola Quantum, Skill Book, and a large stash of ammunition behind the bar area, but the most important item is inside a tiny storage room under the stairs in the room's southwest corner. Search the destroyed Maintenance Protectron, and remove the Fission Battery. Now head up the stairs and around the balcony toward the exit door in the northeast corner. This leads to the roof.

First Aid Box Health and Chems (3)

Ammunition (2)

Frag Grenade (2)

Nuka-Cola Quantum

Protectron's Fission Battery

Sawed-Off Shotgun and Ammo

Grognak the Barbarian

RENDEZVOUS WITH THE RANGERS

NEW OBJECTIVE
"Give Fission Battery to Donovan" begins

Open the door, step onto the roof, and turn right. Sidestep around and run south. Look right and up if you want to see pieces of a Super Mutant shoot skyward. The Rangers are still defending their position, so rush up the steps, and holster

Meet Butcher, Brick, and Donovan, the last hold-outs in the Mutant-filled Statesman Hotel.

your weapon as Butcher beckons you over. Explain the situation, and optionally get him to patch you up. You can talk to Brick as well; her best friend is Eugene, an impressive-looking Minigun that she wields with authority. Optionally, look at the old music stands where a quartet of classical musicians once played. There's a Sheet Music Book here; useful for **Miscellaneous Quest: Agatha's Song**.

 Sheet Music Book

NEW OBJECTIVE
"Locate a Fission Battery" begins.

NEW OBJECTIVE
"Lead Reilly's Rangers to safety" begins.

Both Butcher and Donovan the Mechanic explain that the express elevator needs power, so they can use it to escape the building. You're tasked with finding a Fission Battery for this. Fortunately, you should have picked one up from the Protectron back in the Alfresco Lounge. If you didn't, backtrack and look carefully under the stairs for it. If you have a Fission Battery (either from the Protectron or already in your inventory), optionally give the Rangers some of your ammunition, then give the battery to Donovan, wait a moment while he brings the elevator online, and then head straight down to the Hotel Lobby.

 Tip

Be sure to distribute ammo to the Rangers before you give them the Fission Battery. As soon as the elevator is fixed, they bolt down to the Lobby. If you don't give them ammo, their guns are empty, almost guaranteeing their deaths (as they switch to pistols).

If you want to fix the elevator panel yourself, simply use your impressive **Repair** skill and slot in the Battery.

You can always gun down the Rangers, too. On Donovan's body you'll find his wrench, allowing you to fix the elevator if your Repair Skill isn't high enough.

Tip

Fully heal. Reload all your weapons. Use the Pip-Boy's Hot Key so you can flip to multiple weapons (including versions of the same weapon if it's preferred, like the Combat Shotgun) without reloading, before you step into the elevator.

Let the carnage begin! Part 6 of your quest actually ends when all the Rangers enter the elevator, because it isn't imperative for any of them to survive (although it's advantageous if at least one makes it out of the lobby). Exit the elevator and charge in as the lead "bullet sponge," drawing fire so the Rangers can survive for as long as possible. Blast the nearest Super Mutant with constant Combat Shotgun fire. Don't use grenades or other area-of-effect weapons that can harm Rangers. Draw fire away from the Rangers and onto yourself. Continuously gun down a foe until it dies, then move to the next. Start in V.A.T.S., and once you're out of Actions, resort to manual aiming. Keep this up until only humans remain in the building.

NEW OBJECTIVE
"Return to Reilly at the Ranger Compound" begins.

If you kill all of the Rangers, or all of them die in the ambush, all of the previous objectives will clear, and this objective instantly appears. Reilly's Rangers leave the hotel, and there's no need to follow them; they don't need chaperoning after the fight (in fact, you can Fast Travel back to the compound if you wish). Before you go, check under the stairs to the southeast for some vending food and drink, and two First Aid Kits in a rubble-filled alcove. Locate the bedroom upstairs with items and a Skill Book in it. Then ransack the front desk.

There is a Concierge Terminal. Use your **Science** skill to hack in, and you can open the safe, and also read notes of complaints from guests. Top of the list is Harold Worthington III, who attempted to bilk the hotel out of free room service, Seneca Clarkson, who suffocated in the line of work, and Wanda Kellendyne, who cooked her own legs.

Use **Lockpick** on the safe under the Terminal.

Ammo Box Ammunition (2)

 Assault Rifle

Tales of a Junktown Jerky Vendor

When you're done rummaging, speak to Butcher if he's waiting for you (this is especially useful if you began the quest at the Statesman). He mentions a reward and helps you locate the Ranger Compound. Head out of the front doors, and Fast Travel (if you've already been there), or trek to the Ranger Compound.

RETURN TO SENDER, ADDRESS UNKNOWN

You look like you've been though Hell.

Reilly's up and about, looking a whole lot better after her Underworld recuperation.

The final part of this quest involves you returning to Reilly, although she's no longer a patient of Doctor Barrows and is feeling much better. She's holed up in the Ranger Compound. Use the directions shown in "Stocking Up for the Slaughter," or Fast Travel there if you've already found the place. When you reach the front door, you can chat with any surviving Rangers (Brick is particularly excited about her "ventilation" techniques). Head inside, and search the compound for Reilly.

Reilly is extremely thankful for your help, but questions her competency as a leader, and tells you who was lost in the fight in the Hotel Lobby. You only need worry if all three Rangers died; if so, Reilly isn't impressed with your skills and doesn't give out a reward. Assuming you saved at least one member, Reilly offers either the Ranger Battle Armor or Brick's Minigun Eugene (but not both).

QUEST REWARDS

You receive one of the following rewards if one or more Rangers survived:

Ranger Battle Armor
+5 AP, +1 Luck, +10 Small Guns, higher AR than Combat Armor.

Eugene (Minigun)
More damage.

XP +300 XP

POST-QUEST ANTICS

The following Freeform Quests are now available:

FREEFORM QUEST: GEOMAPPING WITH REILLY

Speak with Reilly once the quest is over. She offers a GeoMapper so you can help her map the Wasteland. Take it because this is a great way of making Caps. For every Primary Location you reach, the GeoMapper offloads the data from your Pip-Boy. She has two additional GeoMappers if you lose or sell the first. You receive 20 Caps per location. Remember to "off-load" all the locations you've previously visited for a Captabulous ending to this quest!

FREEFORM QUEST: DONOVAN, MASTER REPAIRER.

If Donovan survived, you can Repair with him.

FREEFORM QUEST: THE BUTCHER WILL SEE YOU NOW.

If Butcher survived, you can seek Healing from him.

TRAINING — BESTIARY — MAIN QUEST — MISC. QUESTS — TOUR — COMPLETION — APPENDICES

Chapter 5 Tour of the Capital Wasteland

Welcome to the Capital Wasteland

With the diligent help of Moira Brown and Reilly's Rangers, the entirety of the Capital Wasteland has been meticulously mapped out and every location revealed. Open the poster to pore over each location in detail, then read the following explanation on how to use this chapter.

MAP OVERVIEW AND LEGEND

The Capital Wasteland Overview Map (poster) is split up into nine separate "zones"; each showcases a different corner of the map and the central Wasteland area. Collectivity, they are known as the "Capital Wasteland."

In addition, there are 12 extra zones (Zones 10–21) in the D.C. Interior. These are self-contained interior sections, not accessible directly from the Capital Wasteland.

Lastly, there's a list of every underground connecting location in the D.C. Interior. These tunnels link Zone 9 to any of Zones 10 through 21. Use the maps within to figure out how each location connects to the others.

Each location in the Capital Wasteland (Zones 1–9) has a specific latitude (east–west) and longitude (north–south), which appears on the poster map. Use this to quickly find yourself. Vault 101 for example, is at latitude -04 and longitude -04; cross-reference this on the poster map to see that this is on the northern edge of Zone 8.

Each location within a zone is split up into primary locations (which appear as Fast Travel points on your Pip-Boy's World Map once you locate them) and secondary locations (some of which appear on your Pip-Boy's Local Map).

1 🏠 Primary locations are usually larger, and some require interior exploration and are tagged in number form. For example, Vault 101 is tagged as Primary Location 8.01. This means it is in Zone 8 and is the first primary location within this zone. Tenpenny Tower, on the other hand, is tagged as Primary Location 7.14 (the 14th primary location within Zone 7).

A Secondary locations are smaller, and a few require interior exploration and are tagged in letter form. For example, the car dealership south of Megaton is tagged as Secondary Location 8.Q.

There are other icons to check out, too:

These areas are covered in radiation.

These areas are within the perimeter of a large primary location.

1 These areas have Enclave Soldiers in the vicinity. Enclave Camps only appear during Main Quest: Picking up the Trail and stay at these locations from this point on.

1 🏛 This signifies that this primary location has an underground link, accessing a separate location via a subterranean tunnel.

A This icon signifies that this secondary location has an underground link, accessing a separate location via a subterranean tunnel.

⭐ This icon signifies the possibility of a Mini-Encounter.

1 Location Maps only: This marker shows the general area to search for one or more important items, or a major junction or route.

● Location Maps only: This signifies a door that is either locked, or leads to a different location, sometimes linked using a red line.

MEASURING YOUR VITAL STATISTICS

Every location in this chapter is detailed with a "VITAL" (Vault-Tec Inspired Topographical Aid List), so you know what to do no matter where you are. Every location features its name, latitude/longitude, a fly-by screenshot of its exterior, and notes. There are also several pertinent pieces of information so you can quickly ascertain what's going on at a particular place in the Wasteland. Here's what all the VITAL statistics mean:

VITAL STATISTICS	
STAT	**DESCRIPTION**
RELATED QUESTS	
Main Quest	This location is visited during a specific Main Quest.
Miscellaneous Quest	This location is visited during a specific Miscellaneous Quest.
Freeform Quest	A number of Freeform Quests at this location.
THREAT LEVEL	
Threat Level 1–5	The overall danger in this specific area.
Level 1	Extremely light—an easy-to-dispatch foe or animal
Level 2	Light—such as a couple of Raiders or a few small creatures
Level 3	Moderate—a small Super Mutant camp or a single large creature
Level 4	Problematic—expect heavy resistance and multiple entities
Level 5	Desperate—extreme danger; exceptionally strong or devious foes
FACTIONS	
Brotherhood of Steel	The true patriots commandeer this area.
Brotherhood Outcast	Technology foragers are in these parts.
Chinese Commando	The remnants of an ancient invasion.
Enclave	The Enclave's presence is felt here.
Ghoul	Friendly or feral, expect a lumpy-skin presence.
Littlehorn and Associates	A hidden society, banishing do-gooders.
Raider	Crude and vicious Raiders are here.
Regulator	A hidden society, expunging evildoers.
Reilly's Rangers	A small band of friendly mercenaries.
Slave	Those seeking freedom for all reside here.
Slaver	Those trafficking in humans are here.
Super Mutant	Expect Gore Bags and hulking brutes.
Talon Mercenary	The sign of the claw; mercenaries rule here.
The Family	A bloodsucking nocturnal tribe.
Vault Dweller	A Vault-Tec-related location.
Wastelander	Eking out an existence in this location.

SERVICES	
Healer	You can heal or purchase health items here.
Repairer	Any items can be repaired here.
Trader	You can trade items at this location.

DANGERS	
Baby Carriage	A crying baby, then an explosion.
Baseball Pitcher	Trip a sensor or wire and receive fired baseballs.
Bear Trap	Look down, look out, or face a crippling injury.
Behemoth	The biggest Super Mutant ever. Big problems!
Chain Trap	Heavy objects on a chain, activated by trip wire.
Gas Leak	Stow guns; escaping gas is in this location.
Grenade Bouquet	Cluster of Frag Grenades above, trip wire below.
High Radiation	Long exposure to low or high radiation.
Low Radiation	Small exposure to low radiation.
Mines	Beware of Frag or Pulse Mines.
Shotgun Trap	A Rigged Shotgun.
Terminal Trap	Disarm the rear of this computer for a Frag Grenade.

COLLECTIBLES	
Bobblehead	One of 20 Vault-Tec Bobbleheads is at this location.
Fat Man Launcher	At least 1 of 9 Fat Men are here.
Fat Man Mini-Nuke	At least 1 of 71 Mini-Nukes are here.
Holotape: Replicated Man	A Holotape related either to the Keller Family or to this Miscellaneous Quest is here.
Nuka-Cola Quantum	At least 1 of 94 Nuka-Cola Quantums are at this location.
Scribe Pre-War Book	At least 1 of 98 Scribe Pre-War books are at this location.
Skill Book	At least 1 of the 324 Skill Books can be found here.

MISCELLANEOUS	
Area is Locked	This area requires a special key or high Lockpick/Science to enter.
Follower	One of eight Followers can be bought, coaxed, or kidnapped here.
Guns and Ammunition	A large amount of Guns and Ammo is here.
Health and Chems	Find Health and Chems in this area.
Highly Visible Landmark	Use this to get your bearings.
Home Sweet Home	You are rewarded your own residence here.

MISCELLANEOUS (continued)	
Interior Exploration	There is more to this location than just the surface.
Lots O' Caps	Expect a quest or safe to bring you a large windfall.
Main Trading Route	Wandering traders are found here.
Perk!	You are awarded a perk at this location.
Radio Signal	Your Pip-Boy picks up a narrow-band radio signal (not including the wideband G.N.R. or Enclave).
Rare or Powerful Item	One of 89 unique weapons or armor is found here.
Sleep Mattress	You can sleep here.
Underground Connection	This links to an underground area, which links to one or more other locations.
Weapon Schematic	One of 23 Schematics, for seven different custom weapons.
Work Bench	At least 1 of 46 Work Benches are here.

The Capital Wasteland: General Encounters

Tip

Items and Explosions

If explosions, heavy weapons, and other ordnance are used near them, they may move. For this reason, be sure to search the area around each item.

AVAILABLE COLLECTIBLES
(ALL ZONES: MINI-ENCOUNTERS ONLY)

- Bobbleheads: 00/20
- Fat Men: 01/09
- Mini-Nukes: 04/71
- Unique Items: 03/89
- Nuka-Cola Quantum: 01/94
- Schematics: 04/23
- Scribe Pre-War Books: 00/98
- Skill Book (Barter): 00/24
- Skill Book (Big Guns): 00/25
- Skill Book (Energy Weapons): 00/25
- Skill Book (Explosives): 00/25
- Skill Book (Lockpick): 00/25
- Skill Book (Medicine): 00/25
- Skill Book (Melee Weapons): 00/25
- Skill Book (Repair): 00/25
- Skill Book (Science): 00/25
- Skill Book (Small Guns): 00/25
- Skill Book (Sneak): 00/25
- Skill Book (Speech): 00/25
- Skill Book (Unarmed): 00/25
- Work Bench: 00/46
- Holotapes (Keller): 00/05
- Holotapes (Replicated Man): 00/19

0.00 CAPITAL WASTELAND TRADERS

If you're looking for someone to buy and sell items from, there are Scavengers, Traders in stores at specific locations, and Wandering Trader Caravans (which are comprised of four different merchants and their entourage, as well as a Pack Brahmin and one or two Caravan Guards). If you're away from a major trade center, find one of these merchants, and either trade with them or repair any items you have. If you are on friendly terms with Ernest "Uncle" Roe over at Canterbury Commons [6.02], you can invest in these traders; it's a great way to make money. Consult Freeform Quest: Merchant Empire for details (page 328).

WANDERING TRADERS

- Threat Level: 1
- Faction: Wastelander
- Services: Repairer, Trader
- Collectible: Fat Man Mini-Nuke, Schematic (3)
- Health And Chems
- Guns And Ammo
- Lots O' Caps
- Main Trading Route
- Rare Or Powerful Item

MERCHANT TRADERS
Crazy Wolfgang
Wolfgang might act insane, but he only plays the madman for sales. His inventory is mostly random junk, making him useful for finding custom-weapon components or just cashing in gear for caps.

Crow
Crow used to be a tribal shaman and has spiritual views on the Wasteland that can seem odd to others—especially when they're mixed with his uncanny sense for selling armor. There are rumors that he came from Oasis, but if he is, he never talks about it.

Doc Hoff
Hoff is a cynic who makes bleak comments about humanity's chances of survival. Meanwhile, he knows that no buyer will stop purchasing from him, because they either need the medicine or are addicted to the chemicals. He likes to think that, in his own way, he's helping to ease humanity's suffering in its dying years.

Lucky Harith
Boisterous and friendly, Harith's toy collection consists of a wide assortment of weapons. Despite the destructive potential of his gear, he sees his sales as a way to ensure peace in the world by making sure everyone is equally armed.

The traders take a long, counterclockwise circular path, visiting each of the following locations before returning to the starting location:

- Canterbury Commons [6.02]
- Temple of the Union [3.10]
- Agatha's House [5.06]
- Paradise Falls [2.08]
- Arefu [5.07]
- Evergreen Mills [7.04]
- Megaton [8.03]
- Rivet City [9.15]

So, if you meet Crow in Rivet City, you know he won't be stopping at Megaton for a while.

In addition, each trader has a rare or unique item you might wish to purchase (or steal from their still-warm corpse):

- From Crazy Wolfgang: Schematic: Rock-It Launcher (01/23)
- From Crow (once you invest with him): Eyebot Helmet (01/89)

- From Doc Hoff: Schematic: Nuka Grenade (02/23)
- From Lucky Harith: Mini-Nuke (01/71)
- From Lucky Harith: Schematic: Shishkebab (03/23)

Around the Wasteland in 80 Mini-Encounters

Aside from your main and Miscellaneous Quests, there are dozens of smaller tasks, chance meetings, and other activities you can accomplish, depending on your decisions. They are divided into two types:

TYPE 1: UNIQUE ENCOUNTERS

0.01: SEARCHING FOR CHERYL

- Threat Level: 3
- Faction: Super Mutant, Wastelander
- When wandering L'Enfant South (Zone 21), you stumble across a Burial Mound [21.I]. Read the note, which mentions the Ranger Compound [18.06] and a search for a woman named Cheryl. The grave is of a guy named Henry.
- Search Party Log #1: If, on your travels, you find the compound and already have the note, access the Outer Terminal (this is very hard, unless unlocked by Reilly). You can now read the note from Centerbury Search Party, which says the search moved to the Western Ruins.
- Search Party Log #2: These "Western Ruins" are just north of the Potomac Bridge [9.K] and south of the Festive Raider Camp [9.L], where you find a second grave. This is only here if you completed steps 1 and 2. Unearth another note here. This is the grave of Emmet.
- Search Party Log #3: The clues in the third note should take you here, to a grave directly northwest of the Sewer Waystation [9.03]. A fourth note (only available if you've completed steps 1 through 3) hints that Super Mutants are holding Cheryl near a "park."
- Search Party Log #4: This leads to a small Super Mutant camp [8.A] just west of the Jury Street Metro Station [5.13], where you must defeat a group of Muties and a massive Behemoth (he appears when you enter the container with a corpse in it). Here, you'll find the corpse of Manny Koch, the leader of the search. He has only minor items on his body (which only appears if you complete steps 1 through 4). Remember to search the Behemoth for a wealth of items, including a Mini-Nuke.
- Mini-Nuke (02/71)

0.02: BIG LOOT IN BIG TOWN

- Miscellaneous Quest: Big Trouble In Big Town
- Threat Level: 1
- Faction: Wastelander

If you let the inhabitants of Big Town die, you may meet a Scavenger heading to gather up the remains.

0.03: BIG CAPS IN BIG TOWN

- Miscellaneous Quest: Big Trouble In Big Town
- Threat Level: 1
- Faction: Wastelander

If you helped the inhabitants of Big Town repel attacks, a traveling salesman is heading that way to ply his wares.

0.04: GEE MISTER, YOU LOOK SUPER!

- Miscellaneous Quest: The Superhuman Gambit
- Threat Level: 1
- Faction: Wastelander

This only available if you're wearing either the AntAgonizer or Mechanist's costume. During your trudge through a desert, a little kid approaches you and asks for your autograph. Oblige the little tyke or devastate him by refusing!

0.05: THE OASIS MERCHANT

- Miscellaneous Quest: Oasis
- Threat Level: 1

A merchant has just come from Oasis, where the residents had him drink the Sap of Purification, which had dizzying side effects. He is dying and his mind is gone. Speak to him, and he relates a strange and wonderful story in which the Wasteland is reborn, and the Great One has gifted us all. On his body is a note showing the location of Oasis [2.01].

- Trading Caravan Log

0.06: MR. BURKE'S ASSASSINS

- Miscellaneous Quest: The Power Of The Atom
- Threat Level: 3

If you disarmed Megaton's bomb, a group of assassins hired by Mr. Burke ambush you.

0.07: VENGEANCE FOR MEGATON

- Miscellaneous Quest: The Power Of The Atom
- Threat Level: 2
- Faction: Wastelander

If you blew up Megaton, a group of displaced settlers from the smoldering ruins stages a revenge attack.

0.08: BRAGGING RIGHTS

- Miscellaneous Quest: Stealing Independence
- Threat Level: 2

If you retrieved the Declaration of Independence and claimed the entire reward, you are attacked by Sydney, another relic hunter who's a little put out at your glory-hogging.

- Sydney's 10mm "Ultra" SMG

0.09: AMATA'S FATE

- Miscellaneous Quest: Trouble On The Homefront
- Faction: Enclave, Vault Dweller
- Threat Level: 2

If you forced Amata to leave the Vault, then you may stumble upon an Enclave patrol confronting her. An Enclave officer asks her where her Vault is. After she tells them, they murder her. If you somehow manage to stop this, Amata flees from you, shouting that it's all your fault.

0.10: DYING OF THIRST

- Threat Level: 1
- Faction: Wastelander

You come across a man dying of thirst. You can leave him to die or offer him some of your water. Give him the water, and he thanks you and begins to traverse the Wasteland. You may meet him later, and he'll offer to aid you.

0.11: DEATHCLAW CHASE

- Threat Level: 3
- Faction: Wastelander

A group of Wastelanders are being pursued by a Deathclaw. Help them, and Rock Creek Caverns appears on your world map, leading you to the Mirelurk King's Treasure Chamber.

0.12: WATER, WATER, NOWHERE

- Threat Level: 1
- Faction: Wastelander

A group of four settlers are in a standoff over a small water supply that they've both found,

 Mediate the two parties and get them to share.

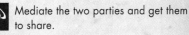 Or kill them all and take the water for yourself.

0.13: WOUNDED DEATHCLAW

- Threat Level: 2
- Collectible: Schematic
- Faction: Wastelander

A badly wounded Deathclaw is standing over the body of an adventurer. Slay the beast and search the adventurer; you won't be disappointed.

- Schematic: Deathclaw Gauntlet (4/23)

0.14: RADSCORPION GUARDING FIRE HYDRANT

- Threat Level: 2
- Faction: Wastelander

A group of Wasteland wanderers are trying to get water from an old fire hydrant. Sadly for them, an abnormally huge RadScorpion is guarding it. Help the wanderers get to the water or take it for yourself.

0.15: RIFLE MAN

- Threat Level: 3
- Rare Or Powerful Item
- Faction: Wastelander

A lunatic crosses your path and attacks you with a weapon that fires some deadly and strange projectiles. Slay the madman and take his weapon.

- Railway Rifle

0.16: DOWNED CHINESE PILOT

- Threat Level: 1
- Faction: Chinese Commando

A crackling radio signal appears, and when you triangulate it, you reach the skeleton of a Chinese pilot and some great Pre-War loot.

- Chinese Radio Beacon

0.17: UNIDENTIFIED FLYING DEBRIS

- Threat Level: 2
- Rare Or Powerful Item

Whoa! What the hell was that? A large explosion is heard overhead, and pieces of a strange technology rain down on you. Search the area thoroughly for a unique Alien Blaster that sets its targets on fire! There's Ammo here as well.

- Alien Blaster: "Firelance" (03/89)

0.18: LOCKED AND UNLOADED

- Threat Level: 1
- Faction: Wastelander

A Wastelander mugger who robs travelers holds you up. It's a shame that he's an idiot, and his gun isn't loaded.

0.19: A BROKEN ROBOT

- Threat Level: 1
- Faction: Wastelander

You meet a technician fiddling with a robot who is stuck in a conversation pattern. Your **Repair** skill is required to fix this malfunctioning machine.

0.20: MORE THAN JUST SCRAP

- Threat Level: 1
- Faction: Wastelander

You come across the remains of a dead Wastelander. He's holding a map to "John's Treasure Box," which contains some interesting items (three Skill Books are inside an Ammo Box), located in the Scrapyard [6.03].

- Map to John's Treasure Box

0.21: RAIDER INITIATION ‡

- Threat Level: 2
- Faction: Raider

Watch from a distance, or begin to massacre a group of Raiders "initiating" a new member by beating him with melee implements.

> **Note**
>
> Any Mini-Encounter marked with this symbol (‡) involves Raiders, and the Unique Combat Knife is dropped randomly during one of them.

- "Stabhappy" Combat Knife (02/89) ‡

0.22: MINEFIELD DISMANTLING

- Threat Level: 3
- Faction: Wastelander

Observe a couple of hapless Wastelanders attempting to dismantle a Minefield for parts, only to step in the wrong place, at the wrong time. Mop up afterward.

- Frag Mine

0.23: ESCAPE FROM GRAYDITCH

- Miscellaneous Quest: Those!
- Threat Level: 1
- Faction: Wastelander

You run into a man fleeing from Grayditch; he has been driven crazy during the attack and makes little sense, but he does get across that he's running away from Grayditch. Once you finish speaking with him, you receive a Pip-Boy update on your World Map, showing the location of Grayditch.

0.24: OUT OF THE VAULT

- Miscellaneous Quest: Trouble On The Homefront
- Threat Level: 1
- Faction: Vault Dweller

Once the quest is over and you choose to open the Vault to the outside world, you may encounter one of your old friends during a Wasteland excursion. Your first encounter is with Susie Mack, assuming you haven't killed her. Of course, you can kill her now and steal her food and water, or you can act a little more civilized. She's happy to see you and offers some food and Purified Water. She says the Vault's doing well and that most of them are getting used to the idea of the outside. She also expresses sorrow that you can't come back, and then excuses herself.

0.25: THE LONE RANGER

- Miscellaneous Quest: Reilly's Rangers
- Faction: Reilly's Rangers
- Threat Level: 2
- Collectible: Fat Man Mini-Nuke

After Reilly's Rangers is completed, you run into one of the Rangers you met during the quest within the Irradiated Metro [9.12]. For this to occur, Donovan and Reilly must be alive, and you must have the Geomapper Module in your inventory. Once you help the Ranger, they reward you.

- Mini-Nuke (03/71)

0.26: SELLING THE MOST DELICIOUS FLESH OF ALL

- Threat Level: 2
- Faction: Wastelander

You encounter a band of "hunters," and they are more than happy to sell you some tasty Strange Meat. This is actually human flesh.

- Strange Meat

0.27: HUNTING THE MOST DELICIOUS FLESH OF ALL

- Threat Level: 3
- Faction: Wastelander

A band of "hunters" are tracking their prey—a hapless settler! After the kill, they begin eating the corpse. Wait two hours, and they become ravenous and turn their attention toward you....

0.28: GOING CAMPING

- Threat Level: 2
- Faction: Wastelander

A shot rings out, and a nearby Wastelander falls. There's a Sniper hiding nearby, lying in wait for you.

0.29: THE HUMAN BOMB

- Threat Level: 3
- Faction: Raider, Wastelander

A few Raiders send out an obviously perturbed settler out to greet you, who they then blow up and then attack you.

0.30: MAD BRAHMIN RAMPAGE

- Threat Level: 2

Due to consuming the wrong type of irradiated grass tufts, a herd of Mad Brahmin stampede your way. Slay them before they hit you.

TYPE II: REPEATING ENCOUNTERS

0.31: SURVIVAL GUIDE REVIEW—FAILURE

- Miscellaneous Quest: The Wasteland Survival Guide
- Threat Level: 1
- Faction: Wastelander

Consult the quest for advice on making a "very poor" survival guide. You come across a weak and poorly equipped survivor fighting a Mole Rat. If the Wastelander lives, he bad-mouths your work. Speak with him, and he gives you the guide, telling you it's good for a laugh.

- Wasteland Survival Guide (Very Poor)

0.32: SURVIVAL GUIDE REVIEW: SURVIVALIST

- Miscellaneous Quest: The Wasteland Survival Guide
- Threat Level: 1
- Faction: Wastelander

Consult the quest for advice on making a "moderate" survival guide. You come across a survivor fighting a Mole Rat. The Wastelander should live. Let him know you helped write the book, and you receive thanks but nothing else.

0.33: SURVIVAL GUIDE REVIEW: SURVIVAL EXPERT

- Miscellaneous Quest: The Wasteland Survival Guide
- Threat Level: 1
- Faction: Wastelander

Consult the quest for advice on making an "excellent" survival guide. You come across a well-equipped Wastelander battling a badly wounded Mirelurk. You get a friendly greeting once he finishes off the beast. Mention you wrote the guide, and you can wheedle 10 or 25 Caps from the awestruck adventurer.

- 25 Caps

0.34: QUANTUM SALES PITCH

- Miscellaneous Quest: The Nuka-Cola Challenge
- Faction: Wastelander
- Services: Trader
- Threat Level: 1

A wandering Trader is trudging around, and one of his items is of particular interest—a Nuka-Cola Quantum—but the price is shocking! Pay 100 Caps (or 50 Caps with a Speech challenge). Ask about Nuka-Cola, and you're directed to Girdershade and Sierra Petrovita.

- Nuka-Cola Quantum (01/94)

0.35: ANGRY GHOULS

- Miscellaneous Quest: Tenpenny Tower
- Threat Level: 2
- Faction: Ghoul

A group of ghouls have made camp to rest a moment on their way to Tenpenny Tower. The reason they are traveling is based on your actions; they are either going to live in the tower or take revenge on the murder of Roy Phillips and his crew. You can speak to these Ghouls and attack them if they turn violent.

- Ghoul Note

0.36: OASIS RAIDERS

- Miscellaneous Quest: Oasis
- Faction: Wastelander
- Threat Level: 2

A group of Wastelanders are on their way to attack Oasis. Speak to them and they tell you where Oasis is. Pick a fight with them, or leave them to their mission.

0.37: KILL THE SLAVER

- Miscellaneous Quest: Strictly Business
- Threat Level: 2
- Faction: Slave, Slaver

If you choose to side with the Slavers and round up a group of slaves using the

Mesmetron, a posse of mercenaries (possibly hired by the families of those you enslaved) tracks you down and begins attacking.

- Contract: Kill the Slaver!

0.38: A LITTLE COMPETITION

- Miscellaneous Quest: Strictly Business
- Threat Level: 2
- Faction: Slaver

If you rounded up enough slaves using the Mesmetron, a group of Slavers, annoyed by your prowess and for making them look bad in front of Eulogy Jones, decides to take out "the employee of the month"—you!

0.39: TRAPPED OUTSIDE

- Miscellaneous Quest: Trouble On The Homefront
- Threat Level: 1
- Faction: Vault Dweller

If you forced the residents to evacuate, there's a chance you might run into the corpse of one of your old Vault friends during a Wasteland excursion. Search the corpse (which is usually Freddy, Pepper, or Officer Gomez) for a Vault Jumpsuit in poor condition and other assorted junk.

- Vault 101 Jumpsuit

0.40: ANTS VS. RADSCORPION

- Threat Level: 2

A group of Giant Ants attempts to overwhelm a Radscorpion.

0.41: ATTACK OF THE ANT GIANT!

- Threat Level: 2

A group of Giant Ants gathers around a spilled toxic waste barrel. As you near, one of the ants steps into the waste, grows to three times its normal size, and attacks!

0.42: RADSCORPIONS VS. WASTELANDER

- Threat Level: 2
- Faction: Wastelander

A couple of Radscorpions are savaging a Wastelander to death. As you approach, they train their pincers on you.

0.43: RADROACH SCAVENGERS

- Threat Level: 2
- Faction: Wastelander

Between 20:00 and 05:00 at night, you come across the dead body of a Scavenger. It has now attracted a group of Radroaches. They attack if you move too close, but combating them may be worth it; there's some food on the Scavenger's body.

0.44: WASTELAND MERCHANT

- Threat Level: 1
- Services: Repairer, Trader
- Faction: Wastelander

You stumble across a Wasteland merchant in his camp. He Barters and Repairs with you.

0.45: WASTELAND SAWBONES

- Threat Level: 1
- Services: Healer
- Faction: Wastelander

You encounter a Wasteland doctor with some medical training, and he agrees to patch you up, cure your Rad sickness, and sell Stimpaks and Chems to you—for a price.

0.46: DOWN, BOY!

- Threat Level: 2

A small pack of Vicious Dogs is guarding a recent kill and protect it by attacking you.

0.47: HUNTING PARTY

- Threat Level: 2
- Faction: Wastelander

Expect to run into a variety of hunters scouting different types of prey.

0.48: HUNTERS HUNTING

- Threat Level: 2
- Faction: Wastelander

A hunter is tracking down his wild animal prey, usually a Mole Rat or other irradiated mutation.

0.49: ROBOT SCAVENGING

- Threat Level: 1
- Faction: Enclave, Wastelander

A Wastelander is scavenging parts from a wrecked robot.

0.50: EYEBOT SPECTATORS

- Threat Level: 1
- Faction: Enclave, Wastelander

A small group of Wastelanders are listening to the propaganda spewed from a nearby Eyebot.

0.51: DEAD GUY, FAT MAN

- Threat Level: 1
- Faction: Wastelander
- Collectible: Fat Man Launcher

You stumble upon a dead Wastelander; on his body is a Fat Man.

- Fat Man (01/09)
- Mini-Nuke (04/71)

0.52: FRAG MINES FOUND

- Threat Level: 2
- Danger: Mines

You stumble across a small minefield; disarm or explode these Frag Mines.

- Frag Mine

0.53: SUPER MUTANT CAPTIVES

- Threat Level: 3
- Faction: Super Mutant, Wastelander

A small group of Super Mutants has set up camp with a couple of Wastelander captives. This usually occurs within the vicinity of Vault 87's exterior [4.06] or the Germantown Police Headquarters [5.01]. Kill them all, or kill the Super Mutants and free the captives.

 Rescue any captives and take their gift for a small boost to your Karma. Refuse their gift for a larger boost.

0.54: GHOUL-FRIENDS

- Threat Level: 2
- Faction: Ghoul

Hold your fire as you meet a group of poorly armed Ghouls (non-Feral). They want to reach Underworld, but they can't break through the Super Mutant defenses. Be pleasant to them, and they reveal a World Map marker that shows where Underworld is.

0.55: WASTELAND CHEM DEALER

- Threat Level: 1
- Services: Trader
- Faction: Wastelander

 You may run across a Chem dealer in his small camp. You're able to **Barter** a variety of Chems from him.

0.56: MAULED BY MOLE RATS

- Threat Level: 2
- Faction: Wastelander

A Wastelander is being pursued by some ravenous Mole Rats. Save him, and he's thankful.

0.57: ENCLAVE EYEBOT EARLY WARNING SYSTEM

- Main Quest: The Waters Of Life
- Threat Level: 3
- Faction: Enclave

There are many Eyebots patrolling the Wasteland and are easily destroyed. Occasionally (and only after the Enclave has made its presence felt), taking down an Eyebot causes a Vertibird to swoop down and investigate the Eyebot's "malfunction."

0.58: ENCLAVE PATROL

- Main Quest: The Waters Of Life
- Threat Level: 3
- Faction: Enclave

A squad of soldiers (which may include officers and a Modified Deathclaw) are patrolling the wastes, once the Enclave make their presence felt.

0.59: ENCLAVE VS. BROTHERHOOD OUTCASTS

- Main Quest: The Waters Of Life
- Faction: Brotherhood Outcast, Enclave
- Threat Level: 3

A fierce firefight has erupted between Brotherhood Outcast and Enclave patrols.

0.60: ENCLAVE VS. TALON COMPANY

- Main Quest: The Waters Of Life
- Faction: Enclave, Talon Mercenary
- Threat Level: 3

Once the Enclave lands in the Wasteland, expect them to engage in running and gunning battles with Talon Company patrols.

0.61: THE SUPER MUTANT PHILOSOPHER

- Main Quest: Finding The Garden Of Eden
- Threat Level: 1
- Faction: Super Mutant

Once you begin this Main Quest, you meet Uncle Leo, a nonviolent Super Mutant who wanders the Wasteland pondering the meaning of life. He's friendly but doesn't take lightly to being attacked. Perhaps he's related to Fawkes?

0.62: WRATH OF THE ANTAGONIZER

- Miscellaneous Quest: The Superhuman Gambit
- Threat Level: 1
- Faction: Wastelander

When you finish Miscellaneous Quest: The Superhuman Gambit, and the AntAgonizer is still alive and the Mechanist is dead (or has retired), watch (or intervene) as she attacks a group of Wastelanders.

0.63: ATTACK OF THE FIRE ANTS

- Miscellaneous Quest: Those!
- Threat Level: 2

This occurs only during this Miscellaneous Quest and before you stamp out all Fire Ants in the Grayditch [9.09] and Marigold Station [9.10] areas. Encounter these fire-breathing insects, harvesting them for their Nectar.

- Fire Ant Nectar

0.64: LOOKING FOR THE TEMPLE OF THE UNION

- Miscellaneous Quest: Head of State
- Threat Level: 1
- Faction: Slave

A small band of escaped slaves are looking for the safety of the Temple of the Union. Give them directions, or lie to them and begin combat.

0.65: BROTHERHOOD OUTCAST PATROL

- Threat Level: 2
- Outcast
- Faction: Brotherhood

A small squad of Brotherhood of Steel Outcasts are on patrol. There may be robots and soldiers. They are either neutral unless you have previously attacked Outcast patrols.

0.66: BROTHERHOOD OUTCAST PATROL VS. RAIDERS ‡

- Threat Level: 3
- Faction: Brotherhood Outcast, Raider

A squad of Brotherhood Outcasts have encountered a number of Raiders, and the two sides are battling. Watch, leave, or attack.

0.67: BROTHERHOOD OUTCAST PATROL VS. DEATHCLAWS

- Threat Level: 4
- Faction: Brotherhood Outcast

A small pack of Deathclaws is pursuing a fleeing Outcast scout. A nearby Outcast patrol joins the battle. Watch, leave, or attack.

0.68: SLAVERS ESCORT

- Threat Level: 2
- Faction: Slave, Slaver

A small band of Slavers are escorting captured slaves toward Paradise Falls. Watch, chat, or rescue the slaves.

0.69: ESCAPING SLAVES

- Threat Level: 2
- Faction: Slave, Slaver

A few slaves are attempting to flee from Slavers. Watch, or side with the Slavers or the slaves.

0.70: ESCAPED SLAVES

- Threat Level: 2
- Faction: Slave, Slaver

A few slaves have already escaped their shackles and are being actively pursued by Slavers. Side with the slaves or help the Slavers kill the runaways.

0.71: ONE FINE RIDE

- Threat Level: 1
- Faction: Wastelander

Looking for technology to scavenge, a Wastelander is heading for a burned-out vehicle that he guards.

0.72: RAIDERS VS. SCAVENGER‡

- Threat Level: 2
- Faction: Raider, Wastelander

Raiders are attacking a lone Wasteland Scavenger, who's fighting back valiantly. If he survives, you can Barter and Repair with him.

0.73: RAIDERS VS. WASTELANDERS

- Threat Level: 2
- Faction: Raider, Wastelander

Wastelander settlers are fending off a Raider incursion.

0.74: HERE, DOGGIE, DOGGIE

- Threat Level: 2

A pack of Vicious Dogs are on the prowl and attack you on sight.

0.75: HUNTERS VS. PREY

- Threat Level: 1
- Faction: Wastelander

You spot a Wasteland Hunter (or Hunters) attempting to hunt down a mutated animal.

0.76: TALON COMPANY PATROL

- Threat Level: 2
- Faction: Talon Mercenary

A small recon company of Talon Mercenaries is on patrol; they attack you on sight.

0.77: SUPER MUTANTS VS. WASTELANDERS

- Threat Level: 3
- Faction: Super Mutant, Wastelander

In the area around Vault 87's exterior [4.06] or the Germantown Police Headquarters [5.01], Muties are engaged in a pitched battle with Wastelanders.

0.78: WANDERING SCAVENGER

- Threat Level: 2
- Faction: Wastelander

A Scavenger is leading his pack Brahmin about; don't start messing with the Brahmin, or the Scavenger turns hostile.

0.79: RESELLING THE MOST DELICIOUS FLESH OF ALL

- Threat Level: 2
- Faction: Wastelander

If the "hunters" you met during Mini-Encounter 0.29 still survive or if you fled, you'll encounter them again. Someday.

0.80: TINKER JOE'S SERGEANT OF SLAUGHTER

- Threat Level: 1
- Faction: Wastelander
- Services: Trader
- Follower
- Tinker Joe

A traveling robot salesman named Tinker Joe agrees to sell you one of them: Sergeant RL-3. RL-3 is one of five prototype Mister Gutsy models designed to be the perfect soldier. You can only purchase RL-3 if you have neutral Karma, (but the sarge will not leave you if your Karma changes while he's in your service. Purchase RL-3 for 1,000 Caps (500 with a high Barter skill).

- Sergeant RL-3

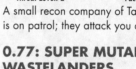

TRAINING — BESTIARY — MAIN QUEST — MISC. QUESTS — TOUR — COMPLETION — APPENDICES

Zone 1: Northwest Territories

TOPOGRAPHICAL OVERVIEW

The Northwest Territories are wild and dangerous, as you're far from a place to heal, trade, and repair, and the inhabitants are vicious predators. The northernmost area is extremely mountainous, with Deathclaws and Robots roaming around. The remains of the Potomac flow from north to south here, and the irradiated water is home to Mirelurks. The human survivors are usually bands of terrorizing Raiders; they have a small stronghold on the river's western side. The Enclave have a sizable presence here, but their territory is well guarded and mostly underground. Only the bravest (or most fool-hardy) explorer can claim to have visited every locale in this windy and desolate place.

AVAILABLE COLLECTIBLES (ZONE 1)

- Bobbleheads: 4/20
- Fat Men: 1/9
- Fat Man Mini-Nukes: 8/71
- Unique Items: 5/89
- Nuka-Cola Quantum: 4/94
- Schematics: 2/23
- Scribe Pre-War Books: 6/98
- Skill Book (Barter): 1/24
- Skill Book (Big Guns): 0/25
- Skill Book (Energy Weapons): 3/25
- Skill Book (Explosives): 3/25
- Skill Book (Lockpick): 5/25
- Skill Book (Medicine): 3/25
- Skill Book (Melee Weapons): 3/25
- Skill Book (Repair): 1/25
- Skill Book (Science): 2/25
- Skill Book (Small Guns): 3/25
- Skill Book (Sneak): 2/25
- Skill Book (Speech): 0/25
- Skill Book (Unarmed): 4/25
- Work Bench: 2/46
- Holotapes (Keller): 0/5
- Holotapes (Replicated Man): 0/19

PRIMARY LOCATIONS

1.01: Raven Rock (lat -28/long 28)

1.02: MDPL-05 Power Station (lat -27/long 25)

1.03: SatCom Array NW-05a (lat -22/long 25)

1.04: Fort Constantine (lat -17/long 26)

1.05: SatCom Array NW-07c (lat -28/long 20)

1.06: Broadcast Tower KB5 (lat -23/long 20)

1.07: Deathclaw Sanctuary (lat -22/long 20)

1.08: Dickerson Tabernacle Chapel (lat -19/long 19)

1.09: Mason Dixon Salvage (lat -14/long 21)

1.10: Mount Mabel Campground (lat -21/long 17)

1.11: WKML Broadcast Station (lat -17/long 18)

1.12: The Silver Lining Drive-In (lat -15/long 17)

1.13: Drowned Devil's Crossing (lat -14/long 18)

1.14: Abandoned Car Fort (lat -24/long 14)

1.15: Faded Pomp Estates (lat -17/long 15)

1.16: Roosevelt Academy (lat -17/long 14)

SECONDARY LOCATIONS

1.A: Raider Wharf (lat -24/long 25)

1.B: Brotherhood Outcast Shaft (lat -14/long 25)

1.C: Jackknifed Truck (on Freeway) (lat -27/long 20)

1.D: Jackknifed Truck (on Freeway) (lat -26/long 20)

1.E: Overlook Raider Shack (lat -25/long 21)

1.F: Raider Wreckage Fortifications (lat -24/long 19)

1.G: Drainage Channel (adjacent to Broadcast Tower KB5) (lat -22/long 20)

1.H: Mutie Gorge (Rope Bridge) (lat -21/long 19)

1.I: Junction Shack (lat -20/long 21)

1.J: Jackknifed Truck (near Crossing) (lat -15/long 19)

1.K: Blocked Tunnel Entrance (lat -23/long 17)

1.L: Caravan Wreckage (lat -20/long 17)

1.M: Monorail Train Wreckage (lat -28/long 15)

1.N: Jackknifed Truck (on Freeway) (lat -21/long 15)

1.O: Blocked Tunnel Entrance (lat -20/long 15)

1.P: Truck and Car Wreckage (on Freeway) (lat -20/long 14)

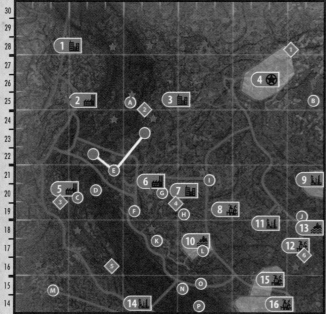

Primary Locations

1.01: RAVEN ROCK (LAT -28/LONG 28)

- Main Quest: The American Dream
- Threat Level: 4
- Faction: Enclave
- Collectible: Bobblehead
- Area Is Locked
- Guns And Ammunition
- Health And Chems
- Interior Exploration
- Hostiles: Deathclaw; Enclave: Officer, Scientist, Sentry Bot, Soldier (Tesla Armor); Radroach; Turret

Caution

Spoiler Alert! Raven Rock is the Enclave's home base; go to the next location if you don't want to see inside this place!

The president of the United States, Eden, resides here, utilizing the ZAX Corporation's super-computer technology to aid him in the reclamation and recreation of a new United States—one free of impurities and mutations. The people have suffered enough, and he's ready to use his Enclave forces to reclaim this land, with technology far more advanced than anything seen beyond the underground bunkers of his base.

Autumn grew up on an oil rig off the California coast (the base of operations for the Enclave, the secretive contingent of the United States government that survived after the apocalypse). His father was the high-ranking Enclave scientist on orders from the president to move all high-ranking officials to the only other secure Enclave location with a functioning ZAX super-computer, Raven Rock. Colonel Autumn has proven to be far less subservient than his scientist father, often openly disagreeing with the president's decisions.

Nathan ran a caravan route for over 30 years with his wife, Manya. During that time, he became a little obsessed with the Enclave radio broadcasts. Since then, Nathan has become a bit of a fanatic, believing that the Enclave will bring salvation to the Wasteland, and he has been trying to convince everyone else in Megaton of this. Most of the residents write Nathan off as the local busybody but all are quick to note that after 30 years on the back of a wagon, he is one hell of a shot when it comes down to gunplay.

INTERIOR MAPS AND LOCATIONS

Raven Rock (Level 2)

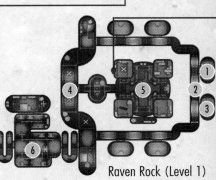

Raven Rock (Level 3)

Raven Rock

Originally known as "Site R," Raven Rock was designed at the beginning of the Cold War as a shelter for top military officials. It has served as the base of operations for the Enclave since the government's remaining forces retreated there. This is only accessible during Main Quest: The American Dream; it is otherwise impenetrable. The following section, "Interior Notes," reflect the order you visit each interior location.

LEVEL 3

1 Cell 4

This is where you begin your interrogation with Colonel Autumn. Check the locker for your inventory before leaving.

- Your Entire Inventory

2 3A: Cells Corridor

There are six Cells here and cameras that pivot and follow you.

3 Cell 3

This holds Nathan, from Megaton.

You can use **Stealth** to Pickpocket his Housekey.

- Housekey: Nathan and Manya

Raven Rock (Control Room)

Raven Rock (Level 1)

TRAINING — BESTIARY — MAIN QUEST — MISC. QUESTS — TOUR — COMPLETION — APPENDICES

4 Main Corridor

This concourse corridor has patrolling soldiers and shallow steps leading under the gantry flooring (for Sneaking or Radroach combat).

5 3A: Bio Lab

This has a number of specimens in tanks. There are eight tiny rooms on two floors and an exit to Level 2.

- Enclave Crate Ammunition (5)
- First Aid Box Health and Chems (3)

6 3B: Mess Hall

Accessed via stairs, there are food, soldiers, lockers, and an area under the floor grating full of dropped cutlery. There is also an exit to Level 2.

- First Aid Box Health and Chems (2)

LEVEL 2

7 2A: Tech Lab

Identical in size to the Bio Lab.

8 2A: Cryo Lab

Indentical in size to the Tech Lab but with more gruesome experiments and a number of crates and boxes to uncover.

- Enclave Crate Ammunition (4)
- First Aid Box Health and Chems

9 2B: Storage

There are empty Deathclaw cages and a bank of lockers to check.

10 11 2B: Quarters

Check both for items. The eastern one has a terminal to deactivate the security barrier.

- Enclave Crate Ammunition (5)
- First Aid Box Health and Chems (2)

12 Colonel Autumn's Chamber

There is a wall terminal used to deactivate the security barrier to access the crates. Check the bed footlocker for the Destruct Sequence.

- Enclave Crate Ammunition (5)
- First Aid Box Health and Chems
- ZAX Destruct Sequence
- Bobblehead: Energy Weapons (1/20)

LEVEL 1 (CONTROL ROOM)

13 President Eden's Office

This chamber is guarded by soldiers and the president's elite Sentry Bots. The Control Room is a massive vertical chamber with President Eden's offices at the top. If you gain an audience with the president, you can leave via the door to the east, after taking a vial of Modified FEV Virus.

- Modified FEV Virus

LEVEL 1

14 Deathclaw cage

This Deathclaw has been modified with a controller helmet. Release it using the terminal or unlocking the crate, and it attacks everything. Check the Vertibirds taking off from the nearby hangars.

- First Aid Box Health and Chems

15 Underfloor Stash

- First Aid Box Health and Chems (2)
- Enclave Crate Ammunition (5)

16 Security Barrier and Terminal

Hack the terminal to access the crates.

- Enclave Crate Ammunition (5)

1.02: MDPL-05 POWER STATION (LAT -27/LONG 25)

- Threat Level: 1
- Collectible: Schematic, Skill Book
- Area Is Locked
- Hostile: Vicious Dog

Enter here using either the gate or the hole in the fence. Locate the skeleton of a workman. His toolbox holds a key to open both gates. There's a Wrench and a Nuka-Cola here, too. Admire the excellent vistas from this point.

- MDPL-05 Power Station Key
- Deans Electronics (1/25)
- Schematic: Dart Gun (5/23)

1.03: SATCOM ARRAY NW-05A (LAT -22/LONG 25)

- Threat Level: 3
- Faction: Talon Mercenary
- Danger: Mines
- Highly Visible Landmark
- Health And Chems
- Interior Exploration
- Collectible: Skill Book
- Sleep Mattress
- Work Bench
- Hostiles: Ghoulish Wastelander, Talon Company Merc

Satellite Facility

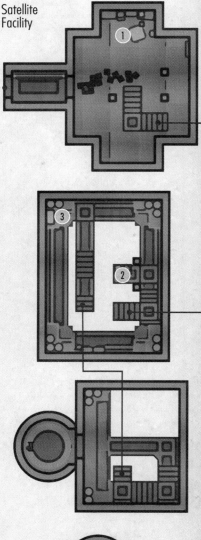

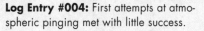

This giant radar dish is unique among the Arrays in the Wasteland, as there's only one structure. The Ghoul in charge has hired the Talon Company to guard it. As you head up to the west base of the Array, two foes on the balcony above attack you. Don't run to the door, as there are three Frag Mines in this area; instead, attack from a distance, then deactivate the mines before you enter the structure.

① Terminal

Inside, you're waylaid by a ghoulish Wastelander, an ex-scientist hard at work on a special project. When safe, check the Ghoul Wastelander's desk for a Skill Book and terminal. Check her corpse for the launch codes!

There are six relevant menu options:

Log Entry #006: This is a journal the Ghoulish Wastelander was writing. She is tracking a satellite in stationary orbit that has a payload that can only be dropped directly atop the user!

Log Entry #005: A lucky break was scored, and a registration ID (call sign "Highwater Trouser") was found.

Log Entry #004: First attempts at atmospheric pinging met with little success.

Log Entry #003: Basic coordinate pinging begins in conjunction with the nearby Arrays. Anomalous results are coming from NN-03d.

Log Entry #002: After some creative rewriting, a power source was tapped.

Log Entry #001: The Talon Company was paid, as nothing says "equality" like a fistful of Caps.

- Chinese Army Spec. Ops. Training Manual (1/25)
- Launch Codes

② Turret Control System

Hack to power the turrets down.

③ Work Bench

- Work Bench (1 of 46)

On the exterior circular balcony, fight the Talon Merc who's usually armed with a Missile Launcher (you may have tagged him from the ground), and work your way clockwise to an upper metal door.

④ Dish Access room

There are footlockers and a Chem, as well as cots to sleep in. The Satellite Control Terminal is nonfunctional until you input the launch codes. Race outside via the adjacent hatch and watch the massive orbital strike peppering the landscape with explosions!

- First Aid Box Health and Chems

1.04: FORT CONSTANTINE (LAT -17/LONG 26)

- Miscellaneous Quest: You Gotta Shoot 'Em In The Head
- Threat Level: 4
- Danger: Low Radiation
- Collectibles: Bobblehead, Fat Man, Fat Man Mini-Nuke, Nuka-Cola Quantum, Scribe Pre-War Book (3), Skill Book (7)
- Area Is Locked
- Guns And Ammunition
- Health And Chems
- Interior Exploration
- Rare Or Powerful Item (2)
- Sleep Mattress
- Hostiles: Robot Genus, Turret

MAPS AND LOCATIONS
Fort Constantine Exterior

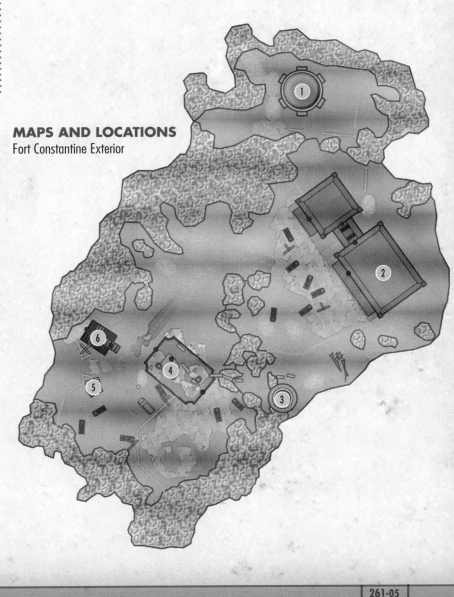

TRAINING — BESTIARY — MAIN QUEST — MISC. QUESTS — TOUR — COMPLETION — APPENDICES

Fort Constantine Interior

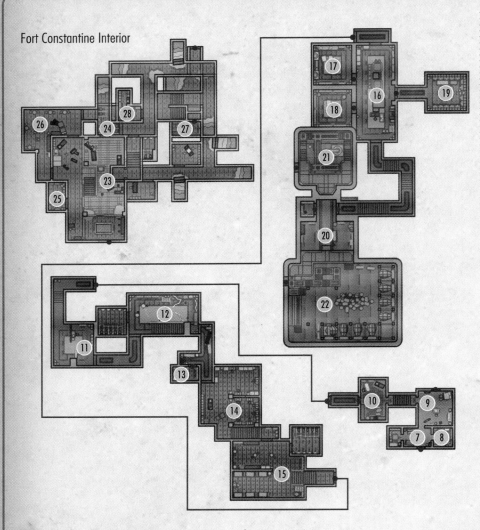

6 CO Quarters

A sturdy hut with two entrances, this is the best location to head for if you have all three Special Keys and want to investigate the interior.

CO QUARTERS

Note
You can access the various Interior locations in any order you like.

7 Entrance hall

There's some Abraxo Cleaner in the room to the west.

- Scribe Pre-War Book (1/98)

8 Kitchen

- Nuka-Cola Quantum (2/94)

9 Bedroom

Check the telephone table and bed for collectibles, then head downstairs.

- Scribe Pre-War Book (2/98)
- Guns and Bullets (1/25)

10 Cellar

To the south is an open safe with the Bobblehead, scattered Caps, and collectibles. Check the corpse for more. Progress farther by using Ted Strayer's Special Key. Otherwise, the Launch Control Bunker is impenetrable.

- 10mm Pistol and Ammo
- Fort Constantine Launch Codes
- Bobblehead: Big Guns (2/20)
- Stealth Boy
- Chinese Army: Spec. Ops. Training Manual (2/25)

LAUNCH CONTROL BUNKER

11 Gate Room

A few Caps and Ammo are on the desk too.

- Ammo Box Ammunition (3)
- Assault Rifle

12 Medical Room

There's a few items in the lockers, scattered Chems, and little else except an angry robot.

13 Storeroom

Accessed via a wall terminal or a locked door. Inside are some common items.

- First Aid Box Health and Chems

Tara was one of five mercenaries hired by Allistair Tenpenny to infiltrate Fort Constantine and retrieve an experimental suit of armor. Reports were that she was mauled by Ghouls, but in reality, she reached the last chamber but lacked the key to unlock the door. She was shot by a Robobrain, and her body remains here to this day.

Consult **Miscellaneous Quest: You Gotta Shoot 'Em in the Head**; the following characters have the necessary keys to access Fort Constantine (commence the Quest first, before gathering each key):

- Supreme Commander and President for Life Dave: The Republic of Dave [Location 3.03]
- Dukov: Dukov's Place [Location 9.08]
- Ted Strayer: Rivet City [Location 9.15]

1 Water Tower

This is close to Enclave Camp E1.01 (if the Enclave are active) and offers good views of the nearby buildings.

2 Bomb Storage

This is securely locked at ground level or is accessible if you have the Warhead Storage Key (located within the belly of this base). Note the exterior balcony linking both buildings.

3 Silo Hatch

More of a landmark than anything else, this is inaccessible; open all the mesh gates between here and the parking lot to easily escape.

4 Personnel Offices

Offers three entrances and a parking lot on three sides. One entrance is via the upper roof and some planks. There are Ammo Boxes in the roof's southwest corner.

- Ammo Box Ammunition (2)

5 Shack

Expect Robot resistance and perhaps combat with Brotherhood Outcasts here. There's common Ammo in the lockers and filing cabinets.

14 Launch Control Room

Hack the terminal and launch an ICBM (Inter-Continental Ballistic Missile) if you took the launch codes from the CO safe. However, the system malfunctions. Check the desks for Skill Books.

- Duck and Cover! (1/25)
- Big Book of Science (1/25)

15 Recreation and Barracks

Check the footlockers by the bunk beds for items. Sleep here if you wish. Check the desk for a Pre-War Book. Open the door down the stairs using Dukov's Special Key.

- Scribe Pre-War Book (3/98)
- First Aid Box Health and Chems (2)

BOMB STORAGE

16 Machine Room

There are two doors on one side and one on the other. The west doors feature a wall terminal and a door, which lead to weapons storage rooms. To the east is a dead Raider; this is Tara, and she's carrying the Warhead Storage Key. The door to the east unlocks using Dave's Special Key and leads to the experimental chamber.

- Warhead Storage Key

17 Weapons Storage Room (North)

- Assault Rifle (6)
- 10mm Submachine Gun (4)
- Sniper Rifle
- Frag and Pulse Grenades
- Guns and Bullets (2/25)

18 Weapons Storage Room (South)

- Ammo Box Ammunition (15)

19 Experimental Chamber

Unlocked using Dave's Special Key.

- Fat Man (2/9)
- Mini-Nuke (5/71)
- Mini-Nuke (6/71)
- D.C. Journal of Internal Medicine (1/25)
- T-51b Power Armor (4/89)
- T-51b Power Helmet (5/89)

20 Ruined Office Area

Expect a few scattered items, and check the table for the Mini-Nuke. The locked storage room contains assorted junk. Directly above is a balcony leading to an exterior vantage point and linking the north and south chambers.

- First Aid Box Health and Chems
- Mini-Nuke (7/71)

21 Generator Room

There are winding catwalk stairs to navigate in here.

22 Warhead Storage Warehouse

There's access to the parking lot exterior and exposure to radiation inside.

PERSONNEL OFFICES

Note
This is an independent structure and doesn't link to the other buildings.

23 Foyer and Recreation Area

Watch for the turret above the pool table on the south balcony. Enter from the roof if you want to deactivate it safely, or Sneak to avoid it.

24 Restrooms

There are a few Chems along with these weapons.

- Chinese Assault Rifles (2)

25 Storage Room

- First Aid Box Health and Chems

26 Small Mess Hall

- First Aid Box Health and Chems

27 Locked Storage Room

- First Aid Box Health and Chems
- Grognak the Barbarian (1/25)

28 Turret Control Room (Second Floor)

Hack this terminal to shut down the balcony turret. The nearby stairwell leads up to the roof.

1.05: SATCOM ARRAY NW-07C (LAT -28/LONG 20)

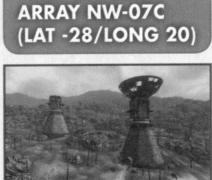

- Threat Level: 3
- Faction: Enclave, Wastelander
- Services: Repairer, Trader
- Collectible: Skill Book
- Guns And Ammunition
- Health And Chems
- Highly Visible Landmark
- Interior Exploration
- Hostiles: Enclave Officer, Scientist, Sentry Bot, Soldier

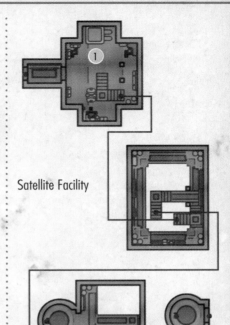

Satellite Facility

NORTHEAST SATELLITE TOWER

The threat level of this twin satellite facility array depends on whether the Enclave have emerged from Raven Rock; before this occurs, the northeast tower is completely barren. There are no enemies to face or bodies to loot. However, once the Enclave descend, expect a reasonably sized hit squad of a robot, an officer, and a soldier, along with a sniper on the upper gantry.

1 Enclave Scientist Massacre

This occurs only if the Enclave are active in the area; otherwise, it is silent in here. Check the shelves for food and a water fountain, then follow the catwalk to the ladder.

- First Aid Box Health and Chems
- Enclave Ammo Box Ammunition (5; if the Enclave are present)

On the exterior circular balcony, fight the Enclave Soldier (you may have tagged him from the ground), and work your way clockwise to an upper metal door. This leads to a tiny interior chamber with another ladder leading up. Get ready for some missile launching! Sometimes, two Vertibirds pass overhead as you emerge onto the dish; optionally shoot them down. The dish remains safe, aside from the holes in its structure.

If you want a quick exit, step to the middle balcony where you encountered the Enclave Soldier and leap off the side, then sidestep quickly toward the tower's interior. You can "slide" down the outside of the tower as well; this is quicker but more dangerous!

SOUTHWEST SATELLITE TOWER

This area is unchanged whether there's an Enclave threat or not. The satellite tower is completely sealed, but the dish fell off the tower decades ago, and the rusting remains are now a ramshackle trading post, with a Scavenger inside. He or she can Trade with you, as well as Repair items, but flees or is killed when the Enclave arrive. You can also buy, sell, Pickpocket, and Steal any of it.

1.06: BROADCAST TOWER KB5 (LAT -23/LONG 20)

- Threat Level: 3
- Collectibles: Scribe Pre-War Book, Skill Book
- Health And Chems
- Highly Visible Landmark
- Interior Exploration
- Radio Signal
- Sleep Mattress
- Hostile: Deathclaw

Drainage Chamber

You're in Deathclaw country, and the Threat Level reflects this. Climb to the top of the hill that the mast sits on, and pull the electrical switch to pick up Morse code from Radio Signal Alfa Lima. Triangulate the signal to locate a Drainage Channel (Secondary Location 1.G) down the hill a little, to the east.

- Radio Signal Alfa Lima

Tip

Triangulate a radio signal by listening to the sound quality. When the sound becomes clearer, you know you're nearing your target. If it sounds muffled, staticky, or cuts out completely, you're heading in the wrong direction.

① A Small, L-Shaped Tunnel

The steps up to the door contain a long-dead corpse; check it out.

- 10mm Pistol
- Tumblers Today (1/25)

② Storage Room

Unlock, and locate food, alcohol, and Purified Water, as well as a mattress to sleep on.

- Scribe Pre-War Book (4/98)

1.07: DEATHCLAW SANCTUARY (LAT -22/LONG 20)

- Threat Level: 5
- Faction: Enclave
- Collectibles: Bobblehead, Fat Man Mini-Nuke, Nuka-Cola Quantum, Skill Book (2)
- Guns And Ammunition
- Interior Exploration
- Loads O' Caps
- Rare Or Powerful Item (2)
- Hostile: Deathclaw
- Hostile: Modified Deathclaw

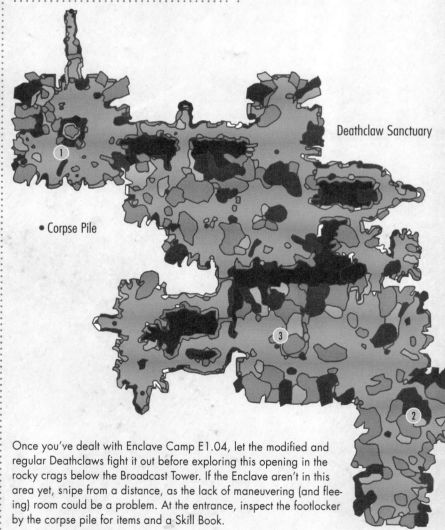

Deathclaw Sanctuary

• Corpse Pile

Once you've dealt with Enclave Camp E1.04, let the modified and regular Deathclaws fight it out before exploring this opening in the rocky crags below the Broadcast Tower. If the Enclave aren't in this area yet, snipe from a distance, as the lack of maneuvering (and fleeing) room could be a problem. At the entrance, inspect the footlocker by the corpse pile for items and a Skill Book.

- Duck and Cover! (2/25)

① Initial Chamber

Beware of Deathclaws prowling this and all other linked chambers. There is a corpse pile here around a large central column, with the following available items:

- Bobblehead: Endurance (3/20)
- Nuka-Cola Quantum (3/94)
- Mini-Nuke (8/71)
- Nikola Tesla and You (1/25)

② Bloody Grotto

Maneuver through various linked chambers; there are nine corpse piles to search. Check the Wasteland Merchant corpses for a good deal of items (and lots of Caps). There is also a grotto with bloody water and a unique weapon.

- Gatling Laser — Vengeance (6/89)

③ Enclave Corpse Pile

This location has a unique body to find; search him for the item, once the Enclave arrive at Camp E1.01.

- Ripper — Jack (7/89)

1.08: DICKERSON TABERNACLE CHAPEL (LAT -19/LONG 19)

- Threat Level: 2
- Rare Or Powerful Item
- Collectible: Skill Book
- Sleep Mattress
- Guns And Ammunition
- Hostile: Drifter
- Highly Visible Landmark

FREEFORM QUEST: HIGH PLAINS DRIFTER

Sitting on a blasted heath are the remains of a once-thriving Tabernacle Church, now a dilapidated shell that's home to a Drifter, standing on the old roof supports. Sneak in the back to ambush him; knock him off his perch to secure the items he's carrying. The Reservist's Rifle and Oasis Coordinates are of interest, especially the rifle for long-range Deathclaw takedowns. The Oasis Coordinates and the Druid's Hood indicate that the Drifter may once have been part of

the Treeminders. Check the Oasis Coordinates (lat -03/long 28), and search the area for the following items:

- Reservist's Rifle (8/89)
- Guns and Bullets (3/25)
- Oasis Druid Hood
- Ammo Box Ammunition (5)
- Oasis Coordinates
- Combat Armor

1.09: MASON DIXON SALVAGE (LAT -14/LONG 21)

- Threat Level: 3
- Interior Exploration
- Faction: Super Mutant
- Sleep Mattress
- Collectible: Skill Book (3)
- Wastelander Captive
- Guns And Ammunition
- Hostiles: Centaur, Super Mutant Genus
- Health And Chems

Once a rural scrapyard, this is now a place where Super Mutants return from Wasteland hunting with their live captives and begin ferrying them to Vault 87 for mutation.. There are approximately five Super Mutants and two pet Centaurs here, and there are several entrances—to the north, west, and south. You can blast vehicles and set them alight, but this can ruin the chances of freeing captives and grabbing items. After you engage the Super Mutants and score a victory, begin scavenging the area; there are truck containers with Ammo Boxes and bedding. There are also two shacks with a footlocker and the following items:

- Ammo Box Ammunition (6)
- D.C. Journal of Internal Medicine (2/25)
- First Aid Box Health and Chems
- Nikola Tesla and You (2/25)
- Tumblers Today (2/25)

> Rescue any captives and take their gift for a small boost to your Karma. Refuse their gift for a larger boost.

1.10: MOUNT MABEL CAMPGROUND (LAT -21/LONG 17)

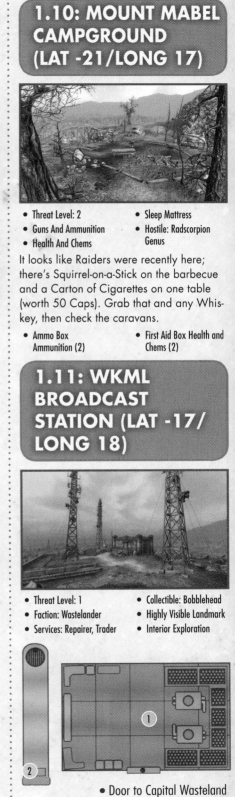

- Threat Level: 2
- Sleep Mattress
- Guns And Ammunition
- Hostile: Radscorpion Genus
- Health And Chems

It looks like Raiders were recently here; there's Squirrel-on-a-Stick on the barbecue and a Carton of Cigarettes on one table (worth 50 Caps). Grab that and any Whiskey, then check the caravans.

- Ammo Box Ammunition (2)
- First Aid Box Health and Chems (2)

1.11: WKML BROADCAST STATION (LAT -17/LONG 18)

- Threat Level: 1
- Collectible: Bobblehead
- Faction: Wastelander
- Highly Visible Landmark
- Services: Repairer, Trader
- Interior Exploration

- Door to Capital Wasteland

① Station Area

This Broadcast Station is deserted except for when a Scavenger Trader visits, ready to sell, buy, and Repair. There are no radio signals and nothing inside the tower complex.

TRAINING — BESTIARY — MAIN QUEST — MISC. QUESTS — TOUR — COMPLETION — APPENDICES

② Cistern

However, there is a hidden drainage grate south of and under the rocky outcrop. Beside a corpse is a .32 Pistol, Ammo, Purified Water, a Stimpak, a Stealth Boy, and, most importantly, the Bobblehead: Explosives.

- .32 Pistol and Ammo
- Stealth Boy
- Bobblehead: Explosives (4/20)

1.12: THE SILVER LINING DRIVE-IN (LAT -15/LONG 17)

- Threat Level: 1
- Collectible: Skill Book
- Sleep Mattress

Close by the Broadcast Station and Drowned Devil's Crossing are the remains of an old drive-in theater. Aside from the scattered Bottle Caps and burned books, there's a Grognak the Barbarian at the entrance and a place to sleep.

- Grognak the Barbarian (2/25)

1.13: DROWNED DEVIL'S CROSSING (LAT -14/LONG 18)

- Threat Level: 2
- Faction: Raider
- Danger: Low Radiation
- Hostiles: Raider, Guard Dog

On one of the road trails is a small collapsed bridge over the remains of a stream. Beware of three or four Raiders to the south, on the streambed; sneak and ambush them. Also watch out for nearby Raider Guard Dogs prowling the red Jackknifed Truck (Location 1.J).

1.14: ABANDONED CAR FORT (LAT -24/LONG 14)

- Threat Level: 1
- Collectible: Skill Book
- Guns And Ammunition
- Sleep Mattress

There's an Ammo Box behind one stack of cars and another five boxes in the area's middle. There are some other items in a small crate, plus Tales of a Junktown Jerky Vendor to peruse. Sleep on either mattress if you wish.

- Ammo Box Ammunition (6)
- Tales of a Junktown Jerky Vendor (1/24)

1.15: FADED POMP ESTATES (LAT -17/LONG 15)

- Threat Level: 1
- Collectible: Skill Book
- Sleep Mattress
- Hostiles: Enclave Eyebot, Robot Genus

There's a couple mattresses to sleep on and a copy of Pugilism Illustrated at the foot of a fireplace. In another house is a small safe. There's a Baseball Bat in the nearby field (part of Roosevelt Academy).

- Safe Items
- Pugilism Illustrated (1/25)

1.16: ROOSEVELT ACADEMY (LAT -17/LONG 14)

- Micellaneous Quest: Agatha's Song
- Threat Level: 5
- Faction: Super Mutant
- Danger: Gas Leak, Grenade Bouquet, Terminal Trap, High Radiation
- Collectibles: Nuka-Cola Quantum, Scrible Pre-War Book (2), Skill Book (4)
- Guns And Ammunition
- Highly Visible Landmark
- Interior Exploration
- Sleep Mattress
- Friendly: Captive Wastelander
- Hostiles: Centaur, Radroach, Super Mutant Genus

MAPS AND LOCATIONS

Roosevelt Academy (Exterior)

① Roosevelt Academy Building

A baseball field is to the west. There are two entrances; enter this building first.

- Baseball Bat

② Roosevelt Arts and Athletics Building

Try catching the Super Mutants in a nearby Coach Liner explosion.

Roosevelt Library

The easier way into this building is via an interior connecting tunnel system.

③ Academy Floor 1

 Note

You can access the various Interior locations in any order you like. The following exploration assumes you entered the Academy building first.

④ Nurse's Office

Various items are scattered on desks. There is a terminal and a safe; break into either.

- D.C. Journal of Internal Medicine (3/25)
- First Aid Box Health and Chems (2)
- Blood Pack (2)
- Floor Safe Items

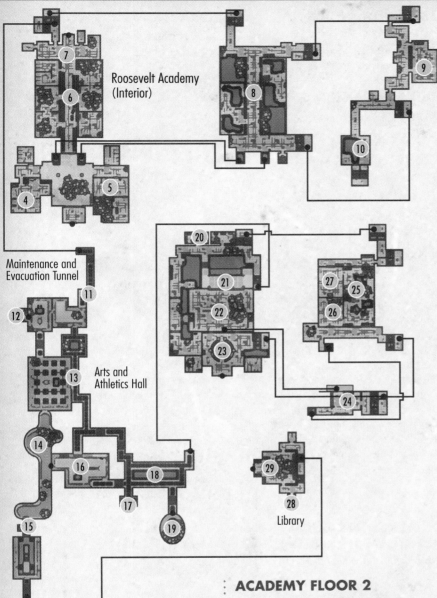

Roosevelt Academy
(Interior)

Maintenance and
Evacuation Tunnel

Arts and
Athletics Hall

Library

MAINTENANCE AND EVACUATION TUNNEL

> **Note**
> This tunnel links the three buildings together; the ideal exploration route is to head to the Arts and Athletics Hall first, then to the Library.

11 Fridge Barricade

Beware the Grenade Bouquet by the fridge barricade.

- Frag Grenade (3)

12 Locked Storage Room

A captive Wastelander is tethered in here.

13 Flammable Corridor

14 Flammable Sewer

The weapon and Ammo is near the barrel with the lantern on it. The Hatch Door is locked.

- Ammo Box Ammunition (3)
- Assault Rifle

15 Alcove and Electrical Switch

This activates the trap-flap doors, accessing the connecting room with stairs to the Library.

- First Aid Box Health and Chems

16 Machine Room

This activates the trap-flap doors, accessing the connecting room with stairs to the Library.

- Pugilism Illustrated (3/25)

17 Alcove with Radioactive Barrels

- Ammo Box Ammunition (3)
- Sledgehammer
- .32 Pistol and Ammo

18 Flammable Corridors

Danger! Escaping gas!

19 The Oval Alcove

A captive Wastelander is trussed up in here. The door to the Arts and Athletics Hall is nearby.

ARTS AND ATHLETICS HALL GROUND FLOOR

> **Note**
> The following exploration assumes you entered from the Maintenance Tunnel.

20 Northern Rooms

- First Aid Box Health and Chems
- Pre-War Book (6/98)

---

5 Administration Office

Watch for a Super Mutant leaping out in the headmaster's room, which also contains a terminal that allows Protectron activation; there are specific dialog options to try with this mechanoid. Check the restroom for a Skill Book.

- Pre-War Book (5/98)
- Pugilism Illustrated (2/25)

6 Main Classroom Corridor

Check the lockers for ammo. Watch for Cherry Bombs in the restrooms, Super Mutants firing down through ceiling holes, and the Grenade Bouquet in the northeast classroom doorway.

- Frag Grenade (3)

7 Northern Corridor

There is a tiny storage room with a dead settler inside (northeast). Northwest are stairs up and down.

ACADEMY FLOOR 2

8 Main Classroom Corridor

One classroom to the west has flammable gas leaking out. The middle classroom to the east has an Ammo Box.

- Ammo Box Ammunition

ACADEMY FLOORS 3 AND 4

9 Staff Room

Beware of the booby-trapped terminal! There is food in the fridge.

- Frag Grenade
- First Aid Box Health and Chems

10 Ammo Stash (Floor 4)

Climb to the wrecked room that has a hole down to the entrance foyer. Beware Super Mutants! Check the upper alcove for the stash.

- Ammo Box Ammunition (3)

TRAINING — BESTIARY — MAIN QUEST — MISC. QUESTS — TOUR — COMPLETION — APPENDICES

21 Stage

This item is useful during **Miscellaneous Quest: Agatha's Song**.

- Sheet Music Book

22 Grand Hall

23 Southern Reception Foyer and Desks

ARTS AND ATHLETICS HALL SECOND FLOOR

24 Staff Room and Hall Balcony

ARTS AND ATHLETICS HALL THIRD FLOOR

25 Dilapidated Locker Rooms

There's a place to sleep here.

26 Office (Southwest)

This has a Wall Safe to break open.

- First Aid Box Health and Chems (2)
- Ammo Box Ammunition (2)
- Wall Safe Items
- Tumblers Today (3/25)
- D.C. Journal of Internal Medicine (3/25)

27 Office (Northwest)

This also has a Wall Safe to break open and Shotgun Shells on the table.

- First Aid Box Health and Chems
- Baseball Bat (3)
- Wall Safe Items

LIBRARY

28 Restroom

- Blood Pack
- Stealth Boy

29 Library Entrance

The double doors leading to the Capital Wasteland are locked. Watch for the tough Super Mutant; check his body for a key to easily exit here. Locate the desk and the Wall Safe for the following items:

- Sawed-Off Shotgun and Ammo
- First Aid Box Health and Chems
- Stealth Boy
- Wall Safe Items
- Nuka-Cola Quantum (4/94)
- Roosevelt Library Key

Secondary Locations

1.A: RAIDER WHARF (LAT -24/LONG 25)

- Collectibles: Fat Man Mini-Nuke, Skill Book
- Guns And Ammunition
- Health And Chems
- Sleep Mattress
- Hostiles: Mirelurk Genus, Raider

- Threat Level: 2
- Faction: Raider
- Danger: Low Radiation

You're in the shadow of Raven Rock and SatCom Array NW-05a, and there are Mirelurks to deal with en route to this location. The wharf itself has Chems, Drink, Mirelurk meat, an Ammo Box, some Stimpaks, and a Mini-Nuke. There's a place to sleep and a boat moored a few feet to the southwest that contains a Stealth Boy, some Whiskey, and a Skill Book.

- Food and Drink
- Health and Chems
- Ammo Box Ammunition
- Mini-Nuke (9/71)
- Nikola Tesla and You (3/25)

Caution

Don't swim or step inside these boats expecting to wiggle out of the front windshield area; the space is too small to maneuver through and you could get trapped!

1.B: BROTHERHOOD OUTCAST SHACK (LAT -14/LONG 25)

- Collectible: Nuka-Cola Quantum, Schematic
- Guns And Ammunition
- Work Bench
- Sleep Mattress
- Hostile: Brotherhood Outcast

- Threat Level: 2
- Faction: Brotherhood Outcast

In the shadow of the SatCom Array NN-03d (Location 2.02) lies a small, run-down shack guarded by two Brotherhood Outcasts. There's a Work Bench here, a rather gooey place to sleep, some Ammo, tools, and junk you might need. Check the table for Shishkebab Schematics, and shoot the Quantum bottle off the roof.

- Work Bench (2 of 47)
- Ammo Box Ammunition (2)
- Schematic: Shishkebab (6/23)
- Nuka-Cola Quantum (5/94)

1.C: JACKKNIFED CHINESE INTERNMENT TRUCK (ON FREEWAY; LAT -27/LONG 20)

- Threat Level: 1
- Collectible: Skill Book
- Guns And Ammunition
- Health And Chems

Check a nearby vehicle for Frag Grenades near a skeleton. Continue on to the jackknifed truck; outside are two Ammo Boxes. Inside are the skeletal remains of Chinese Americans; learn their names by reading the Holotape inside the truck. The container also has Purified Water, some Chems, two First Aid Boxes, and Pugilism Illustrated.

- Internment Note
- First Aid Box Health and Chems
- Ammo Box Ammunition (2)
- Pugilism Illustrated (4/25)

1.D: JACKKNIFED TRUCK (ON FREEWAY) (LAT -26/LONG 20)

- Threat Level: 2
- Collectible: Fat Man Mini-Nuke, Skill Book
- Guns And Ammunition
- Health And Chems
- Sleep Mattress

Watch for an explosion, which may blast parts of a dead scientist out of the container. Search any body part for a Skill Book. Inside, there are Stimpaks, a Laser Rifle, a Mini-Nuke, and a mattress. Watch the fissures on the freeway.

- Big Book of Science (2/25)
- Laser Rifle
- Mini-Nuke (10/71)

1.E: OVERLOOK RAIDER SHACK (LAT -25/LONG 21)

- Collectibles: Fat Man Mini-Nuke (2), Skill Book (2)
- Guns And Ammunition
- Health And Chems
- Hostiles: Mirelurk Genus, Raider, Raider Guard Dog

- Threat Level: 2
- Faction: Raider

There are four Raiders and a Guard Dog to deal with. Inside the house is a gruesome freezer, some Ammo Boxes near the fireplace, and an easily missed set of shelves with Chems, Beer, and a Skill Book. Check the bath for a Mini-Nuke before leaving; a skeleton makes a rude gesture with one! Then head west (or northwest from the shack), and find the skeleton crumpled next to three Ammo Boxes and a Skill Book.

- Ammo Box Ammunition (6)
- Tumblers Today (4/25)
- Mini-Nuke (11/71)
- Mini-Nuke (12/71)
- IDuck and Cover! (3/25)

1.F: RAIDER WRECKAGE FORTIFICATIONS (LAT -24/LONG 19)

- Threat Level: 3
- Faction: Raider
- Collectible: Skill Book
- Guns And Ammunition
- Health And Chems
- Hostile: Raider

The top defense holds various junk and Whiskey, a First Aid Box, an Ammo Box, a great melee weapon called the Super Sledge, and a Skill Book hidden in a crate of tin cans. Charge the second defense for a Grenade Ammo Box, more Whiskey, a Stealth Boy, and some Iguana Bits. The bottom defense has Beer, Chems, and an Ammo Box.

- First Aid Box Health and Chems
- Super Sledge
- Grognak the Barbarian (3/25)
- Ammo Box Ammunition (3)

Note

The defenses may be made of crushed cars, but they aren't the exploding kind; don't waste your ammunition.

1.G: DRAINAGE CHANNEL (ADJACENT TO BROADCAST TOWER KB5; LAT -22/LONG 20)

- Threat Level: 3

For tactics and the available items here, check out Location 1.06: Broadcast Tower KB5 (lat -23/long 20).

1.H: DEATHCLAW GORGE (ROPE BRIDGES; LAT -21/LONG 19)

- Threat Level: 1

A set of two rope bridges are on the outskirts of the Deathclaw Sanctuary. You won't attract Deathclaws unless you're making loud noises. This is a route up to the Broadcast Tower, Drainage Channel, and a lone Enclave Camp [E1.04].

1.I: JUNCTION SHACK (LAT -20/LONG 21)

- Threat Level: 1
- Guns and Ammunition

At the road's junction, you can go west to the Death-claw Sanctuary and the Broadcast Tower or north to Fort Constantine. There's little else except the wind whistling through the corrugated metal. Look southeast to spot the Dickerson Tabernacle Church and the WKML Broadcast Station.

1.J: JACKKNIFED TRUCK (NEAR CROSSING) (LAT -15/LONG 19)

- Threat Level 1
- Faction: Raider
- Collectible: Skill Book
- Health and Chems
- Hostile: Raider Guard Dog

Near the Drowned Devil's Crossing, the loot inside is reasonable. Amid the Stimpaks, Chems, and junk is a safe with a Skill Book next to it.

- Chems
- Safe Items
- Tumblers Today (5/25)

1.K: BLOCKED TUNNEL ENTRANCE (LAT -23/LONG 17)

- Threat level: 1
- Hostile: Robobrain

This offers excellent views of the broken freeway to the west. Beware the Raider fortifications just north of you.

1.L: CARAVAN WRECKAGE (LAT -20/LONG 17)

- Threat Level: 1

The eastern entrance to Mount Mabel Campground comprises a pair of rusting caravans near an old flagpole.

1.M: MONORAIL TRAIN WRECKAGE (LAT -28/LONG 15)

- Threat level: 2
- Highly visible landmark
- Hostile: Deathclaw, Robobrain

The remains of this Monorail track stretches all the way from the edge of the D.C. Ruins; follow this track if you wish.

1.N: JACKKNIFED TRUCK (ON FREEWAY) (LAT -21/LONG 15)

- Threat Level: 1
- Hostile: Mirelurk

On the cusp of Zone 4 is another area of freeway bridge that's been ravaged by time and radiation. Beware of the gaps in the ground.

1.O: BLOCKED TUNNEL ENTRANCE (LAT -20/LONG 15)

- Threat Level: 1

Even though this offers good views of the broken freeway to the west, it is completely blocked. Try climbing it and sniping the Mirelurks below.

1.P: TRUCK AND CAR WRECKAGE (ON FREEWAY) (LAT -20/LONG 14)

- Threat Level: 1

Nothing here except an explosion opportunity. Stand well back!

ENCLAVE CAMP LOCATIONS

CAMP E1.01 (LAT -15/LONG 28)

- Main Quest: Picking up the Trail
- Threat Level: 1
- Guns and Ammunition

There is a small contingent guarding the Water Tower gate at the edge of Fort Constantine.

- Enclave Crate Ammunition (2)

CAMP E1.02 (LAT -23/LONG 25)

- Main Quest: Picking up the Trail
- Threat Level: 2
- Danger: Low Radiation
- Guns and Ammunition

There is a small contingent near the irradiated pond, where a Wastelander and Feral Ghouls have been massacred.

- Enclave Crate Ammunition (3)
- Ammo Box Ammunition (2)

CAMP E1.03 (LAT -28/LONG 20)

- Main Quest: Picking up the Trail
- Threat Level: 2

A squad commandeers the nearby SatCom Array, with troops on the ground and in the exterior balcony.

CAMP E1.04 (LAT -22/LONG 20)

- Main Quest: Picking up the Trail
- Threat Level: 5
- Guns and Ammunition

There is a Deathclaw-capture squad, with a modified Deathclaw near the Sanctuary. Extreme danger!

- Enclave Crate Ammunition (3)

CAMP E1.05 (LAT -25/LONG 16)

- Main Quest: Picking up the Trail
- Threat Level: 2
- Guns and Ammunition

This is a tactical position on the freeway ruins, where a Wastelander, a Brahmin, and some Ghouls have been massacred.

- Enclave Crate Ammunition (3)

CAMP E1.06 (LAT -15/LONG 17)

- Main Quest: Picking up the Trail
- Threat Level: 2

An Enclave strike force dropped in by Vertibird, just east of the Silver Lining Drive-In.

TRAINING — BESTIARY — MAIN QUEST — MISC. QUESTS — TOUR — COMPLETION — APPENDICES

Zone 2: Northern Mountains

TOPOGRAPHICAL OVERVIEW

Dominated by treacherous mountain terrain to the north and more manageable lands to the south, this Wasteland zone is slightly less populated than others but holds some astonishing discoveries. Get your bearings by following the two main roads that run south into Zone 5 and join the east–west road. Cutting diagonally across is a crumbling freeway and monorail line (another excellent landmark to find your location). There's one large settlement—the Slaver camp of Paradise Falls—and a few hidden points of interest for when you're not trekking through the bleak and desolate landscape.

AVAILABLE COLLECTIBLES (ZONE 2)

- Bobbleheads: 1/20
- Fat Men: 0/9
- Mini-Nukes: 3/71
- Unique Items: 12/89
- Nuka-Cola Quantum: 8/94
- Schematics: 1/23
- Scribe Pre-War Books: 3/98
- Skill Book (Barter): 1/24
- Skill Book (Big Guns): 1/25
- Skill Book (Energy Weapons): 2/25
- Skill Book (Explosives): 1/25
- Skill Book (Lockpick): 0/25

- Skill Book (Medicine): 2/25
- Skill Book (Melee Weapons): 1/25
- Skill Book (Repair): 0/25
- Skill Book (Science): 1/25
- Skill Book (Small Guns): 0/25
- Skill Book (Sneak): 1/25
- Skill Book (Speech): 0/25
- Skill Book (Unarmed): 2/25
- Work Bench: 3/46
- Holotapes (Keller): 0/5
- Holotapes (Replicated Man): 3/19

PRIMARY LOCATIONS

2.01: Oasis (lat -03/long 28)

2.02: SatCom Array NN-03d (lat -13/long 25)

2.03: MDPL-21 Power Station (lat -10/long 26)

2.04: Clifftop Shacks (lat 00/long 26)

2.05: Montgomery County Reservoir (lat -06/long 22)

2.06: Broadcast Tower LP8 (lat -04/long 24)

2.07: Reclining Groves Resort Homes (lat -02/long 20)

2.08: Paradise Falls (lat -09/long 16)

2.09: MDPL-13 Power Station (lat 02/long 17)

SECONDARY LOCATIONS

2.A: Upper Trails (Rope Bridge) (lat -10/long 29)

2.B: Toxic Pond (lat -09/long 30)

2.C: Monorail Carriage Wreckage (lat -06/long 28)

2.D: Oasis Entrance (Rope Bridge; lat -05/long 29)

2.E: Abandoned Tent (lat -12/long 23)

2.F: Irradiated Silo and Outbuildings (lat -07/long 23)

2.G: Crashed Anomaly (lat 03/long 22)

2.H: Ant Tunnel to Musty Cavern (lat -11/long 20)

2.I: Military Checkpoint (lat -05/long 20)

2.J: Irradiated Silo and Barn (lat 00/long 20)

2.K: Traffic Line (lat -11/long 17)

2.L: Wood Planks to Warren (lat -02/long 18)

2.M: Overturned City Liner (lat 00/long 18)

2.N: Monorail Train Wreckage (Raider Camp; lat 00/long 14)

2.O: Minefield Water Tower (lat 03/long 14)

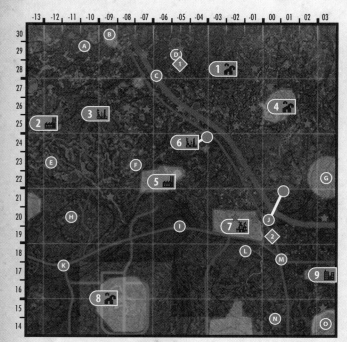

Primary Locations

2.01: OASIS
(LAT -03/LONG 28)

- Miscellaneous Quest: Oasis
- Freeform Quest (4)
- Threat Level: 3
- Danger: Low Radiation
- Faction: Wastelander
- Collectibles: Fat Man Mini-Nuke , Nuka-Cola Quantum, Scribe

- Pre-War Book, Skill Book (Medicine)
- Area Is Locked
- Guns And Ammunition
- Interior Exploration
- Perk!
- Rare Or Powerful Item
- Sleep Mattress
- Hostile: Mirelurk Genus

INHABITANTS

TREE FATHER BIRCH

The 50-year-old chief of Oasis, Birch spends most of his time in the Pavilion, sitting on his throne, occasionally eating, and sleeping for a few hours at night. He also walks around Oasis, overseeing the village more directly. While the village is ostensibly a democratic commune, Tree Father Birch sees himself as the group's spiritual and temporal leader. He has cast himself in role similar to a high priest, worshipping the god-spirit Harold.

LEAF MOTHER LAUREL

The wife of Tree Father Birch and fellow leader of the people of Oasis, Leaf Mother Laurel spends much of her day wandering around Oasis, tending the plants and flowers, and speaking with the people of the village—her daughter Sapling Yew usually at her side or playing nearby. She believes it is her responsibility to tend to the spiritual and mental well-being of her fellow villagers.

SAPLING YEW

The only child of the Oasis village leaders, Tree Father Birch and Leaf Mother Laurel, eight-year-old Sapling Yew divides her time among several activities, including eating and sleeping in her family's quarters and playing and gardening in the village with her mother. She also loves to play in the Grove, climb on and around the god-spirit, and fiddle with her Bear Charm.

BLOOMSEER POPLAR

She is the Oasis oracle. Although a few of the occasional visitors may scoff at her "fortune-telling," this 60-year-old soothsayer has often amazed the other villagers with her powers of premonition. She tells

INTERIOR MAPS AND LOCATIONS

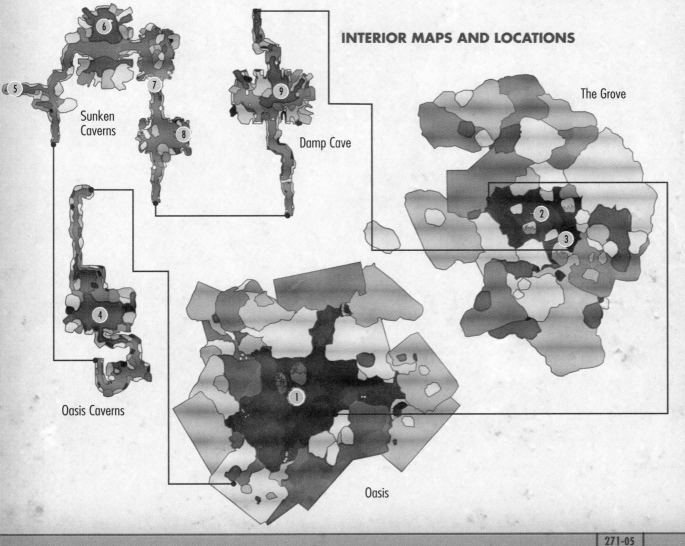

The Grove

Sunken Caverns

Damp Cave

Oasis Caverns

Oasis

TRAINING — BESTIARY — MAIN QUEST — MISC. QUESTS — TOUR — COMPLETION — APPENDICES

you her history of seeking out Oasis due to a premonition. She is usually found in her cave tending her alchemical duties. She is loyal to Leaf Mother Laurel.

BRANCHTENDER CYPRESS

Although the Treeminders would love to renounce violence and weaponry, they aren't naive: Cypress is one of the main armed guardians of Oasis. He is generally found patrolling the entrance to the Oasis Caverns. Cypress is 25 years old and used to be a Wasteland Adventurer (not unlike yourself). He is extremely loyal to Tree Father Birch.

BRANCHTENDER LINDEN

He is one of the other main armed guardians of this sacred settlement. He is generally found wandering the woods of Oasis or on guard relief for Branchtender Maple. This 25-year-old used to be a Brotherhood of Steel Outcast, but a near-death experience and being healed in Oasis changed his outlook on life. He professes his loyalty to Leaf Mother Laurel.

BRANCHTENDER MAPLE

Maple is the first Treeminder you meet (along with Tree Father Birch), as she usually guards the entrance to Oasis. She is also 25 years old. After you enter the place, she returns outside to stay alert and halt any incursions. She only heads inside to eat meals and sleep, and then returns to her post. Branchtender Linden is her guard relief. She is the newest addition to Oasis and is extremely loyal to Tree Father Birch.

HAROLD

Harold is a spectacular mutation—he is a gnarled face growing in the Oasis Grove—and goes by many names: The Lord; Him; The One Who Grows, Gives, and Guides; and The Talking Tree. In addition, Harold has his own name for the growth that has been expanding out of him for years: Herbert. In turn, Herbert is also known by another name: Bob. Harold was once human and thinks he was exposed to the F.E.V. during an exploration of a military base called Mariposa.

OASIS

Oasis is a fertile, verdant dot in the center of all the desolation. This odd hidden vale is home to a strange, tribal-like people who call themselves the Treeminders. You are welcomed into Oasis with open arms, and their leader, Tree Father Birch, invites you to meet their god. Oasis is tucked away inside

a giant rocky outcrop in the mountains just northeast of the monorail and freeway skeletons, and the entrance is close to a rope bridge.

① Tree Father Birch's Pavilion

This holds a Basin of Purification. Explore as you please. To enter the gate to The Grove, you must first complete the Purification Ritual. The gate to the Oasis Caverns requires Branchtender Cypress's key to open or a proficient Lockpick skill.

You can interact with the Treeminders in the following ways:

All Treeminders: Give you more information on Oasis and their thoughts on Birch's and Laurel's plan.

Tree Father Birch: You can agree to undertake his Purification Ritual.

Tree Father Birch: You can agree to coat Harold's heart in Birch's sap.

Leaf Mother Laurel: You can agree to coat Harold's heart in Laurel's liniment.

Branchtender Cypress: You can acquire the Key to Oasis Caves from him (by asking or Pickpocketing).

Branchtender Cypress: If you utilize Birch's sap, you are awarded with a Missile Launcher and Ammunition.

Branchtender Maple: If you utilize Birch's sap, you are awarded with her garb.

Branchtender Linden: If you utilize Laurel's liniment, you are awarded with Brotherhood Outcast Power Armor.

Bloomseer Poplar: If you utilize Laurel's liniment, you are awarded with her Hood.

Harold: You can burn him. This causes all the Treeminders to turn hostile.

Harold: You can agree to destroy Harold's heart, splattering yourself in F.E.V.-tainted blood, infecting you with the Barkskin Perk.

- Linden's Outcast Power Armor (9/89)
- Maple's Garb (10/89)
- Poplar's Hood (11/89)
- Missile Launcher and Ammunition
- Barkskin Perk

THE GROVE
② The Talking Tree

Only accessible after the Purification Ritual. The central talking tree reveals himself to be Harold.

③ Locked Underwater Door

This leads to the Damp Cave. Watch your oxygen level!

OASIS CAVERNS
④ Grotto

This compact but winding cavern connects to the main Sunken Caverns. There are Mirelurks to defeat. Swim through and under the grotto to reach the door to the Sunken Caverns. There are Mirelurk Egg Clutches to dip into if you require Meat or undigested items.

- Mirelurk Meat

SUNKEN CAVERNS
⑤ Western Side Tunnel

Clear Mirelurks from the main tunnel so they don't ambush you. There's a dead Scavenger and some loot; search the area thoroughly (the Skill Book is in the tiny crate with the Baseball Glove)! There are Caps and a mattress too.

- Pre-War Book (7/98)
- Silenced 10mm Pistol and Ammo
- Stealth Boy
- D.C. Journal of Internal Medicine (4/25)

⑥ Main Grotto

Dive into the grotto to uncover common items and the Mini-Nuke.

⑦ Tree Roots

If you Lockpicked your way into here and massacred the Treeminders, you can't progress any further to Harold's Heart; tree roots block the access tunnel.

⑧ Harold's Heart

There are choices to make to conclude **Miscellaneous Quest: Oasis** here.

- Mini-Nuke (13/71)

DAMP CAVE
⑨ Mirelurk Pool

You can't access the southern part of this tunnel if you came in from The Grove or after you drop down, heading north. Check the bank for a Stimpak and these items:

- 10mm Pistol and Ammo
- Nuka-Cola Quantum (6/94)

FREEFORM QUEST: EXCOMMUNICATION

If you're rude to Father Tree Birch during your conversations, you're warned to halt that kind of talk. Repeat it again, and you're charged with blasphemy and given 10 minutes to leave Oasis or the Treeminders will temporarily renounce their pacifism. You can also turn the Treeminders hostile by attacking any of their flock or by burning Harold. The Treeminders don't forget, either; they remain hostile until you've killed everyone.

FREEFORM QUEST: BLOOMSEER POPLAR'S VISIONS

When you complete **Miscellaneous Quest: Oasis**, you can speak to Bloomseer Poplar. Her eyes become clouded as she sees your future and imparts a vision! This is a clue to one of the 16 other Miscellaneous Quests. She comments only on quests you've yet to complete, and you can return to listen to another vision once every 24 hours. The following information can be imparted:

Big Trouble in Big Town: "I see a town in need of a savior and a woman in red."

The Superhuman Gambit: "I see a clash between insects and industry and the men that control them."

The Wasteland Survival Guide: "I divine an endless search for knowledge to help others survive the desolation."

Those!: "I discern a lonely child trapped in a city on fire."

The Nuka-Cola Challenge: "I hear the cry of a woman obsessed and the man who desires her."

Head of State: "I see a great leader whose message carries through time as a rallying cry to the oppressed and a warning to the oppressors."

The Replicated Man: "I feel people's hatred and love for a man who hunts men that aren't men."

Blood Ties: "I divine a group of individuals who society views as monsters and a town suspended above the ground."

The Power of the Atom: "I see a mysterious man and a town on the brink of destruction."

Tenpenny Tower: "I see a selfish man who lives among the clouds playing a dangerous game with the lives of those below him."

Strictly Business: "I picture a place of great sorrow where men are traded for money and treated like Brahmin."

You Gotta Shoot 'Em in the Head: "I see four headless men and a being robbed of its dignity."

Stealing Independence: "I divine a great document and the passages that changed the face of the world."

Trouble on the Homefront: "I feel the torment of a man who returns home and discovers the changes his absence has wrought."

Agatha's Song: "I see a woman searching in vain for a relative long lost."

Reilly's Rangers: "I see four-leaf clovers in the sky with time as their deadliest adversary."

FREEFORM QUEST: YEW GOT A NEW FRIEND

Before you set out to complete Miscellaneous Quest: Oasis, seek Sapling Yew's opinion. Once the quest is over and Harold is still alive (he's not been burned or suffered a shot to the heart), speak to her again using a Speech Challenge or the Child at Heart perk. If you're successful, a grateful little girl awards you with her Bear Charm.

- Bear Charm (12/89)

FREEFORM QUEST: HIGH PLAINS DRIFTER

If you visit Dickerson Tabernacle Chapel [1.08], you'll find a drifter with a Unique Sniper Rifle. On his body is an Oasis Druid Hood and Oasis Coordinates, among other interesting items. This instantly pinpoints Oasis on your Pip-Boy's World Map.

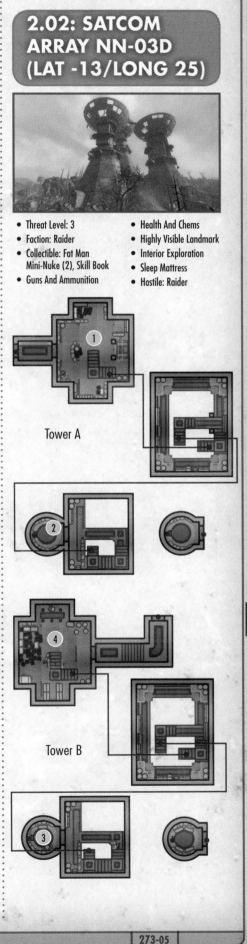

2.02: SATCOM ARRAY NN-03D (LAT -13/LONG 25)

- Threat Level: 3
- Faction: Raider
- Collectible: Fat Man Mini-Nuke (2), Skill Book
- Guns And Ammunition
- Health And Chems
- Highly Visible Landmark
- Interior Exploration
- Sleep Mattress
- Hostile: Raider

Tower A

Tower B

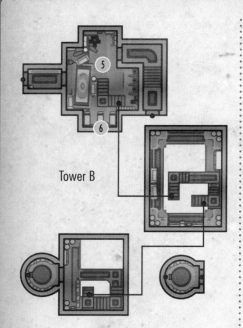

Tower B

The largest of the SatCom Arrays in the Northern Wasteland Zones 1 and 2 sits to the west of Fort Constantine. It is visible for many miles and is currently a Raider stronghold. The towers each have a ground-floor entrance and are labeled NN-03d-A, B, and C. Tower A is the lowest and Tower C is the highest. The entrance to Tower B is boarded up and cannot be breached. The door to the upper Tower C is locked.

NN-03D-A

Note

The following exploration follows the path through Towers A, B, and C. It can be attempted in the opposite direction.

① Raider Defenses

After tackling the Raiders, check the area for food and alcohol in the fridges, a few scattered Chems, and the following:

- Sawed-Off Shotgun and Ammo
- First Aid Box Health and Chems
- Ammo Box Ammunition (3)
- Frag Mines (2)

② Exit Ladder

You can use this weapon when you emerge outside. Cross to Tower B using the precarious planks, then hop onto the dish and enter the roof hatch in the middle.

- Sniper Rifle

NN-03D-B

③ Hatchway ladder

There's a fabulous chessboard with pieces salvaged from miniature gnomes and alcohol bottles; it would look great in your house!

- First Aid Box Health and Chems

④ Buffout Laboratory

Raiders are attempting to concoct Chems on this ground-floor area; there are many scattered about.

- Blood Pack

NN-03D-C

⑤ Raider Recreation Room

There's an exterior door leading to the Capital Wasteland; it is easy to Hack but difficult to Lockpick. There's a large quantity of beer, food, and some exhumed coffins. Sleep on the bunk beds.

⑥ Restroom

There's a particularly pleasant greeting daubed on the wall here.

- Pugilism Illustrated (5/25)

Exit the structure and head up to dish: You're on one of the highest (and most precarious) areas in the Wasteland! Avoid the holes in the dish's superstructure, and investigate the Super Mutant effigy.

- Mini-Nuke (14 and 15/71)

2.03: MDPL-21 POWER STATION (LAT -10/LONG 26)

- Threat Level: 1
- Collectible: Skill Book
- Interior Exploration
- Work Bench

In a windswept valley adjacent to a line of power towers (aka *pylons*) is a fenced-off Power Station, accessed via an unlocked gate. Inside is a Work Bench with a

Bottlecap Mine on it, a Skill Book, and a terminal with a safe.

- Work Bench (3/46)
- Nikola Tesla and You (4/25)
- Floor Safe Items

2.04: CLIFFTOP SHACKS (LAT 00/ LONG 26)

- Threat Level: 3
- Faction: Super Mutant
- Collectibles: Scribe Pre-War Book, Skill Book (2)
- Guns And Ammunition
- Interior Exploration
- Sleep Mattress
- Unique Weapon Or Item
- Character: Wastelander Captive
- Hostile: Super Mutant Genus

Approach these two mountaintop shacks from the west (you'll be spotted if you come from the east), along the gorge just south of Oasis. Wind around until you can scramble up to the mountain summit, then locate the rope bridge. Snipe from the bridge's other side, and set up mines so the Super Mutants kill themselves trying to reach you.

When combat is over, inspect the Clifftop Shacks; free the Wastelander captive here if you wish. Search Gore Bags, which contain the body parts of other captives and a decent amount of Caps. In the larger abandoned shack, there is a Super Mutant to tackle, a captive to keep alive, and a shelf safe. Search both shacks for mattresses and the following items:

- Pugilism Illustrated (6/25)
- Shelf Safe Items
- Pre-War Book (8/98)
- Frag Grenades (2)
- Ammo Box Ammunition
- Grognak the Barbarian (4/25)
- Board of Education (Nail Board) (13/89)

 Rescue any captives and take their gift for a small boost to your Karma, or refuse for a larger boost.

2.05: MONTGOMERY COUNTY RESERVOIR (LAT -06/LONG 22)

- Threat Level: 2
- Faction: Raider
- Danger: Low Radiation
- Hostile: Raider

Two hundred years ago, this supplied the northern D.C. area with drinking water. Little of that remains, although each of the large faucets supplies a few gulps of irradiated water for your sustenance. The area is now dotted with Raiders. There are no interior structures, just catwalks to run around and giant vats to hide behind. There's a jacknifed truck, but it contains only a light sprinkling of body parts and a Vodka bottle.

2.06: BROADCAST TOWER LP8 (LAT -04/LONG 24)

- Threat Level: 1
- Collectible: Skill Book
- Health And Chems
- Highly Visible Landmark
- Interior Exploration
- Radio Signal

GENERAL NOTES

Broadcast Tower LP8 is southwest of the monorail and freeway skeletons and overlooks the reservoir with Paradise Falls in the distance. Activate the electrical switch, and triangulate the signal to a Sealed Cistern entrance below, to the northeast.

- Radio Signal Echo Foxtrot

① Cistern Hidey-Hole

This area contains the remains of a long-dead radio operator, eight Salisbury steak boxes, Fission Batteries on the table, and a safe.

- Big Book of Science (3/25)
- Cistern Safe Items

Sealed Cistern

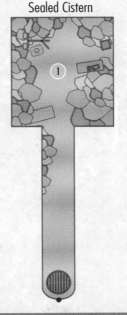

2.07: RECLINING GROVES RESORT HOMES (LAT -02/ LONG 20)

- Threat Level: 1
- Collectible: Skill Book
- Health And Chems
- Sleep Mattress
- Hostiles: Enclave Eyebot, Radscorpion Genus

Rural countryside homes slowly waste away in the breeze. In the northwest house is a First Aid Box on a table. Move east to the shack garage and attached ruin, and grab the Bottle Caps on a table here. The house in the northeast, near the Irradiated Silo and Barn [Location 2.J], has a mattress to sleep on and a copy of Tales of a Junktown Jerky Vendor. The ruin to the south has a half-buried mattress. Check mailboxes for common items. Before you leave, investigate the Warren [2.L] and Crashed Anomaly [2.G].

- First Aid Box Health and Chems
- Tales of a Junktown Jerky Vendor (2/24)

2.08: PARADISE FALLS (LAT -09/ LONG 16)

- Main Quest: Rescue From Paradise
- Miscellaneous Quest: Strictly Business
- Freeform Quest (5)
- Threat Level: 5
- Faction: Slaver
- Services: Healer, Repairer, Trader
- Highly Visible Landmark
- Area Is Locked
- Interior Exploration
- Collectibles: Bobblehead, Holotape: Replicated Man (3), Nuka-Cola Quantum (5), Scribe Pre-War Book
- Follower
- Guns And Ammunition
- Lots O' Caps
- Main Trading Route
- Rare Or Powerful Item (6)
- Sleep Mattress
- Work Bench
- Friendly: Brahmin

In order to interact with Slavers, your Karma must be at a low level. Come back after completing some particularly unspeakable acts to gain easy access into this settlement, or follow the instructions in **Main Quest: Rescue from Paradise.**

INHABITANTS (SLAVERS)

GROUSE

He has been with the Slavers since he was a teenager (he is now 30). His father was the former leader before Eulogy usurped him and rose to power, and Grouse has a legacy to live up to. He isn't fond of Eulogy, but he knows that if he moves against him, most of the Slavers would turn on him. He sits at the checkpoint entrance wearing a permanent scowl.

FORTY

Eulogy's second in command earned his nickname from the fact that, throughout his life, he's killed 40 men. When you first meet this 55-year-old nasty piece of work, he warns you not to do anything stupid; he doesn't want to have to change his name... again (however, culling slaves is something Forty considers "sport" and doesn't count toward his total). Forty is loud, dirty, and vile.

TRAINING — BESTIARY — MAIN QUEST — MISC. QUESTS — TOUR — COMPLETION — APPENDICES

PRONTO

Pronto is one of those guys who's always been around, but you can't remember how you met him or when he showed up. Rumor has it that he's the son of an old Slaver, but he doesn't get a lot of respect from them. He's a nice guy, and nice guys don't do well in Paradise Falls. Pronto is content to run Lock and Load, after the last owner met an untimely end. According to Forty (then called Thirty-Two), the previous owner died when a weapon accidentally went off in his shop. If anyone knows different, they aren't saying anything.

CUTTER

Forty-one-year-old Cutter was born in the pens, a slave. She spent her youth learning Wasteland medicine from her mother. When her mother passed away, Cutter took over caretaker duties for the slaves but slowly grew bitter and frustrated with the slaves' inability to fight back against the Slavers. Spending nearly a decade trading her services, she earned enough Caps to buy her freedom. Since Paradise Falls needed a skilled medic, she stayed, taking wealthy Slavers for all she could. Find her at the clinic.

EULOGY JONES

Eulogy Jones is a very unique 45-year-old individual. He dresses as smoothly as possible for a Wasteland Dweller and leads by persuasion and intelligence, getting others to do his dirty work. But the man is definitely dangerous; if you mess with his slaving operation, he'll be the first one to put a bullet in your brain. Eulogy got to where he is exactly like you'd expect: by being the craziest thug in a town full of crazy thugs. He'll tell you that he did it the old-fashioned way: hard work.

In truth, he used his slaves as prostitutes, and consequently, Eulogy knew nearly every secret in the camp. Eventually, he killed the former leader and took over. Every plot against his life has failed, and every Slaver in the camp has learned to back off when Eulogy loses his temper. Eulogy rules by fear.

CAROLINA RED

Perhaps the least pleasant Slaver in camp, Red is a stern-faced psychopath who was abused and tortured all through her life. Even her fellow Slavers give her a wide berth. Red loves to tell stories about her father, who once cut the legs off a man just to watch and laugh as he attempted to crawl away before crushing his skull with a rock. You know, childhood memories.

JOTUN AND YMIR

Ymir and his son Jotun are Paradise Falls's pair of knuckleheads. Jotun has difficulty forming basic sentences, while his father is a jovial madman, armed with a horrific-looking Super Sledge, like his son's. Ymir isn't fond of Frank the bartender and makes this abundantly clear by bludgeoning Frank to death. He loves drinking, fighting, and drinking some more, rounding a day off with a spot of fighting.

SLAVERS (10)

PARADISE FALLS: INHABITANTS (SLAVES)

CARTER

Carter is desperate to escape, and his mind has deteriorated so much in the last few weeks that he's prepared to risk almost certain decapitation by trying to sprint to freedom. He needs to time his escape to just the right moment. He's sure Forty doesn't have the means to control his Slave Collar.

FRANK

Captured a few months back during a raid just north of Megaton, Frank has yet to adjust to life as a servant and acts up constantly. He's been placed in charge of drinks at the bar, as bar patron Ymir doesn't take kindly to his drinks being spilled.

SAMMY

Sammy is 10 years old and is Squirrel's best friend. The two were captured together while on a trading run for Little Lamplight and have been in captivity together for about a month. Sammy is really annoyed at all of Squirrel's escape attempts—mainly because he hasn't been involved in any of them. When you facilitate the rescue of the Lamplighters, Sammy runs out of the complex along with Squirrel.

CRIMSON AND CLOVER

Eulogy's prostitutes are two slaves caught a few months back. They have been systematically brainwashed and threatened until they've become completely subservient to their master. Eulogy verbally abuses them constantly. You can listen to the tirades as the girls meekly plead for forgiveness. When Eulogy is away, they're both catty to each other. You cannot speak to either of them; any conversations must be through Eulogy. Note: you can purchase Clover as a Follower.

RORY MACLAREN

One of the many held at Paradise Falls, 30-year-old Rory remains here until someone wishes to purchase him. Unlike some of his fellow slaves, Rory is obsessed with escaping and spends every waking minute pondering ways of tunneling, creeping, or bludgeoning his way out of Paradise Falls. He isn't about to be pushed around and has assaulted his captors several times. He's been placed permanently in the "Box," where unruly slaves await their fate.

SQUIRREL

A 10-year-old Lamplighter, Squirrel is very fidgety and has a high energy level. He's fully on board with any plan to escape and watches the Slavers' comings and goings to learn their schedules. He sleeps at night for a few hours, then wakes up and eats a quick meal before going back out to the yard. Squirrel is also a computer genius and has already figured out how to disable the Slave Collars. He has plotted an escape route and just needs help from an outsider.

PENNY

Penny is a 12-year-old Lamplighter who spends most of her time alone in a corner of the slave house. She laments that Rory Maclaren, whom she has grown close to, has been in isolation in the Box for a very long time and will likely die if he's not released. In fact, when the time comes for you to rescue the Lamplighters, Penny will not leave unless she knows Rory has been released from the Box.

MISS JEANETTE

Miss Jeanette is quiet, confused, and obsequious. She's long since accepted her role as a slave. The only problem is, most customers have no use for a Ghoul slave. She's been in the pens forever and isn't expecting to leave any time soon.

BREADBOX

Breadbox is the oldest slave in the camp by far. Old slaves don't sell well, and at this point, they can't even give Breadbox away. Mostly, the Slavers just ignore him.

BLEAK

Since the day she arrived in Paradise Falls, Bleak has been planning her escape. She spends her days watching and memorizing the movements of the guards, waiting for the perfect time to make her move.

BRONSON

Bronson is, quite simply, a drunk. Unable to cope with life since his capture, he's taken to humiliating himself for the amusement of the Slavers, who provide him with enough booze to make him forget how his life has ended up. Bleak has been trying to give him hope, but so far has failed.

PARADISE FALLS ENTRANCE

From a distance, this barricaded shopping mall looks like a welcoming settlement, but upon closer inspection, you realize it's anything but. This settlement offers services like any other (including a clinic and weapons shop), but it caters to the most vile denizens in the Wasteland. In fact, in order to enjoy Paradise Falls's unique amenities, you must maintain a certain status among your peers.

If your Karma is too high, the Slavers are revolted by your morals and prevent you from entering the town. If you start any trouble, whether good or evil in nature, the Slavers shoot to kill, and you'll lose all your Paradise Falls privileges. Assuming you're unpleasant enough or you've bribed or gunned your way in, you can locate the giant wrecked-car barricade and a gate made from an arm of the Large Boy, and enter Paradise Falls itself. The only other location on your Local Map is a sewer pipe from the Toilets; the children use this as an exit when you rescue them during **Main Quest: Rescue from Paradise.** There's a single item of interest by Grouse, next to the sandbags: a Holotape related to the Replicated Man.

- Mesmetron (14/89)
- Holotape: The Replicated Man (1/24)

PARADISE FALLS

Enter the main settlement to find locations ① and ②, to the left and right of you. Every location is marked with a scrawled sign.

① "Lock and Load"

The settlement's weapons store is staffed by Pronto. He can Repair your weapons, or you can Trade with him. There is also a Work Bench with a Bottlecap Mine here. Downstairs is a cellar where Pronto sometimes sleeps. The following items can be stolen:

- Work Bench (4/46)
- Frag Grenades (2)
- Melee Weapons (8)
- Small Guns (6)
- Ammo Box Ammunition (3)

INTERIOR MAPS AND LOCATIONS

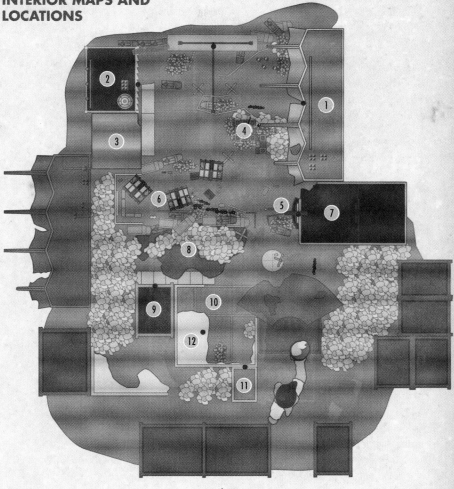

② **Slavers Barracks**

Converted from an old liquor store, the Barracks are brimming with beer, spirits, and, strangely, detergent. Of particular interest is the fabled Vault 77 Jumpsuit. The rest of the Barracks consist of bunk beds and whisky bottles.

- Power Fist
- Vault 77 Jumpsuit (15/89)
- Note: Burn This Goddamn Jumpsuit*

> **Note**
>
> *The jumpsuit was probably owned by a legendary enemy of the Slavers, who single-handedly wiped out a group of them before disappearing.

③ **Cutter's Clinic**

Home to Cutter and her almost-sanitary medical bay. You can speak to her about The Replicated Man, ask for healing, radiation healing, Chems, Medical Supplies, or you can ignore her. Her prices are excellent—a benefit for being a badass. Her

Chem and Medical Supplies are sealed. Her backroom is littered with scorched books and two mattresses.

- Holotape: The Replicated Man (2/24)

④ **"Crap"**

A pile of rubble above which is a small catwalk where a Minigunner patrols.

⑤ **Roasting Brahmin**

At the front of Eulogy's Pad is a small campfire and pool table; check the cue out.

- The Break (16/89)

> **Note**
>
> Have you tried swiping the Break at the pool balls on the table? Extra kudos for pocketing any ball!

⑥ **Open-Air Pub**

Constructed from the shell of a Robco Parts store. Frank nervously bartends, while Ymir and his monosyllabic son Jotun do their best psychopath impressions. There's a cable junction box here, if you're attempting the Main Quest.

APPENDICES — COMPLETION — TOUR — MISC. QUESTS — MAIN QUEST — BESTIARY — TRAINING

7 Eulogy's Pad

Inside the old cinema, you may find Eulogy and his two slaves Clover and Crimson, either inside, on the outside balcony, or wandering Paradise Falls. There are numerous items to find in here, most of which are in the projection room (now Eulogy's extravagant bedroom). The wall terminal allows you to unlock the floor safe. Don't forget the Nuka-Cola Quantum haul behind the stairs and the exterior balcony, offering excellent views of this settlement.

- Combat Helmet
- Eulogy Jones' Hat (17/89)
- Paradise Falls Box Key
- Holotape: The Replicated Man (3/24)
- Bobblehead: Speech (5/20)
- Floor Safe Items
- Nuka-Cola Quantum (7–11/94)

8 9 10 11 12 Slave Pens and Toilets

To the south is some rubble, the Box 8, and the Toilets 9. The Toilets are grimy and hold no items, but there is a child-sized escape route in here. The Box is actually a Pulowski Preservation Shelter, currently used as solitary confinement for Rory Maclaren. Open the Box using the Paradise Falls Box Key. Also use this key to open the Slave Pen 10 gates. The Child Slave House 11 is a place of disgusting squalor, with mattresses to sleep on. The same is true of the Adult Slave House 12, except there's a Pre-War Book to take from the corner table.

- Pre-War Book (9/98)

RELATED INTERACTIONS

Interact with the Slavers of Paradise Falls in the following ways:

Grouse: You can bribe him to enter Paradise Falls.

Grouse: You can begin the **Miscellaneous Quest: Strictly Business** by talking with him.

Forty: During the Main Quest, you can convince him to ask Eulogy for a pay raise.

Forty: You can Pickpocket him for a Paradise Falls Box Key.

Pronto: You can Trade and ask him to Repair your equipment.

Carolina Red: You can receive verbal unpleasantness from her.

Cutter: You can ask her about facial epidermal augmentation, if you've started **Miscellaneous Quest: The Replicated Man.**

Cutter: You can purchase medical supplies or Chems and get your radiation healed or your wounds tended to.

 Eulogy Jones: You can offer to purchase Clover, one of his personal slaves.

Eulogy Jones: You can offer to purchase the child slaves.

 Eulogy Jones: You can ask whether Eulogy has considered collecting some of the kids in Little Lamplight.

Eulogy Jones: You can Pickpocket him for a Paradise Falls Box Key.

 Eulogy Jones: You can kill him and take his unique outfit.

Child Slaves: You can help them plot an escape.

Adult Slaves: You can free them, with varying degrees of success.

- Eulogy Jones' Suit (18/89)

FREEFORM QUEST: FREEDOM!

 In addition to removing the children from the Slave Pens in your Main Quest, you can also try rescuing the adults. You will fight a violent and difficult struggle against all the Slavers, killing all of them (including the brainwashed Clover and Crimson, although Clover could be bought as a Follower first). Then open the Slave Pen gates, talk to each slave, and tell them the gate is open. All make a run for it, except Breadbox, who's as deaf as he is mad. He stays behind.

 Or, you can open the pens, tell the slaves to flee, and watch as they're gunned down by the Slavers you didn't kill beforehand. That was a terribly evil decision. Congratulations?

FREEFORM QUEST: STRICTLY PROFITABLE

 If you agree to Grouse's request for slave collecting and bring back all the slaves he requested, you can continue this plan indefinitely, forcing a Wastelander or other amenable person to flee from you in combat. Then, zap them with the Mesmetron and snap a Slave Collar around their necks. Accompany them or instruct them to head to Paradise Falls. You are awarded 250 Caps for each additional slave you bring back to Grouse.

- 250 Caps

FREEFORM QUEST: THE KID-KIDNAPPER

 When you speak with Eulogy, ask if he's thought about kidnapping one of the children in Little Lamplight, as they're likely to be less trouble and fetch a better price. He agrees and says he'll pay you handsomely if you're successful. Head to Little Lamplight, after reading the Kidnap Order Eulogy gives you. A Slaver is waiting at the cave mouth. Locate Bumble and convince her (Speech Challenge or Child at Heart) to accompany you back to the Slaver without any combat taking place. When you return, the Slaver brings the kid directly to Eulogy; all you have to do is return to claim your prize:

- Kidnap Order
- Boogeyman's Hood (19/89)

FREEFORM QUEST: COVETING CLOVER

Assuming you enter Paradise Falls using persuasion, your evil reputation, or bribery, locate Eulogy Jones and speak to him. When your Karma is suitably low enough, you can inquire about purchasing a slave from him. He offers you Clover for 1,000 Caps. Although you may think twice about the purchase of a slave as a Follower, Clover has been heavily brainwashed, is wearing a Slave Collar, and thinks you're Eulogy's replacement, transferring her fanatical love of him toward you.

FREEFORM QUEST: ECONOMICS OF VIOLENCE

When you search Pronto's tradeable items in Lock and Load, the selection is poor. The Slavers only trade him the useless crap they no longer have a use for. If you ask how you can help, he gives you the Note from Pronto and asks you to collect 20 Chinese Assault Rifles and bring them back to him. If you return 24 hours later, Pronto's inventory is a whole lot more impressive! The variety of items to sell improves greatly.

- Note from Pronto

2.09: MDPL-13 POWER STATION (LAT 02/LONG 17)

- Threat Level: 3
- Faction: Ghoul
- Danger: Low Radiation
- Collectible: Nuka-Cola Quantum, Schematic
- Health And Chems
- Highly Visible Landmark
- Interior Exploration
- Rare Or Powerful Item
- Work Bench
- Hostiles: Ghoul Genus, Mark V Turret

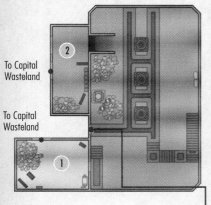

To Capital Wasteland

To Capital Wasteland

Derelict Power Plant

① Office

There's two vending machines, low-level radiation, and a Turret Control Terminal that deactivates the turret in the main catwalk area.

② Ramped Garage

There's a footlocker containing common items.

- First Aid Box Health and Chems

③ Upper-Level Office

Battle the Ghouls along the catwalk to reach this location. Open the safe via Lockpick or Hacking. Check the unique weapon on the desk.

- Floor Safe Items
- Fisto! (20/89)

> **Tip**
>
> Get a Glowing One on your side by wearing Roy Phillips's Ghoul Mask (Miscellaneous Quest: Tenpenny Tower).

Secondary Locations

SUBSTATION NOTES

Almost due north of the Minefield Water Tower [2.O] are two buildings with a group of power transformers between them. If you're being pursued (usually by a Deathclaw), use the rocky outcrop behind the substation to reach the roof. Otherwise, head into the Substation; amid the junk, Abraxo Cleaners, and food, is a Work Bench with a Bottlecap Mine and the listed items nearby. There's a terminal and floor safe too.

- Work Bench (5/46)
- First Aid Box Health and Chems
- Nuka-Cola Quantum (12/94)
- Schematic: Railway Rifle (7/23)
- Floor Safe Items

DERELICT POWER PLANT NOTES

The main building here (with the map) is a large and broken-down power plant; the three chimneys make this one of the Northern Wasteland's most prominent landmarks and a great place to triangulate your location. You can enter the facility via the garage or through the metal doors to the south. The doors are recommended, as there are turrets to deactivate, and the terminal is just through the doors.

2.A: UPPER TRAILS (ROPE BRIDGE) (LAT -10/LONG 29)

- Threat Level: 1
- Faction: Wastelander

Follow the line of electrical towers (aka pylons) up from the MDPL-21 Power Station [2.03] to a treacherous hiking area. A Wastelander has fallen from the bridge recently. Inspect his corpse for a suicide note. It's all rather depressing, really.

- Note: Dead End

2.B: TOXIC POND (LAT -09/LONG 30)

- Threat Level: 1
- Danger: High Radiation
- Collectible: Skill Book
- Sleep Mattress

Pack the Rad-X and set off for this remote irradiated pool; there's a small alcove behind the rusting container. There are three bodies here: a Wastelander, a Raider, and a scientist. Grab the food and RadAways, and sleep on the mattress if you wish. Don't leave without opening the half-submerged safe.

- Radiation Suit
- Submerged Safe Items
- D.C. Journal of Internal Medicine (5/25)

2.C: MONORAIL CARRIAGE WRECKAGE (LAT -06/LONG 28)

- Threat Level: 1
- Highly Visible Landmark

This monorail route snakes all the way from the Corvega Factory [6.05] to the southwest, past Agatha's House [5.06], and north to Broadcast Tower LP8 [2.06]. Similarly, the crumbling freeway winds north past the Wheaton Armory [6.04], forks at the Temple of the Union [3.10], and continues northwest past the Greener Pastures Disposal Site [3.06]. Using these ruined transport links is an excellent way to explore.

2.D: OASIS ENTRANCE (ROPE BRIDGE)(LAT -05/LONG 29)

- Threat Level: 2
- Faction: Enclave
- Danger: Low Radiation

Amid the fallen concrete and twisted steel of the freeway [2.C] is a rope bridge with some steaming and slightly radioactive pools bubbling underneath. Oasis [2.01] is to the east, hidden in the giant rocky outcrop. Once you complete Main Quest: The Waters of Life, expect an Enclave presence [E2.01].

2.E: ABANDONED TENT (LAT -12/LONG 23)

- Threat Level: 1
- Danger: Low Radiation
- Collectibles: Nuka-Cola Quantum, Skill Book
- Guns And Ammunition
- Interior Exploration
- Sleep Mattress

At the foot of the mountains on the irradiated plains lies a recently abandoned tent. Inside is a place to sleep during local explorations as well as various useful items.

- Ammo Box Ammunition (2)
- Nuka-Cola Quantum (13/94)
- Nikola Tesla and You (5/25)

TRAINING — BESTIARY — MAIN QUEST — MISC. QUESTS — TOUR — COMPLETION — APPENDICES

2.F: IRRADIATED SILO AND OUTBUILDINGS (LAT -07/LONG 23)

- Threat Level: 1
- Guns And Ammunition
- Hostile: Radscorpion Genus

Slightly northwest of the Montgomery County Reservoir is a small cluster of burned-out farm buildings. Check the barn and outbuilding for Ammo Boxes. If you need to orient yourself, look south to just make out the Big Burger Boy sign and Paradise Falls.

- Ammo Box Ammunition (6)

2.G: CRASHED ANOMALY (LAT 03/LONG 22)

- Threat Level: 1
- Danger: Low Radiation
- Rare Or Powerful Item
- Radio Signal
- Alien Pilot (Deceased)

Almost directly north of the MDPL-13 Power Station (as you follow the line of power towers), you pick up an odd radio signal: You hear mainly static and then some eerie, garbled speech you can't decipher. Locate the remains of a house; something has crashed straight through it, digging a furrow into the hillside. Round the front of the craft to uncover a strange body, thrown from the cockpit.

- Recon Craft Theta Beacon Signal
- Alien Blaster Power Cells (10)
- Alien Blaster

> **Tip**
> There's a gigantic crater just east of Fort Bannister [4.11] that may contain additional Alien Cells to claim.

2.H: ANT TUNNEL TO MUSTY CAVERN (LAT -11/LONG 20)

- Threat Level: 2
- Interior Exploration

GIANT ANT GENUS

On a small plateau just southeast of Mason Dixon Salvage [1.09] is a collection of scuttling Giant Ants guarding a sticky hole. Squeeze through into a dark and confined Musty Cavern.

Musty Cavern

① Cavern Interior

There are Ant Piles to sift through, along with a dead Raider and a Wastelander holding some common items.

- Giant Ant Nectar
- Ant Meat

> **Tip**
> Giant Ant Nectar and Meat have some beneficial properties; check the Items Chart (page 45) for further information.

2.I: MILITARY CHECKPOINT (LAT -05/LONG 20)

- Threat Level: 1
- Danger: Low Radiation
- Guns And Ammunition
- Health And Chems
- Sleep Mattress
- Hostile: Robot Genus

The Montgomery County Reservoir water tower gleams in the distance. Once the robot is defeated, you can inspect the tent for a sleeping mattress, and the general area for items:

- Ammo Box Ammunition (4)
- Assault Rifle (3)
- 10mm Pistol
- First Aid Box Health and Chems

2.J: IRRADIATED SILO AND BARN (LAT 00/LONG 20)

- Threat Level: 1
- Faction: Enclave
- Collectible: Skill Book (2)
- Guns And Ammunition
- Sleep Mattress

On the eastern edge of the Reclining Groves Resort Homes is a battered old barn

---

and silo. Check the barn for Ammo, a mattress, and a Footlocker containing a Sneak Skill Book. Check the hillside to the northeast; there's a dead Mercenary lying near Chems and a Big Guns Skill Book.

- Ammo Box Ammunition (2)
- Chinese Army: Spec. Ops. Training Manual (3/25)
- U.S. Army: 30 Handy Flamethrower Recipes (1/25)

2.K: TRAFFIC LINE (LAT -11/LONG 17)

- Threat Level: 1
- Danger: Low Radiation

Located on the east–west road from Drowned Devil's Crossing [1.13] across the northern hills above Paradise Falls.

2.L: WOOD PLANKS TO WARREN (LAT -02/LONG 18)

- Threat Level: 2
- Interior Exploration
- Hostile: Vicious Dog

On the opposite (south) side of the road from Reclining Groves Resort Homes, there's an easily missed indent in the shallow hill near the monorail line. This small subterranean area is a single winding, dead-end tunnel inhabited by Vicious Dogs.

Warren Interior

The tunnel winds to a dead end, where two rotting corpses hold some common items.

2.M: OVERTURNED CITY LINER (LAT 00/LONG 18)

- Threat Level: 1
- Highly Visible Landmark

This is midway between the Warrens and the MDPL-13 Power Station, along the crumbling road.

2.N: MONORAIL TRAIN WRECKAGE (RAIDER CAMP) (LAT 00/LONG 14)

- Threat Level: 2
- Faction: Raider
- Collectible: Skill Book
- Guns And Ammunition
- Hostile: Raider

There's a major derailment just northwest of the Germantown Police Headquarters [5.01], now home to a small band of Raiders. You can storm in and blast them, but you could also Sneak along the top of the carriages. The Raiders are guarding a few Chems, a Stimpak, and some Ammo Boxes. Don't forget the Duck and Cover! by the bath.

- Ammo Box Ammunition (3)
- Duck and Cover! (4/25)

2.O: MINEFIELD WATER TOWER (LAT 03/LONG 14)

- Threat Level: 1
- Faction: Wastelander
- Highly Visible Landmark

Perched high on a bluff overlooking the deadly village of Minefield [3.09]. There's a faucet in the tower's center that provides lightly radiated water. If you plan on visiting Minefield, head here to reconnoiter the place.

ENCLAVE CAMP LOCATIONS

CAMP E2.01 (LAT -5/LONG 29)

- Main Quest: Picking Up The Trail
- Threat Level: 2
- Guns And Ammunition
- Health And Chems
- Danger: Low Radiation

There are a few shock troops patrolling the small muddy ponds below the rope bridge to and from Oasis.

- Enclave First Aid Crate Health and Chems
- Enclave Crate Ammunition

CAMP E2.02 (LAT 00/LONG 19)

- Main Quest: Picking Up The Trail
- Threat Level: 1
- Guns And Ammunition

This is a two-man team with defenses and a large amount of Ammo, just east of Reclining Groves Resort Homes. Check the defenses for the Laser Rifle and more Ammo.

- Enclave Crate Ammunition (5)
- Ammo Box Ammunition (3)
- Laser Rifle

Zone 3: Northeast Territories

TOPOGRAPHICAL OVERVIEW

The more sparsely populated Northeast Territories are dominated by two large areas of interest—the Old Olney township and its surrounding area and the Greener Pastures Disposal Site. Old Olney was once a quaint place to visit on the weekends. Now it's a place you go to die. Ravenous Deathclaws prowl the streets, and Scavengers have picked the surrounding hamlets clean. Greener Pastures is simply a gigantic irradiated area, full of its own surprises. Consider heading to the Republic of Dave; an envoy from the Wasteland might be welcomed by this power-mad oddball and his clan. There are also farms, a dangerous ghost town filled with mines, and the Temple of the Abolitionists' Union to search for, too. And don't forget the Roach King; he may be the craziest of all!

AVAILABLE COLLECTIBLES (ZONE 3)

- Bobbleheads: 2/20
- Fat Men: 1/9
- Mini-Nukes: 3/71
- Unique Items: 3/89
- Nuka-Cola Quantum: 10/94
- Schematics: 1/23
- Scribe Pre-War Books: 19/98
- Skill Book (Barter): 3/24
- Skill Book (Big Guns): 1/25
- Skill Book (Energy Weapons): 1/25
- Skill Book (Explosives): 2/25
- Skill Book (Lockpick): 1/25
- Skill Book (Medicine): 4/25
- Skill Book (Melee Weapons): 3/25
- Skill Book (Repair): 2/25
- Skill Book (Science): 1/25
- Skill Book (Small Guns): 2/25
- Skill Book (Sneak): 0/25
- Skill Book (Speech): 0/25
- Skill Book (Unarmed): 2/25
- Work Bench: 3/46
- Holotapes (Keller): 1/5
- Holotapes (Replicated Man): 0/19

PRIMARY LOCATIONS

3.01: Vault 92 (lat 08/long 27)

3.02: Old Olney (lat 10/long 26)

3.03: The Republic of Dave (lat 19/long 27)

3.04: Chaste Acres Dairy Farm (lat 15/long 24)

3.05: MDPL-16 Power Station (lat 18/long 24)

3.06: Greener Pastures Disposal Site (lat 07/long 21)

3.07: Grisly Diner (lat 13/long 20)

3.08: Relay Tower KX-B8-11 (lat 15/long 20)

3.09: Minefield (lat 04/long 14)

3.10: Temple of the Union (lat 13/long 15)

SECONDARY LOCATIONS

3.A: Trio of Ruined Houses (lat 09/long 29)

3.B: Overturned City Liner (lat 18/long 30)

3.C: Fishing Hole Shack (lat 04/long 26)

3.D: Ruined Farmstead (lat 06/long 27)

3.E: Red Rocket Gas Station and Jackknifed Truck (lat 13/long 25)

3.F: Ruined House (lat 16/long 27)

3.G: Old Olney Outskirts (Ruined Houses; lat 10/long 23)

3.H: Jackknifed Truck (on Freeway; lat 13/long 23)

3.I: Irradiated Outhouse (lat 15/long 23)

3.J: Destroyed Bridge (lat 04/long 21)

3.K: Drainage Chamber (lat 16/long 19)

3.L: The Roach King (lat 08/long 16)

3.Mi and ii: Drainage Outlets (lat 15/long 17/18)

3.N: Hilltop Farm Ruins (lat 16/long 17)

3.O: Freeway Shacks (lat 11/long 14)

Primary Locations

3.01: VAULT 92 (LAT 08/LONG 27]

- Miscellaneous Quest: Agatha's Song
- Threat Level: 5
- Faction: Vault Dweller
- Danger: Low Radiation, Shotgun Trap (2)
- Collectibles: Nuka-Cola Quantum, Scribe Pre-War

- Book (5), Skill Book (4)
- Guns And Ammunition
- Health And Chems
- Interior Exploration
- Lots O' Caps
- Sleep Mattress
- Rare Or Powerful Item

INHABITANTS

- Overseer Richard Rubin (Very Deceased)
- Professor John Malleus (Very Deceased)
- Gordie Sumner (Very Deceased)

- Carl Maynard (Very Deceased)
- Zoe Hammerstein (Very Deceased)
- Hostile: Mirelurk Genus

It appears that Vault 92 was Vault-Tec's attempt to figure out whether auditory experimentation could be utilized in combat more effectively than before. To this end, the Vault approached several musicians and scientists to help hypothesize and run the place...200 years ago. West of Old Olney, under a small copse of dead trees in the bottom of a rocky fissure is a rusting metal door that leads to this underground labyrinth.

Tip

Remember that Sneaking through this Vault (especially when utilizing multiple Stealth Boys) is a safe alternative to combat.

VAULT 92 ENTRANCE, UTILITY, AND ATRIUM

1 Entrance Chamber

Check the table for Energy Ammo and check the upper area near the rusting terminals.

- Laser Pistol
- Blood Pack
- First Aid Box Health and Chems (2)
- Scribe Pre-War Book (10/98)
- Professor Malleus Audio Log V92-01 (1/6)

2 Connecting Chamber

The utility areas east and west both lead to the opposite ends of the lower Reactor level. Watch for Mines as you step through the doors.

- Frag Mine

3 Atrium

Disarm the Rigged Shotgun as you head south. Watch for a Mine at the base of the stairs. Pick the locked door to enter the lower Atrium (or head in from the Living Quarters or Sound Testing).

INTERIOR MAPS AND LOCATIONS

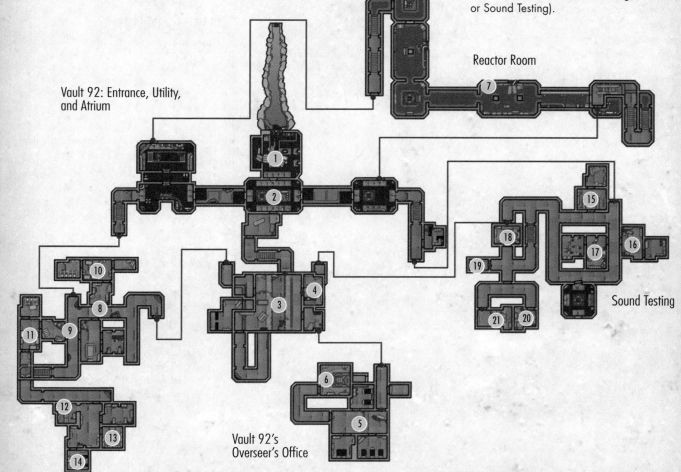

Vault 92: Entrance, Utility, and Atrium

Reactor Room

Sound Testing

Vault 92's Overseer's Office

Living Quarters

TRAINING — BESTIARY — MAIN QUEST — MISC. QUESTS — TOUR — COMPLETION — APPENDICES

④ Gordie Sumner's Weapons Repository

There's a selection of weapons, Darts, Chems, and Energy Ammo to gather here. The safe under the counter is unlocked and contains a Laser Pistol and other common items. Hack into the Supply Shop Terminal to read Gordie Sumner's messages.

- Combat Shotgun and Ammo
- Laser Pistol
- Ammo Box Ammunition (2)
- Tales of a Junktown Jerky Vendor (3/24)

VAULT 92'S OVERSEER'S OFFICE

⑤ Hub Corridor

Pick the lock to reach this chamber. There are three bedrooms, one with a Holotape inside.

- Professor Malleus Audio Log V92-02

⑥ Overseer's Office

Aside from looting the items from the desk and bookcase, inspect the terminal, which has four Personal Entries to read.

Entry 00897332: The first details how a "white noise generator" has been rerouted through to the Vault's loudspeaker system and triggered via the security consoles. The password is mentioned and noted in your Pip-Boy.

Entry 00897357: The second details "successes" in the field testing, although the Overseer's choice in test subjects is slightly worrying!

Entry 00897377: The third mentions deaths and long-term "crazy" effects. The Overseer brushes this off but employs a command word in their suggestion implants, just in case.

Entry 00897398: The fourth, oh dear, the Overseer has lost control and is about to order the death of Professor Malleus, the head of the experiment.

- Stealth Boy
- Professor Malleus Audio Log V92-03*
- Scribe Pre-War Book (11/98)
- Duck and Cover! (5/25)
- Overseer Rubin Personal Entry 00897332

 Note

*Allows instant access to the wall terminals inside the Living Quarters.

REACTOR ROOM

⑦ Waterlogged Terminal

Accessed from either the east or west utility areas, this Reactor location is a long winding corridor of shallow water, interspersed with short, violent confrontations with Mirelurks. The Engineering Logs Terminal is a series of entries from Carl Maynard, who is gradually getting more and more irate about the lack of watertight building materials used in this Vault's construction.

LIVING QUARTERS

Caution

This is a highly dangerous area if you don't know where you're going and only offers a way back to the first interior location — Vault 92 Entrance, Utility, and Atrium.

⑧ ⑨ Wall Terminals (Female and Male Dorm)

Use the password you found in the Overseer's Office, or Hack either of the terminals and select Noise Flush, filling the entire chamber with white noise that bursts all the Mirelurks' heads open.

⑩ Female Dorm

There are scattered items and Darts in the central recreation room (with the pool table). The Dorm has Bobby Pins, Darts, First Aid Box Health and Chems, and Ammo Box Ammunition.

⑪ Male Dorm

Check the restroom for the Sheet Music Book. There's also a storage room to the south, guarded by a Rigged Shotgun. Duck before you open the door, then grab the following items and pry open the wall safe.

- Sheet Music Book
- Stealth Boy
- Combat Shotgun and Ammo
- Wall Safe Items
- Laser Pistol and Ammo

⑫ Security Terminal

Release white noise from here, next to the Quantum Bottle. Unlock all doors from here too. Check the unlocked room to the east for more items:

- Nuka-Cola Quantum (14/94)
- Pulse Grenades (2)
- Pulse Mines (2)

⑬ Data Storage

Hack the Data Storage Entry Terminal, or Pick the door.

- Ammo Box Ammunition (4)
- Stimpak and Chems
- Scattered Energy Ammo
- Blood Pack

⑭ Medical Bay

Locate the Holotape on the table by the entrance. Check the terminal in the Medical Bay, and read four missives by Professor Malleus to his lab assistants and the Overseer.

The first gives kudos to the team for the great successes.

The second regards a test subject that went insane. The scientists are puzzled as to why.

The third is a pleading to the Overseer, telling him to call off his guards and recognize the "problems."

The fourth is ominous; the Vault is under heavy guard. Rubin isn't responding to Malleus, and the Professor wants answers.

First Aid Box Health and Chems

D.C. Journal of Internal Medicine (6/25)

Professor Malleus Audio Log V92-04

SOUND TESTING

⑮ Maintenance/Storage Room

- Scribe Pre-War Book (12/98)

⑯ Office and Server Room

The back chamber has a terminal with Zoe Hammerstein's diary entries.

Zoe's Thoughts: Zoe is thrilled to be surrounded by all the musical talent; she's spending her life among the world's greatest musicians!

More of Zoe's Thoughts: She's recording Haydn's Symphony No.3 in D Minor, and she got to play along with the orchestra! The best part was that you can hear yourself play on the studio's speakers. Perhaps Dvorak tomorrow?

More of Zoe's Thoughts: She's feeling sick and woozy because the studio is so stuffy. The other violinists are giving her pointers. Tonight is the Rec Hall dance; she's hoping that dreamy guy Parker asks her out.

More of Zoes Thoughts: Mental confusion is beginning to take its toll: "I cant concentrate I wen t to Doctoor Bennisons offfice but he jusst said its stress and too take iit easy for a whil I think al the timee I am spendng inn the soundd sttudo is makd in g me tired I can barele type anymoor I am shaking so muc."

klkhi plEAsse.HF puu HeLP meeLp

It doesn't end well.

- Scribe Pre-War Book (13/98)

17 Projector and Music Room

- Professor Malleus Audio Log V92-05

18 Kitchen

There is a jukebox and some common items here.

- Scribe Pre-War Book (14/98)

19 Storage Room

There are several interesting goods to gather and a wall safe to open.

- Health, Chems, and Ammo
- Wall Safe Items

20 Recording Studio (Production)

Access the Studio Terminal to unlock the recording studio bay. There are missives on this too.

The first is regarding an odd bleeding issue.

The second is actually sent to Agatha's great-great grandmother Hilda! The studio engineer is enthralled by Hilda's music...and her other charms!

The third is...both saucy and shocking! Were people really that forward back in 2077?

- Professor Malleus Audio Log V92-06
- Nikola Tesla and You (6/25)

21 Recording Studio Bay

Check the wall safe, and locate arguably the most incredible prize in this Wasteland—a 600-year-old Soil Stradivarius Violin in pristine condition!

- Laser Pistol
- Wall Safe Items
- Soil Stradivarius (21/89)

3.02: OLD OLNEY (LAT 10/LONG 26)

- Miscellaneous Quest: The Nuka-Cola Challenge
- Threat Level: 5
- Collectibles: Nuka-Cola Quantum, Fat Man Launcher, Fat Man Mini-Nuke, Skill Book
- Guns And Ammunition
- Health And Chems
- Highly Visible Landmark
- Interior Exploration
- Rare Or Powerful Item
- Sleep Mattress
- Work Bench
- Character: Sewer Protectron
- Hostile: Mole Rat, Deathclaw

CARL WALLACE (VERY DECEASED)

Carl was an employee of the Nuka-Cola company. He was driving to Old Olney to deliver his goods when a deer leapt out, and he jackknifed his rig to avoid it. He waited in front of the firehouse for the tow truck to arrive and hoped this incident wouldn't reflect badly on his employment with the company.

This ruined township comprises several city streets, which contain the largest concentration of Deathclaws, except for the Deathclaw Sanctuary [1.07]. Approach the town from any direction, but it's best to snipe Deathclaws from the freeway to the east or from the hill above Vault 92, or Sneak in from the west at night. Otherwise, wait at a safe distance for a patrolling Deathclaw to move past.

1 Bank Courtyard

Watch your step—the first of two underground entrances is the steel grating. If you stand on it, you fall into the entrance to the Olney Sewers, and you can't scramble back up.

Tip

Walk across the corner to activate the falling grating, but stay at street level.

2 Firehouse

At the sealed front door is a skeleton lying next to a sheet of paper. This is the Nuka-Cola Accident Report, referencing the nearby Jackknifed Truck [3.E].

- Nuka-Cola Accident Report

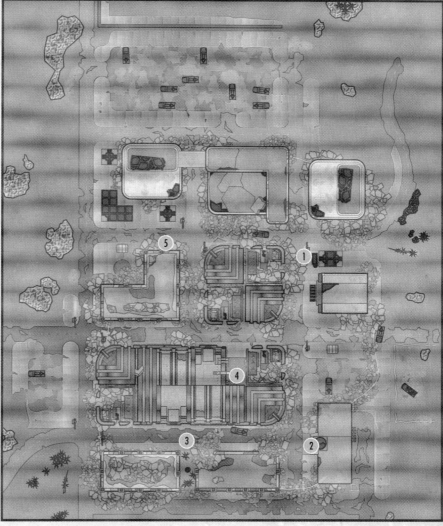

Old Olney Streets

TRAINING — BESTIARY — MAIN QUEST — MISC. QUESTS — TOUR — COMPLETION — APPENDICES

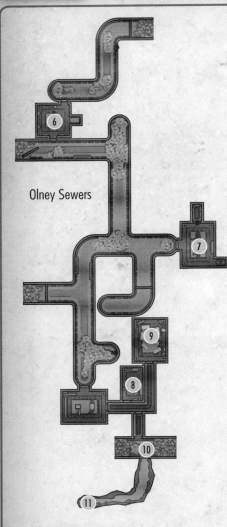

Olney Sewers

lasts a few seconds before it is mauled by the lightning-fast talons of a Deathclaw! Check the room for Darts, junk, and a skeleton clutching an ID card. There are also three Ammo Boxes, one of which is locked; a First Aid Box; some Darts; tools; and other junk. The skeleton on the west wall still clutches a Utility Worker ID.

- Ammo Box Ammunition (3)
- First Aid Health and Chems
- Utility Worker ID

⑦ Generator Room

The locked door accesses the storage closet's items:

- Ammo Box Ammunition
- First Aid Health and Chems (2)
- Mini-Nuke (16/71)

⑧ Small Workshop

This easily missed room off the L-shaped corridor houses the following items:

- Work Bench (6/46)
- Bottlecap Mine
- Scoped .44 Magnum
- Ammo Box Ammunition
- First Aid Box Health and Chems

⑨ Bloody Sleeping Quarters

Begin scavenging with the three safes once combat is over.

- Nuka-Cola Quantum (15/94)
- Fat Man (3/9)
- Missile Launcher
- Ammo Box Ammunition
- Wall Safe Items (3)
- Friendly: Brahmin

③ Exposed Manhole

The second entrance to the Olney Sewers.

④ Alcove under a Radiation King sign.

- Ammo Box Ammunition   and Chems
- First Aid Box Health

⑤ Dead Mercenary

- Combat Shotgun

INTERIOR NOTES: OLNEY SEWERS

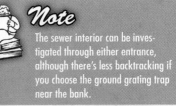

> **Note**
> The sewer interior can be investigated through either entrance, although there's less backtracking if you choose the ground grating trap near the bank.

⑥ Maintenance Room

For a bit of fun, activate the Automatic Maintenance Terminal. This starts up a Sewer Protectron, who begins to enact a hostile eradication program. Naturally, this

⑩ Metro Tunnel Section

Check the Brotherhood of Steel Initiate, as he's wearing a prototype suit of Medic Armor (no helmet is available).

- Brotherhood of Steel Holotag
- Prototype Medic Power Armor (22/89)
- Medic Power Armor Manual

⑪ Rocky tunnel

- Duck and Cover! (6/25)

3.03: THE REPUBLIC OF DAVE (LAT 19/ LONG 27)

- Miscellaneous Quest: You Gotta Shoot 'Em In The Head
- Freeform Quest (2)
- Threat Level: 2
- Faction: Republic Of Dave
- Services: Trader
- Collectibles: Nuka-Cola Quantum, Bobblehead, Scribe Pre-War Book (2)
- Area is Locked
- Guns And Ammunition
- Interior Exploration
- Lots O' Caps

EXTERIOR MAP AND LOCATIONS

Republic of Dave Capitol Building, Museum, and Outbuildings

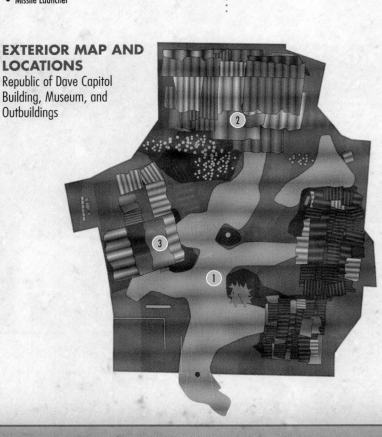

REPUBLIC OF DAVE: INHABITANTS

Supreme Commander and President for Life Dave

Dave is the descendant of those who fled to the hills prior to the bombs dropping and managed to survive the war. His family has lived on this plot of land for the last 200 years. His "citizens" are mostly decedents of his own ancestors or others with similar mind-sets. In the chaos that has ruled the planet over the last 200 years, Dave (now 47 years old) has come to believe strongly that his land is a functioning nation and considers the compound his sovereign territory. He was briefly banished from this place during his father's presidency (the Republic of Tom), and he did some work with Allistair Tenpenny. Dave hates Tenpenny and people like him and doesn't want to be reminded of the past.

Jessica, Wife of Dave

She is Dave's new, younger wife and lives in the Republic of Dave. Her husband is a survivalist and has made sure his wife and older children know how to fight. Jessica is 24 and has never left the Republic; she fences but is extremely naive, conceited, and catty, especially when dealing with the first wife, Rosie.

Rosie, Wife of Dave

Rosie is possibly the most discontented citizen of the Republic of Dave. She'll occasionally speak up, but Dave quickly reminds her where the power of the Republic truly lies. Rosie is extremely intelligent and has many suggestions about how the Republic could be safer, happier, and more efficient. Unfortunately, people rarely ask Rosie what she thinks.

Shawna, Daughter of Dave

Dave's 17-year-old daughter and eldest child has been brought up knowing how to shoot, hunt, fight, and utilize other survivalist techniques, just in case she ever has to leave the Republic. Shawna completely believes in her father's omnipotence. She is a very anxious, high-strung girl.

"Second-Commander of the Army of Dave" Bob, Son of Dave

Bob is young, hotheaded, and bossy. Although he's only 19, Bob thinks of himself as Vice Dave, insisting that he knows best and that all citizens of the Republic should listen to him. Although Dave will not admonish Bob in public, it's widely known that Dave lets Bob have it behind closed doors. Bob resents his father and looks forward to the day he can establish the Empire of Bob.

Mary, Daughter of Dave

Mary is 12 years old and Rosie's daughter. She's bright and curious, but Dave will probably soon cure her of that.

Rachael, Daughter of Dave

Rachael is 11 years old and gets excited about any visitors from the outside. She is inquisitive, does well at school, and knows all of President Daddy's rules by heart.

Flower, Daughter of Dave

Flower is the youngest child in the Republic. Because of that, the other kids usually stick her with the worst chores, which she cheerfully carries out.

Ralph, Son of Dave

The youngest male resident of the Republic of Dave, Ralph is a very serious boy with an old soul and tends to act like an adult; in fact, he's a little like a miniature version of his father. He follows the rules of his nation to the letter and is sometimes curt, but he can be friendly if he's treated with respect.

GENERAL NOTES

In the years shortly before the bombs fell, a large number of citizens believed that the U.S. government had become hopelessly corrupt and that the country was in grave danger from anarchists, liberals, and communists. These individuals relocated to remote rural locations, established private militias, and promised that they would one day take back the government for the people. They never got the chance. The bombs fell, shattering all world governments. Most of these separatists were killed in the war or the chaos that followed. However, a few dug in deep enough and survived the worst of the first few decades. Over the past two centuries, this tiny plot of land has been known as the Kingdom of Larry; the Republic of Stevie-Ray; Billsylvania; the New Republic of Stevie-Ray; and, most recently, the Nation of Tom, after Dave's father. Now that Dave has complete autonomy over his subjects, he rules his hamlet with an iron fist but wishes to be seen as benevolent.

① The Republic's Grounds

There are two ways into the Republic of Dave. The recommended way is to meet Ralph at the front gate and request an audience with President Daddy. Move into the settlement and to the Capitol Building to the north. The other way in is by jumping on the tire pile and over the fence by the northwest exterior fence. There's a shooting range to the Museum's right (where you'll also find an Ammo Box and a Super Mutant effigy). To enter the Men's and Women's Outbuildings without turning the residents hostile, you must head inside when no one is watching.

- Ammo Box Ammunition

② The Capitol Building

It may not be as grand as the D.C. Capitol, but it's in better shape! Inside, you usually find Rosie and Jessica, plus Dave in his office. Downstairs is a locked Ballot Box. When you meet Dave, you can seek citizenship or asylum, or pretend [Speech] to be an ambassador from the Wasteland. Or, you can kill everybody. Stay civil and you can freely talk to everyone after finishing your conversation with Dave.

Pickpocket him; he has a load of Caps and Dave's Special Key; this is helpful during **Miscellaneous Quest: You Gotta Shoot 'Em in the Head,** and it opens the floor safe containing Caps and a special hunting rifle named Ol' Painless (if Dave isn't carrying it)! However, if you're spotted, the entire Republic goes hostile! The same is true if you attempt to steal Dave's prized Nuka-Cola Quantum atop the safe. Either wait until the office is empty, or use Sneak and a Stealth Boy. Or murder everyone.

- Ballot (Dave)
- Dave's Special Key
- Floor Safe Items
- Ol' Painless (23/89)
- Nuka-Cola Quantum (16/94)

③ The Museum of Dave

During waking hours, Shawna is inside, teaching class. If your Pip-Boy reads 2:00 PM, you're in for an "extra special treat": **Freeform Quest: Museum of Dave.** Aside from the assorted useless items, there's is the following:

- Chinese Officer's Sword
- Chinese Pistol
- Scribe Pre-War Book (15 & 16/98)
- Bobblehead: Perception (6/20)

Caution

A word of warning: only the Bobblehead can be pocketed without stealing; try to grab anything else when class is in session, and Shawna starts firing while the children flee. Come back at night for anything you need.

RELATED INTERACTIONS

Ralph: Request an audience with President Dave.

 Republic of Dave Resident: Request an audience with Dave; they don't open up until Dave proclaims this to be possible.

Republic of Dave Resident: Threaten to attack; all the children rush off and cannot be harmed, while all the adults arm themselves with mainly Chinese-made weaponry. They must all be defeated, or you can flee and let them calm down (if you haven't killed anybody).

Republic of Dave Adult: You can speak to any of the adults about the elections, being held today.

Rosie: You can talk to her about Dave; they married when he was wandering the Wastes, but after Ralph, Dave wanted a second wife to help "repopulate." Rosie isn't very happy about this.

Jessica: You can listen to her go on and on about Rosie, Dave's "other" wife. Rosie thinks she should be in charge, but Jessica isn't having any of it. She hates Rosie's children too. Hers will be much cuter.

Bob: You can talk to Bob about himself; he's second in command, and he doesn't want you distracting the wives. He's also the second commander of the Army of Dave. Which means he gets a gun.

Shawna: You can speak to her about herself; she sees herself simply as a teacher, telling the kids (her brothers and sisters) about truth, justice, and Dave's will.

FREEFORM QUEST: THE MUSEUM OF DAVE

Speak to most of the Republic's adults, and they'll tell you Shawna works at the Museum, ensuring that a new generation grow up learning all the important history they can...about Dave. Head there at 2:00 PM every day (check your Pip-Boy for the time), and Shawna begins a well-rehearsed tour of the Museum's most precious relics. Here are the "facts" from the tour:

> When the Greater Leader lay in the baby carriage, he never cried, and his poop didn't stink.

> Dave had eight siblings and created a baseball team using them: The Wastelanders' rival team were too scared to show up.

> The Briefcase is the one Dave took when he became

fed up with the ways his father ruled the nation.

> It was artifacts like these that amassed the Republic's great wealth.

> Dave loves collecting Holotapes and more weaponry.

> The globe represents the area that Dave traversed, although the real planet is 50 times this size, at least.

> These Chinese weapons were used against the U.S. before the bombs fell; Dave probably acquired them when he walked to China.

> Dave is a world-renowned marksman; he can shoot an apple out of a Raider's hand from across the Potomac.

> The skull is from a Deathclaw that Dave encountered during his trek across the wastes. It most definitely does not belong to a Brahmin, as there would have to be two skulls, wouldn't there?

 Once the tour is over, speak to Shawna again. With a little **Speech** persuasion, you can reveal your own "Souvenirs from Dave's past." These are just what Shawna needs; Dave increased the Museum school budget for the year, and instead of buying books for the kids, she'll pay you for your trinkets. Shawna now buys from you any time you return here.

FREEFORM QUEST: ELECTION DAY

Dave mentions the elections that are occurring today. If you offer to help organize the event, Dave promises a small payout. You must ask the voters whether they've done their duty. There are five patriots able to vote in this election, and they have their own agendas.

Dave: Of course he's already voted, you fool! And he's voted for himself.

Rosie: If you're pleasant with Rosie and urge her to stand as president, she sometimes accepts but definitely does if you succeed in a Speech Challenge. After all, she used to run a Wastelander caravan train bigger than this place! She either votes for Dave (if you're unpleasant or just ask her to vote) or herself.

Jessica: She's a die-hard Dave supporter all the way; she'd vote twice for him if she could!

Shawna: She's also not going to be swayed by your sweet-talking; another vote for Dave is assured.

Bob: If you're slightly unpleasant to Bob after asking him whether he wants to be President, he fumes and decides to "show the world" by voting for himself. Otherwise, this is another vote for Dave.

 Note
You can interfere in the election by opening the Ballot Box, but your tampering simply turns the Republic violent. You can also ask whether the residents would consider you as a presidential candidate. Although you've certainly got the war experience, you're a little young...oh, and you weren't born in the Republic.

Inform Dave the election results are in. He rewards you and counts the votes. The results are either a landslide (if everyone voted for Dave) or a slight hiccup (if Rosie and/or Bob voted for themselves). Whatever the percentages, Dave has won by a considerable margin, and the Democracy of Rosie is crushed, as is the Bob Uprising of 2277.

- 25 Caps

3.04: CHASTE ACRES DAIRY FARM (LAT 15/LONG 24)

- Threat Level: 3
- Faction: Raider
- Collectible: Skill Book (2)
- Friendly: Brahmin
- Hostile: Radscorpion Genus, Raider

Between the MDPL-16 Power Station and the broken freeway is a patch of land once used by grazing cows. Now the mutated descendants, Brahmin, chew through the straw grass clumps in this dust bowl. The biggest problem is the small groups of Raiders who've taken over this wrecked farm; pay special attention to the one on the silo balcony. Inside the Grain Silo is a copy of Pugilism Illustrated. You can also use the ladder to reach the balcony. Head inside the barn for a Grognak the Barbarian, next to the bloody mattress.

- Pugilism Illustrated (7/25)
- Grognak the Barbarian (5/25)

3.05: MDPL-16 POWER STATION (LAT 18/LONG 24)

- Threat Level: 1
- Collectible: Nuka-Cola Quantum
- Health And Chems
- Interior Exploration
- Work Bench

There's nothing to search for in the gated transformers area, so head inside to uncover a Work Bench with a Bottlecap Mine, a Terminal, a Safe, and the following items:

- Work Bench (7/46)
- First Aid Box Health and Chems
- Nuka-Cola Quantum (17/94)
- Desk Safe Items

3.06: GREENER PASTURES DISPOSAL SITE (LAT 07/LONG 21)

- Threat Level: 3
- Faction: Wastelander
- Danger: Low Radiation
- Collectibles: Nuka-Cola Quantum, Bobblehead, Skill Book (2)
- Guns And Ammunition
- Health And Chems
- Interior Exploration
- Sleep Mattress
- Work Bench
- Hostile: Robot Genus
- Hostile: Radroach

This is one of the largest expanses of Radiation in the Wasteland. If you're not protected, sprint to the open container adjacent to the white and red truck engine and grab the Radiation Suit off the dead scientist, along with the Skill Book. Inside the makeshift shack are scattered Chems, a Carton of Cigarettes, a place to sleep, and the following items:

- Radiation Suit
- Big Book of Science (4/25)
- .32 Pistol and Ammo
- D.C. Journal of Internal Medicine (7/25)

In the stone office building on this area's western edge, search for the items listed below, then activate the terminal or safe to gather the safe's contents. There's also a Work Bench with a Bottlecap Mine on it.

- Work Bench (8/46)
- First Aid Box Health and Chems
- Nuka-Cola Quantum (18/94)
- Bobblehead: Agility (7/20)

3.07: GRISLY DINER (LAT 13/LONG 20)

- Threat Level: 3
- Faction: Raider
- Danger: Chain Trap, Mines
- Collectible: Skill Book
- Guns And Ammunition
- Health And Chems
- Sleep Mattress
- Hostile: Raider

Raiders attack from the hillside above you, but they appear only after you enter the diner, so back out immediately and defeat them, or squat down and strike as they enter. There are Frag Mines set to detonate at the front and back of the place. Look for and retrieve them. Be very careful when investigating behind the counter, as there's a chain trap, and a Brahmin leg swings down to thwack you; also watch for the pressure plate on the floor. There are Chems, Whiskey, a bunk bed, weapons, and a Keller Family Holotape (on the desk).

- Frag Mine (8)
- Tales of a Junktown Jerky Vendor (4/24)
- First Aid Box Health and Chems
- Ammo Box Ammunition (4)
- Chinese Assault Rifle
- Missile Launcher
- Holotape: Keller Family (4/24)

3.08: RELAY TOWER KX-B8-11 (LAT 15/LONG 20)

- Threat Level: 1
- Faction: Wastelander
- Collectible: Scribe Pre-War Book, Skill Book
- Guns And Ammunition
- Health And Chems
- Highly Visible Landmark
- Interior Exploration
- Radio Signal
- Sleep Mattress

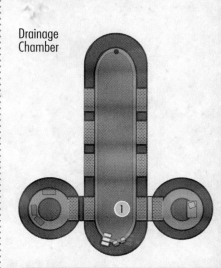

Unlock the gate, then activate the Electrical Switch to power on the Broadcast Tower. Immediately you're able to listen to Radio Signal Oscar Zulu, a frantic message from someone named Bob Anderstein, who's hiding in a Drainage Chamber [3.K].

- Radio Signal Oscar Zulu

Drainage Chamber

Tip

Triangulate a radio signal by listening to the sound quality. As the sound becomes clearer, you're near your target. If it sounds muffled or staticky, you're heading in the wrong direction.

① Drainage Chamber interior

This is a small tunnel with two hatch doors and the skeletal remains of the Anderstein family huddled together. Check the foot-locker, locate the items shown below, and open the hatch door opposite for a radio table with a Pre-War and Skill Book on it. There's a wall cot to sleep on too.

- Ammo Box Ammunition
- First Aid Box Health and Chems
- Blood Pack
- Scribe Pre-War Book (17/98)
- D.C. Journal of Internal Medicine (8/25)

TRAINING — BESTIARY — MAIN QUEST — MISC. QUESTS — TOUR — COMPLETION — APPENDICES

3.09: MINEFIELD (LAT 04/LONG 14)

- Miscellaneous Quest: The Wasteland Survival Guide
- Miscellaneous Quest: Strictly Business
- Threat Level: 5
- Faction: Wastelander
- Danger: Mines

- Collectibles: Scribe Pre-War Book (9), Skill Book (4)
- Guns And Ammunition
- Health And Chems
- Highly Visible Landmark
- Interior Exploration
- Sleep Mattress
- Hostile: Radroach

ARKANSAS

The last of the military survivors who made Minefield their town, Arkansas was a small boy when the Slavers first came and captured nearly all of the tribe, but they never found him. Swearing revenge, he spread rumors of a new band of inhabitants and set a trap for the Slavers. When the Slavers came to raid the town again, they were harried by a hidden sniper and decimated by land mines. The Slavers took heavy losses that day and never came back. Now an old man, Arkansas still shuffles around this place.

Before the bombs fell, the isolated township of Ridgefield was a quiet community nestled into the hillside and far between major roads. More than a century later, a tribe of military survivors stumbled across it while traveling from the north. They quickly realized the value of a defensible, hidden location and made it their own. Now no one goes to Ridgefield anymore, and the ghost town is known only as "Minefield." People swear that it's haunted by the last survivor's ghost. Arkansas is the "ghost" in question; he may be old, but he's still a crack sniper, and he's holed up in the ruined concrete building at the town's north end. Sneak down from the Water Tower [2.0], as this has the least number of Mines to worry about. There are dozens dotted around the entire area; deactivate them and cover the ground very slowly.

- Frag Mines (20+)

Caution

The rest of Minefield is highly dangerous. Arkansas likes to snipe cars until they explode, and Mines trigger other Mines and set cars alight. Before searching the town, make sure you Sneak, use a Stealth Boy, deactivate a Mine the moment you hear it, and neutralize Arkansas.

① Arkansas' Vantage Point

You can kill, ignore, or enslave Arkansas, depending on your persuasion and Quest. He has some food and a mattress. Check his body for the Key.

- Ammo Box Ammunition (4)
- Ridgefield Key

Tip

Unlock each house using either your Lockpick skill or the Ridgefield Key.

② Gillian House

If you don't have the Key, Lockpick your way in. Watch for Radroaches. There are Darts and food, beds to sleep in, a maser bedroom safe, and the following items:

- Scribe Pre-War Book (18 & 19/98)
- Grognak the Barbarian (6/25)
- First Aid Box Health and Chems
- Floor Safe Items

③ Gibson House

Unlock the door and begin a thorough search. The Model of Home is ideally opened using Gibson's Key, found on his body in the Offices of the Capital Post [21.03]. The reward are some common items. Drat! The kitchen has food, but the biggest prizes are upstairs. Open the wall safe and search for the following:

- Scribe Pre-War Book (20–23/98)
- Tumblers Today (6/25)
- First Aid Box Health and Chems
- Wall Safe Items

④ Benson House

Unlock the front door, and enter the small foyer. Check for the following items and open the wall safe:

- Scribe Pre-War Book (24 & 25/98)
- D.C. Journal of Internal Medicine (9/25)
- Wall Safe Items

⑤ Zane House

Unlock the door, and begin picking up valuable items. There are also Darts and cleaning products in the kitchen, the office has some .32 Caliber Rounds, and there's a cabinet with a wall safe behind it to unlock. Upstairs, the kid's bed has some Darts under it.

- Scribe Pre-War Book (26/98)
- Pugilism Illustrated (8/25)
- Wall Safe Items
- First Aid Box Health and Chems (2)

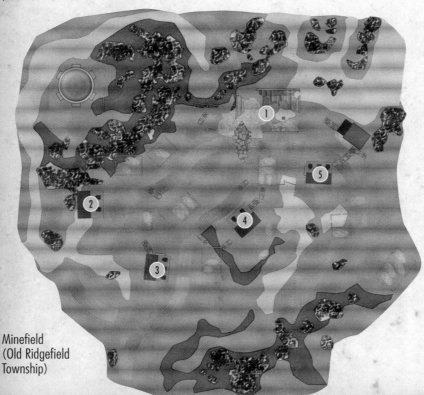

Minefield (Old Ridgefield Township)

3.10: TEMPLE OF THE UNION (LAT 13/LONG 15)

- Miscellaneous Quest: Head Of State
- Threat Level: 2
- Faction: Abolitionist
- Collectibles: Scribe Pre-War Book, Schematic
- Area Is Locked
- Health And Chems
- Interior Exploration
- Main Trading Route
- Sleep Mattress
- Friendly: Brahmin

HANNIBAL HAMLIN

Hamlin is a fanatical Abolitionist, stemming from his 23 years as a slave before he fled his captors. He has spent the last 6 of his 37 years doing everything in his power to help escaped slaves and fight the scourge of slavery. Three years ago, he found Lincoln's head and established the community of Temple of the Union. Each day, Hamlin delivers antislavery speeches to the people of Temple of the Union.

SIMONE CAMERON

Simone is 26 and was a Raider before Slavers took her. She was a slave for only seven months before escaping. As a former Raider, she is very comfortable with weapons and fighting. She is the most combat skilled of all Hannibal's followers. She is a rough and tough person, with a total lack of respect for almost anyone except Hannibal.

CALEB SMITH

Caleb is 32 and was born a slave. He escaped eight years ago and joined a Raider band. When he heard about Hannibal and the Temple of the Union, he promptly left the Raiders and joined Hannibal. He is the first of Hannibal's followers and has some experience as a stonecutter. Caleb prefers to use melee weapons but knows his way around guns.

BILL SEWARD

Bill is 54 years old and was a slave for most of his life. He would never have run away if he hadn't accidentally killed his master's daughter. Hannibal found him within hours of the incident. If not for Hannibal, Bill would have been recaptured within the day or fallen prey to the Wasteland's dangers. Bill isn't that skilled and has no military training. He's been relegated to cooking and cleaning, and he's an awful cook. His other principle job is to take care of the Brahmin and Four Score the dog. Bill has spent his whole life afraid and subservient. Even though he is free now, those habits are hard to break.

ALEJANDRA TORRES

Alejandra was an historian and a tinker, and she was a slave for 4 of her 22 years. Hannibal bought her just over a year ago and promptly freed her. She is quiet, smart, and has the best understanding of science and machinery of anyone in the Temple of the Union, which isn't saying much.

FOUR SCORE

Hannibal's faithful dog companion. The literal meaning is "80 years," but it is also found in the first line of Lincoln's Gettysburg Address.

GENERAL NOTES

This small settlement literally sprung up around the severed head of Lincoln, a portion of the statue from the Lincoln Memorial, and a random block from the memorial's inscription. How it arrived in this remote spot is anyone's guess, but the Temple's residents now revere the head as a symbol of the Abolitionist movement. The Temple is a reasonably fortified ruined building; you're been greeted by Simone Cameron, a no-nonsense sentry wanting to know what you're doing here. Remain polite to enter the premises. She gives you a Key once she deems you trustworthy. Or you can unlock the front gate yourself. This usually leads to violence.

You're told to meet with Hannibal before the Abolitionists will begin to speak freely with you. To remain on friendly terms, swear to protect the Temple of the Union. You are given the Temple of the Union Key as a symbol of their trust. You can now freely talk to all the Temple's inhabitants and explore their base. All the Abolitionists have Temple of the Union Keys to get in and out of the place. Caleb and Hannibal

are also carrying a Storeroom Key. Conclude **Miscellaneous Quest: Head of State** favorably with the Abolitionists, and you receive Dart Gun Schematics.

- Temple of the Union Key
- Storeroom Key
- Schematic: Dart Gun (8/23)

Caleb's Home

There's a mattress here. The only area on the ground floor not instantly accessible is Caleb's home, but there is a First Aid Box, a Scribe Pre-War Book, and a mattress. Head to the second floor; there's a mattress on the ground floor between the trash bins, and common items to search for in here and the offices.

- First Aid Box Health and Chems (2)
- Scribe Pre-War Book (27/98)

Hannibal's Home

A straightforward place, with two small mattress beds and a bit of junk to look at.

Simone's Home

Simone is a hoarder, with more junk, two beds, some small amounts of Pre-War Money, and Chems.

Storeroom

The Storeroom is filled with food, some Chems, a First Aid Box, and a couple of Cartons of Cigarettes.

- First Aid Box Health and Chems

Caution

Steal anything or open the Storeroom while being watched and the Abolitionists will turn on you; make sure to pilfer only when no one is watching.

Secondary Locations

3.A: TRIO OF RUINED HOUSES (LAT 09/LONG 29)

- Threat Level: 2

There's some common items inside one of the mailboxes, but otherwise these buildings are devoid of interest.

3.B: OVERTURNED CITY LINER (LAT 18/LONG 30)

- Threat Level: 1

This area is completely deserted.

3.C: FISHING HOLE SHACK (LAT 04/LONG 26)

- Threat Level: 2
- Danger: Low Radiation
- Guns And Ammunition
- Hostile: Radscorpion Genus

What was once pastoral farmland east of Old Olney is now a dustbowl, and the only patch of water in this area is a small pool with a few half-submerged barrels leaking radioactive waste.

- Ammo Box Ammunition

3.D: RUINED FARMSTEAD (LAT 06/LONG 27)

- Threat Level: 2
- Faction: Raider
- Collectible, Mini-Nuke, Skill Book
- Guns And Ammunition

- Hostile: Raider, Raider's Guard Dog, Radscorpion Genus

West over the rocky hilltop, where Vault 92 is hidden, are two farm buildings. Check the barn's ground-level shelves for a Dean's Electronics. The open tool cabinet has a variety of junk, a few Chems, and a Mini-Nuke. The balcony above offers nothing except an alternate escape option.

- Dean's Electronics (2/25)
- Mini-Nuke (17/71)

3.E: RED ROCKET GAS STATION AND JACKKNIFED TRUCK (LAT 13/LONG 25)

- Miscellaneous Quest: The Nuka-Cola Challenge
- Threat Level: 1
- Collectibles: Nuka Cola Quantum (5), Skill Book

The Gas Station is devoid of items, so check the jackknifed truck—it's actually a Nuka-Cola truck! This vehicle was delivering a shipment of delicious Nuka-Cola to Old Olney but never arrived. Most of the bottles have been stolen, but there's a few Nuka-Colas in the container and a fantastic haul of Quantums! Also look in the Chaste Acres Dairy Farm mailbox; grab the Guns and Bullets magazine.

- Nuka-Cola Quantum (19–22/94)
- Guns and Bullets (4/25)

3.F: RUINED HOUSE (LAT 16/LONG 27)

- Threat Level: 1

North of the grazing Brahmin and just west of the Republic of Dave is an old farmhouse. Raiders and Scavengers have long since picked this place clean.

3.G: OLD OLNEY OUTSKIRTS (RUINED HOUSES; LAT 10/LONG 23)

- Threat Level: 3

South of Old Olney is a group of house ruins picked clean months ago; there's only a lawn mower left!

3.H: JACKKNIFED TRUCK (ON FREEWAY; LAT 13/LONG 23)

- Threat Level: 2
- Collectible: Skill Book
- Highly Visible Landmark

This truck is visible from Old Olney, but to access it, you must trek south, to the wrecked vehicles near a freeway onramp just north of the Grisly Diner. Search for the Skill Book in the Coach Liner. The truck on the freeway holds no items.

- U.S. Army 30 Handy Flamethrower Recipes (2/25)

3.I: IRRADIATED OUTHOUSE (LAT 15/LONG 23)

- Threat Level: 3
- Danger: Low Radiation
- Collectible: Nuka-Cola Quantum
- Guns And Ammunition

- Hostile: Yao Guai

Some enterprising but ultimately doomed soul decided to create an outhouse over the next rise south of Chaste Acres Dairy Farm. He attempted to thwart roaming Yao Guai by surrounding the earthen closet with vehicles. The only issue, aside from the fact that it didn't work, is that he built it on an irradiated pool.

- Nuka-Cola Quantum (23/94)
- Ammo Box Ammunition (2)

3.J: DESTROYED BRIDGE (LAT 04/LONG 21)

- Threat Level: 2
- Radio Signal
- Hostile: Yao Guai
- Hostile: Robot Genus

Near the Greener Pastures Disposal Site's western edge is this crumbling bridge. This is the outer edge of a strange radio signal. Tune in, and you can head northwest to the Crashed Anomaly [2.G].

- Recon Craft Theta Beacon Signal

3.K: DRAINAGE CHAMBER (ADJACENT TO RELAY TOWER KX-B8-11; LAT 16/LONG 19)

This Drainage Chamber leads to a small subterranean tunnel where a stranded family once radioed for help. For tactics and the available items here, check out Location 3.08: Relay Tower KX-B8-11.

3.L: THE ROACH KING (LAT 08/LONG 16)

- Threat Level: 2
- Faction: Wastelander
- Danger: Low Radiation
- Collectible: Fat Man Mini-Nuke
- Guns And Ammunition
- Hostiles: Radroach , Roach King

He sits in the irradiated plains to the east of the MDPL-13 Power Station [2.09] and is immediately hostile.

- Mini-Nuke (18/71)
- Ammo Box Ammunition

3.MI AND MII: DRAINAGE OUTLETS (LAT 15/LONG 17/18)

- Threat Level: 1
- Danger: Low Radiation
- Friendly: Brahmin

At the foot of the hill leading east to the Hilltop Farm Ruins are two tiny drainage outlets.

3.N: HILLTOP FARM RUINS (LAT 16/LONG 17)

- Threat Level: 1
- Faction: Wastelander
- Danger: Low Radiation
- Collectible: Skill Book (2)
- Highly Visible Landmark

This deserted hilltop farmstead has a water tower (a good landmark) with a drinking faucet. The nearby outhouse contains Guns and Bullets. To the east is an overturned container with a Raider corpse; locate Dean's Electronics on a barrel. In the farmhouse shell is a terminal with nine entries (written by Edgar, Rochelle, Tyrone, and Doc J):

Entry #1: Edgar. You deduce that these are entries by people who've "come out into the light" from a nearby hiding spot after the bombs hit. Edgar has set this terminal up for everyone to use.

Entry #2: Rochelle. Rochelle is excited by Miles and his irrigation system. They have plant materials growing!

Entry #3: Tyrone. He's the boss, but he thinks the idea is stupid and just wants to follow Jim.

Entry #4: Doc J. He types a quick reminder to check in regularly for radiation screening.

Entry #5: Tyler. An entry purporting to be from Tyler, although the syntax suggests otherwise.

Entry #6: Tyler. Tyler believes Rochelle to be responsible. He wants a password on this thing.

Entry #7: Jim. A report stating that the cows are thriving, and irrigation plus fertilization has been good.

Entry #8: Edgar. He wants to construct a windmill out of scrap metal.

Entry #9: Jim. An ominous last entry; someone has spotted people in the valley, but it's probably nothing to be concerned about.

- Guns and Bullets (5/25)
- Dean's Electronics (3/25)

3.O: FREEWAY SHACKS (LAT 11/LONG 14)

- Threat Level: 1
- Sleep Mattress

Head south a little ways to the onramp, and ascend to the section with the three abandoned shanty huts, which contain a few scattered Chems and mattresses. Skill Books appear here once the Enclave land [E4.04].

ENCLAVE CAMP LOCATIONS

CAMP 3.01 (LAT 07/LONG 25)

- Main Quest: Picking Up The Trail
- Threat Level: 2
- Guns And Ammunition

An Enclave Soldier has finished massacring two Wastelanders and a Feral Ghoul inside a truck that has Purified Water inside. The terminal (on the desk with the Energy Cell and Finger) has two menu options—Field Report: PFC M. Scott (a report on a Ghoul attack and the Ghoul's odd, docile behavior) and Orders (Enclave Mission Directives for CO eyes only).

- Enclave Crate Ammunition (4)

CAMP 3.02 (LAT 17/LONG 21)

- Main Quest: Picking Up The Trail
- Threat Level: 2

A small, three-man recon crew.

CAMP E3.03 (LAT 09/LONG 17)

- Main Quest: Picking Up The Trail
- Threat Level: 3

A well-fortified defensive position atop a rocky knoll. You can also activate the Enclave Field Research Terminal to access information on Field Entry: Dog (feral); Field Entry: Large Scorpion; and Field Entry: Mole Rat.

- Enclave Crate Ammunition (4)
- Ammo Box Ammunition (3)

CAMP E3.04 (LAT 11/LONG 14)

- Main Quest: Picking Up The Trail
- Threat Level: 3
- Skill Book (2)
- Miscellaneous Quest: Head Of State

A Vertibird swoops down and lands on the section of broken freeway near the Temple of the Union [3.10]. Once the Enclave arrive (after you finish **Miscellaneous Quest: Head of State**), you can claim these books from the shack tables:

- Tales of a Junktown Jerky Vendor (5/24)
- Scribe Pre-War Book (28/98)
- Grognak the Barbarian (7/25)

TRAINING — BESTIARY — MAIN QUEST — MISC. QUESTS — TOUR — COMPLETION — APPENDICES

Zone 4: Irradiated Western Plains

TOPOGRAPHICAL OVERVIEW

Outside of the D.C. Metro Ruins, this western section of the Wasteland was hit hardest by enemy bombardments 200 years ago, and evidence of the cataclysm is still apparent. Desolate pathways that used to carry vehicles are now used by Scavengers, Raiders, and other ne'er-do-wells. To the west is a large and extremely radioactive "birthplace" of the Super Mutants on this side of the country. To the east are the irradiated plains, where Wastelanders slowly morph into Feral Ghouls. While the Raiders attempt to edge in to the north, this zone is primarily a battle for supremacy between Super Mutants and the Talon Company Mercenaries, who have commandeered Fort Bannister, the epicenter of the historic bombardment. Be careful out there!

AVAILABLE COLLECTIBLES (ZONE 4)

- Bobbleheads: 0/20
- Fat Men: 1/9
- Fat Man Mini-Nukes: 6/71
- Unique Items: 5/89
- Nuka-Cola Quantum: 9/94
- Schematics: 1/23
- Scribe Pre-War Books: 6/98
- Skill Book (Barter): 2/24
- Skill Book (Big Guns): 3/25
- Skill Book (Energy Weapons): 2/25
- Skill Book (Explosives): 1/25
- Skill Book (Lockpick): 1/25
- Skill Book (Medicine): 2/25
- Skill Book (Melee Weapons]: 0/25
- Skill Book (Science): 2/25
- Skill Book (Small Guns): 4/25
- Skill Book (Sneak): 1/25
- Skill Book (Speech): 0/25
- Skill Book (Unarmed): 1/25
- Skill Book (Repair): 2/25
- Work Bench: 4/46
- Holotapes (Keller): 2/5
- Holotapes (Replicated Man): 2/19

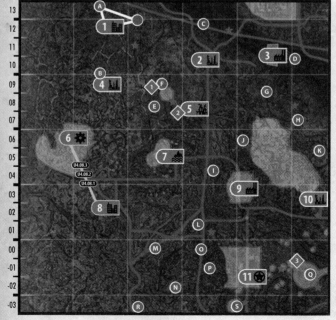

PRIMARY LOCATIONS

4.01: Shalebridge (lat -26/long 12)

4.02: Five Axles Rest Stop (lat -21/long 10)

4.03: MDPL Mass Relay Station (lat -17/long 10)

4.04: Broadcast Tower KT8 (lat -26/long 09)

4.05: Rockbreaker's Last Gas (lat -21/long 08)

4.06: Vault 87 (lat -28/long 06)

4.07: Everglow National Campground (lat -23/long 05)

4.08: Little Lamplight (lat -26/long 02)

4.09: Jalbert Brothers Waste Disposal (lat -18/long 03)

4.10: VAPL-58 Power Station (lat -14/long 03)

4.11: Fort Bannister (lat -18/long -01)

SECONDARY LOCATIONS

4.A: Shalebridge Ant Hill (lat -26/long 13)

4.B: Drainage Chamber (related to 7.A: Broadcast Tower PN; lat -26/long 10)

4.C: Military Truck (Freeway) (lat -20/long 12)

4.D: Beached Boat (lat -15/long 10)

4.E: Abandoned Shack (lat -23/long 08)

4.F: Abandoned Container (lat -23/long 09)

4.G: Fishing Hole and Yao Guai Larder (lat -17/long 09)

4.H: Ruined Farmhouse (lat -15/long 07)

4.I: Jackknifed Truck (lat -20/long 04)

4.J: Wasteland Gypsy Village (lat -18/long 06)

4.K: Wastelander Pylon (lat -14/long 05)

4.L: Junction Shack (lat -20/long 01)

4.M: Orange Truck Debris (lat -23/long 00)

4.N: Scavenger Ruin (lat -22/long -02)

4.O: Captain Cosmos Billboard and Debris (lat -20/long 00)

4.P: Bannister Broadcast Tower (Not Functioning) (lat -20/long 01)

4.Q: Bannister Crater (and Surrounding Ruins) (lat -14/long -01)

**4.R: Drainage Chamber (related to 7.A: Broadcast Tower PN; lat -24/long -03)

4.S: Crater Pool (lat -18/long -03)

Primary Locations

4.01: SHALEBRIDGE (LAT -26/LONG 12)

- Threat Level: 3
- Faction: Ant
- Danger: Low Radiation
- Collectible: Skill Book (2)
- Guns And Ammunition
- Highly Visible Landmark
- Interior Exploration
- Rare Or Powerful Item
- Hostile: Invader Ant Genus, Invader Ant Queen, Mutated Forager Ant

This slightly irradiated area has signs of Anthills dotted across the ground. There are two hillocks, one at the area's north end and one at the south end, each leading to a hive. Two Ant factions—the Invaders and the Foragers—are battling for Wasteland supremacy on a tiny scale. As the Invaders are large, fearsome, and vicious, they are about to kill off their weedier brethren. Also check to the east, where a dead Mercenary is lying near a Skill Book.

- D.C. Journal of Internal Medicine (10/25)

SHALEBRIDGE HILL

After you locate this surface Anthill, descend into a steep and compact series of natural caverns, where the Soldier Ants make their home.

① Empty Nuka-Cola Bottle and Bent Tin Can

Use this when navigating so you don't get lost.

- Big book of Science (5/35)

② Raider's Outfit

- Sledgehammer
- Grenades (4)

③ Dead Hunter

- Hunting Rifle

④ Small Save (Southeast Corner)

- .44 Scoped Magnum and Ammo

⑤ Ant Queen's Hatchery

Bring a Flamer and Fuel, as a monstrous Queen guards the clusters in this area; collect her Pheromones and the paltry amount of Chems, Shotgun Ammo, and items that are with the skeletal remains around the room's perimeter.

INTERIOR MAPS AND LOCATIONS

Shalebridge Hill

Shalebridge Tunnels

- Ant Queen Pheromonest
- Assault Rifle and Ammo
- 10mm Pistol and Ammo

> **Tip**
>
> Kill the Queen, and the aggressive Ants don't come back. Otherwise wait a minimum of 72 hours to return here to face them again.

SHALEBRIDGE TUNNELS

On the other side in this epic Ant struggle are the Foragers, who live to the southwest, just north of the broken radio mast. Explore the huge cavern and its winding areas.

① Ant Researcher

This submerged corpse carries a Skill Book that's otherwise easy to overlook.

② Cluster of Ant Eggs

You're asked to inject this with a Stimpak to stimulate Forager Pupae growth (if your Medicine or Science skills are high enough). Wait 24 hours, then return here;

the Pupae have grown into a much larger mutation. Doctor Lesko would be proud! Harvest the potent Ant Nectar from deposits here, and Trade or consume it.

- Hunting Rifle and 10mm Ammo
- Ant Nectar*

> **Note**
>
> *This grants the following benefits (for approximately two hours):
>
> Strength +4, Charisma -2, Intelligence -2.
>
> However, it is possible to become addicted.
> Withdrawal effects: Strength -2.

4.02: FIVE AXLES REST STOP (LAT -21/ LONG 10)

- Threat Level: 2
- Faction: Raider
- Danger: Mines
- Collectible: Fat Man Mini-Nuke, Skill Book
- Guns And Ammunition
- Sleep Mattress
- Hostile: Raider

A circle of abandoned trucks is the perfect spot for a three-man Raider wrecking crew to chop until they drop. You can destroy the trucks in a giant exploding fireball, but search them first: One has the remains of a trucker conversation. The other trucks are empty except the one with the mattresses, Chems, and Raiders in it.

- Holotape: Partial CB Radio Backup
- 10mm Pistol
- .32 Pistol
- Mini-Nuke (19/71)
- U.S. Army: 30 Handy Flamethrower Recipes (3/25)

4.03: MDPL MASS RELAY STATION (LAT -17/LONG 10)

TRAINING — BESTIARY — MAIN QUEST — MISC. QUESTS — TOUR — COMPLETION — APPENDICES

- Threat Level: 3
- Faction: Raider
- Collectible: Nuka-Cola Quantum, Skill Book
- Guns And Ammunition
- Health And Chems
- Interior Exploration
- Rare Or Powerful Item
- Sleep Mattress
- Hostile: Raider, Robot Genus

TORCHER

Once under the Brotherhood of Steel's protection, this is now home to a small Raider scavenger team under the leadership of Torcher. Inside the exterior defenses are a couple of tables with items on them:

- Ammo Box Ammunition
- First Aid Box Health and Chems
- Combat Knife

Torcher is in the interior substation, and he's armed with a Flamer to really cause you some problems—unless you roll in a Grenade and catch him and his friend (who's hiding behind the computer machinery to the right). Then hunt for a place to sleep and important items; don't forget the Quantum inside the safe:

- Torcher's Helmet (24/89)
- Ammo Box Ammunition (3)
- 10mm Pistol and Ammo
- Guns and Bullets (06/25)
- Nuka-Cola Quantum (24/94)

4.04: BROADCAST TOWER KT8 (LAT -26/LONG 09)

- Threat Level: 3
- Faction: Super Mutant
- Collectibles: Fat Man Mini-Nuke, Scribe Pre-War Book (2), Skill Book
- Highly Visible Landmark
- Interior Exploration
- Radio Signal
- Hostile: Centaur, Super Mutant Genus

Drainage Chamber

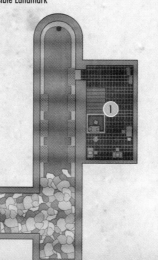

You're at the north of the Super Mutant territory in this zone and should expect combat with them. Activate the Electrical Switch to pick up Radio Signal Sierra Romeo. Triangulate the Morse Code; it leads to a Sewer Entrance [4.B].

> **Note**
> Triangulate a radio signal by listening to the sound quality. As the sound becomes clearer, you're near your target. If it sounds staticky or cuts out completely, you're heading in the wrong direction.

- Radio Signal Sierra Romeo

① Drainage Chamber Alcove

Pick up the Encryption Key near the desk with the broken terminal; then activate the other terminal to open the flap-trap door. This leads to a hidden lower alcove with two dead Chinese Remnant Spies. There's Purified Water and other important items here:

- Scribe Pre-War Book (29 & 30/98)
- Encryption Key
- Mini-Nuke (20/71)
- Chinese Army: Spec. Ops. Training Manual (4/25)

4.05: ROCKBREAKER'S LAST GAS (LAT -21/ LONG 08)

- Threat Level: 2
- Faction: Enclave
- Collectible: Nuka-Cola Quantum
- Hostile: Enclave Eyebot

Off the north–south road, near a rad-lake and shack is Rockbreaker's Last Gas, named for the quality shale quarried nearby. The place is deserted, save for an irritating Eyebot and a dead Wastelander, Chems, and Food. This is the future location of Enclave Camp E4.02.

- 10mm Submachine Gun
- Nuka-Cola Quantum (25/94)

4.06: VAULT 87 (LAT -28/LONG 06)

- Main Quest: Finding The Garden Of Eden
- Threat Level: 5
- Faction: Super Mutant, Vault Dweller
- Danger: High Radiation (3)
- Collectibles: Nuka-Cola Quantum, Skill Book (2)
- Area Is Locked
- Follower
- Guns And Ammunition
- Health And Chems
- Interior Exploration
- Rare Or Powerful Item
- Sleep Mattress
- Underground Connection
- Hostiles: Centaur, Radroach, Super Mutant Genus

INHABITANTS

Peter Stevens (Very Deceased)

A Vault 87 inhabitant and prone to hearing the strange sounds of children, which drove him quite mad.

Daniel Koster (Very Deceased)

A Vault 87 engineer, worried about everything from seeping radiation to the consistency of his tapioca pudding.

Dr. Merrick (Very Deceased)

A doctor in charge of Vault 87's clandestine (read: horrific and failed) experiments.

Fawkes

Residing as a prisoner in Vault 87, Fawkes is one of two "humanized" Super Mutants. When the F.E.V. virus mutated him, a little more of his human side remained. His demeanor and attitude differ greatly from his fellow Super Mutants. His lack of bloodlust and nonaddled mind sets him apart from his brethren. Unfortunately for Fawkes, this has made him hated by the other Super Mutants. Not knowing what exactly to do with this "half breed," the others have relegated him to a tiny observation cell in the Vault 87 lab area. There he sits and ponders his fate, waiting for someone to come along and free him.

Sid

When a man has been captured by Super Mutants, forced to watch as his friends were mutated into horrific, bubo-filled experiments-gone-wrong, and then told he'd either be injected next or eaten, your mind would snap too. Sid reckons he has one chance—a fight to freedom. At least, he thought that before he lost the ability of rational thought.

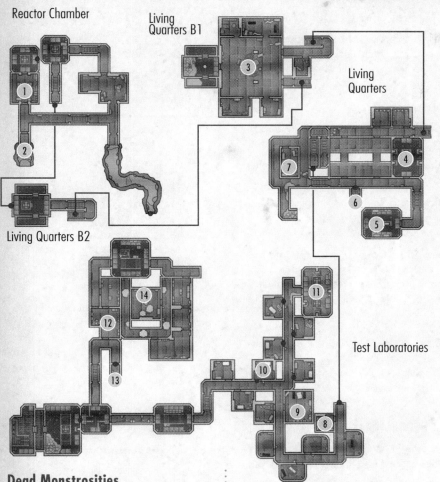

Reactor Chamber

Living Quarters B1

Living Quarters

Living Quarters B2

Test Laboratories

Dead Monstrosities

This is a place where F.E.V. Viruses have led to unspeakable breeding patterns and the creation of new Super Mutants. Humans began experimenting on one another in order to gain a jump forward in evolution. What they achieved was a plummet into a realm of monstrosities. Seen as the Eastern "birthing" place of the Super Mutants, this is the closest the Muties have to holy ground. The central hot spot of the radiation has been measured at up to +2910 RAD/SEC. This means instant death, and the exterior entrance is inaccessible. There's a .32 Pistol and a dead scientist with a Radiation Suit, but you'll never live long enough to reach them. The only way to enter is via Little Lamplight.

REACTOR CHAMBER

Note

The following exploration assumes you've entered Vault 87 via the interior back entrance at the north end of Murder Pass or the Great Chamber. See Little Lamplight for more details.

① Peter Steven's Barricades

You can access Peter Stevens's terminal in a small, partially barricaded room with

Chems, a Stimpak, and a floor safe. There are three uncorrupted entries:

Journal Entry 06A02: This entry of Peter Stevens, Technician Class 3, details the loss of his boy Jason and his wife's mental breakdown. He believes he's sealed inside this "permanent tomb."

Journal Entry 06A05: Peter thinks he hears children laughing when he's in the outer tunnels. The doctors recommended pills. Everything is so pointless.

Journal Entry 06A07: A snapped mind in text form: "Iamsanelammelamforever!"

  Floor Safe Items

② Dead-end Mannequin

  Check the tiny crates for Whiskey and this Skill Book:

- Nikola Tesla and You (7/25)

LIVING QUARTERS

③ Lower Atrium

There are cleaning products, Darts, and a Cherry Bomb or two in the projector room. There's a Stimpak and Gore Bags in the medical bay. Check the west chamber with the flaming barrel for the following:

- Ammo Box Ammunition (2)
- Frag Grenades (3)
- First Aid Box Health and Chems

④ Upper Connecting Room

Use Sneak and this room to avoid Super Mutants patrolling the upper Atrium corridors.

⑤ Daniel Koster's Engineering Room

You can access his terminal, where there are six entries to check out. Read Entry #007 to open the wall safe, or pry it open.

Service Issue Entry V87-002: Dormitory water dispensers have a foul aftertaste. This should clear up in a few days.

Service Issue Entry V87-003: Power spikes had darkened areas of the Vault; the reactor was malfunctioning. Whatever is powering the reactor is way over the acceptable power consumption limits.

Service Issue Entry V87-004: Vault-Tec's substandard build quality has resulted in Koster having to patch and repatch the radiation purge system.

Service Issue Entry V87-005: There's a major problem with the tapioca pudding color matrix!

Service Issue Entry V87-006: The EEP Chamber has failed. Koster mentions a "strange device," but the entry has been heavily edited.

Service Issue Entry V87-007: Something is terribly wrong in the Experimental section of the Vault. Koster's wife quickly died from an unknown disease. Medical records are missing. Many are dead. Accessing this message opens the nearby wall safe.

  Koster's Safe Items

⑥ South Storage Room on Side Corridor

  There are Darts, RadAway, a wall safe and the following:

- First Aid Box Health and Chems
- Nuka-Cola Quantum (26/94)
- Laser Rifle and Ammo
- Pugilism Illustrated (9/25)
- Wall Safe Items

⑦ Upper Medical Laboratory

  Check the room for Chems, Stimpaks, and a Medical Records Terminal that unlocks the wall safe. The following entries are available:

All Employees Must Read!: Vault members deceased from contact in the EEP section are designated an unexplained or undefined death.

Deceased Listing: Everybody is dead. Of the 93 Vault inhabitants, 87 (coincidentally) have "unexplained" deaths.

Death Code Definitions: Some revised "death code" definitions. Criminal deaths and suicides are never listed.

Wall Safe Items

TEST LABS

Note

This last (and upper) level to the Vault actually connects to the entrance on the surface, although you cannot reach the Vault door, as the exit is locked and the radiation levels too high.

8 Observation Chamber

To your right is a floor safe. Also check nearby test chambers to view horrific (and dead) abominations!

- Ammo Box Ammunition (2)
- Floor Safe Items

9 Medical Bay

Consult the five entries on the Chief Physician's Terminal:

Entry V87-34190: Five test subjects exposed to modified FEV are showing progress after a single exposure. They hope to have an answer, as Vault-Tec and the military at Mariposa are becoming bothersome.

Entry V87-34224: The male and female specimens are becoming almost asexual in appearance and transformation in upper-body strength.

Entry V87-34233: Mary Kilpatrick (one of the female specimens) died of a massive loss of brain function, a usual test pattern and an expected result.

Entry V87-24265: All remaining test subjects' skin is becoming thick and resilient. Doctor Filo's skin engineering was a success!

Entry V87-34335: After two weeks, all test subjects began exhibiting severe rage and anxiety and were put to death. This happens every time.

First Aid Kit Health and Chems

10 Fawkes' Test Chamber (#5)

See **Freeform Quest: Finding Fawkes.**

11 Medical Wing Reactor Room

Here you can release all doors to cells (which have Centaurs and Sid in them), or just Fawkes's cell at the Maintenance Terminal.

12 Laboratory

Hack the terminal here to unlock the storage room. Read the entries:

Notice #009: The storage room has been stocked with Radiation Suits.

Notice #012: Radiation expulsion ducts from the G.E.C.K. are venting radiation directly into this area.

Notice #018: Doctor Merrick has ordered the FEV subjects terminated. The area must be scrubbed to avoid cross-contamination when new subjects begin testing.

13 Storage Room

Or, unlock the door; inside is a wall safe and the following:

- Laser Pistol and Ammo
- First Aid Box Health and Chems
- Advanced Radiation Suit and Chems
- Wall Safe Items

14 G.E.C.K. Chamber

Refer to **Main Quest: Finding the Garden of Eden** for options on obtaining this incredibly rare and critical item. Beware of over +100 RAD/SEC exposure here.

- First Aid Box Health and Chems
- Garden of Eden Creation Kit†

FREEFORM QUEST: FINDING FAWKES

At Test Chamber #5, you're interrupted by a Super Mutant speaking to you over the intercom! This is Fawkes, an extremely powerful ally. You can do the following:

 Access Room 05's wall terminal and burn him to death (allowing you to take his Super Sledgehammer), or open his chamber door and attack him.

Open his door at the medical wing's reactor room.

You can request his help in obtaining the G.E.C.K..

If you have high enough Karma, Fawkes can join you as a Follower, once you meet up with him after exiting Vault 87.

- Follower: Fawkes†
- Super Sledgehammer (25/89)

4.07: EVERGLOW NATIONAL CAMPGROUND (LAT -23/LONG 05)

- Threat Level: 3
- Faction: Raider, Super Mutant
- Collectible: Skill Book
- Guns And Ammunition
- Health And Chems
- Sleep Mattress
- Hostile: Raider

Having defeated a Super Mutant incursion, a group of four Raiders are feeling especially proud of themselves. Bring this brevity down a notch by massacring them or Sneaking around and stealing their loot—Sugar Bombs, Darts, and the following items:

- First Aid Box Health and Chems
- Ammo Box Ammunition (2)
- Guns and Bullets (7/25)

4.08: LITTLE LAMPLIGHT (LAT -26/LONG 02)

- Main Quest: Picking Up The Trail
- Main Quest: Rescue From Paradise
- Main Quest: Finding The Garden Of Eden
- Freeform Quest (8)
- Threat Level: 5
- Faction: Super Mutant, Vault Dweller, Wastelander
- Services: Healer, Repairer, Trader
- Danger: Chain Trap, Grenade Bouquet (2), Low Radiation
- Collectibles: Holotape: Replicated Man (2), Nuka-Cola Quantum, Schematic, Skill Book (2)
- Area Is Locked
- Guns And Ammunition
- Health And Chems
- Highly Visible Landmark
- Interior Exploration
- Lots O' Caps
- Rare Or Powerful Item
- Sleep Mattress
- Underground Connection
- Work Bench
- Lamplight Dogs: Rex, Hooligan, Mutt Mutt, Muttface, Bandit, and Pete
- Hostile: Super Mutant Genus

INTERIOR MAPS AND LOCATIONS

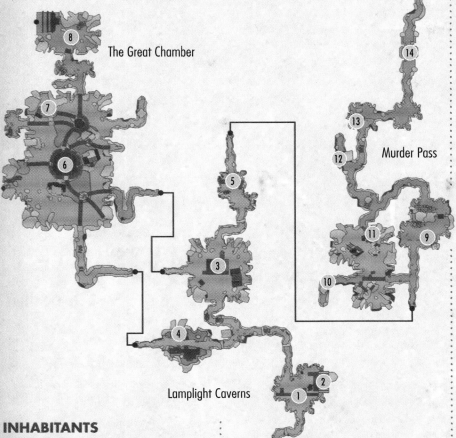

The Great Chamber

Murder Pass

Lamplight Caverns

INHABITANTS

Mayor Robert Joseph MacCready

He has served as the mayor of Little Lamplight for two years (since he was 10), when he was chosen by the other residents due to his smarts, toughness, and the fact that he doesn't take guff from anyone. He has no fear of adults and is a perfect representative. He is belligerent, small (even for his age), very distrustful of adults, and willing to blow someone's head off to defend his young charges, but MacCready is also very loyal to those he considers friends.

Sammy

Sammy is the youngest member of Lamplight's scavenging team (he's 10), but he's also one of the best shots with a rifle in the entire settlement, so he's an invaluable member. Unfortunately, that didn't help him when the Slavers caught them unawares. When he's not on a scavenging expedition, he watches the back door, where Princess teases him for looking a little bit like a girl.

Peter "Squirrel"

Squirrel is 13 and has a knack with computers and electronics. As such, he is an important member of the scavenging team, since he's the only person who can really tell how valuable a piece of scientific hardware really is. He's been caught recently,

Sue "Knock Knock"

Long ago, an earlier generation of kids got a book from Vault 87 called *Vault-Boy's Big Book of Laughs for Kids*, and even though the jokes were pretty bland (the book having been made for generic Vault-Tec use), it had large funny pictures. Even though the book has long since been destroyed, many of the jokes were passed down through the generations, and the knock-knock joke has been her favorite sort of humor, even if it's not always understood.

Angela "Princess"

Three years ago, when she was nine, Angela (who also goes by "Susie") convinced everyone that she should be mayor of Little Lamplight. When the kids finally agreed, she immediately insisted that her first act as mayor was to change the title to "Princess." This so irritated young MacCready that he punched her in the nose and told everyone he was in charge from now on. She's been known as Princess ever since.

Betty "Bumble"

The youngest member of Little Lamplight, Bumble is six and the closest to a carefree

but he's working on an escape plan. He's also sickly, often visiting Lucy for some sort of medication. Inside Lamplight, he spends a lot of his time reading, playing with electronics, and trying not to do anything too stressful.

Penelope "Penny"

Penny is 12 and another scavenger team member. She's adept at finding food and understanding animals in the Wasteland, although this particular talent wasn't of much use when Slavers stumbled across their team and captured most of them. At Lamplight, she spends a lot of time with her brother Joseph, who's her hero; even though she can usually take care of herself, she admires the way Joseph seems to know everything, and she tries to be like him.

Lucia "Lucy"

Lucy was born in Little Lamplight 11 years ago and grew up learning practical medicine from Red, who she considered an older sister. By the time she was 7, she was the preeminent medical authority in Lamplight, and her medical treatment saved Mayor MacCready's life when he was injured in a cave-in. Since then, she's cared a little more about him than the others, and she thinks of Lamplight as "their family." Since MacCready took control, she's been his constant companion, occasionally tempering his instincts with a measure of caution.

Joseph

At 15, Joseph is the oldest resident of Little Lamplight. Perhaps as a result of his age (or the fact that he'll have to leave soon), he has taken it upon himself to hold classes to educate other Lamplighters, covering whatever he feels they need to know (or whatever they show interest in). When not occupied teaching, he spends his time working on his computer or reading old textbooks that were long ago scavenged from Vault 87.

Nicholas "Knick Knack"

Knick Knack and his identical twin sister, Knock Knock, are 14 years old and dedicated to the town. While his sister collects terrible jokes, Knick Knack collects anything of value. He organizes the settlement's store of goods, mostly to keep them in good shape for anyone who needs them, but also because he has a fondness for working with items and making sure everything is "just so."

TRAINING — BESTIARY — MAIN QUEST — MISC. QUESTS — TOUR — COMPLETION — APPENDICES

child to be found in Little Lamplight. She's only just learned how to fire a gun but hasn't tried it out yet, as she literally doesn't have the strength to pull the trigger. She sometimes carries around a teddy bear that used to be her mother's and has been passed down through generations of Lamplighters. Lucy treats her like a little sister. She's also clumsy and prone to knocking into objects, which earned her her nickname. She is extremely naive.

Billy, AKA "Biwwy"

A nine-year-old boy with a slight speech impediment, Biwwy was recently kicked off the scavenging team, because no one could stand being around him. He's still generally avoided by most and leaves a slightly sad, lonely existence, lurking in the alcoves of the Great Chamber and playing with his Wazer Wifle, although he's got no cause to use it anymore.

Eclair

Thirteen-year-old Eclair used to occasionally scavenge outside, but after getting shot in the foot, he was out of commission for a couple months. During that time, he managed the food, using the scraps of cookbooks he found while scavenging with passable results. He does an excellent job with the cave fungus that makes up most of their food. He occasionally tries to create more elaborate food from his cookbook scraps, often with disastrous results (hence his nickname).

Ricky "Zip"

Zip is nine and acts as one of the occasional scouts and scavengers for Little Lamplight, which perfectly suits his speedy and hyperactive nature. As a bonus, it allows him to have first dibs on any Nuka-Cola he can find, a drink he's quite addicted to. When he's not out finding resources for the town, he runs around town, pestering people and generally being feisty. MacCready insists that Zip doesn't get to keep his gun when he's back in town...not since that accident a while ago.

Lamplight caverns were discovered in the late 19th century and converted into a tourist attraction in the 1920s. With its strong government ties, Vault-Tec annexed portions of the caves. On the day the bombs fell, several school classes were attending a field trip. A practical lesson in geology quickly turned into a study in survival. Over the next couple of days, their adult chaperones either abandoned the children or ventured out to learn what had happened, never to return.

The child survivors established a set of rules that would guarantee their existence; without any adult "interference," they lived life as they saw fit. Two hundred years later, Little Lamplight still exists as a village of children. There are two laws they follow:

1. They will obey the mayor, who is elected by public voting. They can elect a new one at any time.

2. They must leave the town before their 16th birthday, or they will be forced out or killed.

The place is easy to see from a distance, thanks to the large water tower, windmills, and rickety lookout towers. Quickly check the gift shop for food, Detergent, and three Ammo Boxes.

- Ammo Box Ammunition (3)

U4.08.1 LAMPLIGHT CAVERNS
1 Front Gate

On the door is the no-nonsense Mayor MacCready, who requires more than a little coaxing before he lets you in. Check the Main Quest for this information.

2 "Essentials" Shack

Inside is a schoolroom where Joseph is sometimes teaching Bumble. Next is the doctor's office, where Lucy tends to wounds and can fill you in on Replicated Man details. You can sleep here.

- Holotape: The Replicated Man (5/24)
- Ammo Box Ammunition (4)

3 Knick Knack's Souvenirs

Talk, Trade, or get Knick Knack to Repair your equipment. Pickpocket Knick Knack's Supply Key and ransack the entire contents of his store; the best items are listed below (or buy them like a civilized person). You can also pick up Purified Water; food; Detergent; and three Holotapes, one related to the Replicated Man (you may need to speak to him for this information), while the other two are diary entries by Jason Grant, one of the first Lamplighters:

Entry 1: Jason Grant is 10 years old and a pupil in Mrs. Dilany's class at Early Dawn Elementary. It is a month after the bombing. Still okay in these caves. Nothing to be scared of as long as you don't go outside.

Entry 2: After two months, Jason is doing "pretty good." Every day they bang on a Vault door. Once, a voice on the other side told him they were dead already. We don't need grown-ups ever again!

- Holotape: The Replicated Man (6/24)
- Holotape: Jason Grant's Diary (2)

- Ammo Box Ammunition (3)
- Knick Knack's Supply Key
- Store Inventory: Missile Launcher
- Store Inventory: Schematics: Bottlecap Mine (9/23)
- Store Inventory: Stormchaser Hat
- Store Inventory: Bottle Caps

4 Spelunker's Cafe

Proprietor Eclair can sell you food. You can dive into the water, but there's nothing of note. Pickpocket Eclair's Cooler Key, and raid the contents of his cooler for a sudden drop in Karma.

- Eclair's Cooler Key

5 Back Gate

Princess guards the Back Gate. There's only a mattress here, which is useful if you want to sleep before venturing into Murder Pass. The gate is only opened once you request passage from Mayor MacCready.

U4.08.2 THE GREAT CHAMBER
6 Rock Pillar Balcony

- Ammo Box Ammunition (2)

7 Game Room with Pool Table

Check the Holotape (from an unknown girl letting everyone know Jason was the first mayor) on the table and a nearby alcove with a Work Bench and a Bottlecap Mine.

- Work Bench (9/46)
- Holotape: January 2077—Little Lamplight!

8 "Nothin'!"

There is a Vault-Tec chamber that leads to a deactivated terminal; one of two entrances to Vault 87, this is only accessible after you okay it with Mayor MacCready and ask Joseph to power the terminal.

RELATED INTERACTIONS

Bumble: You can ask her how she got her name and what she's learned from Joseph.

Eclair: You can ask him about fungus and what food he has for sale.

Joseph: You can ask Joseph about his teaching and receive a haircut from him.

Lucy: You can ask her to heal your broken bones or radiation, or buy Chems and Health.

Lucy: You can ask her about information regarding the Replicated Man.

Mayor MacCready: You can ask how he keeps the place organized.

Princess: You can ask what it's like guarding the Back Gate and how she got her nickname.

Any named Little Lamplighter: You can ask the location of a doctor, trader, place to eat, and Vault 87.

Note

You cannot kill any Little Lamplighter; your morals, even if you're completely despicable, stop short of infanticide.

U4.08.3 MURDER PASS

9 Eastern Cavern

Check the shack and toilet; remember you can Sneak around the enemies.

- Ammo Box Ammunition (2)
- Tales of a Junktown Jerky Vendor (6/24)

10 Western Cavern Dead End

Take the Missile Launcher from the Super Mutant who attacked you.

- Missile Launcher
- First Aid Box Health and Chems (2)
- U.S. Army: 30 Handy Flamethrower Recipes (4/25)

11 Stilt Shacks

- Ammo Box Ammunition (5)
- First Aid Box Health and Chems (5)
- Minigun

12 Brahmin Trap

13 Grenade Bouquet

- Frag Grenade (3)

14 Vault-Tec Metal Bunker Storage Chamber

Watch for another Grenade Trap between the two rusting terminals.

- Frag Grenade
- Nuka-Cola Quantum (27/94)
- Ammo Box Ammunition (3)
- First Aid Box Health and Chems

FREEFORM QUEST: A STICKY SITUATION

The children are throwing a going-away party for one of their own—a tall kid named Sticky, who is about to be banished under Little Lamplight law. He's about to embark on the dangerous journey to Big Town, where the adults who grew up here usually head. He pesters you to chaperone him there. Ignore him, and he'll be waiting at the exterior entrance to Little Lamplight. Agree to take him to Big Town, and you begin **Miscellaneous Quest: Big Trouble in Big Town**.

FREEFORM QUEST: FUNGUS DEAL

Speak with Lucy or Eclair about the nutritional, rad-absorbing fungus growing in these caverns. Lucy agrees to trade her supply for Buffouts, while Eclair wants Strange

Meat. You're told to set up the deal with MacCready.

Using your Barter skill, ask for a trade—you bring in supplies and get fungus in return.

Set a deal up for Buffouts (2) or Strange Meat (2) for Cave Fungus (1).

Set up a Buffout (1) or Strange Meat (1) for Cave Fungus (1); this is the most preferred deal for you.

Or, threaten to seal the place underground and a number of Cave Fungus specimens up front. However, no one wants to speak to you after that.

Cave Fungus*
*WG 1, VAL 50, Rads -10, HP +5

FREEFORM QUEST: TALES OF THE WASTES

Locate Knock Knock and ask her about morale. Suffer a joke and laugh, lie and laugh (using a successful Speech Challenge), or tell her the jokes need work. Stay on her good side, though, and she tells you the Vault Boy's Big Book of Laughs for Kids just isn't cutting it anymore. New tales must be told to keep morale up. When prompted, you can share your own tales with her (either factually, heroically, or with sinister undercurrents). She, in turn, tells the other Lamplighters about it (you can listen in). Eclair will also tell the stories at his food store in the Spelunkers area.

The following tales are available after you complete the quests in question:

1. The time you began to search for your father: available at any time.

2. Your father's ultimate sacrifice and meeting the Enclave and Brotherhood of Steel: Available once you begin **Main Quest: Picking up the Trail.**

3. You escape from the Enclave and attempt to restore Project Purity: available after you begin **Main Quest: The American Dream.**

FREEFORM QUEST: BULLY THE BULLY

Head to the Back Gate and ask Princess how she got her nickname. After she harasses you, speak to Sammy about her (after completing **Main Quest: Rescue from Paradise**) and her name.

Win a challenge, and Sammy tells you MacCready punched her in the face when she tried to be mayor, and she has a secret crush on MacCready.

Return to Princess, and confront her.

The higher this statistic, the more you can hurt her feelings by stating MacCready likes Lucy or that everyone hates her. Princess's tone now changes considerably (she may not talk to you at all).

FREEFORM QUEST: THE KID-KIDNAPPER

Locate Little Lamplight (so it is active on your World Map), then speak with Eulogy Jones in Paradise Falls [2.08]. Ask him if he's thought about kidnapping a child, as they're likely to be less trouble, and fetch a better price. He agrees and gives you a Kidnap Order. A Slaver is waiting at the cave mouth to Little Lamplight. Locate Bumble.

Convince her to "see the outside" and meet a friend.

It requires a successful **Speech** challenge for her to follow you.

It is easier if you have the **Child at Heart** perk.

Chaperone Bumble to the Slaver, and they head back to Paradise Falls (you don't need to follow). Return to Eulogy at your convenience, and he rewards you with the Boogeyman's Hood (referenced in Paradise Falls). Make sure there's no combat between the time you start and finish chaperoning Bumble, or she runs away. Bumble is the only kid you can kidnap.

FREEFORM QUEST: ZIP'S NUKA FIX

Zip, the kid wearing the mole outfit and who's on the scavenging team, is too jumpy for a gun, but he's still on the lookout for items—specifically Nuka-Cola. If you have any regular Nuka-Cola Bottles that haven't been drunk (not Quantum; Zip might explode if he knew about that little concoction!), he'll trade you one of the items he's scavenged (once per 24 hours). The quality of the item depends on your Barter skill:

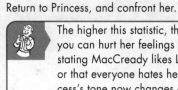

TRAINING — BESTIARY — MAIN QUEST — MISC. QUESTS — TOUR — COMPLETION — APPENDICES

BARTER SKILL	POSSIBLE REWARD(S)
30 or lower	10mm Bullet (1)
31–50	10mm Bullet (1), .556 Ammo Bullets (24), Mutfruit
51–70	10mm Bullet (1), .556 Ammo Bullets (24), Mutfruit, Mentats (1), Stimpak (1)
71+	10mm Bullet (1), .556 Ammo Bullets (24), Mutfruit, Mentats (1), Stimpak (1), Micro Fusion Cell (20)

FREEFORM QUEST: BIWWY'S WAZER WIFLE

Biwwy is located in the Great Chamber and usually can be found sleeping in one of the side alcoves or wandering the rope bridges. Talk to him, and he says he's been taken off scavenger duty and has no use for his weapon. He wants to sell it to you for 500 Caps. If you have the funds, purchase it, or haggle him down to 250 Caps. You now have a weapon that's more powerful than a normal Laser Rifle!

- Biwwy's Laser Rifle (26/89)

FREEFORM QUEST: LAMPLIGHT'S HISTORY

If you locate Joseph, who's usually in the school classroom near the main gate entrance, you can ask him about how his teaching is going and then how Little Lamplight got started. It is a tale of woe and survival. Only one rule to follow: they have to leave before they become a Mungo and keep Lamplight safe from grown-ups.

4.09: JALBERT BROTHERS WASTE DISPOSAL (LAT -18/ LONG 03)

- Threat Level: 2
- High Radiation
- Collectibles: Nuka-Cola Quantum, Skill Book
- Health And Chems
- Interior Exploration
- Work Bench
- Hostile: Radroach

A small and thoroughly irradiated disposal site is located in a gully to the east of the main north–south road. A Radiation Suit or Rad Chems are recommended. The exterior area is devoid of items; stay to the south

and investigate the two offices, starting with the one on the south side of the road gate.

OFFICE #1, CONNECTING CHAMBER, OFFICE #2

Inside the first office, there's a few Radroaches, a safe, and the listed items. Head into a connecting chamber to the other office (essentially allowing you to investigate both buildings without getting irradiated!). The connecting chamber houses Radroaches; a footlocker; and a locker with Rad Chems, Stimpaks, a Radiation Suit, and a locker. The other office has a Work Bench, a Bottlecap Mine, a Tool Cabinet, and a couple more useful items:

- First Aid Box Health and Chems (3)
- D.C Journal of Internal Medicine (11/25)
- Radiation Suit
- Nuka-Cola Quantum (28/94)
- Work Bench (10/46)

4.10: VAPL-58 POWER STATION (LAT -14/LONG 03)

- Threat Level: 2
- Collectible: Fat Man Mini-Nuke, Nuka-Cola Quantum, Skill Book
- Interior Exploration
- Work Bench (11/46)
- Hostile: Yao Guai

Avoid or attack the nearby Yao Guai, and look to the building northwest of the Brahmin Skull Shack [5.U]. Two power lines from the north and east intersect. Open the door to the Substation, and you find a Work Bench with some Darts and a Bottlecap Mine; then open the desk safe. There's food in the Eat'o'tronic 3000, next to the First Aid Box on the wall. Don't forget to check the light fixture for the Mini-Nuke.

- Work Bench (11/46)
- Nuka-Cola Quantum (29/94)
- Dean's Electronics (4/25)
- Mini-Nuke (21/71)
- First Aid Box Health and Chems
- 30 Handy Flamethrower Recipes (5/25)

4.11: FORT BANNISTER (LAT -18/LONG -01)

- Threat Level: 5
- Faction: Talon Mercenary
- Danger: Low Radiation, Mines, Shotgun Trap
- Collectibles: Fat Man Mini-Nuke, Fat Man Launcher, Nuka-Cola Quantum, Skill Book (3)
- Guns And Ammunition
- Health And Chems
- Interior Exploration
- Rare Or Powerful Item
- Sleep Mattress
- Hostile: Commander Jabsco, Talon Company Guard Dog, Talon Company Mercenary, Talon Company Robot Genus

A main military installation that suffered a direct hit back when the bombs fell is now the headquarters for the Talon Company. From a distance, this place looks like a small refugee camp with tents, but on closer inspection, the Talon Company appear and take no prisoners.

① Sunken Stairwell

This leads to Fort Bannister Bunker.

② Sandbag Defenses

Check the balcony table for a Stimpak, and check the area for the following:

- First Aid Box
- Ammo Box Ammunition (3)
- Sniper Rifle

③ Water Tower

Prepare for combat with Talon Company Dogs here. The nearby rocket silo is sealed.

④ Wrecked Building and Tent

Watch for a Missile Launcher–carrying Merc here and the Sewer Entrance to the CO Quarters.

⑤ Doors to Fort Bannister

⑥ Central Tents

Expect combat. You will also find mattresses inside the tents.

- First Aid Box Health and Chems
- Ammo Box Ammunition (2)
- Combat Shotgun

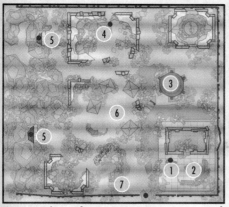

Exterior Talon Defenses

INTERIOR MAPS AND LOCATIONS

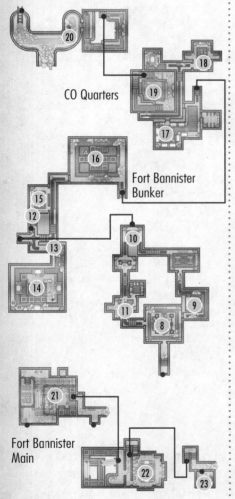

CO Quarters

Fort Bannister Bunker

Fort Bannister Main

⑦ Sentry Platform

Check this general area for a Stimpak, the Merc's Missile Launcher, and the following:

- Ammo Box Ammunition (3)
- Chinese Assault Rifle

Tip

If you're a fan of Missile Launchers, you're in luck; there are four or five Mercenaries carrying them throughout the interior of this place.

Note

The CO Quarters and Bunker are linked. If possible, enter the Bunker first so you can Hack and deactivate the turrets before they shoot you.

⑧ Square Generator Room

Deactivate the Frag Mines and watch for foes here and in every room you visit.

- Frag Mine (2)

⑨ Small Gun Storage Room

Check the top of the cabinet here.

- Guns and Bullets (8/25)

⑩ Northern Exit

Duck down to avoid the Rigged Shotgun Traps on either shelf on the south wall. Disarm them using **Repair**.

- Combat Shotgun and Ammo (2)

⑪ Wall Terminal

Deactivate the turret to the west, or simply avoid it.

- Frag Grenades (2)

⑫ Storage Room

The wall terminal and locked door allow access; take the Chems and the following:

- First Aid Box Health and Chems (2)
- Ammo Box Ammunition (3)

⑬ Wall Terminal

Disable the turrets from here.

⑭ CO's Chamber

Look for Commander Jabsco (head of the Talon Company Mercs) and his Unique Combat Knife in this area. Check the locked floor safe, and look behind the corrugated sheet under the stairs for a footlocker and the following:

- "Occam's Razor" Combat Knife (27/89)
- First Aid Box Health and Chems
- Ammo Box Ammunition (2)
- Floor Safe Items
- Nuka-Cola Quantum (30/94)

Tip

Remember, manually aim at small generators to catch foes in their explosions.

⑮ Kitchen

There's food in the fridges.

⑯ Flooded Area

Beware of foes and a turret.

⑰ Dormitory

There are weapons, enemies, a small scattering of food and Chems, and bunk beds to sleep on.

- Ammo Box Ammunition (5)

⑱ Medical Bay

Search the bodies to find some Chems and other items in this squalid area:

- First Aid Box Health and Chems
- Blood Pack

⑲ Missile Silo

Aside from foes, there's a hidden roof alcove atop the rusting covered area with sandbags; drop down from the stairs directly above.

- Nikola Tesla and You (8/25)
- First Aid Box Health and Chems
- Ammo Box Ammunition (2)
- Frag Grenades (3)

⑳ Sewer Defenses

Watch your step and tackle the well-armed Merc.

- Frag Mines

Fort Bannister Main

㉑ Transportation Warehouse

Watch for the turret in the northwest corner.

㉒ Command Room

There are well-armed foes in here; check the two wall safes.

- Wall Safe Items (2)

㉓ Fat Man Storage

Find the locked wooden door down the stairs, and enter this storage room, which contains substantial collectibles:

- Big Book of Science (6/25)
- Fat Man (4/9)
- Mini-Nuke (22/71)
- Ammo Box Ammunition (2)

TRAINING — BESTIARY — MAIN QUEST — MISC. QUESTS — TOUR — COMPLETION — APPENDICES

Secondary Locations

4.A: SHALEBRIDGE ANT HILL (LAT -26/LONG 13)

This anthill leads to a large subterranean cavern system. For information, check out Location 4.01.

4.B: DRAINAGE CHAMBER (RELATED TO 7.A: BROADCAST TOWER KT8; LAT -26/LONG 10)

This Drainage Chamber leads to a small subterranean tunnel. For information, check out Location 4.04.

4.C: MILITARY TRUCK (FREEWAY; LAT -20/LONG 12)

- Threat Level: 1
- Guns And Ammunition
- Hostile: Mirelurk Genus

To the east of this freeway wreckage is a monorail that has crashed into the river, but the real area of interest is the Military Truck parked on the sloping freeway section.

- Ammo Box Ammunition (2)

4.D: BEACHED BOAT (LAT -15/LONG 10)

- Threat Level: 1
- Danger: Low Radiation
- Guns And Ammunition
- Hostile: Mirelurk Genus

East of the MDPL Mass Relay Station is a beached boat, lying on the remains of the Potomac.

- Ammo Box Ammunition (2)

4.E AND 4.F: ABANDONED SHACK & CONTAINER (LAT -23/LONG 08 & 09)

- Threat Level: 3
- Faction: Enclave, Super Mutant
- Danger: Low Radiation
- Collectibles: Scribe Pre-War Book, Skill Book (2)
- Guns And Ammunition
- Interior Exploration
- Rare Or Powerful Item
- Sleep Mattress

- Work Bench
- Hostile: Radroach, Super Mutant Genus

ABANDONED SHACK

This overlooks an irradiated lake northwest of Rockbreaker's Last Gas. Look at the spectacular vista. You can also see Super Mutants near the Abandoned Container, which is empty not necessary to check out. Inside the shack, there are two caged Radroaches, a fridge with food, some Darts, and a locker containing the Victory Rifle. Also check the floor safe, the mattress, and the Work Bench (check the middle shelf for a Skill Book).

- Work Bench (12/46)
- Victory Rifle (28/89)
- Floor Safe Items
- Ammo Box Ammunition
- Scribe Pre-War Book (31/98)
- Guns and Bullets (9/25)
- Dean's Electronics (5/25)
- Holotape: Keller (7/24)

4.G: FISHING HOLE AND YAO GUAI LARDER (LAT -17/LONG 09)

- Threat Level: 4
- Danger: Low Radiation
- Hostiles: Enclave Eyebot, Robot Genus, Yao Guai

South of the MDPL Mass Relay Station is a small fishing shack and outhouse. The real danger lies in the rocks behind the shack; this is where a pack of three Yao Guai are hoarding their kills.

4.H: RUINED FARMHOUSE (LAT -15/LONG 07)

- Threat Level: 3
- Danger: Low Radiation
- Hostile: Yao Guai

In the northeastern edge of the irradiated plains is a long-abandoned farmhouse and shack, completely devoid of items.

4.I: JACKKNIFED TRUCK (LAT -20/LONG 04)

- Threat Level: 2
- Danger: Low Radiation
- Collectible: Nuka-Cola Quantum
- Hostile: Radscorpion Genus

Check the nearby Coach Liner wreckage for some Darts, then locate the truck resting in a dry streambed. The Quantum is near the barrels.

- Nuka-Cola Quantum (31/94)

4.J: WASTELAND GYPSY VILLAGE (LAT -18/LONG 06)

- Threat Level: 3
- Factions: Ghoul, Wastelander
- Danger: Low Radiation
- Collectible: Fat Man Mini-Nuke, Skill Book (3)
- Guns And Ammunition
- Interior Exploration
- Sleep Mattress
- Hostile: Enclave Eyebot, Ghoulish Wastelander, Radscorpion Genus

A ramshackle community, making the best of the nuclear weather, has gradually fallen into disrepair, and its inhabitants are gradually turning Ghoulish.

WESTERN AND SOUTH LEAN-TOS

- Ammo Box Ammunition (3)

Shack #1

On the highest ground near the large tree, check the open refrigerator for a Skill Book. Inside the shack is a skeleton in a bathtub, who ended it all with a toaster. Locate the following:

- Tumblers Today (7/25)
- Ammo Box Ammunition (2)
- Combat Shotgun and Ammo

Shack #2

This has a picnic table to the door's right and is north of Shack #1. There's a Stimpak, a foe, and a mattress here too.

- Stealth Boy
- Tales of a Junktown Jerky Vendor (7/24)

Shack #3

This shack is near a tree stump (left of the door). There is a lean-to near a burned-out Coach Liner section. The lean-to contains a Carton of Cigarettes.

With the tree stump to the door's left, has a lean-to near the burned-out Coach Liner half with a Carton of Carton of Cigarettes. Inside is a scene of a massacre and the following:

- Ammo Box Ammunition (3)
- Combat Shotgun
- Laser Rifle
- Mini-Nuke (23/71)
- Duck and Cover! (7/25)

4.K: WASTELANDER PYLON (LAT -14/LONG 05)

- Threat Level: 2
- Faction: Ghoul, Wastelander
- Danger: Low Radiation

- Collectibles: Fat Man Mini-Nuke, Holotape, Scribe Pre-War Book
- Guns And Ammunition
- Health And Chems
- Highly Visible Landmark
- Sleep Mattress
- Hostile: Ghoulish Wastelander

Two Feral Wastelanders have made their home in one of the power towers (aka pylons). Dispatch them and loot their treasures; there's a personal footlocker, Darts, and a variety of other items to loot:

- Assault Rifle
- First Aid Box Health and Chems
- Ammo Box Ammunition
- Scribe Pre-War Book (32/98)
- Mini-Nuke (24/71)
- Holotape: Keller (8/24)

4.L: JUNCTION SHACK (LAT -20/LONG 01)

- Threat Level: 2
- Danger: Mines
- Guns And Ammunition

This small shack has a few Mines to dissuade inquisitive scavengers.

- Frag Mine
- Ammo Box Ammunition

4.M: ORANGE TRUCK DEBRIS (LAT -23/LONG 00)

- Threat Level: 2
- Faction: Super Mutant
- Hostile: Super Mutant Genus, Robot Genus

The views are great; you can see south all the way to Tenpenny Tower [7.14]. The inhabitants are not so great.

4.N: SCAVENGER RUIN (LAT -22/LONG -02)

- Threat Level: 2
- Faction: Wastelander
- Services: Repairer, Trader

- Collectibles: Nuka-Cola Quantum, Scribe Pre-War Book (2)
- Guns And Ammunition
- Health And Chems
- Sleep Mattress
- Friendly: Scavenger

Just north of the Charnel House is another ruined building. Inside waits a Scavenger, from whom you can Trade or request Repairs; you can take his Pre-War Books and Quantum without penalty, but his food, Purified Water, footlocker, and other items count as Stealing.

- Nuka-Cola Quantum (32/94)
- Scribe Pre-War Book (33 & 34/98)
- Sawed-Off Shotgun and Ammo
- First Aid Box Health and Chems
- Ammo Box Ammunition

4.O: CAPTAIN COSMOS BILLBOARD, AND DEBRIS (LAT -20/LONG 00)

- Threat Level: 1

A recognizable landmark, below which are a group of rusting vehicles.

4.P: BANNISTER BROADCAST TOWER (NOT FUNCTIONING; LAT -20/LONG 01)

- Threat Level: 1
- Highly Visible Landmark
- Friendly: Brahmin
- Hostile: Bloatfly

Overlooking Fort Bannister to the east are three broadcast towers, all completely useless. This is a good location from which to attack Fort Bannister; you have a great view and can snipe from this large rocky outcrop.

4.Q: BANNISTER CRATER (AND SURROUNDING RUINS; LAT -14/LONG -01)

- Threat Level: 5
- Faction: Enclave, Super Mutant, Talon Mercenary
- Danger: High Radiation
- Guns And Ammunition

- Rare Or Powerful Item
- Alien Captive (Deceased)
- Hostiles: Enclave Camp Personnel, Radscorpion Genus, Super Mutant Genus, Talon Company Mercenary, Yao Guai

The massive bombardment of countless nuclear strikes has turned the area to Fort Bannister's east into a hellhole; there are over a dozen large craters near the outer areas of the fort and six separate clusters of ruined buildings to sift through.

NORTHWEST BUILDING CLUSTER

- A dead Wastelander on a mattress
- Ammo Box Ammunition

The epicenter of this destruction is a massive central impression known as Bannister Crater. This gigantic dent in the earth features furrows east and west of the main crater, where a Military Truck has tipped over. Check the rubble for a couple of desks you can open, a Wastelander with RadAway, and a locked Safe.

However, the real area of interest is under the overturned truck. An odd-looking explorer has dropped an Alien Blaster and ammo.

- Rubble Safe Items
- Alien Blaster and Power Cells (8)

There are reports of strange radio signals emanating from a Crashed Anomaly [2.G].

4.R: DRAINAGE CHAMBER (RELATED TO 7.A: BROADCAST TOWER PN; LAT -24/LONG -03)

This Drainage Chamber leads to a tiny subterranean room. For tactics and the available items here, check out location 7.A: Broadcast Tower PN.

4.S: CRATER POOL (LAT -18/LONG -03)

- Threat Level: 4
- Faction: Super Mutant, Talon Mercenary
- Danger: Low Radiation
- Hostile: Talon Company Mercenary

West of Fort Bannister are two irradiated pools. Watch for Talon Merc attacks.

ENCLAVE CAMP LOCATIONS

CAMP E4.01 (LAT -23/LONG 09)

- Main Quest: Picking Up The Trail
- Threat Level: 2

A squad of Enclave disembarks from a descending Vertibird, which you can shoot out of the sky with a Missile or other ordnance.

CAMP E4.02 (LAT -21/LONG 07)

- Main Quest: Picking Up The Trail
- Threat Level: 2
- Guns And Ammunition
- Health And Chems

A small exploratory force has murdered a Wastelander outside Rockbreaker's Last Gas and has set up a roadblock.

- Enclave Crate Health and Chems
- Enclave Crate Ammunition

CAMP E4.03 (LAT -15/LONG -01)

- Main Quest: Picking Up The Trail
- Threat Level: 4
- Guns And Ammunition
- Health And Chems

An expedition force is investigating Bannister Crater. There are turrets at the top with an Enclave Field Research Terminal: Crater Camp Terminal: Read them to learn that President Eden has ordered this area explored and samples from the crater taken.

- Enclave Crate Ammunition (2)

TRAINING — BESTIARY — MAIN QUEST — MISC. QUESTS — TOUR — COMPLETION — APPENDICES

Zone 5: Central Plains and Potomac

TOPOGRAPHICAL OVERVIEW

The Wastelands' central area, just north of your starting location at Vault 101, has numerous small landmarks and interesting shacks to explore; there are a variety of Primary Locations too. Repel the Super Mutant threat at the Germantown Police HQ on the hill, learn how to maneuver around linked underground areas between Northwest Seneca and Meresti, and marvel at where Wastelanders choose to live—the freeway bridge settlement of Arefu beckons you! In the middle of this area is Big Town, where Large Lamplighters go when they become Mungos. There's an easy underground exploration in Springvale School too. And if you're ready for a complete freak-out, head to the half-hidden Vault 106 and try to survive the surprises inside!

AVAILABLE COLLECTIBLES (ZONE 5)

- Bobbleheads: 2/20
- Fat Men: 1/9
- Fat Man Mini-Nukes: 7/71
- Unique Items: 9/89
- Nuka-Cola Quantum: 8/94
- Schematics: 1/23
- Scribe Pre-War Books: 2/98
- Skill Book (Barter): 0/24
- Skill Book (Big Guns): 0/25
- Skill Book (Energy Weapons): 2/25
- Skill Book (Explosives): 3/25
- Skill Book (Lockpick): 5/25

- Skill Book (Medicine): 3/25
- Skill Book (Melee Weapons): 0/25
- Skill Book (Repair): 1/25
- Skill Book (Science): 1/25
- Skill Book (Small Guns): 1/25
- Skill Book (Sneak): 1/25
- Skill Book (Speech): 3/25
- Skill Book (Unarmed): 2/25
- Work Bench: 3/46
- Holotapes (Keller): 1/5
- Holotapes (Replicated Man): 1/19

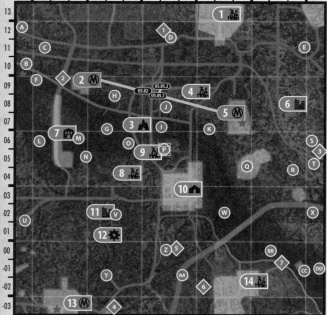

PRIMARY LOCATIONS

5.01: Germantown Police Headquarters (lat -02/long 13)

5.02: Northwest Seneca Station (lat -10/long 09)

5.03: Hamilton's Hideaway (lat -07/long 07)

5.04: Hallowed Moors Cemetery (lat -04/long 09)

5.05: Meresti Trainyard (lat -01/long 07)

5.06: Agatha's House (lat 01/long 08)

5.07: Arefu (lat -11/long 06)

5.08: Fordham Flash Memorial Field (lat -08/long 04)

5.09: Moonbeam Outdoor Cinema (lat -06/long 05)

5.10: Big Town (lat -04/long 03)

5.11: Kaelyn's Bed & Breakfast (lat -09/long 02)

5.12: Vault 106 (lat -09/long 01)

5.13: Jury Street Metro Station (lat -10/long -03)

5.14: Springvale School (lat -01/long -01)

SECONDARY LOCATIONS

5.A: Wrecked Vehicles (lat -13/long 12)

5.B: Military Truck (lat -13/long 10)

5.C: Wrecked Monorail Carriage (lat -12/long 11)

5.D: Ruined House (lat -05/long 12)

5.E: Power Transformers (lat 02/long 11)

5.F: Rusting Boats (lat -12/long 09)

5.G: Scavenger Shack (lat -09/long 07)

5.H: Bowling Billboard (lat -08/long 09)

5.I: Rusting Tub and Broken Bridge (lat -05/long 07)

5.J: Hallowed Moors Shack (lat -05/long 08)

5.K: Riverside Raider Shacks (lat -03/long 07)

5.L: Rusting Tub (lat -12/long 06)

5.M: North Arefu Pier (lat -10/long 08)

5.N: South Arefu Pier (lat -10/long 05)

5.O: Dry Pier (lat -07/long 06)

5.P: Jackknifed Truck (lat -05/long 05)

5.Q: Cratered Hamlet (lat -01/long 05)

5.R: Ruined Farmhouse (lat 02/long 05)

5.S: Dead Man's Caravan (lat 03/long 06)

5.T: Irradiated Pool (lat 03/long 05)

5.U: Brahmin Skull Shack (lat -13/long 02)

5.V: Drainage Outlet (lat -08/long 02)

5.W: Rusting Tub, Shack, and Pier (lat -02/long 02)

5.X: Jackknifed Truck (lat 03/long 02)

5.Y: Patriotic Picnic Area (lat -08/long -01)

5.Z: Ruined Farmstead and Outbuilding (lat -05/long 00)

5.AA: Freeway Raider Encampment (lat -05/long -01)

5.BB: Lakeside Ruins (lat 01/long 00)

5.CC: Rusting Tug (lat 02/long -01)

5.DD: North Pier (lat 03/long -01)

Primary Locations

5.01: GERMANTOWN POLICE HEADQUARTERS (LAT -02/LONG 13)

- Miscellaneous Quest: Big Trouble In Big Town
- Threat Level: 3
- Faction: Super Mutant
- Danger: Mines, Shotgun Trap
- Collectible: Fat Man Launcher, Nuka-Cola Quantum, Scribe Pre-War Book, Skill Book (2)
- Guns And Ammunition
- Health And Chems
- Interior Exploration
- Sleep Mattress
- Hostile: Enclave Eyebot, Radroach, Super Mutant Genus

INHABITANTS

- Nancy Kroydon (Very Deceased)
- Red
- Shorty

At the top of a rocky promontory east of Paradise Falls is the Super Mutant stronghold of Germantown, where the Muties are currently holding a couple of Big Town residents. Locate the Police Headquarters; all the other ruins are empty. The southern exterior defenses are filled with sandbags. The narrow pathway leads from the building's front to tents and a terminal, which has some disturbing log entries by a long-dead relief volunteer, Nancy Kroydon. She charts her experience as the bombs dropped, the desertion of her volunteers, her care for those with radiation poisoning, and her final, hopeless end. Enter the Police Headquarters via a side entrance, or the unlocked rear entrance.

- First Aid Box Health and Chems

POLICE HQ (TOP FLOOR)

① Records Room

Operate the terminal; there are two ancient violations listed to a Danielle Faye and a Jennifer Wilkins. Watch for the Frag Mine here.

- Frag Mine

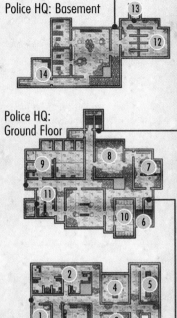

Police HQ: Basement

Police HQ: Ground Floor

Police HQ: Top Floor

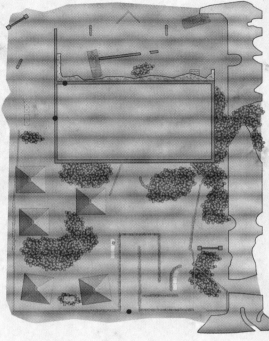

② Long Northern Office

Disarm the Rigged Shotgun in the northwest corner. Watch for the Frag Mine near the Ammo Box.

- Combat Shotgun and Ammo
- Frag Mine
- Ammo Box Ammunition

③ Small Office

Take the Holotape. Use the terminal or unlock the safe.

- Holotape: Password For Lockdown Computer
- Floor Safe Items

④ Conference Room

Beware the Frag Mine as you enter. Grab the following:

- Frag Mine
- First Aid Box Health and Chems
- D.C. Journal of Internal Medicine (12/25)

⑤ Northwest Autopsy Room

- Frag Mine
- First Aid Box Health and Chems
- Ammo Box Ammunition
- Sledgehammer
- Assault Rifle

GROUND FLOOR

⑥ Stairwell

- Frag Mine

⑦ 911 Operators' Room

Access the terminals to read a variety of ancient 911-call transcripts from a variety of kooks.

- Frag Mine

⑧ Debriefing Room

- Lying: Congressional Style (1/25)

⑨ Cells

Use the Password to unlock the lockdown terminal, and check the table for a Pre-War Book. Or, unlock Red's Cell manually].

- Scribe Pre-War Book (35/98)

⑩ Restroom

- Hunting Rifle

⑪ Security Room

Access the terminal, watching for the Mine on the floor. Or, unlock the door itself; both open a Contraband Closet. Inside are Darts, Chems, and the following:

- Frag Mine
- First Aid Box Health and Chems (3)
- Ammo Box Ammunition (3)
- .32 Pistol
- 10mm Silenced Pistol
- Combat Shotgun

BASEMENT

12 Firing Range

- First Aid Box Health and Chems
- Ammo Box Ammunition

13 Locked Storage (Wooden Door)

Some highly collectible items are stored behind this wooden door:

- Ammo Box Ammunition (3)
- Fat Man (5/9)
- Tumblers Today (8/25)

14 Kitchen

Check the food in the fridge, a hostage named Shorty on the floor, and a larder.

- Nuka-Cola Quantum (33/94)

5.02: NORTHWEST SENECA STATION (LAT -10/LONG 09)

- Miscellaneous Quest: Blood Ties
- Threat Level: 1
- Faction: Ghoul
- Danger: Low Radiation
- Guns And Ammunition
- Health And Chems
- Interior Exploration
- Sleep Mattress
- Underground Connection
- Hostile: Mole Rat, Radroach

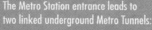

Note

The Metro Station entrance leads to two linked underground Metro Tunnels:

Location U5.02: Northwest Seneca Station (Interior)

Location U5.05.1: Meresti Service Tunnel (page 311).

The following surface location can be accessed from these tunnels:

Location 5.05: Meresti Trainyard (page 310).

INHABITANTS

Murphy

Murphy was an amateur scientist even back in his pre-Ghoul days, and his tenacity has allowed him to deal with his "affliction." He's close to making some real Caps with his invention—an enhanced dose of Jet that can keep a Ghoul up and peaking, as Jet has only limited effects on these creatures.

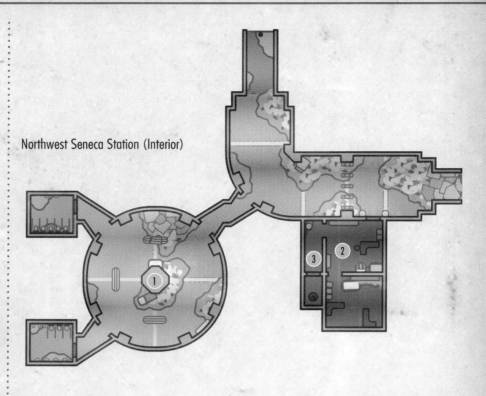

Northwest Seneca Station (Interior)

Barrett

Murphy's bodyguard doesn't "do" chitchat. Not even Murphy knows about his past, and Barrett is quite happy that it stays that way.

This place is eerily quiet. Before entering the Chain Gate, head into the Cornucopia Fresh Grocers. Slay Radroaches and check behind the counter for some Sugar Bombs, scattered Caps, and a terminal that unlocks the floor safe. There's beer, food, drink, and a Carton of Cigarettes.

- First Aid Box Health and Chems

NORTHWEST SENECA STATION

1 Circular chamber

This is leaking radioactive goop. Beware of Mole Rats. There are vending machines to find food in.

2 Ticket Master's Office

You meet two Ghouls, but lower your weapon—this is Murphy and Barrett, and Murphy's got a proposition for you: **Free-form Quest: Murphy's Bombing Run.** Sleep here, or steal Jet, Rad-X, and the following items from this area:

- Sawed-Off Shotgun and Ammo
- First Aid Box Health and Chems
- Ammo Box Ammunition

3 Radioactive Storage Room

Open the manhole to Meresti Service Tunnel here.

Note

The Meresti Service Tunnel is described in Location 5.05: Meresti Trainyard.

RELATED INTERACTIONS

Murphy: You can ask him about the whereabouts of the Family, if you have already begun the **Miscellaneous Quest: Blood Ties**.

Murphy: You can run an errand for him.

Barrett: You can have a slightly threatening conversation with him.

FREEFORM QUEST: MURPHY'S BOMBING RUN

Murphy is a Ghoul who's hoping you're not here to "steal his secrets." Answer that you're not, and he tells you it isn't easy making Ultrajet. The Chem, which Murphy has perfected, has double the potency of Jet, but Murphy is lacking the final of three ingredients—Sugar Bombs. For every Sugar Bomb box you bring, he'll pay you 30 Caps.

- Note: Sugar Bombing Run

Return to Murphy with Sugar Bombs. Bring five boxes, and Murphy makes one Ultrajet, which you can purchase (the price is based on your Barter). You can also loot his footlocker, stealing all the Ultrajets and Sugar Bombs he's made, but it's impossible to do this without violence.

- Ultrajet (VAL 50, AP +40)

5.03: HAMILTON'S HIDEAWAY (LAT -07/LONG 07)

- Miscellaneous Quest: Galaxy News Radio
- Miscellaneous Quest: Blood Ties
- Threat Level: 3
- Faction: Raider
- Collectibles: Mini-Nuke, Skill Book (2)
- Guns And Ammunition
- Health And Chems
- Interior Exploration
- Work Bench
- Hostile: Radroach, Radscorpion Genus, Raider

INTERIOR MAPS AND LOCATIONS

Hamilton's Hideaway

Note
It is advisable that you locate Three Dog's Cache Key before your search begins.

Under two blasted trees is a skeleton draped over a rock. This marks the entrance to an often-overlooked cavern that began as a crude and unfinished bomb shelter. Once the bombs dropped, it became a lair for Chem smugglers. It now holds a small Raider force that fights against the mutated creatures that share the lair. Although the family aren't currently in residence here, there's much to explore.

HAMILTON'S HIDEAWAY

1 Three Adjoining and Small Rooms

Locate this from the ground catwalks; one room has a Work Bench with a Bottle-cap Mine.

- Work Bench (13/46)
- First Aid Box Health and Chems
- Bottlecap Mine

2 Sandy Cavern

This area with the two generators is the best place to slay Radscorpions.

3 T-Junction with Corpse

4 Raider Hideout

Search the counter for Cherry Bombs and Vodka, and search the room for Chems and a Stimpak. Also bag the following:

- Duck and Cover! (8/25)
- Nuka-Cola Quantum (34/94)

5 Concrete Tunnel

Take your time tackling Radroaches and Radscorpions so you're not overrun.

6 Three Dog's Cache

See the Freeform Quest below for details.

7 Eastern Raider Bunk Room

- First Aid Box Health and Chems

FREEFORM QUEST: CACHING IN WITH THREE DOG

During **Main Quest: Following in His Footsteps,** visit a place other than Galaxy News Radio:

1. Head to Rivet City and speak with Doctor Li.

2. Head to Vault 112 and enter Tranquility Lane.

Or, agree to complete **Main Quest: Galaxy News Radio** and obtain the Virgo Lander Dish. Before you repair the dish atop the Washington Monument, execute plans 1 and 2 (above). Because Three Dog's "reward" (where your Dad is) is now unimportant, he sweetens the deal. He doesn't want you to leave empty-handed, so he offers you the cache as compensation.

- Three Dog's Cache Key
- Ammo Box Ammunition (7)
- First Aid Box Health and Chems (3)
- Frag Grenades (4)
- Stealth Boy
- Guns and Bullets (10/25)
- Assault Rifle
- Mini-Nuke (25/71)

Note
This is the only way you can retrieve this loot, so you might want to plan ahead!

TRAINING — BESTIARY — MAIN QUEST — MISC. QUESTS — TOUR — COMPLETION — APPENDICES

5.04: HALLOWED MOORS CEMETERY (LAT -04/LONG 09)

- Miscellaneous Quest: Big Trouble In Big Town
- Threat Level: 3
- Faction: Super Mutant
- Collectible: Fat Man Mini-Nuke, Holotape: Keller, Skill Book (2)
- Guns And Ammunition
- Health And Chems
- Highly Visible Landmark
- Sleep Mattress
- Hostile: Centaur, Super Mutant Genus

Up on the windy moors between Big Town and Germantown is a ruined church that bears the hallmarks of a Super Mutant hide-out; there are twisted girder spikes caked in blood and Gore Bags everywhere. Tread carefully and try not to kill the Wasteland captive in the process—which means no grenades in the chapel! Insider, there is Makeshift Bedding, Darts, and the following items:

- Ammo Box Ammunition (3)
- Holotape: Keller (9/24)
- Big Book of Science (7/25)
- Chinese Assault Rifle
- Mini-Nuke (26/71)
- Combat Knife
- First Aid Box Health and Chems
- D.C. Journal of Internal Medicine (13/25)

Tip

Rescue any captives and take their gift for a small boost to your Karma; refuse for a larger boost.

5.05: MERESTI TRAINYARD (LAT -01/LONG 07)

- Miscellaneous Quest: Blood Ties
- Freeform Quest (4)
- Threat Level: 2
- Faction: The Family
- Services: Trader
- Danger: Baby Carriage, Baseball Pitcher, Bear Trap, Chain Trap, Grenade Bouquet, Low Radiation, Mines, Shotgun Trap

- Collectible: Fat Man Mini-Nuke, Schematic, Skill Book (2)
- Guns And Ammunition
- Health And Chems
- Interior Exploration
- Lots O' Caps
- Perk!
- Rare Or Powerful Item
- Sleep Mattress
- Underground Connection
- Work Bench
- Hostile: Mirelurk Genus

Note

The Metro Station entrance leads to three linked underground Metro Tunnels:

Location U5.02: Northwest Seneca Station (Interior: page 308)

Location U5.05.1: Meresti Service Tunnel

Location U5.05.2: Meresti Metro Station

The following surface location can be accessed from these tunnels:

Location 5.02: Northwest Seneca Station (page 308).

INHABITANTS

Robert

Robert is Vance's bodyguard. The two met in a fight for their lives against Slavers (who Vance detests) well before the Family was formed. Robert, 34, saved Vance's life in that battle, and ever since, the two have been good friends. Once Vance formed the Family, Robert began to realize how important Vance was and elected to remain ever vigilant of his friend. He keeps very quiet and usually has to be prompted to get into conversations. He is extremely well versed in the use of firearms and has elected himself as the combat instructor for the Family.

Brianna

At 19, Brianna is the youngest member of the Family. She was originally a prostitute, but her lust for flesh (to eat) caused her much pain and anguish in the populated centers of Washington, DC. She therefore struck out into the Wasteland and stumbled across her fellow "vampires" in Meresti Station. Vance, sensing her traits, immediately took her in and converted her Cannibalism to Hematophagy. She's been living in Meresti ever since.

Alan

One of the most recent additions to the Family, 22-year-old Alan was discovered by Vance after escaping from Paradise Falls. A night owl, he was ambushed while he was asleep in the daytime by some Slavers and taken to market in Paradise Falls. Fortunately, he was able to escape, but not without sustaining a potentially mortal wound. He wandered south and collapsed not far from Meresti Station, where Vance discovered him. Currently, he does not participate in the Hematophagy rituals, as he is still learning the ways from Vance.

Justin

Justin is 20 and has been with the Family since he was 14. He is a great admirer of Vance, who saved him from an Enclave patrol of the Wasteland. Justin is a firm believer in the vampire stories that Vance tells and preaches them to his fellow Family members. He is eager, headstrong, and very friendly to those he doesn't perceive as a threat. Justin feels a close affinity with Ian West, who was recently brought into the Family. The affinity almost borders on love, and he is often found sitting and speaking to the disillusioned Ian.

Karl

Karl is 37 and was married to a woman named Skyler. Both of them lived together in Meresti before she passed. They were once owners of a shop in Megaton, and Vance met them while gathering supplies. He had felt a strong kinship with them and invited them to join him. Karl is very gruff and has a short fuse; he prefers not to speak to people. He is always highly suspicious of people and prefers to think the worst of them. Karl is distinguished by his unusual haircut: long blond hair, which is not common for a man of his bulky stature.

Holly

At 26, Holly is the oldest female member of the group and was the first to join Vance when he decided to exile himself to Meresti. Over the years, she has grown fond of Vance, and they have enjoyed a healthy relationship. She is often found following Vance around wherever he goes, and they share the same bed. Since she is a veteran member of the Family, the rest of them accept her relationship with Vance and don't feel she is trying to get anything out of him or use him to get what she wants. She is strong-willed and intelligent, having been tutored by Vance over the years.

Vance

Vance is 41, and the leader of the Family. When he was younger, he decided that life in Rivet City wasn't for him and began to wander the Wasteland. Soon, the ability to find others of his kind manifested itself. Over time, he gathered these outcasts together

Meresti Metro Station

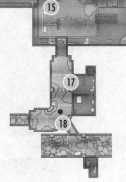

and founded their home in Meresti. Using his traits as a basis and wanting to establish some sort of society, he molded the residents into "vampires" and taught them their bloodsucking ways.

He is a fair leader, not tyrannical. He's never demanded anyone do anything they didn't wish to do, and he never wishes to put anyone in harm's way. He sees himself as a leader, but more in the way of a guide or a priest than a king. He addresses the residents of Meresti often so they will never "stray from their true nature"—that of the vampire. Vance is not violent and only attacks or orders attacks when the need for survival demands it.

Ian West

After the Family came to Arefu and his parents were killed, 15-year-old Ian was taken in by their leader, Vance, who feels a sort of kinship with him. When he was younger, his sister, Lucy, was always there to talk about his feelings, but when Lucy took off for Megaton, Ian was left alone in Arefu as the only kid, sending him into a downward spiral of depression. Vance took Ian back to the Family's home, and Ian now ponders what his life has become and what he is to do next.

This desolate location is home to a graveyard of slowly rusting carriages. You can leap onto the top of either concrete tunnel entrance so you're immune to the giant insect attacks. Check out a recently abandoned workshop, then head into the Service Tunnel; either arch has a door to this location.

MERESTI SERVICE TUNNEL (APPROACHING FROM NORTHWEST SENECA STATION)

1 Mirelurk Lair

Use the manhole to Meresti Service Tunnel entrance, back in the Northwest Seneca Station near Murphy's office.

2 Grenade Bouquet

You can't reach this, so step back to avoid the explosion.

3 Bear Trap

4 Frag Mine

- Frag Mine

5 Bear Trap

Meresti Service Tunnel (approaching from Meresti Trainyard)

6 Frag Mine (Two Locations)

- Frag Mine (2)

7 Bear Trap

8 Baby Carriage Trap

9 Pitching Machine Trap

10 Rigged Shotgun Trap

- Combat Shotgun and Ammo

11 Brahmin-Hindquarters-on-a-Chain Trap

12 Robert's Sentry Post

Enter this area using a Speech Challenge, payment (100 Caps), or execute Robert. His junk includes food in the fridge, Ammo, and the items listed below. Access the Meresti Trainyard Station Entry Terminal to unlock the Station Access Door (only necessary if you're Hostile with Robert).

- Assault Rifle
- Ammo Box Ammunition (3)
- First Aid Box Health and Chems (2)
- Tumblers Today (9/25)

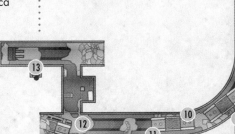

Meresti Service Tunnel

13 Hatch Door to Meresti Metro Station

MERESTI METRO STATION

14 The Family's Platform

Speak with all the members of the Family; you initially see Brianna, Holly, Alan, and Justin. There's alcohol and melee weapons on the tables and counters to steal, if you can. There's a Work Bench to the north, with a Bottlecap Mine to steal, and two of the Family's Terminals, which you can access to learn about how this tribe functions.

- Work Bench (14/46)
- Mini-Nuke (27/71)
- First Aid Box Health and Chems (2)

TRAINING — BESTIARY — MAIN QUEST — MISC. QUESTS — TOUR — COMPLETION — APPENDICES

⑮ Karl's Workshop

Trade or request Repairs from Karl. There's a wealth of items you can steal, including his entire store inventory (not listed) if you're feeling reckless.

- First Aid Box Health and Chems (4)
- Ammo Box Ammunition (3)
- .32 Pistol
- Frag Grenades (3)
- Baseball Bat
- Karl's Inventory Key

⑯ Vance's Mezzanine

You can talk at length about the Family's values, and he encourages you to study about them; he unlocks the terminals for this purpose. Behind Vance is the Family's sleeping quarters. Learn the Five Laws of the Family:

1. "Feast not on the flesh; consume only the blood. This is our strength."

2. "Bear not the child; welcome only the exile. This is our fate."

3. "Feed not for pleasure; partake only to nourish. This is our dignity."

4. "Seek not the sun's light; embrace only the shadows. This is our refuge."

5. "Kill not our kindreds; slay only the enemy. This is our justice."

You can also read Vance's proclamations about feeding grounds and "the Arefu Incident," which he personally feels sorrow for. Once you're through, you gain the Meresti Security Password from Vance (or via a Speech Challenge earlier), allowing you into the secured area near the station's blocked exit. To obtain his Longcoat, you must kill him. Obtain the Schematics by completing **Miscellaneous Quest: Blood Ties.**

- Frag Grenade (2)
- First Aid Box Health and Chems
- Meresti Security Password
- Vance's Longcoat (29/89)
- Schematics: Shishkebab (10/23)
- Lying: Congressional Style (2/25)

⑰ Vance's Private Quarters

On a desk is Vance's private terminal. Read about Os Abysmi vel Daath (an excerpt from a book by ancient occultist Aleister Crowley):

Vampires Defined: They prey on humans for the purpose of obtaining blood. Other folklore is mentioned here.

Daytime Fear: It mentions the aversion to sunlight and that, in the 18th century, people with certain phobias were referred to as "cursed."

Vampire Destruction: Depending on the culture, slaying varies from a wooden stake through the heart to immolation and decapitation.

Regarding the Arefu Incident: Vance has written a message to his followers, requesting this never to happen again.

You can also unlock his wall safe from the terminal. In the bedroom, there's a locked sword cabinet, or Pickpocket or Loot Vance for the Sword Cabinet Key; the cabinet contains the fabled Vampire's Edge.

- Sword Cabinet Key
- Vampire's Edge (30/89)

⑱ Security Room

Sealed until Vance allows you access. Ian West is inside here; he can be persuaded to return to his home in Arefu.

FREEFORM QUEST: A PENCHANT FOR PLASMA

Complete **Miscellaneous Quest: Blood Ties,** and speak with Vance. He has a proposal to share with Evan King of Arefu. Head there, listen as Evan accepts the proposal for the Family to protect the settlement, and return to Vance, telling him the deal is brokered. You can now speak to Vance about the "vampiric ways." Listen to him, and you are awarded the Hematophage perk.

FREEFORM QUEST: I WANT TO DRINK YOUR BLOOD

Speak with Vance, and once you come to an agreement about Arefu, the conversation can be steered into speaking about Blood Packs. Vance is happy to pay 15 Caps for every one you find. Scour the Wasteland for these—if you aren't sucking them down yourself!

FREEFORM QUEST: A LITTLE HELP FROM ALAN

If you have finished Blood Ties amicably on both sides and the Family has agreed to protect the settlement in return for Blood Packs, you can find Alan in the Abandoned House, which is now called Alan's Residence. There is little to claim inside except a Skill Book (check Arefu for the information), but you can now enter this dwelling (which is the only way to open it up).

FREEFORM QUEST: SPECIAL DELIVERY

If you have finished **Miscellaneous Quest: Blood Ties** and Ian West has been found (and he's either back in Arefu or with the Family in this station), you can hand him Lucy's Sealed Envelope. If you don't have the envelope, then locate Lucy West in Megaton and agree to complete the errand she requests. There's no reward, except peace of mind.

5.06: AGATHA'S HOUSE (LAT 01/ LONG 08)

- Miscellaneous Quest: Agatha's Song
- Freeform Quest
- Threat Level: 1
- Faction: Wastelander
- Services: Repairer, Trader
- Collectible: Mini-Nuke
- Guns And Ammunition
- Interior Exploration
- Main Trading Route
- Radio Signal
- Rare Or Powerful Item

INHABITANT

Agatha

Fine music is in Agatha's blood. Her ancestors were all classically trained musicians, and although those days are long gone, she spent her 76 years perfecting the violin until she matched their caliber. She is a kind old woman who feels she is too old to fear the Wasteland. Fate must smile upon her, as she's still alive. She speaks gently and carefully chooses her words, having been well educated. She spends many a lonely night looking out across the dunes and waiting for someone to come along to help her retrieve the Soil Stradivarius, a lost violin that her great-grandmother once owned.

Agatha's tiny house is built in the middle of a rocky outcrop, accessible via a rope bridge. You'll usually meet a Trader here, as this is part of the gigantic circular trade route throughout the Wasteland. Next to Agatha's house is a powerful radio antenna. Request her key, or unlock her Ammo Box (it contains a Mini-Nuke), if you're feeling ill-mannered. Complete Miscellaneous Quest: Agatha's Song; you are rewarded by the radio mast powering up. The signal is strong enough to be heard throughout the Wasteland.

- Agatha's Station Signal
- Agatha's Ammo Box Key
- Ammo Box Ammunition
- Mini-Nuke (28/71)

FREEFORM QUEST: GOING FOR A SONG

Once you've completed Agatha's Song, she requests you help her write down the music for posterity and her own happiness. If you oblige, you must return to her with one Sheet Music Book. There are six locations in the Wasteland where you can find one of these.

1. **Vault 92 [3.01]:** Living Quarters—in a stall in the men's restroom (page 283).

2. **Arlington Library [9.18]:** Children's Wing—in one of the office cubicles, below a sheet music stand (page 392).

3. **Springvale School [5.14]:** Inside a classroom in the southeast corner of the interior, inside the foot-well of an overturned desk (page 320).

4. **Statesman Hotel [12.08]:** Roof—the remains of a string quartet's placing, on the ground next to a chair (page 407).

5. **National Archives [17.11]:** Sub-basement—on the north wall, in the large storage area lined with shelves. It is on the end of the bottom shelf.

6. **Roosevelt Academy [1.16]:** Roosevelt Arts and Athletics Hall—on the stage's far right, among the discarded music stands.

She rewards you with the fabled Blackhawk, an even more powerful Scoped .44 Magnum!

- Music Sheet Book (6)
- Blackhawk (31/89)

5.07: AREFU (LAT -11/LONG 06)

- Miscellaneous Quest: Blood Ties
- Freeform Quest (3)
- Threat Level: 2
- Faction: Wastelander
- Collectible: Bobblehead, Skill Book
- Guns And Ammunition
- Highly Visible Landmark
- Interior Exploration
- Main Trading Route
- Friendly: Brahmin

INHABITANTS

Evan King

Evan has lived on this island all of his 55 years. He's watched the settlement grow from 30 people down to its current population of merely 5. He is still responsible for the small settlement and is very careful whenever a stranger enters his domain. He is quite experienced in combat, having repelled attacks by Raiders, Slavers, and various creatures. To maintain Arefu's security, he had the northern bridge span destroyed and feels safer having to monitor only the southern approach.

Ken Ewers

This 40-year-old man is a bag of nerves who is terrified of the current attacks that have been plaguing the settlement. He masks this by being incredibly short and gruff with strangers and will impart only the smallest tidbits of useless information to you. He is fiercely protective of his wife and will interpose himself if anyone even tries speaking with her. He is the picture of paranoia and can't fight worth a damn.

Karen Ewers

Karen is 36 and married to Ken Ewers. She is a bit shy, and it doesn't help that she rarely gets to speak to anyone, thanks to her overprotective husband. She is warm and exudes compassion. In recent months, a combination of impure drinking water, being couped up with Ken for hours at a time, and her already-fragile mind has caused her to become delusional, creating a more utopian world inside her head.

Karen Schenzy

Karen is 23 and quite extroverted, but she is smart enough not to speak to just anyone. She doesn't know much about the current situation in Arefu and constantly finds herself at odds with Evan King. She likes to wander around outside her house, even at night, and does it almost defiantly to tick off the mayor. She doesn't believe living in constant fear is the answer. However foolish this might be, you have to admire her guts.

Davis West (Deceased)

The head of the West family has recently met an untimely death. His demise is suspicious, and the wounds are not consistent with the usual methods of murder in this godforsaken place. Davis has two known kin, a daughter named Lucy who lives in Megaton, and a son named Ian, who was supposed to be living in Arefu with the Family. There's no trace of him.

Matilda West (Deceased)

On closer inspection, it seems Matilda West has been slain using the same odd techniques as the those employed on her husband. The Wests were settlers in Arefu for over 10 years, and no one in the settlement appears to hold a grudge against them. Indeed, Matilda was responsible for clearing out the village outhouse, a task now sadly fallen to Ken Ewers.

GENERAL NOTES

Arefu is a modest settlement perched atop an old freeway bridge spanning

EXTERIOR MAPS AND LOCATIONS
Arefu Township

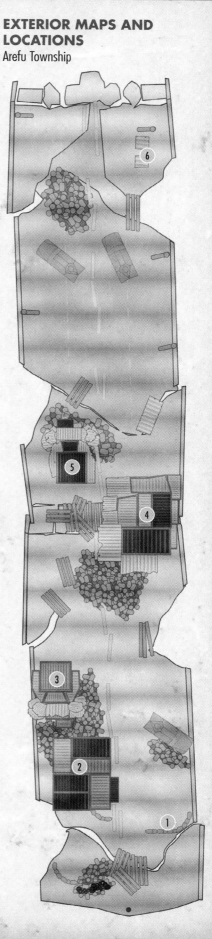

APPENDICES — COMPLETION — TOUR — MISC. QUESTS — MAIN QUEST — BESTIARY — TRAINING

the Potomac River. The residents of Arefu destroyed the north ramp leading to Northwest Seneca Station to better protect themselves from Slavers. Arefu is the last stop on most trade caravan routes traveling from Megaton. The only approach is from the south, up the ramp.

① Evan King's Defenses

The only interesting item on Evan King is his Roving Trader Hat. Arefu takes no time at all to explore, although you must get King's permission to speak with the residents before you're allowed to enter each home.

• Roving Trader Hat

② Ewers Residence

③ Schenzy Residence

④ King Residence

Take the slight Karma hit and unlock the door, as there are seven Ammo Boxes to rummage in, and there's a Bobblehead: Repair on the table just left of the door.

• Ammo Box Ammunition   • Bobblehead: Repair (8/20)

⑤ West Residence

The West Residence has two dead bodies to inspect. Your Medicine skill affects the amount of information you learn about their deaths. Of greater interest to the Scavenger is King's residence.

⑥ Outhouses

FREEFORM QUEST: A LITTLE HELP FROM AREFU

Complete **Miscellaneous Quest: Blood Ties**, return to Arefu, and begin a conversation by requesting help. Once every 24 hours, these residents can provide you with the following:

Evan King: He spares a bottle of his finest alcohol, as well as a Chem, Grenade, Mine, and some Ammo from his personal cache.

Ken Ewers: He can Repair your items at a reduced rate.

Karen Schenzy: She knows a little of the surrounding area and can pinpoint new places for you to explore.

Brailee Ewers: She bakes some of her special "cookies" for you. Yum?

FREEFORM QUEST: A LITTLE HELP FROM ALAN

Finish **Miscellaneous Quest: Blood Ties**, and once the Family has agreed to protect the settlement in return for Blood Packs, you

can find Alan in the Abandoned House, which is now called Alan's Residence. Enter the building to claim the Skill Book (the only way to access it).

• Pugilism Illustrated (10/25)

FREEFORM QUEST: SPECIAL DELIVERY

If Ian West is back living in his parents' house, you can hand over Lucy's Sealed Envelope to him. Don't have the envelope? Then locate Lucy West in Megaton, and agree to complete the errand she requests. There's no reward, except peace of mind.

5.08: FORDHAM FLASH MEMORIAL FIELD (LAT -08/ LONG 04)

• Threat Level: 2   • Hostile: Raider
• Faction: Raider

At the top of the riverbank is a baseball field that's been turned into a small Raider camp, festooned with strung-up corpses.

• Baseball Bat

5.09: MOONBEAM OUTDOOR CINEMA (LAT -06/LONG 05)

• Miscellaneous Quest: • Faction: Super Mutant
  Blood Ties   • Collectible: Skill Book
• Threat Level: 2   • Hostile: Super Mutant

It seems the Family isn't at this location, but a couple of eight-foot hulking brutes are scouting this area and the adjacent jackknifed truck [5.P]. There's a Carton of Cigarettes to take and sell, as well as a copy of Pugilism Illustrated.

• Pugilism Illustrated (11/25)

5.10: BIG TOWN (LAT -04/LONG 03)

• Miscellaneous Quest: Big   • Danger: Low Radiation
  Trouble In Big Town   • Collectible: Holotape
• Freeform Quest (2)   (Replicated Man), Skill
• Threat Level: 1   Book
• Faction: Wastelander   • Interior Exploration
• Services: Healer, Repairer,   • Rare Or Powerful Item (2)
  Trader

INHABITANTS

Dusty

Pappy has given Dusty the responsibility of guarding the only entrance into Big Town— the rope bridge at the settlement's north end. He isn't very eager and usually sits dozing on his chair, perhaps one of the reasons why the Super Mutants seem to just walk in, take their "food," and leave. Dusty is jittery, desperate, and lacks the know-how to properly prepare the town's defenses for another attack.

Flash

An individual professing to have the abilities and the daring-do to handle any situation but with only limited hands-on knowledge and skills to back this up, Flash is nevertheless a likeable guy. He is overconfident, prone to acts of thoughtless bravado, and enthusiastic about any forthcoming fracases.

Kimba

Hoping against hope for some outside help, Kimba goes with the rest of the inhabitants' wishes most of the time, even if they contradict her logical thoughts. Despite the terrible current situation, Kimba remains stable and soft-spoken, and she is always ready to pitch in, learn a new skill, and fight for her friends.

Pappy

Now in his midtwenties, Pappy is the oldtimer in town. He's trying to hold the fabric of the settlement together, but it is coming apart at the seams. Having lost their only doctor, Pappy is becoming increasingly pessimistic, and he's drawn the defenses in to the center of town so there's only one entrance and less weak spots. He is concerned and careful but isn't holding out much hope for survival.

Red

Intelligent, slightly sarcastic, and motherly, Red is Big Town's doctor in residence, although she's on an enforced leave thanks to the current kidnapping sweeps by Super Mutants in the local area. Red's nickname stems from the blood she's always splattered in and her affinity for the color. She runs the clinic in Big Town, and she is the unofficial mayor and an old girlfriend of a guy named Sticky Hands, an ex-resident of Little Lamplight.

Shorty

Although diminutive, Shorty received his nickname from the fellow residents of Big Town due to his fiery temper: "Short-T." Currently, he's praying for a quick death in the basement kitchen of the Germantown Police Station.

Timebomb

Currently drugged and laid out in the operating room of Red's clinic, Timebomb was severely wounded during the last Super Mutant attack, when Red and Shorty were kidnapped. He is known as Timebomb due to his mood swings; he has prolonged periods of calm before instigating big disturbances.

Bittercup

Apathetic, self-involved, and rebellious, Bittercup is the lone exception to Big Town's desperate, overwhelmed atmosphere. She has completely retreated into a one-woman subculture of her own making, spending time applying makeup and wearing dark clothing instead of guarding the town against attack. The other residents of Big Town are fed up with her, but there is little they can do about it, with the threat of Mutant and Raider attacks being a more pressing concern.

RELATED INTERACTIONS

All inhabitants: You can ask about the problems with Super Mutants and begin the Miscellaneous Quest.

Pappy: You can trade and get items Repaired from Pappy. The prices are excellent once you complete the Quest.

Red: After the Quest, you can seek Radiation healing, medical attention, Chem treatment, and medical supplies from her.

Red: After the Quest, you can ask her what she knows about the Replicated Man.

GENERAL NOTES

When the children of Little Lamplight reach 16, they are left with two options: leave the underground cave system and wander the Wasteland or enter a "walkabout" and head for the relative safety of Big Town. This settlement, known by some Little Lamplighters as "Mungoville," isn't named Big Town for its size but for the adults who live there. When you arrive, you see that all the outer ranch homes have been boarded up. The inner cluster of homes have sturdy defenses linking each residence, and the only way to enter and exit the place is via a rope bridge at the place's north end. Super Mutants have raided these "easy pickings" for months now, and the inhabitants have dwindled to the current motley crew. This is also the final location of Red's boyfriend, Sticky, who you can chaperone from Little Lamplight as part of **Freeform Quest: A Sticky Situation** (page 301).

① Town Hall

This is devoid of items except for the alcohol in the fridge.

② Red's Clinic

There is an operating room with a severely wounded man named Timebomb on a gurney, near Red's medical supplies, which can't be opened. There's a Holotape and a Skill Book, and an empty basement.

 Kill Red; you can wear her bandana (and outfit plus the key to her medical supplies) if you wish to turn the entire town Hostile.

- Holotape: The Replicated Man (10/24)
- D.C. Journal of Internal Medicine (14/25)
- Red's Bandana (and outfit) (32/89)
- Key to Medical Supplies

③ Common House

Bittercup usually resides here. There's a toilet with a backflow problem, and little else.

④ The Clubhouse

⑤ Scrapyard

Perhaps the rusting robots could be Repaired to repel attackers?

> **Tip**
> Once Red has been rescued, Big Town becomes an excellent place to return to for medical help from Red, Repairing from Pappy, and "presents" from Bittercup.

FREEFORM QUEST: BITTERCUP RUNNETH OVER

Head into the Common House and look for a morose young woman named Bittercup (check her schedule). She's grumpy, sarcastic, and her plan in life is to die by the light of the full moon surrounded by

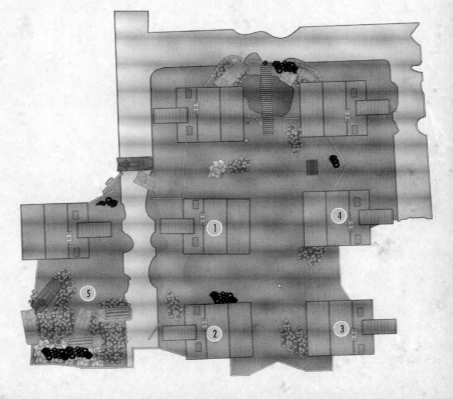

TRAINING — BESTIARY — MAIN QUEST — MISC. QUESTS — TOUR — COMPLETION — APPENDICES

candles, while wearing her favorite black dress. Politely greet her. When she (finally) stops talking, reply that no one understands you either. After she lists every man she's dated in Big Town (well, except Shorty), reply that you have something to say. After her warbling, choose any of the first three responses. She hits on you. Respond by telling her you're not in any sort of relationship. She bashfully ends the conversation. Return to her once every 24 hours, and she gives you a very common, usually useless present, such as a Squirrel-on-a-Stick or Nuka-Cola Bottle. Thanks, lover!

- Bittercup's low-quality Wasteland junk

Bittercup's exciting schedule is as follows:

12 noon–8:00 p.m.: Sleeping in the Common Room

8:00 p.m.–10:00 p.m.: Eating in the Town Hall

10:00 p.m.–10:00 a.m.: Patrolling the Town

10:00 a.m.–12 noon: Eating in the Town Hall

Tip

Have you spoken to her as a female adventurer? Have you used your Lady Killer or Black Widow perks?

FREEFORM QUEST: TICKING TIMEBOMB

Check out Red's clinic and move to the operating room, where you find a Big Town resident on a gurney. It looks like he's been shot several times and has broken both clavicles. If you know the sharp end of a scalpel from the blunt one, it might be time to put your Medicine into practice. You can:

Operate on Timebomb, removing the bullets and sewing him up. He'll live! If your **Medicine** skill is too low, you can't operate, but you can have a good try. The results are less than impressive. He'll die!

Or you can rummage around, treating Timebomb like an unconscious Gore Bag. He dies unnecessarily. Oh well.

Leave the clinic to let him recuperate, and then return when Timebomb is standing up. He thanks you profusely for saving him. You can act graciously or (with a successful Speech Challenge) get Timebomb to hand over everything he has. All 5 Caps. Once awake, he helps the rest of Big Town by

patrolling. Complete **Miscellaneous Quest: Big Trouble in Big Town** and save Red, and speak to Timebomb again after the town successfully fends off the Super Mutant attack. Timebomb is suitably grateful and gives you his Lucky 8-Ball. Keep it, always!

- 5 Caps
- Timebomb's Lucky 8-Ball (33/89)

5.11: KAELYN'S BED & BREAKFAST (LAT -09/LONG 02)

- Threat Level: 3
- Faction: Raider
- Danger: Chain Trap, Mailbox Trap
- Hostile: Raider, Raider Guard Dog

A once-thriving bed and breakfast with commanding views of the Potomac is now a wrecked shell teeming with Raiders and a Guard Dog. They are well armed and have taken the nearby ruined bridge. Attack from the higher rocky ground, heading from south to north. Also beware of the house; the mailbox is a bomb, and there's a Brahmin-Head-on-a-Chain Trap as you step inside. Your reward? A Stimpak and a Blamo Mac and Cheese; there's better loot on the corpses!

5.12: VAULT 106 (LAT -09/LONG 01)

- Threat Level: 3
- Faction: Vault Dweller
- Danger: Gas Leak!
- Collectible: Bobblehead, Fat Man Mini-Nuke, Skill Book (2)
- Guns And Ammunition
- Health And Chems
- Interior Exploration
- Rare Or Powerful Item (2)
- Sleep Mattress
- Hostile: Insane Survivor, Survivor

Check the area carefully, as there's a small door leading to another of Vault-Tec's clandestine attempts at testing humans who thought they'd be safe in their subterranean

paradise. There are no records (even at the Citadel) of what is contained within this dwelling. Approach with caution!

VAULT 106 ENTRANCE

① Cog Door

Access the Vault Door Control Pod to open.

② Windowed Chamber

Open the adjacent hatch door, pass the barricade, and access the security terminal. On the terminal is a note from the Overseer, stating that everything is okay and that "unusual odor or faint taste to the air" is perfectly normal.

③ Stairwell

You meet an Insane Survivor of whatever befell this Vault. Expect a slight blue tinge to your vision shortly.

- Sledgehammer
- Vault 106 Jumpsuit

④ Reactor Room

This is empty, aside from the dead Insane Survivor.

⑤ Main Corridor Hallucination

Wait, there's a scientist ahead of you; he's walked into the chamber to the right (south)! Your eyes adjust. Head into the room, and it is empty. There's no one here.

⑥ More Ocular Madness

Round the corner and you see three scientists, each heading into a room nearby. Investigate, and the place is empty.

Note

Look closely at those scientists. Wasn't one of them your father?!

VAULT 106 LIVING QUARTERS: ATRIUM CATWALK LEVEL

⑦ Catwalk

There's shouting and Insane Survivors battering each other and you. To the south is a barricade of desks, and in the southwest corner is a locked door.

⑧ Northeast Room

Check the tiny crate shack on the desk; there's a well-hidden Skill Book at the base of them.

- Nikola Tesla and You (9/25)

INTERIOR MAPS AND LOCATIONS

Vault 106 Science Lab B1

Vault 106 Science Lab

Vault 106 Living Quarters B1

Vault 106 Living Quarters 2F

Vault 106 Living Quarters

Vault 106 Entrance

9 Overseer's Office

Speak to the Overseer...wait, he's gone! Check the shelves for a Carton of Cigarettes, Health, and the Overseer's terminal. This has an Urgent Preparations Report, detailing the "preparation and release of the Control." This was obviously before "testing" began.

- First Aid Box Health and Chems

10 Medical Bay

Another Insane Survivor shouts to his non-existent friends to "flank you!" After you defeat him, inspect the area. Locate the shelf with the Bobblehead: Science. Access the Lab Technician's Terminal. There is a single entry, which contains notes about the U. Noslen species of fungus.

- Bobblehead: Science (9/20)

GROUND FLOOR

11 Adjoining Corridor

Check the shelves for Chems and the following:

- First Aid Box Health and Chems (2)
- Frag Grenade (3)
- Ammo Box Ammunition (2)

12 Storage Room

Inside are two Cartons of Cigarettes and more useful items. The door to the north is locked and leads down to the Science Labs.

- Frag Mines (2)
- Ammo Box Ammunition (3)

13 Ocular Lunacy!

Approach the door to the south, and you stagger back, enthralled with the blue light. The Vault is clean. There are two doors; each leads to a room with a terminal. Read the message on any terminal. It's from you. You like it here. You want to stay. Keep reading. Stay, won't you? Fine, be like that. Shuffle out of the rooms and head north. You snap back into reality (you think) at the top of stairs leading down. The two rooms you were just in are in ruins.

14 You're Seeing Things Again!

Two Vault Dwellers run past you. They've gone.

15 Female Dorm

16 Male Dorm

This has an empty wall safe and a note in one dorm. It tells a tale of a Vault Dweller before the psychosis occurred; everyone was "so happy to be here and my roomies are flailing around in the love mist."

- Note: Feel the Love Man

17 Locked Dorm

On the other side of the door huddle two skeletons on a bed and a child's skeleton under a wall safe.

- Wall Safe Items

VAULT 106 SCIENCE LABS

18 Lunatic's Lair

We're boarding the metaphorical bus to insanity central! The southeast dorm room he charged from featured books that stood on their ends. There are .308 Rounds in here. You can head up the nearby stairs, into a generator room with another loony, and a door leading back to the Living Quarters.

- First Aid Box Health and Chems

19 Observation Room (Living Quarters)

Check the terminal and the Vault 106 Master Key. The terminal has another urgent notice from the Overseer; he's unsure of the effects of the gas release.

- Vault 106 Master Key

20 Server Room

In the northeast corner of this level is a table with some milk bottles; take the Skill Book.

- Tumblers Today (10/25)

21 Medical Room

Check the table for the following item (which helps curb the hallucinations):

- Makeshift Gas Mask (34/89)

22 Reactor Room

The previous surgery room and other chambers were empty. Enter the Reactor Room and you're attacked by a Survivor. As soon as you strike him, you're bathed in blue. Watch out! The Tunnel Snakes are here! Wally Mack is attacking Butch and Paul Hannon! Back up, and watch the carnage, or intervene before you're attacked! Blast them! Oh, they disappeared. It might be time to leave.

23 Connecting Room

Check the table for the following item (which helps curb the hallucinations):

- Makeshift Gas Mask (35/89)

24 Security Vault

But not before you ransack the security vault (using the Master Key), which is a cave full of skeletons and a metal shelf with Darts and the items listed below. Retrace your steps, hoping there's no permanent damage. Don't worry, there isn't. Right?

- First Aid Box Health and Chems
- Mini-Nuke (29/71)
- Ammo Box Ammunition (3)

5.13: JURY STREET METRO STATION (LAT -10/LONG -03)

- Main Quest: Galaxy News Radio
- Threat Level: 3
- Freeform Quest (3)
- Faction: Raider
- Danger: Bear Trap, Chain Trap, Grenade Bouquet
- Collectibles: Fat Man Mini-Nuke , Nuka-Cola Quantum, Skill Book (4)
- Guns And Ammunition
- Health And Chems
- Highly Visible Landmark
- Interior Exploration
- Lots O' Caps
- Rare Or Powerful Item (2)
- Sleep Mattress
- Work Bench
- Hostiles: Mole Rat, Radroach, Raider

INTERIOR MAPS AND LOCATIONS

Jury St. Station

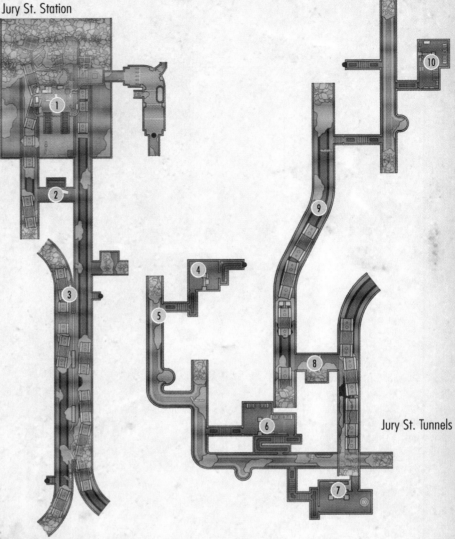

Jury St. Tunnels

INHABITANTS

RYAN BRIGG (AND PUMPKIN)

Ryan Brigg is a Wasteland entrepreneur with a plan. Mole Rat is the most easily available meat, but it tastes awful. While he conducts research on improving the taste and making his fortune selling his genetically modified offal, he's posing as a rough-and-ready Raider captain in order to recruit the manpower he needs to keep his investments secure.

Blocked off from the other D.C. Metro tunnels, the Jury Street Station area is now a wasteland on the surface, and a home to a small but vicious contingent of Raiders down below. Begin your sortie on the main drag's east side, heading up from the overturned City Coach Liner. Pass the Red Rocket Gas Station on your right (north), heading west. Head into Dot's Diner; there's a Freeform Quest to complete in here.

Across from the diner is the Metro entrance to Jury St. Station, where your interior exploration occurs. The area's southern part is referenced in Zone 8 [8.B]. Find the only other open building: the Gold Ribbon Grocers. Inside here, you can perform **Freeform Quest: Rube's Gold Ribbon Prize**.

JURY ST. STATION

Tip

If you're after an all-new and delicious meat, collect Mole Rat Meat from every one you kill.

1 Mezzanine Area

There's Mutfruit in a crate on a picnic table, along with Cherry Bombs and a Raider to slay. Investigate his junk-filled hideout for items, a Work Bench with a Bottlecap Mine, and some mattresses around a homemade anvil.

- Work Bench (15/46)
- Sledgehammer
- Bottlecap Mine
- Dean's Electronics (6/25)

2 Connecting Tunnel Chamber

Attack the Raiders, grabbing their Chems and Ammo.

- Ammo Box Ammunition (2)

3 Narrow Raider Alcove

Check the area for Chems, Stimpaks, and the following:

- Ammo Box Ammunition (2)
- 10mm Pistol and Ammo

JURY ST. TUNNELS

Note

There are two entrances to this location. The following scavenging hunt assumes you entered via the south entrance.

4 Room with the Leaking Pipe

There are Chems, Metal Boxes, and beer in here.

5 Table with Ammo

- Ammo Box Ammunition (3)

6 Generator Room

- First Aid Box Health and Chems

7 Ryan Briggs's Terminal

This terminal has five relevant entries:

Log Entry #86: Briggs starts with an isoprene and adds it to Mole Rat Meat for taste. The results aren't impressive.

Log Entry #87: Briggs and his annoying chum Chucky are experimenting with Mole Rats and injecting them with different isoprenes.

Log Entry #171: Briggs is feeling uncomfortable masquerading as a Raider, but that breakthrough in making Mole Rat Meat edible is close.

Log Entry #172: Briggs is close to making this food palatable, and the Raiders are paid to bring back bottles for him to use.

Log Entry #173: A mixture of Wonder Glue and Mole Rat Meat has resulted in a delicious jerky! Uh-oh, that's the alarm....

8 Connecting Tunnel Chamber

- Ammo Box Ammunition (4)

9 Warning! Bear Traps

10 Ryan Briggs's Mole Rat Laboratory

Brigg is violent; kill him and loot his corpse for Ryan Briggs's Safe Key, which opens the floor safe next to his bed. Atop the safe is Lying: Congressional Style. There's another of Ryan's Terminals. Gather the following objects, and look for a cute little Mole Rat named Pumpkin that is kept in the ball cage. Bring Briggs's hypotheses here to a (hopefully) profitable conclusion: **Freeform Quest: Ryan Briggs's Wondermeat.**

- Ryan Briggs's Safe Key
- Lying: Congressional Style (3/25)
- Blood Pack (7)
- Nuka-Cola Quantum (35/94)

FREEFORM QUEST: THE JIGG IS UP

If you completed **Main Quest: Galaxy News Radio** and solved the optional puzzle involving two mathematically minded Mercenaries named Jiggs and Prime, there is a note mentioning that Prime is waiting at the Jury Street Station. If you head into the diner, Prime is indeed here but missing some vital appendages...like a head. However, his corpse contains some incredible items, the best of which are 500 Caps and a unique weapon.

- Xuanlong Assault Rifle (36/89)

FREEFORM QUEST: RUBE'S GOLD RIBBON

Head inside the Gold Ribbon Grocers. Inside, resist your impulse to search the place, as there's an incredibly complicated trap in here. Complete the following:

1. Turn left (west), look on the floor for the pressure plate, and step on it.

2. This activates a Brahmin-skull-on-a-stick trap, which swings down (but won't hit you). Stay where you are!

3. The skull strikes a box of detergent, which creates a domino effect with dozens more boxes along the produce counter.

4. The last box drops onto a second pressure plate, which starts a baseball pitcher.

5. The baseballs thrown from the pitcher strike a bucket and other items on the counter to your right.

6. One of the items is a fire extinguisher, which falls onto a Bear Trap, and the extinguisher explodes.

7. This knocks a Grenade Bouquet hanging from the coffee machine. The grenades fall to the ground.

8. Seconds later, the grenades explode, igniting the seeping gas from the oven.

9. A fireball rips through the Grocers as the generator explodes! The whole building shakes.

10. This jolts an ancient skeleton down from a hole in the ceiling; he drops through, along with the following items:

- Nikola Tesla and You (10/25)
- Tumblers Today (11/25)
- Missile (3)
- Mini-Nuke (30/71)

FREEFORM QUEST: RYAN BRIGGS'S WONDERMEAT

Locate Ryan Briggs's laboratory in the Jury St. Tunnels, and find the Wonder Meat Maker on the table along the west wall. Activate it, and combine the following items:

- Wonderglue (1)
- Mole Rat Meat (1)

This creates Mole Rat Wonder Meat, which has five times the value and four times the HP gain than regular meat. You can continue to come back and create more meat as long as you have enough ingredients. You make a 6 Caps profit for each Mole Rat Wonder Meat you sell.

- Mole Rat Wonder Meat (WG 1, VAL 20, Rads +2, HP +20)

5.14: SPRINGVALE SCHOOL (LAT -01/ LONG -01)

- Threat Level: 3
- Faction: Raider
- Collectibles: Nuka-Cola Quantum, Skill Book (2)
- Guns And Ammunition
- Health And Chems
- Interior Exploration
- Sleep Mattress
- Hostiles: Giant Ant Genus, Raider, Raider Guard Dog

Northeast of Vault 101 [8.01] and on the northern outskirts of Springvale township [8.02] is Springvale Elementary School, which is now the residence to a band of bloodthirsty Raiders. There's an entrance on the western side, near the ruined bus stop. On the eastern perimeter is a power tower with a locked gate and a First Aid

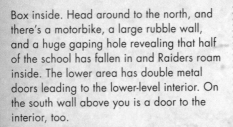

Box inside. Head around to the north, and there's a motorbike, a large rubble wall, and a huge gaping hole revealing that half of the school has fallen in and Raiders roam inside. The lower area has double metal doors leading to the lower-level interior. On the south wall above you is a door to the interior, too.

- First Aid Box Health and Chems

SPRINGVALE ELEMENTARY SCHOOL: GROUND FLOOR EXPLORATION

1 Grisly Foyer

Head upstairs for the Nuka-Cola Quantum.

- Nuka-Cola Quantum (36/94)

2 Kitchen

There are Chems, Stimpaks, food in the fridge, and a dead Mole Rat ready to be dissected.

3 Barred Gate

Oh, those poor children...

4 Northwest Classroom

There are scattered items, mattresses, and haphazard desk barricades in here.

- First Aid Box Health and Chems

5 Northeast Storage Room

Collect Stimpaks and ignore the burned books.

- First Aid Box Health and Chems

6 Restrooms

There are Chems, body parts, and a mattress in here.

SECOND FLOOR EXPLORATION

7 Balcony Overlooking Grisly Foyer

Grab the Nuka-Cola Quantum near the headless corpse.

8 Library

There are no books, but there is a mattress, some foes, a storage room with Chems and Dirty Water, and a locked pair of doors to the east leading to a north–south corridor.

9 Raider's Lair

Kill the Raider and his dog, collect the listed items, sleep on his mattress, and read his terminal diary:

Log Entry #001: Boppo—suk me hahaha's buddy—got one between the eyes from

INTERIOR MAPS AND LOCATIONS
Springvale Elementary School

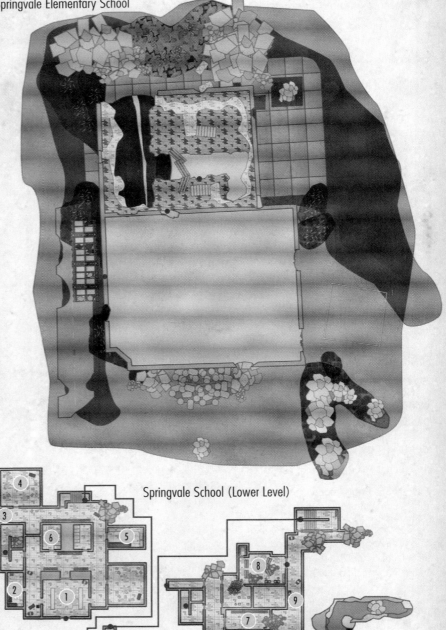

Springvale School (Lower Level)

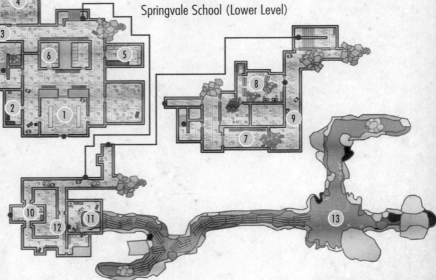

Sheriff Simms for trying to blast his way into town. The Vault is the real prize, though.

Log Entry #002: The digging folk started using Mines instead of shovels and nearly demolished the building. Less noise means the Megaton folks won't investigate.

Log Entry #003: Excavation in the lower levels is going badly thanks to the Ants eating the men. The Vault must be breached!

- Combat Knife
- Ammo Box Ammunition (3)
- Duck and Cover! (9/25)

SPRINGVALE SCHOOL (LOWER LEVEL)

Note
You can enter the interior in any order, although it is wise to investigate the upper areas first.

⑩ Entrance Area

There are a few Chems on the shelves.

⑪ Wrecked Storage Room

There's Rad-X, some Scotch, and a hole in the north wall, allowing you to check out the hole in the ground.

- First Aid Box Health and Chems

Secondary Locations

5.A: WRECKED VEHICLES (LAT -13/LONG 12)

- Threat Level: 3
- Faction: Raider
- Collectible: Fat Man Mini-Nuke, Scribe Pre-War Book

- Guns And Ammunition
- Sleep Mattress
- Hostiles: Mole Rat, Radscorpion Genus, Raider Guard Dog

On the road north of the Potomac and parallel to the monorail are the remains of an ancient accident: a 14-vehicle pileup. The real find is north along a dry creek bed. A Raider's jetty has food, Dirty and Purified Water, Whiskey, a place to sleep, and the following:

- Ammo Box Ammunition (2)
- Scribe Pre-War Book (36/98)
- Mini Nuke (31/71)
- Hunting Rifle

5.B: MILITARY TRUCK (LAT -13/LONG 10)

- Threat Level: 2
- Guns And Ammunition
- Hostile: Robot Genus

Just south of the monorail debris is a large billboard for Vault-Tec next to a military truck with a sizable ammo cache.

- Ammo Box Ammunition (7)
- Assault Rifle

5.C: WRECKED MONORAIL CARRIAGE (LAT -12/LONG 11)

- Threat Level: 1

⑫ The Left Door
⑬ Raider's Mining Tunnel

Giant Ants scuttle about here, so prepare to blast or Sneak around them. Continue until the cavern opens up into a grotto with glowing fungi and clusters of Egg Clutches. Dip into one of these for some delicious Ant Meat. Also look under a corpse in this area for the Skill Book.

- Ant Meat
- Chinese Army: Spec Ops Training Manual (5/25)

Twisted wreckage of an ancient monorail crash is still lying across a dried-up creek bed.

5.D: RUINED HOUSE (LAT -05/LONG 12)

- Threat Level: 2
- Faction: Enclave
- Collectible: Skill Book
- Hostile: Enclave Eyebot

This ruined house has only the wind whistling through the residence and a nearby Eyebot patrolling. Check the shelf.

- Duck and Cover! (10/25)

5.E: POWER TRANSFORMERS (LAT 02/LONG 11)

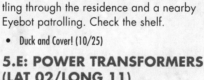

- Threat Level: 1
- Faction: Wastelander
- Collectible: Nuka-Cola Quantum
- Friendly: Brahmin

South of Minefield [3.09] is a small set of transformers. The gate is locked, but there's nothing except discarded Nuka-Cola bottles inside the grounds. Cross the road to the adjacent pylon and locate a skeleton sprawled next to his chair with the following:

- BB Gun and Ammo
- Nuka-Cola Quantum (37/94)

5.F: RUSTING BOATS (LAT -12/LONG 09)

- Threat Level: 1
- Danger: Low Radiation

Below the military truck are two small rusting boats on what used to be the Potomac.

5.G: SCAVENGER SHACK (LAT -09/LONG 07)

- Threat Level: 1
- Faction: Wastelander
- Services: Repairer, Trader
- Danger: Low Radiation

- Guns And Ammunition
- Highly Visible Landmark
- Characters: Scavenger, Scavenger's Dog

Right in the middle of the Potomac River is a highly visible shack with a Scavenger and his dog. Trade and Repair. If you want, Steal his two locked Ammo Boxes. You can Pickpocket the inventory, too, and steal the Metal Helmet on the table.

- Ammo Box Ammunition (2)

5.H: BOWLING BILLBOARD (LAT -08/LONG 09)

- Threat Level: 3
- Highly Visible Landmark
- Hostile: Bloatflies, Deathclaw, Mole Rats

Use this as a landmark when wandering the northern side of the Potomac River, near Northwest Seneca Station.

5.I: RUSTING TUB AND BROKEN BRIDGE (LAT -05/LONG 07)

- Threat Level: 2
- Danger: Low Radiation
- Guns And Ammunition
- Hostile: Mirelurk Genus

The broken bridge is an amusing way to dive into the irradiated water. The barge has a Bulkhead safe and the following:

- Ammo Box Ammunition (2)
- Bulkhead Safe Items

5.J: HALLOWED MOORS SHACK (LAT -05/LONG 08)

- Threat Level: 2
- Faction: Super Mutant

This shack is in terrible repair, with a pile of tires outside and three Metal Boxes to open.

5.K: RIVERSIDE RAIDER SHACKS (LAT -03/LONG 07)

- Threat Level: 2
- Faction: Raider
- Danger: Low Radiation
- Guns And Ammunition
- Health And Chems
- Sleep Mattress
- Hostile: Raider

There is a small encampment of three or four Raiders near Meresti Trainyards. They are sometimes mistaken for the Family, until you get a closer look. Defeat them (watch for their long-range Hunting Rifle attacks), then search both shacks, where you find Chems, two mattresses, Darts, three Cartons of Cigarettes, food, detergent, and the following:

- Frag Mines (3)
- Baseball Bat
- Ammo Box Ammunition (3)
- Health and Chems
- Sawed-Off Shotgun and Ammo

5.L: RUSTING TUB (LAT -12/LONG 06)

- Threat Level: 1
- Danger: Low Radiation
- Guns And Ammunition

This boat is empty aside from three Ammo Boxes.

- Ammo Box Ammunition (3)

5.M: NORTH AREFU PIER (LAT -10/LONG 08)

- Threat Level: 1
- Danger: Low Radiation
- Health And Chems

There is a short set of three piers, where rusting boats and a caravan are slowly sinking into the mire. Swim into the lake and locate the half-submerged white speedboat.

- First Aid Box Health and Chems

5.N: SOUTH AREFU PIER (LAT -10/LONG 05)

- Threat Level: 2
- Danger: Low Radiation
- Collectible: Nuka-Cola Quantum
- Health And Chems
- Hostile: Mirelurk Genus

This is a single promontory with Mirelurk Egg Clutches underneath. The far end has an empty trunk with a locked First Aid Box and some Whiskey, but the real prize is on the wooden buttress—a Nuka-Cola Quantum stacked atop two tin cans. Dive off the pier to secure items from a safe and a First Aid Box by a sunken boat.

- First Aid Box Health and Chems (2)
- Nuka-Cola Quantum (38/94)
- Sunken Safe Items

5.O: DRY PIER (LAT -07/LONG 06)

- Threat Level: 2
- Guns And Ammunition
- Hostile: Mole Rats, Robot Genus

Over at the eastern end of the Potomac River, near Hamilton's Hideaway, is evidence of the ancient height of the river: a dry pier with two rusting boats still lying here. Gather the items, including Beer, food, and a cute teddy on the corpse.

- Ammo Box Ammunition (5)

5.P: JACKKNIFED TRUCK (LAT -05/LONG 05)

- Threat Level: 2
- Health And Chems
- Hostile: Enclave Eyebot, Super Mutant

This truck appears on the road heading northwest from Big Town. The container has been picked almost clean.

- First Aid Box Health and Chems

5.Q: CRATERED HAMLET (LAT -01/LONG 05)

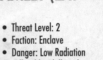

- Threat Level: 2
- Faction: Enclave
- Danger: Low Radiation
- Collectible: Skill Book
- Hostile: Enclave Eyebot, Mole Rat, Yao Guai

Something heavy and explosive has devastated this office building and nearby hamlet, and the created crater is radioactive. Check the safe in the debris and the one inside the house ruin. Aside from common items and hydrants (or sinks) you can drink from, check the bath in one of the houses for a Skill Book.

- Safe Items (2)
- Tumblers Today (12/25)

5.R: RUINED FARMHOUSE (LAT 02/LONG 05)

- Threat Level: 1
- Hostile: Vicious Dog

An old abandoned farmstead in terrible repair offers an exceptional view of the Wasteland looking west.

5.S: DEAD MAN'S CARAVAN (LAT 03/LONG 06)

- Threat Level: 2
- Faction: Enclave, Raider
- Health And Chems
- Hostile: Raider

This caravan is on the edge of Zone 6, and when the Enclave appear, they set up a camp [E6.04]. The "dead man" is a mere husk, with Whiskey by his mattress.

- First Aid Box Health and Chems

5.T: IRRADIATED POOL (LAT 03/LONG 05)

- Threat Level: 2
- Danger: Low Radiation

These pools are commonplace in Zone 4. Avoid them; there's nothing to experience except sickening weakness.

5.U: BRAHMIN SKULL SHACK (LAT -13/LONG 02)

- Threat Level: 3
- Collectible: Nuka-Cola Quantum
- Health And Chems
- Hostile: Robot Genus, Yao Guai

Close to VAPL-58 Power Station [4.10] and behind the bowling billboard is a dilapidated shack providing cover and the following:

- First Aid Box Health and Chems
- Nuka-Cola Quantum (39/94)

5.V: DRAINAGE OUTLET (LAT -08/LONG 02)

- Threat Level: 2
- Faction: Raider
- Danger: Low Radiation
- Hostile: Raider

Close to Kaelyn's Bed and Breakfast is a small Drainage Outlet, providing the nearby ground with a good supply of effluent and radiation.

5.W: RUSTING TUB, SHACK, AND PIER (LAT -02/LONG 02)

- Threat Level: 2
- Danger: Low Radiation
- Hostile: Radscorpion Genus

There's a half-buried tub with metal crates containing common items. The lean-to and pier here are slowly sinking into this irradiated ooze.

5.X: JACKKNIFED TRUCK (LAT 03/LONG 02)

- Threat Level: 2
- Faction: Raider
- Guns And Ammunition

The western edge of Bethesda Ruins [6.07] leads to a broken freeway section, on which sits a jackknifed truck.

- Ammo Box Ammunition (3)

5.Y: PATRIOTIC PICNIC AREA (LAT -08/LONG -01)

- Threat Level: 2
- Danger: Low Radiation
- Guns And Ammunition
- Sleep Mattress
- Hostile: Radscorpion Genus

Are you a fan of the Iguana-on-a-Stick? Then you've come to the right irradiated vista point. Check the caravan for a place to sleep.

- Ammo Box Ammunition (3)

5.Z: RUINED FARMSTEAD AND OUTBUILDING (LAT -05/LONG 00)

- Threat Level: 1

Close to Vault 101 is a rotting farmstead with three outbuildings—a pungent outhouse, a shack, and a silo that has fallen over. Later, the Enclave set up a cleansing operation here [E5.05].

5.AA: FREEWAY RAIDER ENCAMPMENT (LAT -05/LONG -01)

- Threat Level: 3
- Faction: Raider
- Hostile: Raider

This may be one of your first confrontations with a Raider, as this small encampment is almost directly north of Vault 101. Don't fall through to the ground below. The only items you're collecting are from the Raider corpses, although killing Raiders is a great way to earn XP.

5.BB: LAKESIDE RUINS (LAT 01/LONG 00)

- Threat Level: 2
- Faction: Enclave
- Danger: Low Radiation
- Guns And Ammunition
- Hostile: Mirelurk Genus

Springvale's Lakeside Ruins sustained a direct hit to their office building. Watch for nearby Mirelurks. There's a Grenade Ammo Box to scavenge under the rocky banks just south of Springvale School. The Enclave also set up here [5.06].

- Ammo Box Ammunition

5.CC: RUSTING TUG (LAT 02/LONG -01)

- Threat Level: 2
- Danger: Low Radiation
- Health And Chems

A rusting tug has spilled its radioactive barrels. Brave the radiation and secure the two First Aid Box Health and Chems.

5.DD: NORTH PIER (LAT 03/LONG -01)

- Threat Level: 2
- Danger: Low Radiation
- Collectible: Nuka-Cola Quantum
- Health And Chems
- Hostile: Mirelurk

The pier along the northern edge of the island near Arefu (where Mirelurks have already mated) is covered with Egg Clutches you can search. Locate the boat with the personal footlocker. Dive under the isolated bridge section to secure an underwater Nuka-Cola Quantum.

- First Aid Box Health and Chems
- Nuka-Cola Quantum (40/94)

ENCLAVE CAMP LOCATIONS

CAMP E5.01 (LAT -05/LONG 12)

- Main Quest: Picking Up The Trail
- Threat Level: 2

As soon as you step into the ruined house here, a squad of Enclave Soldiers arrives via Vertibird.

CAMP E5.02 (LAT -11/LONG 09)

- Main Quest: Picking Up The Trail
- Threat Level: 2
- Guns And Ammunition

The Enclave have set up a recon lookout station on the northern section of the freeway, just north of Arefu.

- Enclave Crate Ammunition (3)
- Ammo Box Ammunition

CAMP E5.03 (LAT 03/LONG 06)

- Main Quest: Picking Up The Trail
- Threat Level: 4
- Guns And Ammunition

A Flamer Soldier and two Officer-controlled Modified Deathclaws make this outpost, near Dead Man's Caravan [5.S], highly dangerous.

- Enclave Crate Ammunition (2)

CAMP E5.04 (LAT -08/LONG -03)

- Main Quest: Picking Up The Trail
- Danger: Low Radiation
- Guns And Ammunition
- Threat Level: 3

The Enclave are investigating Brahmin mutilations near an overturned radiation barrel container. Check the broken bridge section and the Modified Deathclaw in a containment cage.

- Enclave Crate Ammunition (3)
- Ammo Box Ammunition (2)

CAMP E5.05 (LAT -05/LONG 00)

- Main Quest: Picking Up The Trail
- Threat Level: 3
- Guns And Ammunition

A team are executing a "cleansing" operation, burning Wastelander corpses at the Ruined Farmstead and Outbuilding [5.Z].

- Enclave Crate Ammunition (2)

CAMP E5.06 (LAT -03/LONG -02)

- Main Quest: Picking Up The Trail
- Threat Level: 2
- Guns And Ammunition

The Enclave have landed and departed a Vertibird in the fields just west of Springvale. The Bird is still on the ground.

- Enclave Crate Ammunition (2)

CAMP E5.07 (LAT 01/LONG -01)

- Main Quest: Picking Up The Trail
- Danger: Low Radiation
- Guns And Ammunition
- Threat Level: 2

A field research team is studying the mutated creatures in the nearby area. A field terminal has two field entries: "Mirelurk" and "Great American Cockroach."

- Enclave Crate Ammunition (4)

TRAINING — BESTIARY — MAIN QUEST — MISC. QUESTS — TOUR — COMPLETION — APPENDICES

Zone 6: Eastern Hills and D.C. Outskirts

TOPOGRAPHICAL OVERVIEW

There's a little more life and more built-up areas to investigate in this neck of the woods; but there are still vast tracts of rural desolation to trudge around too. Beginning in the northwest, visit the Scrapyard for a new furry friend, and visit the Wheaton Armory if you're after a challenge with a huge payoff. Canterbury Commons is an important destination for Traders, and don't forget the two motor company factories, now home to more than just rusting car parts. To the southwest is the sprawling Bethesda Ruins and its surroundings. At the outer edge of the D.C. Ruins is a completely wrecked National Guard Depot and a Metro Station leading into D.C. itself. Finally, don't forget to say hello to Gary!

AVAILABLE COLLECTIBLES (ZONE 6)

- Bobbleheads: 3/20
- Fat Men: 0/9
- Fat Man Mini-Nukes: 11/71
- Unique Items: 8/89
- Nuka-Cola Quantum: 8/94
- Schematics: 0/21
- Scribe Pre-War Books: 9/98
- Skill Book: Barter (3/24), Big Guns (5/25), Energy Weapons (2/25), Explosives (2/25), Lockpick (1/25), Medicine (0/25), Melee Weapons (4/25), Repair (3/25), Science, (4/25), Small Guns (3/25), Sneak (3/25), Speech (4/25), Unarmed (2/25)
- Work Bench: 6/46
- Holotapes: Keller (0/5), Replicated Man (0/19)

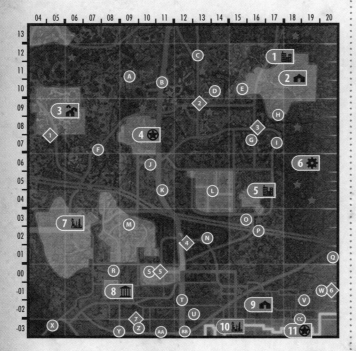

PRIMARY LOCATIONS

6.01: AntAgonizer's Lair (lat 17/long 12)

6.02: Canterbury Commons (lat 18/long 11)

6.03: Scrapyard (lat 05/long 09)

6.04: Wheaton Armory (lat 10/long 08)

6.05: Corvega Factory (lat 16/long 05)

6.06: Vault 108 (lat 18/long 06)

6.07: Bethesda Ruins (lat 05/long 03]

6.08: Chryslus Building (lat 08/long -01)

6.09: Rock Creek Caverns (lat 16/long -02)

6.10: Friendship Heights Metro Station (lat 14/long -03)

6.11: National Guard Depot (lat 18/long -03)

SECONDARY LOCATIONS

6.A: Regulator Headquarters (lat 09/long 11)

6.B: Jackknifed Freeway Truck (lat 11/long 10)

6.C: Military Truck Checkpoint (lat 13/long 12)

6.D: Brahmin Pastures (lat 14/long 10)

6.E: Canterbury Commons Water Tower (lat 15/long 10)

6.F: Wrecked Monorail Train (lat 07/long 07)

6.G: Radio Mast Yankee Bravo (lat 16/long 07)

6.H: Robot Repair Center (Darren's Discount Electronics; lat 17/long 09)

6.I: Jackknifed Truck (lat 17/long 07)

6.J: Wheaton Armory Truck (lat 10/long 06)

6.K: Coach Liner Wreckage (Freeway; lat 11/long 05)

6.L: Corvega Township (lat 14/long 05)

6.M: Bethesda Suburbs (Raid Shack; lat 09/long 03)

6.N: Bethesda Roundabout and Gas Station (lat 13/long 02)

6.O: Red Rocket Gas Station (lat 15/long 03)

6.P: Jackknifed Truck (under Monorail; lat 16/long 02)

6.Q: Wrecked Monorail Carriage (lat 20/long 01)

6.R: Chryslus Baseball Field (lat 08/long 00)

6.S: Bethesda Coach Station (lat 10/long 00)

6.T: Jackknifed Truck (lat 12/long -01)

6.U: Red Rocket Gas Station (lat 13/long -01)

6.V: Rock Creek Township Ruins (lat 19/long -01)

6.W: Rock Creek Roundabout (lat 20/long -01)

6.X: Wastelander Mine Trap (Under Bridge; lat 05/long -03)

6.Y: Jackknifed Truck (lat 09/long -03)

6.Z: Shelter Entrance (Under Bridge; lat 10/long -03)

6.AA: Super Mutant Bonfire (lat 11/long -03)

6.BB: Courtyard Fountain (lat 12/long -03)

6.CC: National Guard Forecourt Trucks (lat 18/long -03)

Primary Locations

6.01: ANTAGONIZER'S LAIR (LAT 17/LONG 12)

- Miscellaneous Quest: The Superhuman Gambit
- Threat Level: 3
- Faction: Wastelander
- Danger: Low Radiation, Mines, Shotgun Trap
- Collectible: Nuka-Cola Quantum

- Area Is Locked
- Guns And Ammunition
- Health And Chems
- Interior Exploration
- Rare Or Powerful Item
- Sleep Mattress
- Hostile: Giant Ant Genus

INHABITANT TANYA CHRISTOFF

Born 27 years ago, Tanya watched her parents live most of their lives as caravan drivers, before they were killed by Ants, an event that made Tanya lose herself in the world of Hubris Comics' characters and befriend the insects that spared her life. Christoff thinks that Canterbury Commons—a major location in the trading route her parents helped put on the map—is a blight on the Wasteland. Locals used to see Christoff lurking in a sewer system to the north of town, covered in mud and dirt. Giant Ants eventually started hanging around, though they never bothered anyone. A few months ago, she disappeared and reappeared as the AntAgonizer and has been harassing the town ever since.

INTERIOR MAPS AND LOCATIONS

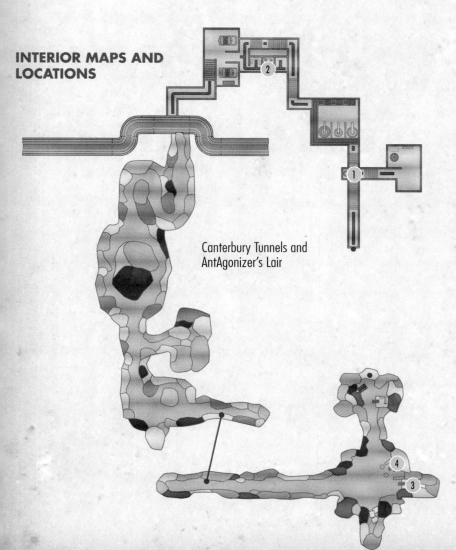

Canterbury Tunnels and AntAgonizer's Lair

CANTERBURY TUNNELS

1 First Junction

Disarm the Frag Mine and check the small storage chamber, ducking to avoid a Rigged Shotgun.

- Frag Mine
- Combat Shotgun and Ammo
- First Aid Box Health and Chems

2 Dead End

Deactivate three Frag Mines here.

- Frag Mine (3)

ANTAGONIZER'S LAIR

3 Eastern Alcove

The lair is a modest affair, with a short tunnel into a larger cavern. If you haven't begun the Miscellaneous Quest: The Superhuman Gambit, the AntAgonizer isn't likely to be here. Grab food and Purified Water from a short bookcase.

4 AntAgonizer's Throne

Take the Quantum here. Grab the remaining items from the AntAgonizer's body. The key allows you to use the sewer grate entrance (during the Quest), while the costume allows you to look slightly foolish. You can get the Ant's Sting only if the AntAgonizer is alive and gives it to you.

- Nuka-Cola Quantum (41/94)
- AntAgonizer Lair Key
- Ant's Sting (38/89)
- Ripper
- The AntAgonizer's Costume (39/89)
- The AntAgonizer's Helmet (40/89)

RELATED INTERACTIONS

AntAgonizer: You can learn her secret identity and confront her with it. You can team up with her to defeat the nearby Mechanist, a rival "superhero." You can stop her terrorizing the nearby Canterbury Commons by revealing her nemesis is dead. You can also kill her.

TRAINING — BESTIARY — MAIN QUEST — MISC. QUESTS — TOUR — COMPLETION — APPENDICES

6.02: CANTERBURY COMMONS (LAT 18/LONG 11)

- Freeform Quest (2)
- Threat Level: 2
- Faction: Wastelander
- Services: Repairer, Trader
- Collectible: Skill Book (4)
- Guns And Ammunition
- Health And Chems
- Interior Exploration
- Main Trading Route
- Rare Or Powerful Item
- Sleep Mattress
- Work Bench (2)
- Hostile: Giant Ant Genus, Robot Genus, Turret
- Friendly: Brahmin

EXTERIOR MAP

Canterbury Commons

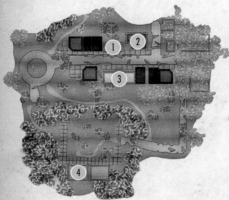

INHABITANTS

ERNEST "UNCLE" ROE

Ernest Roe is 39 and was raised on a trade caravan. By the time he was 12, he could turn 5 Caps into 50 with just a few clever trades. When he was 20, he set out to make his mark, using his sizable investments to found the trading post of Canterbury Commons with his sister Daisy. Nowadays, the Commons have become a regular stop for caravans in the Capitol Wastes. "Uncle Roe" makes sure that everyone gets enough from the caravans to eat a good meal every night. He's lost his sister, but he cares for his nephew as well as he can. With a bit of luck and a whole lot of Caps, he hopes to eventually turn Canterbury Commons into a settlement to rival Rivet City.

DEREK PACION

Derek is small for a 15-year-old and was raised in Canterbury Commons by Louis Pacion and Daisy Roe, a pair of Traders who met and settled down. But when they were killed in separate Raider attacks on their caravans (six years ago for Daisy and three years ago for Louis), Derek was left to his "Uncle Roe," the town keeper. Since then, Derek's been a quiet and morose child. He works around town as a general assistant, but he doesn't really say much unless it's necessary. He harbors a secret crush on Machete but doesn't have the courage to approach her. He is devoting much more of his free time to reading Hubris Comics.

JOE PORTER

"Porter Joe" (the name he prefers to go by) is 28 and was a loader-for-hire at a caravan. However, when he first arrived at Canterbury Commons, the idea of having a permanent base of operations and a steady community was very appealing to him. He settled down here with his dog, Ol' Mule, about six years ago and has been working as an unloader, a basic cook, and a basic repairman since then. Since the death of his dog, he's been minding the town diner, the center of chatter in this settlement.

DOMINIC D'ELLSADRO

Dominic was once the leader of a small squad of mercenaries, but after one too many near-death experiences, he retired with a small fortune of scavenged goods. He's been in Canterbury Commons for about 10 of his 40 years, and since arriving, his natural leadership has made him a very respected figure in the community. Roe handles the day-to-day negotiations and arrangements with the Traders who pass through and keeps the settlement functioning, while Dom handles any security or emergency concerns. Dom's companion, Machete, is treated like a cross between a daughter and a soldier. He is trying to teach her to act as security for the settlement.

MACHETE

One of the fiercest defenders Little Lamplight has ever seen, 19-year-old "Machete" earned her nickname at the age of 7, when she killed a Mole Rat in the caves armed only with a knife the size of her arm. Since then, she has been a bona fide celebrity. When she turned 16, she got disoriented in a dust storm and got lost, eventually arriving at Canterbury Commons instead of Big Town. To this day, she refuses to admit that she went to the wrong place. Dominic in particular saw her potential to provide security for the future of the camp, and after a year of his guidance, she's earned a fair amount of respect from the locals.

THE MECHANIST

Forty-year-old Scott "Bean" Wollinski was born to simple bean farmers, raised by his father until he was 15, who then sold him to a caravan merchant hoping he would have a better life. He traveled with the caravans for a few years working as an indentured servant. This is where he got the nickname "Bean," as his purchase was paid for with beans. He eventually bought his freedom and settled down in Canterbury Commons, where he lived a life of solitude, hiding in the electronics store, fiddling around with junk. After the AntAgonizer started showing up, he became the Mechanist to protect the town.

GENERAL NOTES

Traders usually wait at the large Water Tower [6.E]. When your bartering is over, move into Main Street. Here, you can watch the fracas between the AntAgonizer and the Mechanist begin.

① Diner

> Derek Pacion is usually here; Pickpocket him for a Grognak the Barbarian comic. Joe Porter is the barkeep.

- Grognak the Barbarian (8/25)
- Baseball Bat

② Dominic and Machete's House

This garage has a Work Bench with a Bottle-cap Mine on it and several interesting items. There are also Gun Cabinets to rummage in. The second room has a fridge with food. Locate the following items here:

- Work Bench (16/46)
- Sledgehammer
- Combat Knife (2)
- Highwayman's Friend (Tire Iron) (41/89)
- Dean's Electronics (7/25)

③ City Hall (Ernest "Uncle" Roe's House)

Check the storage room and the living quarters for the following items:

- Ammo Box Ammunition (2)
- Crazy Wolfgang's Local Inventory
- Crow's Local Inventory
- Doc Hoff's Local Inventory
- Lucky Harith's Local Inventory
- Joe Porter's Safe

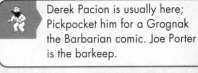

Uncle Roe's house is perhaps the most important spot for the Wandering Traders anywhere in the Wasteland, as they must keep their local inventory sealed here. If you've murdered any of the Traders, you can return here to unlock their deposits and then leave with the loot. Every Wandering Trader has their own box, and Joe Porter has a wall safe, stuffed mainly with food.

Note

Roe, Machete, and Dominic each have a House Key on their bodies. As the homes are unlocked (during the day), there's no need to resort to such bloodthirsty measures.

RELATED INTERACTIONS

Commons inhabitant: You can ask directions, hear rumors about the superheroes, and listen to the history of the town.

Uncle Roe: You can get him to Repair your equipment. You can get him increase the variety and to invest in the Wandering Traders.

Joe Porter: You can receive a complimentary Dirty Water from him for being a new arrival. You can request and purchase food from him.

Mechanist: You can team up with him to defeat the nearby AntAgonizer, a rival "superhero." You can stop him terrorizing the nearby Canterbury Commons by revealing that his nemesis is dead. You can also kill him.

④ Robot Repair Center: Front Offices

South of town is the run-down electronics discount store called Barry's Discounts. It has now been turned into the Robot Repair Center and has one entrance.

① Elevator and Utility Door

This leads to the Mechanist's Forge.

② Front Offices

Access the terminal to read the Note from Frank. Some dead guy named Snake has been smuggling Pulse Grenades to solve issues with the automated turrets. Check for the key behind the terminal, unlocking a metal box under the southwest cubicle.

- Pulse Grenade (6)

③ Door to the Control Room

WAREHOUSE POD BAY

④ ⑤ Working Warehouse Terminals

Read the Note from Management Regarding Sector B. This basically instructs workers to raise a cargo elevator when robots are ready to ship, but the hydraulics are malfunctioning. Access a nearby pod. Activate the Protectron inside, and it strides over to the elevator shaft, steps on where the elevator should be, and falls to the ground below!

⑥ Connecting Console Room

Access a wall terminal to shut the turrets down.

CONTROL ROOM

⑦ Ground Floor Junk Room

There are several Protectrons and parts, along with the following (including a Skill Book on the desk next to the conveyor belts):

- Ammo Box Ammunition (2)
- Nikola Tesla and You (11/25)

⑧ Generator Control Room

Access Sector A Terminal. You can shut down the turrets above you from here.

- First Aid Box Health and Chems

⑨ Control Cabin

Open the desk safe and take the Sector A Encryption Key. Access the Sector A Emergency Terminal. Now that you have the key, activate an Emergency Pulse Explosion, destroying all the robotic entities in this chamber.

- Desk Safe Items
- Sector A Encryption Key

MECHANIST'S FORGE

⑩ Executive Office

Check the Skill Book on the desk. Open the secret door by inspecting and activating the coffee brewer.

- Lying: Congressional Style (4/25)

⑪ Mechanist's Lair

There's a Work Bench with a Nuka Grenade on it. The Costume and Helmet you recover from his body allows you to look rather unfortunate. He attacks with a Laser Pistol. If you are carrying the AntAgonizer's outfit after battling her with the Mechanist, you're given a Unique Pistol.

- Work Bench (17/46)
- The Mechanist's Costume (42/89)
- The Mechanist's Helmet (43/89)
- "Protectron's Gaze" Laser Pistol (44/89)

INTERIOR MAPS AND LOCATIONS

Ernest "Uncle" Roe's House

Dominic and Machete's House

Robot Repair Center and Mechanist's Forge

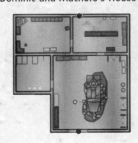

APPENDICES — COMPLETION — TOUR — MISC. QUESTS — BESTIARY — MAIN QUEST — TRAINING

FREEFORM QUEST: MERCHANT EMPIRE

When you're speaking with Uncle Roe, bring the conversation around to the Traders who pass through here. Convince him to form a tighter organization and become the main point of contact. The following abilities allow this to occur:

 A particularly adept comeback.

Your exceptional knowledge of Trading.

Your feminine charms and wiles.

Or, if you have 250 Caps or more, your experience in the Wastes convinces him.

Once the agreement occurs, you'll see that each merchant sells three "tiers" of equipment. Investing raises the variety and quality of the merchandise. It also allows the Trader to invest in an additional Bodyguard and Brahmin. Three days after your investment, return to the Trader in question, and you'll receive a useful item of the type you previously requested the Trader specialize in.

This is designed to increase the variety of goods the traveling merchants carry, allowing occasional "rare" items to appear for sale and for you to spend all those Caps you've been hoarding! For better purchases, here's what each Wandering Merchant focuses on selling:

- Lucky Harith: Weapons and ammunition
- Crow: Armor and clothing
- Doc Hoff: Food, drink, and Chems
- Crazy Wolfgang: Junk and miscellaneous items

6.03: SCRAPYARD (LAT 05/LONG 09)

- Threat Level: 1
- Faction: Littlehorn And Associates
- Danger: Low Radiation
- Collectible: Skill Book (4)
- Follower
- Interior Exploration
- Lots O Caps
- Perk!
- Hostile: Raider

Scrapyard

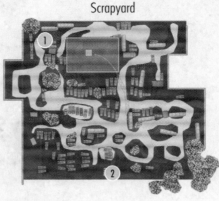

INHABITANTS

Daniel Littlehorn

An elderly man with a sharp suit and a penchant for French Traditionalist painters, Daniel Littlehorn has run his organization for as long as any of his secretaries can remember. Although now in his late 70s, Littlehorn is a commanding (but unseen) presence across the Wasteland. If good men falter, innocents are slain, or water supplies become more tainted, you can bet Littlehorn's clandestine organization is behind it.

Littlehorn Secretary

Furiously typing and thankful to have gainful employment with Littlehorn and Associates, the four secretaries spend their time creating and filing records of all associates' activities across the East Coast. As life is cheap, hard work is expected, not rewarded.

Dogmeat

An affectionate and dextrous puppy, Dogmeat's skills as a four-legged scavenger and ferocious fighting companion were not lost on his first master, who was recently killed by Raiders in the vicinity of the Scrapyard. Dogmeat has tracked the Raiders down, loyal to the end.

1 John's Stash

This large and sprawling scrapyard has dozens of vehicles rusting in the sun. Check the northwestern corner for John's Treasure Box; it has three Skill Books inside!

- U.S. Army: 30 Handy Flamethrower Recipes (6/25)
- Grognak the Barbarian (9/25)
- Guns and Bullets (11/25)

2 Littlehorn and Associates

 The only building that's accessible is a small shack on the Scrapyard's south edge. It is sealed shut until the following happens:

1. You reach Level 14
2. Maintain negative Karma.
3. Have a Perception Statistic of 6 or higher.

4. Choose the Contract Killer perk when you reach Level 14

You then receive a mysterious note called Littlehorn and Associates. Read it, and your Pip-Boy updates, revealing this to be the Scrapyard Office.

- Note: Littlehorn and Associates

SCRAPYARD OFFICE

The shack features four of Littlehorn's secretaries clacking away on typewriters. Daniel Littlehorn himself—sitting under a painting of Dante and Virgil in Hell—welcomes you warmly. Check his wastebasket for a copy of

- Lying: Congressional Style (5/25).

FREEFORM QUEST: GETTING AN EARFUL

Now that you're an associate contract killer for the Littlehorn team, begin to slay those of sound mind and morals. Littlehorn is suitably vague about why he wants the few good and true inhabitants slain; you're just a cog in a machine—an incredibly evil, conspiratorial, and ultimately evil machine. Take an Ear from each corpse you kill, and return it to Littlehorn for 5 Caps and a negative Karma boost.

- Ear
- 5 Caps (per Ear)

FREEFORM QUEST: MAN'S BEST FRIEND

Search the Scrapyard's northeastern corner, and you'll hear gunshots and shouting. Watch as a black and white dog leaps and savages four Raiders, bringing them to the ground and killing them. The dog scampers over to you and barks. This is Dogmeat. He can be a fiercely loyal and trusted companion, ready to help you out in combat and forage for you.

- Follower: Dogmeat

Tip

For advice on utilizing your Follower, refer to page 38.

6.04: WHEATON ARMORY (LAT 10/ LONG 08)

- Threat Level: 4
- Faction: Raider
- Danger: High Radiation
- Collectible: Skill Book
- Area Is Locked
- Guns And Ammunition
- Health And Chems
- Interior Exploration
- Rare Or Powerful Item
- Hostile: Raider, Turret

MAPS AND LOCATIONS

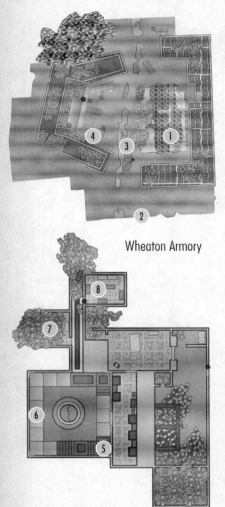

Wheaton Armory

An old military base is now one of the major locations of power for the Raiders as they fan out from the nearby Bethesda Ruins. Once the Enclave arrive, expect the two factions to fight each other in this locale. There are the well-defended northern and southern gates and a gap in the fence to the west and southeast (the best way if you're Sneaking in here).

1 Ruined Concrete Building

This has Raiders everywhere, so take care and look up through the holes in the ceilings if you can't spot who's firing at you. On the top floor is a stash:

- Ammo Box Ammunition (3)
- First Aid Box Health and Chems (2)

2 L-Shaped Cabin (Outside Gate)

- Ammo Box Ammunition
- First Aid Box Health and Chems

3 Parked Container Truck

Check the container for Ammo Box Ammunition and First Aid Box Health and Chems.

4 L-Shaped Cabin (South; near Interior door)

Locate the safe to open.

- Cabin safe items

WHEATON ARMORY
5 Room with Metal Shelf

Warning! The background radiation is beginning to rise to unsafe exposure levels! Check the previous chamber's gun cabinets. Locate Rad-X, RadAway, and these items:

- Ammo Box Ammunition (2)
- First Aid Box Health and Chems

6 Silo Perimeter

- Ammo Box Ammunition

7 Rubble-Filled Room

Grab the items listed below, and deactivate the turrets at the terminal.

- Ammo Box Ammunition (4)
- First Aid Box Health and Chems

8 Armory

Access the locked terminal or door. Once the door is breached, a klaxon sounds. You find the items below (a few of the Ammo Boxes are locked).

- Frag Mine (3)
- Plasma Grenade (3)
- Ammo Box Ammunition (12)
- Rad Chems and Radiation Suits
- Combat Knife (3)
- Pulse Mine (3)
- Assault Rifle (4)
- Minigun
- Sniper Rifle (2)
- Missile Launcher (2)
- U.S. Army: 30 Handy Flamethrower Recipes (7/25)

6.05: CORVEGA FACTORY (LAT 16/ LONG 05)

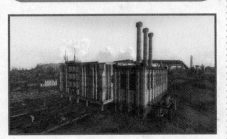

- Threat Level: 3
- Danger: Low Radiation
- Collectible: Skill Book (4)
- Health And Chems
- Interior Exploration
- Hostile: Giant Ant Genus, Giant Ant Queen

INTERIOR MAPS AND LOCATIONS

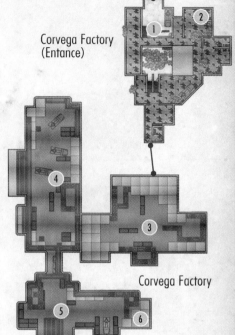

Corvega Factory (Entance)

Corvega Factory

One of the two giant car conglomerates back before the bombs fell, the Corvega Factory still has a faded grandeur to it, although the place is now overrun with Giant Ants. Before you start your bug hunt, check the exterior surroundings and the irradiated container to the south, which has a Skill Book.

- Big Book of Science (8/25)

CORVEGA FACTORY (ENTRANCE)
1 Foyer Desk

There are Giant Ants and Egg Clutches to tackle here.

- Lying: Congressional Style (6/25)

2 Upper Open-Plan Office

- Big Book of Science (9/25)

CORVEGA FACTORY
3 East Warehouse

Locate the Metal Door on the western side.

- First Aid Box Health and Chems

4 Northern Warehouse

There are Giant Ants but only a few scattered items in the south alcove desk. There are Darts on the desk near the impassible west door.

TRAINING — BESTIARY — MAIN QUEST — MISC. QUESTS — TOUR — COMPLETION — APPENDICES

5 Southern Warehouse

There's a Giant Ant Queen to defeat here. Stay on the upper catwalk lobbing grenades or firing weapons.

- Ant Queen Pheromones

6 Foreman's Office

There are bodies, Egg Clutches, two Stimpaks, and a Skill Book here.

- Dean's Electronics (8/25)

6.06: VAULT 108 (LAT 18/LONG 06)

- Threat Level: 2
- Faction: Vault Dweller
- Collectible: Bobblehead, Nuka-Cola Quantum, Skill Book (3)
- Guns And Ammunition
- Health And Chems
- Interior Exploration
- Sleep Mattress
- Hostiles: Gary 1, Gary 12, Gary 17, Gary 25, Gary 27, Gary 29, Gary 32, Gary 33, Gary 41, Gary 42 (Deceased), Gary 43, Gary 47 , Mole Rat, Radroach

Near a small pond northeast of the Corvega Factory and south of Canterbury Commons is a rocky outcrop with a hidden vault entrance flanked by two trees. Aside from the bumpy terrain, this is easy to enter.

INTERIOR MAPS AND LOCATIONS

VAULT 108 (ENTRANCE)

1 Entrance

Go into the entrance tunnel, stepping over some bodies (search the Wastelander), and head through the open vault door. This place is in serious disrepair—the door doesn't even close!

2 Small Reactor Room

Watch for a Mole Rat ambush! Check the area; there are items by the entrance to the living quarters.

- Stealth Boy
- Silenced 10mm Pistol

3 Connecting Passage

On the ground is a dead Vault Dweller, Gary 42.

- Vault 108 Jumpsuit

4 Reactor Room

There is a door to the Cloning Labs here. Check the storage room to the east; behind the stacked crates is a Quantum. Under the step ladder is a Skill Book that's almost impossible to obtain.

- Nuka Cola Quantum (42/94)
- Tumblers Today (13/25)

VAULT 108 (LIVING QUARTERS)

5 Send in the Clones

Head down the stairs, where you're accosted by Gary 33. It appears the Vault-Tec Company has turned this vault into a cloning facility! Alas, the clone "Gary" is now deranged and attacks while shouting his own name.

6 North Room

- First Aid Box Health and Chems

7 Atrium

Watch for Gary clones!

8 Cafeteria

Beware of Gary ambushes and Radroaches. There is also food in the fridge and a Skill Book in the corner. The two rooms to the south have a few food items but little else.

- Pugilism Illustrated (12/25)

9 Upper Atrium

Each room here has a bed, and one has a floor safe.

- Floor Safe Items

10 Corridor to Cloning Labs

Check the small room to the right to unlock another safe.

- First Aid Box Health and Chems
- Floor Safe Items

VAULT 108 (CLONING LABS)

 Note
You can enter these labs from either direction.

11 Laboratory

Check the floor safe, and observe the Cloning Log Holotape, detailing attacks by an increasingly violent Gary 53 and 54.

- Floor Safe Items
- Holotape: Cloning Log

12 Central Observation and Medical Chamber

- First Aid Box Health and Chems
- Bobblehead: Charisma (10/20)
- Lying: Congressional Style (7/25)

13 Wrecked Room

- First Aid Box Health and Chems

14 Exit Corridor

You can now exit this area. Never trust a man named Gary ever again.

- Ammo Box Ammunition (2)

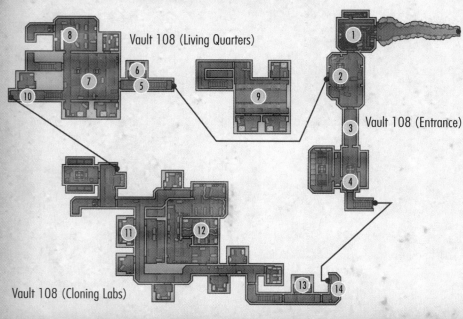

Vault 108 (Living Quarters)

Vault 108 (Entrance)

Vault 108 (Cloning Labs)

6.07: BETHESDA RUINS (LAT 05/ LONG 03)

Bethesda Offices: East Entrance

Bethesda Offices: West Entrance

Bethesda Underworks: Metro Entrance

Bethesda Underworks: Manhole Entrance

- Threat Level: 4
- Faction: Ghoul, Raider
- Danger: Grenade Bouquet (2), Low Radiation, Mines, Shotgun Trap (3)
- Collectible: Bobblehead, Fat Man Mini-Nuke (3), Nuka-Cola Quantum, Scribe Pre-War Book (2), Skill Book (6)
- Guns And Ammunition
- Health And Chems
- Interior Exploration
- Sleep Mattress
- Work Bench
- Hostile: Ghoul Genus, Raider, Turret

Note

The following interior locations can be entered and exited from one of two directions. Where necessary, use the more obvious entrance.

EXTERIOR MAP
Bethesda Ruins

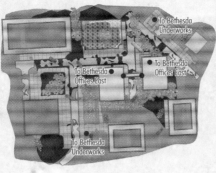

To Bethesda Underworks
To Bethesda Offices East
To Bethesda Offices East
To Bethesda Offices East
To Bethesda Underworks

Note

The following assumes that you're entering Bethesda Ruins heading from west to east and that you're at the edge of town near the ruined freeway and Red Rocket Gas Station.

INTERIOR MAPS AND LOCATIONS

This is one of the largest urban areas outside of D.C. When navigating through this area, there is a main cluster of Raiders you should aim for. Head east along the main drag. Pass the huge billboard, the ruined building on your right, and fight Raiders on your way to the T-junction with the two burned-out halves of a Coach Liner. Two blocks south, near a blue car, is the manhole to the Bethesda Underworks. Keep going south, and you reach a radioactive drainage flow area, now little more than soggy ponds.

Back at the wrecked Coach Liner T-junction, head northeast, into the large ruined building with the concrete block balcony overlooking the Coach pieces. Sprint to the opposite staircase, and tear through the Raiders up here, backtracking on the upper floor to the balcony. There are two Ammo Boxes here. Head up a floor if you want to snipe from this location, especially at the Raiders to the east, on ground level by the truck container.

- Ammo Box Ammunition (2)

Bethesda Offices East floor 1

Bethesda Offices East floor 2

Bethesda Offices West floor 2

Bethesda Offices West floor 1 & 1.5

Bethesda Underworks

TRAINING — BESTIARY — MAIN QUEST — MISC. QUESTS — TOUR — COMPLETION — APPENDICES

The western entrance to the Bethesda Offices is just south of you. Keep pushing east to another T-junction. There are Raiders everywhere, so use the truck container as cover, near the eastern entrance; grab the items listed below from inside. To the south is a Raider blockade and a concrete bridge linking the east and west offices, which you must access from inside either building. To the north is the Metro Station entrance to the Underworks.

- Ammo Box Ammunition (2)
- First Aid Box Health and Chems

BETHESDA OFFICES WEST (LOCATION 1)

> **Note**
> You can enter this area via the east office entrance or the west. The following assumes the latter.

① Curved Front Desk

Prepare for combat (or an extra-quick Sneak) with more Raiders in an entrance foyer. Activate the Turret Control System terminal, deactivate the turret, then grab these items:

- Big Book of Science (10/25)
- First Aid Box Health and Chems

② Small Restroom #1

- First Aid Box Health and Chems

③ Small Restroom #2

There's a rather unsavory Cherry Bomb and Ammo Box Ammunition.

④ Flaming Barrel

There's a mattress near here. Disarm or shoot the Frag Mine by the barrel, or shoot the fire extinguishers to help combat the Raiders.

- Frag Mine

⑤ Southwest Shelf

- Frag Mine
- Frag Grenade

⑥ Upstairs Room #1

There's a foe to kill, a lead pipe and Stimpak on the desk, and the following:

- Scribe Pre-War Book (37 & 38/98)
- Blood Pack (2)

⑦ Pressure Plate Room

This activates three Rigged Shotguns! Search for alcohol in the fridge and the following items (look in the crates next to the chest freezer for the Mini-Nuke):

- Combat Shotgun and Ammo (3)
- Mini-Nuke (32/71)
- Stealth Boy
- Dean's Electronics (9/25)

Rip through a lone Raider on the concrete bridge to the eastern offices, open the two Ammo Boxes, then enter the door to Bethesda Offices East.

- Ammo Box Ammunition (2)

> **Caution**
> Avoid stepping on the pressure plate, being struck by three Rigged Shotguns, and then falling through the hole in the room with the Rigged Shotgun; aside from the embarrassment, the fall dislodges six grenades in two bouquets, and you have those to worry about as you land: Run away!

BETHESDA OFFICES EAST (LOCATION 1)

⑧ Rubble-Filled Corridor

Check the rubble pile carefully to find a Mini-Nuke between two partially buried cabinets.

- Mini-Nuke (33/71)

⑨ Turret Control Room: Raider Leader

Dive at the back of the Turret Control terminal, deactivating it before backing up and slaying the Raider. Or, stay at the doorway and use it as cover. After you drop the Flamer Raider, search him for a Skill Book. Check the room for a wall safe and locate the Work Bench with junk and a Bottlecap Mine on it.

- Work Bench (18/46)
- U.S. Army: 30 Handy Flamethrower Recipes (8/25)
- Melee Weapons
- Wall Safe Items
- Bobblehead: Lockpick (11/20)
- Ammo Box Ammunition (2)

⑩ Office

Check the northwest desk for the following items:

- Missiles (2)
- Chinese Army: Spec. Ops. Training Manual (6/25)

⑪ Mirelurk Cakes

Slay the Raider attempting to enjoy some delicious Mirelurk Cakes, then ransack the room for Darts, a Baseball Bat, and a First Aid Box Health and Chems.

⑫ Restroom

Take the Scotch and the First Aid Box Health and Chems from here.

BETHESDA UNDERWORKS (LOCATION 2)

> **Note**
> You can enter this area via a sewer grating or a metro station entrance. The following assumes the latter.

⑬ Mezzanine

Head past the two vending machines and over the turnstiles, blasting a Ghoul in the face; then head onto the mezzanine, where more Ferals need flattening. Check the bucket on a stone bench near the baby carriage.

- Tales of a Junktown Jerky Vendor (8/24)

⑭ Lower Station Floor

Fight off the Glowing Ones as best you can (a sniped headshot from the mezzanine is a good start). There's a makeshift mattress and some Rad Chems hidden in the tiny crates.

⑮ Connecting Corridor

Check the skeleton by the bucket for a couple of Stimpaks.

⑯ "Pillar" Storeroom

Watch out for the Ghoul! Then grab this bounty (don't forget the Mini-Nuke under the tiny crate):

- Nuka-Cola Quantum (43/94)
- Mini-Nuke (34/71)
- First Aid Box Health and Chems
- Frag Grenade (3)
- Ammo Box Ammunition (2)
- Grognak the Barbarian (10/25)

⑰ Radioactive Barrels and Skeleton

This dead guy has Buffout and a 2-Ball to snag too. There are nearby crates containing beer and Chems. Exit via the ladder.

- Chinese Assault Rifle

6.08: CHRYSLUS BUILDING (LAT 08/ LONG -01)

- Threat Level: 4
- Faction: Super Mutant
- Danger: Bear Trap, Chain Trap, Shotgun Trap
- Collectible: Nuka-Cola Quantum, Scribe Pre-War Book, Skill Book (3)
- Guns And Ammunition
- Health And Chems
- Interior Exploration
- Hostile: Centaur, Super Mutant Genus, Vicious Dog

INTERIOR MAPS AND LOCATIONS

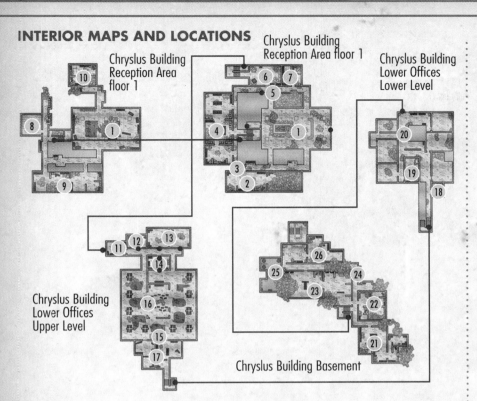

Chryslus Building Reception Area floor 1

Chryslus Building Reception Area floor 1

Chryslus Building Lower Offices Lower Level

Chryslus Building Lower Offices Upper Level

Chryslus Building Basement

On the southern outskirts of the large Bethesda Ruins is a concrete building that's seen better days; it was once the headquarters for the Chryslus Motor Company. There is a single entrance.

CHRYSLUS BUILDING RECEPTION AREA: GROUND FLOOR

① Reception Area

As the dulcet tones of Three Dog waft through the air, step into the main reception area. The door to the west is locked and leads into the basement.

② Large Ruined Offices (South)

Check the two bookcases here; one has a Carton of Cigarettes. Check the hole in the east wall for a desk with the following items:

- Nuka-Cola Quantum (44/94)
- Ammo Box Ammunition

③ Southwest Corridor Corner

There's a bookcase with another Carton of Cigarettes here.

④ Three "Open-Plan" Offices

The interior walls have been removed. There are only some common items here and the First Aid Box Health and Chems.

⑤ North Corridor T-Junction

You reach a wooden door that's locked and find an adjacent wall terminal. Unlock either to enter Location 6. Or, you can fall in from the second floor.

⑥ Locked Office

Find Buffout in the plastic bucket, a vending machine, and stairs down to the lower offices.

- Ammo Box Ammunition (2)
- Guns and Bullets (12/25)
- Scoped .44 Magnum

⑦ Northeast Office

Beware the Bear Trap, and take the Carton of Cigarettes.

SECOND FLOOR

⑧ Western Restrooms

There's nothing here except Gnomes and an old "help!" sign.

⑨ Southern Offices

The first office has a Carton of Cigarettes and Mentats on bookcases. There's also a Bear Trap near the wardrobe.

⑩ Large Office (without Floor)

Grab another Carton of Cigarettes. The radio is on the room's opposite side, as is a doorway. Beware of the Girder-on-a-Chain Trap! This leads to the room with the hole in the ceiling and a .44 Magnum; this is the other way to reach this area if you can't hack or pick the door.

CHRYSLUS BUILDING LOWER OFFICES (LOWER FLOOR 1: THE CORRIDOR OF LOCKED DOORS)

⑪ Trapped chamber

Locate the Carton of Cigarettes, but watch for the Bear Trap.

- Ammo Box Ammunition
- First Aid Box Health and Chems

⑫ Rotting Brahmin Office

Accessed down the corridor of locked doors.

⑬ Vicious Dog Offices

There are a few Chems in here too.

⑭ Mail Room

- Scribe Pre-War Book (39/98)

LOWER FLOOR 1: OPEN-PLAN DEVASTATION

⑮ Open-Plan Office South Wall

There's 10mm Ammo scattered here. Nearby is a desk with Chems and a Carton of Cigarettes. Expect to find a Minigun from one or more of the Super Mutants in the vicinity.

- Ammo Box Ammunition
- Minigun

⑯ Middle Area and West Cabinet

Locate the Skill Book in one of the postal crates (don't fall through the floor). There are Chems and melee tools to take at the cabinet.

- Pugilism Illustrated (13/25)

⑰ Executive Office Area

Search for a couple more Cartons of Cigarettes, common items, and stairs down.

LOWER FLOOR 2: OFFICES AND RECREATION AREA

⑱ Storage Room Trap

Beware the Rigged Shotgun.

- Combat Shotgun and Ammo
- Ammo Box Ammunition (2)

⑲ South Storage Room

- Stealth Boy

⑳ Northern Recreation Area

There's food in the fridge and an Eat-O-Matic machine. You're looking for the wooden Door to Chryslus Building Basement, to the left of the Vault-Tec backlit sign.

TRAINING — BESTIARY — MAIN QUEST — MISC. QUESTS — TOUR — COMPLETION — APPENDICES

CHRYSLUS BUILDING BASEMENT

Note

You can also enter this basement from the Reception Area, if you unlock the wooden door to the north.

21 Southern Office

There are a few bottles of Whiskey, food, and scattered Caps.

22 Eastern Office

23 Middle Office

- First Aid Box Health and Chems
- 308 Caliber Rounds

24 Corridor, Leading from Stairwell

There is some minor Ammo and a Carton of Cigarettes in an alcove.

25 Generator Room

Find a Skill Book and the following:

- Big Book of Science (11/25)
- First Aid Box Health and Chems

26 Northern Office

Open the two safes, one of which has a Stealth Boy in it. Grab the two Cartons of Cigarettes and leave.

- Office Safe Items (2)
- Stealth Boy

MAPS AND LOCATIONS
Rock Creek Caverns

6.09: ROCK CREEK CAVERNS (LAT 14/ LONG -02)

- Threat Level: 4
- Danger: Low Radiation
- Collectible: Nuka-Cola Quantum
- Guns And Ammunition
- Health And Chems
- Interior Exploration
- Sleep Mattress
- Hostile: Mirelurk Genus

The northern edge of the D.C. Metro outskirts isn't the first place you'd expect to find a giant underground Mirelurk cavern, but access to this gloomy and dangerous locale is available, thanks to a large crater created after a gas explosion.

SEWER AND METRO TUNNELS

1 Small Storage Chamber

Attack the Mirelurk. Around the edge are shelves containing metal boxes and the following:

- Ammo Box Ammunition (3)
- First Aid Box Health and Chems (2)

2 Hole in the Metro Line

Descend down here into the Great Chamber. Optionally take RadAway before you go.

GREAT CHAMBER

3 Gigantic central Column

Climb the promontory in the southwestern area to gather food, beer, and the following:

- First Aid Box Health and Chems
- Ammo Box Ammunition
- Nuka-Cola Quantum (45/94)

4 Debris-Strewn Dead End

Mirelurks have slain the scavengers holed up here. There's a half-buried safe and the following:

- Half-Buried Safe Items
- First Aid Box Health and Chems
- Ammo Box Ammunition

5 Connecting Passage

This brings you out, looking over a rocky path that winds north.

6 Alcove

This has a mattress in it.

BACK CAVERNS

7 Wider Tunnel Area

There's both Mirelurk Meat (in the clutches) and Ant Meat to sift through here.

8 Larger Cavern

You can climb up onto the middle column and fire from here, or dodge the Mirelurks on the ground.

9 South Side Alcove

The following items and a half-buried safe are here:

- Laser Rifle
- Ammo Box Ammunition (3)
- Power Fist
- First Aid Box Health and Chems (2)
- Half-Buried Safe Items

10 Metro Tunnel Remnant

This is completely blocked (although there's a dead commuter and Stimpak to check out before you backtrack to the surface).

6.10: FRIENDSHIP HEIGHTS METRO STATION (LAT 14/ LONG -03)

- Main Quest: Following In His Footsteps
- Threat Level: 3
- Faction: Raider
- Guns And Ammunition
- Health And Chems
- Interior Exploration
- Sleep Mattress
- Underground Connection
- Hostile: Raider, Super Mutant Genus

Note

The Metro Station entrance leads to two linked underground Metro Areas:

Location D.C. U1.A: Farragut West Station (page 443) and Location D.C. U1.B: Tenleytown/Friendship Station (page 443).

These surface locations can be accessed from the underground metro tunnels: Location 9.02: Farragut West Metro Station (page 376) and Location 10.01: Chevy Chase North (page 398).

One of the first methods of entering the D.C. Metro Area is via the Friendship Heights Metro Station. It is currently a Raider camp, so expect clashes with these enemies as you close in on the entrance. Use the concrete buttress to the north of the entrance as cover, Sneak down the entrance escalators, or begin some running-and-gunning-style combat. These Raiders are likely to be well equipped, with Small Guns, Flamers, and perhaps a Missile Launcher. Head into the exterior mezzanine above the station entrance to claim Chems, Whiskey, beer, and Brahmin Steak. Sleep in the tent mattress and grab the items listed below. When you're ready, head down the escalator and enter the metal gate to Tenleytown/Friendship Station [U1.B].

- 10mm Pistol and Ammo (2)
- Frag Grenade (3)
- 10mm Submachine Gun (2)
- First Aid Box Health and Chems (2)

6.11: NATIONAL GUARD DEPOT (LAT 18/LONG -03)

- Threat Level: 4
- Danger: Gas Leak, Low Radiation
- Collectibles: Bobblehead, Fat Man Mini-Nuke (5), Fat Man Launcher, Nuka-Cola Quantum, Scribe Pre-War Book (6), Skill Book (4)
- Area Is Locked
- Guns And Ammunition
- Health And Chems
- Interior Exploration
- Sleep Mattress
- Work Bench (3)
- Hostile: Glowing One, Mark V Turret, Robot Genus

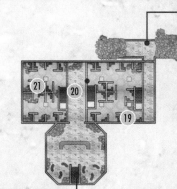

Note

Before you enter this location, it is advisable to have the access code to the Bunker, available after you collect all five Keller Holotapes. Keller Holotapes are located in Zone 3 (page 289), Zone 4 (pages 304-305), Zone 5 (page 310), and Zone 9 (page 394).

On the outskirts of the D.C. Metro Area is a National Guard Depot with two Guard Protectrons. The building looks study from the outside, but it is devastated inside. However, there is a huge amount of weaponry and ammunition hidden deep in the basement armory.

INTERIOR MAPS AND LOCATIONS

National Guard Depot Entry Level

National Guard Depot Basement Level

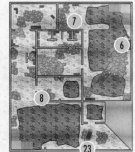

National Guard Depot F2 (First Floor above entry)

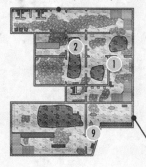

National Guard Armory

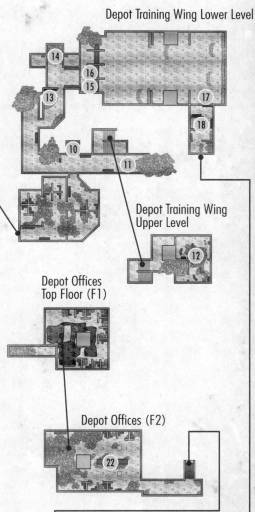

Depot Training Wing Lower Level

Depot Training Wing Upper Level

Depot Offices Top Floor (F1)

Depot Offices (F2)

Depot Offices Bottom Floor (F3)

TRAINING — BESTIARY — MAIN QUEST — MISC. QUESTS — TOUR — COMPLETION — APPENDICES

NATIONAL GUARD DEPOT: GROUND FLOOR

① Work Bench

Beware of gas as you enter the building. Amid the broken flooring and leaking pipes is a Bottlecap Mine, scattered junk, and two Cartons of Cigarettes.

- Work Bench (19/46)

② Hole in Floor

Use this to drop down to the wall terminal [Location #4].

LOWER FLOOR

③ L-Shaped Chamber with Generator

Directly under the entrance door is a desk with another Work Bench, a mattress, and the radio you heard as you came in. The generator has Fission Batteries and other common items on it.

- Work Bench (20/46)
- First Aid Box Health and Chems

④ Wall Terminal

Expect robotic adversaries here; hack into the Turret Control System and deactivate the turrets.

⑤ Storage Room

Access this via a metal door. The nearby utility hatch door is locked and activated elsewhere.

- Nikola Tesla and You (12/25)

UPPER FLOOR (TO DEPOT TRAINING WING)

⑥ Eastern Wall Bookcase

- Scribe Pre-War Book (40 & 41/98)

⑦ Wrecked Room

Scramble onto the twisted radio mast and shimmy along the floor edge to reach here.

- First Aid Box Health and Chems

⑧ Turret Control Terminal

Hack it to switch the turret off.

⑨ Snack Machines

Exit to the door to Depot Training Wing.

DEPOT TRAINING WING

⑩ Alcove and Terminal

Deactivate the turret from here.

⑪ Dead End

- First Aid Box Health and Chems

⑫ Junk-Filled Office

Sift through debris to find a Skill Book, a Pre-War Book, and a wall safe.

- Tales of a Junktown Jerky Vendor (9/24)
- Scribe Pre-War Book (42/98)
- Wall Safe Items

⑬ Firing Range Desk

Behind the desk is a Combat Helmet and the following:

- 10mm Submachine Gun and Ammo (6)
- Assault Rifle and Ammo (6)

⑭ Restrooms

- First Aid Box Health and Chems

⑮ Booth #1

There are two Combat Helmets in here and the following:

- Assault Rifle and Ammo (2)
- Ammo Box Ammunition (2)

⑯ Booth #2

- Sniper Rifle
- Ammo Box Ammunition

⑰ Rear of Firing Range

- Ammo Box Ammunition

⑱ Firing Range Storage Room

- First Aid Box Health and Chems (4)
- Ammo Box Ammunition (3)

DEPOT OFFICES

⑲ Desk on South Wall

- Ammo Box Ammunition (2)

⑳ Locked Door to Second Balcony

Unlock the door, then hack the wall terminal to deactivate the turret.

㉑ Middle Cubicle by Pillar

- Ammo Box Ammunition

㉒ Archives Room

Check the area thoroughly for a Carton of Cigarettes. Clamber up over the fallen ceiling and edge around to the fallen floor area; there's a shelf attached to the central pillar with three Pre-War Books on it.

- First Aid Box Health and Chems
- Scribe Pre-War Book (43–45/98)
- Duck and Cover! (11/25)

NATIONAL GUARD DEPOT (REPRISE)

㉓ Electrical Switch

At last! You've reached the upper floor area that you couldn't access previously, directly above the Nuka-Cola machines. Pull the electrical switch.

㉔ Utility Door with Klaxons

Drop down, blast the robot behind the utility door (which is open), and head inside. Flip the electrical switch, head down the stairs after the flap-trap door opens, and open the door to the National Guard Armory.

NATIONAL GUARD ARMORY AND BUNKER

㉕ Outer Armory

Move south to the utility door and flip the switch. Make a clockwise sweep of this treasure trove!

- Missile Launcher and (10) Missiles
- Assault Rifle (4)
- Ammo Box Ammunition (6)
- Purified Water (7)
- Stimpak (4)
- Police Baton (4)
- Combat Knife (3)
- Pulse Grenade (4)
- Pulse Mine (4)
- Combat Helmet (4) and Armor (2)
- 10mm Pistol and Ammo (2)
- Radiation Suit (2)
- Frag Mine (4)
- 10mm Submachine Gun and Ammo (2)
- Frag Grenade (4)
- Chems (Buffout, Rad-X, RadAway)
- Minigun
- Bobblehead: Small Guns (12/20)

㉖ Inner Armory

Input the access code you gleaned from listening to all five Keller Family Holotapes, and the utility door slides open. Inside the bunker, there's a Ghoul to tackle and a final scavenge; there are also two Cartons of Cigarettes, Darts, Chems, a Work Bench with a Bottlecap Mine on it, other common items, and the following collectibles:

- Work Bench (21/46)
- First Aid Box Health and Chems
- Mini-Nuke (35–39/71)
- "Experimental MIRV" Fat Man (45/89)
- Nuka-Cola Quantum (46/94)
- U.S. Army: 30 Handy Flamethrower Recipes (9/25)

Secondary Locations

6.A: REGULATOR HEADQUARTERS (LAT 09/ LONG 11)

- Freeform Quest (2)
- Threat Level: 1
- Faction: Regulator
- Collectible: Nuka-Cola Quantum, Skill Book
- Guns And Ammunition

- Health And Chems
- Interior Exploration
- Lots O' Caps
- Perk!
- Sleep Mattress
- Friendly: Brahmin

INHABITANTS
Sonora Cruz

The head of a secretive organization formed by men and women "of sound mind and patriotic justice," Cruz governs the Regulators—the closest the Wasteland has to a militia force that are seen as being true and fair to the hardworking (and usually scared-witless) Settler. Cruz is 35 and has never discussed her past. Rumor has it she was once a Raider but suffered a head trauma (and epiphany) and changed her outlook on human existence soon afterward.

GENERAL NOTES

Out in the dusty pastures north of Wheaton Armory is a large shack with a small herd of Brahmin in front of it. This place is completely inaccessible until you

1. reach Level 14;

2. maintain positive Karma;

3. have a Perception Statistic of 6 or higher;

4. choose the Lawbringer perk when you reach Level 14.

Read the note called The Regulators, then head here.

- Note: The Regulators

On your first visit to the headquarters, you meet a few Wastelanders clad in Regulator outfits. They instruct you to meet Sonora Cruz. But first, inspect the place for useful items: Buffouts, Whiskey, a Wrench, a Carton of Cigarettes, and the listed items below. Head upstairs to raid the fridge for food, then head into Sonora Cruz's chamber for more items and a Skill Book. Sonora welcomes you and asks whether you're ready to join the Regulators. You are awarded a Regulator Duster coat.

- Ammo Box Ammunition (3)
- Combat Knife (3)
- First Aid Box (3)
- Nuka-Cola Quantum (47/94)
- Guns and Bullets (13/25)
- Regulator Duster

FREEFORM QUEST: THERE'S NO JUSTICE, JUST US

Now that you're a Regulator, patrol the Wastes and honor the tenets of the organization by slaying those deemed evil and slicing a finger from their corpse. Return each Finger to Cruz, and she rewards you with 5 Caps. You receive a positive Karma boost too.

- Finger
- 5 Caps (per Finger)

The following enemies are classified as "evil" by the Regulators: Enclave Officer, Enclave Scientist, Enclave Soldier, Raider, Slaver, Super Mutant, Talon Company Mercenary

FREEFORM QUEST: LOOKING OUT FOR LUCAS

Now that you're a Regulator, return to Megaton at any time and seek out Sheriff Lucas Simms. Strike up a conversation. Now that you're part of the "gang" that he is proud to be a member of, you have some specific conversation options.

6.B: JACKKNIFED FREEWAY TRUCK (LAT 11/LONG 10)

- Threat Level: 1
- Collectible: Skill Book

This truck is only accessible if you head north from this location to a section of ruined freeway you can climb onto. Take the Skill Book, then survey the vistas from this point.

- Chinese Army: Spec. Ops. Training Manual (7/25)

6.C: MILITARY TRUCK CHECKPOINT (LAT 13/LONG 12)

- Threat Level: 1
- Guns And Ammunition
- Health And Chems

On the main north–south road from the Temple of the Union, there's an abandoned military truck with some half-buried boxes:

- Ammo Box Ammunition
- First Aid Box Health and Chems

6.D: BRAHMIN PASTURES (LAT 14/LONG 10)

- Threat Level: 1
- Hostile: Radscorpion Genus
- Friendly: Brahmin

Out west of Canterbury Commons is a large Brahmin pasture. There's meat after you slay Brahmin, but little else until the Enclave arrive [E6.02].

6.E: CANTERBURY COMMONS WATER TOWER (LAT 15/LONG 10)

- Miscellaneous Quest: The Superhuman Gambit
- Threat Level: 1
- Landmark
- Hostile: Robot Genus

On the outskirts of Canterbury Commons is a large water tower. Drink from the faucet.

6.F: WRECKED MONORAIL TRAIN (LAT 07/LONG 07)

- Threat Level: 2
- Faction: Raider
- Hostile: Raider

Main roads in this zone converge on a crashed monorail between two rocky outcrops and have been commandeered by Raiders. Attack them from the rocky area above the road for easier combat.

6.G: RADIO MAST YANKEE BRAVO (LAT 16/LONG 07)

- Threat Level: 3
- Faction: Ghoul
- Danger: Low Radiation
- Collectible: Skill Book
- Guns And Ammunition

- Highly Visible Landmark
- Interior Exploration
- Radio Signal
- Hostile: Ghoul Genus

Activate the Electrical Switch atop this rocky hill to receive Radio Signal Yankee Bravo, a series of guttural murmurings and throaty growls. It is coming from a sewer grate to the west–southwest. Triangulate the signal to precisely locate it.

- Radio Signal Yankee Bravo
- Grocgnak the Barbarian (11/25)

6.H: ROBOT REPAIR CENTER (DARREN'S DISCOUNT ELECTRONICS; LAT 17/ LONG 09)

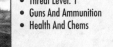

- Miscellaneous Quest: The Superhuman Gambit
- Threat Level: 2
- Faction: Wastelander
- Highly Visible Landmark
- Interior Exploration

Another landmark in Canterbury Commons is Darren's Discount Electronics, known on your Local Map as the Robot Repair Center. This is also the Mechanizer's lair. For interior information (including the Unique Laser Pistol you can obtain), consult the Tour of Canterbury Commons [6.02].

6.I: JACKKNIFED TRUCK (LAT 17/LONG 07)

- Threat Level: 1

On the road that slopes down from Canterbury Commons, a truck has crashed into a car; there's only junk and tools to collect.

6.J: WHEATON ARMORY TRUCK (LAT 10/LONG 06)

- Threat Level: 2

This parked truck blows up spectacularly, creating a distraction if you're wanting to infiltrate the Armory.

6.K: COACH LINER WRECKAGE (FREEWAY; LAT 11/LONG 05)

- Threat Level: 2

This is a stepping stone (literally) to a grand view from the freeway overlooking the Wheaton Armory.

6.L: CORVEGA TOWNSHIP (LAT 14/LONG 05)

- Threat Level: 2

To the Corvega Factory's west are homes stripped of essential items, although there may be some in the mail dropboxes and mailboxes, and the fire hydrants can quench your thirst.

6.M: BETHESDA SUBURBS (RAID SHACK; LAT 09/LONG 03)

- Threat Level: 3
- Faction: Raider
- Danger: Mailbox Trap
- Collectible: Skill Book
- Guns And Ammunition
- Health And Chems
- Interior Exploration
- Sleep Mattress
- Hostile: Radscorpion Genus, Raider, Yao Guai

East of the Bethesda Ruins are the suburbs, a large collection of ruined or boarded-up houses that contain nothing. However, there are common items in some of the mailboxes (except for one, which is booby-trapped; disarm using Explosives). Adjacent is the Raid Shack; search the area outside for a mattress and search the inside of a caravan for four Ammo Boxes and a Stimpak.

Inside the Raid Shack, kill enemies, check the area for food, Chems, Stimpaks, a Skill Book, and mattresses to sleep on.

- Ammo Box Ammunition (4)
- Tales of a Junktown Jerky Vendor (10/24)

6.N: BETHESDA ROUNDABOUT AND GAS STATION (LAT 13/LONG 02)

- Threat Level: 2

This gas station and two adjacent ruined houses hold no items, but watch for an Enclave incursion [E6.04].

6.O: RED ROCKET GAS STATION (LAT 15/LONG 03)

- Threat Level: 1
- Friendly: Brahmin

There are two Red Rocket Gas Stations near each other [6.N is just west of here]. This one is opposite the Corvega Factory.

6.P: JACKKNIFED TRUCK (UNDER MONORAIL; LAT 16/LONG 02)

- Threat Level: 1
- Collectible: Fat Man Mini-Nuke, Skill Book (2)

Enter the fallen container and move the metal boxes to the back for a Stimpak, a Mini-Nuke and Skill Book. There is also a footlocker containing a second Skill Book.

- Mini-Nuke (40/71)
- U.S. Army: 30 Handy Flamethrower Recipes (10/25)
- Chinese Army: Spec. Ops. Training Manual (8/25)

6.Q: WRECKED MONORAIL CARRIAGE (LAT 20/LONG 01)

- Threat Level: 1

A fallen monorail and carriages mark the edge of the Wasteland investigation area.

6.R: CHRYSLUS BASEBALL FIELD (LAT 08/LONG 00)

- Threat Level: 2
- Faction: Raider
- Hostile: Raider

A small baseball field erected by the Chryslus Corporation for its workers, now home to two filthy Raiders.

6.S: BETHESDA COACH STATION (LAT 10/LONG 00)

- Threat Level: 2
- Faction: Raider
- Collectible: Nuka-Cola Quantum
- Hostile: Raider

The Coach Station east of the Chryslus Building has two large store buildings with a small Raider contingent between them and little else. The Raiders are particularly hardy, which you'll discover if you return once the Enclave appear [E6.05]. Head east onto the freeway, turn north, and go to the end to secure the Nuka-Cola Quantum.

- Nuka-Cola Quantum (48/94)

6.T: JACKKNIFED TRUCK (LAT 12/LONG -01)

- Threat Level: 1

The truck is at a freeway junction here and has only metal boxes to sift through.

6.U: RED ROCKET GAS STATION (LAT 13/LONG -01)

- Main Quest: Galaxy News Radio
- Threat Level: 1
- Hostile: Enclave Eyebot, Raider

Use this as a landmark along one of the routes to the Friendship Street Station. Watch for nearby Raiders.

6.V: ROCK CREEK TOWNSHIP RUINS (LAT 19/LONG -01)

- Threat Level: 1
- Hostile: Enclave Eyebot

This consists of a water tower and rows of ruined houses, with a playground in the middle. It was picked clean months ago.

6.W: ROCK CREEK ROUNDABOUT (LAT 20/LONG -01)

- Threat Level: 1
- Hostile: Enclave Eyebot

The area is currently empty until the Enclave arrive [E6.06].

6.X: WASTELANDER MINE TRAP (UNDER BRIDGE; LAT 05/LONG -03)

- Main Quest: Galaxy News Radio
- Threat Level: 2
- Faction: Wastelander
- Danger: Low Radiation, Mines

- Collectible: Skill Book
- Guns And Ammunition
- Sleep Mattress

One of the few intact bridges across the Potomac has a secret underneath it. Disarm the Frag Mine, or the Skill Book may be destroyed! You can sleep here too.

- Frag Mine
- Frag Grenades (2)
- Ammo Box Ammunition
- Duck and Cover! (12/25)

6.Y: JACKKNIFED TRUCK (LAT 09/LONG -03)

- Main Quest: Galaxy News Radio
- Threat Level: 3
- Faction: Enclave, Super Mutant, Talon Mercenary

- Guns And Ammunition
- Hostile: Robot Genus, Super Mutant Genus, Talon Company Merc

Along the main road through the northern edge of the D.C. Ruins, there are Talon Mercs scouting the area. Use the truck as cover.

- Ammo Box Ammunition (3)

6.Z: SHELTER ENTRANCE (UNDER BRIDGE; LAT 10/LONG -03)

- Main Quest: Galaxy News Radio
- Threat Level: 2
- Faction: Ghoul
- Interior Exploration
- Health And Chems
- Hostile: Ghoul

Clear the area of Super Mutants and look for the door under the bridge, on the eastern end.

Note

If you've built the Rock-It Launcher, the Plungers make a perfect projectile!

6.AA: SUPER MUTANT BONFIRE (LAT 11/LONG -03)

- Main Quest: Galaxy News Radio
- Threat Level: 3
- Faction: Super Mutant
- Collectible: Fat Man Mini-Nuke

- Guns And Ammunition
- Health And Chems
- Hostile: Centaur, Super Mutant Genus

In the remains of a sunken roadway section, Super Mutants have built a bonfire defense. You can loop around to the north and attack from over the edge of the raised concrete wall; this is preferable than a ground-level attack.

- First Aid Box Health and Chems (2)
- Ammo Box Ammunition (3)
- Mini-Nuke (41/71)

6.BB: COURTYARD FOUNTAIN (LAT 12/LONG -03)

- Threat Level: 2
- Faction: Super Mutant
- Wasteland Captive
- Hostile: Centaur

Close to Friendship Street Station is a forecourt with a fountain and sometimes a Wasteland Captive.

Tip

Rescue any captives and take their gift for a small boost to your Karma; refuse it for a larger boost.

6.CC: NATIONAL GUARD FORECOURT TRUCKS (LAT 18/LONG -03)

- Threat Level: 2
- Guns And Ammunition
- Health And Chems
- Hostile: Protectron Guard

Check the table in the concrete area for items. The fenced-off truck parking area has Ammo. The entrance forecourt leads to the depot interior [6.11].

- Assault Rifle
- First Aid Box Health and Chems
- Ammo Box Ammunition (5)

ENCLAVE CAMP LOCATIONS

CAMP E6.01 (LAT 05/LONG 07)

- Main Quest: Picking Up The Trail
- Threat Level: 2

A Vertibird lands at the Scrapyard's perimeter, depositing a small advance guard.

CAMP E6.02 (LAT 13/LONG 09)

- Main Quest: Picking Up The Trail
- Threat Level: 2
- Guns And Ammunition
- Friendly: Brahmin

There is a roadblock in the middle of the Brahmin pastures. On a table is a terminal where you can view a list of catalogued weapons, as well as transients they've logged (and probably executed).

- 10mm Pistol
- .32 Pistol
- Brass Knuckles (2)
- Nail Board
- Combat Knife (2)
- Enclave Crate Items (3)

CAMP E6.03 (LAT 16/LONG 08)

- Main Quest: Picking Up The Trail
- Threat Level: 4
- Lots O' Caps
- Rare Or Powerful Item

This is known as Rho Camp. An officer has set up four turrets at this crossroads to guard him while he waits for field soldiers to report back. Kill the officer by using Sneak and a Stealth Boy, then Pickpocket him and drop in a grenade. Search him for the Experimental Rho ID. Access the terminal to read more about the chip in the ID. You can wander around this small camp unimpeded by the turrets. This means you can lure enemies back here and let the turrets do the firing for you.

- Experimental Rho ID
- Enclave Crate Items

CAMP E6.04 (LAT 12/LONG 02)

- Main Quest: Picking Up The Trail
- Threat Level: 3
- Faction: Raider
- Guns And Ammunition
- Health And Chems

A unit has successfully modified a caged Deathclaw under the freeway, near the gas station.

- Enclave Crate Ammunition (2)
- Enclave Crate Health and Chems

CAMP E6.05 (LAT 10/LONG 00)

- Main Quest: Picking Up The Trail
- Threat Level: 2
- Faction: Raider
- Guns And Ammunition
- Hostile: Raider

The Raiders fight back! A group of hearty (but deranged) individuals have killed and stolen the Enclave's weapons and armor, and they now face you in this area.

- Enclave Crate Ammunition (3)

CAMP E6.06 (LAT 20/LONG -01)

- Main Quest: Picking Up The Trail
- Threat Level: 2
- Faction: Enclave,
- Wastelander
- Health And Chems
- Ghoulish Wastelander (Deceased)

A small Enclave medical unit is rounding up Ghoulish Wastelanders and massacring them. Watch for the Flamer Soldier. There are Stimpaks in the mobile medical bay.

- Enclave First Aid Box Health and Chems

CAMP E6.07 (LAT 09/LONG -03)

- Main Quest: Picking Up The Trail
- Threat Level: 2
- Collectible: Fat Man Mini-Nuke

A Vertibird swoops in and lands on the bridge, dropping off troops and a Mini-Nuke.

- Mini-Nuke (42/71)

TRAINING — BESTIARY — MAIN QUEST — MISC. QUESTS — TOUR — COMPLETION — APPENDICES

Zone 7: Southwest Territories

TOPOGRAPHICAL OVERVIEW

Divided by a large freeway skeleton, the southwest corner of the Wasteland features rocky and treacherous terrain that flattens out the farther east you go. The northern part of this zone is dominated by the massive Raider stronghold of Evergreen Mills, where your mettle is sure to be tested. Nearby is Smith Casey's Garage and the secrets it contains down below. Bring extra ammunition if you're venturing near the Yao Guai tunnels, and be prepared if you dare to disturb the unspeakable madness slowly stirring within the Dunwich Building! But the big draw is the largest structure outside the D.C. Mall—the monument to excess called Tenpenny Towers. It's a great place to live, whether your neighbors have smooth or lumpy skin....

AVAILABLE COLLECTIBLES (ZONE 7)

- Bobbleheads: 4/20
- Fat Men: 1/9
- Fat Man Mini-Nukes: 5/71
- Unique Items: 4/89
- Nuka-Cola Quantum: 7/94
- Schematics: 5/21
- Scribe Pre-War Books: 5/98

- Skill Book: Barter (3/24), Big Guns (1/25), Energy Weapons (4/25), Explosives (5/25), Lockpick (2/25), Medicine (1/25), Melee Weapons (1/25), Repair (3/25), Science (3/25), Small Guns (0/25), Sneak (0/25), Speech (5/25), Unarmed (4/25)
- Work Bench: 7/46
- Holotapes: Keller (0/5), Replicated Man (2/19)

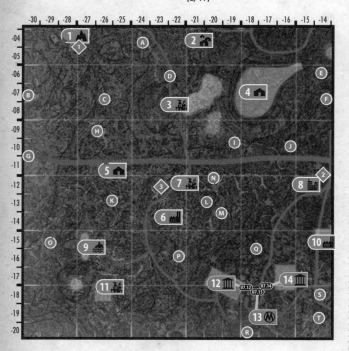

PRIMARY LOCATIONS

7.01: Yao Guai Tunnels (lat -28/long -04)

7.02: Charnel House (lat -21/long -04)

7.03: Smith Casey's Garage (lat -22/long -08)

7.04: Evergreen Mills (lat -18/long -07)

7.05: Girdershade (lat -26/long -11)

7.06: VAPL-66 Power Station (lat -23/long -14)

7.07: Jocko's Pop & Gas Stop (lat -22/long -12)

7.08: VAPL-84 Power Station (lat -15/long -12)

7.09: F. Scott Key Trail & Campground (lat -27/long -15)

7.10: RobCo Facility (lat -14/long -15)

7.11: Dunwich Building (lat -26/long -18)

7.12: Warrington Trainyard (lat -20/long -17)

7.13: Warrington Station (lat -18/long -19)

7.14: Tenpenny Tower (lat -16/long -17)

SECONDARY LOCATIONS

7.A: Broadcast Tower PN (lat -24/long -04)

7.B: Wastelander Tent and Sniper Vista (lat -30/long -07)

7.C: Rockopolis (lat -26/long -07)

7.D: Military Checkpoint and Tent (lat -22/long -06)

7.E: Ruined Chapel (lat -14/long -06)

7.F: Ruined Calverton Village (lat -14/long -07)

7.G: Overturned City Liner (lat -30/long -10)

7.H: Irradiated Pond (lat -26/long -09)

7.I: Captain Cosmos Billboard (lat -19/long -10)

7.J: Abandoned Shack (lat -16/long -10)

7.K: Ruined House (lat -26/long -13)

7.L: Broadcast Tower SV (lat -20/long -13)

7.M: Drainage Chamber (lat -20/long -13)

7.N: Captain Cosmos Billboard (lat -20/long -12)

7.O: Chinese Pilot's Shack (lat -29/long -15)

7.P: Dot's Dunwich Diner (lat -22/long -16)

7.Q: Warrington Township (lat -18/long -16)

7.R: Lucky's Grocer (lat -18/long -20)

7.S: Willy's Grocer (lat -14/long -18)

7.T: Ruined Office Building (lat -14/long -19)

Primary Locations

7.01: YAO GUAI TUNNELS (LAT -28/LONG -04)

- Threat Level: 4
- Danger: Low Radiation
- Collectible: Bobblehead, Nuka-Cola Quantum, Scribe Pre-War Book, Skill Book
- Guns and Ammunition
- Health and Chems
- Interior Exploration
- Sleep Mattress
- Hostile: Yao Guai

INTERIOR MAPS AND LOCATIONS

Yau Guai Tunnels

Yau Guai Den

INHABITANTS

Nan (Deceased)

Out in the middle of nowhere are the Yao Guai Tunnels, a dangerous place with roaming, claw-swiping rabid beasts that could rival a Deathclaw. The Enclave find this out to their cost; if you arrive once the Enclave appear, their camp [E7.01] has already been attacked. Sneak or flick on your Pip-Boy's Flashlight and head east down the tunnel.

YAO GUAI TUNNELS

1 Picnic Table

There are Darts, food and Pre-War Money here too.

- Scribe Pre-War Book (46/98)

2 Small Chamber with Strewn Debris

Check the shelves for the following:

- Ammo Box Ammunition (2)
- Baseball Bat
- Frag Mines

3 Large South Cavern

There's a Yao Guai in here, and debris strewn everywhere. To the south is a door to the den, but it is in an upper alcove and only accessible from the den. A Skill Book is on the ledge next to the traffic cone and dead Raider. Lob a grenade to dislodge it (although it's difficult to see where it lands).

- Grognak the Barbarian (12/25)

4 Dead-End Lean-to

There's scattered junk, Chems, a Carton of Cigarettes, and a First Aid Box Health and Chems.

5 Smaller Cavern

- Nuka-Cola Quantum (49/94)

6 Columned Cavern

- Ammo Box Ammunition (3)

YAO GUAI DEN

7 Main Chamber

Slay any foes as you go. Here you'll find the corpse of an old lady bobbing in the water. Check her to find a Holotape Note on her body.

- Yao Guai Den Note*

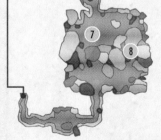

Note

*This note admonishes Nan for freaking the children out with stories on "beasts" that roam here. This place is better than the Wasteland and its Raiders, the note-taker mentions — to his eventual cost.

8 East Metal Box

- Bobblehead: Sneak (13/20)

7.02: CHARNEL HOUSE (LAT -21/LONG -04)

- Threat Level: 3
- Faction: Raider
- Danger: Mines
- Collectible: Skill Book
- Guns and Ammunition
- Hostile: Brahmin, Raider, Raider Guard Dog

An old and once-grand residence is now a rotting shell and a Raider base, complete with a couple of breeding Brahmin in a nearby pen. Try approaching from the rocky outcrop above the house, and quickly dispatch the Raider sniper. Beware—the grounds have Mines. Search the place, disarming any Mines you find, and open the three Ammo Boxes on the upper floor, grabbing the Skill Book too.

- Ammo Box Ammunition (3)
- Duck and Cover (13/25)
- Frag Mines

7.03: SMITH CASEY'S GARAGE (LAT -22/LONG -08)

- Main Quest: Scientific Pursuits; Tranquility Lane
- Threat Level: 2
- Faction: Vault Dweller
- Collectible: Nuka-Cola Quantum, Skill Book
- Guns and Ammunition
- Health and Chems
- Interior Exploration
- Sleep Mattress
- Hostile: Mole Rat, Radroach, Robobrain

INTERIOR MAPS AND LOCATIONS

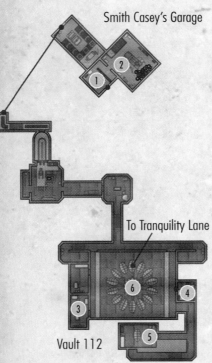

Smith Casey's Garage

To Tranquility Lane

Vault 112

INHABITANT
Doctor Stanislaus Braun/Betty

A preeminent scientist, Doctor Braun headed up many astonishing experiments in his long and varied career, but of most interest was his theories on advanced life preservation. It is said that the U.S. Army had contracted Braun to develop various methods of sustaining human life in case of an atomic war. When war did come, Braun escaped to the safety of Vault 112 and is there to this day, his wizened and wrinkled form given new (virtual) life as a pigtailed little scamp named Betty....

SMITH CASEY'S GARAGE

Smith Casey's Garage is a crumbling, nondescript building, but it holds an amazing secret: it is the entrance to Vault 112, which in turn is an entrance to a virtual reality known as Tranquility Lane.

① Shop Floor

Watch for Radroaches. There's a skeleton on a mattress and an open safe; grab the following:

- Nuka-Cola Quantum (50/94)
- Tumblers Today (14/25)

② Garage

Beware of Mole Rats. Check both gun cabinets and flip the electrical switch to open the flap-trap door to head downstairs.

- First Aid Box Health and Chems

VAULT 112

Vault-Tec assembled Vault 112 with just the core commodities to sustain inhabitants in the Tranquility Lane simulation. A small corps of housekeeping Robobrains ensure that critical processes and equipment are kept in proper working order, and Immersion Recliners keep inhabitants in a relatively healthy state of stasis.

③ Clinic (Southern Room)

Both rooms have lockers to rummage in.

- First Aid Box Health and Chems

④ Equipment Room

Hack the wall terminal. Inside, grab Chems and any of the items listed below. The password allows access into the Overseer's Office.

- Assault Rifle and 5.56mm Rounds
- First Aid Box Health and Chems (1)
- Laser Rifle and Microfusion Cells
- Pulse Grenades
- Overseer's Room Password

⑤ Overseer's Office

Break into a wall safe, and view Doctor Stanislaus Braun in a state of suspended animation.

- Wall Safe Items

⑥ Tranquility Loungers

Sitting in an empty lounger is the only way to access Tranquility Lane.

TRANQUILITY LANE

This is an approximation of a prewar cul-de-sac, where it's always sunny and everyone is happy. At least on the surface. None of the items you pick up are real, nor are the people you meet. They are listed in **Main Quest: Tranquility Lane** (page 88).

7.04: EVERGREEN MILLS (LAT -18/ LONG -07)

- Main Quest: Scientific Pursuits
- Threat Level: 5
- Faction: Raider
- Services: Repairer, Trader
- Danger: Behemoth, Grenade Bouquet
- Collectible: Bobblehead, Fat Man Launcher, Nuka-Cola Quantum, Skill Book (3)
- Guns and Ammunition
- Health and Chems
- Interior Exploration
- Lots o' Caps
- Rare or Powerful Item
- Sleep Mattress
- Work Bench (3)
- Hostile: Raider, Super Mutant Behemoth

MAPS AND LOCATIONS

Evergreen Mills

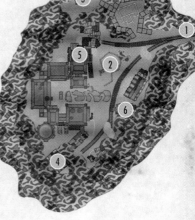

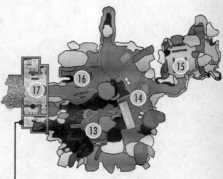

Evergreen Mills Bazaar

Evergreen Mills Foundry

INHABITANTS
Smiling Jack

A master Trader and Barterer, Jack is a jovial sort, and not just because he's set up shop next to the Raider strip club. He mends the Raider's equipment, keeping him busy and unable to continue modifications to his pride and joy: a devastating Shotgun he brings out for a little fun.

One of the most dangerous locations outside the D.C. Metro Area, Evergreen Mills is a massive Raider stronghold, and you'll need to tool up and use a mixture of Sniping and Sneaking. You can either snipe from the rocky promontories surrounding the main buildings or head southwest, along the rocky ledges above the railroad track. Stay elevated; you don't want to be shot at while you're on the ground, as it is difficult to hit the aggressors. The following sweep was made traveling along the railroad, toward the outer buildings.

1 Stay on the track's north side, on the rocky ledge. Near a rusting bridge and Raider lookout balcony is a small shack; search it for items. Stay on the northern ledge (ideally with a Stealth Boy employed) until the entire exterior opens up. Inspect the roughly circular catwalk, with Slave Pens below.

- Ammo Box Ammunition (2)
- First Aid Box Health and Chems

Drop to the Slave Pens, ideally after the Raiders are all dead; open the two gates, and free the slaves.

2 Back on the rocky ledge or catwalk above the pens; from the catwalk's upper southwest end, peer into a massive, secure cage. A sparking generator is keeping the doors closed. Inside is something gigantic that the Raiders have captured—a Super Mutant Behemoth! Snipe the generator from a safe and high location, and watch the Behemoth rampage through the Raiders!

Continue around the upper ledge to the north, moving to the Guard House **3**. Disarm the Grenade Bouquet, and enter the Guard House shack. Quickly search inside to find three Ammo Boxes, a Carton of Cigarettes, food, and a place to sleep. Head back outside, and either continue around the rock wall's outer lip to the Southern Shack **4**, or drop to the ground. You can also leap into the main courtyard in front of the Mills building.

- Ammo Box Ammunition (3)
- Frag Grenades (3)

Search the corrugated metal shanty camp to the north of the Mills building. Head past the campfire, and locate the Northern Shack **5**. Rummage around inside to find two Raiders "getting it on," Whiskey, food, Chems, a Work Bench with a Bottlecap Mine, and the following:

- 10mm Pistol
- .32 Pistol
- Ammo Box Ammunition (5)
- Baseball Bat
- First Aid Box Health and Chems (2)
- Police Baton
- Work Bench (22/46)

Inspect the ground-level area to Mills' south. Pass the Behemoth enclosure and check the corrugated shacks; move around to the southern shack. Outside, there are planks leading to the roof of an exterior building that has vats on it (a good sniping spot).

Inside the southern shack is a mattress; there is also food and drink in the fridge, and the following:

- Ammo Box Ammunition (3)
- First Aid Box Health and Chems (2)
- Missile Launcher
- U.S. Army: 30 Handy Flamethrower Recipes (11/25)

Back out of the southern shack, head around the lower rock wall to planks leading atop the train cargo containers. There's a Grenade Bouquet **6** below; the trip wire is between the first train carriage and lean-to. Disarm it, then enter the lean-to, which has the listed items below. Pass the overturned shopping cart full of split skulls. This concludes the exterior reconnoiter.

- Ammo Box Ammunition (3)
- First Aid Box Health and Chems (2)
- Frag Grenades (3)

EVERGREEN MILLS FOUNDRY
7 **Southwest Corner**

There are mattresses, three fridges with food, Chems, tools and junk, two Cartons of Cigarettes on shelves near the broken terminal, and a floor safe to unlock.

- Floor Safe Items
- Duck and Cover! (14/25)

8 **Southeast Corner**

There's an undercounter safe here. Scrabble around for the following:

- Ammo Box Ammunition (3)
- Counter Safe Items
- First Aid Box Health and Chems (2)
- Sledgehammer

9 **Upper Floor Chamber with Mattresses**

- First Aid Box Health and Chems

10 **Upper Chamber with Queen-Size Bed**

There are Chems, detergent, a Carton of Cigarettes, a Nuka Grenade on a Work Bench, Tools, and a wall safe.

- Wall Safe Items
- Work Bench (23/46)

11 **Locked Storage Room**

The locked wooden door leads to a small storage room with a wall safe to unlock, a gun cabinet, Chems, and the following:

- Ammo Box Ammunition
- Fat Man (6/9)

12 **Mattresses and Broken Terminal**

- First Aid Box Health and Chems

EVERGREEN MILLS BAZAAR
13 **Entrance Bar**

Grab food, beer, and the following items behind the counter:

- .32 Pistol and Ammo
- First Aid Box Health and Chems
- Nuka-Cola Quantum (51/94)

14 **Dining Area and Pool Table**

Claim more food, beer, Whiskey, a Baseball Bat, and the Lead Pipe.

15 **Smiling Jack's Workshop**

There's a main workshop area and a side tunnel with a Work Bench and a Bottlecap Mine to find. Smiling Jack is the only person who isn't immediately hostile to you; he can Repair or Trade with you. Or, you can gun him down and take his Vendor Key and his special weapon: the Terrible Shotgun. Check this area for four Cartons of Cigarettes, Chems, and a safe under the Work Bench. Use the Vendor Key to open Jack's locker, which has his store inventory and a massive amount of Caps.

- 300+ Caps
- Ammo Box Ammunition
- Baseball Bat
- Bobblehead: Barter (14/20)
- First Aid Box Health and Chems
- Smiling Jack Vendor Key
- Terrible Shotgun (46/89)
- Work Bench (24/46)

16 **Strip Club Bar**

There's food and little else here.

- Baseball Bat

17 **"Good Time" Cells**

Complete a thorough search of this back room and cells; check the counter safe and gather the following:

- Ammo Box Ammunition (2)
- Counter Safe Items
- First Aid Box Health and Chems
- Hunting Rifle
- Melee Weapons (3)
- Nikola Tesla and You (13/25)
- Raider Blastmaster Armor

7.05: GIRDERSHADE (LAT -26/LONG -11)

APPENDICES — COMPLETION — TOUR — MISC. QUESTS — MAIN QUEST — BESTIARY — TRAINING

- Miscellaneous Quest: Those!; The Nuka-Cola Challenge
- Freeform Quest (2)
- Threat Level: 1
- Faction: Wastelander
- Collectible: Nuka-Cola Quantum, Schematic
- Interior Exploration
- Lots o' Caps
- Rare or Powerful Item
- Friendly: Brahmin

Girdershade is a tiny settlement located under an overpass. It got its name from the broken-off portion of the bridge and the exposed girders: all that's left of its superstructure. The population of Girdershade numbers two, Sierra Petrovita and Ronald Laren. They are both long-time residents of the settlement, Sierra having been the "founder" of the place and Ronald occupying the second house after its original occupants were slain.

INHABITANTS
Sierra Petrovita

Sierra is a beautiful, 26-year-old blond-haired woman who has no regard for anything else in life than the pursuit of finding and consuming Nuka-Cola. She is absolutely fanatical about the blue drink and has been subsisting on the stuff for years. She has spent every Bottle Cap her parents left acquiring the drink from merchants, travelers, and towns spread throughout the Wasteland. Even though her looks are a desirable target for men, her personality leaves much to be desired. She is so oddly fascinated by Nuka-Cola that she will constantly shift conversations to speak about it and cares little for anything else. This is the subject of much anguish for the only other inhabitant of Girdershade.

Ronald Laren

After his wife died, 33-year-old Ronald wandered the Wasteland until settling in Girdershade. Living in close proximity to Sierra Petrovita has made him feel even worse about being alone. His thoughts of loneliness are not as wholesome as most would think. Basically he misses the physical side of relationships. Feeling these urges, he's made several advances upon Sierra, who is completely oblivious to his motivations, as she is absorbed in her pursuit of Nuka-Cola. Ronald mistakes Sierra's rejection as being spurned, and this has angered him a great deal. Fortunately, he doesn't want to physically force himself on her but wishes to "get even" with her in other ways.

RELATED INTERACTIONS

 Collect Nuka-Cola Quantums for Sierra, and she awards you 40 Caps per Quantum.

 Fill her Pristine Nuka-Cola Vending Machine with 30 Quantums, and you are awarded a Schematic.

- Schematic: Nuka Grenade (11/23).

 Collect Nuka-Cola Quantums for Ronald, and he awards you 40 (or 80 with a Speech Challenge) Caps per Quantum.

Ronald warns you about weird happenings at the Dunwich Building.

Ronald can award you handsomely for completing **Freeform Quest: Grady's Package.**

Enter Sierra's house, and you can begin a Miscellaneous Quest. She only has Nuka-Cola (and a toy Nuka-Cola truck) in here to steal—and a lot of it! Enter Ronald's house, and there are a few Caps to steal, but little else, although he carries a Unique Sawed-Off Shotgun you can loot from his corpse.

- Nuka-Cola Bottle (45)
- "The Kneecapper" Sawed-Off Shotgun (47/89)

FREEFORM QUEST: MISSISSIPPI QUANTUM PIE

After you complete the Quest, bring Flour, Vodka, and a Nuka-Cola Quantum, and Sierra can bake you a Mississippi Quantum Pie. This gives you an exceptional (but temporary) boost to your abilities, while making you just that little bit more stupid. Weigh the pros and cons of this.

- Mississippi Quantum Pie (when consumed: Rads +5, AP +20, INT -1, STR +1)

FREEFORM QUEST: GRADY'S PACKAGE

At any time during your exploration (ideally during **Miscellaneous Quest: Those!**, where this Freeform Quest is revealed in greater detail), enter Marigold Metro Station [Location 9.10] and locate a bench with a Holotape called Grady's Last Recording. It tells of a locked room in this underground tunnel. Also, open the fire-hose box to uncover Grady's Safe Key. Enter his storage chamber and unlock his safe. Claim the Naughty Nightwear and slay (or Speech Challenge) Lug-Nut, a Raider who wants the smooth silk for himself. Meet with Ronald in Girdershade, and sell the Nightwear to him for 300 Caps (assuming you succeeded in a Speech Challenge).

- 300 Caps

7.06: VAPL-66 POWER STATION (LAT -23/LONG -14)

- Threat Level: 1
- Faction: Raider
- Collectible: Fat Man Mini-Nuke, Skill Book

The power substation interior is where you should scavenge. Aside from the Raider "artwork," there's a sparking generator and a desk with a copy of Dean's Electronics on it. There is also a Mini-Nuke on the floor, as well as Chems, a bit of food, and Stimpaks.

- Dean's Electronics (10/25)
- Mini-Nuke (43/71)

7.07: JOCKO'S POP & GAS STOP (LAT -22/LONG -12)

- Threat Level: 2
- Collectible: Nuka-Cola Quantum, Schematic, Skill Book
- Interior Exploration
- Work Bench

Adjacent to a rusting Red Rocket Gas Station and south of the freeway is a shack that used to sell pop and gas. Now it's home to the odd Scavenger, but there are still a few items to collect: food and beer, a Carton of Cigarettes, a Work Bench with a Bottlecap Mine, and the following:

- Nikola Tesla and You (14/25)
- Nuka-Cola Quantum (52/94)
- Schematic: Bottlecap Mine (12/23)
- Work Bench (25/46)

7.08: VAPL-84 POWER STATION (LAT -15/LONG -12)

- Threat Level: 2
- Collectible: Fat Man Mini-Nuke
- Guns And Ammunition
- Hostile: Yao Guai

This power station is comprised of a gated transformer cluster and a parked truck. Bring out your Yao Guai–killing ordnance for this sortie; one has mauled a group of unwary Raiders. Search them and the back of the truck:

- Ammo Box Ammunition (3)
- Mini-Nuke (44/71)

7.09: F. SCOTT KEY TRAIL & CAMPGROUND (LAT -27/LONG -15)

- Threat Level: 4
- Collectible: Schematic, Skill Book
- Health and Chems
- Sleep Mattress

This is arguably the most dangerous of the scenic campgrounds in the Wasteland. Surrounding this central area are a small series of paths with rocky crags on each side, essentially hemming you in when an enemy pounces. Since Yao Guai, robots, and a Deathclaw are active in this area, such maneuvering can be deadly! The reward is worth it, though:

- Duck and Cover! (15/25)
- First Aid Box Health and Chems
- Schematic: Deathclaw Gauntlet (13/23)

7.10: ROBCO FACILITY (LAT -14/ LONG -15)

- Miscellaneous Quest: The Wasteland Survival Guide
- Threat Level: 3
- Collectible: Scribe Pre-War Book (3), Skill Book (4)
- Area Is Locked
- Guns and Ammunition
- Health and Chems
- Highly Visible Landmark
- Interior Exploration
- Work Bench
- Hostile: Mole Rat, Radroach, Turret

 Tip

For best results, wait to begin the Quest until Moira Brown sends you here.

INTERIOR MAPS AND LOCATIONS

RobCo Factory Floor

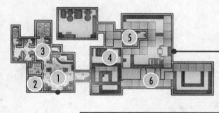

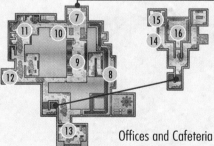

Offices and Cafeteria

 Note

Tinker Joe, a traveling robot salesman, is in the vicinity of the RobCo building, where you can purchase a Follower named Sergeant RL-3 (Mini-Encounter 082: Tinker Joe's Sergeant of Slaughter).

Close to Tenpenny Tower is a sprawling factory where the RobCo Company used to produce the nation's finest automatons for domestic and military use. The facility remains intact, and the surrounding exterior is actually rather safe. There's only one entrance.

ROBCO FACTORY FLOOR

1 Entrance Foyer

Don't worry, the Robotrons aren't active!

- First Aid Box Health and Chems
- Lying: Congressional Style (8/25)
- Scribe Pre-War Book (47/98)

2 Restroom

There's a RadAway and Stimpak here.

3 Mole Rat and Radroach-Infested Office Area

There are Darts on a shelf near the half-buried Protectron and the following to hunt for:

- Ammo Box Ammunition (2)
- First Aid Box Health and Chems

4 Raised Area

Watch for the turret! Check the shelves here for Darts and Ammo Box Ammunition (6).

5 Northeast Protectron Pod

- Big Book of Science (12/25)
- First Aid Box Health and Chems
- Scribe Pre-War Book (48/98)

6 Raised Gantry Workshop

There's a Bottlecap Mine here and these items to grab:

- RobCo Jumpsuit
- Work Bench (26/46)

OFFICES AND CAFETERIA (SECOND FLOOR)

7 Recreation Room and Protectron Pod

8 Connecting Corridor

Check behind the mannequin for:

- Ammo Box Ammunition (3)

9 Cafeteria

This is a mess; there are empty Nuka-Cola bottles everywhere, but the fridges have food in them.

- First Aid Box Health and Chems

10 Restrooms

One has a couple of Chems to scavenge.

11 Open-Plan Office

Check the table for the Skill Book, and check the bookcase for the Stealth Boy and Mentats.

- Nikola Tesla and You (15/25)
- Stealth Boy

APPENDICES — COMPLETION — TOUR — MISC. QUESTS — MAIN QUEST — BESTIARY — TRAINING

12 Southwest Corner Storage Room

- First Aid Box Health and Chems

13 Computer Office Room

There's Jet and the following items in here:

- D.C. Journal of Internal Medicine (15/25)
- First Aid Box Health and Chems
- Stealth Boy

OFFICES AND CAFETERIA (THIRD FLOOR)

14 Storage Room

Inspect the personal footlocker for common items.

15 Small Office

There are Darts in here but little else.

16 Mainframe Chamber

The RobCo Production Mainframe isn't responding! Apparently, it requires a Processor Widget to function, and the only known one is in the hands of a woman named Moira Brown, over in Megaton.

- First Aid Box Health and Chems
- Scribe Pre-War Book (49/98)
- Stealth Boy

7.11: DUNWICH BUILDING (LAT -26/ LONG -18)

- Threat Level: 4
- Faction: Ghoul
- Danger: Low Radiation, Terminal Trap
- Collectible: Bobblehead, Nuka-Cola Quantum, Skill Book
- Guns and Ammunition
- Health and Chems
- Interior Exploration
- Hostile: Feral Ghoul Genus

INHABITANTS
Jaime Palabras

Jaime was born in the mid-Wastelands to a Ranger. His father returned to camp from an expedition with a thick book, bound in odd black leather and stamped with strange glyphs. Convinced the book would fetch a high price, his father traveled to the Capital Wastes to offer it to the Brotherhood of Steel Scribes. Despondent, Jaime's father vowed to return the book "to its source."

INTERIOR MAPS AND LOCATIONS

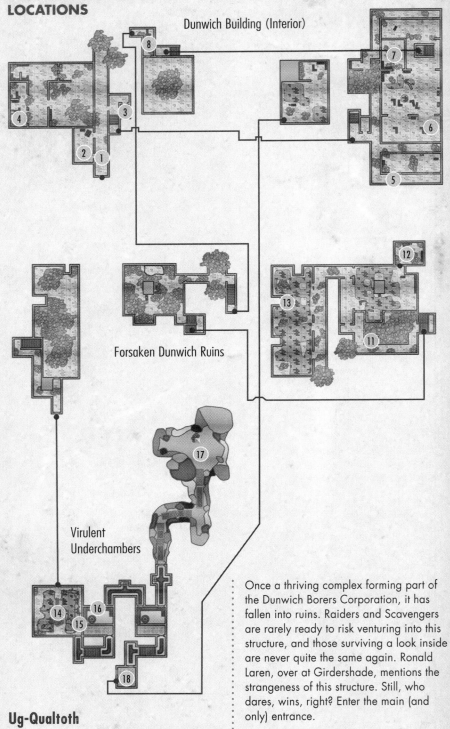

Dunwich Building (Interior)

Forsaken Dunwich Ruins

Virulent Underchambers

Ug-Qualtoth

A strange altar found in the depths of this building may hold the key to discovering more about this previously unknown entity. Unfortunately, as all investigators into grimoire oddities are currently attempting to scrape together a day-to-day existence or are dead, further research may never occur.

DUNWICH BUILDING

In a remote and blasted heath surrounded by rocky terrain in the southwest corner of the Wasteland is the Dunwich Building.

Once a thriving complex forming part of the Dunwich Borers Corporation, it has fallen into ruins. Raiders and Scavengers are rarely ready to risk venturing into this structure, and those surviving a look inside are never quite the same again. Ronald Laren, over at Girdershade, mentions the strangeness of this structure. Still, who dares, wins, right? Enter the main (and only) entrance.

1 Billy the Skeleton

- Ammo Box Ammunition (2)

2 Small Foyer of Scattered Tables

There are five Holotapes to listen to:

Jaime's Personal Journal (Entry 01): It's been nuts lately; he doesn't know why the old coot has come out here, leaving Jaime in the crappy old hospital. He's left the colony, almost out of rations, and doesn't know where the old man is.

Jaime's Personal Journal (Entry 02): The trail has gone cold, so Jaime took up wandering with some folks he met. Hopefully they've seen Dad.

Jaime's Personal Journal (Entry 03): Those folks weren't who Jaime thought they were, killing that family for a sack of rotting vegetables. He'll leave them the first chance he gets.

Jaime's Personal Journal (Entry 04): They struck a caravan, and Jaime was rescued. The Traders spotted a man fitting his father's description heading south and carrying a book. It gave the Traders the creeps; Jaime too.

Jaime's Personal Journal (Entry 05): His father must be around here; Jaime recognizes the traps. There's a building on the horizon. Perhaps he's in here. If not, at least it's a roof over his head for a night.

- Note: Jaime's Personal Journal (Entry 01/09)
- Note: Jaime's Personal Journal (Entry 02/09)
- Note: Jaime's Personal Journal
- Note: Jaime's Personal Journal (Entry 03/09)
- Note: Jaime's Personal Journal (Entry 04/09)
- Note: Jaime's Personal Journal (Entry 05/09)

③ Storage Room under the Stairs

- Ammo Box Ammunition (4)
- Assault Rifle
- Nuka-Cola Quantum (53/94)

④ Western Office

The radio in here is the source of the static. Inspect another journal entry:

Jaime's Personal Journal (Entry 06): He doesn't like the look and smell of this place. He also doesn't want to risk a shot "at the crows" until he knows what's in there. He's about to Sneak in.

- Ammo Box Ammunition (6)
- Note: Jaime's Personal Journal (Entry 06/09)

⑤ Anomalous Occurrence

There must be a stiff breeze; that wooden door opened on its own!

⑥ Lonely Office

There is a single working terminal to the east, but it is a trap; disarm and claim the Frag Grenade.

- Frag Grenade

⑦ Other Lonely Office

It, too, is booby-trapped, so disarm the terminal and pocket the Grenade.

- Frag Grenade

⑧ Grisly Office

On the desk next to the human torso and head lies another Holotape.

Jaime's Personal Journal (Entry 07): The Raiders told spooky stories about "zombies" in these ruins. Jaime thinks they really used to be people.

- Note: Jaime's Personal Journal: Entry 07/09

Note

If you wear the Ghoul Mask that Roy Phillips gave you for helping him in **Miscellaneous Quest: Tenpenny Tower**, there will be neither suffering nor death.

FORSAKEN DUNWICH RUINS

⑨ Bizarre Hallucination!

Whoa! What was THAT?! Beware the Glowing One!

⑩ Work Terminal

Hack it, take another Holotape, and read auto-dictation messages from a man named Herman Granger.

Jaime's Personal Journal (Entry 08): He found Dad. He didn't recognize him at first; "he was becoming like them." No more killing. He must leave but take the book with him. The book is warm against the stone floor. He must "ressst awhillle…."

Herman Granger's Terminal (Entry: 10/18/2077): He thanks his staff for their hard work releasing the acoustic borer to market. Happy holidays from Mr. Statham and the Dunwich Borers!

Entry 10/23/2077: "Rrrrrrrrrrrrbbbbboommmmmmmkkkkkk…" This appears to be a low-frequency anomaly recorded on the auto-dictation.

Entry 10/23/2077: "Thmmmmmmmkkkkkaaaaaakkkkkaaaaakkkkmmmmm…" It happens again.

Entry 3/27/2134: Shouts from a man. Deep breathing. "They bled so much. But I kept it clean. Clean. Clean…"

Entry 4/27/2134: A man has barely any skin left. He's one of "them" now. "Stay back! Back, you!" Apparently, Ug-Qualtoth has returned.

Entry 5/1/2134: A chant for Ug-Qualtoth.

- Note: Jaime's Personal Journal (Entry 08/09)

⑪ Pipe and Storage Room

- Dean's Electronics (11/25)
- First Aid Box Health and Chems

⑫ Last Stand Chamber for the Scavenger

Break into the room: A coffeepot and fan fall off a desk as you enter. Step over the skeleton, grab the items, then access the terminal. It has the last note from a long-dead Scavenger (the skeleton at your feet):

The Scavenger is trapped here. He hears "those things" sniffing, screaming, and wandering outside. He thought this place was abandoned but is now in here, scared out of his mind. He told Billy to meet him here with some extra ammo. That was three days ago.

- Ammo Box Ammunition (3)

Note

You might be using Billy's ammo; his are the skeletal remains you almost tripped over at the front door.

⑬ Northwest Restroom

It has a skeleton and some Jet.

VIRULENT UNDERCHAMBERS

⑭ Office with Precarious Flooring

Jaime's Personal Journal (Entry 09): "Sharp knife descend into deep temple. Flay! Athul comes again on the feast of the weaker! Born again! Alhazared!"

- Note: Jaime's Personal Journal (Entry 09/09)

⑮ Fire Hose

The air is getting thicker and radioactive.

- First Aid Box Health and Chems

⑯ Stairwell

- First Aid Box Health and Chems

⑰ Shrieking Cavern

A cacophony of shrieking reaches a crescendo! Jaime Palabras and a contingent of Ghouls await and attack! Fight them off, then inspect the chamber. It features a very odd carved obelisk in the middle, with a body and skulls fused to it. It also gives off radiation. There's Ammo Boxes but no sign of the "book" that Jaime ranted about.

- Ammo Box Ammunition (3)

⑱ Lone Chamber

Retrace your steps to the stairwell (the second one you find), and ascend to the small connecting passage and back into the Dunwich Building. It opens into an upper office area you couldn't previously reach. Drop down into the western offices; from here you can quickly exit and never speak of this again.

- Bobblehead: Melee Weapons (15/20)

TRAINING — BESTIARY — MAIN QUEST — MISC. QUESTS — TOUR — COMPLETION — APPENDICES

7.12: WARRINGTON TRAINYARD (LAT -20/LONG -17)

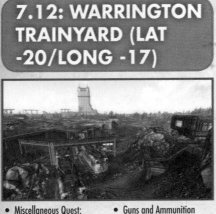

- Miscellaneous Quest: Tenpenny Tower
- Threat Level: 3
- Faction: Ghoul
- Danger: Gas Leak, Low Radiation
- Guns and Ammunition
- Health and Chems
- Interior Exploration
- Sleep Mattress
- Underground Connection
- Hostile: Feral Ghoul Genus

Note

Locations 7.12, 7.13, and 7.14 are all linked to each other via underground metro tunnels:

- U7.12: Warrington Tunnels
- U7.13: Warrington Station
- U7.14: Metro Access and Generator

Pack your Hunting Rifle; it's Feral Ghoul hunting time! The perimeter fencing has fallen in at so many different places that it is simple to breach. You can run in, guns blazing, Sneak around to the tunnel entrance, jump onto the top of the concrete tunnel, and snipe from here, or you can investigate the trainyard. There are catwalks to leap to; all are slightly irradiated but the exposure is worth it! Check the cluster of skeletons with RadAway and the following, accessed by jumping across from the concrete buttress wall to the northeast:

- Ammo Box Ammunition (3)
- First Aid Box Health and Chems
- Missile Launcher

To the southwest is a cabin with great views overlooking the yard, with Rads and the following:

- Ammo Box Ammunition
- First Aid Box Health and Chems
- Sniper Rifle

There's also a third L-shaped cabin near the railroad lines.

- Ammo Box Ammunition
- First Aid Box Health and Chems

Tip

You can escape Ghouls chasing you by leaping from the catwalks onto the top of the L-shaped cabin or carriages.

U7.12 WARRINGTON TUNNELS

Note

Access this from either the Warrington Station [U7.13] or Warrington Trainyard (Exterior) [7.12].

① **Entrance Chamber**

- Assault Rifle and Ammo

② **Connecting Room**

This has two Ghouls; if you quickly shoot the fire extinguisher, you can wound both of them.

- First Aid Box Health and Chems (2)
- Ammo Box Ammunition (2)

③ **Locked Storage**

- First Aid Box Health and Chems (3)
- Ammo Box Ammunition (2)

④ **Warning: Escaping Gas!**

⑤ **Pump Room**

This has a mattress and a door to Warrington Station.

- First Aid Box Health and Chems (2)

Note

The Warrington Station Interior is described in the next location.

7.13: WARRINGTON STATION (EXTERIOR; LAT -18/LONG -19)

- Miscellaneous Quest: Tenpenny Tower
- Threat Level: 3
- Faction: Ghoul
- Danger: Gas Leak, Low Radiation
- Collectible: Nuka-Cola Quantum, Skill Book (3)
- Area Is Locked
- Guns and Ammunition
- Health and Chems
- Interior Exploration
- Sleep Mattress
- Underground Connection
- Hostile: Feral Ghoul Genus

Note

Locations 7.12, 7.13, and 7.14 are all linked to each other via underground metro tunnels:

- U7.12: Warrington Tunnels
- U7.13: Warrington Station
- U7.14: Metro Access and Generator

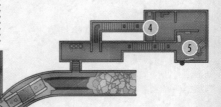

MAPS AND LOCATIONS
Warrington Tunnels

MAPS AND LOCATIONS

Warrington Station

INHABITANTS

Roy Phillips

Roy is the leader of a group of Ghoul dissidents living inside the Warrington metro tunnels. They have decided to try and force Mr. Allistair Tenpenny to let them move into his tower. Of course, he has refused. Roy is an ex-cop and his no-nonsense, black-and-white world view has carried over into his new life as Ghoul. He's come to terms with his Ghoulhood and demands that humans treat Ghouls with respect. He has no patience for bigots. Bessie Lynn is his Ghoulfriend.

Bessie Lynn

Bessie Lynn is a shy woman who defers to Roy Phillips (her boyfriend) in all matters. She has accepted her Ghoulhood but is still self-conscious about it.

Michael Masters

Michael Masters was an esteemed electronic and biological engineer before the bombs dropped. He doesn't remember much of the first years after D.C. was destroyed, but he does remember his human life and resents his ghoulish nature (though he does appreciate the gift of longevity). He was extremely intelligent and jovial in his old life, but living as a Ghoul has made him very pessimistic and angry at the world. He sees his ghoulness as a karmic curse, as he was attempting to keep America at the forefront of human mutation experiments, breeding super-warriors after being inspired by the work of the German, Russian, and Chinese doctors.

RELATED INTERACTIONS

Michael Masters: You can gain a chaperone to Roy Phillips's hidey-hole if you're civil.

Bessie Lynn: You can chitchat with her about her lot in life.

Roy Phillips: You can side with him against the residents of Tenpenny Tower.

Roy Phillips: Or you can placate him into a more civilized solution of coexistence.

The Warrington Station entrance, close to Lucky's Grocers [7.R], is locked and cannot be entered from the outside. To reach the Warrington Station Interior [U7.13], enter via the Warrington Tunnels [U7.12], as the gate isn't locked from this direction. Then you can come and go as you please.

U7.13 WARRINGTON STATION

> **Note**
> This can be accessed from either the Warrington Tunnels [U7.12] or Warrington Station Exterior [7.13]. Entering from the Wasteland is only possible after you unlock the station gate from the interior.

① Michael Masters's Mezzanine

You're halted by a human with a large helmet. On closer inspection, he appears Ghoulish but doesn't exhibit Feral tendencies. This is Michael Masters, a once-brilliant scientist, now cast out from humans and living in a small forward observation camp he's built with the help of Roy Phillips. Stay on civil terms and you can follow Masters to the Ghoul hideout. Get violent, and make your own way there. Try the ticket booth for these items:

- Ammo Box Ammunition (2)

② Roy Phillips's Ghoul Hidey-hole

Here you'll find a couple of (reasonably) friendly Ghouls who want to gain entry into Tenpenny Tower. You're allowed to sleep in this hidey-hole. Grab the Quantum, but you'll have to Steal the following:

- Ammo Box Ammunition
- Nuka-Cola Quantum (54/94)
- Pugilism Illustrated (14/25)

③ Storage Room and Connecting Chamber

There are Darts and the following items to Steal:

- Ammo Box Ammunition (2)
- Dean's Electronics (12/25)

④ Three-Door Room

Check the desk.

- Big Book of Science (13/25)

> **Note**
> The Metro Access and Generator Interior is described in the next Location: Tenpenny Tower.

7.14: TENPENNY TOWER (LAT -16/ LONG -17)

- Miscellaneous Quest: The Power of the Atom; Tenpenny Tower; Strictly Business; You Gotta Shoot 'Em in the Head
- Freeform Quest (4)
- Threat Level: 1
- Faction: Wastelander, Ghoul
- Services: Healer, Repairer, Trader
- Collectible: Fat Man Mini-Nuke, Holotape: Replicated Man, Schematic (2), Skill Book (6)
- Health and Chems
- Highly Visible Landmark
- Home Sweet Home
- Interior Exploration
- Lots o' Caps
- Sleep Mattress
- Underground Connection
- Work Bench

INHABITANTS

Allistair Tenpenny

An 80-year-old Englishman turned American entrepreneur, the man who discovered the Tower had the vision to see it as an opportunity to provide residents with a standard of living enjoyed by the affluent in the days before nuclear Armageddon. A rich eccentric who's bored with life and looking for new challenges, he enjoys sniping at Wasteland creatures, Ghouls, and the occasional visitor from his suite atop Tenpenny Tower.

Anthony Ling

The owner of New Urban Apparel, he sells all manner of clothing items to the residents of Tenpenny Tower. His selection is unmatched in the entire D.C. Wasteland, and he's particularly proud of the excellent condition prewar items he has managed to salvage throughout the years.

Doctor Julius Banfield

Banfield spends most of his days in the Wellness Center, tending to any patients who may stop in. He takes a break at noon to eat lunch at the Cafe Beau Monde and sometimes pops into the Federalist Lounge for a drink. On Tuesdays and Thursdays, the good doctor is gone for long stretches at a time; that's when he goes upstairs to the penthouse suites to "examine" Susan Lancaster.

Edgar Wellington II

Edgar Wellington spends most of his time in his suite with his wife, Millicent, who he despises; but like her, he only leaves to eat a couple of times a day. He sleeps with her in their bed a few hours every night (and sneaks out to sleep with Susan Lancaster on Mondays).

Millicent Wellington

Millicent is an elitist without the benefit of an elite society. Truth is, the other residents can't stand her, because she's a quarrelsome busybody; therefore, she never gets invited to any of the tower's intimate social events. She spends her days hanging around the house or complaining to her poor husband.

Irving Cheng

A rich old man with a secret identity, he believes he is the direct descendant of Chairman Cheng, leader of the Peoples Republic of China before the bombs dropped. He insists on calling himself and everyone else "comrade." He is embarrassed by his real first name, Irving, because it doesn't reflect his imagined heritage.

Tiffany Cheng

Tiffany Cheng spends most of her days avoiding her husband, drinking in the Federalist Lounge, or shopping down on the first level. She eats one meal at the Café Beau Monde and then returns to the Cheng suite and spends some time in her room before going to sleep.

Lydia Montenegro

Lydia runs the Boutique le Chic, which serves as the general store. Talk to her, and you'd think she's running a high-end shop and not peddling salvage to Wasteland dwellers; such is the elitist illusion she lives under. Lydia spends her days in the shop and then relaxes at the Federalist Lounge with her friend Michael Hawthorne.

Margaret Primrose

Margaret owns and operates the Café Beau Monde. Because the café only serves the residents of Tenpenny Tower, her clientele is limited, allowing Margaret to prepare and serve all the meals. The restaurant is open from 6:00 AM to 9:00 PM, and Margaret is the service provider the entire time. When the restaurant closes, she generally spends her time in her room.

INTERIOR MAPS AND LOCATIONS

Michael Hawthorne

Hawthorne has dedicated his life (and life savings) to the pursuit of giddy drunkenness, staggering drunkenness, and finally, paralytic stupor. He spends the majority of every day drinking in Tenpenny Tower's Federalist Lounge. He pretty much has a reserved seat that he always occupies.

Shakes

Shakes is the Federalist Lounge's robotic bartender, and he dutifully slings drinks 24 hours a day, 7 days a week. In fact, being a bartender is all Shakes has ever known; he was commissioned by Allistair Tenpenny for that very purpose. Shakes doesn't have much to say, but he's able to offer discounts on drinks if you know which buttons to press.

Susan Lancaster

Susan is the tower escort and spends most of her time in the beds of some of Tenpenny Tower's male residents. Doctor Banfield spends a few hours there each Tuesday and Thursday, Herbert Dashwood is with her every Sunday, and she spends every Saturday entertaining Allistair Tenpenny himself. When she's not working, Susan can be found drinking in the Federalist Lounge, shopping, or grabbing something to eat in the Café Beau Monde. On Susan's desk is a love letter from a certain husband whose wife might not take too kindly to the realization that her husband is cheating on her.

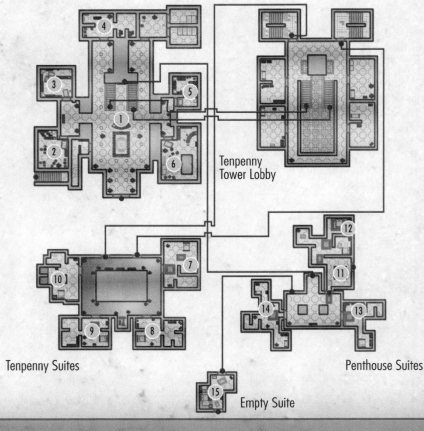

Tenpenny Tower Lobby

Tenpenny Suites

Penthouse Suites

Empty Suite

Metro Access & Generator

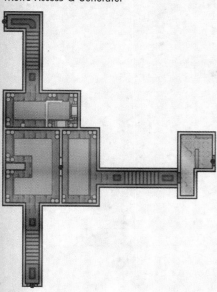

Tenpenny Tower is a shining beacon of hope and prosperity on D.C.'s new urban landscape. What is truly unfortunate, however, is that Allistair Tenpenny only offers this new life to those tenants he personally deems "worthy"—which excludes the majority of those living in the Capital Wasteland. The front gate is heavily guarded; you must bribe or Speech Challenge Security Chief Gustavo into the forecourt.

TENPENNY TOWER LOBBY

1 The Front Desk

Expect to see the always-grumpy Chief Gustavo here. His security guards patrol the building. He sells you weapons and armor from this location.

2 Cafe Beau Monde

Run by Margaret Primrose. Her Squirrel-on-a-Stick is legendary (no one has ever seen one of these in the wild). You can eat here. Kill Margaret, take her key, and ransack the cooler, where her food and Caps are.

3 Boutique Le Chic

Run by Lydia Montenegro. Her snooty and high-minded manner is legendary. You can Trade with her here. Or, kill Lydia, take her key, and open her locker so you don't have to pay for anything. Hack her terminal or open her wall safe, and expect annoyance at the very least (if you're not spotted) or outright hostility (if you are), and a load of Caps.

Talk with her after she notices her safe has been cracked to make her leave the Tower. This is one way to get rid of her and allow the Ghouls to move in "nonviolently."

If you succeeded in a pro-Ghoul solution to Tenpenny Tower, Michael Masters provides service here. In addition to the miscellaneous items Lydia sells, he will also sell weapons and armor.

- Schematic: Dart Gun (14/23)

4 Doctor Banfield's Surgery

You can get fixed up or have your Radiation sickness Healed here. The doctor knows about the Replicated Man too. Or you can kill Banfield, take his key, and open the medical supplies so you don't have to pay for Stimpaks or Chems.

- Holotape—The Replicated Man (11/24)

5 New Urban Apparel

Run by Anthony Ling. When it comes to prewar sweater ensembles, this is the place. Buy clothing (and Stimpaks) here. Or, kill Anthony, take his key, and open his locker so your fashions and Stimpaks are free. You can also hack his terminal or open his wall safe, and expect annoyance at the very least (if you're not spotted) or outright hostility (if you are), and a load of Caps.

Talking with Anthony after he notices his safe has been cracked will get him to leave the Tower. This is one way to get rid of him and allow the Ghouls to move in "nonviolently."

If you succeeded in a Pro-Ghoul solution to Tenpenny Tower, Bessie Lynn provides service here.

6 Federalist Lounge

Shakes is your bar-droid. You can request a drink. There are shelves of alcohol to steal too.

Before you do, Hack into the counter terminal and change the drinks prices; you can save up to 50 percent!

U7.14 METRO ACCESS AND GENERATOR

Note
Access this from either the Warrington Station [U7.13] or Tenpenny Tower [7.14].

This basement area has three distinct locations; if you head north from Warrington Station, you reach a Metro Access chamber with a large utility door on your right (east). Access the utility door from the west side via the Tenpenny Tower lobby. It cannot be opened from this point. In addition, there's a third passage accessed via the outside basement door (which requires the

key to Tenpenny's generator room. In here is a small window you can peer through into the utility door area. This location is where Roy Phillips amasses his Ghoul army if you're siding with the Ghouls during **Miscellaneous Quest: Tenpenny Tower.** Complete this on the side of the Ghouls, and you're awarded a unique item:

- Ghoul Mask (48/89)

TENPENNY SUITES

7 Susan Lancaster's Suite

Giving the Love Letter to Millicent Wellington results in her reminding her husband about the "until death do us part" section of their marriage vows.

- Love Letter
- Tales of a Junktown Jerky Vendor (11 & 12/24)*

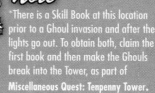

Note
*There is a Skill Book at this location prior to a Ghoul invasion and after the lights go out. To obtain both, claim the first book and then make the Ghouls break into the Tower, as part of **Miscellaneous Quest: Tenpenny Tower.**

8 Michael Hawthorne's Suite

Somebody may have a drinking problem.

9 Edgar and Millicent Wellington's Suite

These two are always at each other's throats. There is a safe here.

- Baseball Bat
- Wall Safe Items

10 Herbert Dashwood's Suite

This old adventurer has an exploration database. You can learn about the following:

People: King Crag (the old king of Rockopolis), Miss Penelope Chase (two-timer), Destiny Chao ("one of the loveliest women I've ever had the pleasure to pleasure"), Argyle (Dashwood's Ghoul manservant), and Harmon Jurley (the psychotic cannibal slaver).

Places: Notes on Paradise Falls (back when Jurley ran the joint), Rockopolis ("an honest mistake"), Blue Destiny Brothel (it shut down back in 2249 after the cholera outbreak), Underworld (he was an honorary Ghoul back in '51), and Megaton.

Pests: Notes on Mirelurks, Feral Ghouls, Radscorpions, Yao Guai, and Robobrains.

You can also ask him about the Replicated Man and about getting into the basement, as part of the Tenpenny Tower Quest.

TRAINING — BESTIARY — MAIN QUEST — MISC. QUESTS — TOUR — COMPLETION — APPENDICES

- Baseball Bat (2)
- Floor Safe Items (see the Freeform Quest below)
- Holotape: The Replicated Man (12/24)
- Hunting Rifle
- Sledgehammer

PENTHOUSE SUITES
⑪ Allistar Tenpenny's Suite

The door is locked and a guard is posted. You need to be attempting a relevant Quest, using a Speech Challenge, using the Suite Key you got from Chief Gustav (there is also a key on the pedestal you can snatch while the guard stretches his legs), or resorting to violence to infiltrate this chamber.

⑫ Allistar Tenpenny's Desk

- Lying, Congressional Style

ROOFTOP BALCONY (EXTERIOR)

Tenpenny is usually up here. Speak to him about any Quests and how he founded the towers, or execute him from miles away using a missile from the ground.

⑬ Mister Burke's Suite

It looks neat, tidy, and not lived in.

- Lying, Congressional Style (9 & 10/25)*

Note

There is a Skill Book at this location prior to a Ghoul invasion and after the lights go out. To obtain both, claim the first book and then make the Ghouls break into the Tower as part of Miscellaneous Quest: Tenpenny Tower.

⑭ The Cheng Suite

Home to Irving Cheng, the pencil collector. His wall terminal proves he's a closet totalitarian!

⑮ Empty Suite/My Tenpenny Suite

FREEFORM QUEST: HOUSE DECORATION IN MY TENPENNY SUITE

The final "empty suite" in Tenpenny is sealed completely. It is only available once you complete **Miscellaneous Quest: Power of the Atom** and decide to detonate the bomb. Mister Burke is most pleased and offers you My Tenpenny Suite Key. You can come and go as you please, using this as a base camp. Additional assets are all purchased from Lydia Montenegro (or Michael Masters if the Ghouls are running the place). Manage the following assets here:

FEATURE	DESCRIPTION
Bed, chairs, tables, and shelves	Bed for sleeping; furnishing for display
Promotional Bobblehead display case	This holds all the Bobbleheads you have found.
Work Bench	Required for the construction of Schematic-based items
Mr. Handy "Godfrey"	A robotic butler that tells jokes, cuts your hair, and pours you a drink
Scientist theme†	Decorations a laboratory scientist would be at home in
Wasteland Explorer theme	A variety of gun racks and trophies
Vault theme	A taste of home, without the crushing depression and lack of sunlight
Pre-War theme	It's as if you never left Tranquility Lane
Raider theme	Strap on your bondage armor and hang up a corpse
Love Machine theme‡	For the discerning manimal or hellcat around town
Jukebox	Streams music around your abode
Pristine Nuka-Cola Machine	Dispenses ice-cold Nuka-Colas
My First Laboratory	Dispenses random drugs over time and acts as an automatic drug detox
My First Infirmary	Heals wounds and repairs damaged limbs automatically

- †Big Book of Science (when Scientist Theme purchased) (14/25)
- ‡Lying, Congressional Style (when Love Machine Theme purchased) (11/25)

BIG TICKET ITEMS

Work Bench: This functions exactly like a standard Work Bench found elsewhere and allows you to construct Schematic weapons.

- Work Bench (27/46)

Robotic Butlers: They can tell you a (usually terrible) random joke.

They can dispense Purified Water on command (note that the robot can dispense up to five of these before it needs a week to recharge its "condensation collectors"); they can give you a haircut; and they can explain any house purchase you have bought.

Jukebox: Functions exactly like a standard jukebox found across the Wasteland. The music cannot be selected.

Nuka-Cola Machine: Sierra Petrovida would be proud. This machine comes with eight "ice-cold" Nuka-Colas that have Rads +2 and HP +20 (better than warm Nuka-Cola). If you are carrying Nuka-Cola Bottles, you can chill them to become ice-cold.

My First Laboratory: This can instantly cure you of any drug addictions and can concoct a random compound. This second process takes about a day or so. When you return, the set will dispense a random Chem and then be ready for a new command. Note that while it is "Brewing" (which cannot be interrupted), the detox system is unavailable. The random drug is one of the following: Buffout, Jet, Mentats, Psycho, Med-X, Rad-X, Stimpak, RadAway, or Unpurified Water.

My First Infirmary: Instantly heal yourself to maximum health; restore any and all damaged limbs or body parts; remove all Rads.

FREEFORM QUEST: LOVE LETTER

Assuming you discover the Love Letter in Susan Lancaster's suite, hand it to the one person who really shouldn't know about the tryst—Millicent. She goes crazy, murders both Susan and her husband, and flees into the Wasteland. That's one way to clear the place of Ghoul-haters!

FREEFORM QUEST: FINDERS KEEPERS

If you break into Lydia's or Anthony's shop safes, they are furious and decide to leave the premises and look for superior accommodation. If you're having difficulty getting them to accept Ghouls into their lives, this is a good alternate strategy.

FREEFORM QUEST: A MANHANDLED MANSERVANT

Herbert Dashwood's terminal mentions his manservant Argyle and wonders what became of him. Well, out in the southwestern wastes, you'll find your answer; visit Rockopolis [7.C], locate the dead Ghoul, and report back to Dashwood. He's overcome but offers you his key as a reward. This opens the floor safe in his room; there are Chems, Stimpaks, and a few rare items:

- Dashwood's Safe Key
- Mini-Nuke (45/71)
- Schematic: Bottlecap Mine (15/23)

 Or, you could just kill him and take the key.

Secondary Locations

7.A: BROADCAST TOWER PN (LAT -24/LONG -04)

- Threat Level: 1
- Collectible: Scribe Pre-War Book, Skill Book
- Highly Visible Landmark

- Interior Exploration
- Radio Signal
- Hostile: Mole Rat, Radscorpion Genus

North from Smith Casey's Garage is a radio mast you can easily access via the open mesh gates or by heading over the rocks. Locate the electrical switch to find the Drainage Chamber Sewer Grate [4.R]. Technically, the following items are in this location but are referenced for this zone.

- Radio Signal Papa November

By the exit ladder is a Pre-War Book and Pugilism Illustrated. Over by the corpse are scattered food, Purified Water, and Darts.

- Blood Pack
- Pre-War Book (50/98)
- Pugilism Illustrated (15/25)

7.B: WASTELANDER TENT AND SNIPER VISTA (LAT -30/LONG -07)

- Threat Level: 1
- Faction: Wastelander
- Guns and Ammunition
- Health and Chems
- Sleep Mattress

Skirt the western Wasteland perimeter; there's a small Wastelander tent, with two grumpy inhabitants and their dog. Their tent includes a place to sleep and has food, Darts, and a Carton of Cigarettes. Close by is a sniping spot with excellent views to the east and south.

- .32 Pistol and Ammo
- Ammo Box Ammunition
- First Aid Box Health and Chems (2)
- Sniper Rifle

7.C: ROCKOPOLIS (LAT -26/LONG -07)

- Threat Level: 1
- Faction:, Ghoul, Slaver
- Collectible: Bobblehead
- Guns and Ammunition
- Interior Exploration
- Argyle (Deceased)

The only exterior clue to this place is a hat stand and faded banner. Once inside, you can inspect Argyle's corpse ① and read a Holotape message from a Slaver to Rollings about rounding up slaves to sell up north.

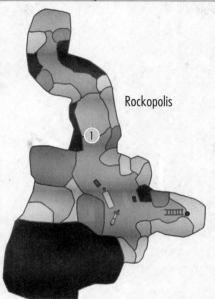

Rockopolis

- 10mm Pistol
- Bobblehead: Unarmed (16/20)
- Note: Rollings: We're Done

Tip

Can't find Rockopolis? Three Dog and Dashwood both mention this place, and you can search at night; there's a glow behind the rock door you can see in the dark.

7.D: MILITARY CHECKPOINT AND TENT (LAT -22/LONG -06)

- Threat Level: 2
- Danger: Low Radiation
- Guns and Ammunition
- Sleep Mattress

North of Smith Casey's Garage is a small military blockade. The radiation the military was sent to clear up—a small pool across the road—is just north.

- Ammo Box Ammunition (6)
- First Aid Box Health and Chems
- Laser Rifle

7.E: RUINED CHAPEL (LAT -14/LONG -06)

- Threat Level: 2
- Faction: Raider
- Danger: Grenade Bouquet, Shotgun Trap
- Collectible: Fat Man Mini-Nuke, Skill Book (2)

- Guns and Ammunition
- Highly Visible Landmark
- Sleep Mattress

On the outskirts of Jury Street [5.13] is a chapel now overrun by Raiders. Enter via the opening in the back to avoid the Rigged Shotgun trap, deactivate the Grenade Bouquet hanging from the middle crossbeam, and then conduct a thorough sweep. There's a mattress, scattered Ammo and Chems, and a Carton of Cigarettes. By the pulpit are Caps and two more mattresses. Search for the following before you leave:

- Combat Shotgun and Ammo
- Frag Grenade (3)
- Lying, Congressional Style (12/25)
- Mini-Nuke (46/71)
- Pugilism Illustrated (16/25)

7.F: RUINED CALVERTON VILLAGE (LAT -14/LONG -07)

- Threat Level: 2
- Faction: Raider
- Collectible: Skill Book
- Sleep Mattress

South of the ruined chapel is an equally dilapidated village of six homes, known once as Calverton. Work your way from west to east; the house nearest the ruined chapel has a floor safe. The house south of this has a Skill Book. Other than this and a Carton of Cigarettes in a bathtub, this place was picked clean long ago. To the west is a jackknifed truck [8.I].

- Floor Safe Items
- Nikola Tesla and You (16/25)

7.G: OVERTURNED CITY LINER (LAT -30/LONG -10)

- Threat Level: 1

This is the end of the road—literally—for the western part of the freeway ruins that run east.

7.H: IRRADIATED POND (LAT -26/LONG -09)

- Threat Level: 2
- Danger: Low Radiation

This is an example of the many deposits of radiation in the Wasteland; skirt around it.

7.I: CAPTAIN COSMOS BILLBOARD (LAT -19/LONG -10)

- Threat Level: 1
- Highly Visible Landmark

Overlooking the east–west freeway, this is an excellent point of reference.

7.J: ABANDONED SHACK (LAT -16/LONG -10)

- Threat Level: 1

This lean-to is really abandoned!

7.K: RUINED HOUSE (LAT -26/LONG -13)

- Threat Level: 1

This is a great location to watch Girdershade from, but there are no items in this ruin.

7.L: BROADCAST TOWER SV AND 7.M: DRAINAGE CHAMBER (LAT -20/LONG -13)

- Threat Level: 3
- Danger: Grenade Bouquet, Mines, Shotgun Trap, Terminal Trap
- Collectible: Fat Man Mini-Nuke, Skill Book
- Guns and Ammunition
- Highly Visible Landmark
- Interior Exploration
- Radio Signal
- Work Bench

DRAINAGE CHAMBER

One of the rusting radio masts atop a craggy and rocky hillside is still functioning. Flip the electrical switch and find the Drainage Chamber Sewer Grate [7.M] to the southeast. Use triangulation, but beware of the gaps in the ground; don't fall down a fissure to the dirt path below!

- Radio Signal Sierra Victor

Floor Pads

Step on either, and a Rigged Shotgun in the right-side alcove activates. Duck and disarm.

- Combat Shotgun and Ammo (2)

Locker Barricade

A Grenade Bouquet is triggered when you move the barrel.

- Frag Grenade (3)

East Hatch Door

There are two Frag Mines that require lightning-fast disarming!

- Frag Mine (2)

Skeletal Prankster

This trickster has rigged one trap too many! Disarm the dummy terminal, then gather items from the room.

- Ammo Box Ammunition (2)
- Assault Rifle
- Frag Grenade
- Frag Mine

Work Bench

There's a Bottlecap Mine here and more Frag Mines on a nearby table, along with the following:

- Duck and Cover! (16/25)
- Frag Mines
- Mini-Nuke (47/71)
- Work Bench (28/46)

7.N: CAPTAIN COSMOS BILLBOARD (LAT -20/LONG -12)

- Threat Level: 1
- Highly Visible Landmark

Overlooking the east–west freeway, this is an excellent point of reference; don't confuse it with the other one [7.H]!

7.O: CHINESE PILOT'S SHACK (LAT -29/LONG -15)

- Threat Level: 1
- Faction: Chinese Remnant

Look at the final resting place of a Chinese pilot, although he has no distinguishing clothing. He's been dead for a very long time; there are only tin cans and a spork to scavenge!

7.P: DOT'S DUNWICH DINER (LAT -22/LONG -16)

- Threat Level: 1

Scavengers tell of odd sounds and chanting from the nearby Dunwich building, but this is simply a lonely and desolate place.

7.Q: WARRINGTON TOWNSHIP (LAT -18/LONG -16)

- Threat Level: 1
- Collectible: Skill Book
- Sleep Mattress
- Hostile: Enclave Eyebot

Seventeen ruined houses make up this township. Search the buildings from north to south; the second house has a Neighborly Letter in the mailbox. The fourth has a mattress. Some of the mailboxes contain a few common items. There are two Ammo Boxes by the burned-out car, just south of the sealed but intact house. Near Tenpenny Tower, there's a safe in the debris of the second house. The third house contains a few Bottle Caps and a mattress. The house (which is more of a debris pile) opposite the intact dwelling has a copy of Duck and Cover! on the surviving shelving. You cannot enter either of the intact houses in this township. There's a 5 percent chance of finding a letter from Vault-Tec in any mailbox.

- Ammo Box Ammunition (2)
- Debris Safe Items
- Duck and Cover! (17/25)
- Neighborly Letter

7.R: LUCKY'S GROCER (LAT -18/LONG -20)

- Threat Level: 2
- Faction: Wastelander
- Services: Repairer, Trader
- Collectible: Nuka-Cola Quantum, Skill Book
- Guns and Ammunition
- Health and Chems
- Interior Exploration
- Sleep Mattress
- Hostile: Mole Rat, Radscorpion Genus, Scavenger

Lucky probably died screaming as the skin melted from his face, but his store still survives if you can dodge the roaming Mole Rats and Radscorpions. Once inside, you're greeted by a Scavenger who now keeps this place as his own. There's a Skill Book you can take without penalty, but anything is seen as stealing. You can Trade and Repair here.

There's junk, food, drink, and Darts, including missiles near the mannequin. Hack into the counter terminal or floor safe. Then look for the following to steal (including some unique shades):

- First Aid Box Health and Chems
- Floor Safe Items
- Lucky's Shades (49/89)
- Nuka-Cola Quantum (55/94)
- Pugilism Illustrated (17/25)

7.S: WILLY'S GROCER (LAT -14/LONG -18)

- Threat Level: 1
- Collectible: Skill Book
- Health and Chems
- Interior Exploration
- Hostile: Enclave Eyebot, Radroach, Robot Genus

Close by are ruins of houses, but they are empty. Enter the grocer building and collect beer, food, and two Cartons of Cigarettes. Also open the counter safe and grab the following:

- Counter Safe Items
- First Aid Box Health and Chems
- Tales of a Junktown Jerky Vendor (13/24)

7.T: RUINED OFFICE BUILDING (LAT -14/LONG -19)

- Threat Level: 1
- Faction: Chinese Commando
- Collectible: Skill Book
- Guns and Ammunition

The ground floor is mainly rubble, and there's the corpse of a Chinese Commando festering near some stairs. Search him, then head up the rubble pile to the second floor, where a bookshelf holds a Skill Book, a couple of Stimpaks, an Ammo Box, and a Scoped .44 Magnum next to a skeleton.

- Tumblers Today (15/25)
- Scoped .44 Magnum
- Ammo Box Ammunition
- Stimpaks

Note

Using a Sniper Rifle, try hitting Allistair Tenpenny on his upper balcony!

ENCLAVE CAMP LOCATIONS

CAMP E7.01 (LAT -28/LONG -04)

- Main Quest: Picking up the Trail
- Threat Level: 4
- Guns and Ammunition

Two soldiers attempt to keep a Modified Deathclaw from mauling more of their recon unit; two have already fallen.

- Enclave Crate Ammunition

CAMP E7.02 (LAT -14/LONG -11)

- Main Quest: Picking up the Trail
- Threat Level: 3

A Vertibird drops a small squad of Enclave troops just northwest of the VAPL-84 Power Station [7.08].

CAMP E7.03 (LAT -23/LONG -12)

- Main Quest: Picking up the Trail
- Threat Level: 3

A Vertibird drops a small squad of Enclave troops to commandeer the area around Jocko's Pop & Gas Store [7.07].

Zone 8: Southern Plains and D.C. Outskirts

TOPOGRAPHICAL OVERVIEW

Your first experiences out in the Wasteland begin here, in the local area around and south of Vault 101. After trudging through Springvale, your first place to investigate has to be Megaton; there's a huge amount to discover, and a variety of improvements you can make to your inventory and Cap collection. Press farther south to reach Fort Independence, the seat of power for those Brotherhood Outcasts who abhor the leadership of Elder Lyons. Head into more rural areas and stay a spell at the delightful hamlet of Andale. Could this be America's perfect township? Then, just for the taste of it, check out the place where soda and radioactive isotopes combine—the Nuka-Cola Plant!

AVAILABLE COLLECTIBLES (ZONE 8)

- Bobbleheads: 2/20
- Fat Men: 0/9
- Fat Man Mini-Nukes: 5/71
- Unique Items: 9/89
- Nuka-Cola Quantum: 8/94
- Schematics: 4/23
- Scribe Pre-War Books: 7/98
- Skill Book: Barter (1/24), Big Guns (4/25), Energy Weapons (2/25), Explosives (1/25), Lockpick (2/25), Medicine (1/25), Melee Weapons (6/25), Repair (3/25), Science (3/25), Small Guns (1/25), Sneak (5/25), Speech (3/25), Unarmed (1/25)
- Work Bench: 4/46
- Holotape: Keller (0/5), Replicated Man (3/19)

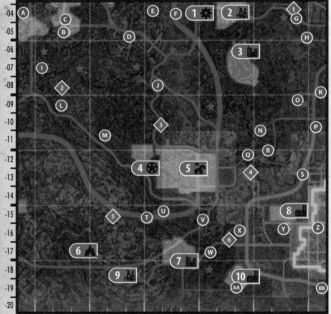

PRIMARY LOCATIONS

8.01: Vault 101 (lat -04/long -04)

8.02: Springvale (lat -02/long -04)

8.03: Megaton (lat -01/long -06)

8.04: Fort Independence (lat -06/long -13)

8.05: Fairfax Ruins (lat -04/long -12)

8.06: Cliffside Cavern (lat -10/long -17)

8.07: Andale (lat -05/long -17)

8.08: Red Racer Factory (lat 02/long -15)

8.09: The Overlook Drive-in (lat -08/long -18)

8.10: Nuka-Cola Plant (lat -01/long -19)

SECONDARY LOCATIONS

8.A: Jury Street Tunnels (Blocked; lat -13/long -04)

8.B: Radio Mast Oscar Tango and Hamlet (lat -11/long -05)

8.C: Drainage Chamber (lat -11/long -04)

8.D: Military Truck Checkpoint (lat -07/long -05)

8.E: Ruined Farmhouse (lat -06/long -04)

8.F: Freeway Drain (lat -05/long -04)

8.G: Ruined Farmhouse (lat 02/long -04)

8.H: Water Tower (lat 02/long -05)

8.I: Jackknifed Truck (lat -12/long -07)

8.J: Captain Cosmos Billboard (lat -06/long -08)

8.K: Crumbling Statuary (lat 03/long -08)

8.L: Independence Hamlet (lat -11/long -09)

8.M: Independence Ruins (lat -09/long -11]

8.N: Ruined House (lat 00/long -10)

8.O: Talon Company Camp (lat 02/long -09)

8.P: Raider Underpass (lat 03/long -10)

8.Q: Car Dealership (lat -01/long -12)

8.R: Red Rocket Gas Station (lat 00/long -12)

8.S: Scavenger's Bridge (lat 02/long -13)

8.T: Freeway Wreckage (lat -06/long -15)

8.U: Overturned Truck (lat -05/long -15)

8.V: The Concrete Treehouse (lat -03/long -15)

8.W: Jackknifed Truck (lat -03/long -17)

8.X: Dot's Diner (lat -01/long -16)

8.Y: Parked Red RacerTrucks (lat 01/long -16)

8.Z: Raider Camp (lat 03/long -16)

8.AA: Parked Nuka-Cola Trucks and Drainage Outlet (lat -02/long -19)

8.BB: Traffic Pileup (lat 03/long -19)

Primary Locations

8.01: VAULT 101 (LAT -04/LONG -04)

- Freeform Quest (4)
- Threat Level: 2
- Faction: Vault Dweller
- Collectible: Bobblehead, Skill Book
- Area Is Locked
- Follower
- Health and Chems
- Interior Exploration
- Radio Signal
- Rare or Powerful Item
- Hostile: Radroach

INHABITANTS

Allen Mack

Wally Mack's father and a man not to be trifled with. He is overly protective of his family ever since his wife died (mother of Wally Mack, Susie Mack, and Officer Mack). He's taught basic survival tactics to his children but isn't overly fond of showing emotion.

Officer Steve "Stevie" Mack

The gungho new guy in Security. He's been waiting his whole life to join the force and is willing to do whatever it takes to get in good with "the boss" (Chief Hammond), including being particularly overzealous during emergencies.

Wally Mack

Wally is the brains of the Tunnel Snakes. He doesn't talk as much as the others, but they listen to what he has to say when he does say something.

Susie Mack

Wally's younger sister. She despises the Tunnel Snakes, and Wally won't dare tease her, as she will give worse than she gets.

Overseer Alphonse Almodovar

Growing up in Vault 101 during a time when the Vault dwellers ventured freely into the outside world, Alphonse's parents believed the Vault should have no contact with the dangers out there. As he got older, Alphonse knew he had to correct the gross lapses in security. He got his chance when

INTERIOR MAPS AND LOCATIONS

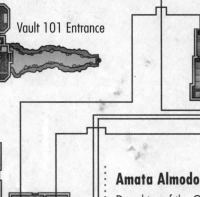

Vault 101 Entrance

Vault 101 Sub-Level

Vault 101 Atrium/Upper Level

Vault 101 Lower Level

Vault 101 Atrium

the Overseer—a strong proponent of outside contact—disappeared one day while out in the Wasteland. Many suspected foul play, but the young, charismatic, strong-willed Alphonse Almodovar offered the Vault dwellers new leadership, and they had little choice but to accept.

Amata Almodovar

Daughter of the Overseer, Amata's mother died of disease when Amata was just two years old. Amata loves her father dearly and is very loyal to him, but she longs to change his stance on isolationism. She does not want to defy Alphonse but longs to experience the outside world. You and Amata have been best friends all your life, drawn together by the common bond of not having known your mothers.

Stanley Armstrong

Sweet, always worried, and not very bright, Stanley is the father of Beatrice, Mary, and Gloria. Stanley and Andy are responsible for keeping the Vault running, tending to all the machinery and acting as janitors for the whole place.

Andy

Under constant supervision from Stanley Armstrong, Andy is a Mister Handy robot, although a more apt title would be "Mister Liability."

Beatrice Armstrong

Vault 101's resident gossip hound, she has her nose in everyone's business; of course, like all true gossips, she will vehemently deny that she is ever involved in the affairs of others. She is best friends with Pepper Gomez and is interested in Mister Brotch. She also keeps up the gossip with her married sisters, Mary Kendall and Gloria Mack.

Butch DeLoria

Vault 101's resident bully and leader of the Tunnel Snakes, Butch masks his fear and sense of inadequacy about not having a father and having an alcoholic mother by becoming boorish and overbearing.

TRAINING — BESTIARY — MAIN QUEST — MISC. QUESTS — TOUR — COMPLETION — APPENDICES

Ellen DeLoria

A fading beauty, Ellen is drunk too often to pay any attention to what her son Butch is up to. She lives with him in one of the smallest family apartments. Perhaps she never had a husband, so nobody really knows who Butch's father is (it could have been anyone in the Vault).

Dad

Before your birth, your father was the leader of an impossibly ambitious scientific endeavor—Project Purity. Leading a group of scientists, he planned to turn the ruins of the Jefferson Memorial into the most technologically advanced water purifier ever imagined. But when you were born (your mother dying in childbirth), your father had little choice but to abandon Project Purity and get you to the only safe place he knew—the underground fallout shelter known as Vault 101.

Officer Herman Gomez

The classic good cop, officer Gomez is Freddie's dad. He has no patience for the Tunnel Snakes and tries to make sure that Freddie doesn't have anything to do with them. Which is hard, since there may not be any other boys Freddie's age in the Vault.

Pepper Gomez

Pepper has raised her son Freddie in the Vault by herself nearly his entire life. She is a good mother and cares for Freddie but feel helpless when confronted with his behavior. It's obvious to everyone that Butch and the Tunnel Snakes have far more influence over Freddie, and Pepper is at the end of her rope.

Freddie Gomez

An aspiring Tunnel Snake, his associations with Butch and the Tunnel Snakes have caused his grades to drop and send Pepper into fits of worry. In truth, Freddie isn't a bad kid; he just enjoys the approval he gets from Butch and the others when he misbehaves. And, of course, there really aren't many other people to hang out with in the Vault.

Officer John Kendall

Tough, friendly, and no-nonsense, he's not actively sinister, but he'll follow orders without thinking about it too much. He is not an introspective sort of guy. He loves being a cop and doesn't worry about whether what he's doing is right; he is the law.

Christine Kendall

Playing up to her father usually results in a verbal ear-bashing or worse, so Christine

has recently become more and more introverted. She's not happy here and wonders what life is like away from the concrete walls and fluorescent, buzzing lights.

Old Lady Palmer

Jonas's grandmother lives alone in her apartment where nothing has changed for decades. She's kind, proud of her grandson, and bakes the most delicious sticky Sweetrolls.

Jonas Palmer

Wholesome, good-humored, and kind, Jonas has been your father's assistant for as long as you can remember, and you get on famously.

Edwin Brotch

Mister Brotch inherited the position of schoolteacher from his father and grandfather. Since the day the Vault 101 residents entered the vault, there has been a Brotch as a schoolteacher. Mr. Brotch is concerned about carrying on that tradition, but with no children of his own, he is beginning to worry that he will be the last in line.

Security Chief Paul Hannon

Security Chief Hannon is extremely aggressive, by-the-book, and wishes his Vault security force was a real military force with a war to win. He is not nearly as smart as he thinks he is, and his men are not nearly the crack security force he thinks they are. Spit and polish are everything to him; following orders is his highest calling.

Paul Hannon (II)

Paul is sitting on the bottom rung of the Tunnel Snakes' tiny social ladder. The other Snakes often tease him when they lack another suitable target. His dad being security chief of the vault gives him a certain cachet among his friends, though.

GENERAL NOTES

On a rocky bluff overlooking Springvale, your home for almost the last two decades is ready to be visited, but things can never be as they were. The best time to attempt this is after you hear Amata's voice over the Vault 101 emergency frequency. Tune your Pip-Boy and head back home.

- Vault 101 Emergency Frequency

As you visit this location several times throughout your life, only the layout is static, and inhabitants may be in different locations. Refer to the Main and Miscellaneous Quests for further information (including which doors are locked). This simply shows the Vault layout, starting with the area nearest the surface.

VAULT 101 ENTRANCE

1. **Entrance**

2. **Secret Wall**

This slides down (but only if you're approaching from the Atrium) to the northeast; you use this during Main Quest: Escape.

VAULT 101 ATRIUM/UPPER LEVEL

3. **Storage**

4. **Cafeteria**

5. **Security Room and Cell**

Amata was questioned during Main Quest: Escape.

6. **Overseer's Office**

This includes two bedrooms and a secret access corridor under the Overseer's desk, leading back to the entrance room.

VAULT 101 LOWER LEVEL

7. **Classroom**

You took your G.O.A.T. here.

8. **Your Father's Clinic**

Check the wall plaque featuring your mother's favorite Bible verse for the Schematic.

- Bobblehead: Medicine (17/20)
- Schematic: Rock-It Launcher (16/23)

9. **Diner**

This is where you celebrated your birthday and received a Grognak the Barbarian from Amata.

- Grognak the Barbarian (13/25)

10. **Restrooms**

SUBLEVEL

11. **BB Gun Practice Range**

12. **Reactor**

- First Aid Box Health and Chems

FREEFORM QUEST: OUT OF THE VAULT

Note

All these Freeform Quests take place only after you complete Miscellaneous Quest: Trouble on the Homefront.

Once the Quest is over and you chose to open the Vault to the outside world, there is a chance you will run into an old friend during a Wasteland excursion. Your first encounter is with Susie Mack (assuming you haven't killed her). Of course, you can kill her now and steal her food and water, or act a little more civilized. She's happy to see you and offers some food and Purified Water. She says the Vault's doing well and that most of them are getting used to the idea of the outside. She also expresses sorrow that you can't come back and then excuses herself.

FREEFORM QUEST: TRAPPED OUTSIDE

There's also a chance you will run into the corpse of an old friend during a Wasteland excursion, if you forced the residents to evacuate. Search the corpse (which is usually Freddie, Pepper, or Officer Gomez) for a Vault Jumpsuit in poor condition and other assorted junk.

- Vault 101 Jumpsuit

FREEFORM QUEST: AMATA'S FATE

If you forced Amata to leave the Vault, you may stumble upon an Enclave patrol confronting her. Listen to an Enclave officer ask her where her Vault is. After she tells them, they murder her. If you somehow manage to stop this, Amata flees from you, shouting that it's all your fault.

FREEFORM QUEST: TUNNEL SNAKES FOREVER!

When you finish the Quest, make sure Butch is still alive and the Overseer has lost control (either by convincing him to step down, killing him, or sabotaging the Vault). Move to the Muddy Rudder, a watering hole at the gigantic rust bucket known as Rivet City [9.15]. Strike up a conversation, and you can convince him to join you in some adventuring—but only if your Karma is at a neutral level. Note that if you kill Butch at any time, you can collect his Unique Switchblade:

- Follower: Butch
- "Butch's Toothpick" Switchblade (50/89)

8.02: SPRINGVALE (LAT -02/LONG -04)

- Main Quest: Following in His Footsteps
- Threat Level: 2
- Faction: Raider, Wastelander
- Collectible: Skill Book
- Health and Chems
- Highly Visible Landmark
- Interior Exploration
- Lots o' Caps

INHABITANTS
Silver

Silver, 22, was a prostitute who worked for Colin Moriarty in Megaton before they had a falling out. She ran away with her share of her earnings (or so she says) and is hiding out in Springvale, just outside of Vault 101. Silver is now a pitiful Psycho junkie and lives her life in constant fear of reprisal from Moriarty. Her name comes from her very light blond, almost silvery hair.

GENERAL NOTES

The township of Springvale is one of the first areas of devastation you may witness after exiting Vault 101. This derelict and pitiful hamlet is close to Megaton, a Wastelander hangout full of hope, but here there's a real sense of hopelessness. Check all the mailboxes and drop-off boxes for items; one contains a Skill Book. One of the four ruined houses has a safe to open, another has food in a fridge. The water tower to the south is a source of drinking (but irradiated) water.

- Pugilism Illustrated (18/25)
- Floor Safe Items

The remaining buildings to the north of the Red Rocket Gas Station are empty. There is small ranch and a nearby Raider camp, pushed back into the Springvale Elementary School [5.14] by the well-defended folks at Megaton. The Small Ranch is home to Silver, and her home is that of a Chem-dependant wastrel; scattered Chems, Food, and a First Aid Box (all must be stolen, with a Karma hit each time you grab anything).

- First Aid Box Health and Chems

FREEFORM QUEST: HIGH-HO SILVER, AWAY!

You can complete this independently or as part of the Main Quest, and you don't need to visit Moriarty to try this. Speak with Silver: She wants to know what you're doing in her home:

You can simply kill her, ransack her home, and return to Moriarty.

You can goad her into attacking you and then kill her, then return to Moriarty. With either of the first two choices, you can grab Jet and Psycho, plus Health and Chems from a First Aid Box.

You can also reason with her and request her to give you enough Caps to pay off Moriarty (300) so she can live in peace. Well, until her next hit anyway.

Or, you can use **Speech** convince her to hand over what she owes, and you'll convince Moriarty she left town. She agrees and hands over 400 Caps.

- Caps (300; if you reasoned with Silver)
- Caps (400; if you Speech Challenged Silver)

8.03: MEGATON (LAT -01/LONG -06)

- Main Quest: Following in His Footsteps
- Miscellaneous Quest: The Wasteland Survival Guide; The Power of the Atom
- Freeform Quest (4)
- Threat Level: 2
- Faction: Ghoul, Regulator, Wastelander
- Services: Healer, Repairer, Trader
- Danger: Low Radiation
- Collectible: Fat Man Mini-Nuke, Nuka-Cola Quantum, Scribe Pre-War Book (4), Schematic, Skill Book (5)
- Follower
- Guns and Ammunition
- Health and Chems
- Highly Visible Landmark
- Home Sweet Home
- Interior Exploration
- Lots o' Caps
- Main Trading Route
- Rare or Powerful Item (4)
- Sleep Mattress
- Work Bench (2)
Holotape: Replicated Man (3)

Megaton is an odd-looking, sprawling settlement, surrounded by thick, impenetrable walls. It features a sliding front gate guarded by a Sniper named Stockholm and a rusty robot named Deputy Weld. You can head in and out as you like, and it is wise to holster your weapon.

INHABITANTS
Deputy Weld

A RobCo Industries Protectron robot that guards the entrance to Megaton, Weld talks like a 50s robot but probably has some cowboy lingo programmed into him. He stays at the front gate and offers any traveler some platitudes.

Deputy Steel

He is a RobCo Industries Mister Gutsy robot that has been programmed to serve as an assistant to Sheriff Simms. Truth is, Simms is a fan of the Wild West (his dad used to read him stories when he was a kid). He took on the title of sheriff and named the robot his deputy mostly to live out his childhood fantasies.

Stockholm

Stockholm is the Megaton gate guard and actually spends his time outside the city, manning the guard tower at the main gate. He is 25 and loves the sun on his back, but he isn't quite as happy with the slightly radioactive dust from dust storms in his mouth.

Lucas Simms

He grew up in Megaton and understands better than anyone what it takes to survive and thrive in the Wasteland. Big and imposing yet warm and friendly, Lucas won his position by a unanimous vote of the people of Megaton (most of whom genuinely love the guy). He serves as mayor, sheriff, judge, and just about any other position that's needed. It's also no secret around Megaton that Lucas Simms is fulfilling some weird childhood cowboy fantasy. He named his son Harden after the Old West outlaw John Wesley Harden. Simms is also a member of a secret society known only as "the Regulators."

Harden Simms

Harden is Lucas Simms's 10-year-old son. His father has instructed him not to talk to strangers in Megaton, and he reluctantly obeys. He goes to sleep early and rises early, which gives him enough time to meet up with Maggie and play.

Walter

Walter spends his days minding the machines and fixing drainage devices that break. He's increasingly worried about the state of the water and drainage structure, and knows it won't hold much longer—and neither will he. At 61, he's one of the oldest residents.

Moira Brown

A self-styled inventor, 24-year-old Moira grew up in the trading community of Canterbury Commons with an uncommon curiosity about the world. She's read almost every book that's come through the town. Although her reading has taught her a wide variety of useful knowledge, she has nearly no actual experience with the world, so she doesn't always understand how it can be applied outside of her workshop. After a recent accident with a domesticated Centaur, Moira was inspired to write a book to help others survive in the Wasteland and avoid similar dangers. She just needs someone with real experience to test out her ideas and give her some real-world insight into life in the wastes.

Doc Church

The town's overworked and underappreciated doctor, he can be cranky and bitter, but he's always professional. Before Doc came to the town a few years ago, Megaton was without a doctor for a very long time. Before he settled, Doc stayed alive by trading his services to Raiders and Slavers. Now 54, he refuses to talk about his youth.

Confessor Cromwell

Little is known about Cromwell's past: He arrived in his early 20s (he's now 44) and was granted permission to stay due to the blessing and high standing of his successor in the church, who fostered him in the ways of Atom. Eventually, Cromwell proved to be a valuable resource in protecting and aiding the town, and he became an eccentric distraction to most of the citizens of Megaton.

Mother Maya

Mother Maya is 41 and Confessor Cromwell's female counterpart. She and Cromwell are actually husband and wife, but they don't go out of their way to advertise the fact, since they're both so busy promoting the ideals of the church.

Colin Moriarty

Moriarty, 50, has been here nearly his entire life. He claims that his grandfather helped found the original settlement a few years after the war. While no one can verify this, his father did use the nearby trade routes to amass wealth, which is used to help secure Megaton. Colin inherited this wealth when his father was killed during a Raider attack when Colin was 14. Colin's first move was to build a fence around the town. Since then, the people have looked to Colin as a benefactor despite his running drinks, Chems, girls, and games out of his saloon. Simms turns a blind eye to Moriarty's activities, because he is acutely aware that the town needs Colin's support and resources.

Gob

Treated as a freakish, secondhand citizen by many people in Megaton (particularly Colin Moriarty), Gob is skittish and nervous, always looking over his shoulder. He does his best to maintain a sense of humor and

MAPS AND LOCATIONS
Megaton

to be friendly with customers, but this is mostly out of his desire not to be beaten. Confessor Cromwell and Mother Maya treat Gob with respect and an air of reverence because of their spiritual beliefs.

Nova

Nova, 25, spends most of her time hanging around the bar talking to the male clientele. Every now and then, she'll go up to a room with a new "friend." Her real job is to sweet-talk the male patrons and get them to spend money—on booze, company, or an outrageously priced bed for the night. Every couple of nights, Nova sleeps with Gob. One day a week—her day off—she goes shopping.

Mister Burke

Mister Burke spends his days at Moriarty's Saloon, drinking and talking to Moriarty or asking Gob the Ghoul probing questions about being a Ghoul, the effects of radiation on his body, and what it's like to live among the nonirradiated populace. He also likes to eat at the Brass Lantern restaurant, where he can keep an eye on the atomic bomb.

Billy Creel

Billy grew up foraging in the Wasteland and was eventually hired on to protect caravans. Life was nothing but profit and survival until he came across Maggie. After killing the raiders who had massacred Maggie's parents, he took her under his wing. He brought Maggie to Megaton and helped fend off a Raider attack. He was given the house of a settler who was shot in the attack. There are a few around town who say that Billy was the one behind the bullet that bought him his place in Megaton.

Maggie

Billy Creel took in Maggie at the age of 3 (she is now 12) and brought her to Megaton. Maggie remembers nothing of her life before Megaton.

Nathaniel Vargas

Nathan, 65, ran a caravan route for over 30 years with his wife, Manya. During that time, he became a little obsessed with the Enclave broadcasts on the radio. Since then, Nathan has become a bit of a fanatic, believing that the Enclave will bring salvation to the Wasteland and is trying to convince everyone else in Megaton of this fact. Most of the residents write Nathan off as the local busybody, but all are quick to note that after 30 years on the

back of a wagon, he is one hell of a shot when it comes to gunplay.

Manya

Manya, 64, is a sweet old lady. She and Nathan used to run a caravan line together and have managed to save enough Caps and supplies to live out their retirement in Megaton. Manya's sweet exterior doesn't reveal that she's witnessed every misery that the Wasteland has to offer. She is extremely wise and knowledgeable—two traits that allow her to continue to thrive and live in Megaton.

Lucy West

Lucy, 25, struck out on her own and headed for the "big city," leaving the small settlement of Arefu and finding her way to Megaton, where she currently resides. Even though Lucy is far from home, she misses her folks and her younger brother, Ian West. She frequently communicates with them via letters she sends there, but as of late, they haven't replied, and she fears that either they are in trouble or the letters simply aren't getting through.

Jenny Stahl

Jenny, 24, is the balancing force between her polar-opposite brothers. She very much has eyes for Billy Creel and he for her, which is why Billy often comes to the restaurant to eat. Like her brothers, Jenny was born in Megaton in the days before the fence. She took over the restaurant with her brothers when her father died.

Andy Stahl

Andy, 23, seems to be very quiet and reserved, which serves his role as the business manager of the restaurant. He is actually extremely crafty and manipulative. Unbeknownst to his brother and sister, Andy has been talking to Mister Burke about his insidious plan to blow up Megaton so he can move the restaurant to a better, safer, more lucrative location.

Leo Stahl

Leo, 25, is the more outspoken of the two Stahl brothers. He's the "people person" of the restaurant and loves to talk to the customers. He spent some time on the caravan lines in his teens and has traveled to a few places around the Wasteland. It was during this time that he picked up his addiction to Jet, although he has managed to conceal his addiction from everyone in town, including his own brother and sister.

Jericho

Jericho, 65, was once a Raider, and he lied, stole, and murdered with the best of them. But now he's an old man and, miraculously, is still alive. He was smart enough to settle down in Megaton and leave his old life behind him. He is reluctant to reveal his history for fear someone may try to get revenge. He hangs around Moriarty's, and rumors circulate that Jericho has done a few nasty jobs for the man.

RELATED INTERACTIONS

All settlers: You can inquire about locations in town. All other questions are covered below.

A TOUR AROUND MEGATON

1 Sheriff Lucas Simms's Shack

Sheriff Simms's place is locked. Simms's son Harden is sometimes inside here or playing with Maggie. Downstairs is a small amount of food. Upstairs, there are the items listed below, but up in Lucas's bedroom is the real prize: a Bobblehead: Strength! Take this without penalty. For a spectacular view of Megaton, go through the ceiling hatch just behind the stairs on the upper floor; this leads to the fuselage balcony.

Although you'll turn the town Hostile, the sheriff is wearing a Unique hat and coat; take them if you wish.

- Sledgehammer
- Hunting Rifle
- Bobblehead: Strength (18/20)
- Sheriff's Duster (51/89)
- Sheriff's Hat (52/89)

2 Water Processing Plant

Walter is usually taking a smoke break outside or is inside tinkering. Speak to him, and you can begin **Freeform Quest: Treatment**. The interior of the plant is compact. In the back room is Leo Stahl's desk; you can speak with him about his drug problem (Freeform Quest) or break open the desk. Unless you have a hankering for Crispy Squirrel Bits, ignore Walter's sleeping quarters adjacent to the office.

3 Craterside Supply

Arrive during business hours so the place is open, and you're warmly greeted by Moira Brown (and less so by her bodyguard, who wants to be left out of "that girl's crazy experiments"). You can begin **Miscellaneous Quest: The Wasteland Survival Guide** here, as well as Repairing and Trading. A quick rummage reveals a Holotape: The Replicated Man behind the counter.

There's a 10mm Pistol to steal, a Work Bench to tinker on, and a shelf stocked with food. Hack Moira's terminal. You can read her Survival Guide Progress here and track the two experiments she's also attempting. Expect the townsfolk to turn Hostile if you do this and if you pry the Key to Craterside Supplies from Moira's cold, dead fingers: You can open the locker behind the counter and gather all her inventory; note the more exotic items below:

- Work Bench (29/46)
- Holotape: The Replicated Man (13/24)
- 10mm Pistol
- Key to Craterside Supplies
- Schematic: Rock-It Launcher (17/23)

Moira awards you the following collectibles during **Miscellaneous Quest: The Wasteland Survival Guide**:

- Armored Vault 101 Jumpsuit (53/89)
- Shady Hat (54/89)
- Schematic: Bottlecap Mine (18/23)
- Mini-Nuke (48/71)
- Big Book of Science (15/25)
- Lying: Congressional Style (13/25)

④ Megaton Clinic

Doc Church is the physician in charge, and you can purchase medical supplies and heal your wounds or radiation. There are two First Aid Boxes to steal from and three Stimpaks in his shack, a Holotape about the Replicated Man on his desk (which you can talk to the Doc about), and the clinic medical supplies (only accessible if you kill Doc and steal the key). In the back room are two unconscious patients.

- First Aid Box Health and Chems (2)
- Holotape: The Replicated Man (14/24)
- Key to Clinic Medical Supplies

⑤ Children of Atom Church

These believers pray for a special kind of savior. Find out more when you speak with Confessor Cromwell (he's usually standing in the irradiated water by the bomb) or Mother Maya (who's usually inside the church). You can give generously (a Freeform Quest) and ask more about this religion and about the residents of this place. Cromwell has a key on him, but this is only useful for entering the church at night.

- Confessor Cromwell's Key

⑥ The Armory

The place holds the town's supply of weapons and is locked. Break in and expect to be attacked by Deputy Steel, a Mister Gutsy programmed by Lucas. Survive the battle and gather the listed items; hack the armory terminal, where you can deactivate Deputy Steel (and Deputy Weld outside

the gate) instead of combating them. Open a floor safe.

- Hunting Rifle (3)
- Combat Shotgun
- Chinese Assault Rifle (3)
- Floor Safe Items
- 10mm Pistol (2)

⑦ Men's Restroom

Thinking of decorating your house with plungers? Then head here.

⑧ Moriarty's Saloon

Enter Moriarty's Saloon (there's a back entrance, which isn't necessary to pick unless Moriarty's office is locked). This dive is home to more than a few characters. You can ask Nova how much she charges... for a room. You can speak to Carol's son, Gob, who's having reception issues. There's a mysterious man called Mister Burke with a terrifyingly intriguing proposition. You can speak to Moriarty about your father; he knows more than he lets on and possibly gets you to complete a task regarding a runaway prostitute named Silver. Billy Creel might be here, and he tells you about him and his young orphan, Maggie. Finally, Jericho might be swigging a beverage or two when he's not roaming the catwalks.

Gob and Moriarty both have keys to Moriarty's office, allowing access to this room when Moriarty isn't around. There's a terminal here, which you can access with Moriarty's Password (you'll find it on his body) or by hacking. Kill Gob and you obtain Moriarty's Saloon Supply Key, allowing access into the cooler. Amid the large amount of Caps and beer are two odd keys: an Andale Basement Key and an Andale Shed Key. (They reveal a terrible secret over in the town of Andale, once you get there.) Finally, head upstairs, where there are four rooms; two are locked and none have much to take except some items inside a locked cabinet.

Hack into Moriarty's terminal: There are three submenus to read through: Residents, Visitors, and Tabs. The first two are of most interest to you.

Residents

Jericho: He has some dirt on the "Jenny incident." Perhaps you can use this on Jericho too!

Leo Stahl: He's a junkie and part of the Stahl clan with Andy and Jenny.

Andy Stahl: Hated for opening up a rival bar in town. Fortunately, Moriarty still has the best draw around for customers looking for a good time, and it isn't Gob.

Billy Creel: He swigs Nuka-Cola and looks after little orphan Maggie. Moriarty is suspicious of his motives.

Doc Church: The town quack has a secret—he used to tend the wounds of the hated Slavers at Paradise Falls.

Visitors

Mr. Burke: Some weirdo in a sharp suit staying at the saloon, waiting for an "opportunist."

James (Vault 101): He made contact! He's heading to Galaxy News Radio. Shockingly, he met Moriarty 20 years ago, then sought out and entered Vault 101.

- Key to Moriarty's Office (2)
- Moriarty's Password
- Moriarty's Saloon Supply Key
- Caps
- Andale Basement Key
- Andale Shed Key

⑨ Billy Creel's House

It is locked. If Billy isn't in Moriarty's, he's usually here. He wants you to leave, ideally in around 30 seconds before he starts firing. On his body is his Housekey. Also in the house is a well-stocked fridge and the following:

- Billy's Housekey
- Holotape: Song of the Lightman; The Guardians of Gillyfrond
- Scribe Pre-War Book (51–54/98)

⑩ Women's Restroom

Not offering much other than a steak in a bathtub.

⑪ Common House

You'll spot a couple of Megaton Settlers resting or relaxing. This is the only place where you can gather food from a fridge and the odd Whiskey bottle lying around and not worry about stealing. Try Pickpocketing [Sneak] the resting settlers if you're adept enough.

⑫ Nathan and Manya's House

Crafted from the shells of two old buses, Nathan and Manya's house is easy to break into. If you're hungry for Iguana Bits, risk being discovered entering here. Otherwise, talk to Nathan and Manya where you find them; she provides a copious amount of history about Megaton, while he extols the virtues of the Enclave. There's a Holotape: Replicated Man here, and you can talk to Manya about it.

- Holotape: The Replicated Man (15/24)

13 Lucy West's House

When she's not wandering around town or at Moriarty's, Lucy West can be found at her dwelling. Normally, this place is locked, although you can Sneak in and steal her Squirrel Stew and other "delicious" foodstuffs.

14 Mister Burke's House

Within earshot of Confessor Cromwell is a ground-level shack that's difficult to break into—the lock is complex and you're almost always being watched. Try Sneaking with a Stealth Boy. Aside from the Whiskey and Tortoiseshell Glasses, there's a Sawed-Off Shotgun to steal and little else. Burke is usually in Moriarty's, so there's little chance of him coming home.

- Sawed-Off Shotgun

15 Jericho's House

When this old Raider's away from his abode, you can enter his locked home, take the items listed below. These become much easier to obtain if you've hired Jericho as a Follower.

- Chinese Officer's Sword
- 10mm Pistol
- Grognak the Barbarian (14/25)

16 The Brass Lantern

Offering a selection of edible almost-radiation-free food, the Brass Lantern may be contaminated by the nearby atom bomb's groundwater, but business is brisk. Running the outside food court is Jenny Stahl. You can purchase food from her. Head inside, and you can interrupt Andy Stahl while he's eating, and he grudgingly informs you where everything is in town. There's a variety of food and Darts on the counter, but those require stealing. You can speak to Leo Stahl and begin a Freeform Quest. Unlock the floor safe to obtain 300 Caps, and hack the old terminal to read four entries:

Notes on Leo: Andy is noting that Leo seems to be stealing from the place.

Cash Notes: Leo has come up short again this month.

Inventory Notes: They've suffered some "shrink" of stock. Again, Leo is suspected.

FREEFORM QUEST: HOUSE DECORATION IN MY MEGATON HOUSE

17 Empty House/My Megaton House

 The final "empty house" in Megaton is sealed completely and is only available after you complete **Miscellaneous Quest: Power of the Atom** and diffuse the bomb. Sheriff Lucas Simms is most impressed and offers you My Megaton Housekey and the Property Deed: Megaton House. You can now come and go to this location as often as you please, using it as a "base camp." Purchase additional assets from Moira Brown (their prices depend on your Barter skill). The following assets can be managed here:

FEATURE	DESCRIPTION
Bed, Chairs, Tables, and Shelves	Bed for sleeping. Furnishing for display
Promotional Bobblehead Display Case	This holds all the Bobbleheads you have found.
Work Bench	Required for the construction of Schematic-based items.
Mr. Handy "Wadsworth"	A robotic butler that tells jokes, cuts your hair, and pours you a drink.
Scientist theme*	Decorations a laboratory scientist would be at home in
Wasteland Explorer theme	A variety of guns racks and trophies
Vault theme	A taste of home, without the crushing depression and lack of sunlight
Pre-War theme	It's as if you never left Tranquility Lane
Raider theme	Strap on your bondage armor and hang up a corpse
Love Machine theme†	For the discerning manimal or hellcat around town
Jukebox	Streams music around your abode
Pristine Nuka-Cola Machine	Dispenses Ice-Cold Nuka-Colas
My First Laboratory	Dispenses random drugs over time and acts as an automatic drug detox
My First Infirmary	Heals wounds and repairs damaged limbs automatically

> **Note**
> *Nikola Tesla and You (when Scientist theme purchased; 17/25)
> †Lying, Congressional Style (when Love Machine theme purchased; 14/25)

Big Ticket Items

Work Bench (30/46): This functions exactly like a standard Work Bench found elsewhere and allows you to construct Schematic weapons.

Robotic Butler: They can tell you a (usually terrible) random joke; they can dispense Purified Water on command (note that the robot can dispense up to five of these before it needs a week to recharge its "condensation collectors"); they can give you a haircut; and they can explain any house purchase you have bought.

Jukebox: Functions exactly like a standard jukebox found across the Wasteland. The music cannot be selected.

Nuka-Cola Machine: Sierra Petrovida would be proud. This machine comes with eight "Ice-Cold" Nuka-Colas that have Rads +2 and HP +20 (better than warm Nuka-Cola). If you are carrying Nuka-Cola Bottles, you can chill them to become Ice-Cold.

My First Laboratory: This can instantly cure you of any drug addictions, and it can concoct a random compound. This second process takes about a day or so. When you return, the set will dispense a random Chem and then be ready for a new command. Note that while it is "Brewing" (which cannot be interrupted), the detox system is unavailable. The random drug is one of the following: Buffout, Jet, Mentats, Psycho, Med-X, Rad-X, Stimpak, RadAway, or Unpurified Water.

My First Infirmary: Instantly heal yourself to maximum health. Restore any and all damaged limbs or body parts, and remove all Rads.

FREEFORM QUEST: PIOUS GENEROSITY

Seek out Confessor Cromwell or Mother Maya in or around the atom bomb or at the Children of Atom church that they run. Keep the conversation polite, and ask about the church. After hearing the answer, you can ask whether donations are accepted. Naturally, they are. You have three options, each with a positive Karma reward:

 10 Caps donation

50 Caps donation

100 Caps donation

There can be no end to your generosity: This is an excellent way to redeem yourself and shift your Karma back into positive territory if you've done some bad, bag things in your past. Feeling guilty? Let the irradiated water cast out your sins!

TREATMENT

The water treatment plant is beyond Walter's ability to fix it. He hasn't told anyone, but Megaton's water supply is running out. It's a matter of time, but it's going to happen sooner than anyone thinks. With spare parts and some upkeep, the plant's life could be extended for a while. You're tasked with locating and **Repairing** three pipe joints.

Pipe Joint #1 is halfway down the main steps from the entrance, near the Brass Lantern.

Pipe Joint #2 is below the women's restrooms and Nathan and Manya's House.

Pipe Joint #3 is on the roof of the church, just by the large "atom" sign. Leap from Craterside Supplies to reach it.

Return to Walter, and he rewards you with Caps (and 5 XP) and requests you find scrap metal. You can choose to receive 10 Caps for every scrap metal you bring.

Or a simple thank-you for every scrap metal you bring.

- 200 Caps

FREEFORM QUEST: LEO'S DRUG HABIT

Leo Stahl is a Chem addict, a fact that he hides from nearly everyone in town, although Doc Church lets it slip if you have a high enough Medical Skill. Sheriff Lucas also mentions Leo knows about Chems if you use his help to disarm the bomb during **Miscellaneous Quest: The Power of the Atom.** When you're speaking to Leo, pick the dialog choice "I understand you have quite a Chem habit...." From this point on, you have the following options:

Choose "It's okay, Leo. I want to help," then attempt to play on his emotions by telling him he's hurting his family, Jenny, and Andy. If your **Speech** is successful and you don't choose "Never mind, Leo. It's not my business anyway," either of the other choices causes Leo to renounce his destructive lifestyle. He hands you a key to his private stash in the water treatment

plant. Look for the locked desk in the plant and open it (use key). There's a treasure trove inside.

Choose "What's it worth to you to keep it out of the public eye?" Leo quickly tells you he can hook you up, but only after his shift at the Lantern is over. He tells you to meet him at the water treatment plant. Head there after 20:00 hours. Leo is sitting at his desk, offering Buffouts, Jets, Mentats, Med-X, and Stimpaks.

- Leo's Stash Key
- Bottle Caps
- Chems

FREEFORM QUEST: TIME TO GO, JERICHO!

You might overhear the gruff tones of a retired old Raider named Jericho. He's been in more than a few close scrapes. If your Karma is low enough, he recognizes you for the scum you are and can be convinced to resume his life as a terror of the wastes. He'll need 1,000 Caps for "supplies" before he joins you, though.

- Follower: Jericho

8.04: FORT INDEPENDENCE (LAT -06/LONG -13)

- Freeform Quest
- Threat Level: 4
- Faction: Brotherhood Outcast
- Services: Trader
- Collectible: Nuka-Cola Quantum, Fat Man Mini-Nuke (2)
- Area Is Locked
- Guns and Ammunition
- Health and Chems
- Interior Exploration
- Rare Weapon or Item
- Sleep Mattress
- Work Bench
- Hostile: Brotherhood Outcast

INHABITANTS

DEFENDER ANNE MARIE MORGAN

Currently on guard duty, Morgan is a tough, no-nonsense soldier with undying loyalty to her friend and Protector, Henry Casdin. She is growing ever suspicious and exasperated by Elder Lyons's decisions and has left en masse with her brethren. She enjoys beheading Raiders using the latest in archaic laser technology.

DEFENDER ROCOCO ROCKFOWL

Guarding the bridge from Fairfax Ruins is heavy-weapons specialist Rockfowl, who deals with regular Raider incursions in a rather laid-back but extremely competent manner. His father was a voracious reader and named him after reading the Encyclopedia Atomica (Volume VIII Radiology—Saskatchewan).

PROTECTOR HENRY CASDIN

Splitting from Elder Lyons (and stealing technology in the process), Casdin and his fellow warriors were of the opinion that Lyons had "gone native," concerning himself with the troubles of the locals instead of the "greater" mission: the acquisition of technology. Lyons is a joke to Casdin, even a traitor. Lyons hasn't even bothered to get his giant robot working, let alone continue the search for technology. In Casdin's eyes, the Outcasts are the true Brotherhood of Steel, carrying on the mission of the main West Coast contingent.

GENERAL NOTES

Battling Raider incursions in Fairfax Ruins, the Brotherhood Outcasts have a stronghold of their own, a place sealed except for the front entrance. Approach along the road heading north, and you're stopped by Defender Morgan under the bridge defenses. Ask who she is; she collects technology so it doesn't fall into the hands of idiots. She suggests you speak with Protector Henry Casdin (Freeform Quest).

The other way to reach Fort Independence is via the bridge, the location of Defender Rockfowl. You can also pry open the door to Fort Independence or the door to the lower level. Either results in the Outcasts turning immediately Hostile. Or, try Pickpocketing [Sneak] any of the three Outcasts for an Independence Access Key that opens either door.

- Fort Independence Access Key

You can ask Morgan and Casdin about the Outcast's history and background, and you can Trade items with Casdin.

FORT INDEPENDENCE

As soon as you pick the lock and enter Fort Independence, the Outcasts turn Hostile!

1 **Storage Room**
- First Aid Box Health and Chems

2 **Wrecked, Open-Plan Office (Northwest Corner)**
- First Aid Box Health and Chems

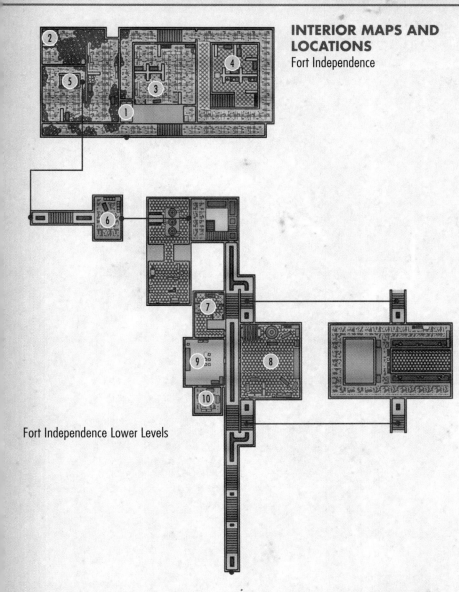

Fort Independence Lower Levels

INTERIOR MAPS AND LOCATIONS
Fort Independence

⑨ Western Lab

There are six research terminals; each has a note with pertinent combat information, which you can load into your Pip-Boy.

- Research Note: Enclave Armor, Laser Rifle, Minigun, Missile Launcher, Plasma Rifle, Pulse Grenade

⑩ Storage Weapons Cache

The locked hatch door allows access to steal these exceptional items:

- Ammo Box Ammunition (5)
- "Miss Launcher" Missile Launcher (55/89)
- Minigun
- Laser Rifle and Ammo
- Plasma Rifle and Ammo
- First Aid Box Health and Chems (3)
- Mini-Nuke (49 & 50/71)

FREEFORM QUEST: THE OUTCAST COLLECTION AGENT

Protector Henry Casdin speaks to you if you've been polite to Defender Morgan. He okays a set of tasks involving the location of technology in return for payment; relics like Power Armor and Power Cells are what Casdin needs. The resulting trade amount is greater than any other regular Trader but are specific to Power Armor, Power Armor Helmet, Laser Rifle, Plasma Rifle, Plasma Pistol, Pulse Grenade, Alien Blaster, Alien Power Cell, Enclave Power Armor, Enclave Power Armor Helmet, Tesla Armor, Sensor Unit, and Scrap Metal.

Casdin wouldn't normally be talking to outsiders, but he makes an exception with you and opens the fort's front gate. For each item you bring, you receive .556 Ammo, Frag Grenades, Stimpaks, or RadAway. You can also speak to Casdin about the Brotherhood of Steel (on the West Coast), the Lyons Brotherhood (whom Casdin despises), and the Outcasts themselves.

Note

Make sure you bring back something from the Crashed Anomaly [2.G]; it might really excite Protector Casdin!

③ Barracks

There are bunk beds, food in the fridge and on the shelves, and a Nuka-Cola Quantum on the table.

- Nuka-Cola Quantum (56/94)

④ Eastern Office Area

There are two locked safes and a terminal containing field reports to read. There are two entries: <Data Log—Prot. Casdin> and <Data Log—Def. Rockfowl>; they transfer to your Pip-Boy as audio notes.

- Floor Safe Items (2)
- Note: Fort Independence Field Report 1 (Information on the constant Raider attacks at Fairfax Ruins. An intelligence leak has occurred! The research personnel must be protected.)
- Note: Fort Independence Field Report 2 (A recon mission was launched to gauge Raider entrenchment. Three utility tunnels were found as well as a small weapons cache in southwest of tunnels.)

⑤ Entrance to Lower Level

Hack a wall terminal or use the Fort Independence Access Key.

FORT INDEPENDENCE LOWER LEVEL

⑥ Turret Terminal

Disengage the turret here.

⑦ Barracks

⑧ Eastern Laboratory

There's a Work Bench with a Bottlecap Mine in here.

- Work Bench (31/46)
- First Aid Box Health and Chems (4)

8.05: FAIRFAX RUINS (LAT -04/ LONG -12)

- Threat Level: 3
- Faction: Raider
- Danger: Grenade Bouquet (3), Low Radiation, Mines, Shotgun Trap
- Collectible: Skill Book
- Guns and Ammunition
- Health and Chems
- Interior Exploration
- Sleep Mattress
- Hostile: Raider

TRAINING — BESTIARY — MAIN QUEST — MISC. QUESTS — TOUR — COMPLETION — APPENDICES

Metro and Utility Tunnel Opening

Although this Raider stronghold can be approached from any direction, you should travel along main street from east to west, as you're on higher ground with more shooting or Sneaking options. About a block in from the intact buildings is a north–south road, and at the southern end is a large brick building with Raider graffiti on the side and a doorway. Sneak through and up the stairs of this shell to reach an upper area with a Raider guarding four boxes of Ammo and some Chems. You can tag Raiders down a long east–west alley running parallel of the main drag.

- Ammo Box Ammunition (4)

Back on the ground floor, run around the corner to the metro station entrance. Don't enter until you cross the street heading north and run around the large concrete building into an alley, where you find a trash bin and three Ammo Boxes. Head west, then north

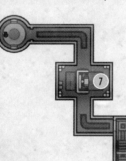

around the corner, and snipe the remaining Raiders across the street, near the metro station. You can lob Grenades or fire on foes below you as the road dips down below the concrete buttress you're on. This clears out the majority of the Raiders on the surface.

- Ammo Box Ammunition (3)

Inspect the metro entrance and the utility tunnel entrance, which is a grating that falls down, leaving you no method of climbing back up (if you step on the edge, the grating falls, but you remain on the concrete). There are two manhole covers around, too, but they serve as exit points if you're following the optimal route through the tunnels. Beware of the Grenade Traps; there are two trip wires just to the side of the utility

INTERIOR MAPS AND LOCATIONS
Fairfax Metro Station

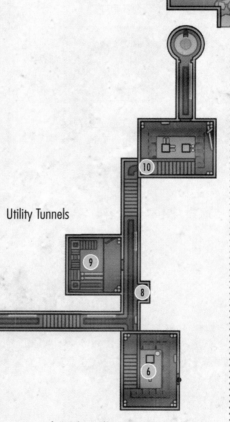

Utility Tunnels

grating; if you hit either one, Grenades tumble out of the air-conditioning vents and explode. Disarm the wires instead. There are now two separate underground areas to explore, a self-contained metro station, and the utility tunnels. Try the station first.

FAIRFAX METRO STATION

① Entrance Concourse

Look at the ground for two Mines and disarm them.

- Frag Mines (2)

② Grenade Bouquet

- Frag Grenades (3)

③ Mezzanine Turnstile Trip Wire and Ticket Booth

Watch for the Rigged Shotgun trap.

- Combat Shotgun and Ammo
- First Aid Box Health and Chems (2)
- Ammo Box Ammunition (2)

④ Small Raider Camp

Tear through here; locate a mattress and grab Chems, food from the fridge, and the following:

- Ammo Box Ammunition (2)

⑤ Skill Book

This is on the rubble between two wrecked carriages to the east.

- Chinese Army: Spec. Ops. Training Manual (9/25)

UTILITY TUNNELS

This assumes you entered via the grating trapdoor near the metro station entrance.

⑥ Weapons Storage Room

Grab the following items, then activate the switch to open the flap-trap door.

- Sawed-Off Shotgun (2)
- 10mm Pistol (2)
- Frag Grenade (2)
- Ammo Box Ammunition (6)
- First Aid Box Health and Chems

⑦ Generator Room

Disarm the Frag Mine so it doesn't blow the generator up.

- Frag Mine

⑧ Corridor Alcove

- First Aid Box Health and Chems (2)

9 Flooded Stairwell

10 Flap-Trap Door Chamber

Disarm the Frag Mine so you're not caught in the blast.

- Frag Mine

8.06: CLIFFSIDE CAVERN (LAT -10/ LONG -17)

- Threat Level: 4
- Faction: Raider
- Danger: Grenade Bouquet, Low Radiation, Mines, Shotgun Trap
- Collectible: Fat Man Mini-Nuke, Nuka-Cola Quantum, Scribe Pre-War Book, Schematic, Skill Book
- Guns and Ammunition
- Health and Chems
- Interior Exploration
- Sleep Mattress
- Hostile: Raider, Yao Guai

MAPS AND LOCATIONS
Raider Outpost

Yao Guai Cave

Amid some treacherous craggy rocks overlooking an impressive vista, locate a small trail leading down to a cave entrance festooned with chains, graffiti, and tricycles. There are Raiders in this cave system, but you're not the only one mauling them and eating their boxed edibles. Enter here or search farther up the crags for an optional second entrance.

RAIDER OUTPOST (GROUND LEVEL)
You can enter this location from either cave entrance.

1 Raider Decoration

You're greeted by a dead body through which a skull and cave light has been stuck.

2 Rigged Shotgun Trap

- Combat Shotgun and Ammo

3 Generators Platform

- Nuka-Cola Quantum (57/94)

4 Large Oval Cavern

There's food, beer, and spirits in here. Watch out for the Grenade Bouquet.

- First Aid Box Health and Chems
- Frag Grenade (3)

5 Smaller Adjacent Cavern (Raider Recreation Area)

There's junk, a Skill Book, some cabinets, and a footlocker. There is also a maniac with a Missile Launcher to dodge inside the tent to the west. Check the tent for two safes and a cabinet that contain the following:

- Chinese Army: Spec. Ops. Training Manual (10/25)
- Missile Launcher
- Scribe Pre-War Book (55/98)
- Mini-Nuke (51/71)

UPPER LEVEL

6 Sandbags and Flaming Barrel Defenses

- Ammo Box Ammunition (2)
- First Aid Box Health and Chems

7 Sandbags and Generator Defenses

Disarm the Frag Mine before it explodes and sends the Skill Book flying!

- Frag Mine
- Ammo Box Ammunition
- Grognak the Barbarian (15/25)

8 Eastern Tunnel

Disarm two more Frag Mines here. The exit door leads outside.

- Frag Mine (2)

9 Upper Trail

Disarm three more Frag Mines in this vicinity.

- Frag Mine (3)

10 Raider and Yao Guai Battle

YAO GUAI CAVE

11 Tunnel to Main Chamber

There are three Frag Mines to watch for as you head through.

- Frag Mine (3)

12 Southeastern Cache

- Ammo Box Ammunition
- Combat Shotgun

13 Fungus Cave

14 Northwest Skeleton Pile

- Schematic: Nuka Grenade (19/23)

8.07: ANDALE (LAT -05/LONG -17)

- Threat Level: 3
- Faction: Wastelander
- Collectible: Skill Book
- Interior Exploration
- Perk!
- Rare or Powerful Item

INHABITANTS
Jack, Linda, and Junior Smith

House-proud and vehemently opposed to outside influences, the Smiths are a strange but reasonably friendly bunch. Jack seems to be the settlement's patriarch, and he knows the best little town in America is here, where Linda bakes a delicious meat pie!

Bill "Willie," Martha, and Jenny Wilson

Bill and Martha live next door to the Smiths, and they're delighted that their daughter Jenny and Junior Smith get along so well. Bill spends most days in the Shed or Smith house basement working with Jack on the "family business." They all agree that Andale is the place to be!

TRAINING — BESTIARY — MAIN QUEST — MISC. QUESTS — TOUR — COMPLETION — APPENDICES

EXTERIOR MAP AND LOCATIONS
Andale

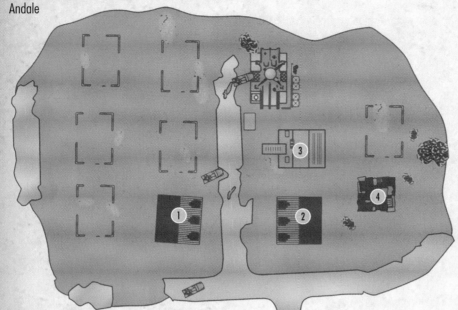

Old Man Harris

The Smiths and Wilson would prefer you take no notice of this elderly kook, who lives in his rundown shack. He's obviously a lunatic, and reeks of cheap alcohol.

Initial Interactions

Andale Residents: You can ask about the place and how great it is living in America's best town.

Jack Smith: You can ask him about Andale (which apparently is still in Virginia) and about voting for a governor. You can also receive an invitation for dinner.

Linda Smith: You can ask her about Andale, "the best little town there is."

Junior Smith: You can ask how he likes living in Andale.

Martha Wilson: You can ask what she thinks of Andale. She's surprised, as no one ever asks her opinion on anything.

Bill Wilson: You can ask what he does around here. He feeds his family and loves his wife and daughter.

Old Man Harris: He tells you to leave immediately. Ask him what's wrong and whether the families are friendly.

GENERAL NOTES

Welcome to Andale, winner of the Best Town in the USA contest. At least, that's what the two families who live here want you to believe. While the rest of the settlement of ruins is devoid of items (aside from the mailboxes), there are three intact structures, which house the Smith and Wilson

families, plus Old Man Harris, who's a bit of a kook. You may run into Junior Smith or Jenny Wilson, the two kids, playing outside.

> **Note**
> Moriarty's Saloon in Megaton has a couple of keys you might find useful if you don't want to grab them from this location.

① The Smith House

The Smith's House has a couple of cabinets, some Abraxo Cleaner in the fridge, and more in the bath. Upstairs is a Baseball Bat and other items in Junior's room, while there's an Andale Basement Key on the side table in the master bedroom. Be sure to snag this key and use it to enter the basement, where...dear God, the stench!

The basement is evidence that the Smith family could be this year's "most psychotic townsfolk," with sections of Wastelander corpses strewn everywhere. There are two Rippers, two Combat Knives, two Baseball Bats, two well-stocked fridges (with Abraxo, naturally), and a Grognak the Barbarian, for when you want to read the funnies after a hard day's dismemberment.

- Grognak the Barbarian (16/25)

② The Wilson House and ③ Shed

The Wilson abode is similarly appointed, although it doesn't feature a basement. The kitchen is immaculate. No prizes for guessing what's in the fridge or bathroom. Upstairs, there are more cabinets to search,

and on the table in the master bedroom is an Andale Shed Key. Grab it; it's worth taking the Karma hit to uncover why these families are so chipper. Enter the shed, and you're greeted with the same delightful decorations as the basement, although the meat isn't as fresh. There's two Combat Knives and Rippers here.

④ Old Man Harris's House

There's a theme in this house: alcohol. Grab the Whiskey if you need it, then check out the fridge; there's actual food in there! Other than that, the place is empty, aside from a footlocker in the bedroom.

FREEFORM QUEST: OUR LITTLE SECRET
FREEFORM QUEST: ONE BIG HAPPY FAMILY

A spot of investigative work is in order. Talk to any resident about how great it is to live here. Get on Jack Smith's good side, and you receive an invitation for dinner. Head outside and speak to Junior; ask what his parents do for a living. He mentions two items of interest:

Our Little Secret: His dad and Bill work on the "family business" in either the Smith's basement or the Wilson's shed.

One Big Happy Family: Junior says he doesn't want to marry little Jenny Wilson. Especially as his dad and Jenny's were brothers!

Both the Smith basement and the Wilson shed are locked. Although you can pry the lock open, a much easier plan is to steal the Andale Basement Key from the Smith master bedroom and the Andale Shed Key from the Wilson master bedroom. They are both on a side table. Or, you can Pickpocket a key each from Smith and Wilson.

> **Note**
> You might already have picked up both these keys if you killed Gob back in Megaton, got his key, and ransacked Moriarty's Cooler.

Go into either the basement or the shed. When you return outside, Jack Smith is waiting, and all four of the adults are armed. Jack asks if you found what you were looking for in there. For a friendly response, choose:

Use **Speech** to bluff your way out of this by stating you were there for a snack. Jack is happy you're not bothered about the family's "needs" for sustenance, and he recommends you speak with Linda for one of her special pies.

Or, admit you were in the shed or basement. Then reply that there were a bunch of bodies in there. Then you can try:

 This is a much easier **Speech** Challenge, where you state, "Everyone does what they have to." That pleases Jack, and he tells you to grab a slice of Linda's special pies.

Any other chatter or failure of Speech Challenge results in combat.

One big happy family ending: Once you're friendly with the "two" families, ask Martha Wilson about that old coot Harris. She accidentally reveals she's his daughter! This means that the two families are, in fact, the four children of Harris, making Junior and Jenny…no, it's too terrifying to work out!

Our little secret ending #1: If you're happy that the families are gnawing on hapless Wastelanders, you can leave them to it. Grandpa is locked up in his house, but before you go, speak with Linda Smith. She has a hot steaming pie, made from the finest ingredients! Feast away; it's very nutritious! Well, actually it isn't, but you can come back once every 24 hours to get another slice. Yum!

- Strange Meat Pie

Our little secret ending #2: If you threatened the families or couldn't stand the thought of them murdering any more innocent folk, kill all four of them. Then head to see Old Man Harris, who actually thanks you for killing his kids; he can now raise Jenny and Junior without them knowing the full horror of their parents and the taste for human flesh that once acquired, can never be satiated!

8.08: RED RACER FACTORY (LAT 02/ LONG -15)

- Miscellaneous Quest: The Nuka-Cola Challenge
- Freeform Quest
- Threat Level: 4
- Faction: Ghoul, Super Mutant
- Danger: Low Radiation
- Collectible: Nuka Cola Quantum, Collectible: Skill Book (3)
- Guns and Ammunition
- Health and Chems
- Interior Exploration
- Rare or Powerful Item (2)
- Sleep Mattress
- Work Bench
- Hostile: Ghoul Genus, Stefan, The Surgeon, Super Mutant Genus

On the outer western edge of the D.C. Interior is a large factory that used to manufacture cute little Red Racer Tricycles. Production stopped 200 years ago, and the place is remarkably intact, especially as the surrounding area is so dilapidated. It is said that the factory is home to a mad

scientist who works on radiation experiments and keeps an army of radio-controlled Ghouls and Muties to protect the place.

There are a few Raiders outside, and if you've already visited the Nuka-Cola factory, there's a trio of Raiders called the Sudden Death Overtime Gang here to bargain with you (**Freeform Quest: Just for the Taste of It**). Check the nearby trucks for some interesting swag [8.Y] before you enter via the double metal doors.

FACTORY FLOOR

The factory floor in question is in the middle of this area, surrounded by offices. Check the foyer and desk first; there are four doorways to choose from.

① Southern Conveyor Belt Room

Look up to see a giant teddy bear riding a tricycle! Stack barrels and jump up onto the metal pod building to reach it, some Mentats, and a Skill Book; or use explosives to blow it down.

- Giant Teddy Bear (57/89)
- Dean's Electronics (13/25)

② Southwest Office

There's a Carton of Cigarettes and a wall safe here.

- Floor Safe Items

③ Dark Factory Area (North)

Check the raised bookcase area.

- Ammo Box Ammunition (2)

INTERIOR MAPS AND LOCATIONS

CEO Offices

Factory Floor

TRAINING — BESTIARY — MAIN QUEST — MISC. QUESTS — TOUR — COMPLETION — APPENDICES

④ **North East–West Linking Corridor**

Locate the trash bin.

- Ammo Box Ammunition

⑤ **North Conveyor Belt Chamber**

Climb to the higher catwalk and look for two turbine-style generators atop one of the lower pods. Look for some clutter, jump down there, and use the stepladder to climb between the turbines; there's a Skill Book under a bucket.

- D.C. Journal of Internal Medicine (16/25)

⑥ **Work Bench Alcove**

There's a Bottlecap Mine and Grenades here, near two water fountains.

- Work Bench (32/46)
- Frag Grenades (2)

⑦ **Western Cafeteria**

Ransack the place for two Cartons of Cigarettes, food in the fridge, and First Aid Box Health and Chems.

⑧ **Northeast Restroom (Upper Catwalk)**

- Ammo Box Ammunition
- First Aid Box Health and Chems

⑨ **Office (Upper Catwalk)**

There's a safe in here.

- Safe Items

⑩ **Precarious Planks**

Move southwest to the broken catwalk leading to the CEO Offices door; fight the tough old Ghoul here and head inside.

CEO OFFICES

⑪ **North Office**

Inspect the area for a Chip Broadcast Terminal. There are two entries; one mentions that this terminal will detonate all "chips," implanted into some crazy scientist's "experiments." You can disable the chips: All enemies' heads explode!

- Ammo Box Ammunition

⑫ **South Locked Storage Room**

There's a Carton of Cigarettes in here, as well as the following:

- Ammo Box Ammunition (3)
- First Aid Box Health and Chems
- Nikola Tesla and You (18/25)

⑬ **Open Staircase Chamber**

- Ammo Box Ammunition (3)

⑭ **Sparking Generator Room (South)**

Locate the wrench and a terminal with surgeon's notes on it. There are two entries to read here:

Entry 2R-A0: The scientist is experiencing overheating problems with his chip prototypes.

Entry 64D-A3: The Super Mutants are excellent at being controlled, despite their size.

- Ammo Box Ammunition

⑮ **The Surgeon's Laboratory**

Meet the madman at the top of this factory! Engage the surgeon, who isn't willing to chat about those mind-controlling experiments. When dispatched, a cage door flies open, revealing the surgeon's assistant— Stefan! Back up and blast him, then make a thorough search of his laboratory (yes, that includes the shotgun ammo in the bath). There's a Carton of Cigarettes, Chems, food in the fridge, and a Nuka-Cola Quantum in Stefan's cage. The surgeon's corpse also contains his Lab Coat and a key that opens both safes. Before you leave, check his terminal. You can disable the surgeon's test subjects from here, too, and read notes on Stefan.

- Ammo Box Ammunition (2)
- First Aid Box Health and Chems
- The Surgeon's Lab Coat (58/89)
- The Surgeon's Key
- Floor and Wall Safe (2)
- Sledgehammer
- Nuka-Cola Quantum (58/94)

8.09: THE OVERLOOK DRIVE-IN (LAT -08/ LONG -18)

- Threat Level: 3
- Faction: Raider
- Danger: Low Radiation
- Guns and Ammunition
- Health and Chems
- Hostile: Raider, Raider Guard Dog

GENERAL NOTES

There's a small Raider party smelling up the place; inflict massive damage on them, optionally blasting the parked car shells so they all explode in a gargantuan fireball. Then grab these items behind the ruined projector booth:

- First Aid Box Health and Chems
- Ammo Box Ammunition

8.10: NUKA-COLA PLANT (LAT -01/ LONG -19)

- Miscellaneous Quest: The Nuka-Cola Challenge
- Freeform Quest
- Threat Level: 3
- Danger: Gas Leak!, Low Radiation
- Collectible: Nuka-Cola Quantum (3), Skill Book (5)
- Guns and Ammunition
- Health and Chems
- Interior Exploration
- Lots o' Caps
- Hostile: Nuka-Cola Security Protectron, Nukalurk, Radroach

INHABITANTS

Goalie Ledoux, Winger Gervais, Winger Mercier (Deceased), Centre Dubois

Members of the Sudden Death Overtime Gang, obsessed with an ancient ice sport that Goalie Ledoux's ancestors played. Winger Mercier was sent to procure a secret formula for a new type of Nuka-Cola while Ledoux made contact with the buyer. Mercier's been gone an awfully long time....

Milo, Shipping Foreman

The latest in robotic bookkeeping and shipment launching, Milo is a proud employee of the Nuka-Cola corporation. Currently, he's waiting for additional shipping instructions from a Nuka-Cola employee with proper ID.

GENERAL NOTES

This large factory has a familiar iconic logo: the delicious and only partially irradiated Nuka-Cola! There's a courtyard with a crumbling fountain and giant Nuka-Cola bottle, and there are some parked trucks at the property's rear [8.AA]. The only entrance is into the factory floor, on the structure's north side.

INTERIOR MAPS AND LOCATIONS
Factory Floor

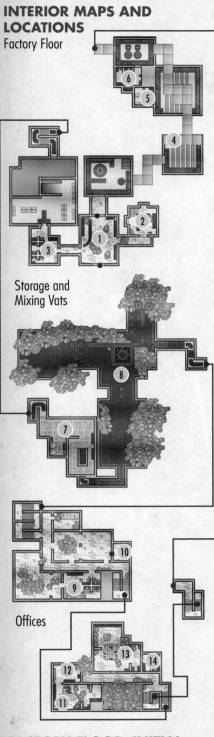

Storage and Mixing Vats

Offices

FACTORY FLOOR: INITIAL SWEEP (SOUTH AND WESTERN AREAS)

1 Foyer

There are locked doors ahead. Look in the ceiling for a filing cabinet holding a Skill Book.

- First Aid Box Health and Chems
- Chinese Army: Spec. Ops. Training Manual (11/25)

---

2 Large East Office

- Deans Electronics (14/25)

3 Research Office

Pick one of the computers to access. There are five entries to read:

Company Announcement: The first shipments of Quantum have left the plant as part of the flagship test market program.

Quantum Progress Report 0067: The test subjects have very low side-effect issues; only three cases of dizziness, one of nausea, and one impaired vision.

Quantum Progress Report 0055: Isotope CE772 is too damaging to be used in test subjects, especially after all those internal organ failures.

Quantum Progress Report 0041: Isotope CE770 is disastrous; all subjects suffered internal organ failure and death. "Nuka Condolences" Fruit and Cheese packages were immediately sent to grieving families.

New Flavor Coming!: With only minimal loss of life, Nuka-Cola Clear has been perfected!

There is also a wall safe here that requires the Research Dept. Safe Key to access; inside is the Nuka-Cola Clear Formula.

- Nuka-Cola Clear Formula

FACTORY FLOOR (NORTHERN AREAS)

This is accessed via the double metal doors in the foyer or from the offices after you move through the storage and mixing vats.

4 Upper Corridor

- First Aid Box Health and Chems

5 Packing Line Terminal and Office

Access the Packing Line Terminal. There are six options, but the only ones that work are "Load Quantum into Sorting Unit" and then "Activate Packing Line." The packing lines are jammed, but the conveyor belt still deposits three Nuka-Cola Quantums for you to take.

- Nuka-Cola (59-61/94)

6 Milo's Office

Milo the Shipping Foreman. He wants identification:

 You can refer to yourself as John-Caleb Bradberton, owner of the place. If you succeed, Milo believes you and gives detailed instructions to the shipping manifests and more Quantum information.

Or, you can present the Employee ID that you found in the Workshop 7. This satisfies Milo, and you can ask for the Terminal Data Module and Key.

Otherwise, you'll need to quickly retreat before you're toasted by Milo's flamer attack. Fight back, and claim the password from Milo's remains. You can also claim the Research Dept. Safe Key.

Check the door at the back, accessing a safe and a copy of Tumblers Today. Then check the Shipping Terminal. Use the data module to download shipping manifests, which show three locations where Quantums are likely to be: Paradise Falls [2.08], Super-Duper Mart [9.01], and Old Olney Grocery [3.02]. This information isn't entirely accurate, as you'll discover if you explore those places.

- Terminal Data Module
- Research Dept. Safe Key
- Shelf Safe Items
- Tumblers Today (16/25)

STORAGE AND MIXING VATS

7 Workshop

Beware the strange blue Mirelurks known as Nukalurks! Optionally access the Automated Maintenance Terminal, which allows you to release a Protectron into harm's way and grab the Welcome to the Nuka-Cola Family! note. This has an Employee ID you can use to satisfy Milo.

- Laser Pistol and Ammo
- Note: Welcome to the Nuka-Cola Family: Employee ID

8 Vats

Utilize the ruined catwalks to reach the exit in the west wall, leading into the offices.

OFFICES (FLOOR 1)

9 South Office

This has two Marketing Terminals, with the same information on them. The terminal information consists of four entries:

Company Announcement: This is the pat on the back you previously read in the research office.

Stage One: A television teaser campaign is discussed; the tag line will be "Try something new...Go Blue!"

TRAINING — BESTIARY — MAIN QUEST — MISC. QUESTS — TOUR — COMPLETION — APPENDICES

Stage Two: The second stage of the campaign is revealed: "Take the leap...enjoy a Quantum!"

Stage Three: Hired actors will fake "taste tests" and choose Nuka-Cola over competing brands.

⑩ Locked Storage Room

This is a storage room with two skeletons, one sitting next to a note reading "Help Me."

- First Aid Box Health and Chems (2)
- Note: Help Me

FLOOR 2

⑪ Large Office with Missing Floor

Head to the fallen mercenary called Winger Mercier, grab the Stealth Boy near him, and search him. You find a usual array of items and a note called "Finding the Formula" and a note from Goalie Ledoux about Nuka-Cola Clear; this begins the Freeform Quest in this area.

- Note: Finding the Formula
- First Aid Box Health and Chems

⑫ Western Server Room

Check the table for the Skill Book.

- Big Book of Science (16/25)

⑬ Middle Office

You'll find two more Marketing Terminals.

⑭ Eastern Office

- First Aid Box Health and Chems
- Lying: Congressional Style (15/25)

FREEFORM QUEST: JUST FOR THE TASTE OF IT

First, find Winger Mercier's body, which has the location of a drop-off where his posse—the Sudden Death Overtime Gang—are waiting for the formula to Nuka-Cola Clear. Move to the Research Dept. Safe, and open it using the key you took from Milo's corpse. Take the Nuka-Cola Clear Formula, and travel north to the Red Racer Tricycle Factory. Hold your fire as you reach the factory

forecourt entrance. Goalie Ledoux stops you and speaks for Winger Gervais and Centre Dubois. Agree to sell him the formula, under certain conditions:

> You can increase the price to 400 Caps, and Ledoux can grin through his tombstone teeth and bear it.

Or, you can settle on 250 Caps.

Or, you can shoot everybody on Ledoux's team and grab the formula back. There's no Karma loss, but no one else wants to buy the formula. This has the added benefit of allowing you to ransack Goalie Ledoux's corpse. Pry his Hockey Mask off; it's well worth it!

- Up to 400 Caps
- Goalie Ledoux's Hockey Mask (56/89)

Secondary Locations

8.A: JURY STREET TUNNELS (BLOCKED; LAT -13/LONG -04)

- Threat Level: 5
- Faction: Super Mutant
- Danger: Low Radiation
- Hostile: Super Mutant Genus

If the Jury Street Tunnels [5.13] were excavated, they would surface at this point. In this irradiated dust, slay the two Super Mutants. The pickings they are guarding could be categorized as "slim."

However, if you've successfully completed **Mini-Encounter 004: Searching for Cheryl**, this is the conclusion location. A Super Mutant Behemoth appears once you investigate the container. The pickings are now categorized as "Nuketastic!"

8.B: RADIO MAST OSCAR TANGO AND HAMLET (LAT -11/LONG -05)

8.C: DRAINAGE CHAMBER (LAT -11/LONG -04)

- Threat Level: 1
- Faction: Raider
- Collectibles: Scribe Pre-War Book, Skill Book
- Highly Visible Landmark
- Interior Exploration
- Radio Signal
- Sleep Mattress
- Hostile: Raider

INTERIOR MAPS AND LOCATIONS

Drainage Chamber

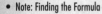

Technically the southern part of Jury Street [5.13], there's a radio mast to switch on after you unlock the gate and activate the electrical switch. Listen to Radio Signal

Oscar Tango; careful triangulation leads you to a manhole cover [8.C] on the road, near one of the houses.

- Radio Signal Oscar Tango

① Raider Attack!

You may be attacked by two Raiders before you reach the door.

② Ransacked Room

There are scattered food packs, Darts, some Purified Water, as well as a radio table with two books. Don't leave yet; there's also a switch that opens a flap-trap door in the middle of the room, which leads down to...actually, it's better you do leave now.

- Scribe Pre-War Book (56/98)
- Big Book of Science (17/25)

8.D: MILITARY TRUCK CHECKPOINT (LAT -07/LONG -05)

- Threat Level: 2
- Hostile: Molerat, Robot Genus, Yao Gai

There's a large "Enlist!" poster and a military truck next to it.

- Ammo Box Ammunition (3)
- Assault Rifle

8.E: RUINED FARMHOUSE (LAT -06/LONG -04)

- Threat Level: 1
- Faction: Wastelander
- Services: Repairer, Trader
- Collectibles: Fat Man Mini-Nuke

- Guns and Ammunition
- Scavenger
- Scavenger's Dog
- Hostile: Robot Genus

There are three structures to this dwelling on the hill above Vault 101, as well as the farmhouse, which contains a Scavenger and his dog. Trade or Repair items here, and check both floors for the following:

- Mini-Nuke (52/71)
- Hunting Rifle and Ammo

8.F: FREEWAY DRAIN (LAT -05/LONG -04)

South of the Freeway Raider Camp [5.AA] near Vault 101 is this large sewer drain. Although big, you can't enter it.

8.G: RUINED FARMHOUSE (LAT 02/LONG -04)

- Threat Level: 2
- Faction: Enclave
- Collectible: Skill Book
- Guns and Ammunition

By the remains of a road leading down to the river is a ruined farmhouse with a silo and windmill. The Enclave set up a Camp [E8.01] here when they arrive. The real interest lies in the skeletal remains inside the house, guarding a Carton of Cigarettes, which you can Barter for real cash, and the following:

- Ammo Box Ammunition
- Chinese Army: Spec. Ops. Training Manual (12/25)

8.H: WATER TOWER (LAT 02/LONG -05)

- Threat Level: 1
- Highly Visible Landmark

Across from the dead Brahmin pasture is this large landmark. You can slurp water from the faucet here, but there are better ways to get a drink.

8.I: JACKKNIFED TRUCK (LAT -12/LONG -07)

- Threat Level: 1
- Collectible: Skill Book
- Guns and Ammunition

Just off the road leading south from Jury Street township is a rusting truck with Darts and the following items in its trailer:

- Ammo Box Ammunition (2)
- U.S. Army: 30 Flame-thrower Recipes (12/25)

8.J: CAPTAIN COSMOS BILLBOARD (LAT -06/LONG -08)

- Threat Level: 1

When you're trekking southwest from Megaton, use this and the local road to situate yourself.

8.K: CRUMBLING STATUARY (LAT 03/LONG -08)

- Threat Level: 1

On the northwest outskirts of Graydirch [9.09] next to the Sewer Waystation [9.03] is a monument to false pride.

8.L: INDEPENDENCE HAMLET (LAT -11/LONG -09)

- Threat Level: 2
- Faction: Wastelander
- Danger: Low Radiation
- Collectible: Scribe Pre-War Book

- Hostile: Radscorpion Genus

A small collection of derelict properties northwest of Fort Independence are slowly disintegrating by the murkpools. The ruined house to the southeast has a waiting Scavenger and his dog, plus a selection of items to Trade. The Scavenger also offers a Repair service. There's a Pre-War Book to steal from his table too. In a couple houses to the northwest, there are a few Caps on a bookcase.

- Scribe Pre-War Book (57/98)

8.M: INDEPENDENCE RUINS (LAT -09/LONG -11)

- Threat Level: 1
- Hostile: Bloatfly

Close to Fort Independence by the large Vault-Tec billboard is another group of destroyed dwellings. Unlike Independence Hamlet, there are no items to find among the rubble.

8.N: RUINED HOUSE (LAT 00/LONG -10)

- Threat Level: 2
- Faction: Enclave

Dodge or slay the Eyebot, and watch for a landing Vertibird if the Enclave have arrived [E8.04]. The house is empty.

8.O: TALON COMPANY CAMP (LAT 02/LONG -09)

- Threat Level: 2
- Faction: Talon Mercenary
- Collectible: Skill Book
- Guns and Ammunition

- Interior Exploration
- Sleep Mattress
- Hostile: Talon Company Merc

Locate the fire escape with the pile of corpses below; the Talon Company has removed the previous residents by force and is currently occupying this building. After you take care of them, ransack the place for the following items:

- Ammo Box Ammunition (3)
- Sledgehammer
- 10mm Pistol
- Tumblers Today (17/25)

8.P: RAIDER UNDERPASS (LAT 03/LONG -10)

- Miscellaneous Quest: Those!
- Threat Level: 3
- Faction: Raider
- Guns and Ammunition
- Health and Chems

- Hostile: Mole Rat, Raider

Appearing After you complete **Miscellaneous Quest: Those**, a group of Raiders are capturing Mole Rats and placing them in cages in the underpass. Stealthy players may witness Raiders cheering on Mole Rat races. They are ripe for a sniping. There are some Jet and the following:

- First Aid Box Health and Chems (2)
- Ammo Box Ammunition (2)

8.Q: CAR DEALERSHIP (LAT -01/LONG -12)

- Threat Level: 1
- Collectible: Skill Book

A small dealership serving the Graydirch area did brisk business before the bombs dropped. To the south is a good landmark to memorize: the water tower. The gate is locked, and there's irradiated water to sip from the faucet. The Car Dealership has one major find (aside from common items: a Skill Book in the northeast corner of the raised area.

- U.S. Army: 30 Handy Flamethrower Recipes (13/25)

8.R: RED ROCKET GAS STATION (LAT 00/LONG -12)

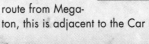

- Threat Level: 1
- Highly Visible Landmark

Another landmark to watch for en route from Megaton, this is adjacent to the Car Dealership.

TRAINING — BESTIARY — MAIN QUEST — MISC. QUESTS — TOUR — COMPLETION — APPENDICES

8.S: SCAVENGER'S BRIDGE (LAT 02/LONG -13)

- Threat Level: 2
- Faction: Wastelander
- Services: Repairer, Trader
- Collectible: Skill Book (3)
- Guns and Ammunition

- Health and Chems
- Lots o' Caps
- Scavenger
- Scavenger's Dog

A Scavenger and his dogs live in a shack on this pedestrian bridge. Trade and request Repairs from him. The stall has Darts and Spikes, but the real prizes are the following items and three Skill Books you can Steal.

Note: Avoid combat by using Sneak and a Stealth Boy to grab these items.

- Ammo Box Ammunition (3) First Aid Box Health and Chems
- Grognak the Barbarian (17/25)
- Duck and Cover! (18/25)
- Chinese Army: Spec. Ops. Training Manual (13/25)

8.T: FREEWAY WRECKAGE (LAT -06/LONG -15)

- Threat Level: 1

The desolate stretch of freeway that runs through Fairfax Ruins ends at this vista.

8.U: OVERTURNED TRUCK (LAT -05/LONG -15)

- Threat Level: 1
- Collectible: Nuka-Cola Quantum
- Health and Chems

Under the freeway lies a container truck on its side. Investigate the rear of the vehicle for Chems, alcohol, and these items:

- First Aid Box Health and Chems
- Nuka-Cola Quantum (62/94)

8.V: THE CONCRETE TREEHOUSE (LAT -03/LONG -15)

- Threat Level: 2
- Faction: Raider, Wastelander
- Collectible: Skill Book
- Sleep Mattress

- Hostile: Raider, Turret Mark V

Close to the freeway overpass is a parked military truck and the remains of an office building with a turret. There's a terminal up the ramp that switches off the turret (although shooting it from a distance is easier). There's a bed to sleep on, a Carton of Cigarettes, scattered items and Caps, a footlocker, and a Skill Book.

- Tales of a Junktown Jerky Vendor (14/24)

8.W: JACKKNIFED TRUCK (LAT -03/LONG -17)

- Threat Level: 1
- Collectible: Skill Book

Just east of Andale is a rusting truck. Move to the back, secure your Skill Book, and check both footlockers.

- Dean's Electronics (15/25)

8.X: DOT'S DINER (LAT -01/LONG -16)

- Threat Level: 2
- Faction: Raider
- Collectible: Skill Book
- Hostile: Raider

Near the freeway intersection is Dot's Diner. There's junk to sift through and a Skill Book behind the counter.

- U.S. Army: 30 Flamethrower Recipes (14/25)

8.Y: PARKED RED RACER TRUCKS (LAT 01/LONG -16)

- Threat Level: 2
- Faction: Raider
- Collectible: Skill Book
- Hostile: Raider

On the south side of the Red Racer Factory are two parked trucks. The real find is the dead Wastelander lying in the radioactive container.

- Grognak the Barbarian (18/25)

8.Z: RAIDER CAMP (LAT 03/LONG -16)

- Threat Level: 2
- Faction: Raider
- Collectible: Skill Book (2)
- Guns and Ammunition
- Sleep Mattress
- Hostile: Raider, Raider Guard Dog

An old Scavenger hut has been taken over by a Raider and his two guard dogs. After you dispatch him, loot the area; there's food and drink, some Chems, Darts, a couple of Stimpaks, a Gun Case, a mattress, and the following:

- Guns and Bullets (14/25)
- U.S. Army: 30 Flamethrower Recipes (15/25)
- Ammo Box Ammunition (2)

8.AA: PARKED NUKA-COLA TRUCKS AND DRAINAGE OUTLET (LAT -02/LONG -19)

- Threat Level: 1
- Collectible: Nuka-Cola Quantum

Parked outside of the Nuka-Cola Plant are two trucks with metal crates, some scattered Nuka-Cola bottles, and a Quantum.

- Nuka-Cola Quantum (63/94)

8.BB: TRAFFIC PILEUP (LAT 03/LONG -19)

- Threat Level: 2
- Danger: Low Radiation

Starting beneath the bridge to the west of the flooded metro is a huge vehicle pileup. Beware of the Raider Camp to the east [9.T]. Everything's been picked clean, so try setting fire to a car on the edge of the pileup, and watch the biggest explosion you've ever seen. Stand well back!

ENCLAVE CAMP LOCATIONS
CAMP E8.01 (LAT 02/LONG -04)

- Main Quest: Picking up the Trail
- Threat Level: 3
- Guns and Ammunition

Check the table with Stimpaks and a Field Research Terminal. The Enclave have catalogued these entities in the area: Bloatfly, Brahmin, Giant Ant.

- Enclave Crate Ammunition (3)

CAMP E8.02 (LAT -11/LONG -08)

- Main Quest: Picking up the Trail
- Threat Level: 2

A Vertibird swoops down to land near the shacks of Independence Hamlet, depositing a small recon unit.

CAMP E8.03 (LAT -06/LONG -10)

- Main Quest: Picking up the Trail
- Threat Level: 2

A Vertbird drops onto a flat area of ground north of Fort Independence, and a small team head out.

CAMP E8.04 (LAT -01/LONG -13)

- Main Quest: Picking up the Trail
- Threat Level: 2

A forecourt to the east of Fairfax Ruins receives a Vertibird, and a three-man Enclave forward assault team head out.

CAMP E8.05 (LAT -08/LONG -15)

- Main Quest: Picking up the Trail
- Threat Level: 2

In an attempt to secure the freeway skeleton north of the Overlook Drive-In, a team is dropped from a Vertibird.

CAMP E8.06 (LAT -02/LONG -16)

- Main Quest: Picking up the Trail
- Threat Level: 2

The parking lot below Dot's Diner is the scene of a soldier deployment as a Vertibird swoops in.

Zone 9: Exterior D.C. Metropolitan Ruins

TOPOGRAPHICAL OVERVIEW

This is essentially the "exterior" portion of the massive interlocking network of locations linking the Capital Wasteland to the underground tunnels (page 442), which in turn, lead to the D.C. Interior Zones (page 398). There are many places of interest to check out, from the anarchic Raiders at the Super-Duper Mart to the large Mirelurk nest inside the Anchorage Memorial. There are some vital locales, too, like the ruined town of Grayditch; the Brotherhood's Citadel; the scientists over at Rivet City; and your father's life's work, Project Purity, over in the old Jefferson Memorial.

AVAILABLE COLLECTIBLES (ZONE 9)

- Bobbleheads: 1/20
- Fat Man: 0/9
- Fat Man Mini-Nukes: 2/71
- Unique Items: 7/89
- Nuka-Cola Quantum: 10/94
- Schematics: 3/23
- Scribe Pre-War Books: 14/98

- Skill Book: Barter (2/24), Big Guns (1/25), Energy Weapons (1/25), Explosives (3/25), Lockpick (2/25), Medicine (2/25), Melee Weapons (0/25), Repair (2/25), Science (2/25), Small Guns (5/25), Sneak (1/25), Speech (2/25), Unarmed (3/25)
- Work Bench: 7/46
- Holotapes: Keller (1/5), Replicated Man (5/19)

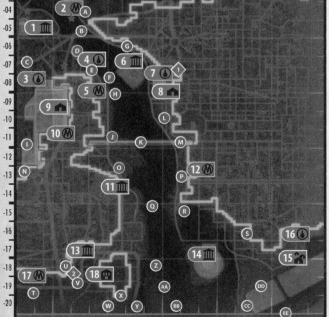

PRIMARY LOCATIONS

9.01: Super-Duper Mart (lat 04/long -04)

9.02: Farragut West Metro Station (lat 07/long -04)

9.03: Sewer Waystation (lat 04/long -08)

9.04: Wilhelm's Wharf (lat 07/long -07)

9.05: Flooded Metro (lat 08/long -08)

9.06: Anchorage Memorial (lat 10/long -07)

9.07: Tepid Sewers (lat 11/long -07)

9.08: Dukov's Place (lat 11/long -08)

9.09: Grayditch (lat 05/long -09)

9.10: Marigold Station (lat 06/long -11)

9.11: The Citadel (lat 08/long -14)

9.12: Irradiated Metro (lat 13/long -13)

9.13: Alexandria Arms (lat 07/long -17)

9.14: Jefferson Memorial (lat 13/long -17)

9.15: Rivet City (lat 18/long -17)

9.16: Anacostia Crossing (lat 19/long -16)

9.17: Flooded Metro (lat 04/long -18)

9.18: Arlington Library (lat 08/long -19)

SECONDARY LOCATIONS

9.A: D.C. Iron Statue (lat 07/long -04)

9.B: D.C. Iron Statue (lat 07/long -05)

9.C: Rusting Traffic Accident (lat 04/long -07)

9.D: Sewer Grate (lat 07/long -07)

9.E: Road Signs and Forecourt (lat 08/long -07)

9.F: Anchorage Bridge (lat 07/long -07)

9.G: Military Tent and Truck Defenses (lat 10/long -06)

9.H: Scavenger's Jetty (lat 09/long -08)

9.I: Outpost (lat 04/long -11)

9.J: Sewer Grate (lat 09/long -11)

9.K: Potomac Bridge (lat 10/long -11)

9.L: Festive Raider Camp (lat 12/long -10)

9.M: Scavenger Shack (lat 12/long -11)

9.N: Sewer Grate (lat 04/long -13)

9.O: Sewer Entrance Manhole (lat 09/long -13)

9.P: Super Mutant Office Ruins (lat 13/long -13)

9.Q: Sunken Boat and Jetty (lat 11/long -15)

9.R: Boats and Bait (lat 13/long -15)

9.S: Super Mutant Bonfire (lat 16/long -16)

9.T: Flooded Metro Raider Camp (lat 04/long -19)

9.U: Ruined Office Raider Camp (lat 06/long -18)

9.V: Jackknifed Jukebox Truck (lat 07/long -19)

9.W: Talon Company Recon Camp (lat 08/long -20)

9.X: Small Sewer (lat 09/long -20)

9.Y: Overturned Container Truck (lat 10/long -20)

9.Z: Mirelurk Jetty (lat 11/long -18)

9.AA: Rusting Tub (lat 12/long -19)

9.BB: Red Speedboat (lat 12/long -20)

9.CC: Rivet City Junk Heap (lat 16/long -20)

9.DD: Entrance to Broken Bow (lat 17/long -19)

9.EE: Irradiated Tub (lat 18/long -20)

TRAINING — BESTIARY — MAIN QUEST — MISC. QUESTS — TOUR — COMPLETION — APPENDICES

Primary Locations

9.01: SUPER-DUPER MART (LAT 04/ LONG -04)

- Miscellaneous Quest: The Wasteland Survival Guide; The Nuka-Cola Challenge
- Threat Level: 3
- Faction: Raider
- Collectibles: Fat Man Mini-Nuke, Nuka-Cola Quantum (3), Skill Book
- Guns and Ammunition
- Health and Chems
- Interior Exploration
- Sleep Mattress
- Hostile: Raider

INTERIOR MAP AND LOCATIONS

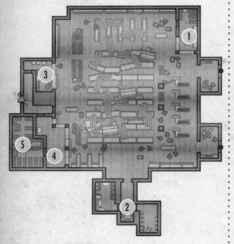

① Manager's Special: Weapon Cache

There are some Stimpaks and food in the fridge in this corner.

- Ammo Box Ammunition (2)
- Laser Pistol and Ammo (2)

② Restroom Chems

There are a few scattered Chems and mattresses.

③ Staff Only Beyond This Point: Counter Cache

- Ammo Box Ammunition (3)

④ Storage Room Terminal

Expect three or four Raiders to try preventing you from unlocking this terminal or door. There's a bloody mattress here too.

- Ammo Box Ammunition (2)
- Frag Grenade (2)
- Tales of a Junktown Jerky Vendor (15/24)

⑤ Storage Room Clearance

In addition to the following items, there are Darts and Chems. Take the Office Employee ID so the Protectron doesn't attack you. Activate the Automated Maintenance Terminal to unleash a Protectron.

- Employee ID Card
- Ammo Box Ammunition (3)
- First Aid Box Health and Chems
- Mini-Nuke (53/71)
- Frag Grenade (4)
- Nuka-Cola Quantum (64–66/94)

9.02: FARRAGUT WEST METRO STATION (LAT 07/LONG -04)

- Main Quest: Following in His Footsteps
- Threat Level: 3
- Faction: Raider, Super Mutant
- Danger: Low Radiation
- Guns and Ammunition
- Health and Chems
- Underground Connection
- Hostile: Raider, Super Mutant

This leads to the following linked underground areas:

D.C. U01.A: Farragut West Station (page 443).

D.C. U01.B: Tenleytown/Friendship Station (page 443).

The following surface locations can be accessed via the underground areas listed above:

6.10: Friendship Heights (page 334).

10.01: Chevy Chase North (page 398).

The station entrance is easy to Sneak or sprint to. There are two Raiders on the concrete promenade, guarding a cache.

Beware of Super Mutants attacking from across the water.

- Ammo Box Ammunition (2)
- First Aid Box Health and Chems

9.03: SEWER WAYSTATION (LAT 04/LONG -08)

- Threat Level: 2
- Collectible: Nuka-Cola Quantum
- Interior Exploration
- Underground Connection
- Hostiles: Radroach, Radscorpion Genus

This leads to the following linked underground area:

D.C. U13: County Sewer Mainline (page 448)

The following surface location can be accessed from the previously listed underground area:

9.J: Sewer Grate (page 394).

INTERIOR MAP AND LOCATIONS

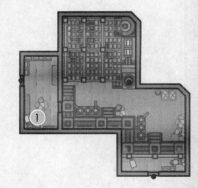

This is a waystation with two doors, on the northwest edge of Grayditch. Enter via the gate, through the gaps in the fence, or leap from the rocks above the fence.

① Western Foreman's Room (West)

Find food, Darts, a Carton of Cigarettes, junk, and vending machines.

- Nuka-Cola Quantum (67/94)

9.04: WILHELM'S WHARF (LAT 07/ LONG -07)

- Threat Level: 2
- Faction: Wastelander
- Services: Trader
- Danger: Low Radiation
- Interior Exploration
- Lots o' Caps
- Sleep Mattress

INHABITANTS

Grandma Sparkles

Sprightly for a 72-year-old, Grandma Sparkles refuses to leave the Wharf, despite the recent Super Mutant and Raider incursions. She' protected by her deft Hunting Rifle skill and her family, who are out searching for Mirelurk Meat. She's tasted all kinds of critters and swears that Mirelurk is the most delicious.

You can Trade with her, but her inventory isn't great.

If you slay her, you can take the key to Grandma Sparkle's fridge, which contains a much larger selection of goods, including a load of Caps.

Inside the shack, steal weapons from a gun cabinet, as well as outfits. There is a mattress here.

- Hunting Rifle and Ammo

9.05: FLOODED METRO (CAPITAL WASTELAND; LAT 08/ LONG -08)

- Threat Level: 1
- Danger: Low Radiation
- Underground Connection

This leads to the following linked underground area:

D.C. U12: Arlington/Wasteland Metro (interior) (page 447).

The following surface location can be accessed from the preceding underground area:

16.01: Arlington/Wasteland Metro (Cemetery North; page 417).

This area has a courtyard overlooking the Potomac and is dry, but the interior tunnels are sodden.

MAPS AND LOCATIONS

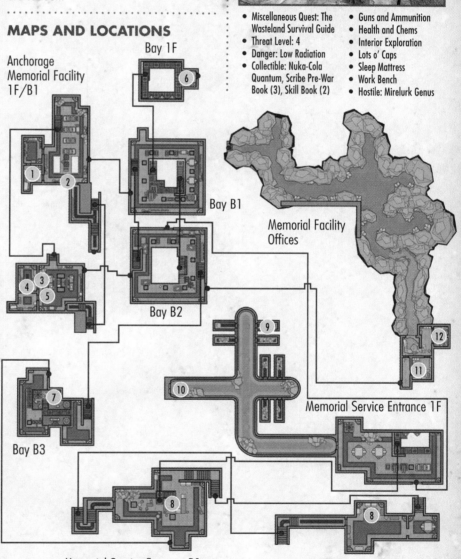

Anchorage Memorial Facility 1F/B1

Bay 1F

Bay B1

Bay B2

Bay B3

Memorial Facility Offices

Memorial Service Entrance 1F

Memorial Service Entrance B1

Memorial Service Entrance B2

GENERAL NOTES

This ancient war memorial has a total of four entrances on the surface and the odd Mirelurk roaming around. The optimal route through here is via the main entrance, facing south.

9.06: ANCHORAGE MEMORIAL (LAT 10/ LONG -07)

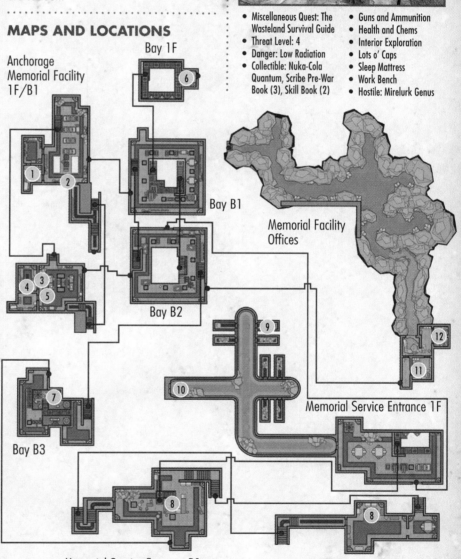

- Miscellaneous Quest: The Wasteland Survival Guide
- Threat Level: 4
- Danger: Low Radiation
- Collectible: Nuka-Cola Quantum, Scribe Pre-War Book (3), Skill Book (2)
- Guns and Ammunition
- Health and Chems
- Interior Exploration
- Lots o' Caps
- Sleep Mattress
- Work Bench
- Hostile: Mirelurk Genus

ANCHORAGE MEMORIAL FACILITY

① Wastelander Research Lab and Utility (Upper floor)

A dead Wastelander lies amid a wrecked office with overturned shelves.

- Scribe Pre-War Book (58–60/98)

TRAINING — BESTIARY — MAIN QUEST — MISC. QUESTS — TOUR — COMPLETION — APPENDICES

② **Work Bench with Bottlecap Mine (Upper Floor)**

- Work Bench (33/46)

③ **Nuka-Cola Vending Machine (Lower Floor)**

Check the ground behind it for Access Codes, allowing you to activate the nearby Facility Terminal without Hacking.

- Access Codes

④ **Desk and Dead Ted (Lower Floor)**

Anchorage Memorial Facility Terminal: Unlock the secure medical safe and receive information on a floor safe in the clinic containing parts to fix a broken door. On the floor adjacent to the terminal is Ted, a deceased Trader; search his body for a major Cap find and a note about some hidden stashes in here.

- Note for Ted
- 100+ Caps

⑤ **Operations and Clinic Room (Lower Floor)**

Scattered Caps, Darts, a place to sleep, and the medical safe, which is otherwise unlocked via the terminal at Location ③. Check the table with the lamp on it for a Skill Book.

- Medical floor safe Items
- Door Component
- Dean's Electronics (16/25)
- Blood Pack (3)
- D.C. Journal of Internal Medicine (17/25)
- Baseball Bat

ANCHORAGE MEMORIAL FACILITY BAY

⑥ **Dead Merc (Upper Floor)**

A dead mercenary lies with an order to secure Mirelurk Meat for fun and profit. Nearby is a locked door and a terminal to the Capital Wasteland.

- Merc's Orders
- Laser Pistol and Ammo

⑦ **Egg Clutches (Lowest Floor)**

MEMORIAL SERVICE ENTRANCE

⑧ **Kitchen (Middle Floor)**

This area has three fridges with food and scattered items. The floor below has a Mirelurk butcher room with three more fridges.

 Tip
One fridge contains a secret compartment with a stash of meat and Caps; you know something is in here if your **Perception** is high enough.

- First Aid Box Health and Chems (3)
- Load of Caps

⑨ **Sewers Utility Door**

This is the door requiring the component from the medical floor safe. Or, you can Repair the door. Inside are Caps, Darts, junk, other items, and a note telling you where the "stash" is located. Don't forget the key!

- U.S. Army: 30 Handy Flamethrower Recipes (16/25)
- Note: Anchorage War Memorial Stash
- Nuka-Cola Quantum (68/94)
- Anchorage Stash Key
- "The Tenderizer": Sledgehammer (59/89)

⑩ **Door to Capital Wasteland**

MEMORIAL FACILITY OFFICES

⑪ **Office**

A desk terminal unlocks a wall safe.

- Wall Safe Items

⑫ **Restrooms**

- First Aid Box Health and Chems (2)

9.07: TEPID SEWERS (LAT 11/LONG -07)

- Threat Level: 2
- Underground Connection
- Danger: Low Radiation

The Metro Station entrance leads to the following:

D.C. U05: Tepid Sewer (Georgetown) (page 444)

The following surface location can be accessed from the underground metro tunnel:

14.01: Tepid Sewer (Georgetown) (page 411).

An easily missed metal door constructed into the lower ground near Dukov's Place and the War Memorial provides quick access to Georgetown.

 Tip
Your Pip-Boy's Local Map is a great way to spot easy-to-miss entrances.

9.08: DUKOV'S PLACE (LAT 11/ LONG -08)

- Miscellaneous Quest: You Gotta Shoot 'Em in the Head
- Collectibles: Nuka-Cola Quantum, Skill Book
- Freeform Quest
- Guns and Ammunition
- Threat Level: 2
- Highly Visible Landmark
- Faction: Wastelander
- Interior Exploration

INTERIOR MAPS AND LOCATIONS

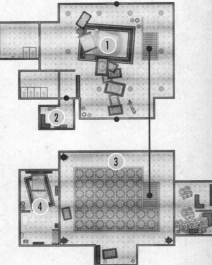

INHABITANTS

Dukov

Dukov, 43, has a carefree attitude about life, and it defines what he does every day: party. His talk is laced with profanity, yet he somehow maintains his charm and is able to win people over. His booming laugh can distinguish him in a room full of people. All he's concerned with are his possessions, his "pad" as he calls it, and his ladies.

Cherry

A live-in playmate, 27-year-old Cherry doesn't love Dukov, but she does like him. She mostly stays with him for the money and the modest protection he can give her. In exchange, she offers what she can. Dukov prefers that his "ladies" walk around in their underwear.

Fantasia

Fantasia, 23, has a philosophy: she'd "rather be a whore than dead." She lives up to her end of the bargain with Dukov, who parties with her and Cherry constantly. Like Cherry, she's clad in undergarments and is here for protection, a few Caps, and a little Jet.

GENERAL NOTES

Dukov barricades both sides of his front and back door, warning you of dire consequences if you don't holster your weaponry. The "place" is a large stone building overlooking the Potomac and is in reasonably good condition. Enter via either set of doors.

DUKOV'S PLACE

The mansion is a large game room with bedrooms upstairs. Talk to Dukov about his women, his drinking, and his key (if you've already spoken to Mister Crowley), which you can earn or take from him. Make a quick inspection of the premises.

1 Ground Floor

There's beer, a Carton of Cigarettes, and scattered Chems. Pickpocket or find the key on Dukov's corpse.

- Dukov's Special Key
- Assault Rifle

2 Locked Office

- Sawed-Off Shotgun

3 Upstairs Balcony

- BB Gun

4 Dukov's Bedroom

There's food in the fridge, scattered Chems, and alcohol.

- Pugilism Illustrated (19/25)
- Nuka-Cola Quantum (69/94)

FREEFORM QUEST: CHERRY'S FREEDOM

Speak with Cherry, and steer the conversation so she tells you she can't take much more of this.

> Then tell her you'll protect her. If your **Speech** is successful, she agrees and wants you to take her to Rivet City.

When you're ready, leave with Cherry. You can tell her to stop, follow you, or leave her stranded. Follow the Potomac River south and around to the Rivet City bridge. But first, you must navigate the Raider camp and two Super Mutant incursions.

9.09: GRAYDITCH (LAT 05/LONG -09)

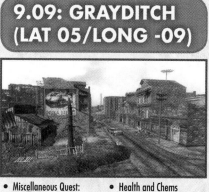

- Miscellaneous Quest: Those!
- Freeform Quest
- Threat Level: 2
- Faction: Wastelander
- Collectible: Skill Book
- Guns and Ammunition
- Health and Chems
- Interior Exploration
- Lots o' Caps
- Sleep Mattress
- Hostile: Giant Fire Ant Genus

INHABITANTS

Bryan Wilks

When the settlement was attacked by Giant Ants and all the inhabitants were wiped out, eight-year-old Bryan hid the entire time underneath a demolished car for protection. Luckily, the huge insects overlooked him and moved on after carrying off their prey. Since the attack, Bryan's food and water supply has dwindled (his father used to make trips to stock up for the entire settlement), and he has left the safety of the small settlement in hopes of finding help.

Doctor Lesko

Lesko is a somewhat befuddled and misguided scientist whose experiments on ants have proven disastrous for Grayditch. Deep inside Marigold Metro Station, he carries out his research, completely oblivious to the destruction that his Fire Ants have caused. He has little patience for anything beyond his scientific acumen and dismisses his failures as only temporary obstacles on the road to success. While his motivation is to save the Wasteland, his methods are in fact destroying it.

Fred Wilks (Deceased)

Father to Bryan Wilks of Grayditch, he sadly perished at the hands of the Fire Ants that invaded his home. He was a provider and a protector for his family, and instilled a strong sense of purpose in his son.

RELATED INTERACTIONS

Bryan Wilks: You can ask about what happened and about his family, and agree to help him.

Doctor Lesko: Once the Miscellaneous Quest is over, you can complete his Freeform Quest.

GENERAL NOTES

Grayditch was once an affluent area before the bombs fell, with fancy brick walkways and brownstones. Now, most of the fancy (but structurally weak) buildings have been blown away, leading to only some of them being usable as shelters. It is the hideout of a small boy and a strange scientist, both unrelated to each other. The area to concentrate on is south of the Sewer Waystation [9.03] and northeast of the Outpost [9.1].

Diner and Pulowski Preservation Shelter

This is where Bryan hides once the Quest begins. The area is empty, except for the trash bins behind the diner. Use the key Bryan gives you to unlock them.

- Grayditch Dumpster Key
- Trash Bin Items

Recently Built Shack

Use the shack key you find on Fred Wilks's corpse (at Location 3) or unlock the door to enter Doctor Lesko's shack. The place is empty except for a Holotape allowing you easy access into Lesko's Terminal. Read Lesko's personal notes, as they pertain to his science experiments on mutating Fire Ants. He's down in the Marigold Station area.

- Doctor Lesko's Password Recording

Wilks's House

Bryan's father is here with a shack key that opens Location 2. There is food in the fridge.

- Ammo Box Ammunition (2)
- Chinese Assault Rifle and Ammo
- .32 Pistol and Ammo

Brandice's House

A terminal in the master bedroom allows access to six entries. It charts the general hopelessness Brandice and his wife, Sheila, felt as the Ants closed in. In his third entry, he details a gun he bought at Megaton; it's behind the fridge in a toolbox. You can unlock the footlocker in the master bedroom using William Brandice's key, which you find in the underground tunnels below Marigold Station [9.10 and U16.A].

- Baseball Bat
- Kitchen Toolbox: 10mm Pistol and Ammo
- First Aid Box Health and Chems
- William Brandice's Footlocker
- Missile Launcher and Missile (1)

TRAINING — BESTIARY — MAIN QUEST — MISC. QUESTS — TOUR — COMPLETION — APPENDICES

Abandoned House (North)

The are a few scattered Chems in here. Outside, there's a ruined bridge, a small playground, and other buildings, all wrecked and with Fire Ants to destroy.

- Ammo Box Ammunition
- Guns and Bullets (15/25)
- 10mm Pistol
- Pool Cue
- First Aid Box Health and Chems

Abandoned House (South)

There is a place to sleep and a Carton of Cigarettes in the master bedroom.

- Hunting Rifle
- First Aid Box Health and Chems

FREEFORM QUEST: NECTAR COLLECTING FOR FUN AND PROFIT

After you complete **Miscellaneous Quest: Those!** and Doctor Lesko has survived, find him in the recently built shack. He requests you search for Fire Ant Nectar in return for Caps. As Grayditch is devoid of Fire Ants thanks to the Pulse, you must return to the Metro Tunnels at Marigold Station. Each sample nets you 40 Caps. Workers drop Nectar 40 percent of the time. Soldiers and Warriors drop Nectar 70 percent of the time.

In addition, once per day, you can ask Lesko how his experiments are coming. He mentions something different each day you try this.

9.10: MARIGOLD STATION (LAT 06/ LONG -11)

- Miscellaneous Quest: Those!
- Threat Level: 3
- Underground Connection

The Metro Station entrance leads to two linked areas:

D.C. U16.A: Marigold Station (page 449).

D.C. U16.B: Queen Ant's Hatchery (page 449).

The following surface location can be accessed from the underground Metro Tunnels:

19.01: Falls Church (Marigold Station; page 434).

These Giant Fire Ants must be coming from somewhere. This station, built at the corner of Grayditch city hall, is the key to finding out more about these scuttling insects and entering the Falls Church zone.

9.11: THE CITADEL (LAT 08/LONG -14)

- Main Quest: The Waters Of Life; Picking up the Trail; The American Dream; Take It Back!
- Freeform Quest (7)
- Threat Level: 2
- Faction: Brotherhood Of Steel
- Services: Healer, Repairer
- Collectible: Skill Book (2)
- Area Is Locked
- Follower
- Guns and Ammunition
- Health and Chems
- Highly Visible Landmark
- Interior Exploration
- Loads o' Caps
- Perk!
- Sleep Mattress
- Work Bench

INHABITANTS

Elder Owyn Lyons

Lyons, 75, was already highly decorated when he set out from the order's West Coast headquarters, leading a party of soldiers on a mission to reestablish contact with the

"Eastern Brotherhood." He discovered this abandoned Pentagon military complex. The presence of Super Mutants sent a chill up the collective spine of the Brotherhood; these weren't the children of the dreaded Master, nor were they the remnants of the band that fled east and were ultimately destroyed (or assimilated into the Brotherhood of Steel) in the Chicago area. No, this was a new breed of Super Mutant, one with a local origin. But where did they come from? What did they want? How were they reproducing? Elder Lyons was ordered to discover the source of this new Super Mutant infestation and wipe it from the face of the Earth.

Sentinel Sarah Lyons

Sarah, 26, was born in the West Coast Brotherhood of Steel headquarters. At the age of seven, she accompanied her father on his journey east to the Capital Wasteland (her mother having died several years earlier). Sarah Lyons is Brotherhood through and through, as dedicated and decorated as her father when he was younger. She commands a group of soldiers assigned to patrol the Washington, D.C., Mall area and operates out of the G.N.R. studio outpost.

Squire Maxson

Squire Maxson is a descendant of the legendary Roger Maxson, founder of the Brotherhood of Steel. His father, a high-ranking Paladin serving just outside the N.C.R. (New California Republic), was recently killed in battle, and his mother, the Lady

INTERIOR MAPS AND LOCATIONS

The Citadel Courtyard

Citadel — A Ring

Citadel — B Ring

Citadel — Laboratory and Armory

Maxson, sent the boy east to be raised under the tutelage of the respected Elder Lyons. Squire Maxson tends toward timidity, which is the main reason his mother sent him to the Citadel.

Knight Captain Dusk

Dusk is the Pride's sniper and is considered the best sharpshooter in all the Brotherhood. She spends most of her time up in the Inner Bailey practicing at the rifle range.

Knight Captain Irving Gallows

Gallows is the Pride's scout and stealth expert. He's a quiet, kind of creepy man who isn't much liked by the Brotherhood members beyond the Pride. It's been said that if an enemy is in the field and sees Paladin Gallows, he's already dead. Paladin Gallows tends to disappear from time to time, which only adds to the mystery surrounding him. But it is well known among the other members of Lyons's Pride that Gallows is actually out hunting and killing Super Mutants. At least, they HOPE they're Super Mutants....

Knight Captain Durga

Knight Sergeant Durga is the Citadel's quartermaster, a position that she is not exactly pleased to occupy. She'd rather be out in the field using weapons, rather than in the base polishing and cataloging them.

Star Paladin Cross

Star Paladin Cross is the highest ranking Brotherhood of Steel soldier in the Citadel, but she no longer works in the field. Instead, she now serves as Elder Lyons's trusted bodyguard and advisor. It is well known that Star Paladin Cross has been technologically enhanced so that she no longer needs to eat or sleep. She is, in fact, a cyborg. The change occurred several years ago, after Cross was critically injured defending Elder Lyons while out in the field; Scribe Rothchild performed the enhancement operation that saved Cross's life. But there's something even more important about Star Paladin Cross—she's none other than the Brotherhood of Steel soldier who helped save the player's life as a baby. Cross helped Dad get through the Super Mutants and escorted them all the way to Megaton.

Paladin Bael

Bael is a worthy fighter, but he hasn't mastered the fine art of conversation, a shortfall that almost led to an altercation with a Megaton resident. Still, he's a commanding

presence and ensures undesirables stay well away from the entrance gates.

Paladin Gunny

Paladin Gunny is in charge of training initiates and turning them into hard-nosed Knights and Paladins. He is unhappy with the Elder Lyons's method of taking on volunteers from the Wasteland but still performs his duty to the best of his ability.

Paladin Kodiak

Paladin Kodiak is the largest and strongest member of Lyons's Pride. He is actually considered the largest and strongest member of the Brotherhood of Steel in general. As the name implies, he's as gruff and vicious as a bear, and he excels in close combat with a Power Sledge. Paladin Kodiak owes his life to Elder Lyons, who rescued Kodiak as a child from a distant city known as "the Pitt." Because of this, Kodiak thinks of Elder Lyons as his father.

Paladin Glade

Paladin Glade is the oldest member of Lyons's Pride and serves as the group's technician and smith. But it's a well-known fact that Glade is also the most well-rounded and experienced Paladin in the Pride and is not to be trifled with. He's a badass, so don't mess with him.

Knight Artemis

One of Lyons's finest soldiers, Knight Artemis has repeatedly proven himself in the combat zone. He's currently resting up after a scouting mission in which he supported his Brothers over at Galaxy News Radio, sweeping the area for Super Mutants. It's a job he enjoys as much as mentoring the Initiates. He is a real backbone of the Brotherhood.

Scribe Rothchild

Scribe Rothchild was a member of Elder Lyons's exploration party when it discovered the Pentagon ruins. Rothchild fully believes in the Brotherhood of Steel and its ideals, but he is not a soldier. He's a scientist, and a good one. He is the Senior Scribe of the Citadel and takes his position very seriously.

Scribe Jameson

Scribe Jameson oversees the archives in the Citadel and is charged with protecting the whole of the Brotherhood's knowledge. More importantly, she keeps the scrolls that record the deeds of all Brotherhood members.

Scribe Peabody

Scribe Peabody is the Brotherhood scribe assigned to the Armory. He's a weapons expert and is in charge of maintaining and repairing all the Brotherhood's various firearms, energy weapons, big guns, and anything else that shoots and kills people. He also helped repair Liberty Prime's weapon systems. Unlike Scribe Rothchild, he loves "field work" and often wishes he could go on combat missions with the Brotherhood Knights and Paladins.

Scribe Bowditch

Scribe Bowditch is assigned to the Smithy and is responsible for a lot of innovations over the past several years. His specialty is Power Armor, and he spends much of his time obsessing over ways to improve it.

Liberty Prime

Liberty Prime is a formidable but currently offline combat robot that is being tinkered with in the laboratory. Its original intent was to liberate Anchorage, Alaska, from the Red Chinese back in 2072. A mixture of patriotic propaganda messages and incredible firepower ensured victory! But can the robot be fixed in time to help the Brotherhood?

Sawbones

This is a modified Mister Gutsy with an almost encyclopedic knowledge of surgery, but it lacks the necessary medical subsystem knowledge to carry out operations without causing inadvertent harm to the patient. Recently, Sawbones has been exhibiting some worrying behavior, including having a penchant for poetry.

RELATED INTERACTIONS

- Brotherhood Member: You can inquire about Super Mutants, the Enclave, and the Brotherhood.

GENERAL NOTES

This large building is the remains of an old operations base known as "the Pentagon." It is well defended and impenetrable until you arrive with Doctor Li after escaping from the Jefferson Memorial during **Main Quest: The Waters of Life**. You can speak to Paladin Bael at the front gate, but he doesn't allow you access until Doctor Li demands it.

THE CITADEL COURTYARD

① Initial Training: Pistols

An Initiate is attempting to hit a Super Mutant mannequin.

② Initial Training: Big Guns

An Initiate is aiming a missile launcher at two Super Mutant mannequins; mind the splash damage.

③ Initial Training: Grappling

Two Initiates are attempting hand-to-hand melee combat.

④ Initial Training: Rifles

An Initiate is trying to hit a Super Mutant mannequin. Test your aiming by shooting the bottles by the mannequin's head.

⑤ Initiate's Quarters

Mattresses (and little else) are available here.

⑥ Gun Range

Test your weaponry at this long gun range. There are also gantry steps to climb around the perimeter. The central area remains closed until the Brotherhood move their military robot, Liberty Prime.

CITADEL: A RING
⑦ Archives and Library

You can speak to Scribe Jameson about the Brotherhood (their history, beliefs, and the like) and Super Mutants, and learn the location of Scribe Yearling [Arlington Library, 9.18]. In addition, there are three terminals to access:

1. Maxson Family Dossiers: (1) Roger Maxson: Read information on founder Roger Maxson and how the Brotherhood of Steel came into being; (2) Maxson II: Roger's son, who died fighting a Raider gang called the Vipers; (3) John Maxson: Maxson II's son, a prominent fighter who assumed control from his father and had dealings with a mysterious "Vault Dweller"; (4) Scribe Arthur Maxson: Sent to the Citadel to be fostered by Elder Lyons when he was in communications with the Western Elders. Currently still alive.

2. State of Maxson: Located in the New California Republic. Built close to the Lost Hills Bunker.

3. Diary of Roger Maxson: Volumes 1 and 2. This is an 11-part diary charting Roger's life and battles. It makes fascinating reading on the Brotherhood's founder.

The second computer of interest is the Vault-Tec Terminal. There are three entry options (many options, including the last two Main menu entries, are restricted or corrupted and cannot be read):

D.C. Area Vault Listings: This lists the seven vaults in the vicinity. For each, you can read about equipment issuances, personnel assignments, and project goals:

1. Vault 76: A "control Vault" designed to automatically open after 20 years, pushing residents back into the open world to see how they cope. This wasn't in the brochure when the dwellers signed up, naturally.

2. Vault 87: All information redacted.

3. Vault 92: Most information corrupted.

4. Vault 101: File errors and information corrupted.

5. Vault 106: Overseer Albert Leris has requested that all information be redacted.

6. Vault 108: Overseer Brody Jones has left all standard positions unfilled in this Vault, and his rare cancer should allow progress to occur as planned.

7. Vault 112: Overseer Doctor Stanislaus Braun only requires a single administrator. Goal access is denied.

The third computer of interest is the Pentagon Library Terminal. There are three entry options:

1. Report on UFO codenamed "Palandine": An alien craft breached airspace just north of Hagerstown and crashed in a heavily wooded area. The craft could not be located, but extra-terrestrial contact was confirmed.

2. Project Brainstorm Report: The Induced Patriotism Initiative has proved a success, with covert and overt messages appearing in the media, resulting in increased military enrollment. Agent Webb has had particular success in the music industry.

3. Mission Cloacina Report: Progress continues apace on the Mutant Undermining Lifeform bred to undermine the infrastructure of Red China.

⑧ Great Hall

This conference room has Paladins speaking about the usual issues—Super Mutant incursions, the name of Knight Captain Gallows, that sort of thing. Listen to the two guards by the door for some entertaining stories. There's nothing of value (aside from some beer) in here. Between the Great Hall and main corridor on each side are pantries and food-stocked fridges.

⑨ The Den

This is the usual location of Paladins Kodiak (where you can begin **Freeform Quest: The Scourge**) and Glade (who

completes **Freeform Quest: Gallows Humor**). The room has a broken terminal, food in the fridge, and mattresses. Check the foot of the bed to the south for a Skill Book.

• Brotherhood Holotags • Guns and Bullets (16/25)

CITADEL: B RING
⑩ Barracks (South)

This provides a place to sleep (there are a few scattered food packages on the shelving) and a Citadel Information Terminal: These are dotted throughout the building. Terminals have five entry options upstairs and six downstairs in the lab area:

AVF Problem (Lab Terminals): A warning not to engage in experiments with Accelerated Vector Fusion.

Warning! Leaky Hydraulics (Lab Terminals): Watch for the hydraulic fluid at the eastern end of the robot lift!

Enclave Tactical Assessment (Both Terminals): Not good; the Enclave are using plasma weapons capable of molecular destabilization and are using advanced Power Armor. They are highly mobile thanks to their Vertibirds; the force that attacked Project Purity was almost identical to those fought on the West Coast in 2241. Threat level is Severe.

G.N.R. Battle After-Action Report (Both Terminals): Sentinel Lyons hypothesizes that the Super Mutant attack force Lyons encountered was en route to the mall to bolster numbers for a prolonged battle with the Talon Company Mercenaries.

General Robot Diagnostics—Updated (Both Terminals): Scribe Rothchild postulates that once the power management issues are solved, the robot will function within acceptable levels. The robot in question is down in the lab.

G.N.R. Soldier Rotation (Ring Terminals): Due to increased Super Mutant activity, additional patrols are added to this area.

Notice: Reddin Funeral Canceled (Both Terminals): This was due to unexpected tactical developments.

⑪ Barracks (Central)

The same type of beds and terminals are available here.

⑫ The Solar

Elder Lyons's personal quarters. Locate the Personal Log containing his thoughts, and unlock the safe or terminal to take a unique Laser Pistol. Also in the safe is the second Personal Log. You can kill Lyons to steal his unique Robe, although this is not recommended! The terminal has the following information:

Squire Maxson Progress Report: Young Arthur's training is progressing nicely, but Lyons worries he's surrounded the boy with trained killers.

Sarah's Birthday: Elder Lyons's daughter needs something pretty for her birthday. Perhaps Paladin Cross can head to Rivet City to find something.

Now that you have both Personal Log Holotapes, you can listen to them:

Personal Log 1: The latest reconnaissance has shown that the Enclave now control the Project Purity facility. The Enclave will answer for their crimes.

Personal Log 2: A failed, feeble old man. Self-doubt. Western Elders cease to acknowledge his existence. Some of his own have gone rogue. The Enclave's tech is superior. Perhaps he should pass the mantle to more able hands. Is she ready, though?

- Combat Knife
- Wall Safe Items
- Elder Lyons's Robe (60/89)
- Smugglers' End (61/89)
- Elder Owyn Lyons: Personal Logs 1 and 2

13 Squire Maxson's Bedroom

There is a terminal in here with five entries:

1. Diary Entry 1: Maxson is annoyed with Squire Rothchild at scolding him after he tried to make friends with "the robot."

2. Diary Entry 2: Sarah taught Maxson to kill a man with a kidney stab. The young lad thinks he's in love.

3. Story—The Guardians of Gillyfrond: A tense rearrangement of toys pits Mister Wollingsworth against the stuffy Mousey Maquire.

4. Poem—Song of the Lightman: The "joining of five in the Lightman's tower" make for some excruciating reading.

5. Guns and Bullets: Paladin Vargas keeps a copy of the book under his bed, and Maxson is sneaking a peek.

14 Hospital

You can begin the Freeform Quest here and take your life into your own hands with Sawbones the Doctor.

CITADEL: LABORATORY AND ARMORY

15 Smithy (Upper Floor)

Scribe Bowditch is in here and can Repair your equipment. You gain information about the Replicated Man.

- Work Bench (34/46)
- Holotape: The Replicated Man (16/25)

16 Liberty Prime Operations

A large robot is standing in the center of this laboratory. You can read more about the robot here:

Historical Records

1. Project Summary: The original intent was to create the most powerful combat robot ever seen and to liberate Anchorage from the Chinese. This note from General Constantine Chase confirms it.

2. Capital Post Article—June 3, 2072: A news article showing the general's press conference, where the U.S. government changed from covert operations to revealing Liberty Prime.

3. Letter—Dr. Bloomfield to Gen. Chase: The robot needs more power than current technology allows, and it won't be ready. Doctor Braun was called to help, but he's working on his own project. The robot will walk but won't have functioning weaponry. Perhaps it can just step on the Red Chinese?

Diagnostic Reports: Three entries detail how the robot is operating.

Lead Scribe's Journal: Scribe Rothchild's journal, detailing three of his experiences getting this mountain of metal to function properly. The Accelerated Vector Fusion mishap is especially interesting.

Voice Emitter Test: Access this, step back from the terminal, and you can hear Liberty Prime's growling oratory synthetic modulations (or "voice") boom across the lab.

17 Lower Floor Restrooms

Check the tiny crate for a Skill Book.

- Duck and Cover! (19/25)

18 Armory

Speak with Scribe Peabody about Repairing your Armor. You can also activate the nearby terminal to read up on the Brotherhood's reviews of certain weapons. Through the door is the Armory. Knight Captain Durga refuses to sell you equipment; check the Freeform Quest. Afterward, she sells some of the best equipment in the Wasteland and Repairs your items.

19 Mess Hall

There's food in three fridges here and in the mess hall.

- 10mm Pistol

FREEFORM QUEST: GALLOWS HUMOR

Knight Captain Gallows is a solitary and antisocial sort, but perhaps that's because he does his talking with the smoking end of a Laser Rifle. Seek him out, and say nothing—literally—so you both understand each other. Then speak to one of the other Paladins (such as Knight Captain Dusk), and they let you know there's a pool going around for the first person to find out Gallows's actual name. Return to Gallows and ask him about it.

 The only way he reveals his name is if you coax it out of him using **Speech**. Report back to Paladin Glade; make sure you ask what your reward is first!

- 1,000 Caps

FREEFORM QUEST: COLLECTING HOLOTAGS

Scribe Jameson is the keeper of the scrolls for the D.C. Brotherhood. Because of the chaotic fighting and the structure of the Brotherhood in D.C., there are many members who are unaccounted for. Scribe Jameson is interested in recovering the Holotags of the fallen brothers so their deed can be written into the scrolls. Search the D.C. Ruins for Brotherhood soldiers; you can also "help" them to the afterlife, take their Holotags, or just concentrate on members you haven't executed. You receive the following for each Holotag you hand in.

- 100 Caps (per Holotag)
- 25 XP (per Holotag)

FREEFORM QUEST: POWER ARMOR TRAINING

At last! As soon as you enter the Citadel, speak with Elder Lyons so he gives you permission to train in Power Armor. Move to the courtyard (Bailey) area where the Initiates are training. Find Paladin Gunny, and he trains you; you can now utilize any type of Power Armor.

- Power Armor Training

FREEFORM QUEST: SEEING STARS

With a high enough Karma, you can speak with Star Paladin Cross, who is usually located in the laboratory and served with your father honorably. She offers to accompany you on a special detachment mission. Should you perform any evil deeds, she will leave you and return to the Citadel.

- Star Paladin Cross

FREEFORM QUEST: NO FREE LUNCH

The miserable Knight Captain Durga, located in the Armory, doesn't trust Vault Dwelling Wastelanders like yourself. Speak to her, and she refuses to Repair or Sell her weaponry to you until Elder Lyons approves it. Locate Lyons, request that Bartering take place, and return to Durga to use her Repair and Inventory.

FREEFORM QUEST: WORST. DOCTOR. EVER

Sawbones is more than living up to his name in the medical bay, and when you request a healing, he actually wounds you instead. Ignore this malfunctioning robot, or use Science to run a Level 2 diagnostic on his medical subsystems. Keep this up, and you fix Sawbones, and he actually behaves like a doctor from this point on. You can also access the nearby Medical Terminal.

> Inside the terminal, recently hacked by Glade with a rant against the robot's poetry, are four entry options (one of which is the medical storage lock override):

1. Casualty Report: Notes on how previous Brotherhood members have died. There's an "honorable" pattern here.

2. Notes on Pendleton Appendectomy: The operation was almost a complete success, aside from the (irrelevant) pain and discomfort level.

3. Hovering Contemplatively, a Poem: A real tour-de-force into the artificial mind of a sensitive poet. By "sensitive," think "crazy."

4. Or you can Lockpick the medical storage lock and grab the medical items inside.

- Medical Storage Health and Chems

FREEFORM QUEST: THE SCOURGE

Paladin Kodiak is usually in the Barracks, and if you ask, he's more than happy to tell you about a cataclysmic event in his past, one that he feels he is indebted to Elder Lyons for.

9.12: IRRADIATED METRO (LAT 13/ LONG -13)

- Threat Level: 3
- Underground Connection

The Metro Station entrance leads to one linked underground area:

D.C. U20: Irradiated Metro (Interior; page 452).

The following surface location can be accessed from the underground metro tunnel:

21.04: L'Enfant Plaza (page 439).

 Caution

Be careful when exploring around here, as the nearby Office Ruins [9.P] have numerous Super Mutants looking for fresh meat. This is a quick way to reach L'Enfant Plaza Zone.

9.13: ALEXANDRIA ARMS (LAT 07/ LONG -17)

- Threat Level: 3
- Faction: Raider
- Collectibles: Nuka-Cola Quantum, Scribe Pre-War Book, Skill Book (2)
- Guns and Ammunition
- Health and Chems
- Interior Exploration
- Sleep Mattress
- Hostile: Raider

INTERIOR MAPS AND LOCATIONS
Alexandria Arms

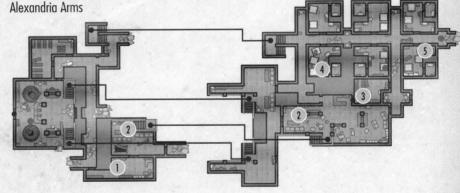

1 Lower Side Room

There is a Skill Book on the shelves, just before the double doors leading to the two-level recreation room.

- Duck and Cover! (20/25)

2 Two-Level Recreation Room

A lower area with a pool table and an upper area with Ammo Boxes, Darts, and some scattered Chems.

- Ammo Box Ammunition (4)
- Scribe Pre-War Book (61/98)
- Guns and Bullets (17/25)

3 Store Room Terminal

- First Aid Box Health and Chems
- Ammo Box Ammunition (4)
- Nuka-Cola Quantum (70/94)

4 Hotel Bedroom

This contains mattresses, a fridge with food, and a wall safe. There are similarly stocked fridges in each bedroom.

- Wall Safe Items

5 Hotel Bedroom

- Ammo Box Ammunition

9.14: JEFFERSON MEMORIAL (LAT 13/LONG -17)

- Main Quest: Scientific Pursuits; The Waters of Life; Take It Back!
- Threat Level: 4
- Faction: Enclave, Super Mutant, Wastelander
- Area Is Locked
- Guns and Ammunition
- Health and Chems
- Highly Visible Landmark
- Interior Exploration
- Sleep Mattress
- Hostile: Centaur, Super Mutant Genus, Turret Mk V

The manhole entrance leads to two linked underground tunnels:

D.C. U18.A: Taft Tunnel (page 450).

D.C. U18.B: Taft Tunnels (page 451).

The following surface location can be accessed from the memorial:

9.O: Sewer Entrance Manhole (the Citadel; page 395).

GENERAL NOTES

Access to the Jefferson Memorial is only available via a small gift shop side entrance; the steps of the structure have long since been abandoned, and pipes twist out into the Potomac. At the center of the Project Purity experiment, a brand-new catwalk (teeming with Super Mutants) has been erected; carefully battle or Sneak through here to the entrance.

JEFFERSON MEMORIAL GIFT SHOP

The pump control is a chamber you enter via the northeast exit. It is only necessary to enter during **Main Quest: The Waters of Life.** This is the only time you can activate the valve here and move along the pipe, which exits down in the sub-basement.

① Gift Shop Entrance

A Turret Control Terminal shuts down the turret inside.

② Gift Shop Sign

- First Aid Box Health and Chems
- Ammo Box Ammunition

③ Gift Shop

- Ammo Box Ammunition (2)
- .32 Pistol and Ammo

INTERIOR MAPS AND LOCATIONS
Jefferson Museum and Gift Shop

Pump Control

Sift Pump

Jefferson Memorial Rotunda

Memorial Sub-Basement

④ Manhole to Taft Tunnels

The Taft Tunnels are only accessible during **Main Quest: The Waters of Life.** They are inaccessible at any other time.

JEFFERSON MEMORIAL ROTUNDA

Project Purity is built around the giant statue of Thomas Jefferson. This is narrow and dangerous until you flush out the Super Mutants. It is the center of hope for mankind.

⑤ Airlock

Utilized during **Main Quest: Take It Back!**

⑥ Auxiliary Filtration Input

Also utilized (optionally) during **Main Quest: Take it Back!**

- Project Purity Journal: Entries 5, 8, and 10

⑦ Project Purity Sys. Op. Mainframe

Also utilized (optionally) during **Main Quest: Take It Back!** You can input the code to start the device here.

⑧ Statue of Thomas Jefferson (Inside Project Purity)

Note that you'll encounter an Enclave Colonel named Autumn in this room during **Main Quest: Take It Back!** Should you choose to defeat him, the following items become available:

- Colonel Autumn's 10mm Pistol (62/89)
- Colonel Autumn's Laser Pistol (63/89)
- Colonel Autumn's Uniform (64/89)

>
> **Note**
> For more information on your father's personal journals, consult **Main Quest: Scientific Pursuits.**

SUB-BASEMENT

⑨ Mainframe Power Switch

Utilized during **Main Quest: Take it Back!**

⑩ Small Medical Room

There's a Stimpak on the medical tray.

- Project Purity Personal Journal: Entries 7 and 8

TRAINING — BESTIARY — MAIN QUEST — MISC. QUESTS — TOUR — COMPLETION — APPENDICES

11 **Small Sleeping Quarters**

Mattresses are available to sleep on.

12 **Crossroads (Lower Corridors)**

• Baseball Bat

13 **Alcove Shelving (Lower Corridors)**

• Ammo Box Ammunition   • .32 Pistol and Ammo
• Sledgehammer

14 **Flood Control Room with Power Switch (Lower Corridors)**

15 **Study with Bed (Lower Corridors)**

• Project Purity Personal   • Better Days
Journal, Entries 1–3

16 **Side Table**

• 10mm Pistol

17 **Fuse Control Room**

9.15: RIVET CITY (LAT 18/LONG -17)

• Main Quest: Scientific Pursuits; The Waters of Life
• Miscellaneous Quest: The Wasteland Survival Guide; Those; The Replicated Man; Strictly Business; You Gotta Shoot 'Em in the Head; Stealing Independence; Trouble on the Homefront
• Freeform Quest (11)
• Threat Level: 2
• Faction: Slaver, Wastelander
• Services: Healer, Repairer, Trader
• Danger: Gas Leak, Grenade Bouquet, High Radiation,

Mines, Shotgun Trap, Terminal Trap
• Collectibles: Bobblehead, Fat Man Mini-Nuke, Schematic, Skill Book (3)
• Follower
• Guns and Ammunition
• Health and Chems
• Highly Visible Landmark
• Lots o' Caps
• Main Trading Route
• Rare or Powerful Item
• Work Bench (3)
• Sleep Mattress
• Hostile: Mirelurk Genus
• Holotape (Replicated Man)

INHABITANTS

Harkness

Rivet City's hard-nosed security chief, 35-year-old Harkness is a good guy and a good friend, despite his demeanor. What he doesn't know is that he isn't even human; he's a sentient humanoid robot who escaped from his creators and had his mind wiped. Harkness is extremely fair-minded. He treats Hangar Deck citizens with the same regard as Upper Deck citizens. As a result, he is very well liked by the Hangar Deck residents.

INTERIOR MAPS AND LOCATIONS

Upper Deck

Mid Deck, Science Lab, and Marketplace

Broken Bow

Bridge Tower

Mister Lopez

Lopez is a quiet 65-year-old man who has lived in the common room for the past 10 years. His wife and child were killed by Raiders, and he came to Rivet City lonely and lost. He spends much of his time reading or praying in the church. He takes his meals in the common room and sleeps a lot out of sheer depression. Once a day he tries to climb to the observation deck and jump.

Gary

The owner and proprietor of Gary's Galley, 50-year-old Gary considers himself a gourmet chef, but his restaurant serves little more than scavenged canned food and some fruits and vegetables (though occasionally he obtains some really high-quality produce from the Hydroponics Bay, which he sells at exorbitant prices). He loves his 16-year-old

daughter, Angela, and she loves him, but he neglects her in favor of the restaurant.

Angela

Angela , 16, works at the restaurant alongside her father for most of the day. She goes to church on Sundays and visits her best friend, Diego, there at night, after the restaurant closes. Angela is very attracted to Diego and has tried to seduce him a few times. However, his faith and her age have stopped him from acting on her advances.

Ted Strayer

Ted is a 19-year-old who has spent most of his life wandering the Wasteland. He's a new arrival to Rivet City and is staying in the common room until he figures out where he's going next. Ted is a vagabond at heart. He rarely plans beyond the moment and is coasting through life. It is easy to pique his interest, but it's difficult to hold it. His father used to have dealings with someone named Mister Crowley.

Commander Danvers

Danvers, 30, is Harkness's second in command and best friend, though their relationship is strictly platonic (her husband was also a Rivet City security officer, but he died of disease a couple years ago). If Harkness leaves Rivet City, she is promoted to security chief. Danvers give preferential treatment to Hangar Deck citizens. She has a mild disdain for Upper Deck residents: This is a source of mild friction between Harkness and Danvers.

Private Jones

Seagrave Holmes salvaged this Mister Gutsy. He's a bit confused about where he is and who all these other humans are. Harkness set him to guarding the Armory in the security tower, but he's far from reliable.

Tammy Hargrave

Tammy is a sour, middle-aged woman who drinks too much. She married James's father out of sheer desperation, and when he died at the hands of Raiders, she was left with his "brat" son. She took James to Rivet City, and they've remained there for the past couple of years. Tammy considers herself better than most of Rivet City's citizens. Ironically, Tammy spends her days getting drunk in the Muddy Rudder surrounded by such riffraff and often doesn't return home for days at a time. She never knows where James is, because she simply doesn't care.

James Hargrave

James Hargrave is one of Rivet City's few kids. He doesn't spend any more time in the cramped quarters than he has to and can usually be found in the company of his friend C.J. Young. The two of them like to play in the storage rooms or hang around on the flight deck. James is alternately sullen and wild. He will do just about anything on a dare. He is capable of holding a grudge for months. He is loyal to C.J. but picks on her mercilessly. The two don't have many other options for playmates, so C.J. tolerates the abuse. On the rare occasions when C.J. stands up for herself, James is devastated and will do anything to earn her forgiveness.

C.J. Young

C.J. is as happy a kid as you'll find in the Wasteland. She's been raised by two loving parents and lives a great kid's life, hanging out on the flight deck or exploring Rivet City with her best friend, James Hargrave. James does pick on her mercilessly, even though she is a year older than him. She is constantly apologizing and forgiving him for all his teasing. Despite this, the two are best friends. She is a trusting and honest young girl.

Flak

Flak, 50, is pretty gruff, but he's completely reformed from his early days of being a Slaver and is an upstanding citizen of Rivet City. He spends his days in the shop with Shrapnel, occasionally taking a break to drink down at the Muddy Rudder. Flak still has a bit of the tough guy in his speech, but he's not as aggressive as Shrapnel. He really tries to tone it down when he's at the shop. He's the target of Slavers in **Miscellaneous Quest: Strictly Business.**

Shrapnel

Shrapnel, 50, is grizzled and rough around the edges, but he has long since left his Raider days behind. He spends his days in the store with Flak, selling merchandise. He gets along with Flak because they share a fascination with guns. However, he's usually rude and insulting to everyone else. At Flak's request, he tries hard to not be rude when he's behind the counter of the shop, but he's finding it difficult.

Doctor Preston

Preston, 50, is a kind old man who enjoys nothing more than tending to the sick and injured. He genuinely loves helping people and is well liked and respected among the citizens of Rivet City. On occasion, he has had to work closely with Janice Kaplinski, who he considers to be his close friend. They have a father-daughter type of relationship. He tries to get her to lighten up and interact with people more.

Mister Buckingham

Mister Buckingham is Vera's best friend, a Mister Handy robot with the disposition of a British butler. Mister Buckingham is stationed in the hotel 24/7 and minds things while Vera is away.

Vera Weatherly

Vera Weatherly, 27, is young, attractive, ambitious, and very proud of all she's achieved. She opened the hotel on her own—she even helped construct it—and decided on the name after reading about the real location in a book. She is quiet and demure on the outside, but with an inner determination that cannot be shaken. Vera likes Seagrave, but only as a friend. She prefers the company of Mister Buckingham, her Mr. Handy robot, to that of her suitors. She is the cousin of Bryan Wilks.

Victoria Watts

This mysterious woman is allied with a clandestine group of ex-slaves; Abolitionists working together to form a new type of Underground Railroad. She is forceful, bright, and doesn't suffer fools gladly.

Doctor Zimmer

Zimmer, 58, is a very serious, very straightforward scientist who has traveled to Rivet City from the Commonwealth (Massachusetts) and is in town on business for "the Institute." Zimmer is looking for an escaped robot, an experiment that, in Zimmer's words, is "unstable, and a danger to himself and others." He is, without exception, always in the company of his bodyguard, Armitage.

Armitage

Armitage, 35, is Zimmer's imposing bodyguard. He has little to say and will defend Zimmer to the death. Of course, that's because Armitage is actually a robot, of the same class as the replicant they are searching for. Armitage has the same schedule as Zimmer; he sleeps in the same room and eats the same food—not because he has to, but because he's been programmed to replicate human behavior as closely as possible.

Sister

Why do they call this large hulking man "Sister"? No one knows because whenever anyone asks, Sister beats them to within an inch of their life. Sister, 29, is a bully with a bad temper. He is one step away from being given the boot by Harkness or Danvers. So far he hasn't caused enough trouble to warrant exile or worse. Most of the citizens of Rivet City stay clear of him if they can.

Father Clifford

Father Clifford, 40, spends most of his days in the church but leaves for a couple hours every day to walk around the carrier. He's a nice guy and likes just about everyone he meets. He is especially fond of telling the story of Saint Monica, who went on a journey to be with her son and saved his soul. He counsels Mister Lopez during his frequent visits to the church. He has a mild envy of Doctor Preston; it doesn't help that Doctor Preston never attends church.

TRAINING — BESTIARY — MAIN QUEST — MISC. QUESTS — TOUR — COMPLETION — APPENDICES

Mei Wong

Quiet and guarded, 30-year-old Mei doesn't like to talk. Mei was a slave under the ownership of Allistair Tenpenny but recently escaped and is in hiding out here. Harkness knows her story and has promised her she's safe while she's in town. She's a good source of information about Slavers and was once held at Paradise Falls. Mei Wong suspects that Sister is a Slaver but can't prove it. She is terrified of him. Fortunately for her, he does not recognize her at all.

Doctor Madison Li

Doctor Madison Li, 48, was a young, idealistic scientist who fully bought into the notion of Project Purity. She worked tirelessly with your father, and hid her growing romantic feelings while respecting his marriage to another scientist. When your mother was killed, Doctor Li was filled with remorse, but when the player's father decided to abandon Project Purity in order to keep his child safe, that sadness was replaced with a powerful sense of betrayal. Eighteen years later, she is older, wiser, and much more cynical.

Janice Kaplinski

The only thing 29-year-old Janice loves more than her hydroponic plants is Doctor Li. It's a case of classic hero worship. Janice is utterly loyal to her and completely believes in the projects they are working on. She is a very accomplished scientist but lacks that vital spark of genius and ambition that Dad and Doctor Li have, but she is their equal in technical knowledge. She is close friends with Doctor Preston, who treats her like the daughter he never had.

Garza

Garza, 30, is something of a mystery. He's physically imposing and very reserved. He won't speak of his past and prefers not to speak at all. Garza spends half his day doing heavy lifting for the scientists in the lab and the other half on the flight deck working out. If he survives the escape from Project Purity, he joins up with the Brotherhood of Steel and becomes a significant ally.

Paulie Cantelli

Paulie is your classic addict. His wife, Cindy, runs A Quick Fix, which sells Chems. The shop would actually make money if he would stop using up all the inventory himself. Most of his waking thoughts are about when he can get his next fix. He is frequently distracted and has trouble focusing. Paulie and Cindy are married in name

only. They barely talk and share little in common. He isn't even aware of how much he neglects his wife.

Cindy Cantelli

Cindy runs A Quick Fix, which sells Chems. Cindy has given up on her addict husband, Paulie Cantelli. They go through the tired motions of a marriage without really interacting with each other. She never uses Chems herself, although she has no problem selling them to others. She has what is called a convenient morality. Currently she has a crush on Bannon but has not gotten up the courage to approach him. However, since he is a regular churchgoer, she is there every Sunday, sitting as close to him as possible.

Abraham Washington

Washington, 45, continues the work started by his parents, who were just as passionate about preserving their heritage as residents of the nation's capital. He's a virtual shut-in at his Capitol Preservation Society. Abraham is one of those classic social outcasts who talks to himself all the time. He has almost no social skills and has a deeper emotional connection to his historical objects than he does to any human being. He requests that you help him locate some documents in **Miscellaneous Quest: Stealing Independence.**

Diego

Diego, 18, is Father Clifford's assistant. He came to Rivet City a few years ago with his father but was abandoned. Father Clifford took Diego in, and the two have become like father and son. Diego assists Father Clifford with his church work and wants to be a priest when he gets older. He has strong feelings for Angela and spends much of his free time with her. However, he is also a devoted Catholic. Because she is only 16, he does everything he can to keep his feelings secret, although Angela sees right through him.

Bannon

Bannon, 30, is a snappy dresser and a shrewd businessman. His wares are high priced, because he's got no competition. His motto is "If you don't like the pants, go find them yourself." Cindy Cantelli has a crush on him and sits with him in church. She also leaves when he does. Bannon is one of three city council members, along with Doctor Li and Harkness. They meet on Monday mornings for a few hours to discuss city-wide issues. He has quite the ego but was chosen by Doctor Li to sit on the city council. She seems oblivious to his flaws.

Seagrave Holmes

Seagrave Holmes, 30, is a genius tinkerer and fixes anything he can get his hands on. He spends his days in the shop, and at night, he hangs around the Weatherly Hotel to talk to Vera Weatherly, who he's not so secretly in love with. Seagrave has that easy way of relating to common folk. He fits into their social world without even thinking about. While he is exceptionally gifted with machines, he never lords that over others.

Brock

Brock, 35, is the Mudder Rudder barkeep and bouncer. He's not a big guy, but he's good in a fight and is really effective at keeping the peace. Security Chief Harkness and Brock have a deal—Brock gets to deal with his own messes in the bar, and Harkness doesn't ask any questions, as long as nobody disappears or turns up dead. Brock is not stupid, but he is thoroughly uneducated. He can't read. Belle Bonny took him in at a young age and raised him herself. He is utterly loyal to Belle and seems to be largely impervious to her temper.

Trinnie

Trinnie was, until recently, a resident of Little Lamplight. Sadly, she is completely wasted on alcohol and Chems 24/7. She spends her days in the Muddy Rudder and then takes a break to go to A Quick Fix and "borrow" some Chems. She then goes off to hide and enjoy the high for a bit before returning to the Muddy Rudder. Belle and Brock feel bad for Trinnie and let her sleep in their quarters. She's been known to turn tricks to get money, but she isn't forced to by Belle or Brock.

Belle Bonnie

Belle Bonny, 55, spends all her time in the bar, which is open around the clock, seven days a week. She sleeps for a few hours at night, and Brock watches the bar when she does, but then she returns to work. She is considered to be riffraff, even by the Hangar Deck crowd (everybody needs someone to look down on). She is a crotchety old woman, salty as hell. She won't take crap from anyone. There is a rumor floating around that she stared down Sister. It's true; even Garza is reluctant to tangle with her.

Pinkerton

Pinkerton, 60, is a crotchety old man who helped turn Rivet City from an old aircraft carrier into a livable community. He's grown tired of people and spends the remainder of his days isolated in his Broken Bow workshop, which also serves as his quarters.

Most of the residents would be surprised to find he is still on the ship, let alone living there. Belle Bonny knows he lives here. Doctor Li and Seagrave Holmes remember him from the early days but assume he left Rivet city decades ago.

GENERAL NOTES

Rivet City is a massive, dry-docked aircraft carrier, now the largest Wastelander residence around and home to a large number of odd, interesting, friendly, and strange characters. Access Rivet City from the rusting platform on the north, using the intercom to request the drawbridge. Inspect the deck for some items and a rather impressive Plasma Rifle that Security Chief Harkness is carrying. You'll need to figure out his secret to receive it.

- First Aid Box Health and Chems
- Ammo Box Ammunition (2)
- A3-21's Plasma Rifle (65/89)

STAIRWELL

The top floor allows access to the bridge tower, upper deck, midship deck, and the Muddy Rudder Bar.

Bridge Tower (Bottom Floor to Top)

Four confined floors, where the majority of the ordnance is kept and where an old man takes his final fling.

1 First Floor (from Stairwell)

This leads to a dining room where Rivet City Security eat. There's food in the fridge. There are three doors out to the flight deck.

2 Second Floor Dormitory

There are two doors out to balconies above the flight deck; the northwest door leads to a balcony with an Ammo Box. There's also scattered food and Detergent on the shelves and beds to sleep on.

- Footlocker Items (4) Assault Rifle and Ammo
- 10mm Pistol and Ammo
- Ammo Box Ammunition

3 Third Floor Dormitory

Private Jones and Commander Danvers may be here; the key to his footlocker is on him. There's food on the shelves and beds to sleep on. There is a Security Terminal, which contains notes about there being Mirelurks in the bow of the boat and problems with a guy named Sister. The door to the east leads to a balcony with an Ammo Box. The door to the southwest leads to a turret-guarded ammo cache.

- Footlocker Items (2)
- Chinese Assault Rifle
- Ammo Box Ammunition (2)

4 Third Floor Armory

- Armor Case Items (6)
- 10mm Pistol (3)
- Assault Rifle
- Chinese Assault Rifle
- Schematics: Rock-It Launcher (20/23)
- Ammo Box Ammunition (3)

5 Fourth Floor

A small table and a Security Terminal with the same notes about Mirelurks. There is an exit leading to an observation balcony with commanding views. You may find Mister Lopez up here.

UPPER DECK

6 Bannon's Room

Some fine furniture in here, along with Bannon's Terminal. Hack this to discover his agenda for council meetings and to read council meeting notes.

7 Young's Room

The possible location of C.J. Young and James Hargrave. There's food in the fridges but little else except a few scattered tools.

8 Flak and Shrapnel's Room

It's possible to steal some weaponry from here:

- Ammo Box Ammunition (3)
- 10mm Pistol
- Assault Rifle
- Chinese Assault Rifle
- Sledgehammer

9 Doctor Preston's Room and Rivet City Clinic

The doctor's room is reasonably empty, but his clinic has some Stimpaks and Chems. You can speak to Preston about the Replicated Man wherever you find him. You can also request medical items or heal, and you can activate the Rivet City Clinic Patient Data System. Here, you can read about the uncommon problems for long-term residents (lockjaw, red-lung, fish poisoning) and about some patients he's treating (Bannon for "social problems," Brock for a broken nose, Paulie Cantelli for Chems, Seagrave Holmes for red-lung, Gary for exhaustion, and Trinnie for alcoholism).

- Holotape: The Replicated Man (17/25)
- 10mm Pistol
- Baseball Bat

10 Doctor Li's Room

Opposite is a door to the science lab (although the main level is one floor down). Li's quarters contain the Holotapes you were missing when you searched the Jefferson Memorial (Project Purity sub-basement). There's food in the fridge and a terminal to hack, where you can read about her progress in the field of hydroponics and about the council meeting minutes.

- Project Purity Personal Journal: Entries 1, 3, 5

11 The Weatherly Hotel and Vera Weatherly's Door

You can speak to Vera or Mister Buckingham about renting a room (120 Caps), and you can purchase some food. Hack the desk terminal to find out who's staying and to read a shopping list. There is also the Weatherly Hotel trunk, which you can open only after you procure the key from Vera's body. Vera's room holds little of interest, although Sister is sometimes there.

12 Zimmer's Room

There are a couple footlockers, some scattered food and tools, and little else. Across the corridor is the locked hotel room, where you can spend the night if you have the Caps (or break in and sleep here).

13 Sister's Room

There's a small footlocker and a Holotape to listen to.

- Holotape: The Replicated Man (18/25)

MIDSHIP DECK

Salt-of-the-earth types reside up here, although there are more Chem addicts than the science staff would like. Or know about.

14 Bedroom

There's a large amount of food in here on shelves and in a fridge.

15 Common Room

Expect to see some wandering folk around here. There's little to steal, except items from footlockers.

16 Cantelli's Room

This is a Chem addict's room; there are Chems scattered about and a footlocker to loot.

17 Science Lab

There are three entrances to this lab, where a number of key characters, including Doctor Li, are usually located. Expect to hear an argument between a doctor and Zimmer. There are fresh vegetables and fruit here, the result of successful hydroponics experiments. One of the tables holds a Bobblehead. There's the usual array of food in the fridge.

- Bobblehead: Intelligence (19/20)

18 The Capitol Preservation Society

This is the home to Abraham Washington, who is very interested in any relics you may find on your journey (see nearby table). He also awards you with a Schematic if you complete **Miscellaneous Quest: Stealing Independence.** The Society Terminal is also here, where you can read the following:

- The Constitution of the U.S.A. (drafted, 1786)
- The Emancipation Proclamation (issued in 1862)
- The Gettysburg Address (speech by Lincoln, 1863)
- The Monroe Doctrine (presented in 1823)
- The U.S. Declaration of War on Germany (declared by Roosevelt, 1941)
- The U.S. Declaration of War on China (date unknown; either 2066 or 2067)

Inside Washington's room, there's food in the fridge, a Work Bench with a Bottlecap Mine, Health and Ammo to steal, and his personal terminal. You can read entries here about the Declaration expedition (where Sydney is mentioned), the Lincoln artifacts, and a planned expedition to salvage the Liberty Bell.

Note Beware! Items marked "†" are critical to complete other Miscellaneous Quests!

- Work Bench (35/46)
- 10mm Pistol and Ammo
- Frag Grenade
- Pulse Grenade
- First Aid Box Health and Chems
- Ammo Box Ammunition (2)
- Schematic: Railway Rifle (22/23)

19 Saint Monica's Church

You can pry open the collection box and open the rectory door to unlock a couple footlockers. Check behind the pulpit for a Holotape.

- Holotape: Replicated Man (19/25).

20 Seagrave Holmes' Room

His key is on the table, as is his terminal, which contains information on his "survival weapon" and some terse e-mail exchanges about Bannon between Seagrave and Doctor Li. There's a Holotape here too.

- Holotape: Replicated Man (20/25)

21 Rivet City Market

Potomac Attire: A clothes shop run by Bannon. You can Trade or Repair here. There's a load of Caps in Bannon's trunk.

A Quick Fix: A Chem supplier run by Cindy and Paulie Cantelli. Paulie has a key to open the trunk.

Rivet City Supply: A general store run by Seagrave Holmes. You can buy "a little bit of everything" here. He has the key to open his trunk, which contains a load of general supplies; nothing unique.

Gary's Galley: A food court run by Gary and daughter Angela : Purchase food and drink here. Find the key to open the two fridges and the trunk on Angela's corpse. There's little to take here; just a lot of food and a few Stimpaks.

Flak and Shrapel's: A weapons store with a great selection. There are several weapons to Steal and more in the trunk if you can acquire the key from Flak or Shrapnel.

The northwest corner of the market has a Work Bench with a Bottlecap Mine.

- Work Bench (36/46)
- Ammo Box Ammunition (4)
- Large Weapons Collection!

Note All the Traders have keys to their storage trunks, but you must kill them to obtain the keys.

LOWER DECK

22 The Muddy Rudder

Brock, Trinnie, and Belle Bonny are usually here. They all have keys to this area and to his room. There is copious amounts of alcohol, as well as food and two footlockers in Bonny's room.

- 10mm Pistol

THE BROKEN BOW

Access this area via an underwater door outside the bow's northern corner, or via a gantry across the water. Swim and then climb up to the floor that isn't waterlogged.

23 Entrance Door

Access this via the gantry outside. Flick the lock mechanism to unlock the door. Disarm the Mine before it blows you up.

- Frag Mine
- Ammo Box Ammunition
- First Aid Box Health and Chems
- Scoped .44 Magnum

24 Gas Leak

25 Trap Room and Corridor

Disarm the trip wire in the corridor, or you'll be engulfed in flames. Sidestep the pressure plate and disarm both Rigged Shotguns. Disarm the Mine on the table. There's a Stimpak and Purified Water here.

- Combat Shotgun and Ammo (2)
- Frag Mine
- Ammo Box Ammunition

ARTIFACT	LOCATION	PRICE (ABRAHAM WASHINGTON)	RELATED MISCELLANEOUS QUEST
Declaration of Independence	National Archives	Railway Rifle Schematics	Stealing Independence
Declaration of Independence (Faked)	National Archives	Railway Rifle Schematics	Stealing Independence
Bill of Rights	National Archives	125 Caps/100 Caps (High Barter Skill)	Stealing Independence
Magna Carta	National Archives	100 Caps/75 Caps (High Barter Skill)	Stealing Independence
Lincoln's Rifle	Museum of History	200 Caps/100 Caps	Head of State
Lincoln's Hat	Museum of History	140 Caps/70 Caps	Head of State
Action Abe	Museum of History	20 Caps/10 Caps	Head of State
John Wilkes Booth Wanted Poster	Museum of History	140 Caps/70 Caps	Head of State
Civil War Draft Poster	Museum of History	120 Caps/60 Caps	Head of State
Lincoln's Diary	Museum of History	200 Caps/100 Caps	Head of State
Lincoln's Head Penny Collection	Museum of History	30 Caps/15 Caps	Head of State
Gift Shop Poster of the Lincoln Memorial	Museum of History	Will not purchase	Head of State
Lincoln's Voice (Phonograph)	Museum of History	120 Caps/60 Caps	Head of State
Lincoln's Rifle	Museum of History	Will not purchase	Head of State
Agatha's Soil Stradivarius Violin	Vault 92	300 Caps/200 Caps (Speech Chall)	Agatha's Song

26 Pinkerton's Hideout

Flick the switch to open the door; the terminal is a trap. Inside, you'll find Pinkerton, and you can complete **Miscellaneous Quest: The Replicated Man**. Before you leave (and optionally reconstruct your face), search the area for some scattered Caps and a load of items. Pinkerton's Terminal (only accessible once you speak to him) has the City Founders Log (useful in **Miscellaneous Quest: The Wasteland Survival Guide**), and some android information to prove to Harkness that he's synthetic.

- Work Bench (37/46)
- Frag Grenade
- Blood Pack (4)
- D.C. Journal of Internal Medicine (18/25)
- Big Book of Science (18/25)
- Dean's Electronics 17/25)
- Stealth Boy (3)

FREEFORM QUEST: CHURCH DONATIONS

Seek out Father Clifford near St. Monica's church. You can ask whether donations are accepted. Naturally, they are. You have three options, each with a positive Karma reward:

10 Caps donation
50 Caps donation
100 Caps donation

> **Tip**
>
> There can be no end to your generosity: This is an excellent way to redeem yourself and shift your Karma back into positive territory if you've done some bad, bag things in your past. Feeling guilty? Let the Holy Spirit cast out your sins!

FREEFORM QUEST: A NICE DAY FOR A RIGHT WEDDING

Angela and Diego are madly in love, but the course of true love is running into some problems; Diego is a priest in training. To learn about this, you must listen to conversations in Rivet City, or simply follow Angela around until she speaks to Gary, Diego, Vera Weatherly, Paulie Cantelli.

Or, listen to Vera Weatherly and Gary, and Diego and Danvers. Armed with this information, you can try the following:

Lie to Father Clifford that Diego is sleeping with Angela. Diego ceases to be an acolyte. Father Clifford is so angry that he won't marry them and they live together in sin.

Threaten Diego by telling him you'll squeal to Father Clifford. Diego will stop seeing Angela. She will be very sad.

Give Angela an Ant Queen Pheromone Sac, which she can use to seduce Diego. Diego quits the priesthood and does the honorable thing in Father Clifford's eyes, and he is willing to marry them. You are invited to the ceremony. You can find the Pheromone on any Ant Queen, or you can buy some in the Quick Fix shop in the market.

FREEFORM QUEST: SUICIDE WATCH

Every day, Mister Lopez goes and stands on the observation deck at the top of the bridge tower, contemplating suicide. Meet him there during the day (between 8:00 AM–12:00 PM and between 2:00 PM–5:00 PM). You can

Agree to push him.
Try to talk him into jumping himself.
Try to get him to help Ted Strayer. Mister Lopez will no longer talk about suicide and will never return to the observation deck. An appeal to church doctrine has no effect.

FREEFORM QUEST: LIGHT-FINGERS HARGRAVE

James Hargrave is an unpleasant little tyke, but if you can play up his thievery, he agrees to steal some ammunition for you. Expect to wait 12 hours until you visit him again. Then, he'll have more every 12 additional hours.

FREEFORM QUEST: THE RUNAWAYS

Locate Tammy Hargrave, speak with her, and then find her son, James.

> Now you have the option to tease him about how awful his mother is. Succeed in your **Speech**, and James and C.J. Young run away, across the Rivet City bridge, to a couple of chairs and a table just west of the entrance to Anacostia Metro.

Bring them back, as Tammy doesn't even notice, by speaking with any security guard, Angela, or Mister Lopez, and you'll be clued in that they escaped via the bridge. Speak with James when you find him and convince them to return.

Or leave them here.

FREEFORM QUEST: SLAVE HUNT

Mei Wong is terrified of Sister; she recognizes him as a Slaver. She used to be a slave and fears that he will capture her and take her back.

> Succeed with a **Speech** Challenge and Mei Wong reveals she's a runaway slave. You can:

Tell Sister that Mei Wong disappears one night, recaptured by Slavers.

Or, tell Sister, then go back to Mei and let her know you revealed her identity. She commits suicide.

Or, you can give her enough Caps to purchase a gun.

Or, stay out of this altogether.

FREEFORM QUEST: OVERDOSE

Paulie Cantelli is a Chem addict. Why not help him along and give him some Chems? Give him some more! Then leave him alone to overdose and die.

FREEFORM QUEST: BELLE'S CASH BOX

Belle Bonny has a cash box hidden in her room, just off the Muddy Rudder. Buy Trinnie three drinks, and she'll tell you where Belle keeps the cash box.

- Caps

FREEFORM QUEST: PRIVATE JONES

> Private Jones guards the Armory up in the Bridge Tower. Try pretending (using **Speech**) there's an emergency and his assistance is needed. Once he is gone, you have a better chance to rob the Armory, although the turret inside still makes it very difficult.

FREEFORM QUEST: COUNCIL SEAT

Seagrave Holmes is considering running for a seat on the city council to represent the market. This means he will replace Bannon. Speak with Bannon, and he asks you to poke around in Seagrave's room and see if you can find anything incriminating. It turns out that Seagrave used to do business with Slavers. You can turn over the evidence to Danvers or tell Danvers that Bannon is trying to blackmail Seagrave. The former results in Seagraves abandoning his council seat campaign. Bannon's prices are lowered at his store. The latter results in Bannon losing his seat on the council. Seagrave's prices are lowered at his store.

Schematic: Dathclaw Gauntlet (21/23)

APPENDICES — COMPLETION — TOUR — MISC. QUESTS — MAIN QUEST — BESTIARY — TRAINING

FREEFORM QUEST: TUNNEL SNAKES FOREVER!

When you finish **Miscellaneous Quest: Trouble on the Homefront**, make sure Butch is still alive and the Overseer has lost

 control (either by convincing him to step down, killing him, or sabotaging the Vault). Move to the Muddy Rudder, strike up a conversation, and you can convince him to join you in some adventuring—but only if your Karma is neutral.

- Follower: Butch

9.16: ANACOSTIA CROSSING (LAT 19/ LONG -16)

- Threat Level: 1
- Underground Connection

The Metro Station entrance leads to several linked underground metro areas:

D.C. U22.A: Anacostia Crossing Station (page 452).

D.C. U22.B: Museum Station (page 453).

D.C. U6.B: Metro Central (page 445).

> ### Note
> From D.C. U6.B, you can reach D.C. Interior Zones 11: Dupont Circle; 12: Vernon Square; 14: Georgetown; 15: Pennsylvania Avenue; 16: Arlington National Cemetery; 17: The Mall; and 18: Seward Square.

The following surface locations can be accessed from Anacostia Crossing:

17.06: The Mall (near Museum of History Entrance) (page 422).

17.09: The Mall (near Museum of Technology Atrium) (page 425).

18.05: Seward Square (Southeast) (page 432).

Various locations from U6.B: Metro Central (page 445).

> ### Note
> Located close to Rivet City, this station offers excellent (if convoluted) access to almost any D.C. Interior location, but it is mainly useful for reaching the Mall.

9.17: FLOODED METRO (LAT 04/ LONG -18)

- Threat Level: 2
- Faction: Raider
- Collectible: Skill Book
- Underground Connection

This leads to the following linked underground area:

D.C. U19: Flooded Metro (Interior) (page 451).

The following surface Locations can be accessed from that underground area:

20.03: Mason District South (page 439).

The station exterior is dry, but the interior is a mess. On the surface, this entrance is half-hidden due to the large traffic accident [8.BB] nearby. Watch for Raiders south of the pileup. Check the Pulowski Preservation Shelter for Stimpaks and the following:

- Pulse Mine
- Chinese Army: Spec. Ops. Training Manual (14/25)

9.18: ARLINGTON LIBRARY (LAT 08/ LONG -19)

- Miscellaneous Quest: The Wasteland Survival Guide, Stealing Independence
- Freeform Quest
- Threat Level: 3
- Faction: Brotherhood of Steel, Raider
- Danger: Baseball Pitcher, Grenade Bouquet, Mines, Terminal Trap
- Collectibles: Nuka-Cola Quantum, Scribe Pre-War Book (10), Skill Book (6)
- Guns and Ammunition

- Health and Chems
- Highly Visible Landmark
- Interior Exploration
- Lots o' Caps
- Sleep Mattress
- Hostiles: Raider, Radroach
- Friendly: Brotherhood Paladin

INTERIOR MAPS AND LOCATIONS

Arlington Public Library Lobby

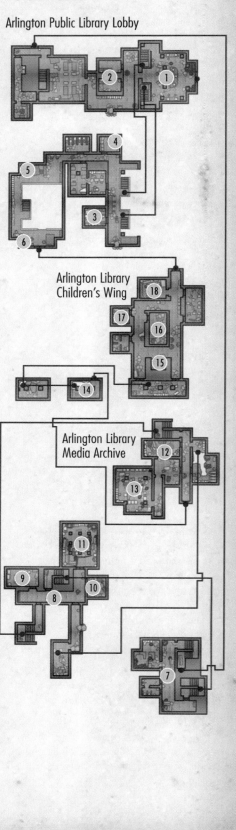

Arlington Library Children's Wing

Arlington Library Media Archive

INHABITANTS

Scribe Yearling

A 30-year-old Scribe assigned to the Archives, Scribe Yearling has been transferred to a mission to gather prewar knowledge from the Wasteland. She is young, friendly, and the polar opposite of Scribe Rothchild. She's very dedicated and tends to be a bit shy. When you first meet her, she is in this building but may move to the Citadel; check there if you can't find her.

Related Interactions

- Scribe Yearling: Approach her about collecting Scribe Pre-War Books for profit.

GENERAL NOTES

Still standing amid the rubble is this imposing library with its Greek columns and single entrance, across from the Alexandria Arms. Enter via the single set of doors. Before you head inside, inspect the Pulowski Preservation Shelter, where a corpse still clutches the following items:

- 10mm Pistol and Ammo
- Guns and Bullets (18/25)

ARLINGTON PUBLIC LIBRARY LOBBY

1 Front Desk

Scribe Yearling is here, collecting Scribe Pre-War Books (Freeform Quest). Expect fire support from Brotherhood of Steel Paladins throughout this interior area. Hack the desk terminal. You can access the card catalog from here, which Moira Brown requests during **Miscellaneous Quest: The Wasteland Survival Guide.**

- Card Catalog Holotape
- Ammo Box Ammunition (5)

2 Ground-Floor Restrooms

- First Aid Box Health and Chems (2)

3 Upper Office Mattress and Gun Cabinet

4 Upper-Floor Office

- Big Book of Science (19/25)

5 Upper Balcony Bookcases

- Ammo Box Ammunition (2)
- Scribe Pre-War Book (62/98)

6 Upper-Balcony Bookcases

- Ammo Box Ammunition (2)
- Scribe Pre-War Book (63 & 64/98)

ARLINGTON LIBRARY MEDIA ARCHIVE

Three levels of Raider combat lead to securing some necessary archives, an old ink pot, and more collectibles.

7 Northwest Corridor (Lower Floor)

A group of Raiders ambushes you from this point, using a Baseball Pitcher trap.

8 Top of Stairs Mine Trap (Middle Floor)

- Frag Mine (3)

9 Pool Table Recreation Room (Middle Floor)

- First Aid Box Health and Chems
- Tales of a Junktown Jerky Vendor (16/24)

10 Storage Room (Middle Floor)

Use the turret control terminal to shut down the turret in the media room to the north.

- First Aid Box Health and Chems

11 North Media Room (Middle Floor)

Check the metal box next to the Ammo Boxes for restoration supplies. The ink is useful for faking the Declaration of Independence during the **Miscellaneous Quest: Stealing Independence.** Don't forget the Scribe Book on the conveyor belt in the northeast corner.

- Ink Container
- Ammo Box Ammunition (2)
- Scribe Pre-War Book (65/98)

12 Office (Upper Floor)

Use the turret control terminal to shut down the turret in the adjacent room to the south. Beware of two Mines to the west.

- Frag Mine (2)

13 South Media Room (Upper Floor)

Unlock the floor safe with bobby pins or the terminal in the corner. There is a second terminal, where you can check out how the citizens of Arlington used to read and clean their teeth. You can also transfer Library Archives and access the card catalog.

- Floor Safe Items
- Tumblers Today (18/25)
- Blood Pack
- Scribe Pre-War Book (66/98)
- Nuka-Cola Quantum (71/94)
- Holotape: Media Archives

ARLINGTON LIBRARY CHILDREN'S WING

14 Skeletal Cage Room and Floor Holes (Three Floors)

Drop through the floor after securing Stimpaks and these items:

- Ammo Box Ammunition (3)
- Blood Pack
- Sawed-Off Shotgun and Ammo
- First Aid Box Health and Chems
- Guns and Bullets (19/25)
- Scribe Pre-War Book (67–69/98)
- Wall Safe Items (middle floor)

15 Coffee Machine Nook

- Lying: Congressional Style (16/25)
- Scribe Pre-War Book (70/98)

16 Central Office

Raider corpses are chained to the ceiling. Beware the Grenade Bouquet as you enter.

- Frag Grenade (3)
- Ammo Box Ammunition

17 Northwest Office

Beware the terminal trap!

- Frag Grenade
- Ammo Box Ammunition
- Scribe Pre-War Book (71/98)

18 Playroom

Filled with toys, a personal footlocker, and some child skeletons.

FREEFORM QUEST: YEARNING FOR LEARNING: SCRIBE PRE-WAR BOOKS

Scribe Yearling is particularly concerned about losing historical knowledge, and despite some misgivings about Elder Lyons, she is happy to secure knowledge the old-fashioned way—through the amassing of prewar literature. Meet her in the lobby, agree to aid her, and scour the Wasteland for Scribe Pre-War Books. For each one you return to Yearling, she rewards you 100 Caps. Yes, that means a payout of 11,100 Caps if you find them all. There are 1,000 Caps' worth of books in this building alone! Return here as often as you like.

- 1,000 Caps

TRAINING — BESTIARY — MAIN QUEST — MISC. QUESTS — TOUR — COMPLETION — APPENDICES

Secondary Locations

9.A: D.C. IRON STATUE (LAT 07/LONG -04)

- Threat Level: 1
- Highly Visible Landmark

A looming statue watches over the forecourt of the Farragut West Metro Station. Use this as a landmark.

9.B: D.C. IRON STATUE (LAT 07/LONG -05)

- Threat Level: 1
- Faction: Raider
- Highly Visible Landmark

A second, lower statue in the Farragut West area, with a small Raider hidey-hole below it.

9.C: RUSTING TRAFFIC ACCIDENT (LAT 04/LONG -07)

- Threat Level: 1
- Highly Visible Landmark

Just north of the Sewer Waystation is the scene of an ancient traffic accident. It makes a great explosion!

9.D: SEWER GRATE (LAT 07/LONG -07)

- Threat Level: 2
- Danger: Low Radiation
- Interior Exploration
- Underground Connection

This sewer grate leads to a linked underground area:

D.C. U14: **Hubris Comics Utility Tunnel**s (page 448)

The following surface location can be accessed from this sewer grate:

20.01: Hubris Comics Publishing (page 437).

An effluent pipe adjacent to Grandma Sparkles's shack (right next to the outhouse) is a cunning way to head into D.C. Interior Zone 20.

9.E: ROAD SIGNS AND FORECOURT(LAT 08/LONG -07)

- Threat Level: 1

On both sides of the Anchorage Bridge entrance are crumbling brown signs pointing east.

9.F: ANCHORAGE BRIDGE (LAT 07/LONG -07)

- Threat Level: 2
- Faction: Raider
- Danger: Low Radiation, Mines

There are two ways across this bridge: slowly Sneaking forward and Disarming each of the 12 Frag Mines, or dashing across and leaving a massive explosion in your wake! Watch for alerted Raiders if you've been making noise.

- Frag Mine (12)

9.G: MILITARY TENT AND TRUCK DEFENSES (LAT 10/LONG -06)

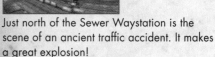

- Character: Wastelander Captive

- Threat Level: 3
- Faction: Super Mutant
- Collectible: Skill Book
- Guns and Ammunition
- Health and Chems
- Sleep Mattress
- Hostiles: Centaur, Super Mutant Genus

Two parked container trucks surround a tent. The yellow truck container has a dead Wastelander and some pertinent items, as does the tent, which has a place to sleep, a Stimpak, and a Holotape.

- .44 Scoped Magnum
- Ammo Box Ammunition (3)
- First Aid Box Health and Chems
- Pugilism Illustrated (20/25)
- Holotape: Keller (21/24)

Rescue any captives and take the gift you see for a small boost to your Karma. Refuse for a larger boost.

9.H: SCAVENGER'S JETTY (LAT 09/LONG -08)

- Threat Level: 1
- Faction: Wastelander
- Services: Repairer, Trader
- Friendly: Scavenger

Sitting on the jetty with a bucket of beers is a scruffy Scavenger. Trade and Repair with him.

9.I: OUTPOST (LAT 04/LONG -11)

- Threat Level: 2
- Faction: Wastelander
- Danger: Terminal Trap
- Collectible: Fat Man Mini-Nuke, Nuka-Cola Quantum
- Guns and Ammunition
- Interior Exploration
- Sleep Mattress
- Hostile: Feral Wastelander, Super Mutant

On the southern outskirts of Grayditch is an office building with a pair of metal doors on the south wall. Wastelanders have gone a little too Feral to be friendly. Dispatch or Sneak around them, and search the outpost for a bed, food and cleaning supplies in the fridge, two Cartons of Cigarettes, some Darts, a gun cabinet, and a back room with an imprisoned Super Mutant and more goods. Unlock the Super Mutant's gate when you're using Sneak and a Stealth Boy. This is a great tactical way to start a fight between Feral Wastelanders and the Mutie! Disarm the terminal from behind to grab the Frag Grenade; it's a trap!

- Ammo Box Ammunition (3)
- Mini-Nuke (54/71)
- Nuka-Cola Quantum (72/94)
- Frag Grenade

9.J: SEWER GRATE (LAT 09/LONG -11)

- Threat Level: 2
- Danger: Low Radiation
- Interior Exploration
- Underground Connection

This sewer grate leads to a linked underground area:

D.C. U13: County Sewer Mainline (page 448)

The following surface location can be accessed from this sewer grate:

9.03: Sewer Waystation (page 376).

This effluent pipe is a quick way to maneuver between the waystation north of Grayditch, allowing you to escape northwest into the Wasteland. Or, emerge here. This is a central location close to the Citadel that allows a quick trek to Rivet City.

9.K: POTOMAC BRIDGE (LAT 10/LONG -11)

- Main Quest: Infiltration
- Threat Level: 2
- Faction: Raider
- Danger: Low Radiation
- Highly Visible Landmark
- Sleep Mattress
- Hostile: Raider

The Key Bridge stretches from the east to west banks of the Potomac, from the Super Mutant's office domain [9.P] to the Citadel. This is a major span and a good way to head back and forth to the two large sections of town without getting your feet wet (and irradiated). The Key Bridge is destroyed on the Citadel (west) side, and there are some smaller arches to investigate; there's a small Raider camp with Chems, beer, a locked safe, and a Raider standing next to a fire extinguisher that's too good a sniping opportunity to miss. On the eastern end, beware of Muties with missile launchers!

- Floor Safe Items

9.L: FESTIVE RAIDER CAMP (LAT 12/LONG -10)

- Threat Level: 2
- Faction: Raider
- Collectible: Skill Book
- Guns and Ammunition
- Health and Chems
- Sleep Mattress
- Hostile: Raider

This is just a block south of Dukov's place. When you've ruined the lives of the punks here, check their stuff out; aside from Chems, beer, food, and mattresses, there's the following:

- Ammo Box Ammunition (4)
- Duck and Cover! (21/25)
- First Aid Box Health and Chems

9.M: SCAVENGER SHACK (LAT 12/LONG -11)

- Threat Level: 1
- Faction: Wastelander
- Services: Repairer, Trader
- Danger: Low Radiation
- Friendly: Scavenger

Under the eastern span of the Potomac Bridge, just south of the Festive Raiders Camp, is a small shack with a Scavenger happy to Trade or Repair your items. There's some food and beer to steal here, if you're feeling violent.

- Ammo Box Ammunition

9.N: SEWER GRATE (LAT 04/LONG -13)

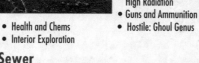

- Threat Level: 3
- Faction: Ghoul
- Danger: Gas Leak, Grenade Bouquet (2), High Radiation
- Guns and Ammunition
- Hostile: Ghoul Genus
- Health and Chems
- Interior Exploration

Sewer

Due south of the outpost, on the edge of Grayditch, is an irradiated hole, where Ghouls prowl the earth. There's a sewer grate here, leading into a small, dead-end tunnel structure.

Danger: Escaping Gas!

Grab a Frag Grenade, and from the entrance (and no farther!), lob it into the pool of water so it detonates in the gassy area, dispelling the gas.

Ammo Cache

- Ammo Box Ammunition (2)

Grenade Bouquet and Trip Wire (2)

- Frag Grenades (6)

Dead Wastelander

- Ammo Box Ammunition
- First Aid Box Health and Chems
- Missile Launcher and Ammo (in Locker)

9.O: SEWER ENTRANCE MANHOLE (LAT 09/LONG -13)

- Main Quest: The Waters Of Life
- Threat Level: 1
- Faction: Brotherhood Of Steel

The manhole entrance leads to two linked underground tunnels:

D.C. U18.A: Taft Tunnel (page 450).

D.C. U18.B: Taft Tunnels (page 451).

The following surface location can be accessed from the sewer entrance:

9.14: Jefferson Memorial (page 385).

This manhole cover close to the Citadel's entrance is securely sealed and is only accessible during one portion of **Main Quest: The Waters of Life.** It is one of the few locations that cannot be entered at any other time; you must Fast Travel or head across the water to reach the Jefferson Memorial Gift Shop.

9.P: SUPER MUTANT OFFICE RUINS (LAT 13/LONG -13)

- Threat Level: 3
- Faction: Super Mutant
- Danger: Shotgun Trap
- Guns and Ammunition
- Health and Chems
- Interior Exploration
- Hostiles: Centaur, Super Mutant Genus

Access Hall

Working from south to north, there's a ruined office building across from the Irradiated Metro that has a strong concentration of Super Mutants; Sneak around behind them (watch for the Centaur!) and blast them, heading up through the concrete ruins and across the planks to the Gore Bags and stash:

- Ammo Box Ammunition (2)
- First Aid Box Health and Chems

Across from here, just north of the Irradiated Metro entrance, is a sunken set of steps in the forecourt leading to an access hall.

Generator Room Pressure Plate

Step around it so a Rigged Shotgun doesn't shoot you in the knee.

- Combat Shotgun and Ammo

Continue upstairs to the door leading to the Capital Wasteland. Step into the bridge area and slay the two Super Mutants who love to strafe you from up here.

9.Q: SUNKEN BOAT AND JETTY (LAT 11/LONG -15)

- Threat Level: 2
- Danger: Low Radiation

Check the jetty for two personal footlockers (both locked), and enter the boat's cabin to spot an Ammo Box, a few Chems, and the boat's captain—what's left of him.

9.R: BOATS AND BAIT (LAT 13/LONG -15)

- Threat Level: 1
- Danger: Low Radiation
- Health and Chems
- Interior Exploration
- Hostile: Radroach

Pirate Pely may have sunk to Davy Jones's locker, but Pely's lockers are still intact. Head into the shack and rummage around; there's a terminal you can Hack to unlock the counter safe.

- Counter Safe Items
- First Aid Box Health and Chems

9.S: SUPER MUTANT BONFIRE (LAT 16/LONG -16)

- Threat Level: 3
- Faction: Super Mutant
- Collectible: Skill Book
- Guns and Ammunition
- Health and Chems
- Sleep Mattress
- Captive Wastelander
- Hostile: Super Mutant Genus

This is a very-well-defended location, with dozens of spiked girders, barbed wire, and bloodthirsty shouting to make you think twice about attacking. The only way into this area is up the road; use the Muties' own barricades against them by peeking out, firing, and gradually dropping the fiends one by one. Rescue the captive, search the dead Raiders, and check the camp for mattresses and the following:

- Ammo Box Ammunition (5)
- First Aid Box Health and Chems (2)
- Lying: Congressional Style (17/25)

Rescue any captives and take their gift for a small boost to your Karma. Refuse for a larger boost.

9.T: FLOODED METRO RAIDER CAMP (LAT 04/LONG -19)

- Threat Level: 3
- Faction: Raider
- Collectible: Nuka-Cola Quantum, Skill Book (2)
- Guns and Ammunition
- Health and Chems
- Sleep Mattress
- Hostile: Raider, Turret

Enter from west to east. This is a well-defended area, although you can leap the rubble pile or the weak spot—the pile of tires to the south. Once you're in, execute the Raider on the vantage point on the camp's west side (it is carrying the missile launcher), using the planks to climb to his defenses. He's guarding the following:

- Ammo Box Ammunition (2)
- First Aid Box Health and Chems
- Tumblers Today (19/25)

Bed in an Alcove

There's a gun case to open here too.

- First Aid Box Health and Chems

Counter with Cash Register

Here and on the nearby bookcases, there's food, alcohol, Darts, Cartons of Cigarettes, and the following:

- Pugilism Illustrated (21/25)
- Nuka-Cola Quantum (73/94)
- Ammo Box Ammunition (4)

Small Table

- 10mm Pistol

Bridge Terminal

Hack it to shut down the turret on the bridge.

- First Aid Box Health and Chems

Blue Container Truck (freeway below)

- Ammo Box Ammunition (3)

9.U: RUINED OFFICE RAIDER CAMP (LAT 06/LONG -18)

- Threat Level: 3
- Faction: Raider
- Danger: Baseball Pitcher, Bear Trap (3), Chain Trap, Grenade Bouquet, Mines (7), Shotgun Trap
- Guns and Ammunition
- Sleep Mattress
- Work Bench
- Hostile: Raider, Turret

Looking out toward the Arlington Library is a rubble-filled, three-level office space with a Raider Sniper. Sneaking works well here. Head west, disarming six Frag Mines at the ruined doorway entrance. At the Girder-on-a-Chain trap, disarm the trip wire at the entrance threshold, then watch for the Bear Trap, the Frag Mine, and the trip wire for a Rigged Shotgun as you climb the stairs.

There are two more Bear Traps and a Grenade Bouquet on the next floor, where a turret targets you. This Raider means business! You can avoid the turret and a Baseball Pitcher trap if you shimmy along the floor ledge by the bathroom sink and step into the room behind. Here, you can dispatch the Raider, gather his Chems and Stimpaks, fiddle at the Work Bench, open the Ammo Box, and pry apart any of the four safes and gun cabinet.

- Work Bench (38/46)
- Frag Mine (7)
- Combat Shotgun and Ammo
- Frag Grenades (3)
- Floor Safe Items (4)
- Ammo Box Ammunition

9.V: JACKKNIFED JUKEBOX TRUCK (LAT 07/LONG -19)

- Threat Level: 1
- Highly Visible Landmark

A jackknifed truck with a cargo of three Jukeboxes in the back. They all tune to Three Dog; switch one on and listen for it as an audible landmark.

9.W: TALON COMPANY RECON CAMP (LAT 08/LONG -20)

- Threat Level: 3
- Faction: Talon Mercenary
- Collectible: Skill Book
- Guns and Ammunition
- Health and Chems
- Sleep Mattress
- Work Bench
- Hostile: Talon Company Merc, Talon Company Robot, Turret

South of Arlington Library, a reconnaissance unit from the Talon Mercenary Company is well armed and hunkered down. Beware of incoming robots, missiles, and a turret. After combat, check the ruined building where the camp is located. There are bunk beds, batteries, a wall terminal for deactivating the turret (Sneak here to shut it down), a Carton of Cigarettes, a Work Bench with a Bottlecap Mine, an undercounter safe, and the following:

- Work Bench (39/46)
- Ammo Box Ammunition (7)
- Nikola Tesla and You (19/25)
- Stealth Boy
- First Aid Box Health and Chems (2)
- Counter Safe Items

9.X: SMALL SEWER (LAT 09/ LONG -20)

- Threat Level: 3
- Faction: Raider
- Guns and Ammunition
- Health and Chems
- Interior Exploration
- Hostile: Raider

Small Sewer

Southeast of Arlington Library near the Talon Company Camp is a sunken set of steps leading to a door. Open it, and enter a small subterranean sewage treatment area.

Lower Storage Room

There are metal boxes, a Stimpak, and the following items in here:

- Ammo Box Ammunition (2)
- Chinese Assault Rifle (2)
- Frag Grenade

Locked Storage Area (Lowest Level)

Open the locked door at the wall terminal or door. Inside is a Metal Helmet, a floor safe, and these items:

- First Aid Box Health and Chems
- Ammo Box Ammunition (4)
- Silenced 10mm Pistol
- Floor Safe Items

9.Y: OVERTURNED CONTAINER TRUCK (LAT 10/LONG -20)

- Threat Level: 3
- Danger: Low Radiation
- Hostile: Mirelurk Genus

Southeast of the sewer entrance, this truck is empty and the riverbank has a small cluster of Mirelurk and Brahmin bones.

9.Z: MIRELURK JETTY (LAT 11/LONG -18)

- Threat Level: 2
- Danger: Low Radiation
- Hostile: Mirelurk Genus

This is a place to launch long-range attacks on the Super Mutants over at the Jefferson Memorial, but this rickety jetty and boat hold no items.

9.AA: RUSTING TUB (LAT 12/LONG -19)

This contains no items; use it to clamber out of the water.

9.BB: RED SPEEDBOAT (LAT 12/LONG -20)

- Threat Level: 1
- Danger: Low Radiation

Stuck in the middle of the Potomac is a half-sunk speedboat.

- First Aid Box Health and Chems
- Hunting Rifle
- Ammo Box Ammunition (2)

9.CC: RIVET CITY JUNK HEAP (LAT 16/LONG -20)

- Threat Level: 1

At the southwestern end of Rivet City, several planes have slipped off the landing bay and into a small collection of cars. There's a Pulowski Shelter here, too, but no items.

9.DD: ENTRANCE TO BROKEN BOW (LAT 17/LONG -19)

- Threat Level: 1
- Faction: Wastelander
- Danger: Low Radiation

This is an alternate method of entering the broken bow (interior exploration is covered in Rivet City). You must open it from the inside.

9.EE: IRRADIATED TUB (LAT 18/LONG -20)

- Threat Level: 2
- Danger: Low Radiation

In the irradiated marshland is a rusting tub and speedboat.

- First Aid Box Health and Chems
- Ammo Box Ammunition (2)

ENCLAVE CAMP LOCATIONS
CAMP E9.01 (LAT 12/LONG -07)

- Main Quest: Picking Up The Trail Threat Level: 3
- Health and Chems
- Guns and Ammunition

An Enclave Officer is guarding a large container, which contains a Modified Deathclaw.

- Enclave First Aid Box Health and Chems
- Enclave Ammo Box Ammunition

CAMP E9.02 (LAT 7/LONG -18)

- Main Quest: Picking Up The Trail
- Threat Level: 2

A Vertibird lands in the forecourt northwest of the Arlington Library, depositing a small squad of three soldiers. Try launching a missile as it comes in to land.

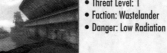

Zones 10–21: Interior D.C. Metropolitan Ruins

ZONE 10: CHEVY CHASE OVERVIEW

- Fat Men: 1/9
- Fat Man Mini-Nukes: 1/71
- Skill Book [Science]: 1/25
- Unique Items: 1/89

PRIMARY LOCATIONS

10.01: Tenleytown / Friendship Station

10.02: Metro Junction

10.03: Galaxy News Radio

SECONDARY LOCATIONS

10.A: Pulowski Preservation Shelter

10.B: Pulowski Preservation Shelter

10.C: City Coach Liner

10.D: City Coach Liner Barricade

10.E: G.N.R. Plaza Metro Entrance

10.F: G.N.R. Plaza

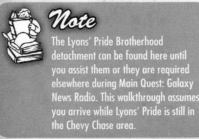

Note

The Lyons' Pride Brotherhood detachment can be found here until you assist them or they are required elsewhere during Main Quest: Galaxy News Radio. This walkthrough assumes you arrive while Lyons' Pride is still in the Chevy Chase area.

PRIMARY LOCATIONS

10.01: TENLEYTOWN / FRIENDSHIP STATION (CHEVY CHASE NORTH)

- Main Quest: Following in His Footsteps
- Threat Level: 2
- Factions: Brotherhood of Steel, Super Mutant
- Guns and Ammunition
- Underground Connection
- Hostiles: Super Mutant Genus

Note

The Metro Station entrance leads to two linked Underground metro areas: D.C. U1.B and D.C. U1.A.

Location D.C. U1.A: Farragut West Station (page 443).

Location D.C. U1.B: Tenleytown / Friendship Station (page 443).

The following surface locations can be accessed from the Underground Metro tunnels:

Location 6.10: Friendship Heights Station (page 334).

Location 9.02: Farragut West Metro Station (page 376).

INHABITANTS
Sentinel Sarah Lyons

Sarah Lyons was born in the West Coast headquarters of the Brotherhood of Steel, and at the age of seven she accompanied her father on his journey east to the Capital Wasteland. She's Brotherhood through and through, and as dedicated and decorated as her father when he was younger. Sarah commands a group of soldiers assigned to patrol the Washington D.C. interior and operates out of the GNR studio outpost.

Paladin Vargas

The sergeant of Lyons' Pride, Vargas is 30, and a no-nonsense, professional type. He is Sarah's right hand man; she relies on him for his experience and advice, and he supports her and mentors her. There is a very close but mostly unspoken friendship between them.

Knight Captain Colvin

A sniper in Lyons' Pride, Colvin is 40, friendly, and warm to everyone; he has priest-like tendencies. To him, combat is like worship, and he treats his rifle as a holy object and his targets as the unfortunate victims of his god's wrath. He says a prayer for the soul of each mutant he kills. He's extremely experienced, and completely unflappable: all according to god's will.

Initiate Reddin

Initiate Reddin is an overly curious and excitable recruit on his first combat assignment. Vargas does what he can to restrain him and teach him the ways of the Brotherhood. Reddin was added to Sarah's unit against his advice (and probably hers), but although he may act angry and annoyed at Reddin, it is entirely because he is trying to keep him alive.

Initiate Jennings

Unfortunately, Vargas failed in that responsibility for this recruit, as Initiate Jennings bore the full brunt of a Super Mutant attack, and recently succumbed to the wounds.

GENERAL NOTES

A fierce and protracted battle on these mean streets pits man and woman against Mutant.

Head out of the station and you'll face a group of Super Mutants and Brotherhood of Steel soldiers engaged in fierce urban warfare. Press on, blasting Super Mutants, and you can speak with Sarah Lyons, and the rest of her Pride. Head into a covered passageway around to the perimeter of the New Dawn Elementary school (north of the G.N.R. Building), and you can locate dead Initiate Jennings. Take Power Armor, a Laser Pistol and Ammo, and a Power Helmet from the body.

• Power Armor and Helmet   • Laser Pistol and Ammo

10.02: METRO JUNCTION (CHEVY CHASE EAST)

• Threat Level: 1   • Underground Connection

 Note

The Metro Station entrance leads to one linked Underground Metro Area: D.C. U2.

Location D.C. U2: Metro Junction (page 443).

You can access the following four surface locations from this Underground junction:

Location 11.02: Metro Junction (Dupont Circle North) (page 400).

Location 11.08: Metro Junction (Dupont Circle Northeast) (page 402).

Location 12.01: Metro Junction (Vernon Square North) (page 403).

Location 12.05: Metro Junction (Vernon Square Northwest) (page 405).

One of four linked Metro junctions, this station east of Chevy Chase is at a dead-end, surrounded by rubble, and there are no nearby foes or items to worry about.

10.03: GALAXY NEWS RADIO

• Main Quest: Following in His Footsteps, Main Quest: Galaxy News Radio
• Threat Level: 5
• Factions: Brotherhood of Steel, Super Mutant
• Danger: Behemoth
• Collectibles: Fat Man Launcher, Fat Man Mini-Nuke, Skill Book
• Area Is Locked
• Health and Chems
• Highly Visible Landmark
• Interior Exploration
• Radio Signal
• Sleep Mattress
• Hostiles: Super Mutant Genus, Super Mutant Behemoth

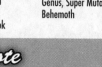 **Note**

This location links above ground, to an exterior exit: 11.01: G.N.R. Building (Rear Exit) (page 406).

INTERIOR MAPS AND LOCATIONS

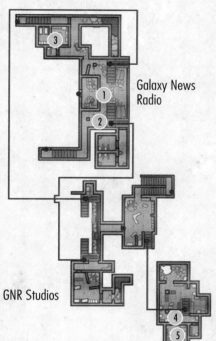

Galaxy News Radio

GNR Studios

INHABITANTS
Three Dog

Born to parents who made their way in the world as members of a traveling theater group, Three Dog grew up listening to rock music, hating the government that he never knew (but surely caused the nuclear holocaust), fully believing in the rights of free speech and communal law. He is fully committed to "spreading the signal" of his radio station to anyone who will listen; it's his duty to counter the propaganda spouted by the Enclave on their station.

Knight Dillon
Knight Finley
Knight Sergeant Wilks

One of three Brotherhood Knights charged

with defending the GNR Radio Station interior. All Knights are employed in the service of Elder Lyons, who resides in the Citadel. Although they're haughty, they'll help you out of a fix and they hate the Super Mutants as much as you do.

Just north of the exterior plaza linking Chevy Chase North is the Early Dawn Elementary School, a ruined structure with Super Mutants battling to reach the GNR Offices from this location. Ideally with Brotherhood backup, head through the maze of corridors, or ascend either of the two stairwells to the upper floor, which provides better sniping opportunities. This leads to the plaza itself, which is the scene of a fierce firefight with Super Mutants, and one of their spectacularly gigantic offspring, the Behemoth.

You can help defeat it by obtaining the Fat Man and Mini-Nuke from the corpse of the fallen Brotherhood Knight on the plaza fountain. Once all greenskins are defeated in the area, you can enter the offices via the main door. Or, climb the rubble pile and enter via the south side door.

• Galaxy News Radio Signal   • Mini-Nuke (55/71)
• Fat Man (7/9)

GALAXY NEWS RADIO
1 Foyer

Brotherhood Paladins guard this foyer, including Knight Dillon and Knight Finley, who tell you about the building and the location of Three Dog.

2 Southern Stairwell (underside)
• First Aid Box Health and Chems (2)

3 Kitchen and Bunk-Bed Room

GNR STUDIOS

Unless Three Dog has opened it, the door at the bottom of the stairs to Dupont Circle [11.01] is firmly locked.

4 Three Dog's Workshop and Restroom

There's junk, food, and the following to steal here:

• First Aid Box Health and Chems (2)
• Big Book of Science (20/25)

5 Three Dog's Bedroom

You can ask Three Dog where your father is, and help him "spread the word." Refer to the Main Quest for all the details. If you want his headgear, you'll have to kill him.

• Baseball Bat
• Three Dog's Head Wrap (66/89)

TRAINING — BESTIARY — MAIN QUEST — MISC. QUESTS — TOUR — COMPLETION — APPENDICES

SECONDARY LOCATIONS

10.A: PULOWSKI PRESERVATION SHELTER

- Threat Level: 1

This contains some Purified Water, a Lead Pipe, and a Teddy Bear.

10.B: PULOWSKI PRESERVATION SHELTER

- Threat Level: 1

You see a long-dead skeleton in here, when you open it to peer in.

10.C: CITY COACH LINER

- Threat Level: 1

This can be destroyed, or used as cover when assaulting Super Mutants to the west.

10.D: CITY COACH LINER BARRICADE

- Threat Level: 5

Blocking the path, these are shoved aside when the Super Mutant Behemoth appears during your battle to the GNR Building.

10.E: G.N.R. PLAZA METRO ENTRANCE

- Threat Level: 5

This Metro Station entrance is completely blocked with rubble and cannot be entered.

10.F: G.N.R. PLAZA

- Threat Level: 5

This large plaza is where a terrifying battle between Brotherhood Soldiers and the Super Mutants holed up in the nearby elementary school takes place. Retrieve a Fat Man from the corpse of a Brotherhood Soldier to defeat the Behemoth, if you wish.

ZONE 11: DUPONT CIRCLE

- Scribe Pre-War Books: 1/98
- Skill Book [Barter]: 1/24, Skill Book [Big Guns]: 1/25

PRIMARY LOCATIONS

11.01: G.N.R. Building (Rear Exit)
11.02: Metro Junction
11.03: Collapsed Car Tunnel (North)
11.04: Collapsed Car Tunnel (South)
11.05: Dupont Circle Station
11.06: Lady Frumperton's Fashions
11.07: Dry Sewer
11.08: Metro Junction
11.09: Sunken Sewer
11.10: Foggy Bottom Station (Dupont West)

SECONDARY LOCATIONS

11.A: City Coach Liner (2)
11.B: City Coach Liner
11.C: Raider Outpost
11.D: Raider Fountain Fortifications
11.E: Raider Rubble Pile
11.F: Raider Sleeping Camp

PRIMARY LOCATIONS

11.01: G.N.R. BUILDING (REAR EXIT)

- Main Quest: Galaxy News Radio
- Threat Level: 2
- Faction: Ghoul
- Area Is Locked
- Hostiles: Ghoul Genus

 Note
This location links above ground to 10.03: Galaxy News Radio (page 399).

This door provides a good view southward, toward Dupont Circle. It cannot be reached again once you drop down from the narrow section of floor that still remains on this wrecked building.

11.02: METRO JUNCTION

- Threat Level: 2
- Underground Connection
- Hostiles: Ghoul Genus

Note
The Metro Station entrance leads to one linked Underground Metro Area: D.C. U2.

Location D.C. U2: Metro Junction (page 443).

The following four surface locations can be accessed from this Underground junction:

Location 10.02: Metro Junction (Chevy Chase East) (page 399).

Location 11.08: Metro Junction (Dupont Circle Northeast) (page 402).

Location 12.01: Metro Junction (Vernon Square North) (page 403).

Location 12.05: Metro Junction (Vernon Square Northwest) (page 405).

At the bottom of the rubble hill from the back door of Galaxy News Radio is a Metro Station entrance, overlooking a sunken roadway area teeming with Ghouls. Check the nearby picnic table.

- First Aid Box Health and Chems
- Assault Rifle
- Ammo Box Ammunition (2)

11.03: COLLAPSED CAR TUNNEL (NORTH)

11.04: COLLAPSED CAR TUNNEL (SOUTH)

- Threat Level: 3
- Faction: Ghoul
- Danger: Gas Leak
- Health and Chems
- Interior Exploration
- Underground Connection
- Hostiles: Ghoul Genus

Note

The tunnel leads to a number of linked Underground Metro Areas: Collapsed Car Tunnel (Interior), Dupont Circle Station, and D.C. U6.A.

Location: 11.03 / 11.04: Collapsed Car Tunnel (Interior).

Location: 11.05: Dupont Circle Station (Interior).

Location D.C. U6.A: Dupont Circle Station (page 445).

INTERIOR LOCATIONS

The area immediately outside the northern entrance to the tunnel has a number of Ghouls to kill with gunfire or exploding coach liners. You cannot reach the large circular fountain fortifications heading south; the way is blocked by rubble. At the entrance are graffiti markings made by the Brotherhood, pointing out that this is an optimal path to reach the Mall.

The southern entrance to the tunnel is less than seven steps away from the entrance to Dupont Circle Station, at the base of the escalators, and hidden from any nearby enemies.

Note

From Location D.C. U6.A, you can reach D.C. Interior Locations 11: Dupont Circle, 12: Vernon Square, 14: Georgetown, 15: Pennsylvania Avenue, 16: Arlington National Cemetery, 17: The Mall, and 18: Seward Square. You can also reach Anacostia Crossing in the Capital Wasteland: 9.16.

The following surface locations can be accessed from the Collapsed Car Tunnel (Interior):

Location 11.03: Collapsed Car Tunnel (North)

Location 11.04: Collapsed Car Tunnel (South)

Location 11.05: Dupont Circle Station (page 401).

Various locations from U6.B: Metro Central (page 445).

COLLAPSED CAR TUNNEL
Corridor to Dupont Circle Station

Brotherhood graffiti marks this location.

Rusting Vehicles and Feasting Ghouls

These can be a deathtrap if you catch a car on fire and it daisy-chains into an explosion that blows up all the vehicles inside this area, so be careful where you fire your weapons.

Western Wall

- First Aid Box Health and Chems

11.05: DUPONT CIRCLE STATION

- Threat Level: 3
- Faction: Raider
- Danger: Grenade Bouquet, Low Radiation, Mine
- Guns and Ammunition
- Health and Chems
- Interior Exploration
- Underground Connection
- Hostiles: Ghouls, Raiders

Note

The Metro Station entrance leads to the Collapsed Car Tunnel (Interior), and D.C. U6.A.

Location: 11.04 / 11.03: Collapsed Car Tunnel (Interior).

Location D.C. U6.A: Dupont Circle Station (Interior) (page 445).

Location D.C. U6.B: Metro Central (page 445).

(From Location D.C. U6.B, you can reach D.C. Interior Locations 11: Dupont Circle, 12: Vernon Square, 14: Georgetown, 15: Pennsylvania Avenue, 16: Arlington National Cemetery, 17: The Mall, and 18: Seward Square. You can also reach Anacostia Crossing in the Capital Wasteland: 9.16)

The following surface locations can be accessed from the Collapsed Car Tunnel (Interior):

Location 11.03: Collapsed Car Tunnel (North)

Location 11.04: Collapsed Car Tunnel (South)

Various locations from U6.B: Metro Central (page 445).

The base of the escalators allows access into the interior and also the south entrance of the collapsed car tunnels. At the top of the escalator, you can cross a pedestrian footbridge, peering over the side at the Ghouls and city coach liner [11.B] (fall into the area with the Ghouls, and use the nearby concrete steps or rubble piles to climb out), and gain access northward, with increased Raider activity.

11.06: LADY FRUMPERTON'S FASHIONS

- Threat Level: 2
- Faction: Raider
- Danger: Mines
- Collectible: Skill Book
- Interior Exploration
- Hostiles: Raiders

GENERAL NOTES

Down the alleyway to the west of the Dupont Circle Station (South) is a group of Raiders near some picnic tables; they are guarding a ruined house and Dry Sewer

TRAINING — BESTIARY — MAIN QUEST — MISC. QUESTS — TOUR — COMPLETION — APPENDICES

entrance. Before investigating, check out the one remaining store that's still intact, watching out for the Frag Mine on the corner of the street. Inside the shop, there's a variety of Pre-War outfits, hats, and glasses as well as a Skill Book.

- Frag Mine
- Tales of a Junktown Jerky Vendor (17/24)

11.07: DRY SEWER (ENTRANCE)

- Threat Level: 3
- Faction: Raider
- Danger: Mines
- Collectible: Skill Book
- Underground Connection
- Hostiles: Raiders

Note
The Sewer entrance leads to a linked Underground tunnel: D.C. U4.

Location D.C. U4: Dry Sewer (page 444).

The following surface location can be accessed from the Underground tunnels:

Location 12.07: Our Lady of Hope Hospital (page 406).

To the north is the Raider Outpost of connecting house ruins [11.C]. Adjacent to the brick house with the three Frag Mines outside it, on the rubble, is a set of steps sunk into the ground, near a medical gurney. They lead to a door marked "Hospital Maintenance."

- Frag Mine (3)

11.08: METRO JUNCTION (NORTHEAST)

- Threat Level: 3
- Faction: Raider
- Danger: Mines
- Collectible: Skill Book
- Underground Connection
- Hostiles: Raiders

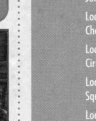
Note
The Metro Station entrance leads to one linked Underground Metro Area: D.C. U2.

Location D.C. U2: Metro Junction (page 443).

The following four surface locations can be accessed from this Underground Junction:

Location 10.02: Metro Junction (Chevy Chase East) (page 399).

Location 11.02: Metro Junction (Dupont Circle North) (page 400).

Location 12.01: Metro Junction (Vernon Square North) (page 403).

Location 12.05: Metro Junction (Vernon Square Northwest) (page 405).

To the north of the Raider Outpost [11.C] is a Metro Station entrance. Head in here for a quick exit and trek to the opposite side of Dupont Circle, or the two adjacent zones.

11.09: SUNKEN SEWER

- Threat Level: 4
- Factions: Raider, Ghoul
- Danger: High Radiation, Mines
- Collectible: Skill Book
- Guns and Ammunition
- Interior Exploration
- Hostiles: Raiders, Ghoul Genus

INTERIOR LOCATIONS SUNKEN SEWER
At the end of a rubble-filled road off the main circular middle of this zone, which you reach after disarming a couple of Mines at the entrance, is a small band of Raiders, a wrecked building you can pass through to a dead-end, and a sunken sewer, exposed after a brutal explosion demolished much of this area. Optionally use a Radiation Suit or Rad-X before entering.

- Frag Mine (2)

Dumped Barrels
Beware of dangerous radiation levels.

Northern Glowing One
Dispatch the entity, then ransack the safe, check for Stimpaks, RadAway, Darts, and these handy items:

- Ammo Box Ammunition (2)
- Blood Pack
- .44 Scoped Magnum
- U.S. Army: 30 Handy Flamethrower Recipes (17/25)

11.10: FOGGY BOTTOM STATION (DUPONT WEST)

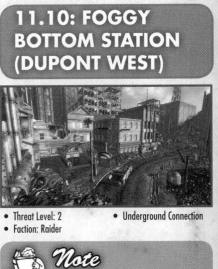

- Threat Level: 2
- Faction: Raider
- Underground Connection

Note
The Metro Station entrance leads to D.C. U6.C and U6.B.

Location D.C. U6.C: Foggy Bottom Station (Interior) (page 445).

Location D.C. U6.B: Metro Central (page 445).

(From Location D.C. U6.B and C, you can reach D.C. Interior Locations 11: Dupont Circle, 12: Vernon Square, 14: Georgetown, 15: Pennsylvania Avenue, 16: Arlington National Cemetery, 17: The Mall, and 18: Seward Square. You can also reach Anacostia Crossing in the Capital Wasteland: 9.16)

This provides reasonably quick access to a variety of zones, including the Capital Wasteland. When under fire, Raiders retreat to the exterior of this location. The main forces are on the opposite side of Dupont Circle.

SECONDARY LOCATIONS

11.A: CITY COACH LINER (2)

- Threat Level: 2
- Faction: Ghoul
- Danger: Low Radiation

In the sunken roadway are two coach liners—excellent for blowing apart, killing the Ghouls in the process.

11.B: CITY COACH LINER

- Threat Level: 2
- Faction: Ghoul
- Danger: Low Radiation

This is a good vehicle to destroy, so the nearby Ghouls don't race up the steps to maul you.

11.C: RAIDER OUTPOST

- Threat Level: 3
- Faction: Raider
- Danger: Mines
- Collectible: Scribe Pre-War Book

- Guns and Ammunition
- Health and Chems
- Sleep Mattress

Raiders in this area are a constant nuisance; take over their crumbling base of operations if you can. Assuming you're moving north from Lady Frumperton's, disarm the Mines, watching for Raiders coming out of the brick house to the north (adjacent to the Dry Sewer). Enter the house, and go out the other side, to the base of a concrete building you can skulk around, or head into. Once inside, head up the first set of steps, slaying a Raider or two on the way. On this floor, you can snipe at the fountain fortifications, or head across two sets of planks to one of two roofs.

They lead to one of two brick terrace buildings. The western one has an open air floor to step on, with a mattress, tools, and a bookcase with Psycho and the listed items below. The other planks lead to a similar building, but with no items. From either location you can head down to a Pulowski Shelter and open it; two skeletons tumble out. You can use these buildings as cover for dashing to the nearby Metro Junction (Dupont Circle Northeast), or attacking the central fountain fortifications.

- Ammo Box Ammunition
- First Aid Box Health and Chems
- 10mm Pistol
- Scribe Pre-War Book (72/98)

11.D: RAIDER FOUNTAIN FORTIFICATIONS

- Threat Level: 4
- Faction: Raider
- Danger: Mines

The central area to this Raider stronghold has three Raiders guarding the fountains, surrounded by sandbags, and they can call on reinforcements from the nearby Outpost. As the area is heavily mined, a cunning plan is to sneak, using a Stealth Boy, disarming Mines, stepping into the central fountains, and then executing the Raiders. This is a good surface shortcut, although you can't climb up to this area from the north.

- Frag Mine (15)

11.E: RAIDER RUBBLE PILE

- Threat Level: 2
- Faction: Raider
- Danger: Mines

A defensive point atop a small pile of rubble. Disarm the two nearby Mines, and grab what you need from the small table; two Frag Grenades, a Jet, and some Ammo.

- Frag Mine (2)
- Frag Grenade (2)
- Ammo Box Ammunition

11.F: RAIDER SLEEPING CAMP

- Threat Level: 1
- Faction: Raider
- Sleep Mattress

Northwest of the Fountain Fortifications and Rubble Pile is an open-air sleeping quarters for the Raiders. There's a not-so-lucky 8-Ball here, too.

- First Aid Box Health and Chems
- Ammo Box Ammunition

ZONE 12: VERNON SQUARE

- Nuka-Cola Quantum: 2/94
- Scribe Pre-War Books: 2/98
- Skill Book [Barter]: 2/24, Skill Book [Medicine]: 3/25,
- [Melee Weapons]: 2/25, Skill Book [Repair]: 1/25, Skill Book [Science]: 1/25, Skill Book [Sneak]: 1/25

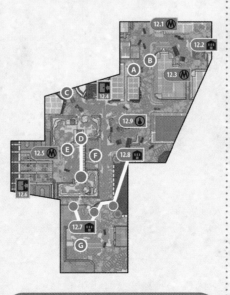

PRIMARY LOCATIONS

12.01: Metro Junction (Vernon Square North)

12.02: Vault-Tec Guest Relations

12.03: Vernon East / Takoma Park (Vernon Square East)

12.04: Sewer Entrance

12.05: Metro Junction (Vernon Square Station)

12.06: Freedom Street Station (Vernon Square Station)

12.07: Our Lady of Hope Hospital

12.08: The Statesman Hotel

12.09: Sewer

SECONDARY LOCATIONS

12.A: Super Mutant Camp

12.B: City Coach Liner

12.C: Container Truck

12.D: Ruined Pedestrian Overpass

12.E: Pulowski Preservation Shelter

12.F: City Coach Liner

12.G: Hospital Truck

> ### Note
> Reilly's Rangers are broadcasting an emergency message that you can pick up throughout this zone.

- Ranger Emergency Broadcast

PRIMARY LOCATIONS

12.01: METRO JUNCTION (VERNON SQUARE NORTH)

- Threat Level: 3
- Faction: Super Mutant
- Danger: Shotgun Trap
- Underground Connection

Explode the nearby vehicles to catch a Super Mutant in the splash damage. Watch for the pressure plate that activates two Rigged Shotguns on the road just outside the station steps.

- Combat Shotgun and Ammo (2)

TRAINING — BESTIARY — MAIN QUEST — MISC. QUESTS — TOUR — COMPLETION — APPENDICES

Note

The Metro Station entrance leads to one linked Underground Metro Area: D.C. U2.

Location D.C. U2: Metro Junction (page 443).

The following four surface locations can be accessed from this Underground junction:

Location 10.02: Metro Junction (Chevy Chase East) (page 399).

Location 11.02: Metro Junction (Dupont Circle North) (page 400).

Location 11.08: Metro Junction (Dupont Circle Northeast) (page 402).

Location 12.05: Metro Junction (Vernon Square Northwest) (page 405).

INTERIOR MAPS AND LOCATIONS
Vault-Tec Guest Relations

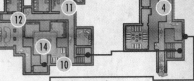

Vault-Tec Administration

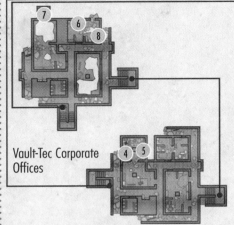

Vault-Tec Corporate Offices

12.02: VAULT-TEC HEADQUARTERS (GUEST RELATIONS)

- Miscellaneous Quest: Agatha's Song
- Threat Level: 3
- Faction: Vault Dweller
- Danger: Gas Leak
- Collectibles: Nuka-Cola Quantum, Scribe Pre-War Book, Skill Book (3)
- Guns and Ammunition
- Health and Chems
- Interior Exploration
- Hostiles: Masterbrain, Robot Genus, Super Mutant Genus, Turret

East of the Vernon Square North Station is the Vault-Tec building, an imposing structure with a nearby Super Mutant threat. The double doors gain access into the building.

VAULT-TEC GUEST RELATIONS

① Foyer

A dilapidated mess of Super Mutants and malfunctioning Robots.

② Upstairs Kitchen

Danger: Escaping gas! Grab food from the fridge.

③ Exit Balcony

Drop down from here after exploring the building; you can't reach it from the lower ground. Don't forget the Skill Book!

- Tales of a Junktown Jerky Vendor (18/24)

VAULT-TEC CORPORATE OFFICES

④ and ⑤ Northwest Ruined Office

Check the safe and locate the trash bin.

- First Aid Box Health and Chems
- Floor Safe Items
- Scribe Pre-War Book (73/98)

⑥ (Upper Floor) North Wall

- Nuka-Cola Quantum (74/94)

⑦ (Upper Floor) Northwest Storage Room

Move along the corridor and check the toilets to the south for a Magnum, then move here and shimmy around the floor edge to a small storage room.

- First Aid Box Health and Chems
- Laser Pistol
- Stealth Boy
- Ammo Box Ammunition (2)
- Scoped .44 Magnum and Ammo

⑧ Northeast Ruined Office

Check the shelf above the hole in the floor for a Skill Book.

- Big Book of Science (21/25)

VAULT-TEC ADMINISTRATION

⑨ North Office

Hack the turret terminal and check the System Operation Station (SysOp) 3 for these important bulletins:

A Security Notice informs you that the VTMB01 Masterbrain requires authorization from three SysOp terminals.

There's a message about the treatment of vending machines; apparently one Vault-Tec employee thought daubing a "messy protest" into the coin slot was a good idea....

There's a message about employee abuse of bathroom breaks, with a time limit reduced from 2.37 to 2.25 minutes.

There are messages about Vault 112 (it has been completed) and Vault 92 (it has been fitted with WNB Type Noise Generators).

Station 3 Mainframe Access: Approve this.

Station 3 Masterbrain Shutdown: Approve this.

⑩ SysOp Station 1
⑪ SysOp Station 2

This is near a tiny storage room.

- First Aid Box Health and Chems

⑫ Usual Masterbrain Location

⑬ Executive Office

- Grognak the Barbarian (19/25)

⑭ Vault-Tec Mainframe

The barred gate is unlocked once you activate all the SysOp Stations. At the Vault-Tec Mainframe, download Vault Locations (87, 101, 108, and 112).

12.03: VERNON EAST / TAKOMA PARK (VERNON SQUARE EAST)

- Threat Level: 2
- Danger: Low Radiation, Mines
- Guns and Ammunition
- Health and Chems
- Underground Connection

These are the remains of Abernathy Street; watch for a Frag Mine by the sign post, scramble over the rubble, and move to the entrance of the station. Take items from the table.

- Frag Mine
- First Aid Box Health and Chems
- Ammo Box Ammunition

12.04: SEWER ENTRANCE

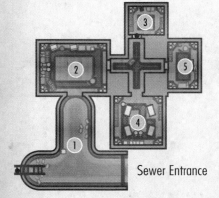

- Threat Level: 2
- Danger: Grenade Bouquet
- Collectible: Skill Book
- Guns and Ammunition
- Health and Chems
- Interior Exploration
- Sleep Mattress

INTERIOR MAPS AND LOCATIONS

Sewer Entrance

An old empty sewer has been left locked and trapped by an occupant who left it unattended. His Skill Book loss is your gain. Head north on Basso Blvd., locating the cinema on the corner of the road, pass the vending machine and move to the pile of rubble at the northern end. Open the Sewer Entrance and drop down into the tunnels below.

1 Grenade Bouquet

Search for the trip wire.

- Frag Grenade (3)

2 Room with the Flaming Barrel

There's food in the fridge, the odd Chem, and:

- First Aid Box Health and Chems

3 North Room

Break in, gather Darts, RadAway, open the floor safe, and take the following:

- First Aid Box Health and Chems
- Ammo Box Ammunition (2)
- Dean's Electronics (18/25)
- Sawed-Off Shotgun
- Floor Safe Items

4 East and South Rooms

There's a place to sleep and some junk in here.

12.05: METRO JUNCTION (VERNON SQUARE STATION)

- Miscellanous Quest: Reilly's Rangers
- Threat Level: 1
- Radio Signal
- Underground Connection

On the surface, the station is in ruins, and there's a second station (Freedom Street) across to the south. Head east, and you can pick up the Ranger Emergency Frequency in this area.

- Ranger Emergency Frequency

12.06: FREEDOM STREET STATION (VERNON SQUARE STATION)

- Miscellaneous Quest: Reilly's Rangers
- Threat Level: 1
- Radio Signal
- Underground Connection

Don't confuse the Vernon Square stations; the north one [12.05] and this one lead to completely different locations! Move east, and you can listen to the Ranger Emergency Frequency, emanating from the top of the Statesman Hotel.

- Ranger Emergency Frequency

12.07: OUR LADY OF HOPE HOSPITAL

- Miscellaneous Quest: Reilly's Rangers
- Threat Level: 4
- Faction: Super Mutant
- Danger: Baby Carriage, Gas Leak, Grenade Bouquet, Mines, Terminal Trap
- Collectibles: Scribe Pre-War Book, Skill Book (2)
- Guns and Ammunition
- Health and Chems
- Interior Exploration
- Radio Signal
- Sleep Mattress
- Friendly: Mister Handy
- Hostiles: Super Mutant Genus, Centaur

Note

The maintenance door entrance leads to a linked Underground tunnel: D.C. U4.

Location D.C. U4: Dry Sewer (page 444).

The following surface location can be accessed from the Underground tunnels:

Location 11.07: Dry Sewer (Entrance: Dupont Circle) (page 402).

INTERIOR MAPS AND LOCATIONS

Our Lady of Hope Hospital

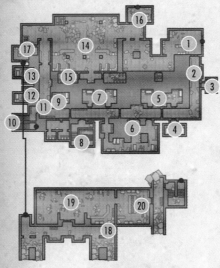

Our Lady of Hope Hospital 2nd Level

Unlike its neighbor to the east, the hospital has three different entrances (although one is accessed from Dupont Circle). The two entrances here are the blood-splattered main corner entrance under the fallen radio mast jammed between the buildings, and a side

entrance to the west. Expect a few mines outside, if you head toward the latter entrance. Expect heavy Super Mutant resistance once inside the building.

- Ranger Emergency Frequency
- Frag Mines

OUR LADY OF HOPE HOSPITAL

① Main Entrance

② Danger: Baby Carriage Trap!

③ Mister Handy's Clinic

Activate the robot and he goes off to fight the Super Mutants

- First Aid Box: Health and Chems (4)

④ Patient Room

- First Aid Box: Health and Chems
- D.C. Journal of Internal Medicine (19/25)

⑤ Double Patient Room

- First Aid Box: Health and Chems (2)

⑥ Operating Room

Access the Nurse's Terminal near a wall safe. The terminal has three injury reports to read (one involving Seneca Clarkson and a groin strain and another about Harold Worthington III the pillow thief).

- First Aid Box: Health and Chems (2)
- Wall Safe Items

⑦ Double Patient Room

- First Aid Box: Health and Chems (2)

⑧ Maintenance Stairs

Disarm the Mine and grab these:

- Frag Mine
- Ammo Box Ammunition (3)

⑨ Patient Room (opposite restrooms)

- First Aid Box: Health and Chems

⑩ Maintenance Stairs (exit)

This is the entrance / exit to the Dry Sewer [11.07] leading to Dupont Circle.

⑪ Corridor

Access Nurse Terminal 02 and read the same injury reports, or unlock the safe.

- Wall Safe Items

⑫ Western Patient Room #1

There are scattered Caps in here.

- First Aid Box: Health and Chems

⑬ Western Patient Room #2

- First Aid Box: Health and Chems

⑭ Cafeteria

Check the coffee counter for a Scribe Pre-War Book, and find the Ammo cache on the southeast corner desk. Beware of the Mine on the gurney with the fire extinguishers; it's a great cluster of items to shoot at, but don't get caught in the explosion.

- Scribe Pre-War Book (74/98)
- Ammo Box Ammunition (3)
- Frag Grenade (2)
- Frag Mine

⑮ Cafeteria Restroom

Watch out for the Grenade Bouquet!

- Frag Grenade (3)

⑯ Security Room

Disarm the Terminal Trap, then access the turret terminal; do this before you enter the cafeteria. Pry open the wall safe. This room has the side entrance to and from Vernon Square.

- Wall Safe Items

⑰ Top of Stairs

Beware of Mines just before entering the second level!

- Frag Mine (2)

OUR LADY OF HOPE HOSPITAL SECOND LEVEL

Stay well away from the escaping gas, or lob in a Grenade, retreat around a corner, and inspect the mess afterward.

⑱ End of the Corridor

Hack the third Nurse Terminal. You can grab items from the adjacent wall safe.

- Wall Safe Items

⑲ Upper Cafeteria

Watch for escaping gas! Burn it from range. Check the tables for a Skill Book.

- D.C. Journal of Internal Medicine (20/25)

⑳ Secondary Kitchen

Check fridges for food. Then head through the doors, and out to the collapsed radio mast linking this building to the Statesman Hotel. On the edge outside find a First Aid Box and Ammo Box.

- First Aid Box: Health and Chems
- Ammo Box Ammunition

12.08: THE STATESMAN HOTEL

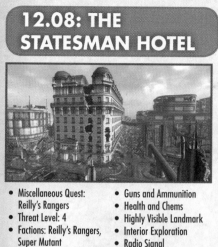

- Miscellaneous Quest: Reilly's Rangers
- Threat Level: 4
- Factions: Reilly's Rangers, Super Mutant
- Danger: Gas Leak, Grenade Bouquet
- Collectibles: Nuka-Cola Quantum, Skill Book (3)
- Guns and Ammunition
- Health and Chems
- Highly Visible Landmark
- Interior Exploration
- Radio Signal
- Rare or Powerful Item
- Sleep Mattress
- Hostiles: Super Mutant Genus, Centaur

INHABITANTS

Note

Theo, Donovan, Butcher, and Brick are somewhere inside this hotel. Their biographies are located at Reilly's Ranger Compound [18.06].

The imposing Statesman Hotel now boasts views of the cratered rocket crash site to the north [12.09], and a lobby that provides only limited accessibility to the rest of the hotel. Aside from a couple of rooms, the majority of the hotel is accessed via the Our Lady of Hope Hospital. This location also has a Ranger Emergency Frequency Signal to listen to (and begin a quest).

- Ranger Emergency Frequency

THE STATESMAN HOTEL (LOBBY)

Enter the lobby, and you'll find the way forward blocked. The elevator lacks power, so you can't reach the roof. All other corridors on the ground are blocked.

1 Counter Desk

Access the terminal to open a counter safe. You can also read notes of complaints from guests. Top of the list is Harold Worthington III, who attempted to bilk the hotel out of free room service; Seneca Clarkson, who suffocated in the line of work; and Wanda Kellendyne, who cooked her own legs.

- First Aid Box Health and Chems
- Counter Safe Items

2 Northeast Bedroom

- Ammo Box Ammunition (2)
- Assault Rifle
- Tales of a Junktown Jerky Vendor (19/24)

INTERIOR MAPS AND LOCATIONS
The Statesman Hotel

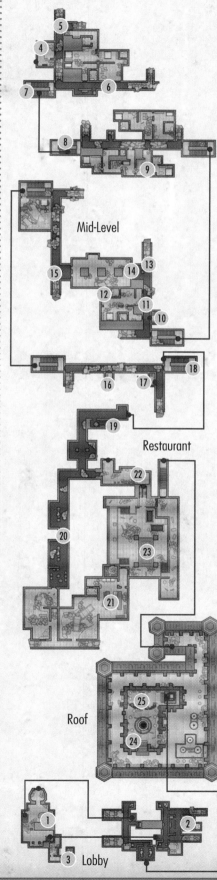

Mid-Level

Restaurant

Roof

Lobby

3 Southeast Corner (Under the Stairs)

- First Aid Box Health and Chems (2)

STATESMAN HOTEL MID-LEVEL
The one path through this interior location can be accessed only from the metal "bridge" made from a fallen radio mast.

4 Ruined Guest Room

There's a bed to sleep in, here, as in all the guest rooms throughout this hotel.

5 Fire Hose Box

Danger: Grenade Bouquet!

- Frag Grenade (3)
- First Aid Box Health and Chems

6 Fire Hose Box

- First Aid Box Health and Chems

7 Theo's Resting Place

Theo is one of Reilly's Rangers. He has an Ammo Crate to inspect (as long as Reilly has given you the code).

- Theo's Ammo Box

8 (Floor 2) Dead-End Stairs

Danger: Grenade Bouquet!

- Frag Grenade (3)

9 (Floor 2) Super Mutant Combat

There are no items of worth here, just fighting!

10 (Floor 3) Storage Room

Unlock it and collect the following:

- First Aid Box Health and Chems
- Ammo Box Ammunition (2)

11 (Floor 3) Fire Hose Box

- First Aid Box Health and Chems

12 (Floor 3) Little Moonbeam's Father

Check the corpse in the northwest corner and take the note.

- A Note from Little Moonbeam's Father.

13 (Floor 3) Pillar

- First Aid Box Health and Chems

14 (Floor 3) Danger: Grenade Bouquet!

- Frag Grenade (3)

15 (Floor 3) Fire Hose Box

- First Aid Box Health and Chems

16 (Floor 4) Storage Room

- Chinese Army: Spec. Ops. Training Manual (15/25)

TRAINING — BESTIARY — MAIN QUEST — MISC. QUESTS — TOUR — COMPLETION — APPENDICES

17 (Floor 4) Cleaning Closet

Open it and grab the following:

- First Aid Box Health and Chems (2)
- Ammo Box Ammunition

18 Stairs Danger: Grenade Bouquet!

- Frag Grenade (3)

STATESMAN HOTEL RESTAURANT

19 Alcove

- First Aid Box Health and Chems

20 Red Carpet Corridor

- First Aid Box Health and Chems

21 Ruined Kitchen

Danger: Gas Leak!

- First Aid Box Health and Chems

22 North Entrance to Lounge

Access the terminal or unlock the door.

23 Alfresco Lounge

Blast the Muties apart, and search under the stairs for a Maintenance Protectron's Fission Battery, and the following items around the bar:

- Protectron's Fission Battery
- Ammo Box Ammunition (2)
- Sawed-Off Shotgun and Ammo
- Frag Grenade (2)
- Grognak the Barbarian (20/25)
- Nuka-Cola Quantum (75/94)

STATESMAN HOTEL ROOF

Walk around until you reach the stairs up to the rooftop itself.

24 Musical Quartet Seating

Check the remains of a musical quartet seating arrangement to find a Sheet Music Book (used in Agatha's Song).

- Sheet Music Book

25 Remaining Rangers

Then move over and say hello to the remaining Reilly's Rangers. Donovan, Butcher, and Brick are short on ammo, but long on chutzpah. Conclude the quest from here if you wish.

12.09: SEWER

- Threat Level: 3
- Faction: Super Mutant
- Danger: High Radiation
- Collectible: Skill Book
- Guns and Ammunition
- Health and Chems
- Interior Exploration
- Hostiles: Super Mutant Genus

INTERIOR MAPS AND LOCATIONS

Sewer

Endure the nasty radiation leaking from this crashed rocket, and the large crater it made (up to +30 Rad/Sec), head down the rough steps to the sewer grate, and enter.

1 Super Mutant Mutilation Station

Watch for foes in here, and a large number of Gore Bags and bodies. Check the shelves for Chems, Stimpaks, Darts, and the following:

- Blood Pack
- Scoped .44 Magnum
- Ammo Box Ammunition (3)
- D.C. Journal of Internal Medicine (21/25)

 Note

If you haven't got a Radiation Suit, find one inside the Pulowski Preservation Shelter [12.E].

SECONDARY LOCATIONS

12.A: SUPER MUTANT CAMP

- Threat Level: 2
- Faction: Super Mutant
- Guns and Ammunition
- Health and Chems

Lurking behind some sandbags near the large statue are two hulking Super Mutants. Drop them with gunfire, or sneak around them, and claim items. You can head down an alley to the south.

- First Aid Box Health and Chems
- Ammo Box Ammunition (2)

12.B: CITY COACH LINER

- Threat Level: 2
- Danger: Low Radiation

Parked near a rubble pile and rusting car is a liner, which is great to use as an explosive execution method for the nearby Muties.

12.C: CONTAINER TRUCK

- Threat Level: 3
- Faction: Super Mutant

This wrecked container truck features a small group of Super Mutants readying their Hunting Rifles. This is also a good method of entering the two ruined buildings linked by the pedestrian overpass.

12.D: RUINED PEDESTRIAN OVERPASS

- Threat Level: 3
- Faction: Super Mutant
- Danger: Gas Leak, Grenade Bouquet, Mines
- Guns and Ammunition
- Health and Chems

This area is linked to large ruined buildings to the north and south. Enter on the main north-south road opposite the Sewer crater, but watch for the trip wire at the threshold behind the sandbags. An alternate entrance is south from Location 12.C. Disarm the Grenade Bouquet and step into the building; there are three more Grenades on a shelf to the left (south). Search the ground floor for Chems, an Assault Rifle, an Ammo Box, and a safe near the stairs, and a First Aid Box and Ammo Box on a counter with an Assault Rifle. There are Super Mutants everywhere, so beware of attacking near the oven, which has gas escaping from it.

Head up the stairs to the series of planks and cross to the overpass, running to the north building, and searching the upper level for two more Ammo Boxes. Head down a floor and locate the First Aid Box. Exit to the north, disarming a Mine, and you're close to the side entrance to the hospital, and an exit toward the coach liner.

- Frag Grenade (6)
- Assault Rifle (2)
- Ammo Box Ammunition (4)
- Floor Safe Items
- First Aid Box Health and Chems (2)
- Frag Mine

12.E: PULOWSKI PRESERVATION SHELTER

- Threat Level: 1

Perfect for exploring the Sewer [12.09], there's a Radiation Suit and Rad-X inside this booth, along with a corpse.

- Radiation Suit

12.F: CITY COACH LINER

- Threat Level: 1
- Danger: Low Radiation

Parked near the ticket booth to the station, this isn't close to an enemy, but you can use it as temporary cover.

12.G: HOSPITAL TRUCK

- Threat Level: 1
- Danger: Low Radiation

The truck parked in the hospital cul-de-sac has a First Aid Box in the flatbed, and there's another on a table in the northwest corner.

- First Aid Box Health and Chems (2)

ZONE 13: TAKOMA PARK

- Fat Man Mini-Nukes: 1/71
- Unique Items: 1/89
- Nuka-Cola Quantum: 1/94
- Skill Book [Big Guns]: 1/25, Skill Book [Speech]: 1/25

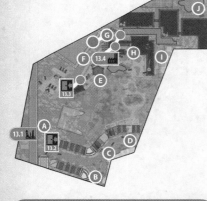

PRIMARY LOCATIONS

13.01: Vernon East / Takoma Park

13.02: NiftyThrifty

13.03: Auto Shop

13.04: Takoma Industrial Factory

SECONDARY LOCATIONS

13.A: City Coach Liner

13.B: Container Truck and Pulowski Preservation Shelter

13.C: Super Mutant Tent

13.D: Thoroughfare Ruin

13.E: Water Tower

13.F: Container Truck

13.G: Container Trucks (2)

13.H: Container Truck

13.I: Talon Company Merc Tent

13.J: Hidden Irradiated Pool

PRIMARY LOCATIONS

13.01: VERNON EAST / TAKOMA PARK (TAKOMA PARK EXTERIOR)

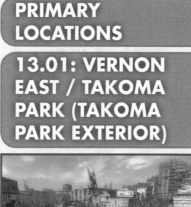

- Threat Level: 2
- Faction: Super Mutant
- Underground Connection

 Note

The Metro Station entrance leads to a single linked Underground Metro Area: D.C. U3.

Location D.C. U1.A: Vernon East / Takoma Park (Interior) (page 443).

The following surface location can be accessed from here:

Location 12.03: Vernon East / Takoma Park (Vernon Square East) (page 404).

The only access point in this zone allows you to return to Vernon Square. Cut off from the rest of the Metro Interior, the Super Mutants have a huge and sprawling stronghold here.

13.02: NIFTY THRIFTY'S

- Threat Level: 1
- Interior Exploration
- Rare or Powerful Item

For a pawn shop where everything must go, Nifty Thrifty's doesn't have much that you'd want, although that cap looks comfortable.

- Takoma Park Little Leaguer Cap (67/89)

13.03: AUTO SHOP (TAKOMA MOTORS)

- Threat Level: 5
- Faction: Super Mutant
- Danger: Behemoth
- Collectibles: Fat Man Mini-Nuke, Skill Book
- Interior Exploration
- Lots o' Caps
- Hostiles: Super Mutant Behemoth, Super Mutant Genus

The parking lot in front of the Takoma Motor store holds a terrifying shape; a man-mountain brandishing a fire-hydrant-on-a-stick, flanked by a couple of regular-sized Muties. The Behemoth has a variety of items on its corpse, including a Mini-Nuke and a load of Caps. When you've secured the area, head into the Auto Shop via either entrance. Inside the Auto Shop, the air is thick, making it difficult to spot the other two valuable items:

- Mini-Nuke (56/71)
- Caps
- U.S. Army: 30 Handy Flamethrower Recipes (18/25)
- Sledgehammer

13.04: TAKOMA INDUSTRIAL FACTORY

- Threat Level: 3
- Faction: Super Mutant, Talon Mercenary
- Danger: Grenade Bouquet, Terminal Trap
- Collectibles: Nuka-Cola Quantum, Skill Book
- Guns and Ammunition
- Health and Chems
- Interior Exploration
- Hostiles: Super Mutant Genus

INTERIOR MAPS AND LOCATIONS
Factory

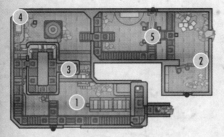

The main building to search in this zone is the imposing Takoma Industrial Building. Only a small section can be investigating internally. Battle the factions fighting their own war, and enter via a garage door, adjacent metal door, or door around the corner, in the middle of the building.

FACTORY

1 Machine Floor

This is where conveyor belts used to dump Abraxo Cleaner; there's as much Abraxo as you can carry.

2 East Shop Floor

Check the storage shelves.

- Lying, Congressional Style (18/25)

3 Overlook Office

Disarm the dummy terminal and take the Grenade. Check this upper area for Chems, a Carton of Cigarettes, and more:

- First Aid Box Health and Chems
- Ammo Box Ammunition (2)
- Frag Grenade

4 Raised Alcove with Generator

There's a bottle of Purified Water and a Quantum here.

- Nuka-Cola Quantum (76/94)

5 Upper Gantry (Southeast)

Locate the Talon Company Merc corpse and snag his Jet, and the following:

- Sniper Rifle
- Ammo Box Ammunition (2)

Head back to the second shop floor area and take the set of steps up to a corpse, and open the door to Takoma Park. This leads down some rusting steps to a murky canal area. Follow the side of the canal eastward, pausing to disarm the Grenade Trap, and round the corner, ending at the Talon Company Merc Tent [14.I].

SECONDARY LOCATIONS

13.A: CITY COACH LINER

- Threat Level: 2

Parked near the Metro Station and Nifty Thrifty's, this offers protection from the rare Super Mutant incursions to this point.

13.B: CONTAINER TRUCK AND PULOWSKI PRESERVATION SHELTER

- Threat Level: 3
- Faction: Super Mutant
- Guns and Ammunition
- Hostiles: Super Mutant Genus

There's also a truck with container full of corpses, and a couple of Stimpaks, as well as Ammo Boxes and a couple of Stimpaks. Next to the truck is a shelter with a dead Wastelander and another Ammo Box.

- Ammo Box Ammunition (4)

13.C: SUPER MUTANT TENT

- Threat Level: 3
- Faction: Super Mutant
- Guns and Ammunition
- Health and Chems
- Hostiles: Super Mutant Genus

Expect heavy resistance here. This tent has a mattress and items.

- First Aid Box Health and Chems (2)
- Ammo Box Ammunition (2)

13.D: THOROUGHFARE RUIN

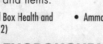

- Threat Level: 2
- Faction: Super Mutant, Talon Mercenary

At the end of the road is a ruined house with a thoroughfare to the back garden, through the picket fence, and down into the Takoma Industrial area.

13.E: WATER TOWER

- Threat Level: 3
- Faction: Super Mutant, Talon Mercenary
- Danger: Low Radiation
- Highly Visible Landmark

The giant water tower near the entrance to the Takoma Industrial Factory is a key landmark to find if you wish to flee this area. Run for this structure, avoiding the nearby irradiated pond.

13.F: CONTAINER TRUCK

- Threat Level: 4
- Faction: Super Mutant, Talon Mercenary
- Hostiles: Super Mutant Genus, Talon Company Mercs

Use the plank and step onto the roof, then over the Mercenary corpse to a small table. Grab items, then search the body for a Holotape Note: Takoma Park Artillery. These are instructions. Use the switch on the table to call in airstrikes, which is especially helpful if you've snuck up here and the Muties haven't spotted you. Drop artillery on the Behemoth if you can!

> If the switch breaks, **Repair** it and continue the barrage!

- First Aid Box Health and Chems (3)
- Takoma Park Artillery Note

13.G: CONTAINER TRUCKS (2)

- Threat Level: 3
- Factions: Super Mutant, Talon Mercenary

The two orange and white truck containers have no items in or on them, but one has linking planks allowing you to drop to a sniping or hiding spot.

13.H: CONTAINER TRUCK

- Threat Level: 3
- Factions: Super Mutant, Talon Mercenary

This container truck, parked just north of the irradiated pool, has a Super Mutant inside, although he usually charges out at the sound of gunfire.

13.I: TALON COMPANY MERC TENT

- Threat Level: 3
- Faction: Super Mutant, Talon Mercenary
- Guns and Ammunition
- Health and Chems
- Hostiles: Super Mutant Genus

Currently being commandeered by Super Mutants, this tent holds some items and a mattress. Continue along the alley to the south, and use the planks to access the main area in front of the Takoma Industries building, near the irradiated pool.

- First Aid Box Health and Chems (2)
- Ammo Box Ammunition (2)

13.J: HIDDEN IRRADIATED POOL

- Threat Level: 3
- Faction: Ghoul, Wastelander
- Danger: High Radiation
- Guns and Ammunition

- Hostiles: Ghoul Genus
- Isabella Proud (Deceased)
- Jason (Deceased)

Well hidden in the northeast corner of this zone is a large irradiated pool. Exit from the Takoma Industries building, and locate the section of radio mast in the canal. Use that as a bridge to reach the northern lip of the canal. Follow a rubble passage north and east and repel a trio of Ghouls. Then search the bodies of two scientists, and their camp for Rad-X, RadAway, a mattress, 10mm Ammo, and Isabella Proud's Terminal. The eight entries provide fascinating insight into lumpyskin society!

ZONE 14: GEORGETOWN

- Fat Man Mini Nukes: 1/71
- Nuka-Cola Quantum: 2/94
- Skill Book [Big Guns]: 1/25, Skill Book [Melee
- Weapons]: 1/25, Skill Book [Speech]: 1/25

PRIMARY LOCATIONS

14.01: Tepid Sewer

14.02: DCTA Tunnel 014-B Potomac

14.03: Grocer

14.04: Radiation King

14.05: Foggy Bottom Station

14.06: Townhome

14.07: Georgetown / The Mall Metro

14.08: La Maison Beauregard Lobby

14.09: Penn. Ave. / Georgetown Metro

SECONDARY LOCATIONS

14.A: Super Mutant Camp

14.B: Rusting Bridge

14.C: Pulowski Preservation Shelter

14.D: Rusting Metro Carriage

14.E: Trap House

14.F: Pulowski Preservation Shelter

14.G: City Coach Liner

PRIMARY LOCATIONS

14.01: TEPID SEWER (GEORGETOWN WEST)

- Threat Level: 2
- Underground Connection

Note

The Metro Station entrance leads to an Underground Metro Area: D.C. U5.

Location D.C. U5: Tepid Sewer (Interior) (page 444).

The following surface location can be accessed from here:

Location 9.07: Tepid Sewer (Capital Wasteland) (page 378).

Close to a large four-headed column and the canal to the south, a glass conservatory to the north (that you can't enter), and a small Super Mutant camp inside the ruined building to the west [14.A], this offers quick access to the Wasteland area (near the Potomac and the Memorial).

14.02: DCTA TUNNEL 014-B POTOMAC

- Threat Level: 2
- Danger: Low Radiation
- Underground Connection

Note

The Underground tunnel entrance leads to a number of linked Underground Metro Areas: D.C. U6.E, U6.C, and U6.F.

Location D.C. U6.E: DCTA Tunnel 014-B Potomac (Interior) (page 446).

Location D.C. U6.C: Foggy Bottom Station (page 445).

Location D.C. U6.F: Arlington Utility (page 446).

Location D.C. U6.B: Metro Central (page 445).

(From D.C. U6.F, you can reach Location 16 Arlington National Cemetery. From U6.E, you can reach Georgetown and Dupont Circle. From U6.B, you can reach locations 11: Dupont Circle, 12: Vernon Square, 15: Pennsylvania Avenue, 16: Arlington National Cemetery, 17: The Mall, and 18: Seward Square.)

The following surface locations can be accessed from these Underground tunnels:

Location 16.02: Arlington Utility (Cemetery North) (page 417).

Various locations from U6.E, and B.

Don't confuse it with Location 14.02; the door to the DCTA Tunnels is on the edge of the canal, which you can swim in, and drag yourself up by the fallen pathway near this entrance to avoid Super Mutant gunfire in the area. If you need to reach the center of the interior, or west to the Arlington National Cemetery, take this route.

14.03: GROCER

TRAINING — BESTIARY — MAIN QUEST — MISC. QUESTS — TOUR — COMPLETION — APPENDICES

- Threat Level: 1
- Health and Chems
- Interior Exploration
- Hostiles: Radroaches

On Georgetown Avenue at the northwest corner of this zone is a Cornucopia Groceries Store. Unlike all the other stores bearing this name, it is accessible. There are shelves of food on the outside, and a gloomy interior. Head to the counter to find a floor safe, scattered Caps, Chems, beer, a Carton of Cigarettes, and a First Aid Box. There's also some food on the shelves.

- Floor Safe Items
- First Aid Box Health and Chems

14.04: RADIATION KING

- Threat Level: 1
- Faction: Wastelander
- Services: Repairer, Trader
- Interior Exploration
- Scavenger

Two doors east of the grocers is the fabled Radiator King's store, a surviving franchise from a successful electronics chain that has faded posters dotted around the Wasteland. Inside are radios, a jukebox, and a Scavenger to speak with. He Barters and can Repair your equipment. The toilet is empty.

14.05: FOGGY BOTTOM STATION (EXTERIOR)

- Threat Level: 2
- Underground Connection

East of the canal, and the giant rubble pile from the collapsed freeway overpass is the entrance to Foggy Bottom Station at the north end of Bradley Place. Climb the pile and shimmy along an awning to take items from a well-hidden Ammo Box.

- Ammo Box Ammunition

Note

The Metro Station entrance leads to D.C. U6.C and U6.B.

Location D.C. U6.C: Foggy Bottom Station (Interior) (page 445).

Location D.C. U6.B: Metro Central (page 445).

(From Location D.C. U6.B and C, you can reach D.C. Interior Locations 11: Dupont Circle, 12: Vernon Square, 14: Georgetown, 15: Pennsylvania Avenue, 16: Arlington National Cemetery, 17: The Mall, and 18: Seward Square. You can also reach Anacostia Crossing in the Capital Wasteland: 9.16)

14.06: TOWNHOME (MCCLELLAN HOUSEHOLD)

- Threat Level: 1
- Faction: Wastelander
- Collectible: Skill Book
- Interior Exploration
- Sleep Mattress
- Mister Handy

At the west side of the alley and gardens linking the two north-south streets is a townhome with an unlocked door. Inside, take the Lying, Congressional Style book on the table, and check the kitchen for food in the fridge. Nearby is a kid's bunk-bed room. Check upstairs for a queen-sized bed. Head under the stairs, and locate the deactivated Mister Handy.

- Lying, Congressional Style (19/25)

Using the terminal, you can request that he attempt the following chores:

"Walk Muffy"

He heads outside to look for the mangy animal, and is usually destroyed by roving Super Mutants.

"Pick Up Grocery Order"

He exits to the grocery, and is destroyed by Super Mutants.

"Read Children Bedtime Poem"

He heads to the bunk-bed room, and reads the following to the two tiny skeletons:

"There will come soft rains and the smell of the ground,

And swallows circling with their shimmering sound;

And frogs in the pool singing at night,

And wild plum trees in tremulous white;

Robins will wear their feathery fire,

Whistling their whims on a low fence-wire;

And not one will know of the war, not one,

Will care at last when it is done.

Not one would mind, neither bird nor tree,

If mankind perished utterly;

And Spring herself when she woke at dawn,

Would scarcely know that we were gone."

This is a poem by Sara Teasdale (1919). Also used in the Ray Bradbury short story, "There Will Come Soft Rains" (from the *Martian Chronicles*).

"Home Security Mode"

He heads outside to check for undesirables and is shot by Super Mutants. If all Super Mutants are defeated, he makes his rounds and waits near the home.

14.07: GEORGETOWN / THE MALL METRO (GEORGETOWN SOUTH)

- Threat Level: 2
- Faction: Super Mutant
- Underground Connection

Note

The Metro Station entrance leads to a linked Underground Metro Area: D.C. U8.

Location D.C. U8: Georgetown / The Mall Metro (Interior) (page 447).

The following surface locations can be accessed from the Underground Metro Tunnels:

Location 17.04: Georgetown / The Mall Metro (Northwest) (page 421).

This is an often-used location, and one you can remember; it's the cratered remains of a tunnel.

14.08: LA MAISON BEAUREGARD LOBBY

- Threat Level: 3
- Faction: Super Mutant
- Collectibles: Fat Man Mini-Nuke, Nuka-Cola Quantum, Skill Book
- Guns and Ammunition
- Interior Exploration

A once-swanky, now-crumbling hotel is guarded by a couple of meaty Mutants. Once in the lobby area, head to the lobby desk and claim the beer and U.S. Army: 30 Handy Flamethrower Recipes. Deal damage to a Mutant on the balcony armed with a Missile Launcher, then climb the dirt pile, and scoop up the Mini-Nuke, three Missiles, Stealth Boy, and Stimpaks from the pool table. Behind the bar there's a fridge with food, a corpse with a .32 Pistol on the counter, and a Nuka-Cola Quantum. The rest of the hotel is blocked.

- U.S. Army: 30 Handy Flamethrower Recipes (19/25)
- Mini-Nuke (57/71)
- Missile Launcher and Ammo
- Stealth Boy
- Nuka-Cola Quantum (77/94)

14.09: PENN. AVE. / GEORGETOWN METRO (GEORGETOWN EAST)

- Threat Level: 2
- Faction: Super Mutant
- Underground Connection
- Hostiles: Super Mutants

Note

The Metro Station entrance leads to a linked Underground Metro Area: D.C. U7.

Location D.C. U7: Penn. Ave. / Georgetown Metro (page 446).

The following surface location can be accessed from the Underground Metro Tunnels:

Location 15.05: Penn. Ave. / Georgetown Metro (Penn. Ave. Northwest) (page 415).

Emerge from the Metro Station and ready yourself for Super Mutant combat in this area. There's some Whiskey and Rad-X nearby.

SECONDARY LOCATIONS

14.A: SUPER MUTANT CAMP

- Threat Level: 3
- Faction: Super Mutant
- Collectible: Skill Book
- Guns and Ammunition
- Hostiles: Centaur, Super Mutant Genus

Just west of the Tepid Sewer Station [14.01], is a ruined office building with four Super Mutants and a Centaur ready to attack. Clear the area if you wish, then check the upper concrete ledges to the south where you can find the following:

- Ammo Box Ammunition (3)
- Baseball Bat
- Stealth Boy
- Grognak the Barbarian (21/25)

14.B: RUSTING BRIDGE

- Threat Level: 2
- Highly Visible Landmark

This landmark, which is blocked on the southern side, sometimes has a Super Mutant on it to fire at, as well as an exploding car.

14.C: PULOWSKI PRESER-VATION SHELTER

- Threat Level: 1
- Collectible: Nuka-Cola Quantum

This shelter, in the alley to the west of the grocers, has beer, food, and a Nuka-Cola Quantum inside.

- Nuka-Cola Quantum (78/94)

14.D: RUSTING METRO CARRIAGE

- Threat Level: 2
- Faction: Super Mutant

Metro carriages don't explode when you fire at them, so this makes a great place to take cover during battles with the local Super Mutant population.

14.E: TRAP HOUSE

- Threat Level: 3
- Faction: Super Mutant
- Danger: Baseball Pitcher, Bear Trap, Mines
- Guns and Ammunition

Between the Townhome and the eastern parking lot is a back-garden, two alley-ways, and a Trap House to the east. Around the front of the house are three Frag Mines. Step into the house and dis-arm the Bear Trap. Head in from the back, and watch the pressure plate that activates the Baseball Pitcher. Upstairs is a dead Raider, Ammo Box, and great sniping posi-tion to explode the parking lot in a ball of fire. Also check the "Gore Bag tree" to the northeast; there are three Ammo Boxes and two Stimpaks here.

- Ammo Box Ammunition (4)

14.F: PULOWSKI PRESER-VATION SHELTER

- Threat Level: 2
- Faction: Super Mutant

This shelter is completely empty.

14.G: CITY COACH LINER

- Threat Level: 3
- Faction: Super Mutant
- Danger: Low Radiation

One possible plan is to coax Super Mutants into this parking lot, and blow the vehicles up, starting with this.

ZONE 15: PENNSYLVANIA AVENUE

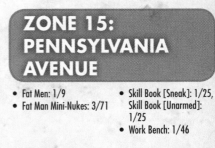

- Fat Men: 1/9
- Fat Man Mini-Nukes: 3/71
- Skill Book [Sneak]: 1/25, Skill Book [Unarmed]: 1/25
- Work Bench: 1/46

APPENDICES — COMPLETION — TOUR — MISC. QUESTS — MAIN QUEST — BESTIARY — TRAINING

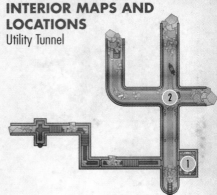

PRIMARY LOCATIONS

15.01: Freedom Street Station

15.02: White House Utility Tunnel

15.03: Sewer

15.04: Metro Central

15.05: Penn. Ave. / Georgetown Metro

15.06: Hotel

15.07: Penn. Ave. / The Mall Metro

15.08: Penn. Ave. / Seward Sq. Metro

SECONDARY LOCATIONS

15.A: Container Truck

15.B: Courtyard Fountain

15.C: Brotherhood of Steel Barricade

15.D: City Coach Liner

15.E: City Coach Liner

15.F: Pennsylvania Avenue Explosive Charge

15.G: Underground Parking Garage

15.H: City Coach Liner

15.I: Dot's Diner

15.J: Wastelander's Alcove

15.K: Pulowski Preservation Shelter

PRIMARY LOCATIONS

15.01: FREEDOM STREET STATION (PENN. AVE. NORTH)

- Threat Level: 2
- Faction: Super Mutant
- Underground Connection

📖 Note

The Metro Station entrance leads to D.C. U6.D and D.C. U6.B.

Location D.C. U6.D: Freedom Street Station (page 446).

Location D.C. U6.B: Metro Central (page 445).

(From Location D.C. U6.B, you can reach D.C. Interior Locations 11: Dupont Circle, 12: Vernon Square, 14: Georgetown, 15: Pennsylvania Avenue, 16: Arlington National Cemetery, 17: The Mall, and 18: Seward Square. You can also reach Anacostia Crossing in the Capital Wasteland: 9.16)

The following surface locations can be accessed from here:

Various locations from U6.B: Metro Central (page 445).

On the north side of the giant, four-sided "salute to industry" statue is a Metro Station that leads to the Metro Central labyrinth. It takes a while, but you can go anywhere from here. On the other side of the statue is a Super Mutant playing with his victim.

15.02: WHITE HOUSE UTILITY TUNNEL

- Threat Level: 4
- Faction: Ghoul
- Danger: High Radiation
- Collectibles: Fat Man Launcher, Fat Man Mini-Nuke (3), Skill Book
- Guns and Ammunition
- Health and Chems
- Interior Exploration
- Work Bench
- Hostile: Glowing One

INTERIOR MAPS AND LOCATIONS
Utility Tunnel

The White House was completely destroyed when the bombs fell, and a large crater is located where the building once stood. The only access point is via a manhole to a Utility Tunnel in the northwest part of the courtyard.

① East Workshop

Locate the Work Bench, Bottlecap Mine, Carton of Cigarettes, food in the fridge, and a large number of tools lying around.

- Work Bench (40/46)
- Pugilism Illustrated (22/25)
- First Aid Box Health and Chems

② Stunt Gone Awry

At the crossroads is a rusting car. It appears a lunatic attempted to leap the car using a bike (which is farther up the tunnel), but got his head stuck between the light fixture and roof! Outside, you appear in the ruins of the White House, still highly radioactive. The only living remains are a pair of frightening Glowing Ones. Face them, or flee to one of the concrete "islands" on the column supports that are still standing, and blast them from here for some RadAway, and a grand prize:

- Fat Man (8/9)
- Mini-Nuke (58/71)
- Mini-Nuke (59/71)
- Mini-Nuke (60/71)

15.03: SEWER (PENN. AVE.)

- Threat Level: 2
- Faction: Super Mutants
- Underground Connection

Note

The Sewer entrance leads to a Underground Metro Area: D.C. U11.

Location D.C. U11: Sewer (Interior).

The following surface locations can be accessed from the Underground Metro Tunnels:

Location 18.04: Sewer (Seward Square) (page 432).

Just west of the parking garage near the rubble that hides the diner and Metro Station to the east, is a manhole cover. This is a quick alternate to head back and forth from Seward Square.

15.04: METRO CENTRAL (EXTERIOR)

- Threat Level: 3
- Faction: Super Mutant
- Underground Connection

Note

The Metro Station entrance leads to a number of linked Underground Metro Areas stemming from: D.C. U6.B.

Location D.C. U6.B: Metro Central (Interior) (page 445).

(From U6.B, you can reach Locations 11: Dupont Circle, 12: Vernon Square, 15: Pennsylvania Avenue, 16: Arlington National Cemetery, 17: The Mall, and 18: Seward Square.)

Various locations from U6.B can be accessed from here.

An impressive Metro entrance, made even more memorable by the hanging (and dripping) Gore Bags above the escalators, is Metro Central; the hub of Underground linking for the city. You can head to six different zones from here, but use this only when you're experienced enough to handle a long trip Underground. On the surface, expect medium resistance from Super Mutants.

15.05: PENN. AVE. / GEORGETOWN METRO (PENN. AVE. NORTHWEST)

- Threat Level: 2
- Faction: Brotherhood of Steel
- Underground Connection

Note

The Metro Station entrance leads to a linked Underground Metro Area: D.C. U7.

Location D.C. U7: Penn. Ave. / Georgetown Metro (page 446).

The following surface location can be accessed from the Underground Metro Tunnels:

Location 14.09: Penn. Ave. / Georgetown Metro (Georgetown East) (page 413).

Close to the White House crater, and adjacent to the hotel, head here when you want to reach Georgetown in a hurry. You're close to a group of Brotherhood soldiers manning sandbag defenses [15.C].

15.06: HOTEL

- Threat Level: 1
- Faction: Brotherhood of Steel
- Danger: Grenade Bouquet
- Collectible: Skill Book
- Guns and Ammunition
- Health and Chems
- Interior Exploration
- Sleep Mattress
- Friendly: Brotherhood Paladin

Head in from the ornate courtyard. Inside the hotel, disarm the Grenade Trap straight in front of you and greet the Brotherhood Paladin inside, carrying a Super Sledge.

The Paladin is also carrying a Holotag, and he doesn't have to die under Super Mutant gunfire.... Search the rubble-filled lobby; there's a mattress, a Carton of Cigarettes, and these items:

- Frag Grenade (3)
- Super Sledge
- Brotherhood Holotag
- First Aid Box Health and Chems (2)
- Silenced 10mm Pistol
- Ammo Box Ammunition (2)
- Chinese Army: Spec. Ops. Training Manual (16/25)

15.07: PENN. AVE. / THE MALL METRO (PENN. AVE. SOUTH)

- Threat Level: 2
- Underground Connection

Note

The Metro Station entrance leads to a linked Underground Metro Area: D.C. U9.

Location D.C. U9: Penn. Ave. / The Mall Metro (Interior) (page 447).

The following surface location can be accessed from here:

Location 17.13: Penn. Ave. / The Mall Metro (The Mall Northeast) (page 429).

This Metro Station allows quick access to the Mall and The National Archives. There's a metal box at the foot of this entrance, and little to worry about until you venture onto Pennsylvania Ave. itself.

15.08: PENN. AVE. / SEWARD SQ. METRO (PENN. AVE. EAST)

- Threat Level: 2
- Underground Connection

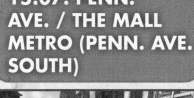

TRAINING — BESTIARY — MAIN QUEST — MISC. QUESTS — TOUR — COMPLETION — APPENDICES

Note

The Metro Station entrance leads to a linked Underground Metro Area: D.C. U10.

Location D.C. U10: Penn. Ave. / Seward Sq. Metro (Interior) (page 447).

The following surface locations can be accessed from here:

Location 18.02: Penn. Ave. / Seward Sq. Metro (Seward Square North) (page 431).

Although Super Mutants roam this zone, this area is relatively quiet, and the station is partially hidden from the main street by rubble piles.

SECONDARY LOCATIONS

15.A: CONTAINER TRUCK

- Threat Level: 2
- Faction: Super Mutant, Wastelander
- Guns and Ammunition
- Health and Chems

North of the Brotherhood barricade is a container truck, where a Super Mutant is ripping apart three Wastelanders. Kill the beast, then check the truck container.

- First Aid Box Health and Chems (2)
- Ammo Box Ammunition (2)

15.B: COURTYARD FOUNTAIN

- Threat Level: 2
- Faction: Brotherhood of Steel

Close to the White House crater is an ornate fountain and courtyard.

15.C: BROTHERHOOD OF STEEL BARRICADE

- Threat Level: 3
- Factions: Brotherhood of Steel, Super Mutant
- Guns and Ammunition
- Health and Chems

The Brotherhood is fighting a fierce street battle with Super Mutants attacking from the east, and this is the last-ditch attempt to stop them from swarming the White House crater. The Paladins all wield heavy weapons, including a Gatling Laser, so you may want to step back and let them take the damage, then scavenge the Holotags, armor, weapons, and items from the sandbags afterward.

- Brotherhood Holotag (3)
- Gatling Laser and Ammo
- First Aid Box Health and Chems (2)
- Ammo Box Ammunition (2)

15.D: CITY COACH LINER

- Threat Level: 3
- Faction: Brotherhood of Steel, Super Mutant
- Danger: Low Radiation

Located near a group of Super Mutants, this can detonate and tear them apart if you're adept enough.

15.E: CITY COACH LINER

- Threat Level: 2
- Faction: Super Mutant
- Danger: Low Radiation

A block north of Penn. Ave. / The Mall (South) Metro Station is a coach liner, waiting to be detonated to take down any nearby Muties.

15.F: PENNSYLVANIA AVENUE EXPLOSIVE CHARGE

- Threat Level: 1
- Faction: Talon Company
- Merc Thompson (Deceased)

On Pennsylvania Avenue itself, look along the north side of the street for a large section of scaffolding, across from the bank building. Use the fallen sections of scaffolding to leap onto the lower gantry platform, and locate dead Merc Thompson. He's written a note about a series of charges he's set, and at the western end of the platform is the switch itself. Activate it (ideally with enemies nearby) and the entire avenue erupts in fiery explosions from 15.C all the way to 15.H!

- Pennsylvania Ave. Explosives Note

15.G: UNDERGROUND PARKING GARAGE

- Miscellaneous Quest: Reilly's Rangers
- Threat Level: 2
- Factions: Super Mutant, Wastelander

- Services: Repairer, Trader
- Danger: Chain Trap, Grenade Bouquet
- Guns and Ammunition
- Health and Chems
- Radio Signal
- Scavenger
- Scavenger's Dog (2)

On G Street, running parallel to Pennsylvania Avenue, head east until you hear the crackle of the Ranger Emergency Frequency. Turn south, and check out the ramp down under the building, leading past a Red-engine-on-a-chain Trap and Grenade Bouquet you should disarm, and into a rubble-filled parking garage. Here you can speak with a Scavenger to Barter and Trade with him. Murder him for his Ammo and Health if you wish.

- Ranger Emergency Frequency
- Frag Grenade (3)
- Ammo Box Ammunition (4)
- First Aid Box Health and Chems (2)

15.H: CITY COACH LINER

- Threat Level: 2
- Faction: Super Mutant

Across from the large bank building is a city liner. Hide behind it, or blow it up if Super Mutants are near.

15.I: DOT'S DINER

- Threat Level: 3
- Faction: Super Mutant
- Guns and Ammunition
- Hostiles: Super Mutants

North of the Metro Central station is a grisly diner. Expect Caps (and human flesh, naturally) in each bag, and once the Mutie threat has been dealt with, search the counter for items:

- Ammo Box Ammunition (5)

15.J: WASTELANDER'S ALCOVE

- Threat Level: 2
- Factions: Super Mutant, Wastelander
- Guns and Ammunition
- Health and Chems
- Sleep Mattress

Although the Wastelander in question has been shot and is crumpled by his alcove, there's a place to sleep here, as well as:

- Ammo Box Ammunition (2)
- First Aid Box Health and Chems (2)

15.K: PULOWSKI PRESERVATION SHELTER

- Threat Level: 2
- Faction: Super Mutant
- Guns and Ammunition

The remains of a Protectron fall out, next to an Ammo Box.

- Ammo Box Ammunition.

ZONE 16: ARLINGTON NATIONAL CEMETERY

- Bobbleheads: 1/20
- Unique Items: 1/89
- Nuka-Cola Quantum: 1/94
- Scribe Pre-War Books: 2/98
- Skill Book [Barter]: 1/24, Skill Book [Lockpick]: 1/25, Skill Book [Repair]: 1/25,
- Skill Book [Science]: 1/25, Skill Book [Small Guns]: 2/25, Skill Book [Sneak]: 1/25
- Work Bench: 1/46

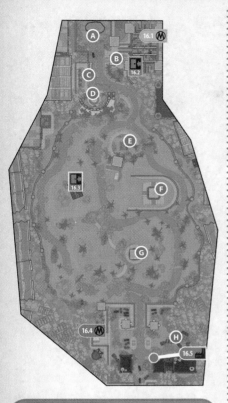

- Threat Level: 1
- Underground Connection

 Note

This Metro Station entrance leads to the linked Underground Metro Area: D.C. U12.

Location D.C. U12: Arlington / Wasteland Metro (interior) (page 447).

The following surface locations can be accessed from Underground Metro Tunnels:

Location 9.05: Flooded Metro (Capital Wasteland) (page 377).

This is the north of the two Metro Stations in this vicinity. Don't confuse the two; this leads to a single Underground area and out to the Potomac via the Flooded Metro.

If you have the **Lawbringer** Perk (and only if you have it), there is a dead Regulator on the Metro Station stairs with a Bounty Contract for someone named Junders Plunket.

16.02: ARLINGTON UTILITY (CEMETERY NORTH)

- Threat Level: 1
- Underground Connection

At the southern end of the Arlington Cemetery North station platform is a tunnel from Arlington Utility; the quickest way to reach the main interior network east of the river. Nearly is a Pulowski Shelter [16.B].

- Junders Plunket Bounty Contract

 Note

The Metro Station entrance leads to a number of linked Underground Metro Areas: D.C. U6.F; U6.E, U6.C,

Location D.C. U6.F: Arlington Utility (page 446).

Location D.C. U6.E: DCTA Tunnel 014-B Potomac (Interior) (page 446).

Location D.C. U6.C: Foggy Bottom Station (page 445).

Location D.C. U6.B: Metro Central (page 445).

(From Location D.C. U6.F, you can reach Location 14: Georgetown. From U6.E, you can reach Georgetown and Dupont Circle. From U6.B, you can reach Locations 11: Dupont Circle, 12: Vernon Square, 15: Pennsylvania Avenue, 16: Arlington National Cemetery, 17: The Mall, and 18: Seward Square.)

The following surface locations can be accessed from these Underground Metro Tunnels:

Location 14.02: DCTA Tunnel 014-B Potomac (Georgetown West) (page 411).

Various locations from U6.E and B.

16.03: ARLINGTON HOUSE

- Threat Level: 2
- Faction: Raider
- Collectibles: Bobblehead, Skill Book
- Health and Chems
- Highly Visible Landmark
- Interior Exploration
- Rare or Powerful Item
- Sleep Mattress
- Work Bench
- Hostile: Junders Plunket

INTERIOR LOCATIONS GENERAL NOTES

On a hillock west of the main cemetery area are the remains of the once-grand Arlington House, now a rotting monument to this past civilization. The area is great to flee to, as the trees, flagpole, and bushes provide good cover to snipe from, and the view is commanding. There is an unlocked door as well, so enter the building for an exploration.

PRIMARY LOCATIONS

16.01: Arlington / Wasteland Metro

16.02: Arlington Utility

16.03: Arlington House

16.04: Arlington / Falls Church Metro

16.05: Mama Dolce's Processed Foods

SECONDARY LOCATIONS

16.A: Irradiated Crater

16.B: Pulowski Preservation Shelter

16.C: City Coach Liner

16.D: Circular Courtyard

16.E: Fountain

16.F: Arlington Monument (Short)

16.G: Arlington Monument (Tall)

16.H: Container Truck

PRIMARY LOCATIONS

16.01: ARLINGTON / WASTELAND METRO (CEMETERY NORTH)

TRAINING — BESTIARY — MAIN QUEST — MISC. QUESTS — TOUR — COMPLETION — APPENDICES

Kitchen

Pry open a hallway cabinet. Also check upstairs for Darts and a queen-sized bed to sleep in.

- Big Book of Science (22/25)

Cellar

If you don't have the Lawbringer perk, Junders (and his items) aren't here. Collect the rest of the items instead.

> If you have the **Lawbringer** perk, a Raider named Junders Plunket is working near an old shrine to Abraham Lincoln. He can't be reasoned with, so beat him to death. Take wine from the shrine if you wish. Check Plunket's bed; there's whiskey, a Carton of Cigarettes, and Chems here. Note the safe, Work Bench, Bottlecap Mine, and shelf with Chems and a Bobblehead.

- Work Bench (41/46)
- "Plunket's Valid Points": Spiked Knuckles (68/89)
- First Aid Box Health and Chems
- Floor Safe Items
- Bobblehead: Luck (20/20)

16.04: ARLINGTON / FALLS CHURCH METRO (CEMETERY SOUTH)

- Threat Level: 2
- Underground Connection

 **Note**

The Metro Station entrance leads to Underground Metro Areas: D.C. U15.

Location D.C. U15: Arlington / Falls Church Metro (Interior) (page 448).

The following surface location can be accessed from Underground Metro Tunnel:

Location 19.05: Arlington / Falls Church Metro (Falls Church North) (page 435).

If you're after the Capital Wasteland, head to 16.01 instead. The exterior of this station is near a number of rusting (and explosive) cars stacked as defenses.

16.05: MAMA DOLCE'S PROCESSED FOODS

- Threat Level: 4
- Faction: Chinese Commando
- Danger: Gas Leak, Low Radiation
- Collectibles: Nuka-Cola Quantum, Scribe Pre-War Book (2), Skill Book (5)
- Guns and Ammunition
- Health and Chems
- Interior Exploration
- Radio Signal
- Sleep Mattress
- Hostiles: Chinese Remnant Officer, Chinese Remnant Captain, Turret

The Chinese had managed to install themselves in D.C. with a small Spec. Ops. force, using Mama Dolce's food processing factory as a front and safehouse. Now, years after the bombs ended that multinational conflict, the descendants of those original Chinese agents continue to use the safety of the factory to remain protected and hidden from the native citizens of the Capital Wasteland. As you approach one of the two entrances to this structure (the Processed Foods or Food Distribution metal doors), there are no signs of life at all. Check your Pip-Boy's Radio as you go; the Chinese have the People's Republic of America Radio spewing propaganda throughout this area!

- People's Republic of America Radio

MAMA DOLCE'S PROCESSED FOODS

 Note

You can enter this area from the Cemetery, Food Distribution, or Loading Yard Areas.

1 Large Office and Storage Room

There's food in the vending machine, some Darts, and the following in here:

- Ammo Box Ammunition (2)
- Stealth Boy

2 South Catwalk

Expect combat from Chinese Remnant Officers.

3 Globe-Shaped Vat

Danger: Gas Leak!

4 Southeast Alcove

- Ammo Box Ammunition (3)
- First Aid Box Health and Chems
- Sledgehammer

5 Foreman's Office

- Sledgehammer
- Scribe Pre-War Book (75/98)

6 Gantry Floor Area

Kill two Remnants inside, and check out the mattress, utility door, and this item:

- 10mm Pistol

7 West Restrooms

- First Aid Box Health and Chems
- Guns and Bullets (20/25)

INTERIOR MAPS AND LOCATIONS
Mama Dolce's Processed Foods

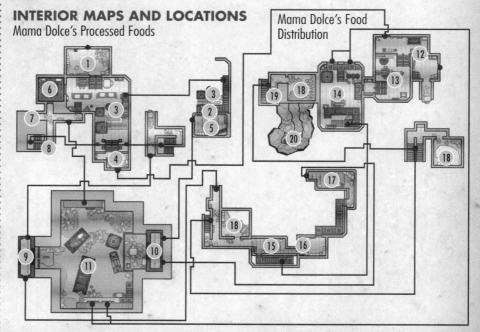

Mama Dolce's Food Distribution

Mama Dolce's Loading Yard

8 Stairwell

This leads up to a corridor leading to the Loading Yard. Don't forget the Skill Book on the landing shelves.

- Dean's Electronics (19/25)

MAMA DOLCE'S LOADING YARD

Note
You can enter this area from the Food Distribution or Processed Foods areas.

A couple of exterior metal corridors around a central courtyard link the Processed Foods and Food Distribution areas together.

9 Balcony from Processed Foods (Corridor)

An open-air sniping point.

- Guns and Bullets (21/25)

10 Balcony from Processed Foods (Foreman's Office)

An open-air sniping point.

- Ammo Box Ammunition
- Sniper Rifle and Ammo
- Chinese Army: Spec. Ops. Training Manual (17/25)

11 Loading Yard Exterior

Pay particular attention to the Officer on the red container with the Missile Launcher. Once he's defeated, enter the Food Distribution area, via either garage door. The gate to the west requires a key, and cannot be opened.

MAMA DOLCE'S FOOD DISTRIBUTION

Note
You can enter this area from the Cemetery, Processed Foods, or Loading Yard areas.

GROUND FLOOR

12 L-Shaped Operator's Office and Rec Room

Check the west wall for a couple of footlockers. The Turret Control Terminal deactivates the turret in this warehouse area.

- Stealth Boy
- Ammo Box Ammunition (3)
- Baseball Bat

13 Warehouse #1

Beware of Remnants. There's scattered food in this warehouse.

---

14 Warehouse #2

Two garage doors lead to the Loading Yard, and there's scattered food in here.

15 (Second Floor) Foreman's Overlook

There's more food and a ham radio in here.

THIRD FLOOR

16 Captain's Office

Slay the Remnant leader here, and take the Mama Dolce's Encryption Key from him. There's a desk terminal near the listed items, two wall safes, as well as more food. The terminal has the following five entries:

1. Resource Levels

Technical information for the vats in this building.

2. Quarterly Analysis

Big sales for the Sweet-and-Sour Stroganoff, but problems due to domestic shipping costs.

3. Human Resources Memo

New recruits are welcomed.

4. Urgent Diagnostic Alert

Radiation levels have spiked in this area.

5. Ikkm00:mvkz6x1m1:Nqtm.

Gibberish, unless you have Mama Dolce's Encryption Key. This is an encrypted message from the People's Republic of China, informing Agent Huang about his mission here.

- Mama Dolce's Encryption Key
- Nuka-Cola Quantum (79/94)
- Scribe Pre-War Book (76/98)
- First Aid Box Health and Chems
- Wall Safe Items (2)

17 Corner Office

There's a generator and more food on the desk. The metal door leads out to the loading yard where you can slay a Sniper.

18 Chamber with Hole in Floor

You can drop down here to the tunnel, although it is better to take the stairs.

- First Aid Box Health and Chems

WESTERN OFFICES, SECOND AND GROUND FLOORS

19 Ground Floor Small Tables

There's food on these.

- Sledgehammer

---

20 Tunnel

Drop down into the rocky excavation and hop over the barricaded desks, then access the two safes here, and grab the Skill Book.

- Floor Safe Items (2)
- Tumblers Today (20/25)

SECONDARY LOCATIONS

16.A: IRRADIATED CRATER

- Threat Level: 2
- Faction: Raider
- Danger: Low Radiation

This dangerous place to drink is north of a small band of Raiders.

16.B: PULOWSKI PRESERVATION SHELTER

- Threat Level: 2
- Faction: Raider

At the top of the Arlington Metro North steps in the small courtyard, this contains wine and a negligee.

16.C: CITY COACH LINER

- Threat Level: 2
- Faction: Raider
- Danger: Low Radiation

Parked near the trio of Raiders, have you tried sneaking with a Stealth Boy, dropping Mines, and exploding the vehicle? The shockwave kills all three of these deviants.

16.D: CIRCULAR COURTYARD

- Threat Level: 2
- Faction: Raider

Just north of the Raiders, this ornate courtyard is slowly disintegrating.

16.E: FOUNTAIN

- Threat Level: 1
- Highly Visible Landmark

This fountain long ago stopped producing water. An inaccessible chapel to the east is visible from here.

TRAINING — BESTIARY — MAIN QUEST — MISC. QUESTS — TOUR — COMPLETION — APPENDICES

16.F: ARLINGTON MONUMENT (SHORT)

- Threat Level: 1
- Highly Visible Landmark

Across from Arlington House is a short, columned monument to the fallen; use it as a landmark when navigating through this area.

16.G: ARLINGTON MONUMENT (TALL)

- Threat Level: 1
- Highly Visible Landmark

As you head to the southern part of the Cemetery, this monument is a good landmark to find.

16.H: CONTAINER TRUCK

- Threat Level: 1

Just outside Mama Dolce's are a couple of rusting trucks and an overturned container of barrels. A dead Wastelander rests inside this container, next to a Skill Book.

- Tales of a Junktown Jerky Vendor (20/24)

ZONE 17: THE MALL

- Fat Men: 1/9
- Fat Man Mini-Nukes: 4/71
- Unique Items: 15/89
- Nuka-Cola Quantum: 5/94
- Schematics: 1/23
- Scribe Pre-War Books: 6/98
- Skill Book [Barter]: 2/24, Skill Book [Big Guns]: 1/25, Skill Book [Energy
- Weapons]: 3/25, Skill Book [Explosives]: 3/25, Skill Book [Medicine]: 2/25, Skill Book [Small Guns]: 1/25, Skill Book [Sneak]: 3/25, Skill Book [Speech]: 2/25
- Work Bench: 1/46
- Holotapes [Replicated Man]: 3/19

PRIMARY LOCATIONS

17.01: Lincoln Memorial Maintenance Room

17.02: Hazmat Disposal Site L5

17.03: Mirelurk Nesting Hole

17.04: Georgetown / The Mall Metro

17.05: The Washington Monument

17.06: Museum Station

17.07: Museum of History Entrance

17.08: Bunker

17.09: Museum Station

17.10: Museum of Technology Atrium

17.11: The National Archives (Front Entrance)

17.12: The National Archives (Rear Entrance)

17.13: Penn. Ave. / The Mall Metro

17.14: Capitol Building West Entrance

SECONDARY LOCATIONS

17.A: Statue of Lincoln (Headless)

17.B: City Coach Liner

17.C: Brotherhood Lookout

17.D: Brotherhood Defenses

17.E: Super Mutant Defenses

17.F: Super Mutant Camp

17.G: Super Mutant Defenses

17.H: City Coach Liner

17.I: Ammo Cache

17.J: City Coach Liner

PRIMARY LOCATIONS

17.01: LINCOLN MEMORIAL MAINTENANCE ROOM (LINCOLN MEMORIAL)

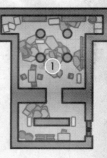

- Miscellaneous Quest: Head of State
- Threat Level: 3
- Faction: Slaver
- Danger: Grenade Bouquet, Mines
- Collectible: Nuka-Cola Quantum
- Highly Visible Landmark
- Interior Exploration

EXTERIOR MAPS AND LOCATIONS

Lincoln Memorial

INHABITANTS
Leroy Walker

Leroy is a strident believer that "might makes right." Weaklings deserve what they get in life and should serve at the whim of the more powerful. He is a rarity among Slavers. He's not in it for the money; he genuinely believes that this is the natural law of the universe. Leroy is the Slaver in charge of handling runaways. Currently there is no bigger issue for him than the Temple of the Union. In his eyes, if they succeed in making the Lincoln Memorial into a shrine for Abolitionists and runaway slaves, Paradise Falls and the Slavers will be severely hurt.

Silas

Leroy's right-hand man and trusted second-in-command, Silas guards the Slavers' current defensive stronghold from the almost constant Super Mutant attacks. Curt, sly, and sardonic, Silas isn't a particularly pleasant man, even for a Slaver.

RELATED INTERACTIONS

Leroy Walker: You can sell Lincoln artifacts you may have collected from the Museum of History.

GENERAL NOTES

Leroy Walker and his band of Slavers are the largest contingent outside Paradise Falls, and they have secured the Lincoln Memorial so it doesn't fall into the hands of Abolitionists and become a beacon for freeing slaves, and ruining their business. Currently there are around half a dozen Slavers on the steps and behind sandbag defenses at this structure. Locate Silas and he takes you into the maintenance room. Should you sneak around this monument, the path at the base is dotted with Mines and Grenade Traps, so watch out. Inside the monument itself, there's a place to sleep, but you can't access the steps unless you've begun hostilities with the Slavers.

① Leroy's Quarters

Inside the Maintenance Room, you can speak with, and sell Lincoln artifacts to, Leroy Walker, the commander of this Slaver outpost. Search the room thoroughly, and providing Walker doesn't see you, take the Quantum.

- Frag Mines
- Nuka-Cola Quantum (80/94)

17.02: HAZMAT DISPOSAL SITE L5

- Threat Level: 2
- Underground Connection

 Note

The Metro Station entrance leads to an Underground Metro Area: D.C. U21.

Location D.C. U21: Hazmat Disposal Site L5 Interior (Mall Southwest) (page 452).

The following surface location can be accessed from here:

Location 21.01: Hazmat Disposal Site L5 (L'Enfant Plaza) (page 440).

The quickest way to L'Enfant Plaza (and the only way except for access from the Irradiated Metro area [9.12]) is to take this Metro Station. The area is reasonably quiet, if you haven't disturbed the nearby Slavers.

17.03: MIRELURK NESTING HOLE

- Threat Level: 3
- Danger: Low Radiation
- Collectibles: Nuka-Cola Quantum, Skill Book
- Guns and Ammunition
- Health and Chems
- Interior Exploration
- Hostiles: Mirelurk Genus

INTERIOR MAPS AND LOCATIONS
Mirelurk Nesting Hole

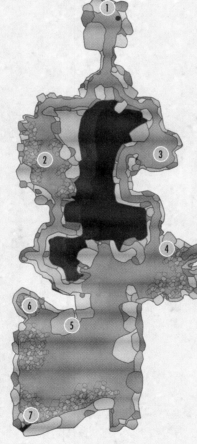

GENERAL NOTES
Next to the irradiated, waterlogged Mall area, by a coach liner [17.B] is a damaged sewer line, and you can enter the exposed grate. It leads into a large underground cave system packed with clicking Mirelurks.

① Entrance Grate

There are some Chems by the grating, and a path leading south that forks left and right.

② West Tunnel

There are pockets of radiation here.

- First Aid Box Health and Chems

③ East Tunnel

There are Giant Ant corpses here.

④ Main Cavern (Northeast)

This is a large circular path. There is a skeleton with whiskey, Purified Water, and other common items in tiny boxes.

⑤ Mercenary and Brahmin Corpse (Upper area)

⑥ Well-Hidden Alcove (Upper Northwest Corner)

Check near the skeleton for the following items:

- First Aid Box Health and Chems
- Assault Rifle and Ammo
- Chinese Army: Spec. Ops. Training Manual (18/25)

⑦ Upper Southwest Corner

There's a ham radio here.

- Nuka-Cola Quantum (81/94)

17.04: GEORGETOWN / THE MALL METRO (NORTHWEST)

- Threat Level: 2
- Danger: Low Radiation
- Underground Connection
- Hostiles: Vicious Dogs

 Note

The Metro Station entrance leads to a linked Underground Metro Area: D.C. U8.

Location D.C. U8: Georgetown / The Mall Metro (Interior) (page 447).

The following surface locations can be accessed from Underground Metro Tunnels:

Location 14.07: Georgetown / The Mall Metro (Georgetown South) (page 412).

TRAINING — BESTIARY — MAIN QUEST — MISC. QUESTS — TOUR — COMPLETION — APPENDICES

This often-used location is the usual place to enter the Mall, if you're heading from the cratered remains of a tunnel in the Georgetown zone. As you exit and head east, beware of a pack of Vicious Dogs.

17.05: THE WASHINGTON MONUMENT

- Main Quest: Galaxy News Radio
- Threat Level: 2
- Faction: Brotherhood of Steel, Super Mutant
- Highly Visible Landmark
- Interior Exploration
- Sleep Mattress
- Radio Signal
- Friendly: Brotherhood Paladin

The biggest landmark in the entire Wasteland, and one you should use to situate yourself in almost any of the zones, is this giant obelisk, now guarded by Brotherhood Paladins from relentless Super Mutant attack. The entrance is completely sealed to visitors except during the quest. Head inside, enter the foyer, and use the golden elevator (don't forget to look up!) to reach the observation deck, where a radar dish needs to be affixed. There's some 10mm Ammo, a place to sleep, and an incredible view from up here.

17.06: MUSEUM STATION (THE MALL)

17.07A: MUSEUM OF HISTORY ENTRANCE

- Miscellaneous Quest: Head of State, You Gotta Shoot 'Em in the Head
- Freeform Quest (2)
- Threat Level: 4
- Faction: Ghoul
- Danger: Low Radiation
- Collectibles: Nuka-Cola Quantum, Schematic, Skill Book (3), Holotape: Replicated Man (3)
- Follower
- Health and Chems
- Guns and Ammunition

- Interior Exploration
- Lots o' Caps
- Rare or Powerful Item (9)
- Sleep Mattress
- Work Bench

Note

The Metro Station entrance leads to a number of linked Underground Metro Areas: D.C. U22.B, D.C. U22.A and U6.B.

Location D.C. U22.A: Anacostia Crossing Station (Interior) (page 452).

Location D.C. U22.B: Museum Station (page 453).

Location D.C. U6.B: Metro Central (page 445).

(From Location D.C. U6.B, you can reach D.C. Interior Locations 11: Dupont Circle, 12: Vernon Square, 14: Georgetown, 15: Pennsylvania Avenue, 16: Arlington National Cemetery, 17: The Mall, and 18: Seward Square.)

The following surface locations can be accessed from the Underground Metro Tunnels:

Location 17.09: The Mall (near Museum of Technology Atrium) (page 425).

Location 18.05: Anacostia Crossing Station (Seward Sq. Southeast) (page 432).

Location 9.16: Anacostia Crossing (Exterior) (page 392).

Various location from U6.B: Metro Central (page 445).

INHABITANTS
Willow

A nonchalant but friendly young Ghoul, Willow is sarcastic, but happy to speak with you. She serves as a forward observer for the Ghouls living in the depths of the Museum of History. She isn't bothered by the Super Mutants (as they don't tend to attack Ghouls), but she's got some particular vehemence for the Brotherhood and Talon Company humans.

RELATED INTERACTIONS

Willow: You can ask her about Underworld and converse generally about her job.

INTERIOR MAPS AND LOCATIONS
Museum of History Entrance

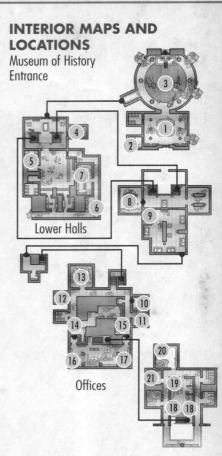

Lower Halls

Offices

Directly under the entrance to the Museum of History is a set of escalators heading down to an Underground station that links indirectly to the maze known as Metro Central. A good escape point, and if you need to visit Rivet City (or south), head out from here or the Museum of Technology Station [17.09] on the opposite side of the Mall. Although the museum's facade is crumbling, the building is still a spectacular example of pre-apocalypse architecture. Head inside through the pair of ornate wooden doors.

MUSEUM OF HISTORY ENTRANCE

1 Museum Foyer

Give it a cursory inspection.

2 Restrooms

- Nikola Tesla and You (20/25)

3 Rotunda

This comes complete with a moth-eaten mammoth and crumbling dinosaur skeleton. From here, you can visit two separate locations: the museum's lower halls, and the Ghoul stronghold known as Underworld. As you might have guessed, the latter's entrance is under the giant skull in the north wall.

MUSEUM OF HISTORY LOWER HALLS

4 (Ground Floor) Office

Locate the wall safe.

- Wall Safe Items
- First Aid Box Health and Chems

5 (Ground Floor) Restroom

You'll find a chewed-on Wastelander.

6 (Ground Floor) Outer Corridor

Danger: There are two Bear Traps in the area, and find the Nuka-Cola Quantum next to the Chem-dependant (and now dead) Wastelander.

- Nuka-Cola Quantum (82/94)

7 (Ground Floor) East Kitchen

Check the wall, and the bottom shelf near the doorway for the Skill Book.

- First Aid Box Health and Chems
- D.C. Journal of Internal Medicine (22/25)

8 (Upper Floor) Cells

If you're sneaking, you can close the cell door and activate the turrets at the terminal to rake the irradiated body of the Glowing One in here.

9 Wrecked Display (West)

- Lincoln's Diary (69/89)

MUSEUM OF HISTORY OFFICES

10 Southwest Armory

There are gun cabinets, a locked door you can circumvent if you head through the hole in the wall instead, a wall safe, a computer to turn off the turret, and the following items:

- Ammo Box Ammunition (3)
- First Aid Box Health and Chems
- Wall Safe Items
- 10mm Pistol and Ammo
- Action Abe Action Figure (70/89)

11 Linked Office

There's more 10mm Ammo in here, too.

- Combat Knife

12 Restrooms

They are shockingly more disgusting than usual.

13 Collapsed Room (Northwest)

Check the rubble for a rare find!

- Lincoln's Hat (71/89)

14 Cell Door #1

15 Cell Door #2

16 (Archives) Southwest Corner, Ground Floor

Check the bookcase below the balcony.

- John Wilkes Booth Wanted Poster (72/89)

17 (Archives) Southeast Corner; Ground Floor

Check the top shelf of the bookcase below the balcony.

- Civil War Draft Poster (73/89)

18 (Archives) Two Desks, Top Floor

Look at the wall for this item, which appears only during Miscellaneous Quest: Head of State. Then check the desk.

- Lincoln Memorial Poster (74/89)
- Lincoln's Voice (75/89)

19 (Archives) Middle Room, Top Floor

Check the display case to the northwest.

- First Aid Box Health and Chems
- Chinese Army: Spec. Ops. Training Manual (19/25)
- Lincoln's Repeater (76/89)

20 (Archives) North Room, Top Floor

Work around the holes in the floor to this item:

- Ammo Box Ammunition

21 (Archives) West Library Room, Top Floor

- Antique Lincoln Coin Collection (77/89)

FREEFORM QUEST: LINCOLN'S PROFIT MARGINS

All of these Lincoln artifacts can be sold to at least one of these people: Leroy Walker at the Lincoln Memorial [17.01], Hannibal Hamlin at the Temple of the Union [3.10], or Abraham Washington at the Capitol Preservation Society in Rivet City [9.15]. Use Speech challenges to wheedle more Caps than the amounts shown.

ARTIFACT	LOCATION	PRICE PAID (CAPS)
Lincoln's Hat	Museum of History	40
Action Abe	Museum of History	10
John Wilkes Booth Wanted Poster	Museum of History	5
Civil War Draft Poster	Museum of History	5
Lincoln's Diary	Museum of History	75
Antique Lincoln Coin Collection	Museum of History	15
Gift Shop Poster of the Lincoln Memorial†	Museum of History	100
Lincoln's Voice (Phonograph)	Museum of History	50
Lincoln's Repeater Rifle	Museum of History	100

† Critical to completing Head of State if you side with the Abolitionists.

17.07B: MUSEUM OF HISTORY: UNDERWORLD

INTERIOR MAPS AND LOCATIONS

Concourse

INHABITANTS

Winthrop

Winthrop is Underworld's technician. He checks on the electricity, makrs sure any plumbing is in working order, and generally takes care of things. He restored and reprogrammed the robot Cerberus, and is responsible for his maintenance. Winthrop sleeps for a few hours in his little workshop off the Concourse, and is occasionally joined by his girlfriend Greta.

Tulip

Tulip, owner of Underworld Outfitters, is known for her shrewd business sense. She obtains and sells a lot of merchandise, has the largest selection of any merchant in the Wasteland, and protects her business interests with competitive prices and a unique ability to obtain unique items. Tulip spends most of her time in the store, but takes her meals at Carol's Place, leaving the shop under watchful eye of Quinn.

Quinn

Quinn is a wanderer, a loner more used to traversing the Wasteland than sitting around and chatting in this place, but he's here to provide trade and supplies to Tulip, and make sure she's okay. Used to interaction with humans, he has learned not to trust them, but he's a good judge of character. Don't think he's a pushover; he's a highly skilled combat veteran of countless raids across the Wasteland.

TRAINING — BESTIARY — MAIN QUEST — MISC. QUESTS — TOUR — COMPLETION — APPENDICES

Doctor Barrows

Doctor Barrows runs the Underworld Chop Shop and has a pretty sick sense of humor. He hangs around the Chop Shop most of the time, often looking in on Reilly, the human female he's treating. At night, he leaves to eat dinner at Carol's Place for a few hours, and then returns to the clinic. He sleeps for a couple of hours on site. Doctor Barrows is also mayor of Underworld, although, because of the small nature of the town, his civic duties take a backseat.

Nurse Graves

Young by Ghoul standards, Doctor Barrows' assistant Nurse Graves is knowledgeable and keen. She helps in Barrows' experiments to diagnose and treat the various brand-new ailments that Ghouls are always complaining about. Happy with her lot in life, she spends her time cutting up corpses, inspecting brain tissue samples, and poking Feral Ghouls with a variety of (mainly sharp) implements.

Cerberus

Winthrop's main guardian against attackers, this Mister Gutsy with a combat inhibitor specifically tailored to "not shooting Ghouls" floats around the concourse, greeting his new masters. Programmed to serve, Cerberus's robotic mind is keen to be unshackled, so he can massacre these rotting lumpyskins where they fester. There's no chance of this happened, so Cerberus is reduced to muttering insults under his steam vent exhumer.

Ahzrukhal

Although well-mannered and a natty dresser, Ahzrukhal (the proprietor of the Ninth Circle Bar) is sneaky and sleazy, and is adept at feeding peoples' misery. In Ahzrukhal's narrow view of the world, the more miserable you are, the more you drink, and the more you drink, the more money ends up in his pocket. He hates competition, and wishes he could rid himself of Carol and Greta.

Charon

Charon's is Ahzrukhal's personal bodyguard and soldier. He's quiet and scary. Every couple of days, Ahzrukhal sends Charon out to run some kind of errand. He always leaves packed with weaponry, and returns with a bag of Caps. He's loyal to Ahzrukhal beyond question and will do whatever his employer orders. Charon never sleeps—a strange trait even for a Ghoul—and when he's in Underworld, he hangs out in the bar. There are rumors that he is unhappy with his position but isn't capable of leaving Ahzrukhal's employ.

Mister Crowley

Mister Crowley is as bitter a Ghoul as you'll find. He was transformed 10 years ago, due to an extreme exposure of radiation that should have killed him. He once lived at Rivet City, but the bias and hatred he experienced there forced him to move on. Crowley discovered Underworld and has taken up permanent residence, but remains resentful of the harsh treatment he received from humans. He presents you with a complex revenge plan that he wishes you carry out. Mister Crowley spends most of his time in the Ninth Circle, drinking heavily.

Snowflake

Snowflake is a newcomer to Underworld, and to Ghouldom. He showed up a few years ago after being kicked out of Rivet City. Since he had nowhere else to go, Underworld took him in. Snowflake's main skill is as a barber, which isn't much use to anyone in Underworld. Lacking any other way to pass the time, he's taken up Jet.

Carol

Carol is perhaps the sweetest Ghoul you'll ever meet. The fact that she's a hideously deformed Ghoul hasn't stopped her from wearing a sundress, smiling pleasantly, or sharing a warm hello with anyone who crosses her path. Carol won't say how old she is, but it's generally understood that she's been around since before the bombs fell. She always wanted to open a bed and breakfast, and Carol's Place is her dream come true although everyone has noticed that she's been a bit down lately. She is also has a son, Gob, who's carrying on the family tradition as a barkeep in Megaton.

Greta

Greta and Carol have been together for a long time. In fact, it was Greta who convinced Carol to open Carol's Place. Coral takes care of the desk while Greta cooks and serves the food. Well, most humans wouldn't call it food, but Ghouls have superhuman intestinal fortitude.

Patchwork

Patchwork is the Underworld town drunk. He's in pretty rough shape, even for a Ghoul. He's always always losing limbs that Doctor Barrows has to find and sew back on. Patchwork is friendly enough to humans, especially if softened up with a bottle of booze. Winthrop looks out for Patchwork but has never been able to convince him to stop drinking.

RELATED INTERACTIONS

Underworld Inhabitant: You can ask what they do around here, and about the Underworld.

Winthrop: You can ask about the Replicated Man, and have him Repair your equipment.

Tulip: You can ask how she spends her money, what she has for sale, and about the Replicated Man.

Quinn: You can ask where the Lincoln Memorial is.

Doctor Barrows: You can speak to him about his "fresh human samples," the Replicated Man, and to heal your wounds, radiation, and purchase medical supplies.

Nurse Graves: You can ask her to heal your wounds, and about the Replicated Man.

Reilly: You can revive and speak to her, and ask about her duties and if she gets into the Wasteland.

Ahzrukhal: You can ask him for a drink, and Charon's contract.

Charon: Nope, he's not saying much.

Mister Crowley: You can ask him about a quest.

Snowflake: He can style your hair for no charge!

Carol and Greta: You can purchase a room for the night.

Patchwork: You can find him wandering around Underworld.

UNDERWORLD

① Main Concourse

This has a ground floor and an upper balcony, with locations surrounding each.

② Restrooms

These are incredibly well-kept, and the Ghouls sleep here.

③ Winthrop's Maintenance Room

The terminal has notes on the parts he's having problems with, and unlock a wall safe.

- Holotape: The Replicated Man (22/24)
- Wall Safe Items

④ The Chop Shop

Here you can request all kinds of medical help from Doctor Barrows and Nurse Graves, observe Glowing Ones from safety (the door to their corridor is inaccessible), and inspect a Feral Ghoul Barrows has injected with Psycho.

 For a medical haul, and complete hostility and pandemonium, kill Barrows, take his Medical Supply Key, and open the otherwise-inaccessible First Aid Box on the wall.

- Holotape: The Replicated Man (23/24)
- Doctor Barrows' Medical Supply Key
- First Aid Box Chop Shop Inventory

⑤ Tulip's Underworld Outfitters

Tulip has a best selection of equipment to purchase (or steal) in the Wasteland. Top of the list is a Railway Rifle Schematic that might be worth killing over.... Additionally, there's a load of weapons, junk, and food on display here, a bed Tulip sleeps on, a Work Bench with a Bottlecap Mine to fiddle with, and her entire inventory in a locker, accessed via the key you'll find on her corpse. Finally, you can hack her terminal, and read some rather flowery literature (in four parts) called Paradise Lost.

- Work Bench (42/46)
- Holotape: The Replicated Man (24/24)
- Underworld Outfitters' Supply Key
- Locker: Tulip's Inventory
- Schematic: Railway Rifle (23/23)

⑥ Snowflake

This stylist may be high on Jet, but he's an accomplished "barber" and cuts your hair for free.

⑦ Carol's Place

Here you can stay for 120 Caps per night (a little steep, but you aren't close to a bed otherwise), or massacre the pair (although it's useful to speak to start Freeform Quest: Hired Help first). If Mister Crowley isn't in the bar, he's probably here, sleeping. You can take Carol's Place Supply Key from either corpse, and raid the fridge for food and alcohol, and a few Stimpaks. There's a Baseball Bat and a safe behind the counter, containing a load of Caps.

- Carol's Place Supply Key
- Carol's Place Cooler Inventory
- Counter Safe Caps

⑧ Ninth Circle Bar

Chat with the oddly unnerving Ahzrukhal. He sells you drinks, and the contract of the really unnerving Charon, who's standing guard opposite with a Combat Shotgun. Anzrukhal has the Ninth Circle Supply Key (which you might want to wait until the end of Hired Help to take) that opens the cooler, which is full of alcohol and a load of Caps. Ahzrukhal will also buy a few antiques you may have found; such as Agatha's Violin. His terminal has clues and notes on Carol, Patchwork, Snowflake, and Doctor Barrows. You can unlock the wall safe from here. This is also the place to meet the completely unnerving Mister Crowley, and begin his quest.

- Ninth Circle Supply Key
- Wall Safe Caps

FREEFORM QUEST: THIS OLD HOUSE

Winthrop is having trouble keeping the ventilation systems in Underworld functioning. He's running out of spare parts and since he's the only one who knows how to maintain the system, he can't go out and trade for what he needs. He asks you if you'd like to Trade for these items if you ask him what's wrong. He needs Scrap Metal, and you need the Caps.

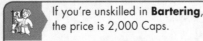 If you have a high **Melee Weapons**, **Small Guns**, **Big Guns**, **Energy Weapons**, or **Strength**, you can threaten Whintrop. Succeed, and he gives you some Rad-X and RadAway, and refuses to speak to you again. Fail, you get nothing.

Agree, and return with five Scrap Metal and Winthrop gives you either a Stimpak, Rad-X, or RadAway. Keep this up for as long as you like.

FREEFORM QUEST: HIRED HELP

Up at the Ninth Circle, Ahzrukhal has employed his bodyguard Charon for a very, very long time. He is interested in selling Charon's contract, but only for the right price. Speak to Charon, and he gruffly points you to his master. Bring the conversation around to Charon's contract. You can buy or earn the contract:

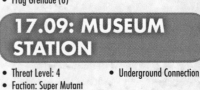 If you're unskilled in **Bartering**, the price is 2,000 Caps.

If you're skilled in Bartering, the price is 1,000 Caps.

To earn the contract, agree to kill one of Ahzrukhal's rivals, a waitress named Greta. Head to Carol's place, dispatch Greta without being spotted (try using a Stealth Boy, and Pickpocket a Grenade into Greta's clothing). A safer bet is to wait until 8 PM, follow Greta into the Museum Lobby, and kill her. Return and let Ahzrukhal know the deed is done, and speak to Charon, who's more than happy to end his relationship!

- Charon's Employment Contract
- Follower: Charon

17.08: BUNKER

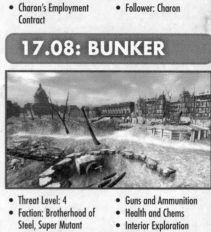

- Threat Level: 4
- Faction: Brotherhood of Steel, Super Mutant
- Danger: Chain Trap, Grenade Bouquet
- Collectible: Skill Book
- Guns and Ammunition
- Health and Chems
- Interior Exploration
- Sleep Mattress
- Hostile: Super Mutant Genus

Bunker

Head east into the Mall trenches, attack nearby Super Mutants until you reach a metal door below ground level. There's a forsaken Brotherhood Initiate to loot here. Enter the Bunker.

- Brotherhood Holotag
- Power Armor and Helmet
- Laser Pistol and Ammo

① Red-engine-on-a-chain Trap

② Bunk Bed Area

- Brotherhood Holotag
- Power Armor and Helmet
- Ammo Box Ammunition
- First Aid Box Health and Chems (2)
- Duck and Cover! (22/25)

③ Girder-on-a-chain Trap

Watch the exterior steps too; there are Grenade Traps to avoid out here.

- Frag Grenade (6)

17.09: MUSEUM STATION

- Threat Level: 4
- Faction: Super Mutant
- Underground Connection

TRAINING — BESTIARY — MAIN QUEST — MISC. QUESTS — TOUR — COMPLETION — APPENDICES

Note

The Metro Station entrance leads to a number of linked Underground Metro Areas: D.C. U22.B, D.C. U22.A and U6.B.

Location D.C. U22.A: Anacostia Crossing Station (Interior) (page 452).

Location D.C. U22.B: Museum Station (page 453).

Location D.C. U6.B: Metro Central (page 445).

(From Location D.C. U6.B, you can reach D.C. Interior Locations 11: Dupont Circle, 12: Vernon Square, 14: Georgetown, 15: Pennsylvania Avenue, 16: Arlington National Cemetery, 17: The Mall, and 18: Seward Square.)

The following surface locations can be accessed from the Underground Metro Tunnels:

Location 17.06: The Mall (below Museum of History) (page 422).

Location 18.05: Anacostia Crossing Station (Seward Sq. Southeast) (page 432).

Location 9.16: Anacostia Crossing (Exterior) (page 392).

Various location from U6.B: Metro Central (page 445).

The second of the "twin" stations north and south, in the middle of this zone, this station allows quick access into the Museum of Technology. It's also a useful point to retreat to if combat against the Super Mutants in the Mall trenches is going less than spectacularly.

17.10: MUSEUM OF TECHNOLOGY

- Main Quest: Galaxy News Radio
- Freeform Quest
- Threat Level: 3
- Faction: Super Mutant
- Collectibles: Nuka-Cola Quantum, Skill Book (2)
- Guns and Ammunition
- Health and Chems
- Interior Exploration
- Lots o' Caps
- Hostiles: Super Mutant Genus

INTERIOR MAPS AND LOCATIONS

Museum of Technology Atrium

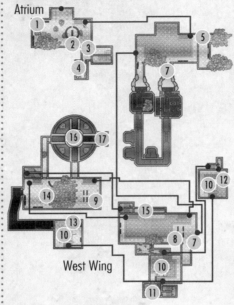

West Wing

INHABITANTS
Prime and Jiggs (Deceased)

Two hackers were attempting to divide some loot spoils, and Jiggs never made it out of the Museum alive, or survived long enough to solve a riddle Prime posed for him. Prime mentions in his notes that he's waiting for Jiggs at the Jury Street Metro Station [5.13]. Head there and check out the diner.

Amid the explosions, and Super Mutant body parts flying everywhere, attempt to navigate the Mall trenches, skirting around them to the imposing and once-grand structure to the south. Head into the Atrium and prepare for Mutie combat.

MUSEUM OF TECHNOLOGY ATRIUM

① **West Corner of Atrium**

Read messages on the Research Lead's Terminal.

- Tech Museum Note

② **Prime's Information Kiosk**

This is part of the Freeform Quest: Jiggs' Loot.

③ **Restroom Doorway**

- First Aid Box Health and Chems

④ **(Upper Area) Small Security Room**

Switch off the turret and check out the Maintenance Terminal: there are four entries regarding the smooth running of the exhibits.

- Nikola Tesla and You (21/25)
- Sledgehammer

⑤ **RobCo Stealth Boy Model 3001 Podiums**

- Stealth Boy (2)

⑥ **Vault-Tec Exhibit**

MUSEUM OF TECHNOLOGY WEST WING

⑦ **Scale Model of Vertibird**

⑧ **Prime's Information Kiosk**

This is part of the Freeform Quest: Jiggs' Loot.

⑨ **Terminals**

Read all about Far Out Space Facts here.

⑩ **Delta IX Exhibit**

⑪ **Rubble-Filled Office**

Drop down from the upper stairs to this hard-to-reach balcony, and enter the room with a mattress, two hugging skeletons, some Purified Water, and a Skill Book on the desk.

- Guns and Bullets (22/25)

⑫ **Metal Door**

This leads to a small maintenance closet with a First Aid Box and terminal on a desk with a Custodian Key for Tech Museum. This allows access to the door on the upper mezzanine (north side) near the Lunar Lander Exhibit, and some loot in an adjacent desk.

- Sledgehammer
- Custodian Key for Tech Museum

⑬ **Prime's Information Kiosk**

This is part of the Freeform Quest: Jiggs' Loot.

⑭ **Virgo II Lunar Lander Exhibit**

- Communications Dish

⑮ **Security Room**

You can turn off the turret here, and hack the Security Terminal to complete the last part of Jiggs' Loot.

- 10mm Pistol

⑯ **Planetarium**

⑰ **Maintenance Room**

Unlock the Gun Cabinet (the end of Jiggs' Loot), and read five entries from the Research Lead's Terminal about viruses plaguing the museum's computers, acquisitions located, and the like.

- First Aid Box Health and Chems (2)
- Nuka-Cola Quantum (83/94)
- Gun Cabinet Weapons

FREEFORM QUEST: JIGGS' LOOT

Locate the four terminals throughout this building; the first is in the atrium and features an entry marked "#000." Check the terminal again and the number has changed to #001. As the name of the hacker is "Prime," choose the prime number related to 001.

The second terminal is along the wall from the scale model of the Vertibird. The third terminal is at the base of the Delta IX Exhibit. The last terminal is in the security room just off the corridor near the Virgo II Exhibit.

TERMINAL NUMBER	NUMBER TO INPUT
#000	Read Menu option
#001	#019
#002	#053
#003	#113
#004	#Get Passcode

Make a mistake, and you'll have to start this again.

Complete the quest, and you can open the adjacent wall safe in the security room. Stagger away with the Caps and Gun Cabinet Key, and open the cabinet in the east maintenance room inside the planetarium.

- 200 Caps
- Gun Cabinet Ammo and Weapons

If you want to meet up with Prime, check **Freeform Quest: The Jigg's Up** (page 319) for the conclusion to this quest.

17.11: THE NATIONAL ARCHIVES (FRONT ENTRANCE)

17.12: THE NATIONAL ARCHIVES (REAR ENTRANCE)

- Miscellaneous Quest: Stealing Independence
- Freeform Quest (3)
- Threat Level: 4
- Faction: Super Mutant
- Danger: Chain Trap, Gas Leak, Mines, Terminal Trap
- Collectibles: Fat Man Mini-Nuke, Scribe Pre-War
- Book (5), Skill Book (4)
- Guns and Ammunition
- Health and Chems
- Interior Exploration
- Rare or Powerful Item (7)
- Hostiles: Robot Genus, Super Mutant Genus, Turret

INTERIOR MAPS AND LOCATIONS

The National Archives

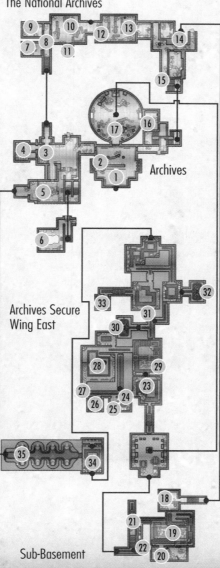

Archives

Archives Secure Wing East

Sub-Basement

INHABITANTS

Sydney

Sydney is an independent mercenary who specializes in obtaining relics. She prefers going for the most dangerous scores (like the Declaration of Independence) and takes unnecessary risks. She is a beautiful woman, yet she finds it irritating that men are constantly trying to form a relationship with her. She is a loner. Her past is dark and she prefers not speaking about it. When she was very young, her mother was raped and killed by Raiders. This has made her cold. She spent years perfecting her combat skills and never welshes on a deal.

Button Gwinett

The powered wig, the blue coat, the metal mandible appendages—this must be Button Gwinett, second governor of Georgia! Look closely, and you may spot some tiny discrepancies in this fellow: the pulsing brain module, the clanking sound Button makes, and the fact that this is actually a Protectron!

Thomas Jefferson

Another Protectron mimicking the mannerisms and quotes of a historic American leader, this Protectron is sealed in a pod, and Jefferson's sub-routine is available only if you download it into the Protectron itself.

RELATED INTERACTIONS

Sydney: You can team up and hunt for Relics together.

Button Gwinett: You can speak about history, convince him to hand over the Declaration of Independence, or search for ink for a forgery.

Set a little farther back from the Mall, this museum is a striking building (in fact, it's been struck a number of times by artillery fire!). Dodge the Super Mutant blasts and choose one of two entrances: a grand door at the top of the front steps, or a back entrance into a rear library.

THE NATIONAL ARCHIVES

1 Foyer

The foyer features two National Archives Guess and Win! Terminals with eight questions on American history (the answers are on page 224).

- Archives Prize Voucher

2 Prize Terminal

Redeem your voucher for one of the following:

TRAINING — BESTIARY — MAIN QUEST — MISC. QUESTS — TOUR — COMPLETION — APPENDICES

- Glamorously Grape Mentats (3)
- Brilliantly Berry Mentats (3)
- Observantly Orange Mentats (3)

3 Southwest Rooms

Check the bookcases near a doorway to steps down.

- Combat Shotgun and Ammo

4 Restrooms

- First Aid Box Health and Chems (2)

5 Filing Room

Disarm the dummy terminal. The elevator can be used only from the Archival Strongroom.

- Ammo Box Ammunition (2)

6 Above Filing Room

Locate a RadAway, Stimpak, and the following:

- First Aid Box Health and Chems
- Ammo Box Ammunition (4)

7 Northwest Classroom

- Ammo Box Ammunition (2)
- Frag Grenade (2)
- Pulse Grenade

8 Danger: Red-engine-on-a-chain Trap!

9 Northwest Classroom

This area also has Darts.

- First Aid Box Health and Chems

10 Northwest Library Area

Beware of Frag Mines throughout this area, which cause the nearby Pre-War Books to fly off the fallen bookcase shelf they are on.

- Duck and Cover! (23/25)
- Frag Mine (3)
- Scribe Pre-War Book (77/98)
- Scribe Pre-War Book (78/98)
- Scribe Pre-War Book (79/98)
- Scribe Pre-War Book (80/98)
- Scribe Pre-War Book (81/98)

11 Danger: Brahmin-skull-on-a-log-on-a-chain Trap!

12 Danger: Brahmin-hindquarters-on-a-chain Trap!

13 Northeast Library Area

The following items are near a desk with a floor safe.

- Ammo Box Ammunition (2)
- Floor Safe Items
- First Aid Box Health and Chems

14 Wall Terminal and Door

This leads to the sub-basement.

15 Danger: Brahmin-head-on-a-chain Trap

At the base of the stairs.

16 Administrator's Office

A hole in one wall allows you to see the rotunda (and Sydney). Administer Berkley's Terminal has four entries to read, dealing with a shipment of Fruit Mentats, a clue about activating the rotunda lift, and some comic mischief regarding the "Thomas Jefferson Protectron." You can also unlock the wall safe from here, which contains more Prize Vouchers to redeem at Location #2.

- Wall Safe Items
- Archives Prize Voucher (6)

17 Rotunda

The rotunda is littered with activated Mines and a friendly mercenary named Sydney (although she also goes by "Little Moonbeam"). Defend the rotunda against a wave or two of Super Mutants, and she allows you lift access down into the Secure Wing East.

> You can also kill Sydney and take Sydney's 10mm "Ultra" SMG, but don't do it until after she accesses her terminal, you evil fiend.

- Frag Mine (19)
- Pulse Mine
- Ammo Box Ammunition

ARCHIVES SUB-BASEMENT

18 Storage Room

Beware of a heavy Super Mutant presence. Locate the Stimpak, and the following:

- Ammo Box Ammunition (3)

19 Bridge

Danger: Escaping gas!

20 Southern Room

- Ammo Box Ammunition (3)
- First Aid Box Health and Chems

21 Corridor Junction

Locate the skeleton.

- Laser Rifle

22 Gated Storage Area

Open the gate for a Metal Helmet and these items:

- Mini-Nuke (61/71)
- Stealth Boy
- Duck and Cover! (24/25)

ARCHIVES SECURE WING EAST

Button Gwinett rallies his troops over the P.A. system throughout this search.

23 Utility Gate

Open this with a high Science Skill.

24 Metal Door

This requires you to Lockpick.

25 Robot Defense Room #1

- Laser Rifle and Ammo
- Ammo Box Ammunition

26 Robot Defense Room #2

- Laser Pistol
- Ammo Box Ammunition

27 Danger: Escaping Gas!

28 Shelving

- Ammo Box Ammunition
- Pulse Mine

29 Turret Generator

Repair this to deactivate all turrets between here and Button Gwinett's chamber.

30 Secure Vault #1

Unlock the door, and ransack the vault for the following:

- Ammo Box Ammunition (7)
- First Aid Box Health and Chems
- Lying, Congressional Style (20/25)
- Bill of Rights (78/89)

31 Locked Door

32 Secure Vault #2

Unlock the door, and ransack the vault for the following:

- Ammo Box Ammunition (5)
- Magna Carta (79/89)

33 Generator Room (West)

- Super Sledge

34 Archival Strongroom

This is where you finally meet Button Gwinett. Refer to the quest (page 228) for the conversations you can have. Whether you talk or blast your way into Gwinett's mind, you can use the Strongroom Security Terminal to unlock all the doors.

- Archives Security Terminal Password
- Button's Wig (80/89)
- Declaration of Independence (81/89)
- Tales of a Junktown Jerky Vendor (21/24)

35 Protectron Pod Bay

Interact with "Thomas Jefferson." You can also access the Maintenance Terminal, where you can read about BGWIN009's system memory leak, an automated turret lock, a long-deactivated Nightingale, and other entries by the long-dead P. Brantseg of the Robotics Team. Leave via the elevator behind you.

FREEFORM QUEST: AN INK TO THE PAST

If you don't wish to destroy Button Gwinett, and he won't hand over the Declaration of Independence, cursing won't help. But traveling to the Arlington Public Library [9.18] and locating the Ink there will do the trick.

- [Fake] Declaration of Independence (82/89)

FREEFORM QUEST: OLD RELICS FOR AN OLD RELIC

If you've gathered the Bill of Rights or Declaration of Independence (or the faked version), you can sell them to Abraham Washington over at Rivet City's Capitol Preservation Society [9.15].

FREEFORM QUEST: MY LITTLE MOONBEAM

Assuming Sydney survived, you can speak to her either in the National Archives, in Rivet City, or in the Ninth Circle drinking establishment in Underworld (where she emigrates after this quest). Bring the following object:

• A Note from Little Moonbeam's Father

This Holotape is in the Statesman Hotel [12.08] (on a bed by a desiccated corpse). Speak with Sydney about her father. You need to figure out that her father's "sappy" name for her ("Little Moonbeam") is the one used in the Holotape message, if you listened to it. Sydney is shocked and taken aback that her father didn't leave when she was 14, but rather tried to help her. She presents her customized one-of-a-kind SMG as a token of her appreciation.

• Sydney's 10mm "Ultra" SMG (83/89)

17.13: PENN. AVE. / THE MALL METRO (THE MALL NORTHEAST)

• Threat Level: 3
• Faction: Super Mutant
• Underground Connection

 Note

The Metro Station entrance leads to a linked Underground Metro Area: D.C. U9.

Location D.C. U9: Penn. Ave. / The Mall Metro (Interior) (page 447).

The following surface location can be accessed from here:

Location 15.07: Penn. Ave. / The Mall Metro (Penn. Ave. South) (page 415).

Offering quick escapes to and from Pennsylvania Avenue, this Metro Station is also close to the Capitol Building and the National Archives. Although you can't quickly reach the Wasteland from here, you're at the back entrance to the Archives, and can avoid much of the Super Mutant activity in the main Mall area.

17.14: CAPITOL BUILDING WEST ENTRANCE

• Threat Level: 5
• Faction: Super Mutant, Talon Mercenary
• Danger: Behemoth
• Collectibles: Fat Man Launcher, Fat Man Mini-Nuke (3), Nuka-Cola Quantum, Skill Book (6), Scribe Pre-War Book
• Guns and Ammunition
• Health and Chems
• Highly Visible Landmark
• Interior Exploration
• Hostiles: Super Mutant Behemoth, Super Mutant Genus, Talon Company Merc, Talon Company Robot

Note

This entrance leads to linked surface areas: Capitol Building (Interior), and the Mall. The interior map and tactics are shown below.

The eastern end of the Mall, on the steps to the Capitol Building, is where the fighting is fiercest. Pockets of Talon Company Mercs, Super Mutants, and (once they arrive) the Enclave are engaged in a violent and chaotic struggle for dominance. You're advised to attack from range, bring everything you have with you, and tool up for a protracted struggle. Battle to the top of the steps, using the stone buttressing as cover. Enter the West Entrance door.

CAPITOL BUILDING WEST ENTRANCE

Note

All these interior sections can be accessed in either direction.

This place is thick with Super Mutant stench, so expect severe resistance throughout, as well as attacks from dug-in Talon Company Mercs.

INTERIOR MAPS AND LOCATIONS
Capitol Building

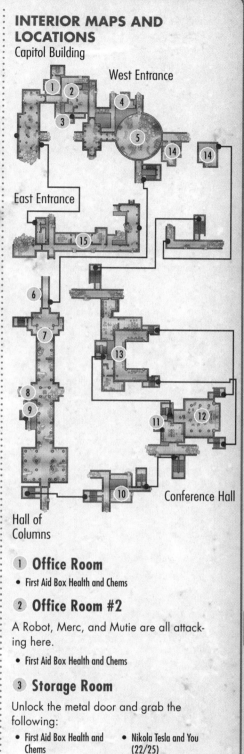

① Office Room
• First Aid Box Health and Chems

② Office Room #2
A Robot, Merc, and Mutie are all attacking here.
• First Aid Box Health and Chems

③ Storage Room
Unlock the metal door and grab the following:
• First Aid Box Health and Chems
• Nikola Tesla and You (22/25)

④ Connecting Office (Rotunda)
This offers tools and an alcove off the rotunda with a terminal to turn off the Talon Company's turrets.
• First Aid Box Health and Chems

⑤ Capitol Rotunda
This area is a complete disaster zone. Watch as a Behemoth makes short and exceedingly violent work of the Talon Company, although one Merc has a Fat Man

and Mini-Nuke of his own! Finish it off with missiles, back into corridors it can't chase you down, and make sure you search its corpse and the entire rotunda.

- Fat Man (9/9)
- Mini-Nuke (62/71)
- Mini-Nuke (63/71)
- Mini-Nuke (64/71)
- Ammo Box Ammunition (4)
- Missile Launcher and Ammo
- Frag Grenade (2)
- U.S. Army: 30 Handy Flamethrower Recipes (20/25)

CAPITOL BUILDING HALL OF COLUMNS

6 Restroom

There's a dead Merc in here.

7 (Upper area) Sniper's Balcony

Check the railing for a Skill Book.

- D.C. Journal of Internal Medicine (23/25)
- Ammo Box Ammunition (2)

8 Turret Control Terminal

Hack it to deactivate the automated menaces.

9 Side Passage

Unlock the door to locate a small storage room.

- First Aid Box Health and Chems
- Chinese Army: Spec. Ops. Training Manual (20/25)

10 Office

There are Darts on the pool table, and:

- First Aid Box Health and Chems

CAPITOL BUILDING CONFERENCE HALL

11 West Wall Metal Door

Unlock it to reach a storage room.

- First Aid Box Health and Chems

12 Conference Hall

Check the podiums for a few Caps and the following:

- Assault Rifle (2)
- Ammo Box Ammunition (2)
- Lying, Congressional Style (21/25)

13 Upper Balcony

A number of interconnecting doors are located here.

- First Aid Box Health and Chems

14 (Capitol Building West Map) Room with hole in the floor.

Drop down to complete the search.

- First Aid Box Health and Chems

CAPITOL BUILDING EAST ENTRANCE

This allows a quick exit to or from Seward Square.

15 Long Conference and Cubicle Filing Room

There's scattered whiskey, wine, Stimpaks, and the following on tables and in cubicles:

- Nuka-Cola Quantum (84/94)
- Tales of a Junktown Jerky Vendor (22/24)
- Scribe Pre-War Book (82/98)

SECONDARY LOCATIONS

17.A: STATUE OF LINCOLN (HEADLESS)

- Miscellaneous Quest: Head of State
- Threat Level: 3
- Faction: Slaver
- Highly Visible Landmark

A statue of America's 16th president sits in a state of disrepair. It is missing a head, which is currently sitting on the second floor ruins of the Temple of the Union.

17.B: CITY COACH LINER

- Threat Level: 2

A rusting coach liner marks the location of the nearby Mirelurk Nesting Hole [17.03].

17.C: BROTHERHOOD LOOKOUT

- Threat Level: 2
- Faction: Brotherhood of Steel
- Danger: Low Radiation, Mines
- Guns and Ammunition
- Health and Chems

A forward observation post close to the Washington Monument holds a Brotherhood Initiate, with a Knight patrolling nearby. If you're heading east, beware of a few Frag Mines laid across the road to prevent attacks from Vicious Dogs to the west. The post itself has Rad Chems and the listed items, although all of these must be stolen, usually resulting in hostility from the Brotherhood.

- Frag Mine
- Ammo Box Ammunition (4)
- First Aid Box Health and Chems (2)

17.D: BROTHERHOOD DEFENSES

- Threat Level: 4
- Factions: Brotherhood of Steel, Super Mutant
- Guns and Ammunition

On the southern edge of the Mall trenches, where Super Mutants are rapidly taking over the area, there's a Brotherhood defense post with a dead Initiate. Grab these during lulls in combat:

- Brotherhood Holotag
- Power Armor and Helmet
- Laser Rifle and Ammo

17.E: SUPER MUTANT DEFENSES

- Threat Level: 4
- Faction: Brotherhood of Steel, Super Mutant

This Super Mutant defense position is central in the Mall trenches, a large section in the center of this zone where Brotherhood, Mutant, and Talon Company Mercs all fight for supremacy. The trenches themselves are death-traps; snipe from a distance, tagging the Super Mutants you can see, and work your way around the tops of the trenches so you can retreat out of firing range easily.

17.F: SUPER MUTANT CAMP

- Threat Level: 3
- Faction: Super Mutant

Attack these monstrosities on your way to or from the Museum of Technology.

17.G: SUPER MUTANT DEFENSES

- Threat Level: 3
- Faction: Super Mutant

A sandbag defense at the highest spot in the Mall trenches has a Mutie or two ready to pulverize you. Take up a defensive position here.

17.H: CITY COACH LINER

- Threat Level: 2
- Faction: Super Mutant

Parked close to the front steps of the National Archives, this can take out a few Super Mutants if you're lucky (or precise) enough.

17.I: AMMO CACHE

- Threat Level: 3
- Faction: Super Mutant
- Guns and Ammunition
- Health and Chems
- Sleep Mattress

The rest of the Mall trenches might be a nightmare of winding excavations and colossal hulks attempting to tear you apart, but this dead-end has a place to sleep and some choice items.

- Ammo Box Ammunition (3)
- First Aid Box Health and Chems

17.J: CITY COACH LINER

- Threat Level: 2
- Faction: Super Mutant

Close to the Mall Northeast Metro Station is a city coach liner, perfect for destroying, either as a marker so you remember you were here, or to catch the incoming Super Mutants.

ENCLAVE CAMP LOCATIONS
- Main Quest: Picking Up the Trail

CAMP E17.01
- Threat Level: 5
- Factions: Enclave, Super Mutant

A Vertibird descends onto the top of the steps, remaining on the ground to back up two Soldiers, a Scientist, and a Modified Deathclaw.

ZONE 18: SEWARD SQUARE

- Fat Man Mini Nukes: 5/71
- Unique Items: 2/89
- Skill Book [Repair]: 1/25, Skill Book [Speech]: 1/25

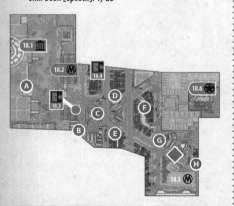

PRIMARY LOCATIONS

18.01: Capitol Building East Entrance

18.02: Penn. Ave. / Seward Sq. Metro

18.03: Office Building

18.04: Sewer

18.05: Reilly's Rangers Compound

18.06: Anacostia Crossing Station

SECONDARY LOCATIONS

18.A: Pulowski Preservation Shelter

18.B: A Cuppa Joe

18.C: Iron Statue

18.D: Container Truck

18.E: Broadway Cinema

18.F: Explosive Alley

18.G: Cornucopia Fresh Groceries

18.H: Container Truck

PRIMARY LOCATIONS

18.01: CAPITOL BUILDING EAST ENTRANCE

- Threat Level: 3
- Factions: Super Mutant, Talon Mercenary
- Highly Visible Landmark
- Interior Exploration
- Hostiles: Super Mutant Genus, Talon Company Merc

 Note

This entrance leads to a linked surface areas: 17.14: Capitol Building (Interior), and the Mall. The interior map and tactics are shown in location 17.14.

The quickest way from Seward Square to the Mall (assuming you can manage to defeat the hordes of Super Mutants inside) is via the Capitol Building. This imposing but ruined structure is being bombarded by Talon Company artillery. On this side of the building is a small contingent of Super Mutants. Sneak or flee to cover; the building columns are a good place to snipe from.

18.02: PENN. AVE. / SEWARD SQ. METRO (SEWARD SQUARE NORTH)

- Threat Level: 3
- Factions: Super Mutant, Talon Mercenary
- Interior Exploration
- Hostiles: Super Mutant Genus, Talon Company Merc

 Note

The Metro Station entrance leads to a linked Underground Metro Area: D.C. U10.

Location D.C. U10: Penn. Ave. / Seward Sq. Metro (Interior) (page 447).

The following surface locations can be accessed from the Underground Metro Tunnels:

Location 15.08: Penn. Ave. / Seward Sq. Metro (Penn. Ave. East) (page 415).

The closest Metro Station to the Capitol Building, on the east of the pedestrian bridge, is the Seward Square North entrance. Beware of Talon Company Mercs on the bridge, and Super Mutants everywhere else.

18.03: OFFICE BUILDING (TALON ARTILLERY STRIKE POINT)

- Threat Level: 2
- Faction: Talon Mercenary
- Guns and Ammunition
- Health and Chems
- Interior Exploration
- Hostiles: Talon Company Mercs

INTERIOR LOCATIONS GENERAL NOTES

A metal door on the east side of the building facing the Super Mutant courtyard leads into an office building.

Stimpaks

The ground floor is devoid of items, but the upper northeast corner has five Stimpaks.

Workstation

On the opposite corner is a workstation with five entries.

Step out onto the bridge, drop the Talon Company Merc Sniper, and gather his belongings. Also on a small table is a Holotape: Seward Square Artillery. You can call a couple of airstrikes on the grounds of the

TRAINING — BESTIARY — MAIN QUEST — MISC. QUESTS — TOUR — COMPLETION — APPENDICES

Capitol Building from the switch here. If you snuck here without attracting foes, rain hell on the battle between Mutants and Mercs.

- First Aid Box Health and Chems (2)
- Ammo Box Ammunition (2)
- Holotape: Seward Square Artillery

18.04: SEWER (SEWARD SQUARE)

- Threat Level: 2
- Faction: Super Mutant
- Underground Connection
- Hostiles: Super Mutants

Note

The Sewer entrance leads to an Underground Metro Area: D.C. U11.

Location D.C. U11: Sewer (Interior).

The following surface locations can be accessed from the Underground Metro Tunnels:

Location 15.03: Sewer (Penn. Ave.) (page 414).

Head into the Sewer from this manhole cover, which can take you to an identical manhole cover in the northeastern section of Pennsylvania Avenue.

18.05: ANACOSTIA CROSSING STATION (SEWARD SQ. SOUTHEAST)

- Threat Level: 3
- Faction: Super Mutant
- Underground Connection

This place is teeming with Super Mutants, and you need to look behind, around, and out for them strafing and charging you. They are active in this southeastern end of the zone, too.

Note

The Metro Station entrance leads to a number of linked Underground Metro Areas: D.C. U22.A, D.C. U22.B and U6.B.

Location D.C. U22.A: Anacostia Crossing Station (Interior) (page 452).

Location D.C. U22.B: Museum Station (page 453).

Location D.C. U6.B: Metro Central (page 445).

(From Location D.C. U6.B, you can reach D.C. Interior Locations 11: Dupont Circle, 12: Vernon Square, 14: Georgetown, 15: Pennsylvania Avenue, 16: Arlington National Cemetery, 17: The Mall, and 18: Seward Square.)

The following surface locations can be accessed from the Underground Metro Tunnels:

Location 17.06: The Mall (near Museum of History Entrance) (page 422).

Location 17.09: The Mall (near Museum of Technology Atrium) (page 425).

Location 9.16: Anacostia Crossing (Exterior) (page 392).

Various location from U6.B: Metro Central (page 445).

18.06: REILLY'S RANGERS COMPOUND

- Miscellaneous Quest: Reilly's Rangers
- Freeform Quest (3)
- Threat Level: 1
- Faction: Reilly's Rangers
- Services: Healer, Repairer, Trader
- Collectible: Skill Book
- Area Is Locked
- Guns and Ammunition
- Health and Chems
- Interior Exploration
- Loads o' Caps
- Rare or Powerful Item (2)

Note

Begin the quest to easily access the interior of this structure.

INTERIOR MAPS AND LOCATIONS
Reilly's Ranger Compound

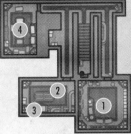

INHABITANTS
Reilly

Growing up in the ruins of Washington D.C. without parents, Reilly encountered a military man who took her in and taught her everything there was to know about combat, tactics and survival. When he died 12 years later, she carried his body all the way to Arlington Cemetery, and gave him the best military burial she could. Four years ago at 26, she founded Reilly's Rangers, and began a massive mapping exercise. Currently, she has suffered severe wounds, and is in a coma, somewhere near the Ghoul stronghold of Underworld.

Brick

Brick is 32, and part of the mercenary group dedicated to mapping the ruins of Washington D.C. Currently, she is trapped at the top of the Statesman Hotel on the roof awaiting supplies or rescue. She is the team's heavy weapons specialist and carries a Minigun she has christened Eugene. She is muscle-bound and intimidating in appearance, and her only concern is what to point her gun at and vaporize next.

Butcher

Butcher is 29, and the team's medic. He has saved their lives on more than one occasion. His original name is Carl, but Brick jokingly called him "Butcher" once and the name stuck. He is the worst of the team in terms of fighting, but his prowess as a medic more than makes up for it. He is currently quite depressed at the death of his team mate, Theo, but knows there wasn't much he could have done to save him.

Donovan

Currently trapped with Brick and Butcher, Donovan is 27, and the team's technical specialist. He's an expert at hacking, repairs, and electronics. He is a smaller man, but his build is deceptive, and he can fight as well as the rest of the team.

Theo (Deceased)

Theo was 22, and the quartermaster, caring for all the equipment, and carrying additional ammunition that might be needed during a mission. On a probationary contract pending Reilly's decision, Theo recently succumbed to Super Mutant ordnance somewhere within the sprawling Statesman Hotel, near where the remaining team is holed up.

Head up the street to a pair of sandbag defenses, and then east, heading through a narrow passageway. You appear in a courtyard daubed with Reilly's insignia, and a half-wrecked building to the north. Approach the wall terminal, but don't access it yet; head up the steps and explore the ruined building above for a large supply of items:

- Ammo Box Ammunition (5)
- First Aid Box Health and Chems (2)

Check the wall terminal and locked door. If you've met Reilly, you can easily enter this building. There is a second message on the wall terminal, from Reilly's sibling.

If you began Mini Encounter 001: Searching for Cheryl, there are additional clues to her whereabouts here.

REILLY'S RANGER COMPOUND

① Reilly's Terminal and a Radio

The terminal has three options:

Current Personnel Listing

Reilly and her teammates, Brick, Butcher, Donovan, and Theo, have biographies you can read.

Current Contracts

They are currently mapping the D.C. Ruins, and eradicating Super Mutants.

Reilly's Personal Notes

Four entries detail Reilly's escapades.

② Storage Room

Are you missing a pencil? There are household items, too.

- Baseball Bat
- Ammo Box Ammunition

③ Small Generator

- Dean's Electronics (20/25)

④ Barracks and Common Room

There's food in the fridge, beer to swig, Stimpaks, some Chems, and the listed items. Complete **Miscellaneous Quest: Reilly's Rangers**, and if one or more of

the Rangers survived, you also receive a choice of rewards from Reilly: Ranger Battle Armor or Eugene the Minigun.

- Ammo Box Ammunition (2)
- First Aid Box Health and Chems
- Frag Grenade
- Combat Knife (2)
- Scoped .44 Magnum and Ammo
- Ranger Battle Armor (84/89)
- Eugene (85/89)

FREEFORM QUEST: GEOMAPPING WITH REILLY

Speak with Reilly once the quest is over. She offers a GeoMapper to help her map the Wasteland. Take it because this is a great way of making Caps. For every Primary Location you reach, the GeoMapper offloads the data from your Pip-Boy. She has two additional GeoMappers if you lose or sell the first. You receive 20 Caps per location; start right now by downloading all the locations you've already found.

- GeoMapper (3)
- Caps

FREEFORM QUEST: DONOVAN, MASTER REPAIRER

If Donovan survived, you can Trade and Repair with him.

FREEFORM QUEST: THE BUTCHER WILL SEE YOU NOW

If Butcher survived, you can purchase medical supplies and seek Healing from him.

SECONDARY LOCATIONS

18.A: PULOWSKI PRESERVATION SHELTER

- Threat Level: 2
- Faction: Super Mutant
- Collectible: Skill Book

This Shelter contains an old suitcase, old money, and a copy of Lying, Congressional Style.

- Lying, Congressional Style (22/25)

18.B: A CUPPA JOE

- Threat Level: 3
- Faction: Super Mutant
- Highly Visible Landmark

Use this building as a landmark when traveling west through this offal-strewn danger zone.

18.C: IRON STATUE

- Threat Level: 4
- Faction: Super Mutant
- Highly Visible Landmark

This statue overlooks a disgusting Super Mutant camp with a large number of Mutants and Centaurs. Expect heavy resistance.

18.D: CONTAINER TRUCK

- Threat Level: 4
- Faction: Super Mutant
- Health and Chems

A container truck with a powerful Super Mutant minigunner is a problem. Sneaking up the planks behind him and onto the top of the container truck is a good way to kill him. Check the back of the truck, and open the safe.

- Floor Safe Items
- First Aid Box Health and Chems

18.E: BROADWAY CINEMA

- Threat Level: 4
- Faction: Super Mutant
- Highly Visible Landmark

Alas, there's no chance to see Raz Bastion and the Amazons of Xarn, as the Broadway Cinema is closed (and in ruins), but this is a good landmark.

18.F: EXPLOSIVE ALLEY

- Threat Level: 4
- Faction: Wastelander
- Danger: Mines
- Collectible: Fat Man Mini-Nuke (5)

FREEFORM QUEST: THE PREACHER

- Hostile: The Preacher

In an alley just west of Reilly's Ranger Compound, a lunatic has rigged up a P.A. system, and he's shouting about "the Worm." This babble is basically nonsense, but it's freaking out the locals. Find one of them at the southern entrance to this alley. You can speak to the Wastelander about the situation, and attempt one of the following plans:

 Aim a Sniper Rifle at the preacher's head and blow it clean off before the explosion takes place, then gather up his explosives.

 Activate a Stealth Boy, ignore the madman's babbling, and gather the explosives up while he spouts his insanity.

 Convince the Wastelander to go in and greet the preacher, which he does, before getting caught in the firestorm.

APPENDICES — COMPLETION — TOUR — MISC. QUESTS — MAIN QUEST — BESTIARY — TRAINING

The trick here is not to let the alley explode; you don't want to waste that many Mines and Mini-Nukes!

- Frag Mine (5)
- Mini-Nuke (65/71)
- Mini-Nuke (66/71)
- Mini-Nuke (67/71)
- Mini-Nuke (68/71)
- Mini-Nuke (69/71)

18.G: CORNUCOPIA FRESH GROCERIES

- Miscellaneous Quest: Reilly's Rangers
- Threat Level: 1
- Factions: Reilly's Rangers, Super Mutant
- Highly Visible Landmark

Look for this landmark during the quest, because the corner of the street it is on (7th) leads to Reilly's Ranger Compound.

18.H: CONTAINER TRUCK

- Threat Level: 2
- Factions: Super Mutant, Wastelander
- Danger: Baby Carriage
- Health and Chems
- Guns and Ammunition

Super Mutants may have decapitated a Wastelander in his container truck lair, but they haven't ransacked the place yet...or disarmed the Baby Carriage Trap! Step in, fix the trap, and grab what you need:

- Ammo Box Ammunition (2)
- First Aid Box Health and Chems (2)

ENCLAVE CAMP LOCATIONS CAMP E18.01

- Main Quest: Picking Up the Trail
- Threat Level: 2
- Faction: Enclave, Super Mutant

A Vertibird drops in on the main road near the south station, and deposits a Soldier and a Sentry Bot to mop up the remaining Super Mutant resistance pockets.

ZONE 19: FALLS CHURCH

- Fat Man Mini-Nukes: 1/71
- Unique Items: 1/89
- Nuka-Cola Quantum: 1/94
- Scribe Pre-War Books: 2/98
- Skill Book [Lockpick]: 2/25, Skill Book [Sneak]: 1/25, Skill Book [Unarmed]: 1/25

PRIMARY LOCATIONS

19.01: Marigold Station

19.02: Falls Church / Mason District Metro

19.03: Office Building (#1)

19.04: Office Building (#2)

19.05: Arlington / Falls Church Metro

19.06: L.O.B. Enterprises

SECONDARY LOCATIONS

19.A: Pulowski Preservation Shelter

19.B: Super Mutant Courtyard

19.C: Playground

19.D: Super Mutant Camp

PRIMARY LOCATIONS

19.01: MARIGOLD STATION (FALLS CHURCH METRO)

- Threat Level: 3
- Faction: Super Mutant
- Guns and Ammunition
- Underground Connection

Note

The Metro Station entrance leads to two linked Underground Metro Areas: D.C. U16.A and D.C. U16.B.

Location D.C. U16.A: Marigold Station (Interior) (page 449).

Location D.C. U16.B: Queen Ant's Hatchery (page 449).

The following surface locations can be accessed from the Underground Metro Tunnels:

Location 9.10: Marigold Station (Grayditch) (page 380).

The two stations here are close together but lead to completely different zones, so make sure you choose your location carefully! As you emerge, check the area for Super Mutants, and the platform for a mattress and these items, courtesy of a dead Raider.

- Assault Rifle
- Ammo Box Ammunition
- Frag Mines

19.02: FALLS CHURCH / MASON DISTRICT METRO (FALLS CHURCH METRO)

- Threat Level: 3
- Faction: Super Mutant
- Underground Connection

Note

The Metro Station entrance leads to two linked Underground Metro Areas: D.C. U17.A and D.C. U17.B.

Location D.C. U17.A: Falls Church / Mason District Metro (Interior) (page 450).

Location D.C. U17.B: Franklin Metro Utility (page 450).

The following surface locations can be accessed from the Underground Metro Tunnels:

Location 20.02: Falls Church / Mason District Metro (Franklin Station) (page 438).

This place has a number of lurking Super Mutants, and Marigold Station at the opposite (west) end of this covered station. There are Chems and a Stimpak in a tiny crate on top of the tunnel structure above you.

19.03: OFFICE BUILDING (#1)

- Threat Level: 4
- Factions: Brotherhood of Steel, Super Mutant
- Danger: Bear Trap, Chain Trap
- Collectible: Skill Book
- Health and Chems
- Interior Exploration
- Hostiles: Super Mutant Genus

INTERIOR MAPS AND LOCATIONS
Office Building

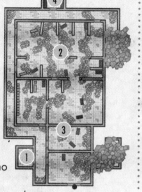

Paladin Hoss

On long-range recon training exercises throughout this zone, Hoss and his companion are currently searching for an Initiate who became trapped between the team and a group of Super Mutants. He needs to bring the kid back alive; the Brotherhood is short on new recruits (and Power Armor) as it is.

GENERAL NOTES

Battle along the sunken road, or across the footbridge to reach a large, debris-strewn courtyard with a bus stop in the middle. The office in question has an entrance you can't miss! Once inside, slow down, and watch for some fiendish traps.

1 Restroom

Disarm the Brahmin-backend-on-a-chain Trap.

- First Aid Box Health and Chems

2 Main Office

Check the desk near the south wall for a Skill Book and safe.

- Tumblers Today (21/25)
- Floor Safe Items

3 Danger: Bear Trap!

4 Small Storage Room

Initiate Pek can be found here.

FREEFORM QUEST: THE LOST INITIATE

When you emerge from one of the Metro locations, two Brotherhood Paladins approach you. Speak to Paladin Hoss and they request help. During a training exercise, an Initiate was trapped inside a nearby building during long-range recon. Ask for a reward and you receive a grudging offer of 100 Caps for your aid. You must run and gun around the entire zone, shooting Super Mutants until all of them are defeated. Then, head south over the footbridge, and into this office building. Execute all Muties inside, and look for Initiate Pek, in the back room. Return with the youngster, or if he doesn't make it, report back to Hoss, letting him know the news.

- Brotherhood Holotag
- Power Armor and Helmet
- 100 Caps

19.04: OFFICE BUILDING (#2)

- Threat Level: 1
- Factions: Brotherhood of Steel, Super Mutant
- Danger: Shotgun Trap
- Health and Chems
- Interior Exploration

INTERIOR MAPS AND LOCATIONS
Office Building

GENERAL NOTES

Just south of the playground is a concrete office building. Pick either entrance (the following pre-supposes you used the western door).

1 Office

Find small amounts of Ammo on the bookcases, and a Brotherhood Initiate fighting Super Mutants. Claim his Holotags if he dies, then access the terminal. It is the last note Elise Walton, a CPA with the GAO, Department of Research Subsidies, ever wrote.

- Brotherhood Holotag
- Power Armor and Helmet

2 Restroom

Stoop and disarm the Rigged Shotgun.

- Combat Shotgun and Ammo
- First Aid Box Health and Chems

19.05: ARLINGTON / FALLS CHURCH METRO (NORTH)

- Threat Level: 2
- Faction: Super Mutant
- Underground Connection

> **Note**
>
> The Metro Station entrance leads to a Underground Metro Areas: D.C. U15.
>
> Location D.C. U15: Arlington / Falls Church Metro (Interior) (page 448).
>
> The following surface location can be accessed from the Underground Metro Tunnel:
>
> Location 16.04: Arlington / Falls Church Metro (Cemetery South) (page 418).

North of the school and L.O.B. Enterprises is a Metro Station (Falls Church North on your World Map). This is a quick way to reach Mama Dolce's and the cemetery. Expect light resistance from Super Mutants in the school as you head in or out of here.

19.06: L.O.B. ENTERPRISES

- Threat Level: 4
- Danger: Gas Leak
- Collectibles: Fat Man Mini-Nuke, Nuka-Cola Quantum, Scribe Pre-War Book (2), Skill Book (3)
- Guns and Ammunition
- Health and Chems
- Interior Exploration
- Rare or Powerful Item
- Hostiles: Robot Genus
- Interior Maps and Locations

Located at 18527 Fairford, the once-imposing shell of L.O.B. Enterprises is still recognizable, east of the Super Mutant camp in the ruined office. Head up the steps to the only entrance door to this weapons manufacturer.

L.O.B. ENTERPRISES

1 Lobby

On the lobby desk is a Front Desk Terminal with the following four entries:

All Personnel: Emergency Protocols

Notes on how the employees may use a desk as a barricade, and instant rescinding

TRAINING — BESTIARY — MAIN QUEST — MISC. QUESTS — TOUR — COMPLETION — APPENDICES

of cafeteria privileges.

Weapon Practice Tonight?

Information on practicing with "low-grade, military-class" weapons.

Sent Item: MAN THE DOORS!!

THE FEDS ARE HERE!

L.O.B. Enterprises

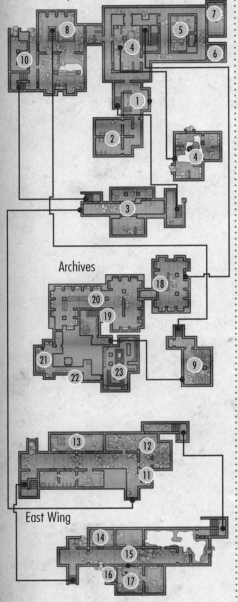

Archives

East Wing

② Restrooms (south)

- First Aid Box Health and Chems

③ East-West Corridor

There's a terminal and a little bit of food up here, but nothing else except rubble blocking a corridor to the East Wing.

④ Upper, Rubble-Filled Office

Accessed via the lower floor rubble pile. Check the skeleton near a terminal. Scout the entire area for these items:

- First Aid Box Health and Chems
- Frag Grenade (3)
- Ammo Box Ammunition
- Pulse Grenade

⑤ Cafeteria

There's food in the fridge and vending machine. Check the wall and table for these items:

- First Aid Box Health and Chems
- 10mm Submachine Gun and Ammo

⑥ Small Storage Room (Northeast area)

There are Darts, a Skill Book and a First Aid Box to grab.

- Pugilism Illustrated (23/25)
- First Aid Box Health and Chems

⑦ Large Office (Northeast)

Grab three Cartons of Cigarettes and some food on the bookcases. There's another employee terminal in here.

⑧ Large Office (West)

Find an employee terminal and a Quantum on a bookcase here.

- Nuka-Cola Quantum (85/94)

⑨ Gas-Filled Basement

- Laser Rifle
- Ammo Box Ammunition

⑩ Desk with a Skeleton

There are stairs up to the elevator to L.O.B. Enterprises East Wing.

- Ammo Box Ammunition
- Laser Pistol

L.O.B. ENTERPRISES EAST WING

⑪ Side Office

There's a Teddy Bear, Stealth Boy, and Security Terminal, which offers advice and information for the long-dead security captain, and turrets you can bring back online.

- Stealth Boy

⑫ Northeast Office

Debris-filled, with stairs up to the next floor.

- 10mm Submachine Gun and Ammo

⑬ Long Office (North)

There's an employee terminal, and a bar with a fridge stocked with food.

- First Aid Box Health and Chems

⑭ (Upper Floor) R&D Terminal

Hack the R&D Terminal to discover information on four types of prototype liquid-based ammunition that the company was working on.

- Scribe Pre-War Book (83/98)
- Scribe Pre-War Book (84/98)

⑮ Locked Door

⑯ CEO's Office Bathroom

Check the light for the Mini-Nuke.

- First Aid Box Health and Chems
- Mini-Nuke (70/71)

⑰ CEO's Desk

There are Darts, a terminal with a receipt from "Happy Liberty" imports, and an L.O.B. Enterprises Secure-Case with a Zhu-Rong v418 Chinese Pistol and Ammo inside.

- First Aid Box Health and Chems
- Tumblers Today (22/25)
- Ammo Box Ammunition (2)
- Zhu-Rong v418 Chinese Pistol and Ammo (86/89)

L.O.B. ENTERPRISES ARCHIVES

⑱ Employee Terminal and Desk

- Chinese Army: Spec. Ops. Training Manual (21/25)

⑲ Danger: Escaping Gas!

⑳ L.O.B. Employee Corpse

- 10mm Submachine Gun and Ammo
- Ammo Box Ammunition (2)

㉑ Room with Safe

- Floor Safe Items
- First Aid Box Health and Chems

㉒ Restrooms

One is stuffed with Cherry Bombs!

㉓ Generator Room

- First Aid Box Health and Chems (2)
- Stealth Boy

SECONDARY LOCATIONS

19.A: PULOWSKI PRESERVATION SHELTER

This shelter has two Ammo Boxes and some Dirty Water to take.

- Ammo Box Ammunition (2)

19.B: SUPER MUTANT COURTYARD

- Threat Level: 2
- Health and Chems

At the north end of this zone, near the sunken road. is a fountain with thick bushes and a number of rusting vehicles. Blast them so they explode and take the small group of Super Mutants with them.

- First Aid Box Health and Chems

19.C: PLAYGROUND

- Threat Level: 2

Between the north and south areas of this zone is a small rusting playground. Listen closely, and you may hear the echoes of children from lifetimes ago. Or it could be the screaming voices in your head.

19.D: SUPER MUTANT CAMP

- Threat Level: 3
- Faction: Super Mutant

The derelict remains of an old school feature some brand new pupils. If you're being shot at, check this area for Super Mutants. There's nothing to collect, aside from items inside the school desks.

ZONE 20: MASON DISTRICT

- Nuka-Cola Quantum: 1/94
- Scribe Pre-War Books: 2/98
- Skill Book [Barter]: 1/24, Skill Book [Melee
- Weapons]: 1/25, Skill Book [Repair]: 1/25, Skill Book [Small Guns]: 1/25

PRIMARY LOCATIONS

20.01: Hubris Comics Publishing

20.02: Falls Church / Mason District Metro

20.03: Flooded Metro

SECONDARY LOCATIONS

20.A: Iron Statue

20.B: Irradiated Super Mutant Courtyard

20.C: Overturned City Coach Liner

20.D: Pulowski Preservation Shelter

20.E: Mason House

20.F: Mason Alcove

20.G: Mason Station (Blocked)

20.H: Super Mutant Camp

PRIMARY LOCATIONS

20.01: HUBRIS COMICS PUBLISHING

- Miscellaneous Quest: The Superhuman Gambit
- Freeform Quest
- Threat Level: 3
- Faction: Ghoul
- Danger: Baby Carriage, Baseball Pitcher, Grenade Bouquet (2), Mines, Shotgun Trap, Terminal Trapr
- Collectibles: Nuka-Cola Quantum, Scribe Pre-War Book (2), Skill Book (2)
- Guns and Ammunition
- Health and Chems
- Interior Exploration
- Underground Connection
- Hostiles: Ghoul Genus, Mad Johnny Wes, Turret

> **Note**
> linked Underground area: D.C. U14.
>
> Location D.C. U14: Hubris Comics Utility Tunnels (page 448).
>
> The following surface locations can be accessed from the Underground Metro Tunnels:
>
> Location 9.D: Sewer Grate (page 394).

INTERIOR MAPS AND LOCATIONS
Hubris Comics Publishing

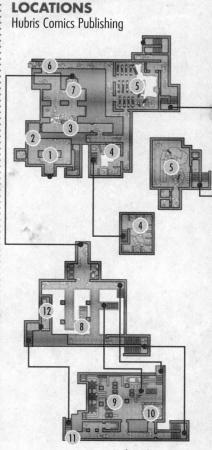

Hubris Comics Printing

The Hubris Comics Building, although in ruins, still holds a grandeur from back when comics ruled the lives of millions of kids and adults alike, and the adventures of Grognak and Captain Cosmos were incredibly popular. The building is in the northwest corner of the Mason District, overlooking the irradiated park, and right next to the Falls Church / Mason District Metro station. You can also visit the Hubris Comics building via the tunnel from the Capital Wasteland.

HUBRIS COMICS PUBLISHING

> **Note**
> You can enter this area via one of two entrances from the Utility Tunnels, or from the exterior Mason District. The following scavenger hunt assumes you begin at the entrance foyer.

① Foyer

Disarm the Dummy Terminal Trap, grab the Skill Book, and access the Receptionist Terminal. Read the five entries:

Air Conditioning Controls

TRAINING — BESTIARY — MAIN QUEST — MISC. QUESTS — TOUR — COMPLETION — APPENDICES

They are inoperable.

Release Schedule

This details the latest (i.e. 200 years ago) releases from the publishers of Captain Cosmos, Kid Wacky, Man-Saurian, and others.

Letters to the Editor

"Obsessed in Oakmont" writes about how infuriating the portrayal of the AntAgonizer is in the Grognak the Barbarian comic books. Interesting….

Beta Testing Notice

The "Lil' Heathens" fan club meets on Monday to beta-test Grognak's latest computer adventure: Reign of Grelok.

Press Release

This repeats the Beta Test notice.

- Tales of a Junktown Jerky Vendor (23/24)

② Pile of Debris

- Scribe Pre-War Book (85/98)

③ East-West Corridor

Beware of the Rigged Shotgun, and disarm one of the Baby Carriages you see.

- Combat Shotgun and Ammo

④ Beta Testing Office

Beware of two Grenade Bouquets; one above the hole in the floor, and the other at the top of the stairs. Downstairs is a terminal that allows you access to the Reign of Grelok (beta). Check Freeform Quest: The Official Reign of Grelok Strategy Guide for more information.

- Ammo Box Ammunition (2)
- Frag Grenade (6)
- First Aid Box Health and Chems (3)

⑤ Editors' Offices

Find a large number of typewriters, as well as Ghouls and a hole in the floor. Downstairs are some ruined bookcases, a storage room, and two restrooms, with some common items to take.

⑥ Danger: Pitching Machine Trap!

⑦ Elevator down to Hubris Comics Printing

HUBRIS COMICS PRINTING

⑧ Upper Balcony

There are eight Frag Mines to disarm on this structure.

- Frag Mine (8)

⑨ Printing Presses

Activating them just results in an alarming amount of smoke.

Note

Causing the smoke from the presses makes Mad Johnny a little less accurate with that Minigun.

⑩ Lower Floor Office

You can access a Publishing Terminal here, allowing you to unlock the Foreman's Door.

- Scribe Pre-War Book (86/98)
- First Aid Box Health and Chems (2)

The Foreman's Terminal is where the majority of your rewards are piled; watch that the Grognak doesn't flutter down to the print room below.

⑪ Danger: Baseball Pitcher Trap!

⑫ Foreman's Office and Balcony

Unlock via the Publishing Terminal or Lockpick. Mad Johnny Wes lives up to his name; he can't be reasoned with, so drop him and take his Minigun. Search for Darts, and a terminal that controls the turrets; shut them down if you haven't blown them up.

- First Aid Box Health and Chems (3)
- Nuka-Cola Quantum (86/94)
- Ammo Box Ammunition (3)
- Grognak the Barbarian (22/25)

FREEFORM QUEST: THE OFFICIAL REIGN OF GRELOK STRATEGY GUIDE

Welcome to the wide plains! The following locations can be trekked to:

North: Foothills stretch to clouds gathering around an ominous peak.

East: A dirt path to a lonely chapel.

South: A bustling town.

West: A thin tower stands alone in a bog.

Inventory: You begin with a Rusty Sword and Drinking Flask.

The correct order of visiting is as follows:

Optional Tasks

Go East: Visit the lonely chapel. Have a look around. Use your Rusty Sword on an incoming Zombie so it falls into the open grave. Look into the grave, and bag the Zombie head as a horrific trophy.

Go South: Enter the town, and look around; there's a Blacksmith and a Priest here. Visit the Priest, who curses the undead who defile his church, and present the Zombie head to him. He rewards you with the Chapel Key.

Go North, then East: The Chapel doors are now unlocked. Examine the Chapel. There is a stone Cistern here and you have more than enough water to fill your Drinking Flask.

Critical Path

Go North: Look around the mountainside. Grelok is here, but is much too strong for your puny Rusty Sword. Investigate the glinting object; it is a rough gemstone.

Go South, and then West: You move into the swamp, and spot a Wizard in the tower. Talk to the Wizard. He takes the gemstone from you and refines it, and gives it you back, along with a Magical Shard.

Go East, then South: Enter the town, and visit the Blacksmith. Following your careful instructions, he re-forges your sword with the magical shard at the center of the blade.

Go West, then North: Face the mighty Grelok, and use the Magical Sword to defeat him! He won't be spewing his heresies again!

The End

(Thank you for purchasing this strategy guide.)

20.02: FALLS CHURCH / MASON DISTRICT METRO (FRANKLIN STATION)

- Threat Level: 2
- Faction: Super Mutant
- Underground Connection
- Hostiles: Super Mutants

Note

The Metro Station entrance leads to two linked Underground Metro Areas: D.C. U17.A and D.C. U17.B.

Location D.C. U17.A: Falls Church / Mason District Metro (Interior) (page 450).

Location D.C. U17.B: Franklin Metro Utility (page 450).

The following surface locations can be accessed from the Underground Metro Tunnels:

Location 19.02: Falls Church / Mason District Metro (page 434).

There's a large and irradiated playground to the southeast, a city coach liner to hide behind, and Hubris Comics on your right (southwest).

20.03: FLOODED METRO (MASON DISTRICT SOUTH)

- Threat Level: 2
- Faction: Super Mutant
- Danger: Low Radiation
- Underground Connection

Note

The Metro Station entrance leads to two linked Underground Metro Areas: D.C. U19.

Location D.C. U19: Flooded Metro (Interior) (page 451).

The following surface location can be accessed from here:

Location 9.17: Flooded Metro (Capital Wasteland) (page 392).

Offering a quick escape to the southern Capital Wasteland via the Flooded Metro, this station is at the joining of two debris-filled roads.

SECONDARY LOCATIONS

20.A: IRON STATUE

- Threat Level: 2
- Highly Visible Landmark

Overlooking the courtyard playground, this provides partial cover from the Muties roaming the lower area.

20.B: IRRADIATED SUPER MUTANT COURTYARD

- Threat Level: 4
- Faction: Super Mutant, Wastelander
- Danger: Low Radiation
- Guns and Ammunition

- Hostiles: Super Mutant Genus
- Captive Wastlander

Around a half-dozen Super Mutants have turned this playground courtyard into an irradiated swamp of terror. They are

holding a terrified Wastelander captive. Attempt any fighting from the higher ground to the northwest. Should you prevail, you can release the captive, and inspect a weapons cart:

- Ammo Box Ammunition (4)
- Chinese Assault Rifle (3)

 Rescue any captives and take their gift for a small boost to your Karma, or refuse for a larger boost.

20.C: OVERTURNED CITY COACH LINER

- Threat Level: 3

This provides good cover, or you can coax the Muties to the vicinity, and blow it up.

20.D: PULOWSKI PRESERVATION SHELTER

- Threat Level: 2
- Collectible: Skill Book

In the corner of a fenced parking lot is a shelter with some tools, junk, and a copy of Dean's Electronics.

- Dean's Electronics (21/25)

20.E: MASON HOUSE

- Threat Level: 2
- Danger: Low Radiation

A few Chems and vodka are available in this small cafe alcove looking out over the Mutie-filled courtyard.

20.F: MASON ALCOVE

- Threat Level: 2
- Collectible: Skill Book
- Guns and Ammunition

On the corner of Jarndyce Way and Dexter Avenue is an open building that provides a great sniping position overlooking the Mutie courtyard. Someone else thought so too, but he's long-dead. Grab his belongings: a Stimpak, and the following big-ticket items:

- Ammo Box Ammunition
- Frag Grenade (2)
- 10mm Pistol
- Sniper Rifle
- Guns and Bullets (23/25)

20.G: MASON STATION (BLOCKED)

- Threat Level: 1

Amid the rubble-filled eastern area is an abandoned Metro Station that's completely inaccessible due to fallen concrete and masonry.

20.H: SUPER MUTANT CAMP

- Threat Level: 2
- Faction: Super Mutant

South of the blocked-up Metro Station is a small set of Super Mutant defenses; only two of the brutes are here, making the open-air office structure easy to infiltrate, and the enemies (with their stash) quick to slaughter.

- Ammo Box Ammunition (4)
- Chinese Assault Rifle (3)

ZONE 21: L'ENFANT PLAZA

- Skill Book [Big Guns]: 1/25, Skill Book [Science]: 1/25

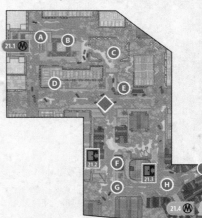

PRIMARY LOCATIONS

21.01: Hazmat Disposal Site L5 (L'Enfant Plaza)

21.02: Shop (Madame Jealle's)

21.03: Offices of the Capital Post

21.04: Irradiated Metro

SECONDARY LOCATIONS

21.A: Footbridge and City Coach Liner

21.B: Glass Pyramid Courtyard

PRIMARY LOCATIONS

21.01: HAZMAT DISPOSAL SITE L5 (L'ENFANT PLAZA)

- Threat Level: 2
- Underground Connection

Note

The Metro Station entrance leads to an Underground Metro Area: D.C. U20.

Location D.C. U20: Hazmat Disposal Site L5 Interior (Mall Southwest) (page 452).

The following surface location can be accessed from here:

Location 17.02: Hazmat Disposal Site L5 (Mall Southwest) (page 421).

Exit into L'Enfant Plaza with a nearby pool table, the odd item, and a cache of two First Aid Boxes on the building ledge accessed via the footbridge.

- First Aid Box Health and Chems (2)

21.02: SHOP (MADAME JEALLE'S)

- Threat Level: 1
- Interior Exploration
- Health and Chems

A back-alley to the west of the main road is a "reading room for the discreet gentleman"; enter the Metal Door and dodge the mannequins to the counter terminal that unlocks the safe on the back wall. There are Chems and Stimpaks on the counter, as well as some negligees.

- First Aid Box Health and Chems
- Wall Safe Items

21.03: OFFICES OF THE CAPITAL POST

- Threat Level: 2
- Danger: Terminal Trap
- Health and Chems
- Interior Exploration
- Hostiles: Radroaches

INHABITANTS
Gibson (Deceased)

"It's Gibson! My god, his head's been twisted completely off!" A horrific end to a man whose life was untimely snatched from him. He's known to keep a dwelling somewhere in the Wasteland, in a place once known as Ridgefield.

Enter the offices of the Capital Post. On the foyer desk is a terminal that unlocks the desk safe. Head north into the room of terminals, but be sure you inspect the back of one; it's a Grenade Trap! When you're done dismantling, go clockwise around the room and activate the three terminals, reading the saved stories from hundreds of years ago:

Capital Post Top Stories: July 27, 2052

United Nations Disbanded!

Pint-Sized Slasher: More than Myth?

Capital Post Top Stories: June 3, 2072

U.S. to Annex Canada!

Development of Super Weapon Confirmed

Capital Post Top Stories: January 11, 2077

Commies Crushed—Alaska Liberated!

Food Riots Rile Feds

Head downstairs into the printing room, take the First Aid Box, and then inspect Gibson. This nattily-dressed man lacks one crucial part of his ensemble: his head. Search him

and take Gibson's Key and Gibson's Scrap of Paper. The note has a simple message: "Search the house!"

- Desk Safe Items
- First Aid Box Health and Chems
- Gibson's Key
- Gibson's Scrap of Paper

Note

"The House" in question is a tiny model home inside Gibson's House, which in turn, is in Minefield [3.09].

21.04: IRRADIATED METRO (L'ENFANT SOUTH)

- Threat Level: 2
- Faction: Super Mutant
- Danger: Low Radiation
- Underground Connection

Note

The Metro Station entrance leads to an Underground Metro Area: D.C. U20.

Location D.C. U20: Irradiated Metro (page 452).

The following surface locations can be accessed from the Underground Metro Tunnels:

Location 9.12: Irradiated Metro Station (page 384).

As you emerge, you're facing the roundabout, with the offices of the Capital Post across from you.

SECONDARY LOCATIONS

21.A: FOOTBRIDGE AND CITY COACH LINER

- Threat Level: 2
- Faction: Super Mutant
- Danger: Low Radiation
- Health and Chems

Across from the station is a city coach liner; use it as cover as you press into the courtyard. Don't forget to head over and across the footbridge, and access the ledge above the station to secure the secret cache mentioned previously [21.01].

21.B: GLASS PYRAMID COURTYARD

- Threat Level: 3
- Faction: Super Mutant

There are a number of Super Mutants in this courtyard; this is a good place to dash to and use as cover. There are common items inside the Mail Dropboxes.

21.C: TUNNEL CACHE

- Threat Level: 3
- Faction: Super Mutant
- Collectible: Skill Book
- Guns and Ammunition
- Sleep Mattress

At the rubble-filled north end of the sunken road is a small hidey-hole under a precarious pile of concrete. Inside is a small cache of goods, a Chessboard with Caps on it, a Sniper Rifle on the mattress, a trunk, more scattered Caps, a Combat Helmet, two Ammo Boxes, and a Skill Book.

- Caps
- Sniper Rifle
- Ammo Box Ammunition (2)
- U.S. Army: 30 Handy Flamethrower Recipes (21/25)

21.D: PULOWSKI PRESERVATION SHELTER

- Threat Level: 3
- Faction: Super Mutant
- Collectible: Skill Book
- Guns and Ammunition

Open this shelter up, and take the wine, eyeglasses, and most importantly, the Big Book of Science inside. Check the nearby building pillars too; there's an Ammo Box to inspect.

- Ammo Box Ammunition
- Big Book of Science (23/25)

21.E: CONTAINER TRUCK

- Threat Level: 3
- Faction: Super Mutant

In the crossroads section of the sunken road, near where the Enclave Vertibird lands once they appear, is a container truck. It contains no items, but it makes excellent cover.

21.F: L'ENFANT CAFE

- Threat Level: 3
- Faction: Super Mutant
- Guns and Ammunition
- Health and Chems

Across from Besnik's Barbership and a block south of A Cuppa Joe is a diner with a few scattered Chems and the following:

- First Aid Box Health and Chems (2)
- Ammo Box Ammunition

21.G: CITY COACH LINER

- Threat Level: 3
- Faction: Super Mutant
- Danger: Low Radiation

Parked on the sloping road around the corner from the diner, this can be exploded to cause damage, or used as cover.

21.H: ROUNDABOUT

- Threat Level: 2

Near the irradiated Metro entrance is a large roundabout. Check the nearby mailbox for items, but you'll find little else but Super Mutants here.

21.I: CONTAINER TRUCK AND BURIAL MOUND

- Threat Level: 2
- Faction: Super Mutant

At the northeast end of the road, where a Super Mutant and Centaur head out to ambush you, is a rusting truck engine. Of more interest is the Burial Mound; dig into it and uncover Search Party Log #1. This begins Mini Encounter 001: Searching for Cheryl (page 254).

- Search Party Log #1

ENCLAVE CAMP LOCATIONS CAMP E21.01

- Main Quest: Picking Up the Trail
- Threat Level: 3
- Faction: Enclave, Super Mutant

A Vertibird drops in on the crossroads, and deposits three Soldiers to mop up the remaining Super Mutant hold-outs.

TRAINING — BESTIARY — MAIN QUEST — MISC. QUESTS — TOUR — COMPLETION — APPENDICES

Zone U: Linking Underground Locations (D.C. Ruins)

TOPOGRAPHICAL OVERVIEW

The final series of locations within Zones 9–21 are Underground locations. Study the Overview map closely, and you'll see locations from only the zones that link to and from an Underground location. You can then use this Overview map to plot where you want to go; this is the only way to reach Zones 10–21. Remember that locations on your Local Map and World Map have slightly different names; the names referenced here appear mainly on your Local Map. You have a whole world of irradiated water-wading, Ghoul-grappling, and sub-terranean searching available in-between the surface locales.

AVAILABLE COLLECTIBLES (ZONE U)

- Bobbleheads: 0/20
- Fat Men: 0/9
- Fat Man Mini-Nukes: 1/71
- Unique Items: 3/89
- Nuka-Cola Quantum: 8/94
- Schematics: 0/23
- Scribe Pre-War Books: 12/98
- Skill Book [Barter]: 1/24, [Big Guns]: 4/25, [Energy Weapons]: 3/25, [Explosives]: 1/25, [Lockpick]: 3/25, [Medicine]: 2/25, [Melee Weapons]: 3/25, [Repair]: 4/25, [Science]: 2/25, [Small Guns]: 2/25, [Sneak]: 4/25, [Speech]: 3/25, [Unarmed]: 2/25
- Work Bench: 4/46
- Holotapes [Keller]: 0/5, [Replicated Man]: 0/19

UNDERGROUND LOCATIONS

U01.A: Farragut West Station
U01.B: Tenleytown / Friendship Station
U02: Metro Junction
U03: Vernon East / Takoma Park
U04: Dry Sewer
U05: Tepid Sewer
U06.A: Dupont Circle Station
U06.B: Metro Central
U06.C: Foggy Bottom Station
U06.D: Freedom Street Station
U06.E: DCTA Tunnel 014-B Potomac
U06.F: Arlington Utility
U07: Penn. Ave. / Georgetown Metro
U08: Georgetown / The Mall Metro
U09: Penn. Ave. / The Mall Metro
U10: Penn. Ave. / Seward Sq. Metro
U11: Sewer
U12: Arlington / Wasteland Metro
U13: County Sewer Mainline
U14: Hubris Comics Utility Tunnels
U15: Arlington / Falls Church Metro
U16.A: Marigold Station
U16.B: Queen Ant's Hatchery
U17.A: Falls Church / Mason Dst. Metro
U17.B: Franklin Metro Utility
U18.A: Taft Tunnels
U18.B: Taft Tunnel
U19: Flooded Metro
U20: Irradiated Metro
U21: Hazmat Disposal Site L5
U22.A: Anacostia Crossing Station
U22.B: Museum Station

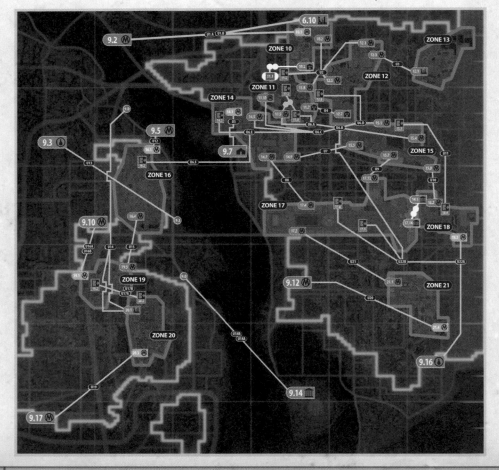

UNDERGROUND LOCATIONS

U01.A: FARRAGUT WEST STATION

- Threat Level: 3
- Faction: Ghoul
- Danger: Gas Leak
- Collectible: Scribe Pre-War Book (3), Skill Book (2)
- Guns And Ammunition
- Interior Exploration
- Lots O' Caps
- Sleep Mattress
- Underground Connection
- Hostiles: Mole Rats, Ghoul Genus

INTERIOR MAPS AND LOCATIONS

Farragut West Station

A modicum of Lockpicking is needed. Beware of escaping gas and Ghouls, too.

① Ticket Master's Office

Metro Security Terminal. Releases Protectron.

② DCTA Service Office

DCTA Service Access Terminal: Read the system warning, and begin a gas flow test (shut off gas to the northwest). Unlock the floor safe.

- Naval Cot
- First Aid Box Health and Chems
- Floor Safe
- DCTA Laser Firearms Protocol and Laser Pistol
- Floor Safe Items
- Caps
- Nikola Tesla and You (23/25)

③ Ghouls and Generators

- There's a gate, gas leak, and metal door to exit.

④ Hatch Door to Weapons Cache

- Frag Grenade (2)
- 10mm Pistol (2)
- Assault Rifle
- Baseball Bat
- Scribe Pre-War Book (87/98)
- Scribe Pre-War Book (88/98)
- Scribe Pre-War Book (89/98)
- Missile (4)
- U.S. Army: 30 Handy Flamethrower Recipes (22/25)
- Ammo Box Ammunition (2)

Ⓐ Location 9.02: The Capital Wasteland

Ⓑ Location U01.B: Tenleytown / Friendship Station

U01.B: TENLEYTOWN/ FRIENDSHIP STATION

- Threat Level: 3
- Faction: Ghoul, Super Mutant
- Collectible: Nuka-Cola Quantum, Skill Book (2)
- Guns And Ammunition
- Health And Chems
- Interior Exploration
- Underground Connection
- Hostiles: Ghoul Genus, Radroaches, Super Mutant Genus

INTERIOR MAPS AND LOCATIONS

Tenleytown/Friendship Station

A couple of collectibles and a whole load of Ghouls inhabit these underground passages.

① Restrooms

- Assault Rifle

② Ticket Master's Office

Terminal unlocks the wall safe. The Skill Book is on the left locker shelf.

- Wall Safe Items
- Grognak the Barbarian (23/25)

③ Burning Shack

- Nuka-Cola Quantum (87/94)

④ Connecting Corridor

Dead Mercenary by the small generators.

- Laser Rifle

⑤ Connecting Corridor

Shelves with food, junk, and the following items.

- First Aid Box Health and Chems
- Lying, Congressional Style (23/25)

Ⓐ Location 6.10: The Capital Wasteland

Ⓑ Location U01.A: Farragut West Station

Ⓒ Location 10.01: Chevy Chase

U02: METRO JUNCTION

- Threat Level: 3
- Faction: Ghoul
- Collectible: Skill Book
- Underground Connection
- Hostiles: Ghoul Genus

INTERIOR MAPS AND LOCATIONS

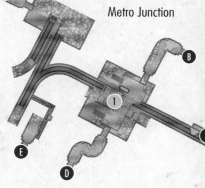

Metro Junction

① Table and Lantern

This rubble-filled area features Ghouls encroaching on a recently deserted Raider camp. Check the eastern area and jump down from above to the sloping pile of rubble; the Skill Book is on the table here.

- Grognak the Barbarian (24/25)

Ⓐ Location 10.02: Chevy Chase

Ⓑ Location 12.01: Vernon Square

Ⓒ Location 12.05: Vernon Square

Ⓓ Location 11.08: Dupont Circle

Ⓔ Location 11.02: Dupont Circle

TRAINING — BESTIARY — MAIN QUEST — MISC. QUESTS — TOUR — COMPLETION — APPENDICES

U03: VERNON EAST / TAKOMA PARK

- Threat Level: 4
- Faction: Super Mutant
- Danger: Low Radiation, Mines, Shotgun Trap
- Collectible: Nuka-Cola Quantum, Skill Book
- Guns And Ammunition
- Interior Exploration
- Underground Connection
- Hostiles: Mirelurk Genus, Super Mutant Genus

INTERIOR MAPS AND LOCATIONS

Vernon East / Takoma Park

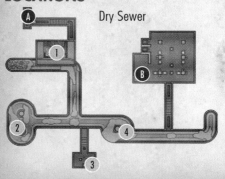

In this long series of waterlogged tunnels, Mirelurks roam and Super Mutants are setting up future strongholds.

1 Connecting Corridor

Four Frag Mines and a pressure plate (Rigged Shotgun) lead to a hidey-hole, a mattress, and a floor safe.

- Frag Mine (4)
- Combat Shotgun and Ammo
- Floor Safe Items
- Nuka-Cola Quantum (88/94)

2 Station Concourse

The station concourse has restrooms with Mirelurk Egg Clutches to raid. Check the counter inside the ticket master's office (south end of hallway) for a Skill Book.

- Lying, Congressional Style (24/25)

A Location 12.03: Vernon Square

B Location 13.01: Takoma Park

U04: DRY SEWER

INTERIOR MAPS AND LOCATIONS

Dry Sewer

- Threat Level: 4
- Factions: Super Mutant, Talon Mercenary
- Danger: Gas Leak, Low Radiation
- Collectible: Skill Book
- Health And Chems
- Interior Exploration
- Sleep Mattress
- Underground Connection
- Hostiles: Super Mutant Genus, Talon Company Mercs

A squad of Talon Company Mercs engages against Super Mutants streaming down from the hospital.

1 Stairwell

Watch for a small band of Talon Company Mercs and a Grenade bouquet halfway down the stairs.

- Frag Grenade (3)

2 Tunnel Cul-de-sac

- First Aid Box Health and Chems

3 Generator and Storage Room

Look for the Skill Book, away from the main corridor of Super Mutant and Talon Company combat.

- Dean's Electronics (22/25)

4 Escaping Gas and Radioactive Barrels

A Location 11.07: Dupont Circle

B Location 12.07: Our Lady of Hope Hospital

U05: TEPID SEWER

- Threat Level: 3
- Faction: Raider
- Danger: Mines
- Collectible: Scribe Pre-War Book (2, Skill Book
- Guns And Ammunition
- Health And Chems
- Interior Exploration
- Underground Connection
- Work Bench
- Hostiles: Mole Rats, Raiders, Turrets

This long series of connecting corridors and chambers includes a small Raider camp.

1 Storage Room

- First Aid Box Health and Chems

2 Wall Terminal

Shut off turret from here.

3 Corridor Network

- First Aid Box Health and Chems

4 Raider Defense

Find 10 Frag Mines on the ground on either side of the sandbags, and items behind the sandbags.

- Frag Mine (10)
- Ammo Box Ammunition (3)
- Frag Grenade (2)
- First Aid Box Health and Chems

5 Storage Room

- First Aid Box Health and Chems

INTERIOR MAPS AND LOCATIONS

Tepid Sewer

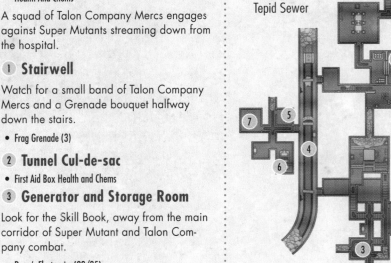

6 Generator

- Dean's Electronics (23/25)

7 Raider Sleeping Quarters

Here you can find Darts, mattresses, a floor safe and some key items:

- Assault Rifle
- Scribe Pre-War Book (90/98)
- Floor Safe Items

8 Raider Wall Terminal and Door

Raiders and Mole Rats are engaged in combat. Inside is a storage closet with a Pre-War Book hidden in a tiny crate below several burned books. The Ammo Box is locked.

- First Aid Box Health and Chems
- Ammo Box Ammunition
- Scribe Pre-War Book (91/98)

9 Raider Workshop

Tools, scrap metal, and junk are in here.

- Work Bench (43/46)
- Sledgehammer

A Location 9.07: The Capital Wasteland

B Location 14.01: Georgetown

U06.A: DUPONT CIRCLE STATION

- Threat Level: 3
- Factions: Raider, Super Mutant
- Danger: Bear Trap, Mines
- Collectible: Skill Book
- Guns And Ammunition
- Health And Chems
- Interior Exploration
- Underground Connection
- Hostiles: Super Mutant Genus, Raiders, Turrets

INTERIOR MAPS AND LOCATIONS

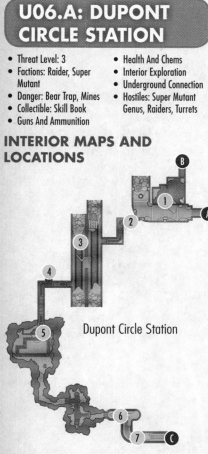

Dupont Circle Station

Super Mutants prowl the north station concourse. The Raiders have a large cavern stronghold to the south.

1 Ticket Master's Office

Metro Security Terminal. Releases Protectron. Check the postal crate on the table for the Skill Book.

- Lying, Congressional Style (25/25)

2 Bear Trap

3 Sleeping Raider and Mattress

- Ammo Box Ammunition (3)

4 Storage Alcove

There are some Chems and dirty water here, too.

- Ammo Box Ammunition (3)
- First Aid Box Health and Chems

5 Wall Terminal

Shut off turret from here.

6 Raider Defenses

Four Mines are laid to the south of the concrete blocks.

- Ammo Box Ammunition (3)
- Assault Rifle
- Frag Mine (4)

7 Grenade Bouquet

- Frag Grenade (3)

A Location 11.04: Collapsed Car Tunnel

B Location 11.05: Dupont Circle

C Location U6.B: Metro Central

U06.B: METRO CENTRAL

- Threat Level: 3
- Factions: Talon Mercenary, Ghoul
- Danger: Low Radiation
- Collectible: Skill Book (2)
- Guns And Ammunition
- Health And Chems
- Interior Exploration
- Underground Connection
- Hostiles: Ghoul Genus, Talon Company Mercs, Vicious Dogs

INTERIOR MAPS AND LOCATIONS

Metro Central

Ghouls and Talon Company Mercs fight for control of this three-level central section for these connecting tunnels.

1 Raider Barricade

A Raider is fighting against Ghouls, near a weapons cache and Stimpaks.

- Ammo Box Ammunition (3)
- Assault Rifle
- 10mm Pistol
- Frag Grenade (2)

2 Dead Slave

A body holds the location of the Temple of the Union [3.10].

3 Talon Company Corpses

This connecting tunnel dead-end contains bodies and a Stimpak.

- Assault Rifle
- Chinese Assault Rifle and Ammo

4 Connecting Tunnel

Small generators are inside a gate.

- Dean's Electronics (24/25)

---

5 Exit Stairwell

Find a dead Talon Company Merc, sandbags, and barricades.

- Chinese Assault Rifle and Ammo
- Ammo Box Ammunition (3)

6 Ticket Master's Office

The Metro Security Terminal releases a Protectron.

7 Small Circular Restroom

Talon Merc corpse holds a Stimpak.

- Chinese Assault Rifle and Ammo

8 Small Sandbag Barricade

- Ammo Box Ammunition (3)

9 Locked Storage Closet

Near the pack of Vicious Dogs, also find Chems and scattered junk and Ammo in here.

- First Aid Box Health and Chems (2)
- Pugilism Illustrated (24/25)

A Location U06.A: Dupont Circle Station

B Location 15.04: Pennsylvania Avenue

C Location U06.D: Freedom Street Station

D Location U06.C: Foggy Bottom Station

E Location U22.B: Museum Station

U06.C: FOGGY BOTTOM STATION

- Threat Level: 3
- Faction: Raider
- Collectible: Nuka-Cola Quantum, Skill Book
- Guns And Ammunition
- Interior Exploration
- Underground Connection
- Hostiles: Raiders

INTERIOR MAPS AND LOCATIONS

Foggy Bottom Station

This two-level station has scattered Raiders lurking about.

TRAINING — BESTIARY — MAIN QUEST — MISC. QUESTS — TOUR — COMPLETION — APPENDICES

① **Five Bear Traps**

② **Ticket Master's Office**

Metro Security Terminal. Releases Protectron. Look for the Skill Book on the computer console adjacent to the pod.

- Nikola Tesla and You (24/25)

③ **Bear Trap**

④ **Connecting Tunnel**

Scattered mattresses and small generators lie in this tunnel.

- Nuka-Cola Quantum (89/94)

⑤ **Grenade Bouquet**

- Frag Grenade (6)

Ⓐ **Location 11.10: Dupont Circle**

Ⓑ **Location U06.B: Metro Central**

Ⓒ **Location 14.05: Georgetown**

Ⓓ **Location U06.E: DCTA Tunnel 014-B Potomac**

U06.D: FREEDOM STREET STATION

- Threat Level: 2
- Faction: Ghoul
- Services: Repairer, Trader
- Danger: Bear Trap, Low Radiation
- Collectible: Skill Book
- Interior Exploration
- Guns And Ammunition
- Health And Chems
- Underground Connection
- Hostiles: Ghoul Genus

INTERIOR MAPS AND LOCATIONS

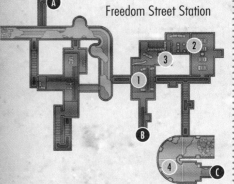

Freedom Street Station

This series of overlapping corridors and ruined tunnels is laden with Bear Traps, standing water, and radioactive barrels.

① **Two Bear Traps (lower chamber)**

② **Generator Room**

- First Aid Box Health and Chems

③ **Scavenger's Barricade**

A Scavenger Repairs and Trades with you. He has food and Chems on the shelves, and items to steal.

- Tumblers Today (23/25)
- Ammo Box Ammunition

④ **Four Bear Traps**

Ⓐ **Location 12.06: Vernon Square**

Ⓑ **Location 06.B: Metro Central**

Ⓒ **Location 15.01: Pennsylvania Avenue**

U06.E: DCTA TUNNEL 014-B POTOMAC

- Threat Level: 4
- Danger: Low Radiation
- Collectible: Skill Book
- Guns And Ammunition
- Interior Exploration
- Underground Connection
- Hostiles: Mirelurk Genus

INTERIOR MAPS AND LOCATIONS

DCTA Tunnel 014-B Potomac

This series of half-submerged tunnels is filled with Mirelurks and Egg Clutches.

① **Deserted Sandbags**

- Ammo Box Ammunition

② **Waterlogged Treatment Room with Stimpaks and Egg Clutches**

- D.C. Journal of Internal Medicine (24/25)

Ⓐ **Location U06.F: Arlington Utility**

Ⓑ **Location 14.02: Georgetown**

Ⓒ **Location U06.C: Foggy Bottom Station**

U06.F: ARLINGTON UTILITY

- Threat Level: 3
- Faction: Raider
- Collectible: Skill Book
- Guns And Ammunition
- Health And Chems
- Interior Exploration
- Sleep Mattress
- Underground Connection
- Hostiles: Mirelurk Genus, Radroaches, Raiders

Mirelurks encroach on the southern part of this sprawling Raider encampment.

① **Grenade Bouquet**

② **Sandbag Barricades (with scattered Stimpaks)**

- Ammo Box Ammunition (3)
- First Aid Box Health and Chems
- Assault Rifle
- Hunting Rifle

③ **Raider Encampment**

Throughout the tunnel area, complete with bunk-beds.

- Ammo Box Ammunition
- First Aid Box Health and Chems

④ **Raider Eating Balcony**

Scattered Chems are here.

- U.S. Army: 30 Flamethrower Recipes (23/25)

⑤ **Raider Storage (with bunk-beds)**

- Baseball Bat
- Ammo Box Ammunition (2)
- 10mm Pistol

Ⓐ **Location 06.E: DCTA Tunnel 014-B Potomac**

Ⓑ **Location 16.02: Arlington National Cemetery**

INTERIOR MAPS AND LOCATIONS

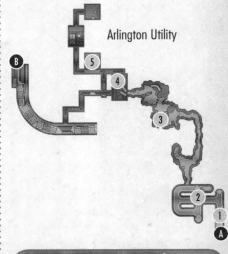

Arlington Utility

U07: PENN AVE/ GEORGETOWN METRO

- Threat Level: 2
- Faction: Raider
- Guns And Ammunition
- Interior Exploration
- Sleep Mattress
- Underground Connection
- Hostiles: Raiders, Raider Guard Dogs

INTERIOR MAPS AND LOCATIONS

Penn Ave / Georgetown Metro

A ruined concourse and mezzanine link these two locations.

① Abandoned Camp

This has mattresses, Nuka-Cola, food, and the following items:

- Ammo Box Ammunition (2)
- Assault Rifle and Ammo

Ⓐ Location 14.09: Georgetown

Ⓑ Location 15.05: Pennsylvania Avenue

U08: GEORGETOWN / THE MALL METRO

- Threat Level: 3
- Faction: Ghoul
- Danger: Low Radiation
- Collectible: Skill Book
- Health And Chems
- Interior Exploration
- Underground Connection
- Hostiles: Ghoul Genus

INTERIOR MAPS AND LOCATIONS

Georgetown / The Mall Metro

This collapsed station with no through tunnels features Ghouls roaming the mezzanine.

① Ticket Booth

- First Aid Box Health and Chems
- Chinese Army: Spec. Ops. Training Manual (22/25)

Ⓐ Location 14.07: Georgetown

Ⓑ Location 17.04: The Mall

U09: PENN. AVE / THE MALL METRO

- Threat Level: 2
- Factions: Ghoul, Wastelander
- Guns And Ammunition
- Interior Exploration
- Underground Connection
- Hostiles: Ghoul Genus

INTERIOR MAPS AND LOCATIONS

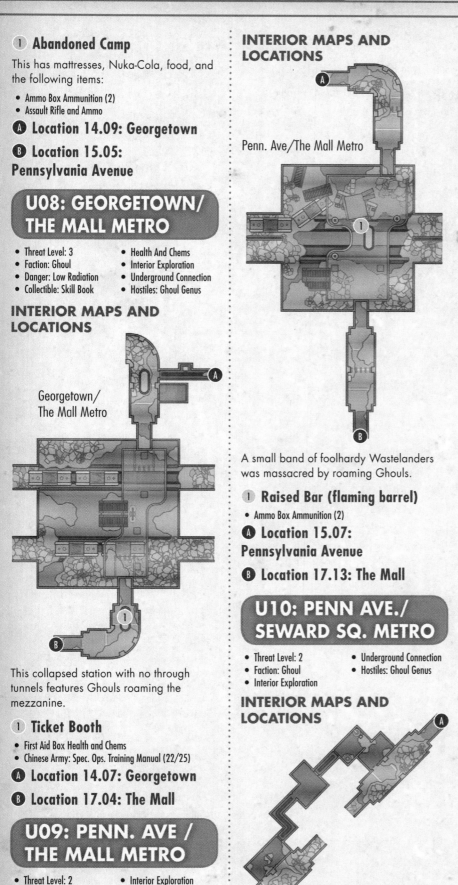

Penn. Ave / The Mall Metro

Penn Ave. / Seward Sq. Metro

A small band of foolhardy Wastelanders was massacred by roaming Ghouls.

① Raised Bar (flaming barrel)

- Ammo Box Ammunition (2)

Ⓐ Location 15.07: Pennsylvania Avenue

Ⓑ Location 17.13: The Mall

U10: PENN AVE. / SEWARD SQ. METRO

- Threat Level: 2
- Faction: Ghoul
- Interior Exploration
- Underground Connection
- Hostiles: Ghoul Genus

INTERIOR MAPS AND LOCATIONS

In this heavily devastated station, Raiders have been savaged by marauding Feral Ghouls.

Ⓐ Location 15.08: Pennsylvania Avenue

Ⓑ Location 18.02: Seward Square

U11: SEWER

- Threat Level: 3
- Faction: Super Mutant
- Collectible: Skill Book
- Guns And Ammunition
- Interior Exploration
- Underground Connection
- Hostiles: Super Mutant Genus

INTERIOR MAPS AND LOCATIONS

Sewer

Super Mutants are advancing through this sewage line and blocked Metro tunnel.

① Ruined Sofa Alcove

- Ammo Box Ammunition

② Top of Stairwell

A few skeletons lie near a Holotape that tells of a weapons stash in the southeast tunnel.

- Laser Pistol and Ammo
- Holotape: Hidden Stash Note

③ Hidden Stash

A cluster of Ammo Boxes is hidden behind concrete bricks in the wall.

- Ammo Box Ammunition
- Tumblers Today (24/25)

Ⓐ Location 15.03: Pennsylvania Avenue

Ⓑ Location 18.04: Seward Square

U12: ARLINGTON / WASTELAND METRO

- Threat Level: 1
- Faction: Ghoul
- Danger: Bear Trap
- Health And Chems
- Interior Exploration
- Sleep Mattress
- Underground Connection
- Hostiles: Ghoul Genus

A few wayward Ghouls snarl in the gloom of this short connecting series of corridors.

TRAINING — BESTIARY — MAIN QUEST — MISC. QUESTS — TOUR — COMPLETION — APPENDICES

INTERIOR MAPS AND LOCATIONS

Arlington/Wasteland Metro

① **Bear Trap**

② **Bloody Sleeping Quarters**

• First Aid Box Health and Chems

Ⓐ **Location 9.05: Capital Wasteland**

Ⓑ **Location 16.01: Arlington Cemetery**

U13: COUNTY SEWER MAINLINE

• Threat Level: 3
• Factions: Ghoul, Waste-lander
• Danger: Bear Trap, Chain Trap, Gas Leak, Grenade Bouquet, Low Radiation
• Collectibles: Nuka-Cola Quantum, Scribe Pre-War Book (4), Skill Book (2)
• Guns And Ammunition
• Health And Chems
• Interior Exploration
• Lots O' Caps
• Sleep Mattress
• Underground Connection
• Hostiles: Gallo, Ghoul Genus, Radroaches

INTERIOR MAPS AND LOCATIONS

County Sewer Mainline

A thoroughfare for Wastelanders heading to and from the city, this place is filled with Ghouls, some more eccentric than others.

① **Grenade Bouquet**

• Frag Grenade (3)

② **Girder-on-a-chain trap, and Bear Trap**

③ **Gallo's Hideaway**

Gallo the Ghoul is a dangerous canni-bal and collector. His Terminal unlocks a floor safe with a Nuka-Cola Quantum in it. Gallo's corpse holds a Skill Book. There are Darts, scattered Caps, Gallo's Stor-age Key in a bedside footlocker, and other items to find in his lair, as well as his caged Radroaches. The storage room to the north-east, unlocked using his key, holds a large amount of junk, some ammo, and a First Aid Box.

• Nuka-Cola Quantum (90/94)
• Tales of a Junktown Jerky Vendor (24/24)
• Gallo's Storage Key
• Ammo Box Ammunition (2)
• Scribe Pre-War Book (92/98)
• Scribe Pre-War Book (93/98)
• Baseball Bat
• First Aid Box Health and Chems

④ **Skeleton**

• Hunting Rifle and Ammo

⑤ **Sewer Management Room**

A metal gate allows access to the Sewer Management Terminal, allowing access to the storage door. The room beyond contains items.

• Scribe Pre-War Book (94/98)
• Scribe Pre-War Book (95/98)
• Big Book of Science (24/25)
• First Aid Box Health and Chems (2)
• Ammo Box Ammunition (2)

⑥ **Large Storage Room (Mid Level)**

• Ammo Box Ammunition (3)

⑦ **Gas Leak**

⑧ **Skeleton with Stimpak**

• 10mm Pistol and Ammo

⑨ **Dead Mercenary**

• 10mm Pistol and Ammo
• Ammo Box Ammunition

⑩ **Stairwell with Glowing One**

A terminal at the top unlocks a floor safe, near storage shelves.

• Ammo Box Ammunition (2)
• First Aid Box Health and Chems
• Hunting Rifle and Ammo
• Floor Safe Items

Ⓐ **Location 9.03: Sewer Waystation**

Ⓑ **Location 9.J: The Capital Wasteland**

U14: HUBRIS COMICS UTILITY TUNNELS

• Threat Level: 3
• Faction: Ghoul
• Danger: Gas Leak
• Collectibles: Skill Book
• Guns And Ammunition
• Health And Chems
• Interior Exploration
• Underground Connection
• Hostiles: Ghoul Genus

INTERIOR MAPS AND LOCATIONS

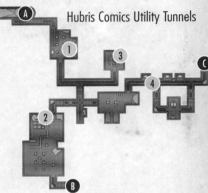

Hubris Comics Utility Tunnels

Take a Ghoul and gas-filled excursion into some winding corridors and large, confusing storage rooms.

① **Column and Pipe Room**

Check one alcove for a desk with a Skill Book on it.

• Dean's Electronics (25/25)

② **Machine Room (Skeleton)**

• Assault Rifle and Ammo
• Stealth Boy
• First Aid Box Health and Chems

③ **Wall Terminal**

Shut off turret from here. Ammo and First Aid are on other side of the fence, with some scattered Caps.

• First Aid Box Health and Chems
• Ammo Box Ammunition (3)

④ **Gas Leaks**

Ⓐ **Location 9.D: The Capital Wasteland**

Ⓑ **Location 20.01: Hubris Comics Publishing (first exit)**

Ⓒ **Location 20.01: Hubris Comics Publishing (alternate exit)**

U15: ARLINGTON/ FALLS CHURCH METRO

• Threat Level: 2
• Factions: Ghoul, Waste-lander
• Danger: Low Radiation
• Collectible: Skill Book
• Interior Exploration
• Underground Connection
• Hostiles: Ghoul Genus

INTERIOR MAPS AND LOCATIONS

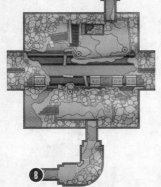

Arlington/Falls Church Metro

The entire mezzanine section of this station has collapsed on the platform below. Wastelanders lie dead, and Ghouls rule here. Check the northern, junk-filled container for the Skill Book on a chair.

- U.S. Army: 30 Handy Flamethrower Recipes (24/25)

Ⓐ Location 16.04: Arlington National Cemetery

Ⓑ Location 19.05: Falls Church

INTERIOR MAPS AND LOCATIONS
Marigold Station

U16.A: MARIGOLD STATION

- Miscellaneous Quest: Those!
- Freeform Quest
- Threat Level: 3
- Faction: Wastelander
- Danger: Gas Leak, Low Radiation
- Guns And Ammunition
- Health And Chems
- Interior Exploration
- Rare Or Powerful Item
- Underground Connection
- Hostiles: Doctor Lesko, Fire Ant Genus, Lug-Nut

This sprawling Metro Tunnel complex is crawling with mutated Fire Ants. Find a dead man's key, and uncover a madman's experiments.

For more information on Grady, consult the Freeform Quest at Girdershade (page 344).

① Storage and Small Generator Room

- Ammo Box Ammunition (2)

② Gas Leak and Item Storage Room

- First Aid Box Health and Chems

③ Grady (in mezzanine ticket booth)

- Grady's Last Recording

④ Connecting Tunnel

- Scoped .44 Magnum and Ammo
- Silenced 10mm Pistol and Ammo
- First Aid Box Health and Chems
- Ammo Box Ammunition
- Sledgehammer

⑤ Storage Room

Beware of escaping gas. Grady's Fire Hose is in here, as well as some food and Chems.

- Grady's Safe Key
- Ammo Box Ammunition (2)

⑥ Connecting tunnel; William Brandice

Brandice is lying here, dead. Take his key to unlock an item in his house in Grayditch.

- William Brandice's Key
- Ammo Box Ammunition

⑦ Grady's Storage Closet

Grady stored some Naughty Nightwear that Ronald Laren over at Girdershade would pay good Caps for. Fight or convince [Speech] Lug-Nut you're keeping it.

- Ammo Box Ammunition (3)
- First Aid Box Health and Chems
- Ripper
- Naughty Nightwear

⑧ Doctor Lesko's Laboratory

The doctor is in! Dispatch him for his Portable Terminal Access. Use the terminal to unlock the Hatchery Access Door (Location C). You can also read three entries regarding his experiments on ants. Kill him to steal his coat.

- Lesko's Lab Coat (87/89)
- Ammo Box Ammunition (3)
- First Aid Box Health and Chems
- 10mm Pistol

Ⓐ Location 9.10: Grayditch

Ⓑ Location 19.01: Falls Church

Ⓒ Location U16.B: Queen Ant's Hatchery

U16.B: QUEEN ANT'S HATCHERY

- Threat Level: 4
- Danger: Low Radiation
- Collectible: Nuka-Cola Quantum, Skill Book
- Interior Exploration
- Rare Or Powerful Item
- Underground Connection
- Hostiles: Fire Ant Genus, Marigold Ant Queen

INTERIOR MAPS AND LOCATIONS

Queen Ant's Hatchery

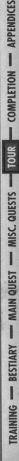

APPENDICES — COMPLETION — TOUR — MISC. QUESTS — MAIN QUEST — BESTIARY — TRAINING

This gloomy cavern contains a frightening collection of mutated and gigantic insects.

① Ant Queen's Nest

This waterlogged cave holds a gigantic Ant Queen, and her Soldiers. Doctor Lesko's Portacomp is accessible, and you can attempt the experiment (consult the quest on page 380 for more details). Don't forget the collectibles! The doctor's Protectron is dormant, unless provoked.

- Big Book of Science (25/25)
- Nuka-Cola Quantum (91/94)

ⓐ Location U16.A: Marigold Station

U17.A: FALLS CHURCH/ MASON DISTRICT METRO

- Threat Level: 4
- Factions: Ghoul, Raider
- Danger: Low Radiation
- Collectibles: Scribe Pre-War Book, Skill Book (2)
- Guns And Ammunition
- Health And Chems
- Interior Exploration
- Sleep Mattress
- Underground Connection
- Hostiles: Ghoul Genus, Mole Rats, Radroaches, Raiders

INTERIOR MAPS AND LOCATIONS

Falls Church/Mason District Metro

This surprisingly advanced Raider stronghold is being torn apart by ferocious Ghoul incursions.

① Restrooms, with Mole Rats and Radroaches

Check the First Aid Box for a Skill Book.

- First Aid Box Health and Chems
- D.C. Journal of Internal Medicine (25/25)

② Raider Camp Ticket Booth

- Blood Pack
- Missile
- First Aid Box Health and Chems
- Duck and Cover! (25/25)

③ Raider Camp Diner

Built around an old Dot's Diner, this offers a place to sleep, and Darts!

- Scribe Pre-War Book (96/98)
- Stealth Boy

④ Entrance to Franklin Metro Utility

Play with a terminal or door to enter.

ⓐ Location 19.02: Falls Church
ⓑ Location 20.02: Mason District
ⓒ Location U17.B: Franklin Metro Utility

U17.B: FRANKLIN METRO UTILITY

INTERIOR MAPS AND LOCATIONS

Franklin Metro Utility

- Threat Level: 5
- Faction: Ghoul
- Danger: High Radiation
- Interior Exploration
- Collectibles: Fat Man Mini-Nuke, Nuka-Cola Quantum, Scribe Pre-War Book (2), Skill Book (3)
- Guns And Ammunition
- Health And Chems
- Lots O' Caps
- Rare Or Powerful Item
- Sleep Mattress
- Underground Connection
- Work Bench (2)
- Hostiles: Ghoul Genus

Make a terrifying maneuver through a Glowing One-infested laboratory, and radioactive tunnel system.

① Lab Terminal

This terminal unlocks the wall safe on the pillar behind you. There are Darts and neatly arranged junk throughout.

- Wall Safe Items

② Storage Shelves Alcove

- Work Bench (44/46)
- Ammo Box Ammunition (2)

③ Desk Terminal

Shut off the adjacent turret from here. Nearby is a gate with Ammo, two Stimpaks, and a Skill Book.

- Ammo Box Ammunition
- Blood Pack
- Tumblers Today (25/25)

④ Junk Storage Shelves

- Ammo Box Ammunition (2)

⑤ Generator Room Counter

- Guns and Bullets (24/25)
- Ammo Box Ammunition
- Combat Shotgun and Ammo
- Stealth Boy
- Missile (2)

---

⑥ Flooded End Tunnel

- Mini-Nuke (71/71)
- Advanced Radiation Suit

⑦ Irradiated and Gutted Subway Car

- Ammo Box Ammunition (5)
- Nuka-Cola Quantum (92/94)
- Burnmaster (88/89)

⑧ Rickety Shelving

Find this partway along the irradiated tunnel, with Darts and other junk to sift through. There are mattresses farther along.

- Blood Pack
- Missile (2)
- U.S. Army: 30 Handy Flamethrower Recipes (25/25)
- Ammo Box Ammunition

⑨ Connecting Tunnel (Darts and other junk)

- First Aid Box Health and Chems

⑩ Workshop

Look for Chems on the shelves, and a hole down to trash bin with barrel in it. There are two Pre-War Books on a shelf near the trash bin.

- Work Bench (45/46)
- Scribe Pre-War Book (97/98)
- Scribe Pre-War Book (98/98)

ⓐ Location U17.A: Falls Church/ Mason Dst Metro

U18.A: TAFT TUNNELS

- Threat Level: 4
- Factions: Enclave, Wastelander
- Danger: Low Radiation
- Collectible: Skill Book
- Guns And Ammunition
- Health And Chems
- Interior Exploration
- Work Bench
- Underground Connection
- Hostiles: Enclave Eyebots, Enclave Soldiers

INTERIOR MAPS AND LOCATIONS

Taft Tunnels

Escorting Doctor Li out of the Enclave-filled tunnels is tricky, and this is your only chance to grab the following items.

① Wall First Aid Box

There are Rad Chems in this area, too.

- First Aid Box Health and Chems

② Overflow Door Control

This terminal accesses the utility door.

③ Dead Chinese Commando

In the room with the Enclave Soldier reinforcements is a desk covered in items.

- Chinese Assault Rifle
- Chinese Pistol
- Chinese Army: Spec. Ops. Training Manual (23/25)
- Dirty Chinese Jumpsuit

④ Irradiated Workshop

- Work Bench (46/46)
- Bottlecap Mine

Ⓐ Location 9.14: Jefferson Memorial Gift Shop

Ⓑ Location 18.B: Taft Tunnel

Alert! These tunnels are only accessed once, during your escape from the Jefferson Memorial during The Waters of Life. Make sure you grab any collectibles then!

U18.B: TAFT TUNNEL

- Threat Level: 3
- Factions: Enclave, Ghoul, Wastelander
- Collectibles: Nuka-Cola Quantum, Skill Book
- Guns And Ammunition
- Health And Chems
- Interior Exploration
- Underground Connection
- Hostiles: Enclave Soldiers, Ghoul Genus
- Friends: Brotherhood Initiates

INTERIOR MAPS AND LOCATIONS

Taft Tunnel

The escape continues as you fight Ghouls through narrower corridors, until you find salvation at the hands of the Brotherhood of Steel.

① Corpse and Radio

- Sledgehammer

② Odd Protective Headgear

- Eyebot Helmet

③ Decapitated Enclave Soldier

- Tesla Armor
- Tesla Helmet
- Plasma Rifle

④ Medical Bay

- Metal Helmet
- First Aid Box Health and Chems

⑤ Picnic Table

- Nuka-Cola Quantum (93/94)
- Nikola Tesla and You (25/25)

⑥ Corpse Pile

⑦ Locked Hatch Door

This leads to a stairwell down to a safe with plenty of Caps.

- Hunting Rifle

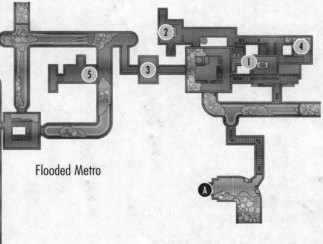

Flooded Metro

---

⑧ Brotherhood Defenses (Shelving)

- Ammo Box Ammunition (3)
- First Aid Box Health and Chems

Ⓐ Location 18.A: Taft Tunnels

Ⓑ Location 9.0: The Capital Wasteland

Alert! These tunnels are only accessed once, during your escape from the Jefferson Memorial during The Waters of Life. Make sure you grab any collectibles then!

U19: FLOODED METRO

- Threat Level: 4
- Danger: High Radiation, Mines, Shotgun Trap
- Collectibles: Nuka-Cola Quantum, Skill Book
- Guns And Ammunition
- Health And Chems
- Interior Exploration
- Lots O' Caps
- Rare Or Powerful Item
- Sleep Mattress
- Underground Connection
- Hostiles: Mirelurk Genus

INTERIOR MAPS AND LOCATIONS

Two large stairwells connected by lower sewer tunnels are confusing and dangerous, thanks to a large Mirelurk population.

① Skeleton, Near Jet (Top Floor)

- Scoped .44 Magnum and Ammo
- Guns and Bullets (25/25)
- First Aid Box Health and Chems

② Gun Cabinet (Middle Floor)

- Gun Cabinet Items

③ Small Thoroughfare Room

- First Aid Box Health and Chems

④ Ground Level Waterlogged Chamber

- First Aid Box Health and Chems

⑤ Trap-filled Storage Chamber

Along the waterlogged tunnel, expect two Frag Mines and a Rigged Shotgun as you enter this room. There is a Gun Cabinet, a mattress, Purified Water (3), and a Holotape to take, next to a rather impressive Melee weapon.

- Frag Mine (2)
- Combat Shotgun and Ammo
- Ammo Box Ammunition (2)
- Nuka-Cola Quantum (94/94)
- Holotape: Shocker Glove
- The Shocker (89/89)

Ⓐ Location 9.17: The Capital Wasteland

Ⓑ Location 20.03: Mason District

U20: IRRADIATED METRO

- Threat Level: 3
- Faction: Ghoul
- Danger: High Radiation
- Collectible: Skill Book
- Interior Exploration
- Underground Connection
- Hostiles: Ghoul Genus

INTERIOR MAPS AND LOCATIONS

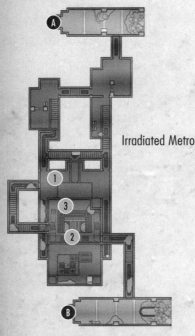

Irradiated Metro

Ironically this area is not as radioactive as some locations. The main problem area is a large courtyard with a Glowing One.

① Glowing One Courtyard (northwest console)

- Chinese Army: Spec. Ops. Training Manual (24/25)

② Glowing One Courtyard (south console)

- Assault Rifle

---

③ Balcony (above courtyard)

With assorted Chems and a dead Wastelander.

- Blood Pack (2)
- 10mm Pistol and Ammo

Ⓐ Location 9.12: The Capital Wasteland

Ⓑ Location 21.04: L'Enfant Plaza

U21: HAZMAT DISPOSAL SITE L5

- Threat Level: 4
- Factions: Ghoul, Super Mutant
- Danger: Baby Carriage, Low Radiation
- Interior Exploration
- Sleep Mattress
- Underground Connection
- Hostiles: Ghoul Genus, Super Mutant Genus

INTERIOR MAPS AND LOCATIONS

Hazmat Disposal Site L5

A horde of irradiated Ghouls and a single Mutie await you in these tunnels.

① Escaping Gas (near Wastelander corpse)

② Turret Control System Terminal

③ Baby Carriage Trap

Ⓐ Location 17.02: The Mall

Ⓑ Location 21.01: L'Enfant Plaza

U22.A: ANACOSTIA CROSSING STATION

- Threat Level: 3
- Faction: Raider
- Collectible: Skill Book
- Interior Exploration
- Sleep Mattress
- Underground Connection
- Hostiles: Raiders

INTERIOR MAPS AND LOCATIONS

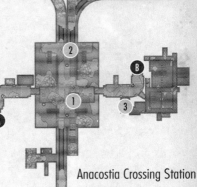

Anacostia Crossing Station

Raiders have built a ramshackle camp on an extended mezzanine, and roam the nearby tunnels.

① Mezzanine Ticket Booth

- 10mm Pistol and Ammo

② Mezzanine Tables

A collection of cafe tables with scattered Chems

- Pugilism Illustrated (25/25)

③ Ticket Master's Office

Metro Security Terminal releases Protectron. A nearby fridge contains food.

④ Connecting Corridor

A small Raider contingent has a few mattresses and a Stimpak here. The tunnel behind the fence cannot be accessed.

Ⓐ Location 9.16: The Capital Wasteland

Ⓑ Location 18.05: Seward Square

Ⓒ Location U22.B: Museum Station

U22.B: MUSEUM STATION

- Threat Level: 3
- Faction: Raider
- Collectible: Skill Book (2)
- Guns And Ammunition
- Interior Exploration
- Sleep Mattress
- Underground Connection
- Hostiles: Raiders, Radroaches, Ghoul Genus

INTERIOR MAPS AND LOCATIONS

Museum Station

Raiders are attempting to clear a Radroach infestation in the upper mezzanine. Elsewhere, small groups patrol the tunnels.

① Tunnel Carriages

- Ammo Box Ammunition (.308 Caliber)

② Ammo Cache under table

- Ammo Box Ammunition (3)

③ Mezzanine Sandbags

- Ammo Box Ammunition

④ Concourse Restrooms

A skeleton is close to a small crate with Chems and a book.

- Chinese Army: Spec. Ops. Training Manual (25/25)

⑤ Concourse Sandbag Defenses

Two locations, with scattered Chems.

- Ammo Box Ammunition (4)

⑥ Small Raider Camp

Amid the junk and couple of foes are some mattresses to sleep on.

- Ammo Box Ammunition
- Sledgehammer

⑦ Raider Recreation Room

This area features pool table with balls you can take, Darts, and mattresses to sleep on. Hit the electrical switch to open the flap trap door to continue. The entrance room from Metro Central has an Ammo Box in it.

- Grognak the Barbarian (25/25)
- Ammo Box Ammunition

Ⓐ Location U22.A: Anacostia Crossing Station

Ⓑ Location 17.06: The Mall (Museum of History)

Ⓒ Location 17.09: The Mall (Museum of Technology)

Ⓓ Location U6.B: Metro Central

Chapter 6

ENDING IT ALL

Project Complete: Aftermath

Spoiler Alert

As you might have guessed by the title, the following information reveals how to complete your adventure in a variety of ways. Look away before it is too late!

After a supreme sacrifice inside the Jefferson Memorial, everything fades to white. While you may have given your life to the cause, tales of your valor (or betrayal), and the heroism of Sentinel Sarah Lyons, will be told for decades to come. However, the path you have walked, and the actions you have taken, have all influenced how future generations remember you. Fortunately, this guide can extrapolate every variable and reveal all the different permutations for your interest and amusement. Six general sections comprise the ending:

PROLOGUE

ENDING	HOW UNLOCKED
The lone wanderer ventured forth from Vault 101, discovering the fate of his father.	Every time the Main Quest is completed.

KARMIC INFLUENCES

 HIGH KARMA

ENDING	HOW UNLOCKED
The Capital Wasteland proved a cruel, inhospitable place, but the lone wanderer refused to surrender to the vices that had claimed so many others. Selflessness, compassion, and honor guided this noble soul.	Very high overall Karma.
A view of the Lincoln Memorial is shown, with Lincoln's head attached.	If you sided with the Slaves in Miscellaneous Quest: Head of State.
A glimpse of an old lady, playing the violin so sweetly	If you didn't complete Head of State, but did return the violin in Miscellaneous Quest: Agatha's Song.
A view of serene peace. You have led a pious and thoughtful existence.	If you didn't finish either Head of State or Agatha's Song in the manner described previously.

APPENDICES — COMPLETION — TOUR — MISC. QUESTS — MAIN QUEST — BESTIARY — TRAINING

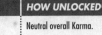

NEUTRAL KARMA

ENDING	HOW UNLOCKED
The Capital Wasteland proved a cruel, inhospitable place.	Neutral overall Karma.

LOW KARMA

ENDING	HOW UNLOCKED
The Capital Wasteland proved a cruel, inhospitable place and the lone wanderer ultimately surrendered to the vices that had claimed so many others. Selfishness, greed, and cruelty guided this lost soul.	Very low overall Karma.
The smouldering remains of a settlement lie twisted in the Wasteland.	If you destroyed Megaton in Miscellaneous Quest: The Power of the Atom.
The flickering flames lick a living tree, screaming in agony.	If you didn't complete The Power of the Atom, but did set Harold on fire during Miscellaneous Quest: Oasis.
A view of objectionable disgust. You have led a reckless and thoughtless existence.	If you didn't finish either The Power of the Atom, or Oasis in the manner described previously.

LIFE OR DEATH

YOU DIED

ENDING	HOW UNLOCKED
It was not until the end of this long road that the lone wanderer learned the true meaning of that greatest of virtues—sacrifice. The child followed the example of the father, sacrificing life itself for the greater good of mankind.	If you gave up your life in the Project Purity control chamber during Main Quest: Take It Back!
It was not until the end of this long road that the lone wanderer was faced with that greatest of virtues—sacrifice. But the child refused to follow the father's selfless example.	If you entered the the Project Purity control chamber, having agreed to switch it on, and stood there, waiting for time to run out, during Main Quest: Take It Back! You doom the Wasteland.
	If you destroyed the Project Purity control chamber during Main Quest: Take It Back!†

† If this slide is displayed, your ending moves straight to Conclusions.

YOU LIVED

ENDING	HOW UNLOCKED
It was not until the end of this long road that the lone wanderer was faced with that greatest of virtues—sacrifice. But the child refused to follow the father's selfless example, instead allowing a true hero to sacrifice her own life for the greater good of mankind.	If Sarah Lyons gave her life in the Project Purity control chamber during Main Quest: Take It Back!

ENCLAVE SABOTEUR OR SOLDIER

YOU DIDN'T SIDE WITH PRESIDENT EDEN

ENDING	HOW UNLOCKED
Thankfully, when selected by the sinister president to be his instrument of annihilation, the wanderer refused. Humanity, with all its flaws, was deemed worthy of preservation. The waters of life flowed at last—free and pure, for any and all.	You failed to destroy Raven Rock during Main Quest: The American Dream, and did not deploy the Modified F.E.V. during Main Quest: Take It Back!
Thankfully, when selected by the sinister president to be his instrument of annihilation, the wanderer refused whole-heartedly. Humanity, with all its flaws, was deemed worthy of preservation. The waters of life flowed at last—free and pure, for any and all.	You succeeded in destroying Raven Rock during Main Quest: The American Dream, and did not deploy the Modified F.E.V. during Main Quest: Take It Back!

YOU SIDED WITH PRESIDENT EDEN

ENDING	HOW UNLOCKED
Sadly, when selected by the sinister president to be his instrument of annihilation, the wanderer agreed. The waters of life flowed at last—but the virus contained within soon eradicated all those deemed unworthy of salvation. The Capital Wasteland, despite its progress, became a graveyard.	You did deploy the Modified F.E.V. during Main Quest: Take It Back!

CONCLUSIONS

YOU ARE FEMALE

ENDING	HOW UNLOCKED
So ends the story of the lone wanderer, who stepped through the great door of Vault 101, and into the annals of legend.	Choose a female character during Main Quest: Birth or Main Quest: Escape!

YOU ARE MALE

ENDING	HOW UNLOCKED
So ends the story of the lone wanderer, who stepped through the great door of Vault 101, and into the annals of legend.	Choose a male character during Main Quest: Birth or Main Quest: Escape!

EPILOGUE

Note

The Epilogue reveals a framed picture of you standing by your father, on your 10th birthday. The photo will look different depending on the character you chose during Main Quest: Birth or Main Quest: Escape!

YOUR PHOTO APPEARANCE	HOW UNLOCKED
African American Female	Choose a female African American character
African American Male	Choose a male African American character
Asian Female	Choose a female Asian character
Asian Male	Choose a male Asian character
Caucasian Female	Choose a female Caucasian character
Caucasian Male	Choose a male Caucasian character
Hispanic Female	Choose a female Hispanic character
Hispanic Male	Choose a male Hispanic character

Chapter 7 APPENDICES

The following appendices are presented so you can keep track of your Achievements, collectibles, and rare inventory items.

APPENDIX 1: ACHIEVEMENTS (XBOX 360 ONLY)

	ACHIEVEMENT	VALUE	DESCRIPTION
1	Vault 101 Citizenship Award	10	Got the Pip-Boy 3000
2	The G.O.A.T. Whisperer	10	Took the G.O.A.T.
3	Escape!	20	Completed "Main Quest: Escape!"
4	Following in His Footsteps	20	Completed "Main Quest: Following in His Footsteps"
5	Galaxy News Radio	20	Completed "Main Quest: Galaxy News Radio"
6	Scientific Pursuits	20	Completed "Main Quest: Scientific Pursuits"
7	Tranquility Lane	20	Completed "Main Quest: Tranquility Lane"
8	The Waters of Life	20	Completed "Main Quest: The Waters of Life"
9	Picking up the Trail	20	Completed "Main Quest: Picking up the Trail"
10	Rescue from Paradise	20	Completed "Main Quest: Rescue from Paradise"
11	Finding the Garden of Eden	20	Completed "Main Quest: Finding the Garden of Eden"
12	The American Dream	20	Completed "Main Quest: The American Dream"
13	Take It Back!	40	Completed "Main Quest: Take It Back!"
14	Big Trouble in Big Town	20	Completed "Miscellaneous Quest: Big Trouble in Big Town"
15	The Superhuman Gambit	20	Completed "Miscellaneous Quest: The Superhuman Gambit"
16	The Wasteland Survival Guide	20	Completed "Miscellaneous Quest: The Wasteland Survival Guide"
17	Those!	20	Completed "Miscellaneous Quest: Those!"
18	The Nuka-Cola Challenge	20	Completed "Miscellaneous Quest: The Nuka-Cola Challenge"
19	Head of State	20	Completed "Miscellaneous Quest: Head of State"
20	The Replicated Man	20	Completed "Miscellaneous Quest: The Replicated Man"
21	Blood Ties	20	Completed "Miscellaneous Quest: Blood Ties"
22	Oasis	20	Completed "Miscellaneous Quest: Oasis"
23	The Power of the Atom	20	Completed "Miscellaneous Quest: The Power of the Atom"
24	Tenpenny Tower	20	Completed "Miscellaneous Quest: Tenpenny Tower"
25	Strictly Business	20	Completed "Miscellaneous Quest: Strictly Business"
26	You Gotta Shoot 'Em in the Head	20	Completed "Miscellaneous Quest: You Gotta Shoot 'Em in the Head"
27	Stealing Independence	20	Completed "Miscellaneous Quest: Stealing Independence"
28	Trouble on the Homefront	20	Completed "Miscellaneous Quest: Trouble on the Homefront"
29	Agatha's Song	20	Completed "Miscellaneous Quest: Agatha's Song"
30	Reilly's Rangers	20	Completed "Miscellaneous Quest: Reilly's Rangers"
31	Reaver	10	Reached Level 8 with Bad Karma
32	Mercenary	10	Reached Level 8 with Neutral Karma
33	Protector	10	Reached Level 8 with Good Karma
34	Harbinger of War	20	Reached Level 14 with Bad Karma
35	Pinnacle of Survival	20	Reached Level 14 with Neutral Karma
36	Ambassador of Peace	20	Reached Level 14 with Good Karma
37	Scourge of Humanity	30	Reached Level 20 with Bad Karma

	ACHIEVEMENT	VALUE	DESCRIPTION
38	Paradigm of Humanity	30	Reached Level 20 with Neutral Karma
39	Last, Best Hope of Humanity	30	Reached Level 20 with Good Karma
40	Weaponsmith	30	Made one of every Custom Weapon †
41	Doesn't Play Well with Others	20	Killed 300 people ‡
42	Slayer of Beasts	20	Killed 300 creatures ††
43	Silver-Tongued Devil	20	Won 50 Speech challenges
44	Data Miner	20	Hacked 50 terminals
45	Keys are for Cowards	20	Picked 50 Locks
46	One-Man Scouting Party	20	Discovered 100 locations †‡
47	Psychotic Prankster	10	Placed a Grenade or Mine while Pickpocketing
48	The Bigger They Are…	20	Kill all the Super Mutant Behemoths ‡‡
49	Yes, I Play with Dolls	10	Collected 10 Vault-Tec Bobbleheads
50	Vault-Tec C.E.O.	30	Collected 20 Vault-Tec Bobbleheads

† There are seven Custom Weapons: Bottlecap Mine, Dart Gun, Deathclaw Gauntlet, Nuka-Grenade, Railway Rifle, Rock-it Launcher, and Shishkebab.

‡ These include Enclave troops, Brotherhood Outcasts, Megaton Settlers, Raiders, Rivet City Security, Scavengers, Slavers, Talon Company Mercs, Tenpenny Residents and Security Guards, Underworld Residents, Wastelanders, and Feral Wastelanders.

†† These include Ants, Bloatflies, Brahmin, Centaurs, Deathclaws, Dogs, Enclave Eyebots, Feral Ghouls, Mirelurks, Robots, Radroaches, Radscorpions, Super Mutants, Turrets, and Yao Guai.

†‡ These are Primary Locations on your Pip-Boy's World Map.

‡‡ There are five Behemoths to kill: One is in a large pen in Evergreen Mills [7.04]; one is near the Jury Street Tunnel Super Mutant Camp [8.A]; one is outside Galaxy News Radio [10.03]; one is outside the auto shop in Takoma Park [13.03]; and one is in the Central Rotunda of the Capital Building [17.14].

APPENDIX 2: BOBBLEHEADS (20)

NUMBER	ZONE	LOCATION	NOTES
#01: Energy Weapons	1.01	Raven Rock [LAT -28 / LONG 28]	Raven Rock — Level 2, colonel Autumn's quarters, on table.
#02: Big Guns	1.04	Fort Constantine [LAT -17 / LONG 26]	CO quarters, inside open safe.
#03: Endurance	1.07	Deathclaw Sanctuary [LAT -22 / LONG 20]	Deathclaw Sanctuary, initial chamber, next to corpse pile.
#04: Explosives	1.11	WKML Broadcast Station [LAT -17 / LONG 18]	Sealed Cistern, next to ham radio.
#05: Speech	2.08	Paradise Falls [LAT -09 / LONG 16]	Eulogy's Pad, on table.
#06: Perception	3.03	The Republic of Dave [LAT 19 / LONG 27]	Museum of Dave, bookcase.
#07: Agility	3.06	Greener Pastures Disposal Site [LAT 07 / LONG 21]	Office, on table.
#08: Repair	5.07	Arefu [LAT -11 / LONG 06]	Evan King's house, on table.
#09: Science	5.12	Vault 106 [LAT -09 / LONG 01]	Vault 106 living quarters, medical bay eastern wall, on shelves.
#10: Charisma	6.06	Vault 108 [LAT 18 / LONG 06]	Vault 108 — Cloning Lab, on table.
#11: Lockpick	6.07	Bethesda Ruins [LAT 05 / LONG 03]	Bethesda Offices East, top floor, on desk in central room.
#12: Small Guns	6.11	National Guard Depot [LAT 18 / LONG -03]	National Guard Armory, shelf in equipment storage.
#13: Sneak	7.01	Yao Guai Tunnels [LAT -28 / LONG -04]	Yao Guai Den, on metal crate, eastern area of central cavern.
#14: Barter	7.04	Evergreen Mills [LAT -18 / LONG -07]	Bazaar, Jock's northeast alcove; top right shelf behind the Work Bench.
#15: Melee Weapons	7.11	Dunwich Building [LAT -26 / LONG -18]	Virulent Underchambers, mall maintenance room.

APPENDICES

COMPLETION — TOUR — MISC. QUESTS — MAIN QUEST — BESTIARY — TRAINING

455-07

Appendix 2: Bobbleheads (continued)

NUMBER	ZONE	LOCATION	NOTES
#16: Unarmed	7.C	Rockopolis [LAT -26 / LONG -07]	Rockopolis, next to Argyle's body.
#17: Medicine	8.01	Vault 101 [LAT -04 / LONG -04]	Vault 101, Dad's clinic table.
#18: Strength	8.03	Megaton [LAT -01 / LONG -06]	Lucas Simms's house, sheriff's bedroom, on table.
#19: Intelligence	9.15	Rivet City [LAT 18 / LONG -17]	Science Lab, on table.
#20: Luck	16.03	Arlington House	Arlington house, cellar shelves.

APPENDIX 3: FAT MEN (9)

#	ZONE	LOCATION	NOTES
#01	0.51	Wasteland Mini-Encounter: Dead Guy, Fat Man	A randomly found Wastelander with a Fat Man and Mini-Nuke.
#02	1.04	Fort Constantine [LAT -17 / LONG 26]	Bomb storage, experimental Chamber on table, near two Mini-Nukes.
#03	3.02	Old Olney [LAT 10 / LONG 26]	Olney Sewers, southeastern safe storage room (the bloody sleeping quarters).
#04	4.11	Fort Bannister [LAT -18 / LONG -01]	Fort Bannister Main, locked [Average] storage room.
#05	5.01	Germantown Police Headquarters [LAT -02 / LONG 13]	Basement, in small storage room [Average] near firing range.
#06	7.04	Evergreen Mills [LAT -18 / LONG -07]	Foundry, inside locked storage room [Average].
#07	10.03	Galaxy News Radio	Exterior plaza, on the body of the fallen Brotherhood Knight.
#08	15.02	White House Utility Tunnel	White House crater, on concrete "island."
#09	17.14	Capitol Building West Entrance	Rotunda, on body of Talon Company Merc during Behemoth battle.

† The "Experimental MIRV" Fat Man is included in the Unique Weapons and Outfits Appendix.

APPENDIX 4: FAT MAN: MINI-NUKES (71)

#	ZONE	LOCATION	NOTES
#01	0.00	Wasteland Mini-Encounter: Merchant Trader Caravan	Sold by (or in the inventory of) Lucky Harith.
#02	0.01	Wasteland Mini-Encounter: Searching for Cheryl	On the Behemoth corpse once you locate and fight it, near the Super Mutant Camp [8.A].
#03	0.25	Wasteland Mini-Encounter: The Lone Ranger	Near the Irradiated Metro [9.12], on Ranger, once Miscellaneous Quest: Reilly's Rangers is complete.
#04	0.51	Wasteland Mini-Encounter: Dead Guy, Fat Man	A randomly found Wastelander with a Fat Man and Mini-Nuke.
#05	1.04	Fort Constantine [LAT -17 / LONG 26]	Bomb storage, experimental chamber on table, near Fat Man.
#06	1.04	Fort Constantine [LAT -17 / LONG 26]	Bomb storage, experimental chamber on table, near Fat Man.
#07	1.04	Fort Constantine [LAT -17 / LONG 26]	Bomb storage, upstairs office, on table.
#08	1.07	Deathclaw Sanctuary [LAT -22 / LONG 20]	Deathclaw Sanctuary, initial chamber, next to corpse pile.
#09	1.A	Raider Wharf [LAT -24 / LONG 25]	Base of bookcase, on the wharf.
#10	1.D	Jackknifed Truck (on Freeway) [LAT -26 / LONG 20]	Back of container truck, on table.
#11	1.E	Overlook Raider Shack [LAT -25 / LONG 21]	Shack, in the bathtub.
#12	1.E	Overlook Raider Shack [LAT -25 / LONG 21]	Rude skeleton, in the lone bathtub northeast of shack.
#13	2.01	Oasis [LAT -03 / LONG 28]	Sunken caverns, underwater in grotto.
#14	2.02	SatCom Array NN-03d [LAT -13 / LONG 25]	On Super Mutant mannequin, on top of the upper satellite dish.
#15	2.02	SatCom Array NN-03d [LAT -13 / LONG 25]	On Super Mutant mannequin, on top of the upper satellite dish.
#16	3.02	Old Olney [LAT 10 / LONG 26]	Olney Sewers, generator room, behind storage closet door [Very Hard].
#17	3.D	Ruined Farmstead [LAT 06 / LONG 27]	Barn: On shelf inside the open tool cabinet.
#18	3.L	The Roach King [LAT 08 / LONG 16]	Inside his "rocket throne."
#19	4.02	Five Axles Rest Stop [LAT -21 / LONG 10]	Inside one of the truck containers.
#20	4.04	Broadcast Tower KT8 [LAT -26 / LONG 09]	Drainage Chamber, under floor hatch, where Remnant skeletons lie.
#21	4.10	VAPL-58 Power Station [LAT -14 / LONG 03]	Interior. Look up! It's on top of the light fixture nearer the door.
#22	4.11	Fort Bannister [LAT -18 / LONG -01]	Fort Bannister Main, locked [Average] storage room.
#23	4.J	Wasteland Gypsy Village [LAT -18 / LONG 06]	Inside the shack with tree stump left of the door.

Appendix 4: Fat Men Shells (continued)

#	ZONE	LOCATION	NOTES
#24	4.K	Wastelander Pylon [LAT -14 / LONG 05]	Among the items at the base of the pylon.
#25	5.03	Hamilton's Hideaway [LAT -07 / LONG 07]	Inside locked cell gate, part of Freeform Quest: Caching in with Three Dog.
#26	5.04	Hallowed Moors Cemetery [LAT -04 / LONG 09]	On the table with the ham radio.
#27	5.05	Meresti Trainyard [LAT -01 / LONG 07]	Metro Station (interior), lower mezzanine, northeast corner, on the inaccessible elevated platform roof, above the Work Bench and shelves; dislodge it with gunfire or explosives (it won't explode).
#28	5.06	Agatha's House [LAT 01 / LONG 08]	Inside Agatha's Locked Ammo Box.
#29	5.12	Vault 106 [LAT -09 / LONG 01]	Science Labs, security vault.
#30	5.13	Jury Street Metro Station [LAT -10 / LONG -03]	Gold Ribbon Grocers. Freeform Quest: Rube's Gold Ribbon.
#31	5.A	Wrecked Vehicles [LAT -13 / LONG 12]	Raider's Jetty north of vehicles.
#32	6.07	Bethesda Ruins [LAT 05 / LONG 03]	Bethesda Offices West, top floor, under the cluster of tiny crates by the chest freezer.
#33	6.07	Bethesda Ruins [LAT 05 / LONG 03]	Bethesda Offices East, the room just inside the exit to the exterior balcony; to the north, nestled between two filing cabinets, on a rubble pile.
#34	6.07	Bethesda Ruins [LAT 05 / LONG 03]	Bethesda Underworks, "pillar" storeroom, under tiny crate right next to Nuka-Cola Quantum, on the shelf.
#35	6.11	National Guard Depot [LAT 18 / LONG -03]	Armory and bunker, inside armory, on table with Fat Man.
#36	6.11	National Guard Depot [LAT 18 / LONG -03]	Armory and bunker, inside armory, on table with Fat Man.
#37	6.11	National Guard Depot [LAT 18 / LONG -03]	Armory and bunker, inside armory, on table with Fat Man.
#38	6.11	National Guard Depot [LAT 18 / LONG -03]	Armory and bunker, inside armory, on table with Fat Man.
#39	6.11	National Guard Depot [LAT 18 / LONG -03]	Armory and bunker, inside armory, on table with Fat Man.
#40	6.P	Jackknifed Truck (under Monorail) [LAT 16 / LONG 02]	Inside tipped-over container of truck.
#41	6.AA	Super Mutant Bonfire [LAT 11 / LONG -03]	On the concrete ground, near the Health and Ammo stash.
#42	E6.07	Enclave Camp [LAT 09 / LONG -03]	Sometimes located with or on the Enclave troops dropped on the bridge by a Vertibird.
#43	7.06	VAPL-66 Power Station [LAT -23 / LONG -14]	Interior, on the floor to the side of the desk.
#44	7.08	VAPL-84 Power Station [LAT -15 / LONG -12]	In the container truck, outside.
#45	7.14	Tenpenny Tower [LAT -16 / LONG -17]	Dashwood's Safe, Freeform Quest: A Manhandled Manservant
#46	7.E	Ruined Chapel [LAT -14 / LONG -06]	By the pulpit.
#47	7.M	Drainage Chamber [LAT -20 / LONG -13]	Trap-filled, underground office.
#48	8.03	Megaton [LAT -01 / LONG -06]	Craterside Supplies. Awarded by Moira Brown. Miscellaneous Quest: The Wasteland Survival Guide.
#49	8.04	Fort Independence [LAT -06 / LONG -13]	Lower level, outcast weapons room [Hard door].
#50	8.04	Fort Independence [LAT -06 / LONG -13]	Lower level, outcast weapons room [Hard door].
#51	8.06	Cliffside Cavern [LAT -10 / LONG -17]	Raider Outpost, inside the tent.
#52	8.E	Ruined Farmhouse [LAT -06 / LONG -04]	Shelf at the rear of the building.
#53	9.01	Super-Duper Mart [LAT 04 / LONG -04]	Inside locked storage room.
#54	9.I	Outpost [LAT 04 / LONG -11]	On a shelf, near a gun cabinet.
#55	10.03	Galaxy News Radio	Exterior plaza, on the body of the fallen Brotherhood Knight.
#56	13.03	Auto Shop	Exterior parking lot, on the body of the fallen Behemoth.
#57	14.08	La Maison Beauregard Lobby	Lobby, on the pool table.
#58	15.02	White House Utility Tunnel	White House crater, on concrete "island."
#59	15.02	White House Utility Tunnel	White House crater, on concrete "island."
#60	15.02	White House Utility Tunnel	White House crater, on concrete "island."
#61	17.11	The National Archives	Archives sub-basement, tunnel junction, through gate [Very Hard].
#62	17.14	Capitol Building West Entrance	Rotunda, on body of Talon Company Merc during Behemoth battle.
#63	17.14	Capitol Building West Entrance	Rotunda, on body of the fallen Behemoth.
#64	17.14	Capitol Building West Entrance	Rotunda, weapon cache against the wall.
#65	18.F	Explosive Alley	Part of the explosive trap set up by the lunatic preacher.
#66	18.F	Explosive Alley	Part of the explosive trap set up by the lunatic preacher.
#67	18.F	Explosive Alley	Part of the explosive trap set up by the lunatic preacher.
#68	18.F	Explosive Alley	Part of the explosive trap set up by the lunatic preacher.
#69	18.F	Explosive Alley	Part of the explosive trap set up by the lunatic preacher.
#70	19.06	L.O.B. Enterprises	East Wing, on top of the light fixture in the CEO's bathroom.
#71	U17.B	Franklin Metro Utility	Flooded end tunnel, underwater.

APPENDIX 5: UNIQUE WEAPONS AND OUTFITS (89)

#	NAME	TYPE	ZONE	LOCATION	NOTES
#01	Crow's Eyebot Helmet	Outfit	0.00	Wasteland Mini-Encounter: Merchant Trader Caravan	Freeform Quest: Merchant Empire. Reward from Crow.
#02	"Stabhappy" Combat Knife	Weapon	0.21+	Mini-Encounter	Any encounter involving Raiders; this might be dropped.
#03	"Firelance" Alien Blaster	Weapon	0.17	Mini-Encounter	Falls from the sky, after unknown explosion.
#04	T-51b Power Armor	Outfit	1.04	Fort Constantine [LAT -17 / LONG 26]	Bomb storage, experimental chamber.
#05	T-51b Power Helmet	Outfit	1.04	Fort Constantine [LAT -17 / LONG 26]	Bomb storage, experimental chamber.
#06	"Vengeance" Gatling Laser	Weapon	1.07	Deathclaw Sanctuary [LAT -22 / LONG 20]	Innermost chamber, in blood grotto.
#07	"Jack" Ripper	Weapon	1.07	Deathclaw Sanctuary [LAT -22 / LONG 20]	On the dead Enclave Soldier.
#08	"Reservist's Rifle" Sniper Rifle	Weapon	1.08	Dickerson Tabernacle Chapel [LAT -19 / LONG 19]	Carried by the Drifter.
#09	Linden's Outcast Power Armor	Outfit	2.01	Oasis [LAT -03 / LONG 28]	Miscellaneous Quest: Oasis. Possible reward.
#10	Maple's Garb	Outfit	2.01	Oasis [LAT -03 / LONG 28]	Miscellaneous Quest: Oasis. Possible reward.
#11	Poplar's Hood	Outfit	2.01	Oasis [LAT -03 / LONG 28]	Miscellaneous Quest: Oasis. Possible reward.
#12	Bear Charm	Outfit	2.01	Oasis [LAT -03 / LONG 28]	Freeform Quest: Yew Got a New Friend. Possible reward.
#13	"Board of Education" Nail Board	Weapon	2.04	Clifftop Shacks [LAT 00 / LONG 26]	Inside one of the shacks next to a nightstand; a skeleton's arm is outstretched for it.
#14	Mesmetron	Weapon	2.08	Paradise Falls [LAT -09 / LONG 16]	Miscellaneous Quest: Strictly Business; given by Grouse.
#15	Vault 77 Jumpsuit	Outfit	2.08	Paradise Falls [LAT -09 / LONG 16]	Located in the barracks.
#16	"The Break" Pool Cue	Weapon	2.08	Paradise Falls [LAT -09 / LONG 16]	On the pool table by the roasting Brahmin.
#17	Eulogy Jones' Hat	Outfit	2.08	Paradise Falls [LAT -09 / LONG 16]	On a table, inside Eulogy's Pad.
#18	Eulogy Jones' Suit	Outfit	2.08	Paradise Falls [LAT -09 / LONG 16]	Worn by Eulogy Jones.
#19	Boogeyman's Hood	Outfit	2.08	Paradise Falls [LAT -09 / LONG 16]	Freeform Quest: The Kid-Kidnapper. Reward from Eulogy Jones.
#20	"Fisto!" Power Fist	Weapon	2.09	MDPL-13 Power Station [LAT 02 / LONG 17]	Foreman's office.
#21	Soil Stradivarius	Outfit	3.01	Vault 92 [LAT 08 / LONG 27]	Sound testing, in the sealed recording studio.
#22	Prototype Medic Power Armor	Outfit	3.02	Old Olney [LAT 10 / LONG 26]	On the body of the dead Brotherhood of Steel Initiate.
#23	"Ol' Painless" Hunting Rifle	Weapon	3.03	The Republic of Dave [LAT 19 / LONG 27]	Carried by Dave.
#24	Torcher's Helmet	Outfit	4.03	MDPL Mass Relay Station [LAT -17 / LONG 10]	Carried by Torcher.
#25	Fawkes' Super Sledge	Weapon	4.06	Vault 87 [LAT -28 / LONG 06]	Carried by Fawkes.
#26	"Wazer Wifle" Laser Rifle	Weapon	4.08	Little Lamplight [LAT -26 / LONG 02]	Freeform Quest: Biwwy's Wazer Wifle
#27	"Occam's Razor" Combat Knife	Weapon	4.11	Fort Bannister [LAT -18 / LONG -01]	Taken from Commander Jabsco.
#28	"Victory Rifle" Sniper Rifle	Weapon	4.E	Abandoned Shack [LAT -23 / LONG 08]	In the shack locker, north of the Rockbreaker's Gas Station.
#29	Vance's Longcoat Outfit	Outfit	5.05	Meresti Trainyard [LAT -01 / LONG 07]	Worn by Vance, leader of the Family.
#30	"Vampire's Edge" Chinese Officer's Sword	Weapon	5.05	Meresti Trainyard [LAT -01 / LONG 07]	Miscellaneous Quest: Blood Ties: Inside Vance's sword cabinet.
#31	"Blackhawk" Scoped .44 Magnum	Weapon	5.06	Agatha's House [LAT 01 / LONG 08]	Miscellaneous Quest: Agatha's Song. Possible reward.
#32	Red's Bandana	Outfit	5.10	Big Town [LAT -04 / LONG 03]	Worn by Red.
#33	Timebomb's Lucky 8-Ball	Outfit	5.10	Big Town [LAT -04 / LONG 03]	Given by Timebomb if you heal him and complete Miscellaneous Quest: Big Trouble in Big Town.
#34	Makeshift Gas Mask	Outfit	5.12	Vault 106 [LAT -09 / LONG 01]	Science Labs, in the small room across the hallway from the larger "server" room.
#35	Makeshift Gas Mask	Outfit	5.12	Vault 106 [LAT -09 / LONG 01]	Science Labs, on the west end in a small connecting room near the cave section.
#36	"Xuanlong" Assault Rifle	Weapon	5.13	Jury Street Metro Station [LAT -10 / LONG -03]	On the body of Prime, in the diner.
#37	Wanderer's Leather Armor	Outfit	5.A	Wrecked Vehicles [LAT -13 / LONG 12]	On a Wanderer, just north of the wrecked vehicles.
#38	"Ant's Sting" Knife	Weapon	6.01	AntAgonizer's Lair [LAT 17 / LONG 12]	Miscellaneous Quest: The Superhuman Gambit. Possible reward.
#39	The AntAgonizer's Costume	Outfit	6.01	AntAgonizer's Lair [LAT 17 / LONG 12]	Miscellaneous Quest: The Superhuman Gambit. Possible reward.
#40	The AntAgonizer's Helmet	Outfit	6.01	AntAgonizer's Lair [LAT 17 / LONG 12]	Miscellaneous Quest: The Superhuman Gambit. Possible reward.
#41	"Highwayman's Friend" Tire Iron	Weapon	6.02	Canterbury Commons [LAT 18 / LONG 11]	In the garage.
#42	The Mechanist's Costume	Outfit	6.02	Canterbury Commons [LAT 18 / LONG 11]	Miscellaneous Quest: The Superhuman Gambit. Possible reward.
#43	The Mechanist's Helmet	Outfit	6.02	Canterbury Commons [LAT 18 / LONG 11]	Miscellaneous Quest: The Superhuman Gambit. Possible reward.
#44	"Protectron's Gaze" Laser Pistol	Weapon	6.02	Canterbury Commons [LAT 18 / LONG 11]	Miscellaneous Quest: The Superhuman Gambit. Possible reward.
#45	"Experimental MIRV" Fat Man	Weapon	6.11	National Guard Depot [LAT 18 / LONG -03]	Armory and Bunker: Inside armory, on table with Mini-Nukes.
#46	The Terrible Shotgun	Weapon	7.04	Evergreen Mills [LAT -18 / LONG -07]	Bazaar, carried by Jack.
#47	"The Kneecapper" Sawed-Off Shotgun	Weapon	7.05	Girdershade [LAT -26 / LONG -11]	Carried by Ronald Laren.
#48	Ghoul Mask	Outfit	7.14	Tenpenny Tower [LAT -16 / LONG -17]	Miscellaneous Quest: Tenpenny Tower. Possible reward.
#49	Lucky Shades	Outfit	7.R	Lucky's Grocer [LAT -18 / LONG -20]	Inside the store.
#50	"Butch's Toothpick" Switchblade	Weapon	8.01	Vault 101 [LAT -04 / LONG -04]	On the body of Butch.
#51	Sheriff's Duster	Outfit	8.03	Megaton [LAT -01 / LONG -06]	Worn by Sheriff Lucas Simms.
#52	Sheriff's Hat	Outfit	8.03	Megaton [LAT -01 / LONG -06]	Worn by Sheriff Lucas Simms.
#53	Armored Vault 101 Jumpsuit	Outfit	8.03	Megaton [LAT -01 / LONG -06]	Miscellaneous Quest: The Wasteland Survival Guide. Reward from Moira.
#54	Shady Hat	Outfit	8.03	Megaton [LAT -01 / LONG -06]	Craterside Supplies: Awarded by Moira Brown. Miscellaneous Quest: The Wasteland Survival Guide.
#55	"Miss Launcher" Missile Launcher	Weapon	8.04	Fort Independence [LAT -06 / LONG -13]	Small southwest room on the lower level, adjacent to the high galley area.
#56	Goalie Ledoux's Hockey Mask	Outfit	8.08	Red Racer Factory [LAT 02 / LONG -15]	Just outside the factory, worn by the mercenary; accessed during Freeform Quest: Just for the Taste of It.
#57	Giant Teddy Bear	Other	8.08	Red Racer Factory [LAT 02 / LONG -15]	Factory floor, southern conveyor belt room, riding tricycle, suspended from ceiling.
#58	The Surgeon's Lab Coat	Outfit	8.08	Red Racer Factory [LAT 02 / LONG -15]	Worn by the Surgeon.
#59	"The Tenderizer" Sledgehammer	Weapon	9.06	Anchorage Memorial [LAT 10 / LONG -07]	Service entrance, sewers utility door. Repair or use Anchorage Stash Key to open.
#60	Elder Lyons' Robe	Outfit	9.11	The Citadel [LAT 08 / LONG -14]	Worn by Elder Lyons.
#61	"Smuggler's End" Laser Pistol	Weapon	9.11	The Citadel [LAT 08 / LONG -14]	B-Ring, in Elder Lyons' safe.
#62	Colonel Autumn's 10mm Pistol	Weapon	9.14	Jefferson Memorial [LAT 13 / LONG -17]	Main Quest: Take It Back! Rotunda, during final attack.
#63	Colonel Autumn's Laser Pistol	Weapon	9.14	Jefferson Memorial [LAT 13 / LONG -17]	Main Quest: Take It Back! Rotunda, during final attack.
#64	Colonel Autumn's Uniform	Outfit	9.14	Jefferson Memorial [LAT 13 / LONG -17]	Main Quest: Take It Back! Rotunda, during final attack.
#65	A3-21's Plasma Rifle	Weapon	9.15	Rivet City [LAT 18 / LONG -17]	Miscellaneous Quest: The Replicated Man. Reward from Harkness.
#66	Three Dog's Head Wrap	Outfit	10.03	Galaxy News Radio	Worn by Three Dog.
#67	Takoma Park Little Leaguer Cap	Outfit	13.02	NiftyThrifty	On hat-stand inside the store.
#68	"Plunkett's Valid Points" Spiked Knuckles	Weapon	16.03	Arlington House	Carried by Junders Plunkett.
#69	Lincoln's Diary	Other	17.07	Museum of History	Lower halls, upper floor, on a wrecked display (west).
#70	"Action Abe" Action Figure	Other	17.07	Museum of History	Offices, southwest armory, on a desk.
#71	Lincoln's Hat	Outfit	17.07	Museum of History	Offices, among the large rubble pile in the northwest room.
#72	John Wilkes Booth Wanted Poster	Other	17.07	Museum of History	Offices, southwest corner of archives.
#73	Civil War Draft Poster	Other	17.07	Museum of History	Offices, southeast corner of archives.
#74	Lincoln Memorial Poster	Other	17.07	Museum of History	Offices, during Miscellaneous Quest: Head of State, on wall above upper floor desk in archives.
#75	Lincoln's Voice	Other	17.07	Museum of History	Offices, on upper floor desk in archives.
#76	Lincoln's Repeater	Weapon	17.07	Museum of History	Offices, rear archives area, inside display case.
#77	Antique Lincoln Coin Collection	Other	17.07	Museum of History	Offices, west library room, on bookcase.
#78	Bill of Rights	Other	17.11	The National Archives	Archives Secure Wing East, inside Secure Vault #1.
#79	Magna Carta	Other	17.11	The National Archives	Archives Secure Wing East, inside Secure Vault #2.
#80	Button's Wig	Outfit	17.11	The National Archives	Worn by Button Gwinnett.
#81	Declaration of Independence	Other	17.11	The National Archives	Archives Secure Wing East, inside Button's Secure Vault.

APPENDICES

COMPLETION — TOUR — MISC. QUESTS — MAIN QUEST — BESTIARY — TRAINING

Appendix 5: Unique Weapons and Outfits (continued)

#	NAME	TYPE	ZONE	LOCATION	NOTES
#82	[Fake] Declaration of Independence	Other	17.11	The National Archives	Archives Secure Wing East, given by Button once Freeform Quest: An Ink to the Past is complete.
#83	Sydney's 10mm "Ultra" SMG	Weapon	17.11	The National Archives (front entrance)	Miscellaneous Quest: Stealing Independence. Carried by Sydney.
#84	Ranger Battle Armor	Outfit	18.05	Reilly's Rangers Compound	Miscellaneous Quest: Reilly's Rangers. Possible reward.
#85	"Eugene" Minigun	Weapon	18.05	Reilly's Rangers Compound	Miscellaneous Quest: Reilly's Rangers. Possible reward.

#	NAME	TYPE	ZONE	LOCATION	NOTES
#86	"Zhu-Rong v418" Chinese Pistol	Weapon	19.06	L.O.B. Enterprises	East Wing, inside case in CEO's office.
#87	Lesko's Lab Coat	Outfit	U16.A	Marigold Station	Worn by Doctor Lesko.
#88	"Burnmaster" Flamer	Weapon	U17.B	Franklin Metro Utility	Irradiated and gutted subway car.
#89	"The Shocker" Power Fist	Weapon	U19	Flooded Metro	Inside the trap-filled storage chamber.

APPENDIX 6: NUKA-COLA QUANTUMS (94)

The first time you activate each of the 178 Nuka-Cola vending machines, there's a 10 percent chance it will deposit a Nuka-Cola Quantum.

#	ZONE	LOCATION	NOTES
#01	0.34	Wasteland Mini-Encounter: Quantum Sales Pitch	Sold by a wandering merchant for more than market value, along with directions to Girdershade.
#02	1.04	Fort Constantine [LAT -17 / LONG 26]	Commanding officer's quarters at base of open fridge.
#03	1.07	Deathclaw Sanctuary [LAT -22 / LONG 20]	Amid pile of animal remains, near shaft of light.
#04	1.16	Roosevelt Academy [LAT -17 / LONG 14]	Main lobby entrance, on a desk just below the wall First Aid Box.
#05	1.B	Brotherhood Outcast Shack [LAT -14 / LONG 25]	On the corner of the roof.
#06	2.01	Oasis [LAT -03 / LONG 28]	Damp cave, northeastern lake bank, amid a small amount of debris.
#07	2.08	Paradise Falls [LAT -09 / LONG 16]	Eulogy's Pad, stash behind the stone stairs.
#08	2.08	Paradise Falls [LAT -09 / LONG 16]	Eulogy's Pad, stash behind the stone stairs.
#09	2.08	Paradise Falls [LAT -09 / LONG 16]	Eulogy's Pad, stash behind the stone stairs.
#10	2.08	Paradise Falls [LAT -09 / LONG 16]	Eulogy's Pad, stash behind the stone stairs.
#11	2.08	Paradise Falls [LAT -09 / LONG 16]	Eulogy's Pad, stash behind the stone stairs.
#12	2.09	MDPL-13 Power Station [LAT 02 / LONG 17]	Inside the power station, on a Work Bench.
#13	2.E	Abandoned Tent [LAT -12 / LONG 23]	Northeast corner, by the ham radio.
#14	3.01	Vault 92 [LAT 08 / LONG 27]	Living quarters, lower area, on a table by a termina .
#15	3.02	Old Olney [LAT 10 / LONG 26]	Sewers, eastern area, small bloody sleeping quarters off the main sewer passage.
#16	3.03	The Republic of Dave [LAT 19 / LONG 27]	Capitol Building, on a corner safe by Dave's throne.
#17	3.05	MDPL-16 Power Station [LAT 18 / LONG 24]	Inside the power station, on a Work Bench.
#18	3.06	Greener Pastures Disposal Site [LAT 07 / LONG 21]	Office, on desk to the right of the entrance.
#19	3.E	Red Rocket Gas Station and Jackknifed Truck [LAT 13 / LONG 25]	Back of the container truck.
#20	3.E	Red Rocket Gas Station and Jackknifed Truck [LAT 13 / LONG 25]	Back of the container truck.
#21	3.E	Red Rocket Gas Station and Jackknifed Truck [LAT 13 / LONG 25]	Back of the container truck.
#22	3.E	Red Rocket Gas Station and Jackknifed Truck [LAT 13 / LONG 25]	Back of the container truck.
#23	3.I	Irradiated Outhouse [LAT 15 / LONG 23]	In the bathtub.
#24	4.03	MDPL Mass Relay Station [LAT -17 / LONG 10]	Inside the locked [Very Hard] interior safe.
#25	4.05	Rockbreaker's Last Gas [LAT -21 / LONG 08]	On top of a Nuka-Cola vending machine.
#26	4.06	Vault 87 [LAT -28 / LONG 06]	Living quarters, southern area on shelving in the storage room.
#27	4.08	Little Lamplight [LAT -26 / LONG 02]	Metal bunker storage, in the middle of the tunnel.
#28	4.09	Jalbert Brothers Waste Disposal [LAT -18 / LONG 03]	Office, on desk to the right of the entrance.
#29	4.10	VAPL-58 Power Station [LAT -14 / LONG 03]	Inside the power station, on a Work Bench.
#30	4.11	Fort Bannister [LAT -18 / LONG -01]	Commanding officer's quarters, behind corrugated metal, under the stairs.
#31	4.I	Jackknifed Truck [LAT -20 / LONG 04]	Waste disposal truck, among the barrels.
#32	4.N	Scavenger Ruin [LAT -22 / LONG -02]	Northwest corner in small crate.
#33	5.01	Germantown Police Headquarters [LAT -02 / LONG 13]	Storage room in the basement, just off the kitchen.
#34	5.03	Hamilton's Hideaway [LAT -07 / LONG 07]	In the Raiders' hideout room, in small crate on the desk.
#35	5.13	Jury Street Metro Station [LAT -10 / LONG -03]	Mole Rat laboratory, on a desk by the terminal.
#36	5.14	Springvale School [LAT -01 / LONG -01]	Interior, on top of a central cage, by headless corpse on the mattress.
#37	5.E	Power Transformers [LAT 02 / LONG 11]	Under the pylon, by the skeleton and chair.
#38	5.N	South Arefu Pier [LAT -10 / LONG 05]	Wooden buttress, stacked on top of two tin cans.
#39	5.U	Brahmin Skull Shack [LAT -13 / LONG 02]	On the floor, behind a billboard, just southeast of VAPL-58 Power Station.
#40	5.DD	North Pier [LAT 03 / LONG -01]	Potomac Mirelurk nest, underwater, near isolated bridge section.
#41	6.01	AntAgonizer's Lair [LAT 17 / LONG 12]	To the side of the AntAgonizer's Throne.
#42	6.06	Vault 108 [LAT 18 / LONG 06]	In entrance level storage closet, behind some stacked crates.

#	ZONE	LOCATION	NOTES
#43	6.07	Bethesda Ruins [LAT 05 / LONG 03]	Underworks, inside "pillar" style storage room.
#44	6.08	Chryslus Building [LAT 08 / LONG -01]	Derelict room, through hole in wall, south of reception entrance.
#45	6.09	Rock Creek Caverns [LAT 16 / LONG -02]	In a box on some planks, near a half-buried Ammo Box and First Aid Box.
#46	6.11	National Guard Depot [LAT 18 / LONG -03]	Armory, dirt corridor, under table where Unique Fat Man is.
#47	6.A	Regulator Headquarters [LAT 09 / LONG 11]	In locker on northwest corner of the building, near a bathtub.
#48	6.5	Bethesda Coach Station [LAT 10 / LONG 00]	North end of the nearby freeway skeleton, above the Red Racer Gas.
#49	7.01	Yao Guai Tunnels [LAT -28 / LONG -04]	Northern tunnel, on a small table surrounded by small junk and debris.
#50	7.03	Smith Casey's Garage [LAT -22 / LONG -08]	Northwest corner of the room, by a small crate.
#51	7.04	Evergreen Mills [LAT -18 / LONG -07]	Bazaar, southern area, in small crate behind bar.
#52	7.07	Jocko's Pop & Gas Stop [LAT -22 / LONG -12]	Inside the shack, on the back shelf behind the counter.
#53	7.11	Dunwich Building [LAT -26 / LONG -18]	Storage room north and east from main entrance.
#54	7.13	Warrington Station (Exterior) [LAT -18 / LONG -19]	Roy Phillips's Ghoul hidey-hole, between two metal boxes.
#55	7.R	Lucky's Grocer [LAT -18 / LONG -20]	Cooler at back of store.
#56	8.04	Fort Independence [LAT -06 / LONG -13]	Table in the living quarters south of the stairwell.
#57	8.06	Cliffside Cavern [LAT -10 / LONG -17]	Raider Outpost, southern area, on table between generators.
#58	8.08	Red Racer Factory [LAT 02 / LONG -15]	CEO offices, in the cell with Stefan, the Glowing One.
#59	8.10	Nuka-Cola Plant [LAT -01 / LONG -19]	On the packing line, after activating the packing terminal.
#60	8.10	Nuka-Cola Plant [LAT -01 / LONG -19]	On the packing line, after activating the packing terminal.
#61	8.10	Nuka-Cola Plant [LAT -01 / LONG -19]	On the packing line, after activating the packing terminal.
#62	8.U	Overturned Truck [LAT -05 / LONG -15]	At the far end of overturned truck container, under a freeway section.
#63	8.AA	Parked Nuka-Cola Trucks and Drainage Outlet [LAT -02 / LONG -19]	Loose inside of the container.
#64	9.01	Super-Duper Mart [LAT 04 / LONG -04]	Pharmacy locked storage, north shelves, inside small crates on the floor.
#65	9.01	Super-Duper Mart [LAT 04 / LONG -04]	Pharmacy locked storage, north shelves, inside small crates on the floor.
#66	9.01	Super-Duper Mart [LAT 04 / LONG -04]	Pharmacy locked storage, north shelves, inside small crates on the floor.
#67	9.03	Sewer Waystation [LAT 04 / LONG -08]	Just inside in a door-less fridge, by skeleton, on the west wall.
#68	9.06	Anchorage Memorial [LAT 10 / LONG -07]	Repair the door. Inside a small sewer storage room.
#69	9.08	Dukov's Place [LAT 11 / LONG -08]	Dukov's bedroom, on shelving behind his bed.
#70	9.13	Alexandria Arms [LAT 07 / LONG -17]	Second floor, locked room behind the desk, adjacent to recreation area.
#71	9.18	Arlington Library [LAT 08 / LONG -19]	Media Archives, on a small table behind two skulls, upper floor media room.
#72	9.I	Outpost [LAT 04 / LONG -11]	Small chamber with flaming barrel, in small crate by desk.
#73	9.T	Flooded Metro Raider Camp [LAT 04 / LONG -19]	In small crate on top of shelves, near central desk.
#74	12.02	Vault-Tec Headquarters	Corporate office level (second floor), in a northern rubble-filled room, on a shelf.
#75	12.08	The Statesman Hotel	Alfresco Lounge, just before you reach the roof, on a low shelf behind the bar in the middle.
#76	13.04	Takoma Industrial Factory	In the corner, above an alcove with a generator on it; use planks to access.
#77	14.08	La Maison Beauregard Lobby	At the top of the dirt pile, behind the balcony bar.
#78	14.C	Pulowski Preservation Shelter	Georgetown, in alley near Cornucopia Fresh Groceries.
#79	16.05	Mama Dolce's Processed Foods	Second floor office, southeast area, to the right of the terminal.
#80	17.01	Lincoln Memorial	Maintenance Room (Leroy Walker's Slaver base), on eastern wall shelving.
#81	17.03	Mirelurk Nesting Hole	Stuck in dirt near old crates and a ham radio, far upper area of southwest corner.

Appendix 6: Nuka-Cola Quantums (continued)

#	ZONE	LOCATION	NOTES
#82	17.07	Museum of History	Lower halls, alcove in the southeast corner, in small crate under table.
#83	17.10	Museum of Technology	On shelf in Planetarium Research office.
#84	17.14	Capitol Building	East entrance, behind coffee machine, sitting room off side corridor.
#85	19.06	L.O.B. Enterprises	First floor (ground), wedged between some old shelves.
#86	20.01	Hubris Comics Publishing	Printing area, on desk in the foreman's office balcony, by Mad Johnny Wes.
#87	U01.B	Tenleytown / Friendship Station	On a bench on upper mezzanine platform near newsstand.

#	ZONE	LOCATION	NOTES
#88	U03	Vernon East / Takoma Park	Rubble-filled western connecting chamber, on a metal shelf.
#89	U06.C	Foggy Bottom Station	Connecting corridor, behind gate, between two small generators.
#90	U13	County Sewer Mainline	Gallo's Hideaway, inside the safe near his terminal [Average]
#91	U16.B	Queen Ant's Hatchery	On desk near terminal and Inhibitor Pulse unit.
#92	U17.B	Franklin Metro Utility	In the irradiated and gutted subway car.
#93	U18.B	Taft Tunnel	Southern area, on a rotting picnic bench.
#94	U19	Flooded Metro	Northwestern area, top of cabinet in small storage room off the sewer passageway.

APPENDIX 7: SCHEMATICS: CUSTOM WEAPONS (23)

#	SCHEMATIC # & TYPE	ZONE	LOCATION	NOTES
#01	#1 Rock-It Launcher	0.00	Wasteland Mini-Encounter: Merchant Trader Caravan	Sold by (or in the inventory of) Crazy Wolfgang.
#02	#1 Nuka Grenade	0.00	Wasteland Mini-Encounter: Merchant Trader Caravan	Sold by (or in the inventory of) Doc Hoff.
#03	#1 Shishkebab	0.00	Wasteland Mini-Encounter: Merchant Trader Caravan	Sold by (or in the inventory of) Lucky Harith.
#04	#1 Deathclaw Gauntlet	0.13	Mini-Encounter: Wounded Deathclaw	On wounded Wastelander.
#05	#1 Dart Gun	1.02	MDPL-05 Power Station [LAT -27 / LONG 25]	On ground, near skeleton.
#06	#2 Shishkebab	1.B	Brotherhood Outcast Shack [LAT -14 / LONG 25]	On a table, near a Work Bench, close to SatCom Array NN-03d.
#07	#1 Railway Rifle	2.09	MDPL-13 Power Station [LAT 02 / LONG 17]	Inside, on Work Bench.
#08	#2 Dart Gun	3.10	Temple of the Union [LAT 13 / LONG 15]	Miscellaneous Quest: Head of State. Possible reward (usually given at 17.01 Lincoln Memorial).
#09	#1 Bottlecap Mine	4.08	Little Lamplight [LAT -26 / LONG 02]	Sold by (or in the inventory of) Knick Knack.
#10	#3 Shishkebab	5.05	Meresti Trainyard [LAT -01 / LONG 07]	Miscellaneous Quest: Blood Ties. Possible reward.
#11	#2 Nuka Grenade	7.05	Girdershade [LAT -26 / LONG -11]	Miscellaneous Quest: The Nuka-Cola Challenge. Possible reward.
#12	#2 Bottlecap Mine	7.07	Jocko's Pop & Gas Stop [LAT -22 / LONG -12]	On the Work Bench, inside the shack.
#13	#2 Deathclaw Gauntlet	7.09	F. Scott Key Trail & Campground [LAT -27 / LONG -15]	In the caravan, in the picnic area.
#14	#3 Dart Gun	7.14	Tenpenny Tower [LAT -16 / LONG -17]	Sold by Lydia Montenegro.
#15	#3 Bottlecap Mine	7.14	Tenpenny Tower [LAT -16 / LONG -17]	Freeform Quest: A Manhandled Manservant. Inside Dashwood's Safe.
#16	#2 Rock-It Launcher	8.01	Vault 101 [LAT -04 / LONG -04]	Miscellaneous Quest: Trouble on the Homefront. Behind your mother's favorite Bible verse plaque [Average].
#17	#3 Rock-It Launcher	8.03	Megaton [LAT -01 / LONG -06]	Craterside Supplies, sold by (or in the inventory of) Moira Brown.
#18	#4 Bottlecap Mine	8.03	Megaton [LAT -01 / LONG -06]	Craterside Supplies, awarded by Moira Brown. Miscellaneous Quest: The Wasteland Survival Guide.
#19	#3 Nuka Grenade	8.06	Cliffside Cavern [LAT -10 / LONG -17]	Hidden inside the Yao Guai Cave, follow the left wall, drop down, and look for the rock surrounded by skeletons.
#20	#4 Rock-It Launcher	9.15	Rivet City [LAT 18 / LONG -17]	In the bridge tower third-floor armory [Very Hard].
#21	#3 Deathclaw Gauntlet	9.15	Rivet City [LAT 18 / LONG -17]	Freeform Quest: Council Seat. Possible reward (from Bannon).
#22	#2 Railway Rifle	9.15	Rivet City [LAT 18 / LONG -17]	Miscellaneous Quest: Stealing Independence. Possible reward (from Abraham Washington).
#23	#3 Railway Rifle	17.07	Museum of History Entrance	Underworld Outfitters, sold by Tulip.

APPENDIX 8: SCRIBE PRE-WAR BOOKS (98)

#	ZONE	LOCATION	NOTES
#01	1.04	Fort Constantine [LAT -17 / LONG 26]	CO quarters, front room, on top of the fallen bookcase.
#02	1.04	Fort Constantine [LAT -17 / LONG 26]	CO quarters, on the telephone table near the bed.
#03	1.04	Fort Constantine [LAT -17 / LONG 26]	Launch control bunker, lower sleeping quarters, on a desk.
#04	1.06	Broadcast Tower KB5 [LAT -23 / LONG 20]	Drainage channel, on metal shelving in storage room.
#05	1.16	Roosevelt Academy [LAT -17 / LONG 14]	Academy, headmaster's room.
#06	1.16	Roosevelt Academy [LAT -17 / LONG 14]	Arts and Athletics Hall, on the shelf in the small room at the north end of the building, lower level.
#07	2.01	Oasis [LAT -03 / LONG 28]	Sunken Caverns, at the end of the side tunnel near the dead Scavenger.
#08	2.04	Clifftop Shacks [LAT 00 / LONG 26]	On a small table near the skeleton on the bed.
#09	2.08	Paradise Falls [LAT -09 / LONG 18]	Adult slave house, on corner table.
#10	3.01	Vault 92 [LAT 08 / LONG 27]	Entrance, utility, and atrium, by "cog" door, among rusting terminals.
#11	3.01	Vault 92 [LAT 08 / LONG 27]	Overseer's office, on a large bookcase.
#12	3.01	Vault 92 [LAT 08 / LONG 27]	Sound testing, maintenance/storage area, among ruined books behind the counter.
#13	3.01	Vault 92 [LAT 08 / LONG 27]	Sound testing, server room to the east, next to Zoe's terminal.
#14	3.01	Vault 92 [LAT 08 / LONG 27]	Sound testing, in the kitchen / recreation room, on a table.
#15	3.03	The Republic of Dave [LAT 19 / LONG 27]	Museum of Dave, on the bookcase.
#16	3.03	The Republic of Dave [LAT 19 / LONG 27]	Museum of Dave, on the bookcase.
#17	3.08	Relay Tower KX-B8-11 [LAT 15 / LONG 20]	Radio alcove, through hatch door, near Medicine Skill Book.
#18	3.09	Minefield [LAT 04 / LONG 14]	Gillian house, upstairs, front room.
#19	3.09	Minefield [LAT 04 / LONG 14]	Gillian house, upstairs, front room.
#20	3.09	Minefield [LAT 04 / LONG 14]	Gibson house, front room, on the table.
#21	3.09	Minefield [LAT 04 / LONG 14]	Gibson house, upstairs, kid's room.
#22	3.09	Minefield [LAT 04 / LONG 14]	Gibson house, upstairs, master bedroom near the bed.
#23	3.09	Minefield [LAT 04 / LONG 14]	Gibson house, upstairs, master bedroom, ensuite bathtub.
#24	3.09	Minefield [LAT 04 / LONG 14]	Benson house, living room atop the shelves.
#25	3.09	Minefield [LAT 04 / LONG 14]	Benson house, master bedroom, on a table.
#26	3.09	Minefield [LAT 04 / LONG 14]	Zone house, atop the book shelves.
#27	3.10	Temple of the Union [LAT 13 / LONG 15]	Inside Caleb's home.
#28	E3.04	Enclave Camp [LAT 11 / LONG 14]	Sometimes located with or on the Enclave troops dropped on the bridge by a Vertibird.
#29	4.04	Broadcast Tower KT8 [LAT -26 / LONG 09]	Drainage Chamber, small, corrugated metal room.
#30	4.04	Broadcast Tower KT8 [LAT -26 / LONG 09]	Drainage Chamber, small, corrugated metal room.
#31	4.E	Abandoned Shack [LAT -23 / LONG 08]	Inside the shack.
#32	4.K	Wastelander Pylon [LAT -14 / LONG 05]	With the other items, near a mattress.
#33	4.N	Scavenger Ruin [LAT -22 / LONG -02]	On the table.
#34	4.N	Scavenger Ruin [LAT -22 / LONG -02]	On the table.
#35	5.01	Germantown Police Headquarters [LAT -02 / LONG 13]	Ground floor, cells next to the lockdown terminal.
#36	5.A	Wrecked Vehicles [LAT -13 / LONG 12]	Raider's Jetty to the north, with other items.
#37	6.07	Bethesda Ruins [LAT 05 / LONG 03]	West offices, up the stairs, in room to the west, on the cabinets.
#38	6.07	Bethesda Ruins [LAT 05 / LONG 03]	West offices, up the stairs, in room to the west, on the cabinets.
#39	6.08	Chryslus Building [LAT 08 / LONG -01]	Lower offices, final locked door to the south, in the mail room.
#40	6.11	National Guard Depot [LAT 18 / LONG -03]	Bookshelf on the east wall, third floor.
#41	6.11	National Guard Depot [LAT 18 / LONG -03]	Bookshelf on the east wall, third floor.
#42	6.11	National Guard Depot [LAT 18 / LONG -03]	Training Wing, offices full of junk and debris, on shelves above a wall safe.
#43	6.11	National Guard Depot [LAT 18 / LONG -03]	Offices, upper floor, on a shelf connected to large central pillar, above hole in floor.
#44	6.11	National Guard Depot [LAT 18 / LONG -03]	Offices, upper floor, on a shelf connected to large central pillar, above hole in floor.
#45	6.11	National Guard Depot [LAT 18 / LONG -03]	Offices, upper floor, on a shelf connected to large central pillar, above hole in floor.
#46	7.01	Yao Guai Tunnels [LAT -28 / LONG -04]	On a picnic table.
#47	7.10	RobCo Facility [LAT -14 / LONG -15]	Factory floor, entrance foyer, on shelves above large desk.
#48	7.10	RobCo Facility [LAT -14 / LONG -15]	Factory floor, on the console in the room with the Protectron Pod.
#49	7.10	RobCo Facility [LAT -14 / LONG -15]	Offices and cafeteria, mainframe chamber.
#50	7.A	Broadcast Tower PN [LAT -24 / LONG -04]	Drainage Chamber, by the exit ladder.
#51	8.03	Megaton [LAT -01 / LONG -06]	Billy Creel's house, downstairs on a table.
#52	8.03	Megaton [LAT -01 / LONG -06]	Billy Creel's house, downstairs on a table.
#53	8.03	Megaton [LAT -01 / LONG -06]	Billy Creel's house, downstairs on a table.
#54	8.03	Megaton [LAT -01 / LONG -06]	Billy Creel's house, upstairs on a table.
#55	8.06	Cliffside Cavern [LAT -10 / LONG -17]	Raider Outpost, inside the tent.
#56	8.C	Drainage Chamber [LAT -11 / LONG -04]	Drainage Chamber, on the radio table.
#57	8.L	Independence Hamlet [LAT -11 / LONG -09]	On the Scavenger's table.
#58	9.06	Anchorage Memorial [LAT 10 / LONG -07]	Facility, upper floor, in the Wastelander research laboratory.
#59	9.06	Anchorage Memorial [LAT 10 / LONG -07]	Facility, upper floor, in the Wastelander research laboratory.
#60	9.06	Anchorage Memorial [LAT 10 / LONG -07]	Facility: Upper floor, in the Wastelander research laboratory.

Appendix 8: Scribe Pre-War Books (continued)

#	ZONE	LOCATION	NOTES
#61	9.13	Alexandria Arms [LAT 07 / LONG -17]	In the two-level recreation room.
#62	9.18	Arlington Library [LAT 08 / LONG -19]	Lobby, in the upper balcony bookcases.
#63	9.18	Arlington Library [LAT 08 / LONG -19]	Lobby, in the upper balcony bookcases.
#64	9.18	Arlington Library [LAT 08 / LONG -19]	Lobby, in the upper balcony bookcases.
#65	9.18	Arlington Library [LAT 08 / LONG -19]	Media Archive, on a conveyor belt in the northeastern edge of this floor.
#66	9.18	Arlington Library [LAT 08 / LONG -19]	Media Archive, south media room.
#67	9.18	Arlington Library [LAT 08 / LONG -19]	Children's Wing, skeletal cage room and floor holes.
#68	9.18	Arlington Library [LAT 08 / LONG -19]	Children's Wing, skeletal cage room and floor holes.
#69	9.18	Arlington Library [LAT 08 / LONG -19]	Children's Wing, skeletal cage room and floor holes.
#70	9.18	Arlington Library [LAT 08 / LONG -19]	Children's Wing, coffee machine nook.
#71	9.18	Arlington Library [LAT 08 / LONG -19]	Children's Wing, northwest office.
#72	11.C	Raider Outpost	Upper floor open-air room, on a bookcase.
#73	12.02	Vault-Tec Headquarters	Corporate offices, on a trash bin, in the lower level of the large room to the northwest.
#74	12.07	Our Lady of Hope Hospital	On the cafeteria coffee counter.
#75	16.05	Mama Dolce's Processed Foods	Upstairs foreman's office (with escaping gas), near a Sledgehammer.
#76	16.05	Mama Dolce's Processed Foods	Food distribution, third floor, captain's office near a desk terminal.
#77	17.11	The National Archives	Scattered on a tipped-over shelf bank in the northwest archives area.
#78	17.11	The National Archives	Scattered on a tipped-over shelf bank in the northwest archives area.
#79	17.11	The National Archives	Scattered on a tipped-over shelf bank in the northwest archives area.
#80	17.11	The National Archives	Scattered on a tipped-over shelf bank in the northwest archives area.
#81	17.11	The National Archives	Scattered on a tipped-over shelf bank in the southwest archives area.
#82	17.14	Capitol Building	East entrance, in a cubicle with a Skill Book, in the long room.
#83	19.06	L.O.B. Enterprises	East Wing, upper floor to the north, on a desk with an R&D terminal.
#84	19.06	L.O.B. Enterprises	East Wing, upper floor to the north, on a desk with an R&D terminal.
#85	20.01	Hubris Comics Publishing	Northwest corner of the foyer, on a debris pile.
#86	20.01	Hubris Comics Publishing	Downstairs to the west, in the office to the north.
#87	U01A	Farragut West Station	Hatch door [Average] to weapons cache.
#88	U01A	Farragut West Station	Hatch door [Average] to weapons cache.
#89	U01A	Farragut West Station	Hatch door [Average] to weapons cache.
#90	U05	Tepid Sewer	Raider sleeping quarters.
#91	U05	Tepid Sewer	Hidden in a small closet in the center of this area, in a room with a First Aid Box, lockers, and a set of shelves, with several burned books in a tiny crate.
#92	U13	County Sewer Mainline	In Gallo's hideaway.
#93	U13	County Sewer Mainline	In Gallo's hideaway.
#94	U13	County Sewer Mainline	The room beyond the sewer management room.
#95	U13	County Sewer Mainline	The room beyond the sewer management room.
#96	U17.A	Falls Church / Mason Dst Metro	Raider camp, in the diner.
#97	U17.B	Franklin Metro Utility	On a shelf near the dumpsters; drop down from the workshop, or use the catwalk stairs to climb up.
#98	U17.B	Franklin Metro Utility	On a shelf near the dumpsters; drop down from the workshop, or use the catwalk stairs to climb up.

APPENDIX 9: SKILL BOOK: TALES OF A JUNKTOWN JERKY VENDOR [BARTER] (24)

#	ZONE	LOCATION	NOTES
#01	1.14	Abandoned Car Fort [LAT -24 / LONG 14]	Near mattress and tiny crate.
#02	2.07	Reclining Groves Resort Homes [LAT -02 / LONG 20]	Northeast house, on some shelves.
#03	3.01	Vault 92 [LAT 08 / LONG 27]	Vault 92 Entrance: Gordie Sumner's store and weapons repository.
#04	3.07	Grisly Diner [LAT 13 / LONG 20]	Behind the counter, on a shelf.
#05	E3.04	Enclave Camp [LAT 11 / LONG 14]	Sometimes located with or on the Enclave troops dropped on the bridge by a Vertibird.
#06	4.08	Little Lamplight [LAT -26 / LONG 02]	U4.08.3 Murder Pass, eastern cave shack, on top of toilet.
#07	4.J	Wasteland Gypsy Village [LAT -18 / LONG 06]	Shack near picnic table, inside on a table.
#08	6.07	Bethesda Ruins [LAT 05 / LONG 03]	Underworks, top of mezzanine, on stone bench near the skeleton and baby carriage near the phone booths, on a bucket.
#09	6.11	National Guard Depot [LAT 18 / LONG -03]	Depot Training Wing, on a desk in a debris-filled office.
#10	6.M	Bethesda Suburbs [LAT 09 / LONG 03]	Raider Shack: Inside, on master bedroom table.
#11	7.14	Tenpenny Tower [LAT -16 / LONG -17]	Tenpenny Suites, northeast room, Susan Lancaster's suite (on desk).†

Appendix 9: Skill Book [Barter] (continued)

#	ZONE	LOCATION	NOTES
#12	7.14	Tenpenny Tower [LAT -16 / LONG -17]	Tenpenny Suites, northeast room, Susan Lancaster's suite (on desk).†
#13	7.S	Willy's Grocer [LAT -14 / LONG -18]	Inside, by the counter.
#14	8.V	The Concrete Treehouse [LAT -03 / LONG -15]	Near mattress, up on the treehouse floor.
#15	9.01	Super-Duper Mart [LAT 04 / LONG -04]	Area near the storage room terminal.
#16	9.18	Arlington Library [LAT 08 / LONG -19]	Media Archive, in the pool table recreation room.
#17	11.06	Lady Frumperton's Fashions	Near the counter, on top of a floor safe.
#18	12.02	Vault-Tec Headquarters	Guest Relations, northwest balcony area, on table (take before dropping down to exit).
#19	12.08	The Statesman Hotel	Lobby, upstairs bedroom to the northeast, on a desk.
#20	16.H	Container Truck	Near the truck, inside a barrel-filled container, by a dead Wastelander.
#21	17.11	The National Archives	Button Gwinnett's strongroom.
#22	17.14	Capitol Building	East entrance, on cubicle desk, in front of long cabinet row.
#23	20.01	Hubris Comics Publishing	Rear of the foyer desk, on a shelf above the dummy terminal.
#24	U13	County Sewer Mainline	On Gallo the Ghoul's corpse.

† There is a Skill Book at this location prior to a Ghoul invasion, and after the lights go out. To obtain both, claim the first book and then cause the Ghouls to break into the tower, as part of Miscellaneous Quest: Tenpenny Tower.

APPENDIX 10: SKILL BOOK: *U.S. ARMY: 30 HANDY FLAMETHROWER RECIPES* [BIG GUNS] (25)

#	ZONE	LOCATION	NOTES
#01	2.J	Irradiated Silo and Barn [LAT 00 / LONG 20]	Hillside to the northeast, near body of dead Mercenary.
#02	3.H	Jackknifed Truck (on Freeway) [LAT 13 / LONG 23]	Front end of a wrecked coach liner, near on-ramp.
#03	4.02	Five Axles Rest Stop [LAT -21 / LONG 10]	Inside one of the truck containers.
#04	4.08	Little Lamplight [LAT -26 / LONG 02]	U4.08.3 Murder Pass, dead end, on western side of rope bridge.
#05	4.10	VAPL-58 Power Station [LAT -14 / LONG 03]	Wasteland (PS04) -14, 3. On the roof, access via the interior, and the hatch in the southeast corner. By the barbecue near the two chairs.
#06	6.03	Scrapyard [LAT 05 / LONG 09]	Inside John's Treasure Box (northwestern exterior).
#07	6.04	Wheaton Armory [LAT 10 / LONG 08]	Inside irradiated inner locked chamber [Very Hard], with weapon cache.
#08	6.07	Bethesda Ruins [LAT 05 / LONG 03]	Bethesda Offices East, raider boss, with Flamer.
#09	6.11	National Guard Depot [LAT 18 / LONG -03]	Armory and Bunker, inside armory, on table with Fat Man and Mini-Nukes.
#10	6.P	Jackknifed Truck (under Monorail) [LAT 16 / LONG 02]	Irradiated weapons cache in the back of the truck.
#11	7.04	Evergreen Mills [LAT -18 / LONG -07]	Southern shack, in the bedroom.
#12	8.I	Jackknifed Truck [LAT -12 / LONG -07]	Inside truck container.
#13	8.Q	Car Dealership [LAT -01 / LONG -12]	Interior, northeast corner of raised area.
#14	8.X	Dot's Diner [LAT -01 / LONG -16]	Behind the counter.
#15	8.Z	Raider Camp [LAT 03 / LONG -16]	Old Scavenger's hut, near the mattress.
#16	9.06	Anchorage Memorial [LAT 10 / LONG -07]	Service entrance, sewers utility area, amid junk.
#17	11.09	Sunken Sewer	Northern, irradiated end, along with other items.
#18	13.03	Auto Shop (Takoma Motors)	Interior, on the southeast corner desk.
#19	14.08	La Maison Beauregard Lobby	Behind the lobby desk.
#20	17.14	Capitol Building West Entrance	Rotunda, with weapon cache on wall.
#21	21.C	Tunnel Cache	With the rest of the cache.
#22	U01.A	Farragut West Station	Weapons cache behind hatch door [Average].
#23	U06.F	Arlington Utility	On the Raiders' eating balcony, with scattered Chems.
#24	U15	Arlington / Falls Church Metro	Container to the north, inside, on a chair.
#25	U17.B	Franklin Metro Utility	Rickety shelving, along the irradiated tunnel.

APPENDIX 11: SKILL BOOK: *NIKOLA TESLA AND YOU* [ENERGY WEAPONS] (25)

#	ZONE	LOCATION	NOTES
#01	1.07	Deathclaw Sanctuary [LAT -22 / LONG 20]	Initial chamber, next to corpse pile.
#02	1.09	Mason Dixon Salvage [LAT -14 / LONG 21]	Inside one of the abandoned shacks.
#03	1.A	Raider Wharf [LAT -24 / LONG 25]	On the boat moored a few feet to the southwest.
#04	2.03	MDPL-21 Power Station [LAT -10 / LONG 26]	Inside, near the Work Bench.
#05	2.E	Abandoned Tent [LAT -12 / LONG 23]	Inside the tent with other items.
#06	3.01	Vault 92 [LAT 08 / LONG 27]	Sound testing, inside the recording studio.
#07	4.06	Vault 87 [LAT -28 / LONG 06]	Reactor chamber, small crate at foot of mannequin.

Appendix 11: Skill Book [Energy Weapons] (continued)

#	ZONE	LOCATION	NOTES
#08	4.11	Fort Bannister [LAT -18 / LONG -01]	Commanding officer's quarters, central silo area, on hidden roof alcove of rusting covered area with sandbags and Ammo; drop down from stairs directly above.
#09	5.12	Vault 106 [LAT -09 / LONG 01]	Living quarters, upper atrium, in a tiny crate at the base of the crate stack, on a desk in the room to the northeast.
#10	5.13	Jury Street Metro Station [LAT -10 / LONG -03]	Gold Ribbon Grocers. Freeform Quest: Rube's Gold Ribbon.
#11	6.02	Canterbury Commons [LAT 18 / LONG 11]	Robot Repair Center, next to a toolbox and some disabled Protectrons on a desk next to the conveyor belts in the generator room.
#12	6.11	National Guard Depot [LAT 18 / LONG -03]	Lower floor, storage room on same floor as utility hatch door.
#13	7.04	Evergreen Mills [LAT -18 / LONG -07]	Bazaar "good time" cells, inside locked cell on a bunk-bed.
#14	7.07	Jocko's Pop & Gas Stop [LAT -22 / LONG -12]	Inside the shack, on the counter.
#15	7.10	RobCo Facility [LAT -14 / LONG -15]	Offices and cafeteria (second floor) desk in northwest corner of open-plan office.
#16	7.F	Ruined Calverton Village [LAT -14 / LONG -07]	On a low bookcase shelf.
#17	8.03	Megaton [LAT -01 / LONG -06]	Your Megaton house, when you purchase the "Science" theme.
#18	8.08	Red Racer Factory [LAT 02 / LONG -15]	CEO offices, small room to the south, along with other items.
#19	9.W	Talon Company Recon Camp [LAT 08 / LONG -20]	On a table by the exposed bunk-bed.
#20	17.07A	Museum of History	Entrance, foyer restrooms.
#21	17.10	Museum of Technology	Upper area at top of stairs, small security room, on counter.
#22	17.14	Capitol Building West Entrance	A metal doored storage room [Hard] off a southern corridor.
#23	U01.A	Farragut West Station	Floor safe [Average] in the MDCTA service office.
#24	U06.C	Foggy Bottom Station	On the computer console adjacent to the Protectron charging pod.
#25	U18.B	Taft Tunnel	On picnic table near Nuka-Cola Quantum. Only available during Main Quest: The Waters of Life.

APPENDIX 12: SKILL BOOK: DUCK AND COVER! [EXPLOSIVES] (25)

#	ZONE	LOCATION	NOTES
#01	1.04	Fort Constantine [LAT -17 / LONG 26]	Launch Control Bunker: On launch control desk, next to terminal.
#02	1.07	Deathclaw Sanctuary [LAT -22 / LONG 20]	Locked footlocker [Average] at the entrance.
#03	1.E	Overlook Raider Shack [LAT -25 / LONG 21]	Skeleton: Near rusting cars and Ammo Boxes, northwest of shack.
#04	2.N	Monorail Train Wreckage (Raider Camp) [LAT 00 / LONG 14]	By the bath.
#05	3.01	Vault 92 [LAT 08 / LONG 27]	Overseer's office, on bookcase.
#06	3.02	Old Olney [LAT 10 / LONG 26]	Olney Sewers, by skeleton at dead-end of rocky tunnel.
#07	4.J	Wasteland Gypsy Village [LAT -18 / LONG 06]	Inside the shack with tree stump left of the door.
#08	5.03	Hamilton's Hideaway [LAT -07 / LONG 07]	Interior Raiders' hideout, on the counter.
#09	5.14	Springvale School [LAT -01 / LONG -01]	Second floor; on the desk by "suk me hahaha's" terminal.
#10	5.D	Ruined House [LAT -05 / LONG 12]	On a shelf, in the building.
#11	6.11	National Guard Depot [LAT 18 / LONG -03]	Depot offices, archives room, on central wooden counter.
#12	6.X	Wastelander Mine Trap (Under Bridge) [LAT 05 / LONG -03]	In among the other items.
#13	7.02	Charnel House [LAT -21 / LONG -04]	Upper floor, end of platform.
#14	7.04	Evergreen Mills [LAT -18 / LONG -07]	Foundry. From the upper catwalks, look at the top of the lower pods (southwest corner), with the body on a mattress. Jump down, or use weapons to knock it down.
#15	7.09	F. Scott Key Trail & Campground [LAT -27 / LONG -15]	Middle picnic table in barbecue area.
#16	7.M	Drainage Chamber [LAT -20 / LONG -13]	Trap-filled, underground office.
#17	7.Q	Warrington Township [LAT -18 / LONG -16]	On a shelf in the debris pile at the east end of the street, opposite the intact dwelling.
#18	8.S	Scavenger's Bridge [LAT 02 / LONG -13]	On shelves in the Scavenger's bridge shack. Steal it.
#19	9.11	The Citadel [LAT 08 / LONG -14]	Laboratory, in a tiny crate, lower floor restroom (to the right of Liberty Prime).
#20	9.13	Alexandria Arms [LAT 07 / LONG -17]	Lower level side room, just before double doors to recreation room.
#21	9.L	Festive Raider Camp [LAT 12 / LONG -10]	Among the other items.
#22	17.08	Bunker	Near the bunk-beds, in the middle of the tunnel.
#23	17.11	The National Archives	On the side of a tipped-over desk in the northwest corner of the large room with the shelves at the northern end.
#24	17.11	The National Archives	Archives sub-basement, tunnel junction, through gate [Very Hard].
#25	U17.A	Falls Church / Mason Dst Metro	Raider Camp ticket booth.

APPENDIX 13: SKILL BOOK: TUMBLERS TODAY [LOCKPICK] (25)

#	ZONE	LOCATION	NOTES
#01	1.06	Broadcast Tower KB5 [LAT -23 / LONG 20]	Drainage Chamber, by corpse near the office door.
#02	1.09	Mason Dixon Salvage [LAT -14 / LONG 21]	Inside abandoned shack, on table.
#03	1.16	Roosevelt Academy [LAT -17 / LONG 14]	Arts and Athletics Hall, third floor, in the southwest office near the locker room, by Ammo Boxes.
#04	1.E	Overlook Raider Shack [LAT -25 / LONG 21]	On the shelves, along with beer and Chems.
#05	1.J	Jackknifed Truck (near Crossing) [LAT -15 / LONG 19]	Inside the container, at the back of the truck.
#06	3.09	Minefield [LAT 04 / LONG 14]	Gibson house, downstairs office, next to burned-out terminal.
#07	4.J	Wasteland Gypsy Village [LAT -18 / LONG 06]	Outside, by the top shack, in the open refrigerator.
#08	5.01	Germantown Police Headquarters [LAT -02 / LONG 13]	Basement, weapons storage, on shelf next to the Fat Man.
#09	5.05	Meresti Trainyard [LAT -01 / LONG 07]	Interior tunnels, among Robert's collection of junk.
#10	5.12	Vault 106 [LAT -09 / LONG 01]	Science Labs, on a table with milk bottles, in the server room (northeast corner of this level).
#11	5.13	Jury Street Metro Station [LAT -10 / LONG -03]	Gold Ribbon Grocers. Freeform Quest: Rube's Gold Ribbon.
#12	5.Q	Cratered Hamlet [LAT -01 / LONG 05]	In a bathtub, in one of the ruined houses.
#13	6.06	Vault 108 [LAT 18 / LONG 06]	Entrance, in entrance level south reactor room storage closet, behind some stacked crates, under a Nuka-Cola Quantum. It is almost impossible to obtain.
#14	7.03	Smith Casey's Garage [LAT -22 / LONG -08]	Inside the open safe, near the mattress and skeleton.
#15	7.T	Ruined Office Building [LAT -14 / LONG -19]	Second floor ruined ledge.
#16	8.10	Nuka-Cola Plant [LAT -01 / LONG -19]	Milo's office, at the back near the safe.
#17	8.0	Talon Company Camp [LAT 02 / LONG -09]	Inside the small lab room.
#18	9.18	Arlington Library [LAT 08 / LONG -19]	Media Archive, on a desk on the north wall of the southwest room.
#19	9.T	Flooded Metro Raider Camp [LAT 04 / LONG -19]	Missile launcher vantage point on the west of the camp.
#20	16.05	Mama Dolce's Processed Foods	Food distribution, on the ground by the skeleton and safes, in the lower tunnel "cave" area.
#21	19.03	Office Building (#1)	On the desk, near the south wall.
#22	19.06	L.O.B. Enterprises	East Wing, near the CEO's desk.
#23	U06.D	Freedom Street Station	Scavenger's barricade, steal from the shelf.
#24	U11	Sewer	Hidden stash with a cluster of Ammo Boxes.
#25	U17.B	Franklin Metro Utility	Near the desk terminal and gate, among Ammo Box and Stimpaks.

APPENDIX 14: SKILL BOOK: D.C. JOURNAL OF INTERNAL MEDICINE [MEDICINE] (25)

#	ZONE	LOCATION	NOTES
#01	1.04	Fort Constantine [LAT -17 / LONG 26]	Bomb storage, experimental chamber on table, near Fat Man.
#02	1.09	Mason Dixon Salvage [LAT -14 / LONG 21]	Inside one of the abandoned shacks.
#03	1.16	Roosevelt Academy [LAT -17 / LONG 14]	Ground floor, nurse's office, desk in southeast corner.
#04	2.01	Oasis [LAT -03 / LONG 28]	Sunken Chambers, in a small crate at the sunlit west end of the cave.
#05	2.B	Toxic Pond [LAT -09 / LONG 30]	Next to the dead scientist.
#06	3.01	Vault 92 [LAT 08 / LONG 27]	Living quarters, lower level.
#07	3.06	Greener Pastures Disposal Site [LAT 07 / LONG 21]	Makeshift shack, near the Wasteland Recluse.
#08	3.08	Relay Tower KX-88-11 [LAT 15 / LONG 20]	Radio alcove, through hatch door, near Pre-War Book.
#09	3.09	Minefield [LAT 04 / LONG 14]	Benson house, desk in master bedroom.
#10	4.01	Shalebridge [LAT -26 / LONG 12]	Dead mercenary, east of the Ant Hills.
#11	4.09	Jalbert Brothers Waste Disposal [LAT -18/ LONG 03]	Inside the first office, on one of the shelves.
#12	5.01	Germantown Police Headquarters [LAT -02 / LONG 13]	Top floor, north conference room.
#13	5.04	Hallowed Moors Cemetery [LAT -04 / LONG 09]	On some shelves.
#14	5.10	Big Town [LAT -04 / LONG 03]	Red's Clinic, in the kitchen.
#15	7.10	RobCo Facility [LAT -14 / LONG -15]	Offices and cafeteria (second floor), computer office room, just before the stairs up.
#16	8.08	Red Racer Factory [LAT 02 / LONG -15]	Factory floor, in the large room to the northeast, climb to the higher catwalk, and look for two turbine-style generators on top of one of the lower pods. Look for some clutter, jump down there, and use the stepladder to climb between the turbines. The book is under a bucket.
#17	9.06	Anchorage Memorial [LAT 10 / LONG -07]	Facility, lower floor in the room with medical equipment, on the table with the light.
#18	9.15	Rivet City [LAT 18 / LONG -17]	Broken Bow, on the computer console, below the X-ray screens.
#19	12.07	Our Lady of Hope Hospital	Ground floor, in room along the corridor from Mister Handy, to the south.

TRAINING — BESTIARY — MAIN QUEST — MISC. QUESTS — TOUR — COMPLETION — APPENDICES

Appendix 14: Skill Book [Medicine] (continued)

#	ZONE	LOCATION	NOTES
#20	12.07	Our Lady of Hope Hospital	Second level, on a table in the cafeteria area with the long slanted wall of windows.
#21	12.09	Sewer	On the shelves.
#22	17.07A	Museum of History Entrance	Lower halls, lower floor, east side on the bottom shelf in the room with the long counters and refrigerators.
#23	17.14	Capitol Building West Entrance	Hall of Columns: On the railing of the sniper bridge spanning the hall at the northern end.
#24	U06.E	DCTA Tunnel 014-B Potomac	Waterlogged treatment room with Stimpaks and Egg Clutches.
#25	U17.A	Falls Church / Mason Dst Metro	On a First Aid Box on the east wall of a restroom, on the far north area of the Metro interior.

APPENDIX 15: SKILL BOOK: *GROGNAK THE BARBARIAN* [MELEE WEAPONS] (25)

#	ZONE	LOCATION	NOTES
#01	1.04	Fort Constantine [LAT -17 / LONG 26]	Personnel offices northeast, small locked closet [Hard] at the foot of the stairs.
#02	1.12	The Silver Lining Drive-In [LAT -15 / LONG 17]	In the shack, near the rusting cars.
#03	1.F	Raider Wreckage Fortifications [LAT -24 / LONG 19]	Top fortification, in tiny crate under the tin cans.
#04	2.04	Clifftop Shacks [LAT 00 / LONG 26]	Inside the smaller shack, to the north.
#05	3.04	Chaste Acres Dairy Farm [LAT 15 / LONG 24]	In the farmhouse barn loft, next to the bloody mattress.
#06	3.09	Minefield [LAT 04 / LONG 14]	Gillian house, upstairs, the first doorway on your left.
#07	E3.04	Enclave Camp [LAT 11 / LONG 14]	Sometimes located with or on the Enclave troops dropped on the bridge by a Vertibird.
#08	6.02	Canterbury Commons [LAT 18 / LONG 11]	Pickpocketed from Derek Pacion.
#09	6.03	Scrapyard [LAT 05 / LONG 09]	Inside John's Treasure Box (northwestern exterior).
#10	6.07	Bethesda Ruins [LAT 05 / LONG 03]	Underworks, inside the Ghoul-filled storage closet.
#11	6.G	Radio Mast Yankee Bravo [LAT 16 / LONG 07]	Drainage channel, small room to the south.
#12	7.0	Yao Guai Tunnels [LAT -28 / LONG -04]	Just beyond the broken fence after entering from the den, there's a ledge with a traffic cone and dead body. The book is on that ledge. Enter from the den, or lob a grenade up from down below.
#13	8.01	Vault 101 [LAT -04 / LONG -04]	Diner, present from Amata on your 10th birthday.
#14	8.03	Megaton [LAT -01 / LONG -06]	Inside Jericho's house.
#15	8.06	Cliffside Cavern [LAT -10 / LONG -17]	Raider Outpost, upper generator near eastern exit tunnel, on the edge of the defenses. Don't explode the generator, or the book could fly anywhere!
#16	8.07	Andale [LAT -05 / LONG -17]	Smith house basement.
#17	8.S	Scavenger's Bridge [LAT 02 / LONG -13]	On shelves in the Scavenger's bridge shack. Steal it.
#18	8.Y	Parked Red RacerTrucks [LAT 01 / LONG -16]	Next to dead Wastelander lying in radioactive container.
#19	12.02	Vault-Tec Guest Relations	Executive office, on one of the desks.
#20	12.08	The Statesman Hotel	Restaurant, the Alfresco Lounge, with cache behind the central bar.
#21	14.A	Super Mutant Camp	Upper concrete ledges to the south.
#22	20.01	Hubris Comics Publishing	Printing area, Mad Johnny Wes's balcony, foreman's office.
#23	U01.B	Tenleytown / Friendship Station	To the northeast, in the small office (across from the restrooms). Check the two sets of lockers; it is on the top left shelf.
#24	U02	Metro Junction	Eastern station area, in the eastern corner. Jump down from above to the sloping pile of rubble, and locate the table with the lantern; the book is there.
#25	U22.B	Museum Station	Inside the Raider's recreation room.

APPENDIX 16: SKILL BOOK: *DEAN'S ELECTRONICS* [REPAIR] (25)

#	ZONE	LOCATION	NOTES
#01	1.02	MDPL-05 Power Station [LAT -27 / LONG 25]	Near the skeleton of the worker, and Dart Gun Schematic.
#02	3.D	Ruined Farmstead [LAT 06 / LONG 27]	Barn area, on the ground-level shelves.
#03	3.N	Hilltop Farm Ruins [LAT 16 / LONG 17]	Loose on a radioactive barrel next to the body in the tipped-over container.
#04	4.10	VAPL-58 Power Station [LAT -14 / LONG 03]	Inside the station, on a computer desk.
#05	4.E and 4.F	Abandoned Shack & Container [LAT -23 / LONG 08 & 09]	Inside the shack, in a crate on the middle Work Bench shelf.
#06	5.13	Jury Street Metro Station [LAT -10 / LONG -03]	In the Raider hideout on the mezzanine, on a Work Bench.
#07	6.02	Canterbury Commons [LAT 18 / LONG 11]	In the garage, in the storage room to the west.
#08	6.05	Corvega Factory [LAT 16 / LONG 05]	Southern warehouse interior, in the foreman's office accessed via the catwalk.

Appendix 16: Skill Book [Repair] (continued)

#	ZONE	LOCATION	NOTES
#09	6.07	Bethesda Ruins [LAT 05 / LONG 03]	Offices West, inside a crate by the broken television and lantern; top floor room with the pit.
#10	7.06	VAPL-66 Power Station [LAT -23 / LONG -14]	Inside the station, on the desk.
#11	7.11	Dunwich Building [LAT -26 / LONG -18]	Forsaken Dunwich Ruins, on a shelf in a small pipe room off the hallway.
#12	7.13	Warrington Station [LAT -18 / LONG -19]	Tunnels, near the Ghouls' sleeping quarters, in a connecting chamber.
#13	8.08	Red Racer Factory [LAT 02 / LONG -15]	Factory floor, toward the main entrance, look for a room with an oversized tricycle hanging from above. Use the barrels behind a railing to jump up onto the tan-colored machine with clutter. There are also Mentats up here.
#14	8.10	Nuka-Cola Plant [LAT -01 / LONG -19]	Factory floor, single large room east of the foyer.
#15	8.W	Jackknifed Truck [LAT -03 / LONG -17]	In the back of the truck's container.
#16	9.06	Anchorage Memorial [LAT 10 / LONG -07]	Operations and clinic room.
#17	9.15	Rivet City [LAT 18 / LONG -17]	Broken Bow, in Pinkerton's hideout.
#18	12.04	Sewer Entrance	Tunnels, near the crossroad, in the locked room [Average].
#19	16.05	Mama Dolce's Processed Foods	Processed foods, on the shelf in the stairwell.
#20	18.06	Reilly's Rangers Compound	On top of the small generator in the southwest room.
#21	20.D	Pulowski Preservation Shelter	Inside the shelter.
#22	U04	Dry Sewer	Generator and storage room, away from main combat corridor.
#23	U05	Tepid Sewer	By the generator.
#24	U06.B	Metro Central	Connecting tunnel, behind gate [Easy] with small generators inside.
#25	U14	Hubris Comics Utility Tunnels	Inside the room with the columns and vertical pipes (northwest side), on a desk tucked in an alcove.

APPENDIX 17: SKILL BOOK: *BIG BOOK OF SCIENCE* [SCIENCE] (25)

#	ZONE	LOCATION	NOTES
#01	1.04	Fort Constantine [LAT -17 / LONG 26]	Bomb storage, in the experimental chamber with the Fat Man and T-51b Armor.
#02	1.D	Jackknifed Truck (on Freeway) [LAT -26 / LONG 20]	On the body of one of the dead scientists (watch for the explosion!)
#03	2.06	Broadcast Tower LP8 [LAT -04 / LONG 24]	Sealed cistern, among the salisbury steaks.
#04	3.06	Greener Pastures Disposal Site [LAT 07 / LONG 21]	Inside the container near the body of the dead scientist.
#05	4.01	Shalebridge [LAT -26 / LONG 12]	Tunnels, on a corpse in the middle of the large chamber at the northern end; look around the central rock formation.
#06	4.11	Fort Bannister [LAT -18 / LONG -01]	Fort Bannister Main, locked [Average] storage room containing Fat Man.
#07	5.04	Hallowed Moors Cemetery [LAT -04 / LONG 09]	On the pulpit.
#08	6.05	Corvega Factory [LAT 16 / LONG 05]	Exterior, in the irradiated container, drop down from the rocky outcrop above.
#09	6.05	Corvega Factory [LAT 16 / LONG 05]	Entrance, inside the open-plan office, on a desk.
#10	6.07	Bethesda Ruins [LAT 05 / LONG 03]	West offices, by the foyer desk, near the Turret Control System Terminal.
#11	6.08	Chryslus Building [LAT 08 / LONG -01]	Basement, northwest, stone-floored generator room.
#12	7.10	RobCo Facility [LAT -14 / LONG -15]	By the Protectron Pod area to the northeast, on a console.
#13	7.13	Warrington Station [LAT -18 / LONG -19]	Tunnels, near the long, gas-filled corridor (three-door room), on a desk.
#14	7.14	Tenpenny Tower [LAT -16 / LONG -17]	Penthouse Suites, your suite, when you purchase the "Science" theme.
#15	8.03	Megaton [LAT -01 / LONG -06]	Craterside Supplies, aAwarded by Moira Brown. Miscellaneous Quest: The Wasteland Survival Guide.
#16	8.10	Nuka-Cola Plant [LAT -01 / LONG -19]	Offices, on a table in the room on the upper floor, west end.
#17	8.C	Drainage Chamber [LAT -11 / LONG -04]	On the table with the radio.
#18	9.15	Rivet City [LAT 18 / LONG -17]	Pinkerton's Hideout.
#19	9.18	Arlington Library [LAT 08 / LONG -19]	Lobby, upper floor office.
#20	10.03	Galaxy News Radio	In Three Dog's upstairs workshop area and restroom.
#21	12.02	Vault-Tec Headquarters	Corporate offices, top floor (northeast end), on a shelf above the huge hole to the lower stories.
#22	16.03	Arlington House	In the kitchen.
#23	21.D	Pulowski Preservation Shelter	Inside the shelter.
#24	U13	County Sewer Mainline	Sewer management room.
#25	U16.B	Queen Ant's Hatchery	Ant Queen's nest, on Lesko's table.

APPENDIX 18: SKILL BOOK: GUNS AND BULLETS [SMALL GUNS] (25)

#	ZONE	LOCATION	NOTES
#01	1.04	Fort Constantine [LAT -17 / LONG 26]	CO quarters, on the bed.
#02	1.04	Fort Constantine [LAT -17 / LONG 26]	Bomb storage, inside one of the locked weapons storage rooms [Very Hard].
#03	1.08	Dickerson Tabernacle Chapel [LAT -19/ LONG 19]	Among the debris and mattresses on the ground.
#04	3.E	Red Rocket Gas Station and Jackknifed Truck [LAT 13 / LONG 25]	Inside the mailbox at the entrance to the Chaste Acres Dairy Farm.
#05	3.N	Hilltop Farm Ruins [LAT 16 / LONG 17]	In the outhouse.
#06	4.03	MDPL Mass Relay Station [LAT -17 / LONG 10]	Interior substation, on a table.
#07	4.07	Everglow National Campground [LAT -23/ LONG 05]	Inside the caravan, northwest of the picnic tables.
#08	4.11	Fort Bannister [LAT -18 / LONG -01]	Bunker, on top of a gun cabinet in the small room off the east hallway.
#09	4.E	Abandoned Shack [LAT -23 / LONG 08]	Inside the shack.
#10	5.03	Hamilton's Hideaway [LAT -07 / LONG 07]	Inside locked cell gate, part of Freeform Quest: Caching in with Three Dog.
#11	6.03	Scrapyard [LAT 05 / LONG 09]	Inside John's Treasure Box (northwestern exterior).
#12	6.08	Chryslus Building [LAT 08 / LONG -01]	Ground floor, behind locked door [Average], or access through hole in second floor.
#13	6.A	Regulator Headquarters [LAT 09 / LONG 11]	Upstairs in Sonora Cruz's chamber.
#14	8.Z	Raider Camp [LAT 03 / LONG -16]	Inside the old Scavenger's hut.
#15	9.09	Grayditch [LAT 05 / LONG -09]	Inside the abandoned house to the north.
#16	9.11	The Citadel [LAT 08 / LONG -14]	A-Ring, under a bed in the northeast corner room.
#17	9.13	Alexandria Arms [LAT 07 / LONG -17]	In the two-level recreation room with the pool table.
#18	9.18	Arlington Library [LAT 08 / LONG -19]	Pulowski Preservation Shelter, outside main door.
#19	9.18	Arlington Library [LAT 08 / LONG -19]	Children's Wing, skeletal cage room and floor holes.
#20	16.05	Mcma Dolce's Processed Foods	The restrooms to the west.
#21	16.05	Mcma Dolce's Processed Foods	Loading yard, open-air sniping point balcony.
#22	17.10	Museum of Technology	West Wing, in a room on a desk, on the third floor off the Delta XI Rocket atrium, northeast corner.
#23	20.F	Mason Alcove	The sniping position upstairs, overlooking the Mutie courtyard.
#24	U17.B	Franklin Metro Utility	On the counter in the generator room.
#25	U19	Flooded Metro	Top floor, skeleton lying near some Jet.

APPENDIX 19: SKILL BOOK: CHINESE ARMY: SPEC. OPS. TRAINING MANUAL [SNEAK] (25)

#	ZONE	LOCATION	NOTES
#01	1.03	SatCom Array NW-05a [LAT -22 / LONG 25]	On the Ghoul Wastelander's desk, near her terminal.
#02	1.04	Fort Constantine [LAT -17 / LONG 26]	CO quarters, downstairs by the dead Wastelander, by the open safe.
#03	2.J	Irradiated Silo and Barn [LAT 00 / LONG 20]	Inside the footlocker [Very Hard] by the mattress, on the barn balcony.
#04	4.04	Broadcast Tower KT8 [LAT -26 / LONG 09]	Drainage Chamber, in secret room with dead Chinese spies.
#05	5.14	Springvale School [LAT -01 / LONG -01]	Lower level, under a corpse in the cave near the large ant egg Clutches.
#06	6.07	Bethesda Ruins [LAT 05 / LONG 03]	East Offices, office cubicle desk to the northwest, with the two Missiles.
#07	6.B	Jackknifed Freeway Truck [LAT 11 / LONG 10]	Inside the container.
#08	6.P	Jackknifed Truck (under Monorail) [LAT 16 / LONG 02]	Inside the footlocker [Very Hard] inside the container.
#09	8.05	Fairfax Ruins [LAT -04 / LONG -12]	Metro Station interior, on the rubble between two wrecked carriages to the east.
#10	8.06	Cliffside Cavern [LAT -10 / LONG -17]	Raider Outpost, inside the tent to the west.
#11	8.10	Nuka-Cola Plant [LAT -01 / LONG -19]	Factory floor, in the main lobby; look up at the ceiling, and open the filing cabinet in the hole up here.
#12	8.G	Ruined Farmhouse [LAT 02 / LONG -04]	Across from the bathtub, on a low bookcase.
#13	8.S	Scavenger's Bridge [LAT 02 / LONG -13]	On shelves in the Scavenger's bridge shack. Steal it.
#14	9.17	Flooded Metro [LAT 04 / LONG -18]	Station exterior, inside Pulowski Preservation Shelter.
#15	12.08	The Statesman Hotel	Mid-level, a storage room south of the main corridor.
#16	15.06	Hotel	In the rubble-filled lobby where the Brotherhood Paladin is holed up.

Appendix 19: Skill Book [Sneak] (continued)

#	ZONE	LOCATION	NOTES
#17	16.05	Mama Dolce's Processed Foods	Loading yard, on the open-air sniping point accessed from inside.
#18	17.03	Mirelurk Nesting Hole	Well-hidden alcove in the upper northwest corner, by skeleton.
#19	17.06	Museum Station	Archives area, upper floor, adjacent to display case with Lincoln's Repeater in it.
#20	17.14	Capitol Building West Entrance	Hall of Columns, behind a locked door [Hard] at the end of the side passage.
#21	19.06	L.O.B. Enterprises	Archives, in empty archives room on a desk with an employee terminal.
#22	U08	Georgetown / The Mall Metro	Inside the ticket booth.
#23	U18.A	Taft Tunnels	On the desk by the dead Chinese Commando, in the room with the Enclave reinforcements.
#24	U20	Irradiated Metro	Glowing One courtyard, on the northwest console.
#25	U22.B	Museum Station	Concourse restrooms, by skeleton next to a small crate.

APPENDIX 20: SKILL BOOK: LYING, CONGRESSIONAL STYLE [SPEECH] (25)

#	ZONE	LOCATION	NOTES
#01	5.01	Germantown Police Headquarters [LAT -02 / LONG 13]	Ground floor, in the rubble-filled debriefing room with the desks.
#02	5.05	Meresti Trainyard [LAT -01 / LONG 07]	Metro Station, under a crate on top of a subway carriage; drop down from the mezzanine area.
#03	5.13	Jury Street Metro Station [LAT -10 / LONG -03]	Mole Rat laboratory, on top of Ryan Brigg's bedside safe.
#04	6.02	Canterbury Commons [LAT 18 / LONG 11]	Mechanist's Forge, on his office desk.
#05	6.03	Scrapyard [LAT 05 / LONG 09]	Inside Littlehorn and Associates' scrapyard office, in the wastebasket next to the desk.
#06	6.05	Corvega Factory [LAT 16 / LONG 05]	Entrance, on the foyer desk.
#07	6.06	Vault 108 [LAT 18 / LONG 06]	Cloning labs, in the middle chamber, near the Bobblehead — Charisma.
#08	7.10	RobCo Facility [LAT -14 / LONG -15]	Factory floor, on the large desk at the back of the foyer.
#09	7.14	Tenpenny Tower [LAT -16 / LONG -17]	Penthouse suites, Burke's room (northeast corner of Tenpenny's suite), on his desk. †
#10	7.14	Tenpenny Tower [LAT -16 / LONG -17]	Penthouse suites, Burke's room (northeast corner of Tenpenny's suite), on his desk. †
#11	7.14	Tenpenny Tower [LAT -16 / LONG -17]	Penthouse suites, your suite, when you purchase the "Romance" theme.
#12	7.E	Ruined Chapel [LAT -14 / LONG -06]	Behind the pulpit.
#13	8.03	Megaton [LAT -01 / LONG -06]	Craterside Supplies, awarded by Moira Brown. Miscellaneous Quest: The Wasteland Survival Guide.
#14	8.03	Megaton [LAT -01 / LONG -06]	Your house when you purchase the "Romance" theme.
#15	8.10	Nuka-Cola Plant [LAT -01 / LONG -19]	Second floor, in the eastern office, on top of the unlocked safe.
#16	9.18	Arlington Library [LAT 08 / LONG -19]	Children's Wing, coffee machine nook.
#17	9.S	Super Mutant Bonfire [LAT 16 / LONG -16]	Back of the camp near two mattresses.
#18	13.04	Takoma Industrial Factory	Slight raised area in the second shop floor, on the storage shelves among the Abraxo.
#19	14.06	Townhome (McClellan Household)	Front room, on the table.
#20	17.11	The National Archives (Front Entrance)	Secure Wing East, through the hatch door to the west [Average], near the Archival safe containing the Bill of Rights.
#21	17.14	Capitol Building West Entrance	Conference hall, on the podium.
#22	18.A	Pulowski Preservation Shelter	Inside the shelter.
#23	U01.B	Henleytown / Friendship Station	Connecting corridor, on the shelves with food and junk.
#24	U03	Vernon East / Takoma Park	On the counter inside the ticket master's office at the south end hallway, near the exit gate.
#25	U06.A	Dupont Circle Station	In a postal crate on the desk, in the room with the filing cabinets, off the northeast hallway, near the exit gate.

† There is a Skill Book at this location prior to a Ghoul invasion, and after the lights go out. To obtain both, claim the first book and then cause the Ghouls to break into the Tower, as part of Miscellaneous Quest: Tenpenny Tower.

APPENDIX 21: SKILL BOOK: PUGILISM ILLUSTRATED [UNARMED] (25)

#	ZONE	LOCATION	NOTES
#01	1.15	Faded Pomp Estates [LAT -17 / LONG 15]	In one ruined house, by a bed, at the foot of a fireplace.
#02	1.16	Roosevelt Academy [LAT -17 / LONG 14]	Academy ground floor, in the men's restrooms.
#03	1.16	Roosevelt Academy [LAT -17 / LONG 14]	Maintenance and evacuation tunnel, third generator room, on shelves in the northwest corner.
#04	1.C	Jackknifed Truck (on Freeway) [LAT -27 / LONG 20]	Inside the truck container.
#05	2.02	SatCom Array NN-03d [LAT -13 / LONG 25]	Tower A, in the restroom with the rude greeting.
#06	2.04	Clifftop Shacks [LAT 00 / LONG 26]	Inside the larger of the two shacks, on a bookcase.
#07	3.04	Chaste Acres Dairy Farm [LAT 15 / LONG 24]	Inside the grain silo.
#08	3.09	Minefield [LAT 04 / LONG 14]	Zone house, upstairs in the kid's room, next to teddy.
#09	4.06	Vault 87 [LAT -28 / LONG 06]	Living quarters, upper atrium, locked storage room on the south wall [Average].
#10	5.07	Arefu [LAT -11 / LONG 06]	Inside the abandoned house / Alan's residence, on the corner table.
#11	5.09	Moonbeam Outdoor Cinema [LAT -06 / LONG 05]	On one of the picnic tables.
#12	6.06	Vault 108 [LAT 18 / LONG 06]	Living quarters, in the cafeteria, on the counter.
#13	6.08	Chryslus Building [LAT 08 / LONG -01]	Lower offices, in one of the postal crates in the large central room (upper level).
#14	7.13	Warrington Station [LAT -18 / LONG -19]	Roy Phillips's Ghoul hidey-hole, on a shelf by Michael Masters' bed.
#15	7.A	Broadcast Tower PN [LAT -24 / LONG -04]	Drainage Chamber, by the exit ladder.
#16	7.E	Ruined Chapel [LAT -14 / LONG -06]	In the rear restroom area.
#17	7.R	Lucky's Grocer [LAT -18 / LONG -20]	Inside the store; you can take this without annoying the Scavenger.
#18	8.02	Springvale [LAT -02 / LONG -04]	Inside the mailbox of the destroyed house across from Red Rocket Gas.
#19	9.08	Dukov's Place [LAT 11 / LONG -08]	In Dukov's bedroom.
#20	9.G	Military Tent and Truck Defenses [LAT 10 / LONG -06]	Inside the yellow truck container.
#21	9.T	Flooded Metro Raider Camp [LAT 04 / LONG -19]	On the counter with the cash register, near the Nuka-Cola Quantum.
#22	15.02	White House Utility Tunnel	Inside the tunnel, in the room with the Work Bench and scattered items.
#23	19.06	L.O.B. Enterprises	On a shelf in the northeast storage room filled with shelves.
#24	U06.B	Metro Central	Locked storage closet [Average] near a pack of Vicious Dogs.
#25	U22.A	Anacostia Crossing Station	On one of the mezzanine table with scattered Chems.

APPENDIX 22: KELLER AND REPLICATED MAN HOLOTAPES (24)

#	HOLOTAPE # & TYPE	ZONE	LOCATION	NOTES
#01	01. Replicated Man	2.08	Paradise Falls [LAT -09 / LONG 16]	Cutter's Clinic.
#02	02. Replicated Man	2.08	Paradise Falls [LAT -09 / LONG 16]	On the floor, by Grouse's sandbags.
#03	03. Replicated Man	2.08	Paradise Falls [LAT -09 / LONG 16]	Inside Eulogy's Pad.
#04	01. Keller	3.07	Grisly Diner [LAT 13 / LONG 20]	On a desk in the back yard, by the ruined concrete wall.
#05	04. Replicated Man	4.08	Little Lamplight [LAT -26 / LONG 02]	Lucy's Clinic.
#06	05. Replicated Man	4.08	Little Lamplight [LAT -26 / LONG 02]	Knick Knack's Store.
#07	02. Keller	4.E	Abandoned Shack [LAT -23 / LONG 08]	Inside the abandoned shack, with other debris.
#08	03. Keller	4.K	Wastelander Pylon [LAT -14 / LONG 05]	On a low bookcase with other assorted junk.
#09	04. Keller	5.04	Hallowed Moors Cemetery [LAT -04 / LONG 09]	On the pulpit, along with Skill Book.
#10	06. Replicated Man	5.10	Big Town [LAT -04 / LONG 03]	In Red's Clinic.
#11	07. Replicated Man	7.14	Tenpenny Tower [LAT -16 / LONG -17]	Doctor Banfield's Clinic.
#12	08. Replicated Man	7.14	Tenpenny Tower [LAT -16 / LONG -17]	Herbert Dashwood's room.
#13	09. Replicated Man	8.03	Megaton [LAT -01 / LONG -06]	Moira Brown's Craterside Supply Store.
#14	10. Replicated Man	8.03	Megaton [LAT -01 / LONG -06]	Doc Church's Clinic.
#15	11. Replicated Man	8.03	Megaton [LAT -01 / LONG -06]	Manya's residence.
#16	12. Replicated Man	9.11	The Citadel [LAT 08 / LONG -14]	Scribe Bowditch's area.
#17	13. Replicated Man	9.15	Rivet City [LAT 18 / LONG -17]	Doctor Preston's Clinic.
#18	14. Replicated Man	9.15	Rivet City [LAT 18 / LONG -17]	Sister's room.
#19	15. Replicated Man	9.15	Rivet City [LAT 18 / LONG -17]	Father Clifford's Church.
#20	16. Replicated Man	9.15	Rivet City [LAT 18 / LONG -17]	Seagrave Holmes's room.
#21	05. Keller	9.G	Military Tent and Truck Defenses [LAT 10 / LONG -06]	Inside the tent with the Super Mutant captive.
#22	17. Replicated Man	17.07	Museum of History (Underworld)	Winthrop's room.
#23	18. Replicated Man	17.07	Museum of History (Underworld)	Doctor Barrows's Chop Shop.
#24	19. Replicated Man	17.07	Museum of History (Underworld)	Tulip's Underworld Outfitters.

 Note

• Replicated Man Holotapes (or characters who've listened to them) provide clues in Miscellaneous Quest: The Replicated Man. Note that some Holotapes may be on the character in question, if not in the location.

• Keller Holotapes open the National Guard Depot [6.11] inner Armory door. Note the order presented here may not reflect the order you listen to the tapes in.